Lecture Notes of the Institute for Computer Sciences, Social Informatics and Telecommunications Engineering   166

More information about this series at http://www.springer.com/series/8197

Alberto Leon-Garcia · Radim Lenort
David Holman · David Staš
Veronika Krutilova · Pavel Wicher
Dagmar Cagáňová · Daniela Špirková
Julius Golej · Kim Nguyen (Eds.)

Smart City 360°

First EAI International Summit, Smart City 360°
Bratislava, Slovakia and Toronto, Canada, October 13–16, 2015
Revised Selected Papers

 Springer

Editors

Alberto Leon-Garcia
University of Toronto
Toronto, ON
Canada

Radim Lenort
Škoda Auto University
Mladá Boleslav
Czech Republic

David Holman
Škoda Auto University
Mladá Boleslav
Czech Republic

David Staš
Škoda Auto University
Mladá Boleslav
Czech Republic

Veronika Krutilova
Mendel University Brno
Brno
Czech Republic

Pavel Wicher
Škoda Auto University
Mladá Boleslav
Czech Republic

Dagmar Cagáňová
Slovak University of Technology
Trnava
Slovakia

Daniela Špirková
Slovak University of Technology
Bratislava
Czech Republic

Julius Golej
Slovak University of Technology
Brno
Czech Republic

Kim Nguyen
University of Quebec's ETS
Montréal
Canada

ISSN 1867-8211   ISSN 1867-822X   (electronic)
Lecture Notes of the Institute for Computer Sciences, Social Informatics
and Telecommunications Engineering
ISBN 978-3-319-33680-0   ISBN 978-3-319-33681-7   (eBook)
DOI 10.1007/978-3-319-33681-7

Library of Congress Control Number: 2016942905

Printed on acid-free paper

This Springer imprint is published by Springer Nature
The registered company is Springer International Publishing AG Switzerland

Preface

SustainableMoG

These proceedings contain revised selected papers form the EAI International Conference on Sustainable Solutions Beyond Mobility of Goods (SustainableMoG 2015). The goal of the conference was to provide a platform for the discussion on achieving a more sustainable balance between economic, environmental, and social objectives in the area of transport, logistics, marketing, and supply chain management. The conference was focused not only on business and industry, but other areas of sustainable mobility. This topic was researched from the Czech, Finnish, German, and Slovak perspective.

Recent sustainable actions in the area of mobility are being implemented as partial solutions, which have a lot of potential but, in the long term, will be depleted relatively quickly. According to the conference participants' opinion, the future lies in a strict adherence to the system approach. This involves not only searching for solutions that take all interrelations of a logistics system into consideration, but also integrating the sustainability with other new logistics and supply-chain management trends, such as leanness, agility, or resilience. The conference SustainableMoG 2015 started the discussion about these challenges.

October 2015   Radim Lenort

MOBIDANUBE

One of the aims of the MOBIDANUBE conference was to strengthen the synergy between researchers and experts from academia, research institutions, and industry to advance the research in the field of mobility opportunities and within the Danube strategy.

The Danube area describes the middle of Europe, the center crossed by the West–East and North–South mobility axes of the continent. Mobility in the Danube region is as such the core of European mobility.

The scientific program for MOBIDANUBE 2015 was prepared to meet the demands of mobility disciplines. Four keynote lectures by internationally recognized experts were on the program. The conference joined individuals from all over the world, all of whom shared a common interest in the area of mobility and the Danube strategy. In particular, we would like to thank the participants for their willingness to share their knowledge, and their latest research results with audience regarding recent developments and the outlook for the future of the field.

The goal of the International Conference on Mobility Opportunities in the Danube Region is to look at major infrastructure platforms, vehicles, people, and freight flowing through an area, which just 25 years ago was still a solid barrier between systems, ideologies, mobility patterns, standards, and mentalities.

The tidal wave of changes, brought about by opening the West–East links and reconnecting Europe, meets the energetic technologic developments in data exchange and communication networking, implementation of AI, vehicle design as well as new patterns of behavior in business and society induced by social media and recent breakthroughs in virtual presence.

All these changes request a comprehensive reflection on current mobility problems, chances, and challenges for a better understanding of the emerging of options and risks, but first of all for inspiring a new outlook.

The 2015 MOBIDANUBE Conference addressed these domains, creating an outlook vision as a base for an integrative strategy of mobility in the Danube region.

October 2015   Dagmar Cagáňová

SmartCityCom

I am honored to present the selected papers form the international conference Social Innovation and Community Aspects of Smart Cities (SmartCityCom 2015). The contributions focus on the current problems of cities and their sustainable development.

The scientific program of the conference created an important opportunity and discussion place for the scientific community and other experts who can contribute to the concept of smart cities development that is now becoming a necessity. The growing population, climate change, energy demands, environmental burdens, and collapsing transport are some of the difficult challenges they have to face.

The application of the concept of sustainable development needs to be based on the position, competencies, and capacities of local governments and their role in achieving goals of sustainable development. The government manages the building of infrastructures, which uses natural resources, and is responsible for the management of waste including its minimization, energy-efficient transport, land use, integrated transport and land use planning, local assessment of environmental impacts and audits, and cooperation with nongovernmental organizations in the implementation of programs to protect the environment, reducing economic and social polarization of society.

The designation of "smart" contributes significantly to the deployment of the latest technologies that serve as sophisticated tools of possible solutions, innovative products, processes, or organizational innovations that reduce environmental costs, increase the acceptance of society and contribute to sustainable development. It should be also noted that the unprecedented and unsustainable urbanization is indeed a manifestation of our economic and social progress, but it also significantly burdens the infrastructure of the planet.

October 2015   Daniela Špirková

SmartCity Toronto

The rapid urbanization of societies globally exacerbates the challenges that cities must face, ranging from basic requirements for food, shelter, health, and mobility to advanced requirements such as providing the resources and services for an informed, productive citizenry. The smart city solutions to these challenges cut across a broad and diverse set of disciplines and they almost always call for an interdisciplinary approach. Information and communications technologies play an enabling, sometimes central, role in these solutions. The SmartCity360 Toronto Conferences were an effort to bring together researchers working across ICT research disciplines addressing the future Smart City.

SmartCity360 Toronto included five conferences addressing urban mobility (SUMS), sustainable cities (S2CT), smart grids SGSC), wearable devices for health and wellbeing (SWIT Health), and big data (BigDASC). In this preface I focus on themes that cut across conferences and that are addressed across multiple conferences. The first theme involves the focus on the personal and individual. Individual persons drive demand in cities for various types of resources, energy, water, food, mobility, etc. and therefore many studies revolve around characterizing the behavior of individuals. Another reason for the focus on individuals is the central role played by the smart phone, and increasingly wearable or specialized personal devices, as the sources of the data streams on user behavior. Privacy is a central concern in this theme. A second theme is the role of wireless networks and sensors in enabling monitoring and actuation in smart cities. These technologies provide the means for collecting data and directing actions to the distributed infrastructure that is inherent in cities and urban regions. These data streams are essential to characterize the consumption and/or generation/capacity of energy, water, GHGs, roads, and so on. A third cross-cutting theme is big data analytics, which plays the key role of discovering, characterizing, and detecting behaviors, anomalies, and other events of interest. The data to understand and predict aggregate behavior in an urban region are only now becoming available, and the promise of addressing global objectives by influencing consumption behavior involving entire urban regions depends on discoveries of patterns and behaviors that are yet to come. A final cross-cutting theme is the support for a broad range of smart city applications and the availability of suitable computing platforms. These platforms must leverage and integrate the capabilities implicit in the aforementioned themes in a manner that enables the desired smart city applications. Taken as a whole, the papers in the SmartCity360 Conferences provide an excellent perspective on the challenges and solution approaches to smart city challenges.

October 2015   Alberto Leon-Garcia

Conference Organization

Sustainable MoG 2015

SustainableMoG 2015 was organized by the Department of Logistics, Quality and Automotive Technology, ŠKODA AUTO University, Czech Republic. The event was endorsed by the European Alliance for Innovation (EAI), a leading community-based organization devoted to the advancement of innovation in the field of Smart Cities, ICT and e-Health and was co-located with the Smart City 360 Summit.

Steering Committee

Imrich Chlamtac	Create-Net, EAI, Italy
Dagmar Cagáňová	Slovak University of Technology, Slovakia
Radim Lenort	ŠKODA AUTO University, Czech Republic
David Holman	ŠKODA AUTO University, Czech Republic

Organizing Committee

General Chair

Radim Lenort	ŠKODA AUTO University, Czech Republic

Program Chair

David Holman	ŠKODA AUTO University, Czech Republic

Web Chair

Pavel Wicher	ŠKODA AUTO University, Czech Republic

Publications Chair

David Stas	ŠKODA AUTO University, Czech Republic

Technical Program Committee

Petr Besta	VSB - Technical University of Ostrava, Czech Republic
David Holman	ŠKODA AUTO University, Czech Republic
Petr Jirsák	University of Economics, Czech Republic
Jakub Jurča	VÍTKOVICE STEEL, a. s., Czech Republic
Radim Lenort	ŠKODA AUTO University, Czech Republic
Andrea Samolejová	VSB - Technical University of Ostrava, Czech Republic

David Vykydal	VSB - Technical University of Ostrava, Czech Republic
Jakub Soviar	University of Zilina, Slovakia
David Stas	ŠKODA AUTO University, Czech Republic
Martin Straka	Technical University of Kosice, Slovakia
Pavel Wicher	ŠKODA AUTO University, Czech Republic

SmartCityCom 2015

Steering Committee

Imrich Chlamtac	Create-Net, EAI
Dagmar Cagáňová	Slovak University of Technology, Slovakia
Daniela Špirková	Slovak University of Technology, Bratislava, Slovakia
Paloma Taltavull de La Paz	University of Alicante, Spain
Erwin Van Der Krabben	Radboud University Nijmegen, The Netherlands
Julius Golej	Slovak University of Technology in Bratislava, Slovakia

Organizing Committee

General Chair

| Daniela Špirková | Slovak University of Technology, Bratislava, Slovakia |

General Co-chair

| Paloma Taltavull de La Paz | University of Alicante, Spain |
| Erwin Van Der Krabben | Radboud University Nijmegen, The Netherlands |

TPC Chair

| Julius Golej | Slovak University of Technology in Bratislava, Slovakia |

Web Chair

| Andrej Adamuscin | Slovak University of Technology in Bratislava, Slovakia |

Publicity and Social Media Chair

| Miroslav Panik | Slovak University of Technology in Bratislava, Slovakia |

Publications Chair

| Julius Golej | Slovak University of Technology in Bratislava, Slovakia |
| Miroslav Panik | Slovak University of Technology in Bratislava, Slovakia |

Panels Chair

Martina Rašticová   Mendel University in Brno, Czech Republic

Technical Program Committee (Scientific Committee)

Stanislaw Belniak   Cracow University of Economics, Poland
Jim Berry   University of Ulster, UK
Dagmar Cagáňová   Slovak University of Technology in Bratislava,
                               Slovakia
Krystyna Dziworska   University of Gdansk, Poland
Maroš Finka   Slovak University of Technology in Bratislava,
                               Slovakia
Petia Genkova   University of Osnabruck, Germany
Jana Geršlová   Technical University of Ostrava, Czech Republic
František Janíček   Slovak University of Technology in Bratislava,
                               Slovakia
Aija Klavina   University of Riga, Latvia
Jana Korytárová   Brno University of Technology, Czech Republic
Lea Kubičková   Mendel University in Brno, Czech Republic
Ramaswami Mahalingam   University of Michigan, USA
Jürgen Mühlbacher   Vienna University of Economics and Business, Austria
Zora Petráková   Slovak University of Technology in Bratislava,
                               Slovakia
Dušan Petráš   Slovak University of Technology in Bratislava,
                               Slovakia
Anna Putnová   Brno University of Technology, Czech Republic
Martina Rašticová   Mendel University in Brno, Czech Republic
Ania Saniuk   University of Zielona Gora, Poland
Petr Štěpánek   Czech Technical University in Prague, Czech Republic
Riccardo Scalenghe   University of Palermo, Italy
Jana Stávková   Mendel University in Brno, Czech Republic
Marcel Ševela   Mendel University in Brno, Czech Republic
Jana Šujanová   Slovak University of Technology in Bratislava,
                               Slovakia
Maurizio Tira   University of Brescia, Italy
Mária Zúbková   Slovak University of Technology in Bratislava,
                               Slovakia
Pavel Žufan   Mendel University in Brno, Czech Republic

MOBI Danube 2015

Steering Committee

Imrich Chlamtac   Create-Net, EAI
Dagmar Cagáňová   Slovak University of Technology, Slovakia
George Teodorescu   Coordinator of the Danubius Innovation Alliance,
                               Institute for Integral Innovation

Organizing Committee

General Chair

George Teodorescu — Coordinator of the Danubius Innovation Alliance, Institute for Integral Innovation

Program Chair

Dagmar Cagáňová — Slovak University of Technology, Slovakia

Program Co-chair

Milan Dado — University of Žilina, Slovakia

Web Chair

Predrag Nikolic — EDUCONS Novi Sad, Serbia

Publicity and Social Media Chair

Alina Raileanu — Danubius University, Romania

Workshop Chair

Jana Šujanová — Slovak University of Technology, Slovakia

Publications Chair

Veronika Krutilova — Mendel University Brno, Czech Republic

Panels Chair

Pavel Žufan — Mendel University Brno, Czech Republic

Tutorials Chair

Andy Pusca — Danubius University, Romania

Technical Program Committee

Mario Valerio Salucci	University of Rome, Italy
Lidia Pavic Rosovic	ODRAZ, EESC Member, Croatia
Milan Dado	University of Žilina, Slovakia
Ana Dragutescu	Association for Urban Transition, Bucharest, Romania
Rob Jeuring	Ecorys Holding Amsterdam, The Netherlands
Predrag K. Nikolic	EDUCONS University, Novi Sad, Serbia
Dušan Petráš	Slovak University of Technology in Bratislava, Slovakia
Never Vrcek	University of Zagreb, Varazdin, Croatia
Milos Cambal	Slovak University of Technology in Bratislava (STU), Slovakia

Krzysztof Witkowski	University of Zielona Gora, Poland
Sebastian Saniuk	University of Zielona Gora, Poland
Michal Balog	Technical University, Kosice, Slovakia
Peter Bindzar	Technical University, Kosice, Slovakia
Martin Straka	Technical University, Kosice, Slovakia
Daniela Spirkova	Slovak University of Technology in Bratislava (STU), Slovakia
Petr Štěpánek	Praha, Czech Republic
Jana Sujanova	Slovak University of Technology in Bratislava (STU), Slovakia
Jaroslav Holecek	Slovak University of Technology in Bratislava (STU), Slovakia
Daynier Rolando Delgado Sobrino	Slovak University of Technology in Bratislava (STU), Slovakia
Giovanni Del Galdo	Fraunhofer, Ilmenau, Germany
Thomas Sporer	Fraunhofer, Germany
Konrad Osterwalder	United Nations University, Tokyo, Japan
Frank T. Anbari	Goodwin College of Professional Studies at Drexel University, USA
Ladislav Janoušek	Zilina University, Zilina, Slovakia
Michael Stankosky	The George Washington University, USA
Pawel Sobcyak	Academy of Business, Olkusz, Poland
Marek Walancik	Wyzsza Szkola Biznesu, Dabrowie Gorniczej, Poland
Joanna Kurowska Pysz	Strada CONSULTING, Bielsko-Biala, Poland
Thomas Palatin	Vienna Business Agency, Vienna, Austria
Walter Mayrhofer	Fraunhofer, Wien, Austria
Ullas Ehrlich	Tallinna Tehnikaulikool, Tallinn, Estonia
Avinash W. Kolhatkar	Jawaharlal Darda Institute of Engineering and Technology, India
Nikolay Madzharov	Technical University of Gabrovo, Dryanovo, Bulgaria
Dorin-Dumitru Lucache	Gheorghe Asachi Technical University of Iaşi, Romania
Cristian-Gyözö Haba	Gheorghe Asachi Technical University of Iaşi, Romania
Florinda Matos	President of the ICAA (Intellectual Capital Accreditation Association), Portugal
Ettore Bolisani	University of Padova, Italy
Ilpo Pohjola	University of Eastern Finland, Finland
Enrico Scarso	University of Padova, Italy
Eduardo Tome	Universidade Europeia, Lisbon, Portugal
Jose Maria Viedma Marti	Polytechnic University of Catalonia, Barcelona, Spain
Malgorzata Zieba	Gdansk University of Technology, Poland
Atul Borade	Jawaharlal Darda Institute of Engineering and Technology, India
Shawn Chen	Sias Group, Inc., China
Małgorzata Zięba	Gdańsk University of Technology, Poland

Florian Marcel Nuta	Danubius University, Romania
Sergey Zapryagaev	Voronezh State University, Russia
Janusz K. Grabara	Polish Journal of Management Studies/Czestochowa University of Technology, Poland
Giorgos Cristonakis	Berlin School of Economics and Law, Germany
Emanuel-Stefan Marinescu	Danubius University, Romania
Yhing Sawheny	Siam University, Thailand
John Kelly	Cascaid, USA
Abdul Dewale Mohammed	The Association of Universities of Asia and the Pacific/ Africa Asia Scholars Global Network, UK
Gabriela Koľveková	Technical University of Košice, Slovakia
Roswitha Wiedenhofer	University of Applied Sciences, Austria
Dr. Carmen Sirbu	Danubius University, Romania
Ania Saniuk	University of Zielona Gora, Poland

SUMS 2015

Steering Committee

Imrich Chlamtac	Create-Net, EAI
Alberto Leon-Garcia	University of Toronto, Canada
Victor Leung	University of British Columbia, Canada

Organizing Committee

General Chair

Victor Leung	University of British Columbia, Canada

Program Chair

Mohamed El-Darieby	University of Regina, Canada

Program Co-chair

Peter Chong	Nanyang Technological University, Singapore
Yaser P. Fallah	West Virginia University, USA
Edith C.-H. Ngai	Uppsala University, Sweden

Publicity Chair

Kaveh Shafiec	Wind River Systems

Web Chair

Kim Nguyen	L'École de technologie supérieure de Montréal, Canada

Technical Program Committee

Nawaz Ali	Khulna University of Engineering & Technology, Bangladesh
Onur Altintas	Toyota InfoTechnology Center
Abdul Bais	University of Regina, Canada
Farshid Hassani Bijarbooneh	Uppsala University, Sweden
Parsad Calyam	University of Missouri, USA
Berk Canberk	Istanbul Technical University, Turkey
Supriyo Chakraborty	IBM, USA
Floriano De Rango	University of Calabria, Italy
Maher Elshakankiri	University of Regina, Canada
Somak D. Gupta	University of California Berkeley, USA
Xiping Hu	University of British Columbia, Canada
Manijeh Keshtgari	Shiraz University of Technology, Iran
Steven Ko	University of Buffalo, USA
Vinod Kulathumani	West Virginia University, USA
Arun Kumar	NTHU Taiwan
Qi Li	Tsinghua University Shenzhen, China
Xi Li	Beijing University of Posts and Telecommunications, China
Xuejun Li	New Zealand
Qiang Liu	National University of Defense Technology
Rongxing Lu	Singapore
Jonathan Petit	University College, Cork, Ireland
Boon-Chong Seet	AUT, New Zealand
Kaveh Shafiee	Wind River Systems
Zhengguo Sheng	University of Sussex, UK
Hnin Yu Shwe	NTU, Singapore
Houbing Song	WVU Institute of Technology, USA
Weibin Sun	Google Inc., USA
Daxin Tian	Beihang University, China
Ke Wang	BUPT, China
Kun Xie	Hunan University, China
Heli Zhang	Beijing University of Posts and Telecommunications, China
Minglong Zhang	CUHK, Hong Kong, SAR China
Yin Zhang	Zhongnan University of Economics and Law, China
Jason Zheng Song	Virginia Tech, USA
Xun Zhou	The University of Iowa, USA

SWIT-Health 2015

Steering Committee

Imrich Chlamtac	Create-Net, EAI
Alberto Leon-Garcia	University of Toronto, Canada
Benny Lo	Imperial College, London, UK

Organizing Committee

General Chair

Benny Lo	Imperial College, London, UK

General Co-chair

Joseph A. Cafazzo	University of Toronto, Canada

Program Chair

Min Chen	Huazhong University of Science and Technology, China
Ilangko Balasingham	Carleton University, Ottawa, Canada

Web Chair

Harshvardhan Vathsangam	University of Southern California, Los Angeles, USA

Publicity and Social Media Chair

Gaetano Valenza	University of Pisa and Harvard Medical School, Italy/USA

Technical Program Committee

Jianqing Wang	Nagoya Institute of Technology, Japan
William Scanlon	Queen's University Belfast, UK
Lorenzo Mucchi	University of Florence, Italy
Thomas Lindh	KTH, Sweden
Josep Miquel	Jornet University at Buffalo, The State University of New York, USA
Matti Hämäläinen	University of Oulu, Finland
Laura Galluccio	University of Catania, Italy
Daisuke Anzai	Nagoya Institute of Technology, Japan
Huan-Bang Li	NICT
Yan Zhang	Simula Research Laboratory
Raul Chavez-Santiago	Oslo University Hospital, Norway
Pål Anders Floor	Norwegian University of Science and Technology, Norway

Kimmo Kansanen	Norwegian University of Science and Technology, Norway
Gill Tsouri	Rochester Institute of Technology, USA
Chunming Rong	University of Stavanger, Norway
Thomas Plagemann	University of Oslo, Norway
Wei Xiang	University of Southern Queensland, Australia
Ying Hu	Huazhong University of Science and Technology, China
Jiafu Wan	South China Unviersity of Technology, China
Yin Zhang	Huazhong University of Science and Technology, China
Kai Lin	Dalian University of Technology, China
Limei Peng	Ajou University, Korea

S2CT 2015

Steering Committee

Imrich Chlamtac	Create-Net, EAI
Alberto Leon-Garcia	University of Toronto, Canada
Bill Hutchison	i-Canada Alliance, Canada

Organizing Committee

General Chair

| Bill Hutchison | i-Canada Alliance, Canada |

Conference Track Chair

| Mohamed Cheriet | Ecole de Technologie Superieure, University of Quebec, Montreal, Canada |

Conference Track Co-chair

| Charles Despins | Prompt Quebec, Canada |
| Réjean Samson | Ecole de Polytechnique of Montreal, Canada |

Conference Track Web Chair

| Kim Nguyen | University of Quebec's Ecole de Technologie Superieure, Canada |

Conference Track Publicity Chair

| Jacques Mc Neil | Prompt Quebec, Canada |

Technical Program Committee

Raouf Boutaba	University of Waterloo, Canada
Cees de Laat	University of Amsterdam, The Netherlands
Charles Despins	ÉTS, University of Quebec, Canada
Rejean Samson	École Polytechnique of Montreal, Canada
Fabrice Labeau	McGill University, Canada
Alex Galis	University College London, UK
Stephane Coulombe	ÉTS, University of Quebec, Canada
Rashid Mijumbi	Universitat Politècnica de Catalunya, Spain
Chamseddine Talhi	ÉTS, University of Quebec, Canada
Tortonesi Mauro	University of Ferrara, Italy
Kim Nguyen	ÉTS, University of Quebec, Canada
Magnus Olsson	Ericsson Research, Sweden
Makan Pourzandi	Ericsson Research, Canada
Tereza Cristina M.B. Carvalho	Universidade de São Paulo, Brazil
Benoit Tremblay	Ericsson Research, Canada
Daniel C. Moura	Instituto de Engenharia Mecânica e Gestão Industrial, Portugal
Ali Kanso	Ericsson Research, Canada
Carol Fung	Virginia Commonwealth University, USA
Abdelouahed Gherbi	ÉTS, University of Quebec, Canada
Walter Cerroni	University of Bologna, Italy
Wessam Ajib	University of Quebec at Montreal, Canada
Weverton Luis da Costa Cordeiro	Federal University of Rio Grande do Sul, Brazil
Mohamed Faten Zhani	ÉTS, University of Quebec, Canada
Paul Steenhof	CSA Group, Canada
Halima Elbiaze	University of Quebec at Montreal, Canada
Reza Farrahi	ÉTS, University of Quebec, Canada
Thomas Dandres	École Polytechnique of Montreal, Canada

SGSC 2015

Steering Committee

Imrich Chlamtac	Create-Net, EAI
Alberto Leon-Garcia	University of Toronto, Canada
Deepa Kundur	University of Toronto, Canada

Organizing Committee

General Chair

Deepa Kundur	University of Toronto, Canada

Program Chair

Hamed Mohsenian-Rad   University of California Riverside

Program Co-chair

Yonghui Li   University of Sydney, Australia
Hao Liang   University of Alberta, Canada
Islam Safak Bayram   Qatar Environment and Energy Research Institute, Qatar
Javad Lavaei   Columbia University, USA
Chris Develder   Ghent University, Belgium
Jiming Chen   Zhejiang University, China
Chen-Ching Liu   Washington State University, USA

Web Chair

Kim Nguyen   L'École de technologie supérieure de Montréal, Canada

Technical Program Committee

Masoud Abbaszadeh   General Electric Global Research
Mahnoosh Alizadeh   Stanford University, USA
Chen Chen   Argonne National Laboratory
Guo Chen   University of Sydney, Australia
Dae-Hyun Choi   Chung-Ang University, South Korea
Ruilong Deng   Nanyang Technological University, Singapore
Darish Fooladivanda   University of Toronto, Canada
Nikolaos Gatsis   University of Texas at San Antonio, USA
Wibowo Hardjawana   University of Sydney, Australia
Miao He   Texas Tech University, USA
Muhammad Ismail   Texas A&M University at Qatar
Melike Erol Kantarci   Clarkson University, USA
Jang-Won Lee   Yonsei University, South Korea
Jin Ma   University of Sydney, Australia
Angelos Marnerides   Liverpool John Moores University, UK
Seyedbehzad Nabavi   North Carolina State University, USA
HyungSeon Oh   University of New York at Buffalo, USA
Yuexing Peng   Beijing University of Post and Telecommunications, China
Shaolei Ren   Florida International University, USA
Petros Spachos   University of Toronto, Canada
Himal A. Suraweera   University of Peradeniya, Sri Lanka
Gregor Verbic   University of Sydney, Australia
Chenye Wu   University of California, Berkeley, USA
Yunjian Xu   Singapore University of Technology and Design, Singapore

Qinmin Yang	Zhejiang University, China
Vahraz Zamani	University of California San Diego, USA
Saman Aliari Zonouz	Rutgers University, USA

BigDASC 2015

Steering Committee

Imrich Chlamtac	Create-Net, EAI
Alberto Leon-Garcia	University of Toronto, Canada
Nick Cercone	York University, Canada

Organizing Committee

General Chair

| Nick Cercone | York University, Canada |

Program Chair

| Ali Tizghadam | University of Toronto/TELUS, Canada |

Program Co-chair

| Fred Popowich | Simon Fraser University, Canada |

Web Chair

| Kim Nguyen | University of Quebec's École de technologie supérieure, Canada |

Technical Program Committee

Lyn Bartram	Simon Fraser University, Canada
Mike Bauer	University of Western Ontario, Canada
Christine Chan	University of Regina, Canada
James Elder	York University, Canada
Esteban Feuerstein	Universidad de Buenos Aires, Argentina
Randy Goebel	University of Alberta, Canada
Ling Guan	Ryerson University, Canada
Vlado Keselj	Dalhousie University, Canada
Marin Litoiu	York University, Canada
Stephen Makonin	Simon Fraser University, Canada
Alan Mackworth	University of British Columbia, Canada
Hausi Muller	University of Victoria, Canada
Bill Oliphant	Fuseforward Systems
Jian Pei	Simon Fraser University, Canada
Stephen Perelgut	IBM Canada University Relations Manager, Canada
Pascal Perez	University of Wollongong, Australia

Eleni Pratsini	IBM Research Dublin, Ireland
Tim Scully	Data to Decisions CRC, Australia
Richard O. Sinnott	University of Melbourne, Australia
Jacob Slonim	Dalhousie University, Canada
Guhno Sohn	York University, Canada
Maria Cristina Soares Guimaraes	ICICT/Fiocruz, Brazil
Renato Rocha Souza	EMAp/FGV, Brazil
	Graham Toppin, Aziiri
Jennifer McArthur	Ryerson University, Canada

Contents

BigDASC

MOBI Danube

Contents   XXXI

SUMS

A Survey on Mobile Sensing Based Mood-Fatigue Detection for Drivers

Wei Tu[1(✉)], Lei Wei[2], Wenyan Hu[3], Zhengguo Sheng[4], Hasen Nicanfar[5], Xiping Hu[5],
Edith C.-H. Ngai[6], and Victor C.M. Leung[5]

[1] College of Computer, Wuhan University, Wuhan, China
twwwheat@gmail.com
[2] College of Computer Science and Electronic Engineering, Hunan University, Changsha, China
f_vice@hnu.edu.cn
[3] School of Computer Science, Carnegie Mellon University, Pittsburgh, USA
huwenyan15@126.com
[4] Department of Engineering and Design, University of Sussex, Brighton, UK
z.sheng@sussex.ac.uk
[5] Department of Electrical and Computer Engineering, The University of British Columbia, Vancouver, Canada
{hasennic,xipingh,vleung}@ece.ubc.ca
[6] Department of Information Technology, Uppsala University, Uppsala, Sweden
edith.ngai@it.uu.se

Abstract. The rapid development of the Internet of Things (IoT) has provided innovative solutions to reduce traffic accidents caused by fatigue driving. When drivers are in bad mood or tired, their vigilance level decreases, which may prolong the reaction time to emergency situation and lead to serious accidents. With the help of mobile sensing and mood-fatigue detection, drivers' mood-fatigue status can be detected while driving, and then appropriate measures can be taken to eliminate the fatigue or negative mood to increase the level of vigilance. This paper presents the basic concepts and current solutions of mood-fatigue detection and some common solutions like mobile sensing and cloud computing techniques. After that, we introduce some emerging platforms which designed to promote safe driving. Finally, we summarize the major challenges in mood-fatigue detection of drivers, and outline the future research directions.

Keywords: Mobile sensing · Mood-fatigue detection · Vehicular sensor application

1 Introduction

With the high-speed of the development of human-centered applications of the Internet of Things (IoT) and the comprehensive application of different kinds of sensor nodes which is represented by mobile nodes, the application of IoT based on mobile sensing is becoming increasingly popular, especially in healthcare.

According to World Health Organization (WHO), approximately 1.3 million people die each year on the world's roads, and between 20 and 50 million sustain non-fatal

© ICST Institute for Computer Sciences, Social Informatics and Telecommunications Engineering 2016
A. Leon-Garcia et al. (Eds.): Smart City 2015, LNICST 166, pp. 3–15, 2016.
DOI: 10.1007/978-3-319-33681-7_1

injuries [1]. One of the main reasons is driver's fatigue driving and negative mood which decrease their vigilance level, because of which about 600 people die on roads everyday [2]. Thus, it is of great importance to detect the mood and fatigue of drivers in real time while driving and take actions according to the vigilance level.

For safe driving, noninvasive techniques are at present being employed to assess a driver's alertness level through the visual observation of his/her physical condition using a camera and related computer vision [3] technologies. Also, corresponding incentive scheme can be taken to make drivers happier and less fatigue, e.g., previous research pointed out that listening to suitable music would not impair driving performance but enhance it [2]. To achieve the aim of assess a driver's mood-fatigue state, two key techniques are of great importance.

The first is mobile sensing which collects necessary data of current driving, including the driver's health data, the car sensors, and the road information. The health data such as the heart rate can be collected by the heart rate sensor, while the car data (e.g., speed, temperature, fuel consumption) can be read by advanced onboard diagnostic port scanners. The environmental data can be collected from the roadside and in-car sensors, news summary, and updates from other drivers. All the input data will be fed into the real-time state analysis module to infer the mood of the driver and the current driving condition [4]. Another is facial expression recognition based mood detection. By catching and processing the real-time photos of drivers' faces, the emotion can be classified into different categories.

In the rest of this paper, Sects. 2 and 3 introduces the current solutions and techniques of mood-fatigue detection and some common solutions, respectively. Then, Sect. 4 describes current platforms for safe driving. Section 5 discusses some technical challenges and future research directions. Section 6 concludes this paper.

2 Mood-Fatigue Detection of Drivers

Mental fatigue is a frequent phenomenon in our daily life, and is defined as a state of cortical deactivation, which reduces mental performance and decreases alertness [5]. The fatigue detection system is critical to prevent the car accident by sounding the alarm to the driver. Besides, the techniques used can also be applied to other similar applications, such as Computer Vision Syndrome [6], human-computer interaction, etc. On the other hand, facial expressions always play a significant role in human communication. Consequently, the technology of mood detection, detect a motion of people by sensors and computer, is essential in HCI (human-computer interaction). As a result, there has been considerable works done on the recognition of emotional expressions. The applications of those researches can be beneficial in improving HCI and applied in various fields like digital camera, Curative effect observation in hospital, etc.

2.1 Fatigue Detection

In earlier years, researchers took direct measures of fatigue, involve self-report of internal states, however there are a number of problems in using any self-report measure due to the influence of demand effects or motivational influences [7]. Therefore, in the recent years, many researchers have focused on the development of monitoring systems using various techniques which are based on physiological signal, such as brain waves, heart rate, pulse rate and respiration. Among these signals, electroencephalogram (EEG) signal was regarded the best way to detect fatigue level of a person [8]. But it is regrettable that these techniques are intrusive. They need to attach some electrodes on the test objective [9, 10] which is not a pleasant experience. Consequently, another technique, which are based on physiological reaction, including head pose, mouth shape, eyes state, increasingly got attentions of researcher. In addition to this, there are some other Fatigue Detection methods based on driver performance, with a focus on the vehicle's behavior including position and headway.

2.1.1 Techniques Based on Physiological Signal

Studies show that physiological signals of a fatigue person are abnormal [11]. For instance, with the increase of fatigue, θ and δ brain waves will increase meanwhile α and β brain waves will decrease [12, 13]. Yeo et al. [14] built an automatic EEG detection system of drowsiness by classifying brain waves based on SVM. Zhao et al. [15] use electroencephalograph to collect the EEG in driving simulation, calculate the distribution of frequency by power spectrum and build a system by neural network. Besides, electrocardiogram signal including HR (Heart Rate) and HRV (Heart Rate Variability) is another important figure in fatigue detection. Patel et al. [16] use HRC as the main parameter to detect the fatigue base on BP neural network and obtained 90 % accuracy. In the researches in Tokyo University, scholars can detect fatigue of test people by contents of alcohol, ammonia and lactate in their sweat.

2.1.2 Techniques Based on Physiological Reaction

Sharma et al. [17] used the amount of pixels in the eye image to calculate the eye state. Sharma converted face images to the YCbCr color configuration. The average and standard deviation of the pixel number in the image is calculated. Then, fuzzy rules [18] are used to identify the eye state. Liu et al. [19] and Tabrizi et al. [20] proposed methods to detect the upper and lower eyelids based on the edge map. The distance between the upper and lower eyelids is used to analyze the eye state. Besides, the head position sensor system MINDS (Micro-Nod Detection System) proposed by ASCI is conceptually designed to detect micro-sleep events occurring in association with head nodding by assessing the x, y, and z coordinates of the head through conductivity measurements [21].

2.1.3 Techniques Based on Driving Behavior

CBerglund et al. [22] established fatigue detection modal which collects data including steering wheel angle, Lane offset, Vehicle lateral sway angle, extract 17 features in a simulative driving experiment and obtained 87 % accuracy. Friedrichs et al. [23] extract 11 fatigue estimative figures from the steering wheel turn angle and the variable of the vehicle crosswise position in their fatigue driving experiments and built several systems by fisher discriminant, k nearest neighbor, Bayes algorithm and neural network.

2.2 Mood Detection

The automated recognition of facial expressions is still a challenge despite its rapid development these years. A mood detection system usually is built on the basic framework of pattern recognition which has three main steps: (1) detection and location of the face, (2) feature extraction and facial representation, (3) classification of emotions. Therefore deriving effective facial representation from original face images is a vital step for successful facial expression recognition. There are two approaches to extract facial features: geometric feature-based methods and appearance-based methods [24].

Authors in [25] proposed a geometric system for breaking down 20 facial appearances with the particular objectives of contrasting, matching, and averaging their shapes. Local feature based algorithms [26] exploits curvelet change in two routes i.e. as a key point finder to extract salient points on the face region. Sparse representation based Face Expression Recognition (FER) strategy [27] lessen the intra-class variety while accentuating the facial expression in a query face image. The authors in [28] propose a deformable 3-D facial expression model and D-Isomap based classification. An enhancement of was proposed by authors in [29]. In this method a novel multi view facial expression recognition technique is displayed.

2.3 Mood-Fatigue Detection for Safe Driving

Since now the mobile sensing can use the growing hardware of sensors to catch the valid data for mood-fatigue detection, there are an increasing number of solutions of mood and fatigue detection for safe driving. Currently, there already have been some in-vehicle technological approaches for safe driving and even addressed on mood and fatigue.

The Driver Fatigue Monitor [30] is a real-time on-board video-based detection system that measures the drowsiness degree of the drivers. It uses the camera catching for the slow eyelid closure. This device shows the driver's drowsiness level with PERCLOS estimation and has a three-state warning mechanism. But it is just good in usage of the night environment because the detection is about the pupil of the eyes, which is easily interfered with the IR illumination by the bright spots from the light reflection.

Thus, the Driver State Monitor [31] improves the estimation skill from PERCLOS to AVECLOS, which is less complex than the PERCLOS. The faceLAB [32] enlarges the detection range from the eyelid to driver's whole behavior including head pose, gaze direction, and eyelid closure. The Drowsy Driver Detection System [33] collects data with all kinds of conditions. It also considers the heartbeat, the pulse rate apart from the eyelid. It has a more integrated detection but still does not go beyond the original detection skills. So as for the algorithm breakthrough on parameters, the RPI [30] uses the Bayesian Networks model to firstly combine the parameters of the face data with algorithm. However, the Artificial Neural Network [34] collects and analyzes the vehicle data only. Without the manual interface and the uncontrollability of the personal behavior, its accuracy of detection can be up to 90 %.

Also, the faceLAB [33] is taken on the eyelid position rather than the bright pupil, but it still does not use the vehicle data, which is just feasible for simulation environment.

Then the Smart Eye [35] uses the 3D technology for driver's head model. The 3D location, the face of the driver's can be captured more accurately with real-time tracking.

As for the nighttime range problem, SMI InSight [36] determines a tracking area on the face for head location, which makes the 24 h operation come true by widely decreasing the reflection influence when in the head and face detection for mood and fatigue judgment. It also conducts researches on the difference between the simulator and real-road environment. The ASL ETS-PC II [37] prefers the bright pupil images, applying itself to the all driving conditions.

Figure 1 shows the structure of data from the camera, sensors and OBD (On-Board Diagnostic) for analyzing mood and fatigue.

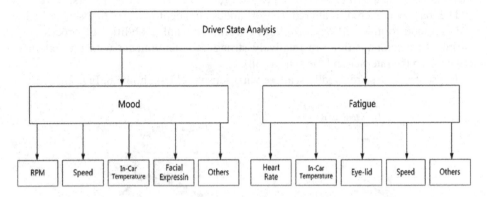

Fig. 1. The structure of data for analyzing mood and fatigue

3   Common Solutions

To support mood-fatigue detection of drivers, several key techniques are necessary. Here we discuss mobile sensing and mobile cloud computing.

3.1   Mobile Sensing

3.1.1   Sensors
Mobile sensing collects data from useful sensors for mood-fatigue detection. These sensors include acceleration sensors, temperature sensors, heart rate sensors and so on. Then the data will be transmitted to upper layer for further processing.

By measuring the acceleration caused by gravity, it can further figure out the angle of inclination relative to horizontal plane; by analyzing the dynamic acceleration, you can work out the way it moves. Acceleration sensors are now necessities in mobile phones. For example, step software like Nike + use the acceleration sensor to calculate the journey while the carrier of the mobile phone is walking or running.

The heart rate is closely connected to one's mood. Heart rate sensors can monitor one's heart rate to track the exercise intensity or different motor and training pattern, and estimate the health data such as the sleep cycle according to the statistics. There are two kinds of heart rate sensors. First is the photoelectric heart rate sensor which makes use of the reflection of the light. Another is the electrode heart sensor which measures the electric potential of the different parts of the human body. Although the former has a relatively low accuracy, it is now used in all mobile terminals due to its small volume. For example, the new Apple Watch embeds four photoelectric heart sensors inside to monitor the wearer's heart rate more accurately.

Just as its name implies, temperature sensors are used for temperature measure and converting it to output signals. In a mood-fatigue detection system, it can help detect the degree of fatigue of drivers.

The OBD can also be viewed as sensors which collect the data of RPM, speed and other state of the car, which will also affect the mood-fatigue state of drivers.

The battery-powered scattered sensor nodes are deployed in the sensor field randomly and form a self-organization network. The sink's abilities of processing, storing and communication are relatively strong. It communicate with the external network like the Internet and the sensor [38].

The sensor nodes are usually scattered in a sensor field as shown in Fig. 2.

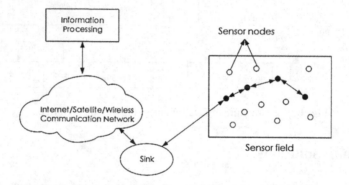

Fig. 2. Sensor nodes in a sensor field

3.1.2   Communication Technology
One of the most important steps of mobile sensing is to collect and transmit the sensing data from the sensors mentioned above. The wireless communication technique plays an important role, especially for IoT, because it gets rid of wiring and is probably the only choice for mobile nodes. Currently common wireless communication techniques include ZigBee, Bluetooth, RFID, NFC, UWB, WiFi and so on.

Table 1 shows the comparisons among different wireless network standards.

Especially, there are some communication protocols designed for vehicles, like Local Interconnect Network (LIN), Controller Area Network (CAN), FlexRay, Media Oriented System Transport (MOST), Low Voltage Differential Signaling (LVDS) and so on.

Table 1. Comparisons among different wireless network standards

	GPRS/GSM	WiFi	Bluetooth	ZigBee
Standard	1Xrtt/CDMA	802.11b	802.15.1	802.15.4
Key application	Sound & data	Web, email, images	Cable replacement	Monitor & control
System resource	16 MB+	1 MB+	250 KB+	4–32 KB
Battery life (days)	1–7	0.5–5	1–7	100–1000
Network size	1	32	7	255/65,000
Bandwidth (KB/S)	64–128+	11,000+	720	20–250
Transmission distance (metres)	1000+	1–100	1–10+	1–100+
Advantages	Large coverage	High rate, flexibility	Low price, convenience	Reliability, low power consumption, low price

Table 2 shows current automotive physical layer technologies [39].

Table 2. Current automotive physical layer technologies

	Bitrate	Medium	Protocol
LIN	19.2 Kbps	Single Wire	Serial
CAN	1 Mbps	Twisted Pair	CSMA/CR
FlexRay	20 Mbps	Twisted Pair/Optical Fibre	TDMA
Most	150 Mbps	Optical Fibre	TDMA
LVDS	655 Mbps	Twisted Pair	Serial/Parallel

3.2 Mobile Cloud Computing for Big Data Analysis

The elastic and customized cloud computing platform can help to finish the processing of big data analysis in an efficient manner. As the statistic about the history of different drivers' mood and fatigue history, then based on the analyzed results, we can provide different customized mobility services to drivers based on their real-time mood-fatigue, e.g., recommend preferable music, recommend shortest routes or most enjoyable routes (e.g., if drivers are not fatigue and enjoying traveling), recommend suitable nearby places for taking a rest (e.g., accommodation, restaurants) that fit for the drivers' preferences.

However, despite the wide range application of cloud computing, it is still in its infancy. Many issues need to be explored. For example, the storage technologies and data management. Current technologies of data management systems are not able to satisfy the needs of big data, and the increasing speed of storage capacity is much less than that of data, thus a revolution re-construction of information framework is desperately needed [40]. Also, current databases are not suitable for data from real world. So it is important to re-organize the data for further use.

Besides, reducing energy consumption is another important issue in cloud computing. It has been estimated that the cost of powering and cooling accounts for 53 % of the total operational expenditure of data centers [41]. In 2006, data centers in the US consumed more than 1.5 % of the total energy generated in that year, and the percentage is projected to grow 18 % annually [42]. The goal is not only to cut down energy cost in data centers, but also to meet government regulations and environmental standards [43].

4 Current Platforms for Safe Driving

Lee and Chung [44] proposed a method (SDSM) for monitoring driver safety levels using a data fusion approach based on several discrete data types: eye features, bio-signal variation, in-vehicle temperature, and vehicle speed. The safety monitoring process involves the fusion of attributes gathered from different sensors, including video, electrocardiography, photoplethysmography, temperature, and a three-axis accelerometer, that are mapped as input variables to an inference analysis framework. A Fuzzy Bayesian framework is intended to indicate the driver's capability level and is updated continuously in real-time. The sensory data are transmitted via Bluetooth communication to the smart phone device. Once the evaluation metric reaches 75 % (in FBN probability expressed as 0.75), a fake call service is initiated along with a loud ringtone and maximum vibration strength to alert the driver of his/her current dangerous driving state.

Suk, and Prabhakaran [45] presented a mobile application for real time facial expression recognition running on a smart phone with a camera (RFER). In order to handle the lower processing power in mobile devices (compared to their desktop counterparts), it proposed some approaches based on a set of SVM classifiers that use ASM features for identifying neutral and peak expression video frames. The accuracy of real-time mobile emotion recognition is about 72 % when this application is running on Galaxy S3 with 2.4 fps.

Hu et al. [3] built a Mood-Fatigue Analyzer (MFA) which collects the real-time sensing data from driver behaviors, cars situation, and outside environment by the mobile device tier, cloud tier, and network tier. Then it analyses the data to get the driver's mood and fatigue degree. Finally, it takes measures to ameliorate the driver's emotion and fatigue status such as play suitable music or give positive reminder.

Other in-vehicle solutions for safe driving include V-Cloud [46], CrashHeip [47], and LCCA System [48]. Compared to solutions which only realize the function of detection and alarming, MFA has an incentive to relieve fatigue and raise a better driving experience when drivers are in a negative situation.

Table 3 shows the comparison among these platforms.

Table 3. Comparisons among different platforms for safe driving

		SDSM	RFER	MFS	V-Cloud	CrashHelp	LCCA
Mood-fatigue state detection	Temperature	✓		✓	✓		
	Humidity	✓					
	Speed	✓		✓	✓		
	Expression	✓	✓	✓	✓		
	Bio-signal	✓		✓	✓		
Location						✓	✓
Alarm		✓		✓		✓	✓
Incentive				✓			

5   Technical Challenges and Future Research Directions

5.1   Energy Constraint of Mobile Sensing Network

The energy consumption is the main problem of the sensor network because the sensor nodes are under an unattended condition for a long time. Thus, effective energy saving strategies are necessary.

At present, the sleeping scheme is the most popular strategy, which means the nodes will sleep when they are spare to save the energy. However, when spare nodes convert to normal state, they will consume much energy. So it is important to convert the state at the appropriate time.

Data fusion is another energy-saving technique. Compared to the energy consumed by computing, communication costs more of it. Adjacent nodes often collect similar or same information and sending this redundant information will impose undue burden on the system. By local computing and fusion, the raw data can be processed in accordance with certain procedures and only necessary information will be sent.

5.2   Facial Expression Recognition

Recognizing facial expression with computers is a very complex problem. Precise facial expression recognition is still a task involving much difficulty. First, existing or user-built facial expression databases are tightly constrained, such as single background, no interference of ornament, little rotation of the face, and no exaggerated expression, etc. The six expressions based on Cascade Classifier can't describe human's complicated and changeable expression accurately. To find a more accurate descriptive approach is a vital problem. Also, current facial expression databases are based on single race. Considering that different race and culture have considerable influence on the understanding of expression. The facial expression databases should vary with different areas.

Currently, there are two main facial expression recognition technique: Feature based techniques and Model based techniques [49]. For feature based techniques, authors in [25] proposed a geometric system for breaking down 20 facial appearances with the particular objectives of contrasting, matching, and averaging their shapes. For model based techniques, authors in [28] propose a deformable 3-D facial expression model and D-Isomap based classification. Different strategies like finding key fiducial point inborn geometries are used. These state-of-art progress has made facial expression recognition more precise and thus improve the performance of mood-fatigue detection system,

5.3   Security and Privacy

As the healthcare related data like the history of the drivers' mood and fatigue would be sensitive, it is of great significance to ensure the data safety and privacy. Unlike traditional security method, security in big data is mainly in the form of how to process data mining without exposing sensitive information of users [40]. Besides, existing security solutions are mostly for static data, while in this case data changes dynamically. To ensure the security and privacy, it is critical to build trust mechanisms at every architectural layer of the cloud [45]. Firstly, the hardware layer must be trusted using hardware trusted platform module (TPM). Secondly, the virtualization platform must be trusted using secure virtual machine monitors [50]. VM (virtual machine) migration should only be allowed if both source and destination servers are trusted. Recent work has been devoted to designing efficient protocols for trust establishment and management [50, 51].

6   Conclusions

The rapid development of IoT has brought revolutionary changes to human life, almost covering every aspect of daily life. More and more IoT applications, systems and services are being deployed. The idea of mobile sensing based mood-fatigue detection of drivers takes the advantage of IoT and potentially provides a seamless solution for safe driving. In this paper, we first introduce the current solutions for mood-fatigue detection. After that, we summarize some common sensors and wireless communication techniques in mobile sensing network and conduct a comparison between them. Furthermore, we specifically describe the way to detect the mood-fatigue status of drivers, and introduce some up to date platforms.

In the future, many challenges need to be explored and addressed, so as to enable the detection of facial expression to be in a more precise manner, e.g., adding the detection of other feature like the mouth [3]. Also, the outside environmental conditions, user behaviors and other factors should be taken into consideration to infer the drivers' mood-fatigue status, and the vigilance level more of them comprehensively and accurately. Furthermore, incentive schemes could be explored to facilitate the collaboration of drivers to promote safe driving together. Moreover, social network can be employed to further improve driving experience [52]. Drivers can share their driving experience or radio music with others who have similar music preferences or experience similar traffic conditions [4].

References

1. World Health Organization, Global status report on road safety (2009). http://www.who.int/violence_injury_prevention/road_safety_status/2009/en/
2. Zwaag, M., Dijksterhuis, C., Waard, D., Mulder, B.L.J.M., Westerink, J.H.D.M., Brookhuis, K.A.: The influence of music on mood and performance while driving. Ergonomics 55(1), 12–22 (2012)
3. Hu, W., Hu, X., Deng, J., et al.: Mood-fatigue analyzer: towards context-aware mobile sensing applications for safe driving. In: Proceedings of the ACM Workshop on Middleware for Context-Aware Applications in the IoT (2014)
4. Hu, X., Deng, J., Zhao, J., Hu, W., Ngai, E.C.-H., Wang, R., Shen, J., Liang, M., Li, X., Leung, V.C.M., Kwok, Y.: SAfeDJ: a crowd-cloud co-design approach to situation-aware music delivery for drivers. ACM Trans. Multimedia Comput. Commun. Appl. 12(1s), 21 (2015)
5. Lal, S.K.L., Craig, A.: A critical review of the psychophysiology of driver fatigue. Biol. Psychol. 55(3), 173–194 (2001)

6. Divjak, M., Bischof, H.: Eye blink based fatigue detection for prevention of computer vision syndrome. In: Proceedings of the Conference on Machine Vision Applications (MVA), pp. 350–353 (2009)
7. Williamson, A., Chamberlain, T.: Review of on-road driver fatigue monitoring devices (unpublished)
8. Lin, C.T., Chen, Y.C., Huang, T.Y., Chiu, T.T.: Development of wireless brain computer interface with embedded multitask scheduling and its application on real time driver's drowsiness detection and warning. IEEE Trans. Biomed. Eng. **55**(5), 1582–1591 (2008)
9. Healey, J., Picard, R.: Smart Car: detecting driver stress. In: Proceedings of the IEEE International Conference on Pattern Recognition, vol. 4, pp. 218–221 (2000)
10. Kircher, A., Uddman, M., Sandin, J.: Vehicle Control and Drowsiness. Swedish National Road and Transport Research Institute, Linkoping (2002)
11. Jap, B.T., Lal, S., Fischer, P., Bekiaris, E.: Using EEG spectral components to assess algorithms for detecting fatigue. Expert Syst. Appl. **36**(2), 2352–2359 (2009)
12. Lal, S.K.L., Craig, A., Boord, P., et al.: Development of an algorithm for an EEG based driver fatigue countermeasure. J. Safety Res. **34**(3), 321–328 (2003)
13. Yeo, M.V.M., Li, X.P., Shen, K., et al.: Can SVM be used for automatic EEG detection of drowsiness during car driving. Saf. Sci. **47**(1), 115–124 (2009)
14. Fang, R., Zhao, X., Rong, J., et al.: Study on driving fatigue based on EEG signals. J. Highw. Transp. Res. Dev. **26**(S1), 124–126 (2009)
15. Pate, M., Lala, S.K.L., Kavanagha, D., Rossiterb, P.: Applying neural network analysis on heart rate variability data to assess driver fatigue. Expert Syst. Appl. **38**(6), 7235–7242 (2011)
16. Sharma, N., Banga, V.K.: Development of a drowsiness warning system based on the fuzzy logic. Int. J. Comput. Appl. Technol. **8**(9), 1 6 (2010)
17. Yao, K.P., Lin, W.H., Fang, C.Y., Wang, J.M., Chang, S.L., Chen, S.W.: Real-time vision-based driver drowsiness/fatigue detection system. In: Proceedings of the IEEE Vehicular Technology Conference, pp. 1–5 (2010)
18. Liu, D., Sun, P., Xiao, Y.Q., Yin, Y.: Drowsiness detection based on eyelid movement. In: Proceedings of the IEEE International Workshop on Education Technology and Computer Science (ETCS), pp. 49–52 (2010)
19. Tabrizi, P.R., Zoroofi, R.A.: Open/Closed eye analysis for drowsiness detection. In: Proceedings of the Workshops on Image Processing Theory, Tools and Applications, pp. 1–7 (2008)
20. Berglund, J.: In-Vehicle Prediction of Truck Driver Sleepiness Steering Wheel Variables. Linköpings Universitet, Linköping (2007)
21. Mattsson, K.: In-Vehicle Prediction of Truck Driver Sleepiness Lane Position Variables. Luleå University of Technology, Södertälje (2007)
22. Zhao, W., Chellappa, R., Rosenfeld, A., Phillips, P.J.: Face recognition: a literature survey. ACM Comput. Surv. **35**(4), 399–458 (2003)
23. Taheri, S., Turaga, P., Chellappa, R.: Towards view-invariant expression analysis using analytic shape manifolds. In: Proceedings of the IEEE International Conference on Automatic Face and Gesture Recognition & Workshops (FG) (2011)
24. Tian, Y., Kanade, T., Cohn, J.: Facial expression analysis. In: Handbook of Face Recognition (2005). Chapter 11
25. Drira, H., Ben Amor, B., et al.: 3D face recognition under expressions, occlusions, and pose variations. Pattern Anal. Mach. Intell. **35**(9), 2270–2283 (2013)
26. Elaiwat, S., Bennamoun, M., et al.: 3-D Face recognition using curvelet local features. Biometrics Compendium **21**(2), 172–175 (2014)

27. Lee, S.H., Plataniotis, K.N., et al.: Intra-class variation reduction using training expression images for sparse representation based facial expression recognition. Affect. Comput. **5**(3), 340–351 (2014)
28. Tie, Y., Cuan, L., et al.: A deformable 3-D facial expression model for dynamic human emotional state recognition. Biometrics Compendium **23**(1), 142–157 (2013)
29. Zheng, W.: Multi-view facial expression recognition based on group sparse reduced-rank regression. Affect. Comput. **5**(1), 71–85 (2014)
30. Qiang, J., Zhu, Z., Lan, P.: Real-time nonintrusive monitoring and prediction of driver fatigue. IEEE Trans. Veh. Technol. **53**(4), 1052–1068 (2004)
31. Edenborough, N., et al.: Driver state monitor from delphi. In: Proceedings of the IEEE Computer Society Conference on Computer Vision and Pattern Recognition (CVPR), vol. 2, pp. 1206–1207 (2005)
32. Machine, Seeing. Seeing Machine's website-FaceLAB (2012)
33. Hopkins, J.: Microwave and Acoustic Detection of Drowsiness (2005). http://www.jhuapl.edu/ott/technologies/technology/articles/P01471.asp
34. Samanta, B., Al-Balushi, K.R.: Artificial neural network based fault diagnostics of rolling element bearings using time-domain features. Mech. Syst. Sig. Process. **17**(2), 317–328 (2003)
35. Smart Eye, A. B. Smart Eye Pro (2011)
36. Ridling, B.L.: Insight and Locus of Control as Related to Aggression in Individuals with Severe Mental Illness SMI (2010)
37. Applied Science Laboratories product information. Provided on CD-ROM by Virginia Salem, Customer Relations, Applied Science Laboratories (2005)
38. Hu, X., Li, X., Ngai, E.C.-H., Leung, V.C.M., Kruchten, P.: Multi-dimensional context-aware social network architecture for mobile crowdsensing. IEEE Commun. Mag. **52**(6), 78–87 (2014)
39. Akyildiz, L.F., Su, W., Sankarasubramaniam, Y., Cayirci, E.: A survey on sensor networks. IEEE Commun. Mag. **40**(8), 102–114 (2002)
40. Hu, X., Chu, T.H.S., Leung, V.C.M., Ngai, E.C.-H., Kruchten, P., Chan, H.C.B.: A survey on mobile social networks: applications, platforms, system architectures, and future research directions. IEEE Commun. Surv. Tutorials **17**(3), 1557–1581 (2015)
41. Hamilton, J.: Low cost, low power servers for Internet-scale services. In: Proceedings of Biennial Conference on Innovative Data Systems Research (CIDR) (2009)
42. Kumar, S., et al.: vManage: loosely coupled platform and virtualization management in data centers. In: Proceedings of the International Conference on Cloud Computing, pp. 127–136 (2009)
43. Zhang, Q., Cheng, L., Boutaba, R.: Cloud computing: state-of-the-art and research challenges. J. Internet Serv. Appl. **1**(1), 7–18 (2010)
44. Lee, B., Chung, W.: A smartphone-based driver safety monitoring system using data fusion. Sensors **12**(12), 17536–17552 (2012)
45. Suk, M., Prabhakaran, B.: Real-time mobile facial expression recognition system - a case study. In: Proceedings of the IEEE Conference on Computer Vision and Pattern Recognition Workshops (CVPRW), pp. 132–137 (2014)
46. Abid, H., Phuong, L., Wang, J., Lee, S., Qaisar, S.: V-Cloud: vehicular cyber-physical systems and cloud computing. In: Proceedings of the ACM International Symposium on Applied Sciences in Biomedical and Communication Technologies (2011). Article 165
47. Schooley, B., Hilton, B., Lee, Y., McClintock, R., Horan, T.: CrashHelp: a GIS tool for managing emergency medical responses to motor vehicle crashes. In: Proceedings of the Information Systems for Crisis Response and Management (ISCRAM) (2010)

48. Chan, L., Chong, P.: A lane-level cooperative collision avoidance system based on vehicular sensor networks. In: Proceedings of the ACM International Conference on Mobile Computing and Networking (MobiCom), pp. 131–134 (2013)
49. Mishra, B., Fernandes, S.L., Abhishek, K., et al.: Facial expression recognition using feature based techniques and model based techniques: a survey. In: Proceedings of the IEEE International Conference on Electronics and Communication Systems (ICECS), pp. 589–594 (2015)
50. Santos, N., Gummadi, K., Rodrigues, R.: Towards trusted cloud computing. In: Proceedings of the Conference on Hot Topics in Cloud Computing (HotCloud) (2009)
51. Krautheim, F.J.: Private virtual infrastructure for cloud computing. In: Proceedings of Conference on Hot Topics in Cloud Computing (HotCloud) (2009)
52. Hu, X., Leung, V.C.M., Li, K., Kong, E., Zhang, H., Surendrakumar, N., TalebiFard, P.: Social drive: a crowdsourcing-based vehicular social networking system for green transportation. In: Proceedings of the ACM MSWiM-DIVANet Symposium, pp. 85–92 (2013)

Straight from the Horse's Mouth: "I am an Electric Vehicle User, I am a Risk Taker." [EV14, M, c. 30]

Eiman Y. ElBanhawy$^{(\boxtimes)}$

Department of Computing and Communication,
The Open University, Milton Keynes, UK
eiman.elbanhawy@open.ac.uk

Abstract. The car has become ubiquitous in late modern society. Electric vehicles (EVs) show potential to reduce environmental burdens of the transport sector. EV-niche market acquires more available and reliable charging infrastructure to support current and potential users. The location-allocation of the recharging facilities is not a new planning problem; however, the planning for newly-adopted low carbon emissions vehicles infrastructure has distinctive design requirements, sociotechnical and demographic factors. This paper reports on the end-user's insight and perceptions. Using ethnographic approach, an interview-based study was carried out addressing 15 EV-users in the North East of England. The sample covered a wide spectrum of active EV-users. Clustering analysis is employed as a dimensional technique for data mining and forming the participants' charging profiles. The model generated 3 clusters; each one is presented and discussed. This study presents a new way of capturing the social aspect of the EV-system and reports on qualitative techniques in EV-context.

Keywords: Electric vehicles · Charging preference · Clustering analysis · Recharging network · EV questionnaire · Narrative analysis

1 E-Mobility System

The reason behind the growth or the lack of the electric vehicle (EV) market is multi-faceted. Many factors are responsible, which vary between socio-technical and psycho-temporal. Individuals and families struggle with the decision of owning an EV due to the different issues related to limited range. Perception of EV-resources and in particular the limited resources (battery) shifts by time and differs between individuals. In recent years, the environmental burden of urban road traffic has been of concern to governments and authorities of developed countries [1] with an increasing interest in mitigating this [2] as well as to develop and (re-) design cities to make them greener [3].

Analysing current systems show cases of variant consumers' profiles and preferences, charging behaviour, and supply and demand records. It provides insights on prices, technologies, investment versus payoff perception, barriers, incentives, and standardization [4]. Moreover, coordinating the charging behaviour EV owners via the potential flexibility of charging time would assist with the great challenge the power system would accommodate with the large scale EV use [5].

© ICST Institute for Computer Sciences, Social Informatics and Telecommunications Engineering 2016
A. Leon-Garcia et al. (Eds.): Smart City 2015, LNICST 166, pp. 16–30, 2016.
DOI: 10.1007/978-3-319-33681-7_2

Despite major technological developments in various EV areas of research, there is a list of issues needs to be addressed. Among these, the need for a reliable and diverse recharging infrastructure, which meets different user mobility demand and charging needs, is placed at the forefront [6]. EV stakeholders have been investing in promoting and introducing EV in their fleets and early adopters [7]. Domestic charging (charging at home using 2.3 kW outlet) has positive values: (i) quiet operation, (ii) zero tail-pipe emissions, (iii) maybe green energy in case of solar panel, and (iv) ease of use. However, the minimum driving ranges that EV user should tolerate in order to obtain these positive attributes and prices are not always convenient and do not meet their everyday mobility demand.

Hence, the importance of non-domestic recharging system arose. The uncertainty of having a reliable and integrated recharging infrastructure (non domestic whether workplace or publically available charging points) slows down the growing trend of smart ecosystems and sustainable urban communities as whole. The strategic locations of charging points (CPs) will help with paving the way for a better electric mobility (e-mobility) market penetration.

2 E-Mobility in the Social Media

The current EV users see themselves as a community; they liaise with each other through Social media suggesting indispensable tools and many phone and computer applications that can help the driver to familiarise with the recharging network and all related issues to EV use. The social Media is used for posting updates and spreading news of interest for any other EV user. Passionate EV users tend to help others benefit from their experience and share pieces of information that can assist them in their daily trip, see Fig. 1.

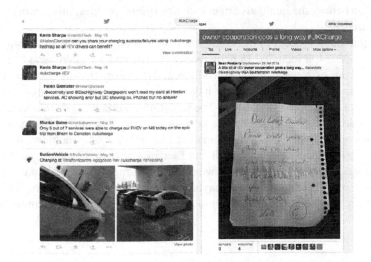

Fig. 1. Twitter: #UKCharge, pieces of information that can assist other EV users and #UKCharge, a tweet shows owner cooperation

Due to the e-mobility network instability, immature monitoring systems and available database, EV drivers always tend to double-check the information from different sources. This happens if the driver is taking a non-routine journey, which requires further planning.

In order to deal with the EV technology, the user attempts to find a mean of communication or interaction with other users to gain reassurance. The use of social Media was and is still one of the tools that EV community uses to interact. It plays a major role in sharing knowledge and experiences among users.

The social mediation evolved by the emergence of EV. Users discuss the social practice especially over social Media. Social influence plays a key role in market dynamics [8], if the hurdles the current users are facing are not resolved, this would result in negative Word of Mouth (WoM) that could lessen EV diffusion in the market [9]. Innovative technology adoption is driven by motivation for purchasing and willingness to pay. Learning processes are a critical dynamic in the spread of new technologies [10]. To advance technologic diffusion beyond the early adopters, EV must appeal to the majority of consumers [11].

3   Methodology – The Interview

In this study we focus on the user's opinion regarding the use of EV. This includes the usability of the car and the infrastructure and preferences. We examine how different age, gender, years driving an EV, driving conditions and styles would affect the use of EV. In order to collect comprehensive opinions, the method employed in this study is an interview. A structured interview was designed and conducted (n = 15). This paper reports on the responses of Newcastle-Gateshead area, in the North East of England. The questionnaire is analysed using narrative analysis for qualitative data and data analytics for quantitative part. Qualitative data includes (purchase process, consumer's perception); whereas, the qualitative data includes (users' profiles, driver workload, and range occurrence).

The requirement process of the users was strictly monitored. The study was carried our in October 2014, it included 15 participants (7 male and 8 female) who live or work in the urban core of Newcastle-Gateshead Area. The selected sample covered a wide spectrum of active EV users who may have access to domestic, workplace or public CPs, users data is provided in Table 1. The selection criteria were developed to ensure that the sample would be representative considering the difficulties of reaching active end users especially when it is a niche market like the current e-mobility market. The participants have been using the EV (Nissan Leaf) for at least 12 months and living or working in the inner urban core of Newcastle. The sample size encompasses private users (own their EVs) and fleet users (maybe used for private purpose). The intention of including fleet users is to get insights into the use of EV from a different angle.

3.1 Sample Size and Recruitment of Participants

A questionnaire-based interview was designed to investigate the EV users preferences and their network spatial awareness of the existing charging infrastructure. Each interview takes approximately 35 min and consists of 4 sets of questions. The interview responses were analysed using content and clustering analyses. In the following lines, each set of questions is presented, followed by analysis. The second part of the article presents the clustering analysis investigating the users profiles and the main predictors that affect the users charging patterns.

Table 1. Participants summary

ID	Ownership	Gender	Age	Home	Mile/day	Home
EV1	Private Car	Male	c. 50	2 years	20 Miles	NE7
EV2	Private Car	Female	c. 30	3 Years	30 Miles	NE21
EV3	Private Car	Male	c. 50	2 years	30 Miles	SR2
EV4	Private Car	Male	c. 50	3 Years	30 Miles	NE25
EV5	Pool Car	Female	c. 30	2 years	30 Miles	DH3
EV6	Pool Car	Male	c. 50	3 Years	20 Miles	NE2
EV7	Pool Car	Female	c. 30	3 Years	10 Miles	NE6
EV8	Pool Car	Female	c. 30	3 Years	10 Miles	NE2
EV9	Pool Car	Male	c. 40	3 Years	40 Miles	NE38
EV10	Private Car	Male	c. 30	3 Years	10 Miles	NE7
EV11	Private Car	Female	c. 40	3 Years	10 Miles	DH1
EV12	Private Car	Female	c. 30	3 Years	20 Miles	NE3
EV13	Pool Car	Female	c. 30	3 Years	20 Miles	NE21
EV14	Private Car	Male	c. 40	1 Year	40 Miles	DL16
EV15	Pool Car	Female	c. 30	1 Year	10 Miles	NE6

3.2 EV Interview: Participant's Profile, Motivation and EV Use

The first set of questions investigated participant's profiles and purchase intention process. The set contains two questions:

1. *Profile: age, gender, home address and work location?*
2. *What motivated you driving an EV? (Private EV users)*

This section aimed at investigating the attitude toward willingness to use an EV. The first question addressed the participants' profiles, responses were tabulated, see Table 2. Gender and age are basic criteria addressing socio-demographic side of EV and non EV mobility studies. Understanding gender differences is essential to policy, marketing, and EV charging infrastructure deployment to ensure that sustainable mobility is appealing and accessible to all users [12, 13]. Gender has been an influential factor that determines the driving habits. The gender dynamics of consumer tastes in the context of EV was addressed in previous studies [14, 15]. In order to explore the possible nexus between the different dependent variables that affect use of EV, the

Table 2. EV participants' age versus gender (n = 15)

Drivers	Male	Female
c. 30	7 %	47 %
c. 40	13 %	7 %
c. 50	27 %	0 %

variables are assessed with respect to the gender. The first variable is the age, see Table 2. The majority of users are senior males and young females.

The second question addressed the decision of electric driving (particularity owning an EV referring to private users). Usually the main intention to purchase is a replacement of an old car or shifting to car as a primary form of mobility [7]. The participants (n = 15) responded to this question differently. Motivations ranged between the environmental concerns of conventional means of transport 40 %, the habit of being a technology geek 8 %, long-term based financial calculations 30 %, the self-satisfaction of being early adopters 12 % or a risk taker (social image) 10 %. The users indicated their opinions about purchase intention process.

> "I had an accident and my car was a total loss. I had a road trip with my friend who has an EV, and guess what, the very next day I decided my next car is NissanLeaf."[EV 2, F, c.30]
> "I am happy to use an EV but still will not buy my own."[EV 6, M, c.50]
> "I would recommend the EV for those who commute short distances to work." [EV 12, F, c.30]
> "I am very passionate about it. I work for a service provider and I can see a very positive future of charging points deployment." [EV 12, M, c.40]

The purchase decision takes time and passes through phases. Based on the interviewers' responses to this question and to the following "Access to charge" question, a flowchart was drawn to illustrate the process and the process may end up purchasing a conventional car. One of the key factors is to have access to charging (domestic) and workplace.

3.3   EV Interview: Access to Charge, Workplace and Charging Frequency

The second set of questions addressed charging preferences and daily trips. The set contains five questions:

3. *Do you have access to domestic charging? Workplace charging? If you do not have access to domestic charging, would you still consider having an EV?*
4. *What is the average of your daily destinations? (Number of destinations you reach-number of trips) Example: 2 destinations (xxxx and yyyy)*
5. *How many times (in days) you drive your EV/week?*
6. *How many times you charge your EV/week?*
7. *What is the usual SOC that you arrive to a charging point? Example: 20 miles left OR 10 % of the battery charge left*

The third question is associated with the purchase intention and process. All private users responded that they would not have contemplated buying an EV if there was no access to a domestic charging. However, this is not the case for all EV users, fleet users have a different opinion.

"I do not worry too much about the non domestic charging, I do the daily trip planning briefly on my head as there are only 3 or four destinations."[EV 1,M, c.50]
"My wife always asks me if I charged my car though she never voluntarily plug it in when both at home".[EV4, M, c.50]
"I drive my EV for everyday use. This does not mean I can only rely on domestic charging."
[EV11, F, c.40]
"I am a fleet user, I never charged at home."[EV13, F, c.30]

The second milestone of the purchase intention process is the workplace charging which was reflected by the respondents' feedback. Recently, workplace charging has gained more attention by the stakeholders and the end-users. After checking the domestic access, the selection of the EV model takes place. By this the attitude phase finishes and the use of EV starts where the driving and charging behaviour commences [16].

"I live 3 miles away from work, I do not have kids at school, and Nissan Office is next my Office, so why to worry? However, if any of these parameters changes, I have no idea what to do."
[EV2, F, c.30]
"I used to charge at home until I know that I may charge at work and even cheaper. Now my domestic charger is the workplace one."[EV14, M, c.40]

The fourth, fifth and sixth questions addressed the number of destinations per day and the use and charge frequency of the EV over the week, see Fig. 2 for a sample of visualization of two participants (private and fleet). The average of weekday-daily destination rate is two (work + school (drop-Off/pickup)); however, the school is on the way home, which does not consume more than two to four miles extra to the road trip.

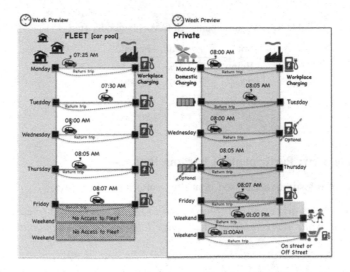

Fig. 2. Visualisation of fleet versus private EV users

The workplace charging practice has a different nature than public recharging network. Employers as public or private bodies, promote an environmental image by providing CPs (workplace CPs) and offers EVs to their employees. This refers to two other types of cars: i) fleet for work use only and ii) fleet for work and private use. The first type is the case of fleet users interviewed. Furthermore, community interest groups like public access car clubs, started to include EVs in their fleet [17]. Car sharing is becoming more and more common. The UK is the largest European carpool representing 12.1 % of the total EU fleet. Charging facilities shared by staff members and visitors requires an internal communication platform. EV4 is a participant who has access to workplace charging facility. There, the EV users communicate with each other to manage the shared charging facilities via internal system. The fifth question addressed the weekly charging frequency. The main differences arose between the private and the fleet users, see Table 3. The private users tend to charge from five to seven times a week (domestic + workplace). Fleet users charge only at workplace with a different frequency depending on the number of users charging the car and their locations. The gender had an effect on participants' responses to SOC related question, see Table 4. The seventh question regarded the usual SoC on arrival.

Table 3. EV participants' charging frequency versus ownership (n = 15)

Charge/W	Private	Fleet
2	0 %	10 %
3	5 %	20 %
4	0 %	0 %
5	15 %	10 %
6	0 %	0 %
7	30 %	10 %

Table 4. EV participants' SoC versus gender (n = 15)

SoC	Male	Female
Below 20 %	7 %	0 %
20 %	7 %	20 %
30 %	20 %	13 %
50 %	13 %	20 %

3.4   EV Interview: Participants' Charging Patterns

The third set of questions addressed charging patterns as follows:

8. *Do you commute across postal zones in NE to reach your work? (please specify the first part of your work address) Example: I live NE4 and commute to work in NE33)*

9. *How can you describe your driving comfort zone? (time, mileage, or area). Example: After commuting "XX" miles, I start to feel worried about my state of charge (Attitude)*

10. *What is the minimum SoC you can tolerate?*

The eight question aimed at identifying the daily-mileage commuted by EV users by counting the number of the postal zones the participants drive through from home (origin) to work (destination). The responses to this question are included in the clustering analysis, which is discussed later in the article. The ninth question is more attitude-oriented, asking the respondents about their range personal preferences. From this perspective, the higher the percentage the individual indicates, the more conservative they are in using their cars (less confident). A further 7 % (males) of respondents reported a wide comfort zone driving an EV. This means tolerating a very low battery (one to two cells charged out of 12 or below 20 % SoC). No occurrence of female respondents expanded their comfort zone to the same extent. The smaller the comfort zone (closer to the origin), the more the female drivers occur. At a small comfort zone circle (equivalent to 50 % charged or more), 20 % was female and 13 % were males, see Table 5.

Table 5. EV participants' charging behaviour versus gender (n = 15)

SoC % left	Comfort Zone	Male	Female
Below 20 %	(1-2 cells)/12 cells	27 %	13 %
20 %	(3-4 cells)/12 cells	13 %	13 %
30 %	(5-6 cells)/12 cells	0 %	20 %
50 %	(7-9 cells)/12 cells	7 %	7 %

The respondents indicated that they would experience severe anxiety by reaching this stage, but it is not on an everyday basis or even weekly. They reported that this only happens when:

"I have been driving my car for 3 years now, I usually reach 15 % charge on my third day on a raw not charging, this happens when I arrive at the workplace to charge. Yes, I do have anxiety by then, but manageable because I know where to charge."[EV4, M, c.50]

"Below 20 %? This never happened to me and I will make sure it does not happen. I will be scared to death."[EV8, F, c.30]

"My anxiety differs. It depends on where I am and how familiar I am with the vicinity (charging points/nearby home charger at friends."[EV11, F, c.40]

"Being down to 20 % SoC is not in my favour. This may take place only if I have strictly necessary trip and will prefer finding alternative charging solutions."[EV11, F, c.40]

"I do not see this possible, having said my routine and charging accessibility. But yes, I will be having a severe anxiety."[EV12, F, c.30]

"It happened once before I installed my domestic charger, and I promised myself it will never happen again. I can not even foresee this as I do not use my car that spontaneously, yet."[EV14, M, c.40]

The tenth question addressed the charging behaviour. The respondent was asked to indicate the minimum SoC ever reached. On the contrary, the lower the percentages the respondents indicated, the more confident they are. This question is addressing their everyday patterns as what is the lowest state they reached spanning their driving experience. This question is different to the usual SoC when arriving at a CP. The latter would indicate when the user tends to charge (whenever possible or when needed). Fleet users didn't reach a low charge due to charging accessibility and limited distances commuted. Additionally, females (13 %) indicated that it was under very special circumstances that they reached this level.

> *"I didn't charge on Monday at the work, I went to pick a friend from Newcastle Airport on Tuesday and was having a meeting outside my company premises on Wednesday. On my way back home after the meeting I was a little bit worried as it was my first time seeing my carwings reading 20 % charged!"[EV 2, F, c.30] (Carwings software is Nissan user interface UI)*

The results showed how different the perception and the actual values can be with regard to minimum SoC, An inconsistency is observed when analysing the interviews. The records of some respondents, who indicated a tolerance to an expanded comfort zone, were inconsistent in terms of minimum SoC. A further 60 % of users have indicated a conservative experienced SoC compared to their indicated comfort zone values. However, two cases (EV2 and EV4) reported that they experienced EV range anxiety (EVRA) [18] as the minimum SoCs they reached were below their comfort zone values. The users justified that these two cases happened under special circumstances. Out of 15 users, 26 % (3 males and 1 female) have inconsistency in their attitude-behaviour process. Although it is based on direct experience (as being active users for more than one year), those users experienced different minimum SoCs than the tolerable values they indicated. This does not mean that the SoC Perception and Action percentages should have been identical. Users at the point of the interview may not have had the chance to experience full electric range although they were willing to. However, the inconsistency, which is referred to, pertains specific cases (EV6, EV9, EV10 and EV15), where the two values showed a significant difference.

3.5   EV Interview: Participants' Perceptions

The fourth set of questions explored the travel demand, flexibility of and willingness to spend time charging an EV over the course of a journey.

11. *In which road trip you usually charge your car? (maybe multiple)*
12. *EV Range: Does the confidence level improve by practice?*
13. *During weekdays, how much time are you willing to spend to charge?*
14. *Is there any time of the day at which you regularly struggle to find an empty CP?*

The eleventh question aimed at identifying (timing/road trip) of the non-domestic charging events made by the participants. The respondents were asked to identify in which trip purpose the charging event likely occurs. As for the non-domestic CPs', 90 % of respondents charge in the morning on their way to work or at noontime at the workplace. The twelfth question ascertained the relationship between the years of driving an EV and the user's confidence of driving an EV. The majority of the

Table 6. EV participants experience versus gender (n = 15)

Drivers	Male	Female
Newly Joined	14 %	13 %
Experienced	29 %	13 %
Early Adapters	57 %	75 %

participants have been driving an EV for 3 years (females and males). Only two participants (male and female) had been driving for one year, see Table 6.

The thirteenth and fourteenth questions were designed to identify the anticipated peak time of charging using the non-domestic network (to be included in the clustering analysis).

4 EV Study Clustering Analysis

The second part of the article discusses the clustering model. A TwoStep analysis was conducted to categorise the (n = 15) users into different groups based on the recorded attributes. Due to the mix of categorical (gender, locations, CPs) and contentious (state of charge, age, years of driving) data types, the TwoStep method was chosen instead of the other two approaches: the hierarchical and k-means. The TwoStep generates a report with some graphs and figures showing the cluster quality, see Fig. 3a. The clustering process took several iterations until the most coherent structure was reached. The decision is made based on the cluster quality, a reasonable number of clusters, and the ratio of clusters' sizes to each other (the biggest to the smallest). The quality should not be poor, and the ratio should not exceed three. As for the predictors (the influential factors affecting the clusters formation), willingness to spend time charging scored the first non-polar attribute that affected the clusters membership formation. The second most influential non-polar predictor was the number of charges/week. The third-ranked predictor was the number of destinations/day, see Fig. 3b.

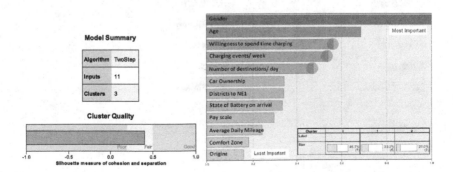

Fig. 3. (a) clustering quality bar, (b) clustering predictors

Frequency of use/week, willingness to spend time charging, domestic or non domestic, and willingness to use *on street* were the points of assessment and evaluation of the formation of the clusters membership. Spatiotemporal analysis of charging patterns was conducted using SPSS Statistics 21 [19]. The model output reflected the traits of the participants and managed to form a heterogeneous three clusters. The first group was termed, "The Risk Takers", see Fig. 4a. It is the second biggest cluster, and contains individuals in the age group of 50–59 years old who had been driving their own EV now for more than three years. The majority were males who usually commute around 30 miles a day. They preferred the *on street* CPs (such as the Grey street one, CP #20059). The number of destinations was two and they lived two miles away from the city centre. This group can tolerate up to 30 % left in their batteries. Users of this group are the lucky few who have access to CPs; however, they can tolerate low charge with a high confidence levels of getting back home safely. The records showed that they charge 5 times a week, however, they drive around the city and reach the CP with only 30 % charged. Those individuals are not happy and willing to spend more time charging; however, they see that investment in RFs is necessary. Compared to other groups, this group considered themselves as risk takers, they tolerate that their SoC being pulled down to 5 % and then they start to worry about finding a CP. The majority of this group lived and worked outside the study area, commuting and passing through every day.

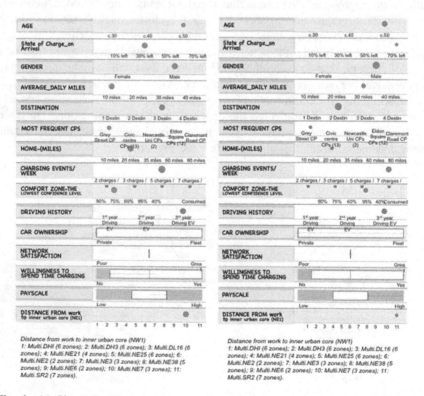

Distance from work to inner urban core (NW1)
1: Multi.DHI (6 zones); 2: Multi.DH3 (6 zones); 3: Multi.DL16 (6 zones); 4: Multi.NE21 (4 zones); 5: Multi.NE25 (6 zones); 6: Multi.NE2 (2 zones); 7: Multi.NE3 (3 zones); 8: Multi.NE38 (5 zones); 9: Multi.NE6 (2 zones); 10: Multi.NE7 (3 zones); 11: Multi.SR2 (7 zones).

Fig. 4. (a) Cluster 1: "The Risk Takers"-SPSS, (b) Cluster 2: "The Old School"-SPSS

The second group was termed "The Old School", see Fig. 4b. The cluster contains individuals in the age group 50–59 who had been driving their own EV for 3 years. The majority were males and they tend to commute around 10 miles a day, two destinations a day and they live 2 miles away from the city centre. It is suggested that this group has low confidence levels. They charged seven times a week and their SoC is always relatively high when they arrive at the CP, 70 % charged. Those individuals are willing to spend more time charging their batteries within the day.

The third group was termed "The Opportunists". The cluster contains individuals in the age group 30–39 who have been driving an EV for three years. They do not own an EV; they go for the work-provided EV car pool option. The drivers of this group are females who commute 10 miles a day on average. The number of destinations was two and they live two miles away from the city centre. The car they use is usually charged at the workplace. This reflects the seven charges a week and explains why the state of charge when arriving at the CP is relatively high, 50 % full of charge. Those individuals were not willing to spend more time in charging their batteries within the day.

5   Commenting the EV Study's Clustering Results

The EV user study presented a new way of investigating the users' charging patterns, spatial awareness, and recharging network recognition. With the clustering analysis, the users' profiles were created and formed into groups with shared characteristics. These clusters may help the stakeholders to elicit the picture of the current system's users and work on satisfying their mobility and charging needs and demand. Each of the three-formed clusters has different paradigms. The Risk Takers are psychologically ready to deal with RA. They are willing to invest on infrastructure; however, they are not willing to spend time on charging especially the *On Street* option unless it is a quick charger. This means that the investment in slow chargers (types 1 and 2) is not in their favour or at least not to their preference, and may result in them not using slow chargers.

The Old School cluster has an issue with the driving pattern. It seemed that they do not expand their comfort zone. This zone is not metric measured; it is about the lowest state of charge at which they are confident to drive their cars. They can only consume up to 30 % of their battery and within the comfort zone. They do not go further than their home, workplace or the zones within which they know they have access to charging. This group is cautious and conservative and do not tend to practise the full electric range.

The third group is The Opportunists, which included those individuals who are the majority of current users. This cluster supports workplace CPs. The Opportunists are aware of the environmental burden of conventional means of transport, they were happy to take initiatives; however, they cannot afford owning a private EV. The way they contribute to the EV market is by car-pooling, using employers fleet and charge at workplace [20].

6 Conclusion

The paper reported on an EV user study. The interview aimed at investigating the users' charging patterns, profiles, each sub-set of questions focused on a particular facet of the e-mobility system of Newcastle-Gateshead area. The interview questions interrogated the driving confidence issue, EVRA, and the associated variables with the use of EV in its urban context. These variables were included in a clustering model, which generated three main clusters of EV users.

The clusters' assessment is articulated in Table 7. It presents the evaluation criteria of the three EV users clusters in relation to the size of each group. The assessment shows the imbalanced state of the e-mobility system of Newcastle-Gateshead area. As per the sample size, only 30 % of the users were happy to practice the full range of the EV and had high confidence level, the risk takers. Those users were not willing to spend time charging, which means they require quick charge (50–250 kw) and may relate to users who tend to top up their batteries on the go using *on street* CPs. Another suggestion is that they stay relatively longer using *off street* CPs (including workplace) in the case of using slow chargers while considering their available time to charge. The Opportunists cluster forms over 50 % of the sample size and this might be an explanation of the e-mobility low market penetration level. They use the non-domestic CPs; however, they tend not to use the publically available CPs as most of their charging events are made at the workplace.

Table 7. EV participants' clusters assessment table

Assessment	The Risk Takers	The Old School	The Opportunistic
Sample size %	30 %	15 %	55 %
Frequency of use/week	80 %	100 %	100 %
Willingness to spend time	Low	High	N/A
Domestic or non domestic	Domestic/On Street	Domestic,workplace,*Off Street*	Workplace
Willingness to use *On street*	Yes, quick charge	Yes	do not own EVs

This leaves only 15 % of the sample size, the Old School cluster, which uses the recharging network relatively more than others. They are willing to spend time charging and invest in installing more CPs. This group is widely spread and they are using both *on* and *off street* CPs alongside the workplace, if any.

To conclude, the paper discussed a selected sample of Newcastle-Gateshead area EV users. Those users vary in their charging preferences and demand, which were associated with their demographics. Although the sample size is statistically small, compared to the available EV owners it is reasonable. The sample covered private and fleet spectrum with different occupation, gender and age ranges. Studying existing system while giving attention to the social aspect interrogates new correlations, provides insights, and justifies the system's dynamics.

For a better diffusion of EV, these clusters should not exist as the way they are. A mix of EV technology literates, who appreciate the long-term benefits of owning an EV and can trust the EV more, is the profile that we should be aiming to have. The Risk Takers need to be merged with the Old School and the Opportunists in order to have a reasonable and stable EV population who are willing to:

- *Pay for a privately owned EV;*
- *Use the recharging network more often and maybe amend their daily routine accordingly;*
- *Spend more time charging;*
- *Expand their comfort zone and experience the full electric range;*
- *Invest in installing slow chargers (quick chargers are too expensive in a larger scale);*

And finally, the contribution of this study can be formulated in two means:

- *Methodological approach: The study provides a methodological approach by employing the presented approach to analyse other existing e-mobility system*
- *Replication: The three clusters can be applied at a wider scale in another similar urban context. A similar urban system may refer to a city with (ex. an organic planned layout with EV population of both private and fleet, and with an existing system including on and off street CPs).*

Acknowledgement. This study is an outcome of a doctoral research that was funded by e-mobility NSR project. The author would like to thank MKSmart project at the Open University for supporting the research and the future work. Previous publications can be found at: https://uk.linkedin.com/pub/eiman-el-banhawy-phd/11/316/36a.

References

1. OLEV: Plug-in vehicle infrastructure grants: the successful organisations. UK (2013)
2. Orsato, R.J.: Sustainability Strategies: When Does It Pay to Be Green?. INSEAD Business Press, Basingstoke (2009)
3. Breithaupt, M.: Towards liveable cities- international experiences. In: The Future of Mobility Options for Sustainable Transport in a Low Carbon Society. Expo (2010)
4. Elbanhawy, E.Y., Dalton, R.: Spatiotemporal analysis of the e-mobility system in Newcastle-Gateshead area. In: 10th International Space Syntax Symposium, SSS10, p. 69 (2015)
5. Guo, Q., Wang, Y.,Sun, H., Li, Z., Xin, S., B. Zhang, "Factor Analysis of the Aggregated Electric Vehicle Load Based on Data Mining," *Energies*, pp. 2053–2070, 2012
6. Brenna, M., Dolara, A., Foiadelli, F., Leva, S.: Urban scale photovoltaic charging stations for electric vehicles. IEEE Trans. Sustain. ENERGY **5**(4), 1949–3029 (2014)
7. Rolim, C., Baptita, P., Farias, T.: Electric vehicle adopters in lisborn: motivation, utilization, patterns and environment impacts. EJTIR **14**(3), 229–243 (2014)

8. Axsen, J., Orlebar, C., Skippon, S.: Social influence and consumer preference formation for pro-environmental technology: The case of a U.K. workplace electric-vehicle study. Ecol. Econ. **95**, 96–107 (2013)
9. Kearney, M.: Electric Vehicle Charging Infrastructure Deployment: Policy Analysis Using a Dynamic Behavioral Spatial Model. MIT (2011)
10. Turrentine, T., Lee-Gosselin, M., Kurani, K., Sperling, D.: A study of adaptive and optimizing behaviour for electric vehicles based on interactive simulation games and revealed behaviour of electric vehicle owners. In: World Conference on Transport Research (1992)
11. Cooper, L.: Electric vehicle diffusion and adoption an examination of the major factors of influence over time in the US market. Haskoli Island (2014)
12. Caperello, N., TyreeHageman, J., Kurani, K.: Engendering the Future of Electric Vehicles: Conversations with Men and Women. Davis (2014)
13. Franke, T., Krems, J.F.: Interacting with limited mobility resources: Psychological range levels in electric vehicle use. Transp. Res. Part A **48**, 109–122 (2013)
14. Hjorthol, R.: Attitudes, Ownership and Use of Electric Vehicles – A Review of Literature Oslo (2013)
15. SwitchEV: SwitchEV Final Report, Newcastle Upon Tyne, UK (2013)
16. Turrentine, T., Lentz, A.: The UC Davis MINI E Consumer Study Authors (2011)
17. CoWheels: Co-Wheels Club (2011). http://www.co-wheels.org.uk/electric_vehicles. Accessed 01 Jan 2015
18. Nilsson, M.: ELVIRA, Electric Vehicle: The Phenomenon of Range Anxiety. Lindholmen Science Park, Sweden (2011)
19. SPSS: SPSS 21 (2012)
20. Elbanhawy, E.Y., Price, B.: Understanding the social practice of EV workplace charging. In: Purba, p. 12 (2015)

Automated Pedestrians Data Collection
Using Computer Vision

Tarek Sayed, Mohamed Zaki[✉], and Ahmed Tageldin

Department of Civil Engineering, University of Bristish Columbia, Vancouver, Canada
{tsayed,mzaki,tageldin}@mail.ubc.ca

Abstract. Active modes of travel such as walking are being encouraged in many cities to mitigate traffic congestion and to provide health and environmental benefits. However, the physical vulnerability of pedestrians may expose them to severe consequences when involved in traffic collisions. This paper presents three applications for automated video analysis of pedestrian behavior. The first is a methodology to detect distracted pedestrians on crosswalks using their gait parameters. The methodology utilizes recent findings in health science concerning the relationship between walking gait behavior and cognitive abilities. In the second application, a detection procedure for pedestrian violations is presented. In this procedure, spatial and temporal crossing violations are detected based on pattern matching. The third study addresses the problem of identifying pedestrian evasive actions. An effective method based on time series analysis of the walking profile is used to characterize the evasive actions. The results in the three applications show satisfactory accuracy. This research is beneficial for improving the design of pedestrian facilities to promote pedestrian safety and walkability.

Keywords: Pedestrian data collection · Computer vision · Road safety · Surrogate measures

1 Introduction

Active modes of travel such as walking are being encouraged in urban cities to project a positive environmental impact and to improve the well-being of the population. However, the physical vulnerability of pedestrians may expose them to severe consequences when involved in traffic collisions. Pedestrians who are jaywalking or engaged in distracted activities such as using their cellphones while crossing a road facility are at the risk of being exposed to unsafe and conflicting situations. In such instances, identifying violations and distraction can provide a reliable surrogate road safety measure, whenever road collisions are attributable to non-conforming behavior. Similarly, pedestrian evasive actions, mainly manifested in the variations of walking behavior can provide useful measures of traffic interactions. Sudden changes of direction, walking speed or even stopping are characteristic actions that pedestrians adopt as strategies to avoid collision. It is therefore suggested that behavioral based traffic conflict indicators can be considered as an alternative to assess traffic safety in less organized, high road

© ICST Institute for Computer Sciences, Social Informatics and Telecommunications Engineering 2016
A. Leon-Garcia et al. (Eds.): Smart City 2015, LNICST 166, pp. 31–43, 2016.
DOI: 10.1007/978-3-319-33681-7_3

user mix driving cultures. However, comprehensive engineering programs can be hindered by limitations in collision data quality as well as gaps in research related to pedestrian behavior and data collection. The analysis of walking gait behavior is an active research area in health science where different methodologies are developed to understand how the walking mechanism changes under varying conditions. The main goal of this paper is expanding the application of computer vision to detect and analyze pedestrian behavior and safety. Several applications are discussed.

The first application examines the possibility of automatically detecting distracted pedestrians on crosswalks using their gait parameters. The methodology invokes recent findings in health science concerning the relationship between walking gait behavior and cognitive abilities. Walking speed and gait variability are shown to be affected by the complexity of tasks (e.g., texting) that are performed during walking. Experiments are performed on a video data set from Surrey, British Columbia. The second case study addresses the automated analysis of pedestrian data collection and conformance behavior. Two types of violations are considered for analysis: spatial and temporal violations. Spatial violations occur when a pedestrian crosses in non-designated crossing regions. Temporal violations occur when a pedestrian crosses an intersection during an improper traffic signal phase. In this analysis, the automated violation detection is performed using pattern matching. The analysis is applied to an intersection with a perceived high rate of traffic conflicts in the Downtown Eastside of Vancouver, British Columbia. The third application addresses the problem of understanding and detecting pedestrian evasive actions during safety critical situations. There is increasing evidence that conventional traffic conflict indicators such as Time-to-Collision (TTC) and Post-Encroachment-Time (PET) lack the ability to describe conflict severity in many traffic environments and may need to be combined with other indicators for safety diagnosis [1, 2]. In this work, a novel method based on time series analysis of the pedestrian walking prolife is used to identify pedestrian evasive actions. The analysis is applied on a data set from Shanghai, China.

This research can benefit applications in several transportation related fields such as pedestrian facility planning, pedestrian simulation models as well as road safety programs.

2   Computer Vision Methodology

The pedestrian analysis methodology uses a video analysis system to automatically detect, classify, and track road users and interpret their movements. The positional analysis of road users requires accurate estimation of the camera parameters. Once calibrated, it is possible to recover real-world coordinates of points in the video sequence that lie on a reference surface with known model (pavement surface). The accuracy of the developed method was examined in [3] and was found to be adequate for positioning slow-moving road users such as pedestrians. The foundation of the tracking system relies on feature-based tracking [4] where important points are tracked on moving objects (Fig. 1.a). The subsequent step is to select a point that moves at similar speed and satisfy other motion constraints to the same coherent object (Fig. 1.b) [4]. Road users are classified into vehicles and pedestrians (Fig. 1.c). The tracking and classification accuracy were presented in [5, 6] and is considered satisfactory.

(a) Features Tracking   (b) Features Grouping

(c) Road-users Classification

Fig. 1. Illustrations for the computer vision based analysis

3 Application 1: Automated Distraction Detection Based on Pedestrian Gait Analysis

This case study uses traffic videos from a location in Surrey, British Columbia. The Surrey data is collected for a major 4-legged intersection. A camera position is used to capture the intersection, as shown in Fig. 2. In this experiment, 50 pedestrians who are looking or typing on their phone are selected along with 98 pedestrians who are not distracted. The selection was performed by a traffic expert using an elaborate and vigilant review to avoid errors in the manual ground truth labeling. Each pedestrian was described by the manual reviewer in detail so that its state could later be compared to the automatically classified one. Figure 2.c illustrates trajectories for distracted pedestrians using their phone while crossing the intersection. For ground truth, the distraction state for each pedestrian is labeled manually based on a good observers' judgment.

(a) Study Location

(b) Video Image with Trajectories

(c) Distraction Tracking Illustrations

Fig. 2. Intersection in surrey, BC

Walking speed is estimated by placing screens around the region of interest and measuring the amount of time it takes for the pedestrian trajectory to cross this region. Walking mechanism can be explained through the spatio-temporal gait parameters (step length and frequency [7, 8]) that can be extracted from the pedestrian trajectories. Step frequency is defined as the number of times a foot touches the ground in a unit of time. The distance between those two instances is defined as the step length. Each pedestrian step is observed to introduce a periodic fluctuation in the speed profile which enables the measurement of the gait parameters such as step frequency and step length. The detection of the dominant periodicities in the speed profile is performed using the power spectral density (PSD) estimation of the speed profile signal [9].

In addition, other gait variables are measured including the walk ratio which represents the relationship between the amplitude and frequency of the rhythmic leg movements when walking. Deviations from the normal walk ratio during free walking may reveal a degree of abnormal walking patterns [10]. Other features include the Acceleration root mean square (RMS A_{rms}) which measures the dispersion of the normalized acceleration profile. The RMS value indicates the degree of gait variability, thus, a higher RMS indicates a higher degree of variability and a lower degree of stability [11]. Acceleration Auto correlation (AAC) measure of the stride similarity and regularity by examining the similarity of the acceleration profile shape. A higher AAC value indicates a greater degree of gait stability [11].

Results Summary. The distraction state estimation is performed using k-nearest neighbors (kNN) classification procedure. KNN assigns a class (state) to a pedestrian based on a majority vote of its k-nearest neighbors; obtained from a training dataset of labeled pedestrians. Pedestrian features data is divided into two subsets; a constraint subset for training and a validation subset for performance evaluation. Maximum correct classification CCR is around 80 % for the different combination of relevant features. The classification performance is also evaluated by means of receiver operating characteristics (ROC), which quantify the trade-off between the detection rate (the percentage of positive examples correctly classified) and the false positive rate (the percentage of negative examples

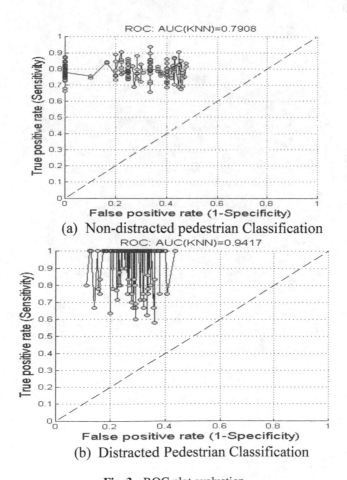

(a) Non-distracted pedestrian Classification

(b) Distracted Pedestrian Classification

Fig. 3. ROC plot evaluation

incorrectly classified). Figure 3 compares the performance of the different runs of the classification with different features selection. Figure 3.a shows a true positive rate (non-distracted pedestrian classified as a non-distracted) of 87 % at a false-positive rate (distracted pedestrian classified as non-distracted pedestrian) of around 0 %. The KNN classification achieved a 90 % correct detection rate at less than 20 % false negative. ROC plot is also shown for the correct distraction classification where a true positive rate (distracted pedestrian classified as a distracted) of 80 % at false positive rate (non-distracted pedestrian classified as distracted pedestrian) of around 10 %. KNN method achieved 100 % correct detection rate at less than 15 % false negative. This result shows the trade-off that is inherently involved in the classification process. A selection of the "best" classifier can then be dependent on the target data collection application. For example, if a practitioner is interested in gathering information about the rate of distracted pedestrians; then the choice of the classifier will rely on the analysis provided in Fig. 3.b.

(a) Satellite View of the Intersection

(b) Video Capture of the Location

Fig. 4. Location characteristics

4 Application 2: Automated Analysis of Pedestrians Non-conforming Behavior at Urban Crossing

In this application, illegal spatio and temporal crossing violations are automatically identified. The site used in this study is a busy eastside downtown signalized intersection located at East Hastings and Main Streets with a mix of business and residential activities. The intersection layout and the lengths of the crosswalk legs are shown in Fig. 4. The intersection was selected because of a perceived high rate of conflicts between vehicles and pedestrians [12, 13]. Some safety countermeasures have already been implemented at the intersection such as reducing the speed limit from 50 km/H (normal posted speed within Vancouver) to only 30 km/H [12].

Violation Detection Procedure: Violation detection starts with identifying a set of movement prototypes that represent what are considered as normal crossing prototypes. Subsequently, a comparison is conducted between a pedestrian trajectory and normal crossing prototypes. Any significant disagreement between both sequences of positions is interpreted as evidence that the given trajectory represents the movement of a non-conforming pedestrian. The longest common sub-sequence algorithm (LCSS) is adopted for the spatial violation detection. More specifically, the comparison relies on an LCSS similarity measure between the movement prototypes and the trajectories to make decision about the classification [14].

The basic idea of the procedure for detecting temporal violations is to identify pedestrian traversing an intersection segment during an improper signal phase. This is performed by automatically recording the temporal and spatial information of each pedestrian and comparing this information against the provided traffic signal cycles and specified screen lines. The first step of the procedure is to draw the boundaries of the intersection segment. The violation detection is then implemented in two consecutive steps. First, the trajectories of the pedestrians crossing the region of interest, at any given time, are identified. This is achieved by intersecting the trajectories coordinates with the intersection segment. The next step is to identify the time period within which the pedestrian trajectories existed in this segment. This period is then compared against the corresponding signal timing phase. If the time period intersects with a phase when the pedestrian is prohibited to cross, then the pedestrian is labeled as violator, otherwise it is labeled as non-violator.

Results Summary. First, the violation classification procedure is applied to estimate pedestrian compliance rate at the intersection. Pedestrians in the scene are tracked and classified according to the methodology developed in the paper. In the 45 min selected video component, a total of 376 pedestrians were tracked. For validation purposes, pedestrians in the scene were manually identified and classified to be used as ground truth. Figure 5(a) and (b) show respectively the trajectories for the normal and spatial violation pedestrians. A high level of crossing violations by pedestrians was detected in the mid-block region (25.5 percent of pedestrians are crossing illegally). As expected, this westbound approach has an increasing number of violations. The performance of the violation detection is shown using the confusion matrix below (Table 1). At 9.31

percent false detection rate (non-violating pedestrian as violating), a 84.5 percent of correct detection rate of true violator can be achieved. The main factor affecting the correct detection rate is pedestrians moving very close to the crosswalk. Those pedestrians were labeled in the ground truth annotation as non-violating pedestrians. However, proximity to the crosswalk resulted in a prototype matching with high score and therefore classified as non-violating.

Table 1. Confusion matrix

Automatic Manual	Normal	Violator
Normal	253	26
Violator	15	82

(a)Non-violating Pedestrians Trajectories

(b) Spatially Violating Pedestrians Trajectories

(c) Trajectories Prototypes

(d) Temporal Violations

Fig. 5. Pedestrians trajectories

Additionally, a manual review of the video was performed and data collection revealed that of the total pedestrians (450 in total) in the scene, 108 were considered violators. Due to the high definition properties of this video, the majority of the spatially violating pedestrians in the scene were tracked (97 as mentioned earlier). Out of 108 total spatially violating pedestrians, only 11 were missed. This is due to missed detection or over-grouping. Over-grouping occurs when several pedestrians share a common trajectory. This can occur when a group of pedestrians are crossing at a fairly close distance with similar walking speed.

The temporally violating pedestrians were 11. Out of those temporally violating pedestrians, 5 were also spatially violating which shows that a large portion of those temporally violating has a tendency to cross in non-designated area. This is likely due to the tendency of the pedestrians to minimize the travel distance. The automated temporal violation methodology detected all the violation correctly with no false detection of non-violator. It is useful to note that the temporal violation accuracy depends on the precision of the camera calibration as well as the provided signal timing. See Fig. 5.d for the spatial distributions of violating pedestrian trajectories.

5   Application 3: Examining Pedestrian Evasive Actions as a Potential Indicator for Traffic Conflicts

This study addresses the problem of understanding and detecting pedestrian evasive actions during safety critical situations. The analysis is demonstrated on a data set collected at a busy congested intersection in the city of Shanghai, China. The intersection has a high mix of different road-users (vehicles, motorcycles, bicycles and pedestrians). The layout of the intersection camera field of view is shown in Fig. 6. Generally, the traffic indicated disorganised road-user behaviour and many conflicts resulting from risky actions and lack of compliance to regulations.

Fig. 6. The layout of the intersection camera field of view

Once the road-users trajectories are extracted, possible conflicts between road-users are detected conflicts between road-users are determined by evaluating if any of their future positions coincide spatially and/or temporally with each other. Time-to-Collision (TTC) and Post-Encroachment-Time (PET) conflict indicators are evaluated as described in [14].

Evasive actions performed by pedestrians are reflected in the pedestrian change of speed or direction. However, these changes are sometimes not apparent in the signal of the pedestrian movement. The ordinal time-series analysis is a complexity measure that can detect qualitative changes of the underlying dynamics in a time series. The ordinal analysis finds a proper abstraction of the pedestrian walking profile that prunes redundant information while retaining qualitative properties relevant to the evasive action analysis. A pedestrian trajectory with varying dynamics will have therefore a varying complexity. The dynamical complexity measured by Permutation Entropy (PE), is the basic Shannon entropy applied with the ordinal patterns as the symbolic words. The formal procedure of the ordinal analysis and permutation entropy procedure is summarized in [15]. This application examines the use of PE in identifying pedestrian evasive actions. PE is adopted to identify behavioural changes in the pedestrian walking pattern at the onset of potential conflicts.

Figure 7 provides illustrations of two different pedestrian situations with vehicles and their corresponding PE profiles. The first is a pedestrian walking normally and then start running as a response to being in a conflict with a turning vehicle shown in Fig. 7a. This pedestrian speed shows the sudden change as a result of the evasive action. This change is reflected in the PE profile as a hard drop. On the other side, the second example shows a steady moving pedestrian maintaining the same walking steps pattern in spite of being in a conflict in Fig. 7b. In this case, the cyclic signal of speed maintains a constant pattern and accordingly there is no change in the PE profile. The PE drop obtained from different pedestrian conflicts can be a good indicator for the evasive action behaviour of pedestrians. The next step is to analyse the PE drop obtained from different conflicts towards the evasive action exerted by the pedestrian.

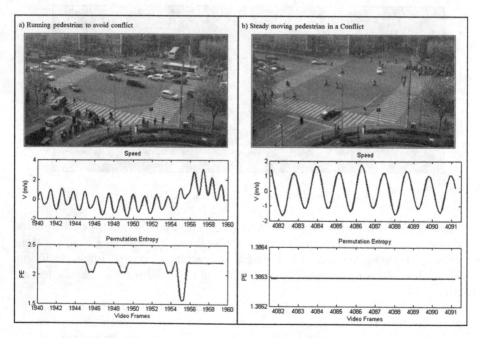

Fig. 7. Pedestrians involved in conflicts and the corresponding speed and permutation entropy profile (a) pedestrian start running to avoid conflict (b) pedestrian moving steady in conflict.

Analysis and Results. In the investigation of the validity of using PE profiles to identify pedestrian evasive actions, the PE is compared to traditional measures of traffic conflicts (e.g. TTC and PET). A sample of 60 pedestrian involved conflicts randomly selected is manually annotated by two traffic safety expert observers. The pedestrian conflicts in the two evasive action groups are compared in terms of severity. The conflicts break-down logically showed that the evasive action group had higher severity conflicts than the no-evasive action group. For both expert results, most highly severe conflicts showed evasive actions in the pedestrian movement. This explains the importance of detecting evasive actions to identify severe pedestrian conflicts.

Calculating the conflict indicators of conflicts in the two groups, evasive action/No evasive action, Fig. 8 shows the means of the different indicators for the two conflict groups. The mean of the PE drop is significantly higher for the evasive action group while for the TTC and PET the mean values are relatively similar. This result is affirmed by the p-value calculated from the Analysis of variance (ANOVA) test performed on

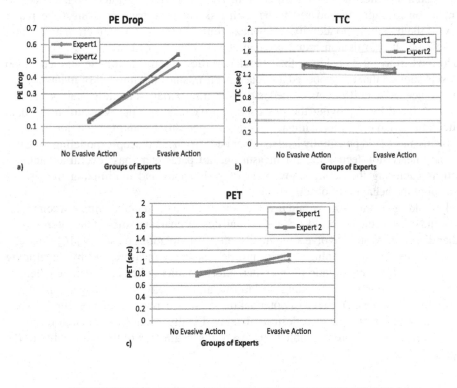

p-value	a) PE Drop	b) TTC	c) PET
Expert 1	0.00007*	0.9489	0.6398
Expert 2	0.00000*	0.6828	0.4333

Statistically significant result at the 5% level

Fig. 8. Difference in indicator means for the evasive action/no evasive action groups and the p-value obtained from the difference in means test between the two groups

the difference between the means of the with/without Evasive Action groups. The difference in the PE case is highly significant at 95 % confidence compared to the TTC and PET. These results show that the PE drop value can differentiate between evasive action and non-evasive action conflicts lacking by conventional proximity measures.

The potential of the newly developed indicator was validated by a set of pedestrian interactions reviewed and ranked by safety experts. Results showed that the PE based indicator can identify pedestrian conflicts that have sudden evasive action. Variations in permutation entropy are shown to be a suitable measuring of the extent of the evasive action better than TTC and PET in less-organized, high road user mix traffic environments.

6   Summary

Recent advances in computer vision encouraged the analysis of safety surrogate measures such as conflict and violation detection. This paper demonstrated the latest development on locations considered to be high risk for pedestrian crossing. The paper showed the possibility to identify safety hazardous situation like distraction and illegal jaywalking. It also demonstrated a technique to identify pedestrian evasive actions performed to avoid collision with vehicular traffic. The results of the studied video datasets showed that the proposed approach is promising. The amount of manual intervention needed to collect data on pedestrians in transportation facilities can be significantly reduced by deploying the proposed approach. Such improvement in the data collection can have significant impact on studying pedestrian walking behavior, crossing decisions and would potentially lead to better pedestrian microscopic modeling. The use of computer vision techniques for measuring gait parameters has several advantages such as capturing the natural movement of pedestrians and minimizing the risk of disturbing the behavior of observed subjects.

Expanding on this work would involve investigating the relationship between violations and other traffic factors like wait-time and design characteristics of the intersection. Other directions would involve studying the effect of violations on safety [16]. This can be made possible by defining severity profiles as safety measure and by developing relationships between violations and other safety conflict indicators. Some challenges remain to be addressed including scalability and the efficient management of the computing resources. One area of potential research is to assess a relationship between the accuracy of tracking and pedestrian density. Finally, more experimental results at different intersections are desirable to have a robust estimation of the practicality of the approach.

References

1. Archer, J.: Indicators for Traffic Safety Assessment and Prediction and Their Application in Micro-Simulation Modelling: A Study of Urban and Suburban Intersections. Royal Institute of Technology, Stockholm (2005)
2. Ismail, K., Sayed, T., Saunier, N.: Methodologies for aggregating indicators of traffic conflict. Transp. Res. Rec.: J. Transp. Res. Board **2237**, 10–19 (2011)

 3. Ismail, K., Sayed, T., Saunier, N.: A methodology for precise camera calibration for data collection applications in urban traffic scenes. Can. J. Civ. Eng. **40**(1), 57–67 (2013)
 4. Saunier, N., Sayed, T.: A feature-based tracking algorithm for vehicles in intersections. In: Third Canadian Conference on Computer and Robot Vision (2006)
 5. Ismail, K., Sayed, T., Saunier, N.: Automated analysis of pedestrian-vehicle conflicts: a context for before-and-after studies. Transp. Res. Rec.: J. Transp. Res. Board **2198**, 52–64 (2010)
 6. Zaki, M., Sayed, T.: A framework for automated road-users classification using movement trajectories. Transp. Res. Part C: Emerg. Technol. **33**, 50–73 (2013)
 7. Hediyeh, H., Sayed, T., Zaki, M.H., Mori, G.: Pedestrian gait analysis using automated computer vision techniques. Transportmetrica A: Transp. Sci. **10**(3), 214–232 (2014)
 8. Hediyeh, H., Sayed, T., Zaki, M.H.: The use of gait parameters to evaluate pedestrian behavior at scramble-phase signalized intersections. J. Adv. Transp. **49**(4), 523–534 (2015)
 9. Messelodi, S., Modena, C.M., Cattoni, G.: Vision-based bicycle/motorcycle classification. Pattern Recogn. Lett. Elsevier **28**(13), 1719–1726 (2007)
10. Sekiya, N., Nagasaki, H.: Reproducibility of the walking patterns of normal young adults: test-retest reliability of the walk ratio (step-length/step-rate). Gait Posture **7**(3), 225–227 (1998)
11. Mizuike, C., Ohgi, S., Morita, S.: Analysis of stroke patient walking dynamics using a tri-axial accelerometer. Gait Posture **30**(1), 60–64 (2009)
12. Cinnamon, J., Schuurman, N., Hameed, S.: Pedestrian injury and human behaviour: observing road-rule violations at high-incident intersections. PLoS ONE **6**(7), e21063 (2011)
13. Zaki, M., Sayed, T., Taggeldin, A., Azab, M.: Application of computer vision to the diagnosis of pedestrian safety issues. Transp. Res. Rec.: J. Transp. Res. Board **2393**(1), 75–84 (2013)
14. Saunier, N., Sayed, T., Ismail, K.: Large scale automated analysis of vehicle interactions and collisions. Transp. Res. Rec.: J. Transp. Res. Board **2147**, 42–50 (2010)
15. Bandt, C., Pompe, B.: Permutation entropy: a natural complexity measure for time series. Phys. Rev. Lett. **88**(17), 174102 (2002)
16. Kattan, L., Acharjee, S., Tay, R.: pedestrian scramble operations: pilot study in calgary, Alberta, Canada. Transp. Res. Rec.: J. Transp. Res. Board **2140**, 79–84 (2009)

5G-Optimizing Network Coverage in Radio Self Organizing Networks by M/L Based Beam Tilt Algorithm

Premkumar Karthikeyan, Nagabushanam Hari Kumar[(⊠)],
and Srinivasan Aishwarya

Ericsson Research India, Tamarai Tech Park, Guindy, Chennai, India
p.karthikeyan@ericsson.com, n.hari.
kumar@ericsson.com, aishwaryasrini94@gmail.com

Abstract. This paper proposes a novel machine learning based antenna beam tilt algorithm for minimizing the overall Poor Signal Strength (PSS) regions / dead zones in the network area considered. Our objective is to provide network intelligence and automation of the optimization of the configurable parameter, azimuth angle of the antenna, to adapt to varying channel conditions and rebalance the entire network so as to provide an optimized level of service to the users. The proposed scheme involves developing a simulation scenario for the existing network and employing machine learning to study the behavior of the network by taking large number of combinations of azimuth angles and corresponding measure of PSS area. Regression analysis and stochastic gradient descent are used to obtain the relationship and the optimized angles for which the PSS area is minimum. Our simulation results demonstrate the reduction in overall PSS area compared to state of art approaches.

Keywords: eNodeB · Azimuth angle · SINR (Signal to Interference Noise Ratio) · Long Term Evolution · Self Optimizing Network · CQI (Channel Quality Indicator)

1 Introduction

With a rapid growth of cellular radio networks and soaring number of mobile users all over the world, there is an increasing demand for enhanced user experience in terms of good coverage and cell capacity. Initial deployment of a radio network includes RF planning. RF Planning is the process of assigning frequencies, transmitter locations and parameters of a wireless communication system to provide sufficient coverage and capacity for the services required. Automatic planning tools are employed to perform detailed predictions of number of sites and site locations, antenna directions and downtilts, neighbor cell lists for each site, mobility parameters for each site, frequency plan and detailed coverage predictions (SINR, CQI and user location). The characteristics of the selected antenna, the terrain, the land use and land clutter surrounding each site, which provide a better estimate of the coverage of the sites are also taken into account in RF planning. Thus, the initially established network is optimum. In due course of time, absorption loss arising due to edifices, interference from the neighboring

© ICST Institute for Computer Sciences, Social Informatics and Telecommunications Engineering 2016
A. Leon-Garcia et al. (Eds.): Smart City 2015, LNICST 166, pp. 44–54, 2016.
DOI: 10.1007/978-3-319-33681-7_4

eNodeBs and other environmental changes cause signal deterioration in certain regions where the Signal to Interference and Noise Ratio (SINR) drops below the desired value. Apart from these reasons, sudden eNodeB failures may also lead to the formation of such regions and the users are affected. Hence, continuous optimization of the network to accommodate the changes in the environment or additional service requirements (e.g. additional coverage or capacity) is inevitable. This process includes collection of measurement data on a regular basis. The data is then used to optimize the parameters (e.g. antenna orientation, downtilt, frequency plan) of existing sites.

1.1 Objective

Present day solutions to reduce dead zone includes installing femtocells, reflectors, manually tilting the antenna etc. Our ultimate goal is to eliminate the manual operational tasks involved in reducing the dead zone, through an automated mechanism called self-optimizing network. Our aim is to provide the maximum possible network coverage to the users in a location considered, irrespective of the environmental and climatic conditions prevailing in that region and thereby increase the number of users and profit for the network operator. The scope of this paper lies in the Self-Optimizing capabilities of the Long Term Evolution, which has been standardized in the 3GPP Release 8 and Release 9.

2 Long Term Evolution – Introduction

LTE stands for Long Term Evolution and it was started as a project in 2004 by telecommunication body known as the Third Generation Partnership Project (3GPP). The main goal of LTE is to provide a high data rate, low latency and packet optimized radio access technology supporting flexible bandwidth deployments. Its network architecture has been designed with the goal to support packet-switched traffic with seamless mobility and great quality of service. LTE is the successor of UMTS and CDMA 2000. It supports flexible carrier bandwidths, from 1.4 MHz to 20 MHz as well as both FDD and TDD.

3 Self Organizing Networks – Introduction

A self-organizing Network is an automation technology designed to make the planning, configuration, management, optimization and healing of mobile radio access networks simpler and faster. SON has been codified within 3GPP Release 8 and subsequent specifications in a series of standards including 36.902. The first technology making use of SON features is the Long Term Evolution. In a typical situation, when the network elements begin to underperform, operators need to manually track down the root cause and develop optimization solutions. With smart SON, operators can sit back and see the network manage itself. SON makes use of the real time radio resource information to provide the required solutions. It makes effective, impactful adjustments to a wide variety of configurable parameters such as antenna tilts, antenna power outputs etc. Based on the functionality of the SON algorithms used, it can be classified into three types – self configuration functions, self optimization functions, self healing functions.

3.1 Self Optimization Functions

Every base station contains hundreds of configuration parameters that control various aspects of the cell site. Each of these can be altered to change network behavior, based on observations of both the base station and measurements at the mobile station or handset. Functions of self-optimization are included in 3GPP Release 9. It includes optimization of coverage, capacity, handover and interference. The algorithm devised falls in this category of SON solutions. It involves optimization of coverage by adjusting the tilt of the antenna. In other words, the azimuth angles of all the eNodeB antenna radiation patterns are adjusted to achieve minimum dead zone region in a network considered (Fig. 1).

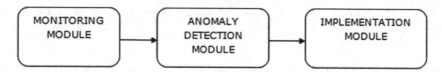

Fig. 1. Self Optimizing Network block diagram

The above diagram illustrates the major modules involved in a self-optimizing network.

- **Monitoring Module:** This module maintains a record of the total number of UEs in its particular cell site, number of neighboring eNodeBs, channel conditions, current location of all UEs, signal strength experienced by each UE in terms of SINR or CQI and other necessary network parameters. This information is constantly sent as feedback to the eNodeBs by the UEs. This data set is the input for the algorithm.
- **Anomaly Detection Module:** As the name implies, this module keeps track of the previous module's record and reports to the administrator if there are any deviations in the network performance parameter values. i.e. if the network performance is poor. In the case considered, this module acts whenever the SINR or CQI value at any particular location in the network approaches a threshold value set by the network administrator.
- **Implementation Module:** Following the data analysis step, optimization algorithm and corrections will be triggered automatically to make decisions on how to operate the system according to user's needs. The implementation module executes the algorithm to optimize the network. It basically involves the creation of virtual simulation scenario for the deviated network using the Vienna LTE Simulator as carried out in the project. The antenna azimuth angle is chosen as the parameter of

configuration for the project. This module uses machine learning principles to obtain the azimuth angles for which the network is optimized i.e. the dead zone region is minimized. In other words, the horizontal tilt of the main lobe is adjusted to cover up the dead zone.

4 Azimuth Angle of Antenna

Azimuth angle is defined as the horizontal angle measured clockwise from the north base line. It is measured in degrees (Fig. 2).

Fig. 2. Azimuth Angle

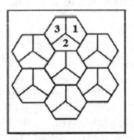

Fig. 3. Network Scenario

Figure 3 shows a simple 7 cell network with hexagonal cells containing 3 sectors with an azimuth span of 120° each. The following table shows sector number and corresponding azimuth angle span (Table 1).

Table 1. Azimuth Angle Span

Sector	Azimuth Angle Span
1	0–120
2	121–240
3	241–360

5 Machine Learning

Machine Learning explores the construction and study of algorithms that can learn from data. Supervised machine learning has been adopted. The existing network is studied by means of setting various azimuth angles to all the base station antennas and the corresponding dead zone measure is obtained. Ultimately, a table of nearly 1800 entries for various combinations of azimuth angles with the dead zone measure is drawn.

5.1 Multi Polynomial Regression

Regression analysis is a statistical process for estimating the relationship among variables. With respect to this paper, there are 21 independent variables which are the azimuth angles and one dependent variable which is the dead zone measure. The data fetched in the previous process is fed as input to the regression algorithm. The output of the algorithm is a polynomial equation that shows the relationship between the independent variables and the dependent variable.

$$y = a1 * x1 + a2 * x2 + a3 * x3 + \ldots\ldots\ldots\ldots\ldots + a21 * x21 \tag{1}$$

where "y" is the dead zone measure, "a1 to a21" are constants and "x1 to x21" are azimuth angle variables.

5.2 Stochastic Gradient Descent

Gradient descent is a first-order optimization algorithm. To find a local minimum of a function using gradient descent, one takes steps proportional to the negative of the gradient (or of the approximate gradient) of the function at the current point and the iteration proceeds until local minimum is reached. The algorithm is illustrated in the following steps.

- The objective function obtained from regression is given as input to the stochastic gradient descent algorithm.
- Choose an initial vector of parameters "x" (x1 to x21) and learning rate "alpha".

  - for i=1,2,3....n
        for r=1,2,3.....21
        g=gradient(x,r);
        xnew = x – alpha*g;
        x=xnew;
       end
      end
    where "i" denotes number of iterations

"r" denotes the subscript of x, for example if r = 2, it denotes the variable x2
"alpha" is the learning rate and its value is 0.05
"g" is the partial first order differentiation of the function with respect to (x, r)

Thus, the output of this algorithm is shown in the figure below.

6   Simulation and Results

The LTE cellular radio network scenario and the algorithm have been coded and simulated using MATLAB 2012a. The following sections describe the steps involved in the algorithm.

6.1   Creation of Virtual Simulation Scenario for Existing Network

The first step involved in this process is to simulate the real time existing network in Matlab. The frequency in which the system is operating is 2 GHz and the system bandwidth is 5 MHz. Totally 7 eNodeBs are established in a region of 1200sqm. The map resolution is 5 pixels per meter and so there are 241*241 = 58081 pixels in the color map. The minimum coupling loss for macro cell urban area is set as 70 dB. The pathloss model used in this simulation scenario for a carrier frequency of 2 GHz is given by the following formula.

$$L = 128.1 + 37.6\log_{10}(R) \tag{2}$$

where L is the pathloss and R is the eNodeB-UE separation in Km. The eNodeB transmit power is 43 dBm/20 W as given in [1]. The UE receiver noise figure is 9 dB as mentioned in Table 12.2 of [1]. Thus, the initial network setup is simulated with the above mentioned parameters and the resultant figures are shown (Figs. 4 and 5).

Figure 6 shows the plot of SINR values at various distances from the eNodeBs. With respect to this paper, the regions where power level is below −98 dBm (blue region in the heat map) are considered as dead zones.

6.2   Multi-polynomial Regression Output

The output of multi polynomial regression is given as follows

$$y = 34.622 * x21 - 11.401 * x20 + 0.133 * x20 * x21\ldots\ldots + 0.1585 * x20^2 \\ + 0.0352 * x21^2 \tag{3}$$

where "y" is the dead zone measure and "x1 to x21" are the azimuth angles.

The following figure shows the correctness of the equation obtained by regression analysis (Figs. 7 and 8).

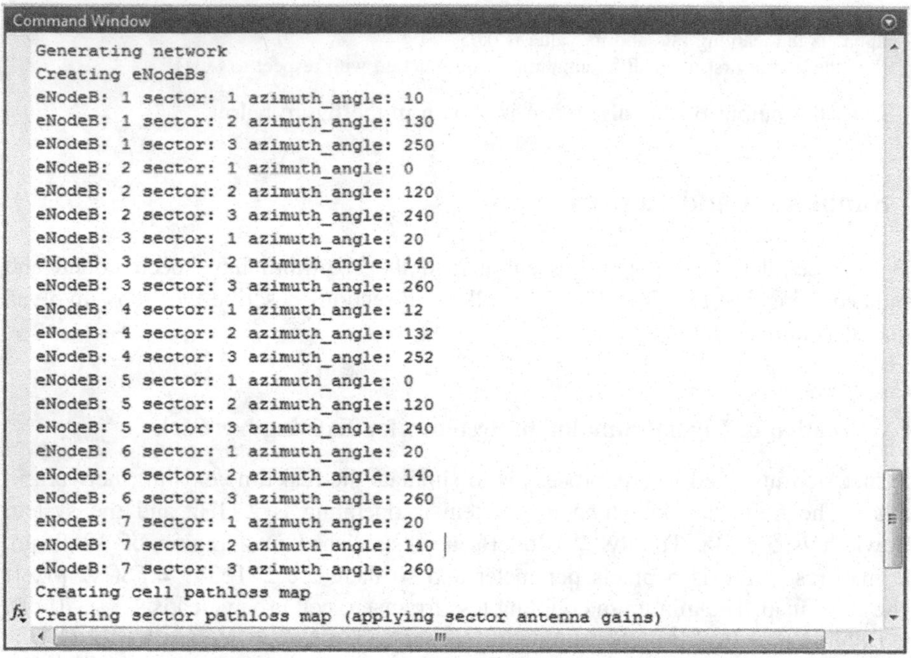

Fig. 4. Azimuth Angles of antennas in existing network

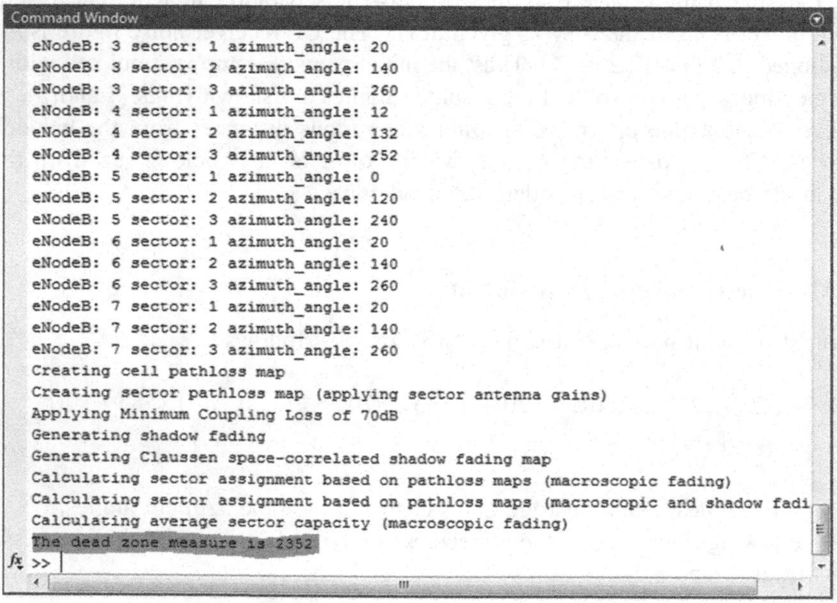

Fig. 5. Dead Zone measure in the existing network

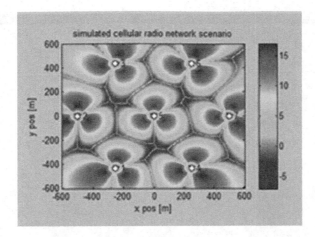

Fig. 6. Color map of the existing network (Color figure online)

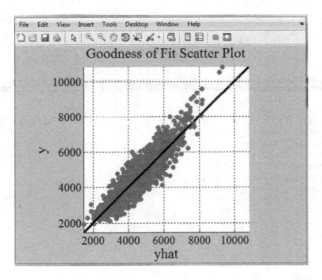

Fig. 7. Goodness of fit

6.3 Stochastic Gradient Descent Output

The angles obtained from the above step are fed into the eNodeBs and the resulting network is shown as simulation results below (Figs. 9 and 10).

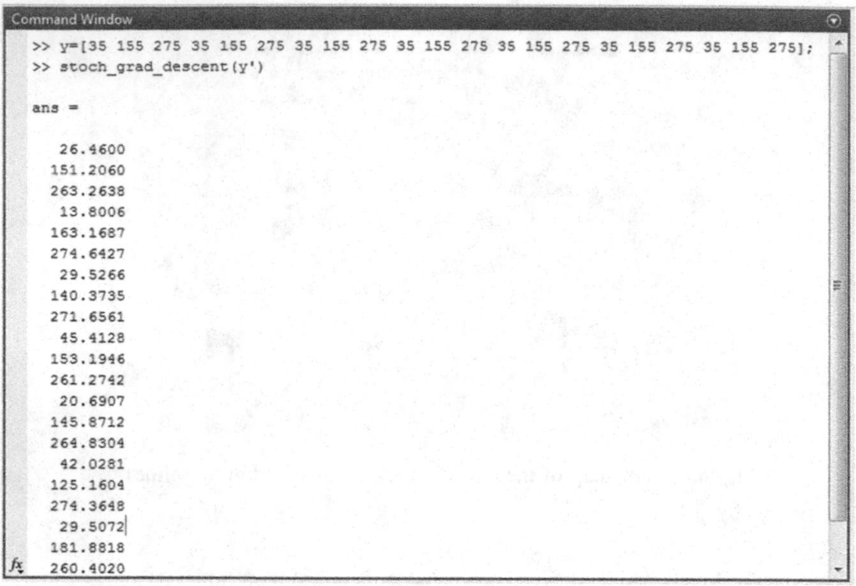

Fig. 8. Output azimuth angles

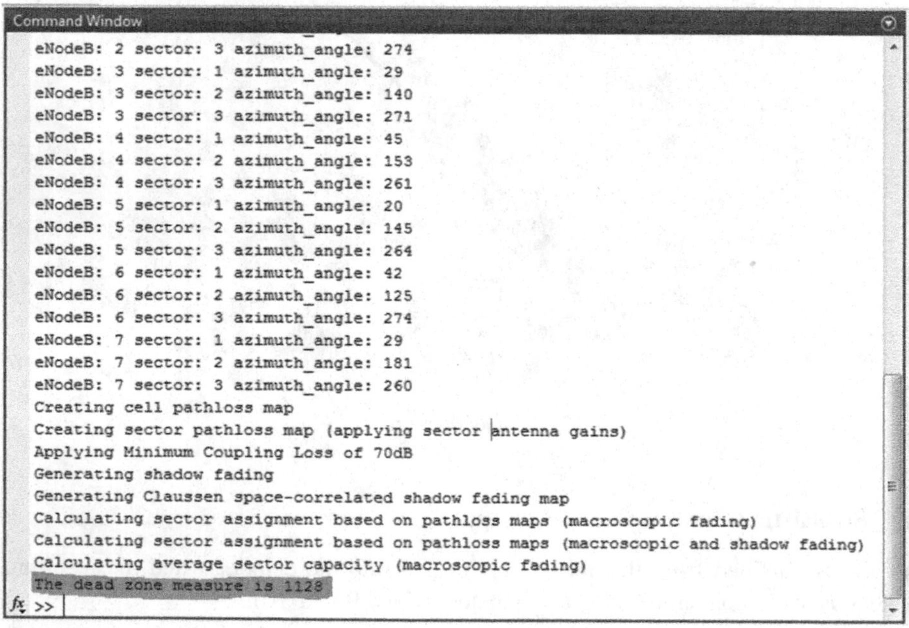

Fig. 9. Dead zone measure of the optimized network

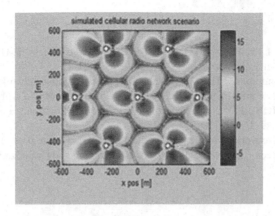

Fig. 10. Optimized network output (Color figure online)

7   Conclusion

This work focuses on the self-organizing networks in LTE to automate the configuration of the antenna parameter, azimuth angle. The proposed machine learning algorithm and researched parameter values help to learn the existing network and establish a relationship among the azimuth angles and PSS measure and thereby finding the azimuth tilts for which the PSS coordinates is minimum. The proposed method can be extended to incorporate various other parameters like power, frequency etc. to improve the optimization for the prevailing network. This is the advantage of the proposed algorithm which involves logical computations rather than technical changes in other parameters of the network.

8   Future Work

Our future work includes implementing the same algorithm in various other channel condition scenarios like cost231, Hata model etc. and make an analysis of the results. Future work also includes considering the configurable parameters other than azimuth angle such as vertical tilt, height of the base station from the ground, number of antennas that can be fired in the array etc. in implementing this machine learning algorithm.

References

1. 3GPP TR 36.942: LTE; Evolved Universal Terrestrial Radio Access (E-UTRA); Radio Frequency (RF) system scenarios (Release 10). v10.2.0, 2011
2. Caminada, A., Gondran, A., Tabia, N., Baala, O.: Self-organizing networks on LTE system: antenna parameters configuration effects on LTE networks coverage with respect to traffic distribution. In: MOBILITY 2013: The Third International Conference on Mobile Services, Resources and Users, IARIA (2013)
3. "Self-Optimizing Networks: The Benefits of SON in LTE", a white paper from 4G Americas
4. Song, L., Shen, J. (eds.): Evolved Cellular Network Planning and Optimization for UMTS and LTE

Understanding Intercity Freeway Traffic Variability at Holidays Using Anonymous Cell Phone Data

Gang Liu, Chenhao Wang, and Tony Z. Qiu[(✉)]

Centre for Smart Transportation, University of Alberta,
9211 116th Street, Edmonton, AB, Canada
{gliu2, chenhao1, tony.qiu}@ualberta.ca

Abstract. Due to the high market penetration of cell phones, the detailed spatial data offer new opportunities for sophisticated applications in traffic monitoring. Previous studies and projects have mainly focused on obtaining location and traffic estimations of individuals using data derived from cell phone networks. Understanding the variability of traffic patterns and congestion characteristics of intercity freeway systems caused by holiday traffic is beneficial, because appropriate countermeasures for congestion mitigation can be prepared and drivers can change their holiday travel schedules accordingly. This study collected 12 months of cell phone data and radar data along a highway in China. The traffic pattern during the Labor Day holiday in 2014 is investigated using the cell phone sample and speed data. The results have the potential to improve freeway operational performance during holiday periods.

Keywords: Intercity freeway · Holiday traffic · Anonymous cell phone data

1 Introduction

As wireless location technology is progressing very quickly, cellular probe technology is becoming a hot topic in the field of traffic engineering. Since cell phones move with people and vehicles, a huge amount of data can be collected at the individual level for estimating traffic-related parameters. Many studies have explored the use of cell phone data to estimate traffic states. Intuitively, monitoring and tracking the movement of cell phones within one wireless network can generate real-time estimated traffic states of the corresponding roadway network covered by the wireless network. For example, measuring the 'speed' of cell phones provides the scope to determine the speed of the vehicles. In past years, a number of simulated studies and field tests have investigated the feasibility of designing and developing a cellular probe-based traffic speed estimation system. Unlike other traffic sensing systems, these techniques rely on the location of the cellular phone over the time period, calibrated using triangulation of the GSM (Global System for Mobile communication) signal strength [1] over time; fingerprint matching of the phone's successive signal strength readings [2]; or the location of the cellular phone handoff between towers [3, 4].

© ICST Institute for Computer Sciences, Social Informatics and Telecommunications Engineering 2016
A. Leon-Garcia et al. (Eds.): Smart City 2015, LNICST 166, pp. 55–65, 2016.
DOI: 10.1007/978-3-319-33681-7_5

Several studies have evaluated traffic patterns using cell phone call data [5–7]. Holiday periods contributed to a large portion of traffic variability (i.e., different traffic congestion patterns in comparison with non-holiday periods) [8, 9]. However, the traffic patterns of the intercity freeway during special holidays have been rarely investigated. Among various statutory holidays in China, the National Day and Labor Day holiday periods were the busiest long-distance travel periods. Heavy traffic congestion and longer delay times are easily created on intercity freeway systems during holiday periods. An understanding of this substantial variation in traffic volume and speed due to holiday events is important for transportation agencies to establish appropriate holiday traffic management plans.

This study evaluates the change in traffic patterns caused by holiday traffic, and discusses how traffic patterns vary each day during holiday periods (before the holiday, during the holiday, and after the holiday). It is anticipated that the findings of this study will help transportation engineers and program managers implement appropriate congestion-related countermeasures for mitigating heavy congestion on a subject roadway during the busiest holiday periods. Drivers can also choose to avoid the congestion and change their holiday travel schedules based on the information about holiday traffic.

2   Literature Review

Based on information from the Bureau of Transportation Statistics, among various statutory holidays in the United States, the Thanksgiving and Christmas/New Year's holiday periods were the busiest long-distance travel periods of the year in 2001 [10]. This report showed that the number of long-distance trips increased by 54 % and by 23 % during the six-day Thanksgiving period and during the Christmas/New Year's holiday period, respectively.

Liu and Sharma analyzed twenty-year data collected by permanent traffic counters on highways in Alberta, Canada. The results of the nonparametric Wilcoxon matched pair test and Friedman method revealed that holidays substantially contributed to the variability of traffic [11]. Later, they showed that the strong directional features of holidays' effects. At the beginning of holiday periods, the volume increases were usually significant at a 95 % confidence level in the outbound direction, as this direction served the traffic from the population center (production area) to the recreation area (attraction area). At the end of holiday periods, significant volume changes were generally observed in the inbound direction, as this direction mainly carried the returning traffic from the attraction area to the production area [9]. Jun investigated the variability of speed patterns and congestion characteristics of interstate freeway systems during holidays. The estimated Gaussian mixture speed distribution showed the potential of improving freeway operational performance evaluation schemes for holiday periods [12].

Several studies investigated using cell phone call data to monitor the traffic speed. In 2003, a researcher from INRETS cooperated with researchers from the University of

California Berkeley to implement a field test on two freeway segments, and the report shows that, comparing the cellular probe data and the loop detector data, little variation occurred within the 32 km freeway segment, while a large variation was observed for the 4 km freeway segment [13]. Smith et al. compared speed estimation of cellular phone–based data with it of a point video sensor for 39 intervals of 10 min (min) each at different freeway locations, and for 35 intervals of 10 min each at different arterial locations. For arterial locations, the average absolute differences between the two measurement methods were 6.8 mph; for freeway locations, those were 7.2–9.2 mph [14]. Steenbruggen et al. reviewed systematically the main studies and projects addressing the use of data derived from mobile phone networks to obtain location and traffic estimations of individuals. They gave several general conclusions: (1) the most studied estimation issues for traffic management purposes were travel speed and travel time; (2) most of the studies focused on stretches of roads, or loops, and not on a road network level; (3) recent studies show more promising results [4].

3   Collection and Characteristics

The studied freeway is the G60 (Shanghai–Kunming Freeway) in China, which starts from Shanghai and ends at Kunming, Yunnan Province, a city that is 2730 km away, southwest of Shanghai. The studied section starts from Hangzhou and ends at Quzhou, as shown in Fig. 1. There are three other big cities along this freeway section: Zhuji, Yiwu, and Jinhua. The analysis is based on cell phone call data from December of 2013 to May of 2014. The information about these five cities is as follows:

- Hangzhou is the largest city of Zhejiang Province in Eastern China. It is the fourth largest metropolitan area in China. During the 2010 Chinese census, the metropolitan area held 21.102 million people over an area of 34,585 km^2.
- Zhuji is a county-level city, located about 40 miles south of Hangzhou. It spans 2,311 km^2 with a population of 1,157,938 inhabitants, according to the 2010 census.
- Yiwu is a city of about 1.2 million people in central Zhejiang province, according to the 2010 census. The city is famous for its small commodity trade and vibrant market, and is a regional tourist destination.
- Jinhua is a prefecture-level city. Its population was 5,361,572, based on the 2010 census, including 1,077,245 in the metro area.
- Quzhou is a prefecture-level city. As of 2010, its municipality registered a population of 2,413,500.

Figure 2 shows the sample number of the corridor on April 26, 28, 29, 30, and May 01 and 04. As May 01 to May 03 is a national holiday, we can see an obvious increase in the sample size on April 30 and May 01. More samples exist for southbound than northbound.

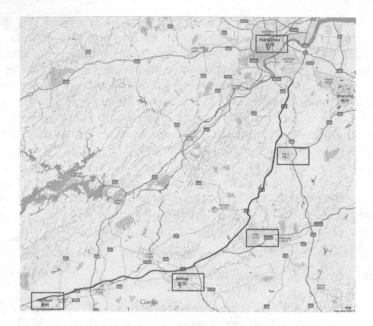

Fig. 1. Schematic diagram of studied freeway section

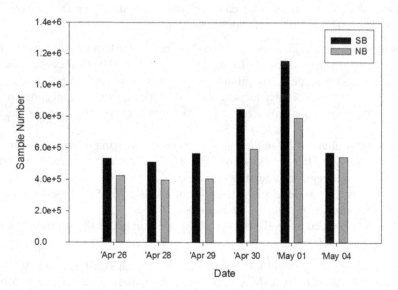

Fig. 2. Sample numbers for different dates

4   Speed Estimation Methodology

Figure 3 shows the system structure of a standard cellular network. A cellular network is a radio network made up of a number of radio cells, each served by a fixed transmitter, known as a base transceiver station (BTS), which is also termed a cell. These cells are used to cover different areas in order to provide radio coverage over an area broader than one cell. Cellular networks are inherently asymmetric with a set of fixed main transceivers each serving a cell and a set of distributed transceivers that provide services to the network's users.

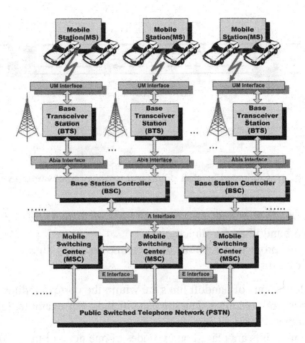

Fig. 3. Architecture of the cellular network

BTSs (cells) are all interconnected, which is the reason why someone can move from one cell to another without losing connection. BTS is the basic geographic unit of a cellular network system, and a city or county is divided into smaller cells, each of which is equipped with a low-powered BTS. The cells can vary in size depending upon the location, terrain and capacity demands, and the size can be several hundred meters or several kilometers. When a cell phone during a call moves from one cell toward another, a base station controller (BSC) monitors the movement, and at the appropriate time, transfers or hands off the phone call to the new cell. Handoff (HO) is the process by which the controller passes a cell phone conversation from one cell to another.

The handoff is performed so quickly that users usually never notice, and the controller records each handoff once it occurs.

Location update (LU) strategy is another mechanism for locating cell phones in the GSM cellular network, and it can handle all cell phones that have been turned on and are in idle status (not on-call). All the cells within the GSM network are grouped into a number of disjointed location areas (LA).

As shown in Fig. 4, a long road segment can be modeled as a straight line, divided into several smaller sections that are connected one by one and separated by the virtual sensor node, and the small segment determined by two consecutive handoff points is

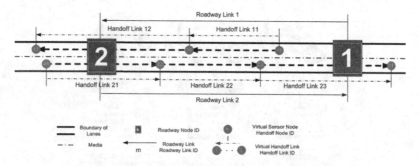

Fig. 4. Calibrated handoff points and two-way roadway links

defined as a handoff link if and only if there exists one actual roadway link that can connect these two handoff nodes directly.

Considering the projection relation between the roadway link and handoff link, there exist three cases:

- The two handoff points of handoff links are within the corresponding roadway link, and the roadway link is longer than the handoff link. For example, refer to handoff link 11 of roadway link 1 in Fig. 4.
- The two handoff points are placed on two sides of one node of the roadway link. For example, see handoff link 21 and 23 of roadway link 2 in Fig. 4.
- The two handoff points are on two sides of the corresponding roadway link, and the roadway link is shorter than the handoff link.

Each virtual sensor link of the virtual sensor network can be described as follows:

$$(H_{from}, H_{to}) = ((ID_{sensor\_from}, Cell_{from\_from}, Cell_{from\_to}), (ID_{sensor\_to}, Cell_{to\_from}, Cell_{to\_to})) \tag{1}$$

The two consecutive handoffs caused by one same cell phone p are called a handoff pair $H_{AB}^p = (ID_{cellphone}, t_{event1}, cell_A, cell_B)$ and $H_{CD}^p = (ID_{cellphone}, t_{event2}, cell_C, cell_D)$, which can determine the unique handoff link, except in cases of a multi-deck bridge or closely parallel roads. It should be noted that $cell_B$ and $cell_C$ are likely the identical cell due to the continuity property of adjacent cells. Given four continuous cells A, B, C, D, if we get the measurement of a HO link from handset p, (H^p_{AB}, H^p_{CD}), where $H^p_{AB} = (p, t_{AB}, A, B)$, $H^p_{CD} = (p, t_{CD}, C, D)$, and $t_{CD} - t_{AB} > 0$, we can easily calculate the moving speed of handset p when traversing the handoff link or location update route identified by H^p_{AB} and H^p_{CD}.

$$v^i_{p0} = \frac{L_{AB-CD}}{t_{CD} - t_{AB}} \qquad (2)$$

And then translate the average HO link speed into the average roadway link speed using the following equation, which integrates the link length adjustment factor α:

$$v^i_p = \alpha\left(H^P_{AB}, H^p_{CD}, l\left(H^P_{AB}, H^p_{CD}\right)\right) \times v^i_{p0} \qquad (3)$$

$$v^i_p = \alpha\left(H^P_{AB}, H^p_{CD}, l\left(H^P_{AB}, H^p_{CD}\right)\right) \times \frac{L_{AB-CD}}{t_{CD} - t_{AB}} \qquad (4)$$

where, L_{AB-CD} is the length of the handoff link.

Meanwhile, the parameter α needs to be chosen in order to minimize the mean squared estimation error. It should be noted that α functions for both the handoff link ID and roadway link ID, so both the roadway link-based speed results and the corresponding HO link-based speed results need to be collected for calibrating the parameters.

5 Results Analysis

Figure 5 shows the temporal variation of the sample number during holidays. Firstly, traffic patterns on April 26, 28, and 29 have a very similar trend, which increases during morning and decreases during evening. Secondly, the sample number starts to increase significantly for April 30, and we can see a much higher sample number on May 01. The reason is that people drive to visit family and friends during the holiday. Thirdly, the increase of the southbound (SB) sample number is much larger than for northbound (NB) traffic, which means more people are traveling outside of Hangzhou to the other four southbound cities. The data clearly show substantial holiday effects on traffic volumes, and the effects are different for outbound and inbound directions.

Figure 6 shows the speed dynamic at one location from April 21 to May 07. The speeds detected by the cell phone and microwave vehicle detector have the same identical trend during holidays, weekends, and weekdays. We can see a clear speed drop on May 01 due to higher traffic volume, especially during the morning.

For further analysis, Fig. 7 shows the speed contour along the studied corridor for May 1. There are obvious congested links and time intervals along the corridor. The northbound and southbound directions show different traffic dynamics. We can see one significant SB congestion in the early morning, at about 3:30 AM.

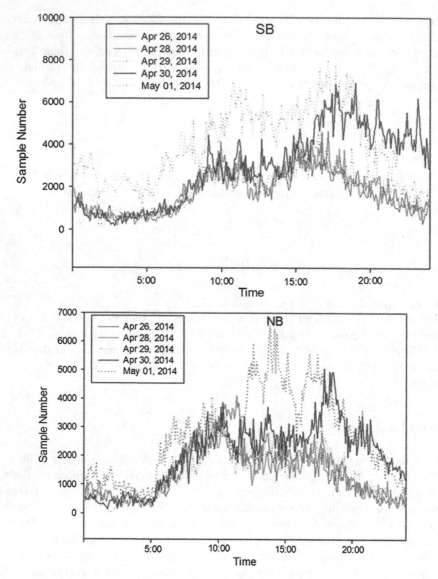

Fig. 5. Temporal variation of the sample number during holidays (Color figure online)

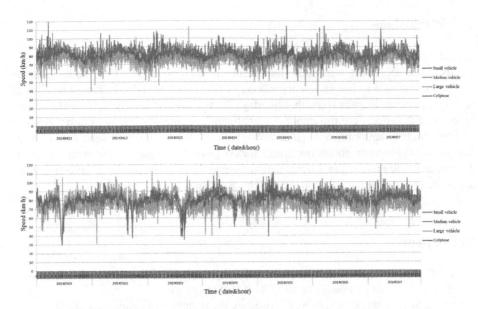

Fig. 6. Speeds (km/h) at one location from April 21 to May 07 (Color figure online)

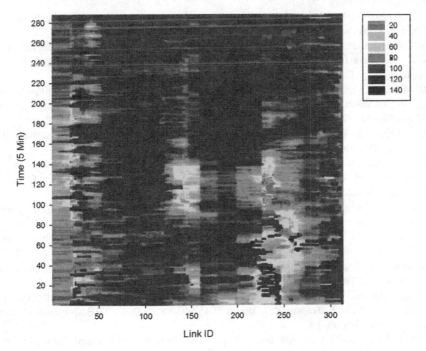

Fig. 7. Speed (km/h) contour along the southbound corridor on May 01, 2014 (Color figure online)

6 Conclusions

Recent studies have showed promising results of using mobile phone data for sophisticated applications in traffic management and monitoring. This study uses the cell phone call data to investigate the effects of holidays (observed in Zhejiang, China) on traffic patterns. Results show that holiday affects daily and hourly traffic volume and speed, and the effects are different for southbound and northbound directions. A good understanding of temporal and spatial traffic patterns due to holiday effects can assist in developing appropriate countermeasures for congestion mitigation. The next phases of the research will include the development of speed distribution model to investigate the trends of speed patterns and congestion characteristics.

References

1. de Frutos, S.H., Castro, M.: Using smartphones as a very low-cost tool for road inventories. Transp. Res. Part C: Emerg. Technol. **38**, 136–145 (2014)
2. Chen, M.Y., Sohn, T., Chmelev, D., Haehnel, D., Hightower, J., Hughes, J., LaMarca, A., Potter, F., Smith, I., Varshavsky, A.: Practical metropolitan-scale positioning for GSM phones. In: Dourish, P., Friday, A. (eds.) UbiComp 2006. LNCS, vol. 4206, pp. 225–242. Springer, Heidelberg (2006)
3. Gundlegard, D., Karlsson, J.M.: Handover location accuracy for travel time estimation in GSM and UMTS. Intell. Transp. Syst. IET **3**(1), 87–94 (2009)
4. Steenbruggen, J., Borzacchiello, M., Nijkamp, P., Scholten, H.: Mobile phone data from GSM networks for traffic parameter and urban spatial pattern assessment: a review of applications and opportunities. GeoJournal **78**, 223–243 (2013)
5. Bar-Gera, H.: Evaluation of a cellular phone-based system for measurements of traffic speeds and travel times: A case study from Israel. Transp. Res. Part C: Emerg. Technol. **15**(6), 380–391 (2007)
6. Liu, H., et al.: Evaluation of cell phone traffic data in Minnesota. Transp. Res. Rec. J. Transp. Res. Board **2086**, 1–7 (2008)
7. Järv, O., Ahas, R., Witlox, F.: Understanding monthly variability in human activity spaces: A twelve-month study using mobile phone call detail records. Transp. Res. Part C: Emerg. Technol. **38**, 122–135 (2014)
8. Cools, M., Moons, E., Wets, G.: Investigating the effects of holidays on daily traffic counts: a time series approach. Transp. Res. Rec. J. Transp. Res. Board **2019**, 22–31 (2007)
9. Liu, Z., Sharma, S.: Nonparametric method to examine changes in traffic volume pattern during holiday periods. Transp. Res. Rec. J. Transp. Res. Board 2049, 45–53 (2008b)
10. Bureau of Transportation Statistics (BTS): America on the Go. US Holiday Travel, US Department of Transportation (2003)
11. Liu, Z., Sharma, S.: Statistical investigations of statutory holiday effects on traffic volumes. Transp. Res. Rec. J. Transp. Res. Board 1945, 40–48 (2006a). TRB, National Research Council, Washington, DC
12. Jun, J.: Understanding the variability of speed distributions under mixed traffic conditions caused by holiday traffic. Transp. Res. Part C **18**, 599–610 (2010)

13. Yim, Y., Cayford, R.: Field operational test using anonymous cell phone tracking for generating traffic information. In: Transportation Research Board 85th Annual Meeting (2006)
14. Smith, B.L., et al.: Final report of ITS Center project: Cell-phone probes as an ATMS tool. University of Virginia Center for Transportation Studies (2003)

Privacy-Enhanced Android for Smart Cities Applications

Matthew Lepinski[1], David Levin[1], Daniel McCarthy[1],
Ronald Watro[1], Michael Lack[2], Daniel Hallenbeck[2],
and David Slater[2(✉)]

[1] Raytheon BBN Technologies, 10 Moulton St., Cambridge, MA 02138, USA
{mlepinski,dlevin,dmccarthy,rwatro}@bbn.com
[2] Invincea Labs, 4350 North Fairfax Drive, Arlington, VA 22203, USA
{mike.lack,dan.hallenbeck,david.slater}@invincea.com

Abstract. Many Smart Cities applications will collect data from and otherwise interact with the mobile devices of individual users. In the past, it has been difficult to assure users that smart applications will protect their private data and use the data only for the application's intended purpose. The current paper describes a plan for developing Privacy-Enhanced Android, an extension of the current Android OS with new privacy features based on homomorphic and functional encryption and Secure Multiparty Computation. Our goal is to make these advances in privacy-preserving technologies available to the mobile developer community, so that they can be broadly applied and enable the impactful social utility envisioned by Smart Cities.

Keywords: Privacy · Cyber security · Encryption · Android · Smart cities

1 Introduction

A key component in the creation of Smart Cities is the deployment of appropriate applications ("apps") on mobile devices. These applications will provide data to Smart Cities systems and also allow users to reap the benefits that Smart Cities have to offer. For example, currently popular mobile phone software for traffic reporting (Waze) and navigation (Google Maps) demonstrate the utility of collecting localized sensor information from the "crowd" and suggest that the impact of future Smart City applications will be proportional to the user base.

Privacy is a fundamental issue to user acceptance of apps that deal with personal information. The details of whether privacy protections are required or optional (or perhaps even prohibited) will vary from country to country. It is our belief that widespread adoption of sensitive applications (such as Government-issued or health-related apps) will be the most successful when they are deployed on a ubiquitous mobile platform and in a manner that enables foundational privacy guarantees.

Raytheon BBN Technologies and Invincea Labs are working together on a new project to define and deploy new privacy-preserving tools on the Android OS, based on recent results in cryptography and human-data interfacing. The project goal is to develop a privacy-enhanced version of the Android OS, PE Android, emulating the

© ICST Institute for Computer Sciences, Social Informatics and Telecommunications Engineering 2016
A. Leon-Garcia et al. (Eds.): Smart City 2015, LNICST 166, pp. 66–77, 2016.
DOI: 10.1007/978-3-319-33681-7_6

path of Security-Enhanced Linux (SELinux), which is now part of the Android OS [1]. The PE Android concept was created to advance the goals of the Brandeis program from the US Defense Advanced Research Project Agency DARPA [2]. The Brandeis concept is that advanced technology now exists to empower human users to much better understand and selectively control the use of their private information.

The acronym for the PE Android project is *PEARLS*, for *Privacy-Enhanced Android Research and Legacy System*. As the name suggest, PEARLS will address privacy enhancements that are deployable on current and future mobile hardware. As a demonstration of the PE Android capabilities, we have designed an enhanced application called RapidGather, an emergency response application that enables rapid, targeted data gathering while ensuring user control over degree of anonymity and data privacy. The goal of PEARLS is to enable effective development of new applications like RapidGather, as well as privacy monitoring tools capable of addressing data theft, driving widespread adoption of privacy-preserving technologies across mobile devices.

2 Related Work

There are two areas of technical advances that are fundamental to the PE Android project: advanced cryptography and sophisticated privacy intent and deployment schemes for Android. We discuss each of these in turn.

2.1 Advanced Cryptography

Since the seminal work of Andrew Yao in the 1980's [3], cryptography has provided techniques for groups of individuals to make effective collective decisions without revealing their specific individual data. The paradigmatic example is the Millionaires' Problem, where Yao shows how two honest individuals can jointly determine which of them is richer without a trusted third party and without revealing any specific information about their actual wealth. This topic area, called Secure Multiple Computation (SMC), has been refined over the years to become very general and much more efficient. Just recently, deployment of SMC to smart phones has been achieved by David Evans' group at the University of Virginia [4].

In addition to SMC, there are new techniques in homomorphic [5] and functional [6] encryption that will support smart cities applications. Homomorphic encryption enables a powerful third party to receive encrypted information from mobile devices, process that information according to a set of rules, and return the updated data to the mobile devices, all without decrypting the data. Functional encryption allows a mobile user to encrypt data that can then be decrypted in multiple contexts. For example, location data can be functionally encrypted so that one set of decryption keys will provide approximate location data while another set will provide exact location.

2.2   Android Privacy Research

The PEARLS team is keenly aware that providing sophisticated privacy options on mobile device can create a complex burden on users for determining the appropriate privacy settings. The new M release of Android is a good step forward in dealing with selective permission sets for conventional apps. Do [7] provides similar capabilities by selectively removing permission-protected functionality from individual apps. Kelly [8] and Felt [9] describe how to create permission settings that are comprehensible to users; Pantel [10] discusses inferring permissions from analysis of user intent. Beyond Android app permissions, other research such as Bugiel [11], has focused on applying lower level mandatory access control over system resources to flexibly augment the permission model. None of these approaches address control over private data that was authorized by the user to be collected by the application, nor apply other privacy preserving techniques such as differential privacy. The closest existing research is Wagner [12], which addresses the privacy of data collected by instrumentation built into the Android OS. Unlike PEARLS, however, this system does not provide specific privacy preserving functionality to individual apps nor provide the user with fine-grained control over their private data.

3   Project Description

PEARLS will enhance the Android platform with a new set of privacy-preserving technologies, including operating system (OS) modifications, graphical user interfaces, and cryptographic libraries. The immediate impact of these enhancements will be to support new privacy-preserving applications, which we will demonstrate by developing RapidGather, a data gathering application for emergency response.

PE Android will extend the Android OS with new privacy constructs to enable the deployment of Smart Cities applications such as RapidGather. Development of PE Android will begin on the PEARLS Research System, a high-performance computing environment where Android virtual machines can be rapidly created, modified, tested, and updated while running on a simulated cellular, Bluetooth, or WiFi network. An Android virtual machine (VM) in the Research System may be instantiated with large amounts of compute power and storage space as needed to effectively test new cryptographic techniques. The VM will be effectively unconstrained by battery life/power consumption or network interference (cell tower congestion, RF interference for WiFi/Bluetooth), and will support emerging and idealized sensor technologies (e.g., the ability to measure human vital signs or radiation, faster refresh rates, etc.).

We will also have the capability to integrate actual mobile devices in real-time with the Research System, as part of the effort to drive PE Android to a performance point where it can be proposed as an addition to the existing Android OS on mobile devices with standard computational power, networking technologies, cell connectivity, and sensor suites (accelerometer, microphone, camera, GPS, etc.), as well as a cloud server backend. Noting that legacy cell phones are a rapidly evolving target, the platform will easily accommodate new hardware and sensors as they become available.

3.1 PE Android-R

The Research System will use a special version of PE Android called PE Android-R (for research) with additional features for the purpose of fast and transparent prototyping. These will include enabling clean state virtual snapshots instead of "factory resets," providing direct access to the system cryptographic keys and sensor outputs, replacing the internal SQLite database with new data storage technologies, and enabling non-native code to run using external virtual resources (e.g., running code written in Haskell or Figaro instead of Java or C/C++). It will also enable extensive instrumentation hooks to accurately measure system performance and metrics. Finally, these additional features will be able to be easily disabled, providing direct compatibility for mobile device deployments and integration testing.

The PEARLS Research System consists of a high-performance virtual emulation platform and simulated environment and user models, and will run PE Android-R, which has additional features for rapid and transparent prototyping.

We will showcase the PEARLS platform with RapidGather, a PE Android app that allows emergency and crisis response teams to gather information quickly and anonymously from citizens at the scene of the event. Currently, it can take days or longer to track down the requisite information, as it depends on people voluntarily coming forward or on wide net investigation by the authorities. In the Boston Marathon bombing, for instance, even though word spread very quickly through radio, television, and social media, it still took days to gather the photos and other information needed to identify the suspects. With RapidGather, the response could be immediate, even as the crisis is unfolding. Authorities could anonymously communicate with RapidGather users in an area of interest and query them for available information, such as sensor data to locate gunshots or the epicenter of an earthquake [13], while providing privacy-preserving mechanisms for user responses.

PE Android will allow developers to create privacy-preserving applications without understanding the underlying primitives. Releasing it into the development community will enable revolutionary advances across a wide range of applications, including dynamic traffic routing and light synchronization, environmental sensing, and medical research. Similar techniques can also be applied to military contexts, such as coalition blue force tracking, where coalition partners could coordinate safe meeting locations without revealing identities. Android has a majority of the smartphone market share, and its potential impact goes beyond the mobile devices themselves to emerging and future capabilities, including the "Internet of Things" and body sensor network health monitoring, since the smartphone is the current locus of control for these emerging applications.

3.2 Crypto Tool Plan

PE Android will enable application users to have unprecedented control over the use of sensitive data by applications on their mobile device. As an example of such a technology, functional encryption can ensure that a user's privacy policy is enforced even when user data resides on an external server [5]. That is, only authorized entities can access user data and such entities can only learn particular functions of the user's data – as specified by the user's privacy policy. By incorporating functional encryption, or a similar technology, into PE Android, an application such as RapidGather can safely store user data on an external server – while maintaining assurance that authorities accessing that data can only learn information about a user that is permitted by the user's privacy policy. For example, a RapidGather user might functionally encrypt geolocation data so as to allow national anti-terrorism authorities to gain access to precise geolocation, while local authorities might only be permitted to derive an imprecise location with a random noise factor applied.

Additionally, PE Android will include a secure multiparty computation (SMC) capability, as this will allow applications to perform computations on data from multiple sources (e.g., multiple user devices, or a user device and an untrusted server) without any party learning another party's input data. For example, an application such as RapidGather could use SMC to enable a set of devices to anonymously aggregate location and sensor data to produce a joint incident report for authorities. Similarly, SMC could be used to perform a joint computation between a server – possessing a message from an emergency authority – and a set of user devices so that only those user devices meeting a certain criteria learn the message from the emergency authority. In recent years, there has been significant progress towards realizing SMC for certain applications on mobile devices [4]. Providing an easily usable SMC capability for any application is an exciting direction for PE Android.

PE Android can support a number of SMC implementations, such as a fully peer-to-peer SMC technology among mobile devices supported by secure out-sourced computation [14] and wireless networking, or a client-server SMC technology that offloads some of the cryptographic computation on one or more untrusted (or partially-trusted) servers [15]. It can also accommodate differential (and other noise-added) privacy approaches through a mediated sensor interface.

PE Android could also accommodate other potential technologies for privacy protection. For example, PE-Android could support differential privacy (or other noise-added) approaches by adding a mediated sensor to the Android platform. Similarly, PE-Android could support private information retrieval (or other advanced client-server technologies) by providing an abstraction layer that allows application developers to query such sophisticated services as simply as they can query traditional application servers.

3.3   Policy Tool Plan

PE Android will enable a broad and granular range of privacy choices, including various computational mechanisms and levels of added noise. These choices, if presented to a user without mediation, would quickly overwhelm them. One of the primary gaps in current Android systems is a lack of user understanding of the Android permissions model [8], which governs what data and functionality an app has access to. In particular, few users pay attention to the permissions during installation or are able to remember what they enabled [9]. This is exacerbated by small screen real estate and limited attention span due to users often being "on-the-go" when installing and using mobile apps. New technologies will close this gap by capturing the user's intention and succinctly displaying to them how their data is being used.

Therefore, PE Android would benefit most from the ability to effectively translate minimal user input to granular privacy policy. It will accommodate both at-installation and interactive mediation of privacy policy and will free users both from the tedium of defining a long privacy policy during app installation (as in Android L) and from constant interruptions from policy pop-ups (as seen on iOS). Useful new technologies would also reason about the impact of computations over the user's data, and mediate those interactions to provide effective policy enforcement. An interactive agent-based or online machine-learning solution that can continuously answer privacy questions, especially as context changes, would be particularly desirable.

We will develop an extensible PE Android Privacy API, which will accommodate a wide variety of interface mechanisms that communicate with and capture privacy intentions of the user, as well as flexibly convey privacy implications of those data choices. For example, this could involve using probabilistically generative models based on historical or societal information to warn users or filter content [17], asking simple policy questions ("yes/no" or "low/medium/high") to develop user models, or applying computational linguistics (such as machine translation or semantic web search [10, 18, 19]) to translate from terse user privacy statements to their implications in the data space and *vice versa*.

For applications such as RapidGather, where individuals may have little prior information in an emergency context to set a precedent, it would be helpful to use information gleaned from other users as well as social norms. For this purpose, we can support systems with various architectures, such as client/server machine learning approaches, or device-hosted autonomous agents that leverage peer-to-peer communication to collectively produce more accurate predictions of user intent. However, due to the potential latency and battery drain introduced by such architectures, external components should not be required to be "always-on."

4 Technical Plan

From "Yelping" a highly-rated nearby restaurant and "Instagramming" dinner to playing Angry Birds on the Uber ride home, mobile apps have transformed society. Their success is due to ubiquitous mobile platforms (Android) tied to distribution frameworks (Google Play) that enable developers to create wide-ranging applications and effectively distribute them. Our goal for PEARLS is to leverage those catalysts so that so that revolutionary advances in privacy-preserving applications can be made via the energetic mobile developer community and applied on a broad scale, thus ensuring the requisite user base to provide impactful social utility while maintaining user privacy.

The core of our extensible PEARLS platform is a privacy-enhanced Android OS fork, PE Android, which enables application developers to use the rich new privacy technologies without needing to understand the underlying cryptographic detail. This includes modifying the Android OS to enable privacy-preserving computation and human-data-interface functionality, integrating best-of-class technologies into main

Android libraries and OS modules, and extending the API to expose those capabilities and support seamless extensibility of new privacy-preserving technology, to include new ways for end users to control what data leaves their device.

We will demonstrate the utility and accessibility of PE Android by developing an emergency response app for it, RapidGather, which enables responders to anonymously communicate with mobile users and privately gather information from them (location, photos, videos, sensor data, etc.) to provide rapid crisis response and save lives. After RapidGather has been successfully prototyped, we will test it with PE Android on current mobile devices in a real urban location.

To achieve widespread adoption and enable practical privacy-preserving computation on everyday mobile devices, we plan to integrate the efficient components of PE Android back into Google's Android Open Source Project (AOSP). Taking inspiration from the successful mainlining of *Security*-Enhanced (SE) Android into Google's AOSP, the PEARLS team will leverage our extensive experience in creating and supporting stable, custom releases of Android on the DARPA Transformative Applications Program, and work with the Android community to effectively mainline PE Android. In parallel, we will also open source PE Android-R, so that the researchers can continue innovating on our system.

Once we have developed alpha versions of PE Android and RapidGather, we will open source them and begin engaging the AOSP project and the Android app developer community to build momentum for our system and solicit feedback from the community. As our code matures, we will submit patches to the AOSP project to be considered for mainlining into the official base. Similar to SE Android, the PEARLS team will provide build support instructions to add PE Android enhancements to the base AOSP tree directly, so that early adopters can start developing new privacy-preserving applications. To mitigate adoption challenges similar to those faced by SE Android, which had very expressive but complex security policies, PE Android will utilize technologies that support the definition of expressive privacy policies without undue developer expertise or effort.

4.1   Privacy-Enhanced Android

Enabling protections for sensitive data can be done in a number of ways on mobile devices. Protecting data at the app level, or through a third-party library, are two methods that can lead to a fractured app ecosystem, with privacy-preserving apps that may be incompatible with each other. However, the PEARLS approach makes modifications at the OS layer to introduce data privacy protections. This approach bakes strong data protection assurances directly into the OS and creates an ecosystem for new applications that can leverage Brandeis data privacy protections. PE Android also integrates the creation and enforcement of privacy policies – governing a user's private, identifiable, and sensitive data, including raw sensor readings – directly into the OS.

The PEARLS team will create PE Android by modifying the OS to provide extensions to the Android runtime API. PE Android will also provide hooks for our CRT partners to easily integrate their technologies into the Android OS. When research and development of PE Android is complete, the PEARLS team will supply patches to the mainline Android OS.

There are a number of areas suitable for extending and adding hooks for Brandeis technologies. As indicated by the dotted lines in the Android Architecture diagram, Fig. 1, the PEARLS team will extend and modify the

- Android Runtime API and core libraries,
- cryptographic libraries,
- *Location* and *Sensor Manager,*
- *Activity Manager* and *Binder,*
- *Surface Manager* and/or *Material Theme.*

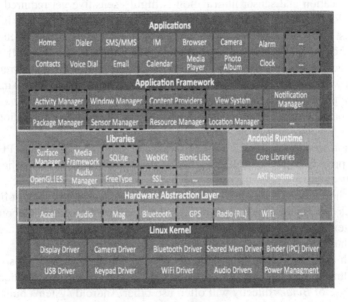

Fig. 1. Locations of PE Android Modifications

Android apps primarily make use of OS services through the Android Java Runtime and core libraries. We will modify the Android Java Runtime to expose the new privacy controls to app developers. The new PE Android Java Runtime API can be exported and used by app developers and other performers until PE Android patches are available and accepted by the Android community. In addition to the Android Java Runtime, we will modify some of the core system *Service* and *Content Provider* classes. For example, will modify the *Contacts Provider* and *Calendar Provider* to ensure data privacy policies are enforced.

Often, Android applications will store private information about the user on the Android device. On Android, the primary means to store and access information is through the use of SQLite databases. To enable existing and future apps to leverage new capabilities, PE Android will provide an interface for app developers to query data from a SQLite database with options such as added noise or cryptographic data transformations.

The Android OS supplies several cryptographic facilities for use by the system including

- the kernel crypto API provided for use by kernel modules,
- OpenSSL libraries for use in native Android binaries, and
- the BouncyCastle implementation of the Java cryptographic extensions.

Additionally, Android supplies its own keystore (either software or hardware backed depending on device) and API to access it. In Android's current state, these cryptographic facilities and keystore may not be enough to support new technologies. Where appropriate, we will add additional primitives and API extensions to PE Android to support new technologies, including extended key management functionality.

Current location and sensor information is highly sensitive yet required for applications like RapidGather. Android apps request the location and sensor information through calls to the *Location Manager* and *Sensor Manager*, which in turn request sensor data from the Android Hardware Abstraction Layer (HAL). We will extend the sensor interface in this framework so that PE Android is aware of the current privacy context, and will provide hooks for adding noise to the location and sensor information coming from the hardware. PE Android can thus enforce mediated access to the sensor information based on the privacy context and obfuscate the sensor information before it goes back to the consumer of the data.

In addition to adding privacy hooks to various Android subsystems, PE Android will allow a privacy policy to be defined, configured, and enforced. This policy can also address theft of private data, by providing users visibility into what is accessing and transferring their private data. The Android *Activity Manager* keeps track of the various running tasks and apps on the system. PE Android will add information about the data privacy context under which a task or app is running so that it can be referenced and used throughout the Android system to help enforce the privacy policy.

One such example is the Android *Binder* driver, which is an Android-specific IPC mechanism that controls most of the data flowing between processes. Applications that don't make use of *Binder* directly will often use other Android systems built on top of *Binder* to send or receive data, like Android *Intents* or *Content Providers*. Since the majority of data passed among Android processes is funneled through the *Binder* driver, it is an ideal place to enforce the privacy contexts of running applications. We will modify *Binder* so that PE Android can pass the privacy context information of the data and ensure that only tasks or applications with the appropriate privacy policy receive the data.

By tracking data throughout the system with privacy policy information, as we propose to do with *Activity Manager* and *Binder*, we can then begin to display the current privacy mode and/or private data that may be emitted from the phone to the end user. We will modify the *Surface Manager* and the *Material Theme* to provide hooks and an API for changing the user interface (UI) based on the privacy mode currently in force. This UI, coupled with privacy policy extensions, will enable application developers to integrate their technologies into the system.

Fig. 2. RapidGather response team (server) interface shows anonymized locations of RapidGather users. Responders can select users to send messages or request information for a region of interest.

4.2   Smart City App: RapidGather

We will showcase the utility of our approach with RapidGather, a Smart City application that leverages mobile crowd sensing to provide rapid emergency response and save lives. Specifically, it enables emergency and crisis response entities (e.g., ambulance, fire, law enforcement) to communicate quickly and anonymously with, and gather data from, mobile users in the midst of unfolding events, while providing users with granular control over how their private information (location, photos, microphone, sensor data, etc.) is used. Since the effectiveness of responding to emergencies or in catching perpetrators is a function of the speed and robustness of the data gathered, RapidGather will greatly enhance the current state of crisis response techniques, and provide natural transitions for other revolutionary advances in public health and safety.

The RapidGather server component will provide a robust back-end and enable authorities to automatically contact an anonymized list of people (e.g. through pub/sub or oblivious transfer mechanisms) who are or were in the location of interest with pertinent alerts ("users in this area have an elevated health risk"), questions ("have you seen license plate XYZ-123?"), and open-ended requests for information ("who has information to share about event X?"). A mockup of the response team server interface that we will develop is shown in Fig. 2, with the icons in the circle representing users with RapidGather-enabled mobile devices at the scene of interest. At a glance, responders can determine how many people are in a chosen area and what information is available, while providing privacy-preserving mechanisms for sending alerts and allowing users to respond with variable granularity.

Data owners will maintain control over their data, with a range of options on the mobile device to elect what information they are willing to share, and the granularity with which it is reported. For example, they could share their general location with varying noise added, depending on population density and their proximity to ground zero for the crisis, or they could allow only some specific function of their location to be securely computed (such as gunshot localization). A mockup of the RapidGather client interface is shown in Fig. 3.

The RapidGather application will leverage PE Android to provide a rich landscape to navigate the range of user privacy options (e.g., translating high-level user concerns to granular privacy policy or using past user behavior to predict intent). It will also support a variety of architectures and mechanisms, such as peer-to-peer secure multiparty computation (e.g., localizing shots fired or aggregating sensor data), functional searches over encrypted data, or outsourced mobile computation through homomorphic encryption, enabling exploration of utility/privacy tradeoffs.

Fig. 3. RapidGather user/client interface

5 Summary

This paper has described the plan for a new extension to Android OS, called PE Android, which includes new data privacy protection and management tools aimed at supporting Smart Cities applications. Our goal for this project is to make the advances in privacy-preserving technologies available to the mobile developer community, so that they can be broadly applied and provide the impactful social utility envisioned by Smart Cities, while maintaining user privacy.

References

1. http://source.android.com/devices/tech/security/selinux/. Retrieved 30 June 2015
2. US Defense Advanced Research Projects Agency: Brandeis, http://www.darpa.mil/program/brandeis. Retrieved 30 June 2015
3. Yao, A.C.: Protocols for secure computations. In: FOCS, 23rd Annual Symposium on Foundations of Computer Science (FOCS 1982), pp. 160–164. doi:10.1109/SFCS.1982.88
4. Huang, Y., Chapman, P., Evans, D.: Privacy-preserving applications on smartphones. In: 6th USENIX Workshop on Hot Topics in Security (HotSec 2011), San Francisco, August 2011
5. Gentry, C.: Fully homomorphic encryption using ideal lattices. In: Symposium on the Theory of Computing (STOC), pp. 169–178 (2009)
6. Boneh, D., Sahai, A., Waters, B.: Functional encryption: definitions and challenges. In: Ishai, Y. (ed.) TCC 2011. LNCS, vol. 6597, pp. 253–273. Springer, Heidelberg (2011)

7. Do, Q., Martini, B., Choo, K.-K.R.: Enhancing user privacy on Android mobile devices via permissions removal. In: 2014 47th Hawaii International Conference on System Sciences (HICSS). IEEE (2014)

8. Kelley, P.G., Consolvo, S., Cranor, L.F., Jung, J., Sadeh, N., Wetherall, D.: A conundrum of permissions: installing applications on an android smartphone. In: Blyth, J., Dietrich, S., Camp, L. (eds.) FC 2012. LNCS, vol. 7398, pp. 68–79. Springer, Heidelberg (2012)

9. Felt, A.P. et al.: Android permissions: user attention, comprehension, and behavior. In: Proceedings of the Eighth Symposium on Usable Privacy and Security. ACM (2012)

10. Pantel, P., Lin, T., Gamon, M.: Mining entity types from query logs via user intent modeling. In: Proceedings of the 50th Annual Meeting of the Association for Computational Linguistics: Long Papers, vol. 1. Association for Computational Linguistics (2012)

11. Bugiel, S., Heuser, S., Sadeghi, A.-R.: Flexible and fine-grained mandatory access control on android for diverse security and privacy policies. In: Usenix security (2013)

12. Wagner, D.T. et al.: Device analyzer: a privacy-aware platform to support research on the Android ecosystem. In: Proceedings of the 8th ACM Conference on Security & Privacy in Wireless and Mobile Networks. ACM (2015)

13. Minson, S.E. et al.: Crowdsourced earthquake early warning. Science Advances 1(3), 10 April 2015. http://advances.sciencemag.org/content/1/3/e1500036

14. Carter, H., Amrutkar, C., Dacosta, I., Traynor, P.: For your phone only: custom protocols for efficient secure function evaluation on mobile devices. Secur. Comm. Netw. 7, 1165–1176. doi:10.1002/sec.851

15. Carter, H., Mood, B., Traynor, P., Butler, K.: Secure Outsourced Garbled Circuit Evaluation for Mobile Devices. In: Proceedings of the 22nd USENIX Security Symposium, August 2013, Washington, D.C. (2013)

16. Bogetoft, P., et al.: Secure multiparty computation goes live. In: Dingledine, R., Golle, P. (eds.) FC 2009. LNCS, vol. 5628, pp. 325–343. Springer, Heidelberg (2009)

17. Peng, H. et al.: Using probabilistic generative models for ranking risks of android apps. In: Proceedings of the 2012 ACM Conference on Computer and Communications security. ACM (2012)

18. Roy, R.S. et al.: Discovering and Understanding Word Level User Intent in Web Search Queries. Web Semantics: Science, Services and Agents on the World Wide Web (2014)

19. Smith, T.F., Waterman, M.S.: Identification of common molecular subsequences. J. Mol. Biol. 147, 195–197 (1981)

Towards Smart City Implementations in Sub-Saharan Africa

The Case of Public Transportation in Ouagadougou (Burkina Faso)

Jonathan Ouoba[1(✉)], Tegawendé F. Bissyandé[2,3], and Cédric Béré[2]

[1] VTT Technical Research Centre of Finland, Espoo, Finland
jonathan.ouoba@gmail.com
[2] SnT, University of Luxembourg, Luxembourg City, Luxembourg
tegawende.bissyande@uni.lu, cedric.bere@gmail.com
[3] University of Ouagadouou, Ouagadouou, Burkina Faso

Abstract. Technological progress, in relation with ubiquitous computing, has put forward the concept of ICT-based smart cities. This concept, which is related to the need of facilitating the daily life of citizens in the concerned cities, relies on the use of existing infrastructures of communication to develop adapted digital services. As such, the implementation of mobile services in the framework of smart cities is equally important in developed countries than in the least developed countries. In the latter (more particularly in sub-Saharan Africa), it is however to be noted that the most advanced technologies of communication are not always available. It thus prevents the immediate deployment of digital systems that are available in developed countries. Obviously, the provision of mobile services dedicated to sub-Saharan areas requires the consideration of the ambient environment in terms of social and technological perspectives. In this paper, we discuss the situation of public transportation in Burkina Faso and the needs of users regarding reliable systems to retrieve transit information. We also provide and evaluate a (realistic) SMS-based solution, leveraging the technological and social specificities of the sub-Saharan context, to enhance the dissemination of information about traffic and buses in the city of Ouagadougou (Burkina Faso).

Keywords: Mobile service · Sub-Saharan Africa · Smart cities · Public transportation

1 Introduction

In recent years, the concept of *smart cities* has been put forward by technological progress. In the context of sustainable development, *smart cities* are meant to offer innovative services based on ICT in the domains of transportation, education, commerce and culture. As such, the reduction of financial costs (in terms of evelopment and deployment of digital services), the preservation of energy and

© ICST Institute for Computer Sciences, Social Informatics and Telecommunications Engineering 2016
A. Leon-Garcia et al. (Eds.): Smart City 2015, LNICST 166, pp. 78–90, 2016.
DOI: 10.1007/978-3-319-33681-7_7

the mobility (services must be accessible in mobility situations) are key points. Especially regarding mobility, most of digital services are in the form of mobile services that citizens can use via their personal mobile devices.

In developed countries, the technological environment favors the development of innovative mobile services by taking advantage of new mobile technologies. Indeed, the availability of high-end mobile devices and the deployment of infrastructures for efficient communications (4G/5G networks, Wi-Fi hotspots with high bandwidth) have obvious advantages. At European level, collaborative projects have then been initiated to tackle issues related to the design of mobile services that are adapted to the environment of potential end-users. A representative example is the Smart Urban Spaces (SUS) project that aimed at defining new mobile e-services in urban contexts. It also aimed at building a network of cities proposing the same set of ICT-based mobile solutions [2].

In countries of sub-Saharan Africa, unlike eveloped countries, the urban environment is not adapted to initiatives such as the SUS project. Concretely, the major part of the population cannot afford to use high-end mobile equipment. Also, investments in terms of infrastructures of communication are not always sufficient. In addition, the use of 3G/4G networks remains a luxury when they are available. This context changes the perspectives in the development of mobile services. It is then necessary to rely on other elements in the design of digital services so that they can be relevant for end-users. Two key elements are to be considered [21]:

- opportunistic and collaborative networking approaches are reasonable as the organization of societies favors long and frequent encounters between citizens [20]
- "cheap" technologies (i.e. technologies that generate no additional cost) must be privileged as people are more willing to use them [12]

Relatively to the previous points, public transportation represents a relevant domain to be explored for the provision of mobile services. Regarding urban areas of sub-Saharan Africa (more particularly in Burkina Faso), the question that we have then chosen to study is the following: **By taking into account the technological/social environment, how to properly disseminate information about traffic and buses to the attention of end-users?** Based on a survey that we have conducted, our approach has first been to analyze the situation of public transportation in Burkina Faso and discuss the needs of users regarding reliable systems to retrieve transit information. Then, we have designed and developed a mobile solution that relies on existing technologies to support the dissemination of information about traffic and buses. This mobile service is to be deployed in the city of Ouagadougou (Burkina Faso).

The remainder of the paper is organized as follows. First, we present the important role of *smart cities* in the context of sub-Saharan regions. Then, we provide general requirements for a system dedicated to the dissemination of information in public transportation (based on feelings and needs of users with the concrete case of the SOTRACO company in Ouagadougou) and we describe the solution (in terms of mobile service) that we propose to solve the problem. Finally, before concluding, we discuss the adoption of the proposed service by highlighting the realistic aspect of our solution and by evaluating the prototype that we have developed.

2 Towards ICT-based Smart Cities in Sub-Saharan Africa

The concept of *smart cities* has drawn much attention in developed countries. In the perspective of sustainable development, the ultimate objective is to implement digital services in order to address economic, environmental and governance issues [23]. In this context, the use of ICT is the privileged option to ease the daily life of citizens regarding the different operations to be performed in urban areas [22]. These operations are made possible by taking advantage of the capabilities of personal mobile devices and the efficiency of communication infrastructures.

In regards with sustainable development, the vital aspect of ICT-based *smart cities* for sub-Saharan countries can be highlighted. The universal scope of the concept allows to affirm its relevance for urban areas of sub-Saharan Africa. Indeed, the natural evolution of societies in all parts of the world (in terms of available technologies) encourage public authorities to provide ICT-based services to their citizens. In addition, the high penetration rate of mobile phones in the populations of sub-Saharan Africa (cf. Sect. 4), even if efficient infrastructures of communication are not always available, offers interesting opportunities for the deployment of mobile services. It is then a question of properly analyzing the technological environment in order to determine the most appropriate combination of technologies that is able to support the development of digital services. It is also a question of properly adapting solutions that have already been deployed in developed countries. More generally, we believe that the concept of *smart cities* is in accordance with the topic of ICT for development (ICT4D). ICT4D aims at leveraging ICT in order to promote sustainable development (to move people out of poverty) with an efficient use of the limited resources that are available in poor countries [16]. In the considered regions, there is thus a need to continue identifying priority areas from a societal point of view so that it is possible to initiate innovative (ICT-based) approaches regarding the provision of appropriate services for a smarter urban environment [12]. In this respect, one of the main topics to be studied concerns the domain of public transportation. The exponential growth of cities in sub-Saharan Africa, partly due to rural exodus and political crises, has led to the disruption of public services. This situation has particularly affected the field of transportation. In most of the cases, the public transportation systems fail to meet the needs of users regarding information about schedules and estimated waiting times at stops. Considering for example a country like Burkina Faso, there are no (real) fixed timetables because of the unreliability of the traffic. In addition, it is not uncommon to read stories in journals about commuters complaining of having waited several hours for a (overcrowded) bus when they could have chosen alternative means of transport if they were informed of the waiting time. In this perspective of implementation of mobile services for *smart cities*, there is an urgent need to provide new solutions to enhance the dissemination of information about traffic and buses. These solutions must be based on the use of technologies that are accessible to the majority of the population. It will allow citizens to adapt their behaviors to the current situation. This could mean that a commuter will decide to stop waiting for a coming bus because it is overcrowded or he will look for alternative means of transport because the estimated waiting time is unusually high.

3 Services for Citizens: Public Transportation Information

3.1 Current Situation and General Requirements

We have carried out a survey among the students of the computer science department at university of Ouagadougou. The aim was to collect the feelings of current/potential/former users within a population which is particularly sensitive to the services provided by public transportation operators (in this case it is the SOTRACO company that operates the network for public transportation in the city of Ouagadougou). The feedback has been collected via a Google form. The results of the survey are presented Fig. 1. Beyond the complaints about the quantity and the quality of the buses, the respondents raised issues concerning the schedules of the buses. Indeed, 97 % of people feel that the waiting times at stops are long or too long and 97 % believe that the (given) timetables are not reliable. Thus, the users "demand" a system so that they can obtain relevant information regarding the estimated transit times of the buses. This analysis is supported by other studies which show that about 70 % of people (in the city of Ouagadougou) are willing to change their travel habits in favor of public transportation provided that improvements are made to the system (especially regarding the compliance of timetables) [18].

From the perspective of end-users, the following points must be considered regarding a system intended to provide information related to public transportation [25]:

- the financial cost for accessing the information should be cheap (for example, it would be a nonsense to pay the same price as the cost of a bus ticket)
- the ease of use and the quick access to the information (so that no complex operations must be performed by the users)
- the relevance of the provided information according to the context (in particular, due to the social organization, the expectations in terms of accuracy of information are somewhat lower in sub-Saharan Africa compared to developed countries)

In our target environment, the option that consists in deploying ICT-enabled equipments at public places is not always reasonable. This situation is linked to the social climate. For example, TV displays at bus stops will probably be

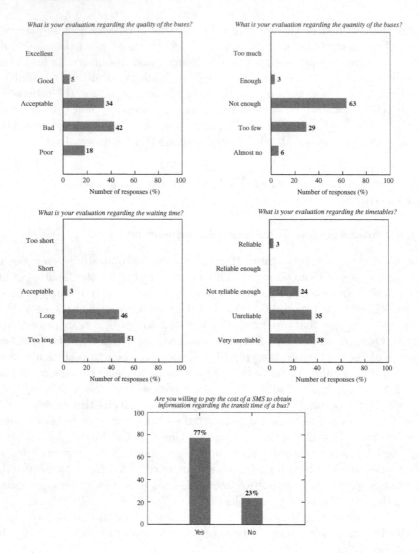

Fig. 1. Feelings of the users regarding the service provided by the SOTRACO company

stolen or broken during the regular strikes. In addition, the high cost of Internet access via personal devices leads to the fact that 3G-based services remain a luxury. In this context, another approach must be considered. It consists in taking advantage of "low-cost" technologies that can be used with the mobile devices of end-users [11, 21].

3.2   Our Proposal for an Information Service

The solution that we propose is adapted to the context of the SOTRACO company (public transportation operator in Ouagadougou). We believe this environment represents the situation that occurs in major cities of West Africa.

As a reminder, the goal is to provide the users of public transportation with up-to-date information about traffic and bus hours.

The Fig. 2 presents an overview of the whole system regarding our solution. The process is as follows:

1. Upon the arrival of a bus at a given stop, the mobile equipment (a mobile phone) of the driver receives a Bluetooth signal from a Bluetooth Low Energy (BLE) beacon[1]. The reception of the Bluetooth signal, which consists of the unique identifier of the BLE beacon, triggers the emission of a message to the SMS platform. This message, which is a SMS, contains the identifier of the bus line (corresponding to the identifier of the BLE beacon) as well as the identifier of the current bus stop and it is used to update obsolete information. In order to enable the automatic initiation of this series of operations, each bus stop is endowed with a BLE beacon that is capable of transmitting Bluetooth data in its immediate environment (an approximate range of 70 m). The Bluetooth data is then automatically captured by the mobile device of the driver when the bus comes close to the considered stop. Subsequently, this action activates a mobile application (running on the mobile phone of the driver) that associates the identifier of the beacon to the identifier of the current bus stop and sends the appropriate message to the SMS platform. It is to be noted that the identifier of the bus line, the connection address to reach the SMS Platform as well as the correspondence between the identifiers of the BLE beacons and the identifiers of the bus stops are preloaded in the application. This preloading is performed before the driver begins his journey.

2. When a user arrives at a bus stop, he taps his NFC-enabled mobile phone to a NFC[2] tag. This action triggers a mobile application (running on the mobile phone of the user) that reads the content of the NFC tag before launching the emission of a message to the SMS Platform. The message, which is a SMS, contains the identifier of the bus line as well as the identifier of the current bus stop retrieved from the tag (it is to be noted that the NFC tag also contains the connection address to the SMS Platform). In return, the SMS Platform sends a message with up-to-date information according to the request (e.g. information about coming buses). In case of change in the available information, the user receives on his mobile phone a notification containing the updated details that are sent by the SMS platform. This option is considered when the change occurs in a relatively short time (not exceeding 5 min for example). An alternative solution for triggering the retrieval of the information about coming buses is to make use of a QR code[3] instead of a

---

[1] BLE beacons are transmitters that use Bluetooth to broadcast small packets of data -http://www.ibeacon.com/what-is-ibeacon-a-guide-to-beacons/.

[2] NFC [15], which stands for Near Field Communication, is a short range wireless technology (about 10 cm) allowing compatible devices to read the content of specific tags (small piece of hardware with electrical circuits).

[3] A Quick Response (QR) code [5] is a type of two-dimensional bar code encoding data and graphically represented (generally) as a set of black squares on a white background.

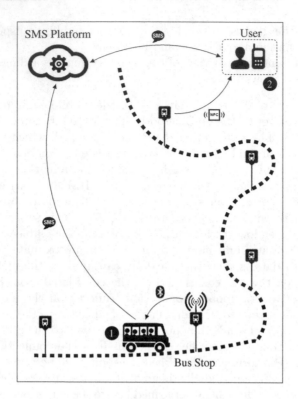

Fig. 2. Keeping commuters up-to-date on bus passage timetables

NFC tag. In this case, the user must "read" the QR code with the camera of his mobile phone. The encoded information is then extracted and the mobile application is activated to perform the requested operations (similarly to the situation in which a NFC tag is used).

According to the description of the process, three main entities are interacting with each other: the SMS Platform, the Mobile Application running on the equipment of the end-user and the Mobile Application dedicated to the equipment of the driver. These entities are illustrated Fig. 3. We detail their main characteristics in the remainder of this section.

SMS Platform. The role of this entity is to receive SMS from different sources, to parse the received messages so that a database can be populated with information regarding bus lines and to answer to requests regarding the information that is stored in the database. The platform, as a traditional SMS platform (i.e. a platform which is able to handle reception and emission of SMS), is accessible via a connexion address which corresponds to a phone number of a mobile operator. The platform also manages the database that stores transit information. Upon the reception of a message, it is parsed in order to be processed according to the following possibilities:

- the message comes from a driver. In this case, the relevant content is inserted in the database to update it with the most recent information regarding a bus line (last stop, transit time at a given stop, current location of the considered bus)
- the message is a request from a user. In this case, the data corresponding to the content of the message is retrieved from the database and it is sent, as a SMS, to the phone number that was used to transfer the request. The transmitted data corresponds to the last time that a bus reached the stop on the concerned line, to the last stop of the approaching bus and to an evaluation of the transit time at the stop of the user (according to the historical data that has been collected)

Mobile Application for the User. The role of this application is to manage the interactions of the user with other entities (or equipments) via NFC and via SMS. The application is able to handle the reading of content stored in a NFC tag (identifier of the bus line, identifier of the bus stop, connection address to the SMS Platform), to format a message with the retrieved information and to send it via SMS to the corresponding platform. The application is also able to handle the reception a message from the SMS Platform (an answer to a request) and to display it for the user. In the case that QR codes are deployed, a module enabling the extraction of data is integrated into the application.

Mobile Application for the Driver. The role of this application is to provide a tool for the driver so that he can transmit information to the SMS Platform (the application works independently and it requires no action from the driver). It concerns the transit times of his bus and its location according to the stops of the journey. The application is then able to handle the reception of signals transmitted by BLE beacons. This data, associated to the preloaded information, is then used by the application to automatically send a message (to the SMS Platform) containing the last stop and the transit time at the stop for the corresponding bus line.

4   Adoption of the Proposed Service

With far more than 650 million users [24], the proliferation of feature-phones and low cost smartphones in sub-Saharan Africa has dramatically increased over the past decade[4]. Moreover, it should be noted that the mobile penetration rate was up to 39 % in 2014 (compared to a global average of 49.9 %) and it is expected to reach 48.7 % by 2020 (compared to a global average of 59.3 %) [10]. It thus highlights the potential of ICT-based systems that rely on the deployment of mobile services. Based on this observation, the following points allow us to anticipate a likely adoption of our solution:

---

[4] According to GSMA (GSM Association), the number of unique mobile subscribers rose from 146 million in 2008 to 347 million in 2014 [9].

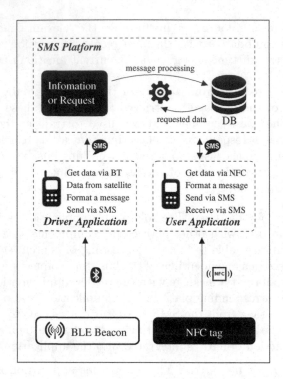

Fig. 3. Overview of the interactions between the entities of the proposed system

- Users increasingly aspire to interact with their mobile phones by taking advantage of productivity and utility applications. This view is supported by a report of a mobile phone manufacturer on *bridging the digital divide* in sub-Saharan Africa [17].
- The availability of feature-phones or low cost smartphones that offer NFC capabilities [1]. This includes for example the Samsung Galaxy Lite S6790, the Alcatel Pop D3 or the Huawei Ascend G300. Obviously, these phones have an affordable price for the people of the concerned areas. It is to be noted that one of the main characteristics of NFC technology is the simplicity of use. Indeed, the user must simply tap his mobile device to the equipment (NFC tags) with which he wants to interact and the corresponding operations are automatically triggered. It is also to be noted that feature-phones and low cost smartphones are equipped with cameras. It then appears realistic to also use QR codes even if this latter option is a little less convenient for end-users (as it has been stated for NFC-enabled ticketing systems [14]).
- In the context of mobile communications, the most popular (and reliable) service in sub-Saharan Africa remains the SMS [3]. Indeed, more than 72 % of the owners of mobile phones use this means of communication on a weekly basis [17]. For the record, the emission of a SMS approximatively costs 0.02

Euro [8] through the networks of the mobile operators in Burkina Faso (compared to the price of a bus ticket which is approximatively set to 0.20 Euro).
- According to the results of the survey that we have carried out, the feelings of users suggest that the people are looking for mobile services dedicated to public transportation. This has to do with the supply of an adapted tool to retrieve relevant information about the traffic of public transportation, especially for the transit time of buses at stops. The survey also suggests that users (more than 75 %, cf. last part of Fig. 1) are willing to pay the *cost of a SMS* in order to get the information they may need. In addition, *SMS Innovation* is seen by the big players as one of the most appropriate means to provide adapted e-services in various domains (e.g. mHealth) for people living in sub-Saharan Africa [6].

We have also performed usability tests with a prototype of our solution. The objective was to collect relevant feedback from potential end-users through the (10-items) questionnaire of the System Usability Scale (SUS) by John Brooke [13]. The System Usability Scale is acknowledged to be an effective tool for the evaluation of perceived usability [7,19]. The group of testers was composed of 34 students of the university of Ouagadougou. Indeed, in the considered environment students represent the type of population that is most likely to use public transportation. As for the prototype, it consists of an Android application that retrieves transit information and a SMS server that performs the operations of the SMS platform. Figure 4 presents screenshots of the mobile application that displays alerts regarding the arrival of a bus. Concerning the scenario of the test, the users simply needed to tap a mobile phone to a NFC tag (or read a QR code) in order to trigger a request (via the emission of a SMS) and they wait to receive in return alerts about transit information. Of course, the Android application was loaded on the mobile phone so that it can interact with the SMS server. By aggregating the answers of the testers (i.e. each set of answers attributes a note on 100), we have obtained an average of 73 out of 100. This result argues in favor of the acceptance of mobile services based on our concept as it corresponds to a good SUS score [4]. As a complement, interviews with the testers have allowed us to get many valuable comments. In particular, we have noted that more than 73 % of the respondents are willing to frequently make use of the proposed service.

The previous elements emphasize the realistic aspect of our system as the social and the technological environment of potential end-users are considered. They also highlight the fact that the system meet the requirements presented in Sect. 3.1. In addition, the implementation of such services may help citizens to benefit from the potential of their mobile equipments and thus make their money worth. However, there is still a challenge in the deployment of the mobile application at the end-user level (i.e. appropriate distribution channel). This topic deserves further studies in order to propose adapted answers. A possible solution will require the establishment of specific customer centers where the people will be able to easily download applications on their mobile phone. Another considerable point concerns the scalability of the system. It should simply be

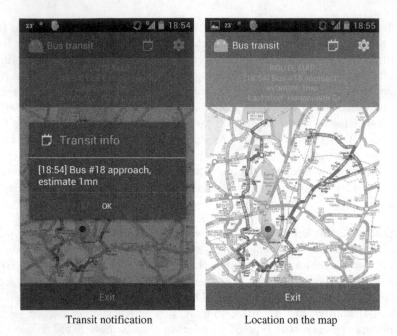

<table>
<tr><td>Transit notification</td><td>Location on the map</td></tr>
</table>

Fig. 4. Reception of alerts within the mobile application of the prototype

pointed that the scalability is an inherent characteristic because of the choices in terms of design and communication technologies. In particular, the use of SMS as the privileged communication carrier is an obvious example. It thus only depends on the level of investments concerning ICT-based infrastructures (e.g. SMS platform).

In view of these observations, a closer cooperation with public authorities is essential to the success of the whole project. As such, we plan to launch a more active phase of the project regarding the collaboration between the university of Ouagadougou and the SOTRACO company (public transportation operator in Ouagadougou).

5   Conclusion

We have proposed a (realistic) system to support the provision of information in public transportation. This system, which is a mobile service, allows the commuters to make use of their mobile equipment to retrieve information about traffic and bus hours. Although initially designed for the public transportation system of Ouagadougou (Burkina Faso), we believe that the solution can be deployed in other cities of sub-Saharan Africa, more particularly in West Africa. The similarity in the structure of the society in these cities allows this extrapolation.

Two main factors militate in favor of the adoption of the proposed service. The sample of opinions that we have collected in Ouagadougou shows the expectations of users. Indeed, they need and they are willing to use such a system of information so that they can adapt their behavior to the current situation (choose to wait or not for a bus depending on the estimated waiting time). In addition, the service is accessible through "cheap" technologies that are commonly used by the people of the concerned regions (SMS) or that generates no additional costs (NFC or QR codes).

It is reasonable to assume that public authorities can afford some investments (regarding systems such as the SMS Platform of our solution). As such, the current work serves as a basis in the collaboration that is to be set up with public authorities in Burkina Faso. This project is part of initiatives intended to improve the experience of citizens regarding the daily operations that they perform. The expected results will provide useful insights to consider in the development of ICT-based smart cities in accordance with the context of sub-Saharan Africa.

References

1. NFC phones: the definitive list. http://www.nfcworld.com/nfc-phones-list/
2. Smart Urban Spaces website, June 2014. http://www.smarturbanspaces.org
3. Cell phones in africa: communication lifeline, June 2015. http://www.pewglobal.org/2015/04/15/cell-phones-in-africa-communication-lifeline/
4. Measuring usability with the system usability scale (sus), June 2015. http://www.measuringu.com/sus.php
5. QR code technology, June 2015. http://qrcodesdoneright.com/
6. SMS innovation and dynamic mobile content drives mHealth initiatives in Africa, June 2015. http://blog.gemalto.com/blog/2014/07/16/sms-innovation-and-dynamic-mobile-content-drives-mhealth-initiatives-in-africa/
7. System usability scale (sus), June 2015. http://www.usability.gov/how-to-and-tools/methods/system-usability-scale.html
8. TELMOB Mobile Operator, June 2015. http://www.onatel.bf/telmob2/prepaye/tarifs-prp.htm
9. The Mobile Economy - Sub-Saharan Africa. Technical report, GSMA (2015)
10. The Mobile Economy. Technical report, GSMA (2015)
11. Anderson, R.E., Poon, A., Lustig, C., Brunette, W., Borriello, G., Kolko, B.E.: Building a transportation information system using only gps and basic SMS infrastructure. In: ICTD, pp. 233–242 (2009)
12. Bissyandé, T.F., Ahmat, D., Ouoba, J., van Stam, G., Klein, J., Le Traon, Y.: Sustainable ICT4D in Africa: where do we go from here? In: Bissyandé, T.F., van Stam, G. (eds.) AFRICOMM 2013, LNICST 135. LNICST, vol. 135, pp. 95–103. Springer, Heidelberg (2014)
13. Brooke, J.: SUS: a quick and dirty usability scale. Usability Eval. Ind. **189**, 4–7 (1996). Taylor and Francis Ltd, London, England
14. Chaumette, S., Dubernet, D., Ouoba, J., Siira, E., Tuikka, T.: Architecture and comparison of two different user-centric NFC-Enabled event ticketing approaches. In: Balandin, S., Koucheryavy, Y., Hu, H. (eds.) NEW2AN 2011 and ruSMART 2011. LNCS, vol. 6869, pp. 165–177. Springer, Heidelberg (2011)
15. Haselsteiner, E., Breitfuss, K.: Security in near field communications (NFC). In: Proceedings of Workshop on RFID Security RFIDSec (2006)

16. Heeks, R.: ICT4D 2.0: the next phase of applying ICT for international. IEEE Comput. **41**(6), 26–33 (2008)
17. Consumer Insight. How mobile phones are playing a key role in connecting people in sub-Saharan Africa. Technical report, Ericsson AB, November 2013
18. Anicha Adéelaïde Alimatou Kadiogo. Modélisation d'un système de transport urbain de personnes en vue d'une amélioration de la mobilité: cas de la ville de Ouagadougou - Modeling a system of urban passenger transport in order to improve mobility: the case of the city of Ouogadougou. Master's thesis, Institut International d'Ingénierie de lEau et de IEnvironnement - 2iE (2014)
19. Bangor, A., Kortum, P., Miller, J.: Determining what individual sus scores mean: adding an adjective rating scale. J. Usability Stud. **4**(3), 114–123 (2009)
20. Ouoba, J., Bissyandé, T.F.: Leveraging the cultural model for opportunistic networking in Sub-Saharan Africa. In: Jonas, K., Rai, I.A., Tchuente, M. (eds.) AFRICOMM 2012. LNICST, vol. 119, pp. 163–173. Springer, Heidelberg (2013)
21. Ouoba, J., Bissyandé, T.F.: Sensing in the urban technological deserts - a position paper for smart cities in least developed countries. In: International Workshop on Web Intelligence and Smart Sensing, IWWISS, Saint-Étienne, France (2014)
22. Ouoba, J., Siira, E.: Many faces of mobile contactless ticketing. In: Proceedings of the Second International Conference on Smart Systems, Devices and Technologies, SMART 2013, pp. 93–98 (2013)
23. Giffinger, R., Fertner, C., Kramar, H., Kalasek, R., Pichler-Milanovic, N., Meijers, E.: Smart cities - ranking of european medium-sized cities. Technical report, Vienna Centre of Regional Science (2007)
24. Sambira, J.: Africa's mobile youth drive change - cell phones reshape youth cultures. Afr. Renew. Afr. Youth Driv. Innov. **27**(1), 19 (2015)
25. Virtanen, A., Koskinen, S.: Public Transport Real Time Information in Personal Navigation Systems for Special User Groups. Technical report, VTT Technical Research Centre of Finland (2004)

Connecting Digital Cities: Return of Experience on the Development of a Data Platform for Multimodal Journey Planning

Jonathan Ouoba$^{(\boxtimes)}$, Janne Lahti, and Jukka Ahola

VTT Technical Research Centre of Finland, Espoo, Finland
jonathan.ouoba@gmail.com, {janne.lahti,jukka.ahola}@vtt.fi

Abstract. The multiplication of real-time data sources in urban areas creates a fragmented environment regarding the supply of mobile services for transportation. Thus, in order to support the deployment of smart mobility services with a more global view of the urban context, the available data must be appropriately handled through dedicated platforms. It is in this context that the Connecting Digital Cities (CDC) project has been initiated at European level. The goal of the project is to deploy a platform that is able to collect, analyze and enrich the relevant information in order to provide a valuable aggregate of real-time data related to urban mobility. This paper presents a first return of experience in the development of this platform. We first provide an overview of the CDC project and we detail the architecture of the platform intended to collect and process real-time data. For validation purposes, we then describe a mobile service for multimodal journey planning that has been deployed to interact with the CDC platform. Finally, we share the lessons learned in terms of reliability of the system and proper integration of the system into urban ecosystems.

Keywords: Digital cities · Smart transportation · Journey planner · Mobile services · Mobility data

1 Introduction

The trend of continuous urbanization and the expansion of cities raise big challenges in the domain of transportation [6]. At a global scale, one million people move to cities every week and it is predicted that urban areas will be home to five billion people in 2020 [15]. This highlights the necessity for ICT-based solutions in order to rationalize the organization of urban spaces and also address issues related to pollution and energy preservation. At European level, many urban mobility services exist to improve the daily life of citizens in the domain of transportation. These solutions take advantage of real-time data provided by different actors of the urban environment. It concerns data from cities (e.g. traffic monitoring), public transportation and private operators (e.g. taxi and parking) that are made available to third parties through open APIs. However, the provided solutions give a fragmented view of urban areas and they are not always

© ICST Institute for Computer Sciences, Social Informatics and Telecommunications Engineering 2016
A. Leon-Garcia et al. (Eds.): Smart City 2015, LNICST 166, pp. 91–103, 2016.
DOI: 10.1007/978-3-319-33681-7_8

complementary to each other. Indeed, due to the multiplication of data sources, they often lack a global view regarding urban mobility data. In addition, new types of information such as crowd-sourced data (accessible for instance via social networks) are too rarely considered.

In this context, EIT ICT Labs[1] is encouraging collaborative initiatives such as the Connecting Digital Cities (CDC) project that are intended to build interoperable solutions to support smart mobility services. This paper presents a first return of experience concerning the CDC project by discussing the following question: **How to appropriately combine real-time data from various sources, hence making it possible to support the development of mobile services for multimodal smart mobility?**

Our approach has been to build a platform with a relevant model from a technical and a business perspective. The remainder of the paper is organized as follows. First, we provide an overview of the CDC project and we detail the architecture of the platform[2] intended to collect and process real-time data in urban environments. Thereafter, we describe the Park&Ride service that has been deployed and evaluated in order to validate the functionalities of the CDC platform. Finally, we share the lessons learned in terms of reliability of the system and business model before concluding.

2   Connecting Digital Cities

2.1   Presentation of the Project

The Connecting Digital Cities project is carried out within the framework of EIT ICT Labs in the category of Urban Life and Mobility. The goal of the project is to deploy a platform that is able to collect, analyze and enrich the relevant information in order to supply a consistent aggregate of real-time data related to urban mobility. The objective is also to develop a set of mobile services making use of the platform so that its efficiency can be illustrated. In others words, this platform is intended to provide a relevant technical layer for supporting the development of transportation services for urban areas. Indeed, the proliferation of data sources makes it difficult to apprehend the whole reality of urban spaces and it leads to the deployment of fragmented mobility services. It concerns data from users (e.g. mobility traces, social networks), data describing the environment (e.g. weather conditions) as well as data produced by public authorities (e.g. public transportation, traffic flow). For interoperability and consistency purposes, it is thus essential to improve the framework to handle (in terms of collection and sharing) multiple sources of real-time information in an urban context. To this end, the straightforward approach consists in building a platform that helps to unify the vision of developers of services regarding the

---

[1] European Institute of Innovation and Technology - http://www.eitictlabs.eu/.

[2] For confidentiality reasons related to the conduct of the CDC project, all technical details are not provided. However, this limitation does not affect the contribution of the paper in regards with the return of experience.

available (real-time) data and the way to use it. This situation illustrates the relevance of the CDC project. The relevance is also reinforced by the actions promoted by EIT ICT Labs in the domain of Urban Life and Mobility [5].

The first phase of the CDC project took place between January and December in 2014. The consortium consists of industrial partners with big players in the domain of ICT-based technology such as Nokia and Thales, research institutes and SMEs offering mobile services for transportation. Three countries were involved, namely France, Finland and Italy. In terms of basis for the work, the project built on top of the results that have been achieved by former initiatives. These initiatives are:

– The ASSISTANT project [2,14] (an European initiative) the goal of which is to improve the mobility of elderly people by providing mobile services allowing them to safely and independently travel with public transportation;
– The SUS project [4,9] (an European initiative) which aims at developing interoperable technology bricks so that it enables cities to easily introduce advanced mobile services in the domain of transportation and tourism [7,8,13];
– The Tivit Digital Services framework which is part of a national project in Finland that aims at supporting the creation of user-driven digital services with the appropriate technological platforms [12].

In terms of architecture and functional characteristics, the next section discusses the approach for designing the CDC platform.

2.2 Architecture of the CDC Platform

As a reminder, the CDC platform is intended to provide a lightweight and service-oriented environment to support the effective development of urban mobility solutions. As such, the main concerns lie in efficiency and scalability. To handle these issues, the platform complies with the reference architecture for Urban Life and Mobility that is defined in the EIT ICT Action Line [5]. The access to the platform is based on the SOA [10] paradigm in order to foster interoperability. It is to be noted that this approach adheres to the principles of the European Interoperability Framework and the European Interoperability Reference Architecture [3].

In a concrete way, the architecture of the CDC system consists of three main layers (as illustrated Fig. 1) that can be described as follows:

– **Data Layer.** This module gathers and organizes the data from external sources. It enables the platform to regularly access remote servers (via HTTP-protocol) in order to collect data (in XML/JSON format) that is published by public/private stakeholders of the ecosystem related to urban mobility. It also ensures that the data is normalized (i.e. it makes use of the norm ISO 8601 [1] as the baseline for timestamps) so that it can be sorted, compared to other information and used by the other layers. Obviously, the pace of updating the data depends on the schedule of the providers. In our context, the Data Layer is able to handle data regarding weather conditions, traffic flows, parking facilities, taxi operators, public transportation and social networks.

- **Analytics Layer.** This module makes use of data collected through the Data Layer in order to discover patterns of urban mobility. It enables the platform to identify eventual traffic disruptions by analyzing the traffic flows, the state of the public transportation network and the relevant posts within social networks. Based on the extrapolation of data history and the anticipation of upcoming events, it also performs forecasts regarding the evolution of traffic flows and the availability of means of transport. Additional information is provided in the Subsect. 3.2 that describes the interaction of the platform with the server of a mobile service.

  The merging of information from multiple sources improves the accuracy of traffic analysis and forecasts as it allows the discovery of significant events that can be "hidden". To this end, this layer is endowed with spatiotemporal Complex Event Processing (CEP) capabilities so that it can perform deductions, analysis and correlations from elementary pieces of information.
- **Interface Layer.** This module provides public APIs so that third parties (e.g. developers, service providers) can take advantage of the analytics capabilities of the CDC platform. The APIs allow third parties to transmit HTTP-based requests specifying an area or a location. The Interface Layer processes these requests and interacts with the Analytics Layer in order to retrieve relevant information. Thus, third parties are able to receive real-time status and forecasts related to urban mobility (in terms of traffic conditions, public transportation) in a given area. This functionality is especially useful for mobile applications dedicated to urban mobility. As they usually rely on back-end systems to meet the expectations of users, it eases the process by merging the source of information.

In addition to these modules, a Registry is integrated to the system[3]. This component provides a comprehensive view of the capabilities of the CDC platform so that it can be effectively used by third parties. Through a web-based environment, it lists the available resources as well as the technical documentation associated to these resources. For evaluation purpose, the Registry also supports feedbacks of users (third parties) regarding the access to the platform.

2.3   CDC Ecosystem

From a business perspective, the potential of the CDC platform is emphasized by the fact that it eases the development of mobility services and it enhances the accuracy of information provided to end-users. Indeed, the capabilities of the platform (data processing and data mining) associated to the provision of public APIs give a simple and customized access to urban mobility data. Then, the service providers (developers of mobility services) can specialize and focus on core business by marketing their own services. We may also mention the public authorities in the list of important actors. Indeed, the public sector can consider the CDC system as an additional tool for planning, collecting and managing mobility issues regarding citizens.

---

[3] This specific module has been developed in the framework of the E015 Digital Ecosystem project [16].

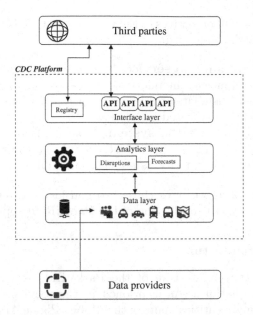

Fig. 1. Architecture of the CDC system

Other business aspects are provided in the Subsect. 3.3 related to the business model of the mobile service (Park&Ride) that has been developed within the CDC project.

3 Multimodal Journey Planner

3.1 Objective and Challenges

In order to illustrate the use of the CDC platform with a concrete case, a service was developed. This service is called Park&Ride and it consists of a mobile application interacting with a backend system to retrieve mobility data. Park&Ride aims at providing an appropriate tool to handle (real-time) multimodal journey planning in specific situations. The main usage scenario is as follows:

- First, the user chooses a destination address that he wants to reach;
- then, the application provides a navigation assistance making it possible to use personal transportation (e.g. private car) and/or monitor the route for traffic disruptions to propose alternative options with public transportation;
- finally, in case the user prefers an alternative solution because of a disruption, the application provides relevant information regarding the parking options and the adequate combination of public transportation to reach the final destination (with a mention of the corresponding walking distance to access public transportation facilities).

In line with the overall objectives of the CDC project, the Park&Ride service must specifically match the following requirements:

- **Quality of information and service.** It represents the added value for the user in terms of relevance of the information.
- **User friendliness.** It is related to the user experience when he interacts with the application via the dedicated interface.
- **Quality in the design of the system.** It concerns the security and the reliability of the system. The design must ensure that the system is resilient to faults while handling connectivity issues with smoothness and responsiveness.

The requirements that we have chosen to consider are returned to in the Subsect. 3.4 dedicated to the evaluation of the Park&Ride application.

3.2 Technical Architecture

Figure 2 illustrates the architecture of the Park&Ride service as well as its links with the CDC platform. As mentioned in the previous section, the service consists of two main entities, namely the Mobile Phone Application and the Park&Ride Server.

The Mobile Phone Application interacts with the Park&Ride Server by forwarding the requests of the user, by collecting the results of the requests and by retrieving relevant data regarding eventual disruptions in the traffic. Upon reception of data from the server, the application notifies the user by displaying the information and it prompts him to take an action (validation of a routing proposal, choice of an alternative solution in case of disruption, etc.). In addition, the Mobile Phone Application contains a map module (maintained by a third party) allowing it to route the user to the destination provided that he wishes to travel either via a private vehicle or via public transportation.

Regarding the Park&Ride Server, it is connected to the CDC platform and it acts as an intermediary for the Mobile Phone Application. The collected data, particularly with regard to the availability of parking lots and the detection of disruption, enables the server to determine the adequate combination (best parking options, transit via public transportation, routing with private vehicle) to reach a given destination. It is to be noted that the Park&Ride Server makes use of external sources in order to access complementary data regarding weather conditions and routing options with public transportation.

The operation of specific modules within the CDC platform, especially the Disruption Checker, the Parking Prediction and the Route Optimizer, completes the description of the technical architecture. These modules are linked to the Park&Ride Server via the Interface Layer of the CDC platform (cf. architecture Fig. 1) and their main characteristics are as follows[4]:

---

[4] It is to be noted that Fig. 2 is simplified as it does not mention the Interface Layer of the CDC platform.

- the **Disruption Checker** identifies the eventual disruptions that occur on a given route. This identification is made possible by the retrieval and the analysis of available data. In our case, this includes public transportation data regarding incidents (delays, service interruption, and accidents), real-time traffic flow in the considered area and activity on social networks (Twitter posts related to the traffic conditions).
- the **Parking Service** collects records related to the evolution of the occupancy rates concerning parking facilities in a given area. Then by extrapolating this data, it estimates the availability of parking lots so that it is possible to propose the best parking options for the considered area.
- the main functionality of the **Route Optimizer** is to identify the best routes to reach a destination. This operation is performed by evaluating, among the matrix of possible routes to a given destination, the minimum of $\{XYZ\}$. X corresponds to the use of a private vehicle (distance, time), Y corresponds to the availability of the associated services (e.g. price and occupancy rate of parking facilities) and as for Z it corresponds to the transit options with public transportation (time, changes, price, walking distances).

According to its original description, the CDC platform operates the internal modules and provides the Park&Ride server with the requested data (historical or real-time) in a normalized standard format.

3.3   Related Business Model

From a business perspective, the use of Park&Ride amounts to considering public transportation as an extension of private means of transport or vice versa. It can

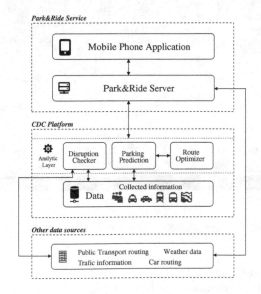

Fig. 2. Architecture of the Park&Ride system

lead to significantly increase the accessibility and the usage of transit networks as well as associated parking areas. Based on this perspective, the most appropriate option is to ensure the development and the deployment of the Park&Ride service through collaborations between public transportation authorities and parking service providers; the main channel to reach the end-user (and "distribute" the service) is the mobile application.

In terms of costs, the resources to mobilize are mainly intended for the deployment and the maintenance of infrastructures for the Park&Ride Server (apart from the development of the mobile application).

In addition, it is to be noted that the Park&Ride service allows suburban/rural users to plan more easily a journey to cities without having to use a private vehicle to go downtown. By leveraging parking information in order to propose public transportation solutions, the system leads to reduce traffic congestion in urban centers. Thus, the demand drops in urban centers regarding the requests for parking. This decrease has the effect of making available more affordable parking options within cities.

3.4   Deployment and Evaluation

The piloting phase of Park&Ride has been carried out in December 2014. It has targeted the city of Helsinki (Finland). The objective was to evaluate the usability and the robustness of the system (supported by the CDC platform) as well as to collect valuable information regarding the feelings of the potential users.

Fig. 3. Screenshots of the Park&Ride application

For testing purposes, a panel of 17 users (an heterogeneous group of voluntary users from diverse backgrounds) was formed among the people working at VTT Technical Research Centre of Finland. These persons were living and working in the area of Helsinki. Each participant was provided with a car and a mobile device (in this case a Nexus 5 smartphone) running the Park&Ride Android application (its interface is presented Fig. 3). The practical set-up of the tests has led to the following process:

- Each participant had to perform a round trip during about 4 h; the journey included the use of the car, the use of parking facilities and the use of public transportation; the users had the flexibility to choose the destination while the starting point was forced for practical reasons.
- The collection of data regarding the perception of users was done through a questionnaire (details of the aspects to be evaluated are given in the results of the evaluation) and phone interviews.

It is to be noted that the test-related operations on the field have taken place during the week of December 1 (2014).

Figure 4 illustrates the perceptions of users (an average that includes the answers of each participant) concerning aspects such as ease of learning to use the service, ease of use, clearness of the provided information, reliability of the information, usefulness of the service and safety related to the use of the service. On the graph, the blue bars represent the navigation when the user drives the car and the red bars represent the other situations (use of public transportation and walking). The rating of the different aspects of the Park&Ride service was supported by the 5-point Likert scale [11]. The value 1 is associated to the worst case while the value 5 is associated to the best (ideal) case.

The graph shows that, for most aspects, a rating greater than 3.5 (or very close to 3.5) is reached. These results (supplemented by the phone interviews) highlight the fact that the system is perceived as being rather reliable (especially in unfamiliar environments) and they also point out the willingness of the participants to use the service in the future. A notable point concerns the relatively low rating of the clearness for navigation in public transportation and during walking phase (an average of 2.5). An analysis of the responses to the questionnaire and the phone interviews have given an insight for an explanation. It appears

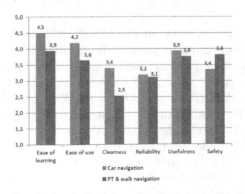

Fig. 4. Evaluation results for the Park&Ride service (Color figure online)

that users, in the context of public transportation, find difficult to understand the flow of information. Due to the various opportunities that are often offered in that phase, the user has to handle a lot of information-rich content.

The evaluation points out the potential of the CDC platform and its suitability for a real urban environment. To further investigate this aspect and complete the previous evaluation, the next section discusses the technical details that have a significant impact on the performance of the CDC platform according to our experience in the CDC project.

4   Return of Experience

In regards to the development and the piloting phase of the platform, we present in this section some reflections and lessons-learned as well as perspectives for the evolution of the CDC framework.

Data Integration. Data integration implied the creation of wrappers for various heterogeneous real-time data sources. The data sources ranged from standardized REST-based APIs to crowd-sourced ones. The development of wrappers is challenging as it requires a precise knowledge of the legacy system for the corresponding data. In our case, the task was especially complex due to the large variation in data types, data models, refresh rates, and storage methods (data dumps vs regular databases). Another challenge was the variation in the quality and the general reliability of crowd-sourced data. For example, during the piloting phase there was several issues in recognizing the right context. E.g. word "Metro" in a Twitter message could mean underground train or downtown as a generic area. Further exploration of this issue is planed.

Presentation and Storage of Data. Designing the object model for the platform was very challenging due the many and varied data sources. It was necessary to normalize certain common attributes, such as the timestamp, which seemed to be different in every data source. We have decided to utilize the ISO 8601 as the baseline for timestamps. We have then implemented converters for each encountered format so that we have the capability to compare, sort, and filter data based on time and date.

Data Provision. During the tests with the Park&Ride mobile application, the most encountered source of problems was the location inaccuracy. The combination of location uncertainties and variations of time lags (because of delays originating from low-quality data links) decreased the quality of the service provided to the users of Park&Ride. Indeed, the handling of multimodal junctions was tricky: How to detect when the user is at the stop or when he has boarded a vehicle? Is the user in the right vehicle? When is the user supposed to get off? In all these cases the location accuracy must be less than ten meters and the real-time data delay (e.g. buses locations) needs to be less than 10 s. These requirements were quite often missed especially in the city center with its "urban canyon" environment. We have thus put a lot of effort on the analysis of the reliability and the accuracy of data sources. We have then been able to provide an estimate that can be injected as metadata, hence enabling the notification of end-users regarding the reliability of information.

Based on the feed-back from developers of mobile applications, we have noticed that the standardized access to real-time data from various sources provided by a centralized platform (i.e. the CDC framework) appears to be valuable. However, there is a trade-off regarding the data when considering the level of processing to perform within the platform. Indeed, raw real-time data has low delays but it requires a lot of data transfer and storage. As for processed data, it is in more compact form but it may limit the potential applicability for developers. The amount of real-time data collected every second by the CDC platform was huge, the storage and the direct distribution of all this raw data was therefore out of question.

Ecosystem of Data Provision. This aspect concerns the adequacy of the CDC platform with the ecosystem related to mobility information. As such, the main issue lies in the fact that data providers are generally local with specificities according to the considered city/area and their systems are (very) proprietary. The data wrapper layer was made as adaptive as possible so that it is relatively easy to implement the integration of new data wrappers to the platform. It was also designed to be lightweight. This approach should simplify the extension of the platform to new cities/areas.

Unreliability of Data Providers. As most of data providers were "loosely-coupled" to the platform, there was no service level agreements (i.e. the supply of data was free of charge). As a consequence, many (unannounced) downtimes occurred. Obviously, downtimes may have cascading effects on other services and their applications. In addition the changes in protocols (e.g. formats of raw-data and interfaces to access data) or even regarding licenses for data usage may happen with short notice. This creates a constant burden relatively to the development of data wrappers as they must be monitored and regularly updated.

Next Steps. According to the feedback from third parties, it is necessary to improve the support for application developers. During this phase of the CDC project, the utilization rate was relatively low for the public APIs (despite appropriate documentation and standardization efforts). The aim is then to produce more mature tools (from a technical perspective) as well as enhanced material in order to ease the use of our APIs within mobile applications.

Based on the analysis of data resulting from Park&Ride pilots, we have noticed additional delays (about 2–5 s) in certain situations. These delays are caused by the data propagation through the layers of our platform and it clearly weakened the user experience. We are therefore looking into more "lighter" and distributed approaches so that in delay-critical cases the real-time data could be directly propagated to the devices of end-users (thus by-passing the analytic layer).

Moreover, there is a clear need to integrate information about ticketing and payment options. It will give the possibility to optimize or sort the routing options according to more (relevant) criteria. Also, the integration of other types of parking places (e.g. satellite parking or road-side parking) in addition to (traditional) large parking facilities would make the system more dynamic in order to better adapt to various contexts.

5   Conclusion

The Connecting Digital Cities project has initiated the development of a data platform intended to provide a valuable aggregate of information related to urban mobility (e.g. traffic, transportation options, crowd-sourced data from social networks). This aggregate is meant to support the implementation of smart mobility services and it is thus made available to service providers through open APIs. The tests that we have carried out in a real urban environment (i.e. city of Helsinki in Finland) have demonstrated the relevance of the platform from technical and business perspectives. These tests essentially involved the deployment of the Park&Ride (multimodal journey planner) service that interacted with the CDC data platform to retrieve consistent mobility data.

However, many efforts are still needed to improve the overall performance of the data platform. As such, the lessons learned in terms of reliability and suitability of the platform have guided the preparation regarding the second phase of the CDC project. This mainly concerns the integration of other types of data (e.g. information about ticketing and payment options as well as details on non-conventional parking places) and the handling of delay-critical situations by directly targeting the devices of end-users when it is relevant. The goal now is to improve the "maturity" of the technical tools in order to increase the use of the public APIs supplied by the CDC platform.

References

1. Data elements and interchange formats - Representation of dates and times. Technical report ISO, International Organization for Standardization (2004)
2. ASSISTANT project, May 2015. http://www.aal-assistant.eu/
3. EIRA, May 2015. https://joinup.ec.europa.eu/asset/eia/description
4. Smart Urban Spaces website, May 2015. http://www.smarturbanspaces.org
5. ULM, May 2015. http://www.eitictlabs.eu/innovation-entrepreneurship/urban-life-mobility/
6. Urban population growth, May 2015. http://www.who.int/gho/urban_health/situation_trends/urban_population_growth_text/en/
7. Chaumette, S., Dubernet, D., Ouoba, J., Siira, E., Tuikka, T.: Architecture and comparison of two different user-centric NFC-enabled event ticketing approaches. In: Balandin, S., Koucheryavy, Y., Hu, H. (eds.) NEW2AN 2011 and ruSMART 2011. LNCS, vol. 6869, pp. 165–177. Springer, Heidelberg (2011)
8. Chaumette, S., Dubernet, D., Ouoba, J., Siira, E., Tuikka, T.: Architecture and evaluation of a user-centric NFC-enabled ticketing system for small events. In: Zhang, J.Y., Wilkiewicz, J., Nahapetian, A. (eds.) MobiCASE 2011. LNICST, vol. 95, pp. 137–151. Springer, Heidelberg (2012)

9. Chaumette, S., Dubernet, D., Ouoba, J., Siira, E., Tuikka, T.: Towards an inter-operability evaluation process for mobile contactless city service. In: Proceedings of the Eighth International Conference on Digital Society, ICDS 2014, pp. 65–70 (2014)
10. Erl, T.: Service-Oriented Architecture: Concepts, Technology, and Design. Prentice Hall PTR, Upper Saddle River (2005)
11. Gwinner, C.: 5-point vs. 6-point Likert Scales. Technical report, Infosurv (2011)
12. Lahti, J., Ahola, J., Ceri, S., Brambilla, M., Celino, I. Zuccal, M.: Empowering digital cities through interconnected services. In: Proceedings of ITS World Congress 2015, October 2015 (to appear)
13. Ouoba, J., Siira, E.: Many faces of mobile contactless ticketing. In: Proceedings of the Second International Conference on Smart Systems, Devices and Technologies, SMART 2013, pp. 93–98 (2013)
14. Siira, E., Heinonen, S.: Enabling the mobility for the elderly: design and implementation of ASSISTANT navigation service. In: Proceedings of 14th International Conference on Mobility and Transport for Elderly and Disabled Persons, July 2015 (to appear)
15. UN-HABITAT and United Nations Human Settlements Programme: State of the World's Cities 2008/2009: Harmonious Cities. The state of the world's cities report, Earthscan (2008)
16. Zuccalà, M., Celino, I.: Fostering innovation through coopetition: the E015 digital ecosystem. In: Cimiano, P., Frasincar, F., Houben, G.-J., Schwabe, D. (eds.) ICWE 2015. LNCS, vol. 9114, pp. 625–628. Springer, Heidelberg (2015)

Development of Route Accessibility Index to Support Wayfinding for People with Disabilities

Jonathan A. Duvall[1,2(✉)], Jonathan L. Pearlman[1,2],
and Hassan A. Karimi[3]

[1] Human Engineering Research Laboratory, Department of Veterans Affairs
Pittsburgh Healthcare System, Pittsburgh, PA 15206, USA
{jad75,jlp46}@pitt.edu
[2] Department of Rehabilitation Science and Technology,
University of Pittsburgh, Pittsburgh, PA 15260, USA
[3] Geoinformatics Laboratory, School of Information Sciences,
University of Pittsburgh, Pittsburgh, PA 15260, USA
hkarimi@pitt.edu

Abstract. Wayfinding is a common task routinely performed by people traveling between unfamiliar locations, but can be a challenge for people with disabilities. In order to be able to travel safely and comfortably, people with physical disabilities depend on the accessibility of the built environment. It is through these accessibility elements that people who use wheelchairs can find their ways in unfamiliar environments. When used by people with disabilities, wayfinding and navigation services must contain accessibility data and support functions to utilize this data. However, while there are standards, such as the Americans with Disabilities Act Accessibility Guidelines, upon which accessibility data can be based or derived, currently there is no automated metric for evaluating the level of accessibility for pathways. To fill this gap, this paper proposes a Route Accessibility Index as a metric for evaluating a pathway's accessibility and discusses its value in a wayfinding case study.

Keywords: Pathway · Sidewalk · Wayfinding · Accessibility · Disability

1 Introduction

The community participation and activity level of people with disabilities (PWDs) is impacted on by the accessibility of the routes they travel over. For instance, studies have shown that power wheelchair (WC) users travel 1.6 km on a normal day. However, in an active and highly accessible environment such as around convention centers and cities where they hold the National Veterans Wheelchair Games (NVWG), power WC users can travel up to almost 8 km per day [1]. A similar study of manual WC users revealed that on typical days they travel 2.0 km, and in a highly accessible setting, such as at the NVWG, they would travel an average of 6.5 km per day; one subject in this study travelled 19.4 km in one day [2].

© ICST Institute for Computer Sciences, Social Informatics and Telecommunications Engineering 2016
A. Leon-Garcia et al. (Eds.): Smart City 2015, LNICST 166, pp. 104–112, 2016.
DOI: 10.1007/978-3-319-33681-7_9

The accessibility of the environment was one of the key factors that influenced the activity level and travel distances in the studies cited above. Accessibility of the built environment is guaranteed by the Architectural Barriers Act of 1968 (ABA) and the Americans with Disabilities Act of 1990 (ADA). The ABA ensures that buildings that are designed, built or altered by federal funding or leased by federal agencies are accessible to the public. The ADA greatly expanded the scope and details of the ABA outside of federally controlled environments. For example, the ADA states that "physical or mental disabilities in no way diminish a person's right to fully participate in all aspects of society." One purpose of the ADA is "to provide a clear and comprehensive national mandate for the elimination of discrimination against individuals with disabilities and to provide clear, strong, consistent, enforceable standards addressing discrimination against individuals with disabilities." [3] Title V of the ADA mandated that the Architectural and Transportation Barriers Compliance Board (Access Board) set up minimum guidelines "to ensure that buildings, facilities, rail passenger cars, and vehicles are accessible, in terms of architecture and design, transportation, and communication, to individuals with disabilities." [3].

The Access Board has established ADA Accessibility Guidelines (ADAAG) for Buildings and Facilities that give specific instructions and limitations about what is considered accessible. There are also many guidelines related to making pathways accessible, for example those by ADAAG (Table 1). The Access Board is currently updating their rules in an effort to make public rights-of-ways (PROW) more accessible for PWDs. These PROW rules will likely be accepted and promulgated and will formalize the rules on many surface characteristics including width, passing spaces, grade, cross slope, curb ramps and surface transitions. They are also looking to include requirements on surface roughness and rollability [4, 5].

Table 1. ADA guidelines

Parameter	Requirement
Clear width	Minimum 36 in
Openings	Maximum ½ in
Obstacle height	
≤ 1/4"	No bevel required
1/4"–1/2"	Must be beveled with Max 1:2 slope max
Ramps max slope	
1:12–1:16	Maximum 30 in high, 30 feet long
1:16–1:20	Maximum 30 in high, 40 feet long
Cross slope	Maximum 1:48

1.1 Monitoring ADAAG Compliance

Unlike roadways, municipalities do not have accurate inventories of the sidewalks locations, curb-cut locations, or information on sidewalk conditions. Consequently, it is unclear whether municipalities are compliant, or, by extension, accessible to PWDs. Some anecdotal information media sources suggest there is widespread non-compliance.

For instance, a recent survey of sidewalks in San Diego, CA indicated that they found 39,000 trip hazards with their survey only about half completed [6].

Many sidewalk surveys and repairs are conducted in response to complaints or incidents that have occurred, such as a trip or fall. Currently, most evaluations are conducted by a technician visiting the location where the complaint was reported, visually inspecting the area, measuring key details with a level and tape measure and taking a photograph. This process is slow and tedious for the technician. In order to make this process more automated and proactive, some automated tools to inventory and evaluate sidewalks have recently been developed [7–9].

Although the required data will exist as several discrete measurements (based on Table 1) along a sidewalk network, so long as it is geo-located (e.g., via GPS), it will afford more sophisticated calculation of route accessibility which can be defined as a cumulative measure of accessibility barriers along a selected route. For PWDs, route accessibility is more important than individual compliance measurements. This is because PWDs have different impairments that make one sidewalk compliance issue more or less impactful on mobility than another. A manual WC user, for instance, would likely be more affected by a non-compliant cross-slope than someone who ambulated but was blind or visually impaired, or even a power WC user. And the cumulative sum or percent of the selected route that has a non-compliance issue that makes it challenging for a certain person would be an important factor in determining which route that person should take.

Route accessibility is naturally tied to wayfinding by PWDs. Almost everyone is familiar with using a routing website or a GPS for traveling with a vehicle and it is expected that the roads on the route provided actually exist and are able to be driven over. This same expectation has not been realized yet for walking directions. Many of the same systems that give driving directions can give walking directions, but it is not uncommon for the sidewalks to be missing or for the condition of the sidewalk to be very poor, since these walking directions are typically based on the road network. Figure 1 shows an example of walking directions using Google Maps and Fig. 2 shows one segment of a route that Google Maps shows for walking directions. For ambulatory

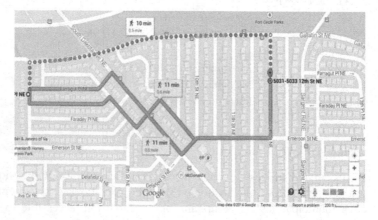

Fig. 1. Example of Google Maps walking directions

Fig. 2. Image showing a possible pathway on Google Maps

people, this does not cause a big concern because they can typically navigate around obstacles. However, for PWDs, specifically WC users, having missing or inaccessible pathways can cause the person to have to backtrack which can cause a great deal of extra time and effort trying to navigate around the problem.

One solution to this problem would be a wayfinding system that could not only give directions, but could also give directions based on route accessibility. Attempts have been made to address this issue using crowdsourced reports [10, 11]. Neis measured the reliability of using volunteered geographic information in OpenStreetMap from WC users to identify characteristics of sidewalks in Bonn, Germany. This data was manually inputted from WC users and then used to identify the best routes for PWDs. For example, a user could specify that they only wanted to travel on surfaces that had inclines less than 5 %. However, one of the limitations identified in this study is the low accuracy and consistency of the data that is being provided by WC users.

This is a promising approach, but the main problem is that the data is not objective or standardized even within a group that has similar mobility abilities. What one person considers inaccessible might be accessible for someone else. This shows a need for more accurate, consistent, and objective data that can be analyzed in a customizable way rather than subjective data that is being self-reported by WC users. In this paper, objective surface characteristic data collected from a small neighborhood are discussed and an approach to determine the most accessible route is presented.

2 Data Collection

The data was collected for a small neighborhood using the Pathway Measuring Tool (PathMeT) [9]. Each segment of a sidewalk (i.e., curb cut to curb cut) was measured individually. The variables collected from this tool include a 2-D surface profile (height changes along a distance travelled), running slope, and cross slope. The profile can be used to determine height changes and roughness. The process for measuring roughness of pedestrian pathways is currently being developed as a standard with ASTM

International [12, 13]. The profile is recorded with approximately one mm resolution and the running slope and cross slope are recorded at 200 Hz. These variables were used in determining the Route Accessibility Index of each pathway. Because the surfaces on which data was collected were not connected, algorithms could not be used to find the shortest routes. Alternatively, three routes were chosen based on visualization of the map and considering small number of street crossings. The three routes that were analyzed are shown in Fig. 3 and combined together they had 24 different sidewalk segments.

The Route Accessibility Index for each surface was determined using Eq. 1 where d is the distance of the surface and the parameter values are maximum height change (HC), average running slope (RS), average cross slope (CS), and average Roughness (RO). Maximum rather than average level changes were used because level changes are not continuous for a surface like the other parameters.

$$d * [(\max \text{HC/HC limit}) + (\text{Ave. CS})/(\text{CS limit}) + (\text{Ave.RS})/(\text{RS limit}) + (\text{Ave.RO})/(\text{RO limit})] \tag{1}$$

The parameter limits would be chosen by the individual that would be finding the most accessible route. In this paper, the limits were chosen to be 10 degrees for cross slope, 15 degrees for running slope, 50 mm for height changes, and 80 mm/m for Roughness.

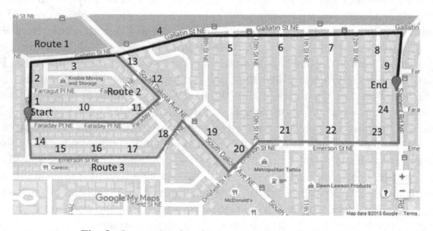

Fig. 3. Image showing three routes chosen for analysis

3   Route Accessibility Index

Table 2 shows the results of all of the pathway segments included in the three routes. For cross slope (CS), running slope (RS) and roughness, the average and maximum of values for each segment are given. For cross slope and running slope, the absolute values of the angles were used in order to have positive angles for both directions. This was done so that for a surface with equal parts of both uphill and downhill slopes, the average slope would not be zero, but would be the average angle away from zero.

Adding the Route Accessibility Indices of all of the segments for the three routes together gives total Route Accessibility Indices of 1086, 1271 and 1424 for routes 1, 2, and 3, respectively. Based on these results, the best route for the user to use would be route 1.

Table 2. Results of Route Accessibility Index analysis

Surface segment	D	CS Ave	CS Max	RS Ave	RS Max	Step Max	RO Max	RO Ave	Path no.	Route Accessibility Index
Units	M	deg	deg	deg	deg	mm	mm/m	mm/m		
1	56.4	2.0	6.3	3.6	8.3	9.9	91.8	45.7	1	68.3
2	49.6	2.5	4.4	5.2	8.1	14.3	98.1	49.4	1	74.5
3	165.0	2.7	7.9	5.9	10.2	9.4	97.4	40.6	1	223.1
4	153.9	2.0	5.9	3.3	7.5	11.5	81.4	39.5	1,2	176.4
5	82.8	2.4	7.8	3.1	5.9	12.2	97.8	47.1	1,2	106.1
6	82.4	2.5	5.4	2.7	5.9	7.2	59.8	43.3	1,2	91.9
7	80.4	1.9	4.7	6.2	8.9	10.3	73.3	40.0	1,2	104.8
8	86.0	3.2	5.9	6.6	11.1	11.9	75.3	51.2	1,2	140.4
9	85.8	1.7	7.7	6.1	8.1	6.6	69.9	36.6	1,2	100.1
10	197.5	3.1	6.9	1.2	4.0	31.7	89.0	43.4	2	310.2
11	69.1	3.9	8.8	2.3	9.3	17.2	96.3	52.8	2	107.1
12	53.5	4.1	6.1	4.1	6.4	13.7	64.9	43.2	2	80.0
13	51.6	2.3	4.4	4.0	6.2	2.9	59.0	39.6	2	54.0
14	53.0	3.2	6.3	1.2	4.6	62.2	85.3	64.0	3	129.4
15	128.9	4.3	9.8	3.4	7.5	21.8	150.1	59.5	3	237.1
16	30.0	2.4	9.3	1.0	4.6	7.8	60.9	50.2	3	33.0
17	70.2	2.3	7.4	1.6	12.1	43.1	76.0	44.3	3	123.4
18	80.6	2.6	5.5	2.5	6.3	21.5	95.4	36.4	3	105.8
19	114.5	2.7	4.6	3.6	12.5	88.9	100.3	37.2	3	315.3
20	41.1	2.4	7.2	1.8	3.9	8.7	124.3	45.7	3	45.5
21	87.0	2.2	5.6	3.1	7.0	13.5	110.9	44.1	3	108.6
22	81.1	2.2	4.4	3.8	9.5	7.4	101.6	66.9	3	118.0
23	71.9	2.5	5.0	4.6	11.0	12.8	83.5	56.8	3	109.4
24	85.8	1.9	4.4	5.5	7.2	8.3	52.6	33.7	3	97.9

4 Discussion

This article shows one way to determine a Route Accessibility Index that can be used as a wayfinding tool for PWDs. The proposed Route Accessibility Index, in its current version, includes cross slope, running slope, height changes, and roughness parameters. The parameters proposed all have to do with the characteristics of a particular pathway segment. The other parameters of a route that could be included, to determine the overall accessibility of a route, are segment width and those that affect the accessibility of getting from one segment to another. Presence and characteristics of curb cuts could also be included to better understand how easy or possible it would be to travel from one route segment to the next. For a comprehensive discussion on the requirements and parameters of sidewalk networks suitable for wheelchair navigation, refer to Kasemsuppakorn and Karimi [14]. For people with visual impairments, the type and presence of crosswalk signals are very important.

Including the data for maximum cross slopes, running slopes, roughness, and height changes also allows a user to determine whether it is even possible to get past the recommended segments. For example, a segment could be very smooth and flat but have one 100 mm height change in the middle of the segment. In this case, the overall route accessibility of the segment could be lower than another route but it could be effectively impassable if the wheelchair user cannot get over that high of a step. This implies that the Route Accessibility Index could be personalized based on information about the pedestrian. Knowing the maximum values of these parameters could help reduce the number of candidate segments for analysis; one parameter's maximum value may make the segment impassable.

A prerequisite for the Route Accessibility Index is having large amounts of data for the potential routes that are being looked at. Currently very few, if any, cities have inventory data on their sidewalks and even fewer have any data of the characteristics of the sidewalks. The Pathway Measurement Tool [9], or similar techniques [7, 8], shows promise for collecting the data and calculating Route Accessibility Index and storing them in a database. However, manually collecting the required data takes a lot of time and resources. This is the main reason why collecting the required data through a crowdsourcing approach has become popular in recent years. As discussed in the introduction, one shortcoming of current crowdsourcing approaches is that the collected data is subjective and there are no agreed upon, specific parameters. Many approaches to collecting objective data using crowdsourcing are currently being developed. Karimi and Kasemsuppakorn have suggested that no single approach can automatically collect all sidewalk data and have proposed a hybrid of three approaches, namely image processing, road buffering, and crowdsourcing, to obtain complete and accurate sidewalk networks [15].

With a large database of data related to surface characteristics, cities and municipalities can take a proactive rather than reactive approach to repairing sidewalks by having a plan in place to repair inaccessible sidewalks before there are incidents or complaints. In this study the limits for the parameters were chosen as if a user had selected what they knew they could safely travel across. For cities, the same data can be considered and the ADAAG standards can be used to determine where the sidewalks are not accessible according to the guidelines.

5   Conclusion and Future Research

PWDs need to know accessible routes to navigate in unknown communities. Typical wayfinding services, such as Google Maps, do not provide suitable solutions for PWDs because their databases do not contain sidewalks, which means their directions are not based on sidewalks and sidewalk conditions are not available. An emerging alternative to the conventional method of assisting in wayfinding and navigation is social network systems. Karimi, Dias, Pearlman, and Zimmerman have discussed the importance and methods of using social networks for sharing and exchanging wayfinding and navigation experiences among PWDs [16]. For another example of a personalized routing technique, based on fuzzy logic, for wheelchair navigation, see Kasemsuppakorn and Karimi [17].

Through a simple experimentation it was shown that the proposed Route Accessibility Index using parameters of sidewalks surfaces can determine the most theoretically accessible routes for PWDs to navigate in unknown areas. The parameters used in this study were cross slope, running slope, height changes, and roughness. Our future research includes improving the Route Accessibility Index as a metric for finding accessible routes by including other parameters such as segment width and those that are used in transition from one sidewalk segment to the next. We also plan to develop an algorithm that can automatically create a connected network of sidewalk segments using the collected data (performed manually in this work) in future.

Acknowledgements. This project was partially funded by the United States Access Board (grants H133E070024 & H133N110011), the Interlocking Concrete Pavement Institute and the Brick Industry Association. The authors of this paper would like to thank the Department of Veterans Affairs for the use of its facilities in conducting this research. The contents of this paper do not represent the views of the Department of Veterans Affairs or the United States Government.

Conflict of Interest. Two of the authors of this paper (Pearlman & Duvall) have equity in, and sit on the Scientific Advisory Board of a company that has licensed the PathMeT technology and evaluates and maps pedestrian pathways for accessibility.

References

1. Cooper, R.A., Thorman, T., et al.: Driving characteristics of electric-powered wheelchair users: how far, fast, and often do people drive? Arch. Phys. Med. Rehabil. **83**(2), 250–255 (2002)
2. Tolerico, M.: Investigation of the Mobility Characteristics and Activity Levels of Manual Wheelchair Users in Two Real World Environments. Rehabilitation Science and Technology. University of Pittsburgh, Pittsburgh (2006)
3. Americans with Disabilities Act (ADA) 42 U.S.C.A Chapter 126 (1990)
4. Americans with Disabilities Act Accessibility Guidelines (ADAAG) 36 480 CFR Chapter 11 (2010)
5. Access Board. Section-by-section Analysis. http://www.access-board.gov/guidelines-and-standards/streets-sidewalks/public-rights-of-way/proposed-rights-of-way-guidelines/section-by-section-analysis
6. Brown, D.: San Diego sidewalks need improvement, group says (2014). http://www.kpbs.org/news/2014/sep/17/san-diego-sidewalks-need-improvement-group-says/ Accessed 16 Oct 2014
7. Beneficial Designs. Public rights of way assessment process. http://beneficialdesigns.com/products/trail-and-sidewalk-assessment-equipment-software/prowap. Accessed 8 Jan 2014
8. Frackelton, A., et al.: Measuring walkability: development of an automated sidewalk quality assessment tool. Suburban Sustain. **1**(1), Article 4 (2013)

9. Sinagra, E., et al.: Development and characterization of Pathway Measurement Tool (PathMeT). In: Transportation Research Board 93rd Annual Meeting Compendium of Papers (2014)
10. Neis, P.: Measuring the reliability of wheelchair user route planning based on volunteered geographic information. Trans. GIS (2014). doi:10.1111/tgis.12087
11. Volkel, T., Weber, G.: A new approach for pedestrian navigation for mobility impaired users based on multimodal annotation of geographical data. Univers. Access Hum.-Comput. Interact. Ambient Interact. **4555**, 575–584 (2007)
12. Duvall, J., et al.: Development of surface roughness standards for pathways used by wheelchairs. In: Transportation Research Record: Journal of the Transportation Research Board, No. 2387, Transportation Research Board of the National Academies, Washington, DC, pp. 149–156 (2013)
13. Duvall, J., et al.: Proposed surface roughness standard for pathways used by wheelchairs. In: Transportation Research Board 93rd Annual Meeting Compendium of Papers (2014)
14. Kasemsuppakorn, P., Karimi, H.A.: Data requirements and spatial database for personalized wheelchair navigation. In: 2nd International Convention on Rehbilitation Engineering & Assistive Technology, Bangkok, Thailand, 13–15 May 2008
15. Karimi, H.A., Kasemsuppakorn, P.: Pedestrian network map generation approaches and recommendation. Int. J. Geograph. Inf. Sci. **27**(5), 947–962 (2013)
16. Karimi, H.A., Dias, M.B., Pearlman, J., Zimmerman, G.: Wayfinding and navigation for people with disabilities using social navigation networks. Trans. Collaborative Comput. **14**(2), e5 (2014)
17. Kasemsuppakorn, P., Karimi, H.A.: Personalized routing for wheelchair navigation. J. Location Based Serv. **3**(1), 24–54 (2009)

Simulating Adaptive, Personalized, Multi-modal Mobility in Smart Cities

Andreas Poxrucker[✉], Gernot Bahle, and Paul Lukowicz

Embedded Intelligence, German Research Center for Artificial Intelligence,
67663 Kaiserslautern, Germany
{andreas.poxrucker,gernot.bahle,paul.lukowicz}@dfki.de

Abstract. Smart, multi-modal transportation concepts are a key component towards smart sustainable cities. Such systems usually involve combinations of various modes of individual mobility (private cars, bicycles, walking), public transportation, and shared mobility (e.g. car sharing, car pooling). In this paper, we introduce a large-scale multi-agent simulation tool for simulating adaptive, personalized, multi-modal mobility. It is calibrated using various sources of real-world data and can be quickly adapted to new scenarios. The tool is highly modular and flexible and can be used to examine a variety of questions ranging from collective adaptation over collaborative learning to emergence and emergent behaviour. We present the design concept and architecture, showcase the adaptation to a real scenario (the city of Trento, Italy) and demonstrate an example of collaborative learning.

Keywords: Multi-agent simulations · Smart urban mobility · Socio-technical systems · Collective adaptive systems · Collaborative learning

1 Introduction

Intelligent, multi-modal transport concepts are widely seen as a key component of smart sustainable cities (see [1–3] for example). Such systems involve a flexible combination of various modes of public transport, individual mobility (from private cars, through private bicycles to walking) and shared mobility (e.g. car sharing, public bicycles etc.).

Within the EU sponsored ALLOW ENSEMBLES project [4] we are investigating adaptive, evolvable, personalized versions of such systems. The key idea is to provide a journey planning system that combines global planning with a decentralized personalization component, taking into account the current conditions in the city. Thus, to get from A to B the system may propose a set of possibilities ranging from a straight forward trip with a private car, through various public transport routes to complex combinations of using a private car, ride sharing, walking, bicycling and taking different public transport offerings. Next each user's personalization component evaluates each route, combining current conditions in the city (weather, traffic situation, how full are buses/trains) with

© ICST Institute for Computer Sciences, Social Informatics and Telecommunications Engineering 2016
A. Leon-Garcia et al. (Eds.): Smart City 2015, LNICST 166, pp. 113–124, 2016.
DOI: 10.1007/978-3-319-33681-7_10

the users preferences (how important is sustainability vs. personal comfort, how much he/she likes to walk, how much he/she dislikes crowds or walking in hot weather etc.) and makes a recommendation.

We assume that the personalization components are adaptive in three ways. First they check how far the users follow their recommendations. Second, during the journey they use sensors to record how far the conditions (travel time, environmental conditions etc.) correspond to the predictions. Third, systems of different users communicate such journey assessments to each other and thus learn from each other. What information is transferred to what other systems is subject to a personal privacy policy and may range from social networks based strategies to proximity (people sharing the same bus or living in the same suburb).

Allowing users' personal systems to control the recommendations fitted to individual preferences and to learn through local interactions controlled by users' privacy policy has a number of advantages. On the other hand predicting the effect of different individual policies on the overall system behaviour and state (traffic jams, total CO_2 output, etc.) is a difficult problem. As the individual systems learn, exchange information and, as a result, recommend various travel options to their owners, they change the travel conditions. Thus, if every system predicts the car to be the best option, streets will fill and traffic jams will arise. If the same bus is recommended to a lot of users, it will be overcrowded. Such obvious effects are made more complicated by the way information spreads, and individual strategies change according to personal policies. Overall we have to deal with a complex dynamic system with non linear dynamics and a variety of potential emergent effects.

In this paper we describe a simulation environment that we have developed to investigate such effects in adaptive, personalized multi-modal transport systems.

1.1 Related Work

Traffic and transportation simulations are a well researched area and many different models exists. Available traffic simulators are commonly classified based on the granularity of the traffic flow model they are based on. Microscopic simulators such as SUMO [5], VISSIM [6], or CORSIM [7] on the one hand model the movement of every single vehicle in great detail. Usually, they also model properties of the transportation network such as lanes of streets or traffic lights. Macroscopic simulations like MASTER [8] or FREFLO [9] on the other hand work with global models of traffic and transportation networks using e.g. differential equations.

The same is true for pedestrian/crowd simulations [10–12]. In general both traffic and pedestrian simulations focus on an in-depth analysis of a particular transportation mode, which is not the focus of this work. In fact, our system could well integrate various more detailed simulation models for traffic and pedestrians if actually needed.

On another end of the spectrum are various agent based modelling techniques for complex social phenomena like [13] for example. Closest to this paper is previous work by our group which investigates collaborative indoor location [14] and learning [15].

2   Paper Contribution

Performing experiments to investigate emergent phenomena of the type outlined in the introduction in large-scale real-world urban mobility systems is hardly ever possible given usual constraints of time and money. A well established methodology is to use what is known about the real world to set up simulations in which interaction effects leading to various emergent effects can be studied.

In this paper, we present our large-scale, multi-agent simulation toolbox to investigate emergent phenomena arising in the context of adaptive, personalized multi-modal urban mobility. The simulator thereby simulates a public transportation system of an urban area and people travelling within this area using different means of transportation. It also incorporates various personalization, decision making and distributed learning strategies. In summary, our simulator has the following main features:

1. **Simulation of a real-world urban mobility system.** In order to generate possible emergent phenomena such as traffic jams or air pollution, it is necessary to simulate a more or less complete urban transportation network. This includes modelling a street network which incorporates a model of *congestion* depending on the movement of the involved entities. Additionally, different means of transportation such as a public transit system are included in order to have travel alternatives. Our simulation uses a model of the urban mobility system of Trento, Italy, as data about the street network, public transportation etc. is available from our partners there from a recent collaboration. We will go into more details about the used real-world data in Sect. 5.
2. **Planning of entity journeys.** In order to let entities perform journeys using different means of transportation, a special planner component is required which allows the planning of multi-modal itineraries. The planner should thereby take the underlying transportation system into account providing not only simple shortest path routings through a street graph, but also multi-modal journeys like walking to a bus stop, getting on the right bus and off again at the correct stop, and walking to the final destination. In our simulation, we use *OpenTripPlanner* [19] which has already been applied in several cities in the world including Trento.
3. **Simulation of entity journeys.** Entities must be able to execute queried journeys in the simulated traffic system. As the transportation network involves means of public transportation, the simulator includes logic to let agents use buses or trains for example. In our current implementation, entities can drive with a car, go by bike, walk, or use means of public transportation as suggested by the planner component.

At this point, it is important to understand that the simulation tool we present in this paper does not claim to be a realistic traffic simulator. The latter are used in traffic engineering and traffic research and have become popular for analyzing and optimizing traffic on the level of a whole city or focusing on a part like a problematic crossing or a roundabout.

Fig. 1. Conceptual architecture of the simulation toolbox. The *NetLogo* multi-agent simulation environment is used as engine driving the simulation. The *DataService* and *PlannerService* are utility components providing information about the underlying transportation network and planning multi-model journeys, respectively.

3   Conceptual Architecture

As depicted in Fig. 1, our simulation tool conceptually consists of three components. The *NetLogo Simulation Environment* [16] is a popular multi-agent time-discrete simulation framework. It is used as an engine driving the step-based execution of the simulator and provides a graphical user interface (see Fig. 2) to interact with the simulation (e.g. starting and stopping the execution), to adjust input parameters, or to observe output parameters during execution.

The *Simulator* is the core component of our tool. It contains the definition of all the models to simulate as well as the specific logic which is executed by every instance of a certain model during every time step. We will explain the modelling in detail in Sect. 4. The simulator is realized as an extension to the NetLogo framework using its rich Java-based extension API. The coupling with

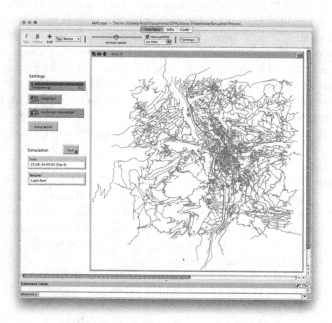

Fig. 2. NetLogo user interface with our simulation loaded.

NetLogo is, however, only loosely with every agent we define in the toolbox being wrapped by a corresponding NetLogo agent. Thus, it would be easy to use another simulation engine if necessary.

The *DataService* component offers an interface to query information about the transportation network of urban mobility system. It provides information about the underlying street network as well as existing public transportation agencies and their routes and schedules. The data provided by the component is thereby read in from a precompiled street graph datastructure and from one or more GTFS [17] datasets which are parsed during instantiation of the service in the beginning.

The *PlannerService* provides multi-modal travel suggestions to persons who want to travel from a certain starting position to a destination. In essence, the *PlannerService* is a client application querying the REST-API of an instance of *OpenTripPlanner* which is, as explained above, a open-source multi-modal journey planner. *OpenTripPlanner* operates on one or more precompiled graphs which are loaded and registered to the service during start-up. The graphs are compiled from *OpenStreetMap* [18] data which allows the planning of journeys based on the street map only (car, walk, and bike) as well as GTFS data for planning itineraries involving public transportation.

To make the journeys proposed by the planner compatible with the underlying transportation system both the *DataService* and the *PlannerService* rely on the same set of basis of data. We will go into more detail about these data in Sect. 5.

4   Modelling

Generally speaking, the simulator relies on a set of models which are instantiated during simulation start-up. The state of these instances is then modified during the actual execution which allows to observe local state changes as well as changes of global system behaviour. In essence, have two types of models: The *environment model* on the one hand models the underlying transportation network including the street network and the public transportation system (see Subsect. 4.1). Models of the *entities* (or *agents* - we will use these terms interchangeable through the rest of the paper) on the other hand represent the actually acting agents (see Subsect. 4.2).

4.1   Environment

In summary, our model of the environment is given by the underlying street map and the public transportation system. The street network on the one hand is modelled as a graph consisting of *StreetNodes* and *StreetSegments* which carry a number of attributes such as the length l and the maximum allowed driving speed v_{max}. In order to realize a model of congestion, every *StreetSegment* keeps track of the number of entities n which are currently travelling on it. Using l, v_{max}, n, and a certain minimum driving speed v_{min} a *possible* driving speed on the segment v_p is computed according to the inverted sigmoid function given by the formula

$$v_p = \frac{v_{max} - v_{min}}{1 + \exp(a * (n/l) - b)} + v_{min} \tag{1}$$

where a and b are two parameters determining how fast the possible speed decreases. v_p is updated once ever time step if the number of entities on a segment has changed. Additionally, we have integrated a model of the weather as a context factor to the environment which also influences the possible driving on a segment which is reduced by e.g. a half in case it is snowing.

The public transportation system on the other hand is given by the routes and schedules of public transportation agencies. All these information is available through the *DataService* component. The current state of the public transportation system during simulation is determined by the state of the entities managing and executing it, which are, in essence, the transportation agencies and buses (see Subsect. 4.2).

4.2   Entities

Transportation Agency. A transportation agency is an entity which manages a set of *routes* specified in the GTFS dataset which is available through the *DataService* component. Every route is defined by a set of stops. A *trip* of a certain route is, in turn, defined by a sequence of stops of the route together with arrival and departure times. Additionally, the shape of every trip, i.e. geographical route is given by a sequence of GPS points which needed to be mapped to the street graph in order to influence buses by congestion as described above. For this purpose, we implemented the heuristics-based map matching procedure described in [20] which maps the GPS point sequences to the respective paths through the street graph. As this procedure is computationally intensive, all trip paths are precomputed and loaded during start-up.

In order to execute the trips of its routes, every transportation agency manages a set of bus agents. During each time step of the simulation, an agency entity checks whether there is a new trip (or possibly several) to depart. In case there is, it assigns the trip to one of its idle buses which then starts to execute it.

Bus. A bus entity executes a trip assigned by the transportation agency it belongs to. During each time step, it moves along the street segments of its current trip resulting from the map matching process described above or waits at a stop to pick up waiting passengers.

Person. The core work-flow person agents execute during simulation is the following: When a person agent wants to go from its current position to a certain destination within the street network, it first sends a request to the multi-modal journey planner. In this request, the agent specifies, among others, its starting position, the destination it wants to reach, the time when the trip should depart, and a number of modes of transportation it wants to use (e.g. walk, car, bus). Based on these request parameters, the planner responds with a set of possibilities satisfying the constraints and preferences specified in the request.

The person then decides on one of the solutions by taking into account a utility ranking derived from estimates for travel time, costs and personal preferences [21] and executes it using the underlying transportation network. In case of the example above, the agent may walk to the given bus station, wait for the correct bus, then enter it and ride to its destination. During its journey, the person keeps track of travel parameters such as time, costs, bus fillgrades etc.

5   Towards a Real-World Simulation

To connect the simulation to the real world, we use real-world data for creating and calibrating our model of the environment and our different agent models. In our concrete case, we use data from the city of Trento. While the intention was not a complete and finely detailed representation of the urban environment (e.g. there are no traffic lights, no car density statistics for individual streets, etc.), we do aim for a realistic representation of behaviour. To that end, we conducted a survey among 15 people living and working in Trento. Participants marked different regions of interest on the map (residential areas, industrial zones, the university). They also specified main routes taken into the and out of the city and typical travel patterns (e.g. rush hours on workdays). Figure 3(a) shows the extracted regions of interest, Fig. 3(b) one possible distribution of agents created based on this partitioning. As a realistic source of weather patterns, we are using historical weather data queried from the wunderground API [22]. This provides an additional context factor influencing entity movement (e.g. when it snows, cars move very slow) which can be learned by the system. Furthermore, an agent is assigned a role which encapsulates different behaviour patterns, e.g. industrial workers, students, elderly (new roles can be added as needed). Based on these roles, a persistent agent population taking into account Trento demographic information is created and used for the subsequent simulation. All agents have a place of residence; some (depending on role) also have a place of work or go to university. Workers for example may travel to their workplace with the aim of being there at a given time, then start their travel home at another fixed time in the afternoon.

6   Example Use-case

Using our real-world setting of Trento described in Sect. 5, we present the results of an early experiment with our simulator investigating its ability to produce emergent phenomena. In this experiment, we rely on a set of assumptions. We define that every person agent of the simulation has a certain preference for going by car p_c and going by bus p_b, respectively, with $p_c + p_b = 1$. We further assume that every person decides on a means of transportation by directly comparing the preferences. If $p_c >= p_b$ the person chooses to go by car and in case $p_c < p_b$ the person decides to use the bus. Additionally, we define that travel time of buses is less affected by traffic than that of cars due to special bus lanes and traffic lights common in Trento.

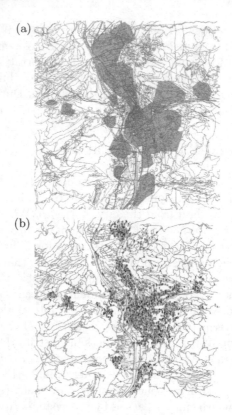

Fig. 3. (a) Partitioning of the city of Trento into different areas e.g. residential, industrial, shopping, or university as an overlay to the street network. (b) Distribution of agents created based on the defined regions of interest.

In this use-case, we want to demonstrate the difference between a traffic system in which entities adapt their preferences only based on their own experiences (scenario 1) and a system in which the agents learn from experience and actively exchange their knowledge when they get spatially close to others (scenario 2). In the first case, agents rely on their own experiences following one simple rule. If they go by car and are late due to heavy traffic (i.e. arrive later than initially predicted by the planner), they decrease their preference for car by a certain value and, in turn, increase their preference to use the bus. Additionally, we keep track of how many times an agent has changed its preferences due to personal experience. In the second scenario, agents also incorporate the knowledge of others whenever they meet using a weighted fusion of self and foreign preferences. Factors taken into account are the number of samples (how often an agent already had a good / bad trip and the (dis)similarity of experiences).

To measure system behaviour in both scenarios, we look at average prior (i.e. predicted by the planner) and posterior (actual simulated) travel time of trips by cars and buses respectively. We also track the average preferences for both car

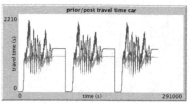

(a) Prior (red) and posterior (blue) travel time by car.

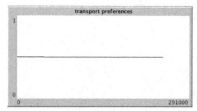

(b) Preferences for bus (red) and car (blue).

Fig. 4. Simulation results for scenario 1 (without knowledge exchange): The actual travel time differs significantly from the estimated one during the rush hour times. However, there is almost no change in the transportation preferences and consequently the posterior travel times look identical during all three days. (Color figure online)

and bus. Figure 4 shows the prior and posterior travel times by car (Fig. 4(a)) and mean transportation preferences averaged over all agents (Fig. 4(b)) for three simulated days. It can be seen that the difference between estimated and actual travel time is especially high during the morning and afternoon rush hours. The peaks in-between are caused by agents representing students who attend their lectures at university which causes high congestion in the university area. Figure 4(b) shows almost no change in the transportation preferences. Consequently, the travel behaviour of the agents does not change and the posterior travel times on subsequent days look almost identical to the first day.

Figure 5 shows the statistics for the second scenario in which agents actually do share information and adapt their preferences based on feedback received from others. In this case, a clear change in preferences is visible. This, in turn, leads to different choices by agents, which generates a shift from cars to buses. This frees up street capacity, reducing difference between predicted and actual travel time.

While this is a rather simple example, it is a show case of the system capabilities. Based on the simulation framework, arbitrary experiments can be designed and deployed quickly. Areas of research that can be explored include:

1. different data exchange strategies, e.g. based on network models, privacy considerations, etc.
2. different knowledge fusion and learning techniques, e.g. graph based models.

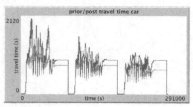

(a) Prior (red) and posterior (blue) travel time by car.

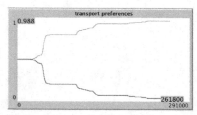

(b) Preferences for bus (red) and car (blue).

Fig. 5. Simulation results for scenario 2 (with knowledge exchange): With agents exchanging knowledge about their prior travel experiences (high delays from traffic jams), the preference for using a car decreases rapidly. The more agents in turn decide to go by bus, the less vehicles are on the streets. Consequently, traffic jams are reduced and the estimated and actual travel time become more aligned. (Color figure online)

3. different ways to automatically rank solutions or even learn user preferences automatically.

All of the above can be represented by different and easily customisable parameters (like we did with travel time).

7   Conclusion and Future Work

In this paper, we have presented a large-scale multi-agent simulation tool for simulating adaptive, personalized, multi-modal mobility in the context of smart cities which can be used, among others, for investigating effects of collaborative agent behaviour on emergent global system properties. The simulator is calibrated using real-world data in an easily customisable way. An early demonstration has been done to show its capabilities. Our next step will be the application of the simulator for investigating collaborative learning techniques based on conditional random fields. We also strive to make the framework open source and public soon so it can be used as a research tool by others.

Acknowledgement. This work has been partially funded by the EU Project ALLOW Ensembles (600792) and Smart Society (600854).

References

1. Carreras, I., Gabrielli, S., Miorandi, D., Tamilin, A., Cartolano, F., Jakob, M., Marzorati, S.: SUPERHUB: a user-centric perspective on sustainable urban mobility. In: Proceedings of the 6th ACM Workshop on Next Generation Mobile Computing for Dynamic Personalised Travel Planning, pp. 9–10. ACM (2012)
2. Motta, G., Sacco, D., Belloni, A., You, L.: A system for green personal integrated mobility: A research in progress. In: 2013 IEEE International Conference on Service Operations and Logistics, and Informatics (SOLI), pp. 1–6. IEEE (2013)
3. Motta, G., Sacco, D., Ma, T., You, L., Liu, K.: Personal mobility service system in urban areas: The IRMA project. In: 2015 IEEE Symposium on Service-Oriented System Engineering (SOSE), pp. 88–97. IEEE (2015)
4. Allow Ensembles. http://www.allow-ensembles.eu
5. Krajzewicz, D., Erdmann, J., Behrisch, M., Bieker, L.: Recent development and applications of SUMO - Simulation of urban MObility. In: International Journal on Advances in Systems and Measurements, pp. 128–138 (2012)
6. Fellendorf, M.: VISSIM: A microscopic simulation tool to evaluate actuated signal control including bus priority. In: 64th Institute of Transportation Engineers Annual Meeting, pp. 1–9 (1994)
7. Halati, A., Lieu, H., Walker, S.: CORSIM-corridor traffic simulation model. In: Traffic Congestion and Traffic Safety in the 21st Century: Challenges, Innovations, and Opportunities (1997)
8. Helbing, D., Hennecke, A., Shvetsov, V., Treiber, M.: MASTER: macroscopic traffic simulation based on a gas-kinetic, non-local traffic model. Transp. Res. Part B: Methodol. **35**(2), 183–211 (2001). Elsevier
9. Payne, H.J.: FREFLO: A macroscopic simulation model of freeway traffic. In: Transportation Research Record (1979)
10. Helbing, D., Buzna, L., Johansson, A., Werner, T.: Self-organized pedestrian crowd dynamics: experiments, simulations, and design solutions. Transp. Sci. **39**(1), 1–24 (2005)
11. Klügl, F., Rindsfüser, G.: Large-scale agent-based pedestrian simulation. In: Petta, P., Müller, J.P., Klusch, M., Georgeff, M. (eds.) MATES 2007. LNCS (LNAI), vol. 4687, pp. 145–156. Springer, Heidelberg (2007)
12. Kster, G., Hartmann, D., Klein, W.: Microscopic pedestrian simulations: From passenger exchange times to regional evacuation. In: Hu, B., Morasch, K., Pickl, S., Siegle, M. (eds.) Operations Research Proceedings 2010, pp. 571–576. Springer, Heidelberg (2011)
13. Epstein, J.M.: Agent-based computational models and generative social science. In: Generative Social Science: Studies in Agent-Based Computational Modeling, pp. 4–46 (1999)
14. Kampis, G., Kantelhardt, J.W., Kloch, K., Lukowicz, P.: Analytical and simulation models for collaborative localization. J. Comput. Sci. **6**, 1–10 (2015). Elsevier
15. Kampis, G., Lukowicz, P.: Collaborative knowledge fusion by Ad-Hoc information distribution in crowds. Procedia Comput. Sci. **51**, 542–551 (2015)
16. Wilensky, U.: NetLogo. http://ccl.northwestern.edu/netlogo/
17. What is GTFS? https://developers.google.com/transit/gtfs/
18. OpenStreetMap. http://www.openstreetmap.org
19. OpenTripPlanner. http://www.opentripplanner.org
20. Marchal, F., Hackney, J., Axhausen, K.: Efficient map matching of large global positioning system data sets: Tests on speed-monitoring experiment in Zrich. Transp. Res. Rec. J. Transp. Res. Board **1935**, 93–100 (2005)

21. Andrikopoulos, V., Bitsaki, M., Bucchiarone, A., Karastoyanova, D., Leymann, F., Nikolaou, C., Pistore, M.: A game theoretic approach for managing multi-modal urban mobility systems. In: 2th International Conference on the Human Side of Service Engineering Human Factors and Ergonomics (2014)
22. Wunderground weather data. http://www.wunderground.com

Feature-Based Room-Level Localization
of Unmodified Smartphones

Jiaxing Shen[1](✉), Jiannong Cao[1], Xuefeng Liu[1], Jiaqi Wen[1], and Yuanyi Chen[2]

[1] The Hong Kong Polytechnic University, Hong Kong, China
{csjshen,csjcao,csxfliu,csjqwen}@comp.polyu.edu.hk
[2] Shanghai Jiao Tong University, Shanghai, China
cyyxz@mail.sjtu.edu.cn

Abstract. Locating smartphone users will enable numerous potential applications such as monitoring customers in shopping malls. However, conventional received signal strength (RSS)-based room-level localization methods are not likely to distinguish neighboring zones accurately due to similar RSS fingerprints. We solve this problem by proposing a system called feature-based room-level localization (FRL). FRL is based on an observation that different rooms vary in internal structures and human activities which can be reflected by RSS fluctuation ranges and user dwell time respectively. These two features combing with RSS can be exploited to improve the localization accuracy. To enable localization of unmodified smartphones, FRL utilizes probe requests, which are periodically broadcast by smartphones to discover nearby access points (APs). Experiments indicate that FRL can reliably locate users in neighboring zones and achieve a 10 % accuracy gain, compared with conventional methods like the histogram method.

Keywords: Room-level localization · RSS · Fingerprinting

1   Introduction

Locating smartphone users in an indoor environment will enable many ubiquitous computing applications, ranging from context-aware applications [1] to location-based services [2,3]. These applications usually require two types of locations, namely geometric locations that are used for mapping and distance-oriented applications; and semantic locations which attempt to represent logical entities and their semantics [4,5]. The concept of semantic location was firstly proposed by HP Labs [6] to address the significant deficiency of geometric locations for providing little context information in mobile web-services. Rooms are typical representation of semantic locations. Getting the room information of users is called room-level localization. Significant as room-level localization is, little attention is paid to this area. Recent research on retail space [7,8] and smart home [9] require room-level localization without modifying users' smartphones, which is both challenging and infusive.

© ICST Institute for Computer Sciences, Social Informatics and Telecommunications Engineering 2016
A. Leon-Garcia et al. (Eds.): Smart City 2015, LNICST 166, pp. 125–136, 2016.
DOI: 10.1007/978-3-319-33681-7_11

Due to the proliferation of WiFi APs, wireless indoor localization methods are becoming increasingly popular and attractive as there are no additional infrastructural costs beyond the wireless APs. Currently, the room-level localization methods can be divided into four categories. The first type utilizes channel state information (CSI) of WiFi to discover users' locations and states [7]. The second type uses geometric localization methods. Examples are deterministic and probabilistic fingerprinting methods [10,11]. The third type regards the room-level localization as a classification problem, e.g., WHAM! [12], a rule-based method [13] and the histogram method used in [9]. The last type integrates WiFi data with other smartphone sensor data to improve localization performance, like Ariel [14] and AurroundSense [15].

However, multiple users result in unpredictable changes of channel states, hence CSI is unlikely to work for a large number of people [7]. Fingerprinting [10,11] requires a large amount of training data, which is too labor-extensive to carry out. Methods mentioned in the third type [9,13] solely rely on RSS feature that attenuates in a highly nonlinear and uncertain way in real situations [16], so it is hard to get high accuracy especially in the case where neighboring rooms have similar fingerprints [12]. It is highly possible that the forth type methods [14,15] are inapplicable as those systems need to install some apps in users' smartphones to collect other sensor data.

To solve these problems, we propose a system called Feature-based Room-Level Localization (FRL), which can accurately and reliably derive smartphone users' locations in the indoor environment. FRL is based on the observation that different rooms have various internal structures and diverse human activities. Therefore, from the observation we extract related features (we call them room features) and combine them with the RSS feature to conduct room-level localization. Simple and direct as the main idea of our solution seems to be, there remains some fundamental challenges to be carefully addressed. First of all, how to acquire WiFi data without modifying users' smartphones? Conventional room-level localization methods often assume the data of users' smartphones are available, but it is not possible to directly access users' smartphones and get the required data in some application scenarios such as locating customers in shopping malls. Besides, how to handle the problem raised by a small amount of training data which downgrades the accuracy of localization models? Most of the fingerprinting methods rely on complete training data to build accurate models. Lastly, how to extract features that relate to internal structures and human activities? Extracting new features is non-trivial task and it usually requires solid observations.

We tackle the first challenge by exploiting probe requests which are periodically broadcast by smartphones to collect WiFi data in a non-intrusive way. As for the second challenge, we apply machine learning methods to derive labels from unlabeled data. When it comes to the last challenge, although it is hard to directly measure internal structures and human activities, different structures result in different RSS fluctuation ranges and different human activities lead to different dwell time. Based on this assumption, we measure RSS fluctuation range and user dwell time from a large amount of estimated labeled data. Dedicated experiments demonstrate the feasibility of combining different features and indicate that FRL has better performance in terms of accuracy than state-of-the-art methods.

The remainder of the paper is structured as follows. We describe the main idea of FRL design in Session 2. Session 3 elaborates on the architecture of FRL and the functionality of different parts. In Session 4, we present a case study in which different methods are applied in a real-world indoor test environment. Session 5 introduces existing and related works. The conclusions are summarized in the last session.

2   System Overview

This paper proposes a system called FRL (Feature-based Room-Level Localization), which combines the RSS feature and room features for room-level localization. FRL utilizes probe requests to periodically collect users' WiFi data as a data sequence. The sequence will be partitioned into snippets based on smoothing and partition rules. Every snippet consists of some data units, for each of which, FRL exploits the histogram method to derive a potential result. After that, FRL uses a voting-based decision fusion strategy for every snippet. If the top two results are neighboring zones and the difference of their votes is under the threshold, then the feature-based localization method will be leveraged to pick up the more possible result.

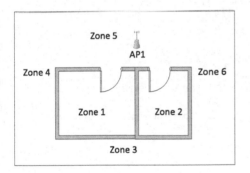

Fig. 1. A example of two rooms

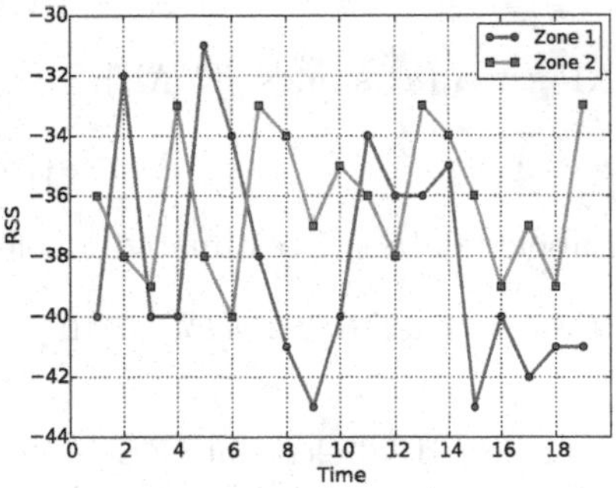

Fig. 2. WiFi data in two rooms

Figure 1 illustrates how FRL works. The floor plan is split into 6 zones with two neighboring rooms (zone 1 is an office and zone 2 is a photocopy room) and two APs. Note that corridors can be represented as more than one zone depending on the need of the application. For each zone, a small amount of (around 10 data units) training data will be collected, i.e., RSS of all APs. Figure 2 is a segment of WiFi data in two rooms. As the RSS feature of two rooms are quite similar and most of them have overlaps, traditional localization methods like [11] or [12] are poor at handling this situation. However, we find that different rooms have diverse internal structure and human activities in those rooms are also different. As the example depicts, zone 1 is large than zone 2, so it is highly possible that the RSS fluctuation ranges of zone 1 are also larger than that of zone 2. Besides, zone 1 is an office where most of the people dwell for hours, while zone 2 is a photocopy room in which people usually only stay for a few minutes. Therefore we conclude that different rooms have different distributions of RSS fluctuation range and user dwell time. Besides, the room features could be used in room-level localization to improve the accuracy. The challenging part is how to extract related features from WiFi data.

3   Design of FRL

FRL consists of two modules (data collection and location inference) and two phases (training phase and testing phase). Figure 3 depicts the overall work flow of FRL. In data collection module, it collects three kinds of data for training and testing. In data processing module, localization models will be built based on the labeled and unlabeled data. The training phase is to extract the binary classifier and smoothing and segmentation rules from labeled data and train feature-based localization method from unlabeled data. The testing phase is to locate users from the collected WiFi data.

Details of data structures are listed below:

– Semantic location set $\mathbb{L}$ (l_i represents i^{th} semantic location):

$$\mathbb{L} = \{l_1, l_2, ..., l_n\}, \ |\mathbb{L}| = n$$

– AP set $\mathbb{A}$ (a_j stands j^{th} AP):

$$\mathbb{A} = \{a_1, a_2, ..., a_m\}, \ |\mathbb{A}| = m$$

– Labeled data $\mathbb{LD}$ (estimated labeled data has the same structure):

$$\mathbb{LD} = \{(time_i, RSS\_vector_i, l_i) \,|\, 0 \leq i \leq p, \, l_i \in \mathbb{L}, \, RSS\_vector_i = (rss_{i1}, ..., rss_{im})\}$$

– Transferred labeled data $\mathbb{TD}$:

$$\mathbb{TD} = \{prob\_vector_i, label \,|\, 0 \leq i \leq p, \, label \in \{true, false\}, \, prob\_vector_i = (p_{i1}, ..., p_{im})\}$$

– Unlabeled data $\mathbb{UD}$:

$$\mathbb{UD} = \{(time_i, mac, RSS\_vector_i) \,|\, 0 \leq i \leq q, \, l_i \in \mathbb{L}, \, RSS\_vector_i = (rss_{i1}, ..., rss_{im})\}$$

– Snippet of unlabeled data $\mathbb{SD}_i$:

$$\mathbb{UD} = \mathbb{SD}_1 \cup \mathbb{SD}_2 \cup ... \cup \mathbb{SD}_k$$

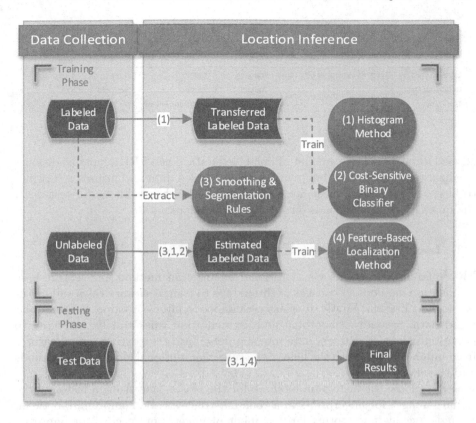

Fig. 3. The architecture of FRL

3.1   Data Collection

As described in Fig. 3, FRL collects labeled data and unlabeled data for training, test data for locating users in real scenarios. To collect the data in a non-intrusive way, FRL exploits probe requests. Probe requests are frames that are broadcast by smart phones to discover nearby APs. Recent research demonstrates great potential of applying this technique in tracking [17,18], crowd density estimation [19,20] and uncovering social relationships [21]. To sniff probe requests, we choose OpenWrt (an embedded operating system based on Linux kernel) as the firmware of the router. After configuration, routers can capture probe requests in the air and store the data on the external storage. Although different smart phones have diverse settings of probe requests [17], generally smartphones will broadcast probe requests every minute. That means in real world, FRL can locate users carrying smartphones every minute, which is adequate for many monitoring applications.

Detailed information of collected data is listed in Table 1. Collecting labeled data requires plenty of manpower, while collecting unlabeled data barely consumes any human resources. Therefore, FRL firstly collects a small amount of

Table 1. Details of collected data

Data type	Structure	Purpose	Required Amount	Manpower	Sampling Rate
Labelled Data	Time, RSS Vector of APs, Label	Training	Small	Needs	4 seconds
Unlabeled Data	Time, MAC, RSS Vector of Aps	Training	Large	No Need	N/A
Test Data		Testing	No Requirement	No Need	N/A

labeled data and a large amount of unlabeled data. Then FRL adopts traditional localization method to estimate labels for unlabeled data and utilizes a classifier to filters out snippets whose accuracy is above the threshold. As for test data, the quantity mainly depends on specific applications.

3.2 Location Inference

FRL inferences locations via traditional localization method and feature-base localization methods. It consists of three steps to train necessary rules and methods for localization. Firstly, it trains a classifier to filter out snippets from unlabeled data. Secondly, smoothing and segmentation rules will be extracted to partition unlabeled and test data into snippets. Lastly, we extract room features from unlabeled data with the help of the rules, conventional localization methods and the classifier.

FRL choose the histogram method, for the reason that using a histogram of signal strength for fingerprints in a zone may offer a good compromise between a single average and storing large number of fingerprints needed for improved accuracy [9]. The method requires a fixed set of bins, i.e., a set of non-overlapping intervals that cover the whole range of the variable from the minimum to the maximum RSS value. The width of the bins, denoted as w, is an adjustable parameter, which affects the performance. The outputs the method is a vector $prob\_vector_i$ indicating the possibilities of all zones.

Then FRL exploits the histogram method to labeled data and Cost-Sensitive Binary Classifier is to identify snippets from unlabeled data over the threshold. FRL gets transferred labeled data after applying the histogram method to labeled data. Based on transferred labeled data, FRL identifies true positive cases, which means real labels and estimated labels are both true. In order to transfer unlabeled data to labeled data with high accuracy, FRL adopts cost-sensitive learning, which makes optimal decision based on a misclassification costs [22].

Smoothing and Segmentation Rules is to remove outliers, smooth data sequence, and partition unlabeled data and test data into snippets. We follow the practice proposed in [12], which declares that a sharp change in signal data indicates that the user is likely to move from one zone to another. In addition, FRL merges small neighboring snippets because localization based on small snippets is not reliable. Figure 4 is an example showing how smoothing and segmentation works. The four cut-off points are chosen according to the accumulative changes

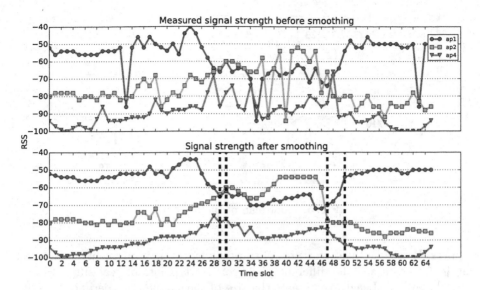

Fig. 4. Example of smoothing and segmentation

of $ap1$, $ap2$, $ap1$ and $ap2$ sequentially in a time window, as their accumulative changes all exceed the predefined threshold.

Feature Based Localization Method provides another way for room-level localization. Feature-based localization method consists of two features, RSS fluctuation range and user dwell time. Both of the two features adopt the histogram method like RSS feature. Basically, FRL uses the result of the histogram method as the final result. If the top two zones of the histogram method are neighboring zones and the difference of their probabilities is below a threshold, then feature-based localization method will be applied to give the final result.

4   Implementation and Experiment Results

FRL is mainly implemented in Python with some C code and shell scripts. The system is tested in our department, in a area of 8 m by 20 m, with 11 zones separated and 3 APs installed, the layout and AP installation are shown as Fig. 5. Basically, $|\mathbb{L}| = 11$, $|\mathbb{A}| = 3$. For labeled data, $|\mathbb{LD}| = 110$, i.e., each zone has 10 training data units. We collect unlabeled data for one week, $|\mathbb{UD}| = 693,231$, including 2, 162 different devices and most of their data sequences are too short to use. For test data, we get four volunteers with smartphones in the test environment for one day and ask them to record their activities (start time, end time, locations). Finally we get 105 snippets and $|\mathbb{TD}| = 1,408$. We compare the performance of FRL with KNN, the histogram method, and the random selection method.

First of all, we leverage test data to evaluate the performance of smoothing and segmentation rules. After applying the segmentation rules, we get 121

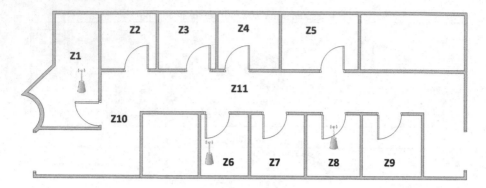

Fig. 5. Floor plan of the test bed

snippets. We define the correctness of snippets by two measurements, offset and length. Offset means the difference between start points of real snippets and derived snippets. Length represents the size of the snippets. Experiment results indicate the rules can identify 85 % the snippets whose errors of offset and length are below 5 %.

Table 2. Comparison of different classifiers

	Cost-sensitive with Random forest	Random forest	Naïve Bayes	Logistic
True positive cases	428	184	132	52
Accuracy	58.24%	71.31%	63.92%	69.03%
Precision	95.54%	41.07%	29.46%	11.61%

Then we use test data to evaluate the performance of the cost-sensitive binary classifier. Among all 1,408 test data units, there are 428 true positive cases, 20 false positive cases, 392 true negative cases, and 568 false negative cases. Table 2 shows detailed information of four classifiers, and the cost-sensitive classifier with random forest outperforms other classifiers in terms of precision and true positive cases. The cost-sensitive classifier improve the precision by increasing the number of true positive cases while reducing the number of false positive cases.

The performance of the system is evaluated by the 1st ranked zone. Due to space limitation, here we only show the final results of those methods. Figure 6 shows the overall accuracy of different methods. It is obvious that among all localization methods, FRL achieves the highest accuracy. FRL targets at the cases where the top two results are neighboring zones and have similar votes. Then it leverages the features of RSS fluctuation range and user dwell time to give the final result. Through the experiments we find that FRL is effective in handling neighboring zone problem and improves the accuracy of such cases by 50 %.

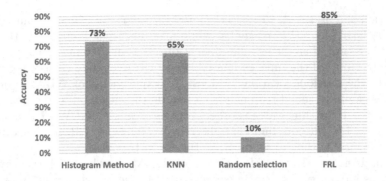

Fig. 6. Results of the experiment

5 Related Works

Currently, room-level localization methods can be divided into four categories. The first type methods rely on channel state information (CSI) of WiFi to discover users' locations and states [7]. These methods even do not require users to carry smartphones, they exploit the information of how a signal propagates from the transmitter to the receiver to locate users. The problem is that multiple people will result in unpredictable changes of channel states, hence it cannot be used to detect large number of users.

The second type focuses on geometric localization approaches, such as deterministic and probabilistic fingerprinting [10,11], that are also applicable for room-level localization determination. This kind of methods work quite well in static environment as it automatically take into account obstacles such as walls and furnitures [9]. On the contrary, dynamic factor cannot be reflected such as the change of layout, the number of people. RADAR [11] is a classic fingerprinting approach. Although it is not intended for room-level localization, the idea is also applicable here. RADAR consists of training phase and testing phase. During the training phase, a fingerprint database will be constructed. In the testing phase, one or more reference points in the fingerprint database will be chosen to estimate the real location. Simple and effective as this approach is, it is barely applied in practice, as constructing fingerprint database is too labor-extensive and boring to be done.

The third type is designed for room-level localization but most of them have troubles in handling neighboring zone with similar fingerprints. Correa et al. [9] utilize k-nearest-neighbor (KNN) with Euclidean distance measurement for indoor localization. According to their experiments, they conclude that only room-level granularity accuracy can be consistently achieved in wireless fingerprinting method. But the accuracy is influenced by the number of people moving around. WHAM! [12] is a nice work utilizing connectivity of semantic locations to resolve localization ambiguities. The system records users' historic location information, when current estimated location(s) are not unique, the system will make a choice based on the relation with previous locations. For example, the last location of a user is A, current estimated locations are B and C, but according to the floor plan, B is reachable while C is unreachable from A, then the system will return B as the estimated location. To some extent, this approach is effective, but most of the time, estimated locations are close to each other and all connect to the previous location. Besides, the experiments of WHAM! indicate it requires carefully tuned parameters to handle the situation where two rooms are separated by a thin wall. Another work is a rule-based WiFi localization method [13]. The authors find that the relative relation of RSS from different APs is more stable then absolute RSS. Based on this observation, they formulate the problem as a Hidden Markov Model (HMM) problem with the semantic locations as hidden states. But in some scenarios, such as shopping malls, with lots of customers moving around, the relative relation is changing frequently over time, thus this method could also be ineffective in real situations.

The forth type methods exploit other smartphones sensor data along with WiFi data to locate users. Ariel [14] utilizes gyroscope to collect WiFi data when users are in still. AurroundSense [15] exploits multiple sensors including the sound sensor, the accelerometer and the camera to construct ambience fingerprints. As it is not possible to get other sensor data without modifying users' smartphones, so these methods are inapplicable.

6   Conclusion

In this paper, we present a system called feature-based room-level localization (FRL). To addresses the deficiency caused by similar fingerprints of neighboring zones, FRL combines RSS feature and room features. In addition, FRL leverages probe requests to locate users without modifying their smartphones. The system is tested in a real scenario of 8 m by 20 m with 9 rooms and 3 APs. Experiments indicate that FRL can achieve a 10 % overall accuracy gain and 50 % accuracy gain in neighboring-zone situations, compared with conventional methods like the histogram method.

Acknowledgment. The research was partially supported by NSFC/RGC Joint Research Scheme under Grant N_PolyU519/12, and NSFC under Grant 61332004.

References

1. Liao, L., Patterson, D.J., Fox, D., Kautz, H.: Learning and inferring transportation routines. Artif. Intell. **171**(5), 311–331 (2007)
2. Zheng, Y., Xie, X.: Learning travel recommendations from user-generated GPS traces. ACM Trans. Intell. Syst. Technol. (TIST) **2**(1), 2 (2011)
3. Farrahi, K., Gatica-Perez, D.: Discovering routines from large-scale human locations using probabilistic topic models. ACM Trans. Intell. Syst. Technol. (TIST) **2**(1), 3 (2011)
4. Hu, H., Lee, D.-L.: Semantic location modeling for location navigation in mobile environment. In: Proceedings of IEEE International Conference on Mobile Data Management, pp. 52–61. IEEE (2004)

5. Kelley, K.J.: Wi-Fi location determination for semantic locations. Hilltop Rev. **7**(1), 9 (2015)
6. Pradhan, S.: Semantic location. Pers. Technol. **4**(4), 213–216 (2000)
7. Zeng, Y., Pathak, P.H., Mohapatra, P., Xu, C., Pande, A., Das, A., Miyamoto, S., Seto, E., Henricson, E., Han, J., et al.: Analyzing shopper's behavior through WiFi signals. In: Proceedings of the 2nd Workshop on Workshop on Physical Analytics, pp. 13–18. ACM (2015)
8. Spink, A., Locke, B., Van der Aa, N., Noldus, L.: Tracklab: an innovative system for location sensing, customer flow analysis and persuasive information presentation. In: Proceedings of the ACM Conference on Pervasive and Ubiquitous Computing Adjunct Publication, pp. 985–990. ACM (2013)
9. Correa, J., Katz, E., Collins, P., Griss, M.: Room-level Wi-Fi location tracking (2008)
10. Roos, T., Myllymäki, P., Tirri, H., Misikangas, P., Sievänen, J.: A probabilistic approach to WLAN user location estimation. Int. J. Wirel. Inf. Netw. **9**(3), 155–164 (2002)
11. Bahl, P., Padmanabhan, V.N.: Radar: an in-building RF-based user location and tracking system. In: INFOCOM, Proceedings of Nineteenth Annual Joint Conference of the IEEE Computer and Communications Societies, vol. 2, pp. 775–784. IEEE (2000)
12. Lee, D.L., Chen, Q.: A model-based Wifi localization method. In: Proceedings of the 2nd International Conference on Scalable Information Systems, p. 40. ICST (Institute for Computer Sciences, Social-Informatics and Telecommunications Engineering) (2007)
13. Chen, Q., Lee, D.-L., Lee, W.-C.: Rule-based WiFi localization methods. In: IEEE/IFIP International Conference on Embedded and Ubiquitous Computing, EUC 2008, vol. 1, pp. 252–258. IEEE (2008)
14. Jiang, Y., Pan, X., Li, K., Lv, Q., Dick, R.P., Hannigan, M., Shang, L.: Ariel: automatic Wi-Fi based room fingerprinting for indoor localization. In: Proceedings of the ACM Conference on Ubiquitous Computing, pp. 441–450. ACM (2012)
15. Azizyan, M., Constandache, I., Roy Choudhury, R.: Surroundsense: mobile phone localization via ambience fingerprinting. In: Proceedings of the 15th Annual International Conference on Mobile Computing and Networking, pp. 261–272. ACM (2009)
16. Pan, J.J., Pan, S.J., Yin, J., Ni, L.M., Yang, Q.: Tracking mobile users in wireless networks via semi-supervised colocalization. IEEE Trans. Pattern Anal. Mach. Intell. **34**(3), 587–600 (2012)
17. Musa, A. Eriksson, J.: Tracking unmodified smartphones using Wi-Fi monitors. In: Proceedings of the 10th ACM Conference on Embedded Network Sensor Systems, pp. 281–294. ACM (2012)
18. Cunche, M.: I know your MAC address: targeted tracking of individual using Wi-Fi. J. Comput. Virol. Hacking Tech. **10**(4), 219–227 (2014)
19. Handte, M., Iqbal, M.U., Wagner, S., Apolinarski, W., Marrón, P.J., Navarro, E.M.M., Martinez, S., Barthelemy, S.I., Fernández, M.G.: Crowd density estimation for public transport vehicles. In: EDBT/ICDT Workshops, pp. 315–322 (2014)
20. Schauer, L., Werner, M., Marcus, P.: Estimating crowd densities andpedestrian flows using Wi-Fi and Bluetooth. In: Proceedings of the 11th International Conference on Mobile and Ubiquitous Systems: Computing, Networking and Services, pp. 171–177. ICST (Institute for Computer Sciences, Social-Informatics and Telecommunications Engineering) (2014)

21. Barbera, M.V., Epasto, A., Mei, A., Perta, V.C., Stefa, J.: Signals from the crowd: uncovering social relationships through smartphone probes. In: Proceedings of the Conference on Internet Measurement Conference, pp. 265–276. ACM (2013)
22. Ling, C.X., Sheng, V.S.: Cost-sensitive learning. In: Sammut, C., Webb, G.I. (eds.) Encyclopedia of Machine Learning, pp. 231–235. Springer, USA (2010)

The Charging Personas of the E-Mobility Users of Newcastle-Gateshead Urban Area

Eiman Y. ElBanhawy[(✉)]

Department of Computing and Communication,
The Open University, Milton Keynes, UK
eiman.elbanhawy@open.ac.uk

Abstract. From a planning and policy making standpoint, the location allocation of electric vehicle (EV) refueling stations is intrinsic problem. The preposition is that the more the charging points are installed, the higher the possibility of potential users gaining confidence in driving their EVs. However, the unplanned deployment of infrastructure may cause a waste of investment. Previous research focused on the domestic charging events and the connection to the grid, slim literature covered the non-domestic charging events and patterns of EV owners. This article develops and identifies the charging personas of EV owners using non-domestic charging points. Spatiotemporal analysis was conducted based on the usage data provided by Charge Your Car (CYC) Ltd. Company, the service provider in Tyne and Wear County. This paper reports on the e-mobility system of a metropolitan area in the North East of England, Newcastle-Gateshead Area. It proposes a methodological approach to analyse current EV users' patterns and assists planning authorities and policy makers in understanding the mobility system hence strategically plan for future EV users.

Keywords: Electric vehicles · Charging network · Charging preference · Comfort zone · User charging personas

1 E-Mobility System

Alternative means of transport have obtained attention in the last decade due to the environmental burden of the transport sector. In the context of urgent challenges presented by carbon reduction targets and air quality goals, Electric vehicle (EV) industry is seen by developed countries to be a viable solution [1]. EVs are currently being discussed intensively around the world especially in European and North-American countries but also emerging economies such as China and India [2]. It is perceived that the electrification of mobility is the most efficient mean of transport compared with Internal Combustion Engine (ICE) vehicles with the smallest CO2 footprint [3–5]. Regardless of the insignificant market share today, automotive companies predict that EVs will progressively gain popularity due to environmental and social-economic factors [12, 13]. In the next 20 years the number of EV, will exponentially increase [8]. The diffusion of purely EVs is on the forefront of the non-conventional power-train technology developments [9]. Stakeholders and EV advocates claim that EVs are winning broader consumer acceptance and the options are

© ICST Institute for Computer Sciences, Social Informatics and Telecommunications Engineering 2016
A. Leon-Garcia et al. (Eds.): Smart City 2015, LNICST 166, pp. 137–150, 2016.
DOI: 10.1007/978-3-319-33681-7_12

growing for potential users to join the market. Nissan reported rising demand for its Leaf from a broader range of consumers [10]. Nissan claims that they are currently beyond the early adopters phase and they are selling for practically minded consumers who are looking at the monthly economic savings of mobility. The opportunities and issues that e-mobility brings will have lifestyle implications for large parts of the population [11]. The wide-scale adoption of privately owned low carbon emission vehicles certainly would provide an improvement [14, 15].

There are many ways and advanced technologies to recharge EVs' batteries: plugged in (domestic/ public), electrified roads, wireless charging stations, wireless charging under the roads [14], and battery swapping [15]. There is a rising demand for Charging Points (CPs) to support the e-mobility system in its urban context. Studies have showed that investments in publically available CPs would better support the EV market. Having an integrated reliable network should promote the EV market as this should slow the rapid increase of the upfront cost of the EV due to the marginal cost of expanding the car range and increasing EV battery capacity [16]. Automotive manufacturers are working on extending the range to 250 miles or more in the EVs. Planners and policy makers have to economically design integrated CPs that can support the demand and secure the way for potential users to join the market.

The non-domestic charging service can be on street or off street CPs. This embraces all publically available CPs, including the shopping centre and workplace car park. The on street one can be like the CP outside the side door of a restaurant and may refer to as "opportunity charge" [17]. This type continues to be rolled out across the UK whether using a pay as you go scheme or the membership scheme [18]. In the North East of England, the charging network is mainly managed and maintained by Charge Your Car Ltd. Company (CYC). Through CYC website and cellphone application, the current state of the CPs can be checked, see Fig. 1.

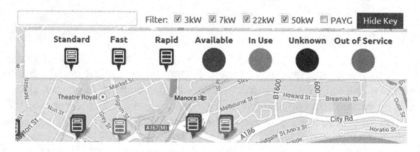

Fig. 1. CP status updates (Color figure online)

CPs are usually 7 kW or 3 kW both with 13 Amp and 32 Amp sockets so they are compatible with all EVs. Drivers can plug in their cars in for approximately 3.5 h if they want to have a full charge as per their battery capacity (Nissan Leaf battery is 21 kW capacity) using a 7 kW charge. The actual charging time will depend upon the on-board type of charger, type and the level of CP including the initial State of Charge (SoC), at arrival.

2 The Consumers and the Myth of the Limited Range

Analysing the behavioural element of an existing EV system and the level of inter-action with the infrastructure, will assist in designing for future EV users [19]. Before reviewing the previous work of the social practice, there are some socio-technical common phrases in the context of EVs that need to be highlighted.

Comfort zone concept is derived from the proxemics approach and it is widely applied in the field of psychology. The proxemics approach is the scenario to social science, which evolves around the spatial behaviour of individuals [20]. The comfort zone of an EV driver is about the individual's psychological boundaries they draw to themselves. [21] explained this zone from a psychological point of view as the comfortable range and [22] defined it as:

> *"the zone (metric, time or defined destinations), within which the driver will not worry about the battery."*

The range of these boundaries is a product of technical awareness, confidence level, mental comfort, analytical thinking, road network layout, and quality of charging services' locations and size. This definition needs to be more precise, as the driver may gain access to non- domestic CP, hence the zone will be expanded.

The definition is to be modified as: the zone (metric, time or defined destinations), within which the EV driver will not worry about the battery with no access to any nearby CP. Figure 2 illustrates the home in the centre (Origin), and the destinations (multiple: school, work, leisure, etc.) are the randomly spotted dots. The EV driver tends to tolerate short trips, which vary from one to another. The origin is the last place that has access to a CP. The first circle from inside is the comfort zone of the users. The road trip can be directed to any of the directions, as the destinations are denoted as black, green, and red circles. The comfort zone is relatively small compared to

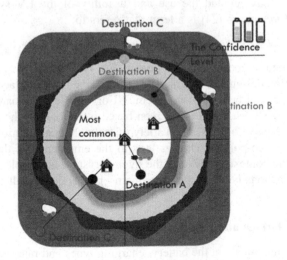

Fig. 2. EV comfort zone (Color figure online)

conventional means of transport. Will remain smaller until the stakeholders and policy makers pick up charging service difficulties.

The comfort zone is coupled with the confidence level of the users, which is the area between the first and the second circle. This area has an irregular curvature shape; it can be extended to cover even beyond the boundaries of the second circle, in which case the confidence level scores the highest levels of certainty. The black circle represents destination A, which is a destination that falls within the comfort zone. The green circle is destination B, which is relatively far compared to destination A, and it might be reached if the comfort zone of the driver is wide enough to reach it. The red circles are the destinations where the EV driver needs to have access to public CPs throughout their road trip. The wider the comfort zone, the less worried the driver would be. To get a wider comfort zone, the routes need to be supported by charging services so as to cover the routes to destination C for instance.

2.1   EV Usability and Technology Affordances

The production of new technology can be divided into a number of periods corresponding to the different social groups [23]. The technology development is a user-centred design based approach, which is driven by the usability, affordances, and difficulties. As per [24], usability refers to:

> "ensuring that interactive product are easy to learn, effective to use and enjoyable from the user' perspective."

User experience (UX) is a phrase that reflects how a product behaves and is used by consumers in the real world, which is central to interaction design. All aspects of the end's user' interaction with a system [25]. Collecting information of a user's performance is a key component of usability testing. Applying this in the e-mobility context, carrying out user studies and analysing real information about users provides insights into the charging behaviour and the use and usability of the EV system (car and infrastructure). Affordance as [24] is a term that refers to:

> "an attribute of an object that allows people to know how to use it."

As [26] simplified its meaning as "to give a clue". Affordance as a term has been used in the interaction design and is being used to describe how interfaces should make it obvious as to what can be done using them. UI or vehicle dashboard, is conceptualised as a perceived affordance, it is a screen-based interface, which is different than real affordance of physical objects. The variety of technological solutions and the link between them and socio-political choices lead to the emergence of the design interventions [23]. In the context of EV use, the overall system is complex with different protocols and interactions between the users themselves and the built environment.

2.2   The User Interface and Mobile Applications

There is basic information about the battery, charging types and rates which the driver should be aware of. Each EV model has its own designed user interface (UI). UIs of

EVs show the charging information, see example of Nissan Leaf, see Fig. 3. The SoC may be in cells or in percentages, see Fig. 3.

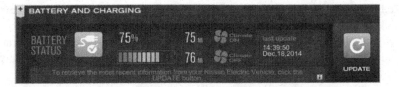

Fig. 3. Nissan Leaf UI showing battery status

This information is fundamental as it justifies the charging patterns and profiles. Starting with the battery, EV battery has 48 modules with 192 cells. An arbitrary display of 12 cells is in the car UI. In case of full charge, the 12 cells will flash in green, the last cell from top displays from 12 % to 15 %, depending on the model. Each following cell displays 8 %–5 % of the charge, depending on the model.

The EV users have different applications on their cell phones to check the charging network, Fig. 4. Each user creates their own collection of applications that covers the mobility demand (e.g., users who do not charge non-domestically, are not keen to install various charging-related applications).

Fig. 4. EV battery arbitrary cells and the percentage display

2.3 The Importance of the Study

Previous studies show that the vast majority of current users rely on domestic charging [27–31]. Even so, in order for EVs to gain widespread consumer adoption, it is critical to have an existing integrated charging infrastructure in urban areas [32]. In order to design an integrated and reliable charging network, a clear understanding of the charging patterns and preferences of privately owned EVs is fundamental. The paper presents the formation of the charging personas based on empirical data (2010–2013). It starts with the relevant work and setting the context for the case study. This is followed by the methodology section introducing the charging preferences and spectra membership and the way the user charging persona (UCP) is developed.

2.4   Related User Studies on Limited Range

Limited range was addressed in 14 studies varied between consumer and EV user, see Fig. 5, highlighting the consumer studies in red and the EV user studies in green. [33] attempted to predict the EV diffusion in the market addressing the range as to evaluate the vehicle attributes. [34] study surveyed the purchase decision and how fundamental is the range to the consumer. For the same objective [35, 36] addressed EV range in their studies investigating the consumer opinions and preferences and what would motivate them to own/lease an EV.

From a different angle, [37] conducted V2G project survey asking the consumers on the minimum acceptable range. [38] asked EV users about the minimum range they accepted or they would have accepted in their EVs. With a different approach, range related questions are addressed in consumer and EV user studies. In the latter, the participants have experienced driving the car and thus the questions relate to the use of EV rather then to predict behaviour. In order to assist Automotive and battery technology providers meet the end user's design needs, [40] surveyed the minimum SoC the users ever reached interrogating the accepted range for their daily use. In brand-perception surveys, the range was addressed to evaluate the user selection criteria as was mentioned by [41] in the USA study. EVREST project [42] surveyed the impact of the EREV on the users acceptance. A further study reported by [43] addressed the range in the Chinese market. The outcomes highlighted it as a barrier to purchase. Finally, the range was surveyed by OFAS [44] when asking the staff members on their individual preferences and how the range and the workplace charging fit within their daily routine.

2.5   The Study Area

Newcastle upon Tyne city is located in the North-East of England. The city is divided into 64 postal districts, see Fig. 6. The inner urban core is mainly the area around the river Tyne, which is defined by the postal district boundaries of NE1 (6 km^2), NE4 (14 km^2), and NE8 (16 km^2). The city has an existing EV charging infrastructure and there are plans to install more CPs around the Newcastle and Gateshead metropolitan

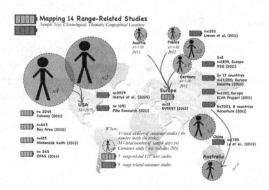

Fig. 5. (Left) Mapping of range-related studies (Color figure online)

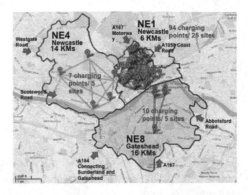

Fig. 6. (Right) CP's distribution Newcastle upon Tyne (CYC) (Source: Google map, 2014)

area over the next two years (2015–2016). According to CYC, 1,500 CPs are installed for the public use [45]. The inner urban core is a hotspot for inhabitants and visitors who are flying or sailing to Newcastle. The majority, 25 CPs are in NE1 and 5 CPs each in NE4 and NE8.

3 Methodology

This study focuses on 395 EV users' records of charging using non-domestic charging points (CPs) between 2010 and 2013. CYC Company retrieves the data from the CPs and generates up to date reports. Based on the data provided, there are four main variables related to charging patterns of individuals, see Fig. 7.

The first behavioural variable measures the time of charging within the day, labelled as Most Frequent Time (M) and it is used to know the busy times of charging (occupation). The Average time spent (A) measures the average time spent by drivers charging their cars using the refueling station (RS). M reflects the peak hour/period where most of the population prefers to replenish their batteries. This is particularly useful when dealing with a big dataset similar to the one used for Newcastle. The first attempt of calculating "M value" is the average time of charging events over a period of time. This is misleading as (M) calculates the most frequent time the users tend to charge their car. To get "M value", the day is to be divided into four time spans, and then the total number of the charging events took place in each period (morning, afternoon, evening and night) is calculated, see Fig. 8 for an example.

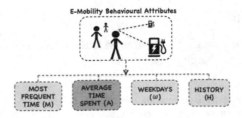

Fig. 7. (Left) E-mobility charging related attributes (measures)

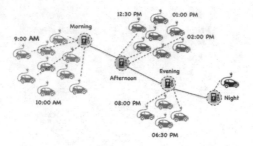

Fig. 8. (**Right**) Most frequent time "M value" visualization. The morning starts from 6 am to 11:59 pm, the afternoon is from 12:00 pm to 5:55 pm, the evening is from 6:00 pm to 11:59 am and the night is from 12:00 am to 5.59 am.

3.1   Charging Personas

[46] created and defined Persona as: a user-centred design method which sets up fictitious characters to represent the different user types within a targeted demographic group that might use a site or product. A persona is a collection of realistic representative information. In this article, the target group is the EV users and the persona as a user-centred design method is employed to characterise the charging spectrums among the group. Charging personas can be defined as:

"EV users have non-linear charging patterns that change on weekly and monthly basis. A charging persona is the charging pattern of a user after tracking their charging records (location and timing) for a period of time not less than 6 months. Charging personas are associated with demographic and socio technical elements."

The charging personas stems from individuals charging preferences. A charging preference can be described as:

"Individual's usual charging pattern that is convenient in terms of time, price, and location. The EV user demands an easy way to publically charge their car in addition to the domestic charging. Depends on the individual mobility demand, the EV owner uses the car in a way that it suits their lifestyle."

To classify the different charging preferences of EV users, CYC dataset (charging sessions of all users for a period of three years and half of operation) is analysed in a way that serves the study objective. From the definition of charging personas, the attributes Most Frequent Time (M) and Average Time Spent (A) are considered.

3.2   Charging Spectra

Prior to integrating the charging measures M and A in an attempt to classify the charging preferences, the charging practice has to be identified. The charging practice can be defined as:

"The common practice of EV drivers using non-domestic charging network where the users charge their cars to commute not a matter of opportunity charging. A creation of charging spectrum that has different patterns. Each spectrum stems from: the desired road trip, initial

SoC (as charging rate differs), confidence level and level of awareness, SoC in relation to the distance to be commuted, charger capacity and the willingness to spend time charging. There are five charging spectra (practices)."

The dataset has been analysed based on the five charging spectra, see Fig. 9.

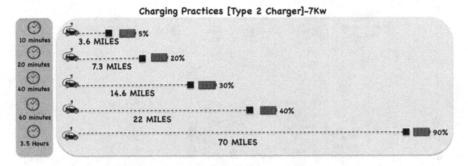

Fig. 9. Charging spectra

The first charging practice is a 10 min-charge, which will top up the battery with enough charge to at least commute around 4 miles in case of using Type 2 charger (in case of Rapid charger, more miles and higher probability to occur in the charging spectrum). Based on the literature and the EV user study, short distance commuters may stop to charge their car for 10 min.

The second charging practice is a 20 min-charge which would be enough to replenish the battery almost 20 % charge (differs based on the initial SoC before charging. The third charging practice is a 40-min charge, which would allow the commuter to drive another 15 miles. The fourth and the fifth charging practices are for those who are willing to spend time charging (one hour up to three hours and a half). The fifth practice is when the drive gets a full charge or 90 % charge (it is advised by battery technology provider to charge the battery only up to 90 % for a better battery lifestyle).

To interrogate the possible charging preferences, the first step is to look for a charging trend that reflects the EV population. An insufficient group of EV users charging their cars in a discrete pattern does not assist the understanding of the charging patterns of current users. For example, a significant group of EV users tend to charge usually at the afternoon, for 15 min using a particular rapid charger in the city centre, will indicate a emergent behaviour.

4   Method: Forming User Charging Persona

Following this line of thought, the analysis is carried out by designing a matrix of four data arrangements, see Fig. 10, creating five user charging personas. The four data arrangements are: M, A, cumulative value of all monthly charging events, and the percentage of the overall EV population. By applying the matrix to the three and half years of operation charging records, the data is administered in a spatiotemporal data analytics (secondary X axis chart) at these five levels of practices. The personas are based on Nissan Leaf model battery capacity and consumption rate. Equation 1 calculates the charging persona membership based on M and A values.

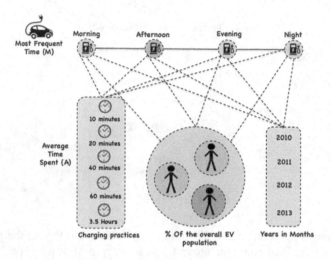

Fig. 10. EV charging personas formation data matrix

$$User\,Charging\,Persona(UCP)$$
$$= INDEX\,(\{BeyondCharging,Superb,TheLuckyYou,GoodEnough,TheTop\},$$
$$MATCH((time\,of\,departure\,(d)$$
$$= -Time\,of\,arrival\,(\delta)),TIME\,(0,\{600,180,60,40,20\}0),-1))$$

Where the time is in minute.

5   Outcome: User Charging Persona (UCP)

This study presents five user-charging personas of Newcastle-Gateshead area. Personas were generated based on the users data. The first persona is "The Top Up" contains those drivers who are willing to spend up to 20 min charging their cars over the daily road trip, see Fig. 11 as an example. This can be down to 10 min, which is sufficient to replenish their batteries and go home safely. A high percentage, 91 %, of this group charges their car for 10 min only. This reflects the reliance on domestic and workplace options. Almost half of the users charge their cars for 10-min in the evenings, which means after work and probably on their way home. The other half is equally distributed over the mornings and the afternoons.

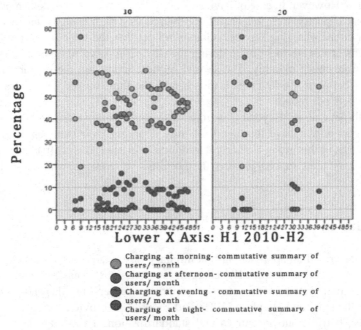

Fig. 11. The Top Up persona visualisation (Color figure online)

The second persona is "The Lucky Charge" and contains those drivers who are willing to spend up to 40 min charging their cars throughout their daily road trips. The analysis showed that the majority of transactions made by this group are ranging between 10 and 19 transactions per month. These records were scored throughout the 3.5 years. This means that this persona barely contributes to the overall charging events. Those users charge their cars in the mornings and the afternoons, in particular in the mornings.

The third persona is "The Good Enough" and contains those drivers who are willing to spend up to almost an hour charging their cars throughout their daily road trips. The analysis showed that the majority of transactions made by this group are ranging between 10 and 19 transactions per month. These records were scored throughout the three years. This means that this group barely contributes to the overall charging events. The EV users with this persona are those who charge their cars at mornings, and afternoons and in particular in the morning.

The fourth persona is "The Superb" which contains those drivers who are willing to fully charge their batteries using RSs. This means that they are so technically oriented and think wisely with respect to electricity. This group does not have a problem with charging. This is due to the high probability of having access to workplace charging (as implied from the charging spectrum), which means that users do not need to worry if they did not charge at home. They save a lot as they probably do not mainly rely on domestic charging, they plan ahead so that they can have full charge which will guarantee a safe daily trip, and also they will ultimately have the longest life time for their batteries. However, in case of having 3 kW CP, this will only replenish 50 percent of the battery capacity. Yet, this is still considered as a high level of dependency and reliance on public charging services. Graphs reflect that the majority of the charging events of this group are more often during the day. Compared to other groups, 50–59 transactions are made monthly. The second highest scores are these charging events that happen between 40–49 times a month and the third ranked scores are over 60 charging events per month.

The fifth persona is "Beyond Charging" and contains those drivers who are using 3 kW chargers and/or have the luxury of fully charging their batteries using it. The charging events of this group are fairly distributed between (20 and 50) charging events monthly. Users tend to charge also in mornings, afternoons while less likely at evenings.

6 Conclusion

This paper described an approach and preliminary observations of EV usage patterns, based on a data collected from EV charging stations in Newcastle-Gateshead Area. Analysing current systems shows cases of variant consumers' profiles and preferences, charging behaviour, and supply and demand records. It provides insights on prices, technologies, barriers and incentives and standardization. The study classified users into different clusters based on usage behaviors (the 5 personas) starting with *The Top Up* to *Beyond Charging*. The study visualised the collective dynamics underlying the dissimilar confidence level and variant comfort zone of the EV-users. The illustration of the UCP shows the non-linear charging patterns of users and how different the users can be when it comes to non-domestic charging. Coupling charging spectra with identified measures formed the membership of the UCP. We contend that range anxiety barely occurs at particular time during the road journey. The EV-drivers do not experience full electric range and they commute known and planned journeys, which makes the event of a "flat battery", is almost impossible.

References

1. Morton, C., Schuitema, G., Anable, J.: Electric Vehicles: Will Consumers get charged up? Open Univ. Milt. Keynes, p. 13 (2011)
2. TUDelft: E-Mobility NSR: Comeprehensive Analysis of European Examples of Schemes for Frieght Electric Vehicles (2014)
3. Egbue, O., Long, S.: Barriers to widespread adoption of electric vehicles: an analysis of consumer attitudes and perceptions. Energy Policy **48**, 717–729 (2012)
4. Frade, I., Ribeiro, A., Gonçalves, G., Antunes, A.P.: Optimal location of charging stations for electric vehicles in a neighborhood in Lisbon, Portugal. Transp. Res. Rec. J. Transp. Res. Board **2252**(1), 91–98 (2011)
5. Logica: Logica annual report 2011, Shaping a sustainable future. Logica, Europe (2011)

6. ElBanhawy, E., Dalton, R., Thompson, E., Kotter, R.: Real-time e-mobility simulation in metropolitan area. In: 30th eCAADe Conference, pp. 533–546 (2012)
7. Cooper, L.: Electric Vehicle Diffusion and Adoption An examination of the major factors of influence over time in the US market. Haskoli Island (2014)
8. Tan, Y., Zhang, Z., Li, J.: An optimised EV charging model considering TOU price and SOC curve. IEEE Transp. Smart Grid 3(1), 388–393 (2012)
9. Dijk, M., Orsato, R.J., Kemp, R.: The emergence of an electric mobility trajectory. Energy Policy 52, 135–145 (2013). no. 2007
10. Frades, M.: Electric Vehicle Consumers-Beyond Early Adopters. Center for Climate And Energy Solutions, Victoria (2014)
11. IET: The Lifestyle Implications of Electric Vehicle Adoption (2011)
12. Anable, J., Skippton, S., Schuitema, G., Kinnear, N.: Who will adopt Electric Vehicles? A segmentation Approach of UK Consumers. Energy Efficiency First Foundation a Low Carbon Society (2011)
13. Graham-Rowe, E., Gardner, B., Abraham, C., Skippon, S., Dittmar, H., Hutchins, R., Stannard, J.: Mainstream consumers driving plug-in battery-electric and plug-in hybrid electric cars. Transp. Res. 46(1), 140–153 (2012)
14. Lindblad, L.: Deployment Methods For Electric Vehicle Infrastructure. Uppsala University (2012)
15. ElBanhawy, E., Nassar, K.: A Movable Charging Unit for Green Mobility. In: ISPRS - International Archives Photogrammetry Remote Sensing and Spatial Information Sciences, vol. XL–4/W1, pp. 77–82, May 2013
16. Chen, T., Kockleman, K., Khan, M.: The electric vehicle charging station location problem: a parking-based assignment method for Seattle. In: The 92nd Annual Meeting of the Transportation Research Board in Washington DC (2013)
17. Conway, G.: The Charging Point (2011). http://www.thechargingpoint.com/knowledge-hub/hot-topics/hot-topics-charging.html
18. CYC: Charge Your Car Ltd. (2010). http://chargeyourcar.org.uk/about/
19. Pasaoglu, G., Zubaryeva, A., Fiorello, D., Thiel, C.: Analysis of European mobility surveys and their potential to support studies on the impact of electric vehicles on energy and infrastructure needs in Europe. Technol. Forecast. Soc. Change 87, 41–50 (2013)
20. Hall, E.T.: The Hidden Dimension, 1st edn. Doubleday, New York (1966)
21. Franke, T., Neumann, I., Bühler, F., Cocron, P., Krems, J.F.: Experiencing range in an electric vehicle - understanding psychological barriers. Appl. Pshychol. 61(3), 368–391 (2012)
22. ElBanhawy, E.Y.: Analysis of space-time behaviour of electric vehicle potential user and commuter. In: ITEC-IEEE (2014)
23. Callon, M.: The state and technical innovation: a case study of the electrical vehicle in France. Res. Policy 9, 358–376 (1980)
24. Preece, J., Rogers, Y., Sharp, H.: Interaction Design, 4th edn, p. 570. Wiley (2015)
25. Nielsen, J., Norman, D.: The definition of user experience. In: The Definition of User Experience (2014)
26. Norman, D.: The Design of Everyday Things. Basic Books, New York (1988)
27. ElBanhawy, E.Y.: Straight From The Horse's Mouth: 'I am an Electric Vehicle User, I am a Risk Taker.' [EV14, M, c. 30]. In: EAI International Conference in Smart Urban Mobility Systems (SUMS) (2015)
28. Cattaneo, M., Ferchow, J., Schulze, A., Koch, C.: Should utilities Build Charging Networks? (2014)
29. Keros, A.: Advanced Vehicle and Infrastructure Policy (2014)

30. Boyce, L.: How much does it cost to charge an electric car, how many times a week would I need to do it and is it worth buying one? The Daily Mail (2012). http://www.thisismoney.co.uk/money/experts/article-2243534/How-does-cost-charge-electric-car-home.html
31. Mcdonald, S.: Practical issue with implementing smart chraging, NAREC. In: e-Mobility project, NSR Programme (2012)
32. Xu, H., Miao, S., Zhang, C., Shi, D.: Optimal placement of charging infrastructures for large-scale integration of pure electric vehicles into grid. Int. J. Electr. Power Energy Syst. **53**, 159–165 (2013)
33. Hidrue, M., Parsons, G., Kempton, W., Gardner, M.: Willingness to pay for electric vehicles and their attributes. Resour. Energy Econ. **33**, 686–705 (2011)
34. Deloitte: UK Electric Car Consumer Survey (2010). http://www.globalwarmingskeptics.info/thread-812.html, http://www.globalwarmingskeptics.info/thread-812.html
35. Lieven, T., Muhlmeier, S., Henkel, S., Waller, J.: Who will buy electric cars? An empirical study in Germany. Transp. Res. Part D **16**, 236–243 (2011)
36. Sahran, Z.: Understanding Electric Car Owners & Potential Electric Car Owners (2013)
37. Bunzeck, I., Feenstra, C.F.J., Paukovic, M.: Preferences of potential users of electric cars related to charging - A survey in eight EU countries (2011)
38. Lesemann, M.: Advanced Electric Vehicle Architectures Collaborative Project, ELVA (2010)
39. Lesemann, M., Funcke, M., Ickert, L., Eckstein, L., Malmek, E.-M., Wismans, J.: Integrated architectures for third generation electric vehicles – first results of the ELVA project. In: EEVC European Electric Vehicle Congress (2011)
40. Mackenzi, D., Keith, D.: To Understand how various factors affect operators' decisions on when and where to charge their plug-in vehicles Survey (2013)
41. Conway, G.: Electric vehicle misconceptions confirmed in survey: Consumer Reports study shows range is still the chief concern (2012). http://www.thechaargingpoint.com/news/Electric-vehicle-misconceptions-confirmed-in-survey.html
42. EVREST: EVREST: Electric Vehicle with Range Extender as a Sustainable Technology (2012). http://www.evrest-project.org/context.php. Accessed 01 Jan 2014
43. Lo, K.: Interested but unsure: Public attitudes toward electric vehicles in China. Electron. Green J. **36**, 1–12 (2013)
44. OFAS: Electric Vehicle Charging Station Survey Report (2014)
45. Wordle, J.: Post Research: An Interview with CYC Infrastructure Director (2014)
46. Cooper, A.: The Inmates are Running the Asylum. SAMS (1999)

SWIT-Health

Segmentation by Data Point Classification Applied to Forearm Surface EMG

Jonathan Feng-Shun Lin[1]([✉]), Ali-Akbar Samadani[2], and Dana Kulić[1]

[1] Department of Electrical and Computer Engineering,
University of Waterloo, Waterloo, ON, Canada
{jf2lin,dkulic}@uwaterloo.ca
[2] Institute of Biomaterials and Biomedical Engineering,
University of Toronto, Toronto, Canada
ali.samadani@utoronto.ca

Abstract. Recent advances in wearable technologies have led to the development of new modalities for human-machine interaction such as gesture-based interaction via surface electromyograph (EMG). An important challenge when performing EMG gesture recognition is to temporally segment the individual gestures from continuously recorded time-series data. This paper proposes an approach for EMG data segmentation, by formulating the segmentation problem as a classification task, where a classifier is used to label each data point as either a segment point or a non-segment point. The proposed EMG segmentation approach is used to recognize 9 hand gestures from forearm EMG data of 10 participants and a balanced accuracy of 83 % is achieved.

Keywords: Motion segmentation · Surface electromyography · Classifiers · Pattern recognition

1 Introduction

Electromyography (EMG), the measure of electrical impulses in the muscles, is a promising approach for gesture recognition [1–3]. In order to utilize EMG-based gesture recognition in naturalistic interactions, the start and end of each gesture must be accurately identified from continuous EMG data; this problem is known as *temporal segmentation*. Segmentation is useful to fields such as human-machine interaction as it breaks down a sequence of complex movements, which may include repetitions of the same gesture, into smaller units, termed *primitives.*

Traditional activity recognition and segmentation techniques employ camera-based systems [4], hand-held inertial measurement units (IMUs) [2] or data gloves [5], but they may not be the most suitable for naturalistic interactions. Camera-based systems require unobstructed line-of-sight, while the form factor of IMUs and data gloves constrict natural hand movements, making them unsuitable for hand gesture recognition. With EMG-based systems, since the electrical impulses

© ICST Institute for Computer Sciences, Social Informatics and Telecommunications Engineering 2016
A. Leon-Garcia et al. (Eds.): Smart City 2015, LNICST 166, pp. 153–165, 2016.
DOI: 10.1007/978-3-319-33681-7_13

that control hand movements flow through the forearm, forearm EMG can be used to detect hand and finger movements [6]. The EMG sensors are placed on the forearm and not the hand, so this approach does not impede finger movement or the performance of any hand gestures, allowing for more natural interactions.

However, EMG data suffers from some key difficulties: (1) EMG signal amplitude is a function of neuronal and tissue conductivity [7]; (2) Water and body fat introduces noise that attenuates the EMG signal [7]; (3) Sensor placement must be consistent between participants for comparison studies; and (4) EMG signals should be normalized to minimize inter-participant variability [8].

Due to these difficulties, to date, EMG has received less attention in the literature on activity segmentation and recognition. Many existing works use manual or semi-automated segmentation to isolate motions of interest, and focus on the classification of the isolated waveforms. In these papers, the segmentation is performed by thresholding on the signal envelope [3], instantaneous energy [2], transient energy [9], root mean square (RMS) [10], ratio of auto-regression parameters [11], and standard deviation [1], or the data is assumed to be pre-segmented [12,13]. Other activity recognition papers produce a class label using a sliding window [6,14]. In activity recognition survey papers, EMG-based activity recognition is either only briefly mentioned [15], or omitted [16], emphasizing the lack of research efforts in this field. However, to the authors' best knowledge, no published work has reported temporal results for temporal segmentation based on surface EMG. Kaur *et al.* [17] applied heuristics and wavelet analysis to needle transducer EMG to isolate action potentials in biceps, but only reported the number of action potential segments denoted by the algorithm and not the temporal accuracy of their algorithm. Carrino *et al.* [18] designed an EMG-based system where the user activates a hand gesture recognition system by first flexing the triceps, then performs the hand gesture. Both the triceps flex and the hand gesture are recognized by linear discriminant analysis. This approach is similar to the work proposed in this paper, but does not report the segmentation accuracy.

This paper explores the efficacy of using EMG signals for detecting the start and the end of hand gestures. To this end, an EMG signal is represented in terms of time and frequency meta-features, and a classifier-based segmentation method [19] is used to detect the start and the end of the active region of the EMG signal. The active region of the EMG signal corresponds to the interval within which a hand gesture is performed. The proposed method classifies individual data points as a *segment point* (p_1) or a *non-segment point* (p_0), and has previously been applied to lower-body [19] joint angle data. This segmentation approach is on-line and generalizes across individuals, using only simple signal preprocessing [19]. In this paper, the classifier-based segmentation method is applied to segment motion data based on associated EMG activities measured from the forearm during the continuous production of hand gestures.

2   Proposed Approach

This paper applies a classifier-based time-series segmentation approach [19] to discriminate between forearm EMG samples corresponding to p_1 (segment) and

p_0 (non-segment) classes. However, using classifiers in this manner to perform segmentation raises several issues: (1) Classifiers do not inherently consider temporal information, which is an important aspect of movement data, (2) appropriate generation of training points is also important, as manually labelled segments typically only specify a single time point to denote the start and the end of a given exemplar, which is not suitable for classifiers, as there is minimum difference between the data point at time t_n and at time $t_{n\pm1}$, and (3) unbalanced p_1 and p_0 data samples. These issues are addressed by employing normalization, manual segment point expansion, input vector stacking and downsampling.

Consideration must also be given for the intrinsic difficulties of utilizing EMG. EMG signals tend to be highly individualistic due to body type and sensor orientation. These issues are addressed by employing normalization, EMG channel remapping, as well as considering EMG features that are channel agnostic or robust against signal noise.

2.1   EMG Features

A large number of typical EMG and signal processing features was examined in order to identify those best suited for segmentation. The features considered were selected due to their prevalence in EMG analysis [7,20], for their ability to extract useful information from a noisy signal, as well as their channel agnostic characteristics to reduce the impact of EMG sensor placement variability. The features examined include RMS EMG, mean absolute value, waveform length, slope sign changes, skewness, kurtosis, channel-pair inner-product, channel-pair angle, RMS ratio and peak-to-peak time between the two most active EMG channels, Hurst exponent, Hjorth parameters, Teager energy, entropy, relative entropy, mutual information, peak frequency, band width, peak width as measured at quarter power point from the peak frequency spectral power, and relative spectral power. These features are computed over moving windows.

The best performing features (See Sect. 3.3) are described below. In the following definitions, $E(t)$ is the raw EMG signal, W_n is the length of the window, t_0, t_1 ... t_n denote entries in the window.

Mean Absolute Value. $MAV = \sum_{t_0}^{t_n} \frac{1}{W_n} |E(t)|$.

The MAV is the sum of the absolute values of the EMG signal over a window, which effectively computes a moving average filter of the EMG signal.

Waveform-Length. $WFL = \sum_{t_0}^{t_n} |\dot{E}(t)|$.

The WFL is the cumulative successive change of the EMG signal over a temporal interval. If a signal fluctuates greatly within a window, WFL is high, while a signal with low WFL does not contain a lot of local variations.

Pairwise Inner-Product. $PIP = E(t)_x \cdot E(t)_y$,

where $E(t)_x$ and $E(t)_y$ refer to specific channels of the EMG. The PIP is calculated by taking the dot product of a moving window between two channels, and captures the interactions between channel-pairs.

Root Mean Square. $RMS = \sqrt{\sum_{t_0}^{t_n} \frac{1}{W_n} E(t)^2}$.

The RMS provides a measure of the signal power.

Teager Energy. $TE = \dot{E}^2(t) - E(t) \cdot \ddot{E}(t)$.

The TE is a local property of the signal, that varies with the amplitude profiles and instantaneous frequency of the signal. TE captures the energy required to generate the signal with various amplitude and frequency specifications. For two signals with similar amplitude profile and different frequency components, the Teager energy returns different values.

2.2   Data Processing

Normalization. The motion exemplars are normalized to reduce the impact of the inter- and intra-participant variability resulting from variations in sensor placement and EMG signal magnitude. For EMG data, a known sync motion is collected for baseline purposes. Sensor placement normalization is carried out by finding the appropriate rotations such that the maxima of the EMG norm of the sync motion are always in a given channel, and applying this rotation to all movements by this participant in a given session.

Magnitude normalization is also important, and a normalization coefficient can be calculated in a variety of different ways: (1) channel-wise normalization, where the coefficient is the maximum magnitude of each channel in each gesture, (2) motion-wise normalization, where the coefficient is the maximum magnitude over all the EMG channels, or (3) participant-wise normalization, where the coefficient is the average of the maximum motion-wise magnitude of different trials of the sync motion. All normalization coefficients are calculated from the absolute value of the raw EMG data.

Manual Segment Point Expansion. Manual segments are required to label the training data and for algorithmic validation. Typical methods to obtain manual segments is by hand annotating the data, by video playback, or via a proxy sensor. For EMG, it can be difficult to determine from the EMG data visually where a primitive begins and ends, so manual segments can be denoted from a secondary sensor, such as from camera data or a data glove. Once the manual segments are created, it is necessary to increase the number of segment training points to balance the training dataset. To this end, an additional n_{exp} points before and after each manually labelled segment point are also labelled as p_1 [19].

Input Vector Stacking. Classifier techniques do not typically consider temporal factors. To consider short term temporal effects, the input vector is stacked, so that a given data point includes data from a few time steps before and after the current data point. That is, $t_{use} = [t_{n-n_{stack}} \cdots t_{n-1}, t_n, t_{n+1} \cdots t_{n+n_{stack}}]$. n_{stack} requires tuning to optimize for the data [19].

Downsampling. In a given dataset, there may be more data points of one class over the other. The number of p_1 and p_0 for each exemplar are noted, and the smallest values are denoted as $p_{1_{min}}$ and $p_{0_{min}}$, respectively. Each exemplar is randomly downsampled without replacement to match $p_{1_{min}}$ and $p_{0_{min}}$, to eliminate the unbalanced dataset.

2.3 Classifier Training and Testing

After the above steps, the individual exemplar features are concatenated into a data matrix, and passed into a two-stage training process, consisting of a dimensionality reduction algorithm and a base classifier. Initial testing showed that, like previous work [19], aggregation techniques such as boosting [21], do not heavily influence accuracy scores. Principal component analysis (PCA) [21] is used for pre-classifier dimensionality reduction on feature sets that produce vectorial datasets, such as the channel-pair inner-product, and is not applied for feature sets that produce scalars. The base classifiers [21] examined are as follows: (1) artificial neural networks (ANN), (2) k-nearest neighbour (k-NN), (3) linear discriminate analysis (LDA), (4) quadratic discriminate analysis (QDA), (5) support vector machine (SVM), and (6) thresholding on magnitude, with the threshold determined by the value that returns the highest training accuracy.

To classify, each set of observation data is processed in a similar fashion as the training data. The input vector is normalized, and n_{stack} is applied. The PCA transformation, as calculated from the training data, is also applied to obtain a low-dimensional representation of the data, if applicable. Unlike the training data, no downsampling is applied to the observation data. For algorithm verification purposes, the ground truth p_1 points are expanded by n_{exp}.

3 Experiments and Results

3.1 Motion Database

The classifiers were trained on a database of 10 participants with a mean age of 26.8 years old, performing 5 repetitions of 9 different hand gesture primitives, denoted as the *individual gesture (IG) dataset*, and tested against separate sequences of continuous motions where the 9 primitives are performed in random order, denoted as the *continuous random (CR) dataset*. For this paper, training data was always drawn from the IG dataset, while testing was always done against the CR dataset. Only 6 of the 10 participants contributed randomized motions sequences. The experiment was approved by the University of Waterloo Research Ethics Board, and consent was obtained from all participants.

A single classifier was created from the different participant and gesture data, and used to test against the observation data to evaluate the classifier's inter-participant and inter-gesture robustness. All processing, implementation, and analysis were done in MATLAB 8.0, along with the LIBSVM Toolbox [22].

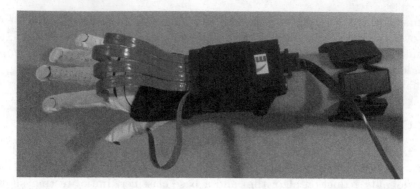

Fig. 1. A participant wearing the Shapehand dataglove from Measurand Inc. (hand and wrist) and the Myo armband from Thalmic Labs Inc. (forearm).

The data was collected by a Myo armband from Thalmic Labs Inc.[1] The EMG armband provides an 8-channel EMG data stream. The armband was placed on the working forearm of the participant, without any specific instructions on armband location or orientation. No conductive paste or other physical attachment site preparation are required when using the Myo. The motion was also collected by a Shapehand dataglove from Measurand Inc.[2] The dataglove provides 15-channel joint angle data, corresponding to each joint in the fingers (Fig. 1). Manual segments were generated by hand annotation on the dataglove data.

The gestures performed were: fist, finger spread, gun, pointing with index finger, pointing with index and middle finger, paddle in, paddle out, snap and thumb-pinky touch. No specific directions on how to perform each motion were given to the participants, so some inter-participant variabilities were observed in how each gesture was executed. Paddle out was used as the sync motion.

3.2 Verification

To calculate the segmentation accuracy, each point in the observation sequence is labelled p_1 or p_0. The number of correctly identified p_1, the true positives (TP), as well as true negatives (TN), false positives (FP), and false negatives (FN), are aggregated together and reported as the balanced accuracy Acc_{Bal}:

$$Acc_{Bal} = \frac{1}{2} \cdot \frac{TP}{TP + FN} + \frac{1}{2} \cdot \frac{TN}{TN + FP}$$

This metric serves as a measure that aggregates both sensitivity and specificity and limits inflated accuracy scores in imbalanced dataset cases.

---

[1] Thalmic Labs Inc., www.thalmic.com.
[2] Measurand Inc., www.shapehand.com.

3.3 Evaluation of Pre-processing Parameters

In this section, the impact of pre-processing parameters on classification accuracy is examined. The thresholding classifier was selected for this experiment as it is the most common current approach [1,3,10]. The window length is generally smaller than during previous experiments [19], so n_{exp} was set to 5. Larger n_{stack} values improve accuracy, so n_{stack} was kept at 15 [19] to balance between runtime and accuracy. Two factors were examined: (1) EMG features: The EMG features specified in Sect. 2.1 were considered. The calculations were performed over a sliding window of length 20 samples (0.067 s) with a window overlap of 10 samples (0.033 s), (2) normalization type: The different normalization methods specified in Sect. 2.2 were considered.

The influence of these factors on segmentation accuracy are reported in Table 1. These results were generated by dividing the IG dataset into two folds of 5 participants each and using each fold to train a separate classifier. Both classifiers were tested against the CR dataset, and the averaged accuracy between the two classifiers was calculated. The table reports the top 5 performing features according to segmentation Acc_{Bal}. The top performing features while using the threshold approach were the TE, WFL, MAV, RMS + PIP (RP), and raw EMG + RMS + PIP (RRP). Other features examined generally require larger windows of the EMG data to be available, and are not suitable for the temporal resolution required for segmentation purposes.

Table 1 shows that channel-wise normalization did not perform as well as the other normalizations, while the other three normalization methods showed comparable results. This is likely due to channel-wise normalization de-emphasizing individual channel differences in the EMG data between the different gestures. Similar results between normalized and non-normalized data could indicate that these features are not sensitive to inter-participant differences in the signal, leading to comparable results between the no normalization case and the normalization cases. Although participant-based normalization did not perform the best in Table 1, its performance was comparable to the other normalization types, it requires the least amount of input from the participant while improving robustness to large inter-personal variability, and will be used as the normalization scheme in subsequent sections.

3.4 Classifier Evaluation

The best features from Sect. 3.3 (TE, WFL, MAV, RP, and RPP) were used to evaluate the impact of classifier choice. The algorithm parameters used were:

- PCA: PCs set by scree plot method at 80 %.
- k-NN: $k = [1, 3]$.
- Soft-margin SVM: Kernel functions tested were linear, polynomial, radial.
- Feedforward ANN: Layout tested are $[10]$, $[10, 10]$, $[10, 10, 10]$.
- LDA, QDA, thresholding: Euclidean distance was used.

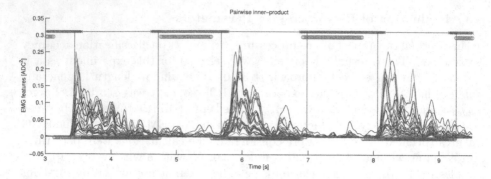

Fig. 2. Segmentation results of a person performing a sequence of random hand gestures, on EMG pairwise inner-product features. The blue rectangles denote the full-motion manual segmentation boundaries. The blue and red lines at the top and bottom denote the classifier p_0 and p_1 for ground truth (blue x) and algorithmic (red circle) segmentation, respectively. (Color figure online)

The results are summarized in Table 2. An illustration of the algorithm segmenting the EMG features can be found in Fig. 2. Similar to Tables 1, 2 was generated by dividing the IG set into two subsets, training a classifier on each subset and averaging the accuracy obtained by each classifier on the testing set. Table 2 shows that ANN and QDA both performed comparatively, showing that both simple and complex classifiers can perform well. In Table 1, the RP was shown to be the best performing feature for participant normalized data, but was outperformed by other features in Table 2.

Table 1. Acc_{bal} scores [%], reported for varying features, after channel, motion, participant or no normalization. The features reported are the top performing features, and are as follows: the Teager energy (TE), waveform-length (WFL), mean absolute value (MAV), the combined features of RMS EMG + inner-product (RP), and the combined features of raw EMG + RMS EMG + inner-product (RRP). Highest Acc_{bal} in each normalization type is bolded. The threshold classifier was used to generate this table, with $n_{exp} = 5$.

Features	Normalization			
	Channel	Motion	Participant	None
TE	72.4 ± 4	74.4 ± 1	73.7 ± 1	73.9 ± 1
WFL	71.6 ± 7	76.2 ± 3	75.3 ± 2	75.6 ± 3
MAV	65.3 ± 12	70.5 ± 8	69.3 ± 9	69.4 ± 9
RP	$\mathbf{73.2 \pm 5}$	$\mathbf{79.0 \pm 0}$	$\mathbf{78.2 \pm 1}$	$\mathbf{78.2 \pm 0}$
RRP	72.4 ± 1	72.4 ± 1	72.4 ± 1	78.0 ± 0

Table 2. Acc_{bal} scores [%], reported for varying classifiers and features. Top scoring classifier from each classifier type is reported. The best performing features are mean absolute value (MAV), and the RMS + inner-product (RP).

Rank	Classifier	Feature	Accuracy
1	ANN, 10^2	MAV	83 ± 6
2	QDA	MAV	81 ± 7
3	SVM, linear	WFL	81 ± 5
4	LDA	RP	80 ± 6
5	k-NN, 3	MAV	78 ± 7
6	Threshold	RP	78 ± 9

3.5   Leave-One-Gesture-Out Analysis

Table 3 reports the inter-gesture generalization results, where the gesture under inspection was left out of the IG dataset using leave-one-gesture-out (LOGO) cross validation. The training data was generated from the same participant as the observation data, and the Acc_{bal} scores were averaged across all participants. The best performing classifier from Table 2, the ANN, was used for this test.

From Table 3, it can be observed that all features tend to perform similarly, with the exception of RRP. Of all the assessed features, RRP contains 44 (8 from raw EMG, 8 from RMS EMG and 28 from the PIP) elements, which is the largest number of elements. The PCA reduction of RRP features might have resulted in overfitting of training data.

Table 3 also provides insight into the generalizability of the proposed approach to unseen motions. Table 3 suggests that the classifier is able to generalize to most new motions. This is a major potential advantage of the proposed approach, eliminating the need for having a fixed set of *a priori* specified motions. However, some motions, such as the fist motion, do not generalize well, and would need to be explicitly included in the training set to improve the segmentation performance.

3.6   Leave-One-Participant-Out Analysis

To evaluate the generalizability of the learned classifier to participants unseen during training, Table 4 was generated by leaving one-participant-out (LOPO) of the training IG dataset, and testing against the data of that individual from the CR dataset. This cross-validation shows that, for most participants, excellent generalization performance is achieved, with classification results comparable to the case when their data is included in the training set. However, for some participants, *e.g.*, participant 9, lower accuracy scores are observed when they are left out, suggesting that their EMG data differs from the other participants. See Fig. 3 for a comparison between participant 4 and 9. An examination into the movements of participant 9 revealed higher variance in both movement and

Table 3. Acc_{bal} scores [%], reported for LOGO cross-validation. The gestures tested were finger spread (FISP), fist (FIST), gun (GUNM), paddle in (PDIN), paddle out (PDOU), pointing with index finger (POIN), pointing with index and middle (POIM), finger snapping (SNAP) and thumb-pinky touch (THPK). The features listed are the Teager energy (TE), waveform-length (WFL), mean absolute value (MAV), the RMS + inner-product (RP), and the raw EMG + RMS + inner-product (RRP). The ANN classifier was used. The best performing feature for each gesture is bolded.

Gesture	FISP	FIST	GUNM	PDIN	PDOU	POIN	POIM	SNAP	THPK
TE	85 ± 7	77 ± 12	**85 ± 7**	82 ± 11	**87 ± 7**	82 ± 7	82 ± 13	78 ± 5	82 ± 11
WFL	86 ± 6	**76 ± 12**	85 ± 8	**83 ± 11**	85 ± 11	**85 ± 8**	86 ± 8	81 ± 6	**83 ± 10**
MAV	**87 ± 6**	76 ± 13	85 ± 8	82 ± 13	83 ± 13	84 ± 10	85 ± 10	**83 ± 6**	82 ± 9
RP	82 ± 9	75 ± 15	85 ± 8	76 ± 12	84 ± 12	85 ± 9	85 ± 9	82 ± 9	81 ± 10
RRP	77 ± 7	69 ± 9	75 ± 8	71 ± 14	78 ± 11	71 ± 9	80 ± 9	70 ± 12	75 ± 9

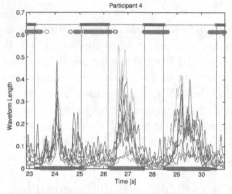

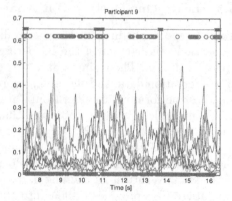

(a) Participant 4, performing pointing with index (23 - 25 sec), pointing with index and middle (26 - 27.5 sec) and paddle out (28.5 - 30.5 sec). This participant obtained a high LOPO score.

(b) Participant 9, performing 3 instances of pointing with index and middle (7 - 10.5 sec, 11 - 13.5 sec, 14 - 16 sec). Note the dissimilarity between the two participant's motions.

Fig. 3. Segmentation results of two people performing a sequence of random hand gestures, with the WFL feature. The blue rectangles denote the manual segmentation boundaries. The blue and red lines at the top and bottom denote the classifier p_0 and p_1 for ground truth (blue x) and algorithmic (red o) segmentation, respectively. The coloured waveforms correspond to different EMG channels and feature elements. (Color figure online)

resting postures, as well as significant differences in the EMG data between these two participants and the other participants, thus causing a degradation in the segmentation performance. Even when participant 9 is included in the training set, the classifier accuracy does not increase, which suggests differences in which the way the gestures were performed between the IG and the CR data for this participant.

Table 4. Acc_{bal} scores [%], reported for LOPO cross-validation. The features reported are the Teager energy (TE), waveform-length (WFL), mean absolute value (MAV), the RMS + inner-product (RP), and the raw EMG + RMS + inner-product (RRP). The ANN classifier was used. The best performing result for each gesture is bolded.

Participant	4	5	6	7	8	9	10
TE	88 ± 0	87 ± 0	86 ± 1	82 ± 1	83 ± 2	71 ± 4	76 ± 3
WFL	**89 ± 1**	91 ± 1	84 ± 1	82 ± 2	83 ± 1	67 ± 4	**81 ± 1**
MAV	89 ± 1	**91 ± 1**	**86 ± 1**	**83 ± 1**	**87 ± 1**	**72 ± 6**	80 ± 2
RP	88 ± 1	90 ± 0	82 ± 1	82 ± 2	85 ± 2	63 ± 5	78 ± 2
RRP	82 ± 1	83 ± 0	81 ± 1	75 ± 2	71 ± 1	59 ± 3	72 ± 3

From Tables 2, 3 and 4, it is noted that different features achieved the highest balanced accuracy score, suggesting that different combinations of features and classifiers can perform well in different situations. The best feature across all three tables is the MAV, with a 82.9 % with the ANN classifier, 86.5 % with finger spread in the LOGO test, as well as achieving 91.4 % with participant 5 in the LOPO test. This could be due to the fact that the MAV removes the high frequency variations and abrupt changes in the signals, whereas features such as RMS may amplify these fluctuations.

4   Conclusion

This paper shows that EMG serves as an interesting and promising measurement system for gesture segmentation, and that the start and the end of the gestures can be identified from continuously measured EMG data, using a classifier based approach. The proposed segmentation method was shown to generalize across gestures. In many cases, participant generalization was observed as well, but the algorithm is limited by inter-participant variances of muscle activity, resulting in differences in the EMG. The proposed method is capable of on-line segmentation, requiring only an observation window of 0.06 s. Various configurations were tested, such as varying normalization methods or classifier combinations, and revealed that the artificial neural network with the moving averaging feature performed best, achieving a balanced segmentation accuracy of 83 %.

For future work, more sophisticated classifiers that aggregate different classifiers and features together will be investigated, to take advantage of the strength of different classifier-feature combinations. An examination of the data shows that a participant is typically in one of three states: resting, gesture onset, and gesture hold. A multi-class segmentation may be able to improve upon the existing p_0/p_1 approach.

Acknowledgement. The authors of this work would like to acknowledge Thalmic Labs Inc. for providing the Myo armband and the data collection codebase. The authors would also like to acknowledge Dr. Pedram Ataee and the Machine Learning team at Thalmic Labs Inc. for their assistance and insights.

References

1. Costanza, E., Inverso, S., Allen, R.: Toward subtle intimate interfaces for mobile devices using an EMG controller. In: SIGCHI, pp. 481–489 (2005)
2. Zhang, X., Chen, X., Li, Y., Lantz, V., Wang, K., Yang, J.: A framework for hand gesture recognition based on accelerometer and EMG sensors. IEEE Trans. Syst. Man Cybern. A **41**, 1064–1076 (2011)
3. Samadani, A., Kulić, D.: Hand gesture recognition based on surface electromyography. In: EMBC, pp. 4196–4199 (2014)
4. Erol, A., Bebis, G., Nicolescu, M., Boyle, R., Twombly, X.: Vision-based hand pose estimation: a review. Comput. Vis. Image Underst. **108**, 52–73 (2007)
5. Sturman, D., Zeltzer, D.: A survey of Glove-based input. IEEE Comput. Graph Appl. Mag. **14**, 30–39 (1994)
6. Phinyomark, A., Quaine, F., Charbonnier, S., Serviere, C., Tarpin-Bernard, F., Laurillau, Y.: EMG feature evaluation for improving myoelectric pattern recognition robustness. Exp. Syst. Appl. **40**, 4832–4840 (2013)
7. Winter, D., Rau, G., Kadefos, R., Broman, H., De Luca, C.: Units, terms and standards in reporting of EMG research. Electromyogr Kinesiol, Technical report (1980)
8. Oberg, T., Sandsjo, L., Kadefors, R.: Emg mean power frequency: obtaining a reference value. Clin. Biomech. **9**, 253–257 (1994)
9. Chen, Z., Wang, X.: Pattern recognition of number gestures based on a wireless surface EMG system. Biomed. Signal Process. **8**, 184–192 (2013)
10. Kim, J., Mastnik, S., André, E.: Emg-based hand gesture recognition for realtime biosignal interfacing. In: IUI, pp. 30–39 (2008)
11. El Falou, W., Duchêne, J., Hewson, D., Khalil, M., Grabisch, M., Lino, F.: A segmentation approach to long duration surface EMG recordings. J. Electromyogr. Kinesiol. **15**, 111–119 (2005)
12. Naik, G., Kumar, D., Palaniswami, M.: Multi run ICA and surface EMG based signal processing system for recognising hand gestures. In: ICCIT, pp. 700–705 (2008)
13. Ahsan, M., Ibrahimy, M., Khalifa, O.: Electromygraphy (EMG) signal based hand gesture recognition using artificial neural network (ANN). In: ICOM, pp. 1–6 (2011)
14. Yoshikawa, M., Mikawa, M., Tanaka, K.: A myoelectric interface for robotic hand control using support vector machine. In: IROS, pp. 2723–2728 (2007)
15. Chen, L., Hoey, J., Nugent, C., Cook, D., Yu, Z.: Sensor-based activity recognition. IEEE Trans. Syst. Man Cybern. C **42**, 790–808 (2012)
16. Lara, O., Labrador, M.: A survey on human activity recognition using wearable sensors. IEEE Commun. Surv. Tutorials **15**, 1192–1209 (2013)
17. Kaur, G., Arora, A., Jain, V.: Comparison of the techniques used for segmentation of EMG signals. In: MACMESE, pp. 124–129 (2009)
18. Carrino, F., Ridi, A., Mugellini, E., Khaled, O., Ingold, R.: Gesture segmentation and recognition with an EMG-based intimate approach - an accuracy and usability study. In: CISIS, pp. 544–551 (2012)

19. Lin, J., Joukov, V., Kulić, D.: Human motion segmentation by data point classification. In: EMBC, pp. 9–13 (2014)
20. Konrad, P.: The ABC of EMG. Noraxon USA, Technical report (2005)
21. Jain, A., Duin, R., Mao, J.: Statistical pattern recognition: a review. IEEE Trans. Pattern Anal. Mach. Intell. **22**, 4–37 (2000)
22. Chang, C., Lin, C.: LIBSVM: a library for support vector machines. ACM Trans. Intell. Syst. Technol. **2**, 27:1–27:27 (2011)

On the Use of Consumer-Grade Activity Monitoring Devices to Improve Predictions of Glycemic Variability

Chandra Krintz[1]([✉]), Rich Wolski[1], Jordan E. Pinsker[3], Stratos Dimopoulos[1], John Brevik[4], and Eyal Dassau[2]

[1] Computer Science Department, University of California, Santa Barbara, USA
ckrintz@cs.ucsb.edu.edu
[2] Chemical Engineering Department, University of California, Santa Barbara, USA
[3] William Sansum Diabetes Center, Santa Barbara, CA, USA
[4] Mathematics Department, California State University, Long Beach, USA
http://www.cs.ucsb.edu/~racelab

Abstract. This paper examines the use of partial least squares regression to predict glycemic variability in subjects with Type I Diabetes Mellitus using measurements from continuous glucose monitoring devices and consumer-grade activity monitoring devices. It illustrates a methodology for generating automated predictions from current and historical data and shows that activity monitoring can improve prediction accuracy substantially.

Keywords: Activity monitoring · Diabetes · Prediction · Decision support

1 Introduction

Ubiquitous mobile Internet connectivity has driven the rapid development of consumer-grade "wearable" devices and monitors that collect data about the wearer, including measurements of movement (or lack thereof), exercise regimes, sleep patterns, vital physiological statistics, activities, and environment. Users employ such data to motivate active lifestyles and to provide new insights into, and decision support for, good health and well-being. Recent technological advances have driven down the cost, size, and ease of use of such devices significantly, making them accessible to a large portion of the population. Such accessibility and potential for widespread use has, in turn, spawned a variety of device options, applications, and analytics technologies.

The goal of our work is to investigate the impact of using activity monitor data to improve the health and well being of individuals with Type I Diabetes

This work has been supported, in part, JDRF grant number 17-2013-473, NSF grants CCF-1539586, CNS-0905237, CNS-1218808, and ACI-0751315, and NIH grant 1R01EB014877-01. We also acknowledge Wendy C. Bevier and Paige K. Bradley for the William Sansum Diabetes Center for their indispensable contributions.

© ICST Institute for Computer Sciences, Social Informatics and Telecommunications Engineering 2016
A. Leon-Garcia et al. (Eds.): Smart City 2015, LNICST 166, pp. 166–178, 2016.
DOI: 10.1007/978-3-319-33681-7_14

Mellitus (T1D). Diabetes is a family of chronic diseases that impacts how the human body produces and uses insulin. When food is eaten, the body digests and converts it to glucose (sugar). The blood glucose levels of individuals with diabetes can vary significantly. If left unchecked and unregulated, *glucose variability* and, in particular, glucose levels outside the normal range can lead to serious complications across the body's systems (vision, hearing, skin, nervous, cardiovascular, and others), which can lead to death.

For this reason, researchers have studied a wide variety of methods for measuring glycemic variability (GV) [1,2,5,9,12,14,15] with the goal of producing a risk index for T1D complications (c.f. Table 1 in Sect. 2) and informing treatment. There is as yet no consensus as to what is the most effective GV risk index, spurring further research and, almost certainly, the definition of new indices in the future.

The American Diabetes Association recommends that people with T1D engage in frequent moderate aerobic physical activity as part of their daily glucose management. However, exercise affects glucose variability and is associated with an increased risk of hypoglycemia (low glucose levels). Hypoglycemia risk is greatest during exercise, 2–3 h following activity, and as a latent effect 12–18 h after the activity [4,7,17]. Currently, people with T1D who perform physical activity must plan ahead of the event to prevent exercise related hypoglycemia. Use of temporary basal rates to reduce insulin delivery, suspension of insulin during and after the event, and carbohydrate intake can prevent immediate glucose drop. This sequence of steps prevents spontaneous activity and requires patients' compliance and significant focus and forethought to prevent adverse events. Thus if GV risk can be predicted automatically from CGM and non-invasive activity monitoring, individuals with T1D can use these predictions to inform their calorie consumption, insulin intake, and exercise decisions.

In this work, we investigate the development of an automated system for predicting next-day GV risk-index values. Our approach combines activity monitoring measurements gathered continuously from consumer-grade devices with blood glucose measurements taken by a continuous glucose monitoring (CGM) device for the same time period. Using Partial Least Squares (PLS) [16] regression, the system generates a model for predicting GV values for the day following a day when activity and CGM measurements have been gathered. .

Rather than focusing on a single GV risk index, however, the methodology chooses the "best" index for a specific individual amongst a set of index choices. The "best" index in our study is the one that exhibits the most predictability (i.e. the lowest prediction error) when its automatically generated model is cross-validated.

Thus the methodology is flexible and adaptive. Each time the data is analyzed, the system may choose a new risk index as being most predictable for a given individual. As new GV indices are developed, they can be added to the suite of indices the system comprises. Similarly, if behavior or physiology changes degrade GV predictability for a given index, the method can determine which new index should replace it as being most predictable.

In this paper, we describe the algorithmic and statistical approaches we use as the basis for this system and detail their function using data gathered from a small clinical study. Our results indicate that the combination of activity data with CGM measurements can improve GV predictability, in some cases substantially.

2   Predicting Glycemic Variability

The goal of the study is to determine the extent to which activity data gathered by consumer-grade activity-monitoring devices (e.g. those manufactured by Garmin [6] or Jawbone [8]) enhance the predictability of glycemic variability (GV) [15]. GV measures and indices are the subject of much research [1,2,5,9,12,14,15]. Rather than choosing a single metric, our approach predicts a set of metrics for each subject to determine which in the set yields the most predictability. That is, rather than attempting to differentiate between the metrics in terms of efficacy, we assume that there is a "best" metric (in terms of predictability) for each subject. Our system automatically identifies this most predictable GV metric from a database of continuous glucose monitoring (CGM) measurements and activity measurements that are gathered on a per-subject basis.

2.1   Data Gathering

In this work, we captured the CGM and activity measurements for seven subjects with T1D during a six-week clinical study. Our study population included adults aged 18–75 years and a mix or those who are typically active and/or perform exercise as part of their weekly routine, and those who are more sedentary, to assess the validity of the algorithms in detecting exercise and determining if any false positive detections occur. Subjects were diagnosed with T1D at least 1 year or more prior to enrollment. The purpose of this is to avoid the transitory "honeymoon" phase in which beta-cells maintain significant insulin production. Subjects had an A1c value less than or equal to 9.5 % at the start of the trial, as chronic hyperglycemia is indicative of problems in addition to T1D, or an inability/unwillingness to effectively participate in self-treatment.

Each subject wore both Garmin and Jawbone activity-monitoring devices simultaneously as well as a a Dexcom [3] CGM device. The CGM device records blood glucose levels every 5 min. However, the Garmin and Jawbone consumer activity devices do not make fine-grained measurements immediately available for download. Instead, the data gathered by each is uploaded to a proprietary service, where it is summarized (either as average or aggregate) on a 24-h basis before it is available for download and analysis. Thus, the minimum future time-frame over which any prediction is possible using these devices as consumer goods is 24 h. We believe that each device stores data at a finer time granularity and that if that data were made available, shorter-term predictions would be possible.

For this study, we aggregate the CGM data on a daily basis (midnight to midnight) so that it matches the time resolution of the activity data. We then predict the next day's GV measurements from each day for which both CGM and activity data are available. Note that, as in any clinical study, the data is subject to some "dropout" – periods of time when one or more measurements are missing. While the duration of the complete study is 6 weeks, only a subset of the period contains complete datasets from the CGM, Jawbone, and Garmin devices. It is from the days in the study when all three measurements are available that we make predictions. Note that only the CGM measurements need be available for the day following a day when CGM and activity data are available. Each GV measure depends only on CGM data. Thus, to validate the predictions, we identify 24-h periods in the data for each subject in which

– CGM measurements, Garmin summaries, and Jawbone summaries are available, and
– CGM measurements are available for the following 24 h period.

The system then predicts GV metrics computed for the following day from the GV metrics and activity data for each day in which the data is available. Table 1 summarizes the GV metrics we consider for each subject.

The activity monitors offer several different measurements of activity, including number of steps taken (pedometer), estimated calories burned, maximum period of activity, and number of sleep hours. Studying these measurements revealed that some of them (e.g., calories) are computed directly from the others arithmetically. Also a cursor inspection of some of the values reveals that they can be unreliable (for example 23 h of sleep in a 24-h period). Table 2 shows the activity measures we believed to be suitable for this study. Note that we were only able to get a pedometer reading from the Garmin device consistently during the study. We include both pedometer measurements because in the case where both Jawbone and Garmin pedometer measurements are available, they differ substantially enough to warrant their inclusion as separate measurements. Also, we made no attempt to "sanity-check" the data to determine whether it is valid. For example, the *acttime* and *inacttime* should sum to 24 h for each day, and they do not. Rather, as long as each measurement seemed "feasible" in isolation, we included it.

3   Prediction Methodology

The basis of the prediction methodology we explore is least-squares regression [16]. Our goal is to determine a linear model with the various regressors (GV and activity measurements for a 24-hour period) that best predicts a specific GV metric for the following day. That is, for a $m \times n$ matrix A consisting of m GV and activity values on each of n days, and a vector $\mathbf{y}$ consisting of n GV values for each succeeding day, we will find the approximate solution $\hat{\mathbf{x}}$ to the (typically overdetermined and unsolvable) equation

$$A\mathbf{x} = \mathbf{y} \tag{1}$$

Table 1. Measures of Glycemic Variability, formulas, descriptions, and citations. We define *daily* as midnight to 11:59:59PM of a given day. BG is blood glucose in mg/dL.

Metric	Formula	Description
bgavg	$\frac{\sum_{i=0}^{n} BG_i}{n}$	Average daily BG [12]
bgmin	$\min_{i=0}^{n} BG_i$	Min daily BG [12]
bgmax	$\max_{i=0}^{n} BG_i$	Max daily BG [12]
drop	$\max_{i=0}^{k} drop(BG)$	Max k daily continuous BG drops
spike	$\max_{i=0}^{k} drop(BG)$	Max k daily continuous BG increases
stdev	$\frac{\sum_{i=0}^{n} |BG_i - bgavg|}{n-1}$	Standard deviation of BG [1, 2, 12, 14, 15]
jindx	$0.001 * (bgavg + stdev)^2$	J-Index: Glycemic control quality metric [15]
covar	$100 * (bgavg * stdev)$	Coefficient of Variation [1]
mag	$\frac{\sum_{i=0}^{n-1} |BG_i - BG_{i+1}|}{24}$	Mean absolute BG difference [15]
range	$bgmax - bgmin$	Min-max BG difference for day [1]
med	$median(BG_1^n)$	Median daily BG [1, 2]
iqr	$Q3(BG_1^n) - Q1(BG_1^n)$	Interquartile daily range (IQR) [1]
low	$\sum duration(< 70)$	Time spent below 70 BG (hypo) [12]
high	$\sum duration(> 180)$	Time spent above 180 BG (hyper) [12]
tg	$low + high$	Time spent outside of BG range (70–180) [12]
mage	$\frac{\sum_{i=0}^{k}(PND_k > stdev)}{k}$	Mean amplitude of glycemic [1, 2, 12] excursions [14, 15] PND = BG peak-nadir differences
mavg	$\frac{\sum_{i=0}^{n} |10*\log BG_i/80|^3}{n}$	M-value: Glycemic control quality metric [1, 15]
mravg	$\frac{\sum_{i=0}^{n} 1000*|\log BG_i/100|}{n}$	MR-value: Weighted average of BG values [2] (control quality metric)
grade	$\frac{\sum_{i=0}^{n} 425*(\log(\log(BG_i*18)+0.16))^2}{n}$	Glycemic risk assessment diabetes equation [14, 15]
modd	$\frac{\sum_{k=d2,t=s}^{dp,e} |BG_{k,t} - BG_{k-1,t}|}{p-1}$ s=midnight, e=11:59:59	Mean of daily differences [2, 14] $p - 1$ consecutive days starting day 2
adrr	$\frac{1}{M} * \sum_{i=1}^{M} (LR^i + HR^i)$	Average Daily Risk Range [2, 14]
	$LR^i = \max(rl_{dayi}(...))$	$TBG_j = 1.509 * ((\ln(BG_j)^{1.084}) - 5.381)$
	$HR^i = \max(rh_{dayi}(...))$	$rl(BG_i) = 10 * TBG_i^2$ if $TBG_i < 0$, else 0
	for days $i = 1 - M$	$rh(BG_i) = 10 * TBG_i^2$ if $TBG_i > 0$, else 0
	and day_i BG values $j = 1 - N$	
lbgi	ADRR only for LR^i only	[2, 14]
hbgi	ADRR only for HR^i only	[2, 14]
conga N	$\sqrt{\frac{\sum_{1}^{k}(DT - AD)^2}{k-1}}$	Continuous overall net glycemic action [2, 15]
	$DT = BG_t - BG_{t-m}$	$AD = \frac{\sum_{1}^{k} DT}{k}$, $m = 60 * N$, $N = 1, 2, 4, 6$ [1, 12, 14]

that is best in the sense that $\|A\hat{\mathbf{x}} - \mathbf{y}\| \leq \|A\mathbf{x} - \mathbf{y}\|$ for all $\mathbf{x} \in \mathbb{R}^m$.

However, direct application of ordinary least-squares (OLS) regression [10] to the problem of predicting next-day GV values is problematic in our setting.

Table 2. Activity measurements and device vendor. Units of time are seconds.

Measurement	Description	Vendor
accttime	Total time active in a day	Jawbone
inacttime	Total time inactive in a day	Jawbone
maxact	Max period of continuous activity in a day	Jawbone
maxidle	Max period of continuous inactivity in a day	Jawbone
jsteps	Steps taken in a day	Jawbone
gsteps	Steps taken in a day	Garmin

While the study spans a 6-week period, each subject did not wear all of the devices (CGM and activity monitoring) each day. Indeed the number of monitored days in the study varies between 28 for subject 001 to 39 for subject 004. With 27 GV metrics and 6 activity measures, the total number of regressors (in this case the m GV and activity measurements represented in the A matrix) is close to the number of measured GV values (one computed for each of the n days during which a subject wore the CGM and activity monitoring devices). Additionally, many of the predictors are correlated with one another, for example *acttime* and *maxact* from Table 2, and these dependencies create instabilities in solutions of linear problems such as the one above. For these reasons, we seek a model that is parsimonious, using a small number of predictors that nevertheless capture most of the predictive power of the entirety.

Partial Least Squares regression (PLS) [16] is a linear regression technique that attempts to identify a smaller number latent factors in the regressor set that best predict the value of the target variable (next-day GV value in our case). It does so by transforming the regressors and the target variable so that the multi-dimensional variance in the transformed regressor space best explains the variance in the transformed target. PLS is often a better choice of technique than Principal Components Regression [11] or Ridge Regression [13] (two related methods) when the goal is to minimize prediction error and the explanatory value of any one regressor is not required.

In this work, we are interested in determining whether an automated technique based on PLS is feasible. To do so, we must define a method for determining the number of latent factors to use in instance of PLS. We use a form of cross-validation (see Subsect. 3.3) to identify the set of factors that results in the minimum prediction error. Specifically, we consider latent factor counts (which we henceforth term "component counts") from 1 to 10 and compute the cross-validation prediction error for each target GV value associated with each count. The component count that corresponds to the smallest prediction error is then selected as the component count to use.

Thus, the PLS method first identifies the component count to use. It then generates a model in the transformed space using this component count constructs a linear model in the untransformed space of the regressors and target variable. In our setting, this linear model takes the values of the regressor variables gathered on a specific day and predicts a specific GV value for the next day.

3.1   Categorization

In examining the data, we observed that several of the subjects experienced "high" and "low" days, particularly with respect to activity. Further, it seemed (by inspection) that the relationship between regressors and predicted GV for the next day differed depending on whether activity levels were "high" or "low".

To test whether predictions are improved by categorization, we also include the possibility of running separate regressions (each using PLS) using only "high" days or "low" days as categorized by a specific regressor. For example, it may be that the `mage` [14, 15] index is more predictable after a day of high activity than it is generally or after a day of low activity. Further, the best activity measure (as reported by the activity device) used to categorize "high" and "low" effectively might vary by subject.

For the purposes of categorization we use one-dimensional k-means clustering. That is, a single metric is clustered into two categories, high and low. The regressors associated with the values in the high category as well as the next-day's target GV metric are extracted. We then use PLS on the extraction to compute predictions of the GV metric on days following a day of high activity. Similarly, the method can automatically extract regressors corresponding to low days so that they may be used separately to make predictions via PLS.

3.2   The Algorithm

As described in Sect. 2, the full regressor set consists of 27 GV metrics and 6 activity measures (c.f. Tables 1 and 2 respectively). Each GV metric can be a prediction target, each regressor can be used to categorize the time epoch into "high" and "low", and there are 7 subjects in the study. The full regression analysis algorithm for data generated by the study is shown in Algorithm 1. The output of the algorithm is a set of linear models (produced on lines 4, 9, and 10 respectively). Each model predicts a different GV metric for a specific subject using either *all* of the regressors (line 4), or based on a categorization into high and low days (lines 9 and 10). The subscripts index each model. For example, the model predicting the *grade* metric for subject 1 using all of the regressors is indexed as $LinearModel_{1,grade,all}$. Similarly, the linear model predicting the *modd* metric for subject 5 using *high* days only and *accttime* to split regressors into high and low sets is denoted $LinearModel_{5,modd,acttime,high}$.

3.3   Evaluating Model Fitness and Predictive Power

The system attempts to identify automatically which model makes the most accurate predictions for each subject, and the specific GV metric that is best predicted by that model. To do so, it uses the regression's R^2 measure to determine the degree to which each linear model explains the variation about the mean value for a specific GV metric. An R^2 value close to 1.0 indicates that almost all of the difference between the observed vales of a GV metric and the values predicted by the model are due to random variation. Alternatively, a value

---

Algorithm 1. Full Regression Analysis Algorithm

1: **for** each subject S **do**
2:     $RegressorSet \leftarrow$ regressors from days with valid data for S
3:     **for** GV in set of GV metrics **do**
4:         $LinearModel_{S,GV,all} \leftarrow PLS(RegressorSet, GV)$
5:         **for** R in $RegressorSet$ **do**
6:             divide R into two clusters using k-means
7:             $HighRegressors \leftarrow$ regressors from days in high cluster
8:             $LowRegressors \leftarrow$ regressors from days in low cluster
9:             $LinearModel_{S,GV,R,high} \leftarrow PLS(HighRegressors, GV)$
10:             $LinearModel_{S,GV,R,low} \leftarrow PLS(LowRegressors, GV)$

---

close to 0.0 indicates that the model does not account for much of the variance in the distribution of GV values. Thus values closer to 1.0 indicate a better "fit" of the model.

For each subject, we concentrate on linear models where the R^2 statistic is greater than or equal to 0.85. The cutoff for deciding whether a fit is good ($R^2 >=$ 0.85) is somewhat arbitrary, indicating that each model under consideration explains at least some of the variance.

To measure predictive accuracy, we compute the root mean square prediction error for each observed value of the specific GV metric under consideration using an "all-but-one" validation strategy (also termed "cross-validation" in some settings). That is, for each linear model for which the R^2 value is greater than or equal to 0.85 (indicating a linear relationship) for a specific GV metric, we

- remove a test value from the set of values gathered for the GV metric
- remove the set of regressors for the day before this test value was recorded
- predict the test value using the PLS algorithm with the remaining regressors and the remaining GV values, and
- record the prediction error as the difference between the predicted GV value and the test GV value

We repeat this procedure making each value in the set of GV values the test value. That is, a prediction error is generated for each value in the set of GV values when the the other values are used to "train" the system. The square root of the mean of the squared prediction errors is the overall cross-validate Root Mean Squared Prediction Error (RMSPE). Smaller RMSPE values indicate more accurate predictions.

Figure 1 depicts the functional decomposition of the automated system. To make a prediction for each subject, the system requires access to a database of previous CGM measurement history and a database of activity measurements. Note that all of the GV metrics described Table 1 can be computed from a single set of CGM measurements. Thus the first step is to convert the history of CGM measurements into a history of GV measurements for each GV metric configured into the system. The GV histories are combined with activity history in Algorithm 1 to create a set of linear models. The system uses a selection

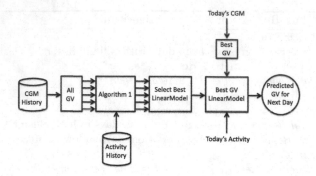

Fig. 1. Functional decomposition of automated prediction methodology

Table 3. Baseline best regression results by subject using GV values only.

Subject	Predicted GV	R^2	Components	Sample Size
001	**covar**	0.88	10	26
002	**mravg**	0.52	10	35
003	**modd**	0.69	10	30
004	**cnga6conga**	0.72	10	37
005	**spike**	0.56	10	33
006	**mravg**	0.71	10	36
007	**addrDRR**	0.80	10	28

mechanism (in this study, it selects the model with the minimum cross-validated RMSPE) to pick the best linear model for the most predictable GV. The current CGM data are converted to this GV metric and combined with the current activity data to predict the next day's GV value. Once the next day's CGM and activity data are available, they can be added to their respective historical databases and the process repeated.

4   Results

We begin with an examination of the effectiveness of the regression technique described in Sect. 3 using GV values only. In this "baseline" analysis, the regressors consist of the 27 GV metrics shown in Table 1. For each subject, we compute the linear model that predicts each of the 27 metrics for the succeeding day and show the model that generates the largest R^2 value for each subject in Table 3. In the table, column 1 gives the subject identifier, column 2 shows the specific GV metric for which the largest R^2 value was generated for that subject, column 3 shows the R^2 value for that metric, column 4 shows the number if principal components, and column 5 shows the sample size (i.e. the number of days n for which there is valid GV data for that subject in the study).

Table 4. Baseline and activity measures in the regressor set, best regression results for GV by subject.

Subject	Predicted GV	R^2	Components	Sample Size
001	covar	0.84	10	26
002	mag	0.76	10	35
003	bgavg	0.76	10	30
004	cnga6conga	0.72	10	37
005	spike	0.65	10	33
006	low	0.73	10	36
007	addrDRR	0.85	10	28

Table 5. Most improved regression predictions of next-day GV by subject for days categorized as "high." Baseline and activity measures are included in the regressor set, only regressions with R^2 greater than or equal to 0.85 are included.

Subject	Category Discriminant	Predicted GV	R^2	RMSPE % Improvement	Components	Sample Size
001	sddev	bgmin	0.99	40 %	10	12
002	gsteps	modd	0.99	36 %	10	16
003	sddev	bgmax	0.95	40 %	6	11
004	hbgi	high	0.99	26 %	10	11
005	covar	covar	0.85	34 %	7	12
006	grade	high	0.99	50 %	10	11
007	inacttime	spike	0.99	41 %	10	13

Note that using GV values alone produces a regression for only one subject (subject 001) with an R^2 greater than 0.85. Using an R^2 cut-off of 0.85 as described in Sect. 3 the results in Table 3 do not indicate a strong linear relationship between current and next day GV measures.

In Table 4 we add to the regressor set the 6 activity measures described previously in Table 2 and repeat the analysis. While only one of the R^2 values reach the 0.85 threshold, comparing Tables 3 and 4 shows that the addition of activity data to GV metric does improve regression fit. Subject 001's R^2 value drops from 0.88 to 0.84 (which is almost above the threshold) while the best R^2 value from each of the other subjects increases with the addition of activity data to the regression.

Also notice that the GV metric exhibiting the best R^2 value changes for three of the subjects (002, 003, and 006) when activity data is introduced. From the results shown in Tables 3 and 4 we cannot conclude (based on R^2 value) that PLS is an effective predictive technique for all subjects and GV metrics. However it does appear that the addition of activity data from consumer-grade activity monitors improves the linear fit generated by PLS with respect to next-day GV when the data is uncategorized.

Table 6. Most improved regression predictions of next-day GV by subject for days categorized as "low." Baseline and activity measures are included in the regressor set, only regressions with R^2 greater than or equal to 0.85 are included.

Subject	Category discriminant	Predicted GV	R^2	RMSPE % Improvement	Components	Sample size
001	drop	**drop**	0.95	50 %	6	13
002	hbgi	**conga 1**	0.99	55 %	10	13
003	conga 4	**mag**	0.99	49 %	7	11
004	tg	**grade**	0.95	41 %	10	14
005	range	**grade**	0.99	54 %	10	15
006	iqr	**drop**	0.99	59 %	9	16
007	tg	**sddev**	0.99	49 %	9	14

4.1   Prediction After Categorization

Separating the per-subject GV and activity measurement data into high and low categories improves regression performance in terms of R^2 value. In Table 5 we show the effect of including activity data on predictability of GV per subject. Each row of the table shows the GV metric (in column 3 in boldfaced type) for which activity data results in the greatest improvement (greatest reduction) of prediction error, as measured by RMSPE (c.f. Subsect. 3.3). Column 2 of the table indicates which GV or activity metric value is best used to categorize the data into "high" and "low" groups of days. Column 4 shows the R^2 value for the PLS, column 5 shows the percentage improvement in RMSPE, column 6 shows the number of principal components, and column 7 indicates the sample size.

Note that we calculate the percentage improvement over *the best* prediction of the GV metric (in terms of RMSPE) that can be made for that individual when activity data is not considered. That is, splitting the data according to the metric shown in column 2 might result in the lowest RMSPE when activity data is considered, but a different split might result in a lower RMSPE when just CGM data is considered. When calculating percentage improvement, we use the lowest RMSPE for the CGM-only comparison across all categorizations and not just the one that minimizes RMSPE when activity data is in the regressor set.

For example, row 1 of Table 5 shows, for subject 001, that activity data improves the RMSPE for the **bgmin** GV metric when the **sddev** metric is used to divide days into those with a high **sddev** score and those with a low **sddev** score. The R^2 value for the PLS on the high data is 0.99 and the improvement in RMSPE for subject 001's **bgmin** GV measure is 40 %. There were 10 components selected for the PLS and 12 days qualified as "high" days in terms of **sddev** (sample size is 12).

Table 6 shows the most improved RMSPE GV metrics for days automatically categorized as "low". From both Tables 5 and 6 it appears that activity data improves PLS predictability when the data is bifurcated for each patient into two categories: "high" and "low". The discriminant that results in the greatest improvement (column 2 in both tables) varies by subject, as does the GV metric that experiences the greatest improvement in predictability.

4.2 Conclusions

The results seem to indicate that activity monitoring via consumer-grade "wearable" devices does improve next-day GV predictability, via PLS, in some measure. While the R^2 values in Tables 5 and 6 are likely overstating the linear nature of the model because the number of PLS components is close to the sample size, the improvement metric is based on cross-validated RMSPE. Further, because each specific split and subsequent regression with activity data in the regressor set is compared to the best cross-validated RMSPE without activity data, we believe that these results show that activity data improves predictability for some of the metrics captured in the study. Also, the specific metric and data categorization that works "best" varies by subject (and indeed may vary by time although our study does not explore time variation). This observation argues for a fully-automated system that can recomputes future GV for each subject when new data becomes available (e.g. every day when the activity devices summarize user measurements).

References

1. Cameron, F., Baghurst, P., Rodbard, D.: Assessing glycemic variation: why, when, and how? J. Pediatr. Endocr. Rev. **7**(3), 432–444 (2010)
2. Czerwoniuk, D., Fendler, W., Walenciak, L., Mylnarski, W.: GlyCulator: a Glycemic variability calculation tool for continuous glucose monitoring data. J. Diab. Sci. Technol. **5**(2), 447–451 (2011)
3. Dexcom. https://www.dexcom.com/. Accessed 25 Mar 2015
4. Ellingsen, C., Dassau, E., Zisser, H.C., Grosman, B., Percival, M.W., Janovic, L., Doyle III, F.J.: Safety constraints in an artificial pancreatic-cell: an implementation of model predictive control with insulin-on-board. J. Diab. Sci. Technol. **3**(3), 536–544 (2009)
5. Farhy, L.S., Ortiz, E.A., Kovatchev, B.P., Mora, A.G., Wolf, S.E., Wade, C.E.: Range, average daily risk range as a measure of Glycemic risk is associated with mortality in the intensive care unit: a Retrospective study in a burn intensive care unit. J. Diab. Sci. Technol. **5**(5), 1087–1098 (2011)
6. Garmin. https://www.garmin.com/. Accessed 25 Mar 2015
7. Gondhalekar, R., Dassau, E., Zisser, H.C., Doyle III, F.J.: Periodic-zone model predictive control for diurnal closed-loop operation of an artificial pancreas. J. Diab. Sci. Technol. **7**(3), 1446–1460 (2013)
8. Jawbone. https://www.jawbone.com/. Accessed 25 Mar 2015
9. Kovatchev, B., Otto, E., Cox, D., Gonder-Frederic, L., Clarke, W.: Evaluation of new measures of glucose variability in diabetes. J. Diab. Care **29**(11), 2433–2438 (2006)
10. Ordinary Least Squares. https://en.wikipedia.org/wiki/Ordinary_least_squares. Accessed 25 Mar 2015

11. Principle Components Regression. http://ncss.wpengine.netdna-cdn.com/wp-content/themes/ncss/pdf/Procedures/NCSS/Principal_Components_Regression.pdf. Accessed 25 Mar 2015
12. Rawlings, R.A., Shi, H., Yuan, L.H., Brehm, W., Pop-Busui, R., Nelson, P.W.: Translating glucose variability metrics into the clinic via continuous glucose monitoring: a graphical user interface for diabetes evaluation. J. Diab. Technol. Ther. **13**(12), 1241–1248 (2011)
13. Ridge Regression. http://ncss.wpengine.netdna-cdn.com/wp-content/themes/ncss/pdf/Procedures/NCSS/Ridge_Regression.pdf. Accessed 25 Mar 2015
14. Rodbard, D.: Interpretation of continuous glucose monitoring data: glycemic variability and quality of glycemic control. J. Diab. Technol. Ther. **11**(1), S55–S67 (2009)
15. Service, F.J.: Glucose variability. J. Diab. **62**(5), 1398–1404 (2013)
16. Tobias, R.D., et al.: An introduction to partial least squares regression. In: 20th Proceedings of Annual SAS Users Group International Conference, Orlando, FL, pp. 2–5. Citeseer (1995)
17. van Heusden, K., Dassau, E., Zisser, H.C., Seborg, D.E., Doyle III, F.J.: Control-relevant models for glucose control using a priori patient characteristics. IEEE Trans. Biomed. Eng. **59**(7), 1839–1849 (2012)

Design and Implementation of a Remotely Configurable and Manageable Well-being Study

Sudip Vhaduri[✉] and Christian Poellabauer

Department of Computer Science and Engineering,
University of Notre Dame, Notre Dame, IN 46556, USA
{svhaduri,cpoellab}@nd.edu
http://engineering.nd.edu/profiles/cpoellabauer

Abstract. Surveys are essential tools for obtaining an understanding of factors impacting a person's physical and mental well-being. Recently, surveys using face-to-face interactions have been replaced with smartphone surveys, with the added benefit of using a phone's sensor and usage data (e.g., locations, apps used, communication patterns, etc.) to collect valuable contextual information. These data collections, especially if longitudinal, often require a certain degree of flexibility and adaptability, e.g., survey questions may change over time or depend on location, demographics, and previous responses. Data collections may also be reconfigured to account for changes in the study goals or to test different intervention techniques. Finally, participant compliance should be monitored and may also lead to modifications in the data collection approach. This paper introduces a data collection tool and study design that not only collects surveys and phone sensor data, but also addresses the need for remote customization, reconfiguration, and management.

Keywords: Data collection · Well-being · Mobile surveys · Smartphone sensing

1 Introduction

1.1 Motivation and Background

Assessment of health and well-being has been an active research area for a long time [1] and researchers have been conducting studies to evaluate how factors such as mood [2], social interactions, sleeping habits, activity levels [3], perceived life satisfaction levels [4], and spiritual beliefs [5] affect the health and well-being of an individual or an entire community. Many prior studies required face-to-face interactions between study coordinator and subject, thereby limiting the geographic reach and the scale of these studies. Over the last few years, such studies have increasingly relied on mobile devices (e.g., smartphones) to support data collections [3,6], thereby enabling large-scale and wide-reaching user studies, while also ensuring increased survey compliance [7].

© ICST Institute for Computer Sciences, Social Informatics and Telecommunications Engineering 2016
A. Leon-Garcia et al. (Eds.): Smart City 2015, LNICST 166, pp. 179–191, 2016.
DOI: 10.1007/978-3-319-33681-7_15

Smartphones also provide other opportunities, e.g., their sensor data (GPS, accelerometer, etc.) can provide additional contextual information that can be essential for better understanding trends and outliers in survey responses (e.g., mood-related survey responses can be different when submitted from home, the workplace, when on vacation, etc.). Further, smartphones also make it easier to collect data over extended periods of time, which is often essential when the goal of such surveys is to capture well-being changes due to infrequent events, seasonal changes, etc. However, data collections using smartphones also face a number of challenges, including the need for parameterization and reconfiguration of the surveys for various reasons. For example, new insights into study design or changes in a study's objectives may necessitate a reconsideration of the survey design and questions. It may also be necessary to structure a study into different phases, each phase with different objectives, therefore, requiring that the surveys change from phase to phase. For example, the first phase could focus on sleep habits only, followed by a phase focusing on physical activities. Survey questions may also have to be configured based on the articipating subjects' demographic information and reconfigured on-the-fly based on subjects' earlier survey responses. As a consequence, this paper introduces a data collection app and study design, primarily intended for well-being studies, that provides the tools needed for remote management and re-configuration of such studies, thereby maximizing their potential values to the researchers responsible for the study outcomes.

1.2 Related Work

The movement from paper-and-pencil surveys to phone-based surveys introduces new challenges and requirements, i.e., researchers have to consider various design issues and usability characteristics [8], including timing characteristics of a user study, such as when to prompt a user for survey responses and when to provide reminders to maximize compliance if needed on top of the existing challenges also found in all forms of surveys, such as wording, question form, contexts, acquiescence response bias, straight-lining versus item specific scales [9,10], unipolar versus bipolar response scales [11], quality, and reliability and accuracy of the information captured [9,10]. User design choices also include the use of colors, fonts, response options and scales, use of images and icons, etc.

Smartphones also provide an exciting opportunity due to their built-in sensors [12], such as GPS, acceleration, proximity, temperature, or pressure, which allow us to automatically capture a wide range of contextual data. Further, other phone-related data, such as battery charge levels, the number of text messages exchanged or phone calls made and received, etc., can also provide important insights into the contexts of the user responding to a survey and can therefore be used to compensate for data collection inaccuracies and biases (such as recall bias, memory limitations, and inadequate compliance that comes from self-reports) [7].

Advances in wearable and pervasive computing technologies [13–15] also provide opportunities for the continuous tracking of various physiological data.

Examples of such sensors include respiratory inductance plethysmography (RIP), electrocardiograph (ECG) and galvanic skin response (GSR). These devices also face various challenges, such as user discomfort and sensing inaccuracies due to improper sensor placement [16], therefore, most studies using such sensors focus on controlled environments (e.g., in laboratories or a doctor's office) instead of collecting data in subjects' home or work environments [3,6]. sensing inaccuracies due to improper sensor placement [16], which demands in person interaction between subject and study coordinator [14,17], therefore, most studies using such sensors focus on simulated or controlled environments (e.g., in laboratories or a doctor's office) for a limited period. Software development kits, such as Apple's ResearchKit also increasingly facilitate the integration of surveys with data collected from physiological sensors using devices, such as Smart Watch, etc.

One of the efforts more closely related to ours was presented in [3], where the authors performed a mobile health study on 48 students for 10 weeks using Android phones. During the study, they continuously captured opportunistic phone sensor data, along with the phone-based user surveys. In this study, subjects are required to respond to surveys immediately upon prompting, which can be difficult in some scenarios, e.g., when the subjects are in exams, sleeping, or driving [17]. While the focus in [3] has been on phone sensing and the use of typical well-being surveys, other efforts suggest that a comprehensive well-being study should also consider life satisfaction [4], spiritual belief [5], and day reconstruction [18] surveys, further demonstrating the need for more comprehensive and flexible data collection tools.

1.3   Contributions

The primary contributions of this paper are (1) the design and implementation of a flexible data collection tool that provides easy remote management and reconfiguration options (Sect. 2), (2) the design of a concrete well-being study using this tool (Sect. 3), and (3) a preliminary analysis of data collected in a brief well-being study performed at the University of Notre Dame (Sect. 4), with a focus on the investigation of changes in sleep habits and mobility levels of students during and after the final weeks of a semester.

2   The WellSense Smartphone-Based Data Collection Tool

2.1   System Architecture

Like other existing data collection applications, the primary goal of *WellSense*, our proposed data collection tool, is to provide a mechanism to perform large-scale well-being studies using modern smartphones. However, WellSense also simultaneously monitors a variety of contextual information (using phone sensors, resources, and usage patterns) and provides mechanisms for remote data collection management, including the ability to redesign and reconfigure an

ongoing study "on-the-fly". Figure 1 shows the high-level system architecture
of WellSense, consisting of a mobile survey and monitoring app, a cloud-based
check-in server and database, and a management web portal. Study participants
will receive survey requests via the mobile app (implemented for both the iOS
and Android platforms) and survey responses are transmitted over the network
to a *check-in server*, which is responsible for processing and storing the incoming
data in a global database, where each subject or device has a unique identifier
and all survey responses are time-stamped. In addition, WellSense also monitors various phone sensors and phone activities that are collected locally on the
mobile device and transmitted to the server via an automatic nightly upload
(i.e., "check-in"). The web portal is the study administrator's primary tool to
manage a study, e.g., to monitor compliance and response rates, but also to
modify study design, including changes to the survey questions, modifying the
timing of survey requests, or the frequency of survey requests. Study participants
may also use the web portal to track their own progress and compliance.

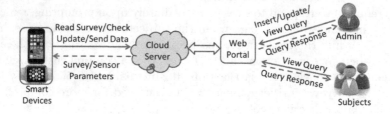

Fig. 1. System diagram of WellSense.

Study participants have full control over which surveys they wish to respond
to, i.e., they can skip entire surveys or individual questions of a survey (e.g., when
a survey may cause emotional distress or privacy concerns). While a survey is
"open", participants can also revise and resubmit their responses. At the end of a
survey, the app informs the participant about the number of questions answered
and skipped and at that point the participant can decide to revisit questions
or to submit the responses. If the survey fails to upload to the server (e.g., due
to a lost network connection), the participant can submit the survey at a later
point, without loss of data. Once a survey has been submitted, all responses,
their corresponding question identifiers, and timestamps, along with a survey
identifier and user identifier are stored on the cloud server. Currently, we use
the Parse (www.parse.com) server, primarily due the ease of integration of the
server with mobile applications. Each survey response is stored as a new row
in the database, together with the identifiers described above. Given survey ID,
question ID, user ID, and timestamps, it is easy for a study administrator to
monitor compliance or to detect patterns that may indicate difficulties in the
study, such as poor response rates for a specific survey or question, which can be
due to the content or the timing of the survey or question. Parse also supports
push notifications, which allows a study administrator to push alerts to one or
more participants, e.g., when their compliance is low.

2.2 WellSense App Design

The primary purpose of the phone-based surveys is to assess the well-being of a subject based on various contexts and activities during different times of the day. For example, to measure the sleep quality of a subject we can administer a sleep survey in the morning that consists of sleep-related questions, such as the number of hours slept, the perceived sleep quality, how many times a participant woke up during the night, etc. However, the survey app is generic enough to be used for any kind of surveys and studies, in the well-being and health domain and beyond.

(a). Google Nexus 5   (b). iPhone 6

Fig. 2. Main menu of the WellSense app on (a) Android and (b) iOS

Figure 2 shows screenshots of the WellSense app for both the Android (Fig. 2(a)) and iOS (Fig. 2(b)) platforms. These screenshots demonstrate two primary design choices:

- **Survey Categories:** Well-being (and other health-related concerns) are affected by a variety of factors, e.g., sleep quality, mood changes, social interactions, and unusual events encountered. Therefore, the app supports the distribution of multiple surveys that fall into one of these categories. Icons are used in addition to textual information to clearly distinguish between different survey categories.
- **Surveys Status and Survey Timing:** On the Android platform, all surveys to be answered during the current day are listed in chronological order and *open surveys* (i.e., surveys waiting for the participant's response) are shown in bold text, while *closed surveys* (i.e., surveys not yet available or surveys that are no longer available for responses) are shown in a gray color and can no longer be tapped. The iOS version uses a slightly different approach: it uses three sections to distinguish between *current* (open), *future* (not yet open), and *past* (already closed) surveys.

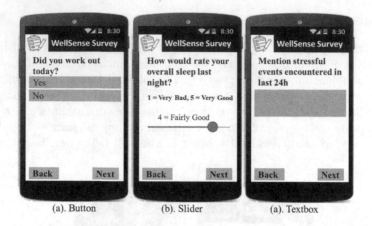

(a). Button   (b). Slider   (a). Textbox

Fig. 3. Response layout for (a) Button, (b) Slider and (c) Textbox questions.

Another design choice is how participants can respond to survey questions and this depends on the type of the question. For example, Fig. 3 shows screenshots of three main types of responses supported in the WellSense app: *buttons*, *sliders* (or scales), and *textboxes*. The textbox input is the most flexible in that participants are able to provide any type of response, while the others have limited input options.

2.3   WellSense Survey (Re)Configuration

Surveys are designed and distributed via the web portal and the Parse-based cloud server. Surveys are stored in the database in a two-level hierarchy. At the first level, survey meta-information, consisting of survey category, identifier, timing (day/time when survey is open), and a boolean field called "active" that allows the study administrator to turn on or off a survey, is stored. Each survey links to information stored at the second level of the hierarchy, including a set of questions (identified by question IDs), response types, and response options. Existing surveys can, therefore, be reconfigured anytime and a subject's WellSense app checks into the server each night (during a randomly selected time between midnight and 6 am) to see if surveys or questions have been added, removed, or modified. In that case, all changes are fetched and the next day's list of surveys will reflect these changes.

2.4   WellSense Survey Notifications

The WellSense app also supports a *notification mechanism*, which can be used to remind participants to respond to open surveys. We call the period when a survey is available for responses the *active period*, e.g., a *sleep quality* survey may have an active period from 7 am to 9 am every morning. During a survey's active period, the phone will generate up to four notifications spaced equally, i.e., an active period of 2 h will generate a notification every 30 min (e.g., a survey with an active period from 10 am–12 pm will trigger notifications at 10 am, 10.30 am, 11 am, and 11.30 am). Once a participant replies to a survey, further notifications for this survey will be suppressed. A participant can choose to respond to a survey either via the app's main menu or by tapping the survey's notification.

2.5 Phone Sensors and Phone Usage Data

Smartphones (and similarly wearable devices) provide an opportunity to collect additional information besides survey responses. Specifically, the sensors built into modern smartphones provide the tools needed to collect information, such as physical activity, location, mobility patterns, social interactions (e.g., using proximity sensors), and heart rate (in the case of wearables). In addition, phone usage patterns and trends can also provide highly valuable context information that can be associated with the changes in survey responses. Such data include browsing histories, communication habits (calls, texting), social networking activities, and app usage. Table 1 shows several examples of data that can be collected on a smartphone. In the case of WellSense, these data are collected from a separate app that runs continuously in the background. This app, called CIMON (Configurable Integrated Monitoring Service) [19], collects data along three axes: (1) system data (that includes information such as battery status or the type of network the phone is currently using for communication), (2) sensors (a phone's built-in sensors), and (3) user activities (such as browsing history, communication, and app usage). CIMON stores all collected data in a database on the phone and uploads these data every night into the server. Similarly to the survey data, all uploads rely on secure handshake protocols and encryption using AES. While the amount of data collected by CIMON can be very large (see sampling rates in Table 1), the data can be extremely useful when analyzing and interpreting survey responses. CIMON also supports *labeling*, which allows participants to log additional contextual information that can be useful for later analysis. For example, a study on the physical activity levels of rehabilitation patients could allow participants to record whenever they perform exercises or

Table 1. Different types of sensor and usage data captured by a phone

Sensor/Data name	Type	Sampling period
Memory, CPU load, CPU utilization, Battery, Network traffic, Connectivity status	System	1 s
Geo-location	Sensor	10 s
Accelerometer, Magnetometer, Gyroscope	Sensor	100 ms
Proximity, Pressure, Light, Humidity, Temperature	Sensor	1 s
Phone activity, SMS, MMS	User activity	1 s
Screen state, Bluetooth, WiFi	User activity	3 min

spend time outside. These labels are considered to be ground truths while performing supervised learning on collected survey and sensor data.

3 Design of a Well-being Data Collection

This section describes the design of a well-being data collection effort built around the WellSense app. The goal of our work is to obtain a better understanding of personal, work-related, social, environmental, and other factors impacting the physical and mental well-being of individuals.

3.1 Pre- and Post-Surveys

For all kinds of data collection efforts, it is very common to perform pre-participation (entry) and post-participation (exit) surveys. Pre-participation surveys can be used to verify that potential study subjects meet inclusion criteria, to ensure a specific desired distribution of the study population, and to establish a baseline for each subject. Exit surveys are often used to gather participants' experiences and feedback for future studies or to collect additional information that was not obtained during the data collection phase.

In our efforts to collect data to study participants' well-being, we utilize two types of surveys in addition to the WellSense data collection (both types are simple web-based surveys; future versions of WellSense will integrate them into the mobile app):

- **Resource Assessment Survey.** The primary goal of this survey is to get an idea of the types of devices used by the subjects, and whether there is any need for resource (e.g., loaner devices). Subjects are also asked for information, such as their class and exam schedules, project deadlines, demographic information, and health issues and concerns (e.g., pre-existing conditions), which provides us with additional context.
- **Pre-Study and Post-Study Surveys.** The primary goal of these surveys is to collect baselines of well-being in terms of current health, fitness, perceived stress, perceived success and satisfaction, loneliness and other social concerns [3], and sleep quality [20] before and after the study.

3.2 Using WellSense for a Well-being Study

The purpose of the phone-based surveys is to assess the well-being of a subject based on various contexts and activities during different parts of the day. Table 2 shows the list of surveys and their question types that we considered in our implementation to capture various contexts and activities that affect personal health and well-being. Table 2 also shows the schedule for these surveys, where "M", "Su" and "S" represents Monday, Sunday, and Saturday, respectively. Apart from "Life Satisfaction" and "Spirituality", all other surveys are answered daily. The "Mood Survey" [2] looks for positive and negative factors impacting mood as well as stress and fatigue levels. While often ignored in other studies, we also consider "Spirituality", since this can also have a great impact on overall well-being.

Table 2. Phone surveys and their schedules

Survey category	Question type and Scale	Day (Time)	Active period (h)
Mood [2]	Rank ordering	M-Su (10 am, 2 pm, 6 pm)	2
Sleep quality [3]	Slider and Likert interval	M-Su (8 am)	3
Social Interaction [3]	Dichotomous, Multiple choice, Bi-polar semantic differential	M-Su (9 pm)	2
Day Reconstruction [18]	Ratio, Open-ended, Multiple choice, Interval	M-Su (10 pm)	2
Life satisfaction [4]	Uni-polar rating	S (12 pm)	12
Spirituality [5]	Uni-polar rating	Su (6 pm)	6

4   Case Study

To test the feasibility and the validity of our remotely configurable and manageable mobile health and well-being approach, we conducted a brief case study on 28 healthy subjects (college students). The study ran for four weeks, covering the end period of spring semester, in order to measure anxiety and stress levels before, during, and after exam time.

4.1   Subjects

Subjects were invited via emails, stating the goals of the study and the requirements for the subjects if they decide to participate (note that no incentives were provided). The study consisted of 12 male and 8 female undergraduate students (average age of 20y 7 m with SD = 8 m) and 7 male and 1 female graduate students (average age of 29y 4 m with SD = 2y 7 m). Only 6 of the subjects used their own phones, all others received loaner devices from our lab. Out of the 28 subjects, 2 used iOS-based devices, all others used Android.

4.2   Method

The study ran over four weeks, where each subject began to use WellSense about 1–2 weeks before finals week and then continued data collection for another 1–2 weeks after finals week. Over the 4 weeks, each subject was required to respond to different types of surveys (as shown in Table 2). They were also asked to provide labels, such as "Meeting", "Entertainment", "Walking", and "Biking". At the same time, the CIMON mobile framework continuously collected various types of phone data (as described in Table 1). In total, more than 17,000 survey responses and over 100 million samples of phone sensor data were collected. A study coordinator frequently monitored the progress of study (i.e., data collection) via the web portal, varied study parameters (such as sampling frequencies, survey administer time and active period, and survey questions), and provided feedback to subjects over email.

4.3   Results

Prior work has shown that sleep patterns can have a significant impact on well-being and health [3,6], therefore, one of our goals is to investigate the sleep patterns captured by the WellSense study. From Fig. 4 (showing the sleep patterns of one specific participant), we can observe that sleep duration falls when class is ending since during that time the subject had three projects and homework deadlines. Sleep duration increases during study days (when students are somewhat more relaxed), but then drops again before the two exams on May 4 and May 5, and finally, go back to normal after exams end.

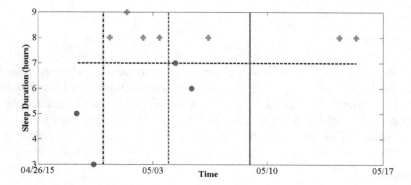

Fig. 4. Sleep duration variation of an individual over the entire study period. The black horizontal dashed line represents the base line of sleep duration (7 h) for the subject based on her response using the PSQI scale [20] in the "Pre-study" survey. The vertical dash-dot black (left most), dashed blue (middle), and solid red (right most) lines correspond to the last day of class (April 29), end of study days and start of exam period (May 3), and end of exam period (May 8) for the Spring 2015 semester. All vertical lines are drawn at 11:55 pm, i.e., at the end of a day. The red colored circles below the horizontal dashed line and green colored plus (+) markers above the horizontal dashed line represent the sleep duration below and above the base line. (Color figure online)

Next, we investigate activity and mobility of subjects. In Fig. 5, we observe low activity and few location changes during exam week. From the "Resource Assessment" survey, we know that this specific subject had an exam from 10:30 am to 12:30 pm on May 8. It seems that before May 8, the subject stayed primarily in his dorm room, preparing for his exam. We observe that from 3:20 pm to 6 pm on May 7, there is no data collected, followed by continuous data streams until midnight that day. It appears that the subject turned off the data collection app, but the phone was still on since the battery level also declined during that period. From May 7 midnight to May 9 at 11 am, we again did not receive any data. This is because the subject had an exam and turned off the phone for all of May 8 until the next morning, since during that period, there was no observable degradation of the battery charge level.

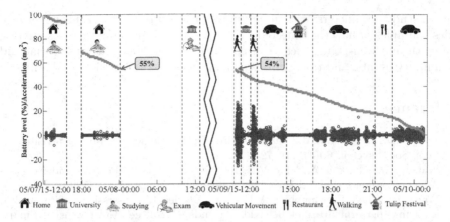

Fig. 5. Variation of battery level (red plus "+" markers) and activity level in terms of magnitude of three axis of acceleration (blue circles) over the study period for an individual. Very low variations of acceleration (**var** ≈ 0) and static geo-coordinates indicate that the subject is not moving; large variations in acceleration, but small changes in location indicate that the subject is walking; small variations of acceleration (**var** > 0), but fast changes in location indicate that the person is moving in a vehicle. (Color figure online)

In Fig. 5, we can also see that on May 9 from 11 am to 11:20 am, the subject was walking from his home to university, spent the time period between 11:20 am and 12 pm at the university, then walked between 12 pm and 12:29 pm, commuted in a vehicle between 12:29 pm and 2:40 pm, participated a festival in Holland, Michigan from 2:40 pm to 4:43 pm (based on GPS coordinates, event calendars, and the subject's "Day Reconstruction" survey), then drove again until 9:17 pm, when the subject spent time at a restaurant in Chicago until 10:30 pm, then finally followed by another drive (towards home) until 12.41 am. The graphs in Figs. 4 and 5) are based on all the surveys that the subjects have taken and the sensor data that their phones have captured. This is an example, showing that the combination of survey data and sensor data can be used to reconstruct a subject's day, providing us with information that can be essential to understand the factors impacting a person's health and well-being.

5   Conclusions

Preliminary analysis from the continuous sensor data and subjects' survey responses shows the feasibility of a remote mobile health and well-being study that does not require fact-to-face interaction between subject and study coordinator. This study can be both managed (i.e., monitoring study progress) and configured (i.e., changing various study parameters) independent from the locations of the subjects. The ability to re-configure an ongoing study provides us (i.e., study administrators/coordinators and researchers) more flexibility to change critical study parameters, without disrupting the study. Further, this paper provides examples of how the collected data can be used to analyze factors relating to health and well-being, such as sleep patterns, mobility patterns, social and community events, and time periods of varying degrees of anxiety and stress.

References

1. Ryff, C.D., Keyes, C.L.M.: The structure of psychological well-being revisited. J. Pers. Soc. Psychol. **69**(4), 719–727 (1995)
2. Watson, D., Clark, L.A.: The PANAS-X: Manual for the Positive and Negative Affect Schedule-Expanded Form. The University of Iowa, Ames (1999)
3. Wang, R., Chen, F., Campbell, A.T., et al.: StudentLife: assessing mental health, academic performance and behavioral trends of college students using Smartphones. In: ACM UbiCompp, pp. 3–14 (2014)
4. Diener, E., Oishi, S., Lucas, R.E.: Personality, culture, and subjective well-being: emotional and cognitive evaluations of life. Ann. Rev. Psychol. **54**(1), 403–425 (2003)
5. Ellison, L.: A review of the Spiritual Well-being Scale. NewsNotes **44**(1) (2006)
6. Lane, N.D., Campbell, A.T., Choudhury, T., et al.: BeWell: sensing sleep, physical activities and social interactions to promote wellbeing. J. Mob. Netw. Appl. **19**(3), 345–359 (2014)
7. Stone, A.A., Shiffman, S., Schwartz, J.E., et al.: Patient compliance with paper and electronic diaries. Controlled Clin. Trials **24**(2), 182–199 (2003)
8. Ji, Y.G., Park, J.H., Lee, C., Yun, M.H.: A usability checklist for the usability evaluation of mobile phone user interface. Int. J. Hum.-Comput. Interact. **20**(3), 207–231 (2006)
9. Krosnick, J.A.: Maximizing questionnaire quality. Measures Polit. Attitudes **2**, 37–58 (1999)
10. Saris, W.E., Revilla, M., Krosnick, J.A., Shaeffer, E.M.: Comparing questions with Agree/Disagree response options to questions with item-specific response options. Surv. Res. Methods **4**(1), 61–79 (2010)
11. Schaeffer, N.C., Presser, S.: The science of asking questions. Ann. Rev. Sociol. **29**, 65–88 (2003)
12. Khan, W.Z., Xiang, Y., Aalsalem, M.Y., Arshad, Q.: Mobile phone sensing systems: a survey. IEEE Commun. Surv. Tutorials **15**(1), 402–427 (2013)
13. Ertin, E., Kumar, S., al'Absi, M., et al.: AutoSense: unobtrusively wearable sensor suite for inferring the onset, causality, and consequences of stress in the field. In: ACM SenSys, pp. 274–287 (2011)
14. Healey, J.A., Picard, R.W.: Detecting stress during real-world driving tasks using physiological sensors. IEEE ITS **6**(2), 156–166 (2005)
15. Mark, G., Wang, Y., Niiya, M.: Stress and multitasking in everyday college life: an empirical study of online activity. In: ACM CHI, pp. 41–50 (2014)
16. Rahman, M.M., Sharmin, M., Raij, A., et al.: Are we there yet? Feasibility of continuous stress assessment via wireless physiological sensors. In: ACM BCB, pp. 479–488 (2014)
17. Sarker, H., Sharmin, M., Kumar, S., et al.: Assessing the availability of users to engage in just-in-time intervention in the natural environment. In: ACM UbiComp, pp. 909–920 (2014)

18. Kahneman, D., Krueger, A.B., Schkade, D.A., et al.: A survey method for characterizing daily life experience: the day reconstruction method. Science **306**(5702), 1776–1780 (2004)
19. Miller, C., Poellabauer, C.: Configurable integrated monitoring system for mobile devices. Procedia Comput. Sci. **34**, 410–417 (2014)
20. Buysse, D.J., Reynolds, C.F., Monk, T.H., et al.: The Pittsburgh Sleep Quality Index: a new instrument for psychiatric practice and research. Psychiatry Res. **28**, 193–213 (1989)

A Novel Wayfinding Service for Empowering Physical Activity

Hassan A. Karimi[1($\boxtimes$)], Janice C. Zgibor[2], Gretchen A. Piatt[3], and Monsak Socharoentum[4]

[1] Geoinformatics Laboratory, School of Information Sciences,
University of Pittsburgh, Pittsburgh, USA
hkarimi@pitt.edu
[2] Department of Epidemiology and Biostatistics, College of Public Health,
University of South Florida, Tampa, USA
jzgibor@health.usf.edu
[3] Department of Learning Health Science, School of Medicine Department
of Health, University of Michigan, Ann Arbor, USA
piattg@med.umich.edu
[4] National Electronics and Computer Technology Center,
Pathum Thani, Thailand
ms@nectec.or.th

Abstract. A wayfinding service for empowering physical activity is presented. The service finds routes that involve multi-modal transportation where walking is always one mode. The service is based on the new concept of multi-modal transportation with multi-criteria walking. A prototype of the service is developed and a new empowerment approach for it is discussed.

Keywords: Physical activity · Wayfinding service · Walking paths

1 Introduction

As the obesity epidemic in the United States continues to worsen (Flegal et al. 2005), the health of communities is increasingly in jeopardy. Approximately 1/3 of Americans are obese [Body Mass Index (BMI) $\geq$ 30 kg/m^2] and nearly 70 % are considered overweight (BMI $\geq$ 25 kg/m^2). Since 1999, a significant increase in BMI was observed for men with a borderline increase among women. These conditions substantially increase the risk for developing type 2 diabetes (diabetes) and/or cardiovascular disease and certain cancers (Pate et al. 1995). There is a significant body of evidence demonstrating the impact of physical activity on reducing body weight. As obesity is a significant risk factor for developing several chronic illnesses (Centers for Disease Control and Prevention 2013a; b), there is a critical need to develop and implement practical, sustainable efforts that focus on increasing physical activity in "real world" community settings in order for patients, healthcare providers, and policy makers to make informed decisions regarding effective approaches to address the epidemic.

One of the most effective methods to combat obesity and prevent other chronic disease is increasing physical activity. Physical activity is an ideal intervention as it can

© ICST Institute for Computer Sciences, Social Informatics and Telecommunications Engineering 2016
A. Leon-Garcia et al. (Eds.): Smart City 2015, LNICST 166, pp. 192–200, 2016.
DOI: 10.1007/978-3-319-33681-7_16

be free or low cost and has demonstrated success. However, little progress is being made to increase physical activity in the United States (Carlson et al. 2010). Approximately 60 % of Americans fail to achieve recommended physical activity goals with little progress noted over the past decade (Carlson et al. 2010). Current evidence-based physical activity guidelines recommend that adults age 18 and older get 2.5 h of moderate intensity or 75 min of vigorous intensity aerobic physical activity per week (Centers for Disease Control and Prevention Division of Nutrition 2011). Despite this evidence, a host of barriers, including time, physical access, financial means, and confidence and enjoyment of the activity keep individuals from engaging in physical activity (Pate et al. 1995). Overcoming these barriers is challenging and short-term physical activity interventions, often, do not lead to long-term sustained physical activity behavior change, largely because of activity not completely being incorporated into day-to-day living. Additionally, successful maintenance of physical activity efforts is highly dependent on improving self-efficacy (or confidence) in a person's ability to be physically active while incorporating social support (Pate et al. 1995).

2 Self-efficacy

Increasing individuals self-efficacy to engage in physical activity is a concept that is deeply rooted in Self-Determination Theory and self-motivation (Williams et al. 1998; Williams et al. 2004). An individual is more likely to be motivated (autonomy motivation) to develop the skills and capacity to self-regulate the behaviors needed to function effectively, if that individual views those behaviors as personally meaningful (Deci et al. 1994). In the context of physical activity, autonomy motivation refers to the extent to which individuals feel they are initiating and valuing specific physical activity behaviors and the type of approach they believe will lead to successful behavior change (Williams et al. 1998). Self-determination theory and autonomy support provide the framework for patient empowerment, which is defined as helping patients discover and develop the inherent capacity to be responsible for one's own life (Anderson et al. 1991). Empowerment plays a key role in enhancing the self-efficacy needed to engage in physical activity in the short and long term and is the theoretical basis for which we developed our prototype, Route2Health.

3 Technology and Social Support

The smart phone is a relatively novel platform through which to deliver empowerment-based physical activity information. It has the advantage of familiarity and flexibility, which are characteristics that may be particularly helpful to socioeconomically or geographically marginalized populations who may not have access to or little spare time to participate in traditional physical activity efforts. Perhaps even more importantly, smart phones provide the capacity to offer an e-community for behavior reinforcement and social support. Online communities are very popular among people with chronic health conditions (Greene et al. 2011), as a source of information as well as emotional support and accountability that comes from connecting with others with similar conditions (Hwang et al. 2010). Zhang et al. (2014) propose an approach to extract community activity patterns using data collected from both the physical world and social networks.

Despite the popularity of navigation services and the importance of physical activity, current navigation services are not designed to assist in improving or monitoring physical activity. Current navigation services operate in the uni-modal transportation mode (i.e., they provide only driving, riding public transportation, or walking) and do not take into account the factors that impact physical activity in finding routes. To fill in this gap, we present a new navigation service, called Route2health, which would be able to: (a) find a route with multi-modal transportation for each trip; (b) include walking always as one mode of transportation; and (c) take specific user's requirements for each walking session so that physical activity is personalized.

4 Route2Health Foundation

The foundation of Route2Health, as a new service, is based on specific models and new algorithms, described in this section.

In the context of this paper, transportation refers to the traveling of people between locations by vehicles or on foot. Transportation can be classified into uni-modal, where only one mode of transportation (e.g., walking, driving) is involved or multi-modal, where more than one mode of transportation (e.g., driving and walking) is involved. Trip refers to transportation from an origin to a destination. Trip can also be uni-modal or multi-modal. Path is a possible physical connection between origin and destination for the purpose of traversing by uni-modal or multi-modal transportation. There could be multiple possible paths for a trip, and travelers usually choose the optimal one, which is the best path with respect to one or more given criteria. Finding an optimal path requires a transportation network containing topological relationships of the real-world transportation infrastructures (e.g., road, bridge, tunnel, intersection, and sidewalk). Transportation networks are modelled as graphs where each node represents a location where travelers must make a traversing decision (e.g., turn left/right, get on/off vehicle, and switch between modes) and a link connects two nodes representing traversable passage (e.g., road segment and sidewalk segment). There is a value quantifying traversing cost associated with each link between its start and end nodes. Examples of traversing costs are distance, time, expense, air pollution, and slope. Transportation networks representing one mode of transportation are uni-modal, and a multi-modal network is formed by combining different uni-modal networks with designated existing or new nodes or links for switching between them.

For calories estimation in Route2Health, we have considered the American College of Sports Medicine's (ACSM)[1] work on amount of calories burned (energy expenditure) for several activities (e.g., walking, running, and stepping) which is formulated in

---

[1] http://www.acsm.org/about-acsm/.

an equation for walking. The ACSM walking equation (Tharrett and Peterson 2012) expresses walking energy expenditure as:

$$EE = (0.1 \cdot S + 1.8 \cdot S \cdot G + 3.5) \cdot BM \cdot t \cdot 0.005 \tag{1}$$

where EE is walking energy expenditure (kilocalories); S is walking speed (meter/minute); G is grade (slope) in decimal form (e.g., 0.02 for 2 % grade); BM is traveller's body weight (kg); and t is walking time (minute). Equation (1) is based on the assumption that the traveller walks at a constant speed during time t, and the slope G is homogeneous. The equation is only accurate for the speed between 60–100 meters per minute (Glass and Dwyer 2007).

Figure 1 illustrates Route2Health algorithm which requires an origin, a destination, body weight, walking distance, and the desired mode of transportation (driving or riding). Walking transfer nodes, located within an acceptable walking distance, are retrieved and used for vehicular and walking path computation. In the absence of walking transfer nodes that satisfy the requested walking distance, the algorithm computes only walking paths that connect the origin and the destination. If walking transfer nodes (parking lots or bus stops) are found, the associated vehicular paths (driving or riding) are computed.

Once vehicular and walking paths are computed, the results (walking paths and vehicular paths) are combined to form multi-modal paths to link the origin, walking transfer nodes, and the destination. The number of walking transfer nodes determines the number of alternate walking paths. Then, based on Eq. (1), the calorie burns for each alternate walking path is estimated. Slope of each segment of a walking path is estimated by using high-resolution Digital Elevation Model (DEM) data. Walking speed is provided by the user, or could be calculated based on walking path distance and estimated duration of walking. For each optimal path, path geometry, travel distance, travel time, and estimated calories burned are presented to the user. Figure 2 shows an example of a route computed for a walking-driving trip and Fig. 3 shows an example of a route computed for a walking-riding trip.

5 Empowering Physical Activity

Theoretical frameworks are usually selected for use in program design and individual practice based on how well they meet one or more of the four purposes detailed below: describing, explaining, predicting, and controlling/influencing health behavior Swanson 2013.

The first purpose of a theoretical framework is to *describe* the phenomena of interest, telling us the way things are, but not why they are the way they are or how they are likely to change. The second purpose of a theoretical framework is *explanation*. While a descriptive framework answers the question, "What is happening?", an explanatory framework answers the question of "Why is it happening?" The third purpose of a theoretical framework is *prediction*. Using data derived from other studies would support a prediction of similar results based on these factors. Finally, a theoretical framework is considered *controlling or influencing* when it has the ability to

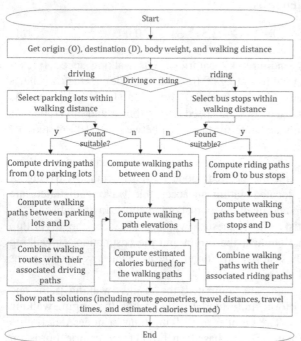

Fig. 1. Route2Health algorithm.

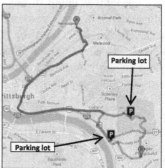

Fig. 2. Example walking-driving route. (Color figure online)

Fig. 3. Example walking-riding route. (Color figure online)

change behavior. The ability of a framework to influence achievement of greater levels of physical activity could be contrasted with a framework that is less useful because it cannot be manipulated to produce better outcomes.

The theory-based framework that we are using for Route2Health encompasses elements of the empowerment approach and self-determination theory and autonomy support (Deci et al. 1994) (Anderson et al. 1995; Williams et al. 1998; Funnell and Anderson 2003; Funnell and Anderson 2004; Williams et al. 2004; Anderson et al. 2009). These elements were combined into a theoretical framework for this project as they complement each other and are proven constructs in successful health behavior interventions. The chosen elements combine strategies for management of the social and behavioral factors associated with physical activity behavior change. Figure 4 depicts the theory-based framework.

6 Team-Based Empowerment for Social Support

An innovative aspect of Route2Health is the use of social media to form teams. Team identification will be encouraged through a process of team naming and an inter-team walking competition to create a collective outcome. Individuals will be able to see not only their own individually tailored messaging and feedback about their walking patterns, but also the percent of their team members who have achieved their physical activity goals for that day and what cumulative percent of goals the team achieved over the month. They will also see this same information for other teams.

We believe that assignment to teams may encourage physical activity behavior change. "Team" behavior differs from "group" behavior in that outcomes are assessed for the team as well as for the individual, and the former is contingent on the latter; in small studies, assignment to teams rather than groups has promoted adherence (Carter 2011). Teams can create camaraderie and accountability. In addition, seeing that most other members of one's team are walking can create a "descriptive norm" that will lead others who are not walking as much to walk more often (Krupka 2009). In a correlational study of a large physical activity program where people voluntarily chose whether to join as part of a team, those who did so continued reporting their activity for longer and reported higher levels of activity when they did so (Richardson et al. 2007; Richardson et al. 2008).

Social media is a novel platform through which to incorporate and study behavior change. Evidence demonstrates that the Internet can be effectively used for weight loss interventions and can be useful in weight loss maintenance (Arem and Irwin 2011) as it has the advantage of familiarity and flexibility, Interviews with users of SparkPeople revealed that some felt that interactions with people on SparkPeople were more helpful than those with real-life friends and family. (Hwang et al. 2010). Evidence also demonstrates that an online community may increase motivation and adherence to online pedometer interventions, potentially through mechanisms above as well as through friendly competitions (Resnick et al. 2010; Richardson et al. 2010). (Consolvo et al. 2006). Route2Health has the potential to build on this above evidence by incorporating physical activity into daily routines, an integral component of making and maintaining physical activity behavior change.

To facilitate team-based empowerment, SoNavNet (Karimi et al. 2009a; Karimi et al. 2009b), a social navigation networking system, will be used. Through SoNavNet, Route2Helath searches for possible recommendations, in particular recommend routes that are, otherwise, not easy to compute, due to lack of modeling and quantifying multiple criteria. An example of how SoNavNet can be used in Route2Health is when a member shares his/her experience about a trip where he/she used a car to drive to a parking lot and walked to and from a destination. In this example, the walking component of the route will be rated by using specific physical activity parameters.

Through the SoNavNet component of Route2Health, specific physical activity parameters of a route can be rated, all possible walking-driving or walking-riding options between origin and destination locations can be searched, and the most optimal (personalized) walking component from among all possible options to find the closest match (recommended by other members of SoNavNet) to a given set of user's criteria can be found.

7 Prototype

A prototype Route2Health has been developed. Figure 5 shows the architecture of the Route2Health application. The architecture is composed of six components: (1) Walking Transfer Selector, (2) Vehicular Path Alternative Generator, (3) Walking Path Alternative Generator, (4) Path Combiner, (5) Objective Function Normalizer, and (6) Multi-Criteria Optimizer. Walking Transfer Selector is the component that collects inputs: origin, destination, and personal walking distance limit. Based on the inputs, Walking Transfer Selector would identify all possible feasible walking transfers. Then based on the origin, the destination, and the identified walking transfers, the relevant walking path alternatives and vehicular path alternatives are computed by Walking Path Alternative Generator and Vehicular Path Alternative Generator, respectively. The path alternatives of the two modes are then combined into a complete path alternative by the Path Combiner. In the Objective Function Normalizer, the path alternatives are quantified using objective functions, and the outputs from the objective functions are normalized. The normalized values are then optimized by the Multi-Criteria Optimizer to obtain the final solution (optimal path).

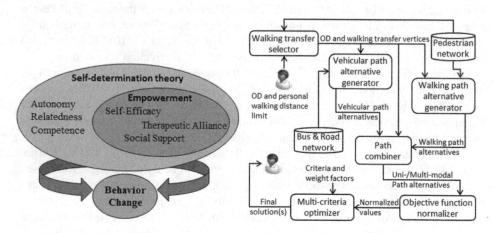

Fig. 4. Theory-based conceptual framework.   **Fig. 5.** Route2Health architecture.

8 Summary

A new service, called Route2Health, is presented where it can be used to empower people in finding optimal routes to improve physical activity. The service is based on the assumption that for any trip there should be a walking component. The MMT-MCW concept is introduced which can find routes that involve multi-modal transportation and find most optimal walking path among the candidate walking paths.

In developed countries, access to the technology may be a limiting factor for dissemination, however an increasing number of people do have access to smart phone technology. Using the technology to track activity and promote positive reinforcement through messaging may increase use. Further, participation in an online community that not only validates the choice of the route but also the advantages and disadvantages of the route for personal goal setting may increase self-efficacy.

References

Anderson, R.M., Funnell, M.M., et al.: Evaluating the efficacy of an empowerment-based self-management consultant intervention: results of a two-year randomized controlled trial. Ther. Patient Educ. **1**(1), 3–11 (2009)

Anderson, R.M., Funnell, M.M., et al.: Learning to empower patients. Diab. Care **14**(7), 584–590 (1991)

Anderson, R.M., Funnell, M.M., et al.: Patient empowerment: results of a randomized control trial. Diab. Care **18**, 943–949 (1995)

Arem, H., Irwin, M.: A review of web-based weight loss interventions in adults. Obes. Rev. **15**(5), 3236–3243 (2011)

Carlson, S.A., Fulton, J.E., et al.: Trend and prevalence estimates based on the 2008 physical activity guidelines for Americans. Am. J. Prev. Med. **39**(4), 305–313 (2010)

Carter, C., Oniecscu, G., Cartmell, K., Sterba, K., Tomsic, J., Alberq, A.: The comparative effectiveness of a team-based vs. group-based physical activity intervention for cancer survivors. Support Care Cancer (2011). epub: 20 September 2011

Centers for Disease Control and Prevention (2013a). http://www.cdc.gov/obesity/data/trends.html#State. Accessed 3 Dec 2013

Centers for Disease Control and Prevention. Obesity: Halting the Epidemic by Making Health Easier At A Glance 2011 (2013b). http://www.cdc.gov/chronicdisease/resources/publications/AAG/obesity.htm. Accessed 3 Dec 2013

Centers for Disease Control and Prevention Division of Nutrition, P. A., and Obesity, National Center for Chronic Disease Prevention and Health Promotion, 1 December 2011. "Physical Activity for Everyone." http://www.cdc.gov/physicalactivity/everyone/guidelines/adults.html. Accessed 13 Jan 2011

Consolvo, S., Everitt, K., et al.: Design requirements for technologies that encourage physical activity. In: CHI (2006)

Deci, E.L., Eghrari, H., et al.: Facilitating internalization: the self-determination theory perspective. J. Pers. **62**, 119–142 (1994)

Flegal, K.M., Graubard, B.I., et al.: Excess deaths associated with underweight, overweight, and obesity. JAMA **293**(15), 1861–1867 (2005)

Funnell, M.M., Anderson, R.M.: Patient empowerment: a look back, a look ahead. Diabetes Educ. **29**(3), 454–460 (2003)

Funnell, M.M., Anderson, R.M.: Empowerment and self-management of diabetes. clinical diabetes. Clin. Diab. **22**(3), 123–127 (2004)

Glass, S., Dwyer, G.B., American College of Sports Medicine (eds.): ACSM's Metabolic Calculations Handbook, p. 19, 26. Lippincott Williams & Wilkins (2007)

Greene, J., Choudhry, N., et al.: Online social networking by patients with diabetes: a qualitative evaluation of communication with Facebook. J. Gen. Intern. Med. **26**(3), 287–292 (2011)

Hwang, K., Ottenbacher, A., et al.: Social support in an internet weight-loss community. Int. J. Med. Inform. **79**(1), 5–13 (2010)

Karimi, H.A., Zimmerman, B., Ozcelik, A., Roongpiboonsopit, D.: SoNavNet: a framework for social navigation networks. In: International Workshop on Location Based Social Networks (LBSN 2009), Seattle, 3–6 November 2009

Krupka, E., Weber, R.: The focusing and observational effects of norms on pro social behavior. J. Econ. Psychol. (2009)

Pate, R.R., Pratt, M., et al.: Physical activity and public health. A recommendation from the centers for disease control and prevention and the American college of sports medicine. JAMA 273(5), 402–407 (1995)

Resnick, P., Janney, A., et al.: Adding an online community to an internet-mediated walking program. Part 2: strategies for encouraging community participation. Med. Internet Res. 12(4), e72 (2010)

Richardson, C., Buis, L., et al.: An online community improves adherence in an internet-mediated walking program. Part 1: results of a randomized controlled trial. J. Med. Internet Res. 12(4), e71 (2010)

Richardson, C., Mehari, K., et al.: A randomized trial comparing structured and lifestyle goals in an internet-mediated walking program for people with type 2 diabetes. Int. J. Behav. Nutr. Phys. Act 16(4), 59 (2007)

Richardson, C., Newton, T., et al.: A meta-analysis of pedometer-based walking interventions and weight loss. Ann. Fam. Med. 1, 69–77 (2008)

Swanson, R.A.: Theory Building in Applied Disciplines. Berrett-Koehler Publishers, San Francisco (2013)

Tharrett, S.J., Peterson, J.A. (eds.): ACSM's Health/Fitness Facility Standards and Guidelines. Human Kinetics, Champaign (2012)

Williams, G.C., Freedman, Z.R., et al.: Supporting autonomy to motivate patients with diabetes for glucose control. Diab. Care 21(10), 1644–1651 (1998)

Williams, G.C., McGregor, H.A., et al.: Testing a self-determination theory process model for promoting glycemic control through diabetes self-management. Health Psychol. 23(1), 58–66 (2004)

Zhang, Y., Chen, M., Mao, S., Hu, L., Leung, V.: Cap: community activity prediction based on big data analysis. Netw. IEEE 28(4), 52–57 (2014)

S2CT

Toward an Architectural Model for Highly-Dynamic Multi-tenant Multi-service Cloud-Oriented Platforms

Adel Titous[✉], Mohamed Cheriet, and Abdelouahed Gherbi

Ecole de Technologie Superieur,
1100, rue Notre-Dame Ouest, Montreal, QC H3C 1K3, Canada
adel.titous.1@ens.etsmtl.ca

Abstract. The characteristics of the Cloud Computing paradigm make it attractive to be used along with other paradigms like mobile and pervasive computing, smart cities, etc. There is a need to develop new platforms in order to take advantage of those converged infrastructures, and to abstract its high heterogeneities and complexities. The design and development of such robust and efficient platforms is challenging, because of the high heterogeneities, complexities and the wide range of features they are supposed to offer.

In this paper, we define some fundamental requirements related to those converged paradigms and infrastructures, and by consequence the requirements for cloud-oriented platforms. We also develop an architectural model, based on a new concept, the semantically defined resource, which is the result of the need to simplify the definition of lightweight services and to introduce more semantics. We also present an example to illustrate how to design architectures basing on the new concept, and how the architectural model can be used concretely.

Keywords: SOA · EDA · SDR · Cloud computing · Semantic web · Converged infrastructures

1 Introduction

The wide adoption of the Cloud Computing (CC) model, and the convergence with other computing paradigms, like mobile computing, introduced some architectural issues. Considering CC as *"a model for enabling ubiquitous, convenient, on-demand network access to a shared pool of configurable computing resources (e.g., networks, servers, storage, applications, and services) that can be rapidly provisioned and released with minimal management effort or service provider interaction"* [1], many aspects must be taken into account when designing and developing cloud oriented platforms for different domains of application. For instance, in [2], Sanai et al. present some important challenges and problems related to the heterogeneity of mobile cloud computing, and present architectural issues as the first requirement, since it is crucial to develop a reference architecture.

© ICST Institute for Computer Sciences, Social Informatics and Telecommunications Engineering 2016
A. Leon-Garcia et al. (Eds.): Smart City 2015, LNICST 166, pp. 203–214, 2016.
DOI: 10.1007/978-3-319-33681-7_17

By cloud-oriented platforms (see Fig. 1) we want to mention platforms to be developed for different domains, as MCC. While the boundaries between the cloud infrastructures and those platforms are not always clear, techniques and principles used to designe the coud-oriented platforms can be applied to design and develop a great part of the cloud infrastructure itself.

So cloud-oriented platforms should comply with different requirements with respect to different application domains, but in general we can distinguish some common fundamental requirements, like the high dynamicity and heterogeneity. Other caracteristics can be defined based on those fundamental requirements. For instance, we can not have efficient elasticity if we do not have adequate dynamicity.

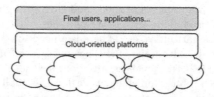

Fig. 1. Cloud oriented platforms

In a such context, the need for an architectural model facilitating the task of design and development of infrastructures is crucial. Several researches tried to take advantage of the Service Oriented Architecture (SOA) to design cloud systems, including [13–15], since SOA is technology-neutral and facilitates the design of large scale distributed systems based on loosely coupled services in highly heterogeneous environments [7,8]. SOA gives answers for some requirements but not for all of them, especially those related to the high dynamicity. Recently some efforts were spent in order to merge SOA with the Event Driven Architecture (EDA) [17,18]. The association between services and events can for example trigger services in response to some events, or produce events by services, which can improve the dynamicity of the classical SOA schema. However, the proposed solutions are restricted to a specific domain, because there is no real fusion between the concepts of services and events, and to our best knowledge, up to now there is no general architectural model, comparable to SOA for example, that can be efficiently applied to a large variety of problems.

On the other hand, the use of ontologies to categorize cloud services is an other track being investigated [3] in order to offer more possibilities to categorize, compare and choose best offered services.

In this paper, we merge all those three tracks into a unique and general architectural model, to be used in the design and development of cloud oriented platforms for different domains.

The remainder of the paper is organized as follows: the second section presents some related works, while the third section presents a brief background.

In the fourth section we define some fundamental requirements that any architectural model for cloud-oriented platforms must satisfy. The section five presents our introduced concept. The section six presents our architectural model. A use case is presented in the seventh section, followed by some discussions in the eight section. A conclusion conclude the paper.

2   Related Works

This section exposes some works in relation with clouds' architectures. Sanaei et al. [2] proclaim powerful dynamic representation and monitoring techniques, especially for heterogeneous wireless environments for cloud-mobile users.

In [3], Di Marino et al. present a semantic representation of services of Openstack platform, using OWL-S.

Celesti et al. [12] give a classification of CC market evolution. In [13] Tsai et al. present the Service Oriented Cloud Computing Architecture (SOCCA). In [15] Zhang and Zhou present the Cloud Computing Open Architecture (CCOA). In [16] Zou et al. assume that the internal structures of private and public clouds are consistent with each other, and present an architecture based on an added layer called cloud bus as an inter-cloud communication middleware.

Zhang et al. [17] develop an event driven SOA for internet of things based on a layered architecture. In [18] Laliwala and Chaudhary develop an Event Driven Service Oriented Architecture (EDSOA). Kim et al. presented ECO, a middleware for cloud of things [19].

Virtualization is another important concern, since it is being used at different levels: servers, storage, networking, etc. In [14] Duan et al. present service-orientation based efforts for networks virtualizations, and show that their are huge ambiguities such as different definitions of QoS, resulting in the absence of a consensus about definition of a network infrastructure description language to describe different networking resources.

3   Background

Some concepts are necessary to understand the work, they are summarized in the following subsections.

3.1   Service Oriented Architecture

SOA is an architectural style that promote service orientation. Thus large softwares can be organized into a collection of interacting services [6], which are autonomuous software packages (similar to classical APIs), and they are described and published in repositories. Tow main actors in SOA: the service provider and the service consumer (see Fig. 2).

Even Web services are the predominant technology used in it's implementation, SOA is technology-neutral, which is one of it's most important features.

Another feature is the abstraction, in a sense where the service consumer has no need to know how the service is implemented, all what he need is the description of the service. Those two features facilitate the design of distributed systems, especially those caracterized by high heterogeneities.

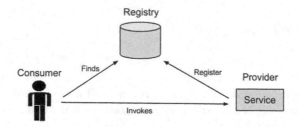

Fig. 2. Service oriented architecture

3.2   Event Driven Architecture

The Event Driven Architecture (EDA) is based on the concept of Events. An event can be any significant change in a given situation, relating to different contexts: overpassing a threshold value, overpassing a certain number of requests, a new situation in the business process, etc. i.e. any significant new situation that may be taken in account through triggering other events or process as a response. for instance, if the quantity of a product in the stock is under the permitted value, this event will not be just written in a file or a database, but will also trigger an ordering process. There are generally two types of events: ordinary and notables, where the last ones are used for signalling more important situations. An EDA is generally built using four layers:

– Event generator: which is the source that has generated the event. If a standard event format is used, the source has to transform the event in the right format before sending it on a channel.
– Event channel: transports events from the source to the event processor.
– Event processor: which process events, sometimes using some established rules. Two types of event processors can be distinguished: the simple ones process each event independently while the complex ones process an event accordingly to the context of prior and future events, possibly using patterns. Some companies like IBM provide complex event processing engines[1].
– Downstream Event-Driven Activity: downstream activities triggered after the processing of the event(s).

---

[1] As WebSpher Event Processing Software.

3.3   Ontologies and Semantic Web

There are many definitions of ontologies in artificial intelligence related literature. In [4] an ontology is defined as *"a formal explicit description of concepts in
a domain of discourse (classes (sometimes called concepts)), properties of each
concept describing various features and attributes of the concept (slots (sometimes called roles or properties)), and restrictions on slots (facets (sometimes
called role restrictions)). An ontology together with a set of individual instances
of classes constitutes a knowledge base"*. Ontologies can be machine readable, in
order to infer new knowledge or, more important in our case, to verify consis-
tencies of informations with the ontology. In the case of Web Services we can
find OWLS, which is based on Web Ontology Language (OWL), a standard of
the W3C [5].

4   The Requirements of Converged Infrastructures

The architecture of a system is the fundamental organization of it's components
and the relations between them, and is developed in response to some constraints and requirements. In the context of converged infrastructures presented
in the introduction, cloud-oriented platforms must satisfy high requirements such
as mobility and dynamicity, where the needs of users change dynamically, and
moreover capabilities of resources also change dynamically.

So the first question to be asked is what are the requirements that the architectural model must satisfy?

First of all, a huge heterogeneity caracterize the converged infrastructures:
different devices from different constructors, networks of sensors, different systems and applications with different requirements, architectures, etc. Thus, an
adequate abstraction is required to overcome this huge heterogeneity and inherent complexity.

The second requirement is the multi-granularity, as the ability to deal efficiently with different levels of granularities, from the finest one to the coarsest
one, since in a such context we can find resources like virtualized devices and
hardware, as well as business related services, usually with coarse granularity.

Finally, we find in [20] a description of volatile systems, characterized by:

- Failure of devices and communication links,
- Changes in the characteristics of communications such as bandwidth,
- Creation and destruction of associations[2] between software components resi-
  dent on different devices.

We can add two characteristics:

- Spontaneous appearance and disappearance of resources, devices and services,
- Dynamic changes in the characteristics and capabilities of resources.

---

[2] Logical communication relationships.

In the remainder of this paper, we use the term of dynamicity to summarize all of those characteristics, which represent our third requirement.

Even SOA provides adequate abstraction power, we think that it has some lacks, especially dynamicity. SOA was developed in the context of companies' information systems, totally different from our context. Also fine-granularity services are not supported as coarse-granularity services. We think that there is a need to make as lightweight as possible the definition and the description of fine-granularity services.

On the other hand, merging SOA and EDA has improved the dynamciity, but do not provide better support for fine-granularity services.

We have developed our model in a fundamentally different way, basing on a new concept, which is in the intersection between SOA, EDA, and Semantics.

5   The Concept of SDR

In order to comply with the context described in section four, we define a new concept based on SOA, EDA and semantics. The idea is to take advantage of SOA, but with improvement of the support for the very-fine granularity services, making their definitions as lightweight as possible by using a formal semantic technique rather than heavy description documents published in a registry. The interaction between providers and consumers is insured by using event processing engines.

Thus, we introduce the Semantically Defined Resource (SDR). An SDR is the abstraction of any resource that architects consider useful in a given context: a distributed object or component, a buffering space, a stack, a processor... etc. Table 1 gives a comparison between SDRs and Services.

Table 1. Services versus SDRs.

Criteria	Services	SDRs
Nature	software	software and hardware
Granularity	varied, but mostly coarse	finest as possible
Description	in repositories	semantic

Maybe in a given context, a resource can be abstracted as an SDR, but in another context the same resource may be integrated with other resources into a more wide scope SDR, in a similar way classes are designed in an object oriented approach.

SDRs are very loose coupled entities, and it is recommended that they have the finest possible granularity, since this will improve modularity and facilitate the maintenance, and augment sharing possibilities, but more important, to fit with the nature of devices available in the converged infrastructures context. Figure 3 present a conceptual diagram of the model: on the right side, there is a layered structure. The first layer is the SDR layer, abstracting different resources, which are defined semantically. Since SDRs may have dependencies in a given situation, the ability to gather them in structures like containers for example is useful, and this is the role of the second layer: the SDR-Containers (SDR-C). Of course, an SDR may be included into more than one SDR-C. It is important to note here that we assume that isolation and security concerns are provided by virtualization technology, or synchronization mechanisms, SDR-Cs deal with slices of resources. Like SDRs, SDR-Cs are defined semantically. The last layer is the Services layer, representing the known SOA services, with one or many related description documents in the registry. Instead of being published in the registry as services, SDRs are defined semantically and managed by the Event Processing Engine.

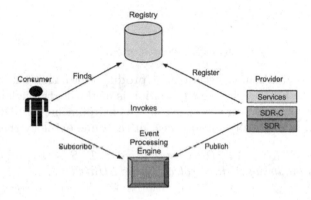

Fig. 3. The complementarity of services and SDRs

6   The Architectural Model

Let introduce some definitions to help the understanding of the model. Let assume that we have a resource with some related characteristics or properties, if the resource is a buffering space for eg. the available capacity is an important related characteristic. $\mathcal{D}$ is a semantic definition of the resource, and $\mathcal{P} = \{p_1, p_2, ...p_n\} \subseteq \mathcal{D}$ the set of its properties.

Definition 1. *(SDR) An SDR is a tuple $< \mathcal{D}, \mathcal{S}, \mathcal{A}, D_{in}, D_{out} >$, where:*

- *$\mathcal{S}$ is the set of states related to the resource.*
- *$\mathcal{A}$ is a set of activities that can change the state of the SDR.*
- *D_{in} are inputs sent by the consumer.*
- *D_{out} are outputs received by the consumer.*

Two states $s_i, s_j \in \mathcal{S}$ are different, if and only if $\exists! \ p \in \mathcal{P}$, where the value of p is different in s_i and s_j. Figure 4 shows the states of a given resource from the perspective of middleware and users, where a resource can be available, not available or available with different states, for eg. the available capacity of the buffer can change dynamically.

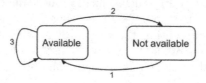

Fig. 4. States of resources

Definition 2. *(Event) An event* $\mathcal{E} \in \mathcal{S} \times \mathcal{A} \times \mathcal{S}$.

Basing on event definition, an event can be produced each time the state of SDR change, i.e. in the Fig. 4 each time a transition is made, i.e. through arc 1, 2 or 3.

SDR-Cs are containers, or virtual execution environments for SDRs, and they are also defined semantically, for instance, in the same ontology than SDRs.

Definition 3. *(SDR-C) An SDR-C is a tuple* $< \mathcal{D}, \mathcal{S}, \mathcal{A}, D_{in}, D_{out}, \mathcal{L}_{SDR} >$, *where* $\mathcal{L}_{SDR}$ *is the list of SDRs involved in the SDR-C.*

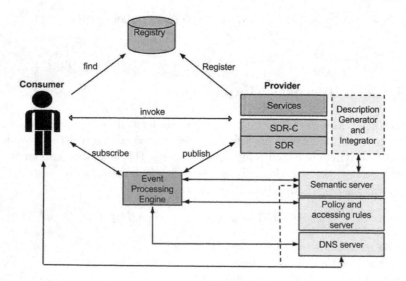

Fig. 5. The architectural model

An SDR-C may contain other SDR-Cs, some added code playing the role of interfaces between SDRs, or to have some special SDRs configurations.

SDR-Cs can be defined as services and published in service registry. It is up to the architect to design his solution basing on needs, and already available SDRs, SDR-Cs and services.

Figure 5 shows the architectural model based on SDRs. The central component is the Event Processing Engine (EPE), which manage and process different events emitted using publish/subscribe communication pattern. Publishers are providers, consumers are subscribers. EPE manage subscribers lists by related event servers, in other words, the event servers life cycle management is performed basing on informations in the semantic server. The model contains also a semantic server containing different semantic definitions (SDRs and SDR-Cs) available for all tenants: the provider, the consumer and EPE. This is because all tenants have to share the same formal definitions of SDRs and SDR-Cs. Because SDRs and SDR-Cs are published on server events, managed EPE, accessing rules must be setted for consumers and providers for accessing different event servers, which motivate the policy and accessing rules server. Finally a DNS server will help to locate different event servers and parts of the middleware.

7   Use Case

The Fig. 6 shows the role of the ontology and event processing engine. Classes in the ontology are used by the event processing engine to create event-servers, in order to manage SDRs. Thus, it may be an event-server for each SDR. Imagine that in a smart house, we need to copy a buffer b1 in another one b2, while b2 is momentarily full, but another buffer b3 is available. We have defined a

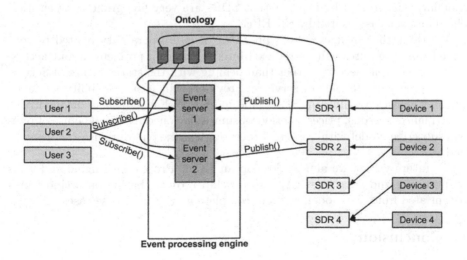

Fig. 6. The roles of the ontology and event processing engine

simple ontology partially represented in Fig. 7 using UML class diagram. The
class `DecodingNode` is composed of a `Buffer` and a `Processor`.

The publisher/subscriber communication paradigm is used: the first event-
server is `BufferServer`, on which b3 is published, the subscriber b1 is notified
about the availability of b3 by `BufferServer` with indication of the size of b3,
b1 will be copied in b3 and unsubscribed from BufferServer. Since b3 is greater
than b1, it will stay published on `BufferServer`, but with an updated size.

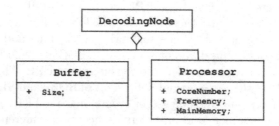

Fig. 7. A part of the ontology

8   Discussion and Future Works

By merging the two architectural paradigms SOA and EDA, and basing on
SDRs, we try to make definition of resources as lightweight as possible, and at
the same time to comply with the fundamental requirements defined in section
four. The abstraction is ensured by using a common semantic definition for the
domain in case of SDRs, and the definition of services in the registry. The multi-
granularity is ensured by the fact that SDRs are very-fine granularity entities.
The dynamicity is ensured by the EPE.

We think that in many cases, problems of inter-operability related to converged infrastructures will be reduced into engineering problems about accessing different event servers, rather than dealing with the static nature of Service
Level Agreements (SLAs) of services. Providers will have possibility to define
different policies for different SDRs, and moreover changing them on the fly for
performances reasons, prices, energy consumption concerns, etc. The use of pub-
lish/subscribe model within Event Processing Engine will diminish the network
load.

As future works, we aim to develop an Event Processing Engine and tools
for providers and consumers. Also to develop projects basing on architectures
instantiated from the model, as more complete and concrete use cases.

9   Conclusion

In this paper, we have proposed an architectural model for cloud-oriented platforms, in order to comply with some fundamental requirements related to the

converged infrastructures. The model can be seen as a refinement of Service Oriented Architecture, merged with Event Driven Architecture, alongside with the use of semantics to define fine-granularity resources. The model is based on the Semantically Defined Resource, the concept introduced in this paper. We think that with an improved dynamicity and efficient mechanisms for very fine granularity resources, the model will offer possibilities for concurrent access to resources, and to define and share different building blocks of highly dynamic platforms, systems and applications through a converged infrastructures environment.

References

1. Mell, P., Grance, T.: The NIST definition of cloud computing. Commun. ACM **53**(6), 50 (2010)
2. Sanaei, Z., Abolfazli, A., Gani, A., Buyya, R.: Heterogeneity in mobile cloud computing: taxonomy and open challenges. IEEE Commun. Surv. Tutor. **16**(1), 369–392 (2014). First quarter
3. Di Martino, B., Cretella, G., Esposito, A., Carta, G.: Semantic representation of cloud services: a case study for openstack. In: Fortino, G., Di Fatta, G., Li, W., Ochoa, S., Cuzzocrea, A., Pathan, M. (eds.) IDCS 2014. LNCS, vol. 8729, pp. 39–50. Springer, Heidelberg (2014)
4. Noy, N.F., McGuinness, D.L.: Ontology development 101: a guide to creating your first ontology, Technical report KSL-01-05, Stanford Knowledge Systems Laboratory (2001)
5. http://www.w3.org/OWL/
6. Buyya, R., Vecchiola, C., Selvi, S.T.: Mastering Cloud Computing Foundations and Applications Programming. Morgan Kaufmann Editions, San Francisco (2013)
7. Erl, T.: SOA Principle of Services Design. Prentice Hall Publishing, Upper Saddle River (2008)
8. Josuttis, N.M.: SOA in Practice. The Art of Distributed Systems Design. O'Reilly, Sebastopol (2007)
9. Shroff, G.: Enterprise Cloud Computing: Technology, Architecture, Applications. Cambridge University Press, Cambridge (2010)
10. Toosi, A.N., Calheiros, R.N., Buyya, R.: Interconnected cloud computing environments: challenges, taxonomy, and survey. ACM Comput. Surv. **47**(1), Article 7 (2014)
11. Petcu, D.: Portability and interoperability between clouds: challenges and case study. In: Abramowicz, W., Llorente, I.M., Surridge, M., Zisman, A., Vayssière, J. (eds.) ServiceWave 2011. LNCS, vol. 6994, pp. 62–74. Springer, Heidelberg (2011)
12. Celesti, A., Tusa, F., Villari, M., Puliafito, A.: How to enhance cloud architectures to enable cross-federation. In: IEEE 3rd International Conference on Cloud Computing (2010)
13. Tsai, W., Sun, X., Balasooriya, J.: Service-oriented cloud computing architecture. In: IEEE Seventh International Conference on Information Technology (2010)
14. Duang, Q., Yan, Y., Vasilakos, A.V.: A survey on service-oriented network virtualization toward convergence of networking and cloud computing. IEEE Trans. Netw. Serv. Manage. **9**(4), 373–392 (2012)
15. Zhang, L.J., Zhou, Q.: CCOA: cloud computing open architecture. In: IEEE International Conference on Web Services (2009)

16. Zou, C., Deng, H., Qiu, Q.: Design and implementation of hybrid cloud computing architecture based on cloud bus. In: IEEE 9th International Conference on Mobile Ad-hoc and Sensor Networks (2013)
17. Zhang, Y., Duan, L., Chen, J.: Event-driven SOA For IoT Services. Int. J. Serv. Comput. **2**(2) (2014). (ISSN 2330–4472)
18. Laliwala, Z., Chaudhary, S.: Event-driven service-oriented architecture. In: 2008 International Conference on Service Systems and Service Management. IEEE (2008)
19. Kim, S.H., Kim, D.: Multi-tenancy support with organization management in the cloud of things. In: IEEE 10th International Conference on Services Computing (2013)
20. Coulouris, G., Dollimore, J., Kindberg, T., Blair, G.: Distributed Systems, Concepts and Design, 5th edn. Addison-Wesley, Boston (2012)
21. Ericsson Mobility Report, November 2014
22. A Conceptual Model for Event Processing Systems. IBM (2010)

Large Scale Energy Harvesting Sensor Networks with Applications in Smart Cities

Hossein Shafieirad[1(✉)], Raviraj S. Adve[1], and Shahram ShahbazPanahi[2]

[1] ECE Department, University of Toronto, Toronto, ON, Canada
{hshrad,rsadve}@ece.utoronto.ca
[2] ECSE Department, University of Ontario
Institute of Technology, Oshawa, ON, Canada
shahram.shahbazpanahi@uoit.ca

Abstract. Wireless sensor networks (WSNs), with a wide range of applications in smart cities (e.g. environmental monitoring, intelligent traffic management, healthcare), have energy self-sufficiency as one of the main bottlenecks in their implementation. Thanks to the recent advances in energy harvesting (EH), i.e., capturing energy from ambient *renewable* sources, it is now a promising solution for low-power and low-rate WNSs. In this paper, we consider two open problems of practical importance to the data quality optimization problem. In this paper, first the probabilistic energy causality constraint for the online consideration of the EH scenarios is proposed. Our realistic assumptions consider causal energy state information, instead of the non-causal cases and the ones based on offline prediction studied in literature. In addition, we propose a novel EH-aware routing protocol, based on opportunistic relaying. This routing protocol is shown to have significant benefits in finding the best path with no prior knowledge of the topology and with minimal overhead, making it an efficient protocol for EH-WSNs.

Keywords: Energy harvesting · Energy outage rate · Probabilistic energy causality constraint · EH-aware opportunistic routing

1 Introduction

Wireless sensor networks with their wide range of applications in smart cities including environmental monitoring, intelligent traffic management, healthcare, target tracking, etc., have received significant attention in the last decade. Some of the most important issues which limit WSNs' functionality are the scale, lifetime, and ease of physical access to replenish their power sources. Therefore energy self-sufficiency is one of the main bottlenecks in the implementation of sensor network applications in smart cities.

Energy harvesting, which is the capture and storage of energy from ambient *renewable* sources, allows for self sustainable and environmentally-friendly operations in low-power wireless sensor networks. This environmental energy

© ICST Institute for Computer Sciences, Social Informatics and Telecommunications Engineering 2016
A. Leon-Garcia et al. (Eds.): Smart City 2015, LNICST 166, pp. 215–226, 2016.
DOI: 10.1007/978-3-319-33681-7_18

(e.g., solar energy, thermal energy, vibration), harnessed at the EH communication nodes, needs to be utilized efficiently for data transmission. The recent advances in EH technologies makes it a promising and viable solution for the aforementioned problems in WSNs.

2   State-of-the-art and Scope

The existing works on EH are classified based on the causal or non-causal knowledge of the energy state information and the channel state information at the transmitter (called ESIT and CSIT, respectively) [1,2].

The related works considering EH in the WSNs are mainly on routing and medium access control (MAC) protocol design, power management, topology design, etc. The main state-of-the-art on the mentioned subjects has considered only the application or network layer without being aware of the other layers' adaptation to EH [3–6].

Different layers are strongly coupled in EH-WSNs while there are only a few works considering cross-layer design problems in such networks. These studies mainly consider the throughput maximization problem while guaranteeing the routing feasibility [7,8].

The main work on EH-WSNs as a cross-layer problem is [9] where the data quality maximization problem in EH-WSNs is considered. [9] uses EH prediction methods instead of considering the causal ESIT which leads to high prediction errors when the energy conditions change significantly. The work also does not provide an efficient routing protocol for the data quality maximization problem considering the EH constraints. In this paper, we consider two open problems in the area of EH-WSNs that help us practically consider the data quality maximization problem in such networks which is an important problem in the applications of EH-WSNs in smart cities.

First, we propose an online scenario, i.e., the causal ESIT case in point to point fading channels and then generalize it to EH-WSNs. We propose a novel problem formulation, in which instead of minimizing the outage probability as is done in [10], we consider the rate maximization problem in [1] but with probabilistic constraints. We show that our problem is non-convex and thus, based on the properties of our problem constraints, we find a convex transformation which results in the optimal solution. The convex transformation of our problem is shown to have a similar form as the problem mentioned in [1]. Therefore, we can find the closed form solution of our problem using the same approach as in [1]. Finally, we compare our results with that of the main EH rate optimization problem proposed in [1] and we quantize loss in the throughput as a result of having only the distribution of the harvested energies.

Second, unlike the work in [9] that deals with the data quality problem, we are also seeking a customized routing protocol, which considers the constraints of EH to maximize data quality in large scale networks as another tool for considering the data quality problem in EH-WSNs. Our proposed protocol considers the packet concatenation and fair bandwidth share as well as decision making based on the EH nature of the network.

The remainder of the paper is organized as follows. The system model and problem formulation are provided in Sect. 3. Then, our online EH scenario is presented in Sect. 4. Section 5 describes the proposed EH-aware routing protocol. Our simulation results are shown in Sect. 6 and finally, Sect. 7 concludes the paper.

3   System Model and Problem Formulation

3.1   System Model

Our system consists of N sensor nodes, one base station (BS), and a user-side application. The sensor nodes are distributed randomly in the monitored area. They harvest energy from the environment and also sense the physical properties of their surroundings. In our model, we consider that the nodes have an infinite battery capacity and a finite buffer for storing the received packets. Each node is assumed to have a fixed transmission region, denoted as R_t. The nodes are randomly distributed inside a circle of radius R.

The user-side application sets constraints on the data in the form of an acceptable error margin and conveys this information to the BS. This is then broadcasted by the BS to the sensor nodes. The sensor nodes sense the physical changes in the environment until the sensed data deviates from the past value by more than the acceptable error margin. This data is then transmitted to the BS. In addition to transmitting its own data, each node also performs the task of forwarding other nodes' data to the BS. Therefore, the total number of messages each node should transmit to the BS in a certain time interval is a function of the error margin and also depends on the routing protocol used in the network. The total number of messages node i transmits during the tth timeslot is denoted as $M(t, e_i)$, where e_i is the error margin defined at this node.

The total energy consumption for each node in a certain time interval is a function of the total number of messages that the node transmits. This has to be less than or equal to the amount of energy harvested by the node in that period of time. Therefore, the EH rate limits the data quality level of the system. Our last term goal is to find the closest we can get to the determined accuracy level while taking into account the EH constraints in large scale EH-WSNs. The energy causality constraint for node i in the data quality maximization problem discussed above is as follows.

$$\sum_{t=1}^{k} M(t, e_i) \times E_p \leq \sum_{t=1}^{k} E_H(t), \ k = 1, 2, \ldots, t_{max}, \tag{1}$$

where $E_H(t)$ is the amount of harvested energy in t^{th} timeslot and E_p is the energy required for transmission of one packet. Note that in the causal ESIT case, $E_H(t)$ is not available for the future timeslots.

3.2 Design Challenges

The randomness in the arrival times and in the amount of energy harvested in addition to fluctuations in the communication channel pose a challenge in the identification of the optimal transmission policy. In order to maintain network connectivity and reliable data delivery, topology design and control across the network is required. Fair bandwidth share is another challenge especially in our case of large scale networks. Nodes which are far from the BS may starve the nodes closer to the BS in order to forward their packets [11]. Since the energy level of each EH node is not high, the nodes closer to the BS do not have enough energy for data transmission which decreases their data quality level. Thus, there is a requirement for an efficient EH-aware routing protocol.

Another challenge due to the energy causality constraint in Eq. (1) is consideration of the causal ESIT. As stated in the previous section, [9] uses prediction methods for this purpose and in the following section, we propose the idea of probabilistic energy causality constraint which helps us consider the online EH scenario for the constraint (1).

4 Online EH Scenario

In this section we propose the probabilistic energy causality constraint as a tool for online consideration of the EH applications.

We propose our online scenario for the rate maximization problem for a single transmitter and a fading channel in a point to point wireless communication system where the harvested energy is harnessed, stored and utilized for data transmission purposes.

We look to maximize the throughput over a finite time horizon and partition this time horizon into M time intervals, where l_i is the length of the ith time interval. The bandwidth is assumed to be sufficiently wide so that we may approximate this slotted time system to a continuous time system. Furthermore, it has been shown that the optimal transmission policy is constant between energy arrivals or change in fading events. Each time interval can, thus, be referred to as a transmission block where the energy arrivals occur at the beginning of the transmission blocks.

Thus, considering the number of channel uses in each block to be large enough [1], the data transmission rate in each block is given by

$$\frac{1}{2} \log \left(1 + |h_i|^2 P_i\right), \tag{2}$$

where h_i is the fading coefficient and P_i is the power allocated to block i. The channel state information, h_i, of the fading channel, is constant over each time interval i and is known at the transmitter. The amount of energy harnessed at the beginning of the time interval, E_i, is random in nature, but constant over the time interval and thus, we model the energy arrivals to be in accordance with a certain probabilistic distribution as only the past and current energy state information (ESI) is known.

We, thus, wish to identify the optimal power, P_i, to be allocated to each time interval subject to causality constraints which dictate that the total power allocated at the end of each interval should not exceed the total energy that is available at that time, which can be shown as follows

$$\int_0^{t_i^e} P(u)du \le \sum_{j=1}^i E_j, \tag{3}$$

where t_i^e is the duration of i energy harvesting timeslots. Because of the concavity of rate in power the transmit power is to be kept constant during each time interval [12], and hence the causality constraints is reduced to

$$\sum_{i=1}^k P_i \le \sum_{i=1}^k E_i, \; k = 1, 2, \ldots, M. \tag{4}$$

4.1   Problem Formulation

The optimization problem for maximizing the total throughput via optimal power allocation subject to energy causality constraints is as follows.

$$\max_{p_i} \sum_{i=1}^M \frac{1}{2} \log(1 + P_i \left| h_i^2 \right|) \tag{5}$$

$$s.t. \; \sum_{i=1}^k l_i P_i \le \sum_{i=1}^k E_i, \; k = 1, 2, \ldots, M.$$

$$0 \le P_i$$

Since the amount of energy harvested is random in nature, we can only consider probabilistic information about the energy. Instead of minimizing the outage probability of the rate as it is done in existing works, we modify to consider probabilistic energy causality constraints where the rate of violation of each constraint is ϵ, which is the energy outage rate. The optimization problem is, thus, reformulated as follows

$$\max_{p_i} \sum_{i=1}^M \frac{1}{2} \log(1 + P_i \left| h_i^2 \right|) \tag{6}$$

$$s.t. \; Pr(\sum_{i=1}^k E_i \le \sum_{i=1}^k l_i P_i) \le \epsilon, \; k = 1, 2, \ldots, M.$$

$$0 \le P_i$$

The time interval lengths, l_i, can be taken to be unity for simplicity.

4.2   Optimal Solution

The objective function in problem (6) is a concave function but the first constraint which is in the form of the CDF of $\sum_{i=1}^{k} E_i$ is not a convex function. The CDF for most distributions is of the form of unimodal distribution functions, i.e., it is convex for some x in the range less than m and concave for $x > m$.

The non-decreasing behavior of CDF makes the probabilistic constraint in problem (6) quasiconvex in nature causing the feasible set of this problem to be convex [13]. However, we propose another method to find the convex transformation of this problem. Based on the non-decreasing behavior of CDF, it is possible to find the inverse CDF using the closed form CDF or the CDF lookup tables. In the following, we consider the case with the harvested energies to be independent and identically distributed (i.i.d.) random variables with exponential distribution. Since the sum of i.i.d. exponential random variables has Erlang distribution, the CDF of the sum of harvested energies is as follows.

$$F(x; k, \lambda) = \frac{\gamma(k, \lambda x)}{(k-1)!},$$ (7)

where $\gamma(.)$ is the lower incomplete gamma function defined as

$$\gamma(s, x) = \int_0^x t^{s-1} e^{-t} \, dt.$$ (8)

The Erlang distribution is a unimodal distribution function. Hence, we should transform the constraint in problem (6) to a convex constraint. The Eq. (7) can be assumed as a function of $\sum_i p_i$. Therefore, the best approach is to find the inverse of the Erlang CDF which results in an affine inequality constraint.

$$F_k(\sum_{i=1}^{k} P_i) \leq \epsilon, \ k = 1, 2, \ldots, M,$$ (9)

where $F_k(.)$ is the CDF of the sum of i.i.d. E_i's, $i = 1, 2, \ldots, k$.

According to the inequality (9), we have

$$\sum_{i=1}^{k} P_i \leq F_k^{-1}(\epsilon),$$ (10)

where $F_k^{-1}(.)$ is the inverse CDF of the sum of i.i.d. E_i's, $i = 1, 2, \ldots, k$.

Given the closed form CDF, it is easy to find the inverse function. Alternatively, because of the non-decreasing behaviour of CDF, we can use the bisection method to find the inverse CDF. Another way of finding the inverse function is to use inverse CDF tables such as the gamma function tables that we used in our simulations.

4.3   Closed Form Solution

After finding the convex form of our optimization problem, now we can obtain the closed form solution by applying the Karush-Kuhn-Tucker (KKT) conditions.

The Lagrangian for (6) using Lagrange multipliers ϵ_i and μ_i can be obtained as

$$L = \sum_{i=1}^{M} \log(1 + |h_i|^2 P_i) - \sum_{j=1}^{M} \lambda_j \left(\sum_{i=1}^{j} P_i - F_j^{-1}(\epsilon) \right) + \sum_{i=1}^{M} \mu_j P_j. \tag{11}$$

Thus, the complimentary slackness conditions can be given by

$$\lambda_j \left(\sum_{i=1}^{j} P_i - F_j^{-1}(\epsilon) \right) = 0, \tag{12}$$

$$\mu_j P_j = 0. \tag{13}$$

It follows that the optimal power for the ith transmission block is

$$P_i^\star = \left[\nu_i - \frac{1}{|h_i|^2} \right]^+, \tag{14}$$

where the water level is given by

$$\nu_i = \frac{1}{\sum_{j=i}^{M} \lambda_j}. \tag{15}$$

The above solution can be obtained using *directional water-filling* algorithm as in [1].

4.4   Updating Scenario

The optimal power allocation, which faces violations, needs to be modified to give the practically achievable alloceted power, that is, one which is in keeping with the causality constraints. The updating scenario we propose here in order to satisfy the energy causality constraint for the optimal allocated power is that for each timeslot j that the energy causality constraint does violate we limit P_j to the total available energy harvested at the jth timeslot.

4.5   Online Scenario in EH-WSNs

The proposed method in this section can be applied as a tool for considering online EH scenario in EH-WSNs since data transmission between two nodes in WSNs can be considered similar to the point to point case. To achieve this objective we just need to change the energy causality constraint in (1) to the probabilistic constraint similar to what we mentioned in the point to point case. Therefore, using the probabilistic knowledge of the harvested energy no offline prediction is required.

5   Proposed Opportunistic Routing

In the previous section we investigated transmission strategies for a single link in the WSN. This section investigates a complementary issue: the route data packets must take to be received at the BS. We propose a new EH-aware routing protocol in order to find the best route from each node toward the BS. As opposed to the other routing protocols applied for EH scenarios which are either only distance-dependent or are just for specific network topologies (e.g., linear, grid), ours considers the remaining energy for each node and the statistics of the channel based on instantaneous channel measurements where nodes are randomly distributed in environment.

Our protocol does not require prior knowledge of the network topology and operates in a distributed fashion. Each EH node is assumed to have a fixed transmission region, a circle of radius R_t. EH nodes are distributed randomly inside a circle of radius R. In addition to transmitting its own data, each EH node is also capable of relaying other nodes' messages to the BS. Each EH node is only aware of its own location and consequently, its distance from the BS. As mentioned in the system model, nodes are battery operated and have a finite size buffer to store packets for future transmission.

Our opportunistic routing protocol exploits the opportunistic relaying scheme proposed and analyzed in [14]. The overall overhead is an important aspect that needs to be taken into account in large scale EH-WSNs. The opportunistic relaying scheme in [14] is based on time and is shown to have the minimal overhead. Each node may have a few neighbouring nodes, i.e., nodes that are present in its transmission region. These neighbouring nodes could be active or in sleep mode (waiting to harvest sufficient energy to transmit data) based on their remaining energy. We define a threshold, E_{th}, so that only those EH nodes with remaining energy more than E_{th} are capable of receiving data (active mode).

Nodes which have a packet to transmit will broadcast it if they have enough energy for data transmission. The active neighbors receive this data and store it in their buffer. Nodes are equipped with an internal timer which starts after they receive data from their neighbours. In our model, as soon as each node receives a message, it goes to the listening mode and starts a timer based on its SNR received at the BS, at each timeslot. Therefore, the timer of the relaying node with the maximum SNR (best end-to-end path between the relaying node and the BS) expires first, thereby choosing the max-SNR node to relay the data (if it has enough energy for data transmission). It then sends a packet to all of its neighbours indicating that they can drop their received data. In this way, the probability of the collision is also decreased.

A node with location vector (a_i, b_i) from the BS and remaining energy E_r should wait T_i seconds after data reception, where T_i is defined as

$$T_i = \frac{\lambda}{SNR_i}, \tag{16}$$

and SNR_i is the signal to noise ratio for the EH node i *at the BS*, and λ is a constant which is defined based on the channel coherence time. For choosing the best path through maximum SNR neighbour selection using the described protocol, not only are the remaining energy of the EH nodes and the channel state information taken into account, but other features like distance to BS are inherently considered.

6   Simulation Results

6.1   Online EH Scenario

In this section we first simulate the rate optimization problem proposed in Sect. 4. The optimal rates have been simulated in order to observe their variation with change in average energy harvesting rate per time interval, using MATLAB CVX toolbox [15].

First, to check the correctness of our model, we simulate random energy arrivals and observe the rate of violation of the causality constraints by the power allocated. The results show that this rate matches the value of ϵ (violation rate) that we set for the probabilistic constraint in our problem thus, justifying the accuracy of the model.

Figure 1 compares the performance of the offline scenario, given in Eq. (5), with our online scenario for ϵ equals to 0.1. In this figure the channel is random fading. The greedy curve is also depicted in the figure, where all the available energy is allocated for data transmission at each timeslot. It can be observed that there is reduction in rate for the reformulated problem due to availability of only probabilistic information regarding the amount of energy as compared to the deterministic scenario addressed in the original problem.

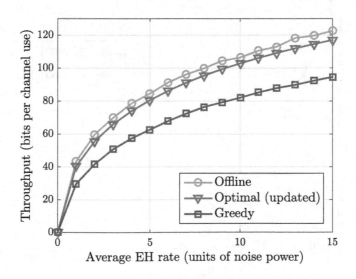

Fig. 1. Comparing achievable rates

6.2 EH-aware Routing Protocol

We simulate our proposed EH-aware routing protocol for different network densities. Our main goal here is to find the expected number of messages transmitted
per node as a function of distance from the BS. This can be used for calculation of $M(t, e_i)$ in the energy causality constraint, mentioned in (1), of the data
quality maximization problem.

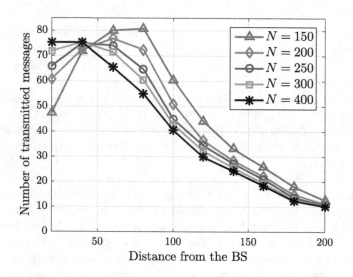

Fig. 2. Opportunistic routing for different network densities

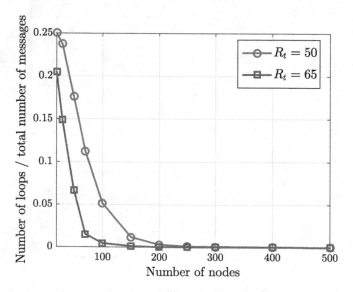

Fig. 3. Number of loops as a function of network density (for nodes with different
transmission regions)

Figure 2 depicts the total transmitted messages versus the distance from the BS. We simulate a network with radius of $R = 200$ and for nodes with transmission region $R_t = 50$. The harvested energy is assumed to have exponential distribution.

We run the routing protocol for 100 timeslots and the total number of the initial messages for each node is considered to be 10 packets that are randomly generated within the running time. We also define a limited buffer size of 20 packets for each node.

Another feature of our proposed protocol is the number of loops that occur during data transmission. We define a loop as the occurrence when a node receives back its own initial transmitted packet as a part of the other nodes' data. Figure 3 demonstrates the number of loops for the EH-aware routing protocol. As we see, for high densities the total number of loops is negligible which means that the protocol works well for large scale EH-WSNs.

7   Conclusion

In this paper, we considered the data quality maximization problem in EH-WSNs. The growing interest in smart cities make the analysis of such networks important. This paper results in a practical framework for the application of WSNs in smart cities. Our realistic assumptions consider causal ESIT instead of non-causal cases and those methods using offline prediction studied in literature. We also propose an EH-aware routing protocol as an efficient routing protocol for the data quality maximization problem in EH-WSNs. To the best of our knowledge, this is the first work on the data quality maximization problem in large scale EH-WSNs as a cross-layer optimization problem considering the causal ESIT knowledge of each node which benefits from an efficient EH-aware routing protocol.

References

1. Ozel, O., Tutuncuoglu, K., Yang, J., Ulukus, S., Yener, A.: Transmission with energy harvesting nodes in fading wireless channels: optimal policies. IEEE J. Sel. Areas Commun. **29**(8), 1732–1743 (2011)
2. Li, H., Xu, J., Zhang, R., Cui, S.: A general utility optimization framework for energy harvesting based wireless communications. IEEE Commun. Mag. **53**(4), 79–85 (2015)
3. Dang, N., Bozorgzadeh, E., Venkatasubramanian, N.: QuARES: quality-aware data collection in energy harvesting sensor networks. In: 2011 International on Green Computing Conference and Workshops (IGCC), pp. 1–9, 25–28 July 2011
4. Hasenfratz, D., Meier, A., Moser, C., Chen, J.J., Thiele, L.: Analysis, comparison, and optimization of routing protocols for energy harvesting wireless sensor networks. In: 2010 IEEE International Conference on Sensor Networks, Ubiquitous, and Trustworthy Computing (SUTC), pp. 19–26, 7–9 June 2010
5. Eu, Z.A., Tan, H.-P., Seah, W.K.: Opportunistic routing in wireless sensor networks powered by ambient energy harvesting. Comput. Netw. **54**(17), 2943–2966 (2010)

6. Eu, Z.A., Seah, W.K., Tan, H.-P.: A study of MAC schemes for wireless sensor networks powered by ambient energy harvesting. In: Proceedings of the 4th Annual International Conference on Wireless Internet, p. 78. ICST (Institute for Computer Sciences, Social-Informatics and Telecommunications Engineering) (2008)

7. Zhang, B., Simon, R., Aydin, H.: Maximal utility rate allocation for energy harvesting wireless sensor networks. In: 14th ACM International Conference on Modeling, Analysis and Simulation of Wireless and Mobile Systems (2011)

8. Fan, K.W., Zheng, Z., Sinha, P.: Steady and fair rate allocation for rechargeable sensors in perpetual sensor networks. In: Proceedings of the 6th ACM Conference on Embedded Network Sensor Systems, pp. 239–252. ACM (2008)

9. Dang, N., Roshanaei, M., Bozorgzadeh, E., Venkatasubramanian, N.: Adapting data quality with multihop routing for energy harvesting wireless sensor networks. In: 2013 International on Green Computing Conference (IGCC), pp. 1–6, 27–29 June 2013

10. Wei, S., Guan, W., Liu, K.J.R.: Outage probability optimization with equal and unequal transmission rates under energy harvesting constraints. In: Global Communications Conference, GLOBECOM 2013, pp. 2520–2525. IEEE, 9–13 December 2013

11. Seah, W.K.G., Eu, Z.A., Tan, H.: Wireless sensor networks powered by ambient energy harvesting (WSN-HEAP) - survey and challenges. In: 1st International Conference on Wireless Communication, Vehicular Technology, Information Theory and Aerospace & Electronic Systems Technology, Wireless VITAE 2009, pp. 1–5, 17–20 May 2009

12. Yang, J., Ulukus, S.: Transmission completion time minimization in an energy harvesting system. In: 2010 44th Annual Conference on Information Sciences and Systems (CISS), pp. 1–6, 17–19 March 2010

13. Boyd, S., Vandenberghe, L.: Convex Optimization. Cambridge University Press, Cambridge (2004)

14. Bletsas, A., Khisti, A., Reed, D.P., Lippman, A.: A simple cooperative diversity method based on network path selection. IEEE J. Sel. Areas Commun. 24(3), 659–672 (2006)

15. Grant, M., Boyd, S., Ye, Y.: CVX: Matlab software for disciplined convex programming (2008)

Applications and Challenges of Life Cycle Assessment in the Context of a Green Sustainable Telco Cloud

Thomas Dandres[1]([⊠]), Reza Farrahi Moghaddam[2], Kim Nguyen[3],
Yves Lemieux[2], Mohamed Cheriet[3], and Réjean Samson[1]

[1] CIRAIG - Polytechnique Montréal, Université de Montréal, Montreal, Canada
thomas.dandres@polymtl.ca
[2] Ericsson Canada Inc., Montreal, Canada
[3] Synchromedia - École de Technologie Supérieure,
Université du Québec, Montreal, Canada

Abstract. An LCA was conducted on a novel Telco-grade cloud technology. Server cloudification has been found to significantly reduce the environmental life cycle impacts as compared to a non-cloud situation. Improving service quality is possible without drastically increasing the life cycle impacts as compared to the non-cloud situation. In this LCA, a novel methodology was used to model electricity flows during ICT use to better reflect the temporal variation in electricity generation by utilities and electricity consumption by ICT. Nevertheless, numerous methodological challenges remain unresolved and more research is required to improve the LCA methodological framework for ICT.

Keywords: Information and communication technologies · ICT · Cloud computing · Life cycle assessment · LCA

1 Introduction: ICT and the Environment

Information and communication technologies (ICT) are pervasive in our society and are often perceived as contributing to our increased overall efficiency in terms of time, money and energy [1–3]. So far, most of the attention has been focused on ICT electricity consumption during use [4–7]. While it is estimated that the global electricity consumption by ICT is constantly rising [4, 8–10], ICT use is expected to slow the increase in future energy demands and thus moderate the emission of greenhouse gases (GHGs) [11, 12]. Nevertheless, electricity consumption by ICT during the use phase is not the only issue. Indeed, the ICT life cycle involves raw materials extraction, manufacturing, handling and shipping of ICT equipment and end-of-life electronic waste management. Moreover, the environmental impacts are not limited to GHG emissions. While climate change is an important issue, resource depletion, ecosystem quality, biodiversity and human health should not be disregarded when evaluating the environmental impacts of ICT. All of these indicators may be taken into account using life cycle assessment methodology (LCA) [13]. Some LCA studies on ICT have revealed that ICT manufacturing generates more impacts than ICT use [14, 15] —or at

© ICST Institute for Computer Sciences, Social Informatics and Telecommunications Engineering 2016
A. Leon-Garcia et al. (Eds.): Smart City 2015, LNICST 166, pp. 227–238, 2016.
DOI: 10.1007/978-3-319-33681-7_19

least represents a significant part of the life cycle impacts [16, 17]. LCA is also used to compare ICT systems and conventional options that provide the same function [18–21]. In these comparisons, reductions in GHG emissions and energy consumption may be achieved with ICT in certain contexts, depending on sensitive parameters including the number of ICT devices considered, the frequency of ICT use, transport distances and the energy mix. However, ICT may cause more metal depletion than conventional technologies [14], thus confirming that the life cycle approach constitutes a relevant method to evaluate ICT. Still, few LCAs have been conducted in the ICT sector and there are many methodological challenges [22], including electricity flow modeling. The issue is addressed in this paper by applying a recent methodological development in LCA to evaluate a new Telco-grade cloud technology.

2 Method

2.1 Life Cycle Assessment

The LCA method has been harmonized in the ISO 14040-44:2006 standard series. It consists in four steps: (1) the goal and scope to define key LCA parameters (e.g. system boundaries, functional unit.); (2) the inventory, which aims to establish the list of all substances extracted and emitted from and to the environment; (3) the environmental impact assessment based on the inventory results and according to several environmental indicators and (4) the interpretation of the LCA results (e.g. contribution and sensitivity analysis, uncertainty assessment and management).

2.2 The Green Sustainable Telco Cloud

The Green Sustainable Telco Cloud (GSTC) is a project led by Professor Mohamed Cheriet at École de technologie supérieure (Université du Québec, Canada) and supported by Ericsson, the Natural Sciences and Engineering Research Council of Canada (NSERC) and the Prompt Consortium (www.promptinc.org) through the Equation Initiative (www.equationict.com), in collaboration with the University of Toronto and Polytechnique Montréal (Université de Montréal). As part of this project, an innovative Telco-grade cloud technology was developed to minimize cloud computing impacts on the environment (see www.synchromedia.ca/node/870 for more information). The principle of the GSTC is to move software applications to the cloud instead of using them directly on the servers: virtual machines are installed on the servers and software applications are then run by the virtual machines.

2.3 Scenarios

In this paper, the deployment of the GSTC is investigated at the Canadian scale. It is supposed that the GSTC technology is installed in three data centres located in the Canadian provinces of Alberta, Ontario and Québec. These regions were chosen for their differences in electricity generation. The energy mix in Alberta is mainly fossil fuel (coal and natural gas) while Ontario is more balanced (nuclear power, fossil fuel (natural gas) and renewable energy (hydropower)) and Québec uses mainly renewable energy (hydropower). Indeed, it is relevant to present the new LCA developments in electricity flow modeling in the context of different mixes. Moreover, the three provincial ICT sectors contribute the most to the gross domestic product of the national ICT sector [23].

In this scenario, the GSTC hosts an instant messaging service (IMS) with three million users. It is assumed that there are one million users in each region and that every user uses the service ten times a day. It is also assumed that the global use of the service during the day is in line with web browsing activity statistics [24], yielding time-dependent service usage during the day (Fig. 1). For the purpose of the calculations, the scenario is modeled for 2011, 2012 and 2013.

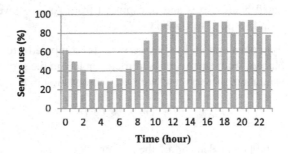

Fig. 1. Service use by time of day

Two types of GSTC configurations are evaluated. In the first case, the GSTC is installed on a single server in each region (scenario 1). In the second case, the GSTC is installed on two servers in each region with the server load equally dispatched between them (scenario 2). The purpose of scenarios 1 and 2 is to evaluate the environmental impacts to enhance the quality of the GSTC service. Finally, a third case is considered: a server running IMS without GSTC technology (reference scenario). This third case is used to assess the benefits and downsides of the GSTC technology as compared to a more conventional technology. In all cases, the servers are Ericsson blade systems (EBS).

2.4   LCA of GSTC

Goal and scope

The purpose of this LCA is to compare different server configurations used to provide an ICT service. Therefore, similar parts of the different life cycles can be excluded from the study. Concretely, this LCA focuses on the servers since the user data transmission and end-user devices are the same in the three scenarios. Data transmission by server synchronization in scenario 2 is included in the system. The functional unit in this LCA is *to provide an IMS service to three million users (locations and user behaviours defined in the scenarios) from 2011 to 2013*. Unlike standard LCAs, the data used to model electricity flows are regionalized and temporally disaggregated to better reflect the reality of electricity generation. Indeed, electricity modeling has been reported as very sensitive in terms of ICT LCA results [15, 25, 26].

Inventory

Manufacturing, handling and shipping. The ecoinvent database [27] is used to model the manufacturing of ICT equipment. Table 1 presents the ecoinvent processes used to model the EBS. For confidentiality reasons, the data used to model the manufacturing phase are not provided. The ecoinvent processes corresponding to the global, China and the rest of world region (GLO, CN and RoW in Table 1 in the Appendix[1]) were selected to prevent the implicit assumption made by ecoinvent that ICT equipment is specifically manufactured in Europe. However, it would be better to use processes corresponding to the Asian region, where the electronic components are expected to be manufactured. In the model, after manufacturing, the electronic components are packaged in corrugated board boxes and transported from Asia to Sweden. Then, the EBS are assembled and shipped to Canada.

Use. The electricity consumption by the servers is computed from an empirical equation (Eq. 1) obtained from energy measurements made on the server while running IMS with different numbers of users and with or without the GSTC [28].

$$P_{server} = P_0 + m \times \% \ CPU. \tag{1}$$

- Where P_{server} is the power demand of the server (W)
- P_0 the power demand of the server (W) when no CPU is used
- m is an empirical constant (W)
- $\%CPU$ is the load of the CPU that depends on the number of users requesting an IMS connection (Rh) and the server capacity to process requests (C_X or C_{GSTC}, see Eq. 3). A load greater than 100 % means more than one CPU is used.

Rh is obtained from Eq. 2:

$$R_h = \frac{N \times D \times L_h}{\sum_{h=1}^{24} L_h}. \tag{2}$$

- Where N is the number of user per server (N = 1,000,000 users)
- D is the number of connection per day per user (D = 10 connections)
- L_h is the service load (%) at hour h (L_h is presented on Fig. 1)
- C_X and C_{GSTC} are empirical constants (%) related to the CPU load and measured while submitting different numbers of requests for IMS connections to the server with GSTC installed (C_{GSTC}) and without (C_X). Then $\%CPU$ can be calculated from Eq. 3:

---

[1] https://dl.dropboxusercontent.com/u/92014052/appendix.pdf.

$$\% \ CPU = R_h \times C_i. \tag{3}$$

Where C_i is C_{GSTC} (scenarios 1 and 2) or C_X (reference scenario).
Finally, Eq. 4 represents the server power demand ($P_{server}(h)$) at hour h:

$$P_{server}(h) = P_0 + m \times \frac{N \times D \times L_h}{\sum_{h=1}^{24} L_h} \times C_i \tag{4}$$

The method developed by Maurice et al. [29] is used to model electricity generation. Historical data are collected from AESO [30] and IESO [31] to model hourly electricity generation in Alberta and Ontario for 2011, 2012 and 2013. Since public historical data on electricity generation in Québec are aggregated at the month level [32], the model developed by Maurice [33] was used to extrapolate hourly electricity generation in Québec. Then, the hourly energy mixes computed using ecoinvent (version 3) processes (see Table 2 in the Appendix) are used to model the impacts of electricity consumption by the server (as presented hereafter, an allocation factor is applied on the term P0).

In scenario 2, the two servers are synchronized. Based on expert assessment, it is estimated that 1 % of the 2 GB server database of IMS users is updated every day. Assuming the synchronization is made every ten minutes, 0.83 MB must be transmitted every hour between the two servers. Then, the value of 2.7 × 10-5 kWh/Gb [34] was used to compute the electricity consumed by data transmission for synchronization.

End of life. As for the manufacturing phase, the modeling of the end of life of the ICT equipment is carried out with ecoinvent. Global region processes were chosen. While the electronic waste is considered to be managed in North America and emerging countries, the global modeling in ecoinvent does not make it possible to assume that the processes occur exclusively in Europe. Moberg et al., who considered Sweden and China for the end of life of mobile phones [15], used a similar approach. The end of life modeling consists in ICT equipment dismantling and recycling (the mass of recycled materials was computed with a model developed by Hischier [35]). Then, an environmental credit (computed in ecoinvent) is given to the recycled materials assuming an equivalent amount of primary production of these materials is avoided. The service life of an EBS is supposed to be five years (based on expert assessment).

Allocation. Different services share some of the ICT equipment considered in the studied systems. Therefore, allocation factors are computed to attribute the environmental impacts of the equipment to each service based on the approach proposed by Vandromme et al. [36].

Server use: The server has several CPU that may be used independently when the GSTC technology is installed on the server. Thus, the base-load electricity consumption (P0) must be allocated between the different services provided by the server. The allocation assumes an average CPU load of 70 % for CPU not used by IMS. Thus, the allocation factor for P0 is provided by Eq. 5:

$$f(h) = \frac{Number\ of\ CPU\ used\ for\ IMS\ at\ hour\ h}{70\% \ \times\ Number\ of\ CPU\ on\ a\ server} \tag{5}$$

In the reference scenario, the server is entirely dedicated to IMS and P0 is not allocated between different services.

Server manufacturing and end of life: An EBS hosts several servers but only one is used to provide IMS in every scenario. In scenarios 1 and 2 (GSTC installed), the allocation is based on the average number of CPU used by IMS during the entire use phase (Eq. 6). In the reference scenario, the allocation is based on the total number of CPU in a server since they are all dedicated to IMS (Eq. 7). In both cases, it is assumed that the remaining CPU of the EBS have an average CPU load of 70 %.

$$f_{GSTC} = \frac{Average\ number\ of\ CPU\ used\ for\ IMS}{70\% \ \times\ Number\ of\ CPU\ of\ the\ EBS} \tag{6}$$

$$f_X = \frac{Number\ of\ CPU\ on\ a\ server}{70\% \ \times\ Number\ of\ CPU\ of\ the\ EBS} \tag{7}$$

Impact assessment method

Impacts were computed using the Simapro (version 8) LCA software [37] and several impact assessment methods in order to include all the environmental indicators recommended by the European Telecommunications Standards Institute [38] and the International Telecommunication Union [39] for ICT studies. The environmental indicators and the corresponding impact assessment methods are listed in Table 3 in the Appendix.

3 Results

Figure 2 presents the GHG life cycle emissions of each scenario. It appears that the GSTC technology leads to a significant reduction in emissions as compared to the reference scenario. This observation is also made for all the other environmental indicators (not shown in Fig. 2). The explanation is that cloud computing (scenarios 1 and 2) makes it possible to use servers for more tasks than in the non-computing situation (reference scenario). Therefore, impacts related to the manufacturing and use of the servers are shared between more services, making the life cycle impacts of IMS lower in the cloud computing situation than in the non-cloud computing situation. It is also observed that, in the cases of Ontario and Alberta, the use phase contributes the most to the server life cycle impacts. In the case of Québec, ICT equipment manufacturing is the main contributor to the servers' life cycle impacts. This result is due to the difference in energy mixes: electricity generation in Ontario (balanced mix) and Alberta (fossil mix) are far more polluting than in Québec (hydro mix) for most environmental indicators. Handling, shipping and end of life contribute minimally to the life cycle impacts in all scenarios for most of the environmental indicators. As expected, the manufacturing phase has significant impacts on the natural resources indicators (mineral resources extraction, land use and water use). The environmental benefits of precious metal recycling appear negligible as compared to the other life cycle impacts of the servers. This may be explained by the weaknesses of the mineral resource indicator in LCA (see Discussion section).

Figure 2 also shows that adding a second server (scenario 2) to improve the quality of service does not significantly impact the life cycle GHG emissions. Indeed, emissions increase by less than 10 % when a second server is added. This result is also observed for other environmental indicators with a similar increase in impacts. These findings are in line with previous GSTC technology assessments in other contexts [29, 33, 36, 40–43].

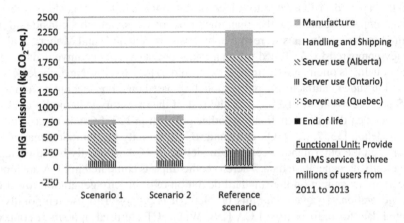

Fig. 2. Comparison of GHG life cycle emissions

4 Discussion

Conducting an LCA on ICT presents many challenges at each methodological step [22, 26]. In terms of the goal and scope, the system borders may be difficult to establish since ICT may provide several different functions. ISO standards recommend avoiding multi-functional process impact allocation by system expansion. In the case of ICT, all of these functions must therefore be included within the system borders. In this study, impact allocation was chosen instead of system expansion because it would have considerably complicated the LCA if the hundreds (if not thousands) of services that may be provided by an EBS were included in the scope of the study. A system expansion would have been better in theory but, from a practical perspective, it may be suitable to do an allocation based on the capacity of the EBS to provide simultaneous services (i.e. an allocation based on the number of CPU used by IMS). The definition of the functional unit may also create an issue in LCA because the impacts attributed to a function provided by an ICT are often strongly related to ICT user behaviours [26], meaning that user behaviours should be included in the functional unit to prevent comparison of LCAs of a same function with different user behaviours. Still, the geographic context and the year of study should also be considered when comparing ICT LCAs.

The life cycle inventory of ICT is problematic due to the lack of accurate data to represent the technologies. Indeed, confidentiality reasons usually prevent LCA practitioners from obtaining specific data from ICT manufacturers. Moreover, even when data is released, the significant number of components made by different electronic manufacturers in a single ICT device makes the ICT data collection for LCA complex. For this reason, few ICT LCAs use manufacturer data and there are very few ICT data in LCA databases [44]. In this study, we used ecoinvent data, which are assumed to be of good quality. However, they are not expected to exactly describe the EBS. Indeed, rapid technological innovation in the ICT sector makes the inventory data obsolete within a couple of years [26, 45]. Also, the manufacturing of ICT equipment involves high purity materials that are known to have major environmental impacts that may not be systematically captured in LCA due to a lack of data [46]. Thus, in this study, the environmental impacts related to the manufacturing phase should be considered very uncertain. Similar conclusions were drawn by Hischier et al. [14] and Moberg et al. [15] when they compared LCAs based on manufacturer data versus ecoinvent data. However, data quality is often an issue in ICT LCA studies [45, 47–49]. Nevertheless, future works will include manufacturing phase modeling based on more specific data to model the EBS and ecoinvent will be used for the rest of the inventory. Malmodin et al. [50] recommend such data combinations. Another problem in ICT LCA is electricity generation modeling [15, 25, 26]. On one hand, ICT electricity consumption may vary in time while, on the other hand, electricity modeling in LCA is usually based on annual average electricity generation data. Therefore, the impacts computed in LCA are more or less uncertain depending on the standard deviation of electricity generation toward the average generation. To overcome this problem, it is proposed to use temporally disaggregated data for retrospective LCA [29]. When ICT are used in a smart context to minimize emissions in real-time, the real-time electric grid is usually considered. However, since the smart management of ICT causes changes in local power demand, the marginal sources of electricity affected by these changes should also be considered. A predictive method based on historical electricity generation data was developed for this purpose and is recommended for the real-time optimization of ICT [42].

As previously mentioned, user behaviours are often reported to be very sensitive in ICT LCA. While it is easy to create a scenario that represents a user behaviour, it is more difficult to make it fit with actual user behaviours. For this reason, ICT LCAs should be seen more as *what if* scenarios rather than *reality* scenarios. The problem of modeling user behaviours may especially occur when a large-scale ICT deployment is evaluated. Indeed, in this situation, all user behaviours should be reflected in the study (assuming the scale is extensive enough to involve all users). Otherwise, the study may diverge from the real potential environmental impacts. One aspect of user behaviours that is known to be problematic in modeling is the rebound effect of ICT use [51–53]. In this study, the user behaviours were characterized only by web browsing activity statistics. The IMS use that would replace other equivalent functions was not evaluated. Since this substitution may be expected to be the same in all scenarios, its omission should not affect the results of the comparison. However, it could be argued that the improved quality of service in scenario 2 would make IMS more competitive with other equivalent services. In that case, the substituted services should be included in the scope of the study. Furthermore, assuming IMS is increasingly used, it would be relevant to evaluate whether IMS is used as an extra service or as a substitute for another service (e.g. cellular telephone conversation or face-to-face meeting). Introducing psychological parameters characterizing the users could improve the accuracy of user behaviour modeling in ICT LCAs. The modeling of the end of life of ICT is challenging in LCA. First, the real outcome for ICT equipment is unclear. The rate of recycling and the mode of recycling (manual or mechanical) are poorly documented. This is partially due to the shipping of electronic waste to emerging countries, where the recycling of valuable products is usually carried out by informal organizations that do not report their activities. Moreover, it is not clear how the environmental credits attributed to recycling should be computed and shared between those providing the materials for recycling and those using recycled materials to manufacture the product [54, 55]. Also, the natural resource depletion indicators are not mature enough to properly represent the impacts of resource depletion [56]. Current methods underestimate the real impact on these indicators. Resolving these two methodological challenges in LCA could possibly increase the positive contribution of electronic waste recycling in ICT studies.

5 Conclusion

LCA constitutes an efficient framework to evaluate the environmental impacts of products and services and was used to study the environmental performance of a new Telco-grade cloud technology. The results clearly demonstrate that server virtualization enhances energy efficiency and multitasking, leading to less significant environmental life cycle impacts as compared to non-virtualized servers. However, conducting LCAs on ICT is challenging due their specificities. The definition of the studied ICT system, the allocation of the impacts of multifunctional equipment, the lack of inventory data and ICT user behaviour modeling remain important issues in ICT LCA. Nevertheless, an increasing number of LCAs are addressing ICT and methodological issues are progressively pinpointed and resolved. In this paper, a new method to model electricity flows during the ICT use phase makes it possible to account for both the geographic and the temporal contexts of ICT electricity consumption.

Acknowledgements. The authors would like to thank NSERC for its financial support under grant CRDPJ 424371-11.

References

1. Bertolini, M., et al.: Lead time reduction through ICT application in the footwear industry: A case study. Int. J. Prod. Econ. **110**(1–2), 198–212 (2007)
2. Gabberty, J.: Management of the productivity of information and communications technology (ICT) in the financial services industry. In: Computational Finance computational Finance and its Applications I and its Applications II: p. 13 (2006)
3. Guerrisi, A., Martino, M., Tartaglia, M.: Energy saving in social housing: an innovative ICT service to improve the occupant behaviour. In: 2012 International Conference on Renewable Energy Research and Applications (ICRERA) (2012)

4. Van Heddeghem, W., et al.: Trends in worldwide ICT electricity consumption from 2007 to 2012. Comput. Commun. **50**, 64–76 (2014)
5. Collard, F., Fève, P., Portier, F.: Electricity consumption and ICT in the French service sector. Energy Econ. **27**(3), 541–550 (2005)
6. Malmodin, J., et al.: Greenhouse gas emissions and operational electricity use in the ICT and entertainment & media sectors. J. Industr. Ecol. **14**(5), 770–790 (2010)
7. Koomey, J.G.: Growth in data centre electricity use 2005 to 2010, pp. 1–24 (2011)
8. Ryen, E.G., Babbitt, C.W., Williams, E.: Consumption-weighted life cycle assessment of a consumer electronic product community. Environ. Sci. Technol. **49**(4), 2549–2559 (2015)
9. Lannoo, B., et al.: Overview of ICT energy consumption. In: Network of Excellence in Internet Science, pp. 1–59 (2013)
10. United States Environmental Protection Agency: Report to Congress on Server and Data Center Energy Efficiency, pp. 1–133 (2007)
11. Thomond, P.: The enabling technologies of a low-carbon economy: a focus on cloud computing. In: GeSI, Microsoft, Johns Hopkins University, think play do, pp. 1–112 (2013)
12. Global e-Sustainability Initiative and The Boston Consuting Group, GeSI SMARTer 2020, Global eSustainability Initiative, pp. 1–87 (2012)
13. Guinée, J.B., et al.: Life cycle assessment: past, present, and future. Environ. Sci. Technol. **45**(1), 90–96 (2011)
14. Hischier, R., Achachlouei, M.A., Hilty, L.M.: Evaluating the sustainability of electronic media: strategies for life cycle inventory data collection and their implications for LCA results. Environ. Model. Softw. **56**, 27–36 (2014)
15. Moberg, Å., et al.: Simplifying a life cycle assessment of a mobile phone. Int. J. Life Cycle Assess. **19**(5), 979–993 (2014)
16. Meza, J., et al.: Lifecycle-based data center design. In: ASME 2010 International Mechanical Engineering Congress & Exposition. Vancouver, British Columbia, Canada (2010)
17. Honee, C., et al.: Environmental performance of data centres - a case study of the Swedish National Insurance Administration. In: Electronics Goes Green 2012 + (EGG), 2012 (2012)
18. Borggren, C., et al.: Business meetings at a distance – decreasing greenhouse gas emissions and cumulative energy demand? J. Cleaner Prod. **41**, 126–139 (2013)
19. Borggren, C., Moberg, Å., Finnveden, G.: Books from an environmental perspective—Part 1: environmental impacts of paper books sold in traditional and internet bookshops. Int. J. Life Cycle Assess. **16**(2), 138–147 (2011)
20. Moberg, Å., Borggren, C., Finnveden, G.: Books from an environmental perspective—Part 2: e-books as an alternative to paper books. Int. J. Life Cycle Assess. **16**(3), 238–246 (2011)
21. Moberg, Å., et al., Effects of a total change from paper invoicing to electronic invoicing in Sweden (2008)
22. Bull, J.G., Kozak, R.A.: Comparative life cycle assessments: the case of paper and digital media. Environ. Impact Assess. Rev. **45**, 10–18 (2014)
23. Statistics Canada: Provincial gross domestic product (GDP) at basic prices, by sector and industry. In: CANSIM (ed.) (2011)
24. Chitika: 24-Hour Examination: Average Mobile and Desktop Usage Rates (2013)
25. Guldbrandsson, F., Bergmark, P.: Opportunities and limitations of using life cycle assessment methodology in the ICT sector. In: Electronics Goes Green 2012 + (EGG), (2012)
26. Arushanyan, Y., Ekener-Petersen, E., Finnveden, G.: Lessons learned – Review of LCAs for ICT products and services. Comput. Ind. **65**(2), 211–234 (2014)
27. ecoinvent Center: Ecoinvent Data - the Life Cycle Inventory Data. Swiss Centre for Life Cycle Inventories, Dübendorf (2007)

28. Farrahi Moghaddam, F.: Carbon metering and effective tax cost modeling for virtual machines (2012)
29. Maurice, E., et al.: Modelling of electricity mix in temporal differentiated life-cycle-assessment to minimize carbon footprint of a cloud computing service. In: ICT4S, Stockholm, Sweden (2014)
30. AESO: Market participant information - Data Requests (2012). http://www.aeso.ca/downloads/Hourly_Generation_by_Fuel.pdf
31. IESO: Generator Output and Capability (2012) cited 2012. http://reports.ieso.ca/public/GenOutputCapability/
32. Government of Canada: Energy Information - Statistics and Analysis (2012). [cited 2013]. http://www.neb-one.gc.ca/nrg/sttstc/index-eng.html
33. Maurice, E.: Modélisation temporelle de la consommation électrique en analyse du cycle de vie, appliquée au contexte des TIC. In: Département de Génie Chimique, Université de Montréal: Montreal, pp. 1–268 (2015)
34. Van Heddeghem, W., et al.: Distributed computing for carbon footprint reduction by exploiting low-footprint energy availability. Future Gener. Comput. Syst. 28(2), 405–414 (2012)
35. Hischier, R.: Composition-Tool-electronics. In: Dandres, T. (ed.) (2014)
36. Vandromme, N., et al.: Life cycle assessment of videoconferencing with call management servers relying on virtualization. In: ICT4S. Stockholm, Sweden (2014)
37. Pre Consultants: SimaPro. Pre Consultants, Amersfoort (2007)
38. European Telecommunications Standards Institute: ETSI TS 103 199 V1.1.1. In: Technical Specification, pp. 1–155 (2011)
39. International Telecommunication Union: Recommendation ITU-T L.1400. In: Telecommunication Standardization Sector for ITU, pp. 1–30 (2011)
40. Vandromme, N.: Modélisation conséquentielle de la consommation d'énergie d'un groupe de servers générant un nuage informatique et attributionnelle des bénéfices de la virtualisation. In: Département de génie chimique, Université de Montréal: Montréal, pp. 1–210 (2014)
41. Dandres, T., et al.: Minimization of Telco cloud emissions based on marginal electricity management. In: ICT4S: Stockholm, Sweden (2014)
42. Dandres, T., et al.: Consideration of marginal electricity in real-time minimization of telco cloud emissions. J. Ind. Ecol. (2015, in preparation)
43. Dandres, T., et al.: Consequences of future data centre deployment on North American electricity generation and environmental impacts: a 2015–2030 prospective study. J. Cleaner Prod. (2015, in preparation)
44. Okrasinski, T., Malian, J., Arnold, J.: Data assessment and collection for a simplified LCA tool. In: Carbon Management Technology Conference (2012)
45. Yao, M.A., et al.: Comparative assessment of life cycle assessment methods used for personal computers. Environ. Sci. Technol. 44(19), 7335–7346 (2010)
46. Higgs, T., et al.: Review of LCA methods for ICT products and the impact of high purity and high cost materials. In: 2010 IEEE International Symposium on Sustainable Systems and Technology (ISSST) (2010)
47. Farrant, L., Le Guern, Y.: Which environmental impacts for ICT? - LCA case study on electronic mail. In: Electronics Goes Green 2012 + (EGG), 2012 (2012)
48. Blazek, M., et al.: Tale of two cities: environmental life cycle assessment for telecommunications systems: Stockholm, Sweden and Sacramento, CA. In: Proceedings of the 1999 IEEE International Symposium on Electronics and the Environment, 1999. ISEE - 1999 (1999)

49. Guldbrandsson, F., Malmodin, J.: Life cycle assessment of virtual meeting solutions. In: EcoBalance 2010, Tokyo, Japan (2010)
50. Malmodin, J., et al.: Methodology for life cycle based assessments of the CO < inf > 2</inf > reduction potential of ICT services. In: 2010 IEEE International Symposium on Sustainable Systems and Technology (ISSST) (2010)
51. Ichino Takahashi, K., et al.: Estimation of videoconference performance: approach for fairer comparative environmental evaluation of ICT services. In: Proceedings of the 2006 IEEE International Symposium on Electronics and the Environment (2006)
52. Takahashi, K.I., et al.: Environmental impact of information and communication technologies including rebound effects. In: 2004 IEEE International Symposium on Electronics and the Environment, 2004. Conference Record (2004)
53. Takahashi, K.I., et al.: Environmental assessment of e-Learning based on a customer survey. In: Fourth International Symposium on Environmentally Conscious Design and Inverse Manufacturing, 2005. Eco Design 2005 (2005)
54. Lee, K.-M., Park, P.-J.: Estimation of the environmental credit for the recycling of granulated blast furnace slag based on LCA. Res. Conserv. Recycl. **44**(2), 139–151 (2005)
55. Frees, N.: Crediting aluminium recycling in LCA by demand or by disposal. Int. J. Life Cycle Assess. **13**(3), 212–218 (2008)
56. Wolf, M.-A., et al.: The International Reference Life Cycle Data System (ILCD) Handbook - Towards More Sustainable Production and Consumption for a Resource-Efficient Europe, pp. 1–72. 2012

M2M Middleware Based on OpenMTC Platform for Enabling Smart Cities Solution

Maman Abdurohman[1](✉), Arif Sasongko[2], and Anton Herutomo[1]

[1] School of Computing (SoC), Telkom University, Bandung 40257, Indonesia
m_abdurohman@yahoo.com, anton.herutomo@gmail.com
[2] School of Electrical and Informatics Engineering,
Bandung Institute of Technology, Bandung, Indonesia
asasongko@gmail.com

Abstract. M2M middleware is needed to avoid silo systems on smart city solutions. The middleware serves as an enabler for the basic process of communication between machines based on the machine type communication. This paper proposes OpenMTC platform as M2M middleware solutions for smart cities. OpenMTC is a platform that communicate data between machine-server-machine without human intervention. Some solutions are implemented on OpenMTC platform such as mobile tracking, early warning of forest fires and water pollutant monitoring systems. The result shows that OpenMTC, empirically, has capability as reliable M2M-Middleware for some smart cities applications.

Keywords: M2M · Middleware · OpenMTC · Smart city

1 Introduction

The era of human-to-human communication may soon decreased and be replaced with machine-to-machine communication. This phenomenon occurs in line with the increasing role of machines in a variety of applications that can not be done manually by humans. BTS information control process, temperature control container, tracking, are some applications that require the involvement of the machine for efficiency.

The sensor has an important role in collecting information from the environment. Through a variety of networks such as wireline and wireless, information collected from the environment to the server for further processing. Data obtained from the sensor can be used for decision making as activates particular actuator or sent to the user as information.

Technology changes the way people view the environment. Smart city is a new concept that is becoming a trend nowadays. This viewpoint is supported by many researchers from the ICT sector, in particular, the infrastructure sector Next Generation Network (NGNI), the Internet of Things (IOT) and Future Internet (FI). This development is supported also by the international standardization body in M2M communication domain, such as: (i) European Telecommunications Standards Institute (ETSI) TC M2M [1–3] on middleware. (ii) 3rd Generation Partnership Project (3GPP) [4] on Machine Type Communication (MTC). (iii) The Telecommunications Industry Association (TIA) [5] established the TR-50.1 Smart. (iv) oneM2M, a consortium of the development of standards to improve the ability of M2M solutions [6].

© ICST Institute for Computer Sciences, Social Informatics and Telecommunications Engineering 2016
A. Leon-Garcia et al. (Eds.): Smart City 2015, LNICST 166, pp. 239–249, 2016.
DOI: 10.1007/978-3-319-33681-7_20

Fraunhofer FOKUS has developed Open Type Machine Communication (OpenMTC) platform based on the ETSI standard [7]. This platform serves as a standard-oriented middleware for M2M applications and services oriented to facilitate research and development of M2M systems [9]. One advantage OpenMTC platform is the availability of a standard application programming interface (API) to access data and information. There are many research and implementation of OpenMTC platform in the real world [8, 9, 11–13].

Smart cities has no definite concept. In terms of information and communication, smart cities can be seen as ICT infrastructure of the city. A town called smart city characterized by an intelligent ICT infrastructure that can improve the control efficiency compared to the manual process. The city's air pollution control, fire control and tracking of vehicles are some examples of processes those would be more efficient by using an intelligent ICT infrastructure such as M2M communication.

Other issues in the smart cities are smart community development and urban planning in favor of nature. Nature is a finite resource that needs to be managed intelligently to sustain support society needs.

There are several stakeholders involved in the development of smart city those are academic, business, community and government. Each stakeholders have important role in developing smart city system.

This paper discusses the role of academic and technology as an enabler to realize smart city environment in terms of M2M communication. M2M communication has a fundamental role to realize the intelligent infrastructure related to the communication between devices. In the smart city there are a lot of devices that communicate each other without human involvement.

OpenMTC platforms need to be tested for implementing different M2M applications with topics related to smart city solution to test the reliability of middleware as M2M communication backbone in smart city.

2   OpenMTC Platform for Smart Cities

Smart City currently widely discussed as a standard concept and also implementation. Smart City definition refers to behavior of a region where some processes of activity are done automatically through communication machine-server-machine without human intervention [9]. M2M communication becomes key enabler to deploy smart city solutions [7, 10]. M2M is a concept that is already designed and standardize by several standard communities, such as ETSI standard for Europe region. This standard body defines M2M system specification as a standard reference for all developers of platform and application [6, 7, 10].

M2M communication has different traffic characteristics based on application needs and prioritization. A M2M platform is needed for enabling those different developments effectively [9–11]. OpenMTC is chosen as M2M platform because of its scalability and compatible with many kinds of sensor system. Figure 1 shows the OpenMTC platform architecture that is developed by Fraunhofer FOKUS based on ETSI M2M Rel. 1. [1–3]. The system is designed as a middleware platform by concerning a variety of sensors, actuators and data transmitter technologies in order to adjust to various use cases.

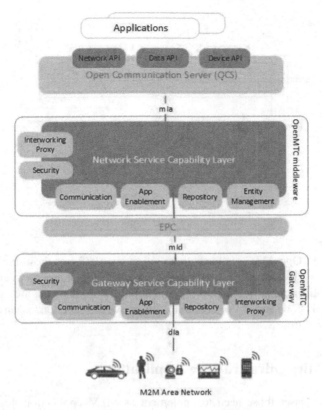

Fig. 1. OpenMTC platform architecture [10]

OpenMTC platform as a middleware has an ability for handling thousands of sensors and actuators rather than one M2M application [9]. The platform communicates various sensor, actuators and user application. OpenMTC Platform is divided into four parts namely M2M Network Area in which devices are located and connected through a variety of networks infrastructure such as Wire line, ZigBee, Wifi, GPRS and Bluetooth [9, 11]. The second is Gateway Service Capability Layer (GSCL) that connects between a Network Area where devices located and a server [9]. The third is Network Service Capability Layer (NSCL) were OpenMTC is implemented as a middleware platform to support user application. The fourth is user application domain [9–11].

OpenMTC platform is designed to be application agnostic, providing a middleware layer for M2M communications [9]. Figure 2 shows the message flow in OpenMTC platform that involves five parts of system namely: devices, sensors, gateway, OpenMTC server and user application. Sensors and devices connect to the system through gateway. Gateway informs OpenMTC server all devices and sensors those connect to the system. Once user applications register and search for devices, OpenMTC server will send all available devices list to them. User applications can choose one of many sensors needed to the gateway. While gateway accepts data from suitable sensors, it will sent notification data directly to application. The user application can send trigger data to actuator device to do something.

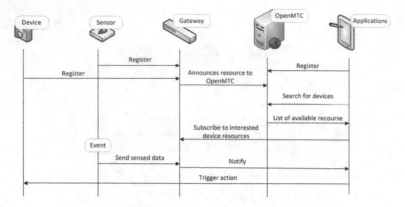

Fig. 2. Message flow of a simple scenario [10]

In addition to OpenMTC platform, there are many platforms those implemented as commercial goods like Axeda. In general both have the same function as an enabler for smart city application as a middleware. In detail both platform are incomparable because OpenMTC designed for laboratory and university version, meanwhile Axeda for commercial purpose.

3   Smart Cities Infrastructure Applications

There are many cases those need to implement as M2M application, four among of many applications are mobile tracking, nature pneumatic pressure monitoring, early warning of forest fires and water pollutant monitoring systems. All application connect to OpenMTC platform using various communication technologies. Those application have been implemented and tested based on OpenMTC platform.

3.1   Mobile Tracking System

First application is mobile tracking system. Figure 3 shows message flow of this application from sensor to gateway, OpenMTC server, and application. Sensors of mobile tracking located on vehicular will register to GSCL gateway and then GSCL will send these data to OpenMTC NSCL. The user application, map application, can search the devices that connected to OpenMTC GSCL [9].

The core server will send information of resources availability that meet the search criteria [9]. The user application sends a request to the GSCL to access required information from the available resource, or subscribe to them, and get notification when sensor data is received by gateway [9]. Sensors send position and time data to gateway. Gateway notifies sensor positions and time to application.

On sensor side, there is one device that collect raw data from sensors and send it the gateway. Figure 4 shows the mobile tracking module that connect to GPS module and GSM module. Mobile tracking system module consists of hardware and software parts.

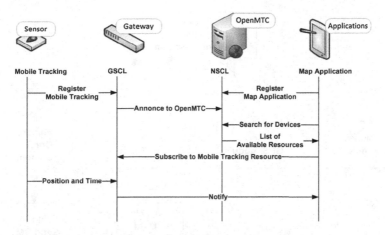

Fig. 3. Message flow of mobile tracking system [9, 11]

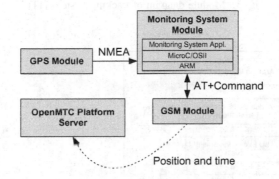

Fig. 4. Mobile tracking module [9, 11]

The microprocessor used in this mobile device is ARM microprocessor with MicroC OS/II-operating system and monitoring application [9]. Figure 5 shows the software modules of tracking system such as GSM and GPS modules, SMS timer, and data processing and SMS sending modules.

GPS module will send longitude, latitude and time data to monitoring system device periodically. Device will send those data to server gateway periodically regarding SMS Timer. Gateway notifies map application and data will showed in the map application that can be accessed by any devices.

3.2 Early Warning Forest Fire System

Early warning forest fire system is a system that monitor and control to avoid forest fire. This system connects many sensors in the forest to monitoring application (Fig. 6) [12].

The system divided into three parts, namely Device app, OpenMTC platforms, and devices other app that allows you to display the data. Device app is a set of sensor networks and gateways are connected to GSCL [12].

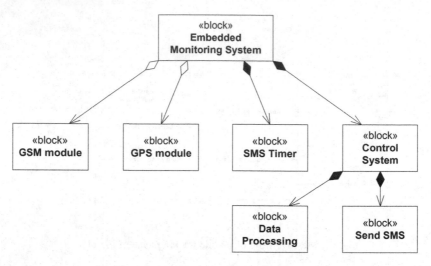

Fig. 5. Module diagram of tracking system [11]

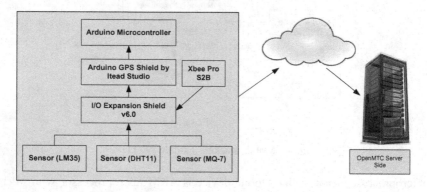

Fig. 6. Diagram of early warning of forest fires system [12]

The sensor network consists of several sensors, microcontrollers, XBee Pro S2B, GPS module, power supply, and I/O expansion shield [12]. The sensor is used to acquire the data early warning of forest fires surrounding environment is processed by the microcontroller and transmitted using XBee Pro S2B module to the gateway. Gateway on device app consists of modules XBee Pro S2B and a computer that acts as the coordinator node for receiving data to be entered into the application on the computer of the sensor device via a ZigBee network [12].

On the other side OpenMTC platform collect the information and send to early warning forest fire system. These information updated periodically regarding the need of user by configuring the timer parameter [12].

3.3   Air Pollution Control System

Air pollution Control System is a system that control number of pollution on the air. Air pollution detection system is divided into 4 parts: M2M Devices, M2M Gateway, M2M and M2M Application Server [13]. M2M Device is a combination device consisting of two sensors (PM and CO), microcontroller, power supply, XBee as an End Node, and Expansion Shield [13]. Expansion Shield is used to connect sensors and XBee with microcontroller (Fig. 7) [13].

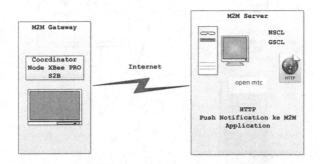

Fig. 7. Diagram of air pollution detection system [13]

M2M Gateway consists of Coordinator NodeXBee and computer. Data sent by the M2M Device through ZigBee networks [13]. The computer will perform the data conversion to XML format base64 to be received by the M2M Server. M2M Server consists of a computer equipped with M2M platform OpenMTC. Air pollution monitoring data into the server will be processed in order to be able to do a push notification to the M2M Application and displayed through the website.

4   Result and Analysis

These analysis to the experiment results have done for evaluating the reliability of OpenMTC as M2M platform on handling the various data coming from various sensors with different types of vendors and communication networks. OpenMTC gateway collects those data in the same way and compatible with various device standards (Fig. 8).

These analysis focusing on evaluation the final result of application on the top of OpenMTC platform those captured at user interface.

These experiments will show the empirical prove and analysis of implementation some application on the top of the OpenMTC platform. All experiments show OpenMTC performance for handling various data from various devices.

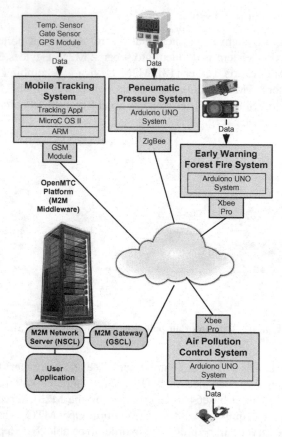

Fig. 8. OpenMTC - M2M middleware implementation

4.1 Mobile Tracking System

On a mobile tracking system: vehicle position obtained from the GPS module. This data is processed in order to obtain the position of the vehicle which is then sent via a GSM module to the server OpenMTC. The data accepted on server side consist of longitude and latitude position and also time stamp when the data captured.

Longitude and latitude position will get as coordinate of the vehicles. The data is displayed in the Google Map. Data taken periodically to show the tracking of vehicles time to time. Figure 9 shows the five points that show the vehicle position in Bandung City, Indonesia.

4.2 Early Warning Forest Fire System

In early forest fire system, the humidity sensor accuracy compared with hygrometer HTC-2 has a difference of ± 0.6435 %. This difference is still within the tolerance value that indicates measuring DHT11 sensor has worked well.

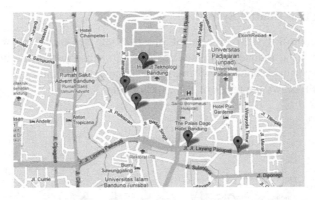

Fig. 9. Map of Mobile Tracking System [9, 11]

Accuracy of temperature sensor is shown by comparison of the infrared thermometer with low temperature difference between the results and the room temperature by 0.9 ° C. The temperature difference is within the tolerance limits indicated temperature sensor LM 35 has worked well.

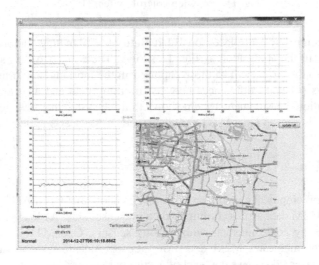

Fig. 10. Early warning forest fire system [12]

Figure 10 shows the result of early warning forest fire system that located on Kamojang forest, Garut, West Java, Indonesia. The sensors put on the tree regarding the safety position, quite high from the land. Monitoring system application will show the forest condition temperature to avoid the overheat temperature of the forest. Once overheat temperature captured by the system, this application will show in the application.

4.3   Air Pollution Control System

Air pollution control system experiment places some sensors in Buah Batu Area, Bandung, West Java, Indonesia. Those sensor set to sense in the morning and afternoon. Those experiment done many times to get the average values or constant condition. Figure 11 shows the result of the experiments.

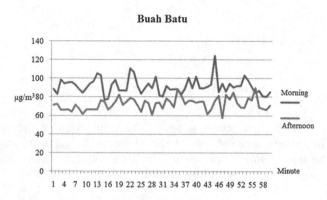

Fig. 11. Pollution control system [13]

Pollution control system placed on Buah Batu area, Bandung, Indonesia and the data will show in the application as Fig. 11 shows. There are two data shown in the user interface application, the data those captured in the morning and in the afternoon. The data shows constants differences between morning data and afternoon data. The results of pollution measurement system shows that the system has detected accurately pollution. Data is sent to OpenMTC and displayed in the user's application.

5   Conclusion

Based on several empirical experiments, the results show that OpenMTC platform can handle all the M2M data well according to data on sensor side. As long as experiments the server gateway could interacts with various sensors. OpenMTC can act as middleware that communicates M2M data from sensors side to user application. Data received on the user side shows the level of accuracy in accordance with the conditions on the ground. These experiments show the proven of OpenMTC as a platform that has good performance in handling the various data M2M. As a discussion, it needs to prove the robustness of OpenMTC platform regarding abundant of smart city data those should be collected from a lot of sensors in the city and communicate it to many user applications.

Acknowledgment. The Authors thank to Research and Public Service Bureau (Direktorat Penelitian dan Pengabdian Masyarakat) of Telkom University for providing and supporting the research financial by Riset Kemitraan scheme and also thank to Unified Communication Lab of

Telkom University, and ELKA Lab STEI – ITB those have supported financially and given sources in this study and also thanks to Alief Pascal Taruna, Muh. Adityawan Syah, Putut Andre, Sidik Prabowo and Ricky Henry Rawung who have helped us in implementing the system.

References

1. ETSI TS 102 689 V1.1.2: Machine-to-Machine communications (M2M); M2M service requirements (2011)
2. ETSI TS 102 690 v1.1.1: Machine-to-Machine communications (M2M); Functional architecture (2011)
3. ETSI TS 102 921 v1.1.1: Machine-to-Machine communications (M2M); mIa, dIa and mId interfaces (2012)
4. 3GPP: System Improvements for Machine-Type Communications, TR 23.888 V0.5.1., July 2010
5. Telecommunications Industry Association. http://www.tiaonline.org/tags/m2m
6. OneM2M. http://www.onem2m.org/
7. OpenMTC. http://www.open-mtc.org
8. Suryani, V., Rizal, A., Herutomo, A., Abdurohman, M., Magedanz, T., Elmangoush, A.: Electrocardiagram monitoring on OpenMTC platform. In: 2013 IEEE 38th Conference on Local Computer Networks Workshops (LCN Workshops), pp. 843–847, 21–24 October 2013
9. Abdurohman, M., Herutomo, A., Suryani, V., Elmangoush, A., Magedanz, T.: Mobile tracking system using OpenMTC platform based on event driven method. In: 2013 IEEE 38th Conference on Local Computer Networks Workshops (LCN Workshops), pp. 856–860, 21–24 October 2013
10. Elmagoush, A., Coskun, H., Wahle, S., Magedanz, T.: Design aspects for a reference M2M communication platform for smart cities. In: 9th International Conference on Innovations in Information Technology, Innovations 2013, Al Ain, UAE, 17–19 March 2013
11. Abdurohman, M., Sasongko, A., Rawung, R.: Mobile tracking system based on event driven method. Appl. Mech. Mater. **321–324**, 536–540 (2013)
12. Herutomo, A., Abdurohman, M., Suwastika, N.A., Prabowo, S., Wijiutomo, C.W.: Forest fire detection system reliability test using wireless sensor network and OpenMTC communication platform. In: 2015 3rd International Conference on, Information and Communication Technology (ICoICT), pp. 87–91, 27–29 May 2015
13. Besari, P.A.L., Abdurohman, M., Rakhmatsyah, A.: Application of M2M to detect the air pollution. In: 2015 3rd International Conference on Information and Communication Technology (ICoICT), pp. 87–91, 27–29 May 2015

Hyper Heterogeneous Cloud-Based IMS Software Architecture: A Proof-of-Concept and Empirical Analysis

Pascal Potvin[1,2]([✉]), Hanen Garcia Gamardo[1,2], Kim-Khoa Nguyen[2], and Mohamed Cheriet[2]

[1] Ericsson Canada Inc., Town of Mount-Royal, Canada
{pascal.potvin,hanen.garciagamardo}@ericsson.com
[2] École de Techologie Supérieure, Montréal, Canada
knguyen@synchromedia.ca, mohamed.cheriet@etsmtl.ca

Abstract. The IP Multimedia Subsystem (IMS) defined by the 3GPP has been mainly developed and deployed by telephony vendors on vendor-specific hardware. Recent advances in Network Function Virtualisation (NFV) technology paved the way for virtualized hardware and telephony function elasticity. As such, Telecom vendors have started to embrace the cloud as a deployment platform, usually selecting a privileged virtualization platform. Operators would like to deploy telecom functionality on their already existing IT cloud platforms. Achieving such flexibility would require the telecom vendors to adopt a software architecture allowing deployment on many cloud platforms or even heterogeneous cloud platforms. We propose a distributed software architecture enabling the deployment of a single software version on multiple cloud platforms thus allowing for a solution-based deployment. We also present a prototype we developed to study the characteristics of this architecture.

Keywords: Cloud computing · Heterogeneous cloud · IMS · NFV · Software architecture

1 Introduction

The IMS [1] is a standardized solution that addresses an operator's need to provide advanced services on top of both mobile and fixed networks. It uses the Session Initiation Protocol (SIP) to establish and manage sessions. Figure 1.A presents a view of the IMS as it is currently standardized. We consider the simplified view of the IMS with its main functions; Call Session Control Functions (CSCF), Home Subscriber Server (HSS), Multimedia Telephony (MMTEL) and Media Resource Functions (MRF) circled in Fig. 1.A. Current IMS deployments are typically done on vendor-specific hardware. For example, Ericsson has a family of hardware platforms [2] for IMS deployment purposes. In other words, IMS functions are customarily deployed on dedicated physical nodes. Figure 1.B shows a possible deployment of the core IMS functionality on server racks.

The Network Function Virtualisation (NFV) standardization effort [3] has recently sought to introduce virtualization platforms for telephony functions and IMS. The NFV

© ICST Institute for Computer Sciences, Social Informatics and Telecommunications Engineering 2016
A. Leon-Garcia et al. (Eds.): Smart City 2015, LNICST 166, pp. 250–262, 2016.
DOI: 10.1007/978-3-319-33681-7_21

standard leverages the evolution of the current (predominantly) vendor-based hardware deployment consisting of Physical Network Functions (PNF) to a vendor-agnostic hardware platform running on virtualized hardware with Virtual Network Functions (VNF). NFV introduces the concept of elasticity for telephony application deployment, allowing a wide range of potential implementations of the elasticity concept from no implementation at all to fully automated.

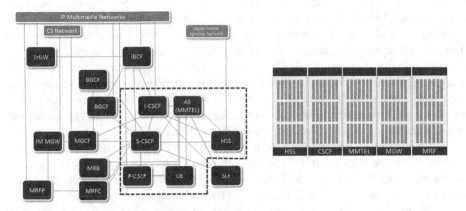

Fig. 1. (A) The IP Multimedia Subsystem (IMS) with the simplified view we consider being circled; (B) A possible IMS deployment on server racks.

Until very recently, the deployment of a VNF was still executed on a per node basis, thus providing coarse scalability and limited elasticity [4]. The problems associated with such coarse scalability are well covered in [5] and the general problem of scaling the IMS [6] is considered in [4, 7]. Prior solutions focused on resource over-provisioning to solve scalability issues leading to poor resource utilization derived from scaling on a per-node basis. A dynamic distribution, or concentration of IMS functionality has been proposed [8], but this still maintains node-based coarse scaling. This approach helps increase utilization but fails to solve the over-provisioning issue. A similar approach, so called "Merge-IMS" [9] proposes a pool of IMS VMs containing CSCF and HSS functionality whereby a specific VM instance is assigned to a subscriber at registration.

Today, Cloud providers usually build their cloud on homogeneous commoditized hardware to reduce acquisition and operating costs. As Cloud technology is being adopted, Telecom vendors might have to deploy their software on an operator's cloud which is very different from one operator to another. Part of the Telecom vendor's software functionality might be better suited for certain types of hardware. Given this, the ability to deploy the same software in a solution-defined heterogeneous pool of computing resources is desirable.

The remaining sections of this paper are organized as follows. Section 2 presents previous work related to our research. Section 3 describes the three main layers of the "Hyper Heterogeneous Cloud" architecture we named Unity: (i) the Unity architecture and the Unity framework, (ii) the re-designed IMS application running on the Unity framework, and (iii) the hardware platform used for our implementation and experimentations. Section 4 describes our experiment and finally in Sect. 5 we discuss our findings and conclusions.

2 Related Work

So far, the definition of "Heterogeneous Cloud" is still unclear. Some authors associate it to the Cloud software stack currently being built by multiple vendors [10] e.g. a management tool from one vendor driving a hypervisor from another. Others associate it to the use of hardware clusters that contain heterogeneous equipment [11, 12] e.g. general purpose computing platforms sitting next to specialized accelerators or mixed-characteristic general computing platforms where some equipment has faster processing, better I/O capacity or provides different memory/storage capacities. Nevertheless, much work has been done on the Heterogeneous Cloud. In [11] the authors propose a solution to schedule tasks to best fit hardware computing resources; in [12] the authors propose a cloud built of a mix of Central Processing Unit (CPU) and Graphical Processing Unit (GPU) based computing resources through virtualization. Another CPU/GPU study [13] looks at how proper allocation and scheduling on such heterogeneous cloud can benefit Hadoop [14] workload.

Unfortunately, to the best of our knowledge, no architecture has yet been proposed for the telecom sector in order to provide portability between multiple cloud environments or to enable solution-oriented heterogeneous cloud deployments. At the same time, no approach has been proposed to distribute and instantiate core IMS functionality in an on-demand, per subscriber and per service basis. This paper is therefore dedicated to address the following questions: (i) Can we define a cloud-based software architecture that can be easily deployed on heterogeneous hardware clusters (containers, virtual machines, bare metal servers clusters, specialized accelerator clusters...)?, (ii) Can we implement an IMS over such an architecture in order to provide on-demand per subscriber and per service functionality?, and finally, (iii) what would be the characteristics of such an architecture and how does it compare to a node-based deployment?

3 Unity Cloud

The "Hyper Heterogeneous Cloud" architecture named Unity that we propose in this paper can be deployed on a set of different hardware infrastructures, using a mix of management tools and a mix of deployment technologies. In other words, part of the deployment may be on Virtual Machines (VMs), on containers and on bare metal to take advantages of the various platforms and their availability. Our goal is to build a system and software architecture which allows a single software base to be deployed on heterogeneous hardware and cloud platforms. Specific requirements are met through deployment configuration rather than a design for a specific platform set.

To study the characteristics of a Hyper Heterogeneous Cloud Deployment Software Architecture, we built a simplified IMS system on a Microservices-based architecture [15].

This gives us the flexibility to distribute the IMS functions on a combination of platforms, through a Descriptor file which defines the available pools of platform resources and the deployment model of the Microservices. The Meta Manager and Orchestrator we built can deploy the functionality on heterogeneous platforms. This approach allows defining Hybrid deployments since the defined platforms could as well be provided by a Public Cloud. The list of Microservices developed for the Unity Cloud and the IMS functionality implemented is detailed later in this paper. We first focus on the software architecture and infrastructure enabling a Hyper Heterogeneous Cloud deployment.

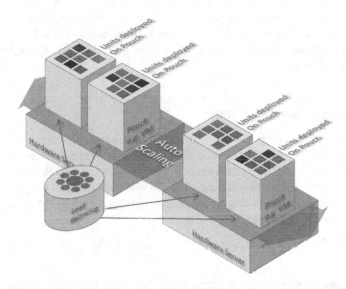

Fig. 2. Distributed deployment of Units on Pouch scaling as needed.

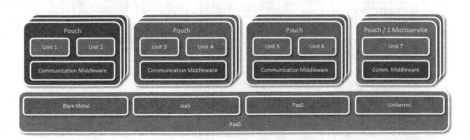

Fig. 3. Concept of Pouch deployed on XaaS.

In this architecture the Cloud platform is responsible for allocating computing, network and storage resources to provide the required telecom functionality on a per-user or per-service basis. In order to cater to the heterogeneity of the platforms

(PaaS, IaaS, BareMetal, etc.) we introduce an abstraction layer which represents an instance of a computing resource on a platform. We define a Pouch (Figs. 2 and 3) as a computing resource combined with a lightweight platform framework. The framework supports functions which are offered as a library to the application code rather than an over the network as a service. The Pouch can be seen as a set of libraries and daemons running on a computing resource to support the Microservices and facilitate access to other services. In practice a Pouch can be a Bare Metal server, a Virtual Machine on IaaS, a Container/job on PaaS, a Microservice on a Unikernel, etc. The number of Microservices and instances held by a Pouch can vary from one to thousands depending on the characteristics of the host where the Pouch is deployed.

One can scale out any number of Pouches on a platform; a Unit which can be assimilated to an actor in the Actor Model and instantiated within a Pouch is able to transparently communicate with other Units within other Pouches through the Communication Middleware.

3.1 The Unity Cloud Architecture

The Unity architecture (Fig. 4) defines a set of functionality or services allowing a Microservices-based application to be deployed on Hyper Heterogeneous Cloud platforms. The Microservices performs a specific task and covers a single scaling domain. For example a Microservice may handle a limited number of related telephony services or the HSS interrogating functionality of an application. The Microservices are deployed as "Units" as follows.

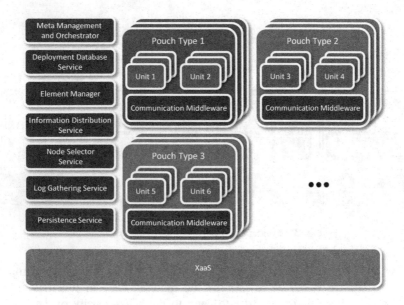

Fig. 4. Unity Cloud Architecture.

Meta Management and Orchestrator (MMO) is responsible for reading the Descriptor file and deploying the appropriate Pouches on the available platform pools. It also monitors usage information from the CMWs via the IDS and instantiates new Pouches to provide elasticity.

Element Manager (EM) is responsible for configuring the Microservices (called Units) running on the Pouches.

Communication Middleware (CMW) forms the basis of the Unity Cloud Architecture; each Pouch is required to run a single instance of a CMW. It manages most basic functionality that is required for the Unity Cloud operation such as Inter-Unit communication, Unit spawning, Pouch monitoring and Unit/Service address resolving.

Node Selector Service (NSS) implements the logic of spreading the Subscribers' service instances on the available Pouches. It ensures that most of the service requests for a Subscriber are made to the same Pouch in order to maximize local memory cache hit.

Information Distribution Service (IDS) allows information exchange based on a publish/subscribe system. Some of the information disseminated through it includes: resource utilization, service/unit resolving updates, system status updates, log levels and log entries, global configuration, etc.

Deployment Database Service (DDS) maintains copies of VM images and service and Microservice binaries that are necessary to deploy software on the Pouches of the system.

Log Gathering Service (LGS) sorts and consolidates the logging information received from the Pouches, Services and Microservices.

3.2   The IMS Telephony Application

To study the advantages of a Hyper Heterogeneous Cloud-based approach (fully distributed and elastic deployment on heterogeneous platforms) versus a Node-based approach (functions constrained to dedicated hardware or virtual machine (VM)) in terms of telecommunication functionality, we built a simplified IMS on the Unity Cloud Microservices-based architecture with the goal of deploying it in a heterogeneous cloud infrastructure. This allowed us to select the distribution of the functions on the physical or virtual platform i.e. IMS functions can be fully distributed on a pool of compute resources (Cloud-based) or on a specific compute resource (Node-based) given a single software base, thus enabling a fair comparison. The simplified IMS functions are split amongst a number of communicating Microservices joined in a complete service chain (or call chain). Figure 5 illustrates how the Microservices are linked in a complete service chain to provide a phone call between two subscribers.

The Microservices (also called Units) developed for the Unity Cloud IMS Telephony Application are listed below with notes as to which of the IMS functions they provide.

SIP Handler (SIPh) implements the SIP processing functions of the P-CSCF and the I-CSCF. It is the first Unit involved in a service setup scenario. It uses the Node Selector Service to figure out where the Call Session Unit should be instantiated and forwards it the received SIP messages.

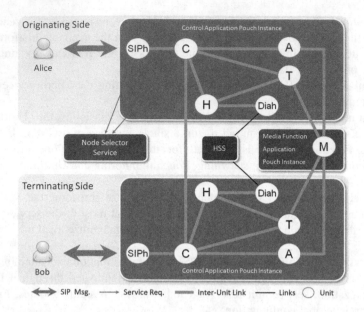

Fig. 5. Microservices involved in a typical two-party call scenario.

Call Session (C) performs the functionality of an S-CSCF. It handles the request coming from the UA, fetches the Subscriber profile based on service triggers and builds the appropriate service chain to provide the requested service. The C Unit is instantiated on request to handle the Subscriber service and is terminated when the service has completed e.g. during a call, it remains active until the SIP Bye message has been acknowledged. The C Unit makes use of the Node Selector Service in order to figure out where the terminating Call Session Unit should be instantiated.

HSS Front-End (H) is used to fetch a Subscriber profile. It is responsible for querying the HSS database in order to get this information.

Diameter Handler (Diah) is used by the H Unit as an interface that implements the diameter protocol towards the HSS in order to fetch a Subscriber profile.

Anchor Point Controller (A) covers the MRFC functionality controlling the Media Processor Unit as needed for the requested service and informs the interested Units of the availability of the functionality in the service chain. The A Unit's main function is to negotiate the media codec so that the UA can properly exchange media with the Media Processor Unit.

Telephony Server (T) provides telephony related features to the Subscriber. As an IMS MMTEL it can listen to DTMF activities to trigger supplementary services like ad-hoc conferences by adding another call leg to the current call. It is created by the C Unit on both the originating and terminating sides based on the Subscriber profile fetched via the H Unit; it connects to the M Unit to receive the media plane telephony events and to control the connectivity of the media plane.

Media Processor (M) is a dialog-based Microservice that handles the media plane of the call through RTP as an IMS MRFP would do. It provides point-to-point connectivity for basic 2-way calls and provides voice mixing in conference calls.

3.3   The Hardware Platform

We deployed our Microservices IMS Telephony application on two distinct platforms. The first deployment platform (Fig. 6.A) is based on a cluster made of eight Raspberry Pi's [16] (RPi). The benefits of this platform are twofold. Firstly, it is a cost effective way to have a 24/7 cloud we can experiment on and secondly, RPi being a simple single core computer, limits the number of variables required to consider while studying the system.

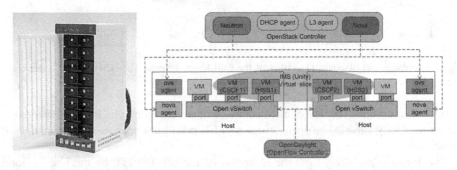

Fig. 6. (A) Eight Raspberry Pi boards Unity Cloud 3D printed Cabinet; and (B) Unity deployment on OpenStack.

The Unity Cloud RPi platform is built of:

- 8 Model B RPi stacked together in a custom made 3D printed cabinet where each RPi is set in a removable sliding tray.
- 8 custom-made RPi Daughter Boards enabling the display of information via 2 RGB LEDs and allowing input via a button.
- 1 Gigabit Ethernet switch providing the backbone network for the system.
- 1 Wi-Fi router providing access to UEs (hosting the UA) and providing the NAS functionality on a USB Storage Device.
- 1 Power Supply for the Cabinet.

The second deployment (Fig. 6.B) is on top of OpenStack deployed on an Ericsson Blade System (EBS) [17] consisting of 8 VMs (2 virtual cores and 2 GB of RAM) deployed on 4 physical blades. An automatic orchestration mechanism is triggered to balance load of the blades though VM migrations.

4 Experimentation

The first experiment is carried out to demonstrate the compatibility and compliance between different cloud-based deployment platforms (RPi cluster and EBS VMs) regarding IMS telephony Microservice functions developed for the Unity Cloud.

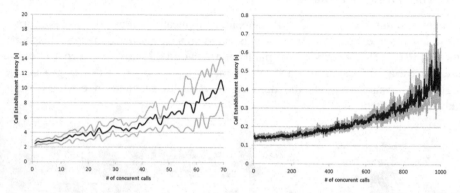

Fig. 7. Average and Standard Deviation of the Call Establishment Latency on RPi cluster (left) and on EBS VMs (right).

Our measurement consists of a collection of in-process logs which are collected in a file on the Unity Cloud. The open-source tool SIPp [18] has been used to generate SIP traffic.

We measure the delay from the reception of the SIP INVITE by the Unity Cloud until it is sent to the terminating UA (Fig. 7). This way we keep the measurement to the portion that is directly dependent on Unity Cloud processing and independent from UA delays. We also take measurements about the average CPU load on all Computing Units (CUs) against the number of concurrent calls being served by the system (Fig. 8). For all measurements we settled on:

- Call Rate: 30 2-way calls establishment / minute
- Call Duration: 3:20 min
- Subscribers: 200 registered users
- Background Registration: 20 re-registration / minute

As shown in Fig. 7, calls could be successfully established in both experimental platforms and the QoS characteristics show similar behavior. QoS characteristics are obviously better on the more powerful EBS but the QoS trend is similar to the RPi cluster. In Fig. 8, we notice similarities in the resource usage profile where average CPU usage increases relatively linearly with the number of concurrent calls.

In order to compare the proposed Microservice-based architecture (where the functions can be fully distributed on the available CUs) to the currently prominent Node-based architecture, (where the functions of a node are bound to a set of CUs) we conducted a set of experiments where the functions developed for the Unity Cloud were statically bound to a specific CU thus replicating the Node-based architecture (Table 1).

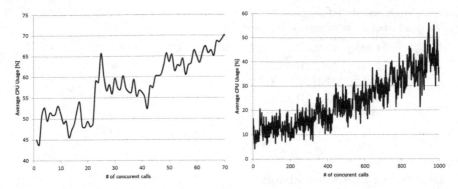

Fig. 8. Overall CPU usage Average for a specific load measured in the number of concurrent calls on the RPi cluster (left) and on EBS VMs (right).

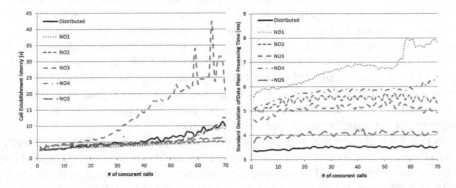

Fig. 9. Call Establishment Latency (left) and Data Plane std. dev. to the 20 ms boundary processing time vs the Number Of Calls (right) for the different experimentation configurations.

In a Node-based architecture the provisioning of the nodes needs to be perfectly engineered. However, since we had only a limited number of CUs available and didn't have proper methods to manually engineer the provisioning, we evaluated a number of configurations. These configurations and their functionality distribution are shown for the 8 available CUs in Table 1.

As shown in Fig. 9 the distributed Cloud-based approach gives similar average control plane QoS characteristics compared to Node-based approach while avoiding the worst case scenario exposed by poorly engineered resource allocation. This is depicted in the Node-based deployment configuration NO3, where the C Unit processing is starved as it is deployed on a single CU. It is worth noting that the Cloud-based approach exhibits the best data plane QoS characteristics compared to all Node-based deployment configurations.

Table 1. Experimental configurations for Node-based measurements: S (SIPh), N (NSS), H (H and Diah), all other Units as previously described.

Config.	CU1	CU2	CU3	CU4	CU5	CU6	CU7	CU8
NO1	SN	H	C	C	A	T	M	M
NO2	SNH	C	C	A	T	M	M	M
NO3	SN	H	C	A	T	M	M	M
NO4	SN	H	C	C	T	MA	MA	MA
NO5	SNH	C	C	T	MA	MA	MA	MA

5   Discussion and Conclusion

Our deployment of a Microservices-based IMS telephony solution on different cloud platforms (RPi cluster and OpenStack/EBS platform) shows that this architecture enables one-time development of the business logic across multiple deployments on various platforms through modification of deployment configuration only. It demonstrates the possibility of defining an architecture supporting Cloud features, especially automatic scaling out of the business logic for the telecom sector. Figures 7 and 8 show that the QoS of the application and platform (e.g., in terms of Call Establishment Delay and CPU consumption) are comparable in both RPi and EBS deployments. A larger number of calls can be handled on the EBS deployment but the trend of QoS characteristics stays the same. This suggests that we achieved our goal of defining a cloud-based software architecture that can be easily deployed on heterogeneous hardware clusters using a single application code base.

In Fig. 9 we observe that accurately allocating resources is required for each node in a Node-based system, and this must be done statically due to the static configuration of the Node-based system. For example, dramatic performance degradation is experienced on NO3 where the lack of resources allocated to the C Unit degrades the control plane latency in a very noticeable fashion. Aside from control plane Unit resource allocation, media plane resource allocation must also be considered. In contrast, the distributed Cloud-based approach allocates the same amount of resources to both media and control plane and also to each unit since distribution is based on CPU usage. As such, we observe better media plane performance and average control plane performance. Using our approach, the Microservices can be distributed and combined without location restrictions on VMs in order to efficiently use the available resources. This is an advantage compared to a Node-based deployment where functionality is bound to specific resources.

In conclusion, a distributed Cloud-based approach can provide automatic platform resource allocation which cannot be easily achieved by a Node-based architecture. Failure to properly engineer node resource allocation in a node-based architecture can lead to major impacts on performance. Node-based deployment also reduces the reliability of the overall system since if a node is deployed on only one CU and it fails, then the whole system fails and the service will remain unavailable until that function is restored. In the distributed cloud-based model, such a failure will terminate the services hosted on a single CU but the system will remain available to provide new service instances spread across other available CUs. The hyper-heterogeneity aspect of the proposed architecture enables us to deploy an application that is designed once across different cloud platforms, thus easing the job of telco vendors to deploy network functions on various operator-owned clouds. The hyper-heterogeneity aspect also allows tailoring of the deployment to take advantage of the benefits of specific platforms for a given application. For example, an accelerator-based cloud might be beneficial for media resource processing functions while a general-purpose cloud might be more appropriate for control information.

In the future it would be interesting to evaluate heterogeneous deployments where a system would be deployed on integrated clusters of different technologies e.g. bare metal server pool used for data plane processing and a VM-based cloud used for control plane processing.

Acknowledgements. This work is sponsored by Ericsson Canada Inc. where we would like to thank the team researchers developing the PoC: Marc-Olivier Arsenault, Gordon Bailey, Mario Bonja, Léo Collard, Alexis Grondin, Philippe Habib, Olivier Lemelin, Mahdy Nabaee, Maxime Nadeau, Fakher Oueslati and Joseph Siouffi.

References

1. 3GPP: IP Multimedia Subsystem (IMS). TS 23.228, v. 10.8.0, December 2013
2. Ahlforn, G., Ornulf, E.: Ericsson's family of carrier-class technologies. ERICSSON REV (ENGL ED) **78**(4), 190–195 (2001)
3. ETSI: Network Function Virtualisation (NFV); Virtual Network Functions Architecture. GS NFV-SWA 001, v 1.1.1, December 2014
4. Agrawal, P., et al.: IP multimedia subsystems in 3GPP and 3GPP2: overview and scalability issues. IEEE Commun. Mag. **46**(1), 138–145 (2008)
5. Glitho, R.: Cloudifying the 3GPP IP multimedia subsystem: why and how?. In: 2014 6th International Conference on New Technologies, Mobility and Security (NTMS). IEEE (2014)
6. Hammer, M., Franx, W.: Redundancy and scalability in IMS. In: 12th International Telecommunications Network Strategy and Planning Symposium, 2006, NETWORKS 2006. IEEE (2006)
7. Bellavista, P., Corradi, A., Foschini, L.: Enhancing intradomain scalability of IMS-based services. IEEE Trans. Parallel Distrib. Syst. **24**(12), 2386–2395 (2013)
8. Dutta, A. et al.: Self organizing IP multimedia subsystem. In: 2009 IEEE International Conference on Internet Multimedia Services Architecture and Applications (IMSAA). IEEE (2009)
9. Carella, G. et al.: Cloudified IP multimedia subsystem (IMS) for network function virtualization (NFV)-based architectures. In: 2014 IEEE Symposium on Computers and Communication (ISCC). IEEE (2014)
10. Wellington, D.: Homogeneous vs. heterogeneous clouds: pros, cons, and unsolicited opinions (2012). http://www.bmc.com/blogs/what-price-homogeneity
11. Xu, B., Wang, N., Li, C.: A cloud computing infrastructure on heterogeneous computing resources. J. Comput. **6**(8), 1789–1796 (2011)

12. Crago, S. et al.: Heterogeneous cloud computing. In: 2011 IEEE International Conference on Cluster Computing (CLUSTER). IEEE (2011)
13. Lee, G., Chun, B.-G., Katz, R.H.: Heterogeneity-aware resource allocation and scheduling in the cloud. In: Proceedings of HotCloud, pp. 1–5 (2011)
14. Hadoop. http://hadoop.apache.org
15. Newman, S.: Building Microservices. O'Reilly Media, Inc, San Francisco (2015)
16. Raspberry Pi. https://www.raspberrypi.org
17. Ericsson BSP 8000. http://www.ericsson.com/ourportfolio/products/bsp-8000?nav=product category008%7Cfgb_101_0538
18. SIPp. http://sipp.sourceforge.net

Micro Service Cloud Computing Pattern for Next Generation Networks

Pascal Potvin[1,2(✉)], Mahdy Nabaee[1,3], Fabrice Labeau[3], Kim-Khoa Nguyen[2], and Mohamed Cheriet[2]

[1] Ericsson Canada Inc., Montreal, Canada
{pascal.potvin,mahdy.nabaee}@ericsson.com
[2] Ecole de Techologie Superieure, Montral, Canada
knguyen@synchromedia.ca, mohamed.cheriet@etsmtl.ca
[3] ECE Department, McGill University, Montreal, Canada
fabrice.labeau@mcgill.ca

Abstract. The falling trend in the revenue of traditional telephony services has attracted attention to new IP based services. The IP Multimedia System (IMS) is a key architecture which provides the necessary platform for delivery of new multimedia services. However, current implementations of IMS do not offer automatic scalability or elastisity for the growing number of customers. Although the cloud computing paradigm has shown many promising characteristics for web applications, it is still failing to meet the requirements for telecommunication applications. In this paper, we present some related cloud computing patterns and discuss their adaptations for implementation of IMS or other telecommunication systems.

Keywords: IP Multimedia System · Cloud computing · Next generation networks · Elastisity and scalability

1 Introduction and Motivation

The increasing demand for telecommunication services has made the providers to invest further in their infrastructure. The cost of upgrading the infrastructure as well as the competition between different providers is resulting in falling revenue obtained from traditional telephony services. This fact has led the providers to look for other revenue sources by offering new multimedia services. However, the rising number of clients and their data usage is increasing the traffic load on the core of telecommunication networks which requires high cost provisioning of the network.

As the main path toward the next generation network, IP multimedia subsystem (IMS) is an architectural framework for end-to-end delivery of multimedia services via IP-based mechanisms [1]. The IMS is built upon Session Initiation Protocol [2] and Real-time Transfer Protocol [3] for control and data planes, respectively. As it is shown in Fig. 1, the main modules in an IMS include Call

© ICST Institute for Computer Sciences, Social Informatics and Telecommunications Engineering 2016
A. Leon-Garcia et al. (Eds.): Smart City 2015, LNICST 166, pp. 263–274, 2016.
DOI: 10.1007/978-3-319-33681-7_22

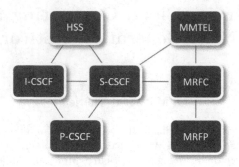

Fig. 1. The main functionalities of the IP Multimedia System: Call Session Control Function (CSCF), Home Subscriber Server (HSS), Multimedia Telephony (MMTEL), and Media Resource Function (MRF).

Session Control Functions (CSCF), Home Subscriber Server (HSS), Multimedia Telephony (MMTEL) and Media Resource Functions (MRF).

The CSCF is the core function in an IMS system, which is in charge of performing the appropriate signaling between the user equipment (UE) and IMS modules. Further, the CSCF handles the establishment and termination of sessions, authentication, security and Quality of Service monitoring. Depending on the specific task of a CSCF unit, it is divided in to Proxy (P), Interrogating (I) and Serving (S) types of CSCF, as shown in Fig. 1.

HSS is the main database unit in IMS, which keeps the profile of all subscribers and the necessary triggers for their policies. MMTEL unit enables end-to-end real time services between the parties for different multimedia contents including real time video, text messaging and file sharing. Finally, MRF (usually divided in control and processing modules) is in charge of delivery of the media services by providing media related functions such as voice mixing for voice content.

Although different resolutions of IMS have been developed for commercial use in the industry, its efficiency and low cost delivery needs further investigation. Especially, the main drawbacks of current IMS infrastructure are manual (human based) scalability[1], lack of elastisity and high deployment and maintenance costs.

Thanks to virtualization techniques, sharing of computing, storage and network resources has been made possible, resulting in the creation and growth of cloud computing [4]. By abstracting the hardware and software, Infrastructure as a Service (IaaS) provides a pool of computing and storage resources which isolates us from the complexity of dealing with individual hardware devices. Meanwhile, since many cloud users have access to these shared computing resources, they can change their subscription volume, resulting in an elastic behavior. Current architectures of cloud computing are designed to provide the best services possible and are failing to provide any telecommunication-level quality of service (QoS) assurances [5].

---

[1] They rely on human operations to deploy further resources to accommodate the increase of demand.

Research on the implementation of IMS core network within the cloud computing infrastructure is in its early stage and there are few competitive published work. The 3GPP standardizing body has attempted to design the IMS such that its main functionalities (especially Call Session Control Function) are to some extent scalable [5] although this limited scalability does not translate in elasticity. A few other works have focused on the scalability of the individual functional units of IMS; for instance, the authors in [6] have addressed the scalability of Home Subscriber Server (HSS) with the aid of concepts in distributed databases. In [7], the authors have proposed a resource allocation which satisfies the time requirements at the level of a telecommunication network. They have accomplished this by using static and dynamic groups for assignment of virtual computation units to the physical computation units.

In this paper, we introduce a new architecture for elastic implementation of IMS which is based on micro services. In contrast with previous work, our new architecture can be implemented on top of different cloud or node based computing services including IaaS and PaaS (Platform as a Service). Further, we propose a mechanism to trigger the allocation of new computing nodes to accommodate overloaded nodes. This will enable us to have automatic scalability and achieve elasticity for the implementation.

In Sect. 2, we describe some of the cloud computing patterns and their application for the IMS. Specifically, we discuss micro service architecture and describe our micro service based architecture for IMS. In Sect. 3, we describe the load balancing mechanism used in our architecture which is followed by our discussion on the automatic scalability of our architecture in Sect. 4. We present some of our experimental results using our proof of concept implementation in Sect. 5. Finally, we present our concluding remarks and future works in Sect. 6.

2   Cloud Computing Scaling Schemes for IMS

One of the main challenges of using cloud architectural patterns is to adapt stateless web technologies for the strictly stateful telecommunication applications. Specifically, we need to adopt mechanisms which enables us to use the current cloud architectures for telecommunication applications with a lot of state information, $e.g.$ the state of SIP handling in IMS. Moreover, we need to study the relation between the cloud related metrics ($e.g.$ load of the units) and the telecommunication related metrics ($e.g.$ Quality of Service). In the remaining of this section, we study some of the conventional architectures for the cloud and discuss their adaptation for our IMS implementation.

In the literature, scaling an application is categorized as three different axes. Running multiple instances of the whole application using a load balancer is referred to as the x axis of scaling. The y axis stands for the splitting of the application into smaller components where each component is a service responsible for a specific functionality. Finally, in the z axis of scaling, the input data are partitioned into different segments where the segments are handled by different computing resource (also called $sharding$).

2.1 Micro Service Architecture for IMS

In the y axis of scaling, the application is decomposed into smaller units, called *micro services*. Decomposing into smaller micro services will enable us to distribute the computational load of the application among different hardware devices or even geographical locations. This will provide the management of computational load and resources with a fine granularity. Further, the micro services architecture will provide a flexibility for deployment by allowing the micro services to be deployed at different computational resources, *e.g.* different virtual machines, platforms, containers or even geographical locations.

On the other hand, having an architecture which is built up from smaller services makes parallel and continuous software development feasible. The ability to reuse micro services for other applications is another advantage of this pattern. Specifically, a micro service implements a small set of functionalities which can be interfaced with other modules of the application via synchronous or asynchronous communication protocols (*e.g.* TCP and UDP). Such an architecture will enable us to deploy (execute) a micro service anywhere without being bound to a specific computing node and therefore achieve a fully scalable architecture.

As shown in Fig. 2, we have divided the IMS functions into smaller micro services where each micro service runs on a *dynamically allocated* computing resource. To establish a call, the originating side will send its INVITE to the load balancer (as the entry point of our IMS). The load balancer will then determine a computing node and create an instance of the C actor (CSCF) to interact with the originating side and handle the call session functions. The Orchestrator (O) is then created by the C and will determine the subscription details for that call session, depending on the subscription policy.

As it is shown in Fig. 2, the H unit is in charge of interacting with the HSS to fetch and update the user profiles via the Diameter stack protocol. The A (Anchor point controller) and T (Telephony server) are in charge of creating and updating the call session settings. Finally, the M unit is the media processor which processes the content of the call sessions (*e.g.* bit rate matching for voice calls).[2]

Splitting the IMS architecture into small units (called micro services) provides us with a lot of flexibility on the deployment of the units. Explicitly, each of the units involved in the establishment of a call session (shown in Fig. 2) can be deployed on a different computing node as they interact together via TCP communication protocol. Hence, the fine granularity offered by our architecture makes it easier to scale the system with the demand (*i.e.* increasing and decreasing the amount of allocated computation resources with the new and terminated call sessions). However, it should be noted that such advantage is achieved by having higher latency in the IMS functionalities.[3]

---

[2] Although the described micro service architecture does not include all of the functionalities in an IMS, it povides a good coverage for most of its functionalities and makes us able to study different aspects of cloud based implementation of IMS, as discussed in this paper.

[3] In Sect. 5, we discuss this further by presenting our experimental results for the latency.

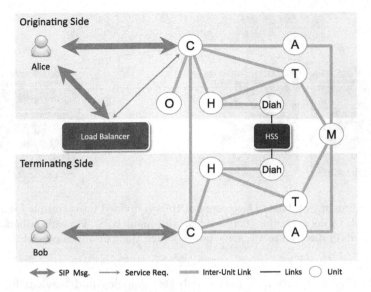

Fig. 2. Micro service implementation of IP Multimedia System: The main functions of IMS are split into smaller micro services, called CSCF (C), Orchestrator (O), Anchor point (A), Telephony server (T), Media processor (M) and HSS front end (H). This allows us to dynamically create micro services for each IMS subscriber or call session.

2.2 Computing Nodes as Pouches

The virtualization platforms have provided us with an abstract encapsulation of computing, storage and network resources. From the perspective of applications (*e.g.* IMS micro services), this encapsulation is similar to a physical computing node like a blade server. However, in practice, it may be a *virtual machine* in OpenStack platform or a *container* in Continuum platform [8]. In general, we call a set of physical or virtual computing resources which are isolated from other sets of resources (for the application), a *pouch*.

The key point in our IMS implementation is the separation of the platform in which a pouch is deployed (or instantiated) and the application micro services. In other words, each of the micro services (discussed in the preceding section) can be run (executed) on a different (type of) pouch, independent of the pouch platform.

2.3 Horizontal Scaling and Sharding Pattern

As the main requirement for scalability, the applications are supposed to work such that adding more computing resources would be the solution to handle further queries, calls or subscriber. A load balancer will then be able to spread the computational load on these computing resources in a way to achieve the quality requirements. Such an architectural pattern has reached its maturity for current web services. However, the stateful nature of telecommunication applications

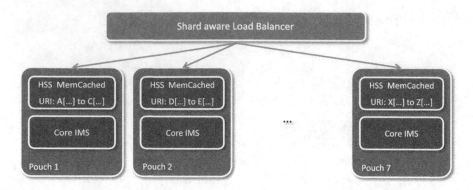

Fig. 3. Sharding of Database: The content of HSS is divided into multiple local caches at each pouch to decrease the query load on the main HSS. The subscribers are (as much as possible) directed to the same pouch which their profile is cached.

requires further adaptation of native web technologies and services for use in telecommunication applications.

One of the key approaches in our design of IMS is based on the concept of sharding where the user database is split into a number of shards (databases). Essentially, at each shard of our IMS architecture, a partition of the user data with the same key is stored (cached). Further, each of these shards are also kept consistent (synchronized) with a centralized HSS entity which results in a smaller number of queries (smaller load) on HSS. Moreover, the key used in the sharding is a hash function of the call session identifier and may be as simple as hard division of first letter of the SIP (Session Initiation Protocol) identifiers (Fig. 3).

The proper design of sharding can help us achieve horizontal scaling and makes us able to recover from computation node failures by creating the cache on a new node. Further, the load balancer will be able to distribute data such that nodes are loaded almost uniformly. The load balancing algorithm used for our IMS architecture is explained in the following.

3   Load Balancing and Scaling

The load balancer goal is to distribute the computational load between the computing nodes and decrease the caching load from HSS. In the following, we describe our proposed load balancing mechanism for IMS.

When a new SIP message is received at the load balancer (entry point in our IMS), it is sent to a randomly picked *rendezvous* load balancer (for example using a round robin mechanism). As shown in Fig. 4, the rendezvous load balancer is then in charge of assigning the computing nodes for handling of SIP message.

The rendezvous load balancers find the computing node by using the highest random weight mapping, introduced in [9]. Specifically, for each computing node, the hash of the combination of originating side URI and computing node

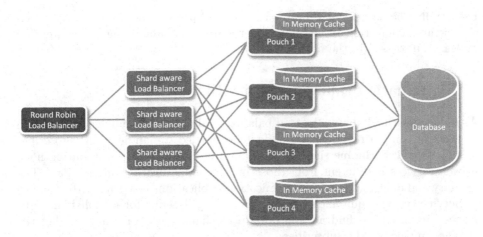

Fig. 4. Rendezvous Load Balancer and Database Sharding: The content of HSS is divided into multiple local caches at each computing node to decrease the query load on HSS. The subscribers are (as much as possible) directed to the computing node where the cache has their profile.

host name (or IP address) is calculated. The combination can simply be the concatenation of the originating URI and host name strings. The computing node with the highest (or alternatively lowest) hash value is then selected for caching of subscriber profile and handling of the call:

$$\text{selected node} = \underset{\text{node } i}{\arg \max} \ \mathcal{H}(< URI > + < host_i >) \tag{1}$$

In (1), $\mathcal{H}(.)$, $< URI >$ and $< host_i >$ represent the hash function, originating side URI and host name of the computing node, respectively. Moreover, $+$ denotes the concatenation operation for two strings.

Since our load balancing algorithm only uses the subscriber URI, all of the calls from the same subscriber are directed to the same computation node. As a result, its user profile does not need to be fetched from the main HSS entity again and can be read from the local cache of that computation node.

Conventionally, multiple instances of HSS with different user profiles were deployed in IMS and a Subscriber Location Function (SLF) was used to direct the calls to their specific HSS unit [1]. In contrast with the SLF mechanism, our approach is designed to minimize the number of database queries out of a pouch. Although the SLF decreases the load on the HSS units, one may still need to make database queries out of the pouch where the computation is done. Further, since the local database queries can be made faster than the external ones (as it does not need to be done via network), our local caching mechanism should be a better alternative for long term handling of a set of stationary subscribers.

In the mentioned algorithm, the rendezvous load balancer may find a computing node which is overloaded and can not handle a new subscriber. In such cases, a busy signal is sent to the management unit and the call session is dropped.

Essentially, the management unit is in charge of preventing such cases by provisioning and monitoring of the computing resources and allocating new computing nodes, as discussed in the next section.

4   Automatic Scaling and Busy Signal

As it was described above, the load balancer will notify the management unit to create new computing nodes if a node is overloaded to handle a new subscriber or call. However, the metrics used to determine the load of a computing node in web services is different from those in telecommunication applications. The primary and final goal in telecommunication applications is to satisfy the Quality of Service (QoS) requirement of the service; *e.g.* latency for establishing calls. Hence, one needs to find an appropriate mechanism to track and predict the changes in QoS for the subscribers.

In our design for IMS, we implemented a *busy signal* mechanism for this purpose which results in dynamic allocation of pouches. Essentially, when a subscriber is directed to a computing node by the load balancer and that node is overloaded, a busy signal would be sent to the management unit and the call session is dropped. Then, the management unit (which can be part of the load balancer functionality) will create a new computing unit and update the record of computing nodes at the rendezvous load balancers. The uniform nature of the hash function ensures that the loads of the computing nodes are distributed almost uniformly. Further, this mechanism prevents the subscribers from being directed to different locations which would result in a large number of queries to the HSS.

The measurements used to determine if a computing node is overloaded have to be carefully chosen and this is still a subject of study in the literature. Notably, the conventional metrics used for measuring the computational load of a node (*e.g.* processing unit load and memory usage) are not directly applicable to the QoS in IMS. Furthermore, the QoS between two subscribers depend on the communication link and network where the traffic travels through. In cases where a computing node is located in a congested part of the network where delivery time of packets is not acceptable, the load balancer will create a new computing node and direct the new subscribers and calls to it.

Although there is still no specific formula to draw QoS conclusions from different metrics representing the condition of the computing nodes, our empirical experiments showed that one has to consider the following to determine if new pouches need to be created:

- the round trip transmission delay between geographically distributed computing nodes and user equipment,
- the processing load (*e.g.* processing unit and memory usage) of individual computing nodes,
- the history of the QoS experienced by different subscribers and their subscription policies.

5   Experimental Results

In this section, we present some of our experimental results, obtained from our implementation. Most of the units in the IMS architecture (shown in Fig. 2) are involved in the establishment of the call sessions. After the call is established, the content of the call (*e.g.* voice) is handled by the media processor (M) unit. Therefore, it need to have a very small number of interactions with the other units which may affect the computational performance of the media processor. As a result, we focus on the call establishment process and evaluate the performance of our architecture in terms of the latency in the establishment of a call.

We have implemented and deployed our micro service IMS application on a cluster of Raspberry Pi, as a proof of concept. Our cluster is built of eight model B Raspberry Pi [10] which are put together similar to a cabinet of blade servers. Each Raspberry Pi is considered as a pouch and they are linked together by using an Ethernet switch. One of the pouches is used to host the load balancer as the entry point of the SIP messages which is used by the SIP client at the beginning of their SIP signaling.

Our experiments are done by making a number of SIP calls via our IMS implementation. Specifically, we put a maximum of 80 concurrent calls to the system with a constant rate of 30 calls per minute. After a call is established, it lasts 300 s and then it is terminated. The calls are made between different pairs of subscribers and only carry voice content. In Fig. 5, we have depicted the call establishment latency for each call. In this figure, the vertical axis represents the delay in seconds and the numbers on the horizontal axis correspond to the order in which the calls are placed.

As it is shown in Fig. 5, the call establishment latency is around 2 s which is in a comparable range with the the results in [11]. However, as the number of concurrent calls on the system increases, the load on the system is increased which results in higher call establishment delays. Especially, this happens for calls which are initiated late during our experiments. The high latency values for the establishment of late calls is mainly because the pouches are overloaded by

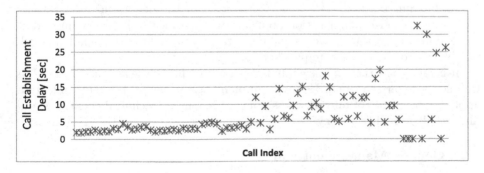

Fig. 5. Call establishment latency for different calls: The latency increases when the load on the system (number of concurrent calls) increases.

the actors corresponding to the other previous calls. Specifically, the concurrent C, A and T processors, created for different call sessions, put a lot of load on Raspberry Pi's which may result them not to be able to handle the new call establishments with a reasonable latency.

6   Conclusion and Discussion

In this paper, we discussed some of the cloud computing patterns and studied the possibility of applying them to the IP multimedia system. Specifically, we described a new cloud based architecture for implementation of IMS where the system is split in a number of micro services. Such micro service based architecture made us able to adopt automatic scalability to achieve elasticity for the IMS. We also proposed to use local caching as an effective approach to reduce the number of queries to the main HSS unit which is a major bottleneck in the IMS architecture. Further, we discussed rendezvous load balancing in order to achieve uniform load distribution among the computing nodes and reduce the communication overhead by handling the calls of a subscriber at the same computing node (and take advantage of local caches). In the following, we discuss some of the important aspects of our work in progress.

6.1   Computing Node Failure

Traditional implementation of telecommunication functionalities on dedicated hardware does not provide a mechanism for automatic recovery and migration. As a result, the recovery of failed devices only has to rely on manual (human assisted) maintenance and operation. This fact requires the telecommunication equipment to have a very high *mean time between failures*.

The isolation of pouches and the IMS micro services allows us to move the deployed micro services to a new instantiated pouch in case of a failure. This advantage of cloud computing has introduced a change in the definition of reliability for the systems. Since the cloud platform provides us with a large pool of pouches (or virtualized computing nodes), the frequency of happening of a failure is not a critical factor for cloud based implementations. However, the new mindset requires a low *mean time to recovery* for the new cloud based implementations of telecommunication applications. Specifically, it is now important to be able to create new pouches and move the functionalities of the failed pouch (or device) to the new create pouches.

It is fair to say that this new mindset is mainly due to the advance of *stateless* web services on the cloud. However, implementing *stateful* telecommunication applications on top of fully stateless pouches has many technical challenges and may result in higher latency.

6.2   Generic Management Unit

In Sect. 4, we discussed automatic scaling using application related parameters (*e.g.* QoS) to achieve elastisity in our architecture. Isolation of the IMS application functionalities from the cloud management unit is one of the interesting features in development of generic cloud management with automatic scalability for telecommunication applications. To develop such generic architecture, we need to find an appropriate figure which is independent of the application layer and is capable to reflect the level of used resources by the application. Having such generic figure, the management unit will be able to increase or decrease the number of pouches, allocated for the application with the changes of the load (*e.g.* number of requested call establishments in IMS).

6.3   Elastisity-QoS Trade-Off

The advantages of resource sharing has drawn attention to design of elastic architectures to carry telecommunication applications. In such architectures, low amount of available computing resources may result in bad or unacceptable QoS level. Especially, when the time required for creating (or allocating) new computing nodes is long or the increasing rate of the load on the system is high, the performance of telecommunication applications may be affected.

To address this issue, a safe bound is usually considered between the number of allocated pouches and the number of required pouches to handle the current load. This safe bound will be able to accommodate the new incoming requests (*i.e.* new call establishment requests from UEs) until new pouches are allocated for the IMS application layer.

The size of this safe bound (more precisely the number of extra-allocated pouches) specifies the chance of being overloaded (and hence receiving a busy signal for a new call). Specifically, a small number of extra-allocated pouches will increase the likelihood of falling in a busy situation. On the opposite side, picking a large number of extra-allocated pouches is inefficient and move us far from having an ideal elastic deployment. In summary, there is a trade-off between the experienced QoS and the level of elastisity that we can achieve and it is controlled by allocating an appropriate number of extra-allocated pouches. In practice, this task can be done by studying the statistics of the subscriber requests and analyzing the latency of different parts of the implementation.

Acknowledgments. This work was supported by Ericsson Canada Inc and MITACS Canada through a MITACS Accelerate partnership program between Ericsson Canada Inc and McGill University. We would also like to thank the team of dedicated researchers, Marc-Olivier Arsenault, Gordon Bailey, Mario Bonja, Leo Collard, Philippe Habib, Olivier Lemelin, Maxime Nadeau, Fakher Oueslati and Joseph Siouffi, for their endeavoring effort in developing our proof of concept implementation.

References

1. Poikselkä, M., Mayer, G., The, I.M.S.: IP Multimedia Concepts and Services. Wiley, New York (2013)
2. Handley, M.: SIP: Session Initiation Protocol (1999). http://tools.ietf.org/html/rfc2543.html

3. Schulzrinne, H.: RTP: a transport protocol for real-time applications (1996). https://tools.ietf.org/html/rfc1889
4. Buyya, R., Vecchiola, C., Selvi, S.T.: Mastering Cloud Computing: Foundations and Applications Programming. Newnes, Boston (2013)
5. Glitho, R.: Cloudifying the 3GPP IP multimedia subsystem: why and how? In: 6th Conference on New Technologies, Mobility and Security, pp. 1–5. IEEE (2014)
6. Yang, T., Wen, X., Sun, Y., Zhao, Z., Wang, Y.: A new architecture of HSS based on cloud computing. In: 13th International Conference on Communication Technology, pp. 526–530. IEEE (2011)
7. Lu, F., Pan, H., Lei, X., Liao, X., Jin, H.: A virtualization-based cloud infrastructure for IMS core network. In: 5th International Conference on Cloud Computing Technology and Science, vol. 1, pp. 25–32. IEEE (2013)
8. Apcera Continuum (2014). http://www.apcera.com/continuum/
9. Thaler, D., Ravishankar, C.V.: A name-based mapping scheme for rendezvous. Technical report, University of Michigan, November 1996
10. Raspberry Pi Model B (2014). https://www.raspberrypi.org/products/model-b/
11. El Mahdi Boumezzough, M., Idboufker, N., Ait Ouahman, A.: Evaluation of SIP call setup delay for VoIP in IMS. In: Guyot, V. (ed.) ICAIT 2012. LNCS, vol. 7593, pp. 16–24. Springer, Heidelberg (2013)

SGSC

Economic Analysis of Chemical Energy Storage Technologies

Parvez Ahmed Khan and Bala Venkatesh[(✉)]

Centre for Urban Energy, Ryerson University, Toronto, ON, Canada
{pkhan, bala}@ryerson.ca

Abstract. Smart Grid Technologies are set to transform electric power systems and energy storage is a key tools that will enable this transformation. Energy storage provides innumerable services such as energy arbitrage, frequency regulation, transmission and distribution system deferral, etc. In electric power systems, asset procurement is based upon investment models that ultimately minimize net amortized annual asset costs to supply a unit of electric energy. Accordingly, energy storage procurement is also scrutinized for cost-effectiveness. This paper provides cost effectiveness of different electrical energy storage technologies when used for single and multiple energy storage services. Different popular economic parameters like Net Present Value, Internal Rate of Return, Cost-Benefit Ratio, etc. are estimated to find out cost effectiveness of the technologies.

Keywords: Evaluation · Time value · Discounting · Pay-back period · Debt-service coverage · Net present value · Internal rate of return · Weighted average cost of capital · Benefit-cost ratio · Viable

1 Introduction

Energy exists in different forms in the universe and among those, some can be consumed directly and some by transforming into another useable form. Some of the transformation process could be controlled depending on demand or loads and others could not be controlled, that is, once the process is started, it goes continuously till the input(s) are available and don't depend on demand or loads. Without storage, energy generation must equal energy consumption. Energy storage transfers a part of the generated energy (excess of loads) at one time so that excess energy can be used at another time [1].

Due to different environmental factors and scarcity of non-renewable energy sources, increase in energy generation from renewable sources becomes obvious. But these types of energy generation are by nature intermittent and unpredictable, and the supply of renewable energy resources fluctuate independently from demand. This creates imbalances within the system and develops risk of not meeting the demand by supply. Energy storage is being considered as a solution to maintain the energy balance within the renewable energy system with consistency [2]. Thus, significant contribution of renewable energy to sustainable energy use will require considerable further development of cost-effective energy storage technologies [3].

© ICST Institute for Computer Sciences, Social Informatics and Telecommunications Engineering 2016
A. Leon-Garcia et al. (Eds.): Smart City 2015, LNICST 166, pp. 277–291, 2016.
DOI: 10.1007/978-3-319-33681-7_23

1.1 Energy Storage Services and Benefits

Up to mid-1980s, energy storage was used only to time-shift from coal off-peak to replace natural gas on-peak so that the coal units remained at their optimal output as system load varied. But till now about 17 services under 5 categories have been identified which these emerging energy storage technologies could provide [1].

Among these 5 categories, bulk-energy services are the most important. Bulk-energy services include electric energy time-shift (arbitrage) which involves charging of the storage system during off-peak periods or by storing excess energy produced by renewable sources during their pick production hours and utilizing the stored energy as and when needed [1]. Such service of energy storage also helps deferral and/or reduction of developing new generation capacity.

Ancillary services are the second most important services that energy storage can provide which include maintaining grid frequency known as regulation service; maintaining smooth operation of an electric grid through spinning, non-spinning, and supplemental reserves; voltage support to manage reactance at the grid level; black start service to provide an active reserve of power and energy within the grid which can be used to energize transmission and distribution lines and provide start-up power to bring power plants on line after a catastrophic failure of the grid; and other uses like load following/ramping support for renewables and frequency response [1]. Spinning, non-spinning, or supplemental reserve is the reserve capacity required for smooth operation of electric grid during unexpected failure of some portion of the normal electric generation resources and hence being considered the most important among ancillary services of energy storage [1]. This type of service requires larger size of energy storage like bulk-energy services and hence can be integrated in the same storage system.

Other categories of energy storage services are transmission infrastructure services (transmission upgrade deferral, transmission congestion relief, etc.); distribution upgrade deferral and voltage support; and customer energy management services (maintain power quality, reliability, retail energy time-shift and demand charge management) [1]. These types of transmission and distribution services can be performed by adding a relatively small size of energy storage within the grid system.

1.2 Electrical Energy Storage Technologies

Several electricity storage technologies are currently under commercial operation and a considerable number of emerging technologies are anticipated to be available within the next two to three years. One of the most popular storage technologies is Pumped Hydroelectric energy storage. This is a large, mature, and commercial utility-scale technology currently being used at many locations around the world. Compressed Air energy storage is also commercially available technology being used for large scale applications.

Besides, the above technologies' chemical storage or battery is the most popular and frequently used method of energy storage. Most of the batteries fall into the two main types; flow batteries and normal cell batteries.

Flow batteries are generally used for large scale applications. In these types of batteries, the electrolytes are kept separately in reservoir tanks and moved into the electrochemical cell using pumps. These batteries are deemed 75–85 % efficient and have a long life span [1]. Due to the fact that the electrolytes are stored separately, very little self-discharge occurs. But these batteries are quite costly as they require other components, such as pumps to move the electrolytes between the reservoirs and the electrochemical cell [1]. Vanadium Redox batteries (VRB), Iron-chromium batteries (Fe-Cr) and Zinc-bromine batteries (Zn-Br) are among the emerging technologies in this field [1].

Cell batteries are another type of chemical storage in which storage is achieved through electrochemical accumulators. There are a wide range of technologies used in the fabrication of accumulators (lead–acid, nickel–cadmium, nickel–metal hydride, nickel–iron, zinc–air, iron–air, sodium–sulphur, lithium–ion, lithium–polymer, etc.). The main assets of this storage are their energy densities (up to 150 and 2000 Wh/kg for lithium) and maturity of the technologies [1]. Their main inconvenience, however, is their relatively low durability for large-amplitude cycling (a few 100 to a few 1000 cycles) [3]. Sodium-sulphur batteries (NaS), Sodium-nickel-chloride batteries (NaNiCl$_2$), Zinc-air batteries (Zn-Air) and Lead-acid family of batteries are among

Table 1. Maturity level of different chemical storage technologies

	NaS	NaNiCl$_2$	VRB	Fe-Cr	Zn-Br	Zn-Air	Lead-Acid
Maturity Level	A	C	B	E	D	E	C

A: Significant recent commercial experience; B: Pre-commercial; C: Demonstration;
D: Demonstration trial; E: Laboratory

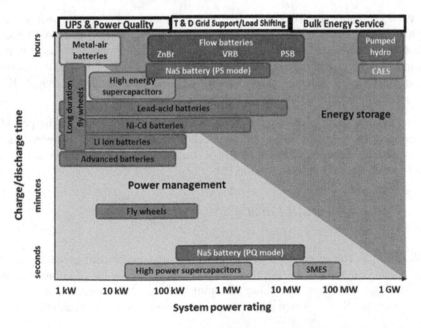

Fig. 1. Position of different energy storage technologies [14]

popular choices for energy storage [1]. Table 1 below shows the maturity level of different chemical storage technologies mentioned above.

Among others, hydrogen fuel-cells, super-capacitor and fly-wheel energy storage technologies are also commercially available but till now these are being used as small range energy storage.

1.3   Suitability of Different Energy Storage Technologies

Not all the technologies are suitable for all type of energy storage services due to their different energy density, power and discharge time. Figure 1 shows the power-energy relationship of different energy storage technologies and their suitability in different categories of storage services. From Fig. 1, it is obvious that CAES and Pumped Hydro are capable of discharge times in several hours with correspondingly large sizes (+1000 MW). In comparison of these technologies, flywheels and various chemical storages (batteries) are positioned around lower power and shorter discharge times [1].

2   Literature Review

To analyze the cost effectiveness, different economic & financial analyses are being done. In some cases, time value of money is taken into consideration but in some cases it is ignored to simplify the calculation depending on the context.

2.1   Economic Evaluation without Considering the Time Value of Money

Time value of money is an important element on financial and economic analysis, even though in some situation it is reasonable to deal with the face value of monetary amounts and ignore time value i.e. discounting of the face value. The most popular economic tool in this category is Simple Pay-back Period [4]. Beside this, the financers are also interested in another yearly indicator called Debt-service Coverage Ratio. These indicators are discussed briefly below:

Simple Payback (SP). Simple payback in economic analysis refers to the period of time required for the return on an investment to repay the original investment. Shorter payback periods are preferable than longer payback periods [4]. The following Eq. (1) is used to calculate the payback period [5]:

$$Payback\,Period = n_y + \frac{(CFn_{y+1} - CFn_y)}{CFn_{y+1}} \tag{1}$$

Where, n_y = The number of years after the initial investment at which the last negative value of cumulative cash flow occurs, CFn_y = The value of cumulative cash flow at which the last negative value of cumulative cash flow occurs, and CFn_{y+1} = The value of cash flow at which the first positive value of cumulative cash flow occurs.

Debt-Service Coverage Ratio (DSCR). The Debt-service Coverage Ratio (DSCR) is the ratio of cash available to meet the obligations of debt and repayment amount of debt which includes interest, principal and lease payments. It is a popular benchmark used to measure the ability of a creditor to produce enough cash to cover its all types of debt payments. The higher this ratio is, the easier it is to find out and convince a financer. It is generally calculated by using the following equation [6]:

$$DSCR = \frac{Cash\ available\ to\ meet\ debt\ of\ obligations}{Total\ of\ debt\ of\ obligations} \tag{2}$$

If the debt coverage ratio is less than one, it means that the income that the business/entity property generates or supposed to generate is or will not be enough to cover the debt obligations after meeting its operating expenses.

2.2 Economic Evaluation Taking Time Value of Money into Consideration

This type of evaluation starts with the premise that the value of money is declining over time and therefore, the values in the future should be discounted relative to the present. The most popular economic tools in this group are Present Net Value (NPV), Internal Rate of Return (IRR) and Benefit Cost Ratio (BCR) [4, 5].

Net Present Value (NPV). To find out NPV total of discounted present value of cash inflows is subtracted from the total of discounted present value of the cash outflows. If the NPV of a prospective project is found positive, then it is considered to be economically viable. However, if it is negative, then the project should probably be rejected, as the project will not be able to return the minimum attractive rate of return (MARR) [5]. The following equation is being used to estimate NPV of a project [5].

$$NPV = \sum_{n=0}^{m} \frac{CFn}{(1+i)^n} \tag{3}$$

Where, 'n' is the number of year from 0 to life of the project (m), 'CF_n' is cash flow for the year 'n' and 'i' is the weighted average cost of capital (WACC) also known as discount rate.

WACC of a project can be calculated by using the following equation [4]:

$$WACC = \sum_{n=0}^{m} \left[\left\{ (1 - Taxrate) \times I_d \times \frac{D_n}{D_n + E_n} \right\} + \left(I_e + \frac{E_n}{D_n + E_n} \right) \right] \tag{4}$$

Where, I_d is cost of debt or external capital, I_e is cost of equity or internal capital, D_n is amount of external capital at year n and E_n is amount of internal capital at year n.

Internal Rate of Return (IRR). The internal rate of return on an investment or project is the annualized effective compounded return rate or the rate of return that makes the

Net Present Value (NPV) of all cash flows (both positive and negative) from a particular investment equals to zero. Internal rates of return are commonly used to evaluate the desirability of investments or projects. The higher a project's internal rate of return, the more desirable it is to undertake the project. The project with the highest IRR would be considered the best and undertaken first [5].

If 'n' is the period (n = 0 to N where N is equal to the economic life of the project), CF_n is the net cash flow from the project at any period of 'n' and NPV is the net present value of the project and 'r' is th internal rate of return (IRR), then the value of 'r' i.e. the IRR can be found by solving the following equation [5]:

$$NPV = \sum_{n=0}^{m} \frac{CF_n}{(1+r)^n} = 0 \tag{5}$$

Benefit-Cost Ratio (BCR). Benefit-cost ratio (BCR) is the ratio of monetary value of the benefits of a project to its costs [4, 6]. All benefits and costs are expressed in discounted present value at WACC. If BCR of a project stands > 1 then project is considered as economically viable since this indicates that the present value (PV) of all benefit will be more than the costs [4, 6].

$$BCR = \frac{\sum PV \text{ of benefits}}{\sum PV \text{ of costs}}. \tag{6}$$

3   Results and Discussions

Economic viability of any project depends on the location where it is going to be set-up. If the main input of the project is coming from that location and the output is also consumed to the same or adjacent location like an energy storage project, then the location becomes a major driver of economic viability of such project. This report analyzed the economic viability of chemical energy storage technologies considering Ontario, Canada as the location of projects.

Cost of a project has also an important role on overall project viability. The following figures (Figs. 2 and 3) are showing the present value installed cost in $/kw of chemical storage technologies for spinning and bulk energy services (units of 50 MW) and utility transmission and distribution services (units of 1 MW) as estimated by Sandia National Laboratories, USA (SAND2013-5131) [7].

The popular economic tools as mentioned above are calculated for different types of chemical storage of energy for a combination of bulk storage and an ancillary service (Spinning service), and transmission and distribution (T&D) services. Economic evaluation for a mix of services (bulk, T&D and frequency services) are also done by preparing an MS excel spread sheet. The basic information regarding cost of system, system's performance like depth of discharge and average O&M costs are taken from the SANDIA Report (SAND2013-5131) [7]. Rests of the required information are taken from the web site of IESO and other related web sites.

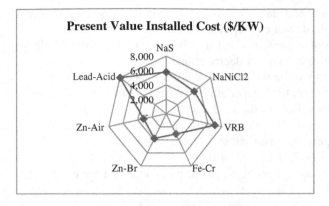

Fig. 2. Present value installed cost for bulk energy services [7]

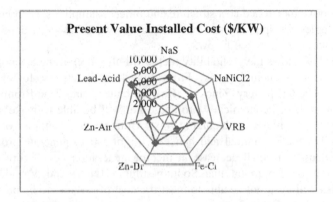

Fig. 3. Present value installed cost for T&D services [7]

Assumptions:

a. Average market rates (last 4-months) of different energy storage services are being taken as sale price of the services [9]
b. Energy Price will be at $ 135.00 per MWh which is little less than present threshold price for demand response [9]
c. System Capacity will be 50 MW for bulk services, 1 MW for T&D services and 3 MW for frequency regulation
d. Discharge duration will be within 5 and 6 h per cycle and total 365 cycles per year for bulk and T&D services and 1 h per cycle with 3650 cycles per year in case of frequency regulation [7]
e. Round trip AC/AC efficiency for Bulk, T&D and Frequency regulation services will be 75 %, 80 % and 90 % respectively with 100 % depth of discharge in each case
f. The Energy Storage System will be charged during the off-peak hours when the electricity is the cheapest and here it is considered at $ 0.03/kWh (weighted average in 2013 was $ 0.026) [10]

g. No repair & maintenance will be required in first 5-years and after that, it will cost about 0.1 % of total cost of system every year

h. Useful life of the systems will be 15-years and the project will flow straight line method for calculation of depreciation

i. The projects will be financed by at 50: 50, Debt – Equity ratio

j. Cost of debt will be 5 % per annum (Average yield in Govt. bonds over 10 years– 2.85 %, Prime Rate in Banks–3 %) [8]

k. Debt repayment will be made by 10 equal yearly instalments

l. Cost of equity is considered at 7 % per annum [11, 12]

m. Corporate Tax Rate 27.5 % [13]

n. Operating costs, battery replacement costs and time are considered as it shown in SANIDA report [7].

3.1 Spinning and Bulk Energy Services

Based on the above mentioned cost structure and other assumptions, economic analysis of the technologies for spinning and bulk energy services has been done, results of which are shown and discussed below.

Figure 4 below shows the profitability (net profit after tax) of the technologies after meeting all expenses including tax. From Fig. 4, it is clearly found that only Iron-Chromium (Fe-Cr) battery, Zinc-Air (Zn-Air) battery, and Zinc-Bromine (Zn-Br) battery systems will be economically profitable i.e. will be able to make some profit after meeting all obligations including tax. But, as the amount of profit of Zinc-Bromine battery is minimal and hence it might fail to generate profit if small increase in expenses or small decrease in income generation occurs. From the fore-casted results, it is also found that Sodium-sulphur (NaS) and Vanadium Redox (VRB) batteries will even not be able to meet the cost of services to be provided from its generated revenue (Gross Profit of these two systems are negative).

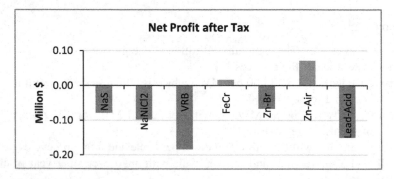

Fig. 4. Net Profit after Tax of different chemical storages for spinning reserve and bulk energy services

If we look at the Debt-service Coverage Ratio (DSCR) of the technologies as shown in Fig. 5, it is found that only Iron-Chromium battery and Zinc-Air battery have DCSR greater than one which means that only these systems will be able to meet the

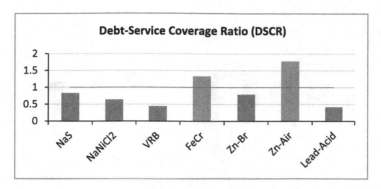

Fig. 5. Debt-service coverage ratio (DSCR) of different chemical storages for spinning reserve and bulk energy services

financial liabilities against the debt though it is considered that debt will only be 50 % of total cost. Though Net Profit after Tax of Zinc-Bromine battery is found positive but the DCSR is below one which indicates that this technology might earn some profit but will not be able to repay the debt (including principal repayment).

From the rest of figures (Figs. 6, 7, 8 and 9) shown below, it is found that in overall consideration only Iron-Chromium (Fe-Cr) battery and Zinc-Air (Zn-Air) battery systems will be economically feasible at present conditions (the IRR of these systems are higher than WACC, their NPVs' are positive, Payback Period are less than 15 years and the BC Ratios are greater than one). Though Zinc-Bromine (Zn-Br) battery system has positive retained earnings, DSCR greater than one and payback period is less than 15 years, but still it is not economically feasible as the IRR is less than WACC, NPV is negative and BC ratio is less than one. Hence, we can say that at the set assumptions only Iron-Chromium Battery and Zinc-Air Battery systems are economically feasible. All other technologies are not found economically feasible in overall consideration as due to higher capital cost of the systems (due to higher capital cost depreciation expenses of these technologies are more than 70 % of revenue generation).

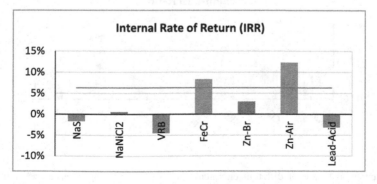

Fig. 6. Internal rate of return (IRR) of different chemical storages for spinning reserve and bulk energy services

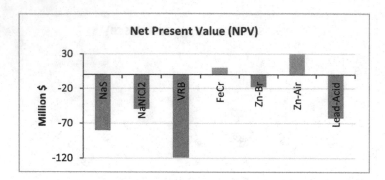

Fig. 7. Net present value (NPV) of different chemical storages for spinning reserve and bulk energy services

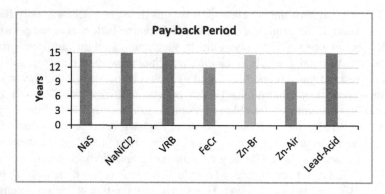

Fig. 8. Pay-back period of different chemical storages for spinning reserve and bulk energy services

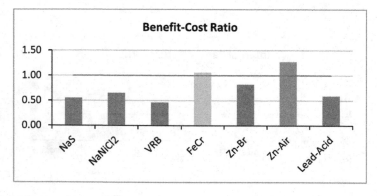

Fig. 9. Benefit-cost ratio of different chemical storages for spinning reserve and bulk energy services

3.2   Utility Transmission and Distribution Services

Based on the above mentioned cost structure and other assumptions, economic analysis of the technologies for utility transmission and distribution services have been done, results of which are shown and discussed below.

Figure 10 below is showing the profitability (net profit after tax) of the technologies after meeting all expenses including tax. From Fig. 10 it is clearly found that only Iron-Chromium (Fe-Cr) battery and Zinc-Air (Zn-Air) battery systems will be economically profitable in case of utility transmission and distribution (T&D) services (Net Profit after Tax of these technologies are positive). But, as the amount of profit of Iron-Chromium (Fe-Cr) battery will be very low and hence it might fail to generate profit if small increase in expenses or small decrease in income generation occurs.

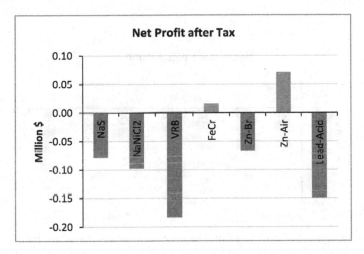

Fig. 10. Net profit after tax of different chemical storages for utility transmission and distribution services

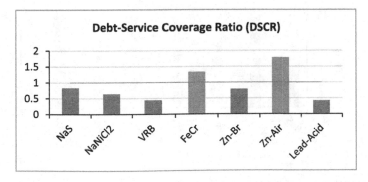

Fig. 11. Debt-service coverage ratio (DSCR) of different chemical storages for utility transmission and distribution services

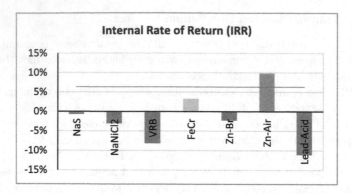

Fig. 12. Internal rate of return (IRR) of different chemical storages for utility transmission and distribution services

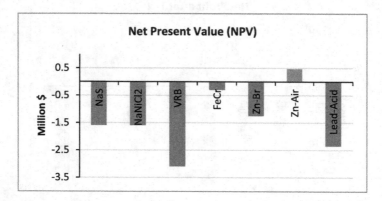

Fig. 13. Net present value (NPV) of different chemical storages for utility transmission and distribution services

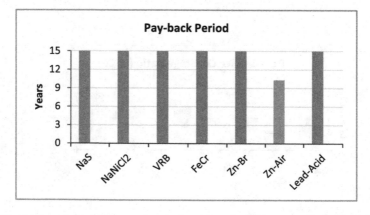

Fig. 14. Pay-back period of different chemical storages for utility transmission and distribution services

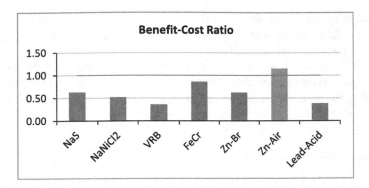

Fig. 15. Benefit-cost ratio of different chemical storages for utility transmission and distribution services

From Fig. 11 below it is found that debt-service coverage ratio (DSCR) of only Zinc-Air battery id greater that one i.e. only this technology will be able to meet the financial liabilities against its debt. Though Net Profit after Tax of Iron-Chromium (Fe-Cr) battery is found positive but its DCSR is below one which indicates that this technology might earn some profit but will not be able to repay the debt.

From the rest of figures (Figs. 12, 13, 14 and 15) shown below, it is found that in overall consideration only Zinc-Air (Zn-Air) battery technology will be economically feasible at present conditions (the IRR of these systems are higher than WACC, their NPVs' are positive, Payback Period are less than 15 years and the BC Ratios are greater than one). Though Iron-Chromium (Fe-Cr) battery system has positive net profit after tax but still it is not economically feasible as its DSCR is less than one, IRR is less than WACC, NPV is negative, pay-back period is more than 15-years and BC ratio is less than one. Hence, we can say that at present condition only Zinc-Air battery technology is economically feasible.

3.3   Combination of Multiple Services

To see the economic aspects of the technologies when some of those will be combined to provide more than one energy storage services, we forecasted the results considering

Table 2. Economic indicatore of combination of multiple energy storage services

Indicators	Results
Net Profit after Tax ($ /Yr)	5,338,268
Debt-Service Coverage Ratio (Times)	2.05
Weighted Average Cost of Capital (WACC)	6.27 %
Internal Rate of Return (IRR)	13.55 %
Net Present Value (NPV)($)	54,093,970
Modified Internal Rate of Return (MIRR)	9.36 %
Pay-Back Period (Years)	8.31
Benefit-Cost Ratio	1.28

a combined system of 3–technologies (Iron-Chromium for mainly for bulk services, Zinc-Air for T&D services and Li-ion for frequency regulation). Summary of results are shown in the following table (Table 2).

From all the above, it is revealed that if a combined system is made for multiple energy storage services the system becomes more feasible economically (DSCR, IRR, NPV, MIRR, Payback period and BC ratio all are better in case of combined system then the other two cases) than the individual systems.

4 Conclusion

From all the above shown economic analysis, it is revealed that only two chemical storage technologies (Iron-Chromium (Fe-Cr) battery and Zinc-Air (Zn-Air) battery) will be economically feasible at present condition. Some of the technologies like Lead-Acid batteries and Vanadium Redox Batteries are very far from economic feasibility (even gross profit of these technologies is found negative). It is also found that a combined system for multiple energy storage services will be more feasible than a system designed for single service. The technologies which are found more economically attractive are still at laboratory or early stage of demonstration trials. So, it is expected that with further research and development of these technologies and commercialization, their reliability and the overall cost of the technologies will decrease further and these energy storage technologies will become more economically attractive.

References

1. Sandia National Laboratories: DOE/EPRI 2013 Electricity Storage Handbook in Collaboration with NRECA, USA, Sandia Corporation, United States Department of Energy (SAND2013-5131) p1-110 (2013)
2. Coppez, G., Chowdhury, S., Chowdhury, S.P.: The importance of energy storage in renewable power generation: a review. In: EPEC2010, 45th International Universities' Power Engineering Conference, Cardiff, Wales, 31st August - 3rd September 2010 (2010)
3. Ibrahima, H., Ilincaa, A., Perronb, J.: Energy storage systems—Characteristics and comparisons. Sci. Dir. Renew. Sustain. Energy Rev. 12(2008), 1221–1250 (2008)
4. De Gramo, E., Sullivan, W.G.: Engineering Economy, 9th edn. Macmillan, New York (1993)
5. Vanek, F.M., Albright, L.D.: Energy System Engineering Evaluation & Implementation. The McGraw-Hill Companies, Inc., New York (2008)
6. Wikipedia, The Free Encyclopedia: Debt Service Coverage Ratio (2013). http://en.wikipedia.org/wiki/Debt_service_coverage_ratio. Accessed 11 April 2014
7. Sandia National Laboratories: DOE/EPRI 2013 Electricity Storage Handbook in Collaboration with NRECA, USA, Sandia Corporation, United States Department of Energy (SAND2013-5131). Appendix-B (2013)
8. Bank of Canada: Selected Bond Yields (2014). http://www.bankofcanada.ca/rates/interest-rates/canadian-bonds/. Accessed 29 March 2014

9. The Independent Electricity System Operator (IESO): Daily Operating Reserve Prices, year-to-date. http://www.ieso.ca/Pages/Power-Data/Price.aspx. Accessed 27 March 2014
10. The Independent Electricity System Operator (IESO): Price Overview (2014). http://www.ieso.ca/Pages/Power-Data/Price.aspx. Accessed 27 March, 2014
11. Scotia Bank: Returns from Scotia Canadian Equity Funds (2014). http://www.scotiabank.com/ca/en/0,,736,00.html. Accessed 29 March 2014
12. Royal Bank of Canada (RBC): RBC Funds (2014). http://fundinfo.rbcgam.com/mutual-funds/rbc-funds/performance/default.fs. Accessed 29 March 2104
13. KPMG: Federal and Provincial Territorial Tax Rates for Income Earned by a General Corporation Effective, 1 January 2104. http://www.kpmg.com/Ca/en/IssuesAndInsights/ArticlesPublications/TaxRates/federal-and-provincialterritorial-tax-rates-for-income-earned-gen-corp-2014.pdf. Accessed 29 March 2104
14. INM – Leibniz Institute for New Materials (2014). http://www.leibniz-inm.de/forschung/grenzflachenmaterialien/energie-materialien/. Accessed 30 May 2015

Trends in Short-Term Renewable and Load Forecasting for Applications in Smart Grid

Dongchan Lee[✉], Jangwon Park, and Deepa Kundur

University of Toronto, Toronto, ON M5S 3G4, Canada
{dongchan.lee,jangwon.park}@utoronto.ca, dkundur@comm.utoronto.ca

Abstract. The development of smart grid paradigm enabled greater integration of renewable energy sources into the generation mix based on the renewable and load forecasting. This paper presents a review of applications and recent development in short-term forecasting methods for smart grids. We look at the characteristics and limitations of the methods and how they are used to improve the performance of smart grids. While the existing forecasting methods such as time series models and artificial intelligence have been successful, we focus on the new applications that rise in smart electric grid. There is an increasing interest in using distributed generation such as in microgrids, and as a result, the demand for forecasting at distribution system level is growing.

Keywords: Load forecasting · Renewable forecasting · Demand response · Microgrid · Energy management system · Neural network · Support vector machine · Smart grid

1 Introduction

Accurate forecasting of demand and supply is a critical component of operation and planning of power systems. Historically, load forecasting has played an important role in power system operation, and thus it has been a popular topic for research especially with the growing interest of integrating renewable energy sources. Load forecasting is typically divided into short term forecasting, which is less than a day ahead, and mid to long term forecasting, which is more than a day ahead. While unit commitment, economic dispatch and maintenance schedule rely on the short term forecasting, transmission planning, generation mix, and long term outage planning rely on long term load forecasting. In this paper, we will focus on short term forecasting methods, which contribute to the operation of the grid.

Generation from renewable energy sources is uncertain in nature because they are intermittent primary sources. Therefore, increased penetration of renewables has introduced high volatility and uncertainty into the system, and the need for accurate supply and demand forecasting is growing. Wind and solar energy have been the two most dominant intermittent renewable energy sources, and the

© ICST Institute for Computer Sciences, Social Informatics and Telecommunications Engineering 2016
A. Leon-Garcia et al. (Eds.): Smart City 2015, LNICST 166, pp. 292–300, 2016.
DOI: 10.1007/978-3-319-33681-7_24

forecasting methods have been developed separately based on their characteristics. Wind power generation is highly dependent on wind speed, and the solar power generation is highly dependent on solar irradiation.

This paper reviews the current demand in renewable and load forecasting for smart grid applications and existing methodologies in forecasting. We pay particular attention to the recent development in smart grid technologies to identify the current trend in their need of supply and demand forecasting. We start with Sect. 2 where we formulate the general problem of load and renewable forecasting and the characteristics that distinguish the problem. In Sect. 3, we identify the applications of forecasting in smart grids and explore the current needs in terms of accuracy and duration. Section 4 reviews the state of the art forecasting methods, and the trend and future needs will be discussed in Sect. 5 followed by the conclusion.

2   Problem Formulation

The renewable and load forecasting problem is predicting the future condition $\mathbf{y} - [y_1 \ y_2 \ ... \ y_m]$ based on input parameters $\mathbf{x} = [x_1 \ x_2 \ ... \ x_n]$, which often involve weather indices, time, any special events, etc. The problem usually involves a set of parameters $\mathbf{w}$ that characterize the predictor $\hat{\mathbf{y}} = f(\mathbf{x}, \mathbf{w})$. The objective is to minimize the forecast error,

$$\min d(\mathbf{y}, \hat{\mathbf{y}}) \tag{1}$$

where $d(y, \hat{y})$ defines the pre-defined distance between data y and $\hat{y}$. For example, this distance can be the square of the difference or absolute value of the difference. The problem resembles the classical machine learning problem, and thus the machine learning algorithm has been a popular tool for renewable and load forecasting. There are some unique characteristics that are only inherent in energy system forecasting problems:

1. Energy forecasting requires a number of exogenous variables that are difficult to capture with the provided data. Weather conditions, unprecedented events and human behaviour are difficult to quantify with only few variables.
2. Renewable and load require time series forecasting. The generation and load change over continuous time, and the forecast has to be made in discrete time with fixed or various time steps depending on its application.
3. Power system is a critical infrastructure where reliability should be one of the most prioritized objectives. The forecast error should be small enough so that it does not affect the security of the system.

Forecasting, when inaccurate, can threaten the reliability of the system, and thus is important for decision making of the system operators. Smart grid brings many features that will benefit the system operation, but it will introduce greater vulnerabilities at the same time. In the next section, we will look at how the forecast fit into the smart grid applications and their impact on the grid.

3   Applications of Forecasting in Smart Grid

Smart grid introduced many applications where load and renewable forecasting is required. The observability of the state are the input variables for the control and dispatch of power systems, and therefore, the performance of applications have a strong link to the performance of the forecast.

3.1   Demand Response

Contrary to the conventional economic dispatch in transmission system, the demand response attempts to match the load to supply [1,2]. Demand response uses planned contracts or price incentives to reduce the consumption when the supply is insufficient. Since the required capacity of demand response depends on the renewable supply and the load, the forecast is a valuable piece of information to make plans ahead of time. The main purpose of demand response is the peak reduction, which requires the forecast of the amount of deficient supply and the time when the electricity would peak. The implementation of demand response in buildings and home energy management is done at the residential level with decision support system and home automation [3]. Forecasting is often done for the aggregate load and resources, but there is a growing need for forecast at the local level [4]. In the case of controllable loads, the load control depends on the forecast, requiring the control strategy to be robust against forecast error [5]. Many of the demand response are aware that the forecasts are subject to error, and thus robustness against forecast error is an important objective in designing the demand response program. Demand response could utilize real-time pricing where load forecasting becomes critical to balance the market [6]. In addition, demand response is usually used for short-term or real-time applications, and the forecast value is required at anytime from hours to day ahead [3].

3.2   Microgrid Energy Management System

Microgrid is a low voltage power system that allows easier integration of renewable energy sources. The energy management system of the microgrid assigns real and reactive power references to the generators and controllable loads, and for long-term energy balance, the EMS requires the day-ahead forecast of renewable generation and load [7]. The main challenge in microgrid management is that the power output fluctuates with the changing weather conditions, which tampers the power quality of the grid. Reliable and economical operation of microgrids requires coordination among the distributed generators, which also accounts for the uncertainty. The uncertainty in microgrid is higher than the bulk power system, so the role of forecast becomes more crucial [8]. The forecast value is mostly used in their tertiary control, which determines appropriate unit commitment and dispatch for the resources. In fact, most energy management system for microgrid include forecast modules [9], and improved accuracy and reliability of forecast will strengthen the security and resilience of the microgrid.

3.3   Control of Energy Storage

Energy storage is identified as one of the key technologies that will enable large integration of renewable energy sources. Energy storage can compensate for the errors in the forecast and maintain a certain level of reserves [10]. The purpose of energy storage is to increase reliability and reduce the penalties from the forecast errors. The management of energy storage includes the prediction layer where the renewable and load forecast are used to estimate the status [11]. The charging and discharging depends on both the current status and the predicted load and supply profile because the capacity of energy storage is limited. The energy storage needs to forecast the time the supply is expected to be deficient, and it needs to be charged ahead of the expected time. In the next section, we review the existing forecasting methods and their appropriate applications.

4   Renewable and Load Forecasting

The load and renewable forecasting requires the researchers to deal with the unpredictability of the natural and human behaviour. Many papers have addressed these challenges in uncertainty with various methods including time series models, artificial neural network, support vector machine and hybrid models. In this section, we will explore the techniques that are recently developed and used in smart grid.

4.1   Time Series Models

Time series models use a sequence of data points over a time interval to make predictions for the future. One of the most well known time series models is the auto regressive (AR) model where the output variable depends linearly on the data previously taken over time. In [12], a method of predicting the photovoltaic (PV) generation using an Bayesian AR model is presented. The paper first chooses an analytical expression of the probability density function (pdf) of the hourly clearness index and defines an AR time series model to represent the relationship between the pdf parameters, meteorological variables, and the clearness index. While the conventional time series approach does not consider the weather data [13], the Bayesian AR model is able to incorporate weather data such as clearness index, ambient temperature, relative humidity, wind speed and cloud cover. Finally, through the Monte Carlo simulation procedure, the model generates the predicted pdf of the PV's active power. Similarly, the method proposed in [14] predicts short term solar power generation using adaptive linear time series models based on recursive least squares (RLS). It accomplishes this by first normalizing solar power with the clear sky model and employing the AR and the AR with exogenous input (ARX) models. The paper introduces adaptivity to consider the snow cover, leaves and dirt on the panel, etc. Several works including [15,16] have also reviewed the application of AR models for the purpose of solar forecasting.

Other methods of time series analysis include auto regressive moving average (ARMA) models, which are general cases of the AR and moving average (MA) models. ARMA models consist of both the AR and MA models and forecast future values based on the linear combination of the past values and errors. [17] presents a method of integrating the ARMA models with a Kalman filter to ensure accuracy in predicting the time distribution of solar radiation and ambient temperature. It adjusts the climatic parameters at every five minute intervals based on their acquired values and their last prediction errors. Auto regressive integrated moving average (ARIMA) models are presented in [18] to predict sub-hourly and hourly PV arrays power output.

The time series model is a dominant technique in short term solar forecasting because it is flexible in handling a wide range of different time series patterns. The short term weather is likely to be dependent on the previous weather condition, so it is especially attractive for modeling solar irradiance. However, time series models show deficiency in modeling holidays, weekends, and seasonal changing periods [13,19], and currently, it is not widely used in load forecasting or wind forecasting, which constantly changes.

4.2 Artificial Neural Networks

Artificial neural networks (ANN) are inspired from the human brain and how it processes information. In our brain, the neurons are the basic units that receive, process and output response. Similarly, ANNs define the activation functions that receive linear combination of the data with weight **w**. ANNs are organized in multiple layers that use *hidden variables*, which are not directly observed, but are used in the computation. There has been a great success with ANNs in renewable and load forecasting [13,20]. In [21], solar irradiation and wind velocity are taken as inputs to predict the maximum power generation of PV systems, and in [22] solar irradiation and air temperature are considered. ANN is also a popular method in short term wind power forecasting because wind often experiences high variation over a short period of time [23,24]. However, the performance of ANNs significantly drops as the prediction lead period increases. The major application where ANNs showed most success is the load forecasting, which predicts the peak load, valley load, and total load [13,19]. Accuracy and reliability make it very attractable for applications in smart grid [6,25].

The main advantage of ANN is that it does not require specific model based on knowledge, and the historical data is directly linked to the output [19]. It accounts for non-linearity among data and is able to detect all possible interactions between predictor variables. However, NNs also present the problem of over-fitting, requiring much computational resources and time, missing an exact rule for setting the number of hidden neurons, having poor scalability, and lacking the ability to generate explanations for their results [26,27]. These are classical problems in ANN for other applications, and there are methods such as cross-validation and regularization to overcome the problem of over-fitting.

4.3   Support Vector Machine

Support vector machines (SVM) are machine learning techniques of inferring a function from a set of training data associated with learning algorithms which analyze data and recognize patterns. SVMs are typically used for classification and regression analysis, and has been a popular tool for load forecasting. [28] proposes a method of using linear least squares regression and SVM with site-specific forecast data from National Weather Service to derive prediction models for solar power at individual smart homes. [29] proposes daily peak load forecasting model for smart meters based on the technique of support vector regression (SVR) using least squares. The authors mention that their method can potentially be used by utility companies in their large-scale load forecasting application. [30] reports that high accuracy can be achieved with SVM for distribution system energy forecasting. The paper also looks at the extension of their method for determining optimal demand response and anomaly detection in energy usage.

SVM accounts for non-linearity among data by finding a hyperplane that could divide the data points into different spaces. The accuracy of SVM depends on the selection of kernel function and parameters, which transform the input space to the high-dimensional feature space [28]. Although SVM may have advantages in accuracy, it requires great computational resources and time in both training and testing, as well as the parametrisation of kernel functions [26].

4.4   Hybrid Models

In order to take advantage of different methods, many researches have been done to develop and test hybrid models or a combination of known methods to improve the efficiency and accuracy of load forecasting. In [26], a post-processing method is employed to overcome the shortcomings of the conventional methods in efficiency, flexibility, and scalability. Their post-processing method attempts to identify the appropriate techniques to be applied in different circumstances for better performance. Similarly, [31] proposes a hybrid model of wavelet transform, firefly algorithm, and fuzzy ARTMAP to achieve significant improvement in lowering mean average percentage error compared to various other single or hybrid forecasting models. [32] performs similar tasks of improving accuracy by combining regression tree and Gaussian Process to accurately predict maximum daily temperatures, which are vital in handling demand response and PV.

The hybrid models address new challenges that rise in smart grid by introducing variables that were not considered conventionally. For example, as consumers gain the ability to manage their consumption, new considerations such as the effect of electricity prices on consumer behaviour require a new framework that can successfully account for this price-demand relationship. [33] proposes such a model which combines multi-input multi-output forecasting engine with data mining algorithms to make joint price and load predictions. Hybrid models consider the complex relationships among the variables, which could improve the accuracy. While hybrid models can improve the accuracy and flexibility in forecasting, they depend on the combination of methods or the overall framework and require much computational resources.

5   Discussion

We have explored smart grid applications, which make use of renewable and load forecasts, and the existing forecasting methods. Fundamentally, the applications such as demand response and energy management of microgrid depend on the forecast to plan the operation. Although the demand of accurate and reliable forecasting methods is always high, developing a single perfect forecasting method that works best in all situations is practically impossible due to the volatility of nature. This paper reviewed existing methods for forecasting in power systems and their advantages and disadvantages. Hybrid models seem to be promising in increasing accuracy by taking advantage of different methods, but they will come at the expense of simplicity.

The principles and techniques used for forecasting did not significantly change with the advent of smart grids. However, many recent papers suggest that the power system is going in the direction of local distributed network such as microgrid, and the development of forecasting methods should accompany the current needs. There is a growing demand for distributed forecasting where the forecast is required at the household level, and it will require an efficient and reliable forecasting methods.

In addition, we have seen that the performance of forecasting is fundamentally dependent on and limited by the historic data. It is important to test and evaluate the methods for the data from various case studies to overcome the issue of data-dependency. In order to overcome this issue, we have seen the research effort for the algorithm to be robust and adaptive to change in variables.

6   Conclusion

Reliable and accurate forecasting of renewables and load is an essential component in the development of smart grids. This paper presented an overview of applications and current forecasting methods to review the current demand and trend in the field. We explored the requirements and desirable characteristics of each application and also looked at the traits of the existing methods.

While many of the work showed success in various applications, there is still a need for developing forecast models at the distribution system level. In addition, we require standard test cases and numerical examples to clearly illustrate the performance difference between developed methods. A more standardized procedure will enable direct comparison of the methods and numerical characterization of the forecasting techniques.

References

1. Albadi, M.H., El-Saadany, E.F.: Demand response in electricity markets: an overview. In: Power Engineering Society General Meeting, pp. 1–5. IEEE, June 2007
2. Lee, D., Kundur, D.: An evolutionary game approach to predict demand response from Real-Time pricing. In: IEEE Electrical Power and Energy Conference (EPEC), London, Canada, October 2015
3. Siano, P.: Demand response and smart grids a survey. Renew. Sustain. Energy Rev. **30**, 461–478 (2014)
4. Moslehi, K., Kumar, R.: Smart grid - a reliability perspective. In: Innovative Smart Grid Technologies (ISGT), pp. 1–8, January 2010
5. Huang, K.-Y., Chin, H.-C., Huang, Y.-C.: A model reference adaptive control strategy for interruptible load management. IEEE Trans. Power Syst. **19**(1), 683–689 (2004)
6. Chan, S.C., Tsui, K.M., Wu, H.C., Hou, Y., Wu, Y.-C., Wu, F.F.: Load/price forecasting and managing demand response for smart grids: methodologies and challenges. IEEE Sig. Process. Mag. **29**(5), 68–85 (2012)
7. Kanchev, H., Lu, D., Colas, F., Lazarov, V., Francois, B.: Energy management and operational planning of a microgrid with a pv-based active generator for smart grid applications. IEEE Trans. Ind. Electron. **58**(10), 4583–4592 (2011)
8. Olivares, D.E., Mehrizi-Sani, A., Etemadi, A.H., Canizares, C.A., Iravani, R., Kazerani, M., Hajimiragha, A.H., Gomis-Bellmunt, O., Saeedifard, M., Palma-Behnke, R., Jimenez-Estevez, G.A., Hatziargyriou, N.D.: Trends in microgrid control. IEEE Trans. Smart Grid **5**(4), 1905–1919 (2014)
9. Motevasel, M., Seifi, A.R.: Expert energy management of a micro-grid considering wind energy uncertainty. Energy Convers. Manage. **83**, 58–72 (2014)
10. Daz-Gonzlez, F., Sumper, A., Gomis-Bellmunt, O., Villaffila-Robles, R.: A review of energy storage technologies for wind power applications. Renew. Sustain. Energy Rev. **16**(4), 2154–2171 (2012)
11. Sechilariu, M., Wang, B., Locment, F.: Building integrated photovoltaic system with energy storage and smart grid communication. IEEE Trans. Industrial Electron. **60**(4), 1607–1618 (2013)
12. Bracale, A., Caramia, P., Carpinelli, G., Di Fazio, A.R., Ferruzzi, G.: A bayesian method for short-term probabilistic forecasting of photovoltaic generation in smart grid operation and control. Energies **6**(2), 733 (2013)
13. Park, D.C., El-Sharkawi, M.A., Marks II, R.J., Atlas, L.E., Damborg, M.J.: Electric load forecasting using an artificial neural network. IEEE Trans. Power Syst. **6**(2), 442–449 (1991)
14. Bacher, P., Madsen, H., Nielsen, H.A.: Online short-term solar power forecasting. Sol. Energy **83**(10), 1772–1783 (2009)
15. Inman, R.H., Pedro, H.T.C., Coimbra, C.F.M.: Solar forecasting methods for renewable energy integration. Prog. Energy Combust. Sci. **39**(6), 535–576 (2013)
16. Martn, L., Zarzalejo, L.F., Polo, J., Navarro, A., Marchante, R., Cony, M.: Prediction of global solar irradiance based on time series analysis: application to solar thermal power plants energy production planning. Sol. Energy **84**(10), 1772–1781 (2010)
17. Chaabene, M.: Measurements based dynamic climate observer. Sol. Energy **82**(9), 763–771 (2008)

18. Hassanzadeh, M., Etezadi-Amoli, M., Fadali, M.S.: Practical approach for sub-hourly and hourly prediction of pv power output. In: North American Power Symposium (NAPS) pp. 1–5, September 2010
19. Lu, C.N., Wu, H.-T., Vemuri, S.: Neural network based short term load forecasting. IEEE Trans. Power Syst. **8**(1), 336–342 (1993)
20. Hippert, H.S., Pedreira, C.E., Souza, R.C.: Neural networks for short-term load forecasting: a review and evaluation. IEEE Trans. Power Syst. **16**(1), 44–55 (2001)
21. Hiyama, T., Kitabayashi, K.: Neural network based estimation of maximum power generation from pv module using environmental information. IEEE Trans. Energy Convers. **12**(3), 241–247 (1997)
22. Ioakimidis, C.S., Eliasstam, H., Rycerski, P.: Solar power forecasting of a residential location as part of a smart grid structure. In: Energytech, 2012 IEEE, pp. 1–6, May 2012
23. Wu, Y.-K., Hong, J.-S.: A literature review of wind forecasting technology in the world. In: Power Tech, 2007 IEEE Lausanne, pp. 504–509, July 2007
24. Potter, C.W., Negnevitsky, M.: Very short-term wind forecasting for tasmanian power generation. IEEE Trans. Power Syst. **21**(2), 965–972 (2006)
25. Zhang, H.-T., Xu, F.-Y., Zhou, L.: Artificial neural network for load forecasting in smart grid. In: 2010 International Conference on Machine Learning and Cybernetics (ICMLC), vol. 6, pp. 3200–3205, July 2010
26. Borges, C.E., Penya, Y.K., Fernandez, I.: Optimal combined short-term building load forecasting. In: Innovative Smart Grid Technologies Asia (ISGT), 2011 IEEE PES, pp. 1–7, November 2011
27. Tu, J.V.: Advantages and disadvantages of using artificial neural networks versus logistic regression for predicting medical outcomes. J. Clin. Epidemiol. **49**(11), 1225–1231 (1996)
28. Sharma, N., Sharma, P., Irwin, D., Shenoy, P.: Predicting solar generation from weather forecasts using machine learning. In: 2011 IEEE International Conference on Smart Grid Communications (SmartGridComm), pp. 528–533. IEEE (2011)
29. Aung, Z., Toukhy, M., Williams, J., Sanchez, A., Herrero, S.: Towards accurate electricity load forecasting in smart grids. In: The Fourth International Conference on Advances in Databases, Knowledge, and Data Applications, DBKDA (2012)
30. Yu, W., An, D., Griffith, D., Yang, Q., Guobin, X.: Towards statistical modeling and machine learning based energy usage forecasting in smart grid. SIGAPP Appl. Comput. Rev. **15**(1), 6–16 (2015)
31. Haque, A.U., Mandal, P., Meng, J., Pineda, R.L.: Performance evaluation of different optimization algorithms for power demand forecasting applications in a smart grid environment. Procedia Comput. Sci. **12**, 320–325 (2012). Complex Adaptive Systems 2012
32. Singh, A.K.: Smart grid load forecasting. Int. J. Eng. Res. Appl. (IJERA) (2012)
33. Motamedi, A., Zareipour, H., Rosehart, W.D.: Electricity price and demand forecasting in smart grids. IEEE Trans. Smart Grid **3**(2), 664–674 (2012)

An Overview of Smart Grids in the GCC Region

İslam Şafak Bayram[1](✉) and Hamed Mohsenian-Rad[2]

[1] Qatar Environment and Energy Research Institute and College of Science
and Engineering, Hamad Bin Khalifa University, Doha, Qatar
ibayram@qf.org.qa
[2] Department of Electrical Engineering, University of California, Riverside, USA
hamed@ece.ucr.edu

Abstract. The members of the Gulf Cooperation Council (GCC),
namely Qatar, Bahrain, Saudi Arabia, Kuwait, Oman, and United Arab
Emirates (UAE), are facing challenges to meet the growing electricity
demand and reduce the associated hydrocarbon emissions. Recently, there
has been a pressing need for a shift towards smart power grids, as smart
grids can reduce the stress on the grid, defer the investments for upgrades,
improve the power system efficiency, and reduce emissions. Accordingly,
the goal of this paper is to delineate an overview of current smart grid
efforts in the GCC region. First, we present a detailed overview of the current state of the power grids. Then, we classify the efforts into three broad
categories: (i) energy trading and exchange through GCC interconnection;
(ii) integration of renewable resources; and (iii) demand side management
technologies for shaping the demand profile.

Keywords: Smart grids · Gulf Cooperation Council · Qatar · Bahrain ·
Kingdom of Saudi Arabia · Kuwait · Oman · United Arab Emirates (UAE)

1   Introduction

Over the last few years, the fast-growing energy needs in the GCC region has
intensified a central challenge: how to reduce the cost power systems operations
and minimize the hydrocarbon emissions. As the significant portion of the GCC
economies relies on oil and gas reserves, the GCC governments show growing
amount of interest to diversify their economies for the post-carbon era. To that
end, there has been a substantial amount of interest in the integration smart
grids. Overall, there are three primary group of interest: (1) energy exchange
among neighboring states to improve power system stability; (2) integration of
renewable resources to reduce carbon emissions; and (3) demand response programs to shape the load profile and lessen the cost of system operations. One
essential element of such efforts is the GCC Interconnection Grid that connects
the power systems of six member countries. The integration is expected to transform the region into a significant energy hub, and the network is envisioned to
expand to other parts of the world, e.g., sell electricity to North African Countries
and Southern Europe. The GCC members are endowed with a significant portion

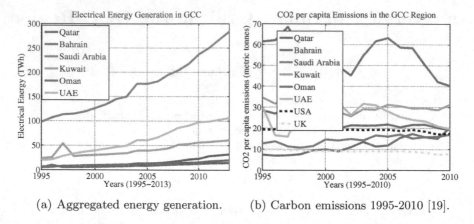

(a) Aggregated energy generation.   (b) Carbon emissions 1995-2010 [19].

Fig. 1. Energy demand and the population growth over the years. (Color figure online)

of the world's hydrocarbon resources: 33.9 % of the proven crude oil and 22.3 % of the proven natural gas resources reside in the region. Owning such abundant resources have boosted the economies and transformed the region within a mere of two decades into the world's wealthiest nations (in term of GDP per capita). In addition to the economic boom, high fertility rates, increasing population of expats, and the desire for a better standard of living have lead to a steady rise in electricity demand. The trajectory depicted in Fig. 1a shows the enormous energy demand in each country. Also, there has been a tremendous population increase respect. For instance, the population of Qatar is almost tripled within the last two decades. Moreover, gross domestic product per capita is an important determinant of energy usage. The GDP growth, not only increase the energy demand, but also rendered the region among the most carbon-intensive countries in the world. According to 2010 World Bank data, Qatar, Kuwait, Oman, and UAE are the top four nations with the highest emissions per capita [19] and an overview of carbon emissions is depicted in Fig. 1b.

Another primary driver behind the rise in energy consumption is that GCC governments provide substantial subsidies both in electricity and oil tariffs. This policy serves as a means to redistribute the wealth among the citizens. However, reduced tariffs have lead to several adverse impacts. First, low prices translated into over-consumption of energy resources. The majority of the residential energy is consumed for air-conditioning and potable water, the bulk of which comes from energy-intensive desalination of sea water. Second, the GCC governments are facing a fiscal pressure as the volatility in the international markets combined with the foregone export revenues due to over-consumption fuels represent a sizable portion of the national budgets [7]. Third, the increasing levels of carbon emissions due to high consumption raises economic concerns.

The aforementioned issues have pressed the GCC members to reform the power systems through smart grids. In order to provide the motivation for smart grids, in Sect. 2 we give an overview of the current power grids. Then, in the next three sections we present a systematic the overview of GCC interconnection grid, renewable energy integration efforts, and current demand side management programs in the region.

2 Current Power Grid Operations

2.1 Overview

The first GCC power grids were built in the early 50s when there was a need for electricity for oil drilling. With the incline of the oil prices, the region gained significant financial wealth, and the modern power grids were built in the 80s. Compared to western grids, the GCC grids are younger and equipped with modern components. On the other hand, the region often experiences excessively hot days during summers. In such periods, the demand for cooling raises tremendously thus leading to regional blackouts and threatens the security of the supply. Hence, system operators are continuously seeking ways to expand the system capacity to secure the supply.

Even though the region was served by vertically integrated utilities, typically owned by the governments, the GCC members are reforming the sector by unbundling the power generation, transmission, and the distribution segments. This will encourage private sector investments, which will allow the private sector to generate and sell electricity to the customers [3]. The primary drivers of this transformation are the need for improved operational efficiency and the fact that the private sector can quickly respond to economic and technological changes. The Sultanate of Oman is leading the privatization process. Oman is the first member country that allows independent system operators to generate and sell electricity to government authority, which handles transmission and distribution lines.

Table 1. Percentage of generation mix in the GCC. Natural Gas (NG) and Oil are considered.

	Qatar	Bahrain	Saudi Arabia		Kuwait		Oman		UAE	
	NG(%)	NG(%)	NG(%)	Oil(%)	NG(%)	Oil(%)	NG(%)	Oil(%)	NG(%)	Oil(%)
1996	100	100	44.15	55.85	62.43	37.57	82.55	17.45	96.63	3.37
2000	100	100	46.03	53.97	32.92	67.08	82.83	17.17	96.91	3.09
2004	100	100	56.95	43.05	27.68	72.32	82.00	18.00	97.66	2.34
2008	100	100	48.83	51.17	35.65	64.35	97.83	2.17	98.29	1.71
2012	100	100	44.69	55.31	36.22	63.78	97.58	2.42	98.62	1.38

The electricity dispatch curve is also an important parameter for the smart grid operations. Since, the oil and natural gas reserves are abundant in the region, the power generation depends entirely on these two sources. In Table 1, we present the generation mixture of the member countries over the years. The table reveals an interesting fact that the cost of producing electricity is quite different among the members. For instance, Qatar and Bahrain have plenty of natural gas

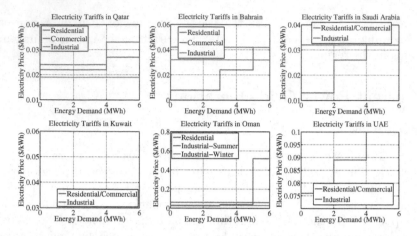

Fig. 2. Electricity tariffs obtained from Qatar [12], Bahrain [13]. Saudi Arabia [14], Kuwait [15], Oman [17], UAE [16]. (Color figure online)

resources, hence hundred percent of the electricity is generated by fossil fuels. On the other hand, countries like Saudi Arabia and Kuwait produce a significant portion of the electricity through diesel generators. Considering the cost and negative environmental impacts of such generators, the interconnection of power grids would provide a good level of savings. For instance, Kuwait and Saudi Arabia could purchase electricity from Qatar and eliminate the need for running diesel generators. Moreover, the GCC members are seeking ways to accommodate the growing demand in through diversifying their generation portfolio. United Arabic Emirates is building nuclear power plants to be operated by 2017 [20] in order to meet the 7 % annual demand growth. Also, Qatar, Saudi Arabia, and UAE have put goals to integrate gigawatt level solar farms. The details will be given in the next section.

2.2   Pricing and Customer Types

The electricity tariffs are the primary control mechanisms to shape the customer demand profile. In the business of electric utilities, the unit electricity cost is calculated through locational marginal prices (LMP) that takes into account various factors such as generator type and cost, distances to load, etc. LMP reflects the marginal cost of supplying an increment of load at each node. LMP are determined in the wholesale market via a bidding structure and details can be found in [9].

The pricing in the GCC region, however, is lower than the marginal prices as the governments provide subsidies to redistribute the wealth to the citizens. For instance, according to [7] the total subsidies in 2011 for electricity exceeded 29 billion Dollars in the GCC region. By considering the populations across the nations, the yearly subsidy per capita can be found as 556.5, 1510.1, 166.9, 1206, 522.28, and 770.81 US Dollars for Bahrain, Kuwait, Oman, Qatar, Saudi Arabia,

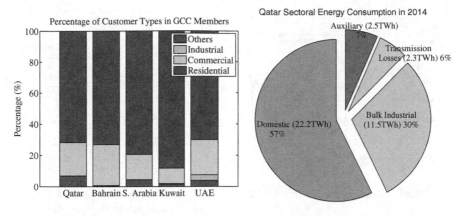

(a) Percentage of customer types [1].   (b) Energy consumption by sector in Qatar (2014).

Fig. 3. Customer types and sectoral energy usage (Color figure online)

and UAE, respectively. The current electricity prices are publicly available on the utility of each country, and we present an overview of the prices in Fig. 2. In the case of Saudi Arabia, for example, the electricity cost is one-fifth of the average US prices. Also, in the State of Qatar, the power consumption of the local citizens are entirely subsidized by the government.

Traditionally electric utilities serve three different customer types namely, residential, commercial, and industrial. The customer types are differentiated by the amount of energy/power requirements and demand curves. As depicted in Fig. 3a, residential customers constitute the vast majority of the meters. This is mainly because the industry is limited to oil and gas and severe weather and limited water resources restrict the agricultural activities. Unlike industrial and commercial customers, the energy demand of residential customers has high variability. This behavior increases the power system operating cost and reduce system utilization. Hence, this state of affairs contain an enormous potential for demand response programs for peak shaving.

Subsidized energy can, however, lead to a range of unintended adverse impacts, as it distorts price signals for consumers, with serious consequences for energy efficiency and the optimal allocation of resources. Low tariffs have lead to over-consumption of energy resources. The majority of the residential energy is consumed for air-conditioning and potable water, the bulk of which comes from energy-intensive desalination of sea water. Moreover, the GCC governments are facing a fiscal pressure as the volatility in the international markets combined with the opportunity cost incurred of exporting over-consumption fuels represent a sizable portion of the national budgets [7].

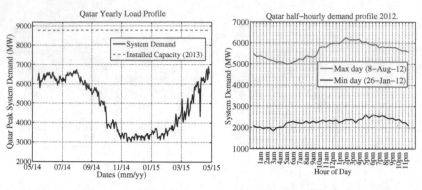

(a) Qatar demand profile in year 2014.   (b) Qatar hourly load profiles for max and min usage days in 2012.

Fig. 4. Increasing energy demand in the GCC (Color figure online)

2.3   Load Profile

The country load profiles, daily, monthly, or yearly contain valuable information on the applicability of the potential smart grid applications. In the case of GCC members, the load profiles reveal how much energy can be exchanged and determine the potential integration renewables and demand response technologies.

Currently, there is no publicly available load profile data in any of the member states. However, the electric utility of Qatar regularly share the peak system usage on their social media page. Hence, we developed a simple data scraping software to collect the data for the last twelve months. We present the yearly load profile of Qatar in Fig. 4a. It can be seen that the peak demand occurs in August when the school season starts and there is a high demand for air conditioning. Moreover, the work in [21] states that there is a linear correlation between the daily peak temperature and the daily peak consumption for days that are warmer than 22°C. Moreover, the seasonal gap between the winter and the summer demand leads to unused system capacity that can be used trade electricity between neighboring countries. This is better depicted in Fig. 4b, where we show the half-hourly demand profile of two sample days from 2012: the first one is the day with the peak system demand (August, 8, 2012) and the second is the day with the lowest customer demand (January, 26, 2012). The results show that there is a high potential to employ demand response techniques to control electricity consumption, especially for the air conditioning load.

3   GCC Interconnected Power Grid

3.1   Overview

The interconnection of GCC power grids can be viewed as the first major smart grid activity. The main drivers of the interconnection grid are: (1) cost efficiency;

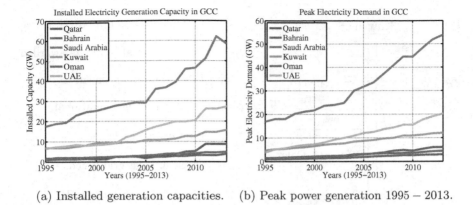

(a) Installed generation capacities.   (b) Peak power generation 1995 − 2013.

Fig. 5. Increasing energy demand in the GCC (Color figure online)

(2) shared spinning reserves; (3) deferred and reduced capacity investments; (4) lower carbon emissions; and (5) development of power markets. The growing energy demand (almost 10 % annually) and the sudden demand surges frequently threaten the supply thus requiring costly investments. For example, in Fig. 5a we present the steady increase in generation capacity expansion for each country. Consequently, as shown in Fig. 5b the peak electricity demand increases and leads to higher operation cost. Furthermore, according to the study conducted in [3], there would be a need to invest one hundred billion Dollars to meet the growing demand of GCC over the next decade.

On the other hand sharing generation and transmission resources can alleviate the upgrade requirements. Hence, the interconnection is of paramount importance. The architecture of the GCC interconnected grid presented in Fig. 6a and the milestones of the project is given in Fig. 6b. Currently, member states are in the phase of creating a power market for energy trading. The real challenge in developing this platform is to find right pricing schemes as the subsidies vary significantly across the region. The benefits of the interconnection grid summarized next.

3.2   Benefits

The benefits of the GCC interconnection grid is multifaceted. From an economic standpoint, the benefits include improved supply security, higher energy efficiency and savings through sharing spinning reserves. Also, the interconnection will reduce additional investments, and operational and maintenance cost. For instance, if Saudi Arabia can reduce total installed capacity by 2 GW, the total savings could be more than $309 million [3]. Also, it is estimated that there will be a $180 million US Dollars of savings in fuel operating costs from the entire region.

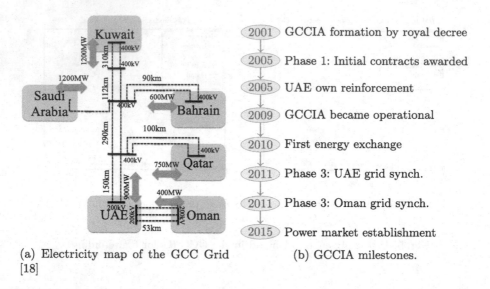

(a) Electricity map of the GCC Grid [18]

(b) GCCIA milestones.

Fig. 6. GCC interconnection grid overview

Moreover, in the case of emergencies the interconnection can provide energy supply. In fact, the security of power supply is one of the primary motivations behind the interconnection grid. According to [6], the GCC power network has prevented 250 sudden power loss incidents among the various member states. The GCC grid can also help to reduce the carbon emissions caused by the using crude oil. Countries such as Kuwait and Saudi Arabia can purchase electricity produced from natural gas, nuclear power, or solar from other countries. Also, with the help of the proper regulations, independent power producers already started to generate profit through energy exchange. Moreover, the member states are considering to create an energy market that can trade electricity with countries like Egypt, Jordan, Iraq, Lebanon, Syria, and Turkey.

3.3 Current Status

Since 2009, the GCC members invested around $1.2 billion US Dollars to build 900 km long 400 kV transmission lines and 9 substations with the same capacity. From 2009 to 2012 GCC interconnection grid has been operational and it has improved the security and reliability of the network. According to GCC Interconnection Authority 2012 annual report, more than 700 incidents occurred between 2009 and 2012. In Fig. 7b, we present the number of mutual support instances among the member states. Notice that Oman is excluded from the lists as Oman was not connected to the network until 2011. Mainly, the interconnected grid ensured that the system operates at the right frequency and voltage standards. Moreover, it prevented the system from demand disconnections. For this reason, member states exchange energy through high transmission lines. For instance

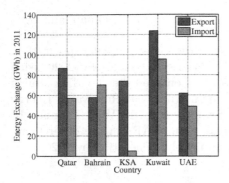
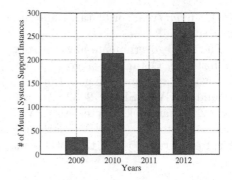

(a) Energy exchange for system support during 2011.

(b) Number of mutual support instances.

Fig. 7. The operation of GCC interconnection grid for power system stability. (Color figure online)

in 2011, 680 GWh of energy was exchanged between the members and Fig. 7a shows the amount of energy exports and imports of each GCC member.

4   Renewable Energy Integration

The GCC region is endowed with one of the world's most abundant solar resources and the integration of renewable energy has attracted systematic interest by the governments. The main drivers behind the solar energy are to minimize the electricity generation and reduce the carbon emissions. For end-users, solar generation is expected to have two applications. In the first one, consumers can install PV panels to their rooftops and generate electricity for domestic usage and sell the excess power back to the grid. Recently, UAE became the first GCC member to allow customers to employ solar rooftops.

One key issue is that the region demographics include a significant number of remote scatters farms and villages. Typically these locations operate off-grid and burn diesel generators, as the integration of the main grid is not economically viable. Hence, the second application would be to run solar panels in off-grid mode that will eliminate the need for burning crude oil.

4.1   Goals & Potential Analysis

The Global Horizontal Irradiance (GHI) defines the average electricity generated from Photovoltaic systems. The measured GHI for the GCC members are 2140, 2160, 2130, 1900, 2050, and 2120 kWh/m^2/year for Qatar, Bahrain, Saudi Arabia, Kuwait, Oman, and UAE respectively. Concentrating Solar Thermal Power (CSP) systems are also widely used for solar energy generation. For CSP technology, Direct Normal Irradiance (DNI) is used to define the average electricity generation. The measured DNI is 2000, 2050, 2000, 1900, 2200, and

$2200\,\mathrm{kWh}/m^2$/year for Qatar, Bahrain, Saudi Arabia, Kuwait, Oman, and UAE respectively.

The GCC governments have set solar penetration goals for solar integration. For instance, Qatar has a goal of putting 1 GW solar panels by 2020 using Photovoltaic systems. Kingdom of Saudi Arabia, on the other hand, is aiming to build 41 GW CSP by 2032. According to International Renewable Energy Agency, Kuwait seeks to create 10 MW Photovoltaic and 50 MW CSP. Similarly, Oman aims to put 700 MW solar capacity by 2020. UAE, on the other hand, seeks to generate 15 % of the total demand from solar generation by 2020.

4.2   Barriers

Even though the region has a high potential for solar integration, the afore-mentioned goals cannot be achieved without addressing the following issues. The first problem is with the materials of the PV panels. The efficiency of the crystalline silicon-based photovoltaic solar cells degrade with high temperature and the current technology does not perform well in the region. Hence, there has been a growing research and development interests in the region to develop new materials for PV panels for in high-temperature conditions which will also improve solar economics in the region. Another barrier to solar integration is the soiling of PV panels due to dust deposition. This is a significant factor as the region frequently experiences sand storms and the performance of the solar systems degrade significantly. For instance according to a study conducted at Qatar Foundation (QF) [22], the power loss is around $10-15\,\%$ per month on average. Similarly, research activities in QF include developing anti-dust tech-nologies such as hydrophobic coatings, robotic cleaners, and electrical shields. Currently, renewable energy integration is very limited in the region because the cost of renewable energy systems compared to conventional electricity gen-eration methods is still very costly. Hence, there is pressing need to create new policies and incentives to push the solar generation into mainstream acceptance. Also, utilities need to create a common standards and regulations and need to consider the effects of solar integration once the GCC grid is fully operational.

5   Demand Side Management

Demand side management (DSM) refers to a set of rules and policies that aim to optimize the energy consumption at the end-user side. The most popular DSM programs that have been used in practice include energy efficiency, dif-ferential tariffs (e.g., time-based tariffs, dynamic pricing), and demand response programs. Such programs are also becoming popular in the GCC region, as DSM programs can shave the peak demand and reduce the cost of system operations.

The aforementioned subsidies provided by the governments have been dis-couraging the investments to efficient infrastructures. Nevertheless, the GCC members recently started to invest in energy efficiency programs in buildings and transportation systems. For instance, Qatar has launched a new energy conservation program called Tarsheed, aiming to improve the energy consumption in residential and commercial buildings. Similarly, in 2012 Saudi Arabia launched the Saudi Energy Efficiency Program in order to enhance the consumption. Similar efforts are carried out in UAE: Dubai initiated a demand-side management committee to reduce energy demand by 30 % by 2030. Similarly, Sharjah of UAE has started a peak load reduction program that enforces citizens to turn off non-essential appliances during peak hours. The GCC members are gradually transforming their transportation systems from oil-based to electric-based [24,25]. Dubai is installing 100 charging stations. Qatar is considering to employ electric vehicles for public transportation for the Fifa 2022 World Cup.

Smart meters and advanced metering infrastructures are critical enablers of demand side management. Qatar utility company Kahramaa already started to deploy 17000 smart meters in Doha teamed up with Siemens for the smart meters [2]. For the case of Oman, the work presented in [23] shows that the long-term benefits of load management outweighs the required investments.

One essential characteristic of the region is that the vast majority of the energy is consumed at residential units, mostly for air-conditioning. Hence, with the help of the communication and sensor technologies, utilities can employ direct load control mechanisms to adjust the load while providing a good level of comfort. Also, the integration of social sciences could help to reduce the peak usage. Peer pressure is one of the most effective methods of reducing electricity consumption. For instance, a social study in California tries to motivate customers to reduce their consumption by comparing the individual bills with the average consumption of their neighbors. This method enables customers to reduce their consumption by 1.5 to 3.5 %. Our final recommendation is for coupling the solar generation with energy-intensive water desalination process.

Recently, the deregulation of electricity markets has provided end consumers with new opportunities to directly offer their load flexibility as a market product. For example, in the U.S., large consumers such as industrial units or commercial buildings are already eligible to participate in both the day-ahead and real-time wholesale markets, e.g., in California [26]. Such market participation is facilitated by submitting *demand bids*. As it is recently shown in [27], DSM can be co-optimized with demand bidding, leading to significant reduction in energy expenditure of time-shiftable and other flexible loads. Similar opportunities could be pursued in the near future in the GCC region once the GCC interconnection wholesale electricity market becomes operational, see Sect. 3.

6   Conclusion

In this paper, we provided an overview of the GCC power grid and smart grid efforts. We showed that the interconnection of the grid would improve grid stability, lead to efficient resource usage, and reduce the operation cost. The integration of abundant solar resources and the implementation of DSM programs can be very useful to substitute diesel generators at remote farms and villages.

References

1. El-Katiri, L., Husain, M.: Prospects for Renewable Energy in GCC States-Opportunities and the Need for Reform. Oxford Institute for Energy Studies (2014)
2. Abdalla, G.: The Deployment of advanced metering infrastructure. In: IEEE First Workshop on Smart Grid and Renewable Energy, Doha, Qatar (2015)
3. Al-Asaad, H.: Electricity power sector reform in the GCC region. Electricity J. **22**(9), 58–64 (2009)
4. Shaahid, S.M., El-Amin, I.: Techno-economic evaluation of off-grid hybrid based hybrid energy system photovoltaic-diesel-battery power systems for rural electrification in Saudi Arabia. A Way Forward for Sustainable Development, Renewable and Sustainable Energy Reviews **13**(3), 625–633 (2009)
5. May, P., Ehrlich, H.C., Steinke, T.: ZIB structure prediction pipeline: composing a complex biological workflow through web services. In: Nagel, W.E., Walter, W.V., Lehner, W. (eds.) Euro-Par 2006. LNCS, vol. 4128, pp. 1148–1158. Springer, Heidelberg (2006)
6. Al-Ebrahim, A.: Super grid increases system stability. In: Transmission and Distribution World (2012)
7. Charles, C., Moerenhout, T., Bridle, R.: The context of fossil-fuel subsidies in the GCC region and their impacts on renewable energy development. International Institute for Sustainable Development (2014)
8. Foster, I., Kesselman, C.: The Grid: Blueprint for a New Computing Infrastructure. Morgan Kaufmann, San Francisco (1999)
9. Kassakian, J., Schmalensee, R.: The Future of the Electric Grid: An Interdisciplinary MIT Study. Massachusetts Institute of Technology, Cambridge (2012)
10. Czajkowski, K., Fitzgerald, S., Foster, I., Kesselman, C.: Grid information services for distributed resource sharing. In: 10th IEEE International Symposium on High Performance Distributed Computing, pp. 181–184. IEEE Press, New York (2001)
11. Foster, I., Kesselman, C., Nick, J., Tuecke, S.: The physiology of the grid: an open grid services architecture for distributed systems integration. Technical report, Global Grid Forum (2002)
12. Qatar General Electricity and Water Corporation. http://www.km.com.qa/
13. Electricity and Water Authority of Bahrain. http://www.mew.gov.bh/
14. Saudi Electricity Company. http://www.se.com.sa/
15. Ministry of Electricity and Water of Kuwait. http://www.mew.gov.kw/
16. Abu Dhabi Water and Electricity Company. http://www.adwec.ae/
17. Electricity Holding Company. http://www.electricity.com.om/
18. Gulf Cooperation Council Interconnection Authority. http://www.gccia.com.sa/
19. The World Bank. http://data.worldbank.org/indicator/EN.ATM.CO2E.PC
20. Emirates Nuclear Energy Cooperation. http://www.enec.gov.ae/
21. Gastli, A., Charabi, Y., Alammari, R., Al-Ali, A.: Correlation between climate data and maximum electricity demand in Qatar. In: IEEE GCC Conference and Exhibition, Doha, Qatar (2013)
22. Guo, B., Javed, W., Figgis, W., Mirza, T.: Effect of dust and weather conditions on photovoltaic performance in Doha, Qatar. In: IEEE First Workshop on Smart Grid and Renewable Energy, Doha, Qatar (2015)
23. Malik, A., Bouzguenda, M.: Effects of smart grid technologies on capacity and energy savings - a case study of Oman. Energy **54**, 365–371 (2013)
24. Bayram, I.S., Michailidis, G., Devetsikiotis, M.: Unsplittable load balancing in a network of charging stations under QoS guarantees. IEEE Trans. Smart Grid **6**(3), 1292–1302 (2015)

25. Bayram, I.S., Tajer, A., Abdallah, M., Qaraqe, K.: Capacity planning frameworks for electric vehicle charging stations with multiclass customers. IEEE Trans. Smart Grid **6**(4), 1934–1943 (2015)
26. Mohsenian-Rad, M.: Optimal demand bidding for time-shiftable loads. IEEE Trans. Power Syst. **30**(2), 939–951 (2015)
27. California ISO. http://www.caiso.com/1c78/1c788230719c0.pdf

Smart Grid for Smart City Activities in the California City of Riverside

Hamed Mohsenian-Rad[1(✉)] and Ed Cortez[2]

[1] Department of Electrical and Computer Engineering,
University of California, Riverside, CA 92521, USA
hamed@ece.ucr.edu
[2] Riverside Public Utilities, Riverside, CA 92522, USA
ecortez@riversideca.gov

Abstract. In this paper, we overview various urban smart grid development activities in the City of Riverside in Southern California. Challenges and opportunities as well as potentials for university-industry collaborations are discussed. The following smart grid topics are covered: energy efficiency and demand response, renewable power generation, energy storage, electric vehicles, and monitoring and automation.

Keywords: Smart grid · Smart city · City of riverside

1 Introduction and Background

A "smart" city uses information and communication technologies (ICT) to enhance energy, water, transportation, public health, public safety, and other key services to make the urban environment more sustainable, increasing quality of life, and improving efficiency of urban infrastructure and operation. A smart grid, c.f. [1,2], sits at the heart of the smart city paradigm to ensure sustainable and resilient delivery of energy to support the many functions of all other critical urban services under normal and extreme operational conditions [3].

In this paper, we overview some of the recent and ongoing smart grid development activities and their related challenges in the City of Riverside in the State of California in the United States. With a total population of 321,786, Riverside is the 12th most populous city in California and the 59th most populous city in the United States [4]. Riverside is part of the Greater Los Angeles metropolitan area in Southern California. It has a semi-arid Mediterranean climate. The average high temperature is more than +30 degrees Celsius during June, July, August, and September. The average low temperature is less than +10 degrees Celsius during December, January, February, and March [5].

The City of Riverside is served by the Riverside Public Utilities (RPU), which is a municipal electric and water utility company: http://www.riversideca.gov/utilities. The service area for RPU is 82 square miles. RPU serves electricity to over 107,000 metered electric customers and water to over 65,000 metered water customers [6]. The RPU subtransmission network is shown in Fig. 1. In total,

© ICST Institute for Computer Sciences, Social Informatics and Telecommunications Engineering 2016
A. Leon-Garcia et al. (Eds.): Smart City 2015, LNICST 166, pp. 314–325, 2016.
DOI: 10.1007/978-3-319-33681-7_26

RPU has 14 substations, 91 circuit miles of transmission lines, and 1,323 circuit miles of distribution lines [7]. The RPU substransmission system is connected to the California grid at the 230 kV Vista substation that is operated by Southern California Edison (SCE). The RPU historical peak demand is 612 MW that was recorded on September 14, 2014 during a summer heat wave [7].

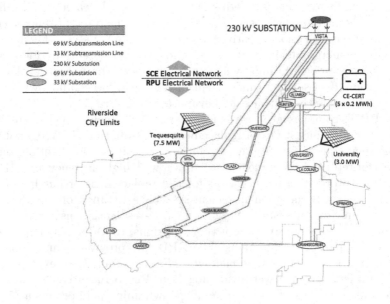

Fig. 1. The RPU subtransmission system [8].

In the sections that will be followed, we will briefly summarize some of the key smart grid activities in the City of Riverside. Specifically, the following smart grid topics will be covered: energy efficiency and demand response, renewable power generation, energy storage, electric vehicles, and monitoring and automation.

2   Energy Efficiency and Demand Response

Demand Side Management (DSM) is a global term that includes a variety of activities that aim at changing the *level* or *timing* of electricity demand among consumers [9]. The former often involves programs that seek to improve energy efficiency of appliances, equipment, etc. The latter often involves demand response (DR) programs that seek to alter electric users' normal consumption patterns in response to changes in the price of electricity, or to incentive payments designed to induce lower consumption at peak hours and when the system reliability is at risk. The United States National Assessment of Demand Response Potential report has identified that DR programs have the potential to reduce up to 20 percent of the total peak load demand in the U.S. [9,10].

RPU has developed a portfolio of programs for its residential and small commercial customers to encourage energy conservation and to meet its long-term energy reduction goals. Some of the current residential energy efficiency programs include: (1) air conditioning rebates for new or replacement units: offering incentives for replacement or installation of central HVAC (heating, ventilating, and air conditioning) units and/or room units with high efficiency equipment; (2) energy star appliance rebates: offering incentives for replacement or installation of qualifying home appliances, such as energy star refrigerators; (3) home energy analysis and weatherization incentive rebates: offering an analysis of home energy that identifies energy efficiency measures and savings, potentially following by a whole house approach to improving energy efficiency through attic insulation, duct insulation, duct sealing, window replacement, window shading, whole house fans, programmable thermostats, and evaporative coolers [11].

Also, RPU's commercial energy efficiency programs include: (1) air conditioning rebate: offering incentives for replacement or installation of HVAC units with high efficiency equipment; (2) energy efficiency incentives for lighting: offering incentives for replacing older inefficient lighting with high efficiency units [12–14]; (3) efficient motors: offering incentives for the replacement or purchase of new premium motors; (4) energy management systems assistance: offering incentives for energy management system upgrades for non-residential customers.

Besides the above energy conservation programs, RPU has also implemented various demand response programs. The RPU DR programs can be classified into three groups: *off-line, online manual, online automated*. An example offline DR program is the Pool Saver Swimming Pool Pump Incentive that is offered to residential customers. This program offers swimming pool owners a $5 credit on their monthly electric bill for setting their pool pump timers to operate at off-peak hours. The typical peak hours are identified as 12:00 PM to 8:00 PM.

An example online manual DR program is the Power Partner Program [15]. It was initially put in place in response to the temporary closure of San Onofre Nuclear Generating Station, a key Southern California energy resource. This program has since been used by RPU to reduce the demand on the regional energy grid and lessen the likelihood of temporary planned outages, e.g., during the heat wave in September 2014 when RPU reached its record high demand, see Sect. 1. In this program, local businesses are encouraged to sign up to be Power Partners, and agree to shed or shift a specific amount of their energy use during peak demand times when requested from July through September, or when they are notified by RPU. All RPU commercial electric customers with peak demands of at least 150 kilowatts per month (about the size of a small restaurant or larger) are eligible to participate in this program. During the heat wave in September 2014, the power reduction notifications were sent by RPU, in form of emails and phone calls, to several Power Partners, including the University of California at Riverside (UCR), which is one of the largest RPU customers. The notification was then disseminated among the university faculty, staff, and students.

Finally, RPU has also implemented online automated DR programs, e.g., in form of non-flat pricing tariffs. Specifically, RPU currently practices *peak pricing*

(PP) and *time-of-use pricing* (ToUP) programs, which are among the most effective pricing models in smart grid, c.f. [16]. Peak pricing is mainly intended for commercial customers. Specifically, RPU uses *automated meter reading* (AMR), c.f. [2,17], to monitor the electric load on 15-min intervals. The program allows non-residential customers the ability to view, via the Internet, their usage patterns [11]. As for time-of-use pricing, it is available to both commercial and residential customers. The rates depend on both *season* and *tier*, as follows [18]:

- Summer On-Peak:
  - Tier 1 (0–145 kWh): 18 cent per kWh,
  - Tier 2 (over 145 kWh): 45 cent per kWh.
- Summer Off-Peak:
  - Tier 1 (0–1125 kWh): 8.5 cent per kWh,
  - Tier 2 (over 1125 kWh): 12 cent per kWh.

- Winter On-Peak:
  - Tier 1 (0–60 kWh): 20 cent per kWh,
  - Tier 2 (over 60 kWh): 35.5 cent per kWh.
- Winter Off-Peak:
  - Tier 1 (0–500 kWh): 9.5 cent per kWh,
  - Tier 2 (over 500 kWh): 15.2 cent per kWh.

Note that, the above tier-based rates have inherently incorporated the idea of inclining block rates (IBRs) into the basic ToUP tariff, see [16].

3   Renewable Power Generation

The County of Riverside is home to San Gorgonio Pass Wind Farm, which is the second largest wind farm in California with a nameplate capacity of 615 MW [19]. The County of Riverside is also home to the Joshua Tree Solar Power Plant, which is one of the largest solar farms in the world with a nameplate capacity of 550 MW [20]. However, within the City of Riverside, the existing and planned renewable energy generation installations are primarily solar and in the following two forms: *behind-the-meter* installations and small *solar farms*.

As of 2014, the total installed behind-the-meter capacity of solar panels in the City of Riverside has been 13 MW [7]. This number is expected to grow significantly over the next few years. RPU does not operate behind-the-meter solar panels. However, RPU does offer to purchase electricity from the owners of behind-the-meter solar panels once they sign and execute a Power Purchase Agreement (PPA) with RPU. The purchase is at an applicable price for metered energy delivered on a Time-of-Delivery (TOD) basis. The TOD time periods are defined in form of *on-peak*, *mid-peak*, and *off-peak* hours [21]:

- Summer:
  - On-Peak: 12:00 PM to 6:00 PM on weekdays,
  - Mid-Peak: 8:00 AM to 12:00 PM and 6:00 PM to 11:00 PM on weekdays,
  - Off-Peak: All other hours on weekdays and any hour on holidays.

– Winter:
  • On-Peak: 5:00 PM to 9:00 PM on weekdays,
  • Mid-Peak: 8:00 PM to 5:00 PM on weekdays,
  • Off-Peak: All other hours on weekdays and any hour on holidays.

There are currently two solar farms under construction in the City of Riverside. The locations of these projects are marked in Fig. 1. The Tequesquite Landfill Solar PV Project is a 7.5 MW solar farm that is being built on the decommissioned Tequesquite landfill, east of Downtown Riverside. The point of interconnection for this solar farm is a primary 12 kV at Mountain View substation. The University Solar PV project is a 3 MW solar farm that is being built on the campus of the University of California at Riverside [22]. The point of interconnection for this solar farm is a primary 12 kV at University substation.

From a distribution system planning viewpoint, RPU has identified three barriers to the study of integrating large PV systems: (1) inadequate tools that simulate high-penetration levels; (2) inaccurate models, due to limited availability of data; (3) limited accuracy of measured data sources [7]. Nevertheless, RPU has recently conducted a solar integration analysis at its Circuit 1364, where the Tequesquite Landfill Solar PV Project will be interconnected. It is identified that during off-peak hours in winter, the 7.5 MW PV exceeds the load on the circuit, causing *reverse power flow* into the substation and *voltage increase* along the distribution feeder. This problem is illustrated in Fig. 2, where the voltage versus the distance from substation is plotted under typical one-direction power flow assumption as well as for the actual case in presence of a large solar farm. RPU is currently working on improving the existing distribution infrastructure by reconduction, load transformation, and capacitor bank relocation [7].

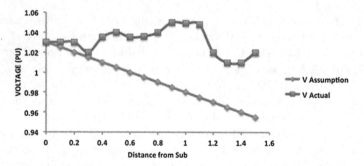

Fig. 2. Voltage as a function of distance to substation in presence of a large solar farm.

4   Energy Storage

The large-scale deployment of energy storage systems is one of the priority areas to build a smart grid, as identified by the U.S. Department of Energy and the National Institute of Standards and Technology [23,24]. The applications of grid-scale battery systems are diverse and include peak-load shaving, synchronous reserve, non-synchronous reserve, voltage support, and frequency regulation [25].

RPU has recently funded two battery energy storage projects in the City of Riverside to demonstrate peak-load shaving. In general, peak-load shaving can target reducing the load at the *meter level* [26,27], *feeder level* [28,29], and *grid level* [30–32]. The current battery energy storage projects in the City of Riverside address the first two cases. Specifically, RPU has funded Pacific Energy Inc. with a project entitled "Demand Response and Peak Shaving Advanced Energy Storage System" to address peak-load shaving at meter level. RPU has also funded the University of California at Riverside with a project entitled "Monitoring and Control of PVs and Energy Storage Systems at a 12 kV Industrial Substation" to address peak-load shaving at feeder level.

The goal in the Pacific Energy battery project is to design, implement, and test a 100 kWh peak-shaving, advanced energy storage system to be integrated into an existing commercial building utilizing lithium ion batteries, advanced controls and measurement equipment. The objective is to reduce the peak-to-average ratio in the load of a commercial building. This project uses a 100 kW inverter which allows charging or discharging the battery system in one hour.

The goal in the UCR battery project is to assess feasibility and test the idea of conducting peak-load shaving (congestion control) at Circuit 1224 in Hunter substation using the energy resources, namely batteries and solar panels, at the UCR College of Engineering - Center for Environmental Research and Technology (CE-CERT). The location of this project is marked in Fig. 1. The size of the battery system in this project is 1 MWh. It is divided into two 500 kWh battery stations, where each station uses a 100 kW inverter to charge and discharge the batteries. Accordingly, the battery system in this project can support 200 kW power for five hours. The battery system in this project is also connected to three solar PV units, with a total power generation of 480 kW.

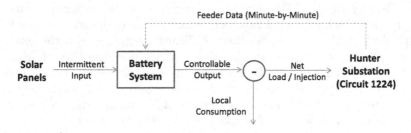

Fig. 3. The operational block diagram in the UCR battery project. Power flow is shown with solid line. Information flow is shown with dashed line.

The block diagram of the UCR battery project is shown in Fig. 3. A unique feature of this project is the communications between the battery controller and the RPU Supervisory Control and Data Acquisition (SCADA) system. Specifically, the RPU SCADA system sends a stream of minute-by-minute measurements from Circuit 1224 to the battery controller. This data stream, which provides various measurements including the feeder load, allows the battery system to adjust its output in response to congestion or other events on Circuit 1224.

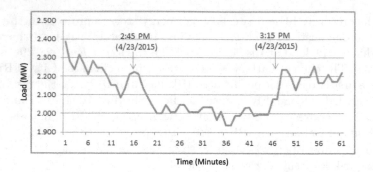

Fig. 4. The load on Circuit 1224 during an experiment in the UCR battery project.

The results for a recent experiment in the UCR battery project is shown in Fig. 4. In this experiment, which was done on April 23, 2015, the two battery stations at the CE-CERT facility were charged during the typical RPU off-peak hours from 10:00 PM to 6:00 AM. After that, the battery control system was programmed to discharge both stations at their maximum discharge rate from 2:45 PM to 3:15 PM, resulting in injecting 200 kW power into Circuit 1224 for a duration of 30 min. We can see in Fig. 4 that the load on Circuit 1224 dropped by 200 kW at 2:45 PM and then it went back to its normal trend at 3:15 PM. The signature of the battery discharge is evident in this figure.

5   Electric Vehicles

Transportation electrification is another priority area to build a smart grid, as identified by the U.S. Department of Energy and the National Institute of Standards and Technology [23,24]. Increasing the use of electric vehicles (EVs) is particularly critical for the Southern California region due to the severe air pollution in the Greater Los Angeles area that includes the City of Riverside. In 2013, the Los Angeles-Long Beach-Riverside area ranked the 1st most ozone-polluted city, the 4th most polluted city by annual particle pollution, and the 4th most polluted city by 24-h particle pollution [33]. Among other factors, motor vehicles are the main sources of air pollution in this region [34].

Due to the above concerns, and also partly because of the high price of gas in California, the State of California is currently the largest plug-in car regional market in the country, with almost 143,000 units sold between December 2010 and March 2015, representing over 46 % of all plug-in cars sold in the United States [35,36]. The exact number of electric vehicles in the City of Riverside is not currently known; however, it is known that over 5500 electric vehicles are owned in the County of Riverside, where the City of Riverside is the county seat [37]. Compared to over 200,000 total registered vehicles in County of Riverside [38], this suggests an EV penetration rate of about 2.7 %.

Given the still-low penetration of electric vehicles, the impact of EVs on the RPU power network is currently negligible. However, the role of EVs and their charging load may gradually start to become significant when it comes to urban distribution system planning. For example, as of June 2016 and according to Charge Point, there are 55 Level 2 and three Level 3 DC Fast charging stations installed in the City of Riverside: www.chargepoint.com. The typical charging load of Level 2 and Level 3 chargers are 3.3 kW and 50 kW, respectively. As for the Level 1 residential chargers, the typical charging load is 1.2 kW [39].

The studies on the integration of EVs into smart grid often address two different directions. First, there are studies that examine the adverse impact of EV charging load on distribution feeders, e.g., with respect to increasing power loss, line overflow, and substation congestion [40–43]. Second, there are also studied that examine the new opportunities that the EVs may offer to better operating the electric grid. In fact, while PEVs are expected to provide economic and environmental benefits to the transportation sector, they may also have a lot to offer to the electric grid, in particular at the distribution level, whether as a potential source of energy storage or as a means to improve power quality and reliability. The possibility of using PEVs to discharge electricity back to the grid has been studied in vehicle-to-grid (V2G) systems [44–49]. More recently, it has been have shown that PEVs may also offer reactive power compensation, not only in a V2G mode but also during a regular charging cycle, with minimum impact on the EV battery lifetime [50–54].

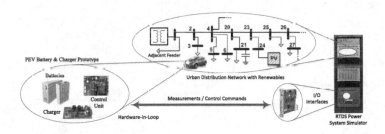

Fig. 5. The setup of the EV integration testbed at UCR Smart Grid Research Lab.

To study the impact of EVs on urban distribution networks, the Smart Grid Research Lab at the University of California at Riverside is currently building a hardware-in-loop (HIL) EV smart grid integration testbed using the RTDS Real-time Digital Power System Simulator (www.rtds.com), as shown in Fig. 5.

6   Monitoring and Automation

Monitoring and communications is the heart of the smart grid paradigm [1, 2]. For example, a critical component in the UCR battery project that we discussed in Sect. 4 is the live data stream that is provided to the battery controller from the RPU SCADA system. This is done by establishing a secure FTP connection between UCR and the City of Riverside. Currently, the following quantities are measured and streamed from Circuit 1224 on a minute-by-minute basis:

- Active Power
- Reactive Power
- Apparent Power
- Voltage Magnitude
- Average Phase Current
- Neutral Amps.

A one day sample of the above data streams is shown in Fig. 6. As explained in Sect. 4, the primary data that is currently used in the UCR battery project is the Active Power measurement. However, in the future, other data types such as voltage and reactive power can also be integrated into the analysis to investigate the impact of battery operation on, e.g., voltage regulation.

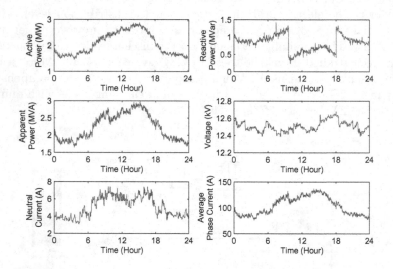

Fig. 6. Sample SCADA data at RPU Circuit 1224 on May 28, 2015.

RPU is also currently in the process of installing a few micro Phasor Measurement Units (PMUs) [55] across its distribution networks. Micro-PMUs allow recording detailed measures for AC power at high time resolutions. Some of the applications of micro-PMUs include topology detection, state estimation, performance evaluation, and fault detection at distribution level. The RPU mirco-PMU project is in partnership with the California Institute for Energy and Environment and Lawrence Berkeley National Lab, see [56] for details.

7   Conclusions

Sitting at the heart of the smart city paradigm, a smart grid can bring new opportunities to urban environments to improve stainability and infrastructure efficiency and reliability. The City of Riverside in Southern California has particularly taken important steps towards developing an urban smart grid foundation, through private-public partnerships and university-industry collaborations. In this paper, an overview of some of the existing and emerging smart grid development activities in the City of Riverside was provided, covering different smart grid topics, including energy efficiency and demand response, renewable power generation, energy storage, electric vehicles, and monitoring and automation.

References

1. Ipakchi, A., Albuyeh, F.: Grid of the future. IEEE Power Energy Mag. **7**(2), 52–62 (2009)
2. Farhangi, H.: The path of the smart grid. IEEE Power Energy Mag. **8**(1), 18–28 (2010)
3. Geisler, K.: The relationship between smart grids and smart cities. In: IEEE Smart Grid, May 2013
4. http://quickfacts.census.gov/qfd/states/06/0662000.html
5. http://www.ncdc.noaa.gov/cdo-web/datatools/normals
6. http://www.riversideca.gov/utilities/admin-executive.asp
7. Cortez, E.: Challenges and solutions for large-scale PV integration on RPUS distribution system, March 2015
8. Riverside Public Utilities: Initial study/Final mitigated negative declaration subtransmission project, July 2009
9. Loughran, D.S., Kulick, J.: Demand-side management and energy efficiency in the United States. Energy J. **25**(1), 19–43 (2004)
10. Palensky, P., Dietrich, D.: Demand side management: demand response, intelligent energy systems, and smart loads. IEEE Trans. Ind. Inf. **7**(3), 381–388 (2011)
11. Summit blue consulting: evaluation, measurement and verification plans for Riverside Public Utilities, March 2010
12. Rubinstein, F., Kiliccote, S.: Demand responsive lighting: a scoping study, LBNL-62226, Berkelry, CA (2007)
13. Raziei, A., Mohsenian-Rad, H.: Optimal demand response capacity of automatic lighting control. In: Proceedings of the IEEE PES Conference on Innovative Smart Grid Technologies (ISGT), Washington, DC, February 2013
14. Husen, S.A., Pandharipande, A., Tolhuizen, L., Wang, Y., Zhao, M.: Lighting systems control for demand response. In: Proceedings of the IEEE PES Conference on Innovative Smart Grid Technologies, Washington, DC, January 2012
15. http://www.riversidepublicutilities.com/powerpartners.asp
16. Mohsenian-Rad, H., Leon-Garcia, A.: Optimal residential load control with price prediction in real-time electricity pricing environments. IEEE Trans. Smart Grid **1**(2), 120–133 (2010)
17. Mahmood, A., Aamir, M., Anis, M.I.: Design and implementation of AMR smart grid system. In: Proceedings of the IEEE Electric Power Conference, Vancouver, BC, October 2008
18. http://www.riversideca.gov/utilities/elec-provrate.asp
19. http://www.awea.org/resources/statefactsheets.aspx
20. http://www.usatoday.com/story/tech/2015/02/10/worlds-largest-solar-plant-california-riverside-county/23159235/

21. Riverside public utilities: Feed-in Tariff (FIT) for renewable energy generation facilities, January 2011
22. http://ucrtoday.ucr.edu/19743
23. United States Department of Energy, The smart grid: an introduction (2010)
24. National Institute of Standards and Technology: NIST framework and roadmap for smart grid interoperability standards, Release 3.0, September 2014
25. Byrne, R., Loose, V., Donnelly, M., Trudnowski, D.: Methodology to determine the technical performance and value proposition for grid-scale energy storage systems. Sandia National Lab, Report (2012)
26. Raziei, A., Hallinan, K.P., Brecha, R.J.: Cost optimization with solar and conventional energy production, energy storage, and real time pricing. In: Proceedings of the IEEE Conference on Innovative Smart Grid Technologies, Washington, DC, February 2014
27. Lee, J., Jo, J., Choi, S., Han, S.B.: A 10-kW SOFC low-voltage battery hybrid power conditioning system for residential use. IEEE Trans. Energy Convers. **21**(2), 575–585 (2006)
28. Chen, S.X., Gooi, H.B., Wang, M.Q.: Sizing of energy storage for microgrids. IEEE Trans. Smart Grid **3**(1), 142–151 (2012)
29. Sechilariu, M., Wang, B., Locment, F.: Building integrated photovoltaic system with energy storage and smart grid communication. IEEE Trans. Ind. Electr. **60**(4), 1607–1618 (2012)
30. Mohsenian-Rad, H.: Optimal bidding, scheduling, and deployment of battery systems in California day-ahead energy market. Accepted for Publication in IEEE Transaction on Power Systems, February 2015
31. Mohsenian-Rad, H.: Coordinated price-maker operation of large energy storage systems in nodal energy markets. Accepted for Publication in IEEE Transaction on Power Systems, April 2015
32. Akhavan-Hejazi, H., Mohsenian-Rad, H.: Optimal operation of independent storage systems in energy and reserve markets with high wind penetration. IEEE Trans. Smart Grid **5**(2), 1088–1097 (2014)
33. http://www.stateoftheair.org/2013/city-rankings/most-polluted-cities.html
34. http://www.epa.gov/region9/socal/air/index.html
35. Ohnsman, A.: Californians propel plug-in car sales with 40 % of market, Bloomberg News, September 2014
36. http://www.hybridcars.com/californians-bought-more-plug-in-cars-than-china-last-year
37. http://www.kesq.com/news/truth-behind-valley-electric-vehicle-charging-stations/31002754
38. http://www.city-data.com/county/Riverside_County-CA.html
39. Nicholas, M.A., Tal, G., Woodjack, J.: California statewide charging assessment model for plug-in electric vehicles: learning from statewide travel surveys. Technical report, University of California at Davis, January 2013
40. Fernandez, L.P., Enagas, S.A., Roman, T.G.S., Cossent, R., Domingo, C.M., Frias, P.: Assessment of the impact of plug-in electric vehicles on distribution networks. IEEE Trans Power Syst. **26**(1), 206–213 (2011)
41. Clement-Nyns, K., Haesen, E., Driesen, J.: The impact of charging plug-in hybrid electric vehicles on a residential distribution grid. IEEE Trans. Power Syst. **25**(1), 371–380 (2009)
42. Green, R.C., Wang, L., Alam, M.: The impact of plug-in hybrid electric vehicles on distribution networks: a review and outlook. Renew. Sustain. Energy Rev. **15**(1), 544–553 (2011)

43. Akhavan-Hejazi, H., Mohsenian-Rad, H., Nejat, A.: Developing a test data set for electric vehicle applications in smart grid research. In: Proceedings of the IEEE Vehicular Technology Conference, Vancouver, BC, September 2014
44. Han, S., Han, S.H., Sezaki, K.: Development of an optimal Vehicle-to-grid aggregator for frequency regulation. IEEE Trans. Smart Grid 1(1), 65–72 (2010)
45. Kumar, P., Kar, I.N.: Implementation of vehicle to grid infrastructure using fuzzy logic controller. In: Proceedings of IEEE Transportation Electrification Conference and Expo, Dearborn, MI, June 2012
46. Ma, Y.C., Houghton, T., Cruden, A.J., Infield, D.G.: Modeling the benefits of Vehicle-to-grid technology to a power system. IEEE Trans. Power Syst. 27(2), 1012–1020 (2012)
47. Ota, Y., Taniguchi, H., Nakajima, T., Liyanage, K.M., Baba, J., Yokoyama, A.: Autonomous distributed V2G (Vehicle-to-grid) satisfying scheduled charging. IEEE Trans. Smart Grid 4(1), 559–564 (2012)
48. Singh, M., Kumar, P., Kar, I.N.: Coordination of multi charging station for electric vehicles and its utilization for vehicle to grid scenario. IEEE Trans. Smart Grid 4(1), 434–442 (2012)
49. Wu, C., Mohsenian-Rad, H., Huang, J.: Vehicle-to-Aggregator interaction game. IEEE Trans. Smart Grid 4(1), 434–442 (2012)
50. Kisacikoglu, M.C., Ozpineci, B., Tolbert, L.M.: Examination of a PHEV bidirectional charger system for V2G reactive power compensation. In: Proceedings of the IEEE Applied Power Electronics Conference (APEC), Palm Springs, CA, February 2010
51. Mitsukuri, Y., Hara, R., Kita, H., Kamiya, E., Hiraiwa, N., Kogure, E.: Voltage regulation in distribution system utilizing electric vehicles and communication. In: Proceedings of the IEEE T&D Conference, May 2012
52. Wu, C., Mohsenian-Rad, H., Huang, J.: PEV-based reactive power compensation for wind DG units: a Stackelberg game approach. In: Proceedings of IEEE Smart Grid Comm, Taiwan, November 2012
53. Wu, C., Mohsenian-Rad, H., Huang, J., Jatskevich, J.: PEV-based combined frequency and voltage regulation for smart grid. In: Proceedings of IEEE Conference Innovative Smart Grid Technologies, Washington, DC, January 2012
54. Wu, C., Akhavan-Hejazi, H., Mohsenian-Rad, H., Huang, J.: PEV-based P-Q control in line distribution networks with high requirement for reactive power compensation. In: Proceedings of the IEEE PES Conference on Innovative Smart Grid Technologies, Washington, DC, February 2014
55. http://www.powersensorsltd.com/PQube
56. von Meier, A., Culler, D., McEachern, A., Arghandeh, R.: Micro-synchrophasors for distribution systems. In: Proceedings of IEEE Conference on Innovative Smart Grid Technologies, Washington, DC, February 2012

Power Consumption Scheduling for Future Connected Smart Homes Using Bi-Level Cost-Wise Optimization Approach

Mohammad Hossein Yaghmaee[1,2(✉)], Morteza Moghaddassian[2],
and Alberto Leon Garcia[1]

[1] Department of Electrical and Computer Engineering,
University of Toronto, Toronto, Canada
hyaghmae@um.ac.ir,
alberto.leongarcia@utoronto.ca
[2] Department of Computer Engineering,
Ferdowsi University of Mashhad, Mashhad, Iran
morteza.moghaddassian@stu-mail.um.ac.ir

Abstract. Future smart-home functionalities enable users to manage their home appliances through a single application by connecting home appliances through an integrated platform and server. In the smart home, a Home Energy Management System (HEMS) is necessary to monitor, control and optimize electrical generation and consumption. On the other hand Demand Response (DR) provides an opportunity for consumers to play a significant role in the operation of the electrical grid by reducing or shifting their electricity usage during peak periods in response to time-based rates or other forms of financial incentives. In this paper we propose an autonomous Demand-Side Management (DSM) model to control the residential load of customers equipped with local power storage facilities as an auxiliary source of energy. In our proposed model the power consumption level of local devices, the amount of power being demanded from both local storage facilities and local utility companies are scheduled using a bi-level quadratic optimization approach of a well-defined convex cost function. Therefore we show that this goal can be fulfilled with a bi-level scheduler unit installed inside the smart meters. In addition our proposed model can also achieve the global optimal performance in terms of energy minimization cost at the Nash equilibrium of a formulated non-cooperative game. We also extend our DSM model to a two tiers cloud computing environment in which both customers and utility companies participate on it.

Keywords: Smart home · Home energy management systems · Demand-side management · Local storage facilities · Bi-level quadratic optimization

1 Introduction

The Smart Grid (SG) is a modernized electrical grid that uses Information and Communications Technology (ICT) to gather information from different parts of power network. This information is used to monitor and control the generation, transmission and

© ICST Institute for Computer Sciences, Social Informatics and Telecommunications Engineering 2016
A. Leon-Garcia et al. (Eds.): Smart City 2015, LNICST 166, pp. 326–338, 2016.
DOI: 10.1007/978-3-319-33681-7_27

distribution equipment. The SG improves the efficiency, reliability and sustainability of the power grid. It has some unique benefits including: more efficient transmission of electricity, quicker restoration of electricity after power disturbances, reduced operations and management costs for utilities, lower power costs for consumers, reduced peak demand, increased integration of large-scale renewable energy systems, better integration of customer-owner power generation systems and improved security.

A key element of the SG is the availability of a sophisticated Advanced Metering Infrastructure (AMI), capable of real-time communication with the utility company. AMI is an advanced system, incorporating two-way communications to the SG with intelligent applications and communication infrastructure. Using AMI capabilities, it is possible to establish two-way communication between customers and utilities. Smart meters are used to send customer consumption information to the utility and receive control data and price information from the utility. Currently most electricity consumption is in the residential and commercial buildings. Homes and working environments are now isolated, energy-consuming units with poor energy efficiency and sustainability. Based on the Smart Home (SH) concept, these units can be transformed into intelligent networked nodes where a significant part of the energy is locally produced by renewables.

In Fig. 1(a) some applications of smart grid are shown. In Fig. 1(b) an overall view of a smart home is depicted. As shown in this figure, the Home Energy Management System (HEMS) is a proprietary hardware and software system that monitors, controls and optimizes electrical generation and consumption. Smart plug is a WiFi-enabled plug that connects home appliances to the power line and control them remotely.

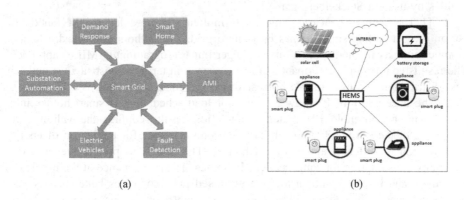

(a)   (b)

Fig. 1. (a) Smart grid applications (b) A smart home

The demand for more electricity has also been growing with the increasing trend in using more electrical devices. It has been changed significantly by the recent advancements in technology and the advent of plug-in hybrid electric vehicles (PHEVs) [1]. Therefore besides allocating more sources of energy to generate electricity, many utility companies try hard to make sure that they can manage the demand for more electricity by the adaptation of well-established demand-side management programs (DSM). These programs will establish practical methods to manage the demand for electricity at the customer side. For this reason, intricate models have been employed which are aimed at reducing consumption or simply shifting it from peak-time hours to non-peak hours during the day. For example in Direct Load Control (DLC) programs, the utility company will manage the customers' consumption level by directly controlling their appliances [2, 3]. However this method ignores the end customers/users' privacy. Therefore a better alternative is the employment of dual or multiple tariffs energy cost systems [4, 5]. In this approach the utility company differentiates between peak-time hours and off-peak hours by applying different consumption costs respectively. Moreover in most of the recent demand-side management programs, the main goal has been on the development of robust models in which the total demand of customers will be reduced at peak-time hours to reduce the cost of power generation [6]. In the next section, some related work in this area is discussed.

2 Related Work

During the past few years, much research has been devoted to DSM programs. Most use optimization techniques and game theory to design an optimized DSM program. There is a rich literature on autonomous demand-side models to manage the demand at the customer side by minimizing the cost of power generation or maximizing the customers' utility [7–9]. However in these models the only entity to generate power is the local utility company. In contrast a recent study has employed a DSM model with multiple utility companies in which customers benefit from maximizing their own utilities by using a Stackelberg game [10].

In [11], a mathematical programming formulation is presented for the fair distribution of cost among smart homes in a micro grid. The authors developed a lexicographic minimax method using a mixed integer linear programming (MILP) approach. The results confirm the performance of the approach in terms of cost savings and fair cost distribution among multiple homes. In [12], a robust approach is developed to tackle the uncertainty of PV power output for load scheduling of smart homes integrated with a household PV system. Simulation results confirm the validity and advantage of the proposed approach. [13] Presents methods for prediction of energy consumption of different appliances in homes. The aim is to predict the next day electricity consumption for some services in homes. The performance of the predictors is studied, and has been shown that the proposed predictor gives better results than other approaches. The authors of [14] present and analyze online and offline scheduling models for the determination of the maximum power consumption in a smart grid environment. Each load model is associated with a proper dynamic pricing process to provide consumers with incentives to contribute to the overall power consumption reduction. The evaluation of the load models through simulation reveals the consistency and the accuracy of the proposed analysis. [15] Deals with the performance analysis of a Global Model Based Anticipative Building Energy Management System (GMBA-BEMS) for managing household energy. The model has been developed in MATLAB/Simulink and evaluated. In [16] an innovative method to manage the appliances on a house during a demand response event has been proposed. A case study with different scenarios has been presented considering a demand response with different durations. Results confirm that the power consumption is reduced. The authors in [17] propose a hierarchical architecture for the utility-customer interaction consisting of sub-components of customer load prediction, renewable generation integration, power-load balancing and Demand Response (DR). A real-time scheduling problem is defined and solved. In [18] a Mixed Integer Linear Programming (MILP) model to schedule the energy consumption within smart homes by coupling environmental and economic sustainability in a multi-objective optimization with ε-constraint method has been developed.

As it can be inferred, in most of the DSM programs, the residential power generation and storage facilities are not considered as active entities in the development of the DSM models. However they can be significantly beneficial in the reduction of residential loads in peak-time hours to help local utility companies to provide more reliable services and reduce costs [19]. Moreover we note that in a recent study, it has been shown that the use of a residential Energy Consumption Scheduler (ECS), a strictly convex cost function and in a non-cooperative distributed game among customers with two-way data and energy communication capabilities, can result in global minimized energy cost at the Nash equilibrium of the formulated game [9]. This approach consider the appliances in two distinct groups of shiftable and non-shiftable devices. The ECS units inside of each smart meter will schedule the consumption level of shiftable devices by minimizing the value of a convex cost function to reduce the demand for electricity during peak-time hours in order to reduce the global cost of power generation.

In this paper we will define an autonomous consumption model that will not only keep the properties of the latter referenced model, but will also consider the local power generation and storage facilities as a substitute source of available power to address the increasing need of customers to consume electricity during the day.

3   System Model

In this section we described out proposed power system model and the properties of the cost function. We will explain how the schedulers minimize the cost of power generation, and introduce our proposed bi-level cost-wise optimization approach.

3.1   Power System

We consider N customers who are connected to each other using smart meters and a two-way data and power communication link. It is also assumed that each smart meter can communicate with the local utility company through the same link. Moreover it is considered that customers can demand for electricity from only one utility company. Each customer is equipped with local power generation and storage facilities which are connected to the smart meters using a separate data and power communication link as shown in Fig. 2.

Throughout the paper, N denotes the set of customers/users that are connected to the grid. For each customer $n \in N$, we also define the vector l_n to denote the total load of each customer at each hour. Therefore the total daily load of each customer can be shown by the vector $l_n = \{l_n^1, l_n^2, \ldots, l_n^h, \ldots, l_n^{24}\}$ where h denotes any hour from the set of hours $H = \{1, 2, \ldots, 24\}$. Therefore based on the above definition we can calculate the total hourly load of the grid as [9] $L_h = \sum_{n \in N} l_n^h$ and the peak-time hour and the average load level in the local grid will also be calculated as [9] $L_{peak} = max_{h \in H} L_h$ and $L_{avg} = \frac{1}{24} \sum_{h \in H} L_h$, respectively. There is also another important factor in any power system which is called peak-to-average ratio (PAR) that can be also calculated as follows [9]:

$$PAR = \frac{L_{peak}}{L_{avg}} = \frac{24 \, max_{h \in H} L_h}{\sum_{h \in H} L_h} \tag{1}$$

Generally lower PAR is preferred due to the impacts of higher PAR values in the increase of global cost of power generation.

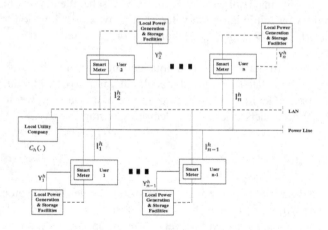

Fig. 2. Block diagram of the proposed system model

3.2   Smart Meter Functionality and Design

As it is shown in Fig. 2, each customer is connected to the grid by the use of a smart meter. We then assume that each smart meter is equipped with two different schedulers, Energy Consumption Scheduler (ECS) and Battery Consumption Scheduler (BCS). The ECS unit is considered to be level one scheduler and is designed to schedule the consumption pattern of shiftable devices to reduce the total load at peak-time hours during the day, as in the referenced model [9]. The BCS unit is also considered to be level two scheduler and is designed to schedule the amount of power being demanded from local storage facilities and the local utility company at the same time.

Smart meters hold a vector $X_{n,a}$ for each appliance to keep track of their consumption pattern during the day. Therefore $X_{n,a} = \left\{ X_{n,a}^1, X_{n,a}^2, \ldots, X_{n,a}^h, \ldots, X_{n,a}^{24} \right\}$ where $n \in N$ is the users' index and $a \in A_n$ indicates any appliances from the set of users' n appliances $A = \{a_1, a_2, \ldots, a_m\}$. Moreover smart meters will also keep track of the amount of power that can be consumed from the local storage facilities by considering a vector $Y_n = \{y_n^1, y_n^2, \ldots, y_n^h, \ldots, y_n^{24}\}$.

Therefore in our proposed model the vector l_n which denotes the hourly consumption level for each user during the day is rewritten as $l_n = \left\{ \left(x_n^1 - y_n^1 \right), \left(x_n^2 - y_n^2 \right), \ldots, \left(x_n^h - y_n^h \right), \ldots, \left(x_n^{24} - y_n^{24} \right) \right\}$ where each $l_n^h = \left(x_n^h - y_n^h \right)$ denotes the hourly aggregated demand of local appliances x_n^h minus the amount of power that can be consumed from the local storage devices y_n^h. Moreover it is important to know that the smart meter will schedule the consumption pattern of each appliance separately using the ECS scheduler and then the hourly aggregated load of the local appliances will be sent to the BCS scheduler for further optimization as shown in Fig. 3. This is done to keep the feasibility of the method to schedule the customers' appliances and to provide all the appliances with the chance of consuming energy from local generation and storage facilities in an optimized manner. Therefore we can calculate the hourly consumption level of local appliances as $X_n^h = \sum_{a \in A_n} x_{n,a}^h$.

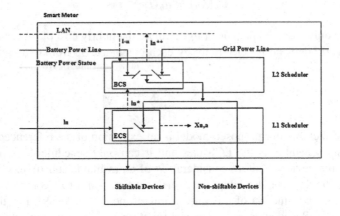

Fig. 3. Block diagram of smart meters showing the ECS and BCS functionalities in our proposed model.

As it is depicted in Fig. 3, the vector $X_{n,a}$ is held in the local memory of ECS unit and is scheduled when an update occurs by user. Then the vector l_n is sent to BCS unit. In BCS unit the vector Y_n is kept in the memory and is used to calculate vector l_n. Moreover the vector Y_n is updated once an optimization is done in BCS units. Therefore the BCS unit schedules the amount of power consumption from local storage facilities to determine the amount of power that should be demanded from both the local utility company and local storage facilities. The hourly demand of electricity from local utility company can be calculated as $L_h = \sum_{n \in N} (X_n^h - Y_n^h)$ where X_n^h is the sum of all the $x_{n,a}^h$ for any customer $n \in N$. For the sake of efficiency, it should be mentioned that the BCS units will also keep track of the amount of power being generated each hour by local power generation facilities and the state of the local storage devices in appropriate vectors $P_n = \{p_n^1, p_n^2, \ldots, p_n^h, \ldots, p_n^{24}\}$ and $B_n = \{b_n^1, b_n^2, \ldots, b_n^h, \ldots, b_n^{24}\}$, respectively.

3.3   Energy Cost Function

As it is already mentioned in Sect. 1, we consider a strictly convex cost function as given below [9]:

$$C_h(L_h) = a_h(L_h)^2 + b_h(L_h) + c_h \tag{2}$$

which is used by thermal generators and has two important properties that makes it an interesting candidate to be employed in such models.

Firstly, the quadratic cost function is increasing and secondly the cost function is strictly convex.

However in this model for the sake of simplicity the values for parameters b_h and c_h are considered to be zero. Therefore the cost function is simplified as follows:

$$C_h(L_h) = a_h(L_h)^2 \tag{3}$$

Where the only essential parameter to calculate the hourly cost of power generation is the total hourly demand for electricity by each customer. So from expression (3) we have:

$$C_h(L_h) = a_h\left(\sum_{n\in N}\sum_{a\in A_n} x_{n,a}^h\right)^2 \tag{4}$$

Due to the fact that our proposed model is an extension of the referenced model in which the only scheduler is the ECS unit and it can only schedule the consumption level of shiftable devices with no consideration of an available substitute local energy source during the day, we also adopt the same cost function for ECS units, since there is no changes in the function of this unit in our proposed model [9]. For the sake of consistency, we will also adopt the same cost function in BCS unit, however we should investigate the same properties for the proposed cost function when another variable Y_n is added and the result shows that the cost function is also convex when another variable is considered in the model $(C_h\left(\theta\widehat{L}_h + (1-\theta)\tilde{L}_h\right) < \theta C_h\left(\widehat{L}_h\right) + (1-\theta)$ $C_h\tilde{L}_h)$ and will be suitable to be used in our model [20, 21]. We then propose the following cost function to be employed in BCS unit.

$$C_h(L_h) = a_h\left(\sum_{n\in N}\binom{h}{n} - \sum_{n\in N}(Y_n^h)\right)^2,$$
$$C_h(L_h) = a_h\left(\left(\sum_{n\in N}(X_n^h)\right)^2 + \left(\sum_{n\in N}(Y_n^h)\right)^2 - 2\left(\sum_{n\in N}(X_n^h)\sum_{n\in N}(Y_n^h)\right)\right) \tag{5}$$

As in the referenced model, in our proposed model the price tariffs are also supposed to be adequate enough to differentiate between peak-time hours and the rest of the day. So for the sake of consistency, we also adapt the same values of 0.2 Cents during the morning until 8 am and 0.3 Cents for 8 am to 12 pm. The same negative values are used for the power consumption level from local storage facilities.

3.4   Cost Optimization Problem

Previously it has been shown that the cost function of expression (3) is strictly convex when the only variable for calculating the value of cost function is X_n and is convex when the variables X_n and Y_n are considered to calculate the value of the cost function. Therefore the target cost function (3) can be suitable for use in both ECS and BCS units for the purpose of power generation cost optimization. To do this, we can formulate the cost optimization problem in each scheduler (optimization level) by considering the task that is assigned for each of them. Therefore by considering the task of ECS unit we can formulate the optimization problem which is executed by each ECS unit as below:

$$minimize_{x_n \in X_n, \forall n \in N} \sum_{h=1}^{24} C_h\left(\sum_{n \in N} \sum_{a \in A_n} x_{n,a}^h\right) \tag{6}$$

After optimizing X_n by ECS, the BCS unit run the following optimization problem to find the optimized values of Y_n:

$$minimize_{y_n \in Y_n, \forall n \in N} \sum_{h=1}^{24} C_h\left(\sum_{n \in N} \left(x_n^{*h} - y_n^h\right)\right) \tag{7}$$

where X_n^* is the optimized value of X_n which is obtained from expression (6). Each smart meter schedules the consumption level of its local plugged-in appliances at first (level one optimization) and then schedules the amount of available power in the local storage facilities to minimize the daily cost of power consumption (level two optimization). Then each smart meter broadcast the optimized vector $l_n^{**} = \{(x_n^{**1} - y_n^{**1}), (x_n^{**2} - y_n^{**2}), \ldots, (x_n^{**h} - y_n^{**h}), \ldots, (x_n^{**24} - y_n^{**24})\}$ to other smart meters to inform them of its statue. In this way users play a non-cooperative game with each other to minimize the global cost of power generation in the local grid [9]. Therefore to solve the mentioned problem using the distributed approach, expressions (6) and (7) are rewritten as:

$$minimize_{x_n \in X_n, \forall n \in N} \sum_{h=1}^{24} C_h\left(\sum_{a \in A_n} x_{n,a}^h + \sum_{m \in N/\{n\}} l^{**h}\right) \tag{8}$$

$$minimize_{y_n \in Y_n, \forall n \in N} \sum_{h=1}^{24} C_h\left(\left(x^{*h} - y_n^h\right)\right) + \sum_{m \in N/\{n\}} m^{**h} \tag{9}$$

4 Simulation Results

In this section, by using computer simulation, we evaluate the performance of our proposed model and compare its performance with the referenced model and the normal consumption pattern in which customers have no participation in any cost reduction program. Therefore in our simulation, we consider 100 customers/users that are signed up to use our cost-wise optimization service. For each user we have considered 10 appliances with shiftable and non shiftable operations. We also consider that each customer is equipped with the average of 10 square meters of photovoltaic cells to generate electricity. Note that the scheduler does not aim to change the amount of daily energy consumption $(En, a = \sum_{h=1}^{24} x_{n,a}^h)$, but instead to systematically manage and shift it to minimize the energy consumption cost (Fig. 4). We also defined soft but adequate constraints for the optimization vectors $x_{n,a}^h$ and Y_n^h in each level as mentioned before.

In addition, in an interesting result, we note that by scheduling the amount of power consumption from local storage devices in BCS units, the fluctuations in the amount of hourly demands for electricity will be answered by local storage facilities rather than the local utility company that will lead to a more smoothened power demand from the local grid as shown in Fig. 5.

It also has to be mentioned that as it is expected, the value of PAR is decreased in both referenced and proposed models in comparison to the normal model in which customers have no participation in any consumption scheduling program. Results confirm that the value of PAR for normal, referenced and proposed models are 1.98, 1.27 and 1.4, respectively. As it can be inferred, the cause of increment in the value of PAR in the proposed model in compare to the referenced model is the higher rate of reduction for average value of total demand in the grid than the reduction rate of the maximum value of that after the level two optimization. This would be the result of power consumption from local storage facilities.

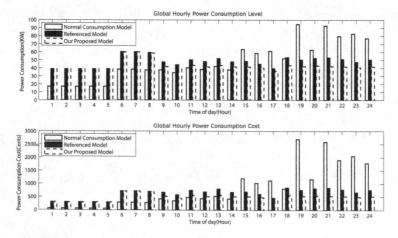

Fig. 4. The total hourly power consumption level (top) and consumption cost (down) in the grid, a comparison between normal, referenced and proposed models.

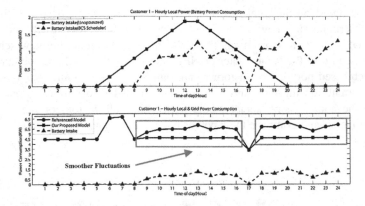

Fig. 5. Hourly comparison of consumption level from local storage facilities (top) and comparison of hourly consumption level of referenced and proposed model (down)

5 Extension to Cloud Computing Environments

The advent of AMI has increased the level of data collection dramatically. There are different sources of "Big Data" in utilities which use smart grid applications in their networks. Some of these sources are: smart meters, grid equipment, off-grid data sets, home devices and substation sensors. To cover the processing and storage requirements of new smart grid applications, cloud computing is a good solution. Recently cloud computing has received attention for smart grid applications [22–24]. Most smart grid applications need reliable and efficient communications system. This can be met by utilizing the cloud computing model. As investigated in [24], cloud computing brings some opportunities for smart grid applications. Flexible resources and services shared in network, parallel processing and omnipresent access are some features of cloud computing that are desirable for smart grid applications.

Using the processing and storage capabilities of the cloud computing, it is possible to solve expression (6) and (7) centrally. We believe the reference model [9] has the following major problems: (1) We should classify all customers in some clusters with N users and provide communication protocol for all of them. (2) We need sophisticated HEMS or smart meter to run the optimized problems. This has more cost for the users. (3) The security is a major problem. If a hacker access the smart meter, he/she can change all users' consumption and scheduling information, and broadcast wrong information for the other users in the cluster. So the user privacy still remains a main challenge. By developing the Internet of Thing (IoT) technology, it is possible to connect each customer appliance to the cloud and control and schedule it centrally. As shown in Fig. 6 the proposed demand side management program can be implemented in a two tier cloud computing environment such as SAVI network [25]. The local edge cloud is responsible to store the load consumption information of customers. The DSM program is run at local edge cloud to optimize power consumption of local customers and minimize the customer's cost. At the core cloud all information from edge cloud are collected. Using this information it is possible to predict the total demand load in the network. Based on the total load and the amount of generated power, the utility company determines the new price. The new price is forwarded to the edge cloud which the DSM program is running. The DSM program compute the new scheduling pattern and send it to the smart meter or HEMS to be applied to the home appliances. Using a web based portal, any customer can login to the system and gets information about the current consumption and cost. It is also possible to remotely control some devices in the home. Using social media networking, all customers can share their usage information and compare their power consumption and costs together.

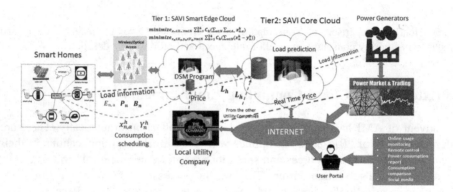

Fig. 6. Extension of the proposed model in SAVI cloud

6   Conclusion and Future Works

In this paper we proposed an autonomous model to schedule the consumption level of customers who are equipped with local power generation and storage facilities in a way that the global optimal performance in terms of energy minimization cost can be achieved. The proposed model has been designed to schedule both the consumption level of local appliances and the amount of power consumption level from local storage devices simultaneously by the use of a bi-level optimization approach. Moreover by the consideration of soft but adequate constraints on the optimization vectors the stimulation results indicate that the proposed model can reduce the cost of power generation in the local grid to a more interesting level in compare to the normal and referenced consumption model which led us toward a more reliable grid as an important energy infrastructure in future smart cities. We believe using cloud computing benefits, it would be possible to design and implement an optimized demand side management program that both customers and utility companies participate on it.

References

1. Han, S., Han, S., Sezaki, K.: Estimation of achievable power capacity from plug-in electric vehicles for V2G frequency regulation: Case studies for market participation. IEEE Trans. Smart Grid **2**(4), 632–641 (2011)
2. Ruiz, N., Cobelo, I., Oyarzabal, J.: A direct load control model for virtual power plant management. IEEE Trans. Power Syst. **24**(2), 959–966 (2009)
3. Weers, D., Shamsedin, M.A.: Testing a new direct load control power line communication system. IEEE Trans. Power Deliv. **2**(3), 657–660 (1987)
4. Centolella, P.: The integration of price responsive demand into regional transmission organization (RTO) wholesale power markets and system operations. Energy **35**(4), 1568–1574 (2010)
5. Herter, K.: Residential implementation of critical-peak pricing of electricity. Energy Policy **35**(4), 2121–2130 (2007)
6. Palensky, P., Dietrich, D.: Demand side management: demand response, intelligent energy systems, and smart loads. IEEE Trans. Ind. Inform. **7**(3), 381–388 (2011)
7. Caron, S., Kesidis, G.: Incentive-based energy consumption scheduling algorithms for the smart grid. In: 2010 First IEEE International Conference on Smart Grid Communications (SmartGridComm), pp. 391–396 (2010)
8. Fan, Z.: Distributed demand response and user adaptation in smart grids. In: 2011 IFIP/IEEE International Symposium on Integrated Network Management (IM), pp. 726–729 (2011)
9. Mohsenian-Rad, A.-H., Wong, V.W., Jatskevich, J., Schober, R., Leon-Garcia, A.: Autonomous demand-side management based on game-theoretic energy consumption scheduling for the future smart grid. IEEE Trans. Smart Grid **1**(3), 320–331 (2010)
10. Maharjan, S., Zhu, Q., Zhang, Y., Gjessing, S., Basar, T.: Dependable demand response management in the smart grid: A Stackelberg game approach. IEEE Trans. Smart Grid **4**(1), 120–132 (2013)
11. Zhang, D., Liu, S., Papageorgiou, L.G.: Fair cost distribution among smart homes with microgrid. Energy Convers. Manage. **80**, 498–508 (2014)
12. Wang, C., Zhou, Y., Jiao, B., Wang, Y., Liu, W., Wang, D.: Robust optimization for load scheduling of a smart home with photovoltaic system. Energy Convers. Manage. **102**, 247–257 (2015)
13. Arghira, N., Hawarah, L., Ploix, S., Jacomino, M.: Prediction of appliances energy use in smart homes. Energy **48**, 128–134 (2012)
14. Vardakas, J.S., Zorba, N., Verikoukis, C.V.: Scheduling policies for two-state smart-home appliances in dynamic electricity pricing environments. Energy **69**, 455–469 (2014)
15. Missaoui, R., Joumaa, H., Ploix, S., Bacha, S.: Managing energy smart homes according to energy prices: analysis of a building energy management system. Energy Build. **71**, 155–167 (2014)
16. Fernandesa, F., Moraisa, H., Valea, Z., Ramos, C.: Dynamic load management in a smart home to participate in demand response events. Energy Build. **82**, 592–606 (2014)
17. Li, D., Jayaweera, S.K.: Distributed smart-home decision-making in a hierarchical interactive smart grid architecture. IEEE Trans. Parallel Distrib. Syst. **26**(1), 75–84 (2015)
18. Zhang, D., Evangelisti, S., Lettieri, P., Papageorgiou, L.G.: Energy consumption scheduling of smart homes with microgrid under multi-objective optimization. In: 12th International Symposium on Process Systems Engineering and 25th European Symposium on Computer Aided Process Engineering, Copenhagen, Denmark, 31 May–4 June 2015
19. Li, N., Chen, L., Low, S.H.: Optimal demand response based on utility maximization in power networks. In: Power and Energy Society General Meeting, 2011 IEEE, pp. 1–8 (2011)

20. Yang, X.-S.: Engineering Optimization: An Introduction with Metaheuristic Applications. Wiley, New Jersey (2010)
21. Boyd, S., Vandenberghe, L.: Convex Optimization. Cambridge University Press, New York (2014)
22. Markovic, D.S., Zivkovic, D., Branovic, I., Popovic, R., Cvetkovic, D.: Smart power grid and cloud computing. Renew. Sustainable Energy Rev. **24**, 566–577 (2013)
23. Sheikhi, A., Rayati, M., Bahrami, S., Ranjbar, A.L., Sattari, S.: A cloud computing framework on demand side management game in smart energy hubs. Electrical Power Energy Syst. **64**, 1007–1016 (2015)
24. Yigit, M., Gungor, V.C., Baktir, S.: Cloud Computing for Smart Grid applications. Comput. Netw. **70**, 312–329 (2014)
25. Smart Applications on Virtual Infrastructure (SAVI). http://www.savinetwork.ca

Wind Resource Assessment of the Metropolitan Area of Barcelona

Guillaume Caniot[1](✉), María Bullido García[1], Stephane Sanquer[1],
Starsky Naya[2], and Emili del Pozo[2]

[1] Meteodyn, 14 Bd Winston Churchill, 44100 Nantes, France
{guillaume.caniot,maria.bullido-garcia,
stephane.sanquer}@meteodyn.com
[2] Barcelona Regional, Carrer 60, 25-27, Edifici Z. 2a Planta,
Sector A., 08040 Barcelona, Zona Franca, Spain
{starsky.naya,emili.pozo}@bcnregional.com

Abstract. Large cities are engaged in reducing CO_2 emissions with the help of renewable energy. The aim of this study is to assess wind energy production over the 640 km^2 of the Metropolitan Area of Barcelona (AMB in Catalan) in order to set up small wind turbines to be connected to the smart grid. Buildings will create wind acceleration, recirculation areas, blocking effects. CFD software Urbawind models the wind inside this complex urban canopy. The work has been commissioned by the Sustainability Plan and the Environmental Services of the Metropolitan Area of Barcelona.

Keywords: Numerical simulations · Wind resource assessment · Renewable energy · Urban · Small wind turbines

1 Introduction

The Metropolitan Area of Barcelona (AMB in Catalan) has developed a Sustainability Plan for 2014–2020.

In order to develop installation of wind turbines in urban areas, five potential barriers has been identified [1]: Safety (fatigue resistance, braking redundancy...), Wind Resource, Turbine technology (noise, vibration...), Building interactions (resonance frequencies between building and turbine, mechanical and electrical integration), Non-technical obstacles (safety hazards during installation, operations and maintenance...).

In the present paper, we will focus on wind resource assessment in order to guide the deployment of wind turbines in urban environments.

Most of the small wind turbines are designed for rural areas where low turbulence intensity and high mean speed occur. Whereas built environment is characterized by high turbulence intensity and low mean wind speed. Inadequate sitting of small wind turbines could lead to turbine failure and potential liabilities. Thus it is important to provide a good estimation of the wind resource at different heights for developers. In order to bring out characteristics of wind flow in an urban environment, a specific wind model dedicated to urban areas is used. Unlike other meso-scale models, each building of the urban fabric was modeled and exists as a proper 3D geometry in the computation.

© ICST Institute for Computer Sciences, Social Informatics and Telecommunications Engineering 2016
A. Leon-Garcia et al. (Eds.): Smart City 2015, LNICST 166, pp. 339–347, 2016.
DOI: 10.1007/978-3-319-33681-7_28

The final goal was, therefore, to detect areas (this is to say roofs or open fields or agricultural lands) to install a small wind turbine suitable for a particular wind potential and to assess the wind energy available for each building owner or to the electrical grid.

2 Wind Resource Assessment Methodology

The methodology [2] consists in:

1. Transferring wind data from a weather station to 200 meters high area over the AMB thanks the CFD software Topowind [3] taking into account the effect of topography (elevation and terrain roughness of the site) (Fig. 1)

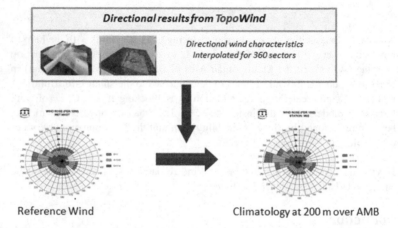

Fig. 1. Transfer of wind rose from the weather station (Reference Wind) to the local area at 200 m high (Color figure online)

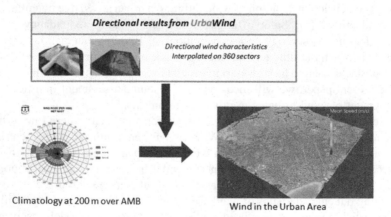

Fig. 2. Transfer of wind rose from climatology at 200 m high over AMB to the urban area (Color figure online)

2. Computing the wind flow inside the urban area taking into account the effect of the elevation and the buildings in 3D thanks to UrbaWind [4] (Fig. 2)

2.1 Transfer of the Reference Climatology Above the Metropolitan Area of Barcelona

The selected wind reference is from a weather mast located near the shore at Sirena (41°20'28.29"N, 2° 9'57.99"E, H = 10, Port of Barcelona). The wind speed histogram and wind rose observed at the station are included hereunder (Fig. 3).

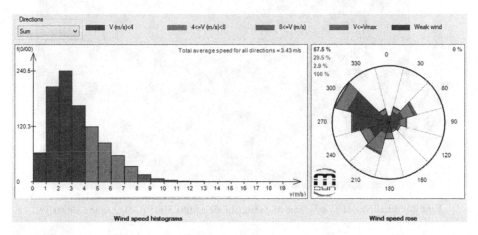

Fig. 3. Wind Rose and histogram of the wind reference at Sirena (Barcelona). Data source: Port of Barcelona (Color figure online)

Orography data is extracted from the NASA database (SRTM). Roughness is computed from Corine Land Cover database (2006).

TopoWind, commercial software [5], performs the transfer of the wind characteristics from the wind reference to the 200 m high area above the AMB.

With a horizontal resolution of 25 m, the mesh size is about 20 Million cells for a computational time of 5 h per direction. The directional resolution is 20°, leading to 18 directions. As an example of these computations, a mapping of the resulting wind speed coefficients for one synoptic wind direction is shown in Fig. 4.

The wind speed coefficient is defined as the horizontal mean speed divided by a wind at 10 m height. The obtained wind characteristics over the AMB were used as the input in the subsequent micro-scale downscaling carried out to include the urban local effects (Fig. 4).

2.2 Computation of the Wind Characteristics in Urban Area

Barcelona Regional, an urban development agency provides the entire numerical model of the 640 km² AMB's urban area. The whole area has been split in small parts with

Fig. 4. Wind Speed Coefficient mapping for direction 300° (Color figure online)

overlapping pats in order to suit the wind model requirements. It includes CAD of the building and orography. For the buildings, Barcelona Regional developed some scripts for GIS and RHINO-Grasshopper in order to get 3D building geometry joining 0.5 m resolution LiDAR data with Cadastre data. For the terrain it has been used an original 2 m orography data resolution.

Vegetation is not taken into account because, inside the urban canopy, its effect on the small wind turbines is negligible compared to the effect of the buildings.

The CAD of the building includes roof superstructures such as chimneys and shed dormers.

The 10 m horizontal resolution of topography maps was fine enough to catch slopes over 2.5 % responsible for wind acceleration (Fig. 5).

One single simulation of the entire area entails 1.7 TB of RAM. In order to be able to run such a simulation on a standard cluster, the area is split in smaller domains. The AMB is divided then into 138 sub-areas of 2.5 km × 2.5 km each.

An overlapping area of 450 m is added to each border to ensure better wind characteristics thanks to the extra roughness on the ground. Thus each computed sub-area has a 3.4 km × 3.4 km total surface (Fig. 6).

Once the wind characteristics is computed at 200 m high area over the AMB, UrbaWind transfers the wind inside the urban area taking into account the effect of the elevation and the buildings.

Fig. 5. Sample of buildings and topography - Source: Barcelona Regional

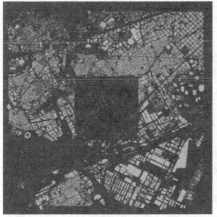

Fig. 6. 3.4 km × 3.4 km domain (red area) - Source: Barcelona Regional (Color figure online)

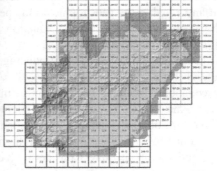

Fig. 7. AMB divided into 138 small areas - Source: Barcelona Regional

UrbaWind solves the Navier-Stokes equations with a one-equation turbulence model, where the turbulent length scale L_T varies linearly with the distance to the nearest wall [6].

Boundary conditions are automatically generated. The vertical profile of the mean wind speed at the inlet is divided in three layers: logarithmic profile within the surface layer; in the Ekman layer wind speed profile is a logarithmic function of geostrophic

Fig. 8. Non-homogeneous result at the border for mean wind speed

wind speed; at the upper limit of the surface layer and above the ABL the wind speed is constant and equal to the geostrophic wind speed.

The geostrophic wind speed is a function of ABL height and the wind speed at 10 m high in open land.

A 'Blasius' law is modeled by introducing a volume drag force in the cells lying inside the obstacle.

The equations resolution is based on a finite volume method with a rectangular multi-bloc refined mesh. A very efficient coupled multi-grid solver is used [7].

The mesh resolution is about 1.0 m around the buildings and close to the ground leading to a number of cells of about 10 million per direction. The computational time for one direction is about 1 day. Considering 8 directional computations for each of the 138 sub-areas, the total computational time is about 1104 days. Three computers with 8 processors 2.4 GHZ Intel Xeon each helps to reduce the computation time to 3 months (efficiency in parallel of 50 %) (Fig. 7).

Once all sub-areas are completed, the results at the borders can be non-homogeneous and present discontinuities (Fig. 8).

Those discontinuities appear when there is a roughness difference between two sub-areas. In fact for an Urbawind directional computation, the roughness inlet is limited to 4 different profiles (Water, Open country, Small density city, and High density city) whereas in reality the value of the roughness could be different. The wind characteristics at the exit of a sub-domain take into account the real roughness of the city. Therefore a wind speed difference between the outlet of a sub-area and the inlet of the adjacent one may come out (Fig. 9).

In order to smooth results between two neighboring sub-areas, a box average over three points is performed.

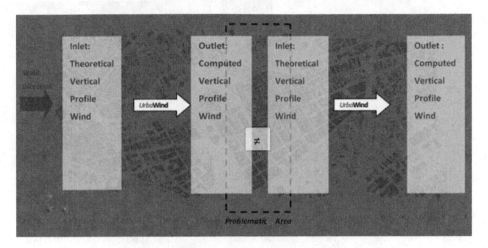

Fig. 9. Discontinuity between two areas

3   Results

Mean Annual Wind Speed and Mean Annual Energy Production for a TechnoWind 1 kW wind turbine are computed on various mappings at 10 m, 20 m, 30 m, 40 m and 50 m above the ground with a horizontal resolution of 10 m (Figs. 10 and 11).

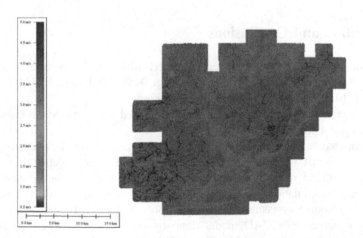

Fig. 10. Mean Annual Wind Speed Atlas at 20 m high (Color figure online)

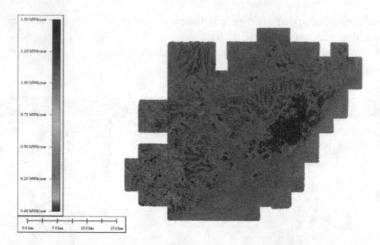

Fig. 11. Mean Annual Energy Production Atlas at 20 m high (Color figure online)

Table 1. Comparison between computed mean speed and measured mean speed.

Station	Height	Mean speed measured	Mean speed computed	Difference
El Prat de Llobregat	10 m	3.0 m/s	2.6 m/s	0.4 m/s
Barcelona - Zona Universitaria	10 m	2.1 m/s	2.1 m/s	0.0 m/s
Barcelona - el Raval	30 m	2.0 m/s	1.7 m/s	0.3 m/s
Vallirana	10 m	1.9 m/s	2.5 m/s	-0.6 m/s
Castellbisbal	10 m	2.4 m/s	2.2 m/s	0.2 m/s
Badalona - Museu	33 m	2.7 m/s	2.8 m/s	-0.1 m/s
Barcelona - Observatori Fabra	10 m	4.7 m/s	4.3 m/s	0.4 m/s

4   Validation and Conclusions

A cross-validation of the numerical results is performed thanks to seven weather stations located in the AMB. The period starts from 04/01/2011 until 12/31/2012 with a time step of 30 min to 1 h depending on the station.

The difference between measured and computed wind speeds remains under 0.4 m/s except for the station of Vallirana.

The computed values underestimate the mean speed recorded at the weather station.

For the station of Vallirana, the mast is located near some vegetation.

Higher computed results can be explained because of the non-existence of the vegetation in the simulation, which leads to an over-estimation of wind speed.

The wind resource assessment of the Metropolitan Area of Barcelona is computed thanks to the large scale CAD model done by the Barcelona Regional and CFD software such as TopoWind and UrbaWind (Table 1).

Because small wind turbines usually require a minimum of 4 m/s annual mean velocity to start working, 20 m height for wind turbine location is a minimum for wind energy production. In fact about 5 % of the Metropolitan Area of Barcelona reaches the minimum mean velocity criteria at 20 m hub height. For higher hub heights, the percentage of exceeding the minimum velocity criteria will increase.

References

1. Smith, J., Forsyth, T., Sinclair, K., Oteri, F.: Built-Environment Wind Turbine Roadmap (No. NREL/TP-5000-50499). National Renewable Energy Laboratory (NREL), Golden, CO (2012)
2. Delaunay, D., Chantelot, A., Guyader, T., Alexandre, P.: Meteodyn WT: An automatic CFD software for wind resource assessment in complex terrain. In: EWEC 2004 Wind Energy Conference, London (2004)
3. TopoWind: www.meteodyn.com/wp-content/uploads/2012/10/TopoWind-tecnical-document-ation.pdf
4. UrbaWind: www.meteodyn.com/wp-content/uploads/2012/06/UrbaWind-Software.pdf
5. Kalmikov, A., Dupont, G., Dykes, K., Chan, C.: Wind power resource assessment in complex urban environments: MIT campus case-study using CFD Analysis. In: AWEA 2010 WINDPOWER Conference, Dallas, USA (2010)
6. Fahssis, K., Dupont, G., Leyronnas, P.: UrbaWind, a computational fluid dynamics tool to predict wind re-source in urban area In: International Conference of Applied Energy, Conference paper, Singapore (2010)
7. Ferry, M.: New features of the MIGAL solver. In: Proceedings Phoenics Users International Conference, Moscow (2002)

User Behavior Modeling for Estimating Residential Energy Consumption

Baris Aksanli[⊠], Alper Sinan Akyurek, and Tajana Simunic Rosing

University of California San Diego, La Jolla, CA 92093, USA
{baksanli,aakyurek,tajana}@ucsd.edu

Abstract. Residential energy constitutes a significant portion of the total US energy consumption. Several researchers proposed energy-aware solutions for houses, promising significant energy and cost savings. However, it is important to evaluate the outcomes of these methods on larger scale, with hundreds of houses. This paper presents a human-activity based residential energy modeling framework, that can create power demand profiles considering the characteristics of household members. It constructs a mathematical model to show the detailed relationships between human activities and house power consumption. It can be used to create various house profiles with different energy demand characteristics in a reproducible manner. Comparison with real data shows that our model captures the power demand differences between different family types and accurately follows the trends seen in real data. We also show a case study that evaluates voltage deviation in a neighborhood, which requires accurate estimation of the trends in power consumption.

Keywords: Residential energy · Modeling · Appliance · User activity

1 Introduction

Residential energy accounts for 38 % of the total energy consumption in the US, with millions of individual consumers [10]. Although the other components, such as commercial or industrial, are well-investigated, residential energy has not been studied extensively until recently. Due to high potential of savings, many researchers have started to focus on methods to minimize the residential energy consumption. These studies target heating, air conditioning and ventilation (HVAC) units, appliances, and electric vehicles (EVs). The new technologies, such as home automation kits, smart meters, controllable appliances, provide constant monitoring and detailed energy usage breakdown in the houses, making it easy to deploy energy-aware solutions. The studies show that it is possible to obtain significant savings by cleverly adjusting the power demand, and these savings can easily add up to correspond millions of dollars savings.

Despite the effectiveness of energy-aware residential solutions, it is not easy to test them on a larger scale. Residential buildings have a dominant human factor. Many of the energy-aware mechanisms are designed to perform uniformly

© ICST Institute for Computer Sciences, Social Informatics and Telecommunications Engineering 2016
A. Leon-Garcia et al. (Eds.): Smart City 2015, LNICST 166, pp. 348–361, 2016.
DOI: 10.1007/978-3-319-33681-7_29

regardless of different compositions of families leading to variations in habits and energy usage. Thus, we cannot expect that the outcomes (e.g. savings) will be the same for different households. It is also important to see the overall effect of these mechanisms on the electrical grid, when several houses are applying them simultaneously. This aspect is important for utilities, that want to predict the energy demand ahead of time to match supply and demand. To reflect the human element, the differences across the demand profiles of individual houses should be considered. Previous studies use either real [3] or generated traces [15] for this purpose. The former requires equipment installation across many houses, which has high cost. It is not generalizable and the traces cannot be used to create statistically correlated, new traces. The latter increases the scalability of representing houses, but requires careful modeling for the human element.

This paper presents a user-behavior model to estimate the energy consumption of a house. Our model is based on detailed activity sequences of household members and the connections between these activities and appliances. We use two publicly available data sets, American Time Use Survey (ATUS) and Residential Energy Consumption Survey (RECS) to account for user activity and appliance usage habits. ATUS contains detailed activity responds from more than 10000 individuals over one year and RECS has statistics from more than 110 million households, both from entire US. Our model develops hierarchical activity graphs for each individual and probabilistically determines the appliance usage events. When creating power profiles for the houses, we consider the characteristics of the inhabitants and show the relationships between these and the house power demand. We compare our model against real house traces from Pecan Street database [11]. The power profiles we generate follow the trends in real traces, e.g. matching the peak demand times and frequencies. We show the importance of this with a case study, where we evaluate voltage deviation in a neighborhood. We use a grid simulator [2] to compute the deviation values and show that our model captures the high deviation events with high accuracy.

2   Related Work

User behavior modeling studies estimate appliance and plug load energy consumption in residential houses. Previous studies construct models based on historical activities [6,12,15], using commonly available activity data sets such as ATUS [17] data. They group the activities into meaningful clusters and create user categories based on people's age, gender, employment status, and the number of other household members. Other studies use similar survey data from France [4], UK [7] and Spain [14]. These studies also use machine learning methods such as Markov chains [12], neural networks, Bayesian networks, and decision trees [4] to determine the activity chains, i.e. which activity is more likely to follow another. These models rely only on activity data, thus cannot capture the dynamic relationship between activity sequences and appliance usages.

Using these data sets, previous studies determine which activities are related to appliances either manually [12] or by using another data set [15] (RECS [8]).

After this linking, they estimate the starting time of appliances (such as washer, dryer, dishwasher) and the operating conditions of bigger units (e.g. refrigerator, HVAC, lighting, etc.). The house energy consumption is then simply aggregation of all the individual appliances and plug load units. By disaggregating the total energy consumption, previous studies can apply different mechanisms (such as appliance rescheduling, controlling HVAC and lighting parameters, etc.) to participate in demand response programs ultimately to save energy [16] and electricity cost [18]. There are also the widely-used residential energy databases, REDD [13] and Smart* [3] that show the disaggregated energy consumption of several houses over a couple of months. To get detailed user behavior models, the researchers use the disaggregated appliance consumption to deduce the user behavior or occupancy [5]. The main disadvantage of this approach is that there is no real information in the data set on what the users were actually doing and thus have to be mostly guessed. Different than previous studies, we use high granularity user activity data to represent the relationship between users and appliances. We create power profiles not just for individuals but also for families and a neighborhood with several families. We verify our model using real data from Pecan Street, and show that our traces are highly correlated with real data.

3   User Behavior Modeling with Activity Graphs

In this section, we first develop a graph-based model to represent the chain of user activities. Our main goal is to probabilistically capture the time-series nature of user behavior. These probabilities depend on several people-related and non-people-related variables. The former include the number of other household members, people's gender, age, employment status, etc. whereas the latter have time of day, day of week, etc. We use these variables to calculate the probability of an event that would follow another event at a given time.

User activities are the main events in a house that trigger energy consumption. We define user activity as a set of actions associated with one or multiple appliances over a time period. For example, cooking is an activity that includes all actions between getting into the kitchen and cleaning the dishes. During this activity, the user might use several appliances such as refrigerator, oven, microwave, etc. The exact set of appliances associated with an activity changes among different activity

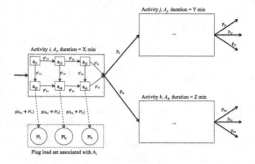

Fig. 1. Activity graph structure

ity changes among different activity instances. All activities have a duration associated with them. The day of a person is divided into discrete activity blocks. The next step is determining the chain of activities for a user. We model the next activity for a given one probabilistically, which depends on a similar set of variables as described earlier. Using this information, we build activity graphs, where the nodes are the activity blocks (with inner graphs as actions for a specific activity) and the edges are the activity transitions. The graph is designed to be cyclic with sleeping activity as the reference node. The formal construction of the activity graph includes the following steps (following Fig. 1):

1. The activity graph is a directed graph and with activity blocks $\{A_i | 1 \leq i \leq N\}$, where N is the number of activities, as the nodes and transitions between the activities as edges. The activity blocks are shown by big rectangles and the transitions are the directed edges between them in Fig. 1.
2. Each activity, A_i, is followed by a set of activities $\{A_j | 1 \leq j \leq N_i\}$ where each transition $(A_i \rightarrow A_j)$ has a probability, p_{ij}. Thus, $\sum_{j=1}^{N_i} p_{ij} = 1$. This makes sure that the activity chain never ends.
3. Each activity, A_i, consists of a sub-graph, with nodes as the actions of that activity, a_{ik}, and the edges are the transitions between the actions. The actions are shown by the smaller rectangles in the activities and the transitions are the directed edges between the smaller rectangles in Fig. 1. The transitions can result in another action but also the end of that activity. The probability of transition from a_j to a_k in A_i is denoted by p^i_{jk}. The probability of transition from a_j to the end of A_i is shown by p^i_{jt}, where the sub-index t corresponds to activity termination. Similar to 2, $\sum_{k=1}^{N_j} p^i_{jk} = 1$, where N_j is the number of transitions that can follow a_{ij} in A_i.
4. For each activity A_i, there is an appliance set associated with it $Ap_i = \{Ap_{ij} | 1 \leq j \leq n_i\}$, where n_i is the number of appliances in set Ap_i. This set contains the individual appliances Ap_{ij}, whose operation can be triggered by the actions of A_i. We follow a probabilistic approach for the appliance triggering. The probability of a_{ij} triggering appliance Ap_{ik} is $p(a_{ij} \rightarrow Ap_{ik})$. These relations are shown by dotted lines in Fig. 1. For these probabilities, we do not require any probability summation to be equal to 1 because an action (or a set of actions) does not always trigger an appliance.
5. Our appliance definition suits most of the plug loads with ON/OFF states. These are discrete appliances [18]. This might now work for some appliances with continuous energy draws, e.g. refrigerator, HVAC, and lighting.

Refrigerator: The power consumption follows a duty cyclic behavior, except when its door is opened. This is mostly observed during a cooking activity. We model the refrigerator power consumption as a constant addition to the aggregated house consumption, with higher value during cooking activities.

Lighting: We breakdown the lighting into individual rooms and associate them with activities when performed in the relevant room. We also set time-of-day as another constraint for room lights to be ON.

HVAC: The operation of HVAC is correlated with user preferences [18]. Since its temperature settings affect its active power consumption, we cannot assume an ON/OFF model. As developing a new HVAC manager is not

Table 1. List of activities, actions and associated appliances

Activities	Actions	Appliances
Sleeping	N/A	N/A
Personal grooming	Showering, bathing, brushing teeth, hair drying, shaving	Electric razor, electric toothbrush, hair dryer, bathroom lights
Cooking	Preparing food, eating, cleaning kitchen, washing dishes	Microwave, stove, oven, refrigerator, dishwasher, water heater, kitchen lights
Cleaning	Laundry, interior cleaning, exterior cleaning	Washer, dryer, vacuum cleaner, room lights
Entertainment	Watching TV, using computer	TV, computer, any other small entertainment device, e.g. x-box, playstation, etc., room lights
Working at home	Using computer, reading, writing	Computer, room lights
Going to work	N/A	N/A

in our paper's scope, we adopt the methodology in [18], which models the correlation with user preferences for scheduling and temperature settings.

6. We model the activity graph as cyclic. We select one activity as the starting activity of a day where at the end of the day, that activity is repeated. We choose the sleeping activity for this purpose, but another repeating activity can be used.

4   Activity Graph Construction

This section shows how we calculate the activity graph parameters. There is a separate graph for each individual, thus we estimate the parameters separately for different classes of people. To meet our classification needs, we use ATUS data [17]. It has more than 10000 participants from different parts of the society and includes their detailed activity information, which corresponds to the actions/activities in our graphs. ATUS does not have any details about appliance usages. We use another data set, RECS [8], which surveys more than 110 million households and has statistics regarding the families, the types and numbers of appliances used, and how frequently they use the appliances. We get the higher level family and appliance statistics from RECS and connect them with the lower level, individual activity data from ATUS.

Activity-Related Parameters. These parameters correspond to the physical characteristics of user actions and activities.

Table 2. Example action duration values for different groups of individuals

User group	Action	Average duration (min)	Action	Average duration (min)
< 18 y/o	Sleeping	360	Preparing food	22
≥ 18 y/o working male	Sleeping	325	Preparing food	31
≥ 18 y/o working female	Sleeping	322	Preparing food	32
≥ 18 y/o unemployed female	Sleeping	333	Preparing food	35
< 18 y/o	Eating	28	School	207
≥ 18 y/o working male	Eating	34	Work	197
≥ 18 y/o working female	Eating	33	Work	188
≥ 18 y/o unemployed female	Eating	33	Job search	96

Set of Activities: The ATUS data set does not make a distinction between actions and activities. It provides the information of what a user does. It classifies the activities hierarchically, which helps us determine the set of actions vs. activities. The first column of Table 1 shows the list of main activities we find.

Set of Actions for a Given Activity: These actions are determined manually found from ATUS. The difference between actions and activities are based on the activity tiers (1, 2, 3) reported in ATUS. The second column of Table 1 shows the actions included in different activities. We increase the granularity of user events mainly to understand and study what actions may lead to appliance usage or to another action that might result in appliance usage. Without this, the exact properties of an appliance usage event can be missed.

Durations of Actions: Since the action duration varies among individuals, we use statistical distributions to represent these durations, and sample a value from those distributions to assign an action duration. We use the activity duration information from ATUS to construct these distributions. We cannot create a separate distribution for each person or use a single distribution for everyone. Instead, we create multiple distributions to account for different user groups for each action. Table 2 shows example values for action durations for different groups. Based on the average values, each action instance samples a value from an exponential distribution with the corresponding average. We obtain these averages based on the weight values assigned to the individuals based on demographic representations by ATUS data set.

Duration of Activities: Since an activity is a composite (of individual actions) object, we compute its duration as the total duration of its individual actions.

Appliance-Related Parameters. These parameters show the list of appliances and how they are associated with specific actions and activities, determined by the statistical data from RECS. We then manually select the appliances associated with a given activity, shown in Table 1. An appliance may not be used for each instance of the activity it is associated to (probabilistic relation).

Probability-Related Parameters. These parameters determine both the possible transitions between actions and activities, forming the connections in the activity graph, and the probabilities of appliance usage events based on user actions. These parameters depend on two factors (1) user gender and age, (2) user employment status. We also consider time of day and day of week information because the activities a user performs change highly based on time of day (morning vs. evening) or day of week (weekday or weekend). In this paper, we do not make the distinction between days of week but consider time of day differences.

Action Transition Probabilities: These are based on the observed user actions and how frequently they follow each other. For each action in an activity, we count the number of actions following a given action to calculate the transition probabilities, as shown in Eq. 1. Since these probability values change for each user group and time of day, we calculate separate values accordingly. We use discrete time-of-day classification, i.e. morning, noon, and evening.

$$p(a_{ij} \rightarrow a_{ik}) = p^i_{jk} = \frac{\text{\# action transitions from } a_{ij} \text{ to } a_{ik} \text{ in activity } A_i}{\text{\# total transitions from } a_{ij} \text{ in activity } A_i} \quad (1)$$

The special case occurs when the activity that a specific action belongs to terminates. Equations 2 revises 1 by counting the instances where an action a_{ij} in an activity A_i is followed by an action A_{kl} in another activity A_k.

$$p^i_{jt} = \frac{\text{\# transitions from } a_{ij} \text{ to } a_{kl} \text{ from } A_i \text{ to } A_k, i \neq k}{\text{\# total transitions from } a_{ij} \text{ in activity } A_i} \quad (2)$$

Activity Transition Probabilities: These are computed similarly to the previous case, except we consider when an activity ends rather than single actions. The transition probabilities are computed in Eq. 3, which is calculated for each user group. To simplify and obtain a more compact model, we consider activity transitions independent of the actions finishing an activity. We compute the next activity independent of the last action of the current activity.

$$p(A_i \rightarrow A_j) = p_{ij} = \frac{\text{\# activity transitions from } A_i \text{ to } A_j}{\text{\# total activity transitions from } A_i} \quad (3)$$

Appliance Triggering Probabilities: We use the appliance usage frequency information from RECS to deduce the probability of using an appliance given the current action/activity. For example, assume that the *cooking* activity takes place twice in the activity graph of a user. But not all the kitchen appliances are used in all the *cooking* activity occurrences. According to RECS, 8.7 % of the households use the oven twice a day, 17.3 % use it once whereas 34.6 % use it only a few times a week. The appliances that RECS has these data stove/oven, microwave, dishwasher, washer, dryer, portable loads. We determine these probabilities based on the family size, e.g. single vs. couple, with or without children. We demonstrate how we construct families from individual people in the next section. We first calculate the average usage frequency of a given appliance and

Table 3. Example appliance triggering probabilities

Activity appliance couples	Family types				
	Single male	Single female	Couple	Couple +1 child	Couple + 2 children
p(cooking → oven)	0.13	0.15	0.21	0.25	0.28
p(cooking → microwave)	0.52	0.53	0.49	0.51	0.51
p(cooking → dishwasher)	0.12	0.13	0.27	0.31	0.39
p(cleaning → washer)	0.26	0.33	0.59	0.76	0.91
p(cleaning → dryer)	0.23	0.28	0.52	0.67	0.81

Table 4. Family distribution percentages (%) of ATUS and RECS data sets

	Single male	Single female	Couple	Couple - 1 kid	Couple - 2 kids	Couple - 3 kids	Couple - 3+ kids
RECS	9.87	13.18	33.53	17.14	14.47	7.11	4.70
ATUS	17.85	22.07	26.73	12.29	13.93	5.15	1.98

then deduce the probability based on the time frame of this average. We use one week as the time frame to compute these averages using RECS data set. Similar to ATUS, we leverage pre-computed sample weights RECS provides to calculate average values. We compute the appliance triggering probabilities for different family sizes for a given activity as follows:

$$p(A_i \rightarrow PL_j | \text{family type } t) = \frac{\text{average usage of } PL_j \text{ of family type } t}{\#\text{instances of } A_i \text{ over the time frame}} \quad (4)$$

where PL_j is a specific appliance, t is an enumeration for family types. The number of instances of A_i is counted based on the activity-appliance couples. For example, possible number of *cooking* instances in a week is 21, whereas this number is 7 for *cleaning*. Table 3 shows some examples of these values.

Combining Activity Graphs. We construct different families based on ATUS and RECS and first analyze the family statistics. We specify family types as single (male or female) and couple (no child, 1–2–3 or more children) as in Table 4. These percentages are calculated based on only the listed family types, which span more than 85 % of the survey respondents. The family types are distributed based on the numbers presented in Table 4 over all the houses. We obtain the final percentages as the average values between ATUS and RECS. We also specify the employment status of the adults in Table 5 for different family types, gathered from ATUS as the duration of *work* activity is modeled using it.

Next, we combine the the activity graphs of individuals. If each graph is mutually exclusive, we can simply add up the power profile of each person to obtain the total consumption. But multiple instances of a single appliance

Table 5. Employment percentages (%) of the adults

	Single man	Single woman	Couple	Couple - 1 kid	Couple - 2 kids	Couple - 3 kids	Couple - 3+ kids
Male	54.1	N/A	92.93	95.74	94.7	95.21	95.85
Female	N/A	42.88	84.86	97.91	82.08	65.47	55.96

can coincide. Thus, we cannot simply add up the consumption values. To solve this, we adopt a first come first serve solution. Assume that person x's activity graph leads to starting Ap_i at time t, where Ap_i has been in use by person y, which started at time $t - \delta$. If $\delta \leq \frac{d_i}{2}$, where d_i is the execution duration of Ap_i, the new instance of Ap_i is assumed as concurrent and discarded. If $\delta > \frac{d_i}{2}$, the incoming instance is scheduled to be executed after the current instance of Ap_i finishes.

5   Evaluation

This section first presents the power profiles we generate for families and then shows a case study for a neighborhood with 50 houses covering a range of families. The family types include single adults (male or female), couples without and with 1 or 2 children. The appliance power consumption values, shown in Table 7, are taken from Home Appliance Energy Use data from General Electric [9]. Profiles are generated for 5 days to observe the daily changes. We use residential power traces from Pecan Street database [11] to evaluate the effectiveness of our model. We gather these traces for corresponding family types. We match the time frames of the traces to the time frames of the generated traces. We select 5 consecutive days for each family type, randomly between 01–01–2014 and 06–01–2014. Table 6 shows the summary of our data sources and how we use the data. We incorporate multiple data sources (ATUS, RECS and GE) to build our user behavior model and compare it against the real power traces from Pecan Street database. It is difficult to directly compare the exact values in generated vs. real power traces since (1) the data we build our model on does not have direct correspondence with Pecan Street database (activities + appliance statistics vs. energy traces), (2) ATUS and RECS data spans the entire country, whereas Pecan Street has data only from Austin, TX, (3) the appliance power ratings from GE and Pecan Street do not match. Appliance power data from many houses in Pecan Street are missing. Although the exact values may not match, our model still accurately finds the peak demand times for both individual houses and a neighborhood with several houses. We scale the appliance ratings based on the peak values observed in generated vs. real traces and show that our model is more accurate if the correct appliance ratings are used.

Individual Power Profiles. Figures 2 and 3 show the power profiles of single male and female houses. The first and second figures show generated and real

Table 6. Data sources and usage purposes summary

Data source	Usage purpose	Data size	Data span
ATUS [17]	Modeling activities	10000+ participants/year	Entire US
RECS [8]	Modeling appliance usage	110+ million participants	Entire US
General electric [9]	Appliance power ratings	N/A	N/A
Pecan street Inc. [11]	Verification of power profiles	778 houses	Austin, TX

Table 7. Appliance power consumption values [9]

Appliance	Power (W)	Appliance	Power (W)	Appliance	Power (W)
Central HVAC	3000–5000	Hair dryer	1500	Dryer	3400
Vacuum cleaner	500	Oven	3000	Laptop	100
Dishwasher	1500	Washer	500	LCD TV	210
Microwave	1500	Toaster	1100	Lights	50–100/room

traces. Both adults are assumed to be working full-time. The generated traces match the times of the power spikes of the real traces, where exact values do not match due to the reasons listed previously. The generated traces demonstrate more spikes and higher maximum power consumption for female adult households, which is also visible in the real traces.

Figures 4, 5 and 6 show the power profiles of couples with 1 child, 2 children with the mother is working and stay-at-home (with and without HVAC). These profiles show similar peaks, all higher than the couples only case as the families with children use the appliances more often and spend more time at home. The difference arises in terms of the frequency of peaks. In the case with stay at home mother, we see the duty cycle behavior of HVAC spread throughout the day. The appliances are not used only in the evenings but also during the day. Most of the washer, dryer, dishwasher instances occur during the day because the appliance usage probabilities are higher for the stay at home mother during the day. The maximum power demand never exceeds 8 kW since the appliance operations do not coincide. In the case with working mother, appliances accumulate in the evenings, leading to a larger maximum power demand, around 12 kW.

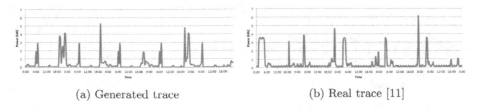

(a) Generated trace   (b) Real trace [11]

Fig. 2. Single male house power profile

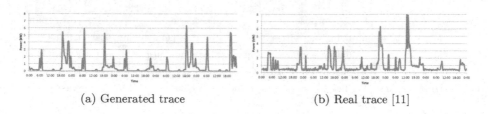

(a) Generated trace   (b) Real trace [11]

Fig. 3. Single female house power profile

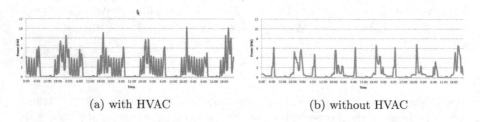

(a) with HVAC   (b) without HVAC

Fig. 4. Generated power traces for couples with 1 child

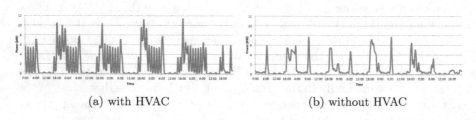

(a) with HVAC   (b) without HVAC

Fig. 5. Generated power traces for couples with 2 children - mother is working

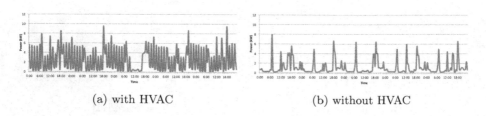

(a) with HVAC   (b) without HVAC

Fig. 6. Generated power traces for couples with 2 children - mother is not working

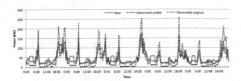

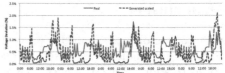

Fig. 7. Total power consumption   **Fig. 8.** Max voltage deviation

Case Study: Neighborhood Energy Analysis. One of the strengths of our model is that it can capture the nuances between the power profiles of different family types and show when the maximum power draws are likely to occur. This is an important and very useful capability when studying the effects of total power consumption during peak periods [2]. By creating several, reproducible power traces, we significantly increase the scalability of such system analyses and reduce the complexity to evaluate several cases with many homes.

Figure 7 shows the total power consumption of a neighborhood with 50 houses. The numbers of different family types are calculated based on Table 4. Comparing the real (straight) and generated (dotted) traces, we see that our model matches the times of peak spikes, but not the exact values due to (1) different appliance power ratings and (2) various small plug loads not included in our model as we either could not associate any user activity with them or did not find any usage data for them in large, long-term ATUS and RECS data sets. We scale values based on the maximum observed in generated vs. real traces and add an offset to account for the various plug loads. We show this new trace with the dashed line in Fig. 7. The scaled trace matches the peak power times and obtains 38 % absolute mean error, with minimum 0.25 % error. This shows that our model becomes more accurate once appliance power values closely match the original appliances used. We also compute the correlation coefficient between generated and real traces. This coefficient is between 0.1–0.3 for individual houses, 0.45 for the neighborhood with original generated traces and 0.62 with scaled generated traces. Our values have strong correlation with real traces for aggregate consumption, by correctly detecting the power spikes.

We use this neighborhood profile to study voltage deviation. Deviation values elevate with increased total consumption [2], thus, it is imperative to correctly estimate both the times and the magnitude of the spikes. We use the grid simulator in [2] to compute the deviation values. We get the physical circuit as a subset from one of EPRI's openly released test circuits [1]. Figure 8 shows the maximum deviations for both real and generated (scaled) traces. The deviation values show significant correlation with the spikes in Fig. 7. Our traces match these high deviation events (captures 5/5), which generally occur during the evenings. During these events, we get little or no error in voltage deviation.

6   Conclusion

Residential sector is a significant portion of the overall energy consumption in the US. Recent studies propose several energy-aware automation and scheduling solutions to address this. However, they need power profiles from a diverse set of houses to test these solutions. To achieve this, we propose a user behavior model to estimate the power demand of a house. We consider the features of both users and appliances to create diversity across neighborhoods. We can form several house profiles with different energy needs in a reproducible way. We compare the traces we generate against real data from Pecan Street. Our model matches the trends observed in real data for both individual houses and a neighborhood with 50 houses, by accurately estimating appliance usage times and thus peak power times. We also show the effects of peak power spikes with a grid simulator. Our model detects the high voltage deviation events observed with real data.

Acknowledgment. This work was supported in part by TerraSwarm, one of six centers of STARnet, a Semiconductor Research Corporation program sponsored by MARCO and DARPA.

References

1. EPRI test circuits. http://svn.code.sf.net/p/electricdss/code/trunk/Distrib/ EPRITestCircuits/Readme.pdf
2. Akyurek, A.S., Aksanli, B., Rosing, T., S2Sim: smart grid swarm simulator. In: International Green and Sustainable Computing Conference (IGSC). IEEE (2015)
3. Barker, S., Mishra, A., Irwin, D., Cecchet, E., Shenoy, P., Albrecht, J.: Smart*: An open data set and tools for enabling research in sustainable homes. In: SustKDD 2012 (2012)
4. Basu, K., Hawarah, L., Arghira, N., Joumaa, H., Ploix, S.: A prediction system for home appliance usage. Energy Build. **67**, 668–679 (2013)
5. Chen, D., Barker, S., Subbaswamy, A., Irwin, D., Shenoy, P.: Non-intrusive occupancy monitoring using smart meters. In: ACM Buildsys (2013)
6. Chiou, Y.: Deriving us household energy consumption profiles from american time use survey data a bootstrap approach. In: 11th International Building Performance Simulation Association Conference and Exhibition (2009)
7. Collin, A.J., Tsagarakis, G., Kiprakis, A.E., McLaughlin, S.: Multi-scale electrical load modelling for demand-side management. In: IEEE PES ISGT Europe (2012)
8. U.S. E.I.A. Residential energy consumption survey (2009)
9. General electric. http://visualization.geblogs.com/visualization/appliances/
10. Center for climate and energy solutions. Energy and technology (2011). http:// www.c2es.org/category/topic/energy-technology
11. Pecan street Inc. Dataport (2015)
12. Johnson, B.J., Starke, M.R., Abdelaziz, O., Jackson, R.K., Tolbert, L.M.: A method for modeling household occupant behavior to simulate residential energy consumption. In: Innovative Smart Grid Technologies Conference, IEEE PES (2014)
13. Kolter, Z., Johnson, M.J.: REDD: a public data set for energy disaggregation research. In: Workshop on Data Mining Applications in Sustainability (2011)

14. López-Rodríguez, M.A., Santiago, I., Trillo-Montero, D., Torriti, J., Moreno-Munoz, A.: Analysis, modeling of active occupancy of the residential sector in spain: an indicator of residential electricity consumption. Energy Policy **62**, 742–751 (2013)
15. Muratori, M., Roberts, M., Sioshansi, R., Marano, V., Rizzoni, G.: A highly resolved modeling technique to simulate residential power demand. Appl. Energy **107**, 465–473 (2013)
16. Neill, D.O., Levorato, M., Goldsmith, A., Mitra, U.: Residential demand response using reinforcement learning. In: IEEE SmartGridComm (2010)
17. Bureau of Labor Statistics. American time use survey (2014)
18. Venkatesh, J., Aksanli, B., Junqua, J., Morin, P., Rosing, T.: Homesim: comprehensive, smart, residential electrical energy simulation and scheduling. In: International Green Computing Conference (IGCC). IEEE (2013)

Secure Management and Processing
of Metered Data in the Cloud

Bokun Zhang, Pirathayini Srikantha$^{(\boxtimes)}$, and Deepa Kundur

University of Toronto, Toronto, ON, Canada
{bokun.zhang,pirathayini.srikantha,dkundur}@mail.utoronto.ca

Abstract. The recent cyber-physical integration in the electric power grid provides unprecedented insights and management capabilities to the grid operator. Devices such as smart meters have been widely deployed in urban cities and produce granular user consumption information that can be used for many useful applications such as demand response. Efficiently managing and processing this expansive sensitive data in a secure manner is a challenging task. We address this in this paper by leveraging on light-weight encryption and the cloud services. Results indicate that our proposed solution is economical and eliminates many of the issues associated with relying on third party services for data management.

Keywords: Cloud · Homomorphic encryption · Security · Demand response

1 Introduction

The advanced metering infrastructure (AMI), a component of an Electric Power Utility (EPU), is comprised of smart meters equipped with bi-directional communication capabilities [1]. Smart meters residing at the local premises of thousands of energy consumers generate and transmit local energy consumption data to the EPU at a daily basis. This process generates vast amounts of data which is typically used by the EPU for efficient and convenient billing. As many valuable insights can be drawn from this data, the EPU and many third party solution providers can utilize this information for many other useful applications. One particular example of such an application is real-time demand response. Statistics such as average energy consumption extracted from this metered data can be used in real-time demand response (DR) for reducing peak aggregate power consumption in the system. Real-time applications such as DR require these statistics from metering data generated at high frequencies [2]. Hence, an extremely efficient data management system equipped with significant storage and computational capabilities is imperative to enable these real-time applications.

Managing and performing computations on data at such a large scale in an economical manner is not an trivial task. The cloud provides vast amount of storage and powerful computational resources on-demand with no need for

© ICST Institute for Computer Sciences, Social Informatics and Telecommunications Engineering 2016
A. Leon-Garcia et al. (Eds.): Smart City 2015, LNICST 166, pp. 362–373, 2016.
DOI: 10.1007/978-3-319-33681-7_30

advanced commitment. This inherent flexibility renders the cloud to be a practical and viable option for meter data management [3]. However, the cloud has many security issues that must be carefully dealt with by the EPU due to the revealing nature of meter data. Techniques based on energy signatures can be used to infer the daily activities of a consumer from his or her metered data [4].

As the EPU will not be able to ascertain the security statuses of physical servers used in the cloud, sensitive data can be exposed to data leakage and loss of integrity due to unresolved vulnerabilities in the cloud environment [7]. In order to overcome these issues, it is necessary to apply additional processing to ensure that this data cannot be compromised while residing on a third party infrastructure like the cloud. One approach will be to store data in encrypted form at all times on the cloud. However, typical encryption techniques impose difficulties with being able to leverage the vast amount of computational resources available in the cloud for data analytics.

In the existing literature, many proposals discuss potential solutions for cloud security issues. Reference [13] suggests processing sensitive data via homomorphic encryption technology to promote security. However, this solution supports limited functions, such as data aggregation. Reference [14, 15] propose schemes that utilize the Paillier scheme to obtain sums of meter measurements at the neighborhood level in order to address privacy issues. Again, this imposes limitations on the processing capabilities on encrypted data. In [16], Goh's encryption scheme is leveraged to perform homomorphic operations for statistical data analysis in smart grid system. This is associated with possible efficiency and functionality issues. All of these results indicate that although homomorphic encryption consists of many attractive properties for ensuring security and integrity, there are unresolved issues associated with efficiency and functionality.

In this paper, we present a cloud-based solution that focuses on the use of Paillier encryption for storing and processing meter data in a secure and an efficient manner while also addressing limitations in basic computational features supported by this encryption scheme. Simulations are used to infer the efficiencies of these three methods. Then, we address potential issues with metered data synchronization in the cloud due to latencies in data transmission.

2   Homomorphic Encryption

In this section, we provide a brief background on homomorphic encryption. Homomorphic encryption allows basic mathematical operations to be performed directly on cipher-text. Even though these operations are applied on cipher-text, these are also reflected in the plain-text [6]. For example, suppose that an addition operation on two cipher-text units which are the encrypted versions of two numbers, say 3 and 4. When the resulting cipher-text is decrypted, the value 7 will be obtained. This is extremely advantageous as there is no need to decrypt cipher-text for computations that involve elementary mathematical operations. This homomorphic property can be expressed as:

$$f(Encode(m)) = Encode(f(m)) \tag{1}$$

where $Encode(x)$ is the homomorphic encryption function, $Decode(x)$ is the homomorphic decryption function, m is the plain-text and $f(.)$ represents the function that performs a mathematical operation on $(.)$.

The various types of mathematical operations $f(.)$ that allow the homomorphic property in Eq. 1 to hold depends on the type of homomorphic encryption utilized. There are two main types of homomorphic encryption schemes widely used in the literature. These are the fully homomorphic encryption (FHE) and Paillier encryption (PE) schemes.

2.1   Fully Homomorphic Encryption

FHE scheme supports a broad range of mathematical operations that include division, etc. Although this scheme supports all of the mathematical operations required for our purposes, major issues that render it unsuitable for real-time large data sets include: slow processing speed, complex cipher-text noise reduction functions and tremendous memory storage space [6,8,9,11]. FHE supports many additional features that are typically not necessary for energy applications.

2.2   Paillier Encryption Scheme

The PE scheme is a light-weight factoring based, asymmetrical encryption technology used typically in electronic money and voting system applications [10]. It supports homomorphic addition and a relative homomorphic multiplication property. These PE homomorphic operations are expressed as follows:

$$\text{Addition: } Add(c1, c2) = Encode(m1 + m2, pk) \tag{2}$$

$$\text{Multiplication: } Mult(K, c1) = Encode(K * m1, pk) \tag{3}$$

where pk is the public key, $m1$ and $m2$ are plain-text values, $c1$ and $c2$ are cipher-text values corresponding to the plain-text, and K is an integer. The relative multiplication property, as it is evident from 3, is restrictive. One operand must be an integer (i.e. both operands cannot be cipher-text values and the non-ciphertext operand cannot be a fraction). Hence, it is not possible to perform averaging, which is a very common computation in energy applications such as DR, using this relative multiplication operation. As the PE scheme is light-weight, it is well-suited for processing vast amounts of data in the cloud. In order to overcome the limitation of not being able to use the division operation, in Sect. 3, we propose three methods that enable division possible. These can be applied to obtain general statistical metrics such as averaging via the basic operations supported by the PE scheme.

3   Extended Cipher-Text Operations for PE

Here, we propose the following three methods that extend aggregation operations in PE: direct send back, data amplification-grouping and multiplier amplification. Although our focus is on averaging operations, these methods can be easily extended to other operations such as division on cipher-text, etc. Our primary goal is to design a light-weight scheme for averaging computations on large data sets in a quick and efficient manner. To assess this, we also include comprehensive results that compare key metrics such as latency and complexity of our proposed extensions.

3.1 Direct Send Back

For an averaging operation, many additions must be performed and only one division operation is required. The direct send back method involves a two step process. First, the *Add* operation in the PE scheme can be applied within the cloud to the cipher text corresponding to the data set of interest. Then information including this result and the number of entries that have been added can be sent to the client. The client can then decrypt the cipher-text and directly apply division operation to obtain the average value. Although this is a viable option as data is not decrypted on the cloud, there are two main issues associated with this approach. Firstly, the computational process is partially completed by the client and this is not desirable as division is a computationally intensive task. Cloud resources can more effectively perform this operation than the client. Also, the aggregated value can be very large and communicating this to the client can cause issues such as transmission delays. Moreover, there are security concerns with this approach. Revealing the size of the data set to the client can expose demographic information.

3.2 Data Amplification and Grouping

This is our second proposal which utilizes the modular inverse concept in lieu of the division operation for averaging. This allows us to use the relative multiplication and modular operations supported by PE to perform division indirectly. However, modular inverses are associated with some limitations and we show that with additional processing on data via grouping and amplification, these can be overcome.

As mentioned in the background section, PE does not support direct division or relative multiplication of a cipher-text with a float value. Suppose that b and N are relatively prime. Then, the modular inverse $modInv(b)$ of b with respect to N satisfies $b * modInv(b) = 1 (mod\ N)$. $modInv(b)$ is an integer. A division operation $\frac{a}{b}$ can be effectively replaced by the modular inverse as follows if certain conditions are met:

$$\frac{a}{b} \equiv a\ modInv(b)\ (\text{mod}\ N)$$

The first condition is that $N \geq \frac{a}{b}$ and we satisfy this condition by setting N to be the public key pk used to encrypt the data set (as $pk \gg \frac{a}{b}$). The next requirement is the existence of the modular inverse. The modular inverse of b modulo pk exists if and only if

$$gcd(b,\ pk) = 1$$

In PE, the public key pk is the product of two non-even prime numbers. If b is an even number, then the above condition is satisfied for $N = pk$. However, it is not possible to force b to be an even number as for our averaging application, b represents the total number of data values composing the data set that we are averaging. In order to resolve this issue, we group the data values in the data set so that the number of data values composing each subset is even. This guarantees the existence of the modular inverses required to compute the averages of data values in these groups. Next, we discuss how we propose to divide the data set into groups containing even number of data values.

Let b be the total number of data values composing the data set of interest. b can be represented as a binary number as follows:

$$b = \sum_{i=0}^{\lfloor log_2 b \rfloor} c_i * 2^i$$

where $c_i \in \{0, 1\}$ is the bit corresponding to the ith significant digit of the binary representation of b. The data set originally containing b data values can be considered to be a composition of several smaller groups where the ith group (which exists if $c_i = 1$) consists of 2^i data values. In Fig. 1, an example of this data grouping is illustrated for a data set comprising of 1173 elements.

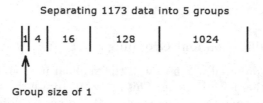

Fig. 1. Grouping of data values in a data set

The averaging of each group i can be applied directly on the cipher-text by first summing all cipher-text values in this group to obtain S_i. Before applying $mult(S_i, modInv(2^i))$, it is necessary to check if S_i is exactly divisible by 2^i. Otherwise, the modular division will fail to produce the correct value. In order to ensure that this condition always holds, an amplification is applied to S_i by multiplying this value with 10^i so that now $S_i * 10^i / 2^i$ will always be exact. $A_i = S_i * 10^i / 2^i$ can now be obtained from the cipher-text values in the cloud via these homomorphic encryption operations: $A_i = Mult(Mult(S_i, 10^i), modInv(2^i))mod(pk)$. Averages computed for all groups are compiled into a list $L = \{[A_0, Encode(0), c_0], \ldots, [A_i, Encode(i), c_0], \ldots, [A_{\lfloor log_2 b \rfloor}, Encode(\lfloor log_2 b \rfloor), c_0]\}$. This list is then sent to the client. The client will decrypt L and perform a weighted average $\sum_{i=0}^{\lfloor log_2 b \rfloor} \frac{c_i * A_0}{5^i}$ to recover the final average.

With this particular proposal, we have demonstrated how the traditional division can be replaced with the modular division after some additional processing. Bulk of resource intensive operations are performed on the cloud. However, there still exists the issue of exposing the total number of value points in the data set to the client as the binary representation of the size of the data set is appended to L.

3.3   Multiplier Amplification

Another simpler alternative that does not require exposing the total number of data points in the set is presented next. Suppose the sum of all data points in the set is S, then the average of this set is $\frac{S}{b}$. Amplifying $\frac{1}{b}$ by 10^n, setting $P_n = \lfloor \frac{1}{b} * 10^n \rfloor$ preserves a precision of n digits. Now, the relative multiplication operation can be applied to S and P_n which results in T_n. The value pair $[T_n, n]$ is then sent to the client who can now recover the final average by applying $decode(T_n, n)$ and dividing this value by 10^n. Although this is much more simpler and maintains privacy, the cipher-text transmitted to the client will typically represent a large value.

3.4   Time Latencies of PE

In order to establish the performance of each of the above methods, the homomorphic encryption project (THEP), made available by Pwnhome Research [12] is utilized in our test cases implemented in Java. In our algorithm implementations, we use Java's building-in BigInteger class to store and process the plain and cipher text. Our test client consists of a CPU i5-4200U that operates at 1.6GHz. Before characterizing the performance of our proposed algorithms, we first present the latencies for various PE functions.

Key Generation. First, we assess the time required to generate a pair of keys of constant length. This generation process is repeated 20 times and the average of this time values are presented in Table 1.

Table 1. Average time for key generation

Key length	256 bit	800 bit	1024 bit
Time consumption	125 ms	188 ms	216 ms

It can be concluded from the above set of results that the time complexity for key generation increases with the size of the key.

Encryption Speed. Next, we assess the complexity of encrypting data with PE. Since a longer key translates to greater security, we use a key length of 1024 bit for testing purposes in the remainder of this section. In the set of

Table 2. Encryption speed of data

Message length	32 bit	64 bit	256 bit	512 bit
Time consumption	13.0 ms	14.7 ms	15.9 ms	17.6 ms

results in Table 2, 100 randomly generated plain-text data of the same size are encrypted.

It is evident from the above set of results that even though the message size is doubling, the time required for encryption increases only slightly.

Decryption Speed. Here, decryption is applied on 100 randomly generated plain-text messages as in the above. The average time required for decryption is presented in Table 3.

Table 3. Decryption speed of data

Message length	32 bit	64 bit	256 bit	512 bit
Time consumption	12.3 ms	12.1 ms	12.5 ms	11.4 ms

The time required for decryption remains almost constant regardless of the size of the data being decrypted.

Proposed Algorithm. Finally, we present the time complexity of applying our three proposed algorithms on the client side for computing the average of a data set containing 750,000,000 values where each is of length 256 bits. This data set consists of 12 groups where the ith group is of size 2^i. The average time required for the client to recover the final averaged value is listed in Table 4.

Table 4. Client side latency for recovering final average

Method	Direct send back	Data grouping and amplification	Multiplier amplification
Time consumption	24.46 ms	156.08 ms	24.37 ms

It is clear that the data grouping and amplification method results in the most computational latency on the client side. The direct send back and multiplier amplification methods have similar performances. Although the data grouping and amplification method makes an interesting connection to modular mathematics and is tailored around the PE scheme, it requires excessive resources at the client side. As our goal is to minimize resource allocation on the client side, this will not be a suitable algorithm. Since, the multiplier amplification is the least revealing and the fastest, it is most suited for our purpose.

4   Data Transmission Synchronization

Data generated from the metering infrastructure is encrypted via PE at the smart meter and is transmitted to the cloud in the encrypted form. This start-to-end encryption has been proposed in works such as [14–16]. For applications such as real-time demand response, averaging operations are performed on meter data transmitted in the order of minutes [2]. Communication latencies can cause this encrypted data to be unordered. Hence, when these arrive at the cloud, it is not possible to identify precisely the time at which data has actually been generated at the smart meter as this information is encrypted. An example of this issue is illustrated in Fig. 2. In this figure, although the data is generated by the slow and fast client at the same time, the data from the fast client always arrives much earlier than the slow client. If the averaging window is small, then the information from the slow client will not be representative of the averaging window.

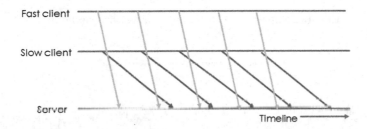

Fig. 2. Example of desynchronization of data values

We define a bucket to be a period of time in which we take the average of data points from a particular meter and an example is presented in Fig. 3. Hence, incorrect ordering within this time frame is tolerated.

We explore the tolerance to error of the averaging function for various averaging bucket sizes. Load profiles of 30 homes are generated over a 24 h period. All load generation parameters are obtained from [5] for Ontario. Figures 4 and 6

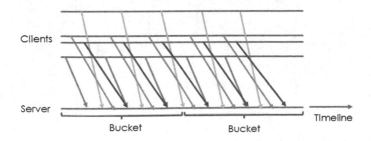

Fig. 3. Illustration of a bucket

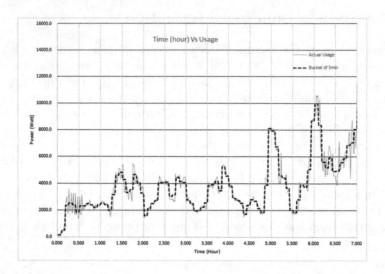

Fig. 4. Comparison of averaging during off-peak hours

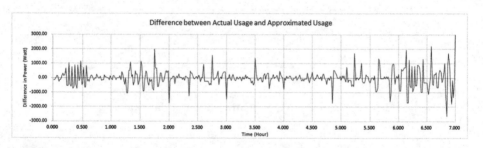

Fig. 5. Error between actual average and approximated average during off-peak hours

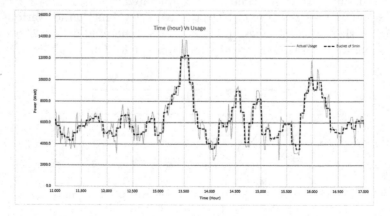

Fig. 6. Comparison of averaging during on-peak hours

illustrate the average load profiles of 30 homes for off-peak and on-peak periods respectively. Each one of these graphs contains the actual average load profile obtained from perfectly synchronized data points and the approximated average using a bucket that is 5 min in length. Errors resulting from the approximation is illustrated in Figs. 5 and 7.

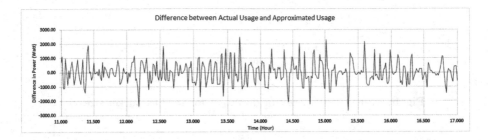

Fig. 7. Error between actual average and approximated average during on-peak hours

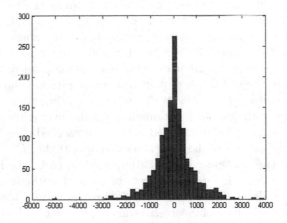

Fig. 8. Error distribution

The distribution of error over a day is illustrated in Fig. 8. This distribution curve is very similar to a normal distribution with a mean of approximately 0 W and a standard deviation of 799 W. Next, Fig. 9 presents a scatter plot containing the standard deviation of error for various bucket sizes. A line of best fit reveals that the general trend of error standard deviation is that it is logarithmically increasing with the bucket size. This log function has a coefficient of determination of 0.98.

All results presented in this section provide interesting insights on the impact of the bucket size on errors introduced into the computations. Smaller the bucket size, the smaller is the variation in error around the mean 0.

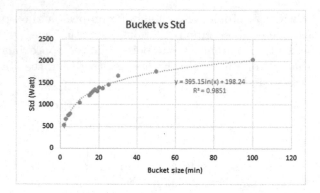

Fig. 9. Best-fit curve for error deviation for various bucket sizes

5   Conclusions

In this paper, we explore how sensitive meter data can be stored and processed securely in the cloud for applications such as demand response that perform basic analytics on this data in real-time. As vast amounts of meter data are generated and processed daily for these applications, it is necessary to utilize a light-weight encryption scheme that protects the data from issues such as leakage and integrity which are especially of concern when a third party infrastructure is used for managing this data. Homomorphic encryption is a suitable candidate for this as it enables the utilization of powerful computational capabilities of the cloud without exposing actual data to the external environment. PE is a light-weight scheme but with limited functionality. As the averaging operation is a common computation applied to metered data, we presented three methods that leverage on existing features of the PE scheme to support this. Of these methods, we have identified the multiplier amplification method to be the least intrusive for clients. Next, we investigate how latency introduced in the transmission and storage of encrypted data can affect the actual representation of the system state. In order to reduce the impact of incorrect ordering, the data values from a single source are averaged over a time window (i.e. bucket). We show that the error of the approximated system represents a normal distribution and more specifically, the error deviation increases logarithmically with the bucket size.

References

1. BC Hydro's Smart Metering Program - Program Overview for Key Account Customers. BC Hydro PDF, British Columbia
2. Srikantha, P., Kundur, D.: A novel evolutionary game theoretic approach to real-time distributed demand response. In: IEEE Power Engineering Society General Meeting (PES GM), July 2015
3. Rong, C., Nguyen, S.T., Jaatun, M.G.: Beyond lightning: a survey on security challenges in cloud computing. Comput. Electr. Eng. **39**(1), 47–54 (2013)

4. Ruzzelli, A., Nicolas, C., Schoofs, A., OHare, G.: Real-time recognition and pro-filing of appliances through a single electricity sensor. In: Seventh IEEE Communications Society Conference on Sensor Mesh and Ad Hoc Communications and Networks, pp. 1–9 (2010)
5. Srikantha, P., Rosenberg, C., Keshav, S.: An analysis of peak demand reductions due to elasticity of domestic appliances. In: Proceedings of the 3rd International Conference on Future Energy Systems: Where Energy, Computing and Communication Meet. ACM (2012)
6. Craig, G.: Fully homomorphic encryption using ideal lattices. In: STOC, vol. 9 (2009)
7. Murrill, B.J., Liu, E.C., Thompson, R.M.: Smart meter data: privacy and cyber-security. In: Congressional Research Service, Library of Congress (2012)
8. Halevi, S., Shoup, V.: Bootstrapping for HElib. In: Oswald, E., Fischlin, M. (eds.) EUROCRYPT 2015. LNCS, vol. 9056, pp. 641–670. Springer, Heidelberg (2015)
9. van Dijk, M., Gentry, C., Halevi, S., Vaikuntanathan, V.: Fully homomorphic encryption over the integers. In: Gilbert, H. (ed.) EUROCRYPT 2010. LNCS, vol. 6110, pp. 24–43. Springer, Heidelberg (2010)
10. Paillier, P.: Public-key cryptosystems based on composite degree residuosity classes. In: Stern, J. (ed.) EUROCRYPT 1999. LNCS, vol. 1592, p. 223. Springer, Heidelberg (1999)
11. Wang, W., et al.: Exploring the feasibility of fully homomorphic encryption. IEEE Trans. Comput. **64**(3), 698–706 (2015)
12. Pwnhome. The Homomorphic Encryption Project. Vers. 0.2. Computer software. Pwnhome(2011)
13. Tebaa, M., El Hajji, S., El Ghazi, A.: Homomorphic encryption applied to the cloud computing security. In: Proceedings of the World Congress on Engineering, vol. 1 (2012)
14. Garcia, F.D., Jacobs, B.: Privacy-friendly energy-metering via homomorphic encryption. In: Cuellar, J., Lopez, J., Barthe, G., Pretschner, A. (eds.) STM 2010. LNCS, vol. 6710, pp. 226–238. Springer, Heidelberg (2011)
15. Li, F., Luo, B., Liu, P.: Secure information aggregation for smart grids using homomorphic encryption. In: First IEEE International Conference on Smart Grid Communications, pp. 327–332 (2010)
16. He, X., Pun, M.O., Kuo, C-C.J.: Secure and efficient cryptosystem for smart grid using homomorphic encryption. In: Innovative Smart Grid Technologies (ISGT), IEEE PES. IEEE (2012)

A Secure Cloud Architecture for Data Generated in the Energy Sector

Michael Pham-Hung, Pirathayini Srikantha$^{(\boxtimes)}$, and Deepa Kundur

University of Toronto, Toronto, ON, Canada
{michael.pham.hung,pirathayini.srikantha,dkundur}@mail.utoronto.ca

Abstract. In urban cities, intelligent devices such as smart meters are deployed extensively and these provide comprehensive real-time snapshots of energy consumption patterns to the electric power utility (EPU). This data can be leveraged by the EPU, other third-party solution providers or consumers themselves to make informed and smart decisions that enable sustainable power consumption. However, managing vast amounts of meter data generated at a regular basis in a secure and economical manner is not a trivial task. We propose a cloud-based architectural model that leverages recent developments in standardized data access and encryption techniques to enable flexible, secure and economical management of energy data. We also present a prototype of a mobile application that performs analytics on meter data to provide information to consumers that will incentivize more sustainable power consumption patterns.

Keywords: Cloud services · Green button standard · Security · Homomorphic encryption

1 Introduction

Today's grid is a cyber-physical system consisting of many interconnected intelligent devices that perform measurement and actuation in real-time. Information and tools made available by these devices allow both the power supplier and consumer to make informed decisions on sustainable energy management. The advanced metering infrastructure (AMI) is a critical component of the electric power utility (EPU) composed of smart meters that are equipped with bi-directional communication capability [9]. These transmit local energy usage measurements of thousands of consumers to the EPU at a daily basis. This data is not only convenient for billing consumers, it contains interesting insights on energy consumption patterns that can be leveraged by the EPU, third party solution providers and the consumers themselves to promote sustainable power consumption behaviour. In order to glean these insights, this data must be effectively stored, managed and processed. This represents a significant challenge for the EPU as metered data is vast and is continually generated at a fast pace. Significant resources are necessary to store and manage data at this scale and using

© ICST Institute for Computer Sciences, Social Informatics and Telecommunications Engineering 2016
A. Leon-Garcia et al. (Eds.): Smart City 2015, LNICST 166, pp. 374–383, 2016.
DOI: 10.1007/978-3-319-33681-7_31

in-house methods for this purpose is not economical. A very viable alternative for the EPU is the cloud.

The cloud provides on-demand access to storage and computational resources without prior commitment. Moreover, pricing models of cloud services are extremely economical. Although the cloud consists of many features that address most needs of the EPU for handling metered data, security is a primary concern. As the cloud providers do not reveal details on the internal workings of their infrastructure, the EPU cannot ascertain the security level of the system (i.e. unpatched vulnerabilities, etc.). Security is an important consideration for the EPU as metered data can be analyzed to reveal confidential information of consumers. We propose a cloud-based architectural model with a central focus on security. Main components of our proposed model include additional processing of metered data via homomorphic encryption prior to cloud storage and the integration of the Green Button standard that provides interfaces for accessing authorized data with privacy considerations in tact. In order to demonstrate how our proposed architecture provides means for secure data management and processing, we present a mobile application prototype that can be provisioned by the EPU to encourage sustainable energy consumption based on analytics performed on metered data managed by our cloud model.

2   Background

In this section, we provide a brief background on the Green Button standard, homomorphic encryption and cloud services.

2.1   Green Button Standard

The Green Button initiative provides interfaces that can be used to access available metered data in a standardized manner by solution providers and consumers. Privacy is incorporated into this standard as any data obtained via Green Button excludes Personal Identifiable Information (PII) [1]. Only meter measurements obtained within a specified time interval is provided without including information of its origins. Utility providers are already using smart meter data for billing purposes. However, proprietary protocols have been used to access this data. This makes data sharing extremely challenging. The green button standard provides a universal format that allows consumers to gain access to their data through the use of the *Download my Data* (DmD) interface. Apart from being able to view their own data, consumers are able to authorize access to their data for usage by third party solution providers via *Connect my Data* (CmD) interface. These features promote privacy and security. The proposed architectural model revolves around the Green Button standard as the cloud will be able to gain access to standardized formatted data from EPU companies through these interfaces and this data can then be processed by third parties to infer interesting estimations and models without impinging on consumer privacy.

2.2   Homomorphic Encryption

Homomorphic encryption represents a group of semantically secure encryption functions that allow certain algebraic operations on the plaintext to be performed directly on the ciphertext. Mathematically, given a homomorphic encryption function E( ), and two messages $x, y \in N$, we are able to compute $E_k(x \star y) = E_{k1}(x) \circ E_{k2}(y)$, without knowing the plaintext x, y or the private key [8]. Ideally, a fully homomorphic encryption allows any function E( ) to be computed on ciphertext, however these schemes, such as Gentry, are hugely inefficient [15]. More practical schemes, such as Pailler's scheme, are partially homomorphic [14]. These schemes can only compute a limited amount of functions on ciphertext, however are much more efficient and therefore practical.

2.3   Cloud Services

According to the National Institute of Standards and Technology (NIST), cloud computing systems enable convenient, on-demand network access to a shared pool of configurable computing resources and services (e.g. networks, servers, storage, applications) that can be rapidly provisioned and released with minimal management effort or service provider interaction [2]. The attractiveness of cloud computing, specifically the *Infrastructure as a Service* (IaaS) model, stems from its scalability and economic viability. There is potential to obtain access to a vast amount of computing services according to the needs of clients without up-front commitment [3]. In this paper, we are focusing on the IaaS cloud service which is typically provided by a third party cloud provider.

With the vast and increasing amount of data that the energy sector generates and processes, an economically viable option for utilities is to outsource computation and storage to cloud providers. However, there are a few concerns listed in the following that must be addressed by the utilities prior to fully engaging in cloud services.

Forensic Accessibility: Metered data contains highly revealing private information of consumers. For example, energy signatures can be applied to metered data to determine the occupancy and activities of a home [11]. When handling sensitive consumer data, utilities must be prepared to provide logs and forensic records for regulatory compliance purposes. It will be impossible for cloud providers to provide this information without exposing their internal architecture and algorithms. This lack of transparency renders significant difficulties for the power EPU sector as it is accountable for the protection and integrity of the data it stores [4].

Multi-tenancy: The method by which data is distributed across the cloud is completely under the control of the cloud provider. In a multi-tenant public cloud system, data is typically spread across multiple physical servers that may be shared with other users. Any unresolved vulnerabilities in the virtual environment that divides physical resources can be exploited by other tenants to access data in an unauthorized manner [5].

Resource Location: End-users use the services provided by the cloud providers without knowing exactly where the resources for such services are located. The physical systems supporting the cloud can possibly reside in other legislative domains. As local laws apply, exposure to possible issues that affect the integrity and privacy of data maybe inevitable.

Authentication and Trust of Acquired Information: Since data is stored within a third party infrastructure, it possible for information to be altered without the owner's consent. Authenticity and integrity of data must be guaranteed [4].

These security issues can be overcome by integrating standard interfaces for data access and incorporating additional layers of security to data prior to cloud deployment in a practical manner. The proposed architecture will preserve privacy and data integrity.

3   Related Work

Many industries have recently begun adopting cloud computing to share data in a quick and cost-effective manner.

In the health care industry, data sharing is essential for health problem detection, solution identification and medical resource allocation. Reference [6] proposes a solution for preserving the privacy of medical records stored within the cloud. Their approach involves vertical partitioning of their data into plaintext, anonymized and encrypted sections. The data owner can then authorize the merging of the partitioned data to improve medical search or analysis. As an added level of security, their proposal also allows for a hybrid method to check the integrity of data due to different requirements between data owners and recipients. Such a comprehensive solution for metered data adds significant complexity and can introduce difficulties maintaining a standard method for data access.

In the energy sector, research is plentiful in exploring how the smart grid can be combined with the cloud. One solution proposes the use of a cloud architecture that provides a platform in which third parties are allowed access to Green Button Data and development tools to provide further analysis of energy usage data [7]. These tools allow users to gain valuable information from the usage data with analysis and results aiming to reduce costs for both the users and the suppliers themselves. This paper, in contrast, proposes a security based cloud architecture that leverages standardized protocols to access sensitive data while preserving privacy and integrity.

In terms of security, reference [8] provides an excellent example of an encryption model, however it is currently not integrated with green button services. Through the use of homomorphic encryption, they suggest encrypting data starting from the smart meter to maintain anonymity. Homomorphic encryption allows data to be encrypted and have plaintext algebraic functions performed on the cipher text. This ensures that all smart meters participate in the aggregation while simultaneously maintaining user privacy. Within this paper, such a model is assumed to exist and this paper incorporates the encryption scheme to improve the security of our proposed architectural model.

4 Proposed Architecture

The main focus of our proposed smart grid cloud architecture is to provide a secure solution to store and organize EPU data. Revolving around the Green Button standard format, the cloud will be able to utilize existing DmD and CmD interfaces along with added security features to improve the integrity and usability of data.

As clouds provide resources that otherwise would have been too costly to manage internally, access to ample resources such as storage on the fly becomes trivial. With the use of the cloud, EPU companies certified by Green Button will be able to store information within a database residing in the cloud. Utilities, consumers and third parties, with authorization, will then be able to access this data from the past or present. Green Button data is stored in Extensible Markup Language (XML) which can be easily accommodated by databases.

The cloud is also able to provide access to powerful computational resources. One of the main activities that the utilities and third parties accessing the data will perform is executing various computations for further analysis. Therefore, within the proposed architecture, a separate computational component in the cloud is available for this purpose. As comprehensive powerful features such as these are provisioned by the cloud, all major operations can be executed on the cloud.

Before storing data, our model encapsulates this data with an added security layer via homomorphic encryption. This addresses many of the security and privacy issues raised earlier. As all stored data is stored as encrypted cipher-text, data will not be subjected to privacy issues due to leakage. The major attractiveness of homomorphic encryption is that mathematical operations can be directly performed on the cipher-text (i.e. there is no need to decrypt data). Since all processing of metered data involve computations, these can be performed on the cloud in the encrypted state. In other words, during the lifetime of the data, third parties hosting the cloud will never be able to gain access to the content of the data as data is never decrypted on the cloud. Figure 1 illustrates the important components of our proposed architecture.

Each process in Fig. 1 is labelled and described in detail in the following:

1. Since 2010, every home in Ontario has been installed with a smart meter [9]. Not only do smart meters measure energy and gas usage, but they are able to store and send measurement data to EPU companies.
2. Assuming that the model referenced in [8] exists, homomorphic encryption is applied to all information gathered from the smart meters. The secure data transfer is visualized in orange.
3. Utility companies (Toronto Hydro etc.) convert data received from the meters into the Green Button Standard format [1].
4. The cloud will actively gather data by using Green Button's "Download my Data" and "Connect my Data" interfaces and possibly a third interface to gather the completely anonymous data.
5. The web server will act as the wrapper and the communicating point between the cloud, users and EPU companies.

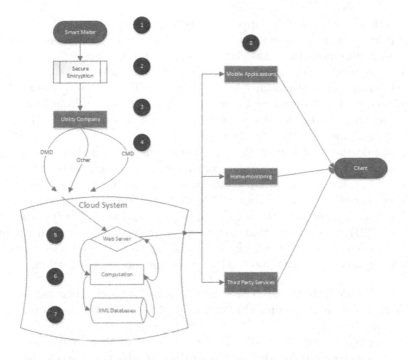

Fig. 1. Proposed architecture model

6. Computations on data before or after storage are executed by computational applications installed in the cloud.
7. The cloud will store data within an XML database. Every set of data will be tagged/labelled with parameters such as location for different types of computation and aggregation.
8. This data can be accessed by third party entities which can perform necessary operations on data in the cloud and then use these in applications that for example promote sustainable use of energy.

We are in the process of implementing a testbed modelling this cloud architecture at a smaller scale. We have used only open-source software to implement the entire testbed. Usage data is generated from Green Button's Sandbox which is populated with sample personal data [1]. The cloud itself is managed by the open source software Cloudstack [13]. The database and querying component is supported by the Basex XML Database engine.

5   Mobile Application

5.1   A Proof-of-Concept

In order to demonstrate the practicality of the proposed cloud-based smart grid data management architecture, we propose a mobile application that accesses data according to the architecture illustrated in Fig. 1.

The main motivation of this application is to encourage sustainable behaviour with respect to energy consumption. The application also serves as a proof-of-concept that illustrates the possibilities of useful applications which can access data in a manner that maintains security and privacy. This application will be deployed via the Android platform to ensure portability and convenience. It will be developed on the Android environment with the use of Android Studio. The end-product will then be tested along with the test-bed cloud which will simulate the interactions between the two entities.

The application will collect the aggregate consumption data of the user's neighbourhood, compute the average consumption rate and then compare this with the user's usage via a simple interface. The aggregation will be able to operate on anonymous data using the proposed cloud architecture at a time scale that matches the rate at which data is produced (e.g. hourly). Users will receive a real-time rendering that compares their consumption with the average consumption in their neighborhood. Following is a detailed overview of the processes required for typical interactions with the mobile application:

1. Users will supply their log-in credentials into the single time log-in screen of their mobile application. This will implicitly evoke the DmD and CmD interfaces.
2. User supplied information will then be delivered to the cloud's web server. Data sets authorized for the user according to the postal code associated with the user's residence is fetched via DmD from the XML database in the cloud. This information is still encrypted. In the case of this application, Paillier homomorphic encryption suffices due to the low complexity of the computational requirements of this application [14].
3. Using the computation component, aggregation operations are performed on the rendered data sets to obtain average consumption at the geographical location corresponding to the user.
4. The geographical average consumption and the user's consumption data are then sent via the web server to the user's device.
5. The user's device then decrypts and plots both sets of data, highlighting the differences between these. To ensure users are enticed to alter their behaviour, the graph will include a dynamic vertical scaling in order to ensure that the differences are displayed prominently to the user. Green and red trend lines will show the user the time periods at which their consumption rate is above or below average.
6. Also displayed within the application is an estimate of the amount of savings the user has been able to achieve from his or her typical energy consumption.

In Fig. 2, there are two illustrations of the Graphical User Interface (GUI) of the mobile application. The first is the primary screen the user sees after logging in. This screen is labeled as the "SAVE" screen. The "SAVE" screen provides users with a quick summary of their progress towards more sustainable power consumption behaviour: a positive value indicates that they are well on track of achieving their goals. Additionally, the "SAVE" screen presents advice/tips to the user on how they can lower their energy consumption rates. This advice is dynamic and is based on energy signatures that can be used to detect and suggest the conservation steps that can be taken by the user. Also, this advice is tailored to various periods in a day (i.e. expensive during peak and inexpensive off-peak hours).

The second screen, labelled as "COMPARE", provides a graphical rendering that compares the differences between the user's usage and the average power consumption in the system. The user will also be able to view other data within Green Button. The user's usage trend is colored in the illustration provided in Fig. 2. This color can change depending on whether the user's trends are above or below the geographical average depicted in black. In Fig. 2, the user's consumption is illustrated in red where the application informs the user that their consumption rate is greater than the average. When the user consumption rate is green, this indicates that the user's consumption is well below the average and this is desirable. The colored cues provide an intuitive visual for users to interpret their data. The graph rendering is therefore dynamic and interactive. The user is able to pan in and zoom out for further analysis of their consumption.

On both screens, two buttons are present to show the user which screen they are on. The screens are labelled respectively with the depressed and bold button showing the current screen.

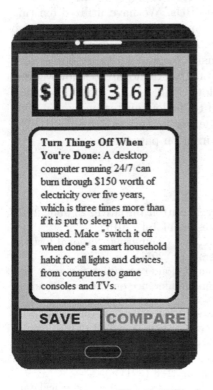 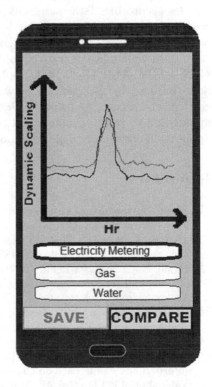

Fig. 2. GUI of mobile application prototype

Applications similar to the one proposed in this paper can be shown to encourage purely sustainable behaviour in the long-run with appropriate incentives. For instance, work in [12] evokes evolutionary game theory to prove that with appropriate incentive mechanisms in place, consumers can be induced to select more profitable actions (i.e. sustainable behaviour) with a probability of one. As future work, we intend to deploy this mobile application to the public and analyze whether this is indeed true in a realistic setting.

5.2 Our Contributions

The proposed cloud architecture provides a secure access point to data custodians, retail customers and third parties, revolutionizing the Green Button standard. The main purpose of the mobile application is to test the architecture and evoke each process flow. The mobile application provides an example of the possibilities the architecture provides for analysis and comparison tools without compromising personal information.

6 Conclusions

In this paper, we have proposed a comprehensive cloud-based architecture that enables secure big data management for the EPUs. We have utilized existing standards to enable universal accessibility for authorized clients. We have also proposed additional processing of data with homomorphic encryption to securely store data while also capitalizing on the extensive computational resources provided by the cloud. Our mobile application prototype demonstrates how various flows induced by interactions between the cloud, the EPU and the client are efficient and secure. As future work, we intend to deploy our testbed and mobile application to real consumers and analyze whether incentives displayed by the application effects any impact on power consumption patterns.

References

1. Green Button Data, An Overview of the Green Button Initiative, 25 June 2015. http://www.greenbuttondata.org/learn/. Accessed 14 July 2015
2. Mell, P., Grance, T.: The NIST Definition of Cloud Computing. National Institue of Standards and Technology (NIST), Gaithersburg (2011)
3. Ugale, B.A., Soni, P., Pema, T., Patil, A.: Role of cloud computing for smart grid of india and its cyber security. In: International Conference on Current Trends in Technology, pp. 1–5 (2011)
4. Rong, C., Nguyen, S.T., Jaatun, M.G.: Beyond lightning: a survey on security challenges in cloud computing. Comput. Electr. Eng. **39**(1), 47–54 (2013)
5. Simmhan, Y., Kumbhare, A.G., Cao, B., Prasanna, V.: An analysis of security and privacy issues in smart grid software architectures on clouds. In: IEEE 4th International Conference on Cloud Computing, pp. 1–8 (2011)
6. Yang, J.-J., Li, J.Q., Niu, Y.: A hybrid solution for privacy preserving medical data sharing in the cloud environment. Future Gener. Comput. Syst. **43**, 74–86 (2015)

7. Ballijepalli, V.M., Khaparde, S.A.: Smart grid standards conformed cloud based demand side management tools. Int. J. Eng. Res. Technol. (IJERT) 1(5), 7 (2012)
8. Li, F., Luo, B., Liu, P.: Secure information aggregation for smart grids using homomorphic encryption. In: First IEEE International Conference on Smart Grid Communications, pp. 327–332 (2010)
9. Hydro One, Smart Meter, Hydro One. http://www.hydroone.com/myhome/myaccount/mymeter/pages/smartmeters.aspx. Accessed 21 July 2015
10. Gens, F.: IDC eXchange, 2 October 2008. http://blogs.idc.com/ie/?p=210. Accessed 20 July 2015
11. Ruzzelli, A., Nicolas, C., Schoofs, A., O'Hare, G.: Real-time recognition and profiling of appliances through a single electricity sensor. In: Seventh IEEE Communications Society Conference on Sensor Mesh and Ad Hoc Communications and Networks, pp. 1–9 (2010)
12. Ramchurn, S.D., Vytelingum, P., Rogers, A., Jennings, N.: Agent-based control for decentralised demand side management in the smart grid. In: 10th International Conference on Autonomous Agents and Multiagent Systems (2011)
13. A. S. Foundation, Apache Cloudstack. https://cloudstack.apache.org/index.html. Accessed 29 July 2015
14. Paillier, P.: Public-key cryptosystems based on composite degree residuosity classes. In: Stern, J. (ed.) EUROCRYPT 1999. LNCS, vol. 1592, pp. 223–238. Springer, Heidelberg (1999)
15. Gentry, C.: Fully homomorphic encryption using ideal lattices. In: STOC, vol. 9, pp. 169–178 (2009)

Network-Aware QoS Routing for Smart Grids Using Software Defined Networks

Jinjing Zhao[1(✉)], Eman Hammad[2], Abdallah Farraj[2], and Deepa Kundur[2]

[1] National Key Laboratory of Science and Technology
on Information System Security, Beijing, China
jinjing.zhao@utoronto.ca
[2] Department of Electrical and Computer Engineering,
University of Toronto, Toronto, Canada
{ehammad,abdallah,dkundur}@ece.utoronto.ca

Abstract. We consider the problem of quality of service (QoS) routing for smart grids using software defined networks (SDN). The SDN framework enables an efficient decoupled implementation of dynamic routing protocols that is aware of the communication network status. In this work we consider the varying delay status of the communication network along with other network parameters such as links throughput. The routing problem is formulated as a constrained shortest path problem. The results for a test case of the New England test power system are shown.

Keywords: Constrained shortest path · Quality of service · Routing · Software defined networks · Smart grid

1 Introduction

One of the coupled interactions in the smart grid is between communication network infrastructure and cyber-enabled control; in this context many works have considered the quality of service (QoS) of the communication infrastructure that is involved in the system control [1–3]. Previous works studied delay-sensitive control functions that require QoS guarantees or best effort and consequently formulated the routing problem in smart grid systems as a QoS routing problem. In [2] an enhanced genetic algorithm with ticket-based flooding discovery is proposed for a QoS routing in the smart grid. QoS routing problem is also considered in [1] in the context of demand-response; where the authors develop a QoS metric based on the impact of some constraints on the pricing-based control, and propose a greedy algorithm to solve for the shortest path under the defined QoS metric. In addition to the QoS studies, recent research work have tried to address denial of service (DoS) attacks on communication networks using different approaches including potential games, flocking based routing, and genetic algorithms in order to avoid the links that are under attack [4].

© ICST Institute for Computer Sciences, Social Informatics and Telecommunications Engineering 2016
A. Leon-Garcia et al. (Eds.): Smart City 2015, LNICST 166, pp. 384–394, 2016.
DOI: 10.1007/978-3-319-33681-7_32

Dijkstra algorithm can be used for finding the shortest paths between nodes in a graph; it is widely used in network routing protocols, most notably in Intermediate System to Intermediate System (IS-IS) [5] and Open Shortest Path First (OSPF) [6]. In Dijkstra algorithm, each network link has a cost value to present its status, and this cost is used to calculate the shortest path. In practical implementations of the Dijkstra algorithm, link costs are assigned in a simple approach due to the hardship of obtaining useful link status updates automatically and dynamically for the whole network. For example, a link cost in OSPF is defined as the reference bandwidth divided by interface bandwidth which leads to a static cost value [6]; however, in other cases, link cost is defined simply as 1 reducing the shortest path weight to a hop count.

The software defined network (SDN) framework provides an approach to solve for the shortest path based on dynamic link statuses through SDN's high network monitoring capability. Many useful link information (for example, link type, ownership, bandwidth, delay and historical data) can be collected by the SDN controller and used in the routing algorithm enabling more reliable, safe and efficient paths.

Enabled by the SDN framework, the implementation of the double constrained QoS routing in the SDN framework takes advantage of the dynamic communication network state. A dynamic delay cost matrix is obtained using regularly-updated link delay statistics. The constrained shortest path (CSP) algorithm is evaluated by the SDN controller and corresponding routing entries are respectively pushed to related forwarding switches.

The main contributions of this work include the following:

1. We formulate a multi-constraint routing problem for network-status aware routing.
2. We model and simulate the smart grid communication network using software defined networks.

The remainder of this paper is organized as follows: the problem setting is presented in Sect. 2, double constrained shortest path problem is discussed and the derivation of QoS constraints and related cost metrics are presented in Sect. 3, a background on software defined networks is provided in Sect. 4, and implementation details are provided in Sect. 5. Section 6 investigates the performance of the proposed framework and some test cases are considered. Conclusions and final remarks are discussed in Sect. 7.

2   System Model

Let N denote the number of nodes in the power system; for this discussion let N refer to number of buses in the power grid. Then, without loss of generality, we can assume a communication network connecting the N buses in a topology that parallels that of the electrical grid. This assumption is justified based on a mix of fiber optic and Ethernet physical-media communication networks.

Consider a graph representation of the corresponding communication network. The weighted undirected graph model $G(V, E, w)$ describes an N-node and M-link network, where the node set $V = \{v_1, \ldots, v_N\}$ and the edge set $E = \{e_{ij}, i, j = 1, 2, \ldots, M\}$ denote the buses and communication links, respectively. The weight w on the edge between two nodes is defined as the cost of the corresponding communication link. Then, the adjacency matrix A can be defined as

$$A_{i,j} = \begin{cases} w_{ij} \ i \neq j, \text{ for } (i, j) \in E \\ 0 \quad \text{otherwise.} \end{cases} \tag{1}$$

Consider next the routing problem of communication data between a source node s and destination node t in the graph G. The shortest path route between the pair can be found using various algorithms. Due to its simplicity and optimality, Dijkstra-based routing algorithm has long been the most used algorithm to arrive at the shortest path.

Within the smart grid, cyber-enabled control systems require information delivery between relevant nodes with certain delay requirements; as an example, the IEC 61850 GOOSE messaging specifies the message delay constrains for performance class P2/3 to be within 3 ms [7]. Accordingly, if we define the delay cost matrix A_d, then the problem of finding paths that satisfy the delay constraints can be formulated as a CSP problem. When there are more than one constraint, the CSP problem is often called a multi-constraint shortest path (MCSP) problem. Further, CSP and MCSP problems are proved to be NP-hard; yet, many algorithms have been developed to find a feasible or a set of feasible solutions [8].

It is essential to distinguish between the nature of the constraints and their interdependencies, as this will dictate if the constraints can be combined (in an additive way) into a single constraint. To illustrate this idea, consider packet-drop and link congestion, where an interdependence between the two constrains can be observed; a similar relation could be observed between congestion and communication delay. This approach can be abstracted by considering only one constraint or by constructing an additive combination of the two constraints as one with proper scaling.

In the context of smart grid systems, networked sensory and control impose many constraints on data communications; nevertheless, we are interested with how SDN can facilitate an efficient dynamic delay aware protocol with other constraints. Additionally, the SDN framework allows us to obtain a dynamic delay cost matrix sampled from the network at pre-defined intervals. If T_{sd} is defined as the sampling time, then the dynamic delay cost matrix is defined as $A_d^i = A_d(T_{sd}.i)$.

3   Constrained Shortest Path Problem

Given a network $G(V, E)$, assume every link $L_{u,v} \in E$ has two weights $c_{uv} > 0$ and $d_{uv} > 0$ (denoting, cost and delay). For source and destination nodes (s, t)

and maximum delay $T_{max} > 0$, let $\mathbf{P}_{st}$ denote the set of paths from s to t. Further, for any path p define

$$c(p) = \sum_{(u,v)\in p} c_{uv}$$
$$d(p) = \sum_{(u,v)\in p} d_{uv}. \tag{2}$$

CSP problem seeks to arrive at the shortest path between s and t nodes with a certain link cost c. However, when the path is constrained by more than one constraint, the problem is termed an MCP problem. Given that there are multiple paths between s and t, a modified MCP problem, often called the multi-constrained optimal path (MCOP) problem, is defined where the goal is to retrieve the shortest path among a set of feasible paths. Furthermore, restricted shortest path (RSP) problem is a special case of MCOP problems where the goal is to find the path with the least cost among the set of feasible paths that satisfy one constraints; for example, a constraint on T bounds the maximum path delay [9].

A feasible path $s \rightarrow t$ is defined as path p_{st} that satisfies $d(p_{st}) \leq T_{max}$. let $P_{st}(T_{max})$ be the set of all feasible paths from s to t. Then, the CSP problem can be formulated as an integer linear program (ILP) with a set of zero-one decision variables x_{uv}. For each link $(u, v) \in E$; define $x_{uv} = 1$ if the link is in path p, and $x_{uv} = 0$ otherwise. The problem of finding the minimum-cost feasible path can be formulated as an integer linear program as [8–10]

$$\text{minimize} \quad \sum_{(u,v)\in E} c_{uv} x_{uv}$$
$$\text{subject to} \sum_{v\in V} x_{uv} = \sum_{v\in V} x_{vu}, \forall u \in V \setminus \{s,t\}$$
$$\sum_{v\in V} x_{sv} = 1 \tag{3}$$
$$\sum_{u\in V} x_{ut} = 1$$
$$x_{uv} \in \{0,1\}, \forall (u,v) \in E.$$

If the integrity condition $x_{uv} \in \{0,1\}$ is relaxed into $x_{uv} \geq 0$ then the dual of the relaxed problem (a Lagrangian dual problem) is constructed [8,10]. The dual will include $s \rightarrow t$ paths and a multiplier $\lambda \geq 0$. For a link (u,v), let the aggregated cost c_λ be defined as $c_{uv} + \lambda d_{uv}$. Additionally, for a given λ, aggregated cost of the p is annotated $c_\lambda(p)$. Then, $L(\lambda)$ is defined as

$$L(\lambda) = \min\{c_\lambda(p)|p \in \mathbf{P}_{st}\}. \tag{4}$$

Let p_λ denote the path from s to t with the minimum aggregated cost with respect to a given λ. Then, $L(\lambda) = c_\lambda(p_\lambda) - \lambda T_{max}$, and the dual of the relaxed problem can be described as

$$L^* = \max\{L(\lambda)|\lambda \geq 0\}. \tag{5}$$

Algorithm 1. LARAC Algorithm

PROCEDURE LARAC(s, t, d, T)
$p_c :=$ Dijkstra(s, t, c)
if $d(p_c) \leq T$ **then**
   return p_c
$p_d :=$ Dijkstra(s, t, d)
if $d(p_d) > T$ **then**
   return "there is no solution"
loop
   $\lambda := \frac{c(p_c) - c(p_d)}{d(p_d) - d(p_c)}$
   $r :=$ Dijkstra(s, t, c_λ)
   if $c_\lambda(r) = c_\lambda(p_c)$ **then**
      return p_d
   else if $d(r) \leq T$ **then**
      $p_d := r$
   else
      $p_c := r$
END PROCEDURE

As previously pointed out, this is an NP-hard problem, where usually algorithmic approaches have successfully arrived at feasible solutions. The Lagrangian Relaxation Based Aggregated Cost (LARAC) algorithm developed in [10] solves the integer relaxation of the CSP problem. The LARAC algorithm is proven in [8] to be equivalent to Minimum Cost Restricted Time Combinatorial Optimization (MCRT) problems; further, the authors establish the generality of the LARAC algorithm for solving combinatorial problems involving two metrics. As shown in Algorithm 1, the LARAC algorithm presents an efficient procedure to arrive at an optimal λ and to terminate the search.

4   Software Defined Networks

Software defined networking offers the potential to change the traditional way networks operate. Current communication networks are typically built from a large number of network devices, with many complex protocols implemented on them. Operators in traditional communication networks are responsible for configuring policies to respond to a wide range of network events and applications. Consequently, network management and performance tuning is quite challenging and error-prone [11].

SDN provides a new toolkit and perspective for approaching many problems in smart grid communication network. Recent works have started to explore the potential of SDN in smart grids. In [12], Sydney et al. present a prototype that integrates a 4-bus power grid testbed with an OpenFlow network. Further, Goodney et al. propose in [13] an efficient multicast SDN system that connects high-rate PMUs and data subscribers with different data rate requirements. Moreover, an integrated SDN with IEC-61850-based substation automation systems is proposed in [14,15] to facilitate and improve the networking of intelligent electric devices (IEDs) in a substation. In addition, Kim *et al.* propose in [16] using OpenFlow switches to form virtual local area networks (VLANs) for multiple grid applications with different QoS requirements. Zhang *et al.* also discuss in [17] three use cases of SDN applications in smart grids; specifically, content-based data exchange, virtual networks for distributed energy resource (DER) aggregation, and smart building management. Furthermore, Molina *et al.* discuss in [14] an OpenFlow's fast failover mechanism upon the detection of node failures in the application of SDN to IEC-61850-based substations. Finally, Dong *et al.* explain in [18] some of the challenges in applying SDN to improve smart grid resilience.

4.1 SDN Architecture

SDN is an approach to networking that allows network administrators to manage network services through abstraction of lower-level functionality. This is done by decoupling the system that makes decisions about where traffic is sent (the control plane) from the underlying systems that forward traffic to the selected destination (the data plane). An SDN network comprises of two main components:

- SDN Controller: the controller is a logically centralized function that determines the forwarding path for each flow in the network. A network is typically controlled by one or a few controllers.
- SDN Switch: SDN switches constitute the network data plane. The logic for forwarding the packets is determined by the controller and is implemented in the forwarding table at the switches.

The SDN architecture is designed to provide dynamic, manageable, cost-effective and adaptable networks. Within the SDN framework, network applications can obtain detailed traffic statistics from network devices and thus construct an up-to-date global network view. One common standard for the implementation of software defined networks is OpenFlow [19]. The OpenFlow standard defines a communication protocol between network switches forming the data plane and one or multiple controllers forming the control plane.

4.2 Implementation

Our SDN system setup is built using free open source tools. We use Floodlight v1.0 [20] as the SDN controller and Mininet 2.2.0 [21] as the SDN switches. Floodlight is an Apache-licensed, Java-based OpenFlow SDN Controller. Mininet can create a realistic virtual networks. The SDN controller can communicate with the switches via the OpenFlow protocol through the abstraction layer present at the forwarding hardware.

The architecture of the test SDN network is illustrated in Fig. 1 and is comprised of Floodlight controller and Mininet switches, and an OpenFlow controller typically manages a number of switches. Every switch maintains one or more

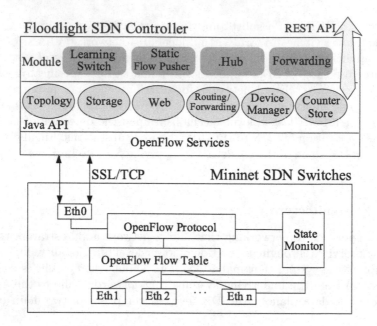

Fig. 1. Network architecture

flow tables that determine how packets belonging to a flow will be processed and forwarded. Communication between a controller and a switch happens via the OpenFlow protocol, which defines a set of messages that can be exchanged between these entities over a secure channel. The state monitor module can be used to collect switch state and transmit it to the controller.

5   Smart Grid

We consider the New England 10-generator 39-bus test power system; we develop a communication network that parallels that of the power grid. The New England power system and its candidate communication topology are shown in Fig. 2. The communication topology is based on the assumption of installing a network forwarding switch at every bus.

5.1   Network Topology

We consider a network where a centralized SDN controller computes the forwarding table for a set of SDN forwarding switches. Each bus can be considered as an SDN switch. In addition to forwarding packets, the SDN switches do some simple traffic measurement which they forward to the controller. The SDN controller uses this information along with routing rules defined by the protocol to dynamically change the forwarding tables at the switches in order to adapt to changing network link conditions.

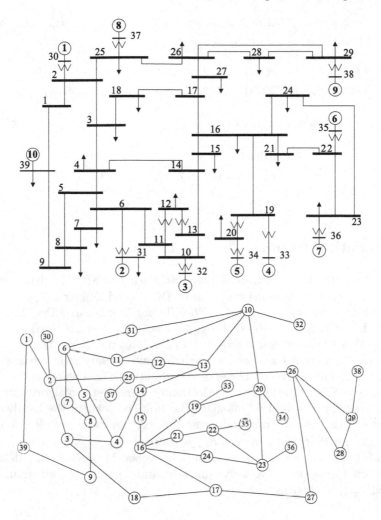

Fig. 2. New England test power system and its proposed communication network

5.2   Environment

The test environment is built using Floodlight v1.0 as the SDN controller [20], and Mininet 2.2.0 is used to implement the SDN switches network topology [21]. We utilize Iperf and jperf as test tools for collecting network performance statistics. Iperf [22] is a commonly-used network testing tool that can create Transmission Control Protocol (TCP) and User Datagram Protocol (UDP) data streams and measure the throughput of a network that is carrying them. Iperf has a graphical user interface (GUI) frontend called jperf [23]. The simulation environment runs on a Windows 7 64-bit machine with a 2.53-GHz Intel Core i5 CPU and 8-GB RAM.

Table 1. Example of different paths between DCSP and Dijkstra algorithms

Algorithm	$11 \rightarrow 31$	$1 \rightarrow 38$	$22 \rightarrow 24$
DCSP	{11, 6, 31}	{1, 2, 25, 26, 29, 38}	{22, 21, 16, 24}
Dijkstra	{11, 10, 31}	{1, 2, 25, 26, 29, 38}	{22, 23, 24}

Table 2. Processing time of random-chosen pairs (ms)

Algorithm	$11 \rightarrow 31$	$1 \rightarrow 38$	$22 \rightarrow 24$
DCSP	20.149	20.932	20.233
Dijkstra	20.145	20.915	20.227

6 Simulation Results

We consider a Double Constrained Shortest Path (DCSP) algorithm, and we compare the network performance between DCSP and Dijkstra algorithms in a smart grid communication network with different link bandwidths. The DCSP algorithm tries to achieve the best throughput within the maximum delay restrictions. The Dijkstra algorithm in Floodlight calculates the shortest paths between source and destination based on one metric, and usually it is the hop count (number of links in the path). The end-to-end network bandwidth and delay are measured to compare the network performance using the two algorithms.

Link bandwidth is used to calculate the link cost, where the bandwidth of each link bw_{ij} is assigned randomly within a certain range say $[2 - 4.5]$ Gbps in this case. Further, the link cost c_{bw}^{ij} is defined as $c_{bw}^{ij} = 4.5 - bw_{ij}$; higher bandwidth links have lower link cost, and vice versa. Meanwhile, link delay cost d_{ij} is collected from the network dynamically, and a parametric maximum delay is defined $T_{max} = 1000$ ms.

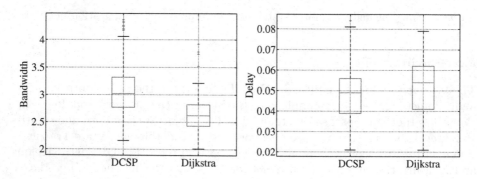

Fig. 3. Bandwidth and delay performance comparison of DCSP and Dijkstra algorithms

Random pairs of source and destination nodes (s, t) are selected (from a combination of 38×38), where for each pair both DCSP and Dijkstra algorithms are run. Statistics show that there are 228 different paths (119 undirected paths) between DCSP and Dijkstra among the total 1444 paths. Table 1 shows a random subset of 3 different (s, t) pairs with the calculated paths using DCSP and Dijkstra algorithms. In addition, Table 2 shows processing time for calculating the routes.

Finally, the set of affected paths was run for duration of 30 s during which bandwidth and delay was calculated using iperf and ping every 10 s. Numerical results are shown in Fig. 3 where DCSP algorithm has better performance both in network bandwidth and delay compared to that of Dijkstra algorithm.

7   Conclusions

In this work, we investigate the QoS routing problem with added constraints for smart grids using software defined networks. We consider the delay of the communication network of the smart grid along with other network parameters such as links throughput. The routing problem is formulated as a constrained shortest path problem. Numerical results for a test case of the New England test power system are shown.

References

1. Li, H., Zhang, W.: QoS routing in smart grid. In: IEEE Global Telecommunications Conference (GLOBECOM), pp. 1–6 (2010)
2. Zaballos, A., Vernet, D., Selga, J.M.: A genetic QoS-aware routing protocol for the smart electricity networks. Int. J. Distrib. Sens. Netw. **2013**, 1–12 (2013)
3. Pavlidou, F.-N., Koltsidas, G.: Game theory for routing modeling in communication networks a survey. J. Commun. Netw. **10**(3), 268–286 (2008)
4. Zhu, Q., Wei, D., Basar, T.: Secure routing in smart grids. In: Workshop on Foundations of Dependable and Secure Cyber-Physical Systems (FDSCPS), pp. 55–59 (2011)
5. Network Working Group, RFC 1195 use of OSI IS-IS for routing in tcp/ip and dual environments. Available at. https://www.ietf.org/rfc/rfc1195.txt (1990). Accessed 9 June 2015
6. Network Working Group, RFC 2328 OSPF version 2. Available at. https://www.ietf.org/rfc/rfc2328.txt (1998). Accessed 9 June 2015
7. Hohlbaum, F., Braendle, M., Alvarez, F.: Cyber security practical considerations for implementing iec 62351. ABB Technical Report (2010)
8. Xiao, Y., Thulasiraman, K., Xue, G., Jüttner, A.: The constrained shortest path problem: algorithmic approaches and an algebraic study with generalization. AKCE Int. J. Graphs Comb. **2**(2), 63–86 (2005)
9. Kuipers, F., Van Mieghcm, P., Korkmaz, T., Krunz, M.: An overview of constraint-based path selection algorithms for QoS routing. IEEE Commun. Mag. **40**(12), 50–55 (2002)

10. Jüttner, A., Szviatovski, B., Mécs, I., Rajkó, Z.: Lagrange relaxation based method for the QoS routing problem. In: Twentieth Annual Joint Conference of the IEEE Computer and Communications Societies (INFOCOM), vol. 2, pp. 859–868 (2001)
11. Nunes, B., Mendonca, M., Nguyen, X.-N., Obraczka, K., Turletti, T.: A survey of software-defined networking: past, present, and future of programmable networks. IEEE Commun. Surv. Tutorials **16**(3), 1617–1634 (2014)
12. Sydney, A., Ochs, D.S., Scoglio, C., Gruenbacher, D., Miller, R.: Using geni for experimental evaluation of software defined networking in smart grids. Comput. Netw. **63**, 5–16 (2014)
13. Goodney, A., Kumar, S., Ravi, A., Cho, Y.H.: Efficient PMU networking with software defined networks. In: IEEE International Conference on Smart Grid Communications (SmartGridComm), pp. 378–383 (2013)
14. Molina, E., Jacob, E., Matias, J., Moreira, N., Astarloa, A.: Using software defined networking to manage and control IEC 61850-based systems. Comput. Electr. Eng. **43**, 142–154 (2015)
15. Cahn, A., Hoyos, J., Hulse, M., Keller, E.: Software-defined energy communication networks: from substation automation to future smart grids. In: IEEE International Conference on Smart Grid Communications (SmartGridComm), pp. 558–563 (2013)
16. Kim, Y.-J., He, K., Thottan, M., Deshpande, J.G.: Virtualized and self-configurable utility communications enabled by software-defined networks. In: IEEE International Conference on Smart Grid Communications (SmartGridComm), pp. 416–421 (2014)
17. Zhang, J., Seet, B.-C., Lie, T.-T., Foh, C.H.: Opportunities for software-defined networking in smart grid. In: International Conference on Information, Communications and Signal Processing (ICICS), pp. 1–5 (2013)
18. Dong, X., Lin, H., Tan, R., Iyer, R.K., Kalbarczyk, Z.: Software-defined networking for smart grid resilience: opportunities and challenges. In: ACM Workshop on Cyber-Physical System Security, pp. 61–68 (2015)
19. Open networking foundation, software-defined networking: the new norm for networks. ONF White Paper (2012)
20. Project Floodlight. Available at. http://www.projectfloodlight.org/floodlight/ (2015). Accessed 9 June 2015
21. Mininet. Available at. http://mininet.org/ (2015). Accessed 9 June 2015
22. iperf.fr, Iperf. Available at. https://iperf.fr/ (2015). Accessed 9 June 2015
23. xjperf. Available at. https://code.google.com/p/xjperf/ (2015). Accessed 9 June 2015

Self-healing Restoration of Smart Microgrids in Islanded Mode of Operation

M. ZakiEl-Sharafy and H.E. Farag[✉]

Electrical Engineering and Computer Science, Lassonde School of Engineering,
York University, Toronto, ON, Canada
Eng.mzaki@hotmail.com, hefarag@cse.yorku.ca

Abstract. This paper proposes a new algorithm for optimum self-healing restoration of a smartmicrogrid operating in islanded mode of operation. The objective of the proposed algorithm is to optimize the topological structure of the islanded microgrid system (IMG) via: (1) maximizing the served load after the fault isolation; and (2) minimizing the switching operation costs. The proposed algorithm takes into consideration the system operational constraints in all operating conditions. The new algorithm accounts for droop controlled IMG special operational characteristics. The problem is formulated as a multi-objective optimization problem and solved using Ant Colony Optimization Algorithm. The proposed algorithm has been implemented in MATLAB environment and several case studies have been carried to test its effectiveness.

Keywords: Ant colony optimization algorithm · Islanded microgrid · Droop control · Power system restoration

1 Introduction

One of the most problems in the self-healing of the distribution system is the service restoration for a faulted area. When a fault takes place in distribution systems it affects the system reliability and the customer's satisfaction. As such to ensure a maximum reduction in the system reliability, the faulted area must be detected and isolated [1]. After the fault isolation, the Distribution Network Operator (DNO) reconfigures the distribution network to restore the outage (i.e. system restoration process) [2]. The main objective of the system restoration is to restore the out of service loads by transferring the power to them through alternative paths with minimum losses or to transfer these loads to other feeders. Due to delays in the outage processing and the required time for service crews, an outage time from minutes to several hours might be yielded [2]. This slow response in service restoration of conventional distribution networks remarkably affects the system reliability.

Nowadays, driven by technical, environmental and economical benefits, distribution networks are currently undergoing a profound paradigm shift towards active networks. Such networks are characterized by multidirectional power and information flow due to the integration of high penetration levels of distributed generation (DG) accompanied with advanced metering, communication and control technologies. The integration of DG units and other emerging components can have an impact on the practices used in distribution systems. Therefore, various operational strategies are expected to face numerous challenges. With the high degree of complexities that is accompanied with the transformation of distribution networks, DNO might no longer able to detect and isolate faults and/or restore the outage loads using the human operator's experimental rules. This in turn necessitates the need for implementing automated self-healing mechanisms in active distribution networks. There are many artificial intelligence methods that have been proposed in the literature to restore radial distribution systems [3–10].

The widespread implementation of DG units in distribution systems makes them capable of supplying all or most of their local power demands; which initiated the concept of microgrids. Microgrids are localized grids that are typically implemented in local areas (e.g. cities, towns, or villages) and capable of disconnecting from the traditional power grid to operate in island (i.e. able to operate in grid-connected and off-grid modes) [11, 12]. Because they are able to continue operating while the main grid is down, microgrids help mitigate grid disturbances to strengthen the grid resilience and customers' reliability [13, 14]. Further, under the smart grid paradigm, microgrids would be able to facilitate seamless integration for high penetration and wide variety of DGs, energy storage technologies and demand response [15, 16]. Interestingly, the concept of microgrids in energy sector is also interrelated to the recent vision of smart cities. Where, the development and implementation of "smart" microgrids is a key component in enhancing the livability, workability and sustainability, which are identified as the pillars of smart cities. For these reasons, microgrids can be identified as the building blocks of both smart power grids and cities.

Given the special control features and operational characteristics of islanded microgrids (IMG), the state-of-the-art self-healing restoration of distribution networks should be adopted to take IMG deployment into consideration. Up to the authors' knowledge, there is no previous work that addressed the problem of self-healing restoration in IMG. In this work, a new algorithm for self-healing restoration of IMG is proposed. Appropriate power flow models for DGs have been incorporated in the optimization problem to provide proper representation for microgrid components during islanded mode of operation. Ant Colony optimization has been utilized to solve the problem and several case studies have been conducted in order to validate the proposed IMG restoration algorithm.

2   Operation Mechanism of Islanded Microgrids

The majority of DG units forming microgrids are interfaced via dc-ac power electronic inverter systems. In islanded mode, droop control that enables active and reactive power sharing through the introduction of droop characteristics to the output voltage frequency and magnitude of dispatchable DG units is usually applied. In this section, a review for droop-based control scheme in IMG is presented.

2.1   Transmission Line Power Transfer Theory

The active and reactive power transfer in transmission lines is based on the operation characteristics of synchronous generators, where it depends on the voltage and the phase angel at both sending and receiving bus sides. The active power and reactive power flowing into the transmission line at the sending end can be given as follows:

$$S_i = P_i + jQ_i = u_i I^* = u_i \left[\frac{u_i - u_j e^{-j\gamma}}{jX} \right]^* \tag{1}$$

$$P_i = \frac{u_i u_j}{X} \sin\gamma^* \tag{2}$$

$$Q_i = \frac{u_i(u_i - u_j \cos\gamma)}{X} \tag{3}$$

where; P_i is the active power at line i, Q_i is the reactive power at line i, S_i is the total complex power at line i, u_i is the voltage at sending side, u_j is the voltage at receiving side, I is the current flow in the line, γ is the power angle, and X is the line inductance. In transmission lines, the power angle is very small, therefore it can be assumed that $\sin\gamma = \gamma$ and $\cos\gamma = 1$. Accordingly, one can observe that the active power is strongly dependent on the power angle, while the reactive power is strongly dependent on the voltage of the sending and receiving ends. Therefore the frequency droop can regulate the active power and the voltage droop can regulate the reactive power. From the above discussion, the inverters in IMG are controlled to imitate the behaviors of synchronous machines by applying the following droop equations:

$$F - F_0 = -K_p(P - P_0) \tag{4}$$

$$u - u_0 = -K_q(Q - Q_0) \tag{5}$$

where, F is the system Frequency, u is the voltage magnitude, F_0 is the nominal system frequency, u_0 is the nominal voltage magnitude, P is the inverter output of active power, Q is the inverter output of reactive power, P_0 is the momentary set point for the active power of the inverter, Q_0 is the momentary set point for the reactive power of the inverter, K_p is the frequency droop coefficient, and K_q is the voltage droop coefficient.

2.2   Voltage and Frequency Control

Figure 1(a, b) shows the power sharing of two inverters based on droop control. Let's assume that the frequency droop coefficients of the two inverters are k_{P1} and k_{P2}, and the output active power of the two inverters are P_{10} and P_{20} at the nominal frequency of the grid f_0, respectively. When the load increases, the two inverters change their output power and the system frequency is changed from its nominal frequency to f_1. Such change in active power can be formulated mathematically as follows:

$$\Delta P_1 = P_{11} - P_{10} = -\frac{1}{K_{p1}}(f_1 - f_0) \tag{6}$$

$$\Delta P_2 = P_{21} - P_{20} = -\frac{1}{K_{p2}}(f_1 - f_0) \tag{7}$$

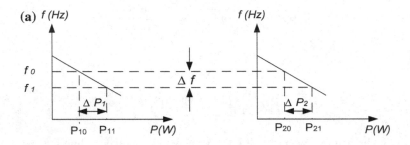

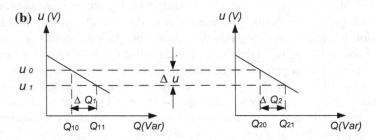

Fig. 1. (a): Power sharing in droop control: $(P{-}f)$ characteristics (b): Power sharing in droop control: $(Q{-}U)$ characteristics

Similar to (6) and (7), the two inverters share the reactive power demand. As shown in Fig. 1, the active and reactive power sharing is mainly governed by the static droop coefficients of active and reactive power, where

$$\frac{\Delta P_1}{\Delta P_2} = \frac{k_{P2}}{k_{P1}} \tag{8}$$

$$\frac{\Delta Q_1}{\Delta Q_2} = \frac{k_{q2}}{k_{q1}} \tag{9}$$

Equations (8) and (9) are used as virtual communication mediums among the inverters in order to represent the active and reactive power sharing between the DGs. For n droop-controlled DG units, (10) and (11) below are met

$$\Delta P_1.k_{P1} = \Delta P_2.k_{P2} = \cdots = \Delta P_n.k_{Pn} \tag{10}$$

$$\Delta Q_1.k_{q1} = \Delta Q_2.k_{q2} = \cdots = \Delta Q_n.k_{qn} \tag{11}$$

Here it is noteworthy that the aforementioned analysis is under the strong assumption that the DG units are highly inductive due to the coupling inductor used in the DG interface. If the system is resistive, however, the equation will be given by (P–f) and (Q–U) instead.

3   Problem Formulation of Service Restoration in IMG

The problem of self-healing restoration in IMG is formulated in this section as an optimization problem as follows:

3.1   Objective Functions

The main objective functions in the restoration are maximizing the restored load (12) and minimizing the number of switching operations (13).

$$max \sum\nolimits_{x \in D} L_X \cdot j_X \tag{12}$$

$$min \sum\nolimits_{X \in D} SW_X \tag{13}$$

where;

L_X: The load at bus no. X, j_X: The binary decision whether the load at bus X is restored ($j_X = 1$: resorted, $j_X = 0$: not restored), D: The set of all de-energized loads, SW_X: Representation of the switching operation in bus X ($X_X = 1$: the switch state is changed, $X_X = 0$: no change occurs in the switch state).

3.2   Constraints of the IMG Service Restoration Problem

In the self-healing restoration process for the IMG system, the constraints can be represented as follow:

(1) **The Voltage level:** for every bus load at the distribution system the voltage level must be maintained to be within range of ± 5 % from the p.u. value.

$$u_{min} \leq u_X \leq u_{max} \tag{14}$$

where; u_{min} And u_{max}: Minimum and maximum voltage levels at bus X respectively (95–105 %), u_X: The voltage level at bus X

(2) **Power Balance Equations:** The Active and reactive power balance between supply and demand.

$$P_i\left(|u_i|, |u_j|, \partial_i, \partial_j, w\right) - PG_i(w) + PL_i(|u_i|, w) \cong 0 \tag{15}$$

where; PG_i: The total active power from supply, PL_i: The total active power demanded at the load, P_i: The total active power at bus i, ∂_i: Phase angle at bus i, ∂_j: Phase angle at bus j.

$$Q_i\left(|u_i|, |u_j|, \partial_i, \partial_j, w\right) - QG_i(|u_i|) + QL_i(|u_i|, w) \cong 0 \tag{16}$$

where; QG_i: The total Reactive power from supply, QL_i: The total Reactive power demanded at the load, Q_i: The total Reactive power at bus i

(3) **Droop-controlled DG units constrains:** The capacity of DG units and the limits of the droop parameters (Kp, Kq, w^*, u^*)

$$P_{Gi} \leq S_{Gi,max} \tag{17}$$

$$Q_{Gi} \leq \sqrt{\left(S_{Gi,max} - (P_{Gi})^2\right)} \tag{18}$$

$$0 \leq Kp_i \tag{19}$$

$$0 \leq Kq_i \tag{20}$$

$$59.5\,\text{HZ} \leq w^*_i \leq 60.5\,\text{HZ}(w_{max}) \tag{21}$$

where; P_{Gi}: Generated active power from DG i, Q_{Gi}: Generated Reactive power from DG i, $S_{Gi,max}$: MVA rating of DG i, Kp and Kq are the droop control setting for the DG i, w^*_i is the requested frequency for the DG to reach it's sharing level (same as the system frequency), finally the voltage level for the DG bus is the same as (14).

(4) **Feeder line current limits** should be also taken into consideration as follows:

$$I_{min} \leq I_j \leq I_{max} \tag{22}$$

where; I_{min} and I_{max} are the minimum and maximum current level of the line respectively, I_j is the current level of line j.

4 IMG Self-healing Restoration Based on ACO

The ant colony optimization is a stochastic population based heuristic algorithm which is equivalent to the behavior of the ant or bee in there colony in the real life [17]. ACO is widely used in solving the problem of self-healing restoration in active distribution networks. ACO can also be used to solve the problem of self-healing restoration in IMG, where the outage buses findits own feeder bus as follows [7]:

$$P_{ij} = \frac{(\tau_{ij})^{\alpha}(\eta_{ij})^{\beta}}{\sum_{s \in allowed\,k}(\tau_{is})^{\alpha}(\eta_{is})^{\beta}} \tag{23}$$

where; P_{ij}: The probability of the ant to move from point i to j, τ_{ij}: The quantity of remnant pheromone on the trail from i to j, η_{ij}: The desirability of the trail which is $1/dis\tan ce$, β: The parameters that control the relative importance of the trail pheromone versus the desirability of the trail. When all ants have completed a tour, the pheromone trails are globally updated using the global pheromone-updating rule (24). The aim of the pheromone update is to increase the pheromone values associated with good or promising solutions, and to decrease those that are associated with bad ones based on (25).

$$\tau_{ij} = (1 - \rho)\tau_{ij} + \Delta\tau_{ij}. \tag{24}$$

where, ρ is the evaporation of trail pheromone between i and j and $\Delta\tau_{ij}$ is the pheromone left on trail ij by current optimal solution given as follows:

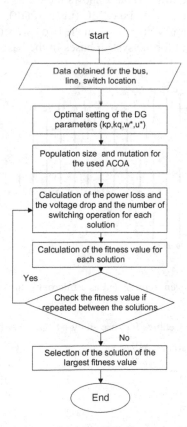

Fig. 2. Flowchart for the proposed self-healing restoration process in IMG

$$\Delta\tau_{ij} = Q/L_S \qquad\qquad (25)$$

where, Q is a constant and L_S is the tour length of the ant s to the whole trip. The optimum solution is obtained; after a number of iterations, comparing the probability of each path with each other, and by choosing the one with the highest probability. Where the total self-healing restoration process can be represented as shown in Fig. 2.

5   Simulation and Results

The 33-bus distribution test system shown in Fig. 3 has been used in this work to test the effectiveness of the proposed self-healing restoration algorithm in IMGs. As shown in the figure, four dispatchable DGs are installed. According to the droop settings of DG units, two base case studies have been carried out during the normal operation of IMG. In the first case study, a capacity-basedpower sharing of DG units has been implemnted. In this case, the staticdroop coeffecients of the DG units are calculated in proportion to the capacities of DG units. Table 1 shows the droop settings in the first case study. In the second case study, the droop settings of the DG units are optimally selected to minimize the total system losses of the IMG. Table 2 shows the droop settings for optimal power sharing during the normal operation of the IMG (i.e. no fault). Table 3 presents the total system losses and the minimum voltage level in the two case studies. Figure 4 shows the voltage magnitude in per unit for the system buses in the base case studies. The results

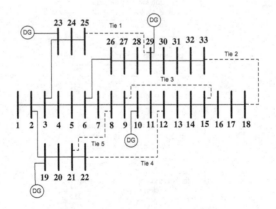

Fig. 3. The 33 IEEE-bus system represented as a microgrid in islanded mode of operation

Table 1. Droop settings for case study #1: capacity-based sharing

DG#	Bus location	Rating MVA	k_P	k_q	u^* (p.u.)	w^* (p.u.)
1	10	2	0.0027/2	0.05/2	1.01	1
2	29	2	0.0027/2	0.05/2	1.01	1
3	23	2	0.0027/2	0.05/2	1.01	1
4	19	2	0.0027/2	0.05/2	1.01	1

Table 2. Droop settings for case study #2: optimal power sharing

DG#	Bus location	Rating MVA	k_P	k_q	u^* (p.u.)	w^* (p.u.)
1	10	2	0.0014/2	0.025/2	0.9856	1.0044
2	29	2	0.0014/2	0.025/2	1.01	1.0001
3	23	2	0.0019/2	0.032/2	0.9895	1.0073
4	19	2	0.0016/2	0.029/2	0.9956	1.0067

Table 3. Steady state system losses and voltage in normal operation

Steady state	Case study 1	Case study 2
Total system losses	0.111MVA	0.106MVA
Min. voltage level	0.951 p.u.	0.951 p.u.

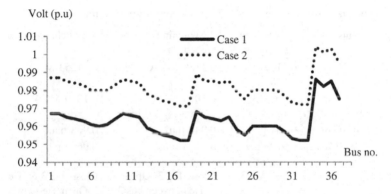

Fig. 4. Voltage profile of the islanded microgrid during normal operation

show that optimal power sharing of droop-controlled DG units reduces the system losses and enhances the voltage profile significantly.

The above case studies have been repeated in the self-healing restoration process. It is assumed that a fault occurs between bus 10 and bus 11, where the loads from bus 11 to the downstream is out of service and need to be restored. According to the topology of the studied system, it can be noticed that Tie 2, 3 and 4 are only the candidate paths in order to restore the faulted area, where only one switching operation of them can be used to satisfy the restoration problem. However, when the losses minimization is taken into account, there might be several required switching actions. To determine the optimal switching actions for maximizing the load restoration, minimization the system losses, minimizing the switching operation and satisfying the operation constraints, the proposed ACO needs to be executed.

After the occurrence of the faulted area, the restoration process is carried by the ACO to choose from different switching actions to restore the faulted area, which can help the microgrid operator to take appropriate decision. The challenge in the self-healing restoration is thus prevailing in taking an optimal decision that is a trade-off between the minimum losses and the number of switching operations, where as the number of switching operation increases the total cost of the restoration process is also increased. In this work a limit of 3 switching operations has been assumed in order to study the impacts of the number of switching operations on the solution of the optimization problem. Here it is noteworthy that in the 2nd case study, the restoration process is also achieved by using ACO while in this case the new droop setting for the DGs that can optimize the system operation is applied (i.e. For each candidate solution (i.e. configuration), a nonlinear optimization problem is solved to determine the droop settings of DG units).

Table 4 shows the results of the proposed self-healing restoration process in the two case studies with different switching operation. Figures 5 and 6 show the total system losses and the voltage profile in the two case studies with different switching operation. As shown in the results, the optimal power sharing among the droop-controlled DG

Table 4. Results of the proposed self-healing restoration process in IMG

Comparison points		1 Switching Operations	2 Switching Operations	3 Switching Operations
Total system losses	1st Case	0.1139 MVA	0.1139 MVA	0.11253 MVA
	2nd Case	0.109713 MVA	0.1089 MVA	0.1089 MVA
Min. voltage level	1st Case	0.951 p.u.	0.949 p.u.	0.948 p.u.
	2nd Case	0.9708 p.u.	0.9696 p.u.	0.9675 p.u.
Switching action	1st Case	Close Tie 3	Close Tie 3, Open Tie between bus 3 and 23	Close Tie 3 & Tie 1, Open Tie between bus 28 and 29
	2nd Case	Close Tie 3	Close Tie 3, Open Tie between bus 3 and 23	Close Tie 3 & Tie 1, Open Tie between bus 26 and 27

units in IMG will enhance the system losses. Further, as depicted in the results, the voltage profile for the buses has been significantly improved.

As shown in Fig. 5, the minimum voltage occurred in all switching scenarios in case study 2 is within the range of the voltage constrains. However, in some switching operation scenarios, in the 1st case study, the voltage magnitude violated its lower bound, which is a critical state for the total system. The DNO can use the obtained results to compromise between the total losses and the cost of the switching operation.

A key factor that needs to be taken into account in the self-healing restoration process is the time of execution. Where, it is critical to restore the faulted loads as quick as possible. In the proposed algorithm, the number of iterations that has been taken in this process to restore the loads was found to be 9 iterations for the ACO to take the

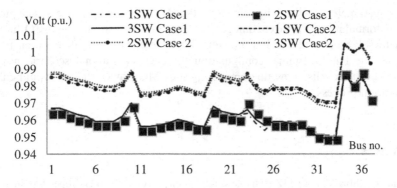

Fig. 5. Voltage profile for all restoration scenarios

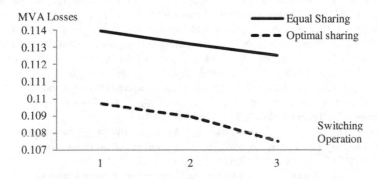

Fig. 6. Pareto optimal front for the total system losses

decision in all possible switching actions, and 3 to 12 iterations for the power flow for every nominated configuration for the system. The processor used to conduct the simulation was Intel® Core ™2 Duo CPU P8700 @ 2.53 GHz with system type of 32-bit operating system and the installed memory was 4.00 GB. Where at this specs the duration time taken from the ACO to propose the suitable configuration was 115.25 s. The obtained execution time of the proposed self-healing restoration process is acceptable to the microgrid operator in order to do the switching actions in the system.

6   Conclusion

In this paper a new algorithm has been proposed for the optimum self-healing restoration of a microgrid operating in islanded mode. The proposed algorithm aims to maximize the capacity of the restored load. In addition, the proposed algorithm aims to choose the optimum configuration that compromises the trade-off of between two objective functions; namely number of switching and the system losses. Two different operational control schemes (without and with optimal power sharing) have been implemented in the proposed algorithm to account for the impacts of the selection of the droop parameters on the enhancement of the IMG restoration process. The problem has been formulated as a mixed integer nonlinear optimization. The ACO has been utilized to solve the optimization problem. To handle the trade-off between the two objectives, the Pareto optimal configuration for each operational scenario has been determined. The results show that optimizing the IMG power sharing would enhance its restoration process.

References

1. Faria, L., Silva, A., Vale, Z., Marques, A.: Training control centers' operators in incident diagnosis and power restoration using intelligent tutoring systems. IEEE Trans. Learn. Technol. 2(2), 135–147 (2009)
2. Oualmakran, Y., Melendez, J., Herraiz, S.: Opportunities and challenges for smart power restoration and reconfiguration smart decisions with smart grids. In: 2011 11th International Conference on Electrical Power Quality and Utilisation (EPQU), pp. 1–6 (2011)
3. Prakash, M., Pradhan, S., Roy, S.: Soft computing techniques for fault detection in power distribution systems: a review. In: 2014 International Conference on Green Computing Communication and Electrical Engineering (ICGCCEE), pp. 1–6 (2014)
4. Sujil, A., Agrwal, S.K., Kumar, R.: Centralized multi-agent self-healing power system with super conducting fault current limiter. In: 2013 IEEE Conference on Information & Communication Technologies (ICT), pp. 622–627 (2013)
5. Zidan, A., El-Saadany, E.F., El Chaar, L.: A cooperative agent-based architecture for self-healing distributed power systems. In: IEEE Conference on Innovations in Information Technology (IIT), pp. 100–105 (2011)
6. Gonzalez, R.O., Gonzalez, G.G., Escobar, J., Barazarte, R.Y.: Applications of Petri nets in electric power systems. In: Central America and Panama Convention (CONCAPAN XXXIV). IEEE, pp. 1–6 (2014)
7. Abd El-Hamed, M.Z., El-Khattam, W., El-Sharkawy, R.: Self-healing restoration of a distribution system using hybrid fuzzy control/ant-colony optimization algorithm. In: 2013 3rd International Conference on Electric Power and Energy Conversion Systems (EPECS), pp. 1–6 (2013)
8. Karn, R., Kumar, Y., Agnihotrim, G.: Development of ACO algorithm for service restoration in distribution system. Int. J. Emerging Technol. 2(1), 71–77 (2011)
9. Mustafa, M., El-Khattam, W., Galal, Y.: A novel fuzzy cause-and-effect-networks based methodology for a distribution system's fault diagnosis. In: 2013 3rd International Conference on Electric Power and Energy Conversion Systems (EPECS), pp. 1–6 (2013)
10. Malakhov, A., Kopyriulin, P., Petrovski, S., Petrovski, A.: Adaptation of smard grid technologies. In: 2012 IEEE International Conference on Fuzzy Systems (FUZZ-IEEE), pp. 1–6 (2012)
11. Cheng, S., Junyong, L., Yang, J., Ni, Y., Xiang, Y., Zhu, X., Tian, H.: Optimal coordinated operation for microgrid with hybrid energy storage and diesel generator. In: 2014 International Conference on Power System Technology (POWERCON), pp. 3207–3212 (2014)
12. Jouybari-Moghaddam, H., Hosseinian, S.H., Vahidi, B., Rad, M.G.: Smart control mode selection for proper operation of synchronous distributed generators. In: 2012 2nd Iranian Conference on Smart Grids (ICSG), pp. 1–4 (2012)

13. Ashabani, S.M., Mohamed, Y.A.-R.I.: New family of microgrid control and management strategies in smart distribution grids—analysis, comparison and testing. IEEE Trans. Power Syst. **29**, 2257–2269 (2014)
14. Etemadi, A.H., Davison, E.J., Iravani, R.: A generalized decentralized robust control of islanded microgrids. IEEE Trans. Power Syst. **29**(6), 3102–3113 (2014)
15. Lee, D.-L., Wang, L.: Small signal stability analysis of an autonomous hybrid renewable energy power generation/energy stroge system Part I: time domain simulation. IEEE Trans. Energy Convers. **23**(1), 311–320 (2008)
16. Miao, Z., Domijan, A., Fan, L.: Investigation of microgrids with bothinverter interfaced and direct AC connected distributed energy resources. IEEE Trans. Power Delivery **26**(3), 1634–1642 (2011)
17. Hlaing, Z.C.S.S., Khine, M.A.: Solving traveling salesman problem by using improved ant colony optimization algorithm. Int. J. Inf. Educ. Technol. **1**(5), 81–87 (2011)

Energy Efficient Data Centres Within Smart Cities: IaaS and PaaS Optimizations

Corentin Dupont, Mehdi Sheikhalishahi$^{(\boxtimes)}$, Federico M. Facca,
and Silvio Cretti

Create-Net, Trento, Italy
{cdupont,msheikhalishahi,ffacca,scretti}@create-net.org

Abstract. Data centres are power-hungry facilities that host ICT services and consume huge amount of the global electricity production. Consequently, in the last years, research trends in the field focused on mechanisms able to reduce the overall consumption of a data centre so as to reduce its energy footprint. In this paper, we argue that the data centres for city needs should be located physically in the smart city, in order to address smart city needs, and serve citizens without any latency. Furthermore, those data centres should strive to make their energy footprint greener, i.e. consume more renewable energy. We present the concept of Service Flexibility Agreement (SFA), an extension of the traditional SLA able to qualify the flexibility of applications deployed in a smart city cloud environment. In particular, we detail preliminary models able to exploit this flexibility in order to increase the ratio of renewable energy consumed. The introduction of new solutions, such as containers and platform as a service (PaaS) in cloud data-centres also opens new challenges and opportunities. We describe how the combination of PaaS and IaaS cloud layers provide the needed flexibility to support the SFA.

Keywords: Platform as a Service · Energy management · Flexibility · Scalability

1 Introduction

Data centers are one of the largest and fastest growing consumers of electricity in the United States. In 2013, U.S. data centres consumed an estimated 91 billion kilowatt-hours of electricity – enough electricity to power all the households in New York City twice over – and are on-track to reach 140 billion kilowatt-hours by 2020[1]. However, a recent study [1] showed that, while still growing, the current energy consumption of data centres (DCs) is less than previously excepted. Electricity used in US DCs in 2010 was significantly lower than predicted by the EPAs 2007 report to Congress on DCs. There is a combination of factors explaining this slow down, among which the application of new energy policies in DCs. For example, consolidation techniques to reduce the power of servers in a

---

[1] http://www.nrdc.org/energy/data-center-efficiency-assessment.asp.

© ICST Institute for Computer Sciences, Social Informatics and Telecommunications Engineering 2016
A. Leon-Garcia et al. (Eds.): Smart City 2015, LNICST 166, pp. 408–415, 2016.
DOI: 10.1007/978-3-319-33681-7_34

DC are nowadays adopted in several cloud management solutions. As important energy consumers, it is also important that the energy management and policies of DCs prioritize the consumption of renewable energies over brown energies. However, the main problem with the utilization of renewable energies is that they are very variable in time. To adapt to such energies, we need to adapt and shift the workload of applications. This means reducing the workload when there is less renewable energies available, for example.

Beyond that, the technological landscape is changing. DCs can now host more than simple virtual machines. New "virtualization" techniques such as containers are appearing on the scene, and Platform-as-a-Service solutions are more and more used on top of Infrastructure-as-a-Service solutions. PaaS management frameworks model the architecture of applications and provide management functions to scale up and down multi-tier applications. Some frameworks allow to automatize this process: Cloudify[2], for example, provides a language for auto-scaling. This language defines Key Performance Indicators (KPIs) and thresholds that will trigger the scaling operations. For example, in the case of a 3-tier Web server application, it is possible to describe that if the latency in serving the pages goes over a certain threshold, a new front-end VM should be launched. As such, the "intelligence" of PaaS management frameworks can be easily employed to apply energy management policies taking into account application SLAs and their architecture. Following this reasoning, we believe that the combined management of PaaS and IaaS may bring new opportunities in energy policies management.

However, when it comes to the adaptation of applications workload to dynamic power budgets, we think that a piece is missing. Indeed, currently PaaS frameworks have no way to lower or postpone workload in a reasonable way when there is no renewable energy or energy is too expensive, for instance. PaaS models can be enhanced to better describe the flexibility of applications and allow to perform optimizations at smart city DC level, such as increasing the renewable energy usage.

Thus, in this paper we propose the concept of Service Flexibility Agreement (SFA). The SFA is an extended Service Level Agreement (SLA): it includes a description of the flexibility of an application. While the SLA usually defines only minimum levels of resources that an application should be guaranteed to have, in the context of flexible applications, this is not enough: for example some applications can accept to have a temporarily reduced performance or shifted activities. Similarly, some applications would benefit from a temporary increase of allocation of resources when renewable energies are available. The SFA defines a simple interface to describe this flexibility in terms of resource allocated over time, with possible deviations. Thanks to the SFA, an energy-aware PaaS framework is able to dynamically reconfigure applications or single layers (e.g. scale-up and down) to comply with a given energy budget (e.g. the amount of green energy available at a given moment in time). Finally, changes occurring at the level of the PaaS framework can be exploited by an underlying IaaS framework: the information sharing between the two improves the energy usage.

---

[2] http://www.gigaspaces.com/cloudify-cloud-orchestration/overview.

With the aim of addressing climate change, increasing the EUs energy security and strengthening its competitiveness, the EU has created the set of targets known as 20–20–20 for its climate and energy policies. Due to the trend of further urbanization, Smart Cities are one of the key enablers of the 2020 targets. It is expected that the urbanization concentrates the energy consumption in the city and Smart Cities are one way to decrease and optimize this consumption and therefore increase the energy efficiency. Therefore it will need new processes and innovation concepts at city level.

For some years there was a tendency to move DCs outside the cities, to locations where space is not an issue and the electricity infrastructure is not challenged by other large consumers. Furthermore, the selected locations had a cold climate (i.e. Finland, Iceland), in order to save on the cooling expenses. However, lately we see the trend of DCs moving back into the vicinity of cities because of issues like network latency and due to the increased density of racks and modularity of whole DC sites. DCs that are separate departments inside a company can be integrated into the smart city energy management. This allows a better control for the Smart City in terms of management, energy consumption, renewables, data security/privacy and governance.

This data is more and more processed in the Cloud. So DCs located in the city near the base station means more responsiveness and less losses. Similarly, the concept of "cloud edge" or mini-cloud located near a base station or a sensor network in a smart city where a sensor network is deployed can benefit from this approach.

2   Service Flexibility Agreement

In current PaaS architectures, the framework grants a certain flexibility to applications. For example, an application can ask the PaaS framework to spawn more or less VMs or Linux containers[3] according to its needs. However, the flexibility is entirely controlled by the application and/or the application owner. The intuition behind SFA is to delegate some of the flexibility control to the PaaS framework while still guaranteeing the end user satisfaction. With respect to a traditional SLA, the SFA adds a few new dimensions: the possibility for the required resources to vary in time, plus the possibility to qualify violations of the required performance.

As shown in Listing 1 and also represented graphically in Fig. 1, for each time frame of a day the SFA defines a recommended business performance (RecoBP, in red in the figure). The business performance is one of the KPIs of the application. For example, for a Web server it is the number of pages served per minutes, for a video transcoding service it will be how many videos can be transcoded per minutes.

We then define a concept called "Happy points", noted "H". This is an abstraction of the end-user satisfaction. An application having zero Happy points

---

[3] http://docs.cloudfoundry.org/concepts/architecture/warden.html.

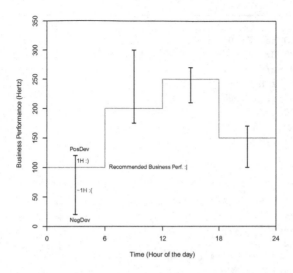

Fig. 1. Service Flexibility Agreement representation

means that the end user is reasonably satisfied. An application being allocated exactly the number of resources corresponding to the RecoBP collects 0 Happy points. This situation corresponds to the traditional SLA threshold. The positive and negative deviations (PosDev and NegDev) declared in the SFA are then the way that each application "reacts" to being given more or less resources than the RecoBP. Indeed, some applications such as video transcoding can benefit from receiving temporarily more resources because they can process more videos and thus make their end user happier. This kind of application reacts linearly to the amount of resources it is allocated. On the other hand, an application such as a web server typically have a "turning point" in their relation between performance and resources. Indeed, giving them less that a certain level of resources (such as the number of front-end VMs) will start to augment the latency in delivering web pages, thus making the end-user unhappy. On the contrary, giving them more than that level of resources will not have any perceptible impact on the end user, as the latency is already small. This is represented by the vertical deviation bars in Fig. 1: the length of the bar represents the amount of Happy points that the application will win/lose when given more/less performance than the recoBP, respectively. In this example, at 10 O'clock, if the PaaS framework allocates the resource corresponding to the recommended business performance of 200 Hz, the application will collect 0 Happy points. If the application gets 300 Hz, it will get 1H, and one more Happy point for each 100 Hz above that. Conversely, if it gets less than the recommended 200 Hz, it will loose Happy point at the rate of one happy point per 25 Hz.

```
SFA:
  - Time: 00:00 to 05:59
    RecoBP: 100 Hz
    PosDev: 20 Hz/H
    NegDev: 80 Hz/H
  - Time: 06:00 to 11:59
    RecoBP: 200 Hz
    PosDev: 100 Hz/H
    NegDev: 25 Hz/H

WorkingModes:
  - WMName: WM1
    actuator: 'cf scale myApp -i 3'
    defaultPower: '300 W'
    maxBusinessPerf: '100 Hz'
  - WMName: WM2
    actuator: 'cf scale myApp -i 5'
    defaultPower: '500 W'
    maxBusinessPerf: '150 Hz'
```

Listing 1: SFA example

We further define the various Working Modes (WM) of an application. A WM corresponds to a set of resources allocated by the PaaS to an application. We associate to each WM its typical power consumption and the maximum business performance it can offer. In practice, a WM corresponds to a number of VMs or Linux Containers, each running instances of the application. Using the SFA, it is now possible to compute the number of Happy points provided by each WM for each time slot.

3   Interaction Among IaaS and PaaS Layers

In novel PaaS frameworks, application scaling is performed by launching more containers. Each container is an instance, or worker, of the application. Containers run in a VM, controlled by an underlying IaaS framework. To save energy, those VMs are traditionally consolidated on a part of the servers of the DC, which permits to switch off unused servers and thus save energy. Using the SFA, it is now possible to predict the amount of resource that an application will need, together with the possible deviations. This will allow to optimize VMs by consolidating containers in them and at a second level optimize servers by consolidating the VMs. VMs and containers movements should be minimized to preserve the energy efficiency. However to achieve this we need to enhance the interaction between the IaaS and PaaS. There are essentially two types of information that need to be exchanged:

- VMs grouping
- VMs life-time

The PaaS layer has a certain degree of knowledge about the architecture of deployed applications. If an application is composed of several containers forming the different layers, it is beneficial to keep them together on the same VMs as much as possible, because they will probably have the same life cycle. Those containers will probably exchange a lot of information among them. Furthermore, they will be switched off together when the application is terminated. This justifies to keep them together on the same VM or group of VMs as much as possible.

Knowing the VM life-time (an estimated duration that the VM will be kept running before being switched off) is important for the IaaS layer when optimizing the energy consumption of a DC through VM consolidation. Indeed, migrating a VM to consolidate it is an investment, and if the VM is about to be terminated soon, this investment is lost. In PaaS environments, the VM life-time is determined by the life-time of the underlying containers. This life-time should be calculated by the PaaS framework and transmitted to the IaaS framework. Of course, the IaaS layer shouldn't be aware of the applications running in the DC, as it is not its role and would furthermore break the separation of concerns between the IaaS and the PaaS. The sharing of VMs grouping and VMs life-time does not break the separation of concerns between IaaS and PaaS, because they are expressed in terms of the IaaS VMs only.

4 Design and Optimization

The SFA is used in the communication between an application and the underlying PaaS framework (while the SLA, on the contrary, is used for the communication between the DC and its clients), as shown in Fig. 2.

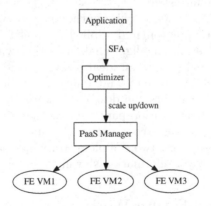

Fig. 2. SFA block diagram

In practice, we add a component in the Cloud Foundry stack called the "Optimizer". This component accepts commands from the application load balancer. Instead of just scale-up/scale-down commands as it is the case currently, we include a recommended scaling level, together with a positive deviation and a negative deviation, as described in Sect. 2. This will let the Optimizer to optimize the full PaaS layer according to multiple criteria: (1) the energy consumption in the DC, (2) the global happiness of the applications (as the sum of all happy points granted to applications) and finally (3) the usage of renewable energies. Using the SFA, the Optimizer is able to find the correct trade-offs that will allow it to comply which energy budgets while maximizing the overall end-user happiness in the DC.

5   Related Works

VM consolidation approaches to reduce energy consumption at IaaS layer have been explored in many recent papers [2–6].

In addition, there are energy efficient solutions based on scaling operations (scale up/down application) based on applications performance metrics. Although these proposals reduce the energy footprint of applications and cloud infrastructures, they do not model the applications performance trend to finely define a trade-off between applications Quality of Service and energy footprint.

Autonomic Computing has been exploited in the design of cloud computing architectures in order to devise autonomic loops aiming at providing coordinated actions among cloud layers for efficiency measures, turning each layer of the cloud stack more autonomous, adaptable and aware of the runtime environment [7,8].

In order to reach a global and efficient state due to conflicting objectives, autonomic loops need to be synchronized. In [7], authors proposed a generic model to synchronize and coordinate autonomic loops in cloud computing stack. The feasibility and scalability of their approach is evaluated via simulation-based experiments on the interaction of several self-adaptive applications with a common self-adaptive infrastructure.

In addition to elasticity, scalability is another major advantage introduced by the cloud paradigm. In [9], automated application scalability in cloud environments are presented. Authors highlight challenges that will likely be addressed in new research efforts and present an ideal scalable cloud system.

[10] proposes a co-design of IaaS and PaaS layers for energy optimization in the cloud. The paper outlines the design of interfaces to enable cross-layer cooperation in clouds. This position paper claims that significant energy gains could be obtained by creating a cooperation API between the IaaS layer and the PaaS layer. Authors discuss two complementary approaches for establishing such cooperation: cross-layer information sharing, and cross-layer coordination.

6   Conclusion and Future Work

The PaaS Cloud paradigm and the corresponding frameworks are currently developing at high-speed within smart cities. As shown in this paper, they provide new opportunities for energy optimization. We presented the SFA, a concept able to describe the flexibility of applications within smart cities. This format includes the trade-off between the amount of resources allocated to a PaaS scalable application, the resulting performance and the corresponding user experience, in a simple way. This allows the PaaS framework to perform multi-criteria optimizations such as lowering the global energy consumption of the data centre in a smart city, using more renewable energies and increasing the application user satisfaction. As future work, we will design the proposed API and components within the CloudFoundry framework.

Acknowledgments. This work has been carried out within the European Project DC4Cities (FP7-ICT-2013.6.2).

References

1. Koomey, J.: Growth in Data Center Electricity Use 2005 to 2010. Analytics Press, Oakland, 1 August 2010 (2011)
2. Cardosa, M., Korupolu, M.R., Singh, A.: Shares and utilities based power consolidation in virtualized server environments. In: Proceedings of the 11th IFIP/IEEE Integrated Network Management (IM 2009), Long Island, NY, USA, June 2009
3. Schröder, K., Nebel, W.: Behavioral model for cloud aware load and power management. In: Proceedings of HotTopiCS 2013, 2013 International Workshop on Hot Topics in Cloud Services, pp. 19–26, ACM, May 2013
4. Hermenier, F., Lorca, X., Menaud, J.-M., Muller, G., Lawall, J.: Entropy: a consolidation manager for clusters. In: Proceedings of the 2009 ACM SIGPLAN/SIGOPS International Conference on Virtual Execution Environments, VEE 2009, pp. 41–50. ACM (2009)
5. Sheikhalishahi, M., Wallace, R.M., Grandinetti, L., Vazquez-Poletti, J.L., Guerriero, F.: A multi-capacity queuing mechanism in multi-dimensional resource scheduling. In: Pop, F., Potop-Butucaru, M. (eds.) ARMS-CC 2014. LNCS, vol. 8907, pp. 9–25. Springer, Heidelberg (2014)
6. Dupont, C., Hermenier, F., Schulze, T., Basmadjian, R., Somov, A., Giuliani, G.: Plug4green: a flexible energy-aware vm manager to fit data centre particularities. Ad Hoc Netw. **25**, 505–519 (2015)
7. Alvares de Oliveira Jr., F., Sharrock, R., Ledoux, T.: Synchronization of multiple autonomic control loops: application to cloud computing. In: Sirjani, M. (ed.) COORDINATION 2012. LNCS, vol. 7274, pp. 29–43. Springer, Heidelberg (2012)
8. de Oliveira, F.A., Ledoux, T., Sharrock, R.: A framework for the coordination of multiple autonomic managers in cloud environments. In: 2013 IEEE 7th International Conference on Self-Adaptive and Self-Organizing Systems (SASO), pp. 179–188, September 2013
9. Vaquero, L.M., Rodero-Merino, L., Buyya, R.: Dynamically scaling applications in the cloud. SIGCOMM Comput. Commun. Rev. **41**(1), 45–52 (2011)
10. Carpen-Amarie, A., Dib, D., Orgerie, A.-C, Pierre, G.: Towards energy-aware IaaS-PaaS co-design. In: SMARTGREENS 2014, pp. 203–208 (2014)

BigDASC

Sipresk: A Big Data Analytic Platform for Smart Transportation

Hamzeh Khazaei[(✉)], Saeed Zareian, Rodrigo Veleda, and Marin Litoiu

School of Information Technology, York University, Toronto, ON, Canada
{hkh,zareian,rveleda,litoiu}@yorku.ca

Abstract. In this paper, we propose a platform for performing analytics on urban transportation data to gain insights into traffic patterns. The platform consists of data, analytics and management layers and it can be leveraged by overlay traffic-related applications or directly by researchers, traffic engineers and planners. The platform is cluster-based and leverages the cloud to achieve reliability, scalability and adaptivity to the changing operating conditions. It can be leveraged for both on-line and retrospective analysis. We validated several use cases such as finding average speed and congested segments in the major highways in Greater Toronto Area (GTA).

Keywords: Smart transportation · Data analytics platform · Traffic data · Adaptive systems

1 Introduction

The effective movement of people and vehicles has long been critical to economies and qualities of life worldwide. Inefficiencies cost money, increase pollution and take time away from peoples lives. The problem is, the supply of transportation infrastructure grows more slowly than demand. Cars can be built more quickly than roads. Cities grow faster than highways can be expanded. Even if there were a limitless supply of money and personnel for road construction, many areas are already built out. That is why the transportation industry is turning to data analytics to find smarter ways to use the resources that exist, reduce congestion, and improve the travel experience [4].

Researchers have modelled different aspects of transportation using travel surveys, fluid flow model or game theory. With the emergence of new data sources, such as traffic sensors, cameras, GPS-devices and cell phones, opportunities have emerged for near real-time and at-rest data analytics [15].

The velocity and magnitude of data varies across sources. For example, loop detector sensors, embedded in the Highways of Greater Toronto Area (GTA) collect data at every 20-s intervals. Meanwhile, the social activity varies during the day. The data exists in a variety of forms including numerical, textual and visual either in structured or un-structured fashion. The data is collected over

© ICST Institute for Computer Sciences, Social Informatics and Telecommunications Engineering 2016
A. Leon-Garcia et al. (Eds.): Smart City 2015, LNICST 166, pp. 419–430, 2016.
DOI: 10.1007/978-3-319-33681-7_35

years, and is voluminous in size. Managing and mining this data is truly a big data problem [10].

The analytics, e.g. average daily traffic and congested segments, are of immediate interest to ministry of transportation, various municipalities and transportation planners. Meanwhile, data mining might benefit a wider audience by predicting traffic congestion, uncovering timings of various hot spots and/or suggesting fastest route [19].

In this paper, we present a big data analytics architecture, Sipresk, that is tailored to transportation data and adaptation. Sipresk is not an acronym and it means "Swallow" (the bird) in the old Persian language. The architecture is an instantiation of the conceptual architecture presented by some of the current authors in [19]. More specifically, Sipresk has a multi-tier architecture including, data, analytics and management components. Data layer ingests data from multiple sources, performs en route data processing with user-specified plug-ins, and normalizes it for analytical jobs. The analytical layer supports three types of job analytics: (a) interactive processing, (b) batch processing, and (c) graph processing. Sipresk requires to handle large magnitude of data and number of users. Therefore, a MAPE-K loop based solution [23] is employed to keep the Sipresks performance at an optimal level, for example, scaling out in times of high load. We realize an instance of Sipresk to shed some lights on congested segments and average daily speed in Ontario's highways.

The rest of the paper is organized as follows. In Sect. 2 we highlight the functional and non-functional requirements of Sipresk. Section 3 specifies the characteristics of available traffic data and the data management component. In Sects. 4 and 5, we describe our analytic engine and the management system. We present a case study on loop detectors data by leveraging Sipresk platform in the Sect. 6. Section 7 surveys related research and Sect. 8 concludes the paper.

2   Functional and Non-functional Requirements of Sipresk

There are different types of users that pose different questions to a transportation analytics platform such as Sipresk; Shtern et al. [19] classify them into four categories:

1. Transportation Manager
   - How was the traffic on the highways yesterday?
   - Which regions saw the worst traffic yesterday?
2. Traffic Engineer
   - Which loop detectors are malfunctioning?
   - Which locations do congestion occur and what time?
   - How do congestions start and spread?
3. Planner Researcher
   - What will be the traffic volume in future?
   - Where will the future bottlenecks be? How can they be addressed?
   - How will the hybrid cars effect the environment?
4. Policy Maker

- What are the suitable toll charges on the highways?
- How much more should heavy vehicles pay relative to cars?

In order to answer above type of questions, we design Sipresk in a way that can support spatiotemporal, graph, periodic, statistical, prediction and fusion queries as highlighted in [19]. These queries can be mapped into 4 classes of workloads, namely batch, interactive, stream and graph processing that must be supported by Sipresk. The characteristics of traffic data and the functional requirements impose the following non-functional requirements on Sipresk:

- **Scalability and Elasticity**: handle constantly increasing size of traffic data, and varying number of users.
- **Efficient range scans**: provide efficient range scans to support data aggregations.
- **Low-latency of storage and access**: offer low-latency between storage of a data source sample, and availability for analysis through specialized interfaces.
- **Autonomic management**: adapting to unpredictable changes and optimizing its performance by self-awareness, auto configuration, recovering from failures, and protecting itself from malicious users.
- **High Availability**: provide high availability to support real-time data ingestion and online statistics.

3   Data Management Subsystem

Table 1 presents the available traffic data in GTA, Ontario, Canada. Sipresk provides storage and analytics capabilities on all available data. In this work we leverage the loop detectors data to answer the interested questions. For a detailed description of data refer to [15, 19].

The data management layer pools the data from CVST platform [3, 20] that collects traffic data directly from multiple sources. The acquired data is then processed according to user specified plug-ins and is stored in HBase or HDFS (as the data warehouse) depending on the data type and size. Data with small size is stored in HBase while large payloads go directly into HDFS. For example, speed metrics can be stored in HBase. Meanwhile, videos can be stored directly in HDFS, while any meta-data extracted during the pipeline processing is also stored in HBase.

We chose HBase for our warehouse because HBase supports high access throughput, strictly consistent reads and writes, and efficient range scans. It also provides low latency of storage and access [2]. Hsu et al. [8] have used HBase to create spatial indexes, a main requirement for efficient spatial queries. However, HBase supports only one index. To overcome this shortcoming, we use Solr[1] to generated additional indexes on data which are then stored back into HBase.

We provide on demand analytic datastores, e.g., key-value, document, wide column or graph stores for research projects on top of the warehouse. The type of

---

[1] http://lucene.apache.org/solr.

Table 1. Available traffic data in GTA

Data source	Data format	Data type	Description
Loop detector sensors	Structured	Numerical	Average speed and traffic flow per 20-s
Traffic cameras	Unstructured	Video	Blob of video in stream format
Mobile devices (GPS/Bluetooth)	Structured	Numerical	Location and speed via cellular network
Toronto traffic survey	Structured	Text/Numerical	This survey has a very large sample size resulting in interviews with hundreds of thousands of households
Incident reports	Structured	Text/Numerical	Witness reported issues
Public transportation	Structured	Numerical	Tabular schedules of public transportation
Media outlets	Semi-structured	Text/Numerical	e.g., radio stations reports, CP24
Social nedia	Unstructured	Text	Crowd reported information

analytic datastore is dependent on target queries and the nature of the research project data. For example we may create a key-value storage for loop detectors data for Winter of 2014. This layered architecture is mainly adopted for the sake of isolation, performance, scalability and availability. By doing so, each project has the full access to the data in the most appropriate datastore technology. Figure 1 shows the concept of our adopted layered architecture.

4   Analytic Subsystem

The analytic engine in Sipresk is based on Sahara project, which is the data processing component in OpenStack[2] foundation. It can deliver different types of data processing clusters based on Apache Spark or Hadoop ecosystems. The analytic engine consists of modellers, graph processing, real-time processing, batch processing and machine Learning algorithms at large scale. The analytic engine provides high-level interfaces to analyze traffic related problems.

For instance, in case of a Spark[3] cluster deployment, R[4] gives the user the capability to construct statistical and prediction models from the traffic data; MLlib allows analysts to detect patterns and build classters over data; GraphX provides the ability to perform iterative graph processing at large scale such as calculate travel time on a route; Spark SQL and Spark Streaming provide fast real-time and batch processing in memory. In case of a hadoop-based clusters, corresponding tools will be available for above mentioned type of analytics. Figure 2 shows the high level architecture of Sipresk.

---

[2] http://www.openstack.org.

[3] https://spark.apache.org.

[4] http://www.r-project.org.

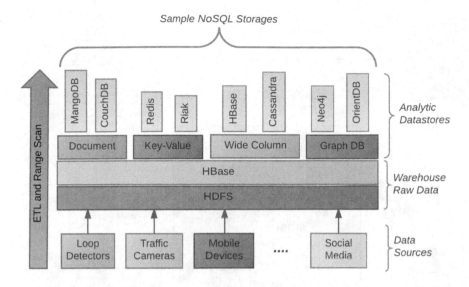

Fig. 1. Layered data management platform.

5 Management Subsystem

We expect very large data sizes and varying number of users, and the need of platform to adjust to changing demands. Therefore, a management system based on the MAPE-k loop [9] is an integral part of the platform. The manager monitors the analytic engine and data management layer, analyzes the current conditions, plans actions to take the platform to desirable state, and executes the corresponding actions. It may acquire, adjust or release resources from the cloud.

We leverage our in-house implementation of MAPE-K methodology, K-Feed (Knowledge-Feed) [23], to manage both data management and analytic engine. K-Feed monitors the platform closely and gathers the performance metrics. It analyzes these collected metrics in real-time and acts when certain type of conditions are met. For example, if aggregated CPU utilization stays high (e.g., > 60 % for 2 min) in HBase regional servers or in workers in Spark cluster, it will add one node to the pool to bring the platform to normal condition. In addition to reactive adaptation, K-Feed also is able to provide proactive adaptation by doing statistical modeling on the performance metrics data. Figure 3 shows the high level architecture of K-Feed.

6 Case Study

The traffic congestion is a major issue for GTA. In this section, we use Sipersk to investigate the major highways of Toronto and characterize the average speed and occupancy during the year of 2014 and first 4 months of 2015. This is just a

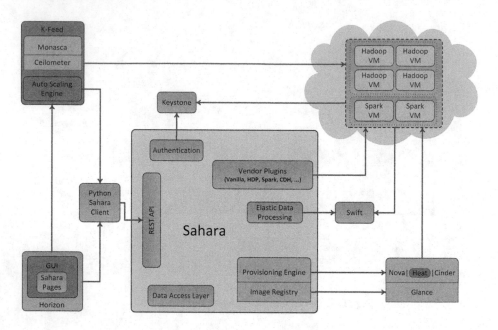

Fig. 2. Analytic engine in Sipresk.

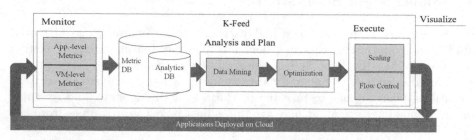

Fig. 3. High level architecture of K-Feed [23].

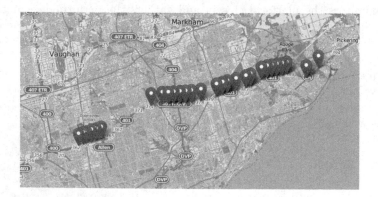

Fig. 4. Congested points in 401 East, aggregated for Wednesdays in October 2014, during morning rush hours.

Fig. 5. Congested points in 401 West, aggregated for Wednesdays in October 2014, during evening rush hours.

use case of Sipresk capabilities for smart transportation. Specifically, we perform an analytical study to answer the following questions:

1. What are the congestion points in GTA's highways during morning and evening rush hours?
2. What was the average speed for highways 401, 404, 400, 407, DVP and QEW during the last 16 months? We are interested in daily average speed for congested segments of the above highways.

   Our analysis is conducted on the data collected from the sensors embedded in the highways of GTA. In the CSV format, the size of data is 30 GB for the whole year of 2014 and the first 4 months of 2015. We conduct the study using a customized deployment of Sipresk on SAVI [18] cloud. SAVI is an OpenStack-base academic cloud platform being leveraged by many Canadian universities.

   We use a HBase cluster as the analytics datastore on top of our warehouse; the data cluster consists of 8 VMs with the flavour of "m.large" (i.e., 4 vCPU, 8 GB RAM, 80 GB disk) grouping in 2 master and 6 worker nodes. The HDFS capacity in the cluster is 406.2 GB of usable space. We use Apache Spark stand alone deployment as the analytic engine. It comprises of 3 "m.xlarge" (i.e., 8 vCPU, 16 GB RAM, 160 GB disk) including one master and 2 slave nodes. For the management system, i.e., K-Feed, we deploy two "m.medium" instances; one for the monitoring purpose and collecting performance metrics and the other one for analysis, planning and execution of the outcome commands. All nodes in Sipresk platform are running Ubuntu 14.04 LTS as the underlying operating system.

   Once Sipresk is instantiated, the analyst can focus on the tasks she/he is interested. We, for example, have been able to carry out various and extensive

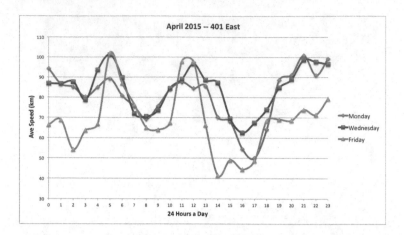

Fig. 6. Average speed for congested points in 401 East during April 2015.

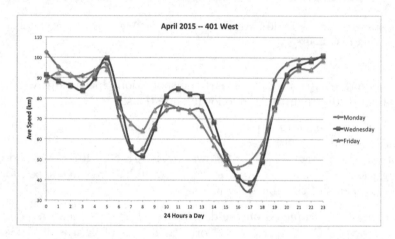

Fig. 7. Average speed for congested points in 401 West during April 2015.

analytics on loop detector data and detailed next. We define a point in highways as congested, if it's average speed is less that 60 % of the average speed in the whole highway (i.e. the segment of highways that is instrumented by loop detectors). Using this definition, we identified the congested points in GTA highways for each day during the whole data set. Then we aggregated results for each month (e.g. obtaining the average speed for all Fridays in January) in order to reduce the noise and avoid rare congestions (e.g. an accident casing the congestion). We did this analytics for the whole year of 2014 and the first 4 months of 2015. However, due to space limit, we only show two samples of our results (Figs. 4 and 5) here. The extra results can be found in the Adaptive Systems Research Lab (ASRL) portal[5].

---

[5] http://www.ceraslabs.com/people/hamzeh/bigdasc2015paper.

We also identified the daily average speed for congested segments in the highways for the entire data set. Then, we aggregated weekdays for each month and visualized the average speed for the 24 h of that day. Figures 6 and 7 show the average speed for Mondays, Wednesdays and Fridays in April 2015. For extra results corresponding to other months and weekdays, please refer to the ASRL portal specified above.

7   Related Work

In this section we survey the recent works in analytics of transportation data and related research in big data analytics in the area of smart cities.

Mian et al. proposed a platform to support analytics over traffic data [15]. The platform includes multiple engines to support various types of analytics and processing ranging from text searching to route planning. However, they used Matlab as their analytic engine that made their case study limited to three months. Also the data layer proposed in this work is not extendable for supporting different data type as well as research projects. In this work, our goal was to relax these limitations.

Zareian et al. [23] proposed a monitoring system for performance analysis of applications deployed on cloud. Their platform K-Feed, can perform at scale monitoring, analysis, and provisioning of cloud applications. It supports both proactive and reactive scalability. We use K-Feed in Sipresk as the management system.

Shtern et al. [19] propose a conceptual architecture for a data engine, Godzilla, to ingest real-time traffic data and support analytic and data mining over transportation data. They specified the requirements and specifications of a multi-cluster approach to handle large volumes of growing data, changing workloads and varying number of users. We incorporated some of the specifications and design patterns mentioned in this work to realize and deploy the Sipresk. Sipresk is a concrete architecture and implementation.

There are about 1,600 loop detector sensors and 200 cameras located in the highways of northern Belgium. The measurements, collected at the frequency of 1 m, are stored into a central database in the raw, unprocessed and non-validated form [14]. The California Freeway Performance Measurement System (PeMS) has about 26,000 loop detector sensors collection data at 30 s interval into an Oracle database system [21]. The type of analytics that they are doing on these two projects is not clearly known.

The city of Bellevue has about 180 loop detector sensors, and the data captured is available in CSV files at every minute interval. GATI system [22] downloads the traffic data from the Bellevue data server and stores it in a MySQL database system. Hoh et al. [7] and Lo et al. [13] collect traffic data by probing GPS-equipped vehicles, and store it in a Microsoft SQL Server and PostgreSQL respectively.

The above systems usually collect data from a single source, which has structured type, and is stored in a relational database system. The traditional database systems have limitations over horizontal scalability [1]. The above systems display the collected data on a map, estimate travel times, or show current traffic conditions in a web-browser or over cell phones.

In contrast, our data platform will collect data from multiple sources, which have multiple types, and would be stored in a scalable NoSQL layer. The vision is to provide a comprehensive analytic platform for traffic analysts by offering multiple interfaces. Data from multiple sources can be combined to lead to new insights. For example, it will be possible to study effects of introducing new toll charges on traffic volumes and reaction of traveler using the tolled highways. However, developing efficient and scalable platforms for Big Data is actively being researched [2,5,11,12]. Building such a platform is a multi-facet problem, and we provide examples of research in addressing a particular aspect of the problem.

Rabkin et al. [16] explores the reasons for the downtime of a Hadoop cluster. They discover misconfiguration to be the biggest reason for failures. Heger [6] presents a methodology to tune a Hadoop cluster for varying workload conditions. Meanwhile, Rao et al. [17] explores the performance issues of Hadoop in heterogeneous clusters and suggest possible ways to address the issues. Rabkin et al. and Rao et al. explores methods to reduce downtown and improve performance. We incorporate their ideas to create a smart deployer for Sipresk platform.

We also see several commercial solutions such as Google[6] and Inrix[7] mainly focus on providing predefined traffic analytics and reports accessible through dashboards and/or APIs. However, our work focuses on providing a generic platform that enables ad-hoc analytics over traffic data.

8   Conclusion

In this paper, we presented a big data platform, Sipresk, to support analytics over large traffic data. Sipresk supports various types of analytics on different data sources. It can adapt to the changing environment – workload, failure, networking and the like – by leveraging a MAPE-K loop based solution. In addition we implemented and deployed an instance of Sipresk to provides insights on highways traffic in GTA. We specified the congested points in all highways and also depicted the average speed in those congested segments for the last 16 months.

As the future work, we plan to extend our analytics to the rest of available traffic data in order to answer other research questions mentioned in Sect. 2. In particular, we are interested in building statistical models for predicting the traffic condition in GTA for near future.

Acknowledgments. This research was supported by the SAVI Strategic Research Network (Smart Applications on Virtual Infrastructure), funded by NSERC (The Natural Sciences and Engineering Research Council of Canada) and by Connected Vehicles

---

[6] https://support.google.com/maps.
[7] www.inrix.com.

and Smart Transportation (CVST) funded Ontario Research Fund. We acknowledge the contribution of the ONE-ITS platform in providing access to aggregated of-line traffic data. We also would like to thank Brian Ramprasad for his help in deployment of HBase clusters and Yan Fu for her help on data collection.

References

1. Abadi, D.J.: Data management in the cloud: limitations and opportunities. IEEE Data Eng. Bull. **32**(1), 3–12 (2009)
2. Borthakur, D., Gray, J., Sarma, J.S., Muthukkaruppan, K., Spiegelberg, N., Kuang, H., Ranganathan, K., Molkov, D., Menon, A., Rash, S., et al.: Apache hadoop goes realtime at facebook. In: Proceedings of the 2011 ACM SIGMOD International Conference on Management of data, pp. 1071–1080. ACM (2011)
3. CVST. Connected Vehicles and Smart Transportation, June 2015. http://cvst.ca
4. Dirks, S., Gurdgiev, C., Keeling, M.: Smarter cities for smarter growth: how cities can optimize theirsystems for the talent-based economy. IBM Institute for Business Value (2010)
5. Hayes, M., Shah, S. Hourglass: a library for incremental processing on hadoop. In: 2013 IEEE International Conference on Big Data, pp. 742–752. IEEE (2013)
6. Heger, D.: Hadoop performance tuning-a pragmatic & iterative approach. CMG J. **4**, 97–113 (2013)
7. Hoh, B., Gruteser, M., Herring, R., Ban, J., Work, D., Herrera, J.-C., Bayen, A.M., Annavaram, M., Jacobson, Q.: Virtual trip lines for distributed privacy-preserving traffic monitoring. In: Proceedings of the 6th International Conference on Mobile systems, Applications, and Services, pp. 15–28. ACM (2008)
8. Hsu, Y.-T., Pan, Y.-C., Wei, L.-Y., Peng, W.-C., Lee, W.-C.: Key formulation schemes for spatial index in cloud data managements. In: 2012 IEEE 13th International Conference on Mobile Data Management (MDM), pp. 21–26. IEEE (2012)
9. Kephart, J.O., Chess, D.M.: The vision of autonomic computing. Computer **36**(1), 41–50 (2003)
10. Kitchin, R.: The real-time city? big data and smart urbanism. GeoJ. **79**(1), 1–14 (2014)
11. Konstantinou, I., Angelou, E., Boumpouka, C., Tsoumakos, D., Koziris, N.: On the elasticity of NoSQL databases over cloud management platforms. In: Proceedings of the 20th ACM International Conference on Information and Knowledge Management, pp. 2385–2388. ACM (2011)
12. Lane, N.D., Miluzzo, E., Lu, H., Peebles, D., Choudhury, T., Campbell, A.T.: A survey of mobile phone sensing. IEEE Commun. Mag. **48**(9), 140–150 (2010)
13. Lo, C.-H., Peng, W.-C., Chen, C.-W., Lin, T.-Y., Lin, C.-S. Carweb: a traffic data collection platform. In: 9th International Conference on Mobile Data Management, MDM 2008, pp. 221–222. IEEE (2008)
14. Maerivoet, S., Logghe, S.: Validation of travel times based on cellular floating vehicle data. In: Proceedings from 6th European Congress and Exhibition on Intelligent Transport Systems and Services (2007)
15. Mian, R., Ghanbari, H., Zareian, S., Shtern, M., Litoiu, M.: A data platform for the highway traffic data. In: 2014 IEEE 8th International Symposium on the Maintenance and Evolution of Service-Oriented and Cloud-Based Systems (MESOCA), pp. 47–52. IEEE (2014)
16. Rabkin, A., Katz, R.H.: How hadoop clusters break. IEEE Softw. **30**(4), 88–94 (2013)

17. Rao, B.T., Sridevi, N., Reddy, V.K., Reddy, L.: Performance issues of heterogeneous hadoop clusters in cloudcomputing (2012). arXiv preprint arXiv:1207.0894
18. SAVI. Smart Applications on Virtual Infrastructure. Cloud platform, June 2015. http://www.savinetwork.ca
19. Shtern, M., Mian, R., Litoiu, M., Zareian, S., Abdelgawad, H., Tizghadam, A.: Towards a multi-cluster analytical engine for transportation data. In: 2014 International Conference on Cloud and Autonomic Computing (ICCAC), pp. 249–257. IEEE (2014)
20. Tizghadam, A., Leon-Garcia, A.: Connected Vehicles and Smart Transportation - CVST Platform, June 2015. http://cvst.ca/wp/wp-content/uploads/2015/06/cvst.pdf
21. Varaiya, P.: Reducing highway congestion: an empirical approach. Eur. J. Control **11**(4), 301–309 (2005)
22. Wu, Y.-J., Wang, Y., Qian, D.: A google-map-based arterial traffic information system. In: Intelligent Transportation Systems Conference, ITSC 2007, pp. 968–973. IEEE (2007)
23. Zareian, S., Veleda, R., Litoiu, M., Shtern, M., Ghanbari, H., Garg, M.: K-feed, a data-oriented approach to application performance management in cloud. In: 2015 IEEE 8th International Conference on Cloud Computing (CLOUD), June 2015. IEEE (2015)

Day-Ahead Electricity Spike Price Forecasting Using a Hybrid Neural Network-Based Method

Harmanjot Singh Sandhu[1(✉)], Liping Fang[1], and Ling Guan[2]

[1] Department of Mechanical and Industrial Engineering,
Ryerson University, Toronto, Canada
{harmanjotsingh.sandh,lfang}@ryerson.ca
[2] Department of Electrical and Computer Engineering,
Ryerson University, Toronto, Canada
lguan@ee.ryerson.ca

Abstract. A hybrid neural network-based method is presented to predict day-ahead electricity spike prices in a deregulated electricity market. First, prediction of day-ahead electricity prices is carried out by a neural network along with pre-processing data mining techniques. Second, a classifier is used to separate the forecasted prices into normal and spike prices. Third, a second neural network is trained over spike hours with selected features and is used to forecast day-ahead spike prices. Forecasted spike and normal prices are combined to produce the complete day-ahead hourly electricity price forecasting. Numerical experiments demonstrate that the proposed method can significantly improve the forecasting accuracy.

Keywords: Neural network · Price spikes · Day-ahead forecasting · Electricity market

1 Introduction

A competitive generation sector and open access to transmission systems are two common aspects of various competitive electricity markets around the world. However, depending on the market design and organization of the different electricity markets, there is considerable diversity in implementation. The competitive electricity markets from different jurisdictions may be categorized as single settlement markets or as two or multi-settlement markets [1]. The single settlement market is also known as a real time market in which the electricity prices are settled on hourly, half-hourly, or five minute bases depending on the demand and available supply. On the other hand, in a two settlement or multi-settlement market, settlement of prices for demand and supply depends on day-ahead and real-time operation of the market. In a two settlement market, prices are determined by a forward market for day-ahead consumption and generation of electricity and a real time market which is used to cover the differences between the proposed and actual consumption and generation. The problem of price spikes has been reported in almost all the electricity markets around the world. The main reason for the price spikes is the complexities and uncertainties in the power grid

[2]. However, the severe nature of the occurrence of spikes may differ depending on the structure and operation of a market.

Price forecasting is important to power suppliers for short-term and medium-term planning in setting rational offers and signing bilateral contracts. Moreover, electricity prices in the open market greatly influence generation expansion plans in long-term planning. Therefore, forecasting of electricity prices is an important and challenging task and has gained momentum during recent years [3, 4]. Accurate forecasting of electricity prices is very useful for generators and consumers to determine their offers and bidding strategies. In the case of load management programs, independent system operators (ISOs) and large wholesale consumers can use forecasting information to look for reliable options to reduce system demand and high electricity prices during peak hours.

In this study, the Ontario wholesale electricity market is explored. The Ontario electricity market is interconnected with the neighbouring electricity markets of New York, New England, Midwest, and Pennsylvania-New Jersey-Maryland (PJM) [5, 6]. It is considered to be one of the most volatile electricity markets in the world due to its single settlement operation [7]. The occurrences of price spikes depend upon the volatile nature of the market. Hence, price forecasting in the Ontario electricity market is challenging.

The problem of price spike forecasting has been studied for different electricity markets of the world, using various methods. Most of these studies use support vector machine (SVM) and neural networks (NNs) [8–11]. In Zhao et al. [8], occurrences of price spikes from the national electricity market (NEM) in Australia are predicted using a support vector machine and probability classifier. These predicted spikes are combined with normal price forecasts to generate the overall price forecasting. Amjady and Keynia [9] report a wavelet transform method to construct the set of candidate inputs along with feature selection techniques for the forecasting process and probabilistic neural network (PNN) has been used to predict price spikes for the Queensland and PJM electricity markets. In Baez-Rivera et al. [10], price spike forecasting of the PJM electricity market is obtained by using radial basis neural networks. In a study by Wu et al. [11], the occurrence of price spikes for a regional electricity market in China is predicted with a Bayesian expert classifier while day-ahead hourly spikes are forecasted using SVM and artificial neural networks.

In addition to SVM and NNs, Christensen et al. [12] uses an autoregressive conditional hazard (ACH) model to forecast half-hourly ahead price spikes in the NEM Australia. Eichler et al. [13] extend the work by Christensen et al. [12] and employ a dynamic logit model to represent price spike forecasting for the NEM Australia. Lu et al. [2] and Zhao et al. [14] utilize a statistical approach to identify spikes and data mining techniques for spike forecasting for the NEM Australia. Although many studies have demonstrated good work on price spike forecasting, a significant improvement in forecasting accuracy is still needed. Furthermore, most of the studies for price spike forecasting have been carried out for the Australian electricity market, and no study on price spike forecasting for the Ontario wholesale electricity market has been reported. As pointed out by Zareipour et al. [7], the Ontario electricity market operates in real time only and is very volatile. Accordingly, the main objective of this paper is to develop techniques to forecast day-ahead spike prices for the Ontario electricity market with high forecasting accuracy.

In recent studies, neural network techniques have gained popularity for handling non-linear relationships accurately. Neural networks do not need prior information and depend on the processing of available data. Neural networks are capable of handling large classes of functions and are known as universal approximation models [15]. In this paper, a hybrid method based on neural networks and data mining techniques at the pre-processing stage is used to predict day-ahead price spikes and combined with the forecasted normal prices to achieve overall day-ahead price forecasting. Many features are responsible for variations in electricity prices. Some of these important features are demand, temperature, humidity, time of consumption, and type of generation facility available. In the current study, normal prices are forecasted with a method proposed by Sandhu et al. [16]. In the next step, a second neural network is trained over spike hours prior to the forecasting day in the same year and from the previous two years with data values of demand, temperature, dew point temperature and relative humidity. Spike prices over these hours are used as respective target values to compare the forecasted and actual values. Hence, day-ahead spike forecasting is achieved with reduced errors with this trained neural network. The first neural network used to forecast the normal prices in Sandhu et al. [16] is called as Network 1 (or Net 1) in the current study, while the second neural network used to forecast day-ahead spike prices in this work is called Network 2 (or Net 2).

The present paper is organized as follows. Section 2 describes the proposed method for spike price forecasting. Results and discussion are presented in Sect. 3. Section 4 concludes the paper.

2 Proposed Method for Spike Price Forecasting

2.1 Electricity Price Spikes

Spikes in the electricity market may be considered as random events. Many studies in the past have shown encouraging results on the spike forecasting and discussed the reasons for occurrence of spikes [2, 8–14]. Mainly spikes occur if the available supply is less than demand or if the reserve margin is very low. There are many short-term factors, such as breakdown of generators operating at low cost, transmission line constraints, generation capacity constraints, and weather conditions like temperature, humidity and dew point temperature, affecting the occurrence of spikes. There are also long term factors, such as hikes in gas and oil prices, shutting down of generators due to ageing, government policies, inflation rates, and economic growth.

Electricity market spikes may be divided into three categories: high spikes (if the prices are much higher than the average prices), negative spikes (if the prices are below zero), and jump spikes (if there is a significant change in the prices at time '$t + 1$' from price at time 't'). In the Ontario electricity market, if the demand is less than the supply electricity prices are negative and buyers are paid for energy consumption. Spikes may occur for several hours but normally not for more than a day.

In this study, high spike prices are analyzed and forecasted day-ahead over a day for the Ontario electricity market. As shown in Table 1, the number of electricity price spike hours in Ontario is increasing every year. Hence, to fulfil the demand during these spike hours new generation facilities may be needed. These facilities are operative only for a few hours for a few days in a year, but have a significant impact on increases in electricity prices. In the Ontario electricity market, historical prices, demand, temperature, dew point temperature and relative humidity data are selected as important features for forecasting price spikes. These features are available for public access on the Independent Electricity System Operator (IESO) website at ieso.ca.

Table 1. Number of spike hours and spike days from 2009 to 2014.

Year	Number of spike hours	Number of spike days
2009	21	12
2010	44	25
2011	61	36
2012	58	33
2013	73	67
2014	122	95

The historical price data are obtained for the Ontario wholesale electricity market for 2011 and the mean 'μ' and standard deviation 'σ' are calculated. Then the price spike threshold for 2012 is calculated as $\mu + 2\sigma$ [2, 8]. The threshold level is computed as $71.26/MWh for 2012 and prices above this threshold are considered spikes. When prices are forecasted to be above this threshold by the neural network presented in Sandhu et al. [16], the second neural network is utilized to predict the spike prices. The threshold for 2012 is calculated from the mean and standard deviation of the prices in 2011. Similarly, the threshold for 2013 can be computed from the mean and standard deviation of the prices in 2012.

2.2   Flow Chart of the Proposed Method

A hybrid neural network-based method is proposed in the present study to forecast the electricity price spikes over a day. In the first step, a neural network (called Network 1 or Net 1) along with the data mining techniques at the pre-processing step presented by Sandhu et al. [16] is used to forecast the day ahead prices for a forecasting day. The mean absolute percentage errors (MAPEs) are often large at spike hours. In the next step, as shown in Fig. 1, a classifier is employed to classify the forecasted prices to be below, above or equal to the threshold price. The prices above or equal to the threshold are considered as spike prices. In the third step, in order to improve the accuracy of forecasting, a second neural network (called Network 2 or Net 2), as shown in Fig. 2, is used to forecast the spike prices and the overall forecasting is achieved by combining the results of two networks. Network 2 is trained with discrete values over the spike hours from the same year prior to the forecasting day and from the previous two years

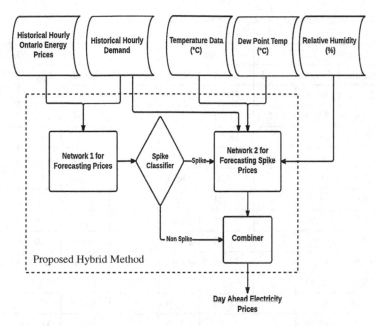

Fig. 1. Flow diagram of day-ahead electricity price spike forecasting.

with price, demand, temperature, dew point temperature, and relative humidity data. Dew point temperature is the absolute measure of moisture in the air and at the dew point temperature water vapor will condense. On the other hand, the relative humidity gives an expression for air saturation at a given temperature. As an example, to forecast the spikes for January 3, 2012, spike hours for January 2 and January 1, 2012 from the same year are identified and spike hours over all 365 days in 2011 and 2010 are identified as the spike hours from the previous two years. Training dataset, to train Net 2, consists of these identified spike hours. Spikes do not occur continuously, therefore, the training dataset for Net 2 consists of these discrete hours. Hence, prices above the threshold level, as forecasted by Network 1, are re-forecasted by Network 2 trained

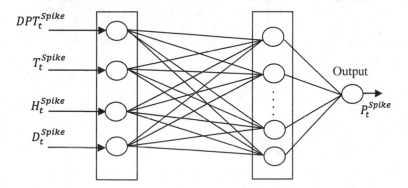

Fig. 2. Proposed network 2 for spike price forecasting

Table 2. Forecasting day-ahead electricity prices and spikes using neural networks.

Hour	January 3, 2012			June 20, 2012			June 28, 2012		
	Actual	Net 1	Net 2	Actual	Net 1	Net 2	Actual	Net 1	Net 2
1	28.34	30.25		20.28	22.89		14.17	14.41	
2	27.69	30.14		21.64	23.28		16.64	15.89	
3	25.31	28.79		18.59	20.16		12.47	13.34	
4	25.22	28.65		19.5	20.48		12.65	13.43	
5	25.88	28.72		16.4	18.24		13.06	12.78	
6	26.66	28.97		20.34	19.63		4.38	4	
7	31.16	33.59		27.24	24.87		15.8	15.68	
8	34.77	36.87		31.15	28.55		21.06	20	
9	35.89	37.29		47.59	41.98		22.71	21.9	
10	33.82	36.37		56.88	52.86		28.24	25.2	
11	32.96	36.16		38.29	45.19		31.31	31.9	
12	29.05	33.29		50.51	49.55		29.16	31.73	
13	31.62	34.57		88.81	76.49	82.59	31.5	31.42	
14	31.48	34.46		66.28	70.7		30.7	31.04	
15	47.13	38.97		108.24	88.92	99.28	38.82	37.44	
16	44.83	37.86		44.68	68.49		93.76	78.79	84.12
17	58.15	45.78		95.06	81.59	86.87	100.1	91.36	96.82
18	115.2	79.46	92.76	95.79	86.79	91.36	71.86	76.77	73.23
19	91.28	76.89	86.79	97.89	89.26	93.08	45.37	42.19	
20	135.3	94.79	119.4	62.7	79.83	72.89	44.38	46.21	
21	124.7	93.23	115.4	46.38	58.22		47.15	45.6	
22	41.33	78.49	82.37	28.95	38.76		56.56	53.58	
23	32.09	70.12		26.06	32.11		31.39	36.06	
24	29.16	62.79		24.13	27.14		21.7	20.42	

(*Continued*)

Table 2. (*Continued*)

Hour	July 6, 2012			July 17, 2012			July 18, 2012		
	Actual	Net 1	Net 2	Actual	Net 1	Net 2	Actual	Net 1	Net 2
1	21.13	23.59		28.44	26.33		32.93	30.36	
2	20.92	22.89		25.88	24.26		27.42	28.13	
3	19.87	22.09		24.99	24.11		26.32	27.04	
4	17.43	19.38		23.79	24.06		25.67	26.11	
5	16.55	19.24		23.94	24.08		25.94	26.15	
6	18.93	20.63		24.18	24.12		25.47	25.83	
7	24.39	21.94		25.33	24.49		26.03	25.94	
8	25.16	23.88		28.32	26.79		27.46	26.97	
9	30.47	27.49		32.39	29.86		27.34	26.94	
10	59.01	42.68		65.05	48.22		31.9	31.18	
11	107.06	75.21	87.27	87.79	67.59		35.54	34.22	
12	77.16	79.96	80.76	120.4	79.46	90.27	41.12	39.25	
13	119.04	97.26	112.76	138.3	86.33	115.5	71.91	66.43	
14	96.24	89.57	101.25	103.3	75.22	99.56	32.05	34.21	
15	96.33	90.29	99.87	105.1	76.43	101.7	43.46	41.83	
16	94.72	89.64	98.59	144.3	89.76	129.4	89.15	73.58	74.82
17	93.17	89.88	97.92	147.7	95.78	135.8	97.32	79.85	85.24
18	64.23	80.29	75.29	149.2	103.7	139.5	30.31	32.59	
19	43.37	69.58		148.2	103.5	140.8	29.2	31.08	
20	88.85	82.59	86.24	96.49	90.78	112.7	31.66	31.88	
21	86.84	82.05	85.46	69.71	78.65	82.49	30.82	31.09	
22	53.9	78.91	62.34	39.28	68.46		25.26	27.16	
23	53.17	62.15		41.45	68.78		22.88	23.54	
24	22.36	32.65		35.51	54.12		20.74	21.82	

(*Continued*)

Table 2. (*Continued*)

Hour	4-Aug-12			24-Aug-12		
	Actual	Net 1	Net 2	Actual	Net 1	Net 2
1	27.44	26.49		25	24.85	
2	26.45	26.13		21.71	22.36	
3	27.47	26.89		18.64	18.78	
4	27.32	26.88		13.79	14.91	
5	25.37	26.03		19.17	19.89	
6	24.32	25.79		19.35	17.83	
7	25.77	26.11		18.3	19.22	
8	23.79	25.31		20.89	20.65	
9	24.81	25.46		22.67	22.32	
10	45.76	38.47		23.4	23.28	
11	58.58	42.19		26.88	25.79	
12	54.06	41.27		25.31	25.98	
13	84.14	67.49		31.56	29.65	
14	92.38	76.49	85.46	31.76	31.75	
15	100.75	85.64	92.37	77.52	54.27	
16	162.07	134.25	149.66	135.9	118.6	129.3
17	157.31	130.46	148.55	97.72	121.8	106.4
18	94.57	104.79	97.65	28.91	38.53	
19	109.79	118.34	112.43	28.47	28.6	
20	151.33	142.24	148.79	25.73	26.76	
21	49.97	94.37	79.58	22.65	23.79	
22	25.89	76.28	59.48	26.43	24.96	
23	23.77	69.42		20.62	23	
24	23.33	62.72		22.36	22.14	

with discrete values at spike hours. Spike prices forecasted by Network 2 are then combined with the previously forecasted prices of Network 1 to achieve the complete day-ahead electricity price forecasting to improve accuracy.

Network 2, as shown in Fig. 2 is used to forecast spike prices at 't' hour. Input features applied to Network 2 are DPT_t^{Spike}, T_t^{Spike}, H_t^{Spike} and D_t^{Spike} as dew point temperature, temperature, relative humidity and demand at spike hour 't', respectively. The output of Network 2 is the forecasted spike hour price P_t^{Spike} at hour 't'. Hidden neurons are increased from seven neurons in Network 1 to twelve neurons in Network

2 because of the increase in the number of input features. The other training parameters of Network 2 are kept the same as in Network 1.

3 Results and Discussion

The proposed spike price forecasting method uses the historical data available to the public from the Ontario electricity market at ieso.ca. A detail description of the Ontario electricity market is available in Zareipour et al. [4]. Previous studies on forecasting prices for the Ontario electricity market are mostly focused on normal price forecasting [17–20]. The proposed method presented in Sect. 2 is utilized to forecast spike prices for the Ontario electricity market. Eight spike days in 2012 are selected for numerical experiments. The forecasting results are given in Table 2.

As discussed in Sect. 2, the neural network developed by Sandhu et al. [16] is first used to forecast electricity prices during these selected days. The results are given under the column entitled "Net 1". The prices above the 2012 threshold of $71.26/MWh are highlighted in Table 2. As can be seen, the spike hours, the forecasted prices deviate from the actual prices significantly. Next step, Network 2 is used to forecast prices over the spike hours for the selected days. These forecasting results are given in the column entitled "Net 2". The proposed method combines the results from Network 1 and Network 2 to form the complete day-ahead price forecasting for each day. The MAPEs are calculated for these selected days in 2012, as shown in Table 3. As can be seen, the MAPEs are significantly reduced from Network 1 to the proposed method. An overall average MAPE value of 11.76 % for eight selected days in 2012 is achieved.

Table 3. Comparison of methods in terms of MAPE.

Day	Network 1	Hybrid neural network-based method
January 3, 2012	26	20.2
June 20, 2012	14.8	11.6
June 28, 2012	6.87	5.15
July 6, 2012	15.6	11.2
July 17, 2012	27.9	14.7
July 18, 2012	6.9	6.1
August 4, 2012	24.1	17.2
August 24, 2012	11.02	7.96
Average MAPE	**18.57**	**11.76**

Forecasting for normal prices and spike prices is demonstrated for eight different days from the summer and winter seasons in 2012. Day-ahead hourly forecasting for January 3, 2012 is shown in Fig. 3 and the overall MAPE value for the day is decreased from 26 % to 20.2 %. The forecasting results are obtained with two neural networks trained for normal and spike price forecasting. As can be seen, at spike hours, the results from the proposed hybrid method follow the actual prices much closer.

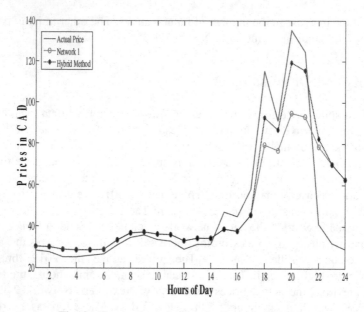

Fig. 3. Forecasting of prices for January 3, 2012.

Figure 4 illustrates normal and spike price forecasting for a summer day, July 17, in 2012, over the period of 24 h, with an overall improvement of MAPE from 27.9 % to 14.7 %. In a similar manner, hourly forecasted normal and spike prices have been obtained over all the selected days and the results are shown in Table 3.

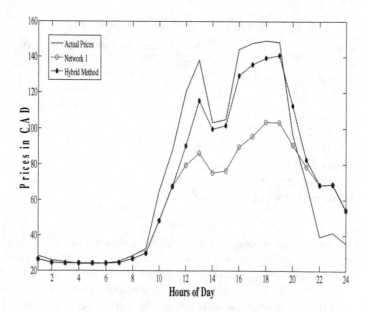

Fig. 4. Forecasting of prices for July 17, 2012.

It is observed that the first neural network, developed in a previous study by Sandhu *et al.* [16], is capable of forecasting day-ahead electricity prices with high accuracy for the low and medium price ranges. However, forecasting errors increase significantly as prices pass the threshold level defined by $\mu + 2\sigma$. These prices are considered as spikes and the second neural network, trained over the spike hours prior to the forecasting day in the same year and from the previous two years, is able to forecast spike prices. The proposed hybrid neural network-based method, combining results from the first and second neural networks, improves the overall forecasting accuracy.

4 Conclusion

A new approach for forecasting hourly normal and spike prices has been presented for the Ontario wholesale electricity market. Two feed forward neural networks trained differently are used along with a spike classifier to forecast day-ahead electricity prices. Forecasting experiments are carried out for eight different days, from different seasons, in 2012. Numerical experimental results show that the first neural network is able to predict electricity prices with high accuracy for the low and medium price ranges. However, with jumps in price, the forecasted prices deviate from the actual prices significantly and accuracy decreases. The prices above the pre-defined threshold level are known as spikes. The second neural network trained with historical spike hours from the same year and from the previous two years reduces forecasting errors over the spike hours. Experiments show that the overall MAPE is improved from 18.57 % to 11.76 %, an improvement of 36.7 % by the proposed hybrid neural network-based method. It is also observed from the 2012 data from the Ontario wholesale electricity market that spikes occurred when the demand was high and most of the spikes occurred during the summer season.

References

1. Veit, D.J., Weidlich, A., Yao, J., Oren, S.S.: Simulating the dynamics in two-settlement electricity markets via an agent-based approach. Int. J. Manage. Sci. Eng. Manage. **1**(2), 83–97 (2006)
2. Lu, X., Dong, Z.Y., Li, X.: Electricity market price spike forecasting with data mining techniques. Int. J. Electr. Power Syst. Res. **73**(1), 19–29 (2005)
3. Mandal, P., Senjyu, T., Urasaki, N., Funabashi, T., Srivastava, A.K.: Short-term price forecasting for competitive electricity market. In: Proceedings of the 38th North American IEEE Conference on Power Symposium, pp. 137–141. Carbondale, U.S., 17-19 September (2006)
4. Zareipour, H., Canizares, C., Bhattacharya, K.: The operation of Ontario's competitive electricity market: overview, experience and lessons. IEEE Trans. Power Syst. **22**(4), 1782–1793 (2007)
5. Hong, Y.Y., Hsiao, C.Y.: Locational marginal price forecasting in deregulated electricity markets using artificial intelligence. Proc. Inst. Elect. Eng. Gen. Transm. Distrib. **149**(5), 621–626 (2002)

6. Mandal, P., Srivastava, A., Park, J.-W.: An effort to optimize similar days parameters for ANN-based electricity price forecasting. IEEE Trans. Ind. Appl. **45**(5), 1888–1896 (2009)
7. Zareipour, H., Bhattacharya, K., Canizares, C.: Electricity price volatility: the case of Ontario. Energy Policy **35**(9), 4739–4748 (2007)
8. Zhao, J.H., Dong, Z.Y., Li, X., Wong, K.P.: A framework for electricity price spike analysis with advanced data mining methods. IEEE Trans. Power Syst. **22**(1), 376–385 (2007)
9. Amjady, N., Keynia, F.: Electricity market price spike analysis by hybrid data model and feature selection technique. Int. J. Electr. Power Syst. Res. **80**, 318–327 (2010)
10. Baez-Rivera, Y., Rodriguez-Medina, B., Srivastava A.K.: An attempt to forecast price spikes in electric power markets. In: Proceedings of 38th North American Conference on Power Symposium, pp. 143–148. Carbondale, U.S., 17-19 September (2006)
11. Wu, W., Zhou, J.-Z., Mo, L., Zhu, C.: Forecasting electricity market price spikes based on bayesian expert with support vector machines. In: Li, X., Zaiane, O.R., Li, Z.-h. (eds.) ADMA 2006. LNCS (LNAI), vol. 4093, pp. 205–212. Springer, Heidelberg (2006)
12. Christensen, T.M., Hurn, A.S., Lindsay, K.A.: Forecasting spikes in electricity prices. Int. J. Forecast. **28**(2), 400–411 (2012)
13. Eichler, M., Grothe, O., Manner, H., Tuerk, D.: Models for short-term forecasting of spike occurrences in Australian electricity markets: a comparative study. J. Energy Markets **7**(1), 55–81 (2013)
14. Zhao, J.H., Dong, Z.Y., Li, X.: Electricity market price spike forecasting and decision making. IET J. Gener. Trans. Distrib. **1**(4), 647–654 (2007)
15. Zhang, G.P., Qi, M.: Neural network forecasting for seasonal and trend time series. Eur. J. Oper. Res. **160**(2), 501–514 (2005)
16. Sandhu, H.S., Fang, L., Guan L.: Forecasting day-ahead electricity prices using data mining and neural network techniques. In: Proceedings of the 11th International Conference on Service Systems and Service Management, pp. 1024–1029, Beijing, China, June 25-27 (2014)
17. Aggarwal, S.K., Saini, L.M., Kumar, A.: Day-ahead price forecasting in Ontario electricity market using variable-segmented support vector machine-based model. Electr. Power Compon. Syst. **37**, 495–516 (2009)
18. Azmira W.A.R., Rahman, T.K.A., Zakaria, Z., Ahmad, A.: Short term electricity price forecasted using neural network. In: Proceedings of the 4th International Conference on Computing and Informatics, pp. 103–108, Sarawak, Malaysia, 28-30 August (2013)
19. Mandal P., Haque, A.U., Meng, J., Martinez, R., Srivastava, A.K.: A hybrid intelligent algorithm for short-term energy price forecasting in the Ontario market. In: Proceedings of the IEEE General Meeting of Power and Energy Society. p. 7, San Diego, CA, US, July 22–26 (2012)
20. Shrivastava, N.A., Ch, S., Panigrahi, B.K.: Price forecasting using computational intelligence techniques: a comparative analysis. In: Proceedings of the International Conference on Energy, Automation and Signals (ICEAS), pp. 1–6, Bhubaneswar, Odisha, December 28-30 (2011)

Transportation Big Data Simulation Platform for the Greater Toronto Area (GTA)

Islam R. Kamel[1(✉)], Hossam Abdelgawad[1,2], and Baher Abdulhai[1]

[1] Civil Engineering Department, University of Toronto, Toronto, Canada
islam.kamel@mail.utoronto.ca,
hossam.abdelgawad@alumni.utoronto.ca,
baher.abdulhai@utoronto.ca
[2] Faculty of Engineering, Cairo University, Giza 12631, Egypt

Abstract. This paper presents how big data could be utilized in preparing for smart cities. Within this context, smart cities require intelligent decisions in real time, while processing large amount of data. One big component that relates to smart cities in ITS applications is using artificial intelligent techniques that rely heavily on simulation environments for the evaluation and testing of ITS strategies. In this paper, we present a model for the GTA transportation network. While the model enables big data transportation applications to run in real time, its building process implied intensive work with big data. Within this paper, we show the structure, the calibration, and the outputs of the model. Moreover, some applications, which use the proposed model, are presented. These big data applications are a step towards the smart city of Toronto. Finally, we conclude with some thoughts of future work and the next generation of big data models.

Keywords: Big data · Smart city · Traffic simulation · Intelligent Transportation Systems · Greater Toronto Area

1 Introduction

Big data is typically characterized by three dimensions, widely known as 3Vs: volume, velocity, and variety as first defined by [1]. As such, dealing with big data implies processing very large volumes of fast generated data coming from multiple sources. Since then researchers have been expanding the definition of the basic 3Vs to include many other Vs, including: veracity, visualization, and value of data [2]. Additionally, the quality, readability, and contents of data are essential as the data itself. Having a lot of data generated at high speed from different sources is worthless, if it is of a low quality. This why research emphasizes the need to measure the veracity of data by determining how much one can trust the data. Even trustworthy data may be useless, if it remains in its raw format without being processed and visualized. Visualization is always seen to be a challenge when dealing with big data as it is challenging to summarize several variables with a lot of details in a graph or chart. The value of data is another basic dimension in characterizing big data. Although the data in its raw format may not be of a great value, rigorous analysis (descriptive, exploratory, and statistical) is what gains the data its value.

© ICST Institute for Computer Sciences, Social Informatics and Telecommunications Engineering 2016
A. Leon-Garcia et al. (Eds.): Smart City 2015, LNICST 166, pp. 443–454, 2016.
DOI: 10.1007/978-3-319-33681-7_37

Another dimension, which is somehow related to the *variety* or *veracity* of data, is the *variability* of data [3]. It defines the variance in the meaning of data. The meaning of data should be extracted from the whole context around it, just like words which have different meanings according to the context they are used in. In summary, to date, various definitions of big data result in 7 Vs as follows: *Volume, Velocity, Variety, Veracity, Visualization, Value,* and *Variability*.

This increasing interest in big data is witnessed across many fields worldwide. In two years (from 2011 to 2013), the generated data worldwide was almost doubled (from 1.8 to 4 ZB) [4]. These massive volumes of data exist almost everywhere around us; generating a lot of opportunities and challenges. Examples include technological industries and social networks, such as: *Facebook* deals with 30+ PetabyteS of user-generated data and receives 100 TB of data daily; *YouTube* handles more than 48 h uploads every minute; and *Twitter* estimated the number of tweets in early 2012 to be 175 million tweets daily. Examples also include other industries, such as retail companies: *Walmart* handles every hour more than 1 million customer transactions and imported them into databases estimated to contain more than 2.5 PB of data [5].

Big data in transportation is no different from the above trends. Collected data and traffic network conditions, especially those indicating traffic conditions and public transit status, is growing rapidly within the field of Intelligent Transportation Systems (ITS). For instance, traffic loop detectors in the Netherlands generate approximately 80 million records daily [6]; while the Greater Toronto Area (GTA) alone generates around 35 million traffic loop detection readings [7]. Crowd sourcing traffic data generate a significant portion of data in transportation (e.g., Waze: the largest community-based traffic and navigation mobile application [8]; and Roadify: the largest mobile application for transit information [9]). These data sources provide real-time traffic and transit information to enable travellers make better real-time informative decisions.

The intelligent use, analysis, and visualization of the previous data sources, combined with information and communication technologies (ICT) aim at building smarter cities. While there is no specific definition to the term smart city; it could be characterized by: (1) efficiently using the existing infrastructure, such as roads, by harnessing artificial intelligence techniques and data analytics; (2) effectively engaging with residents through e-Participation to improve the decision making process; and (3) intelligently responding to any changes or system disturbances in real-time.

From a transportation perspective, efficient and fast traffic simulation modelling of the transportation network enables real-time simulation of the system and application of smart artificial intelligence techniques to the transportation system. Not only that building and calibrating these simulation models require big data, but also these models themselves can generate a significant amount of data with various frequencies, and varieties; i.e., another source of big data.

To that effect, the motivation of this research is to shed some light into the big data sources that could be harnessed to build large-scale simulation platforms to enable ITS applications and smart cities; and to illustrate how simulation models themselves could be the source of generating big data. These models – along with the data used to build and calibrate them, and the data to be generated from their use in ITS applications – form a key component of smart cities as they replicate the dynamic and stochastic transportation system in a simulation environment.

2 Big Data in ITS

Big data in transportation and smart cities is related to the use of artificial intelligence and digital technology in order to improve the performance of the existing services and to achieve the optimal usage of the infrastructure. This is exactly the definition of the ITS. In this section, we show how big data is a core part of ITS using a few examples. For instance, the advances in ICT and automobile manufacturing sectors have motivated the ongoing research on connected vehicles. With the number of vehicles reaching 1.18 billion vehicles in 2013 (25 % increase from 2006) [10], the emergence to the smart connected vehicles becomes a must rather than a choice. In fact, most modern smart cities have the minimum required intelligent infrastructure to be compatible with these connected vehicles. According to [11], a connected vehicle today has about 40 microprocessors and hundreds of sensors, and generates more than 25 GB of data per hour. Considering only 1 % penetration of the 1.18 billion vehicles above could easily translate to 280 PB of data per hour. With this potential massive set of data, a number of questions arise: Could it be processed and analyzed in real-time? What are the travel patterns and sensory information that could be inferred from this data? Could this data be integrated with other sources such as weather and social media? The answer to these questions could open up new possibilities and applications that would easily change the ITS and transportation systems all together.

Another recent example of big data in transportation is the naturalistic driving study, which is part of the Strategic Highway Research Program 2 (SHRP 2) experiments. In this single study, large volumes of data from more than 3000 drivers in the United States were collected to better understand drivers' behaviors and hence improve the safety on the roads [12]. The collected data includes: driving, driver, crash, and roadway data obtained by cameras and sensors installed in the vehicle and attached to the driver. In 2014, the collected data was estimated to exceed 4 PB from multiple sources with about 5.4 million trips covered representing about 3,958 vehicle-years of data.

As discussed earlier, simulation platforms are integral part of enabling ITS applications in both real-time and off-line testing and modelling of smart cities. The next section discusses a case study of developing an enabling big data simulation platform for the Greater Toronto Area (GTA).

3 Big Data Simulation Platform for the GTA

Although developing a traffic simulation model to test what-if scenarios is becoming a best practice and known among the research community; we approach the simulation platform in this paper as an enabler for big data applications in traffic and ITS. In this section, we present a big data simulation platform for the GTA, which includes: a simulation-based dynamic traffic assignment (DTA) model, a set of analytics, and of a lot of data collected from multiple sources within the region. This platform is an important step towards the smart city of Toronto; the digital city that utilizes all available data to improve the traffic and safety conditions on its roads. Currently, this platform is being used in many applications, such as minimizing evacuation travel time in case of severe disasters, implementing dynamic congestion pricing over some corridors in the GTA, and deciding optimal investment decisions for regional transportation planning projects. In this section, we present the structure of the proposed model, how it was built, and its outputs. Thereafter, the calibration of the model is presented, showing the different criteria used to adjust the parameters of the model. Finally, the section concludes with a brief discussion on the challenges and data issues faced during building, calibrating, and using the model.

3.1 Model Input Data: Volume, Variety, Veracity and Value

A number of data sources have been used to build the DTA model. It started with a comprehensive GIS database from Land Information Ontario (LIO) warehouse as shown in Fig. 1. The model covers more than 7000 km^2 and consists of 26,446 links, including all highways and major arterials in the GTA, and 14,228 nodes, including 830 signalized intersections.

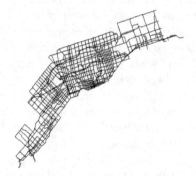

Fig. 1. The GTA network obtained from LIO

Although that the value of the GIS database was great to form the basis for the model geometry, it suffered from a number of missing items that accentuate the need to further refine the data and complete the missing data. The following are tasks to illustrate the effort required to refine the data for such big area: encoding locations and timing of 800+ signalized intersections; defining location of thousands of off and on ramps to the highway network; preventing U-turn movements at the signalized intersections; and checking the number of lanes and geometry of more than half the network.

3.1.1 Travel Demand and Traffic Zones

After the network geometry was prepared, the travel demand data has to be prepared and fed into the simulation model. For such big area, the number of trips travelled across the region is captured through the Transportation Tomorrow Survey, which is one of the largest surveys in North America [13]. The travel demand is then translated to form of trips from origins to destinations (OD matrices). To reflect on the volume and frequency of the demand data, an OD matrix with 2.25 million cells (1500 origins to 1500 destinations) has to be generated each 15 min, for the AM peak period (from 6 AM to 10 AM); resulting in 36 million OD cell records fed into the simulation model. During this period, about 2 million trips traverse the GTA network and their individual traces are stored in a min per min basis.

Quality and veracity of the demand data are vital to ensure the accuracy of the simulation model. To that effect, two issues arose after extracting the TTS demand data. *First*, the number of generated trips every 15 min exhibited significant flip-flopping demand pattern due to the fact that travelers have a tendency to report their departure time on a half-hour basis, instead of using the exact time 15 min interval. To resolve this issue, the OD matrices were filtered through a mathematical procedure to generate a smooth demand curve while maintaining the same total number of trips as shown in Fig. 2.

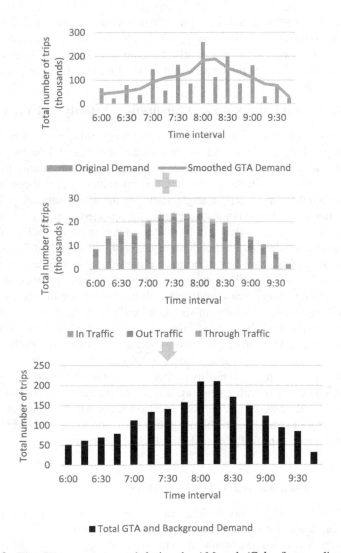

Fig. 2. The GTA travel demand during the AM peak (Color figure online)

Second, the TTS demand matrices did not consider the fact at 6 AM there is traffic in the network, the so-called background demand. This background demand shall include three types of trips: (1) from outside the GTA to the core of the network, (2) from the GTA to outside the network, and (3) from and to zones outside the GTA but passing through some routes within the network. To resolve this issue, a model of the Greater Toronto and Hamilton Area was simulated to get information about vehicles that meet the above conditions and the simulation results were analyzed to find the path for each vehicle, which can be traversed to find out the number of vehicles/trips in each category. Figure 2 shows the background demand during the AM peak and the total number of extra OD trips added to each time interval. About 260,000 trips have been added to the original demand. The total smoothed demand of the GTA, including these trips, is shown in Fig. 2, and estimated as 1.9 million trips.

The above input data examples clearly demonstrate the *v*olume and *v*ariety of the required data to develop the basic geometry and demand of the simulation model; but what is probably more important is to reflect on the additional significant effort exerted to deal with issues related to the *v*eracity and *v*alue of the data to the application at hand.

3.2   Model Output Data: Volume, Visualization, Velocity and Variability

Using the simulation modelling platform, various types of outputs can be generated: at the network-level, e.g., total travel time, travelled distance, and time lost in traffic; and corridor and facility level, e.g., speed over a link, queue length at an intersection, and travel path of a vehicle. Simulation outputs vary in *v*olume and *v*elocity. For instance, while the total travel time is only a single value for the whole network produced at the end of the simulation, traffic counts over links are reported minute by minute for each single link. In the GTA model, this translates to 1.6 million readings for only one measure that characterizes traffic each hour of the simulation (i.e., traffic counts or flows on links). Considering other key performance measures; such as average speed, free flow speed, traffic density, toll revenues, and queues of vehicles; this data could easily result in 10 million readings each hour; 40 million readings for the morning rush hour; and 240 million readings for a day of simulated traffic data for the GTA. Additionally, detailed vehicle trajectory data are available for each vehicle. The spatio-temporal paths of vehicles generate more than 17 million node-arrival time pairs each hour, and are updated almost second by second. A sample of vehicles' paths is shown in Fig. 3. Although the large *v*olume and *v*elocity of this fast-produced traffic data poses a number of challenges associated with extracting useful information and making informative decisions in real time, it also introduces an opportunity for data analytics and visual-ization techniques to translate this humongous set of data to meaningful information in an intuitive manner, especially for real-time ITS applications.

3.3   Model Calibration and Validation: More Vs

After defining the model inputs, building the model, and extracting model outputs and measures, the calibration and validation of the model cannot be overemphasized. The calibration process consisted of multiple interrelated steps, including: a comparison

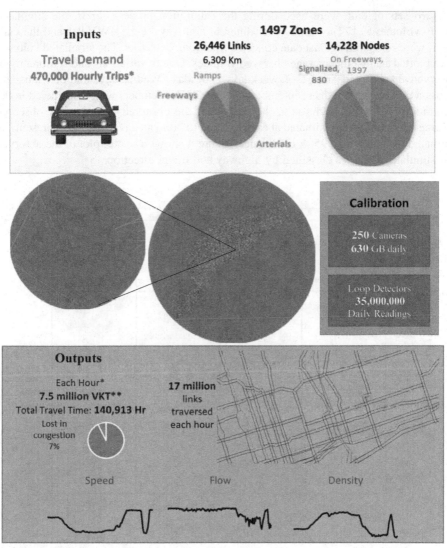

Fig. 3. Inputs and outputs of the GTA model, and calibration data

between observed and simulated measures, such as traffic speed and volume, to evaluate the accuracy of the model; and tweaking some specific parameters, e.g., traffic flow model parameters, OD matrices, and network geometry-related parameters, to improve the calibration results. Figure 3 shows the various inputs and outputs of the model, and sources of data used in calibration of the model, e.g., loop detectors with readings updated every 20 s for each single lane, camera feeds from about 250 different locations, hundreds of daily Twitter reports, and google maps.

Two sets of data were used during the calibration process. *First*, the simulated hourly volumes at 177 locations over different highways, e.g., HWY401 and the Gardiner, were compared against data collected from loop detectors. The simulated volumes were plotted against the average observed volumes. Due to variations and seasonality of observed data, a wide range of weekdays (Tuesday, Wednesday, and/or Thursday) across a number of months (September, October, or November) were considered in the calibration process. In addition to the average of the observed volumes, the observed volume variations were estimated at each location to build an envelope that represents an estimated interval with a 95 % confidence. Figure 4 shows a scatter plot of the observed and simulated volumes classified by highway and travel direction.

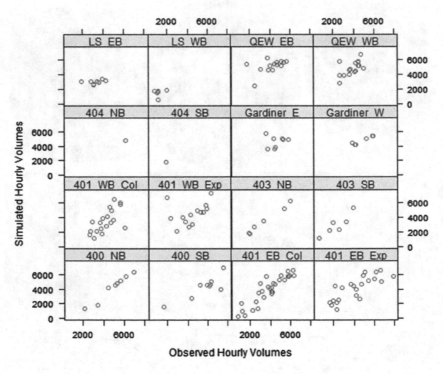

Fig. 4. Scatter plot of the observed and simulated hourly volumes

Second, observed speeds are compared against simulated speeds. Like the traffic volumes, the observed speeds were obtained from detectors every 20 s. The comparison was held between the simulated speeds, and the average observed speeds and their envelopes which are defined as intervals contain the average speed at confidence level of 95 %. The results showed that simulated speeds follow a similar pattern as this of the observed speeds as shown in Fig. 5.

Afterwards, some OD trip demand tables were adjusted to ensure calibrated speeds and flows/volumes. More than 1300 trips travelling during the AM peak were analyzed to obtain their origins and destinations. These OD pairs were adjusted (increased/decreased) based on how much they affect the traffic flows and speeds across

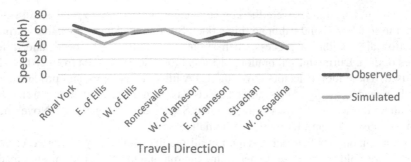

Fig. 5. Lake shore Blvd EB: observed and simulated speeds (Color figure online)

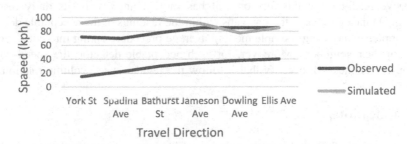

Fig. 6. Gardiner expressway WB: speeds before demand calibration (Color figure online)

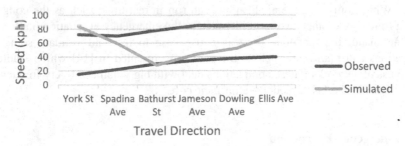

Fig. 7. Gardiner expressway WB: speeds after demand calibration (Color figure online)

key corridors throughout the network. Sometimes additional demand imposes more traffic and therefore creates realistic congestion such as the case of the Gardiner WB. The simulated speeds before and after demand calibration are plotted with the observed speed envelope in Figs. 6 and 7, respectively.

3.4 Data Issues and Challenges

As discussed above, a number of data challenges were faced while dealing with this big data simulation platform for the GTA. The GTA network contains thousands of links and nodes, and millions of vehicles. Not only the volume of data, size of the network, and variety of data sources were the key challenges; but also the veracity and value of the data used to build and calibrate this model. Similar challenges appeared during the calibration and validation process, such as large volumes, high speed, and different' sources of data. During the calibration, historical loop detectors data from 2010 to 2012 were used. These loop detectors cover the GTA highway network and produced about 40 million readings a day. These large datasets has been filtered to get only traffic speed and volume during weekdays within months: September, October, and November, to match the travel demand fed into the simulation.

As a common problem in big data, not all readings are always reported correctly. Hence, a threshold has been set to determine the maximum number of missing readings which maintain the data quality at an acceptable level. The threshold was set such that a detector will be excluded either if it is down for more than a minute, i.e., three successive readings are missing, or if it has more than 5 % of its daily readings missing. On the other hand, the few gaps within the readings of the acceptable detectors were supplemented using a simple moving average procedure taking into consideration values of their neighbors. Moreover, for each acceptable detector, the speed-volume relationship is checked to verify that it follow the regular speed-volume relation.

4 Applications

The proposed platform is currently being used in some real applications and will be used in more applications in the next few years. In this section, we give a brief overview on the applications that have used and are currently using the proposed GTA model. While some of these applications can run in real-time, such as the congestion pricing framework; others work offline, such as the emergency evacuation platform. On the other hand, the model is used as a use case to test and validate some other applications and platforms, such as the platform presented in [14] which studies the robustness of networks. These applications deal with big volumes of very frequent data as they contain the GTA model within their core.

4.1 Emergency Evacuation

In [15], authors presented a multi-objective optimization framework for emergency evacuation and tested it with the city of Toronto as a use case. This platform minimizes the in-vehicle travel time, the at-origin waiting time, and the fleet cost in the case of mass evacuation. It has been tested for evacuating more than 1 million persons from Toronto based on travel demand extracted from TTS-2001. A lot of changes have occurred through the last decade, and the TTS-2001 dataset became obsolete. Hence, the evacuation platform is currently running using the new simulation GTA model presented in this paper. The new application run aims to produce up-to-date results match the current population of Toronto and to test a different implementation scheme of the evacuation platform where it runs on a virtual infrastructure.

In the current version of the evacuation platform, the optimization is done by Genetic Algorithm (GA) which runs on different virtual machines on the NSERC strategic network for Smart Applications on Virtual Infrastructure (SAVI). It is a network that provides various applications with a flexible platform where they can run and redistributed over different virtual machines [16]. Each generation within the GA includes performing 20 simulation runs and analyzing their results. These results are in order of and millions of data records. Within each simulation run, the GA produces new pattern for travel demand by assigning different departure time for each vehicle. That includes making trip plans for millions of vehicles simultaneously.

4.2   Robust Network Design

Robust network design is widely used in many fields studying the optimal design of different network layouts that can handle the impacts of any disturbance in the network, such as weather conditions and incidents in transportation networks, excessive noise in communication networks, cyber-attacks on computer networks, and even disturbances in financial networks. The framework presented in [14] studied different robust network designs especially for transportation networks. The simulation test network started with a proof-of-concept network, and the research now has been extended to improve the performance of the simulation in [17] and was tested using the proposed GTA model. This paper presents new solutions to speed up the DTA simulation of transportation networks, especially for large-scale applications. Hence, the authors used our big data GTA model as an example of large transportation networks to test the efficiency of their algorithm.

4.3   Congestion Pricing

Dynamic congestion pricing is an ongoing research in the transportation group at University of Toronto. Unlike other congestion pricing policies, researchers at University of Toronto are working on an optimization platform that finds the optimal dynamic toll on roads to maximize the social welfare [18]. Unlike the emergency evacuation application, the dynamic pricing platform is intended to be a real-time application, which makes intensive analysis and optimization on larger volumes of data within timing constraints. In addition to the optimization, it analyzes the simulation results to get information about vehicles paths, traffic volumes and speeds, travel time, and toll revenues. Using the GTA model, the application sets dynamic tolls on the GTA's roads, while analyzing about 10 million of data records per hour.

5   Next Generation ITS and Big Data

The transportation applications illustrated above are just examples of how big data could be utilized given current data needs and simulation requirements. Such applications, which deal with big data nowadays, cannot be compared to the future applications of ITS and the expected sizes of data they will deal with. As expected by many experts, the future revolution in ITS will be the emergence of autonomous (driverless) vehicles. These self-driving vehicles are seen to be the next generation of the connected vehicles. Although some technologies already exist and some samples of these vehicles are currently under test, this is a tiny fraction of what will be available in the future.

While connected vehicles are still driven by humans and only use communication technologies to improve their efficiency and safety, driverless vehicles will be fully automated. Instead of the 25 GB generated by each connected vehicle today, the generated data from autonomous vehicles will be hundred fold greater.

Like the existing transportation applications, these future projects will soon require trustworthy models that can deal with these expected big volumes of data. Those models will be the future of existing models, such as the GTA model presented in this paper. They have to deal with very dynamic environments including tremendous volumes of data on both micro and macroscopic levels.

References

1. Laney, D.: 3D Data Management: Controlling Data Volume, Velocity, and Variety. META Group Inc., Stamford (2001)
2. Quinn, E.: Discovering big data's value with graph analytics. White Paper, Enterprise Strategy Group (2013)
3. Understanding big data: the seven V's. http://dataconomy.com/seven-vs-big-data/
4. Podesta, J., Pritzer, P., Moniz, E.J., Holdren, J., Zients, J.: Big Data: Seizing Opportunities, Preserving Values. Executive Office of the President, Washington (2014)
5. A comprehensive list of big data statistics. http://wikibon.org/blog/big-data-statistics/
6. Daas, P., Loo, M.: Big data (and official statistics) (2013)
7. Browse traffic loop detectors by list (ONE-ITS). http://128.100.217.245/web/etr-407/trafficreports2
8. Waze mobile. https://www.waze.com/
9. Roadify. http://www.roadify.com/
10. Statista Inc.: Number of passenger cars and commercial vehicles in use worldwide from 2006 to 2013 (in millions). http://www.statista.com/statistics/281134/number-of-vehicles-in-use-worldwide/
11. Hitachi Data Systems: The Internet on Wheels. Technical report (2014)
12. Campbell, J.L.: SHRP2 naturalistic driving study: data collection is complete - now what? In: Northwest Transportation Conference (2014)
13. Data Management Group at UofT: Transportation Tomorrow Survey. http://dmg.utoronto.ca/transportation-tomorrow-survey/tts-introduction
14. Koulakezian, A., Abdelgawad, H., Tizghadam, A., Abdulhai, B., Leon-Garcia, A.: Robust network design for roadway networks unifying framework and application. IEEE ITS Mag. 7(2), 34–46 (2015)
15. Abdelgawad, H., Abdulhai, B., Wahba, M.: Multiobjective optimization for multimodal evacuation. J. Transp. Res. Rec. 2196, 21–33 (2010)
16. Kang, J.-M., Lin, T., Bannazadeh, H., Leon-Garcia, A.: Software-defined infrastructure and the SAVI testbed. In: 9th International Conference on Testbeds and Research Infrastructures for the Development of Networks & Communities (Tridentcom) (2014)
17. Koulakezian, A., Graydon, W. E., Abdelgawad, H., Chiu, Y.-C., Abdulhai, B., Leon-Garcia, A.: Speedup of DTA-based simulation of large metropolises for quasi real-time ITS applications. In: IEEE 18th International Conference on ITS (2015)
18. Aboudina, A., Abdulhai, B.: Win-win dynamic congestion pricing for congested urban areas. In: ITS Canada - ACGM (2012)

Appliance Water Disaggregation
via Non-intrusive Load Monitoring (NILM)

Bradley Ellert[✉], Stephen Makonin, and Fred Popowich

Simon Fraser University, Burnaby, BC V5A 1S6, Canada
{bellert,smakonin,popowich}@sfu.ca

Abstract. The world's fresh water supply is rapidly dwindling. Informing homeowners of their water use patterns can help them reduce consumption. Today's smart meters only show a whole house's water consumption over time. People need to be able to see where they are using water most to be able to change their habits. We are the first to present work where appliance water consumption is non-intrusively disaggregated using the results from a non-intrusive load monitoring algorithm. Unlike previous works that require the installation of water sub-meters or water sensors, our method does not. Further, our method uses low-frequency data from standardized meters and does not rely on labelled data. We modify the Viterbi Algorithm to apply a supervised method to an unsupervised disaggregation problem. We are able to achieve very high accuracy results having mean squared errors of under $0.02\,\mathrm{L}^2/\mathrm{min}^2$.

Keywords: Water disaggregation · Water conservation · Non-intrusive load monitoring · NILM · Smart homes · Sustainability

1 Introduction

Globally we have become concerned with the cost of consuming energy and the lack of supply. Many studies have emerged that investigate ways to reduce consumption. Computational methods such as non-intrusive load monitoring (NILM) allow us to understand how appliances consume power [5]. Cities are increasingly becoming concerned with fresh water, where demand is also exceeding supply. Soon every house will have a water meter, if they do not already. We have the means to disaggregate appliance power usage using NILM and we demonstrate a computational method to take those disaggregation results to essentially disaggregate the water usage of appliances. This allows homeowners to understand how much water is consumed by appliance use and by human use. It is the human consumption (e.g. showering, bathing, lawn watering) that can be targeted for conservation and motivate behaviour change in our societies.

Household water consumption can be viewed as a hierarchy (Fig. 1). In the broadest sense, it can be broken down based on the agent causing the consumption: human use, appliance use, and leaks. Human use refers to fixtures that can be used for variable lengths of time with varying flow rates, such as showers and

© ICST Institute for Computer Sciences, Social Informatics and Telecommunications Engineering 2016
A. Leon-Garcia et al. (Eds.): Smart City 2015, LNICST 166, pp. 455–467, 2016.
DOI: 10.1007/978-3-319-33681-7_38

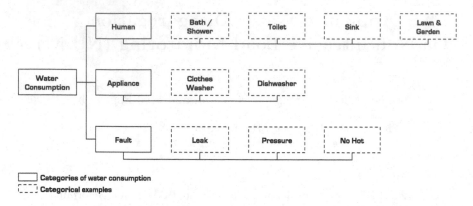

Categories of water consumption
Categorical examples

Fig. 1. Within the three sub-categories of household water consumption for households there are many examples of how water is consumed. We focus on appliances that consume water. By subtracting appliance consumption, we can inform homeowners of the amount of consumption that can be changed due to behaviour or habit.

sinks. Appliance use refers to machines that follow cycles with fixed patterns after being initiated, such as (clothes) washing machines and dishwashers. Our work focuses on finding events of this latter variety, as they can be correlated with energy consumption. Certain household water-users can be more difficult to classify. For example, toilets could be considered *appliances* as they are constrained to consuming fixed amounts of water. However based on our definition of correlating with electricity consumption, toilets fall under human use.

In this paper, we present an algorithm for disaggregating appliance water use from main water meter data given disaggregated electricity data. This allows low-frequency, unlabelled data to be used to build a model specific to each household. Domain knowledge about the general consumption patterns is not needed, as this information is learned from smart meter data. By not relying on generic ontological information, the system does not make incorrect assumptions about different makes and models of appliances and is able to be used on future appliances that may follow unforeseen patterns. This represents the first water disaggregator that has the potential of providing homeowners with detailed appliance water use information outside of a controlled setting without the need for tuning by a trained professional or the installation of non-standard metering equipment. By developing this technology alongside NILM, we open the door to a symbiotic relationship between these common related tasks, instead of relying on more obscure sensor data.

2   Previous Work

Household water disaggregation is still quite a young topic, and therefore relatively few papers have been published on the topic. Table 1 summarizes the previous work in the field of household water disaggregation. We discuss each in detail below.

Table 1. The major previous works in household water disaggregation.

Name	Group	Dates	Contribution	Measurement
Trace wizard	Aquacraft	1996 – 2004	Seminal papers	Flow rate
NAWMS	UCLA	2008	Flow rate estimate	Vibration
WaterNILM	MIT	2014	Single sensor	Vibration
HydroSense	Washington	2009 – 2014	Consumer feedback	Pressure
WaterSense	U.Va	2011 – 2013	Motion detectors	Flow rate
DSCRDM	Virginia Tech	2011 – 2013	Low sample rate	Flow rate

The first true method for water disaggregation was developed by Aquacraft, a water management company based in Boulder, Colorado [1] which performed flow trace analysis using a largely manual process. A flow trace is simply a plot of water flow rate over a period of time. This information was collected using a retrofit device that attaches to a water meter and logs flow rate every 10 s by measuring changes in magnetic field. Signature traces were first collected for each fixture and appliance in each house followed by technicians who manually labelled future examples by hand. Eventually a set of heuristics was developed to automatically categorize based on flow rate and duration. Dishwashers and washing machines were noted as difficult to disaggregate because they often co-occurred with miscellaneous faucet use. Flow trace analysis is limited to determining the fixture class (e.g. toilet, sink) of an instance of water use. Recently, the trend has been to focus on finer grained disaggregation down to the level of specific fixture (e.g. kitchen sink, bathroom sink).

NAWMS (Nonintrusive Autonomous Water Monitoring System) is the first method to demonstrate disaggregation down to the level of individual pipes [6]. The authors show that flow rate can be estimated based on pipe vibration readings collected at a frequency of 100 Hz using individual accelerometers. The flow rate of the water main was monitored to fit a model that used a cubic root curve. Although the error rate was just over 1 %, these results only serve as a proof of concept, as their approach was not able to scale up, requiring dozens of sensors in a realistic setting.

More recently, WaterNILM (Non-Intrusive Load Monitoring) applied a similar physical architecture to a real-world setting [12]. The authors developed a technique requiring only two accelerometers (12 kHz–16 kHz) for an entire house. One was installed downstream from the water meter and the other at the outlet of the hot water tank. These readings are down-sampled to 4 kHz and the stream is segmented into 0.75 s chunks. Models were built using labelled data to create clusters. In the best case, they were able to achieve a misclassification rate under 2 %. However, addressing simultaneous water use requires training examples of each possible combination in question. Further, true disaggregation is not performed, as only the combined labels were identified as the source.

HydroSense introduced a simple single point sensor for whole house water pressure that took readings at a rate of 1 kHz [4]. This sensor was attached to an unused outside tap to infer approximate flow rate. In each home hand-labelled data was collected. Baseline static water pressure was measured and pressure signatures were taken for each valve (hot and cold) on each fixture using their proprietary HydroSense unit. Valve events were classified as open or close based on the change in pressure or the average derivative if the pressure did not exceed a fixed threshold. Valve events were associated with individual fixtures by their similarity to other events in the same home via a trained classifier. Average home error rates were reported to be around 5 %. However, this method was very sensitive to the location where the pressure sensor was installed. This process required the installation of a pressure sensor and labelled training data to train the classifier – a very expensive procedure.

Other than the original flow trace analysis, the previously mentioned methods relied on sensors that monitored a house's plumbing. WaterSense instead utilizes data captured by motion sensors to help with water disaggregation [13]. Unlike the previous approaches where supervised learning was required, WaterSense claimed to be unsupervised. The house's water main is monitored at a frequency of 2 Hz and motion detectors were read once every 7 s. Motion sensors were installed in three rooms with water fixtures (two bathrooms and kitchen). Water meter samples discovered using edge detection were clustered into rooms based on the temporal proximity of motion sensor readings. Toilets are differentiated from sinks simply by having an average flow rate greater than 0.3 kL/hr and a duration greater than 30 s. Accuracies between 80 %–90 % were reported. This approach only focuses on the *human* side of our hierarchy defined in Fig. 1. The *appliance* side used flow trace analysis. The need for additional water monitoring devices is reduced but the installation of motion sensors is required.

The aforementioned methods rely on moderate- to high-frequency sampling to allow for the detection of rising and falling edges in water usage data. Corresponding to a real-world setting with commodity hardware and privacy concerns, it makes sense to restrict oneself to lower frequency data streams. Unfortunately, this makes the problem of water disaggregation much more difficult with the loss of event granularity.

DSCRDM (Deep Sparse Coding Based Recursive Disaggregation Model) formulates the problem by iteratively decomposing the aggregate water reading one device at a time [2]. After the first device has been separated, the second device is disaggregated from the residual, and so on until one device remains. Using the flow trace data from an Aquacraft study [10], they were able to achieve F-measures of: above 70 % for the shower, 35 % for the toilet, and 45 % for the washing machine. Sampling at such a low frequency means that the results are more useful for seeing longterm consumption rather than the consumption while a specific appliance/faucet is being used.

Water disaggregation has been dominated by studies that rely on high-frequency data, proprietary meters, and/or labelled datasets. The focus has been on disaggregating subtleties in human use before more fundamental parts of the problem have been solved. In contrast, we use low-frequency data (per minute) from standardized meters and do not rely on labelled data to disaggregate appliance water use from household water data. Note, smart meters report readings at $\frac{1}{8}$ Hz within the house.

3   Our Approach

We leverage data from electricity disaggregation to help with water disaggregation. Given the electrical state of a water-consuming appliance and the whole house water meter reading, the goal is to build a model that can predict the amount of water used by the appliance. Figure 2 shows an outline of our NILM system.

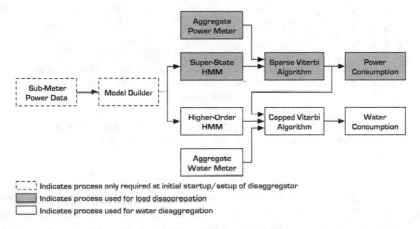

Fig. 2. A block diagram depicting how water disaggregation is a part of a whole NILM process. NILM appliance classification is used by the water disaggregator to disaggregate that appliance's water consumption.

3.1   Disaggregating Electricity

In [7], a method for non-intrusive load monitoring is provided. By quantizing the electricity readings of an appliance based on peaks in its probability mass function (PMF), the time series can be viewed as a list of discrete state transitions. These states may correlate to different functions of the appliance. For example, in the dishwasher, one may represent the electricity consumed when the water pump is on, while another may represent the electricity consumed when the heating element is on.

For our purposes, we assume we have a method for obtaining the series of states an appliance transitions through, given the series of whole house electricity readings. The method described in [7] determines the entire house's superstate (a combined state representing the state of each appliance simultaneously) at once. A Hidden Markov Model is built that takes the whole house's electricity reading as input and produces the house's superstate as output.

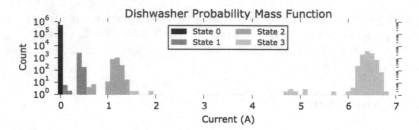

Fig. 3. Dishwasher PMF with unnormalized counts to depict the scale of the dataset used. Most of the time the dishwasher is in the OFF state. When it is ON, it is in one of three other distinct states.

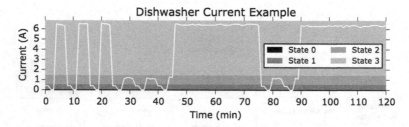

Fig. 4. Current (A) readings for one dishwasher example. States emerge from peaks within the histogram. The exact current reading does not matter, but rather the state the dishwasher is in.

To build and test our model we used The Almanac of Minutely Power Dataset (AMPds) [9]. AMPds is a standardized, low-frequency dataset capturing meter information from a household in the Greater Vancouver region of British Columbia, Canada. It is designed with disaggregation in mind, providing data for electricity, water, and natural gas. Compared to other datasets for this purpose, this data is of extremely high quality and has been cleaned to ensure that different researchers will be working from the same starting point. The dataset contains two years of data from the beginning of April 2012 to the end of March 2014. Meters read in at a rate of once per minute. This means there are over one million records for each meter. In addition to the main electricity meter there are 20 sub-meters (one of which is for the dishwasher), resulting in over 20 million total electricity records. The electricity readings are taken by two DENT PowerScout 18 units.

To test our model, we just use the sub-metered ground truth current to determine the appliance's state. States are assigned by using peaks in the appliance's PMF to discretize the raw current reading. Figure 3 shows the PMF for the dishwasher's current reading which are algorithmically determined [7]. Note that the logarithmic scale means that readings of 0 far outnumber other readings. This is the OFF state. When this appliance is ON, three additional distinct peaks form. Using this method on an example dishwasher run from AMPds, we obtain Fig. 4.

3.2 Disaggregating Water

For water there are only meters for the main and the instant hot water unit, resulting in over two million total water records. Elster/Kent V100 water meters are used to take the water readings. Each record includes a pulse counter (litres), the average rate (litres per minute), and the instantaneous rate (litres per minute). This means there are over three million data points for each water meter, resulting in over six million water data points total. For our purposes we only need the average flow rate, which can also be determined directly from the change in the pulse counter, since we are measuring in L/min and pulses are recorded once per minute. Water readings are collected in half-litre pulses. For the first few months of AMPds, the water meters were only set to pulse at every gallon (3.785 L). Due to this, we only consider the second year of AMPds.

Figure 5 shows the whole house water readings during the example from Fig. 4. Looking at the state changes alongside, a clear pattern emerges. In the case of the dishwasher, water is used in spurts of roughly 3 L over the course of two minutes. We can clearly see that only using an appliance's electrical state and the whole house's water consumption from a few points in time is necessary to provide a good indication of whether the water use is due to the appliance in question or from something else in the house.

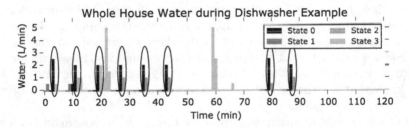

Fig. 5. Whole house water readings for one dishwasher example. Circled amounts are from the dishwasher consuming water – a repeating pattern of 2 L followed by 1 L.

Hidden Markov Models (HMMs) are designed to capture these kinds of relationships. Our solution requires some modifications to the traditional formulation. Like an unsupervised scenario, we do not have labelled data to train with. Unlike an unsupervised scenario, we have some prior knowledge about the output we are looking for (i.e. each appliance's water use is bound above by the whole house's water reading). Machine learning methods use HMMs for efficiently modelling and learning patterns in state transitions over time [11]. They rely on the Markov assumption that a state at a given point in time being dependent on all previous states can be simplified to only being a conditional probability on a single previous state. A standard HMM can be defined as HMM $= \{h, o, \mathbf{S}, \mathbf{T}, \mathbf{E}\}$, where h is the number of possible hidden states, o is the number of possible observed states, $\mathbf{S}$ is the start probability vector (of length h), $\mathbf{T}$ is the transition probability matrix ($h \times h$), and $\mathbf{E}$ is the emission probability matrix $(h \times o)$. Where there exists a finite sequence of hidden states, $H = (h_0, h_1, h_2, \ldots, h_T), h_t \in 0..h - 1$, and a finite sequence of observed states, $O = (o_0, o_1, o_2, \ldots, o_T), o_t \in 0..o - 1$, both of length T. In a first-order HMM, the probability of being in a given hidden state at time t is only conditioned on the hidden state at time $t - 1$. The probability of seeing a given observed state at time t is only conditioned on the hidden state at that time.

In the problem we are trying to solve, we know the appliance is in the OFF state (State 0) outside of the extracted samples regardless of the representation we choose. We prepend a 0 hidden state to H and a 0 observed state to O to simplify the start probabilities. With this $\mathbf{S} = [1]$, a simple one-element vector since the probability of starting in state 0 is 100 %. This simplifies things when we look at higher-order models later.

3.3   Capped Viterbi Algorithm

The Viterbi Algorithm is a dynamic programming solution to the problem of finding the most likely sequence of hidden states corresponding to a sequence of observed states [3,14]. Running through the steps of the algorithm can be visualized with a trellis diagram. At each point in time, only the most likely path leading there needs to be considered.

For our particular problem, we know the electrical state of the appliance and the whole house water reading at each point in time. We want to find the disaggregated water reading for the appliance in question. Since we do not have sub-metered water data, we cannot use a standard supervised learning method. Conversely, we do not want to use a standard unsupervised learning method, because we have prior knowledge about the disaggregated water reading. That is, we know that it must be in half-litre increments and is bound above by the whole house water reading.

To utilize this information, we formulate the model as we would if we were learning the whole house water reading given only the electrical state of one appliance. This means the hidden states are the range of possible whole house water readings in half-litre increments and the observed states are the appliance's electrical states. Since we already have both of these pieces of information, we can use a supervised training method. The intuition behind this is that we are purposely *under-fitting* the data in the hopes that we are left with only the disaggregated reading we are looking for when predicting. Instances where the appliance in question is the only thing consuming water (i.e. the whole house water reading is exactly the desired answer) are more consistent with each other and train the model to ignore noise from the rest of the house.

Not only do we have access to the true hidden labels at training time, but we also know them for the sequences we want to predict. Of course we do not want our model to outright see this information, as this would just leave us with the whole house water readings we already know. Instead, we provide this information as a *hint* to the Viterbi Algorithm.

We call this variant the Capped Viterbi Algorithm. In addition to the sequence of observed states O, our algorithm takes as input a sequence of upper bounds (or *caps*) on the hidden states $C = (c_0, c_1, c_2, \ldots, c_T), c_t \in 0..h - 1$. For the problem at hand, this is the whole house water meter reading (which is used as H when training). Pseudocode for the Capped Viterbi Algorithm is as follows:

```
input:  C = (c_0, c_1, c_2, ..., c_T)  // the sequence of caps
        O = (0, o_0 , o_1 , o_2 , ..., o_T)
        S = [s_j]
        T = [t_(i,j)]
        E = [e_(j,n)]
Output: H = (h_0, h_1, h_2, ..., h_T)
for j in S do
  H[j] = ();  // the most likely sequence H ending in j
  P[j] = s_j*e_(j,0); // P[x] is the probability of H[x]
end
for t = 0 to T do
  for j = 0 to c_t do  // where c_t is the current cap
    newP[j] = max_(i in P) P[i]*t_(i,j)*e_(j,o_t);
    newH[j] = H[argmax_(i in P) P[i]*t_(i,j)*e_(j,o_t)] + j;
  end
  P = newP;
  H = newH;
end
return H[argmax_(i in P) P[i]]
```

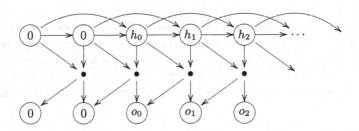

Fig. 6. Our modified second-order HMM. The relationship with the observed states is not a standard second-order HMM. Bullets line up with t where emission pairs are taken into account when predicting the optimal hidden state sequence.

A simple first-order model is not able to capture the relationships in our dataset. Using a second-order model variation, we get $\mathbf{T}$ being a $h^2 \times h$ matrix and $\mathbf{E}$ being an $h^2 \times o^2$ matrix where $t_{(i_2,i),j} = P(h_t = j | h_{t-2} = i_2, h_{t-1} = i)$ and $e_{(i,j),(m,n)} = P(o_{t-1} = m, o_t = n | h_{t-1} = i, h_t = j)$. Figure 6 shows the modified model. Compare this to a standard second-order model where the emission matrix is the same as in a standard first-order model. In our case, pairs of hidden states emit pairs of observed states.

This is easily generalized to higher-order models. There are h^T possible sequences of hidden states for a given sequence of observed states. The standard first-order Viterbi algorithm finds the optimal sequence by only looking at h possibilities for each hidden state at each point in time. This results in an $O(h^2T)$ running time. Generalizing to order-n models, it looks at h^n possibilities for each hidden state at each point in time, giving a running time of $O(h^{n+1}T)$.

The Capped Viterbi Algorithm reduces the search space by only looking at $\prod_{x=t-n}^{t-1} c_x \leq h^n$ possibilities for each hidden state up to $c_t \leq h$ at each point in time. In the worst case $C = (h, h, \ldots, h)$, keeping the $O(h^{n+1}T)$ running time. Empirically the running time is much less than this, as usually little to no water is being used in the house relative to the highest recorded water consumption. The running time is also kept low by only keeping track of subsequences with non-zero probabilities. This is especially significant in higher-order models where $\mathbf{T}$ is quite sparse.

To ensure there is at least one possible path with a non-zero probability at each point in time, we ensure that every entry in the 0 column of $\mathbf{T}$ is non-zero (i.e. every row can transition to the OFF hidden state). This maintains the sparsity of $\mathbf{T}$ while allowing any path to *zero-out*. $\mathbf{E}$ is smoothed by averaging out the 0 and 1 counts in each row before normalizing. Effectively, the singular counts are spread out to emissions with no count. The intuition behind this is that the number of fluke single observations give an indication of the probability of a previously unseen emission. In cases where there are no 1 counts, all of the 0 counts are set to 1.

4   Experimental Results

Here we provide the results of a formal evaluation of the performance of our model on AMPds. By hand-labelling the dishwasher water data, we are able to conduct a quantitative analysis. 185 dishwasher runs were extracted from the second year of AMPds. These were divided into 10 sets with 18 or 19 samples each. 10-fold cross-validation was used to evaluate the performance of first-order,

Table 2. Results of different n-order HMMs. Disaggregation in not performed in the first row where the aggregate water reading is just assumed to be the dishwasher.

Order	Explained variance	Mean squared error (L^2/min^2)	Training time (μs per point)	Testing time (μs per point)
—	−33.648582	9.238157	—	—
1	0.000000	0.249550	3.70	55.1
2	0.932241	0.015590	7.75	94.1
3	**0.938049**	**0.014253**	**32.5**	**113**
4	0.902036	0.022544	195	125

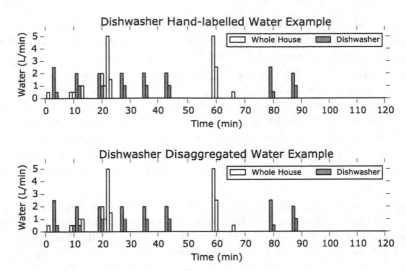

Fig. 7. Results example: (top) hand-labelled ground truth for one dishwasher example, and (bottom) output of third-order HMM on this example. The labeller was able to use knowledge from nearby actions to more accurately label difficult cases; e.g. there are multiple ways to determine 3 L in the second burst of water.

second-order, third order, and forth-order models. The results[1] are presented in Table 2 along with average running times per data point.

The first-order model is not able to capture any of the relationships in the dataset, as shown by the Explained Variance of 0. In fact, it just labels the dishwasher's water consumption as 0 L at every point in time. This acts as a good baseline because it shows that even only looking at times when the dishwasher is running, most of the time it is not consuming water. A mean squared error of $0.25\,L^2/min^2$ is trivial to achieve.

As expected, the second-order model performs considerably better. The third-order model shows minor improvements over this. Once we reach the fourth-order model, we begin to see diminishing returns. This is due to the extreme sparsity of such a high order model. Note that the testing time (Capped Viterbi Algorithm) does not grow exponentially as with the training time (including smoothing).

Figure 7 (top) shows the hand-labelled ground truth for the example from Figs. 4 and 5. The output of the third-order model when run on these examples is shown in Fig. 7 (bottom). We are able to almost capture the exact water usage.

5   Conclusion

The field of household water disaggregation has tended towards studies that focus on teasing out low-level differences between similar fixtures. In doing so,

---

[1] Classification measures [8] were not used. As NILM has predetermined classification for us, we only need to measure the amount of error in our results.

non-standard sensors must be introduced to collect additional data. By situating the problem in terms of a hierarchy, we were able to pinpoint the level to which disaggregated water information is helpful to homeowners.

This work is the first to present non-intrusive water disaggregation using the results from a non-intrusive load monitoring algorithm. There is no need to install water sub-meters to build a model of water consumption. Further, our work allows a data model to be built that does not require tuning by an expert. Our water disaggregator achieves very high accuracy results having mean squared errors of under $0.02L^2/min^2$. Future work may include combining our method with other aforementioned methods to disaggregate human water usage.

Acknowledgments. Research was supported by NSERC, including an Alexander Graham Bell Canada Graduate Scholarship, and a number of awards given by SFU's Dean of Graduate Studies: a Provost Prize of Distinction, a C.D. Nelson Memorial Graduate Scholarship, and a Graduate Fellowship.

References

1. DeOreo, W.B., Heaney, J.P., Mayer, P.W.: Flow trace analysis to assess water use. J. Am. Water Works Assoc. **88**(1), 79–90 (1996)
2. Dong, H., Wang, B., Lu, C.T.: Deep sparse coding based recursive disaggregation model for water conservation. In: Proceedings of the Twenty-Third International Joint Conference on Artificial Intelligence, pp. 2804–2810 (2013)
3. Forney Jr., G.D.: The viterbi algorithm. Proc. IEEE **61**(3), 268–278 (1973)
4. Froehlich, J., Larson, E., Campbell, T., Haggerty, C., Fogarty, J., Patel, S.N.: HydroSense: infrastructure-mediated single-point sensing of whole-home water activity. In: Proceedings of the 11th International Conference on Ubiquitous Computing, pp. 235–244 (2009)
5. Hart, G.W.: Prototype nonintrusive appliance load monitor. MIT Energy Laboratory and Electric Power Research Institute Technical report (1985)
6. Kim, Y., Schmid, T., Charbiwala, Z.M., Friedman, J., Srivastava, M.B.: NAWMS: nonintrusive autonomous water monitoring system. In: Proceedings of the 6th ACM Conference on Embedded Network Sensor Systems, SenSys 2008, pp. 309–322. ACM, New York (2008)
7. Makonin, S., Bajic, I.V., Popowich, F.: Efficient sparse matrix processing for nonintrusive load monitoring (NILM). In: 2nd International Workshop on Non-Intrusive Load Monitoring (2014)
8. Makonin, S., Popowich, F.: Nonintrusive load monitoring (NILM) performance evaluation. Energy Effi. **8**, 1–6 (2014)
9. Makonin, S., Popowich, F., Bartram, L., Gill, B., Bajic, I.V.: AMPds: a public dataset for load disaggregation and eco-feedback research. In: Electrical Power & Energy Conference, pp. 1–6 (2013)
10. Mayer, P.W., DeOreo, W.B., Opitz, E.M., Kiefer, J.C., Davis, W.Y., et al.: Residential End Uses of Water. American Water Works Association, Denver (1999)
11. Rabiner, L.: A tutorial on hidden markov models and selected applications in speech recognition. Proc. IEEE **77**(2), 257–286 (1989)
12. Schantz, C., Donnal, J., Sennett, B., Gillman, M., Muller, S., Leeb, S.: Water non-intrusive load monitoring. IEEE Sens. J. **PP**(99), 1 (2014)

13. Srinivasan, V., Stankovic, J., Whitehouse, K.: WaterSense: water flow disaggregation using motion sensors. In: Proceedings of the Third ACM Workshop on Embedded Sensing Systems for Energy-Efficiency in Buildings, BuildSys 2011, pp. 19–24. ACM, New York (2011)
14. Viterbi, A.J.: Error bounds for convolutional codes and an asymptotically optimum decoding algorithm. IEEE Trans. Inf. Theory **13**(2), 260–269 (1967)

Seismic Source Modeling by Clustering Earthquakes and Predicting Earthquake Magnitudes

Mahdi Hashemi[✉] and Hassan A. Karimi

Geoinformatics Laboratory,
School of Information Sciences, University of Pittsburgh,
135 North Bellefield Avenue, Pittsburgh, PA 15260, USA
m.hashemi1987@gmail.com, hkarimi@pitt.edu

Abstract. Seismic sources are currently generated manually by experts, a process which is not efficient as the size of historical earthquake databases is growing. However, large historical earthquake databases provide an opportunity to generate seismic sources through data mining techniques. In this paper, we propose hierarchical clustering of historical earthquakes for generating seismic sources automatically. To evaluate the effectiveness of clustering in producing homogenous seismic sources, we compare the accuracy of earthquake magnitude prediction models before and after clustering. Three prediction models are experimented: decision tree, SVM, and kNN. The results show that: (1) the clustering approach leads to improved accuracy of prediction models; (2) the most accurate prediction model and the most homogenous seismic sources are achieved when earthquakes are clustered based on their non-spatial attributes; and (3) among the three prediction models experimented in this work, decision tree is the most accurate one.

Keywords: Clustering · Prediction · Seismic source · Earthquake · Big data

1 Introduction

The study of earthquake ground motions and associated hazards and risks play an important role in sustainable development especially in earthquake-prone areas such as southwestern United States [1, 2]. Reliable evaluation of seismic hazards and risks is a foundation for all earthquake mitigation plans, upon which decision makers can prepare for earthquakes in an optimal way. The first step in any seismic hazard analysis is earthquake source modeling [3, 4]. A single earthquake source is supposed to be uniform in terms of earthquake potential, i.e., the chance of an earthquake of a given magnitude occurring is the same throughout the source. Sources may be linear or areal [4] and are usually used to generate hazard maps and estimate the probability of earthquakes of different magnitudes [5]. Large collections of historical earthquakes have made it possible to construct these sources more efficiently. Seismologists usually determine the boundary of seismic sources manually based on historical earthquakes and tectonic features [6–8] with no standard or automatic method in place. However, as the size of historical earthquake databases grows, the manual delineation of source

© ICST Institute for Computer Sciences, Social Informatics and Telecommunications Engineering 2016
A. Leon-Garcia et al. (Eds.): Smart City 2015, LNICST 166, pp. 468–478, 2016.
DOI: 10.1007/978-3-319-33681-7_39

boundaries becomes more cumbersome and less accurate. This calls for development of approaches to automate the same process.

Anderson and Nanjo [2] clustered earthquakes based on their distance in space and time and proposed an optimal distance and time interval, obtained experimentally, for clustering earthquakes. Zmazek et al. [9] used a decision tree to predict the radon concentration in soil based on environmental variables. They found that the accuracy of their prediction model changes during seismically active periods comparing with seismically inactive periods. They proposed to predict the time of earthquakes based on this observation. Hashemi and Alesheikh [10] used spatial data mining techniques and indices to reveal the characteristics of earthquakes. They clustered earthquakes around a fault in one class and showed that the earthquake magnitudes in each class are neither spatially correlated nor have any spatial trend, though the earthquakes themselves are strongly clustered at multiple distances. They suggested, as future research, developing prediction models of earthquake characteristics.

The work in this paper is focused on developing a methodology for generating areal seismic sources based on historical earthquakes. Different from previous approaches, the proposed methodology benefits from hierarchical clustering technique [11–13] and is for the purpose of automating the process. Faults, tectonic features and linear sources are not considered in this work. Three clustering approaches are explored:

(a) hierarchical clustering only based on non-spatial attributes,
(b) hierarchical clustering only based on location, and
(c) hierarchical clustering based on all attributes.

The purpose of clustering is to categorize similar events together. When events are earthquakes, this process coincides with the purpose of seismic source modeling. Thus, assuming similar earthquakes are clustered correctly, one should be able to develop more accurate prediction models in each cluster than without clustering. The proposed prediction model in this work aims to predict the magnitude of an earthquake based on its other characteristics. A different prediction model is required for each cluster. Assuming the first clustering approach (a above) results in n clusters, there should be n prediction models, one for each cluster. Consequently if the second and third clustering approaches (b and c above) result in m and k clusters, respectively, there should be m prediction models for the second one and k prediction models for the third one. Decision tree, SVM and kNN [11–13] are three different prediction models experimented in this work, resulting in a total of $3 \times n \times m \times k$ different prediction models. These prediction models are evaluated using 10-fold cross validation. The accuracy of a prediction model not only reveals the strength and suitability of the applied prediction model (decision tree, SVM or kNN), but also demonstrates the effectiveness of clustering in producing homogenous seismic sources. Thus, by comparing and analyzing the evaluation results, suggestions are made at the end of this article regarding appropriate clustering approaches and prediction models for earthquakes. Figure 1 shows the process of clustering earthquakes and predicting earthquake magnitudes used in this work.

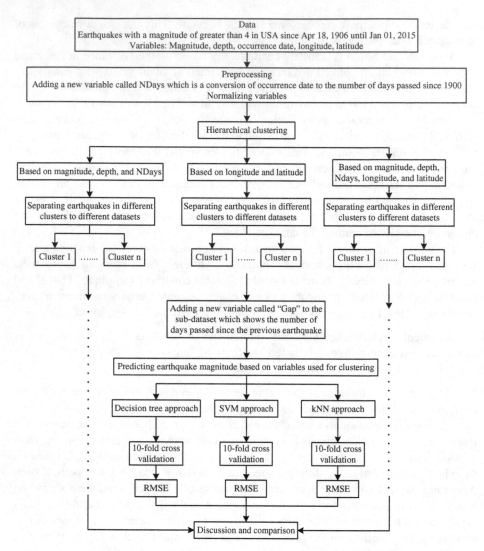

Fig. 1. Process of clustering earthquakes and predicting their magnitudes.

2 Data

Earthquakes with a magnitude of greater than 4 in the United States between April 18, 1906 and January 1, 2015 were downloaded from the United States Geological Survey (USGS) website [14]. This is the longest time range available in the database at the time of writing this article in January 2015. The dataset contains 5,368 earthquakes. Table 1 shows the description of each attribute in the dataset [15].

Although the occurrence dates of earthquakes are available in the original dataset, they are formatted here as the number of days passed since 1900 and called NDays in

Table 1. Available attributes for earthquakes.

Variable	Description
Longitude	Decimal degrees longitude. Negative values for western longitudes
Latitude	Decimal degrees latitude. Negative values for southern latitudes
Magnitude	The magnitude for the event
Depth	Depth of the event in kilometers

the dataset. Since all earthquakes in the dataset have occurred after 1900, all values for this variable are positive.

An important step before clustering data points or developing prediction models is normalizing variables. To normalize a variable (e.g., Magnitude in the dataset), the values are transformed to a normal distribution with a mean of zero and standard deviation of one. Equation 1 shows this normalization where $\bar{x}$ is the mean and s is the standard deviation of data.

$$\hat{x} = (x - \bar{x})/s \tag{1}$$

This step is important because if the range of one variable is much larger than the range of other variables, it will dominate the clustering and prediction process. By normalizing all variables to the same scale, their contribution in the clustering and prediction models is homogenized.

3 Clustering

Hierarchical clustering technique is chosen for clustering earthquakes because unlike k-means technique it is not sensitive to initial seeds [11]. The distance between two clusters during hierarchical clustering can be calculated using different methods. Average-link method is chosen here because unlike single-link and complete-link methods it is less sensitive to outliers. However, both advantages (not being sensitive to initial seeds and being less sensitive to outliers) come with computational cost [12, 13].

The earthquakes are clustered in 10 classes. If a class contains only one earthquake, that earthquake is eliminated and the clustering process is repeated until each cluster contains more than one earthquake. This iterative elimination process helps filter out outliers.

3.1 Clustering Based on Non-spatial Variables

The earthquakes are clustered based on their magnitude, depth and occurrence date, i.e., earthquakes which have close magnitudes, depths and occurrence dates are more probable to be in the same cluster. At the first iteration, three clusters contained only one earthquake. These three earthquakes were removed and the clustering process was repeated. In the second iteration, there was one cluster with one earthquake. This earthquake was eliminated. In the third iteration, all clusters contained more than one earthquake.

3.2 Clustering Based on Spatial Variables

The earthquakes are clustered based on their location (longitude and latitude). There is no need to normalize the variables (columns) for this clustering because the distances in longitude and latitude are compatible with and compensate each other. The resultant clusters contained more than one earthquake in the first iteration.

3.3 Clustering Based on All Variables

The earthquakes are clustered based on their magnitude, depth, occurrence date, longitude, and latitude. At the first iteration, three clusters contained only one earthquake. These three earthquakes were removed and the clustering process was repeated. In the second iteration, all clusters contained more than one earthquake.

4 Earthquakes Clusters and Magnitude Prediction

Since the prediction model is developed for earthquakes in each cluster independently and separately, earthquakes in each cluster are moved to a new dataset. Thus, the number of sub-datasets is equal to the number of clusters, the union of sub-datasets is the original dataset and the intersection of sub-datasets is empty.

One of the variables required for predicting the magnitude of earthquakes is the number of days passed since the last earthquake. We call this variable "Gap" and add it to each sub-dataset separately. To calculate Gap, first the sub-dataset is ordered in an ascending order based on NDays. NDays is representative of the earthquake occurrence date as the number of days passed since 1900. Gap for an earthquake is equal to its NDays subtracted by the NDays of its immediate predecessor in the sub-dataset. Since Gap cannot be calculated for the first earthquake, it is removed from the sub-dataset.

A prediction model is developed for each sub-dataset to predict the magnitude based on other predictors. The prediction model for the sub-dataset is evaluated using 10-fold cross validation and root mean square error (RMSE) is calculated to evaluate the accuracy of the prediction model. As mentioned before, there are 10 sub-datasets for each dataset, each includes earthquakes of a specific cluster. Consequently, there will be 10 different prediction models with 10 different RMSEs. However, to achieve a single RMSE for the entire dataset (including 10 sub-datasets), the weighted average of these 10 RMSEs is calculated. The weight is the number of earthquakes in the sub-dataset. Three different prediction models are experimented: decision tree, SVM, and kNN.

5 Results

Figures 2, 3, and 4 show the size of each cluster (logarithmic scale) in three different clusterings explained in Sect. 3. The cluster sizes are closer to each other in Fig. 3 compared to the other two cases in Figs. 2 and 4. This observation shows that earthquakes are distributed in a few clusters almost uniformly in terms of their locations, though, in terms of their magnitude, depth and occurrence date, most earthquakes (80 %) are in one class while the rest of them are distributed in nine other classes.

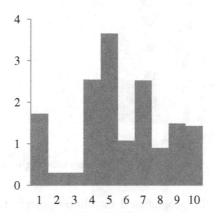

Fig. 2. Size of each cluster (log 10 scale) when clustering based on non-spatial variables.

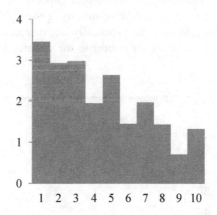

Fig. 3. Size of each cluster (log 10 scale) when clustering based on location.

Figures 5, 6, and 7 show the spatial distribution of earthquakes colored based on their clusters. In Fig. 5, earthquakes are colored based on non-spatial attributes (magnitude, depth, and occurrence date) clusters. In Fig. 6, earthquakes are colored based on location clusters. In Fig. 7, earthquakes are colored based on all variables clusters. Lines in these figures are faults. When earthquakes are clustered based on their non-spatial attributes, the geographical distribution of clusters seems random and does not follow the location of faults. In other words, the earthquakes of one cluster may be located in different parts of the region. On the other hand, when earthquakes are clustered only based on their locations, clusters follow the faults. This is compatible with the concept that earthquakes are stacked around faults [10]. Finally, when both spatial and non-spatial attributes of earthquakes are taken into account for clustering,

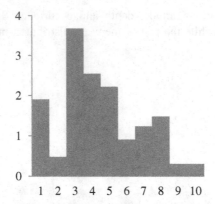

Fig. 4. Size of each cluster (log 10 scale) when clustering based on all variables.

additional factors affect the geographical distribution of clusters. In areas with low seismicity (lower number of earthquakes), most earthquakes belong to one cluster and there are rarely earthquakes of other clusters. However, in areas with high seismicity, such as southwestern U.S., earthquakes of different clusters are stacked together. This observation shows that in areas with low seismicity, geographical location of earthquakes dominates the clustering but in seismically active areas, with dense historical earthquakes, other non-spatial attributes dominate the clustering.

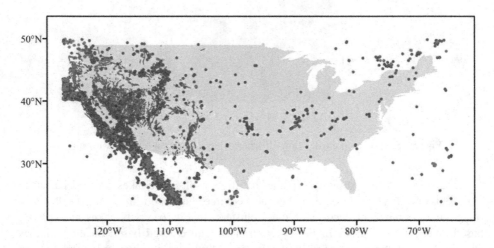

Fig. 5. Clustering earthquakes based on non-spatial attributes.

The results for different prediction models and clustering criteria are shown in Table 2. The RMSE (last column in the table) indicates the accuracy of the prediction model. This RMSE is obtained through 10-fold cross validation. Following are the steps to calculate the RMSE of 0.329 in the first row of Table 2:

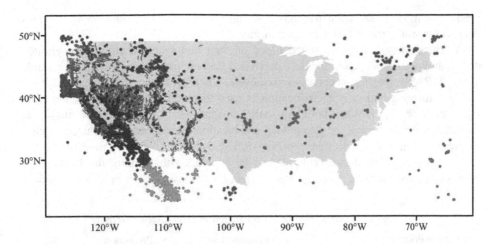

Fig. 6. Clustering earthquakes based on location.

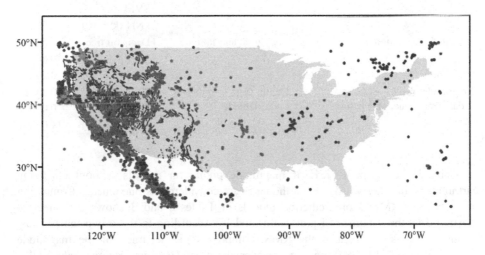

Fig. 7. Clustering earthquakes based on all attributes.

- Obtain the earthquake clusters (10 in total) based on magnitude, depth, and occurrence date.
  - Develop one prediction model for each of these 10 clusters.
  - Evaluate each prediction model using 10-fold cross validation and calculate a RMSE.
- Calculate the weighted average of ten RMSEs which is 0.329.

The accuracy measure (RMSE) is affected by variables considered for clustering and the prediction model. According to Table 2, kNN is obviously not a good prediction model because its RMSE is much larger than the RMSEs for the other two prediction models. Decision tree has a slightly smaller RMSE than SVM. Besides, decision tree is a much faster prediction model than SVM [11–13].

When earthquakes are clustered based on their non-spatial attributes (magnitude, depth, and occurrence date) and only depth and Gap are used to predict the magnitude, the least RMSE (highest accuracy) is achieved. When earthquakes are clustered based on their location and only their location is used to predict the magnitude, the worst accuracy is observed. When both non-spatial attributes and location of earthquakes are considered for clustering and depth, Gap and location of earthquakes are used together to predict their magnitude, the observed RMSE is close to the average of the two previous cases. With these results, it can be concluded that taking the locations of earthquakes into account has an adverse effect on accuracy of the prediction model.

Table 2. Results of different prediction models after clustering.

Clustering criteria	Variables used in prediction of magnitude	Prediction model	RMSE
Magnitude, depth, and occurrence date	Depth and Gap	Decision tree	0.329
		SVM	0.339
		kNN (k = 10)	6.905
Longitude and latitude	Longitude and latitude	Decision tree	0.541
		SVM	0.564
		kNN (k = 10)	8.262
Magnitude, depth, occurrence date, longitude, and latitude	Depth, Gap, longitude and latitude	Decision tree	0.4386
		SVM	0.460
		kNN (k = 10)	11.068

Table 3 shows the RMSE of magnitude prediction models without clustering earthquakes. In other words, all earthquakes are considered as one cluster. Comparing the accuracy (RMSE) of prediction models in Tables 2 and 3 shows the effect of clustering on the accuracy of prediction models. According to these two tables, clustering earthquakes decreases the RMSE (improves the accuracy of the magnitude prediction model) by 30 % on average over all cases. This observation confirms that clustering earthquakes has been partly successful in generating homogeneous seismic sources. Clustering earthquakes based on their non-spatial attributes (magnitude, depth, and occurrence date) results in the least RMSEs over all different prediction models compared to clustering earthquakes based on spatial or all criteria. In other words, clustering earthquakes based on non-spatial attributes produces the most homogenous hazard zones.

Table 3. Results of different prediction models without clustering.

Variables used in prediction of magnitude	Prediction model	RMSE
Depth and Gap	Decision tree	0.502
	SVM	0.527
	kNN (k = 10)	10.143
Longitude and latitude	Decision tree	0.545
	SVM	0.571
	kNN (k = 10)	13.884
Depth, Gap, longitude and latitude	Decision tree	0.505
	SVM	0.526
	kNN (k = 10)	13.765

6 Conclusions and Future Directions

The most accurate earthquake magnitude prediction model is obtained when the earthquakes are clustered based on their depth, occurrence date and magnitude and the predictors in the prediction model are depth and Gap (number of days passed since the last earthquake in a specific cluster). Adding location of earthquakes to the clustering criteria and predictors weakens the prediction model. Among the three prediction models experimented in this work to predict the magnitude of earthquakes, decision tree was 95 % more accurate than kNN and 4 % more accurate than SVM in terms of RMSE.

Clustering earthquakes reduced all RMSEs by 30 % on average which shows clustering earthquakes, as proposed in this work, is a potential approach in producing homogenous seismic sources which can later be used for producing hazard maps. It is also shown that clustering earthquakes based on their non-spatial attributes (magnitude, depth, and occurrence date) produces the most homogenous seismic sources compared to other clustering criteria.

Clustering earthquakes based on their non-spatial attributes (magnitude, depth, and occurrence date) resulted in one large cluster and many small clusters. Clustering inside the largest cluster was considered, discarding the other small clusters. However, the results are not shown in this article because it resulted in one very large cluster and other very small clusters. This observation implies that the actual clusters are circularly nested inside each other and cannot be separated using regular k-means or hierarchical clustering approaches. However, this hypothesis requires further investigation and is a future research direction.

References

1. Scholz, C.H.: Large earthquake triggering, clustering, and the synchronization of faults. Bull. Seismol. Soc. Am. **100**(3), 901–909 (2010)
2. Anderson, J.G., Nanjo, K.: distribution of earthquake cluster sizes in the western united states and in japan. Bull. Seismol. Soc. Am. **103**(1), 412–423 (2013)

3. Cornell, C.: Engineering seismic risk analysis. Bull. Seismol. Soc. Am. **58**, 1583–1606 (1968)
4. Reiter, L.: Earthquake Hazard Analysis, Issues and Insights. Columbia University Press, New York (1990)
5. Anagnos, T., Kiremidjian, A.S.: A review of earthquake occurrence models for seismic hazard analysis. Probab. Eng. Mech. **3**(1), 3–11 (1988)
6. Hashemi, M., Alesheikh, A.A., Zolfaghari, M.R.: A spatio-temporal model for probabilistic seismic hazard zonation of Tehran. Comput. Geosci. **58**, 8–18 (2013)
7. Erdik, M., Biro, Y.A., Onur, T., Sesetyan, K., Birgoren, G.: Assessment of earthquake hazard in Turkey and neighboring regions. Ann. Geofis. **42**(6), 1125–1138 (1999)
8. Erdik, M., Demircioglu, M., Sesetyan, K., Durukal, E., Siyahi, B.: Earthquake hazard in marmara region, turkey. Soil Dyn. Earthq. Eng. **24**, 605–631 (2004)
9. Zmazek, B., Todorovski, L., Džeroski, S., Vaupotič, J., Kobal, I.: Application of decision trees to the analysis of soil radon data for earthquake prediction. Appl. Radiat. Isot. **58**(6), 697–706 (2003)
10. Hashemi, M., Alesheikh, A.: Spatio-temporal analysis of Tehran's historical earthquakes trends. In: Geertman, S., Reinhardt, W., Toppen, F. (eds.) Proceedings of Advancing Geoinformation Science for a Changing World, pp. 3–20. Springer, Utrecht, Netherlands (2011)
11. Ledolter, J.: Data Mining and Business Analytics with R. Wiley, Hoboken (2013)
12. Conway, D., White, J.: Machine Learning for Hackers. O'Reilly Media, Sebastopol (2012)
13. Liu, B.: Web Data Mining: Exploring Hyperlinks, Contents, and Usage Data. Springer, Heidelberg (2007)
14. United States Geological Survey (USGS) (2015). Retrieved from http://earthquake.usgs.gov/earthquakes/search/
15. United States Geological Survey (USGS) (2015). Retrieved from http://earthquake.usgs.gov/earthquakes/feed/v1.0/glossary.php

Restaurant Sales and Customer Demand Forecasting: Literature Survey and Categorization of Methods

Agnieszka Lasek[1]([✉]), Nick Cercone[1], and Jim Saunders[2]

[1] Department of Electrical Engineering and Computer Science,
Lassonde School of Engineering, York University, 4700 Keele Street,
Toronto, ON M3J 1P3, Canada
alasek@cse.yorku.ca, ncercone@yorku.ca
[2] Fuseforward Solutions Group, 671J Market Hill, Vancouver, BC V5Z 4B5, Canada
jim.saunders@fuseforward.com

Abstract. Demand forecasting is one of the important inputs for a successful restaurant yield and revenue management system. Sales forecasting is crucial for an independent restaurant and for restaurant chains as well. In the paper a comprehensive literature review and classification of restaurant sales and consumer demand techniques are presented. A range of methodologies and models for forecasting are given in the literature. These techniques are categorized here into seven categories, also included hybrid models. The methodology for different kind of analytical methods is briefly described, the advantages and drawbacks are discussed, and relevant set of papers is selected. Conclusions and comments are also made on future research directions.

Keywords: Restaurant sales forecasting · Guest count prediction · Forecasting survey · Revenue management · Yield management

1 Introduction

Demand forecasting is one of the important inputs for a successful restaurant yield revenue management system. Sales forecasting is crucial for an independent restaurant and for restaurant chains as well.

The sales transaction data collected by restaurant chains may be analyzed at both *the store level* and *the corporate level*. At the level of single store, exploring the large amounts of transaction data allows each restaurant to improve its operations management (e.g., labor scheduling) and product management (e.g., inventory replenishment, product preparation scheduling), and in consequence reducing restaurant operating costs and increasing quality of serving food. Whereas at the corporate level, extraction of relevant information across the restaurants can greatly facilitate corporate strategic planning. Management can assess the impact of promotional activities on sales and brand recognition,

© ICST Institute for Computer Sciences, Social Informatics and Telecommunications Engineering 2016
A. Leon-Garcia et al. (Eds.): Smart City 2015, LNICST 166, pp. 479–491, 2016.
DOI: 10.1007/978-3-319-33681-7_40

assessment of business trends, conduct price elasticity analysis and measure brand loyalty [17].

There do not exist any review of forecasting methods for the restaurant industry. The aim of this paper is to survey and classify restaurant sales forecasting techniques published over the last 20 years.

Historically, forecasting of restaurant sales has been judgemental based. This technique is still often used by the majority of the restaurant industry. Judgemental techniques consist of an intuitive forecast based on the manager's experience. But restaurant sales forecasting is a complex task, because it is influenced by a large number of factors, which can be classiffied as: time, weather conditions, economic factors, random cases etc. This makes judgemental techniques inaccurate. A wide variety of models, varying in the complexity form has been proposed for the improvement of restaurant forecasting accuracy.

The rest of this paper is organized as follows. Section 2 contains basic information on yield management for restaurants. Based on literature review we specified seven categories of restaurant forecasting techniques: multiple regression; Poisson regression; exponential smoothing and Holt-Winters model; AR, MA and Box-Jenkins models; neural networks; Bayesian network; and hybrid methods. They are arranged in roughly chronological order and discussed in Sect. 3. Section 3 is divided into nine subsections, one subsection for each category of restaurant forecasting techniques, the eighth subsection describes application of Association Rule Mining for the restaurant industry and ninth subsection is a summary of all described methods. Every subsection provides a brief verbal and mathematical description of each technique and gives a literature review of a representative selection of publications in the given category. Section 4 presents the discussion of advantages and disadvantages of each of methods. Section 5 includes summarizing of our research and some remarks.

2   Revenue Management

Revenue management (RM) is the application of information systems and pricing strategies to allocate the right capacity to the right customer at the right place at the right time [6]. The determination of "right" entails achieving both the most revenue possible for the restaurant and also delivering the greatest value or utility to the customer [8].

In practice, revenue management means determining prices according to forecasted demand so that price-sensitive customers who are willing to purchase at off-peak times can do it at lower prices, while customers who want to buy at peak times (price-insensitive customers) will be able to do it [9].

A pioneer in Revenue Management was airline industry [19]. Other examples of industries in which RM is implemented nowadays are hotel industry, car-rental industry, tour operators, restaurants and many others.

One critical element in a strategy for Restaurant Revenue Management is to predict future demand. Restaurant managers have always struggled with the question of how many guests will show up this day. Customer demand varies by the time of year, month, week, day and by the day part. Restaurant demand may be higher on weekends (especially on Fridays and Saturdays), during holidays, summer months, or at particular periods as lunch or dinner time. Restaurant operators want to be able to forecast time-related demand so that they can make effective pricing and table-allocation decisions [8].

Sales forecasting is the answer to the question how high will be sale under certain circumstances. The circumstances includes the nature of sellers, buyers, and the market (e.g., competitors). Thus, important factors are historical sales data, promotions, economic variables, location type or demographics of location. All variables that are useful in predicting demand are listed in Table 1. A multicriteria decision-making method used to rank alternative restaurant locations was presented in [30]. In [25] important attributes for restaurants customers were presented, what can help in determination and prediction customers' intentions to return.

Table 1. Variables that can be used as predictors

No	External variable	Range or an example of the variable
1	Time	Month, week, day of the week, hour
2	Weather	Temperature, rainfall level, snowfall level, hour of sunshine
3	Holidays	Public holidays, school holidays
4	Promotions	Promotion/regular price
5	Events	Hockey games, other
6	Historical data	Historical demand data, trend
7	Macroeconomic Indicators (useful for monthly or annual prediction)	CPI, unemployment rate, population
8	Competitive issues	Competitive promotions
9	Web	Social media comments, social media stars
10	Location type	Street/shopping mall
11	Demographics of location (useful for prediction by time of a day)	The average age of customers

3   Literature Review

3.1   Multiple Regression

Multiple regression is a simple, yet powerful technique used for predicting the unknown value of a dependent variable X_t from the known value of two or more explanatory variables (predictors) $V_1, ..., V_k$. The equation for multiple regression is:

$$X_t = \alpha_0 + \alpha_1 V_{1t} + ... + \alpha_k V_{kt} + \varepsilon_t,$$

where ε_t is the error. Coefficients $\alpha_1, ..., \alpha_k$ can be estimated using least squares to minimize sum of errors [7].

For example, multiple regression models can be used in econometrics, where regression equation(s) model a casual relationship between the dependent variable (e.g., restaurant sales) and external variables such as disposable income, the consumer price index, unemployment rate, etc. One of the advantages of econometric models created for predicting restaurant sales is that the researchers can logically formulate a cause and effect relationship between the exogenous variables and future sales/demand. Econometric models have however some drawbacks. Geurts and Kelly [10] noticed that the future values of the independent variables themselves have to be predicted, what can cause data in an econometric model to be inaccurate and the model to be weak in its ability to forecast. Also the relationship found between the dependent and independent variables may be pretended or their causal relationship can change over time, causing the need for constant update, or complete redesign model.

An example of using multiple regression is presented in [13]. The purpose of this study was to identify the most appropriate method of forecasting meal counts for an institutional food service facility. The forecasting methods included naive models, moving averages, exponential smoothing methods, Holt's and Winter's methods, and linear and multiple regressions. The result of this study showed that multiple regression was the most accurate forecasting method.

Also in [14] multiple regression model was used to demonstrate its potential for predicting future sales in the restaurant industry and its subsegments. Authors considered in this study the macroeconomic predictors such as percentile change in the CPI, in food away from home, in population, and in unemployment. They collected data from 1970 to 2011 from a variety of sources, including the NRA, the USDA, the Bureau of Labor Statistics, and the US Census Bureau. The model, trained and tested on aggregated data from the past 41 years, appears to have reasonable utility in terms of forecasting accuracy.

In [15] authors used several regressions and Box-Jenkins models to forecast weekly sales at a small campus restaurant. The result of testing indicates that a multiple regression model with two predictors, a dummy variable and sales lagged one week, was the best forecasting model considered.

Regression model was also used in a specific situation described in [5], where the restaurant was open and close during different times of the week or year.

3.2   Poisson Regression

Restaurant guest count is an example of variable, that takes on discrete values. When the dependent variable consists of count data, there can be used Poisson regression. This method is one from a family of techniques known as the generalized linear model (GLM). The foundation for Poisson regression is the Poisson distribution error structure and the natural logarithm link function:

$$ln(X) = \alpha_0 + \alpha_1 V_1 + ... + \alpha_k V_k,$$

where X is the predicted guest count, $V_1, ..., V_k$ are the specific values on the predictors, ln refers to the natural logarithm, α_0 is the intercept, and α_i is the regression coefficient for the predictor V_i.

The method is used e.g. in [2,32]. In [28] authors noticed that Poisson Regression can be used to predict the number of customers being served at a restaurant during a certain time period.

3.3   Box-Jenkins Models (ARIMA)

Time series models are different from Multiple and Poisson Regression models in that they do not contain cause-effect relationship. They use mathematical equation(s) to find time patterns in series of historical data. These equations are then used to project into the future the historical time patterns in the data. The autoregressive model specifies that the output variable depends linearly on its own previous values. The autoregressive model of order p $AR(p)$ for time series X_t is defined as:

$$X_t = c + \sum_{i=1}^{p} \varphi_i X_{t-i} + \varepsilon_t$$

where $\varphi_1, \ldots, \varphi_p$ are the parameters of the model, c is a constant, and ε_t is white noise. ε_t are generally assumed to be independent identically distributed random variables (i.i.d.) sampled from a normal distribution with zero mean [8].

Other common approach in time series analysis is a moving-average model. The notation $MA(q)$ indicates the moving average model of order q:

$$X_t = \mu + \varepsilon_t + \theta_1 \varepsilon_{t-1} + \cdots + \theta_q \varepsilon_{t-q}$$

where μ is the mean of the series, the $\theta_1, \cdots, \theta_q$ are the parameters of the model and the $\varepsilon_t, \cdots, \varepsilon_{t-q}$ are white noise error terms [8].

AR and MA models were used to make a prediction for many different time series data. One of the example is presented in paper [12], which is the first research looking into the casino buffet restaurants. Authors examined in this study eight simple forecasting models. The results suggest that the most accurate model with the smallest MAPE and RMSPE was a double moving average.

Another tool created for understanding and predicting future values in time series data is model $ARMA(p,q)$, which is a combination of an autoregressive (AR) part with order p and a moving average (MA) part with order q. The general $ARMA$ model was described in the 1951 in the thesis of Peter Whittle [11]. Given a time series of data X_t, the $ARMA$ model is given by the formula:

$$X_t = c + \varepsilon_t + \sum_{i=1}^{p} \varphi_i X_{t-i} + \sum_{i=1}^{q} \theta_i \varepsilon_{t-i}.$$

where the terms in the equation have the same meaning as above.

An autoregressive integrated moving average $ARIMA$ model is a generalization of an autoregressive moving average $ARMA$ model. $ARIMA$ models

(Box-Jenkins models) are applied in some cases where data show evidence of non-stationarity (stationary process is a stochastic process whose joint probability distribution does not change over time and consequently parameters such as the mean and variance do not change over time).

The first step in developing $ARIMA(p, d, q)$ model is to determine if the time series is stationary and if there is any significant seasonality that needs to be modelled [18].

3.4   Exponential Smoothing and Holt-Winters Models

Exponential smoothing, proposed in the late 1950s, is another technique that can be applied to time series data to make forecasts. Whereas in the simple moving average the past observations are weighted equally, exponential smoothing uses exponentially decreasing weights over time. The more recent the observation the higher the associated weight. For the sequence of observations $\{x_t\}$ begins at time $t = 0$, the simplest form of exponential smoothing is given by the formula:

$$s_0 = x_0; \quad s_t = \alpha x_t + (1 - \alpha)s_{t-1}, \ t > 0$$

where α is the smoothing factor, and $0 < \alpha < 1$.

Triple exponential smoothing (suggested in 1960 by Holt's student, Peter Winters) takes into account seasonal changes and trends. Seasonality is a pattern in time-series data that repeats itself every L periods. There are two types of seasonality: "mutiplicative" and "additive" in nature. For time series data $\{x_t\}$, beginning at time $t = 0$ with a cycle of seasonal change of length L, triple exponential smoothing is given by the formulas:

$$F_{t+m} = (s_t + mb_t)c_{t-L+1+(m-1)modL}$$

$$s_0 = x_0; \quad s_t = \alpha \frac{x_t}{c_{t-L}} + (1 - \alpha)(s_{t-1} + b_{t-1})$$

$$b_t = \beta(s_t - s_{t-1}) + (1 - \beta)b_{t-1}$$

$$c_t = \gamma \frac{x_t}{s_t} + (1 - \gamma)c_{t-L}$$

where F_{t+m} is an estimate of the value of x at time $t + m, (m > 0)$, α is the data smoothing factor, β is the trend smoothing factor and γ is the seasonal change smoothing factor, $0 < \alpha, \beta, \gamma < 1$, $\{s_t\}$ represents the smoothed value of the constant part (level) for time t, $\{b_t\}$ estimates of the linear trend for period t and $\{c_t\}$ represents the sequence of seasonal factors.

Exponential smoothing was one of the most common and simple methods for food and beverage sales forecasting (e.g., [23,24]). The results of the study [16] show that for the actual sales in the restaurant, located in a medium size university town, Box-Jenkins and exponential smoothing models performed as well or better than an econometric model. Since time series models are usually more economical in terms of time and skill levels of the users, the results of this study is important for forecasting in the restaurant industry.

Interesting case of big data mining project for one of the world's largest multi-brand fast-food restaurant chains with more than 30,000 stores worldwide is illustrated in [17]. Time series data mining is discussed at both the store level and corporate level. To analyze and forecast large number of data researchers used Box-Jenkins seasonal ARIMA models. Also an automatic outlier detection and adjustment procedure was used for both model estimation and prediction.

3.5   Artificial Neural Networks

All the forecasting methods we have discussed in previous subsections have the same strategy: make a functional assumption for the relationship between the observed data and various factors and then estimate the parameters of this function. In contrast, neural network methods, inspired by research on the human nervous system, use interactions in a network architecture to automatically estimate the underlying unknown function that best describes the demand process. ANNs are systems of connected "neurons", where the connections have numeric weights that can be tuned based on historical data, what makes that neural networks are adaptive to inputs and capable of learning.

Article [20] compares artificial neural networks and traditional methods including Winters exponential smoothing, Box-Jenkins ARIMA model, and multivariate regression. The results indicate that on average ANNs are more successful compared to the more traditional statistical methods. Analysis of experiments shows that the neural network model is able to capture the trend and seasonal patterns, as well as the interactions between them. Despite many positive features of ANNs, constructing a good network for a given project is a quite difficult task. It consists of choosing an appropriate architecture (the number of hidden layers, the number of nodes in each layer, the connections between nodes), selecting the transfer functions of the middle and output nodes, designing a training algorithm, selecting initial weights, and defining the stopping rule.

Fuzzy neural network with initial weights generated by genetic algorithm can be found e.g., in [3]. In the study [22] authors combined an artificial neural network and a genetic algorithm to design and developed a sales forecasting model. They collected sales data from a small restaurant in Taipei City and used them as the output for the forecasted results while associated factors including seasonal impact, impact of holidays, number of local activities, number of sales promotions, advertising budget, and advertising volume were chosen as input data. Firstly, this approach applies the ANN to select the relevant parameters of the current sales condition as the input data. Then it uses a genetic algorithm to optimize the default weights and thresholds of the ANN. Researchers used empirical analysis to examine the effectiveness of the model. The results indicate that this is a scientifically practical and effective sales forecasting method that can achieve rapid and accurate prediction.

3.6 Bayesian Network Model

Paper [26] proposes a service demand forecasting method that uses a customer classification model to consider various customer behaviors. A decision support system based on this method was introduced in restaurant stores. Authors automatically generated categories of customers and items based on purchase patterns identified in data from 8 million purchases at a Japanese restaurant chain (48 stores, data from 5 years). They produced a Bayesian network model including the customer and item categories, conditions of purchases, and the properties and demographic information of customers. Based on that network structure, they could systematically identify useful knowledge and predict customers behavior. Details of this demand forecasting technique are given in [29].

3.7 Hybrid Models

In the literature there is also proposed a hybrid approach to sales forecasting for restaurants. It is often difficult in practice to determine whether one specific method is more effective in prediction then the other. Thus, it is difficult for

Table 2. Summary of sales/demand forecasting methods

Method	Description	Examples of papers
Multiple regression	Multiple Regression uses least squares to predict the unknown value of a dependent variable from the known value of two or more explanatory variables (predictors)	[5, 10, 12–15]
Poisson regression	Poisson regression uses the Poisson distribution error structure and the natural logarithm link function	[28]
Box-Jenkins model (AR, MA, ARIMA)	The autoregressive model specifies that the output variable depends linearly on its own previous values. The simple moving average weights the past observations equally	[15, 18]
Exponential smoothing and Holt-Winters models	Exponential smoothing uses exponentially decreasing weights over time	[13, 16, 17, 23, 24]
Artificial neural networks	ANNs use interactions in a network-processing architecture to automatically identify the underlying function that best describes the demand process	[3, 22]
Bayesian network model	Bayesian Network can represent the probabilistic relationships between the variables	[26, 29]
Hybrid model	Hybrid models combine 2 different models in one	[1, 21]
Association rules	Association Rules algorithms find frequent patterns in the data	[4, 27, 31]

researchers to choose the right technique for their unique situations. Usually, different models are tested and the one with the most accurate result is selected. However, the final chosen model is not always the best for the future use. The problem of model selection can be facilitated by combining methods [21].

Researchers use hybrid model in many different areas of forecasting. As an example of a hybrid system with excellent performance can be shown the application on daily product sales in a supermarket proposed in [1]. Authors combined ARIMA models and neural networks to a sequential hybrid forecasting system, where output from an ARIMA-type model is used as input for a neural network.

For restaurant industry a hybrid methodology that combines both ARIMA and ANN models is proposed in [21]. Experimental results with real data sets indicate that the combined model can be an effective way to improve forecasting accuracy achieved by each of the models used separately.

3.8   Association Rules (Market Basket Analysis)

In this subsection we want to mention an additional method which can help in restaurant forecasting. In [4] there is studied the problem of mining association rules which holds either in all or some of time intervals. As an example there are considered association rules in a given database of restaurant transactions.

In [27] authors applies a simplified version of market basket analysis (MBA) rules to explore menu items assortments, which are defined as the sets of most frequently ordered menu item pairs of an entre and side dishes. In some cases, MBA does not provide useful information if data item is the name of goods. In [31] authors proposed a new MBA method which integrates words segmentation technology and association rule mining technology. Characteristics of items can be generated automatically before mining association rules by using word segmentation technology. This method has been applied to a restaurant equipped with electronic ordering system to give recommendations to customers, where the experiments were done. The experiment results show that the method is efficient and valid.

4   Discussion of Methods and Data Mining Algorithms

The summary of all approaches is presented in Table 2.

It is difficult for forecasters to choose the right technique for their unique situations. Typically, a number of different models are tried and the one with the most accurate result is selected. Below, in Table 3 there is a brief description of the advantages and disadvantages of methods of demand and sales prediction. In our opinion techniques that take into account external factors mentioned in Table 1 are the best. Not only the choice of method but also preparing the relevant data affects the high efficiency of the model.

Table 3. Advantages and disadvantages of sales/demand forecasting methods

Method	Input Data	Output	Advantages	Disadvantages
Multiple Regression	Exogenous variables such as disposable income, the consumer price index, unemployment rate, personal consumption expenditures, housing starts.	E.g., restaurant sales/ customer demand	+ the decision maker can logically formulate the model based on a cause and effect relationship between the causal variables and future sales	- Multiple regression analysis can fail in clarifying the relationships between the predictor variables and the response variable when the predictors are correlated with each other. - The relationship found between the dependent and independent variables may be spurious or can change over time, making it necessary to constantly update or totally redesign the model.
ARIMA (Box-Jenkins models)	Historical time series demand/ sales data.	Long-term or short term predictions of future demand/ sales.	+ Do not need any external data.	- The input series for ARIMA needs to be stationary, that is, it should have a constant mean, variance, and autocorrelation through time.
Exponental smoothing model, Holt-Winters models	Historical time series demand/ sales data.	Long-term or short term predictions of future demand/ sales.	+ Exponential smoothing generates reliable forecasts quickly, which is a great advantage for applications in industry. + Do not need any external data.	- Method is influenced by outliers (sales/demand that are unusually high or low).
Bayesian Network Model	Particular set of variables.	The probability of the variable, e.g. high sale.	+ All the parameters in Bayesian networks have an understandable interpretation.	
Neural Networks	E.g., associated factors including seasonal impact, impact of holidays, number of local activities, number of sales promotions, advertising budget, and advertising volume can be used as input data. All the training and test data used in this study are required to be pre-processed. The input and output data used for training and the input data used for testing have to be pre-processed so that the data were mapped between [1,-1].	Sales amount can be chosen as the output data for the forecasted results. An inverse transformation should be conducted on the results of the simulated forecast to restore the actual value of the forecasted sales condition.	+ Have high tolerance of noisy data. + Ability to classify patterns on which they have not been trained. + Can be used when there is little knowledge of the relationships between attributes and classes. + They are well-suited for continuous-valued inputs and outputs, unlike most decision tree algorithms. + Are parallel; parallelization techniques can be used to speed up the computation process. + Can model complex, possibly nonlinear relationships without any prior assumptions about the underlying datagenerating process + Overcome misspecification, biased outliers, assumption of linearity, and re-estimation.	- Neural networks involve long training times and are therefore more suitable for applications where this is feasible. - They require a number of parameters that are typically best determined empirically, such as the network topology or structure. Constructing a good network for a particular application is not a trivial task. It involves choosing an appropriate architecture (the number of hidden layers, the number of nodes in each layer, and the connections among nodes), selecting the transfer functions of the middle and output nodes, designing a training algorithm, choosing initial weights, and specifying the stopping rule. - Neural networks have been criticized for their poor interpretability.
Association Rule Mining (Market Basket Analysis)	Transactional database (TDB) or Relational database (RDB). Given a minimum support (min_{sup}) and a minimum confidence (min_{conf}).	All association rules that satisfy both min_{sup} and min_{conf} from a data set D.	+ Association rules that satisfy both min_{sup} and min_{conf} can help with discover factors which influence high/low demand.	

5   Conluding Remarks

Demand prediction plays a crucial role in planning operations for restaurant's management. Having a reliable estimation for a menu items future demand is the basis for other analysis. Various forecasting techniques have been developed, each one with its particular advantages and disadvantages compared to other approaches. The evolution of the respective forecasting methods over past 20 years has ben revealed in the paper. A review and categorization of consumer restaurant demand techniques is presented in the paper. Techniques from a range of methodologies and models given in the literature are classified here into seven categories: (1) multiple regression, (2) Poisson regression, (3) exponential smoothing and Holt-Winters model, (4) AR, MA and Box-Jenkins models, (5) neural networks, (6) Bayesian network, and (7) hybrid methods. The methodology for each category has been described and the advantages and disadvantages have been discussed. This paper conducts a comprehensive literature review and selects a set of papers on restaurant sales forecasting. It is almost universally agreed in the forecasting literature that no single method is best in every situation.

Acknowledgments. This work was supported by a Collaborative Research and Development (CRD) grant from the Natural Sciences and Engineering Research Council of Canada (NSERC), grant number: 461882-2013.

References

1. Aburto, L., Weber, R.: A sequential hybrid forecasting system for demand prediction. In: Perner, P. (ed.) MLDM 2007. LNCS (LNAI), vol. 4571, pp. 518–532. Springer, Heidelberg (2007)
2. Coxe, S., West, S.G., Aiken, L.S.: The analysis of count data: a gentle introduction to poisson regression and its alternatives. J. Pers. Assess. **91**(2), 121–136 (2009). doi:10.1080/00223890802634175
3. Kuo, R.J.: A sales forecasting system based on fuzzy neural network with initial weights generated by genetic algorithm. Euro. J. Opera. Res. **129**(3), 496–517 (2001)
4. Li, Y., Ning, P., Wang, X.S., Jajodia, S.: Discovering calendar-based temporal association rules. Data Knowl. Eng. **44**(2), 193–218 (2003)
5. Morgan, M.S., Chintagunta, P.K.: Forecasting restaurant sales using self-selectivity models. J. Retail. Consum. Serv. **4**(2), 117–128 (1997)
6. Smith, B.C., Leimkuhler, J.F., Darrow, R.M.: Yield management at American airlines. Interfaces **22**(1), 8–31 (1992)
7. Hastie, T., Tibshirani, R., Friedman, J.: The Elements of Statistical Learning Data Mining, Inference, and Prediction. Springer Series in Statistics. Springer, New York (2008)
8. Kimes, S.E., Chase, R.B., Choi, S., Lee, P.Y., Ngonzi, E.N.: Restaurant revenue management applying yield management to the restaurant industry. Cornell Hospitality Q. **39**(3), 32–39 (1998)

9. Kimes, S.E., Wirtz, J.: Revenue management: advanced strategies and tools to enhance firm profitability. Found. Trends Mark. **8**(1), 1–68 (2015)
10. Geurts, M.D., Kelly, J.P.: Forecasting retail sales using alternative models. Int. J. Forecast. **2**(3), 261–272 (1986)
11. Whitle, P.: Hypothesis Testing in Time Series Analysis, vol. 4. Almqvist & Wiksells, Uppsala (1951)
12. Hu, C., Chen, M., McCain, S.-L.C.: Forecasting in short-term planning and management for a casino buffet restaurant. J. Travel Tourism Mark. **16**(2–3), 79–98 (2004)
13. Ryu, K., Sanchez, A.: The evaluation of forecasting methods at an institutional foodservice dining facility. J. Hospitality Financ. Manage. **11**(1), 1–4 (2003)
14. Reynolds, D., Rahman, I., Balinbin, W.: Econometric modeling of the U.S. restaurant industry International. J. Hospitality Manage. **34**, 317–323 (2013)
15. Forst, F.G.: Forecasting restaurant sales using multiple regression and box-jenkins analysis. J. Appl. Bus. Res. **8**(2), 2157–8834 (1992). ISSN: 2157-8834
16. Cranage, D.A., Andrew, W.P.: A comparison of time series and econometric models for forecasting restaurant sales. Int. J. Hospitality Manage. **11**(2), 129–142 (1992)
17. Liu, L.-M., Bhattacharyya, S., Sclove, S.L., Chen, R., Lattyak, W.J.: Data mining on time series: an illustration using fast-food restaurant franchise data. Comput. Stat. Data Anal. **37**, 455–476 (2001)
18. George, B., Gwilym, J.: Forecasting and Control. Holden-Day, San Francisco (1970)
19. Talluri, K.T., van Ryzin, G.J.: The Theory and Practice of Revenue Management. Springer Science+Business Media Inc., Heidelberg (2005)
20. Alon, I., Qi, M., Sadowski, R.J.: Forecasting aggregate retail sales: a comparison of artificial neural networks and traditional methods. J. Retail. Consum. Serv. **8**, 147–156 (2001)
21. Zhang, G.P.: Time series forecasting using a hybrid ARIMA and neural network model. Neurocomputing **50**, 159–175 (2003)
22. Chen, P.-J., Lao, C.-Y., Chang, H.-T., LoCho, Y.: A study of applying artificial neural network and genetic algorithm in sales forecasting model. J. Convergence Inf. Technol. (JCIT) **6**(9), 352–362 (2011)
23. Miller, J.J., McCahon, C.S., Miller, J.L.: Foodservice forecasting using simple mathematical models. J. Hospitality Tourism Res. **15**(1), 43–58 (1991)
24. Miller, J.J., McCahon, C.S., Miller, J.L.: Foodservice forecasting: differences in selection of simple mathematical models based on short-term and long-term data sets. J. Hospitality Tourism Res. **16**(2), 93–102 (1993)
25. Qu, H.: Determinant factors and choice intention for Chinese restaurant dining: a multivariate approach. J. Restaurant Foodservice Mark. **2**(2), 35–49 (1997)
26. Koshiba, H., Takenaka, T., Motomura, Y.: A service demand forecasting method using a customer classification model. In: CIRP IPS2 Conference (2012)
27. Ting, P.-H., Pan, S., Chou, S.-S.: Finding ideal menu items assortments: an empirical application of market basket analysis. Cornell Hospitality Q. **51**(4), 492–501 (2010)
28. Sellers, K.F., Shmueli, G.: Predicting censored count data with COM-Poisson regression, Working Paper. Indian School of Business, Hyderabad (2010)
29. Ishigaki, T., Takenaka, T., Motomura, Y.: Customer-item category based knowledge discovery support system and its application to department store service. In: IEEE Asia-Pacific Services Computing Conference (2010)
30. Tzeng, G.-H., Teng, M.-H., Chen, J.-J., Opricovic, S.: Multicriteria selection for a restaurant location in Taipei International. J. Hospitality Manage. **21**(2), 171–187 (2002)

31. Wen-xiu, X., Heng-nian, Q., Mei-li, H.: Market basket analysis based on text segmentation and association rule mining. In: First International Conference on Networking and Distributed Computing (2010)
32. Wulu Jr., J.T., Singh, K.P., Famoye, F., Thomas, T.N., McGwin, G.: Regression analysis of count data. J. Ind. Soc. Ag. Statistics **55**(2), 220–231 (2002)

Visualizing a City Within a City – Mapping Mobility Within a University Campus

Dirk Ahlers$^{(\boxtimes)}$, Kristoffer Gebuhr Aulie, Jeppe Eriksen, and John Krogstie

NTNU – Norwegian University of Science and Technology, Trondheim, Norway
{dirk.ahlers,john.krogstie}@idi.ntnu.no

Abstract. Urban mobility analysis usually examines large cities or even regions. We take another angle and examine a university campus as a city within a city to focus on small-scale and hyperlocal characteristics. The campus mobility data exhibits a high spatial and temporal granularity that we use to drive analyses and visualizations towards the aim of campus analytics. We describe the abstraction approaches and visualizations used towards the development of our tool and share initial results of campus analytics.

Keywords: Visualization · Visual analytics · Mobility · WLAN localization · Object traces · Campus analytics

1 Introduction

The analysis of urban mobility can be used to understand behavior and improve services, transportation, and area use. In this paper, we present a system for visual analytics of people's movements on a large university campus. A campus can be understood as a miniature city embedded in a city. In our case, we model the campus as a combination of multiple large-scale places with indoor localization infrastructure.

The system serves as a proof-of-concept for several building-related analyses in a campus scenario. Current use cases and applications include improved awareness of building usage including use of labs, lecture halls, reading rooms; learning and possible improving routes on campus; improvement of services and their locations; energy savings for a sustainable campus; and research investigating the characteristics of human mobility on campus-like structures. We use the campus as a lab infrastructure to test approaches that we later consider to scale to a city level as part of the smart cities infrastructure. For the presented application, we work together with stakeholders from the university's building management and scheduling offices to finetune application scenarios of building use on campus. Our approach to smart city mobility analysis on campus is to support stakeholders in making sense of the huge amounts of positioning data by reducing and abstracting it in a way that facilitates visual analytics with a *campus analytics* approach.

© ICST Institute for Computer Sciences, Social Informatics and Telecommunications Engineering 2016
A. Leon-Garcia et al. (Eds.): Smart City 2015, LNICST 166, pp. 492–503, 2016.
DOI: 10.1007/978-3-319-33681-7_41

In the growing interest areas of smart cities, urban computing [13], and mobility analysis, much work has been done on the basis of mobile phone call data records (CDR) or social networks. For example, [10] describe trajectory analysis and show the existence of regularity and similarity of individual's mobility patterns. [5] look at aggregate mobility and transportation patterns with a broad set of methods. These scenarios usually are using individual's traces to gain aggregate knowledge over cities or regions.

We are in a privileged position where we can have access to mobility data at both a high temporal and spatial resolution, thus delivering much finer grained analyses that only times of calls or tweets. Compared to CDRs, WLAN trilateration has a much higher spatial and temporal granularity, but usually a much lower coverage. This makes it viable to look at smaller populations or smaller areas, complementing city-level approaches and instead, aggregate on an intracity level. In our case, we can only cover a limited area of the city, but in the form of a self-contained campus it is functionally closed and is a high density area of people's movements.

In related work, [2] describe visual analytics tools for transportation patterns on a regional regional scale and [4] follow a visual analytics approach on an urban scale for land use analysis. We are scaling this down to a campus, similar to [9] who analysed a year of mobility data. [12] examines how indoor location influences information needs, based on access to a WLAN network and also to Web traffic over the network inside a mall. We only look at mobility data without traffic content at the scale of a larger set of buildings.

We do not aim to track actual persons, therefore we use device movement as a proxy for people's movement and operate on anonymous data that we aggregate. The smartphone ownership in Norway is above 75 %, and we estimate it even higher in the student and staff population of the university. Additionally, some feature phones also are WLAN-enabled. The multi-device ownership (tablets, notebooks, etc.) rate is also high. This means that we are able to capture a majority of people in the device tracking. At the same time, for this reduction in sampling bias we also get a certain number of cases where we track multiple devices belonging to the same person, thus increasing bias towards multiple device owners by double counting. Because usually people take their devices with them if they move, the proxy assumption holds. Investigating these issues are part of future work combined with deeper accuracy evaluation.

In our approach we use a stacked campus movement abstraction. It comprises the steps of all device positions, extracted movement heatmap, inter-building movement matrix visualization, and specific use-case functionality. The logical steps we take are position gathering, movement extraction, building graph extraction, and visualization. The present paper includes results of two theses [3,7] done in collaboration with NTNU and Wireless Trondheim.

We start by describing the setup of data collection and our data set in Sect. 2, describe our visual analytics approach and data processing in Sect. 3, present results in Sect. 4, and discuss limitations and future work in Sect. 5 before closing in Sect. 6.

2   Data Set

NTNU together with Wireless Trondheim and Mazemap is employing a WLAN infrastructure in the city center and the campuses, which is set up as a living lab [1]. In this work, we are focusing on Gløshaugen, the biggest campus of NTNU. Existing work on this infrastructure for example enables campus wayfinding [6] or an estimation of available reading rooms for students [8].

The WLAN infrastructure at NTNU employs a Cisco MSE (mobility services engine) controller with a location engine that derives device positions by trilateration over the access points [11]. The coverage is based on the roughly 1800 access points on 350000 sqm of campus. The tracking is based on passive location sensing, i.e., any device with enabled WLAN can be tracked, by means of its probe requests. These are transmitted by the devices at varying intervals, which sets the sampling rate usually to less then 60 s. Thus stickiness is a lesser issue as even when the device is not yet connected to a closer access point, it will already be sensed. The system is setup to provide coverage mainly indoors, but also covers outdoor areas close to buildings. Therefore it captures most indoor but also some outdoor movement.

An abstraction and processing layer is deployed on top of this. The data we can gather is already processed/abstracted and anonymized, and we do not have access to raw data. Other data that would be available on the backend is stripped out or otherwise unavailable, for example the device type or model as well as any traffic over the WLAN network. The output we can access contains data points that consist of an anonymized device ID, coordinate pair of latitude and longitude, a hierarchical description of the position, a timestamp, accuracy measure, and a salt timestamp. The anonymization uses a hashing function on the MAC addresses of devices to generate a random ID. This changes regularly by changing the salt of the hash. It thus ensures that a single device cannot be tracked over an extended period of more than one day. For this reason the salt timestamp is included in the data record. As long as the timestamp has not changed, an ID continuously identifies the same device. For internal university use of the data, this process was approved by the The Norwegian Data Protection Authority. We also feel that privacy is important especially for such high-granularity data. Our approach thus uses not individual, but general patterns.

The hierarchy description contains three items: campus name, building name, and floor, for example *Gloshaugen > IT-Vest > 1. etasje* or *Gloshaugen > Sentralbygg II > 13. etasje*. Further details such as mapping to individual rooms are not included in the data, but can be map-matched later [6,8]. The accuracy gives the estimated radius of error for each measurement. The average indoor accuracy is about 5–10 m, outdoors this can be higher as positions are estimated close to the buildings. For the visualization, we already have tailored digital maps, building models, and positions available [6].

For initial data collection and partition, we use a fixed window of one day starting at midnight. Compared to other city scenarios, this is sufficient for the campus area, where there is usually very little activity at night. We are currently using a collection of historic data, but the system could easily be adapted to handle live data. We define a trace as a sequential list of positions for a single device that contains at least two positions and is delimited either by the end of day or by a 1-h timeout with no further data points. There are about 43000 devices per day with 3.2 million position measurements available for the campus with a captured historical dataset of two months.

3   Approach for Visual Analytics

Our approach uses visual analytics of the position data of the devices on campus, with gradually refined data processing steps. We start with simple device positions, then animate them over time, then derive movement data and finally move to a graph-based analysis.

The first iteration is an animation of density heatmaps over all data. It shows changes in the device density, which could be interpreted as movement, but is difficult to analyze. Of course, areas filling up or emptying out can easily be identified. But for example, slight fluctuations between densities in neighboring buildings could mean few movements or larger reciprocal movements happening between these two buildings. This means there is a need to extract the movement as a derivative and possibly also make out the trajectories of movements. As we do not only have point clouds, but stable randomized IDs over a certain period, we can extract device traces.

In a heat map visualization of movement data, trajectories are abstracted in a non-directional heat map. In a graph-based approach, directional inter-building traffic can be analyzed. This manages to integrate two complementary geospatial dimensions. First, it uses plain geospatial data in the form of coordinates, second, it uses a conceptual view by abstracting and mapping positions to buildings and generate a building graph. The visualization of movement instead of raw position achieves two things. First, it obviously filters out those devices that do not move. Second, it allows to see where the movement takes place and at what magnitude (as an aggregated temporal view). The standard heatmap can make it difficult to distinguish between static and moving devices if they do not move far beyond the kernel bandwidth or radius. Thus, this shows the areas where movement takes place, and together with a temporal dimension can derive the direction. For more abstract analysis that is difficult to visualize as heatmaps, we chose an abstraction to buildings as functional areas with a graph-based approach.

3.1   Extraction of Movement

When at rest, devices will be located at similar positions because the trilateration is done via probe requests to any base station picking up the signal. Detected movement correlates highly with actual device movement. But on the individual level, there may be slight deviations during movement about the exact position. Yet, the indoor accuracy is usually within 5–10 m.

To abstract the data and filter out jitters in the positions, we apply a simple track smoothing with a distance filter and then consider a device in movement

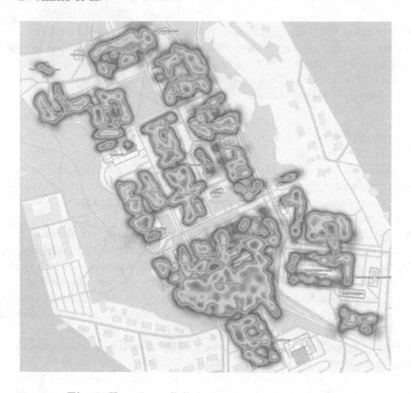

Fig. 1. Heatmap of all device positions on campus

only if its position differs by a determined threshold of 10 m from its previous position. Data points matching these conditions are then considered as in movement and are visualized. This can be used to show the movement and intensity in different time periods.

3.2   Extraction of Inter-Building Movement

The next step is to go beyond positional movement data and look at trajectories on campus. We chose to abstract movement to a building level, or rather, to movement between buildings. To this end, we build an inter-building movement matrix. Movement between floors was not yet considered. Device traces between buildings are counted to build a building movement graph.

As we already have the building names in the position data, we do not need a map matching or clustering approach. Thus the building extraction is rather trivial. In the WLAN setup, a device does not actually have to enter a building to be registered or even to connect. This is of course desirable to deliver at least partial outdoor coverage. For example, if a person walks along the outside of a building, the device can still be registered by the access points within, thus registering the device to that building. We do no further mapping or snap-to-building, so we may capture some outdoor positions as well.

To model device movement between buildings, we have experimentally implemented two approaches. For the 'all-movement' approach, all movement in the location traces between buildings is considered. This means that whenever we see a device in a building A and later in its location trace in another building B, we count one movement from A to B in the building movement matrix. Each device's location trace is iterated to capture all these events. The most obvious limitation of this approach is that it will cut apart longer trajectories between buildings of there are other buildings on or along the way. Thus, a movement does not mean that the registered destination of a movement is actually the destination of the user moving around campus. It may just lie on the way and be either bypassed or passed through to the true destination. This is especially the case for centrally located building on campus that have a lot of through traffic.

To counteract this and filter out buildings that were only passed on the way, we attempt to identify movements with a defined origin and destination. The improved 'start-stop' approach delivers better results towards the extraction of the true user-intended destination of a movement. The approach does not currently consider movements outside the system boundary, for example, users entering or leaving the campus. Again, each location trace is iterated. While a group of three subsequent positions are at rest, a halt is assumed. After a halt, when three subsequent positions have a distance to each other of more than 10 m, they are considered in movement and a movement origin is registered in the current building. When a halted stated is detected in the further iteration of the trace, this is registered as the destination and a movement between the two buildings is generated.

4   Results

We share our insights into the use of these campus mobility visualizations. We are able to generate heatmaps with very high spatial resolution that allow to analyze movement even in small indoor structures. Mapping all devices as in Fig. 1 shows the full amount of position data for a morning. It can be zoomed in to enable drill-down, and the heat map parameters can be adapted to change the visualization. The mapped positions follow largely the buildings on campus and their expected traffic densities. In the static view, there is limited information to be gained, but we can animate this map over time to show changing densities, which makes this already a useful tool.

However, as noted above, it is difficult to make out movements in this mapping, as there is a lot of ambiguous fluctuation. In the following we take the next step of our approach and use only extracted movement.

If we use the visualization of extracted movement to move through a typical day, the first thing to note is that there is a reduction in density of the data points which allows a more focused view of only movement. As an example, we show the evolution of the movement on campus for one morning. We use only selected time slices to show the most distinctive visualizations. We can see daily patterns revolving around campus structures and lectures. From 8:00–9:00 there

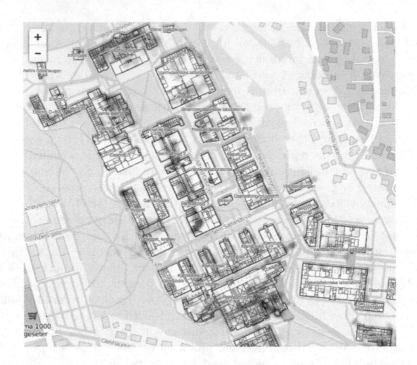

Fig. 2. Evolution of a morning: movements 8:00–9:00

Fig. 3. Evolution of a morning: movements 9:45–10:00

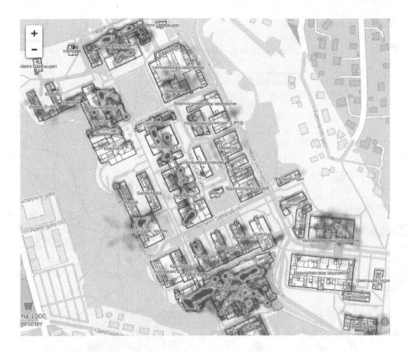

Fig. 4. Evolution of a morning: movements 11:00–12:00

is little movement overall when the first lectures of the day start (Fig. 2); at 9:45–10:00 there is a slight increase due to the end and the start of the second lectures (Fig. 3) and at 11:00–12:00 the campus really comes to life (Fig. 4). There is one obvious pattern that the early morning is not a preferred time for users to arrive on campus. Lunchtime sees highly increased movement as people move from lecture halls or labs to the canteens.

For the time being, this visualization cannot yet fully distinguish between a lot of local movement and longer trajectories, however, the former will halt once in a while while the latter continues stronger and thus delivers more movement density.

For a more detailed view into the longer trajectories, we can switch to the building graph view. In the default state, it shows the contribution of each building to the overall movement by the size of the overlaid bubble plot as in Fig. 5 and provides numerical data on hovering.

Furthermore, the underlying origin-destination building matrix can be explored for each building as shown in Fig. 6, which shows the movement from or to all other buildings, in this case limited to the top-5 connected nodes which again show their weight when hovering. This can also be viewed as the raw matrix and further processed in other tools. We provide a sample of the matrix for the top-k buildings regarding traffic count in Table 1. One result that can be derived for example is that movement is correlated with building size, i.e., there is more movement inside and to/from larger buildings. Another quite interesting

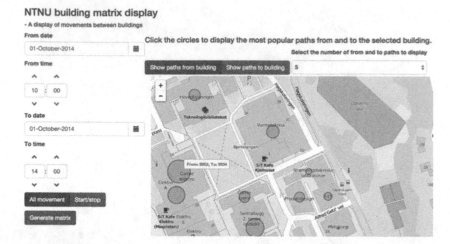

Fig. 5. Visualization of building traffic embedded into the application with a selection of interaction and analysis tools

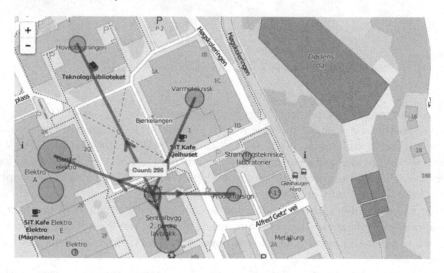

Fig. 6. Visualization of the origin-destination building matrix: top-5 destinations of traffic flow from the Gamle Kjemi building

finding is that there seems to be a lot of reciprocal movement between buildings. The matrix is not fully symmetric, but the numbers of ingoing and outgoing trajectories are strongly correlated over different periods during the day. This is surprising because it means that buildings have the same average usage over the day and that also the initial movement of people onto the campus (which we do not capture in the matrix) is well distributed over all buildings. What we of course also see is that some buildings act as hubs for movement, either by their central location or by housing a canteen.

Table 1. Selection from the building matrix of the top 8 building traffic counts for a 4 h period

From \ To	Gamle Elektro	Realfagbygget	Sentralbygg I	Sentralbygg II	Elektroblokk A	Kjemi 3	Gamle Fysikk	Driftssentralen
Gamle Elektro	0	36	33	153	1308	24	220	4
Realfagbygget	46	0	255	85	22	660	152	402
Sentralbygg I	35	165	0	1083	12	255	321	3
Sentralbygg II	83	80	1031	0	21	27	215	0
Elektroblokk A	1245	7	16	38	0	6	83	3
Kjemi 3	23	800	316	26	7	0	209	3
Gamle Fysikk	234	187	270	157	80	284	0	5
Driftssentralen	1	482	7	8	3	7	3	0

Switching between the two modes of inter-building detection, it is also possible to distinguish those buildings that are mostly passed by and whose WLAN contributes strongly to the outdoor coverage. These disproportionately lose traffic when switching to the start-stop method.

5   Limitations and Future Work

As discussed before, the access points are only indoors, so there is no full view of the campus, but outdoor is covered close to buildings. However, the accuracy of the localization is much higher indoors than outdoors and often outdoor positions get localised indoors. A classification of these cases is not directly obvious from the data, but may be explored in future work. An interesting aspect is that the system can be used to detect outdoor events based on the detected (indoor) positions. Figure 7 shows the movement during a career day for students. The event took place in a large industrial tent on the large square in the North of the campus. No positions were located on the square, but there is much higher movement in all neighboring buildings as compared to the normal day in Fig. 4.

Issues of data sparsity for outdoor areas and some erroneous attributions will need to be improved when looking at higher granularity estimates, for example at room level and to better separate functional areas. Finding the entrance points into buildings and including movements crossing the system boundary

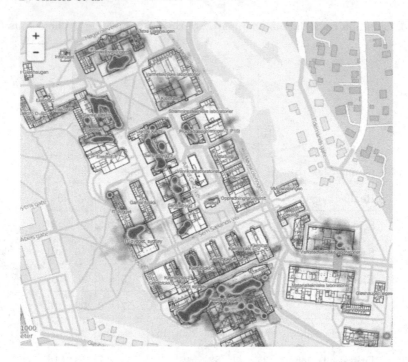

Fig. 7. Influence of (outdoor) events on indoor detected mobility: movements 11:00–12:00 of a student event in a temporary industrial tent on the square in the Northeastern part of the campus

(when people enter or leave the campus) will help in a detailed understanding of movement and transportation. We also aim to more fully utilize the height information of floors inside buildings to improve the mobility models towards three dimensions.

Another point is the improvement of the movement extraction and classification and the use of more complex data mining approaches to drive the visualizations. For added accuracy of the origin-destination matrix, we plan several improvements on the movement extraction. For example, the assumed pattern underlying the approach does not always hold and may not always be representative of actual movements. It filters out well those buildings that are merely bypassed, but when users go through a building, they may not always exhibit a consistent movement with stopping at doors or other bottlenecks, reading bulletins or meeting friends. Incidentally, the identification of bottlenecks inside buildings is another application scenario that we are working on. Additionally, considering different timings or inconsistencies of probe requests and devices that go 'dark' intermediately should also improve the measure. Finally, we will develop a stronger focus on the temporal aspect by providing additional analysis beyond time selection or animation.

6   Conclusion

We have presented our approach of campus analytics to use WLAN localization to derive movement patterns on a university campus. We have shown that the localization is sufficiently accurate to build this type of application and employ smart city analyses also on this smaller scale. Having mobility data available at very high spatial and temporal granularity makes this a very rich data source. Results show that both heat map and building graph mobility visualization can provide value to stakeholders and that patterns of movement can be identified. Further development of the NTNU campus visualization application will improve the developed methods and integrate additional modes of analysis towards using the campus analytics as a contribution for smart cities.

References

1. Andresen, S.H., Krogstie, J., Jelle, T.: Lab and research activities at wireless trondheim. In: 4th ISWCS (2007)
2. Andrienko, G., Andrienko, N., Wrobel, S.: Visual analytics tools for analysis of movement data. SIGKDD Explor. Newsl. **9**(2), 38–46 (2007)
3. Aulie, K.G.: Human Mobility Patterns from Indoor Positioning Systems. Master's thesis, Norwegian University of Science and Technology, Trondheim, Norway (2015)
4. Bak, P., Omer, I., Schreck, T.: Visual analytics of urban environments using high-resolution geographic data. In: Painho, M., Santos, M.Y., Pundt, H. (eds.) Geospatial Thinking. LNGC, vol. 0, pp. 25–42. Springer, Heidelberg (2010)
5. Becker, R., Cáceres, R., Hanson, K., Isaacman, S., Loh, J.M., Martonosi, M., Rowland, J., Urbanek, S., Varshavsky, A., Volinsky, C.: Human mobility characterization from cellular network data. Commun. ACM **56**(1), 74–82 (2013)
6. Biczok, G., Diez Martinez, S., Jelle, T., Krogstie, J.: Navigating MazeMap: indoor human mobility, spatio-logical ties and future potential. In: PerMoby 2014 (2014)
7. Eriksen, J.B.: Visualization of Crowds from Indoor Positioning Data. Master's thesis, Norwegian University of Science and Technology, Trondheim, Norway (2015)
8. Gao, S., Krogstie, J., Thingstad, T., Tran, H.: A mobile service using anonymous location-based data: finding reading rooms. Int. J. Inf. Learn. Technol. **32**(1), 32–44 (2015)
9. Ghosh, J., Beal, M.J., Ngo, H.Q., Qiao, C.: On profiling mobility and predicting locations of wireless users. In: REALMAN 2006, pp. 55–62. ACM (2006)
10. Gonzalez, M.C., Hidalgo, C.A., Barabasi, A.L.: Understanding individual human mobility patterns. Nature **453**(7196), 779–782 (2008)
11. Little, J., O'Brien, B.: A Technical Review of Cisco's Wi-Fi-Based Location Analytics. Technical report, Cisco (2013)
12. Ren, Y., Tomko, M., Ong, K., Bai, Y.B., Sanderson, M.: The influence of indoor spatial context on user information behaviours. In: Workshop on Information Access in Smart Cities. ECIR 2014 (2014)
13. Zheng, Y., Capra, L., Wolfson, O., Yang, H.: Urban computing: concepts, methodologies, and applications. ACM Trans. Intell. Syst. Technol. **5**(3), 38:1–38:55 (2014)

BIM for Corporate Real Estate Data
Visualization from Disparate Systems

S. Lazar and J.J. McArthur[✉]

Department of Architectural Science, Ryerson University,
350 Victoria Street, Toronto, ON, Canada
{s.lazar, jjmcarthur}@ryerson.ca

Abstract. Corporate Real Estate (CRE) management has several functional components, which are often owned by different departments and stored on different data management systems. A Building Information Modelling (BIM) centralized software framework is an efficient way to document, manage, share, analyze and present information used in CRE management operations and provide a single source of truth to allow evidence-based decision-making regarding individual buildings as well as property portfolios. This paper explores previous examples from the literature and presents a case study whereby BIM models were created for two existing small commercial offices to display information related to corporate real estate management, facility management and space use, building operations and maintenance, and thermal comfort and complaint tracking. These case studies demonstrate the data visualization benefits of this tool within this context and its potential for scaling to the portfolio level, as information in each of these models can be interfaced with its associated centralized data management system.

Keywords: Building Information Modeling · Corporate real estate · Lease management · Facilities management · Multi-system data visualization

1 Introduction

Building Information Modeling is effectively a database of building information, both geometric and non-geometric, with a 3D interactive graphical user interface (GUI) that allows user navigation and access to this data within an object-based virtual environment. As has been noted by some authors [1], it is often difficult for facilities managers to switch between text-based data from their Facility Management systems and the physical nature of either drawings or the built environment. Because of its information-rich and graphical nature, BIM provides a promising platform to merge these two types of data to support CRE activities.

BIM is commonly used for the design and construction of buildings, and substantial research has been published regarding data management in these contexts (e.g. [2–4]). Applications to facilities and asset management and real estate are topics of current research [5–9]; for a comprehensive review of BIM applications for existing buildings, the reader is further referred to [10].

© ICST Institute for Computer Sciences, Social Informatics and Telecommunications Engineering 2016
A. Leon-Garcia et al. (Eds.): Smart City 2015, LNICST 166, pp. 504–516, 2016.
DOI: 10.1007/978-3-319-33681-7_42

At the core of the traditional approach to BIM FM model development is the creation of an as-built model, and the subsequent addition of operations data and information to this model. This process of adding additional information to a BIM model results in the creation of multi-dimensional models, (referred to as "4D", "5D", etc.), which has proven to be a highly efficient way of documenting all aspects of a building through its life cycle [6]. Unfortunately, the creation of as-built BIM models has proved to be a barrier to adoption of BIM in FM, particularly for existing buildings due to the resource cost [10] and similarly, the constant update of such BIM models has proved a further hindrance to adoption [11]. Previous research aimed to minimize these barriers by using a simplified BIM model for data visualization [9]. That model was developed incrementally and iteratively to incorporate use cases driven by the stake-holders, and was focused on an institutional (university campus) context.

The purpose of this paper is to demonstrate how this simplified BIM model provides an efficient platform for data visualization for Corporate Real Estate (CRE) applications and presents two case study examples where BIM models were created for existing commercial offices of a financial services company (referred to herein as "FinCo"). In these examples, information related to CRE management, facility management and space use, building operations and maintenance, and thermal comfort/complaint tracking are displayed in a common user interface. Because these functions tend to be contained in organizational "silos", the associated data is typically not readily available across departments. The use of BIM to store a read-only copy of this data thus provides benefit to those individuals requiring data from multiple systems to support organizational decision-making. In this paper, these individuals will be referred to as end-users and are seen as the primary drivers of the information content of the platform. Note that FinCo does not conduct their own construction activities, but rather hires this out to third parties (as is common for corporate tenants) and thus this element is beyond the scope of the case studies. For a recent case study where this is not the case, the reader is encouraged to refer to [12].

2   Context

The ability to create simplified visual representations of data is a key benefit of BIM within the facilities management context. These representations allow end-users a simpler but more comprehensive means of understanding the relationships between building elements and processes, which is required to resolve maintenance and operations functions by building experts [7]. Critical to the CRE context are two key elements of BIM: the ability for multiple users to interface with the same model simultaneously, and the ability to interface multiple data systems with a single model. This data integration allows a simplified and efficient means of inputting and disseminating information across different software through BIM plug-ins and API scripts [5, 7, 13], and the use of a single model, particularly one that could be accessed within an Augmented Reality context on a mobile device (as proposed conceptually in [1]) further increases its potential use as a core facilities management tool.

The research presented herein recognizes the current research on data integration with existing FM software, database functions in BIM for asset management (i.e. inventory and building condition assessment), and the use of 3D representation as a means of visual analysis and navigation [6, 7, 14, 15], and builds on it by demonstrating how such use cases could be implemented using this simplified BIM model approach, reducing the barrier to adoption noted previously.

3   Case Studies

To explore the range of applications within the Corporate Real Estate (CRE) context, two case studies were undertaken in cooperation with FinCo, a large tenant occupying over 150 small facilities and five large office towers across Canada. Each considered a single small retail office and together they represented the archetypes representative of FinCo's small office portfolio, namely tower (Facility A) and walk-up (strip mall; Facility B) occupancies. For each case study, a BIM model was created based on available data and supplemented by site surveys and meetings with CRE leasing, sustainability, and data management system staff. The detailed creation of these models is further discussed in Sect. 3.1 while the use case development and interfaces with existing systems are discussed in Sects. 3.2 and 3.3, respectively.

Previous research on a similar project in the institutional sector [9] informed the BIM model development process for this research. Based on that experience, three key concepts were drivers for this methodology:

1. The effort/reward relationship must be balanced to make BIM model development both financially feasible as well as useful
2. Data must be added incrementally based on end-user needs to maximize the benefit of the model to the user and engage buy-in
3. Existing data management systems are not to be replaced by the BIM model; rather, the BIM model pulls data from multiple systems using API scripts and allows this "central" model to act as an information portal for all systems, eliminating the need for additional data management and maintenance of the model.

3.1   Building the BIM Model

The three dimensional models were created in Autodesk Revit^{TM} and produced from the as-built CAD drawings of the facilities provided by FinCo. Because these were limited to FinCo-occupied spaces, the remainder of the building was modeled with minimal detail to show the location of the leased space but no other details (Fig. 1).

Base Geometry and Equipment. 2D architectural drawings were provided by FinCo and these were used to create the floor plans and base geometry (wall, door and window locations, etc.). To minimize effort in modeling, data not relevant to the CRE systems was not modeled in detail but were included as assigned attributes, e.g. partition types and fire ratings, and captured either in notes, tags, schedules or as parameters thereby providing pertinent information without having to expend effort to create a full "as-built" detailed model. This reduced the total data content of the model significantly and optimized the model.

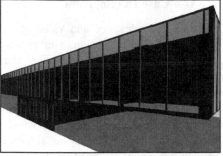

Fig. 1. 3D modeled in Revit views of the FinCo facilities used in study illustrating the base geometry elements to construct the BIM models. Facility A (left) shows a top view into the occupied floor and Facility B (right) shows the front façade.

Because FinCo either outsources maintenance (in walk-up units) or it is provided by the landlord (tower units), detailed construction and operation information for equipment is less important than details indicating who to contact in case of equipment failure. As a result, only the primary equipment was modeled using manufacturer "families" (data-rich objects containing equipment construction and performance data) and was enhanced with information more relevant to facility management systems, as discussed in Sect. 4.3. The detailed design of the air distribution systems were considered minimally relevant for the end-user and were thus not modeled as data rich objects; they were included as reference, however, in the form of a 2D drawing overlay on the ceiling, as shown in Fig. 2. This allows system information to be readily accessible while minimizing effort and model size. In addition to this system data, detailed architectural elements such as stairs and handrails were also displayed using the 2D overlay. This reduced the expended effort for such elements that offer no significant value to the corporate system database.

Fig. 2. Partial reflected ceiling plan of Facility A showing base geometry with overlaid 2D CAD data shown in grey.

3.2   Use Case Development

To ensure the relevance and value of this research to the end-users, the study was carried out in collaboration with representatives of various departments including facilities management, space planning and real estate management. This is the iterative process (Fig. 3) by which through a dialogue with FinCo, the most critical data would be added to the model in essentially what is a process of layering information onto the model. This process would commence with the creation of the level of data being the basic geometry, walls and openings which define space, followed by other components which FinCo would identify as significant for the company to garner information pertinent for management of the facilities.

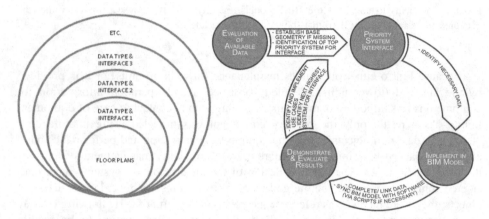

Fig. 3. Incremental data increase *(left)* and iterative process to identify, implement and evaluate use cases based on critical management needs *(right)* [9].

3.3   External Software and Data Manipulation

The BIM model is linked to multiple facility management systems as indicated conceptually in Fig. 4. Each interface is either defined as a "PUSH" interface (where data is pushed from the BIM model to the central data management systems to update geometric information) or a "PULL" interface, where this data is pulled from the central systems for visualization at the site level.

Input Information (PULL): Using the base model outlined above various analysis and reports are able to be generated from data stored in existing CMMS software being used by FinCo. Information stored in work orders or maintenance logs can be associated with the digital space or component. In the models used for FinCo one of the variables which was explored was comfort and occupant complaints. Within the models the rooms were provided with a complaint parameter that would be linked to the data provided from the complaint log. By linking the external log data to the model each log entry would be pulled into the model once synchronized via a program plug-in. In this way the floor plans can be automatically colour coded to indicate either the type of complaint logged or the frequency of complaints within the room.

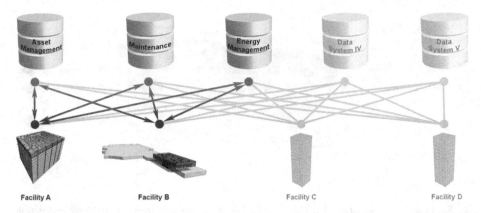

Fig. 4. Each facility BIM model interfaces with the full range of corporate data management systems, allowing the visualization of all data relevant to that facility from a range of systems as well as the potential to update all systems based on renovations or changes in space leased at the facility. (Color figure online)

Output Information (PUSH): In addition to data being parametrically manipulated to visually illustrate differing conditions and properties of various spaces and components, specific information was also directly identified in customized tags. By adding information to tags, component information is provided within the context of its location within the building. In the study models the mechanical roof top units were tagged with custom tags. It was important to FinCo to have information such as the service contractor contact information, service dates, warrantee status and manufacturer and model information easily identified within their physical context.

Data within the model can also be pushed into other software as an input. Data derived from the components or the geometry (e.g. example room areas) is used within FinCo's existing CMMS. FinCo's current software utilizes polylined CAD drawings to generate areas needed to allocate space within the facility and further across its extensive portfolio. As Revit inherently produces this information based on the modeled geometry, it can be automatically pushed into their current software once synchronized with any proposed layout produced in Revit. As Revit can produce multiple iterations, this increases the information the external software is able to receive and compare to ensure the best possible scenario is achieved.

Figure 5 illustrates both the PUSH and PULL data interfaces within each BIM model.

4   Results and Discussion

Three case studies were considered in this research: space management, complaints visualization, and equipment maintenance. These are described in Sects. 4.1, 4.2 and 4.3. Section 4.4 discusses how these case studies combined can contribute to more effective evidence-based decision-making.

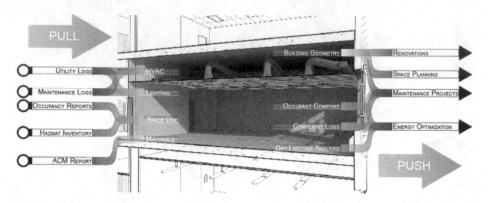

Fig. 5. Types of information that can be pulled into and pushed from the BIM by interaction with external software [9].

4.1 Space Utilization

A significant amount of effort is expended by FinCo on managing space use. FinCo's current software has the capacity to group/classify space based on variables the company assigns (Fig. 6). This serves as a powerful tool which has been customized to assist in the space allocation process of various individual spaces, group spaces, department spaces, etc., by comparing spatial needs against actual physical space. The software is capable of interpreting other variables which are essential to occupancy usage. Safety is an example of one parameter used within the software. It is able to identify where offices held by special safety personnel are required to be within the facility. BIM can be set up in a similar fashion by tagging each space with multiple space properties such as occupant type, space classification, department or fire evacuation zone. However it would be more efficient to utilize their existing software setup and pull these data points from the central facility management system (FM Interact, which is Revit-compatible) into the BIM model. This would take advantage of the existing software capabilities and BIM's ability to manipulate the layout which the space management software is not able to. This would be a powerful tool for proposing space changes during renovations for example. If the BIM model is updated to reflect the revised layout, this data transfer can be reversed, updating the room areas in the central system without undertaking the manual polyline-generation exercise that is now required for updating the data.

4.2 Comfort Complaints

Four key types of comfort complaints had been noted through site surveys and discussions with FinCo staff: thermal comfort (hot), thermal comfort (cold), air quality (odor and/or lack of fresh air), and acoustics (excessive noise and/or vibration).

In cases where thermal comfort has been historically identified as a problem in a specific area of the building this can be tracked through a running counter of complaints associated with each space type and thus assist in the diagnosis of the problem.

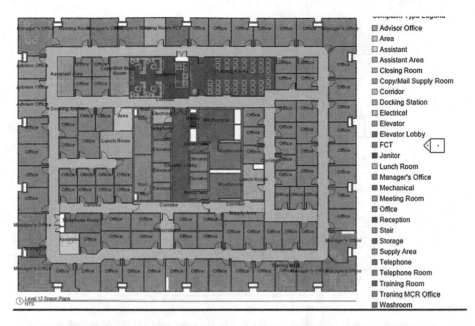

Fig. 6. Sample space management output from BIM model. (Color figure online)

By visualizing the extent of the area affected and how often individual spaces within that area log complaints, patterns of proximity to the building envelope, identification of a zone being served by a particular mechanical unit or an issue with the mechanical distribution system within the area may become apparent to maintenance staff reviewing the complaint log in conjunction with this contextual colour coded overlay (Fig. 7).

4.3   Maintenance and Operations

At Facility B, FinCo is responsible for managing their site systems and equipment. The company identified the management of the maintenance and operations records of recently installed roof top units as critical to its facilities management operations. The determined best method to document the units was using the manufacturer created Revit family. The model provided detailed visual representation and operational data with little effort. Unit variables were input into the family to reflect as built specifications. Pertinent data for the units was displayed in two ways: as 2D/3D drawings or in schedule format. The drawings gave the units their contextual locations within the facility. The units were identified with custom tags containing the unit name, make and model as well as the contracted maintenance representative information, latest service date and warrantee status. The information included in this tag was that deemed most important for quick reference required by FinCo. Additional information was available in drawing views. The detailed properties and unit capacities are visible through the BIM user interface. The schedules contain all operational and service information available on the units. External documentation such as manuals and service reports were available for the units by way of hyperlinks from the schedule (Fig. 8).

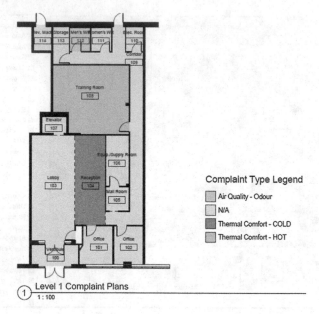

Complaint Type Legend

- Air Quality - Odour
- N/A
- Thermal Comfort - COLD
- Thermal Comfort - HOT

Level 1 Complaint Plans
1 : 100

Fig. 7. Example of complaint overlay display to inform lease renewal decision-making. (Color figure online)

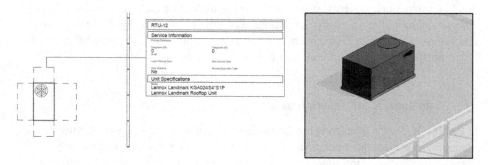

Fig. 8. Example of equipment and maintenance data visualization (rich data tag on left; 3D view to serve as reference on right)

4.4 Applications of Data Visualization in Corporate Real Estate

The value of readily available visual data for quick reference and analysis is evident in the examples above. This however is only one step beyond FinCo's current usage of their existing software. Where BIM can become an even more powerful tool for data analysis is through the flexibility with which a multiplicity of data can be integrated and captured in a single snapshot, within a Smart Cities context. This functionality can be used in energy analysis that not only takes into account detailed information provided in modeled components and systems that would typically be analyzed but also offers the capacity to overlay existing operations data, energy reports and payments from utility providers, occupancy usage, etc., onto that analysis. For example, consider the complaint log scenario described previously where there are recurring thermal comfort issues. In such a facility, the Sustainability Director would like to investigate measures by which to reduce the overall energy performance. The BIM model in this instance would be able to illustrate the heating and cooling loads through a contextual environmental analysis, the types of equipment and electrical loads within the individual space, complaints related to energy related components, typical office occupancies and billing records from the utility providers. These utility reports might indicate usage greater than expected from the loads produced by the components shown in the model. The difference that can be discerned from the overlaid information would be the highlighted thermal complaints indicating that in a large area of the facility the occupants are cold and supplement their temperature using small electric space heaters. By including all data in the visualization, information that may not typically be considered by a department can provide evidence to support improved decision-making.

Another application for consideration is lease renewal. Consider the scenario where the real estate team in the second facility has a need to modify the space. Using the BIM model for multi-system visualization, existing occupants, area requirements, existing room geometry, and existing structural and building service information can inform the basis for revision or renovation. By overlaying complaint information and work order logs on the facilities management and space data, issues related to thermal comfort or excessive noise could identify mechanical equipment in need of replacement as a condition of lease renewal, or could inform a reduced floorplate selection avoiding those areas where such historical complaints exist.

In accordance with the results of an industry survey [5], one of the issues faced within the process was a reluctance to introduce BIM as the core component among the collection existing facilities management software. The current software used by FinCo does offer the capacity to display simple 2D visualization of various data sets through custom queries. While the existing software is unable to overlay information to the extent proposed within a BIM central framework it is sufficient for FinCo's current operations. As a pilot it is difficult to ascertain the type of information that is critical for collection which would result in the most valuable use. This is a significant obstacle given the fact that the buildings being modeled have not undergone recent renovation and the availability of accurate documented information is very limited. What further complicated the collection of data was the current way in which various reports and logs were documented and stored. For example the existing documentation used for work orders is carried out using a Microsoft Excel spreadsheet document. The way in which work orders are documented consists of a minimal number separated values which include a date, an incident number, its status and a general description. The details which are necessary to assign as parameters to modeled elements are included in one unseparated value documented in the description. Simply put in order for the existing work order logs to be of value within the proposed BIM central framework the description must be further broken down into a format that can be pulled into the BIM model upon synchronization. Therefore to implement the BIM framework would necessitate a modification to some of the existing management protocols. Based on these issues, the effort that would be required to implement the framework to produce data may be considered questionable relative to the value of the BIM framework versus the existing software framework. While the type of data available will affect the feasibility of implementing the framework into existing building the issue is nonexistent with new or recently renovated facilities.

What is most significant about this approach to framework utilization is that it is meant to supplement existing software and procedures. By reusing the existing data and merely manipulating how it is presented a much greater depth of insight and analysis can be had. Further to this the BIM model is used to eliminate data entry overlap and make documentation more efficient and less prone to error [13]. While the possibilities of this application have been seen for these two test facilities, the potential for use for a complete portfolio of facilities would seem almost limitless. For example an energy analysis inventory on all facilities could become the primary selection criteria used to determine the priority sequence of capital renovation projects for all facilities. This would promote a more sustainably responsible corporation and lower overall energy operational costs. In this way the centralized software would allow a scaled approach for large scale data comparison across all properties similar to the data overlays generated within the individual BIM facility models. With this broad adaptation of the data provided by the BIM framework, an organization would be better equipped to manage its facilities to align with its overall goals as per [8].

5   Recommendations and Conclusions

The various FM and BIM software available each hosts a diverse selection of tools and capabilities for creating, storing, manipulating and presenting data. While these tools are powerful by themselves, the potential attainable through using the various systems together in an efficient workflow increases the processing and analyzing of information. Because multiple data sets can be overlaid into a single visual workspace, facilities managers and other operations personnel are able to consider multiple types of data simultaneously, increasing their capacities to analyze complex elements and processes by discerning relationships and patterns between the data which may be missed [7] and supports evidence-based decision-making in the portfolio. Herein lies the hidden value of BIM as the central hub within which a dialogue between existing FM software can be used as illustrated in the scenarios above.

In addition to the increased analytical capabilities, the BIM central framework offers greater efficiency in data sharing [13]. Because the BIM software acts as a pointer to the original data source, there is minimal data entry required to maintain the model, reducing known barriers to adoption of BIM in this context [11], and eliminating the risk of accidental data over-writes. Where calculations occur within the software, data entry is mostly eliminated. This significantly reduces the effort to maintain the BIM model and makes much greater use of the available data by maximizing information distribution efficiency.

The value of a BIM central platform is that it does not change the information or processes currently employed in facilities management but rather allows the visualization of multiple systems. This reduces the effort required to input data, while disseminating information effectively and increasing an organization's capacity for evidence-based decision-making. The ability to overlay and visualize different data sets using information-rich tags is necessary to understand how data is related and is essential in order to understand those relationships as data accumulates. Because of its intrinsic ability to combine data in this way, BIM is a powerful tool for data management. Looking from the building to the portfolio scale and beyond, these case studies have demonstrated the potential for BIM as a data visualization tool for real estate management.

Moving to the city - or Smart City - data increases exponentially, and this type of visualization approach provides insight for an owner with multiple sites to inform decision-making using large quantities of data. This ability to utilize simplified visual navigation and representation provides significant scaling potential as it would allow the visualization and synthesis of large amounts of information within complex networks. Additional case studies expanding this research to the portfolio scale would confirm this potential benefit and as such provides a promising avenue of further exploration.

Acknowledgments. The authors wish to thank the Financial Company who provided access to their facility data and insight into their data systems to facilitate this research.

References

1. Irizarry, J., Gheisari, M., Williams, G., Roper, K.: Ambient intelligence environments for accessing building information: a healthcare facility management scenario. Facilities **32** (3/4), 120–138 (2014)
2. Karan, E., Irizarry, J., Haymaker, J.: BIM and GIS integration and interoperability based on semantic web technology. J. Comput. Civ. Eng. **30**(10), 1–11 (2016). doi:10.1061/(ASCE) CP.1943-5487.0000519. 04015043-1-11
3. Lawrence, M., Pottinger, R., Staub-French, S.: Coordination of data in heterogenous domains. In: 2010 IEEE 26th International Conference on Data Engineering Workshops (ICDEW). IEEE (2010)
4. Nepal, M.N., Staub-French, S., Pottinger, R., Webster, A.: Querying a building information model for construction-specific spatial information. Adv. Eng. Inform. **26**(4), 904–923 (2012)
5. Sillanpaa, E., Sillanpaa, I.: Developing the elements of information integration in the real estate and user services. Facilities **33**(7/8), 485–501 (2015)
6. Becerik-Gerber, B., Jazizadeh, F., Li, N., Calis, G.: Application areas and data requirements for BIM-enabled facilities management. J. Constr. Eng. Manage. **138**, 431–442 (2012)
7. Motamedi, A., Hammad, A., Asen, Y.: Knowledge-assisted BIM-based visual analytics for failure root cause detection in facilities management. Autom. Constr. **43**, 73–83 (2014)
8. Ebinger, M., Madritsch, T.: A classification framework for facilities and real estate management: the built environment management model (BEM2). Facilities **30**(5/6), 185–198 (2012)
9. McArthur, J.J.: A Building Information Management (BIM) framework and supporting case study for existing building operations, maintenance and sustainability. In: International Conference on Sustainable Design, Engineering and Construction, Proc. Eng., 118C, pp. 1115–1122. Elsevier, London (2015)

10. Volk, R., Stengel, J., Schultmann, F.: Building Information Modeling (BIM) for existing buildings — literature review and future needs. Autom. Constr. **38**, 109–127 (2014)

11. Lin, Y.-C., Su, Y.-C.: Developing mobile- and BIM-based integrated visual facility maintenance management system. Sci. World J. **2013**, 124249 (2013). doi:10.1155/2013/124249

12. Neath, S., Hulse, R., Codd, A.: Building information modelling in practice: transforming Gatwick airport, UK. In: Proceedings of the Institution of Civil Engineers, 167.2, pp. 81–87 (2014)

13. Cirincione, J., Bacharach, S.: Data standards and service standards helping businesses in real estate, mortgage, appraisal, and related industries function more efficiently. J. Real Estate Lit. **15**(1), 127–137 (2007)

14. Arayici, Y., Onyenobi, T., Egbu, C.: Building Information Modelling (BIM) for Facilities Management (FM): the mediacity case study approach. Int. J. 3-D Inf. Model. **1**, 55–73 (2012)

15. Mahdjoubi, L., Moobela, C., Laing, R.: Providing real-estate services through the integration of 3D laser scanning and building information modelling. Comput. Ind. **64**, 1272–1281 (2013)

A Naive Bayesian Classification Model for Determining Peak Energy Demand in Ontario

Bon Ryu[⊠], Tokunbo Makanju, Agnieszka Lasek, Xiangdong An, and Nick Cercone

Department of Electrical Engineering and Computer Science,
Lassonde School of Engineering, York University, Toronto, ON, Canada
bonryu2@yorku.ca

Abstract. In the Canadian Province of Ontario, electricity consumers pay a surcharge for electricity called the Global Adjustment (GA). For large consumers, having the ability to predict the top 5 daily energy demand hours of the year, called 5 Coincident Peaks (5CPs), can save millions of dollars in GA costs, and help decrease peak energy usage. This paper presents a Naive Bayesian classification model for predicting the 5CPs. The model classifies hourly energy demand as being a 5CP hour or not. The model was tested using hourly energy demand for the province of Ontario over a 21 year period (1995–2015). Classifying a day as a 5CP hour containing day yielded a mean precision and recall of 0.49 (0.18) and 0.88 (0.23) (Standard deviation is in brackets), respectively. Targeting the 5CP hours to within three candidate hours of potential 5CP containing days yielded a mean precision and recall of 0.47 (0.19) and 0.83 (0.22), respectively.

Keywords: Global adjustment · Energy · Demand · Peak · Prediction · Naive Bayesian · Classification

1 Introduction

In the Canadian province of Ontario, electricity consumers pay above the market price for energy (price has units of $/energy unit, and energy has units of watt-hr, e.g. kilowatt-hr or KWHr). The additional price of energy, referred to as the *Global Adjustment* (GA) rate, is the difference between the market price and the guaranteed prices paid to regulated and contracted generators [2,6]. The GA rate applied to consumers depends on their classification as a *Class A* or a *Class B* customer. Class A customers are the largest energy consumers with top average hourly energy demands of 5 megawatts (MW) or higher, and they pay GA costs through the *Industrial Conservation Initiative* (ICI), established by the *Independent Electricity System Operator* (IESO[1]) [7].

---

[1] The IESO is a crown corporation whose mandate is to oversee the health and efficiency of the electrical grid. They are tasked with several responsibilities, such as ensuring adequate supply of electricity, and promoting the decrease of peak energy usage.

© ICST Institute for Computer Sciences, Social Informatics and Telecommunications Engineering 2016
A. Leon-Garcia et al. (Eds.): Smart City 2015, LNICST 166, pp. 517–529, 2016.
DOI: 10.1007/978-3-319-33681-7_43

The ICI program encourages Class A consumers to shift energy use away from the **5 Coincident Peak (5CP)** hours of the year. Henceforth we define 5CP as the top 5 daily maximum energy demands of a fiscal year and **peak** as one of the 5CPs. Demands are reported hourly and have units of Watts. A daily maximum is simply the maximum province wide demand for a given day. The term "Coincident" is in reference to the multiple sources of demand in Ontario during a single hour. Each of the 5CPs are daily maximum demands and must happen on different days of the fiscal year [7].

Each fiscal year (from May 1st to April 30th), the IESO maintains a table sorted by the top 10 daily maximum energy demands of the fiscal year, aggregated for all of Ontario [7]. For each row in the table, the hour for which the energy demand occurred is also recorded. Furthermore, each row in the table has an associated total Ontario wide GA cost for Class A customers [6]. At the end of the fiscal year, a Class A customer pays a percentage of this cost for the first five rows in the list (i.e. the 5CP hours), equal to the percentage of the total Ontario demand they were responsible for during those five hours.

For a given year, the total GA cost incurred by a Class A customer can be worth millions of dollars. Thus, a Class A customer can have very large savings if they can ramp down their energy usage during the 5CP hours.

In this study, we present a *Naive Bayesian Classification Algorithm* to classify hourly energy demands as a peak ($peak$) or non-peak ($peak^c$) based on the definitions outlined in the ICI program. In this context, one is actually predicting which hour will be one of the 5CP hours of the year. This is very different from traditional peak demand forecasting algorithms which attempt to predict a numerical value of demand during predetermined hours of the day.

1.1 Related Work

Currently, we are aware of only one other study in literature that aims to solve the exact same Ontario peak prediction problem [8]. In the paper, Jiang et al., modify and test a few different algorithms from literature that solved similar problems [5]. They refer to these algorithms as the following: "Californias Critical Peak Pricing, "Stopping", and "Optimization". They compared these adapted algorithms with their own novel method, which they called "Probabilistic" and report as the best performer.

Their novel algorithm utilized 14-day ahead daily maximum demand predictions from the IESO (let us call this dataset the **14-DayAhead-Dataset**). For each day of the fiscal year, their algorithm takes the maximum predicted demand for the next day (from the *14-DayAhead-Dataset*), and calculates the probability of that demand being within the top 5 of all daily maximums since the start of the fiscal year until 14 days ahead. If this probability is above some static threshold τ_p, they classify the next days maximum demand to be a one of the 5CPs for that year.

The algorithm calculates probabilities based on some probability theories (*e.g.* order statistics, distribution of differences, *etc.*), as well as employing simple IF statements to increase or decrease a demand threshold. Their logic however, requires setting a static value for "extreme temperature". At the same time, their static threshold for probability, τ_p, should be adjusted to acquire acceptable *precision* and *recall*. (See Subsect. 2.4 for definitions of Precision and Recall).

Since the 14-DayAhead-Dataset only exits for 2006 and on-wards, they used 2006 as a training set for their initial demand threshold, and tested on years 2007 to 2013. These test years only had summer peaks; a fact that will be important in comparing our own algorithm to this previous work.

1.2 Motivation

In this study, we attempt to solve this problem by classifying hourly energy demands with a Naive Bayesian Classification model. The intention was to create an algorithm that does not heavily depend on heuristic thresholds. In addition, from a machine learning perspective, we preferred an approach that can easily accommodate many variables as inputs, and which has the potential for testing the best combination of inputs.

The results of the initial model were reported in a previous work [3], which had the limitations of discretizing continuous variables, and not predicting winter coincident peaks. The current version of the model solves these issues.

Furthermore, we wished to train and test our model on more years, including those that have winter peaks. The occurrence of winter peaks is a very real possibility and we wanted a model that could easily accommodate such occurrences.

2 Methods

2.1 A Naive Bayesisan Classifier to Classify Energy Demand as Peaks or Non-peaks

In a Naive Bayesian classification model [11], variables used as inputs create a vector,

$$\boldsymbol{x} = (a, b, c, d, e, f) \tag{1}$$

$\boldsymbol{x}$, is also called a *tuple*, and the elements, a to f are called *attributes*.

Using Bayes theorem, the model calculates the following two conditional probabilities that an hourly demand is a *peak* or $peak^c$, given a tuple $\boldsymbol{x}$.

$$P(peak|\boldsymbol{x}) = \frac{P(\boldsymbol{x}|peak)P(peak)}{P(\boldsymbol{x}|peak)P(peak) + P(\boldsymbol{x}|peak^c)P(peak^c)} \tag{2}$$

$$P(peak^c|\boldsymbol{x}) = \frac{P(\boldsymbol{x}|peak^c)P(peak^c)}{P(\boldsymbol{x}|peak)P(peak) + P(\boldsymbol{x}|peak^c)P(peak^c)} \tag{3}$$

The left hand side of the equations are called posterior probabilities, and there are only two because we only have two classifications, *peak* and $peak^c$. Their sum equals 1, and the final classification of an hourly demand corresponds to whichever posterior probability is largest.

$P(peak)$ is the probability of a peak. Let N_{train} be the number of training years. Since there are only five top-5 peak demands in a year and demand is reported hourly,

$$P(peak) = \frac{\# \text{ of Peaks}}{\# \text{ of training hours}}, \tag{4}$$

$$\# \text{ of Peaks} = 5N_{train}, \tag{5}$$

$$\# \text{ of training hours} = \sum_{year_i \,\in\, training\ year} \# \text{ tuples in } year_i \tag{6}$$

The probability of a non-peak is simply

$$P(peak^c) = 1 - P(peak) \tag{7}$$

The following conditional probabilities are called *likelihoods*:

$$P(\boldsymbol{x}|peak) = \prod_{A=a..f} P(A|peak) \tag{8}$$

$$P(\boldsymbol{x}|peak^c) = \prod_{A=a..f} P(A|peak^c) \tag{9}$$

where A is a variable for a specific attribute from a to f.

To train the classification model, one first partitions the training tuples into a set of peaks ($\{peak\}$) and non-peaks ($\{peak^c\}$) based on prior knowledge of how to classify them (i.e. $\boldsymbol{x} \in \{peak\}$ **IF demand is top-5**, else $\boldsymbol{x} \in \{peak^c\}$).

For each discrete attribute that has disjoint bins, one calculates the conditional probability of a tuple belonging to each bin by simply counting. *E.g.* If A is *discrete*,

$$P(A = A_{bin1}|peak) = \frac{\#(\{peak\} \cap \{\boldsymbol{x}|\boldsymbol{x}_A \in A_{bin1}\})}{\#\{peak\}} \tag{10}$$

$$P(A = A_{bin1}|peak^c) = \frac{\#(\{peak\} \cap \{\boldsymbol{x}|\boldsymbol{x}_A \in A_{bin1}\})}{\#\{peak^c\}} \tag{11}$$

In Sect. 2.3, we describe how the likelihoods for the continuous variables were calculated.

2.2 Data Sources and Software Tools

The attributes used to train the Naive Bayesian classification model prototype were Ontario energy demand, hour of the day, day type (*e.g.* holiday or workday), temperature, humidex, and windchill. Historical demand data from May 1st, 1994 April 30th, 2015 is publicly available and were obtained from the IESO [1].

Unfortunately, we were not able to acquire the historical 14-DayAhead-Dataset from the IESO, which Jiang et al. says exists for 2006 onward. Currently, on a real-time hourly basis, the IESO provides hourly predictions up to 7 days

Table 1. Attributes for the Naive Bayesian Classification Model. For continuous attributes, the bandwidths used for Gaussian kernel density estimations of PDFs are shown. The estimation algorithm was developed by Kristan *et al.* [9]

Discrete attribute	#Bins	Bins
Hour of day	24	1, 2, 3, ... , 24
Day type	6	Weekend or holiday, workday Monday, workday Tuesday, workday Wednesday, workday Thursday, workday Friday

Continuous attribute	PDF	Bandwidth
Temperature	$P(Temperature\|peak)$	Automatic
	$P(Temperature\|peak^c)$	Automatic
Humidex	$P(Humidex\|peak)$	2
	$P(Humidex\|peak^c)$	0.35
Windchill	$P(Windchill\|peak)$	Automatic
	$P(Windchill\|peak^c)$	0.35
Normalized Demand (NormDem)	$P(NormDem\|peak)$	Automatic
	$P(NormDem\|peak^c)$	Automatic

in advance but we could not to the best of our abilities locate such information for past days and years.

Hourly weather data was obtained for the Toronto Buttonville Airport from the climate website of the government of Canada [4]. Raw data was originally imported into a MYSQL database with php scripting. The rest of the work such as querying, model creation, training, and testing were all done in MATLAB [10]. All work was performed on a machine with an Intel Core i5 M 540 CPU, with 8 Gb of ram.

2.3   Attributes and Training

Discrete Attributes. Since peaks also never occurred during the weekends or holidays, the attribute *day type* was designed to differentiate between weekends/holidays, and workday weekdays. *Hour of day* is also an important attribute for the model since high energy demands usually occur during specific hours. Both these attributes had naturally occurring discrete bins.

Continuous Attributes. To avoid the issue of binning continuous attributes, Gaussian Kernel Density Estimation (KDE) was used to estimate probability density functions (PDF). A MATLAB implementation was borrowed from

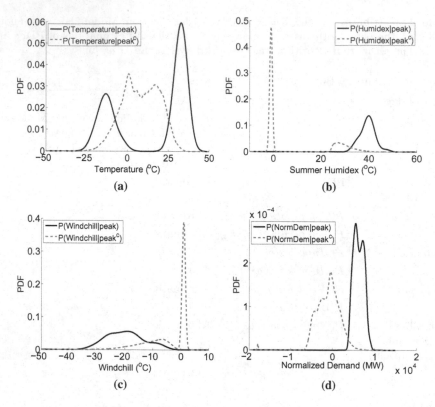

Fig. 1. Example of Gaussian kernel density estimations of continuous attribute PDFs. The PDFs above were derived by training on all years except for 1997. (a) Temperature, (b) Humidex, (c) Windchill, (d) Normalized Demand (NormDem).

Kristan *et al.* [9]. Gaussian KDE involves treating each count of a histogram as a normal Gaussian (i.e. a Gaussian kernel), adding all the kernels, and dividing the resulting function by the number of kernels added in order to re-normalize. Kristan *et al.*'s implementation automatically estimates the bandwidth of the Gaussian kernels to be added (**bandwidth** is a smoothing parameter that modifies the widths of the kernels). This automatic estimation had to be manually adjusted for a few of the distributions, to achieve relatively smooth PDFs. For the sake of helping readers reproduce our results while using Kristen *et al.*'s algorithm, the set bandwidths are listed in Table 1. The PDFs of the continuous variables used for test year 1997 is shown as an example in Fig. 1.

Temperature is an important continuous attribute. High and low temperatures are correlated with summer and winter peaks, respectively. As an additional way of helping differentiate between peaks and non-peaks, we also used humidex and windchill, which are indices that combines the effects of high temperatures with humidity and wind speed, respectively.

There were no humidex values below 25 °C, and no winchill values above 0 °C, and empty humidex and windchill values only existed for $peak^c$ tuples. During pre-processing, empty humidex and windchill values were assigned a value of -1 and 1, respectively. This simplified our code by allowing the KDE algorithm to take care of maintaining the relative size of the empty and non-empty domains of the $peak^c$ PDFs. The exact values assigned to the empty values are not important as long as the ratio $P(A|peak)/P(A|peak^c)$ approaches zero somewhat monotonically, as the humidex and windchill approaches the assigned values from their non-empty domains.

Normalizing Demand. To decrease the variance in the demand *probability distribution functions* (PDFs), the demand is normalized by subtracting from each fiscal year's demand data, the average maximum daily demands of the first 15 working days of the fiscal year. Thus the demand data from all the years are shifted to a common starting point (i.e. to zero), to remove the effects of different baseline demands of different years. Luckily no peaks have ever occurred during the first 15 days of May. Thus in real-time use of the algorithm, this process should not negatively affect the detection of summer peaks.

2.4 Testing and Evaluation

Since we could not obtain the historical 14-DayAhead-Dataset from the IESO (as mentioned previously in Subsect. 2.2), during testing we used the actual historical hourly demand for the testing years. This is a limitation of this current study, which we hope to address in the future by at the very least downloading prediction data on a daily basis and estimating the predicted demand with a random error term.

We did however, test on many years of historical data (*i.e.* for fiscal years ending in 1995 to 2015), whereas in literature [8], tests were only done for 2005 on-wards. Since there were 21 full years of demand data, the model was trained 21 times, each time excluding a desired testing year, and testing on the excluded year.

To help compare the best performing peak prediction algorithms in literature [8] with ours, we compute similar metrics such as precision and recall.

Evaluation Metrics. Precision is the number of true positives (TP) divided by the total number of positive predictions, which is the sum of true positives and false positives (FP). Precision is also know as positive predictive value.

$$Precision = \frac{\#\text{True Positives}}{\#\text{True Positives} + \#\text{False Positives}} = \frac{TP}{TP + FP} \quad (12)$$

Recall is the number of true positives (TP) divided by the number of actual positives (AP), which is the sum of true positives and false negatives (FN). Recall is also known as *sensitivity*.

$$Recall = \frac{\#\text{True Positives}}{\#\text{Actual Positives}} = \frac{TP}{TP + FN} \tag{13}$$

Note that the set of tuples counted as TP or FN make up the set of peaks, $\{peak\}$, and $TP + FN = \#$Actual Positives $= 5$. FN and True Negative counts (TN) are not reported, but they are simply the complements of TP and FP, respectively.

2.5   Prediction Time-Frame: 24 Hrs, 3 Hrs, and 1 Hr

In the work by previous authors, predictions of peaks are performed to classify an entire day as a peak day or not, and precision and recall is calculated only on daily peak predictions [8].

In the current study, we go a step further and attempt to predict whether or not a peak occurs among the Top 3 hours of the day, or during a single hour. Let these three additional prediction types be called *3 Hr*, and *1-Hr* predictions. The following describes what constitutes a TP or FP for these different prediction types. Let the prediction of a *peak* and *peak^c* be labeled as `true` and `false`, respectively.

Daily Peak Prediction. A Daily Peak is simply an entire day that is labeled as `true` because it contains at least a single hourly tuple whose value of $P(peak|\boldsymbol{x})$ is greater or equal to 0.5. If an actual *peak* occurs on this day, then increase TP by 1. If an actual *peak* does not occur on this day, then increase FP by 1.

3-Hr Peak Prediction. Once a Daily Peak is predicted, look at the *three hours with the highest values* of $P(peak|\boldsymbol{x})$, and label these three hours as `true`. If an actual *peak* occurs during one of the three hours, then increase TP by 1. If an actual *peak* does not occur during one of the three hours, then increase FP by 1.

1-Hr Peak Prediction. Once a Daily Peak is predicted, look at the *hour* with the highest value of $P(peak|\boldsymbol{x})$, and label this hour as `true`. If an actual *peak* occurs during this hour, then increase TP by 1. If an actual *peak* does not occur on this hour, then increase FP by 1.

3   Results

True positive count (TP), false positive count (FP) count, precision (Eq. 12) and recall (Eq. 13) were computed for all 21 test years, and are displayed in Table 2. This table compares the precision and recall for the three different prediction types mentioned above.

Precision for daily predictions ranged from 0.25 and 1.00, and was below 0.4 for five out of the 21 test years (1996, 1998, 2003, 2006). The low precision for these years mean that the FP count was high compared to the TP count.

Table 2. TP, FP, Precision, and Recall for all 21 testing years. Fiscal year ends are from 1995 to 2015. Color scales were generated in Microsoft Excel. The blue scale is between 0 and 5, red scale is between 0 and 12, and green scale is between 0.0 and 1.0. #S Pks and #W Pks stand for number of actual summer and winter peaks, respectively.

Test Year	#S Pks	#W Pks	TP Day	TP 3-Hr	TP 1-Hr	FP Day	FP 3-Hr	FP 1-Hr	Precision Day	Precision 3-Hr	Precision 1-Hr	Recall Day	Recall 3-Hr	Recall 1-Hr
1995	0	5	5	5	3	4	4	6	0.56	0.56	0.33	1.0	1.0	0.6
1996	0	5	3	3	1	9	9	11	0.25	0.25	0.08	0.6	0.6	0.2
1997	0	5	2	2	1	2	2	3	0.50	0.50	0.25	0.4	0.4	0.2
1998	1	4	1	1	1	3	3	3	0.25	0.25	0.25	0.2	0.2	0.2
1999	1	4	5	5	5	6	6	6	0.45	0.45	0.45	1.0	1.0	1.0
2000	3	2	5	5	5	7	7	7	0.42	0.42	0.42	1.0	1.0	1.0
2001	2	3	3	3	2	0	0	1	1.00	1.00	0.67	0.6	0.6	0.4
2002	5	0	5	3	2	5	7	8	0.50	0.30	0.20	1.0	0.6	0.4
2003	5	0	5	4	4	11	12	12	0.31	0.25	0.25	1.0	0.8	0.8
2004	2	3	5	5	5	6	6	6	0.45	0.45	0.45	1.0	1.0	1.0
2005	1	4	5	5	4	5	5	6	0.50	0.50	0.40	1.0	1.0	0.8
2006	5	0	5	5	3	10	10	12	0.33	0.33	0.20	1.0	1.0	0.6
2007	5	0	5	5	3	8	8	10	0.38	0.38	0.23	1.0	1.0	0.6
2008	5	0	5	5	4	7	7	8	0.42	0.42	0.33	1.0	1.0	0.8
2009	5	0	5	5	2	2	2	5	0.71	0.71	0.29	1.0	1.0	0.4
2010	5	0	5	5	4	2	2	3	0.71	0.71	0.57	1.0	1.0	0.8
2011	5	0	5	4	2	6	7	9	0.45	0.36	0.18	1.0	0.8	0.4
2012	5	0	4	4	1	6	6	9	0.40	0.40	0.10	0.8	0.8	0.2
2013	5	0	5	5	4	7	7	8	0.42	0.42	0.33	1.0	1.0	0.8
2014	5	0	5	4	1	4	5	8	0.56	0.44	0.11	1.0	0.8	0.2
2015	2	3	4	4	2	1	1	3	0.80	0.80	0.40	0.8	0.8	0.4
min	0	0	1	1	1	0	0	1	0.25	0.25	0.08	0.20	0.20	0.20
max	5	5	5	5	5	11	12	12	0.19	0.20	0.16	0.29	0.29	0.30
mean	3.19	1.81	4.38	4.14	2.81	5.29	5.52	6.86	0.49	0.47	0.31	0.88	0.83	0.56
σ	2.01	2.01	1.13	1.12	1.40	2.88	3.00	3.04	0.18	0.19	0.15	0.23	0.22	0.28

Recall for daily predictions was very high for all 21 years except for three: 1996, 1997, and 1998. Recall was 1.0 for all but 6 of our 21 test years. Of these six test years, two had recalls of $0.8 = 4/5$ (2012 and 2015), two had recalls of $0.6 = 3/5$ (1996 and 2001), one had recall of $0.4 = 2/5$ (1997) and finally one had recall of just $0.2 = 1/5$ (1998).

As expected, making daily predictions yielded the highest precision and recall, compared to targeting a smaller time-frame of prediction (*e.g.* 3 h or 1 h). Performance was not as good for the 3-Hr and 1-Hr peak predictions methods, which were preliminary attempts to hone in on smaller prediction time-frames. The authors have yet to investigate all possible methods of targeting smaller prediction time-frames, and are hopeful that further study will be fruitful.

Table 3. Precision and Recall averaged across 7 years from **2007 to 2013**, inclusively, for the three different prediction types. σ is standard deviation. The results of the daily predictions of the "Probabilistic" algorithm from literature [8] are displayed for comparison. The green color scale was generated in Microsoft Excel and is between 0.0 and 1.0

	Precision				Recall			
	Daily	Probab-ilistic	3-Hr	1-Hr	Daily	Probab-ilistic	3-Hr	1-Hr
min	0.38	0.40	0.36	0.10	0.8	0.8	0.8	0.2
max	0.71	0.71	0.71	0.57	1.0	1.0	1.0	0.8
mean	0.50	0.55	0.49	0.29	0.97	0.94	0.94	0.57
σ	0.14	0.11	0.14	0.14	0.07	0.11	0.09	0.22

Additionally, precision and recall of the Daily predictions were averaged for years 2007 to 2013 to help compare with the results in literature [8], and these results are show in Table 3. As previously mentioned, the "Probabilistic" algorithm in literature made daily predictions and was tested on data for fiscal years 2007 to 2013 [8]. The average precision, recall, and their corresponding standard deviations of the "Probabilistic" algorithm are shown in Table 3 for comparison with our Daily peak predictions. In Table 3, the minimum and maximum precision values were estimated from the plots given in literature, and the fact that their minimum and maximum precisions as fractions must have numerators (TP in Eq. 12) of 4 or 5.

The current model, had slightly higher recall and slightly lower precision in comparison to the model in literature. Furthermore, both the Daily and 3-Hr prediction methods had high recall for many years for which winter peaks existed. Years with winter peaks were not tested in literature.

4   Discussion

In making daily peak predictions, the Naive Bayesian Classification algorithm had a precision and recall that is comparable to work by previous authors [8]. The model was tested on many more years, however, and was trained and tested on years with winter peaks, which was not previously done. While the results are good, there is still potential for even better performance.

4.1   Low Recall for 1996, 1997, 1998

Low recall (0.6 or less) for the test years 1996, 1997, and 1998 likely cannot be attributed to whether the low recall test years had more winter peaks since both summer and winter peaks occurred commonly during many years for which the model performed with perfect recall. Most likely the issue is related to the normalization procedure described in Sect. 2.3. The procedure was carried out to eliminate the effects of large differences in baseline demand from year to year, and help line up the demand thresholds from one year to the next.

The point was to decrease the variance in the demand and increase the separation of the peak and non-peak distributions. For the testing years in question, this procedure may have been insufficient, or it may have inadvertently shifted the testing years' demand thresholds away from the average demand threshold of the training years.

4.2   Demand Threshold Prediction

The current model does not predict a demand threshold, and the authors believe that incorporating an adaptive estimation of the demand threshold (i.e. the midpoint between the 5th and 6th top demand) may solve the low precision and recall problems during a few of the years.

Most of the algorithms tested in literature are demand threshold prediction algorithms [8], and any such algorithms can be incorporated to the current one in the following way. Every time a demand is being tested, one could shift the test demand value by the same amount one would shift the current demand threshold to line it up with the intersection of the *peak* and *peak^c* PDFs in Fig. 1d. The more accurate the estimation, the better the model would perform. Even if the estimation is not perfect, the other attributes may be just extreme enough to push the classification to be a peak (or mild enough to push the classification to be a non-peak). Even without a threshold demand prediction incorporated into the model, the model works fairly well. Thus, any demand threshold predictions that works better than no prediction, would likely improve the current model.

If there exists an algorithm that can predict the threshold perfectly, then the problem is solved completely. However, this is very unrealistic and the best one can do is predict the threshold as well as possible. Then, in the case of the Naive Bayesian algorithm, use other attributes to take the final step in deciding if a peak will occur.

4.3   Testing on Years with Winter Peaks

The current model benefited from experimenting and training on years with winter peaks such as the years previous to 2006 as well this past fiscal year ending in April 2015. It has been tested and shown to work well for many years with summer and/or winter peaks. The previous authors did not train nor test on years with winter peaks because predicted day ahead Ontario demands were only available from 2006 to 2013 when winter peaks did not occur [8].

4.4   Testing on Actual Versus Predicted Demand Data

A limitation of the current study is that the current model was tested on actual demand data, due to the authors being unable to acquire daily historical *predicted* demand (*i.e. the 14-DayAhead-Dataset*). Our Daily Prediction method (see Subsect. 2.5) may perform poorer using such demand data. In that regard, we commend the work of the previous authors who managed to test their model on day ahead predicted demand [8].

Due to using actual demand data for testing, the 3-Hr and 1-Hr peak predictions were designed to not utilize the knowledge of the highest hourly demand of the day. If the 14-DayAhead-Dataset can be used for testing, then knowledge of the predicted maximum demand hour can be used. This would likely increase the precision and recall of the 3-Hr and 1-Hr prediction methods closer to that of the Daily prediction method.

5   Conclusion and Future Work

The Naive Bayesian Classification Model was successfully trained and tested 21 times. The mean precision and recall of Daily classifications were 0.49 (0.18) and 0.88 (0.23), respectively[2]. Predicting whether a peak will occur in a smaller time-frame is more difficult. When the model was used to choose three hours of a potential peak day as candidates for the top 5 yearly peak hours, the mean precision and recall were 0.47 (0.19) and 0.83 (0.22), respectively. The results are promising and with some additional work, the authors are confident that the model's statistical evaluation metrics will improve significantly.

6   Future Work

Besides incorporating a demand threshold prediction algorithm to the current model, further testing of the model will involve acquiring and testing on predicted demand data. At the very least, testing will use estimated predicted demand, which can be derived by considering the standard deviation of predicted demand with respect to actual demand. Past weekly and current daily predicted demand can be downloaded easily from the IESO. Once such testing is possible, we will also optimize methods of predicting peaks within the smaller time-frames of one, two, and three hours.

This study is part of a much larger project that will involve integrating many different algorithms to a common cloud based big data server and visual analytics system. One of goals of the project will be to help different types of Ontario energy consumers reduce peak energy usage as well as decrease overall energy consumption.

Acknowledgments. This work was supported by a Collaborative Research and Development (CRD) grant from the Natural Sciences and Engineering Research Council of Canada (NSERC), grant number 461882-2013. The authors of this work thank their collaborative development partner Fuseforward Solutions Group. The authors also thank Ricky Fok for suggesting the use of Kristan *et al.*'s kernel density estimation algorithm.

---

[2] Standard deviation is in brackets.

References

1. IESO Data Directory. http://www.ieso.ca/Pages/Power-Data/Data-Directory.aspx. Accessed 27 July 2015
2. Office of the Auditor General of Ontario - Report on Renewable Energy initiatives. http://www.auditor.on.ca/en/reports_en/en11/303en11.pdf. Accessed 30 June 2015
3. An, X., Cercone, N.: A statistical model for predicting power demand peaks in power systems. In: Proceedings of the 12th International Conference on Fuzzy Systems and Knowledge Discovery, pp. 1022–1026 (2015)
4. Environment Canada: Climate Data - Environment Canada, October 2011. http://climate.weather.gc.ca/. Accessed 01 July 2015
5. Gallagher, S.H.: Electric Demand Response Tariffs Clean-Up. http://www.pge.com/nots/rates/tariffs/tm2/pdf/ELEC_3221-E.pdf. Accessed 06 July 2015
6. IESO: IESO Global Adjustment. http://www.ieso.ca/Pages/Ontario%27s-Power-System/Electricity-Pricing-in-Ontario/Global-Adjustment.aspx. Accessed 30 June 2015
7. IESO: IESO Global Adjustment, for Class A customers. http://www.ieso.ca/Pages/Participate/Settlements/Global-Adjustment-for-Class-A.aspx. Accessed 30 June 2015
8. Jiang, Y.H., Levman, R., Golab, L., Nathwani, J.: Predicting peak-demand days in the Ontario peak reduction program for large consumers. In: Proceedings of the 5th International Conference on Future Energy Systems, e-Energy 2014, pp. 221–222. ACM, New York (2014). http://doi.acm.org/10.1145/2602044.2602076, Accessed 30 June 2015
9. Kristan, M., Leonardis, A., Skoaj, D.: Multivariate online kernel density estimation with Gaussian kernels. Pattern Recognit. 44(1011), 2630–2642 (2011). http://www.sciencedirect.com/science/article/pii/S0031320311001233, Accessed 09 July 2015
10. MATLAB: version 7.8 (R2009a). The MathWorks Inc., Natick (2009)
11. Russell, S., Norvig, P.: Artificial Intelligence: A Modern Approach. Prentice-Hall, Englewood Cliffs, New Jersey (1995)

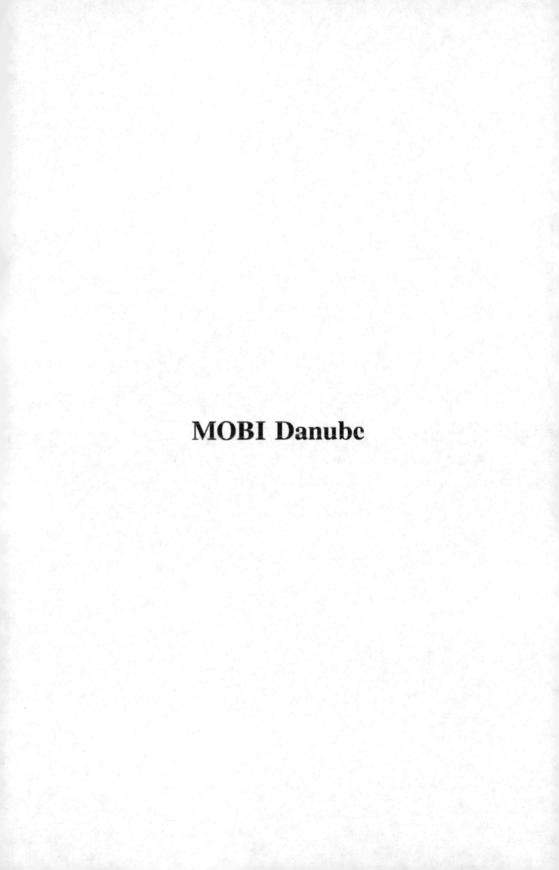

MOBI Danube

Eco-Innovation in Manufacturing Process in Automotive Industry

Martin Spirko[1], Daniela Spirkova[2(✉)], Dagmar Caganova[3],
and Manan Bawa[3]

[1] Faculty of Electrical Engineering and Information Technology,
Slovak University of Technology in Bratislava,
Ilkovicova 3, 812 19 Bratislava, Slovakia
martinspirkol@gmail.com
[2] Institute of Management, Slovak University of Technology in Bratislava,
Vazovova 5, 812 43 Bratislava, Slovakia
daniela.spirkova@stuba.sk
[3] Faculty of Materials Science and Technology in Trnava, Slovak University
of Technology in Bratislava, Paulinska 16, 917 24 Trnava, Slovakia
{dagmar.caganova,manan.bawa}@stuba.sk

Abstract. One of the current problems of the global nature is environmental pollution caused by industrial production. Nowadays, we know many advanced hi-tech materials and production methods in the car industry, but when it comes to such innovations, the environment is often forgotten. Therefore it is necessary to find a solution that technological innovations in automobiles will go hand in hand with innovations of emission reductions in manufacturing process. One of ways to achieve a reduction of emissions and prevent leakage of harmful substances is to change the structure of the different principles in the production process (substitute auxiliary compounds, change amount of the compounds, the expansion of the recycling process). The aim of this paper is to highlight the innovation of the manufacturing processes in the automotive industry in order to reduce emissions and save the environment and partially point out also the innovated products of the manufacturing process.

Keywords: Environment · Sustainability · Manufacturing process · Automotive industry

1 Introduction

Decrease of fossil fuel reserves, environmental and human health damage as well as the ethical dimension of the problem related to that whether we have the moral right to extract and burn all the oil need to think about changing the status quo. Efforts to change requires new technologies which require a new way of thinking.

European cities are home of 70 % of the EU population which forms more than 80 % of EU GDP. Mobility within cities is still more complicated and inefficient. Road transport has become the largest polluter of the environment in urban areas, while emissions from transport grow every year [1].

© ICST Institute for Computer Sciences, Social Informatics and Telecommunications Engineering 2016
A. Leon-Garcia et al. (Eds.): Smart City 2015, LNICST 166, pp. 533–540, 2016.
DOI: 10.1007/978-3-319-33681-7_44

Automotive companies are beginning to recognize the new situation that calls for faster implementation of eco-innovation in manufacturing processes, which will be related to the production of new fuels and lower consumption of vehicles. There are still more and more examples. Toyota is already selling models in Japan with consumption of 4 l/100 km. In Brazil, several million cars runs on ethanol. Shell has built its own division specialized in the renewable energy sources. BP became one of the world's most successful manufacturers of solar panels and General Motors are trying to introduce higher tax on gasoline. All this can be included in innovative approaches in manufacturing processes.

2 Problem Identification

Eco-innovations are normally defined as innovations whose primary purpose is to reduce damage to the environment and the nature by various scientific disciplines, such as institutional and evolutionary economics, industrial economics, system analysis and operation research, knowledge management, organizational change management and so on [2].

The term "eco-innovation" refers to innovative products, processes or organizational innovations that reduce environmental costs, increase the acceptance of society and contribute to sustainable development. The concept is often used in conjunction with "eco-efficiency" and "eco-design" and also covers ideas related to environmentally friendly technological advances and socially acceptable, innovative ways towards sustainability [3]. Eco-innovations reduce material requirements, use closed material flows, or create respectively use new materials. They also focus on reducing energy demand, or create respectively use alternative energy sources, reduce overall emissions released into environment or existing environmental burdens and health risks in order to support the idea of healthy lifestyles and sustainable consumption [4].

The automotive and transport industry has taken steps to reduce CO_2 emissions and other environmental impacts, notably those associated with fossil fuel combustion. Combined with the growing demand for mobility, particularly in developing economies, many eco-innovation initiatives have focused on increasing the overall energy efficiency of automobiles and transport, while heightening automobile safety. Eco-innovations have, for the most part, been realized through technological advances, typically in the form of product or process modification and re-design, such as more efficient fuel injection technologies, better power management systems, energy-saving tires and optimization of painting processes. Yet, there are indications that the understanding of eco-innovation in this sector is broadening.

For example, the introduction of new legislative requirements for motor vehicle emissions in the United States in 1993 intensified pressures on the automotive industry to reduce the environmental impact from the use of automobiles. In response, a number of steelmakers from around the world joined together to create the Ultra-Light Steel Auto Body (ULSAB) initiative to develop stronger and lighter auto bodies. From this venture, the ULSAB Advanced Vehicles Concept (ULSAB-AVC) emerged. The first proof-of-concept project for applying advanced high-strength steel (AHSS) to automobiles was conducted in 1999. By optimizing the car body with AHSS at little additional cost compared to conventional steel, the overall weight saving could reach nearly 9 % of the total weight of a typical five-passenger family car. It is estimated that for every 10 % reduction in vehicle weight, the fuel economy is improved by 1.9–8.2 % [5]. At the same time, the reduced weight makes it possible to downsize the vehicle's power train without any loss in performance, thus leading to additional fuel savings. Owing to their high- and ultra-high-strength steel components, such vehicles rank high in terms of crash safety and require less steel for construction.

The iron and steel industry's continuing R&D efforts in this area also stem from its attempt to strengthen steel's competitive advantage over alternatives such as aluminum. The Future Steel Vehicle (FSV) is the latest in the series of auto steel research initiatives. It combines global steelmakers with a major automotive engineering partner in order to realize safe, lightweight steel bodies for vehicles and reduce GHG emissions over the lifecycle of the vehicle [6].

Innovation plays a key role in moving manufacturing industries towards sustainable production. Evolving sustainable manufacturing initiatives – from traditional pollution control through cleaner production initiatives, to a lifecycle view, to the establishment of closed-loop production – can be viewed as facilitated by eco-innovation. Figure 1 provides a simple illustration of the general conceptual relations between sustainable manufacturing and eco-innovation. The steps in sustainable manufacturing are depicted in terms of their primary association with respect to eco-innovation, i.e. with innovation targets on the left and mechanisms at the bottom. The waves spreading towards the upper right corner indicate the path dependencies of different sustainable manufacturing concepts.

While more integrated sustainable manufacturing initiatives such as closed-loop production can potentially yield higher environmental improvements in the medium to long term, they can only be realized through a combination of a wider range of innovation targets and mechanisms and therefore cover a larger area of Fig. 1.

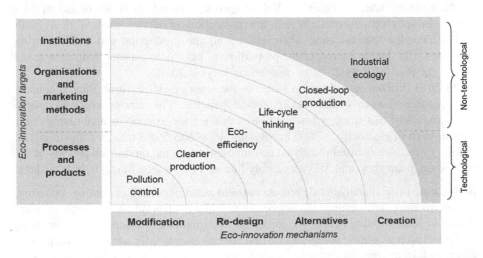

Fig. 1. Conceptual relationships between sustainable manufacturing and eco-innovation [6]

These complex, advanced eco-innovation processes are often referred to as system innovation – an innovation characterized by fundamental shifts in how society functions and how its needs are met [7]. Although system innovation may have its source in technological advances, technology alone will not make a great difference. It has to be associated with organizational and social structures and with human nature and cultural values. While this may indicate the difficulty of achieving large-scale environmental improvements, it also hints at the need for manufacturing industries to adopt an approach that aims to integrate the various elements of the eco-innovation process so as to leverage the maximum environmental benefits. The feasibility of their eco-innovative approach would then depend on the organization's ability to engage in such complex processes [6].

3   Results and Discussion

"Ecological modernization" – understood as systematic eco-innovation and its diffusion – has by far the largest potential to achieve environmental improvements. In general, the market logic of modernization and competition for innovation combined with the market potential of global environmental needs serve as important driving forces behind "ecological modernization" [8]. In recent times, however, additional factors like rising energy prices or fears from climate change have favored the rise of this innovation-based approach to environmental policy.

Environmental strategic visions and plans of automotive companies are generally based on the following key objectives:

- non-waste production technologies,
- reduction of emissions throughout the life cycle,
- reduction in fuel consumption and alternative sources of propulsion,
- replacement of non-recyclable materials,
- reducing the consumption of energy and water in the production process.

As a model case, we chose the Volkswagen Group, which is one of the world's largest automotive concerns. Within the protection of environment it deals with environmentally relevant issue where belong all the production and manufacturing processes with the aim to reduce the proportion of key environmental indicators at the end of the year 2018 by 25 % in comparison to year 2010.

In 2013, Volkswagen Slovakia joined to the strategy called Think Blue to achieve with production even greater environmental benefits. The seriousness Volkswagen approaches how this strategy has real results that are for example annual savings of 1 million kWh of electricity, 77.000 m^3 of natural gas and 595.8 tons of CO_2 (in 2013). In this context, we focused mainly on eco-innovations in the production process of the body shop, paint shop and SUVs assembly line at Volkswagen Slovakia in Bratislava.

Bodyshop. In the manufacturing process are used techniques such as welding, soldering, gluing, riveting and bolting. An important technique of bonding is energy efficient resistance spot welding. There are used also environmentally friendly manufacturing processes such as gluing using solvent-free adhesives and laser welding - energy efficiency of laser aggregates is very high. Several machines in the manufacturing process are

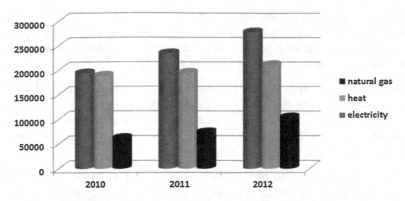

Fig. 2. Lowering values of energy indicators in Volkswagen Slovakia [9]

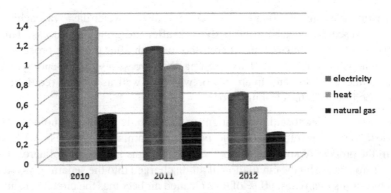

Fig. 3. Energy indicators in MWh/vehicle [9]

powered hydraulically. The relevant units are equipped with sump, which protect the subsoil in the event of malfunction against leaking hydraulic fluid. Welding smoke is suctioned and before being discharged into the environment is filtered through appropriate filtering equipment that removes polluting particles. Metals residues that remain from the production of car body are transported for recycling (Figs. 2 and 3).

Laser soldering. Impact on energy savings has also soldering of roof welds with side body parts, which is performed by a laser beam with more options of metal soldering. It can bond work pieces on the surface or create deep welds. The surface of the soldered joint is smooth and clean. Using the proper soldering wire will reduce the need for subsequent treatment of products. The source of this laser beam is so-called diode laser, which in comparison to the previous generation of arc lamp is 8-times more effective and has 33 % lower power consumption.

Degreasing and cleaning aluminum parts. Aluminum is still more frequently used in order to reduce the weight of SUVs. This lightweight material brings along also some technologies, such as degreasing and washing. After welding, the parts must be precisely degreased and washed. For this process is used special equipment for cleaning and degreasing. Its daily shutdown for 12 h can save up to 20 % of electricity.

Gelling devices. In the manufacturing of bodyworks are used two methods of curing of adhesives - infrared and induction. With infrared curing, burned infrared lamps have to be changed more often. On the other hand, the deployment of induction gelling devices for rear hood will save an average of 360 lamps per year.

Paint shop. The paint shop handles large amounts of material, water and energy. In the manufacturing process, the generation of emissions is limited by using separators and filters. Furthermore, the emerging waste water is treated and purified before discharge into the recipient. This area has therefore, in the whole manufacturing process of vehicles, the greatest relevance to environmental protection.

Material savings. By using the new technology EcoBell 3 is achieved saving of 70 % of varnish while achieving perfect adhesion of varnish to the body and less waste from the captured varnish. Eco LCC technology enables savings of up to 10 ml when changing paint colors in robot's spray nozzle.

Water savings. Saving of 30–60 m^3 of demineralized water/day was achieved by omitting the process of washing the bodywork after the grinding process. This technology uses a closed compartment where robotic brush after grinding process dedusts and cleans the whole bodywork. This cleaning /1} process also saves energy, which is required for the transport and treatment of water as well as energy required for the drying the bodywork after cleaning process.

Emission savings. Electrostatic separation, or E-Scrub, is a new technology for separating waste varnish resulting from the bodywork varnishing. Varnish which is not applied in the process of spraying the bodywork, remains in the form of aerosols in the air. These aerosols are by the circulation of air discharged into the separating system that disposes the varnish particles. 90 % of thus cleaned air becomes the circulation air again.

Waste savings. The main advantage of innovative varnishing process while maintaining the quality, one color layer - filling layer has been left out. The function of the filler is integrated into the base paint. Reduction of the whole process of applying the filler is significant both in terms of reducing the incidence of hazardous waste as well as reducing vehicle weight by 0.5 kg [9].

Assembly of a vehicle refers to the connection of the bodywork with a drive unit (motor), attachment parts and mounting modules, which is all carried out on partially automated assembly lines. During vehicle assembly arises waste from packaging in which parts were packed. This waste is as a priority used again, respectively it is recovered as secondary material. By separation, adhesive residues and cleaning cloths containing solvents are separated from recyclables.

Reduction of CO_2 emissions. For the control of quality and noise of vehicles are used vibrating rollers that simulate driving on the road. 90 % of finished of New Small Family vehicles drive on vibrating rollers, which means annual savings of 96 tons of CO_2 emissions.

Saving water in water tests. Water tightness tests for vehicles are carried out in monsoon conditions. Vehicles are in the water test tunnel exposed to a strong pressure of water from different spots. This process uses only technical water, not drinking water.

Innovations in the manufacturing process have a positive impact on the environment and saves energy that can be used somewhere else. For example, this energy can be used to power products from this innovated manufacturing process. It should be noted that innovation of the manufacturing process must be reflected in its final products - automobiles. When you take it from a different perspective that environmentally friendly manufacturing process would makes automobiles that produce high emissions, what all the eco-innovations of manufacturing would be for?

The final product of these innovations is an environmentally friendly automobile what is also positive to the final consumer - very low emissions which means low fuel consumption. When mentioning very low fuel consumption, most people will think of an automobile that in one side has a very low fuel consumption but on the other side the performance probably will not be much impressive, because a lot of people still have the one old rule in their minds - the higher the performance, the higher the fuel consumption. This is not currently true. Volkswagen AG came up with a solution that is not only highly environmentally friendly, but has a performance the end user will be pleasantly surprised with. As an example of one of those solutions, We would like to mention particular automobile model - Volkswagen Golf GTE. Golf GTE is powered by a turbocharged petrol engine in a combination with an electric motor. These two power units together give the automobile power of 204HP/150 kW. Acceleration from 0 to 100 km/h in 7.6 s, fuel consumption of 1.5 l/100 km and produces only 35 g/km of CO_2 emissions, which is a very favorable combination.

4 Conclusion

In the article we have dealt with eco-innovations in automotive industry on the example of the Volkswagen Group. For eco-innovation is considered every innovation, which can reduce the exploitation of natural resources and release of harmful substances in the whole life cycle. We can find eco-innovation in presented company either in the all manufacturing sectors (body shop, paint shop, assembly line etc.) as well as in new manufactured vehicles. The introduction of 'Think Blue. Factory' (strategy of sustainable production of vehicles), had a significant impact on the increase of eco-innovations in the vehicle manufacturing while the production adapted to it in all its stages. Volkswagen Slovakia produces environmentally friendly vehicles through green technologies. This confirms that technical progress is indeed inextricably linked to increasing of competitiveness, but it can also represent significant environmental protection.

References

1. Spirkova, D., Golej, J., Panik, M., Spirková, D., Golej, J., Panik, M.: The issue of urban static traffic on selected examples in bratislava in the context of economic sustainability. In: Conference proceedings of 2nd International Conference on Traffic and Transport Engineering (ICTTE), Belgrade, Serbia (2014)

2. Carrillo-Hermosilla, J., Gonzaléz, P., Könnölä, T.: Eco-Innovation: When Sustainability and Competitiveness Shake Hands, 1st edn. Palgrave Macmillan, New York (2009)
3. Eco Innovations - how eco ideas become a reality. http://www.greenbeings.com.au
4. Leskova, A.: Politika eko-inovácií a jej prejavy v automobilovom priemysle. Technicka univerzita Kosice (2009)
5. World Steel Association: An Advanced High-Strength Steel Family Car, Environmental Case Study: Automotive. Worldsteel, Brussels (2008)
6. OECD: Sustainable Manufacturing and Eco-Innovation. Synthesis Report. Framework, Practices and Measurement
7. Geels, F.W.: Technological Transitions and System Innovations: A co-evolutionary and socio-technical analysis. Edward Elgar, Cheltenham (2005)
8. Jänicke, M.: Ecological modernisation: new perspectives. J. Cleaner Prod. **16**(5), 477–482 (2007)
9. Environmental Report 2013. Volkswagen Slovakia (2013)

Knowledge Management in the Marketing Mix of Small Food Businesses

Michal Pružinský[✉]

Faculty of Business Economy with Seat in Košice, University of Economy
in Bratislava, Tajovského 13, 041 30 Košice, Slovak Republic
michal.pruzinsky@euke.sk

Abstract. The types of industries are more or less lucrative for expansion in national even international markets. Regardless of whether a decision is made for expansion it is part of the globalization and internationalization that affects all businesses [1]. New markets are often geographically distant, and therefore businesses (especially small), enter them carefully and only rarely [2]. Even in the food penetrating the international markets is not easy. The starting point for the analysis of Company Frozen Feedstock was to search the situation and propose the measures and steps for enterprise in order to be sustainable and able to expand. We collected data for a period over five years. The goal of contribution is to make proposals on increased investment in marketing mix, changes in hiring and training sales representatives and suppliers of raw materials based on the findings of knowledge management.

Keywords: Knowledge · Knowledge management · Marketing mix · Competitive advantage · Market · Customer

1 Introduction

Peter Drucker expressed marketing saying: "The aim of marketing is to make selling superfluous. The aim is to know and understand the customer so well the product or service will satisfy him and themselves before" [3]. Marketing therefore is defined as social and management process in which individuals and groups obtain through creating and exchanging products and value what they need and want. We are often confused with the concept of marketing sales. In fact, the act of marketing meets before the sale, but also beyond. This is about a combination of several activities (e.g. market research, product development, distribution, pricing, advertising, personal selling), whose mission is to understand, serve and satisfy customer needs and simultaneously fulfil the goals of the company. The essence of marketing is a simple idea that is true in all professions. According Lauterborn success is based on understanding the needs and wishes of the area, and creating ideas, services or products that they fulfill the needs and wishes [4]. Enterprises that fail to meet the needs and desires of others cannot succeed. In a market economy, enterprises must constantly monitor changes and developments in the market to maintain and improve its position compared to its competitors. Owners and managers manage companies so as to respond effectively and at the same time strengthened its market position. The main aim of this paper is to

© ICST Institute for Computer Sciences, Social Informatics and Telecommunications Engineering 2016
A. Leon-Garcia et al. (Eds.): Smart City 2015, LNICST 166, pp. 541–550, 2016.
DOI: 10.1007/978-3-319-33681-7_45

assess a specification of the existing marketing mix food business and troubleshooting based on the evaluation of internal information and business data from the Slovak Statistical Office. Examination of the attributes and draft amendments to the marketing mix in selected business carried out based on the evaluation of the success of sales analysis of selected accounts.

2   Methodology

Within this chapter we present information characterizing the company, the methods and procedures of the matter. To meet the objective we used pair wise method such as induction and deduction, analysis and synthesis, and other empirical methods. The data we have obtained from the primary and secondary sources. The primary sources were interviews with the owner of the business and production workers. We obtained valuable information from the drivers of refrigerated vehicles. Informal interviews were conducted with the use of prepared questioned issues. By observing the production processes to understand the relationships between them. Part of the data we have drawn on the company web site. Most important, the data of internal accounting documents of the company. Secondary sources of data and information were publications in the field of marketing mix and the web site of the Statistical Office of the Slovak Republic.

2.1   Characteristics of the Company Frozen Feedstock

Our contribution was developed based on input information from food plant that we named for the purpose of this contribution Frozen Feedstock. The enterprise is in the market for more than 20 years. Its leadership has extensive experience in the field of competition for the customer. It is a manufacturing company whose main business is the production and sale of frozen bakery products and confectionery, as well as other semi-taking efforts to introduce and provide additional services.

Production and distribution is focused on frozen puff pastry dough manufactured in a state of deep shock freezing when freezing temperature is −40° C. The production range is divided into sweet, salty, multigrain, cereal pre-baked, ordinary bread, and pre-baked frozen breaded and frozen confectionery products.

2.2   Characteristics of the Vision and Mission of the Food Business

The vision of the company is to establish themselves closer to foreign markets and subsequent expansion into Asia with maintaining the current volume of deliveries to Slovak and European consumers. Mission of the company is to produce frozen bakery products to a wide network of customers, intermediary consumers a varied menu of confectionery and bakery products. In addition to the production of bakery and confectionery products business offers relating to marketing and technological equipment – electric hot air oven for baking frozen products. The enterprise is successful in central and western Slovakia. Fiercer competition in Eastern Slovakia required fulfilling an important goal – denser meet demand in Eastern Slovakia.

3 The Results

Company Frozen Feedstock operates mostly in Eastern Slovakia. The company makes business within the Košice region demographic conditions. For the enterprise as such, the common Slovak economic conditions, as customers are active across the country. According to the Statistical Office of the Slovak Republic in the city where the headquarters of the firm is situated live more than 23,000 residents and across whole district 106,000 people. 41 % of the population lives in the cities of the district. 59 % of it lives in rural areas. Of working age (15–64 years) there are 74,679 inhabitants. Life expectancy of men is 68.82 and 77.59 years for women.

3.1 Business Marketing Environment

Macro environment factors during three years changed slightly with small fluctuations. Demographic changes alone do not cause changes within the period in social environment. The most significant factors affecting may affect the operation of the company's purchasing power. In sensitive economic environment due to customers' nationwide spectrum we review in our contribution data from all over the country. In 2014, Slovakia had 2,715,000 economically active people, of which 2,329,000 employed and 386,000 unemployed. There are significant differences in household income by regions. In the Western Slovakia the average monthly disposable income of households was in 2013 € 635.56. In central Slovakia, it was € 614.98 and in eastern Slovakia just above € 600. This is related to consumption. Monthly household expenditure on food and non-alcoholic beverages were on average € 75.42 in the West, € 73.94 in Mid and € 65.62 in East of Slovakia. This confirms that the East is purchased and probably consumes less. Despite these data it does not make venture differences in the prices of products for the region. Ecological (natural) environment affects mainly raw materials that are inputs into the production process. Energy costs for the Company Frozen Feedstock are highest and therefore the most substantial component of the environment. The legal framework within which the company operates is defined primarily by Trade Act, the Commercial Code and a number of laws, decrees and regulations governing sanitary conditions and standards in the food industry.

Company uses the services of agents. The plant has concluded agreements with several dealers, who operate in the defined territory of Slovakia. The suppliers are an important factor in the microenvironment. Among the largest suppliers of Company Frozen Feedstock includes:

- ZEELANDIA Ltd. (Košice - pastry supplier of raw materials for bakers and confectioners).
- AGROREAL a.s. (Streda nad Bodrogom - agricultural primary production).
- LASTONHILL Ltd. (Rimavská Seč).
- OMEGA Slovakia s.r.o. (Vrútky).
- PURATOS zrt. - Establishment (Hungary).

Customers are those who buy the product. Company Frozen Feedstock operates mainly in the market intermediaries and partly in the consumer market. Among the customers for our consideration there are companies, mainly:

- Bakeries and mini-bakeries.
- Sweets.
- Food, hypermarkets.
- Restaurants and pizzerias.
- Refreshment stands.

Enterprise had the largest share (96 %) of its sales on the Slovak market in 2014. For exports to the EU venture it earned 0.6 % of sales and 3.4 % of revenues came from exports to countries outside the European Union. The main competitors of the company with a similar range of products that the Slovak market expanded come mainly from Hungary, Poland and Slovakia offering customers products at lower prices. The company employs 33 people, of which 20 are production employees, one working in management, and administration of 3, other 3 in the sales department and 6 as freezer lorry drivers.

3.2   Market Segmentation Business

Market segmentation reflects homogenous groups that differ from each other their needs and buying behaviour and which can be modified to operate shopping mix [5].

Table 1. Enterprise customer segments and their characteristics

Segment No.	Name of segment segment	Segment characteristics	Segment determining factor
1	Large and regular consumers (75 %)	Goods are generally not processed for the final consumer, they are demanding the durability and storage	The quality and durability of the product, timely delivery, ancillary services
2	Occasional and regular consumers (20 %)	Products offer customers processed, ready for consumption	Quality, shelf-life and the possibility of processing
3	Individuals and households (personal collection) (5 %)	Priority is low cost, the possibility of storing and home baking	Price, taking in small amounts and taste

Source: own processing

Segmentation and the characteristics of individual groups we mentioned in Table 1. Although the company does not prefer any segment and acts not only on one target market, the data in the table shows that the majority of business customers (75 %) are regular and large consumers. Individuals and households collected only 5 % of production, so we will not examine targeting.

3.3   Product Mix Company Frozen Feedstock

By marketing mix we understand the qualitative and quantitative mix of marketing tools in time. In the literature we often meet with the following tools of marketing mix 4P termed: Product, Price, Place (distribution policy), and Promotion (some people say marketing communication). We visualized Product mix the Company Frozen Feedstock in Fig. 1. It consists of all product lines, namely concerning product groups for which the selected characteristics similar to all products of this group. We examined the different levels of the selected product **Amarelle grid**. The core of the product (its basic utilitarian effect) due to which the product the customer buys, a saturated or real treat you. **Amarelle grid**, as well as other products, are packaged and sold in plastic bags of 50 and 100 pieces designed for wholesale and for retail customers can stick packaging of this product.

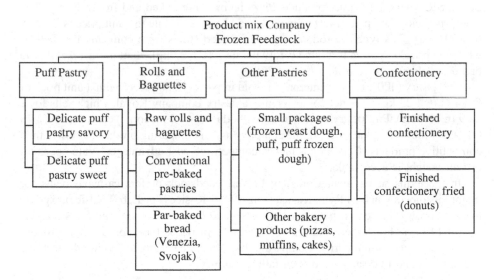

Fig. 1. Product mix Company Frozen Feedstock. Source: own processing

Extended product represents additional services. When of Products Company Frozen Feedstock then enterprise offers a range of services, among which we select:

- Technological equipment borrowed from customers.
- Training purchasers of the right technology training.
- Delivery of promotional items with a company logo, baking paper or baking sheet. Development HACCP33 (food safety system based on prevention according to Law

no. 152/1995 on foodstuffs, as amended, and the Codex of food of the Slovak Republic. HACCP system is mandatory for all producers and people handling food).

All these services are provided free of charge by the enterprise, which is indicative of high levels of provision of additional services. This is confirmed by the fact that the company appreciates the customer and it has a positive effect on building long-term and trusted relationships with customers. The value of additional services is times higher than the value delivered frozen product.

Price is from a macroeconomic perspective, the basic mechanism which indicates to balance supply with demand in the market. For the customer the cost amount of funds that must give up acquiring the product. Manufacturer and seller for the price of a single component of the marketing mix to generate income for the company. Pricing policy includes various discounts, conditions and maturity dates and credit possibilities. Company Frozen Feedstock creates the price of its products mainly on the costs. It covers, for example raw material prices, energy cost of running production, and wages of employees. Enterprise monitors prices of competitors, but of crucial importance in pricing are the costs of production and operation of the company.

We compared prices of selected products of the enterprise with chain Tesco Stores SR. There are similar products Pizza hams – pre-baked and frozen pastry. The enterprise sells Ham pizza (430 g) in packs of 12 pieces, while the unit price is € 1.598 (€ 3.716/kg). This type of product is sold by Tesco stores from company Dr. Oetker, while the price of a pizza is around € 2.49 per item (€ 6.07/kg). Ham pizza Tesco Value brand is sold at a price of € 1.79 (€ 4.26/kg).

Puff pastry (400 g) of the enterprise is sold in packs of 20 pieces with a unit price of € 0.492 (€ 1.23/kg). Product comparison is a pastry company Royal, which sells for € 0.59 (€ 1.48/kg). Puff pastry marketed as Svoboda (Eng. "Freedom") costs € 1.39 (2.78 €/kg). It follows that the prices of the company are in comparing products at lower than competitive products. Company achieves competitive cost advantages. Value per unit or unit weight is acceptable.

In the terms of payment Company Frozen Feedstock prefers cash payments for major customers (such as Ryba Košice (Eng. "Fish Košice") or Labaš Košice) exposes the enterprise invoice and payment shall be made by wire transfer. Invoices are due within 14 days. For larger volumes of business it provides the opportunity for longer term agreements with maturity. Comparing data „income statement" within the last five years, we found that sales have been falling slightly.

Table 2. Development of revenues from sales of own products according to the "profit and loss"

	Year 2010	Year 2011	Year 2012	Year 2013	Year 2014
Revenue [EUR]	1 092 012	1 008 039	991 137	953 218	901 012

Source: own processing

The objective reason for the decline in production is the economic crisis at the end of the first decade of the 21st century. The consequent increases in prices of production inputs imply the increase in sales prices. In Table 2 we introduced the development of sales revenues. The turnover of the company divided by product lines offers us a detailed and transparent information about the importance of individual components of the product mix on overall turnover. In Table 3 we reported data on the turnover of the undertaking for the period 2010–2014.

Table 3. Turnover product lines during the years 2010 to 2014 in EUR

Product lines	2010	2011	2012	2013	2014
Puff pastry	425 100	415 051	329 879	289 994	295 415
Rolls and Baguettes	94 432	106 972	145 995	162 827	133 075
Other pastries	357 005	289 014	218 111	289 987	275 110
Confectionery	215 478	197 002	297 152	215 410	197 412

Source: own processing

3.4 Distribution

This component of the marketing mix means in English "place" as "site" or "Distribution Policy" addresses where and how the product will be sold. It involves determining the distribution channels, the sales range and the actual transport to the customer. To Company Frozen Feedstock customers mainly include bakeries, pastry shops, restaurants and food shops. Company has in Slovakia a number of contractual agents who in this area, inter alia, also perform activities related to the distribution policy. The role of the agent is therefore an analysis and control culture point of sale product the Company Frozen Feedstock, as corporate objectives, among others, building its reputation. Sales representatives teach (train) customer on proper product preparation technology Training of sales representatives still act only within the premises of the Company Frozen Feedstock and is performed by the director and owner of the company.

Company previously operated own sale of products, but with the advent of large retail chains (e.g. Kaufland, Lidl or Tesco) was forced to close shop. It is now possible to purchase the products by employees at the enterprise premises. It follows that the company performs the sale of direct selling channel i.e. it sells directly to the consumer and uses the sale through one or more intermediaries. Shares of distribution channels in total turnover in 2014 we stated in Table 4.

Table 4. Turnover by individual distribution channels in 2014

Distribution channel	Turnovers [EUR/2014]
Direct sales	102 586
One broker	425 928
More intermediaries	372 444
TOTAL	901 012

3.5   Marketing Communications

Marketing Communications (promotional mix) expresses the target reach potential customers in order to familiarize recipient of the message with the product business and its advantages, and ultimately his "convictions" of the suitability and relevance purchase a particular product. Company Frozen Feedstock gains new customers mainly through sales representatives. They actively seek and reach potential customers directly, usually in their operation (e.g. at the bakery, candy store). Vehicles are identified business advertising stickers. The resources available to invest in additional services to customers prioritize enterprise's products in search engines agile management of its website in English, French and German, as well as distributing advertising materials for its customers. Funds that enterprise in the years 2010–2014 spent on the purposes of marketing communication we stated in Table 5.

Table 5. Cost of marketing communication in the years 2010–2014

Year	2010	2011	2012	2013	2014
Costs [EUR]	3 298	1 876	2 612	1 928	1 526

Source: own processing

From the data it is clear that the enterprise marketing communication carried out prudently. In percentage terms, the share of sales € 901,012 in 2014 was only 0.17 % advertising.

According to the company management experience any problems in the market, so its main effort should be to develop a strategy to maintain market position and formulate a new sales strategy. Defensive Strategy should help to create resources for the subsequent transition to a growth strategy with expansion into foreign markets.

4   Discussion and Conclusions

The company offers a wide range of products. Of the products most sold item product line is "puff pastry" and sold at least "common bread". Puff pastry is involved in the undertaking's overall turnover more than 30 % in 2011 alone it was 41.1 % and in 2014 it was 32.79 %. Although the "common bread" has the smallest share of turnover recorded an increase in sales. When in 2010 it was only 8.65 %, in 2014 this figure was 14.77 %.

By comparing the "profit and loss" for the period 2010–2014, we found a downward trend in sales of products. However, the company reported a profit in each year of the period. Price of the company products is competitive; even there exists a possibility of slight increases. By comparison, we found that randomly selected products "ham pizza" and "pastry" sold the holdings surveyed are cheaper for the customer. We see the possibility of optimizing the review of trading partners and finding competitive advantage through such raw material suppliers who would be able to offer the same quality, better prices, and thus the company would reduce production costs and increase their profits.

Distribution production business is satisfactory; the company has its own means of transport. We found deficiencies in marketing communication. Enterprise uses it partially. Although the company has its own web site, it does not have e-shop for registered wholesale customers. Business representatives should not hinder the creation of orders for service or signing new contracts in finding new customers because they would have registered themselves via the website of the company. Direct selling in the factory is not enough in the public consciousness or potential consumers in the vicinity. We recommend investing in five large billboards that would be at the entrance to the largest cities in Slovakia and informed about the food business and its products. Should this form has made a positive impact, i.e. increased sales, also do so in border areas in the language of the country. Presenting on charity events can raise awareness of the company and its products, which could also lead to an increase in sales, while the company built the team and its reputation. The costs of marketing communication in 2014 decreased compared to 2010 by 46.27 %.

Company after realization of the above proposals has the option of its revenue from sales to increase and streamline the activities of commercial agents. Selects its dealers should pay more attention to business, and conduct professional training as their share of the distribution company attaches great importance.

5   Conclusions

The contribution aimed to assess a specification of the marketing mix production Company Frozen Feedstock, exploring the attributes of the selected company for the evaluation of the success of sales and formulate recommendations and proposals for improvement of the prior marketing mix. Based on the results of the analysis of management interviews, observations and comparisons, we propose measures which the company will raise awareness about its products and services offered to customer, which can lead to increased profits and achieving competitive advantage.

Assessment of the marketing mix implies that the company operates in its own premises, transport production to realize its own transport, and has 20 years of experience in the market, a wide range of products and numerous awards. It is ineffective marketing communications, to which the enterprise does not invest even 1 % of annual sales. We recommend increasing the percentage of funds for marketing communications.

The competition is gaining momentum and has global dimensions. Opportunities in the domestic markets are declining, and therefore businesses must aggressively expand into international markets. Evaluation of the results of the company according to data from accounting documents for the last five years have provided the basis for several proposals that could help the company in further developing and achieving profitability.

Acknowledgement. The paper conducts research in area of Sustainable development of higher education in the fields of management in the frame of VEGA project No VEGA č.1/0708/14.

References

1. Bobenič Hintošová, A.: Medzinárodný manažment, 1 vyd. Vydavateľstvo EKONÓM, Bratislava (2008)
2. Csikósová, A., Mihalčová, B., Antošová, M.: International Business, First edn. VŠB Ostrava – Technical University of Ostrava, Ostrava (2015)
3. Kotler, P., et al.: Moderní marketing, 4 evropské vydání. Grada Publishing, Praha (2007)
4. Lauterborn, B.: New Marketing Litany: Four Ps Passé: C-Words Take Over. Advertising Age **61**(41), 25–26 (1990)
5. Lieskovská, V., et al.: Marketing. Vydavateľstvo EKONÓM, Bratislava (2009)

Some Reflections on the Determinants of ICT Usage

Menbere Workie Tiruneh[1,2(✉)]

[1] Vysoká škola manažmentu,
Panónska cesta 17, 85104 Bratislava, Slovakia
mworkie@vsm.sk

[2] Institute of Economic Research, Slovak Academy of Sciences,
Sancova 56, 811 05 Bratislava, Slovakia

Abstract. This paper sheds some light on the Networked Readiness Index (NRI) compiled by the World Economic Forum and discusses the sources of cross-country variations in the European Union based on the 2013–2014 period. The results based on NRI reveal that the highest variation – measured by standard deviation – is in Economic impacts, Business usage, Political and regulatory environment, and in Infrastructure. There is a clear endogeneity problem though as all the pillars that make-up the NRI are somewhat intertwined. The results seem to signal there is a substantial cross-country variation in both ICT usage and the resulting benefits, which goes against the assumptions that EU is a homogenous economic club with significant convergence criteria. The results also suggest that the catch up process in ICT usage require an improvement in building ICT infrastructure and effective use of ICT primarily by the business sector. This goes against the remarkable success EU has achieved in terms of real income convergence during the past 18 years or so.

Keywords: Information and communication technologies · Network readiness index · Correlation

1 Introduction

The expansion of the ICT sector manifests itself in various ways that include but is not limited to the use of ICT by individuals, businesses as well as governments; the price of ICT, which determine its affordability; and social and economic impacts of ICT usage [3]. While progress has been made in ICT usage both globally in general and in the European Union in particular, there are cross-country variations (as indicated by the World Economic Forum ICT Report) when it comes to the level of ICT usage, the infrastructure to facilitate the use of ICT as well as the subsequent economic benefits. As argued by the World Economic Forum's annual ICT Report, high-quality regulatory and business environment is critical in order to fully leverage ICTs and generate impact. This paper empirically discusses selected determinants of ICT usage in the European Union and points out the complementarity nature of various indicators (pillars) that make up the Networked Readiness Index. In addition the paper also explores the social and economic benefits of investing and using ICT based on a cross-section of 28 EU member states during the 2013–2014 period.

© ICST Institute for Computer Sciences, Social Informatics and Telecommunications Engineering 2016
A. Leon-Garcia et al. (Eds.): Smart City 2015, LNICST 166, pp. 551–558, 2016.
DOI: 10.1007/978-3-319-33681-7_46

2   An Empirical Insight into the Determinants of ICT Usage

The benefits of effective ICT usage are broader and multifaceted. The Global Information Technology Report assesses the state of networked readiness of 143 economies using the Networked Readiness Index (NRI). As indicated by the Global Information Technology 2001–2002 Report, Networked Readiness is considered as *"the degree to which a community is prepared to participate in the Networked World"* (p. 11). According to NRI, the ranking is based on a composite indicator made up of four main categories (subindexes), 10 subcategories (pillars), and 53 individual indicators distributed across the different pillars. We summarize the subdexes and subcategories in Table 1.

There are several questions that may arise following the subindexes and corresponding sub-categories summarized in Table 1. First, how accurate the data compilation is given the fact that some of the data are generated through a survey? This may be even a more serious problem for developing countries with significant data quality problem. Second, is it really possible to isolate the subindexes and sub-categories from each other? In fact, the underlined indicators are intertwined with each other which may signal a significant endogeneity problem and therefore measurement error. Nonetheless, the data are still helpful to get some picture on ICT advancement and to make cross-country comparison in ICT performance overtime.

Table 1. Subindexes and corresponding sub-categories in the NBI

A. Environment subindex	B. Readiness subindex	C. Usage subindex	D. Impact subindex
Political and regulatory environment (9 indicators)	Infrastructure (4 indicators)	Individual usage (7 indicators)	Economic impacts (4 indicators)
Business and innovation environment (9 indicators)	Affordability (3 indicators)	Business usage (6 indicators)	Social impacts (4 indicators)
	Skills (4 indicators)	Government usage (3 indicators	

Author's modifications based on The Global Information Technology Report 2015: ICTs for Inclusive Growth (2015)

3   The Determinants of ICT in the European Union

The effective use of ICT is constrained by many factors that include affordability, infrastructure and regulatory environment, among other things. Studies indicate a significant cross-country variation in ICT usage in spite of the overall advancement in the sector in the past decades. As indicated by the World Economic Forum Global ICT Report [3], while *"there are as many mobile subscriptions as (the number of) human beings on the planet, but half of the world's population do not have mobile phones and 450 million people still live out of reach of a mobile signal"*. This is something that has come to be known as the *digital divide* with all the undesirable consequences to the socio-economic advancement of technologically lagging countries.

While the cross-country variation across EU member states is not as dramatic as one witnesses on the global level, there are nonetheless some noticeable differences in both ICT usage level as well as ICT infrastructure in the EU. Table 2 shows the correlation matrices of the ten pillars that make up the Networked Readiness Index for the panel of EU member States (2013–2014). The list of countries and their codes are in the appendix. While the correlations indicate statistically significant relationships across pillars, the link between pillar four (affordability of ICT) seems to be either not correlated with the rest of the pillars or only partially correlated with them. This may signal that ICT affordability may not be the most difficult challenge for this group of economies.

Table 2. Correlation matrices of NRI (EU cross-section, 2013–2014)

	Pillar_1	Pillar_2	Pillar_3	Pillar_4	Pillar_5	Pillar_6	Pillar_7	Pillar_8	Pillar_9	Pillar_10
Pillar_1	1									
Pillar_2	0.782*	1								
Pillar_3	0.793*	0.608*	1							
Pillar_4	0.334	0.295	0.263	1						
Pillar_5	0.718*	0.722*	0.658*	0.342	1					
Pillar_6	0.859*	0.682*	0.771*	0.338	0.528*	1				
Pillar_7	0.924*	0.734*	0.829*	0.411*	0.712*	0.879*	1			
Pillar_8	0.859*	0.726*	0.618*	0.383*	0.620*	0.758*	0.765*	1		
Pillar_9	0.926*	0.810*	0.819*	0.359	0.732*	0.896*	0.952*	0.825*	1	
Pillar_10	0.823*	0.778*	0.613*	0.335	0.597*	0.765*	0.762*	0.955*	0.816*	1

Author's computations

The asterisk, * indicate significance level at 5 %.

Likewise, the standard deviation in Table 3 suggests that the highest cross-country variation in the European Union has been captured in pillar one (Political and regulatory environment), pillar three (infrastructure), pillar seven (Business ICT usage) and pillar nine (Economic impacts). This may signal EU member states are still heterogeneous in their economic parameters and technological infrastructure in spite of the convergence criteria and EU-wide funds designed to help poor countries to catch up with richer ones.

4 The Economic and Social Impacts of ICT Usage: An Empirical Exploration

It is recognized that widespread ICT usage by businesses, governments, and the population at large is a precondition for all the subsequent benefits and opportunities accompanying the payoffs from ICT usage. This has been confirmed by the nearly perfect correlation between the NRI's usage and Impact subindexes (Table 2). From the correlation matrices we may infer that pillar seven (business ICT usage) has been

Table 3. Descriptive statistics

Variable	Obs	Mean	Std. Dev.	Min	Max
pillar_one	28	4.4760	0.8561	3.1772	5.8176
pillar_two	28	4.8450	0.3508	4.2072	5.4152
pillar_three	28	5.6452	0.8292	4.1143	6.9996
pillar_four	28	5.6141	0.6633	3.8219	6.6898
pillar_five	28	5.7096	0.3436	5.0708	6.5301
pillar_six	28	5.6156	0.6550	4.4566	6.8298
pillar_seven	28	4.4711	0.8664	3.3836	5.9006
pillar_eight	28	4.3972	0.7132	3.1113	5.4704
pillar_nine	28	4.3283	0.8690	3.0709	6.0749
pillar_ten	28	4.8569	0.6630	3.8030	6.0716

Author's computations

statistically significantly correlated with all the other variables. Past studies confirm the powerful economic impact of ICT usage on organization level. ICT enable firms to introduce organizational changes in the areas of re-engineering, decentralization, flexible work arrangements, outsourcing, lean production, and teamwork and customer relation [1]. There is strong evidence that the share of workers using computers is positively related to productivity performance, where a 10 % percentage point increase in the share of workers using computer is associated with a 1 % percentage point increase in probability of productivity improvement.

In the same token, the role of ICT usage on the firm level tends to foster productivity and accelerate efficiency. The research conducted based on a survey of 482 companies of which 148 are listed or traded Over- the- counter (OTC) in Japan confirms that firms with higher level of information technology and higher human capital tend to have higher productivity than those with lower information technology and human capital [2].

On the macroeconomic level there is a bulk of theoretical and empirical literature that deals with the role of human capital accumulation both for effective use of information technology and for long-term growth:

- First, production and diffusion of technology is impossible without human capital accumulation [4].
- Second, a larger stock of human capital makes it easier for nations to imitate new ideas developed elsewhere, which helps to accelerate the catch-up process.

The school of thought that advocates the role of human capital and technological progress for both economic development and competitiveness is classified as Endogenous growth theory. In this regard, Romer [5], Lucas [6], among others argue that human capital is a fundamental input into the research sector, where current research has a positive spillover for the productivity of future research and that technology (such as ICT) is considered as endogenous, therefore complementary to advancement in technology and human capital are highly intertwined. One major conclusion in this respect is that the cost of inventing a new product declines as society accumulates more ideas.

This goes against the neoclassical assumption where the steady state of output per worker depends on savings and growth rate of population, while the growth rate of output per worker depends only on technological progress that is determined exogenously [7]. Therefore, economic policy does not play any substantial role in the catch up process and poor countries unconditionally converge to the income per capita of richer ones due to the declining marginal productivity of capital.

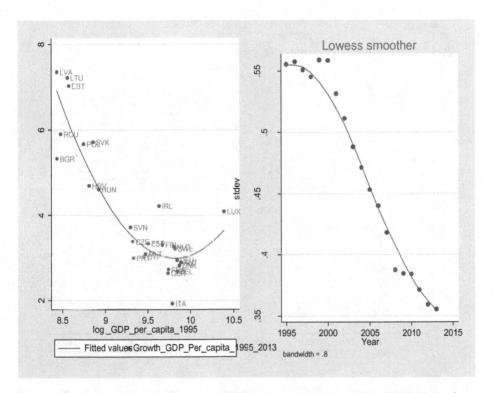

Fig. 1. Real GDP per capita convergence in the European Union (1995–2013) (Color figure online)

However, the empirical evidence for unconditional convergence for a larger group of world economies has been rather weak and there is an empirical evidence for conditional convergence, hence controlling for initial conditions and investment into both physical as well as human capital and vector of policy variables. The results for EU member states indicate a successful convergence in real income per capita, hence poorer EU members having grown faster than richer ones in the past 18 years or so (Fig. 1, left quadrant). This has also been confirmed by declining standard deviation in real income per capita indicating a decline in the dispersion of income per capita across EU member states in the same years (Fig. 1, right quadrant).

The success story in remarkable income convergence in the European Union does seem to be the case when it comes to technology readiness index. From Fig. 2 and

Table 2 it is possible to infer that the level of ICT usage tend to have a significant subsequent economic benefits, while the social impact of ICT usage does not seem to have a clear relationship. The link between ICT usage both by individuals, businesses and governments has on average a strong (and almost linear) relationship with subsequent economic benefits as indicated in Table 1 and Fig. 2.

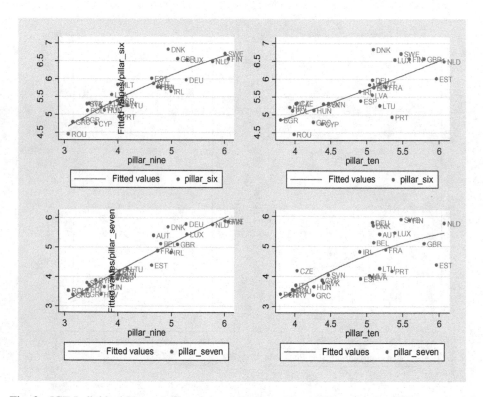

Fig. 2. ICT Individual Usage (pillar_six) and Business Uage (pillar_seven) and Economic and Social Impacts (2013–2014) (Color figure online)

Table 4. ICT Usage and economic and social impacts (based on a cross-section of EU member states, 2013–2014)

	Pillar_six	Pillar_seven	Pillar-eight	Pillar_nine	Pillar_ten
Pillar_six	1				
Pillar_seven	0.8794*	1			
Pillar_eight	0.7584*	0.7655*	1		
Pillar_nine	0.8965*	0.9526*	0.8254*	1	
Pillar_ten	0.7658*	0.7628*	0.9552*	0.8160*	1

The asterisk, * indicate significance level at 5 %.
Author's computations

From Fig. 1 and Table 2 it is possible to infer that the level of ICT usage tend to have a significant subsequent economic benefits, while the social impact of ICT usage does not seem to have a clear relationship. The link between ICT usage both by individuals, businesses and governments has on average a strong relationship with subsequent economic benefits as indicated in Table 1 and Fig. 1. However, the results also suggest business use of ICT (pillar_seven) has a more powerful economic impact (pillar_nine) while government use of ICT (pillar_eight) has a significantly higher social impact (pillar_ten). The results seem to be intuitive as much of government use of ICT is primarily to deliver public service and the social impact is a desired outcome (Table 4).

5 Concluding Remarks

This brief empirical discussion and previous other studies suggest that global competition is likely to be determined primarily by competitive rather than comparative advantages. In this regard, innovation and use of technology that include ICT remain the major source of sustaining competitiveness. The results also seem to indicate that the pillars of the global Networked Readiness Index are complementary and intertwined and therefore could be misleading if not handled and interpreted with appropriate amount of caution. The results also suggest that while EU seems to be quite a homogeneous economic club from various perspectives, including real income convergence, it appears the degree of cross-country variation is significantly high when it comes to Networked Readiness Index suggesting the prevalence digital divide in the European Union albeit its relatively smaller scale compared to the global digital divide. This may signal possible new convergence criteria in Networked Readiness Index for EU member states in order to reduce the scale of the current *digital divide* across countries.

Appendix

Table: List of countries and their codes included in the study

Country	Code	Country	Code	Country	Code
Austria	AUT	Germany	DEU	Poland	POL
Belgium	BEL	Greece	GRC	Portugal	PRT
Bulgaria	BGR	Hungary	HUN	Romania	ROU
Croatia	HRV	Ireland	IRL	Slovak Republic	SVK
Cyprus	CYP	Italy	ITA	Slovenia	SVN
Czech Republic	CZE	Latvia	LVA	Spain	ESP
Denmark	DNK	Lithuania	LTU	Sweden	SWE
Estonia	EST	Luxembourg	LUX	United Kingdom	GBR
Finland	FIN	Malta	MLT		
France	FRA	Netherlands	NLD		

References

1. Surendra, G., Wulong, G.: The effect of organizational innovation and information and communications technology on firm performance. Int. Prod. Monit. **9**, 37–51 (2004)
2. Bresnahan, F.T., Boynjolfsson, E., Lorin Hitt, H.L.: Information technology, workplace organization and the demand for skilled labor: firm-level evidence. Q. J. Econ. **117**(1), 339–376 (2012)
3. Dutta, S., Geiger, T., Lanvin, B.: The Global Information Technology report (2015). http://reports.weforum.org/global-information-technology-report-2015/
4. Nelson, R.R., Phelps, S.P.: Investment in humans, technological diffusion, and economic growth. Am. Econ. Rev. **56**(1/2), 69–75 (1966)
5. Romer, M.P.: The origins of endogenous growth. J. Econ. Perspect. **8**(1), 3–12 (1994)
6. Lucas, E.R.: On the mechanics of economic development. J. Monetary Econ. **22**, 3–42 (1988)
7. Solow, R.: A contribution to the theory of economic growth. Q. J. Econ. **70**(1), 65–94 (1956)

Social Media Communication: Re-creating the Context of Social Gaming

Predrag K. Nikolic[1(✉)] and Jelena S. Stankovic[2]

[1] Faculty of Digital Production, EDUCONS University,
Vojvode Putnika 87, 21208 Novi Sad, Serbia
predragknikolic@gmail.com
[2] Faculty of Business, Singidunum University,
Danijelova 32, 11000 Belgrade, Serbia
jstankovic@singidunum.ac.rs

Abstract. As social media communication represents an important platform for environmental innovations and service design necessary for creating sustainable living environment and leverage users mobility, in this paper we investigate, by using data from three experiments, how human communication and engagement in social gaming can be utilized in such new contexts, for the purpose of service innovation, brand and service design, building sustainable living environments and well-being, such as smart initiatives. Experimental research data collection had been done during three social media activation Coca-Cola Hellenic 45 Years in Serbia, Smoki Smokic Pirate Adventure, and Kraft Sport Game Campaign.

Keywords: Social media communication · Social gaming · Brand and service design · Service innovation · Sustainable living environments · Smart initiatives · Social networks

1 Introduction

Social media refers to "mobile and web-based technologies to create highly interactive platforms via which individuals and communities share, co-create, discuss, and modify user-generated content" [1]. According to Kaplan and Haenlein [2] it is important that decision makers keep trying to identify ways in which social media applications such as Wikipedia, YouTube, Facebook, Second Life, and Twitter can make difference for their users and the society in general. Among others, they involve the best practices in social media environment, to create a positive impact on people and their working and living society such as eco-friendly environment, "going green" etc. [3].

People are getting more and more familiar with modern communication gadgets, mobile applications, instant message transmission and exchange. According to global statistics, 29% of total population (around 2,08 billion) utilize Social Media [4], while 52% of total online population uses two or more Social Media sites [5]. On the other hand, according to Global Fortune 500 firms [6], all together with older tools (LinkedIn, Twitter, Facebook, YouTube, and corporate blogs) companies are embracing new social media (Foursquare, Instagram, Google+, Pinterest) using actively at least one of them, with the purpose of exchanging information and engaging in different

© ICST Institute for Computer Sciences, Social Informatics and Telecommunications Engineering 2016
A. Leon-Garcia et al. (Eds.): Smart City 2015, LNICST 166, pp. 559–571, 2016.
DOI: 10.1007/978-3-319-33681-7_47

activities. That refers not only to the importance of Social Media platforms in defining and re-defining communication and collaboration in working and living environment, but also to the possibilities for online user engagement expand toward new ways of communication, with huge potentials to affect and re-create the context of the networked users involvement, relationship development and user mobility.

2 Social Gaming and Service Innovation

Although it is most commonly considered that online gaming tends to isolate players from their social environment, researches showed that establishing relationships between players [7], their involvement in social community, making friends, and exchanging personal information online, is of a high importance [8]. Social gaming helps not only creation of social interactions, social engagement, and social experience through entertainment as a major source of enjoyment and pleasure in contemporary societies [9], but it also represents the source for encouraging users to participate in joint initiatives and creative processes by producing and distributing information through collaborative exchange, such as writing, content sharing, social networking, social bookmarking, and syndication [10].

Unlike playing games in solitude, social gaming refers to playing online games which enable or require social interaction and engagement between players [11]. Interactions among players, even considered as "weak ties", may contribute to social and emotional well-being [12]. Furthermore, social gaming could contribute in measuring the extent to which players are capable to exploit the potentialities of single or multiple social media platforms [11]. Data gathered from players through such gaming platforms could be valuable source of information for human-centered service design as well as to enhance living environments and upgrade existing services. The network of relationships created among players represents the true resource of knowledge which ultimately provides "the creative potential for "innovation" – the so-called "core competency" [13].

3 Related Works

The most significant "core competence" [13, 14] of social gaming, as the platform for service innovation and design in comparison with other forms of social environments, is the sense of competition and belonging among players. In addition to that, collaboration and cooperation also have been distinguished as the key effects of gameplay [15]. Based on that, Voida, Carpendale and Greenberg [15] classify social games into three categories: competitive, cooperative and collaborative. Competitive games require players to oppose one another in the game; in cooperative games players' goals are neither directly opposed nor completely aligned, while in collaborative games players win or lose together because they share the same goals [16].

The study Voida, Carpendale and Greenberg [15] was carried out on 36 players, recruited in 12 groups of different age, with the purpose of understanding massively multiplayer online games in sense of competition, cooperation, and collaboration of participants during playing console games. The goal was to better understand individual - and group-oriented practices in social gaming. One of the factors distinguished as crucial for collaboration and conversation among players, was group cohesion. No matter the type of the game - competitive, cooperative, or collaborative – cohesion among the groups was important to be achieved. Also, establishing social relationships was classified as of high importance of players' well-being and identity. The research, Voida, Carpendale and Greenberg [15] identified four classes of practices in group playing: presence of shared awareness, reinforcing shared history of playing, sharing in period of success and failure, and engaging in interdependence and self-sacrifice. Both group- and individual-oriented gaming practices were present in competitive, cooperative, and collaborative games.

4   Social Gaming Honeycomb

Given the fact that services dominate contemporary market, creating about 70% of the global aggregate production and employment [17], one can easily conclude that providing upgraded service is required in business and living environment. Heaving in mind that service innovation presents an idea that leads to performance enhancements considered to be new benefits [18], we believe that social gaming, as a source of service innovation, has the potential to create various sustainable social environments which differ from each other based on the type of services and benefits offered. In that sense the important role has the so-called "honeycomb" framework (Fig. 1) [1] that refers to and defines the particular social media functionality or seven social media building blocks [1]:

- **Identity** representing the extent to which users reveal their identity in a particular social media setting;

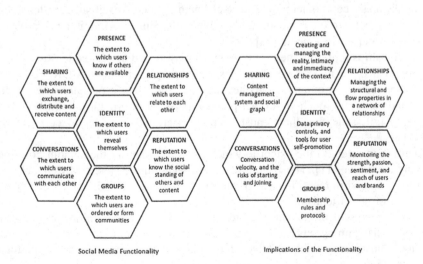

Fig. 1. The honeycomb framework

- **Conversations** representing the extent to which users communicate with each other in the social media setting;
- **Sharing** representing the extent to which users exchange, distribute, and receive content;
- **Presence** representing the extent to which users can know if other users are available in the social media setting;
- **Relationships** representing the extent to which users can be related to other users;
- **Reputation** representing the extent to which users can identify the standing of others, including themselves, in a particular social media setting, and
- **Groups** representing the extent to which users can create communities and sub-communities.

Each of the seven elements can be analyzed in detail so to provide a better understanding of players' experience during social game, and, furthermore, possible implications on the society and the quality of living environment.

Identity implications serve as tools for self-promotion. Social gaming, as a platform for expressing players' act of competing and rivalry for supremacy, promotes users' playing achievements and their personal profiles. According to Kaye and Bryce [8], the degrees of autonomy and competence of players determine the degree of game enjoyment.

Conversations refers to conversation velocity, and risks of starting or involving in conversation. "Social-oriented players" [19–22] emphasize social factors as key element of social behavior and communication. There has been established the relationship between social factors in gaming and enjoyment [8, 23, 24], as well as between the time spent playing and social motivators [25].

Sharing refers to establishing new contents and social relations during play. Smyth [26] suggests that playing in so called Massive Multiplayer Online Role-Playing Games – MMORPG [27] creates feeling of shared online media space among players and has positive social outcomes, in comparison with individual playing experience.

Presence refers to the extent to which other players are available. Unlike individual gaming, the presence of other players in social gaming provokes greater excitement due to highly competitive environment and individual's ability to monitor other players' performance and achievements [28].

Relationships represent the extent to which players can be related to other players. The importance of making relationships between players in MMORPG [7, 29], involved in social community, motivates players' enjoyment especially when making friends and getting in touch with other players' personal information online [8]. Nardi and Harris [30] state that there must be players around in order to compete even individually.

Reputation refers to the extent to which users can identify the standing of others, including themselves [1]. The feeling of social belonging [31] sets MMORPG as the social media environment in which players show higher enjoyment and greater acquisition of new friendships.

Groups represent the extent to which users can form communities and sub communities. Social gaming sets itself as a specific social media environment, characterized by game amusement which is affected by players' performance and game-related self-efficacy [32].

In social gaming, players' engagement and existence of online communities and "clans", with the emphasis on making online friendships, has been found as one of the key motivational factors, especially for playing MMORPGs [33]. Comparing to other social media networks, we found that social gaming could be addressed to its own honeycomb frameworks of building blocks. As source for the comparison analysis we used functionality blocks of the following networks: YouTube, LinkedIn, Foursquare, and Facebook (Fig. 2) [1]. Based on their honeycomb frameworks, presented social media platforms tend to concentrate on three or four primary blocks [34]. LinkedIn shows the identity as the greatest social media functionality, followed by relationships and reputation. Foursquare displays presence as the greatest social media functionality, followed by relationship and identity. YouTube distinguishes sharing as its greatest social media functionality, followed by conversations, groups and reputation. Facebook is undoubtedly well known for making relationships, which is followed by presence, identity, conversation, and reputation of its users.

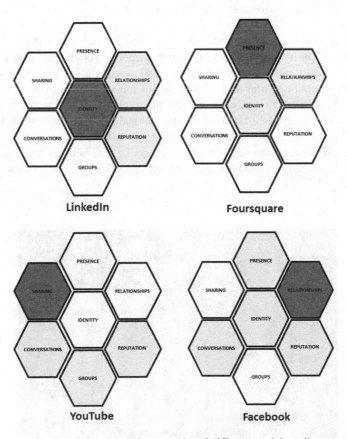

Fig. 2. Honeycomb frameworks of different social media

5   Research Approach

In three research experiments we were analyzing players' behavior during their participation in social gaming, in sense of their engagement during play, the decisions they made while making relationships with other players, and the implications of their decisions and presented behavior. Our research experiments included Social Media Activation 45 Years of Coca-Cola in Serbia, Smoki Smokic Pirate Adventure, and Kraft Sport Game Campaign. We will also present the goals and expected outcomes of our ongoing project Twix "Pick a Side, Twix is back" Theoretical framework has been based on Activity and research methodologies from user-centered design process [35, 36]. The goals of the experiment were to:

- describe group behavior and participation of the players;
- analyze social interactions, relationships, and participating in playing;
- understand established relationships through social engagement and potentials for further usage in service design and smart innovation implications.

6   Research Experiments and Results

The idea of the first experiment, Facebook activation 45 Years of Coca-Cola Hellenic company promotion in Serbia, was to organize corporate social responsible campaign with the purpose of involving and uniting local communities in Serbia to support development of public fitness zones. The social media campaign was executed on Facebook and lasted for two months, supporting competition among municipalities. It ended as one of the regional most successful campaigns ever, with over 1,7 million votes and 200,000 weak ties participant collected, so called fans, during activation period [37]. The results showed the power of social interactions and social media, proving that the feeling of belonging can be initiated through community well-being intentions (Fig. 3).

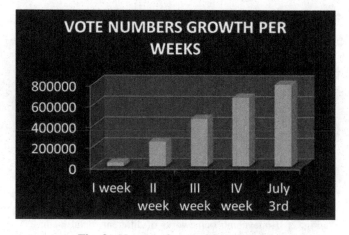

Fig. 3. Vote number growth per weeks

The social gaming moment of this activation was seeded in the group competing elements, spontaneously developed between participants throughout campaign period. The increase of the collected votes in the first four and a half weeks of the activation was much greater than expected. There was 36.153 votes in the first week, followed by the increase to 236.721 during the second week, and peaking 795.725 votes in the first week of July [37]. The activation rules included lower interaction complexity, minimizing engagement difficulties, reducing steps in the process of voting, enabling multiple voting, maximizing sharable opportunities and possibilities for exposing leadership in the game. Our design system was based on simplicity and provocation that participants are engaged on something they are doing for their local community well-being (Fig. 4).

Fig. 4. The Coca Cola game interface with listed participant municipalities

Qualitative results for the research were collected from comments left by participants on Facebook pages and other social media channels, while quantitative data were collected from activations database. Our prediction was that the players would online cooperate and make relationships. But, through the time, online relationships established by players moved on offline in a form of organized online groups' initiatives (e.g. organizing street stands to provide support to potential players offering help with logging in, voting, etc.). Even more, the players started to spread the eco-system themselves by making video tutorials, starting blogs, inviting people to vote. We found out that the crucial factor for the social interaction and engagement was emotional attachment to the belonging community and the strong and respectable organization to trust behind the activation. Not only the participants were playing individually on everyday bases but they started to organize themselves in groups on daily routine, to vote for their local community and to win the prize – fitness zone in their neighborhood. Apart from sharing and obviously relationships, in case of Activation 45 Years Coca-Cola in Serbia we distinguished identity of participants, conversation, and groups' coherence as the most important engagement needs/social media building blocks for the particular social game players.

Second experiment was executed for the Smoki Smokic online campaign, the sub brand of regional emotional consumer goods brand Smoki, where the main interaction and engagement hub has been online game named Smoki Smokic Pirate Adventure (Fig. 5). The idea was to increase product sale with strong support from digital communication channels. It was a regional campaign which embraced 6 neighbor countries. The game was designed for individual gaming experience and an only indirect connection with other players was leaderboard with the list of top players. The fact that game had regional character was crucial for spontaneous social interactions establishment. It started on the Smoki Facebook page as spontaneous sharing of tutorials, how to win the game between players, and, eventually, ended with creation of secret codes they used in the game in order to reveal their location and belonging to certain socio-cultural communities.

Fig. 5. Smoki smokic pirate adventure online game

After revealing their identity and belonging to certain groups it was easy to transform individual playing experience into social gaming. Throughout the time communication established over the brand, Facebook page evolved into between countries competition and, eventually, became platform for new relationship development and interpersonal and international joint initiatives. This experiment showed to us that people are in need of social interactions and even not initially planned relationships between players were spontaneously established on available social media platform. According to this we could say that social network infrastructure developed in the last 10 years fundamentally changed the way we are playing online, as if no other way of gaming exists anymore then social gaming. In case of Smoki Smokic online game, reputation and identity of the players were important engagement factors, since the players were highly competitive. Also, group power and coherence as well as establishing relationships should be considered in this case as crucial social media building blocks.

Our third experiment was Kraft Sport Game Campaign. Sport is traditional Hungarian countline brand, energy bar that satisfies the need for mental boost because it provides tasty energy. The task of our campaign was to create integrated campaign for Sport autumn promotion, and lasted for ten weeks, from August to October 2010. The rules of the game were simple: potential players were supposed to buy Sport bar, register with a code on brand site or on Facebook, play the game, collect the points, redeem the points for prizes and win the prize.

Among the key goals there were two: rising brand awareness and increasing product sale. Kraft Sport Game Campaign made a great success. We managed to reach players commitment, focusing more on converting visitors of the sites into players. There were 72 615 registrations made, with 353 919 chocolate bars redeemed. It was important that we attracted people to play the game and to commit to the brand. Frequent Players achieved long-term relationships with the brand established, and also among themselves. Frequent code uploads contributed offline sales of the Sport chocolate bar.

Although gamers were encouraged to communicate during the game, they also found their motivation to communicate through the social networks. Furthermore, after the end of the campaign, the players continued to communicate, which showed us that the social game was the trigger for establishing and building their future relationships and even virtual communities. In case of Kraft Sport Game Campaign, the game itself became the communication platform. Based on that, we concluded that the social game can actually exceed the goal of the competition itself – the game became the factor of group cohesion. There were established such good relationships among the players throughout the game campaign, that once the campaign was over, the participants continued to log in and communicate about different things. That was the anomaly that we did not count with at the beginning of the campaign, which eventually changed the context of the social game itself (Fig. 6).

Fig. 6. Sport game virtual room for socialization

Our third experiment, Kraft Sport Game Campaign, showed that social gaming has the potential to surpass and exceed its own goal, and to become the community on its own, created by the players themselves. Unlike two previously mentioned experiments, in Kraft Sport Game Campaign players actually changed the context of social gaming - from competition to collaboration, from the goal of winning the prize to the social platform suitable for starting initiatives, making decision important for achieving community goals, with potentials for smart initiatives or projects aimed to contribute livability and sustainability of the environment.

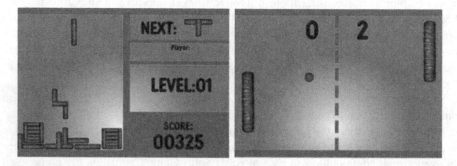

Fig. 7. Twix internal campaign

In case of Kraft Sport Game Campaign, reputation and identity of the players were strong engagement factors, followed by making intensive conversation and establishing long-term relationships which contributed enhancing group power and coherence.

Our recent ongoing project is Twix "Pick a Side Twix is Back" (Fig. 7), which purpose is to make employees of the organizations aware of the upcoming national

Fig. 8. Proposed honeycomb of social gaming

product campaign and, based on that, to make them start getting in touch and making relationships among themselves. In this experiment, we have moved the game from the external to the internal environment, observing participants behavior and changes in their communication. Our presumption is that the employees, involved in the social game, would accept the game as the cohesive platform for tightening the relationship between employees and provoke their broader engagement, such in social corporate responsibility initiatives and contributing the well-being of the communities they live in.

7 Conclusions

With the three experiments, we were investigating players' engagements in social games and the possibilities to use social games as platforms for extending players' cooperation and collaboration for more realistic purposes, such as contributing sustainable living environments and users' mobility.

The case of Coca Cola experiment, social media was the place of collaboration, while the site itself served only as a support. Players built new type of relationships, united for the common cause. The social game served for expanding players' communication platform, while the distinctive sense of competition, cooperation and collaboration among the players was showed. In second experiment, Smoki Smokic Pirate Adventure Game, there was obvious that the players actually dislocated their communication platform – they played the game on one platform, and transferred the communication to another. Competition among themselves was present, but collaboration was nurtured over the Facebook, long after the campaign was over. In the third experiment, Kraft Sport Game Campaign, it became obvious that the social game became more than just the playing platform. It served as the trigger, in the best possible way, for upgrading collaboration among the players. Game involvement was important, but not sufficient for the participants, because they showed they were motivated to engage themselves, share information, and start to believe in their own common goals, more than in promotion of the brand or the purpose of the game.

Upon the outcomes of all three experiments, we also concluded that presented social games share the same "honeycomb" social media building blocks, and the same strongest functionalities which characterize social gaming media environment (Fig. 8). First of all identity of the players, then relationships established among the players, and last, but not the least, group coherence needed for achieving long-term goals of the social game players: individual contribution to group sessions; the group contribution to individual sessions; the correlation between generated creative artefacts; the possibility to control created collective artefact.

References

1. Kietzmann, J.H., Hermkens, K., McCarthy, I.P., Silvestre, B.S.: Social media? get serious! understanding the functional building blocks of social media. Bus. Horis. **54**, 241–251 (2011). Elsevier

2. Kaplan, A.M., Haenlein, M.: Users of the world, unite! the challenges and opportunities of social media. Bus. Horis. **53**(1), 59–68 (2010). Elsevier

3. Agarwal, S., Datta, A., Nath, A.: Impact of green computing in it industry to make eco-friendly environment. J. Global Res. Comput. Sci. **5**(4), 5–9 (2014)

4. Kemp, S.: We are Social, January 2015. http://www.slideshare.net/wearesocialsg/digital-social-mobile-in-2015. Accessed 14 Aug 2015

5. Perez, S.: Pew: Facebook User Growth Slowed As Others Gained, But Still Has Most Engaged Users (2015). http://techcrunch.com/2015/01/09/pew-facebook-user-growth-slowed-as-others-gained-but-still-has-most-engaged-users/. Accessed 2 Aug 2015

6. Barner, N.G., Lescault, A.M.: The 2014 Fortune 500 and Social Media: LinkedIn Dominates As Use of Newer Tools Explodes, UMass Darthmouth (2014). http://www.umassd.edu/cmr/socialmediaresearch/2014fortune500andsocialmedia/. Accessed 4 Aug 2015

7. Filiciak, M.: Hyperidentities: postmodern identity patterns in massively multiplayer online role-playing games. In: Wolf, M.J.P., Perron, B. (eds.) Video Game Theory Reader, pp. 87–102. Routledge, New York (2003)

8. Kaye, L.K., Bryce, J.: Putting the "fun factor" into gaming: the influence of social context on experiences of playing videogame. Int. J. Internet Sci. **7**(1), 23–36 (2012)

9. Ritterfeld, U., Cody, M., Vorderer, P.: Serious Games: Mechanisms and Effects. Routledge, New York (2009)

10. Thackeray, R., Neiger, B.L., Hanson, C.L., McKenzie, J.F.: Enhancing promotional strategies within social marketing programs: use of web 2.0 social media. Sage J.: Health Promot. Pract. **9**(4), 338–343 (2008)

11. Aichner, T., Jacob, F.: Measuring the degree of corporate social media use. Int. J. Market Res. **57**(2), 257–275 (2015)

12. Sandstrom, G.M., Dunn, E.W.: Is efficiency overrated? minimal social interactions lead to belonging and positive affect. Soc. Psychol. Person. Sci. **5**, 436–441 (2014)

13. Kandampully, J.: Innovation as the core competency of a service organisation: the role of technology, knowledge and networks. Eur. J. Innov. Manage. **5**(1), 18–26 (2002)

14. Prahalad, C.K., Hamel, G.: The core competence of the corporation. Harward Bus. Rev. **33**, 79–91 (1990)

15. Voida, A., Carpendale, S., Greenberg, S: The individual and the group in console gaming. In: CSCW, pp. 371–380, Savannah, Georgia, USA, 6–10 February 2010

16. Zagal, J.P., Rick, J., Hsi, I.: Collaborative games: lessons learned from board games. Simul. Gaming **37**(1), 24–40 (2006)

17. Wölfl, A.: The Service Economy in OECD Countries. Working Paper, 2005/3, OECD – Directorate of Science, Technology and Industry and Office of the U.S. Trade Representative. U.S. Submits Revised Service Offer to the WTO. Press Release. Executive Office of the President, Washington, D.C. (2005)

18. Berry, L.L., Shankar, V., Parish, J.T., Cadwallader, S., Dotzel, T.: Creating new markets through service innovation. MIT Sloan Manage. Rev. **47**(2), 56–63 (2006)

19. Bartle, R.A.: Designing Virtual Worlds. New Riders, Berkeley (2004)

20. Bartle, R.A.: Hearts, clubs, diamonds and spades: players who suit MUDs. J. MUD Res. **1**(1), 19 (1996). http://www.mud.co.uk/richard/hcds.htm. Accessed 10 Aug 1996

21. Yee, N.: Motivations of play in online games. CyberPsychol. Behav. **9**, 772–775 (2007)

22. Yee, N.: The demographics, motivations and derived experiences of users of massively multiuser online graphical environments. Presence: Teleoperators Virtual Environ. **15**(3), 309–329 (2006)

23. Ryan, R.M., Rigby, C.S., Przybylski, A.: The motivational pull of video games: a selfdetermination theory approach. Motiv. Emot. **30**, 347–363 (2006)

24. Tamborini, R., Bowman, N.D., Eden, A., Gizzard, M., Organ, A.: Defining media enjoyment as the satisfaction of intrinsic needs. J. Commun. **60**(4), 758–777 (2010)
25. Williams, D., Yee, N., Caplan, S.: Who plays, how much and why? debunking the stereotypical gamer profile. J. Comput. Mediat. Commun. **13**, 993–1018 (2008)
26. Smyth, J.M.: Beyond self-selection in video game play: an experimental examination of the consequences of massively multiplayer online role-playing game play. CyberPsychol. Behav. **10**(5), 717–721 (2007)
27. Cole, H., Griffiths, M.D.: Social interactions in massively multiplayer online role-playing gamers. CyberPsychol. Behav. **10**(4), 575–583 (2007)
28. Kraft, P., Schjelderup-Lund, H., Brendryen, H.: Digital therapy: the coming together of psychology and technology can create a new generation of programs for more sustainable behavioral change. In: Kort, Y.A., IJsselsteijn, W.A., Midden, C., Eggen, B., Fogg, B. J. (eds.) PERSUASIVE 2007. LNCS, vol. 4744, pp. 18–23. Springer, Heidelberg (2007)
29. Ng, B.D., Wiemer-Hastings, P.: Addiction to the Internet and online gaming. Cyberpsychol. Behav. **8**(3), 110–113 (2005)
30. Nardi, B., Harris, J.: Strangers and friends: collaborative play in World of Warcraft. In: Proceedings: ACM Conference on Computer Supported Cooperative Work, pp. 149–158. ACM Press, New York (2006)
31. Griffits, M.: Computer game playing in early adolescence. Youth Soc. **29**(2), 223–237 (1997)
32. Trepte, S., Reinecke, L.: The pleasures of success: game-related efficacy experiences as a mediator between player performance and game enjoyment. CyberPsychol. Behav. Soc. Netw. **14**(9), 555–557 (2011)
33. Van Looy, J., Courtois, C., de Vocht, M.: Player identification in online games: validation of a scale for measuring identification in MMORPGs. In: 3rd International Conference on Fun and Games, New York (2010)
34. Smith, G.: Social Software Building Blocks (2007). http://nform.ca/publications/social-software-building-blocks
35. Ascott, R.: Telematic Embrace: Visionary Theories of Art, Technology, and Consciousness. University of California Press, Berkeley (2003)
36. Stenslie, S.: Virtual Touch, Ph.D. dissertation. Oslo School of Architecture and Design. Oslo, Norway (2010)
37. Nikolic, P.K.: Social media interactions and online games - building up new human relationships in danube region. J. Danubian Stud. Res. **5**(2), 208–221 (2015)

The Requirements to Develop a Competency Model for the Position of a Team Leader in Industrial Enterprises in Slovakia

Barbora Sokolovská[1,2]([✉]), Dagmar Cagáňová[1,2],
and Kristína Kašníková[1,2]

[1] Faculty of Materials Science and Technology in Trnava,
Slovak University of Technology in Bratislava, Bratislava, Slovakia
{barbora.sokolovska,dagmar.caganova,
kristina.kasnikova}@stuba.sk
[2] Institute of Industrial Engineering and Management, Trnava, Slovakia

Abstract. In the selection process of a team leader, competency models find their application, which guarantee the occupancy of this position by a person, who is actually able to perform this role. This paper aims to highlight the requirements to develop a competency model for the position of a team leader. The paper presents the results of a questionnaire survey, which was aimed at industrial enterprises in Slovakia. These results confirmed that a competency approach is not a common fact in industrial enterprises and also that industrial enterprises are interested in the development of a competency model for the position of a team leader and its consequential usage in the selection of a team leader. These findings represent a great challenge to improve human resource management in industrial enterprises in Slovakia, but also in developed Danube region as a part of Danube strategy.

Keywords: Team · Teamwork · Competency · Competency model · Team leader · Industrial enterprise

1 Introduction

In current global business environment almost all enterprises have the same conditions for their operation – capital, sources, environment; therefore competing with competitors is very difficult. Enterprises have to seek to differentiate from their competitors and thereby gain a competitive advantage. Most enterprises do not realize that this can be achieved just by their workforce [15].

In modern management the idea of the team is increasingly rising in prominence. Consultants in the area of management propose restructuring of enterprises and institutions in favour of strengthening teamwork, directors of organizational boards draw the attention to the importance of the team for the whole enterprise and senior managers encourage their younger colleagues to develop teamwork at their departments. Team has become a recognized basic unit of organization of work [3].

© ICST Institute for Computer Sciences, Social Informatics and Telecommunications Engineering 2016
A. Leon-Garcia et al. (Eds.): Smart City 2015, LNICST 166, pp. 572–583, 2016.
DOI: 10.1007/978-3-319-33681-7_48

And for this there are many reasons. Teams have a huge potential. Researches suggest that in all types of enterprises or organizations, whether in the public or private sector, teamwork improves work ethic and reduces employee turnover [3].

In the enterprise, which strives to apply teamwork, people work more effectively, experience lower stress and make more effort. They stay in the enterprise longer and they are absent from work for a shorter period of time. They contribute with new ideas and seek to develop in their work. The result is a smoother operation of the enterprise or institution that at the same time saves money and is more competitive [3].

Of course, not every enterprise that will apply teamwork has significant results. Some enterprises have introduced teamwork and revealed no major differences. But one thing is certain: *If the teamwork is applied correctly, it will lead to fundamental changes* [3].

The study of literature concerned with teams and also the experience of practitioners leads to the realization that the atmosphere in the team and performance of the team is extremely important to the way it is led [4]. Achievements thus depend on the personality of a leader and leadership styles, which they use [2]. However, there are many other factors, that affect the way of leadership – the kind of task, a little or a lot of time to complete the task, the nature of employees, previous experience of leader, etc. [14].

Practice shows that even highly developed teams, which already work very cooperatively, have not developed without a leader. When everyone feels responsible for everything and work is not divided according to the tasks and abilities, the team will become unproductive [10].

It follows that whether it is the newly established or developed team, each needs to have a leader. Sufficient attention must be given to the selection of the team leader. The authors of the paper claim that it is mainly about finding qualities, abilities, skills and knowledge, hence it is necessary to identify the leader's competencies.

The competency approach started to be expressively applied in the area of selection of employees, their development, their evaluation and in managing their career [7].

The authors of the paper emphasize mainly the application of a competency approach in the area of selection of employees, thus they focus on the use of the competency model in the selection of a suitable candidate for the position of a team leader.

1.1 Team and Teamwork

The current market environment and, particularly, changes in the economic area and entrance of mostly Western European enterprises to the Slovak market, have brought the necessity to solve many tasks through teamwork. This change is related to the necessity of rapid, the most effective solutions with minimal error rate in the final decision [2].

Therefore teamwork in recent years became common in various areas [19].

People, who are good and acquainted in their field, can prove a lot – but not everything. There are still tasks, which an individual alone is not able to do, in which they are dependent on knowledge, cooperation and ideas of others. Perhaps in any sphere it does not work without teamwork [11].

The authors of the paper identify with the definition of Duchoň and Šafránková [2], who define teamwork as a set of values that encourage certain ways of behaviour, e.g. listening to others, cooperative response to the ideas of others, expressing doubts in favour of the others and also in favour of fulfilment of the tasks, help the needy members and recognition of interests and achievements of others.

The concept of teamwork differentiates from the common cooperation in work groups. The essence of teamwork is to transfer responsibility to work teams so they can perform their tasks, without the fact, they would still have to ask higher components of the enterprise for approval. This means that teams must be sufficiently authorized to be able to make independent decisions in daily practice, and must have sufficient power to be able to ensure the proper fulfilment of the tasks [2]. In principle, a purpose of teamwork is delegation and authorization [3].

Teamwork is used in all situations, where a comprehensive and synergistic approach to solving the problem is needed [2].

We can talk about the teamwork, as a specific form of work organization, if its basic conditions or characteristics are fulfilled. These include [19]:

- assignment of common tasks or goals;
- association of people with different professional knowledge and experience.

In addition to the mentioned basic conditions or characteristics of teamwork, certain assumptions have to be created for its successful operation [21]:

- **to want** – the employee must want to do something, prepare, improve, organize, i.e. the employee is motivated to carry out the activities;
- **to be allowed** – the employee must have sufficient powers to carry out these activities;
- **to know and prove** – the employee needs to have not only professional, but also organizational knowledge and abilities to know and prove to do something, improve and organize.

The authors of the paper state that teamwork brings many benefits, whether for the enterprise or for co-operating employees themselves. People will learn to participate in the successes and also failures, gain a sense of fellowship and take collective responsibility. Consequently, the enterprise will be more competitive; it will achieve higher performance and become more attractive for potential employees, as well as for potential partners in the business.

The application of teamwork thus brings the necessity of team creation in enterprises. In Table 1, the authors of the paper provide definitions of the concept of team according to different authors.

A team is a very good tool for solving the difficult tasks and problems, for searching for new ways in project style of work [9], because the use of groups and teams gives an advantage for achieving a certain type of synergy. Employees [17]:

- produce a higher quality of outputs than either working alone (combination of effort);
- learn from each other;
- together correct errors and immediately solve arose problems;
- share knowledge, tasks and objectives.

Table 1. Definitions of the team according to different authors [own elaboration]

Year	Author	Definition
2005	Střížová	Team is a group of people, who complement each other by their knowledge and skills, they are committed to a common purpose, they dedicate to the common work goals, for which they are mutual responsible, they combine skills, experience and perspectives of different people and thus they carry out more performance than individuals working alone or in large groups, they respond flexibly to changing events and requirements, they adapt to new information and tasks faster, more accurately and effectively than individuals acting in a network of large-scale organizational links.
2008	Duchoň and Šafránková	By team, we understand three or more individuals, who are in mutual interaction and have a feel of a common identity, a common consciousness of "we". They all are trying to achieve the same goal. They respect mainly unwritten norms or rules, under which they voluntarily will work and act.
2009	Mohauptová	Team is a clearly defined whole of cooperating people with time limited goal, limited size, clear rules and roles and characteristic process of work.

Often in connection with the effectiveness of the team, the equation of synergy can be seen, which should tell us that nothing beats the work of a team [9].

- **Synergetic equation of a team (the equation of the effectiveness of team): $1 + 1 = 3$**

The team achieves better results, than the individuals could achieve by themselves [9]. Two people together do more work than either alone. Mutual integration and usage of the talent in the team brings added value, which is worth to experience. It is not only the contribution of result, but also the contribution of the feeling. Mostly, people in a team feel the application, they are important to the others and they have a feeling of appreciation. Their motivation and commitment for the team is increasing [10].

- **The equation of work of several individuals (the equation of efficiency of a group): $1 + 1 = 2$**

The group has the same results as if the individuals work alone [9]. Two people together do the work of two people. There is no added value in the cooperation. If such added value does not arise, the cooperation will die and cease after time. Everyone does their own things [10].

- **The equation of an ineffective team: $1 + 1 = -1$ or $1 + 1 < 2$**

Even this variant may occur. The team is less productive than the individuals themselves. Employees would operate more effectively, if they did not seek to cooperate [9]. Two people together do less work than either alone. This is a description of many workplaces and it is a real disadvantage of the effort of cooperation [10].

The authors of the paper state that the benefit of team as a form of work organization stems mainly from the above mentioned synergy. The people in the team are open to different opinions and ideas, they are not afraid to present them in front of the other team members, and hence there may arise entirely new ways how to fulfil the tasks, how to cooperate and how to achieve the goal faster and more effectively.

1.2   Competency and Competency Model

The term competency is currently often used not only in the professional literature, but also in practice. But what does this term mean [1]? Although the term competency is naturalized in our vocabulary, its use and importance, which professional and general public attach to it, differ [20].

The term competency is usually used **in two basic meanings** [1].

The first meaning and interpretation of the concept of competency is often associated with the performance of profession or in general with work activity and it is traditionally used to label the power to make decisions and responsibilities for the consequences of made decisions following from this power. It follows that competency is in this case the term semantically related to other terms such as power, influence or positional or formal authority [18]. It can therefore be concluded that competency is power, authorization, scope of powers usually given by some authority or belonging to some authority [2]. Competency in this meaning is possible to move on someone [1].

The second meaning of this term refers to the fact that competency is the ability to perform some activity, to be able to perform it, to be qualified in the concerned area on the basis of the necessary knowledge and skills [2]. Competency is therefore the expression of the general ability to adequately evaluate the situation (by far not only work situation) and be able to adapt own behaviour to it or be prepared (know) to respond to the situation [18]. A competency can be understood as specific set of knowledge, skills, experience, methods and procedures, but also, for example, attitudes, which the individual uses for successful solving of different tasks and life situations and which enable the individual's personal development and fulfilment of life aspirations [20].

The concept of competency as ability was brought into the managerial practice by R. Boyatzis in the work "Competent manager" [5].

Each author, dealing with the issue of competencies, firstly defines this concept. The authors of the paper offer in the following Table 2 an overview of definitions of the concept of competency by different authors, whereby definitions are listed in ascending order according to the year.

A person in order to perform successfully individual tasks, needs to have desirable competencies [12]. Competent is the one, who usually handles efficiently different tasks and situations [20]. A competent employee is therefore the one, who, on one hand, has the assumptions (knowledge, skills, abilities, characteristics, attitudes) for achieving performance (i.e. he is able for performance) and, on the other hand, really achieves required performances [12]. For better illustration serves Fig. 1.

If the employee is competent, thus they fulfil the assigned role well or on an excellent level, it means that they fulfilled three assumptions [2]:

Table 2. Definitions of competency according to different authors [own elaboration]

Year	Author	Definition
1982	Boyatzis	Competency is the ability of a person to behave in a certain way corresponding with the requirements of work in the parameters given by the environment of the enterprise and thus bring the desired results.
2006	Hermochová	Competency is a set of required characteristics of employees, which are deduced from the nature of work tasks and situations peculiar for particular workplace or work position in the enterprise.
2010	Bartoňková	Competency is a set of knowledge, skills, experience and characteristics, which supports the achievement of the objective.
2011	Steigauf	Competency is personal provable task-specific and transferable knowledge and skill for the particular goal or task. Competency is acquired in the course of time.
2013	Procházka, Vaculík, & Smutný	Competency is a summary of knowledge, skills, abilities and other characteristics, which a person needs to achieve a good work performance.

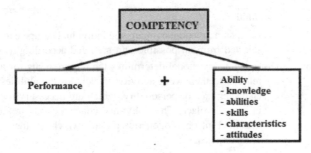

Fig. 1. Competency [12]

- the employee is internally provided with characteristics, abilities, knowledge, skills and experience, which he necessarily needs for such behaviour;
- the employee is motivated to use such behaviour, thus they see value in the desired behaviour and are willing to invest necessary energy in this direction;
- the employee has a possibility to use such behaviour in the particular environment.

While the first assumption concerns the skills and knowledge, which can be relatively easy to develop, the second one has an entirely different nature. It is affected more difficult, because it is about motives, attitudes, values, beliefs and philosophy of life. This area belongs to the stable components of human personality. The third assumption included into the list is maybe a little surprisingly. It is related to the external conditions and not to the personality of employee. However, these significantly affect both above mentioned areas [8].

In order for an employee to be competent, all three conditions have to be fulfilled simultaneously. The absence of whichever of them block competent performance. In this sense, all three conditions are equivalent. If the employee really wants to deliver a good performance and also such performance is required, but they lack, for example, skills, they will not reach the expected result. If they are not motivated, they will not make an effort to use the skills, even if they have them at their disposal. If the environment does not allow them to use the competencies, even the fact that they are capable and willing, will not help them [8].

In the following, the authors of the paper discuss the competency model and its possibilities of application in practice.

Competency models are used in increasingly more enterprises. These are mainly enterprises with foreign participation. In Slovak enterprises a competency model can be rarely encountered and also there is relatively little professional literature, which addresses to this issue [6].

Firstly, it is necessary to define what the concept of competency model means. The following Table 3 offers an overview of definitions of competency model from the perspective of different authors.

Table 3. Definitions of competency model according to different authors (Source: own elaboration)

Year	Author	Definition
2006	Hroník	A competency model contains the individual competencies, which are selected from all possible and arranged according to some key.
2010	Kocianová	A competency model determines the requirements for a person in relation to their work activity; it includes the abilities and characteristics of personality, which are necessary for performance in the workplace. The individual characteristics are generally classified into homogeneous groups, which are then referred to as competencies.
2013	Procházka et al.	A competency model is a set of competencies associated with a particular position or role within the enterprise.

There are universal competency models, models of managerial competencies and models for certain work activities, for example, models of competencies of sellers [7]. Hroník [5] points out to the fact that the more the model is universal, the more it can unify, but less differentiate.

The most common domain of utilization of competency models is the area of leadership and management of human resources. Competency models are successfully used for planning of recruitment of employees, selection of employees and their evaluation, management of performance and development of employees and they are used due to their contribution for individuals (leaders) as well as for the enterprise [13].

Contribution of the competency model for an individual [13]:

- it includes the experience and view of other leaders;
- it specifies a set of useful patterns of behaviour;
- it is a tool, which managers can use for their development;
- it defines a framework, which can help to choose leaders, develop and understand their effectiveness.

Contribution of the competency model for an enterprise [13]:

- it allows to openly communicate important patterns of behaviour of leaders;
- it helps to distinguish the performance of individuals;
- it connects the behaviour of leaders with the strategic direction and goals of the enterprise;
- it provides integrative model of leadership, which is relevant to many positions and situations.

In identifying desirable competencies of the leader, it is necessary to take into consideration the fact that we are looking for such competencies, which are causally related to the efficient and/or standard or exceptional performance of the work. A practical tool, which can be used in the process of cognition of the key competencies are competency models [13].

It is very difficult – but not impossible – to create a comprehensive or general model of competencies [20].

The authors of the paper emphasize the fact that competency models are increasingly coming to the forefront in enterprises. This actuality has for the consequence mainly their wide use and benefits not only for enterprise, but also for employees.

The authors of the paper claim that the competency model is a set of competencies, which employees must have to be able to perform the work on the particular work position with the desired results. A competency model then not only helps to choose suitable candidates for work positions in the enterprise, but also serves to plan their further development.

2 Method of Research

In the following part of the paper, the authors present the method of research, which was used during writing this paper.

The authors of the paper used a questionnaire survey. It is a pilot survey, which is a part of the dissertation thesis conducted at the Institute of Industrial Engineering and Management, Faculty of Materials Science and Technology, Slovak University of Technology. The dissertation thesis is focused on addressing the issue of leadership in teams and competencies of the team leader.

A pilot survey was conducted through questionnaire survey, which was aimed at industrial enterprises in Slovakia. The questionnaire was made with the application GoogleDocs. It consisted of eight questions, while the first three were designed to obtain basic information about the enterprise – size, subject of business activity and branch of industry. Another five questions served to obtain the information concerning leadership, teamwork and competency model in the particular enterprise.

Data collection took place in the time period from 6.12.2014 to 31.12.2014. The questionnaire was sent to email addresses of 515 respondents, while 55 questionnaires were returned completed. The return thus constitutes 10.68 %.

In the following chapter, the authors of the paper connect the theoretical backgrounds, which were previously mentioned, with the important results of the questionnaire survey conducted by the authors of the paper.

3 Results of the Questionnaire Survey

In the paper, the authors specifically focus on four questions from the questionnaire survey. In the following text, gradually explained and also graphically illustrated are the answers of the respondents to the selected four questions.

The first of the selected four questions was focused on the importance of teamwork in the enterprise. It is positive that almost all, i.e. 53 respondents, consider work in teams in an enterprise as important. Only two respondents were unable to answer this question, which may be caused due to the fact that these enterprises do not apply work in teams and therefore the respondents cannot assess its importance to the enterprise.

Another question served to investigate the opinion of respondents on whether the performance of the team is affected by the way a leader leads their team. Everyone, i.e. 55 respondents, answered this question clearly yes.

Through the next question, the authors of the paper sought to determine whether enterprises use a competency model in the selection of the team leader. 18 respondents claimed that they use a competency model and 10 respondents answered negatively. 27 respondents were not able to express their opinion, which may be caused due to the fact that the respondents did not have sufficient information to answer this question. The percentage expression of the answers of respondents is shown in Fig. 2.

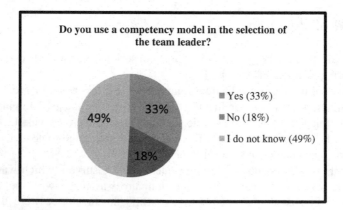

Fig. 2. The answers to the question: Do you use a competency model in the selection of the team leader? [own elaboration] (Color figure online)

Through the last of the four selected questions, the authors of the paper identified whether enterprises would be interested in the creation of a competency model for the position of a team leader. More than a half, i.e. 31 respondents, would welcome the creation of a competency model for a team leader. 7 respondents rejected this option and 17 of them were not able to express to this question, which may be caused due to the lack of information to answer this question. The percentage expression of the answers of respondents is shown in Fig. 3.

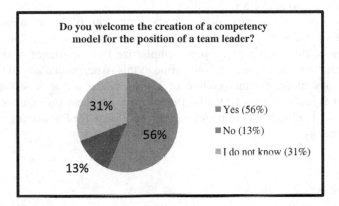

Fig. 3. The answers to the question: Do you welcome the creation of a competency model for the position of a team leader? [own elaboration] (Color figure online)

In the following chapter, the authors of the paper summarize the answers of respondents to the selected four questions and draw conclusions.

4   Discussion

The purpose of the paper was not only to determine what importance is attached to teamwork in industrial enterprises in Slovakia, but also to verify whether enterprises use a competency model in the selection of suitable employees on the position of a team leader.

In the previous chapter, the authors presented the results of the questionnaire survey. These results confirmed that teamwork has its application in industrial enterprises and employees really considered it as an important form of work organization. Among respondents, there was a clear consensus in the opinion on the fact that the performance of a team is affected by the way a leader leads his team. Such a clear consensus among respondents, however, was not in the area of using a competency model. More than a half of respondents were unable to answer this question and 18 % of respondents claimed that they do not use a competency model in the selection of a team leader. From the answers to this question, therefore, the authors can deduce that the competency approach is not a common fact in industrial enterprises in Slovakia. For further research, it is a positive finding that more than a half of the respondents would welcome the creation of a competency model for the position of a team leader. Thus, it makes sense to deal with the issue of leadership in teams and competencies of a team leader further.

From the findings it followed that teamwork has its application in enterprises, therefore it is very important to ensure the effective functioning of teams. This can be achieved by choosing a suitable employee on the position of a team leader. The best tool for this is precisely the competency model, and therefore the authors of the paper recommend using a competency model for ensuring the selection of a suitable employee on the position of a team leader.

The authors of the paper acknowledge some limitations of the conducted research, such as the low return of completed questionnaires, which can distort the results.

Nevertheless, the authors of the paper emphasize the importance of the obtained information and they recommend devoting time to this issue, particularly to the creation of a competency model for the position of a team leader to facilitate the industrial enterprises in Slovakia to choose the best employees for these positions according to possibly the most consistent criteria. It is a great challenge for Danube region as a part of Danube strategy.

References

1. Bartoňková, H.: Enterprise Education. Strategic Approach to the Education of Employees. Grada Publishing, Praha (2010)
2. Duchoň, B., Šafránková, J.: Management – The Integration of Hard and Soft Elements of Management. C. H. Beck, Praha (2008)
3. Hayes, N.: The Psychology of Teamwork – Strategy of the Effective Leadership of Team. Portál, s.r.o, Praha (2005)
4. Hermochová, S.: Teambuilding. Grada Publishing, Praha (2006)
5. Hroník, F.: The Evaluation of Employees. Grada Publishing, Praha (2006)
6. Hroník, F.: Development and Education of Employees. Grada Publishing, Praha (2006)
7. Kocianová, R.: Personal Activities and the Methods of Personal Work. Grada Publishing, Praha (2010)
8. Kubeš, M., Spillerová, D., Kurnický, R.: Managerial Competencies – Abilities of Exceptional Managers. Grada Publishing, Praha (2004)
9. Mohauptová, E.: Teambuilding – The Way to the Effective Cooperation. Portál, s.r.o, Praha (2009)
10. Mohauptová, E.: Team Coaching. Portál, s.r.o, Praha (2013)
11. Mühleisen, S., Oberhuber, N.: Communication and Other Soft Skills – Soft Skills in Practice. Grada Publishing, Praha (2008)
12. Pilařová, I.: How to Effectively Evaluate Employees and Improve their Performance. Grada Publishing, Praha (2008)
13. Procházka, J., Vaculík, M., Smutný, P.: The Psychology of the Effective Leadership. Grada Publishing, Praha (2013)
14. Sokolovská, B., Cagáňová, D.: Leadership styles from the perspective of employees of industrial enterprises. In: Proceedings of Young Science 2014, Bratislava, Slovakia, 12th November 2014. Croatian Quality Managers Society, Zagreb, Croatia, pp. 96–107 (2014)

15. Sokolovská, B., Cagáňová, D., Čambál, M., Saniuk, A.: Intellectual capital of employees as a competitive advantage of an enterprise. In: Proceedings of the 6th European Conference on Intellectual Capital, ECIC 2014, Trnava, Slovakia, 10th–11th April 2014, pp. 399–407 (2014)
16. Steigauf, S.: Leadership or What do not they Teach you at Harvard. Grada Publishing, Praha (2011)
17. Střížová, V.: Organization, Information, Management. Vysoká škola ekonomická, Praha (2005)
18. Tureckiová, M.: The Key to the Effective Leadership. Unlock the Potential of your Co-workers. Grada Publishing, Praha (2007)
19. Urban, J.: How to Handle 10 the Most Difficult Situations of Managers. Grada Publishing, Praha (2008)
20. Veteška, J., Tureckiová, M.: Competencies in Education. Grada Publishing, Praha (2008)
21. IPA Slovakia. Teamwork, 24 January 2007. http://www.ipaslovakia.sk/sk/ipa-slovnik/timova-praca

Traffic Signs in Urban Logistics with the Use of RFID Technology

Michal Balog[(⊠)], Erik Szilagyi, and Miroslav Mindas

Faculty of Manufacturing Technologies with Seat in Presov,
Technical University of Kosice, Bayerova 1, Presov, Slovakia
{michal.balog,erik.szilagyi,miroslav.mindas}@tuke.sk

Abstract. Increase of the traffic safety is one of the most important issues for most countries. Our goal is to introduce the concept of the traffic sign recognition system based on radio frequency identification, which presupposes a significant increase of the traffic safety. The concept of the solution is a prerequisite for marking traffic signs with RFID transponders, on which is entered information about specific traffic signs. A vehicle equipped with RFID components for reading the transponder can read the traffic signs and offers the opportunity to inform the driver about significance of the specific traffic signs. By using this technology it is possible to minimize human error while driving and with a support system this solution can offer secondary audio-visual and real-time information about the actual situation on the road with the possibility of interference in control of the vehicle.

Keywords: Urban logistics · RFID · Traffic signs

1 Introduction

Transportation is one of the basic sectors that significantly affect the socio-economic development and growth of living standards. In passenger transport quality depends largely on satisfying the everyday needs of citizens, such as the level of accessibility to work, schools, shops, accessibility to social care and leisure activities. On the quality of freight transport impact factors such as: speed, safety, punctuality and timing of delivery date. That is why the use of modern technologies in the field of transport and urban logistics is a global trend. Most often the application delivers the benefits associated with electronic data processing, which may be inputs (after the evaluation) for decision making processes of the security elements of transport infrastructure.

1.1 Logistics of the Region

The concept of regional logistics can be defined as that part of logistics, which is focused on events in the region and accepts all the attributes of the logistics. Its outputs constitute competitive advantages of the region, such as: efficient supply in the region, quality logistics services, favorable structure of the business environment and healthy business environment, transportation availability and serviceability in the region and

© ICST Institute for Computer Sciences, Social Informatics and Telecommunications Engineering 2016
A. Leon-Garcia et al. (Eds.): Smart City 2015, LNICST 166, pp. 584–591, 2016.
DOI: 10.1007/978-3-319-33681-7_49

quality infrastructure. City logistics expresses the part of the regional logistics, which is oriented to the organization of traffic in space and time of social and material flows, ensuring maximum orientation in production areas, economic and social throughout the city with maximizing satisfaction. Its activity is concentrated on traffic - movement of goods and people in larger cities, where today there is a need of solving often acute. In rush hour, in traffic accidents or during events with greater accumulation of people and consequently also cars, these events can lead to absolute disablement transport infrastructure, thereby hindering the overall running of the city. Need to address the role of urban logistics was established gradually in major cities (the capital) with a high concentration of transport [1].

Due to rising motorization already smaller cities have now traffic problems already depending on the quality of transport infrastructure and transport organization. Twist in the relatively calm traffic situation in the region came after EU accession, which brought increased migration of the population and its subsequent concentration at the sites, which offering higher job opportunities. Consequently the creation of a new urban centre various linked to essential historical estates, bringing a further increase of traffic. Under the increase of individual transport especially, is also signed by easier availability of passenger cars (leases, loans, jumble sale, etc.) The structure of the control system of urban logistics formulates clear ties for the further development of the logistics system and updating the applied technologies to the definition of possible overall benefit. The structure of the control system defines the formal relationship between all major- individual elements and objects, along with other subsystems and components and determines the rules of their operation. The structure of the control system of urban logistics defines a scheme in which they a recreated technical specifications and interface design of the overall system [2] (Fig. 1).

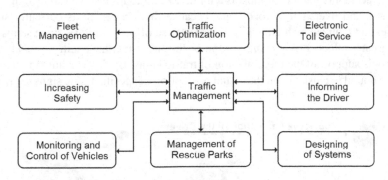

Fig. 1. The structure of management system of urban logistics [2]

1.2 Accidents

The unresolved logistical transport processes in smaller cities is often a source of collisions and subsequent congestions, which often leads to a complete meltdown of transport. In larger cities congestions are occurring without collision situation and mostly during the morning or afternoon peak hours. An important and primary role of urban logistics is a search - optimizing transport infrastructure, i.e. search for the optimal topology transport network (optimization of transport routes, modes of transport in that area). While city logistics addresses route optimization in relation to cultural and social centre, manufacturing companies, shops, schools etc. Major transport problems faced by cities in the region are unresolved key problems of traffic, then thereto unresolved population mobility in their activities. Lacking respectively sub standard urban areas which would help to relieve the city centre from excess traffic. Another parameter which is strongly linked to the intensity of road transport, quality transport infrastructure and unsolved transport logistics is accident rate, which is in the region's roads considerably high. In the view of the frequency of transport is high incidence of road accidents recorded on local roads [2] (Fig. 2).

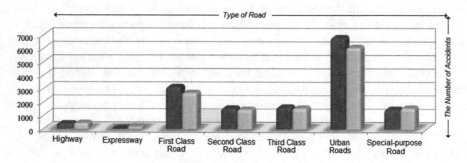

Fig. 2. Accident rate in Slovakia according to the type of road in the periods 01.01-31.12.2012 (red colour) and 1.1-31.12.2013 (yellow colour) (Color figure online)

Traffic accidents that occur most often due to failure to observe traffic signs due to carelessness and oversight of road signs because drive a vehicle is currently still the greatest extent realized by human [2]. The existence of supporting safety systems while driving greatly affects driving safety. One of the areas that have still not been solved complexly is support of the identification of traffic signs. By this is a human interaction in driving bound exclusively on the visual perception of specific traffic signs [2] (Fig. 3).

Fig. 3. The current state of the process of identifying road signs by drivers

In 2005, the Government adopted Resolution no. 445 Transport Policy of SR 2015, which defines a global objective and a number of specific objectives that include specific measures in the transport sector in Slovakia to ensure the sustainable development of mobility, conceived as long-term satisfaction of increasing needs of the society in the required time and quality while reducing the negative effects of transport on the environment. In the so-called Operational Transport Program (OTP), it is one of the activities to support the development of intelligent transport systems and create conditions for broader application of information and communication systems and technology (ICT) to transport.

Nowadays, there are many similar systems concepts, especially in applications for road transport. Most of them use built-in camera inside the vehicle with the on-board computer, which processes visual stimuli and chosen way warns the driver about the current situation. Systems based on the principle of camcorders are dependent on the weather and daylight. Rain, fog and poor lighting make it impossible correct interpretation in these systems. The use of ICT allows very significantly reduce the negative effects arising from the operation of transport systems, positively affects the economics of the transport organizations and services, not just reduces the demands on public resources, but also on the resources of other entities transport and transportation process and enables them to rational decision-making. It also has a positive impact on improving safety and traffic flow [3].

The core elements of comprehensive solutions are intelligent transport systems (ITS), which aim to:

- increasing the safety of road-transport process
- improving the efficiency and quality of service expressed the time saved on transport;
- reducing negative impacts on the environment;
- reducing transport energy intensity;
- increasing access to transport information between all entities of transport and shipping process for their rational decision making;
- enhancing the quality of transport infrastructure and reduce costs entered into the construction of new transport infrastructure.

Our proposed solution contained in this publication provides a method for reducing respectively eliminating the possibility of overlooking road signs using a wireless identification technology, known as RFID technology.

2   RFID Technology

The principle of radio frequency identification is based on the use of wireless non-contact radio frequency electromagnetic fields to transfer data for purposes of automatic identification and tracking RFID tags placed on objects. Radio frequency identification (RFID) is formed by components developed for wireless identification.

The basic components of an RFID system are:

- Middleware consists of the control computer, database information and communication infrastructure;
- RFID reader that contains a transmitter and receiver circuit with a decoder and an antenna. Complementary solution can also be read out by integrated operating system with basic software functionality;

- RFID antenna realizing transmitting and receiving radio waves
- Transponder or the so-called RFID tag, consisting of the chip (an electronic memory circuit), and in the case of the active antenna or the semi passive tag may contain its own power supply. For these components it is then projected proper packaging structures depending on the purpose of use [4] (Fig. 4).

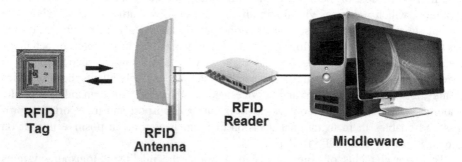

RFID Tag

RFID Antenna

RFID Reader

Middleware

Fig. 4. The basic decomposition of elements of the RFID system

Communication between the components of RFID technology most often occurs on frequencies:

- Low frequency at 125-134 kHz;
- High frequency at 13.56 MHz;
- Very high frequency at 868-956 MHz;
- Microwaves at 2.45 GHz.

By type of power of the RFID transponders is possibly their classification on passive and active transponder. Passive RFID transponder does not have its own energy sources, and its functionality depends on the power of RFID antennas. Through antenna is generated an electromagnetic field, which serves as a power source for the RFID transponder, and also as a channel of communication between these elements [5, 6]. The active RFID tag is designed not only for the identification of objects but also to ensure the various measured physical parameters such as temperature, pressure etc. It includes power supply and thus it can monitor parameters and enhance the impact of the antenna. The applicability of the RFID system is very large, but in each application requiring the use of a system of elements that are adapted on given conditions and its efficiency can provide a full functioning of the system as a whole. Each element of an RFID system is therefore defined by the values of the reference parameter [7].

2.1 Application of RFID Tags on Traffic Signs

The principle solution is based on the appropriate application of RFID system into the microenvironment of transport infrastructure including the identification of traffic signs drivers. The present situation in which is the perception of traffic signs subjective by the driver, causing a risk of overlooking traffic signs which can ultimately give rise to negative events in the transport communications. The introduction of the scheme provides secondary support system for perception, respectively, identification of traffic signs, which consists in electrisation of the elements participating in the aforementioned process through RFID components. System design lies in integration of RFID reader and middleware together into an integrated control unit, whose task is to manage the system itself and evaluate the collected data. Application of RFID the antenna is proposed solution to the front of the vehicle body to ensure the most appropriate position with respect to the direction of reading. We propose to fit traffic signs with preprogrammed RFID tags, which will contain information about specific traffic signs (Fig. 5).

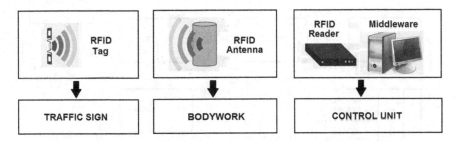

Fig. 5. Location of the RFID components with respect to the elements involved in the process design of identifying traffic signs

This solution after proper configuration of individual elements ensures electronic data collection on traffic signs. This data will provide space for the possibility of using this information both to familiarizing the driver with the closest traffic signs through visualization display supplemented by sound acquaintance, respectively interact to drive a vehicle in the form of speed reduction or stopping of the vehicle (Fig. 6).

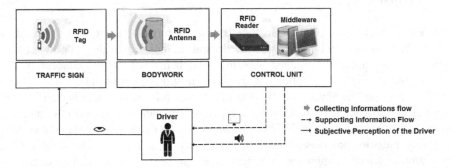

Fig. 6. Visualization of course of proposed process of informatization recognition traffic signs

Middleware system includes a database of traffic signs. Incoming vehicle equipped with RFID reader reads the RFID tag placed on traffic signs and on the evaluation of the appropriate code identifying the meaning traffic signs. At this point, the system notifies to the driver importance of the traffic signs visual way on display PC board, respectively additional display device and sound notification.

In the following scheme is presented draft of implementation of the RFID elements in the current concept of selected elements of a motor vehicle and their activity in interaction with other elements (Fig. 7).

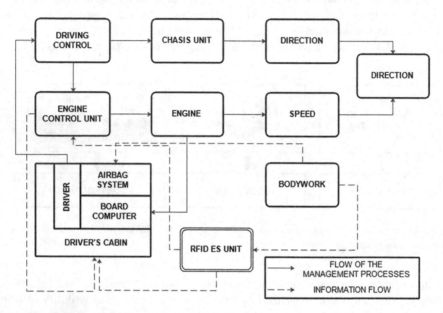

Fig. 7. The current concept of selected elements of a motor vehicle and their activity in interaction with other elements

3 Conclusion

Positive effects of this application include increasing transport safety. The application provides benefits in addition to normal traffic and the benefits of the simplification of control of the vehicle by disabled persons, as it benefits from the concept of this solution consists in the elimination and prohibition of driving a vehicle. These may be people with visual impairments in the form of colour blindness. There is also of great importance in the field of urban logistics. It actively participates in their communities, and helps to solve the basic problems of its functionality outside and inside the system. Increasing pressure on transport logistics in urban areas confirms the need for the application of scientific approach to designing of transport systems and their operation. The problems of urban logistics are almost identical worldwide. The difference lies mainly in the size of served area, density, density and quality of transport infrastructure. The needs to address the problems are also common since the advent of individual motorized transport as well as the distribution of goods by means of automobile transport devastates the environment.

Acknowledgement. Research reported in this paper was supported by EU Structural Funds within the project "Promotion & Enhancement of Center for Research on Transportation" ITMS code 26220220160.

References

1. Balog, M., Straka, M.: Logistické informačné systémy. Epos, Košice (2005)
2. Balog, M.: Mestská logistika ako súčasť logistiky regionálneho rozvoja. Habilitačná práca. Tuke Fberg, Košice (2009)
3. Gála, L., Pour, J., Šedivá, Z.: Podniková informatika. Grada, Praha (2009)
4. Pour, J.: Informační systémy a elektronické podnikání. VŠE, Praha (2002)
5. Sweeney, P.: RFID ForDummies. Wiley, Indianapolis, Indiana (2005)
6. Finkenzeller, K.: RFID Handbook. Wiley, New Jersey (2003)
7. RFID Journal, http://www.rfidjournal.com/article/articleview/1337/1/129/

Informatization of Rail Freight Wagon by Implementation of the RFID Technology

Michal Balog[(⊠)] and Miroslav Mindas

Faculty of Manufacturing Technologies with Seat in Presov, Technical
University of Kosice, Bayerova 1, 080 01 Presov, Slovakia
{michal.balog,miroslav.mindas}@tuke.sk

Abstract. This paper deals with the informatization of railway freight wagon
using elements of IoT for monitoring the technical condition of selected elements of the chassis. The introduction is devoted to the current state of the issue
of maintenance of rail freight wagons. The core of the paper is a technical
solution for collecting, storing and analyzing data about the technical condition
of the chassis with the use of RFID technology. Where are described each joints
of technical solutions. Further discusses about the detailed monitoring of an
error condition of bearing chamber by using RFID technology. In the conclusion
is evaluated the technical solution using elements of the IoT and its possible
impact on the safety of rail freight transport.

Keywords: RFID technology · IoT · Rail freight wagon

1 Introduction

RFID technology (Radio Frequency Identification) is one of the automatic identification systems to be used to generate, collect and speed up the processing of information,
increased accuracy and automation of data processing [1]. Development of RFID
technologies and possibilities of its use are unlimited nowadays. The proof is the
ever-increasing expansion of RFID technology which can be applied in almost every
sector, at almost any product or material, or component. Appreciation of use in rail
traffic with the application of RFID technology on wagon components, apart from the
safety aspects is the financial effect of which brings the RFID application [2]. By
utilizing this technology for checking the technical condition of the wagon we can
avoid huge disaster caused by poor technical condition of the wagon, this prediction
brings in the long term the return of initial investments, reduce costs and improve
competitiveness [3].

1.1 The Current State of the Rail Freight Wagons Maintenance

In current practice there is frequent occurrence of accidents, failures and downtime in
railway transport, which are due to poor technical condition of rail freight wagons [4, 5].
The main cause is poorly controlled technical state of wagons, unsystematic maintenance and low prevention arising from non-existent records of technical and operational

© ICST Institute for Computer Sciences, Social Informatics and Telecommunications Engineering 2016
A. Leon-Garcia et al. (Eds.): Smart City 2015, LNICST 166, pp. 592–597, 2016.
DOI: 10.1007/978-3-319-33681-7_50

parameters of railway wagons (speed, traveled distance, load respectively overloading of the wagons, etc.). This condition is acute and increasing of accidents and collisions at rail is getting worse. In consequence, considerable funds currently spent on repairs and maintenance such as vehicle fleet as well as the railway line itself and intangible assets (stations, demolished trolley, etc.). As a consequence of this state, the cargo companies devote substantial funds just for repairs and maintenance of the vehicle fleet as well as the railway line itself and immovable assets (stations, demolished trolley, etc.) [6, 7]. They are often accompanied by the loss of human lives. Considerable damages are also caused by essential operational restrictions on transport road due to its damage and subsequent long and difficult repairs. To remedy these deficiencies are in practice implemented solutions that deal with emergency situations, but not with the underlying causes. By the traffic tracking and timely scheduled maintenance of vehicle fleet we can come to the stage of preventing the entry of problem vehicles to the transport route and thus eliminate risk situations to a minimum [8].

2   Disclosure of the Technical Invention

A prerequisite for establishing intelligent wagons is suitable communication system in which sensors are connected to the system using a wireless connection. Smart wagon represents utilization of sensors, controllers, software, RFID technology and many other equipment necessary for setting up such a wagon. This technology will allow for monitoring of specific components and parts in the wagon, which might affect the running of the operation.

RFID technology can be used for gathering all the information about the freight wagon, given that is necessary to apply RFID tags resistant to the external environment. In the RFID tag can be encoded complete information on the wagon (identification interoperability, state code, custom wagon number, check digit), due to the use of this system, we can easily identified wagon. RFID technology can be used for gathering all the information about the freight wagon, given that is necessary to apply RFID tags resistant to the external environment. Using of these parameters, we can easily read from the database the essential characteristics of the wagon (the wagon length over buffers, weight of an empty wagon, loading capacity, loading length, etc.). By encrypting of electronic consignment note to the RFID tag, we can identify the sender, recipient and payer type of goods, the total weight.

Principle of technical solution consist in installation of information technology elements based on RFID technology, for each railway wagon in operation, which is requesting entry to the transport route. Using elements of RFID technology placed on the wagon, we can create the conditions that will be monitored, registered and assessed all preselected operating parameters. Based on this controlled and continuously evaluated parameters it will be possible to scheduled maintenance, continuously monitor the technical condition of the rail freight wagons, but also indicates breakdowns in real time. Signalization of the malfunction in real time enables the restriction of the operation of the damaged railway wagon, respectively immediate withdrawal from service of serious damaged wagon. Thus equipped wagons will be subject to scheduled maintenance by the amount of driven kilometres, by wear of critical nodes of wagons respectively according to the quantity of the transported material, but also indicate unequally placed load on the wagon or overloaded wagon. Application of the components based on RFID technology for railway wagon allows uniquely identify and transfer the operating parameters of the rail system to the internal information systems, which will greatly simplify the operation of rail transport, statistical evidence, monitoring the technical condition of railway wagons and subsequent maintenance planning.

RFID tags with sensors enables the measurement of physical parameters, including temperature, pressure, as well as measuring the thickness of material wear, vibration or correct load distribution between the axles of the wagon to avoid overloading the wagon [9]. RFID technology itself is not to able measure these values, but may be connected to other elements which are designed to measure these quantities. Currently, these sensors are integrated in specialized RFID tags (Fig. 1 shows an example). Measured values that are stored in the internal memory of the label are immediately available for user. With the use of appropriate IoT applications, it is possible to monitor and analyse these information in the online mode. By using these marks with the sensors, it would be possible to monitor the operating parameters. Real-time monitoring would create ideal conditions for ensuring greater operational safety and enhance the quality of customer service by enabling online monitoring of current position of the rail freight wagon.

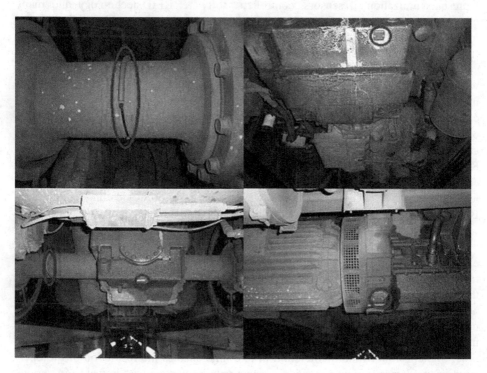

Fig. 1. Example of using RFID technology with integrated sensors for rail freight carriage.

2.1   Examples of Practical the Realization

Figure 2 provides examples of the invention embodiments. It shows the overall sche-matic arrangement of mutual relations and its functional parts. A smart wagon with electronic control of the technical condition is a classic railway wagon accompanied by a data switchboard **1**, which receives information from rotational-speed sensor **2**, from the temperature sensor **3**, from the pressure sensor **4**, from the wear sensor of the braking block **5**, position sensor of the brake cylinder **8** and weight sensor of the cargo **9**. Data switchboard **1** communicates with the support of the service block **6** with technical service depot and operating through block **7** railway operation while driving (train driver in the locomotive or operation staff of the railway station). Data switchboard 1 is with the wireless (radio-electronic) joints **10** connected to the speed sensor 2, with wireless joint **11** connected to the temperature sensor 3 and wireless joint **12** is connected to a pressure sensor 4. At the same time is data switchboard connected with the support of the wireless joint **13** to the wear sensor of the braking block 5, wireless connection **14** is connected to the position sensor 8 of the brake cylinder and with wireless joint **15** connected to the sensor 9 of the cargo. With the support of the wireless joint **16** is a data switchboard 1 connected to the service block 6 and with wireless connection **17** con-nected to the operating unit **7**.

Activity of the railway wagon with electronic control of the technical condition-classic railway wagon equipped with components of IoT and RFID technologies consist in that the data switchboard takes and stores all data from the sensors 2, 3, 4, 5, 8 and 9 and informs technical service in depot and railway operation staff about the technical state of the wagon, with the support of the service block 6, it means their checkpoints while driving. Based on this data you can evaluate the technical condition of the rail freight wagon and to limit respectively prevent (according to severity of the disorder) its further operation in transport. In data switchboard 1 are pre-set marginal parameter of status of each sensor 2, 3, 4, 5, 8 and 9 and also recorded operating parameters of the wagon (its individual nodes) and their changes. Thus prepared railway wagon is eligible for smooth and safe ride without endangering its surroundings.

Operation of the smart wagon with electronic control of the technical condition is as follows:

- Data switchboard 1 collect through sensors 2, 3, 4, 5, 8 and 9 all information about technical condition of the wagon, position of the cargo and information about all operating parameters of the wagon and also attached identification numbers respectively distinguishing marks of the wagon to those data.
- Through the rotational-speed sensor 2 the switch board evaluated parameters (speed of the wagon, mileage driven and the state of rotation of the measured running gear of the wagon). The data are used for failure free operation tracking, but at the same time allowed on the basis of driven kilometers to schedule the different types of repairs (current repair or general repair) in order to prediction of accidents and collisions during the operation.
- Via temperature sensor 3 the data switchboard monitors and evaluates the tem-perature of critical nodes of the wagon and hence its ability to operate and

simultaneously informs the driver and railway service personnel of the need to intervene immediately and prevent possible accidents and subsequent damages in full operation in the case of overheating monitored components.

- Through the pressure sensor 4 monitors response and ability to operate of the braking system.
- Via wear sensor of the braking block 5 (brake pad wear) monitors the operability of the wagon in terms of eligibility of the braking system and also indicates the need of their early exchanges for technical personnel.
- Via position sensor of the brake cylinder 8 is monitored and evaluated its position. In case of a negative signal from one of the brake cylinders the data switchboard limits respectively disables the start of the train until the fault is if not impossible Starting with the train until the fault is eliminated.
- Weight sensor of the cargo 9 monitors, evaluates and indicates congestion of the wagon and also uniformity of cargo storing.

Due to the fact that the interoperability of rolling stock is not given sufficient attention, occur in railway operations to frequent collisions respectively accidents, what can prevent just the systematic monitoring and recording of technical condition of the wagons. The solution is applicable in all companies operating rail transport.

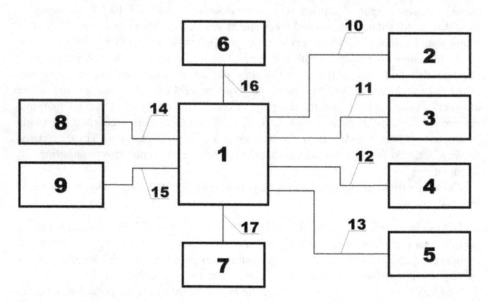

Fig. 2. Functional block configuration of devices and their interconnections of the smart wagon.

3   Conclusion

The article points out the need to speed up and improve the quality and competitiveness of rail freight. The greatest advantage of RFID applications is that it brings the possibility of reducing accidents and improves information flow. Based on the analysis of technical condition, it can be assumed as long or how many kilometers will be able wagon fully operable. On this basis, it is possible to eliminate situations that might arise from bad technical condition of the wagon. The aim is to build a functional and modern network of information flows and data collection, that will be used by operators of railway lines, logistics companies as well as customers themselves, which will be managed everything from maintenance to transportation.

Acknowledgement. Research reported in this paper was supported by EU Structural Funds within the project "Promotion & Enhancement of Center for Research on Transportation" ITMS code 26220220160.

References

1. Finkenzeller, F.: RFID Handbook, 2nd edn. Wiley, New York (2003)
2. Modrak, V., Semanco, P., Straka, M.: Applying RFID for synchronization of factory floor. In: Modrak, V., Semančo, P., Balog, M. (eds.) Research in Engineering and Management of Advanced Manufacturing Systems, pp. 137–142. Trans Tech Publication, Pfaffikon (2014)
3. Kostial, I., Dorcak, D., Sindler, V., Spisakk, J., Glocek, J., Lisuch, J.: Process approach to the process control. In: Proceedings of the 2012 13th International Carpathian Control Conference (ICCC), article no. 6228669, pp. 364–369 (2012)
4. Modrak, V., Knuth, P.: Architecture design and implementation of RFID based academic library. Res. J. Appl. Sci. **7**(1), 21–28 (2012)
5. Suhairy, S.A.: Prediction of ground vibration from railways. In: SP REPORT 2000, vol. 25, pp. 1–102. Swedish National Testing and Research Institute, Borås (2000)
6. Umble, E.J., Haft, R.R., Umble, M.M.: Enterprise resource planning: implementation procedures and critical success factors. Eur. J. Oper. Res. **146**, 241–257 (2003)
7. Hou, H., Ma, L.: The relationship management of information system outsourcing provider perspective. In: 17th International Conference on Industrial Engineering and Engineering Management, pp. 1760–1763. IEEE, Xiamem (2010)
8. Andrea, M., Dagmar, C., Peter, K.: Production system control labs and new methods of education based on IT. In: Zhang, Y. (ed.) Future Wireless Networks and Information Systems. LNEE, vol. 142, pp. 77–84. Springer, Heidelberg (2012)
9. Angeles, R.: RFID technologies: supply-chain applications and implementation issues. Inf. Syst. Manage. **22**, 51–65 (2005)

Development of Costs of Living in the South Moravian Region of the Czech Republic, and Affordable Housing

Pavel Zufan[(⊠)]

Faculty of Business and Economics,
Mendel University in Brno,
Zemedelska 1, 613 00 Brno, Czech Republic
pavel.zufan@gmail.com

Abstract. The paper focuses on analysis of the development of the costs of living of the South Moravian households in the period of 2008–2014, throughout which there was noted an apparent increase. The paper analyses the structure of costs, changes of the shares of the partial components (rent, electricity, gas, heat and hot water), and comments on the changes. Taking into account the development of incomes of the households the paper presents a calculation of the impacts of possible governmental support for two key social groups requiring attention of the society – young people below 35 years of age, and retired people over 65 years of age. This calculation comes from the current structure of costs, and compares the conditions of two different levels of mortgage (100 % and 70 % of the price of a flat) without any support, with the development of costs under the conditions of governmental support in the form of subsidy for "entry housing" currently amounting for CZK 600 thous. (EUR 22 thous.), which shows to be on the edge of comparability with rental housing.

Keywords: Housing policy · Costs of living · Household incomes · Affordable housing · Structural changes of costs of living · Entry housing

1 Introduction

Strategic goals set forth by the Lisbon strategy [1] include "modernizing the European social model, investing in people and combating social exclusion". This is further addressed by country strategies, and also projects into the approaches regional and municipality representatives adopt in order to achieve this goal, and to promote social inclusion.

Housing represents one of the key issues for young people and their families, i.e. those without a credit history or sufficient savings for a down payment. As far as the right to adequate housing is included (even though indirectly) in the basic human rights [2], the European social charter [3] binds national governments to "support economic, legal, and social protection of family life through such measures as family subsidies, tax measures, providing housing for families, support of newlyweds, and other suitable measures".

© ICST Institute for Computer Sciences, Social Informatics and Telecommunications Engineering 2016
A. Leon-Garcia et al. (Eds.): Smart City 2015, LNICST 166, pp. 598–604, 2016.
DOI: 10.1007/978-3-319-33681-7_51

This paper aims on examination of the real situation related to this right looking at the situation of NUTS III region of South Moravia, where it examines the income and living costs conditions, and shows the impacts of the current policy on the availability of affordable housing. Considering the potentially endangered groups (young people below 35 years of age with the income lower than 0.8 multiple of the median income in the country), the population in South Moravian region represents about 24 % of households (43 thousand).

Compared with other European countries, the situation of the Czech Republic is not bad. Looking at the overcrowding indicator, Czech Republic ranked 22nd within the EU countries, in 2012 [4]. What represents certain risk, though, is the structure of costs households spend, and share of the rents on the total costs of living, where there are some notable differences.

Rents represent the major part of the housing costs in the EU, but in the Czech Republic they only account for some 21 % [5].

Czech households spend about 18 % of their income on direct costs connected with housing [5], but concerning the overall housing costs, they are on the top of EU (together with Slovakia), spending 26 % of their incomes [6].

Table 1. Structure of housing costs of South Moravian households [CZK per month per household]

	2008	2009	2010	2011	2012	2013	2014
Household net incomes	23 418	24 793	27 762	29 424	29 370	30 206	30 368
Housing costs of which:	4 333	4 824	5 006	5 199	5 398	5 596	5 574
- rent	917	1 047	1 141	1 179	1 207	1 230	1 147
- electricity	1 164	1 294	1 341	1 389	1 434	1 486	1 433
- gas	784	911	857	898	960	1 015	1 394
- heat and hot water	598	644	700	715	738	762	602
- Other	870	928	967	1 018	1 059	1 103	998
Hous. c. [% of income]	16.2	16.5	16.7	17.3	18.2	18.6	17.8
Rent as % of hous. c.	21.2	21.7	22.8	22.7	22.4	22.0	20.6

Source: CZSO [5]

According to the McKinsey Global Institute [7], the accessible housing policy has to come from a rational set of criteria – their setting on a high level can rather deepen the problem than solve it.

Another complicating factor is that the housing market has to be approached as a whole due to the fact, that a transfer of higher income groups to new flats/houses opens the housing capacity for the lower income groups [8]. Job distance and service availability can also represent a risk factor – the policy should not lead to creation of isolated communities of lower-income citizens [9].

2 Materials and Methods

Given the aim of the paper, the author comes from the data on the housing costs in South Moravia, current governmental support of accessible housing, and current interest rates of mortgages in the Czech Republic, projecting it to the reality of households, and their spending under selected model situations.

This study comes from the generally defined and used standard of total costs of housing amounting for max. 30 % of the household income [7]. Given the data in Table 1, this standard is met in the current situation of an average South Moravian family.

Criteria used in the model (see Tables 1 and 2):

- Maximum monthly income of the target group (0.8 multiple of the income median) – CZK 24 294.
- Actual monthly housing costs – CZK 5 574.
- Acceptable share of housing costs on the household income – 30 %.
- Acceptable monthly costs of housing – CZK 7 288.
- Average price of new flat – CZK 34 759 per square meter.
- Target area of a new flat – 40 m^2.
- Mortgage interest rate – 3.00 % [5].
- Governmental support – CZK 600 000 [3].

Table 2. Input data

Average price of new flat [CZK.m^{-2}]	34 759
Median income [CZK per month]	30 368
80 % of the median income [CZK per month]	24 294
Acceptable costs of housing [CZK per month] (30 % of income)	7 288
Average interest rate of mortgage [%]	3

Source: CZSO [5]

Based on these indicators, there is calculated the projection of the current conditions into the situation of the households, and compared with the target values of the maximum acceptable housing costs for the target group. Modelled situations include:

1. Full mortgage.
2. Necessary mortgage with the governmental subsidy for accessible entry housing currently amounting for CZK 600 000 [3].
3. Entry housing subsidy minimum – calculated as the amount, under which the monthly costs of a 30-year mortgage still enable to keep the housing costs on the target level (30 % of the household income).
4. Entry housing subsidy maximum – calculated as the amount, under which the monthly costs of a 15-year mortgage still enable to keep the housing costs on the target level (30 % of the household income).

After this analysis, there is done a projection of the development of the income and cost situation in the next two years (till 2016), under the conditions of their continual change amounting for the geometric average of the development in the previous 7 years (2008–2014), and the situation is re-considered.

3   Results and Discussion

Description of the current situation based on the model criteria is given in Table 3. This shows that the current level of governmental support of entry housing (CZK 600 000) does not reach the level of accessibility required by the given criteria of keeping the costs under 30 % of the household income for a 40 m^2 flat, unless the households have at least CZK 112 thous. (711 567 – 600 000) of their own savings for a down payment. Given the average price of new flats in 2013 (CZK 34 759 per square meter of a new flat [5]), the current support represents a significant help, but does not enable to reach the set targets even under the conditions of a 30-year mortgage. This would be reached only if the support is increased by 18.6 % - to CZK 711 567, as shown in Table 3.

Table 3. Resulting situation of the model application under different mortgages

	40 m^2 * 34 759 CZK. m^{-2} = CZK 1 390 360			
Repayment period [years]	15	20	25	30
Full mortgage	CZK 1 390 360			
Monthly repayment	9 602	7 711	6 593	5 862
Total costs of housing	15 176	13 285	12 167	11 436
Difference against acceptable costs	7 660	5 769	4 652	3 920
Entry housing subsidy of CZK 600 000	CZK 790 360			
Monthly repayment	5 458	4 383	3 748	3 332
Total costs of housing	11 032	9 957	9 322	8 906
Difference against acceptable costs	3 516	2 442	1 806	1 391
Entry housing subsidy minimum (CZK 711 567)	CZK 678 793			
Monthly repayment	4 688	3 765	3 219	2 862
Total costs of housing	10 262	9 339	8 793	8 436
Difference against acceptable costs	1 826	903	358	0
Entry housing subsidy maximum (CZK 975 953)	CZK 414 407			
Monthly repayment	2 862	2 298	1 965	1 747
Total costs of housing	8 436	7 872	7 539	7 321
Difference against acceptable costs	0	−563	-896	−1 114

Source: Own calculations

Given the average growth of household incomes of 4.43 % in the previous 7-year period, and the average growth of the housing costs in the same period reaching 4.29 %, the situation should be slowly improving (given that the incomes are expected to grow faster than the costs). Therefore, the minimum level of support required to reach the set conditions would decline to less than CZK 647 thous. in 2016 – see Table 4.

This calculation comes from the stable costs of new flats, which is not realistic, though. Development on the construction market, on the other hand, is difficult to predict, as far as the number and character of the variables is further complicated with potential influence of regulatory forces and public administration measures in connection with construction of blocks of flats designated for the entry housing.

Described situations represent impacts of a selected set of criteria, which have to be discussed. When determining the needed amount of support, governments have to come from the income situation, calculate the acceptable share of housing costs, and based on the market conditions decide on the minimum required support. This is influenced by the type of housing, its construction or purchase costs, and the overall situation on the market, considering also a possible involvement of the governments in the house construction and facility management. There are numerous ways how to approach this issue, and the calculations in this paper can serve as a model providing methodology of a part of the calculations.

Table 4. Expected development in 2016

Flat price	40 m^2 * 34 759 CZK. m^{-2} = CZK 1 390 360			
Repayment period [years]	15	20	25	30
Entry housing subsidy minimum (CZK 646 745)	CZK 743 615			
Monthly repayment	5 135	4 124	3 526	3 135
Total costs of housing	11 197	10 186	9 588	9 197
Difference against acceptable costs	2 001	989	392	0
Entry housing subsidy maximum (CZK 936 379)	CZK 453 981			
Monthly repayment	3 135	2 518	2 153	1 914
Total costs of housing	9 197	8 580	8 215	7 976
Difference against acceptable costs	0	−617	−982	−1 221

Source: Own calculations

4 Conclusion

This paper focused on examination of the situation in affordable housing in South Moravia, where it examined the income and living costs conditions, and showed the impacts of the current policy on the availability of affordable housing. It concluded, that the current governmental support of initial housing does not assure meeting the conditions of enabling the target group to reach affordable housing under the conditions of housing costs lower than 30 % of their household incomes.

When determining the target group of support beneficiaries, there are four necessary steps governments have to take [7]:

- Defining target group – in this paper the young people below 35 years of age with the income lower than 0.8 multiple of the median income in the country.
- Defining eligibility criteria – not considered in this paper.
- Defining ranking mechanism – not considered in this paper.
- Determining the support beneficiaries obtain – main focus of this paper.

Determination of the amount of support is shown under the described assumptions, which can be easily changed and "re-modelled". One of the key components of a smart city – smart living [9] – also has a dimension of enabling an affordable housing, which was addressed in this paper.

When looking at the technical issues and innovations, we cannot forget about the socio-economic impacts of the new solutions, and their possible (and very welcome) assistance in addressing the emanating problems. As far as the customer focus is very much applicable also in these conditions, innovative approaches to addressing the mentioned issues become a very important opportunity – technological opportunities enable closer involvement of customers in designing the solutions, so that an overall satisfaction is reached. In this connection we can mention an apparent connection of housing policy with other items of smart cities [10] – Smart government (Information, communication and technology enabled government; Participation and corporation of citizens to the government), Smart utility (Efficient use of utilities), Smart economy (Public private partnership, Highly productive and sustainable economy), Smart environment (Renew and recycle), Smart living (intelligent living).

References

1. European Council: Presidency conclusions (2000). http://www.consilium.europa.eu/uedocs/cms_data/docs/pressdata/en/ec/00100-r1.en0.htm. Accessed 25 Aug 2015
2. United Nations High Commissioner for Human Rights, The right to adequate housing, fact sheet number 21 (Rev. 1), May 2014
3. Ministry of labor and social affairs. European charter. http://www.mpsv.cz/files/clanky/1218/esch.pdf. Accessed 25 Aug 2015
4. Eurostat – Population and housing census. http://ec.europa.eu/eurostat/web/population-and-housing-census/statistics-illustrated. Accessed 25 Aug 2015
5. Czech statistical office: Household Income and Living Conditions (2014). https://www.czso.cz/csu/czso/household-income-and-living-conditions-2014. Accessed 25 Aug 2015
6. OECD Better Life Index. http://www.oecdbetterlifeindex.org/topics/housing/. Accessed 25 Aug 2015
7. McKinsey&Company: A blueprint for addressing the global affordable housing challenge. McKinsey Global Institute. www.mckinsey.com/mgi. Accessed 25 Aug 2015

8. Bertaud, A.: Land markets, government interventions, and housing affordability, Wolfensohn Center for Development at Brookings working paper number 18, May 2010
9. ADCC Infocad (2015). http://www.adccinfocad.com/smart_city_and_data_organisation.html
10. What is a smart city: Business standard (2014). http://www.business-standard.com/article/opinion/vinayak-chatterjee-what-is-a-smart-city-114121501181_1.html

Importance of Internet of Things and Big Data in Building Smart City and What Would Be Its Challenges

Manan Bawa[✉], Dagmar Caganova, Ivan Szilva, and Daniela Spirkova

Faculty of Materials Science and Technology in Trnava,
Institute of Industrial Engineering and Management, Slovak University
of Technology in Bratislava, Trnava, Slovakia
{manan.bawa, dagmar.caganova, ivan.szilva,
daniela.spirkova}@Stuba.sk

Abstract. Cities are regarded as the backbone of the country's economy and sustainability. To make a city 'smart', we need to build upon the strategies which could mitigate city's current issues and avert future problems which are driven by the urban society and its rapid expansion. According to the UN urbanization report (2011), urban cities occupy 2 % of the earth's total area and still they are responsible for the 70 % of the global energy consumption and emission of greenhouse gases. The cities will need to attend to these global facts and take upon bigger challenges of fulfilling the essential needs of water, food and shelter, providing necessary public services like utility, security, and mobility and importantly managing scare resources. IoT and big data with their innovating techniques and advancing technology provides those critical tools which helps to address these topics and lay down the foundation for next generation smart cities.

Keywords: Smart city · Internet of things (IoT) · Big data · Innovation · Cloud computing

1 Introduction

The world is moving towards extreme urbanization and we need to build our cities around it to sustain the needs and requirements of this urban population. According to UN world urbanization perspective (the 2011 revision), 50 % of the current world population lives in the cities and towns and by 2050 the percentage will rise to 70 %. The word 'city' may not exist from the vantage point of a traditional economist, as they might believe city means higher cost of living, land, goods, etc. Moreover, air and water pollution, toxic emissions due to the greenhouse gases, sewage overflows and different kind of viruses, flu's and diseases floating around are common problems faced by the people living in the city. In 2013, poor air quality shut down the Harbin city in China with population of 11 million and also affected Beijing the capital city of China [1]. However, still 70 % of the world's GDP runs on the economic growth of the cities.

© ICST Institute for Computer Sciences, Social Informatics and Telecommunications Engineering 2016
A. Leon-Garcia et al. (Eds.): Smart City 2015, LNICST 166, pp. 605–616, 2016.
DOI: 10.1007/978-3-319-33681-7_52

'Smart City' is the term we are going to hear a lot in the coming years. Research at MIT media lab predicted in the future, the modern cities will account for about 80 % of wealth creation and approximately 90 % of global population and the total energy consumption will keep increasing every year. Our objective should be to improve our understanding of the cities and also to develop new and better strategies with the help of innovations and emerging technology for the creation of new cities. Rather than focusing separately on individual functions like – Energy, Transport, Food, Water, Shelter, etc. smart cities should set up a collective approach where a central nervous system with latest technology, using internet of things and big data should be created. This central hub will maintain and sustain all functionalities of public health, food, education, work and even government stability.

The idea behind the smart city initiative is to use innovation in advancing technology and focus on data collection and analysis to make the internet of things and big data a reality into environment where we live in. Every city is a part of complex ecosystem where lot of planning is required for instance to develop data driven systems for transport, efficient energy use and law enforcement to improve the lives of the society. Decision making in most situations may be politically driven, hence the derived data is inevitably human and sometimes analogue. For our purpose we need digital data and with the IoT devices and big data tools we will produce intelligent data which will be able to send and receive information in both direction and be able to interact using smart systems to our smart phones, wearable glasses, watches and other devices and most importantly machines and devices will be able to communicate to each other [2].

2   Smart City

In this digital world our lives are driven by the advancements of computing which has already brought us the social web, the internet, smart phones and more recently internet of things and now we are witnessing this idea of digitalization has started shifting to our cities [4]. We are seeing that tremendous amount of people are moving from rural to urban areas for opportunity to work, to access better education, be part of digital and global economies along with other facilities and services for improved quality of life [5]. Supporting such a movement requires innovative ideas and ways to manage current resources and at the same time think and build upon the future, which has led to the idea of technologically driven interconnected city referred as 'Smart City'.

Figure 1 shows the concept or provides an overview of smart cities, where every key aspect from energy to mobility of the city is integrated together using latest and innovative technologies to make them smart. Figure 2 below, lays out some of the essential terms and tools used for building an advanced next level city. In next couple of sections the authors will discuss the significance of these tools and will also touch upon why and how they need to be interconnected for achieving the goal of structuring a sustainable and a superior smart city.

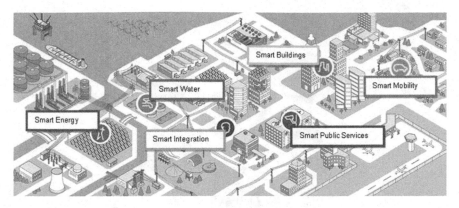

Fig. 1. Concept of the smart city [3]

Fig. 2. Smart city and its tools [6]

2.1 Components and Features of Smart City

Population is migrating from rural areas to cities and urban regions at a very high pace as a result city has to grow in every aspect to maintain harmony and to generate socio-economic and environmental balance among the inhabitants. The premier aim of the city to rise to the status of a 'Smart City' is to make the life easier for its people [7]. In doing so, city will have to incorporate certain essential components and establish vital features to its periphery. According to the authors of the paper some of the critical components and features for building a smart city are given below. Figure 3 shows the pictorial representation of the components and the features and Table 1 describes the key areas, benefits and the resources required for building a smart city.

Smart Government – *Information, Communication and Technology Enabled Government* [8]: To succeed with the smart city concept the government first has to enable the smart government tag upon itself, which means adopting the information, communication and technology platform to integrate the various aspects of key government functionalities to the public which is speedy, transparent and accessible to all.

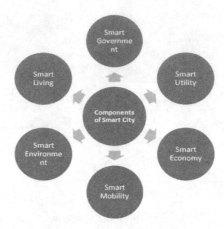

Fig. 3. Components and features for building a smart city [7]

Safety and Security of the Citizen: Safety and security is a very high priority for the government to its citizens and any concerns especially due the alarming and disturbing news on the safety of women and road rages gives sleepless nights to the police. The use of video CCTV cameras in all public areas, man-less verified access, smart centres for surveillance and robot controlled patrolling, and intelligent data to identify the emergency before it happens and at the same time inform the rapid response team to mitigate any emergency situations should be some of the parameters for the government to incorporate.

Participation and Corporation of Citizens to the Government: Government driven mobile applications and web portals should be made responsive to the citizens to participate and help the police and authorities to solve any local issues. A new electoral structure should be carefully designed with the help of latest technologies to enable elections online or to book the voting slots using smart technology.

Smart Utility – *Efficient use of Utilities* [8]: With large amount of population moving to the urban regions, utility becomes a major concern. City will have to clearly look into innovative ways to mitigate the utility scenario by using modern advancements like – smart utility grids, internet powered smart energy meters, buildings running on solar power, efficient usage of energy using sensor enabled technology, using scientific ways for waste disposal and effluent recycling, garbage trucks to be made aware using mobile application to the locality that requires waste collection, use of renewal energy like wind and water and its conservation.

Smart Economy – *Private and Public Partnership:* Healthy and secure economy should be the motto for a smart city, which will require partnerships between private and public sectors. These two sectors working together will not only keep the financials strong but also help in efficient delivery of the agreed services [8].

Highly productive and sustainable economy: Smart economy is about thinking smarter and creating novel and innovating ideas to generate new and successful revenue

Table 1. Key areas, benefits and resources required for a smart city [7]

Smart city – components and features	Key areas	Benefits	Resource requirements
Smart government	Information, communication and technology driven government	Increased safety and security	Government started initiatives – open data, smart city, energy conservation
	Digital presence	Improved and transparent policies	Skills and experience to build and manage smart city (IoT and big data)
	Open communication for everyone	Real time and quick services	
Smart utility	Smart grid	Cleaner, healthier and greener cities	Creating network for managing electricity distribution, water supply, gas distribution and waste management systems via central cloud server
		Solar panels on individual houses and buildings	
	Zero waste and green initiative	Availability of clean water and uninterrupted power	
	Round the clock water & electricity supply	Services available online using technology	
	Using renewable sources of energy – solar power	Recycle and reuse	Smart meters, grids, devices, etc.
	City waste and sanitation management	Improved quality of life	Modern utility to enable a more reliable, efficient and resilient future
Smart economy	New revenue models	Increase in GDP and per capita income	National hubs
	Biggest financial hub		Skill development
	Competitive pricing	Partnership between public and private	Innovation and entrepreneurship
	International and local investments	Greater employment opportunities	Trade centers
Smart mobility	Intelligent transport system	Clean energy	Technological Infrastructure
		Hybrid, solar and electric technology	
	Real time data capture	Cleaner and efficient fuel	
	Big data analysis	Efficient and elegant design	Smart hardware – sensors, cameras, etc.
	Internet of things		Smart software's and tools – mobile applications, designs, web portals

(Continued)

Table 1. (*Continued*)

Smart city – components and features	Key areas	Benefits	Resource requirements
Smart environment	Green and clean environment	Technology and network enabled houses	Government initiatives – greener public transportation system, cycle paths, etc.
		Efficient urban planning	
	Use of renewable and recyclable materials	Control over energy consumption	
	Smart homes and buildings	Reduction of waste generation	Central hub for all urban planning – energy distribution, waste disposal, transportation, etc.
Smart living	Intelligent devices	Increased safety	Advancement in technology
	Automation systems	Improved health	
	Education facilities for everyone	Increase in life expectancy	Smart data analysis using big data and its features
	Wi-Fi and internet availability everywhere	Better education to all	Creating networked world with sensors using IoT and controlled by cloud servers

models. Smart means producing improved products and services at a competitive price and the aim would be to influence government to implement a range of policies to make the economy more dynamic.

Smart Mobility – *Urban Transportation:* Big data and internet of things can capture real time data and help manage the road traffic using the video cameras and sensors. Social media and mobile applications can help avoid road blocks by updating information about accidents or potential traffic jams. Concept behind smart mobility is to use latest techniques and innovate designs developed by vehicle manufacturers like electric and hybrid cars, solar powered cars with solar cells on the rooftop, highly efficient and intelligent vehicles etc.

Smart Environment – *Green Transportation:* Use of urban public transport system which contains all different mode of transportation's schedules which links even to the remotest location and is connected to the cloud network, minimizing the use of private vehicles, changing the fuel technology to use electric or hybrid techniques and build bicycle paths and promote cycling are some of the features for smart environment.

Renewable and recycle: Thoughtful measurements should be taken by the government for creating an habitable environment for its citizens like smart tags can be implemented on the products which are recyclable by the manufacturers and by default it highlights itself as a mandatory recyclable item, thinking of innovative ideas in the field of biodegradable packaging, using sensors and internet of things which connects to the central server in the cloud to notify the nearest garbage pickup truck when the bins are full.

Smart Living – *Intelligent Living:* Modern homes equipped with intelligent devices and automation systems are the key to smart living. With internet of things a network of devices like washing machines and refrigerator and systems like central heating, air conditioners and home theatre can all be connected together via a cloud and they all can interact and communicate with each other and can be controlled with a mobile application by the owner [9].

3 Internet of Things

The internet of things can be defined as a system where all the machines and devices are connected to a network and have a central server or a cloud server, which has the capability to monitor and control everything on the network [10]. All these gadgets will have their own unique internet protocol (IP) addresses and all of them can see, communicate and exchange information among each other [11]. With IoT traditional systems which used to work independently like in the case of home and industry automation such as fire alarm system, motion detection and access control, surveillance system, HVAC and energy management system, etc. can all work, interact and talk with each other using propriety protocols and standards over a network. IoT is the foundation for a smart city, as all the equipment can sense the complexity of the environment and they can communicate and exchange information as required.

It is very hard to estimate the exact size of IoT as numerous embedded devices like machines, automation devices, sensors, radio frequency identification tags, and many more other devices are all linked together on to a network. It is believed that with this tremendous rate of growth of internet of things, it will soon exceed the size of the internet (in terms of number of nodes) and it will keep growing at a rate of billions of devices per city.

Two crucial features of IoT includes sensor networks and cloud computing. A sensor network is a web of sensors which are used for monitoring, transmitting, analyzing and recording different conditions [12]. Sensor detects via a sensor node and each node consists of a specialized transducer, microcontroller, transceiver, and a power supply [11]. Transducer converts physical sensations for example pressure, vibrations, humidity, temperature, vital body functions, etc. to an electrical signal and microcontroller at the same time processes and stores these signal [12]. The transceiver, acts both as a transmitter and receiver and when it receives a command from the central computer, it transmits the stored output to the computer for analyzing. Power is required for the sensor to operate which is usually supplied by the grid or it has a battery onboard.

Another important feature of IoT is that all information or the data from the embedded devices gets stored on to a central cloud server. Users can access the information from anywhere from the world using their smart phones, tablets, laptops, smart watches, etc. from the cloud in a form of an application which is usually hosted as software as a service (SaaS) [13]. Cloud computing also acts as a service for storing, sharing, computing, and analyzing the data.

A very vital component for the IoT network is the software design, as it brings life to the hardware and completes the whole network cycle. The software architecture is divided into three functional layers namely – data format, application/transport layer and network layer [14]. Figure 4 shows the internet of things protocol used for each functional layer for constrained nodes and for constrained networks.

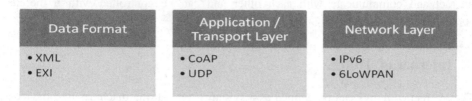

Fig. 4. IoT protocols for each functional layer [14]

Data Format: With internet of thing there are specific data requirements for generating and supporting messages for all the devices embedded in its network. The common languages for data exchange are extensible mark-up language (XML) and efficient XML interchange (EXI). The size of the XML files can become too large and with limited capacity for the devices onboard to handle such large data, the complexity can increase [15]. These issues are resolved when use EXI format and that's why authors of the paper proposes to use EXI format, additionally all constrained devices can interpret EXI format hence making the devices a multipurpose IoT node [16].

Application/Transport Layers: Internet traffic is mostly transported at the application layer by hypertext transfer protocol (HTTP) over transmission control protocol (TCP) protocol, however the complexity of HTTP and no scalability of the TCP protocol with the constrained devices make it unsuitable for IoT environment [14]. The constrained application protocol (CoAP) transported over user datagram protocol (UDP) helps overcome the above mentioned problem and provides a reliable solution [17] and they can be easily interoperate with HTTP.

Network Layer: World wide web consortium (W3C), has recently declared the internet protocol version 4 (IPv4) standard, which is the most popular addressing technology has exhausted all its address blocks [14], however we have internet protocol version 6 (IPv6) standard which provides 128 bit address field and helps assigns a unique address to all possible nodes in the IoT network [18]. The issue with using IPv6 it is not fully compatible with the capabilities of all the constrained nodes [14], therefore the authors of this paper recommends adopting IPv6 over low power wireless personal area network (6LoWPAN) standard which is derived from the IPv6 and UDP header which works over low power constrained networks [19, 20] ideal for IoT.

4   Big Data

Data plays a vital role in the concept of smart city as massive amount of data is streamed though different kinds of network and even with IoT's cloud technology for storing, analysing and processing the data, it is still very complicated to convert the data into useful or intelligent form [11]. Big data with its innovative approach which aims for creating data driven processes and its leveraging advancements in data analysis and technology offers some promises.

Big data can be defined as a medium for collection and storage of data so humongous and complex that it is not possible to use traditional data and management tools for processing and analyzing of the data. There are three V's to the concept of big data – volume, variety and velocity, as shown in Fig. 5 below. City generates large **volume** of data with a vast range and **variety** and the decisions needs to be made at a very high **velocity** [21]. It is a challenge for the smart city to collect, store, process, analyze, share and visualize huge amount of data coming from all different sources and convert the information into useful and meaningful form. More than 80 % of data is unstructured, variable in nature and come in many formats – documents, emails, images, videos, GPS coordinates, sensor data, etc. however it is also predicted by the data scientists that with smart city, sensor data will hit the crossover point with the unstructured data from the social media [22]. These data streams are all in real time and changes very constantly and rapidly.

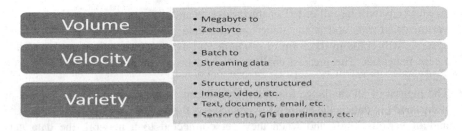

Fig. 5. The three V's of big data [23]

Big data provides flexible model to store, analyze and process data of any shape and size. It can receive data from number of channels and offers innovative tools and latest techniques to explore and convert the incoming data into intelligent and meaningful form. The most sophisticated tools out in the current market which can handle big data are Hadoop and NoSQL technologies. Also there are other open source solutions available which fulfil the requirements of big data. These tools are secure and they can work with any size, variety and scale of data. NoSQL technology has gained high popularity in the world of big data and it has four different varieties – key value, document store, wide column and graph database [23]. It can process complex and multiple data arriving from social media, sensor, linked data, etc. along with its relationships. Big data has some challenging software requirements for its processes, here are few of the requirements –

- The data storage should be redundant, reliable, and could store data for very long time
- Data processing and analyzing should be fast
- Tool should share the information in real time and with multiple locations

- Should have fast response and allows the users to navigate through the information with no delays
- It should be scalable to the needs for the user and the society.

5   Challenges

In coming days the country's economic progress and status would be measured by the sustainable development of their smart cities. The cities will be filled with IoT devices and big data technology – smart and urban mobility, smart buildings running smart meter, monitoring security, running elevators, etc., smart traffic, use and tracking renewable items, etc. Therefore, it will be safe to say that we exist in a networked world, and so do our cities.

However, there are many challenges to reach to the goal of creating a smart city and it can create a havoc situation for the people, society, government, and even for the country's growth and economy. According to the authors of the paper, few of the critical challenges which needs to be addressed now are discussed below –

- A smart city will be full of IoT enabled devices and different systems which run on various platforms and at the same time the data generated by these devices and systems will come in the form of different variety, velocity and volume over different networks. The greatest challenge would be to integrate the either city to a network.
- The biggest of all challenge for smart city concept, which ties mainly to internet of things and big data is the concerns over security, the IoT devices contains lot of data and of various kinds and when they get connected to a network the data gets communicated to the central server (cloud), which increases its vulnerability to the next level. As the amount and value of data increases with time, the targets for the attacks also get multiplied with the same number [24]. The attackers and the hackers can steal all the private information, may be they can also manipulate information and even can damage its integrity.
- The lack of standards in the field of internet of things and big data are another set of challenges for the progress of smart city. There are lot of concepts out there however not many of them are designated to form a standard yet. Therefore, there are no real standards to follow for some of the critical functionalities in terms of IoT and big data like – how to handle data, how to adapt to the real values, and how to transmit, store, analyze and most importantly secure the information.

6   Conclusion

Smart city is a great initiative and making it a reality requires development of all the components and sectors associated with and around it. Many key features and requirements of smart city including smart government, smart mobility, smart living, smart utility and others, all play a very critical part in the designing, planning and development of a city. It provides enormous benefits to the people and the society and even though intelligent city has very contingent resource requirements. The big players and the government understands the importance of urban city and are putting the right step forward to implement it and this can seen from the fact that it is estimated by the industry analysts that smart city will represent around USD 40 billion in the market by the year 2016.

Internet of things is the brains of the smart city concept as it provides all the essential hardware and software to manage the city efficiently and improve the quality of life. Big data is the heart of the smart city as it promises to generate intelligence from the data collected from IoT enabled devices and other data streams. There are still lot of unknowns and challenges like security, privacy, data management and analysis that needs to be addressed and attended too, however if the city needs to be smarter, show progress, be more competitive and have sustainable development they need to leverage to the advancements of IoT and innovative techniques of big data to succeed towards their goal of building smart city.

References

1. A truly smart city is more than sensors, big data and an all-seeing internet (2014). http://www.theguardian.com/sustainable-business/2014/nov/21/smart-city-sensors-big-data-internet
2. How big data and the internet of things create smarter cities (2015). http://www.forbes.com/sites/bernardmarr/2015/05/19/how-big-data-and-the-internet of things-create-smarter-cities/
3. Schneider Electric (2014). 2014.gogreeninthecity.com/smart-cities.html
4. Kennedy, D., Gross, P., Sing, N., Dawes, G., Lee, D.: Smart Cities and Big Data, Deloitte & Touche (2015)
5. Lall, S.V., Agarwal, O.P., Lozano-Gracia, N., Dowall, D., Klein, M., Wang, H.G.: Connecting & Financing Cities - Now, Priorities for City Leaders, p. 132. The World Bank, Washington, D.C. (2013)
6. Wave Group. http://blog.thewavegroup.com/a-smart-difference-traditional-smart-cities/
7. ADCC Infocad (2015). http://www.adccinfocad.com/smart_city_and_data_organisation.html
8. What is a smart city: Business standard (2014). http://www.business-standard.com/article/opinion/vinayak-chatterjee-what-is-a-smart-city-114121501181_1.html
9. Ellermann, H.: What is Smart? Creating a Cyber-Physical World, Germany Trade & Invest (2015)
10. Shelby, Z., Bormannc, C.: 6LoWPAN: The Wireless Embedded Internet. Wiley, Hoboken (2009)
11. Pawar, S.P.: Smart citied with internet of things (sensor networks) and big data. In: ASM'S IBMR, Chichwad, Pune, India (2015)
12. Wireless Sensor Network (WSN). http://searchdatacenter.techtarget.com/definition/sensor-network
13. Hassan, M.M., Song, B., Huh, E.N.: Framework of sensor – cloud integration opportunities and challenges. In: Proceedings of the 3rd International Conference on Ubiquitous Information Management and Communication, New York, USA (2009)
14. Zanella, A., Vangelista, L.: Internet of things for smart cities. IEEE Internet Things J. 1(1), 22–32 (2014)

15. Efficient XML Interchange (EXI) Format 1.0, 2nd edn. World Wide Web Consortium (2014). http://www.w3.org/TR/exi/
16. Castellani, A.P., Bui, N., Casari, P., Rossi, M., Shelby, Z., Zorzi, M.: Architecture and protocols for the internet of things: a case study. In: Proceedings of 8th IEEE International Conference Pervasive Computer Communication Workshops (PERCOM Workshops), Germany, pp. 678–683 (2010)
17. Constrained application protocol (CoAP), draft-ietf-core-coap-18 (work in progress) (2013). http://tools.ietf.org/html/draft-ietf-core-coap-18
18. Internet Protocol, Version 6 (IPv6) Specification. https://www.ietf.org/rfc/rfc2460.txt
19. Transmission of IPv6 packets over IEEE 802.15.4 networks. http://tools.ietf.org/html/rfc4944
20. Compression format for IPv6 datagrams over IEEE 802.15.4-Based Networks (2011). http://tools.ietf.org/html/rfc6282
21. Big Data: All roads lead to smart cities. http://en.blogthinkbig.com/2014/05/21/big-data-smart-cities/
22. Sensor networks top social networks for big data. Knowingly Inc. (2010). http://www.bloomberg.com/bw/technology/content/sep2010/tc20100914_284956.html
23. Zaslavsky, A., Perera, C., Georgakopoulos, D.: Sensing as a service and big data. In: Proceedings of the International Conference on Advances in Cloud Computing (ACC), Bangalore, India (2012)
24. Smart Cities', IoT's Key Challenges: Security, Lack of Standards (2015). http://www.darkreading.com/endpoint/smart-cities-iots-key-challenges-security-lack-of-standards/d/d-id/132

Socio-Economics Aspects of Housing Quality in the Context of Energy Poverty

Daniela Spirkova[1](✉), Maria Zubkova[1], Janka Babelova[2], and Dagmar Caganova[3]

[1] Institute of Management, Slovak University of Technology in Bratislava, Vazovova 5, 812 43 Bratislava, Slovakia
{daniela.spirkova,maria.zubkova}@stuba.sk
[2] UCJ LFUK, Comenius University in Bratislava, Sasinkova 4/a, 811 08 Bratislava, Slovakia
jbabelova@stonline.sk
[3] Faculty of Materials Science and Technology in Trnava, Slovak University of Technology in Bratislava, Paulínska 16, 917 24 Trnava, Slovakia
dagmar.caganova@stuba.sk

Abstract. Energy poverty is a term that is used for energy shortages in terms of providing electricity, heat, cold, etc. and it primarily means a limited or no access to these resources in the context of lack of necessary infrastructure, inability to connect to the transmission system, low income households etc. It is a problem that has a significant impact on the development and formation of young people. Quality of life is closely linked to housing and housing is determined by other factors, and energy poverty can be regarded as one of the most important factors. The aim of this paper is to name the energy poverty as an important determinant of the social dimension of housing quality, which may be a negative boundary element to the social exclusion of people.

Keywords: Housing quality · Social exclusion of people · Energy poverty

1 Introduction

Energy poverty is an acute problem not only in developing countries but also in several European countries. As depicted in Fig. 1, energy poverty is caused by an interaction between high energy bills, low income and poor energy efficiency, in addition to supplementary determinants such as housing tenure and quality of energy supply [1].

The term energetic poverty is meant as inability of the population to pay bills for energy in the household. Nowadays one of the official and publicly accessible sources of measurement of the energetic poverty is in this view the EU-SILC survey investigating the share of population, which cannot afford to keep adequate warmth in the house. In the Slovak Republic such measurements have been done since 2004, but they are based on subjective evaluation of respondents. Among EU countries Slovakia belongs to countries in danger of energetic poverty. Up to 2008 energetic poverty in Slovakia lowered due to economic growth. However, since 2009 under the influence of world economic crisis it has been already growing while the most endangered are mainly households with low income.

© ICST Institute for Computer Sciences, Social Informatics and Telecommunications Engineering 2016
A. Leon-Garcia et al. (Eds.): Smart City 2015, LNICST 166, pp. 617–626, 2016.
DOI: 10.1007/978-3-319-33681-7_53

For example, Great Britain (as example of the country that is still in this field) operates with the term of so-called 'fuel poverty'. Energetically/fuel poor is, according to their approach, the household, which needs for purchase of fuel more than 10 % of their disposable income. But this is just fuel used for transport. Involving of expenses on petrol and oil into energetic poverty is quite problematic, because from objective point of view we should also implement fuel paid indirectly via services of public transport and also it is not always possible to distinguish which part of expenses on transport is inevitable for provision of basic life needs (as e.g. inevitable travelling to work related to unavailability of work closer to home) and which part is created by upmarket services (as travelling for fun or holiday to from the view of needs inadequate destinations). If we, according to English methodology, (10 % limit of expenses in proportion to net income) evaluate also energetic poverty of bill payment for household, an average Slovak citizen should be considered as energetically poor even in the long term view (during 10-year followed period) as it is also seen in Fig. 2.

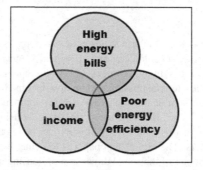

Fig. 1. Causes of energy poverty [2]

Legislative Aspects. In the Slovak legislation this term is defined in the Law No. 250/2012 Coll., As amended: "energy poverty refers to a condition where the average monthly household expenditure on electricity, gas, steam for heating and domestic hot water make up a significant share of the average monthly income of the

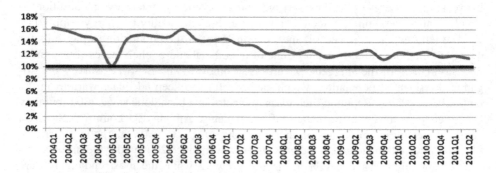

Fig. 2. The share of household expenditures on energies to their net income [6]

household." Energy poverty means difficulty or inability to ensure suitable temperature conditions (according to the World Health Organization for a comfortable temperature in the living room considered 21 °C and in other rooms, 18 °C), as well as the difficulty or inability to have other essential energy services for a reasonable price [3]. It is alarming that (according to the International Energy Agency) currently almost 1.4 billion people do not have access to electricity. Consequences of energy poverty [2]:

- damp and mouldy living conditions,
- an increased risk of heart disease,
- school absences due to worsened asthma [4],
- reduced food intake – "heat or eat",
- dangerous coping strategies such as fuel disconnection.

One of the ways how to measure the poverty as well as energetic poverty is the view on the growth of indebtedness or savings of the population (expressed as a difference between net income and net expenditures). It might be widened also with the share (or volume) of their expenditures on so-called 'luxury' products and services (as e.g. expenses on holidays and so on). This approach results from assumption, that 'poor households' will restrict the above mentioned expenditures as the first and they will not increase their savings.

2 Theoretical Basis and Methodology

Housing is closely linked to the quality of life and the right to live is a fundamental human right. It creates conditions for improving the quality of life, utilizing the potential of the territory and to attract skilled labour into urban areas. Ensuring of these needs would probably alleviate poverty (including energy) and social exclusion which is still in many European countries a significant challenge. This implies that housing is one of the fundamental rights and the approach to this right determines access to other basic rights and to live in dignity [5]. Housing problem in terms of social aspects can be divided into two main levels:

- problem of citizens who are not able to "get" flat,
- problem of people who have flat, but not have enough funds to cover fees associated with its use.

As shown, the support issue is not only the financing of housing, but also access to the apartment itself. The economic situation in individual households is largely affected by the deregulation of rents and housing-related services. Following this dominant trend of the economic efficiency of housing is necessary to create adequate living conditions for weaker social communities, for example, young families, families with several children, elderly or severely disabled persons. However, this trend means another rent increases and also increase in charges for services related to housing, including charges for heat, gas, electricity - the overall increase of expenses related to housing (see Fig. 3). It must be said that energy poverty is a consequence not only of low income but also high energy consumption. Without creating the appropriate compensatory measures in social policy this actually means disproportionate impacts on low-income groups.

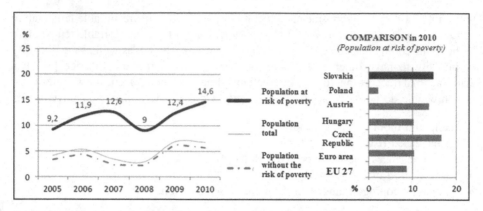

Fig. 3. Proportion of population with arrears for housing [6]

In literature as well as in practice in many European countries, including the Czech Republic and Slovakia, we meet with two basic definitions of social housing. They differ from each other by ways of housing financing, type of user and standard equipment. This means that social housing can be defined as "housing for households with clearly defined (low to zero) income".

To better understand the adverse situation where the low-income groups are situated, it is necessary to characterize another term - "social exclusion". This term in Western European countries had begun to be used in the Eighties and Nineties mainly due to substitute the term "poverty". It should be emphasized that this term insufficiently takes into account quality criteria of social relations and implies a lack of material resources. Nevertheless, social exclusion is closely linked to poverty. Some authors argue that poverty hinders the realization of civil and social rights, which is precisely the result of social exclusion. Other authors consider social exclusion as an extreme form of poverty. For example in the 1993, Maastricht Treaty defined the fight against social exclusion as one of the main objectives of social policy of the European Union [7].

Social exclusion is undoubtedly associated with economic exclusion, which presents limited access to primary as well as secondary labour market, energy poverty, concluding the life chances and so on. From the available analysis it is clear that in socially excluded localities, unemployment rate is over 90 % while individuals living in such areas are limited to contact with people who are in a similar social situation.

The most important tool how to measure energetic poverty is a statistical survey. The results of subjective measurement of poverty might be helpful when evaluating the time development or when comparing between particular countries. The main disadvantage of this approach is the fact that fully objective formula for measurement of poverty would be very complicated if it took into consideration all differences which exist in different demands of inhabitants for material needs, different price levels in the regions or in different property of individuals. So in practice these formulas are limited to quite simple calculations in every country. On the basis of such simplified calculations and objective data subsistence minimum is defined and each year up-dated.

It is calculated on the basis of statistic data of growth in net income per capita as well as living costs of low income households. Other simplified mechanism used for measurement of poverty on the basis of objective data is the indicator of relative poverty derived from comparison with other citizens.

The European Commission approaches to energy poverty through the European Platform against Poverty and Social Exclusion, which is a specific instrument 2020 strategy. In fact, energy poverty can cause that households remain without heating or cooling, without hot water, light and other basic household needs, which is a serious form of shortage. The European Union currently does not have consistently defined energy poverty, on which basis the specific and common European policy aimed at this acute problem would be gradually established. On the other hand, within the European Union there is still no uniformed methodology which would measure energy poverty. Still however, there predominates an opinion that it is a condition where the cost of energy for households makes up a significant share of disposable income. That is closely related to the risk that a household can be disconnected from the system or network.

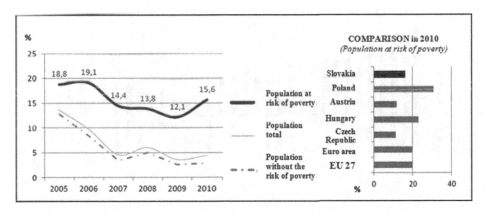

Fig. 4. Proportion of the population that cannot afford to keep their home adequately warm [6]

Expert analyses show that 40 million EU citizens suffer from "serious material deprivation". From a demographic point of view, the most vulnerable group are children. Children from poor households have worse conditions for the development of their personality in terms of the availability and use of technical and technological capabilities, education, finding job and application and in life. In Europe, energy poverty appears by a growing number of people (project of the European Fuel Poverty and Energy Efficiency, 2009), who have difficulty of paying for energy or the energy is available only to a limited extent, because they have a low income. Flats where they live are without insulation and therefore they do not sustain heat, have inefficient equipment (heating, cooking, hot water) or energy prices are very high (see Fig. 4). Budgets of households, which are often far from urban centres and where the job often depends on the transport link, is often burdened by mobility. This applies to the elderly, single-parent families, the unemployed, welfare recipients, etc. The consequences are different - poor mobility impact on employment, inadequate heating affects sanitation, health (dilemma "heat or food", respiratory diseases etc.) and often leads to increased mortality, high indebtedness, social and geographic isolation.

It follows that energy poverty is a negative determinant of weakness, which is associated with other factors, where difficulties act as upward spiral and beset the people in general poverty. In 2013, 122.6 million people, or 24.5 % (Fig. 5) of the population in the EU-28 were at risk of poverty or social exclusion (AROPE), compared with 24.8 % in 2012. This means that these people were at least in one of the following conditions [8]:

- at-risk-of-poverty after social transfers (income poverty);
- severely materially deprived or
- living in households with very low work intensity.

The reduction of the number of persons at risk of poverty or social exclusion in the EU is one of the key targets of the Europe 2020 strategy.

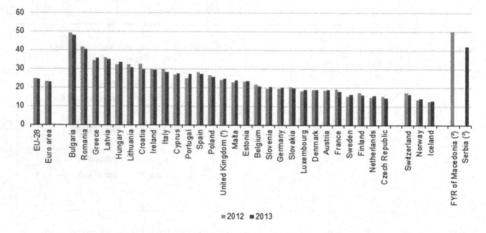

Fig. 5. At-risk-of poverty or social exclusion rate, 2012 and 2013 (%) [8]

The at risk of poverty or social exclusion figure, for the EU-28 average, calculated as a weighted average of national results, masks considerable variation between EU Member States.

In 2013, more than a third of the population was at risk of poverty or social exclusion in five EU Member States: Bulgaria (48.0 %), Romania (40.4 %), Greece (35.7 %), Latvia (35.1 %) and Hungary (33.5 %). At the other end of the scale, the lowest shares of persons being at risk of poverty or social exclusion were recorded in Sweden (16.4 %), Finland (16.0 %), the Netherlands (15.9 %) and the Czech Republic (14.6 %).

Overall, the at risk of poverty rate has slightly decreased at EU-28 level between 2012 and 2013 by 0.3 pp. The risk of poverty or social exclusion rose by 2.1 pp in Portugal and 1.1 pp in Greece and Hungary, decreasing by 2.7 pp in Croatia and 1.7 pp in Lithuania [8].

European statistics also shows that 40 million citizens in EU suffer from "serious material deprivation". Of the 500 million citizens of the EU, 116 million are "at risk of poverty or social exclusion". Young people, migrants and parents - single parents are in the vulnerability of persistent poverty the most. One of the most affected post-communist countries is Romania. Three million of the 19.6 million Romania's population lives in absolute poverty and 40 % of the population in relative poverty.

Absolute poverty - is a condition that is characterized by a severe lack in meeting basic human needs, including food, safe drinking water, sanitation, health, housing, education and information. This type of poverty depends not only on income but also on access to social security - Program of Action, Chap. 2.

Relative poverty - is a condition where people do not have sufficient resources to provide that right kind of diet, participation, welfare and benefits, which are customary in the respective community. Such an understanding is very close to understanding of the poverty in the EU. This concept is used in developed countries.

Surveys show that in Romania, but also in some other countries (such as Latvia and Lithuania), the poorest households spend a smaller share of financial resources on energy than households with higher incomes. This is due to the fact that in these countries, more residents live in one room, who share the cost of energy. In those countries with lower standards of living are therefore energy demand per capita lower, and therefore they appear as countries with lower energy poverty as developed countries of the EU. In 2005, per capita devolved 1.5 rooms in EU26 countries. In Romania and Latvia, however, it was only 0.9 rooms (at least from the current whole EU). It was followed by Bulgaria, Lithuania, Hungary, Poland and Slovakia (1.0 room per capita).

Since 1997, UN experts have introduced the method of detection level of human development using human development index (HDI - Human Development Index). This evaluation builds on the fact that the poor is not only a person who has a low income, but also takes into account the chances of survival and education. The Human Development Index is composed of three sub-indicators:

1. life expectancy, measured by expected length at birth,
2. educational attainment, measured by a combination of literacy (2/3) and the combined enrolment ratio in primary, middle and high school (1/3),
3. standard of living, measured by real GDP per capita in USD, converted through purchasing power parity.

Index determines the minimum and maximum values for each parameter. The resulting index value ranges from 0 to 1 and for each indicator were prepared fixed minimum/maximum values:

- life expectancy at birth: minimum 25 years, maximum 85 years,
- adult literacy rate 0 % and 100 %,
- real GDP per capita in USD, 100 USD and 40 000 USD.

The problem of poverty cannot be understood as only a problem of poverty, but in a broad sense as a problem of social inequality and unavailability of social goods (jobs, education, housing, health care and ensuring the opportunity of participating on the life of society).

In order to solve energy poverty, the European Union established general approaches in the form of direct and indirect support:

- social subsidy programs (direct support),
- social tariff system (indirect support),
- improving the energy efficiency.

3 Results and Discussion

Solving the energy poverty in European countries is addressed in different ways. Energy-poor customers in Bulgaria, Netherlands and Sweden, for example, get help from the energy supplier in way that energy supplier must inform the social or nursing service before disconnecting from the energy. In Finland and Sweden social care services pay invoices for energy, in Bulgaria and Norway poorer citizens get energy contribution. In Finland, Ireland and Slovenia, protection of energy-dependent citizens is ensured in a way that the disconnection from energy is forbidden in the case of chronically ill customers. So-called social tariffs are in Belgium, Spain, France, Italy, Portugal and Romania. Special fares on the initiative energy companies are in the UK.

Criteria for EU energy poverty are also different. Is it for example enlistment of citizens to social services (Hungary, Bulgaria), old age and disability (Belgium, Greece, Ukraine), low family income (Czech Republic, France, Greece, Great Britain), chronic disease (Finland, Hungary, Ukraine), multiplicity families (Hungary, France, Great Britain), and unemployment (Finland).

Slovakia. Based on analyses of the Regulatory Office for Network Industries Slovak Republic is clear that also in Slovakia there is quite a lot of households at risk of energy poverty. The most vulnerable Slovak households (under EU SILC 2012), at different breakdown of households (according to the number of dependent children, age):

- 2 adults + more than 3 dependent children 35.1 %,
- 1 adult with at least 1dependent children 27.5 %,
- Single household up to 65 years 24.1 %,
- Older than 65 years 7.8 %,

According to age the most risky were children up to 17 years, the number of at-risk-of-poverty persons gradually decreasing with the age. According to economic activity under the EU SILC 2012 the risk of poverty threatens unemployed persons the most, almost 44.6 % out of them [9].

It can be stated that energy poverty is primarily the result of combination of the following factors:

- income level,
- level of energy prices,
- level of energy performance of buildings and homes,
- level of use of energy-saving devices - e.g. gas boilers, solar panels,
- household appliances with higher energy class and below,

- small willingness of customers to manage their consumption (shift the consumption off the peak).

In this field, the Slovak Republic has prepared a number of solutions, from which we can select the most significant:

- reflect the solution of energy poverty into social policy,
- establish a system of monitoring socially vulnerable population groups, focus on the efficiency of spending their income from the social sphere,
- ensure the efficiency and targeting of social welfare and contributions,
- create models of housing optimization of residents in proportion to their income and needs,
- adopt legislative measures to address energy poverty etc.

In June 2014, the Slovak government approved the Conception of protection of consumers in energy poverty under which a household is in energy poverty if it meets the condition that disposable average income is lower than minimal disposable monthly income. The limit of minimal disposable monthly income is given as a multiple of actual electricity and gas prices and minimal energy costs of household depending on number of its members, the nature and use of energy.

The Conception implements minimal energy consumption only by example. Actual energy prices depending on the nature and use of energy and relevant supply and distribution tariffs are regulated. Households may choose tariff depending on amount of consumption and day time.

"The substantial share of" average monthly income of household is a regulated price of electricity and gas multiplied by regulated (predefined) energy consumption of the household. Analysis of share of energy expenditures on household income is not a part of the Conception and that is the reason why today it is not possible to estimate the share of households in energy poverty.

4 Conclusion

Energy poverty should be regarded as a social phenomenon that is gaining prominence at the level of the entire European Union. Despite the fact that energy poverty does not yet have a precise definition, non-governmental organizations, however, consider this condition when households pay for energy more than 10 % of their income. Joining together the terms "housing" and "energy poverty" has a negative effect on quality of life, level of utilization of technical and technological possibilities in relation to education and personal development particularly with children and adolescents.

References

1. Thomson, H., Snell, C.: Quantifying the prevalence of fuel poverty across the European Union. Energy Policy **52**, 563–572 (2013)
2. Thomson, K.H., Snell, C.: Energy poverty in the EU, Policy Brief. The University of York (2013)

3. Holiencik, J.: Energy poverty in Slovakia. In: Power Engineering 2014, Tatranske Matliare (2014)
4. Free, S., et al.: More effective home heating reduces school absences for children with asthma. J. Epidemiol. Commun. Health **64**, 379–386 (2010)
5. Spirkova, D., et al.: Housing and Housing Policy - Development, Determinants of Housing Development and New Approaches to Rental Housing Policies in Slovakia. Slovak University of Technology, Bratislava (2009)
6. Valentovic, M., Kavicky, R., et. al.: Energy povety in Slovakia. Analyses and studies. M.E.S. A._10, Consulting Group (2011)
7. Mareš, P.: Chudoba, marginalizace, sociální vyloučení. Sociologický časopis **36**(3), 285–297 (2000). Praha
8. Eurostat statistics: People at risk of poverty or social exclusion. http://ec.europa.eu/eurostat/
9. Strakova, D.: Energy poverty in Slovakia. http://www.regulatoryreview.sk

SustainableMoG

Identification of Key Supply Chain Elements from the Supply Chain Resilience Viewpoint Using the Computer Simulation and Design of Experiments

Radim Lenort[1(✉)], Pavel Wicher[1], Eva Jarošová[1], Marek Karkula[2],
David Staš[1], and David Holman[1]

[1] ŠKODA AUTO University, Na Karmeli 1457,
293 01 Mladá Boleslav, Czech Republic
{lenort,wicherl,yjarosova,stas,holman}@is.savs.cz
[2] Faculty of Management, AGH University of Science and Technology,
Gramatyka 10, 30-067 Krakow, Poland
mkarkula@zarz.agh.edu.pl

Abstract. Today's supply chains must face a wide spectrum of factors causing their disruption. The concept of supply chain resilience is response to this situation. Utilization of suitable decision support techniques is necessary to manage the supply chain resilience effectively. One of the key question in supply chain resilience management is to find such combination of investments to increasing the resilience of single supply chain elements to obtain maximal financial benefit for the whole supply chain. The aim of this article is to find an approach for identification of such supply chain elements, which are the most important for resilience of researched supply chain. The paper analyze possibilities of using computer simulation and design of experiments techniques for reaching the aim. Suitability of these techniques is confirmed on the supply chain model, which was created for that purpose.

Keywords: Supply chain resilience · Computer simulation · Design of experiments

1 Introduction

Today's supply chains must face a wide spectrum of factors causing their disruption. According to the World Economic Forum (WEF) [1], the major ones include: natural disasters, extreme weather changes, conflicts and political troubles, terrorism and sudden radical changes of demand. The concept of supply chain resilience is response to this situation.

The supply chain resilience is defined as follows - it is: (1) the ability of a system (supply chain) to return to its original state or move to a new, more desirable state after being disturbed [2], (2) the ability to bounce back from large-scale disruptions [3], (3) being better positioned than competitors to deal with – and even gain advantage from - disruptions [4], (4) the ability to maintain output close to potential in the

© ICST Institute for Computer Sciences, Social Informatics and Telecommunications Engineering 2016
A. Leon-Garcia et al. (Eds.): Smart City 2015, LNICST 166, pp. 629–639, 2016.
DOI: 10.1007/978-3-319-33681-7_54

aftermath of shocks [5]. The main idea of these definitions is to create such a supply chain that is not vulnerable to serious disruptions.

According to kinds of disruptions identified by WEF and mentioned resilience definitions, authors of the article define the supply chain resilience as the ability of a supply chain to return to its original state in case of its serious disruptions.

Utilization of suitable decision support techniques is necessary to manage the supply chain resilience effectively. One of the key question in supply chain resilience management is to find such combination of investments to increasing the resilience of single supply chain elements (subjects or groups of subjects) to obtain maximal financial benefit for the whole supply chain. Trade-off between investments and benefits resulting from increasing the supply chain resilience is investigated.

The aim of this article is to find an approach (using suitable quantitative techniques) for identification of such supply chain elements, which are the most important for resilience of researched supply chain. Even relatively small investments to these elements ensure relatively high benefits for the whole supply chain.

2 Methodological Basis

Computer simulation and Design of experiments were used as a methodological basis for reaching the research aim.

2.1 Computer Simulation and Its Utilization in Supply Chain Management

The computer simulation is defined as a numerical technique used to simulate a real system by means of an experimental model, with dynamical processes ongoing within the system factored in, in order to identify the behavior and effect thereof on the system operation [6].

The selection of computer simulation as a useful tool for an analysis of the supply chain resilience is motivated by its successful application in the sphere of simulation of supply chain management [7, 8, 9]. There is only a limited number of research works dealing directly with the computer simulation of resilient supply chains. On the basis of a critical evaluation of these studies, authors can say that the utilization of computer simulation in modelling of supply chain resilience is still in the initial research state [10] and developed own computer simulation-based model to eliminate the identified shortcomings [11]. The model will be described in the experimental part of the article.

2.2 Design of Experiments and Its Utilization in Computer Simulation

Design of experiments (DOE) refers to the process of planning, designing and analyzing the experiments so that valid and objective conclusions can be drawn effectively and efficiently. In order to draw statistically sound conclusions from the experiment, it is necessary to integrate simple and powerful statistical methods into the experimental design methodology. This indicates that there are two aspects to any experimental problem: the design of the experiment and the statistical analysis of the data. These two subjects are closely related because the method of analysis depends directly on the design employed. DOE methods have three basic principles, namely randomization, replication and blocking, which can be utilized in the experiments to improve the efficiency of experimentation and reduce or even remove experimental bias. [12, 13].

Basically, there are three main types of problems to which DOE is applicable. The first type is screening. Screening is used to identify the most influential factors, and to determine the ranges in which these should be investigated. The second type is optimization, which aims to find out the combination of important factor resulting in optimal operating conditions. The third type is robustness testing, which examining sensitivity. All of these types are used in the industrial practice to improve products and processes. [14].

One of the important areas where the DOE is used is a computer simulation. Systematized DOE can be used for improvement of understanding and utilization of computer simulation experiments. It is increasing the transparency of simulation model behavior and the effectiveness of reporting simulation results. Lorscheid et al. propose a systematic procedure for applying DOE principles for a more standardized computer simulation research process [15].

3 Experimental Work

Experimental work was divided into five steps: (1) Mental model preparation, (2) Computer simulation model construction, (3) Determination of supply chain performance, (4) Design of experiments, and (5) Key supply chain elements identification.

3.1 Mental Model Preparation

The model was created on the basis of a supply chain from automotive industry because [11]: (1) the automotive industry is central to Europe's prosperity, (2) the automotive industry is a representative of global supply chains (worldwide), which contains all kind of elements from supplier of steel materials and other components trough manufacturing plants to distribution network, (3) these supply chains are affected by all major disruptions defined by the WEF, (4) the automotive industry is the leader in supply chain management.

To verify the computer simulation and the design of experiments are suitable techniques for identification of the most important supply chain elements from the resilience viewpoint, the model was designed in such way, the key elements to be obvious prior to the techniques utilization. If the results from application of the computer simulation and the design of experiments meet presumed outputs, the selected approach can be considered as right.

Structure and relations among single elements of the modelled supply chain are given in Appendix 1.A. Each element represents group of companies in the entire region, because a crucial disruption affects not only one company, but the whole region.

Regions 1 and 2 contain suppliers and logistics service providers (LSP) from larger distances. Therefore, their deliveries are consolidated in a cross-docking center in the region 4 and sent to production plants in the region 5 through a LSP. Suppliers from the region 3 deliver to a relatively short distance, again through LSPs. Suppliers from the region 4 are situated close to production plants. Producers are active on two markets. Market 1 is a part of the more distant region 6, which is supplied by an importer. Market 2 represents customers situated relatively close to the production plants.

The model is balanced as far as its capacity. Sum of the suppliers' capacity is equal to the producers' capacity and the total market demand. This capacity is lowered by occurrence of significant disruptions, i.e. there is lowering the supply chain performance and incomes.

The model uses JIT supply chain strategy. The individual links in the supply chain can be arranged in a series or in a parallel form. A disruption of a link in the series part of the supply chain will reduce the performance of this whole part.

To have presumed outputs for verification of the selected approach, the model assumes:

- Disrupted are all supply chain elements.
- Impact of any disruption on each element is identical (disruption parameters are set at each element in the same way).
- There is such solution for each element, which is able to eliminate any impact of disruptions completely.
- Investments for elimination or lowering the disruptions' impacts are for each element identical too.
- Suppliers' capacities in various regions are the same, similarly the capacities of PLSs in the region 5 and of both markets.
- Shutdown of suppliers from one region doesn't mean a total stopping of the production plants, but only reducing their production to the capacity of the suppliers from remaining regions.

With respect to these assumptions, the key elements are predetermined by the supply chain structure. The most crucial element from the resilience viewpoint are production plants, which process all material flows. As next key elements can be seen elements from region 4 and elements, which are situated after the producers.

3.2 Computer Simulation Model Construction

Simulation model in software DOSIMIS-3® (dynamic, stochastic, and discrete event simulation tool) was created on the basis of the mental model (see Appendix 1.B).

The whole capacity of the supply chain is 500 000 tons per year. The simulation step is one week and the simulated period is 20 years. The capacity of the elements and the performance of the whole chain are measured in tons per week.

Disruption parameters of each supply chain element (parameters were selected on the basis of [16]) are as follows: (1) disruption periodicity (time interval between disruptions) varies from 1 to 3 years according to uniform distribution, (2) disruption time period (time interval between disruption beginning and capacity recovery) varies from 30 to 90 days according to uniform distribution, (3) disruption capacity loss (the number of tons lost at the outset of the disruption) is assumed in the amount of 100 % (total capacity loss), (4) disruption profile (the shape of the disruption capacity loss from beginning to end) is represented in Fig. 1.

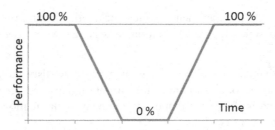

Fig. 1. Used disruption profile.

The model uses the loss of unrealized production caused by a disruption as a supply chain performance measure. This loss is represented by unsold tons per 20 years. A disruption in any element evokes stopping or strong limiting the other supply chain elements. To demonstrate it, an example of the whole supply chain performance fluctuation in simulated period is given in Fig. 2.

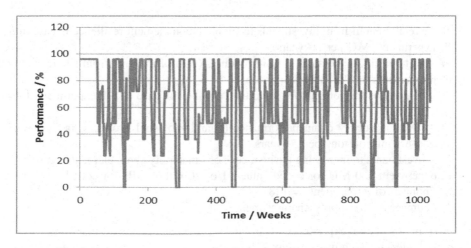

Fig. 2. Supply chain performance fluctuation in one simulation run [17].

3.3   Determination of Supply Chain Performance

Average supply chain performance for defined above assumptions is the main input value for identification of the key supply chain elements. The value was determined as average from 30 simulation runs and it is app. 6.7 million tons per 20 years. It means only app. 67 % performance of the supply chain in comparison with its theoretical capacity (without occurrence of any disruptions) of 10 million tons per 20 years.

3.4   Design of Experiments

To determine simulation experiments, which make identification of the key supply chain elements possible, fractional factorial design 2^7 were used with coding as follows:

1. Code −1: the given supply chain element is exposed to disruption with periodicity from 1 to 3 years according to uniform distribution and time period from 30 to 90 days according to uniform distribution. Investment to elimination of the disruption impact in this element is zero.
2. Code 1: the given supply chain element isn't disrupted at all, i.e. the disruption periodicity is set on a value higher than 20 years. Investment of 20 billion MU is expected to eliminate any disruption.

Software Minitab was used to generate 128 experiments. All experiments were conducted using simulation model created in DOSIMIS-3®. Overall benefit from investments to supply chain element resilience was calculated for each experiment according the following formula:

$$B_i = m(Q_i - Q_a) - \sum_{j=1}^{k} I_{ij} \quad \text{for } i = 1, 2, \ldots, n \tag{1}$$

B_i – overall benefit from investments to supply chain element resilience in case of i-th experiment (MU per 20 years)
M – unit margin of the supply chain products (sum of margins from single supply chain elements) = 90 000 MU per ton
Q_i – quantity of the sold supply chain final products in case of i-th experiment (tons per 20 years)
Q_a – average supply chain performance (quantity of sold products) in the initial state = 6.7 million tons per 20 years
I_{ij} – investments to increasing the resilience of j-th supply chain element in case of i-th experiment = 0 MU for coded value −1 or 20 billion MU for coded value 1
n – number of experiments = 128
k – number of the supply chain elements = 15

List of profitable experiments (sum of investments is lower than profit from increased sales) is given in Appendix 2. It is obvious from the results the Plant element (Production plants in the region 5 is the most important supply chain element, because at all experiments is coded value 1. It means if the supply chain should reach profitable resilience, it should invest to eliminating the disruption impacts in production plants primarily. On the contrary, investments to increasing the resilience of suppliers and their LSPs aren't effective. These preliminary conclusions were verified statistically in the next step.

3.5 Key Supply Chain Elements Identification

Analysis of variance (ANOVA) in statistical software Minitab was used to determine statistical significance of the single supply chain elements for the overall benefit from investments to supply chain element resilience B_i. Significance level α for P-value was set to 0.05. Statistical significance was confirmed at all supply chain elements. For final selection of key elements was used Pareto chart of standardized effects (see Fig. 3).

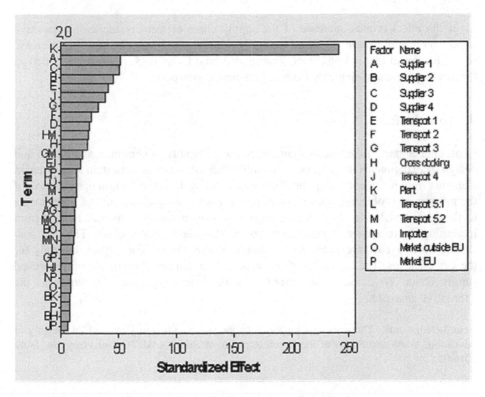

Fig. 3. Pareto chart of the standardized effects.

The most statistically significant is the element Plant, which is followed by Supplier 1, Supplier 3, Supplier 2, Transport 1, Transport 4, Transport 3, Transport 2, Supplier 4, and Cross docking. However, sign plus and minus at the single effects must be taken into consideration (see Table 1).

Table 1. Results from ANOVA.

Element	Effect	P-value
Plant	46.68	0.000
Supplier 1	−9.89	0.000
Supplier 3	−9.84	0.000
Supplier 2	−8.73	0.000
Transport 1	−7.93	0.000
Transport 4	7.45	0.000
Transport 3	−6.37	0.000
Transport 2	−5.11	0.000
Supplier 4	−4.64	0.000
Cross docking	4.36	0.000

If the effect is plus, increase of the supply chain element resilience has positive impact on overall benefit B_i. While the effect is minus, the impact is opposite (decrease of the B_i). From that reason, Plant, Transport 4, and Cross docking were identified as the key supply chain elements from the resilience viewpoint.

4 Conclusion

Experimental part of the research confirmed the suitability of computer simulation and design of experiments techniques for identification of the most important supply chain elements from resilience viewpoint. Future research work is focused on optimization of the investment problem. In other words, the aim is to find such amount of investments to the identified key supply chain elements to obtain maximal overall benefit from increasing the resilience of these elements for the whole supply chain. The first possibility how to reach the aim is to use design of experiments once again, but only for the key elements. The limitation of this approach is number of elements in researched supply chain. To eliminate the problem, authors apply genetic algorithms as the alternative approach.

Acknowledgments. The work was supported by the specific university research of Ministry of Education, Youth and Sports of the Czech Republic at SKODA AUTO University No. SGS/2015/02.

Appendix 1: Supply Chain Model

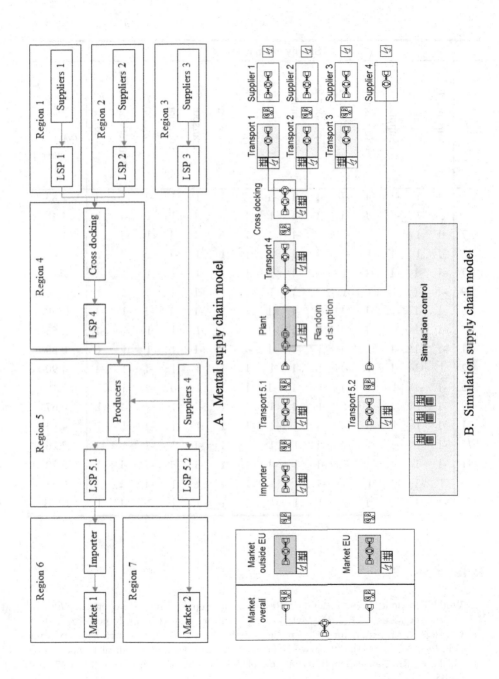

A. Mental supply chain model

B. Simulation supply chain model

Appendix 2: List of Profitable Experiments [17]

	Supply chain elements															
i	Supplier 1	Supplier 2	Supplier 3	Supplier 4	Transport 1	Transport 2	Transport 3	Cross docking	Transport 4	Plant	Transport 5.1	Transport 5.2	Importer	Market outside EU	Market EU	B_i (MU per 20 years)
3	-1	1	-1	-1	-1	-1	-1	-1	-1	1	1	1	-1	-1	-1	1.83
4	1	1	-1	-1	-1	-1	-1	1	1	1	-1	1	1	-1	1	3.48
7	-1	1	1	-1	-1	-1	-1	-1	1	1	-1	-1	1	-1	-1	1.42
11	-1	1	-1	1	-1	-1	-1	-1	1	1	1	-1	1	-1	1	5.43
17	-1	-1	-1	-1	1	-1	-1	1	1	1	1	1	1	1	-1	23.91
29	-1	-1	1	1	1	-1	-1	1	1	1	-1	1	1	1	1	5.86
33	-1	-1	-1	-1	-1	1	-1	-1	1	1	-1	-1	-1	1	-1	17.96
37	-1	-1	1	-1	-1	1	-1	-1	-1	1	1	1	1	1	-1	4.63
41	-1	-1	-1	1	-1	1	-1	-1	-1	1	-1	1	1	1	1	0.88
42	1	-1	-1	1	-1	1	-1	1	1	1	1	1	-1	1	-1	4.90
45	-1	-1	1	1	-1	1	-1	-1	1	1	1	-1	-1	1	1	2.19
59	-1	1	-1	1	1	1	-1	1	1	1	-1	1	-1	-1	1	0.67
71	-1	1	1	-1	-1	-1	1	1	1	1	1	1	-1	1	1	4.83
75	-1	1	-1	1	-1	-1	1	1	1	1	-1	1	-1	1	-1	7.26
81	-1	-1	-1	-1	1	-1	1	-1	1	1	-1	-1	-1	-1	1	5.70
90	1	-1	-1	1	1	-1	1	1	1	1	1	1	-1	-1	1	0.53
97	-1	-1	-1	-1	-1	1	1	1	1	1	1	1	1	-1	1	12.51

References

1. World Economic Forum: Building Resilience in Supply Chains: Report, http://www3.weforum.org/docs/WEF_RRN_MO_BuildingResilienceSupplyChains_Report_2013.pdf
2. Christopher, M., Rutherford, C.: Creating supply chain resilience through agile six sigma. Crit. Eye, 2–28 (2004). http://www.sclgme.org/shopcart/documents/critical_eye.pdf
3. Sheffi, Y., Rice, J.: A supply chain view of the resilient enterprise. MIT Sloan **47**, 8–41 (2005)

4. Sheffi, Y.: Building a resilient supply chain. Harvard Bus. Rev. Supply Chain Strategy **1**, 1–4 (2005)
5. Duval R., et al.: Structural Policies and Economic Resilience to Shocks. http://ssrn.com/abstract=1002508
6. Malindzak, D., Straka, M.: The methodology for the logistics system simulation model design. Metallurgija **49**, 348–352 (2010)
7. Campuzano, F., Mula, J.: Supply Chain Simulation: A System Dynamics Approach for Improving Performance. Springer, London (2011)
8. Cigolini, R., et al.: Linking supply chain configuration to supply chain performance: a discrete event simulation model. Simul. Model. Pract. Theor. **40**, 1–11 (2014)
9. Ramanathan, U.: Performance of supply chain collaboration – a simulation study. Expert Syst. Appl. **41**, 210–220 (2014)
10. Lenort, R., Grakova, E., Karkula, M., Wicher, P., Staš, D.: Model for simulation of supply chain resilience. In METAL 2014: 23rd International Conference on Metallurgy and Materials, pp. 1803–1809. TANGER, Ostrava (2014)
11. Wicher, P., Staš, D., Karkula, M., Lenort, R., Besta, P.: A computer simulation-based analysis of supply chains resilience in industrial environment. Metalurgija **54**, 703–706 (2015)
12. Montgomery, D.C.: Design and Analysis of Experiments. Wiley, New York (2008)
13. Antony, J.: Design of Experiments for Engineers and Scientists. Elsevier, London (2014)
14. Eriksson, L. (ed.): Design of Experiments: Principles and Applications. MKS Umetrics AB, Umeå (2008)
15. Lorscheid, I., Heine, B.O., Meyer, M.: Opening the 'black box' of simulations: increased transparency and effective communication through the systematic design of experiments. Comput. Math. Organ. Theor. **18**(1), 22–62 (2012)
16. Melnyk, S.A., Rodrigues, A., Ragatz, G.L.: Using simulation to investigate supply chain disruptions. In: Zsidisin, G.A., Ritchie, B. (eds.) Supply Chain Risks, pp. 103–122. Springer Science and Business Media, New York (2009)
17. Grakova, E.: Metodika uplatnění počítačové simulace pro řízení odolných dodavatelských řetězců v průmyslu. Dissertation thesis, VSB – Technical University of Ostrava, Ostrava (2015)

Traditional Cost Accounting as the Key Obstacle to Reach Sustainable SCM Solution in the Industry of the 3rd Millennium

Jiří Michna, David Holman$^{(\boxtimes)}$, Radim Lenort, David Staš, and Pavel Wicher

ŠKODA AUTO University, Na Karmeli 1457,
293 01 Mladá Boleslav, Czech Republic
michna.jiril@gmail.com,
{holman,lenort,stas,wicherl}@is.savs.cz

Abstract. Competitive long term market position cannot be reached by a particular solution in terms of low price or high quality or just innovative products. A system solution fulfilling the current customer demand should be based on the respectful utilization of scarce resources. 20th century creates successful production and accounting systems unique for the industrial development. Traditional cost accounting (TCA) was developed to work with the traditional mass supply chain management concept of customer satisfaction. To successful cost efficiency measuring of the Sustainable SCM concept in the industry of the 3rd millennium, new accounting methods must be used.

Keywords: Lean accounting · Lean productivity · Competitiveness in automotive SCM

1 Introduction

Reaching twice as much more productivity – number of personnel, profit margin, twice as better quality, means to implement the Toyota Production System (TPS) [1]. From 1990 when productivity and quality were discovered by James Womack, The Machine that changed the world, TPS tools and principles have been performed in countless optimization in production or supply chain management (SCM). TPS, generally known as Lean [2] became the source of productivity improvement in the whole range of automotive producers. After more than 20 years of TPS implementation in the automotive industry, the productivity of TOYOTA Motor Corporation has exceeded its competitors still twice over.

The objective of the Lean manufacturing system is to identify and eliminate the processes, resources which do not add value to a product. Eliminating waste in manufacturing however cannot be achieved solely through efforts in manufacturing. It requires changes in other functions such as product design, materials section, marketing etc. [3]. The main difference between the previous Mass production system, whose efficiency goal was "Producing More" was replaced by a "Consuming Less" Lean attitude which could

© ICST Institute for Computer Sciences, Social Informatics and Telecommunications Engineering 2016
A. Leon-Garcia et al. (Eds.): Smart City 2015, LNICST 166, pp. 640–647, 2016.
DOI: 10.1007/978-3-319-33681-7_55

be understood as an economic dimension of Sustainable development [4]; a part of Sustainable SCM solution in the 3rd millennium.

The selling volumes of numbers one and two, TOYOTA Motor Corporation and VOLKSWAGEN, enable an interesting comparison in productivity results of the whole automotive makers after more than 20 years of implementation of TPS tools and principles. Number of employees or profit margin presented in Table 1, shows big difference, although the production volumes are almost the same. The number of employees can be influenced by in/out sourcing the SCM activities. For a proper comparison of the automotive producer's results there must be used a more strict indicator of the total cost. The profit margin is an indicator of how well the company controls costs. It measures profit as a percentage of the selling price or revenue.

Table 1. Toyota, VW – efficiency comparison 2013

Automotive producer	Number of sold cars	Number of employees	Profit margin (%)
TOYOTA	9.98	330 000	8.8
VW	9.70	550 000	2.9
Δ (%)	−3	−40	303

The transition to Lean as the reaction of the different market condition was presented either as an evolutionary step followed by another competitive concept LARG SCM [5, 6] or revolutionary or paradigmatic change which must be followed by a transition in productivity understanding, traditional cost accounting, perception of value added and management [7]. A detailed analysis of traditional cost accounting bottleneck for successful implementation of Lean in industry is the goal of this article.

2 Traditional Cost and Lean Accounting Differences

Lean accounting has been defined in 2005 by the lean accounting summit as a response to the need to support lean efforts [8]. It differs from traditional cost accounting in several areas. The first difference is in the data sources that are used, which is shown in Table 2.

Table 2. Data source differences

Cost accounting	Lean accounting
Production data	Production data
Financial data	Financial data
	Market data

As a result of a broader data base, the concept and tools of lean accounting is different from traditional cost accounting as it is shown in Table 3.

Table 3. Utilization of different tools

	Cost accounting		Lean accounting	
	Management	Control	Management	Control
Strategic level	Company P&L		Value stream value × cost analysis, process KPI	Company P&L
Tactical level	Cost centre P&L			Value stream P&L
Operative level	Variance analysis		Production cell process KPI	

Authors of lean accounting argue that traditional cost accounting creates barriers to successful transformation of a lean manufacturing system [9, 10]. To be able to support the lean transformation and the customer focused management, different methodology must be used as shown in Table 4.

Table 4. Lean accounting transformation methodology

	Cost accounting	Lean accounting
Cost subjects	Cost centres	Value streams
Cost pricing	Standard prices/real prices	Real prices
Cost subjects revenues	Cost of production taken over from foregoing subject	Value created for customers/selling price
Inventory increase effect	Cost reduction	Cost up
Capacity	Volume of production	Uptime
Profit calculation	Revenue − (Direct + Indirect cost − Δ Inventory)	Revenue − Cost per period

Main and most frequently reported benefits [9, 10] of lean accounting are:

1. Faster data rate and simplicity.
2. Easy to understand.
3. Ability to quantify the financial impact of lean improvements.
4. Support of lean decisions.

To confirm benefits 3 and 4 a theoretical model of production control transformation, which was measured by selected comparable instruments of both the accounting methods had to be created.

3 Theoretical Model Description

The theoretical model illustrates the transformation of the production from mass to lean with production at full capacity of 10 units sold and at half capacity of 5 units sold. To increase the conclusiveness, simplistic assumptions had to be made [11], the most important assumptions being listed below:

1. Distribution of customer orders is linear: one order per one time unit.
2. The selling price is equal to the market price.
3. There is one employee in each department with uniform wage.
4. The fixed assets are uniform in all departments and the depreciation calculation is uniform.
5. All products are made in 100 % quality.
6. Standard prices are equal to real prices.
7. The length of the accounting period is set as the length of the production process.
8. There is no work in progress at the end of the accounting period.
9. After five orders, mass production creates a forecast of five other orders (Figs. 1 and 2).

3.1 Model Visualization

The benefits of the transformation in the model are:

1. Shorter lead time
2. Planning department elimination.

Table 5 shows the effects of the transformation of production - 10 pcs to the P&L in traditional accounting cost centers in comparison with lean accounting value x cost analysis.

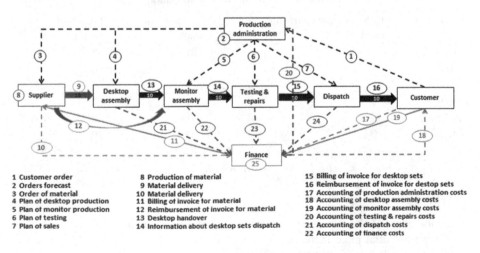

1 Customer order	8 Production of material	15 Billing of invoice for desktop sets
2 Orders forecast	9 Material delivery	16 Reimbursement of invoice for destop sets
3 Order of material	10 Material delivery	17 Accounting of production administration costs
4 Plan of desktop production	11 Billing of invoice for material	18 Accounting of desktop assembly costs
5 Plan of monitor production	12 Reimbursement of invoice for material	19 Accounting of monitor assembly costs
6 Plan of testing	13 Desktop handover	20 Accounting of testing & repairs costs
7 Plan of sales	14 Information about desktop sets dispatch	21 Accounting of dispatch costs
		22 Accounting of finance costs

Fig. 1. Mass production model

As shown in Table 5 the traditional cost accounting is able to track only the transfer of employee from the planning department to the sales department as profit of the main production and the loss of sales. In contrast, lean accounting is able to trace the value added by shortening the delivery time and improving customer support. The allocation of value added to processes can be calculated according to following formula:

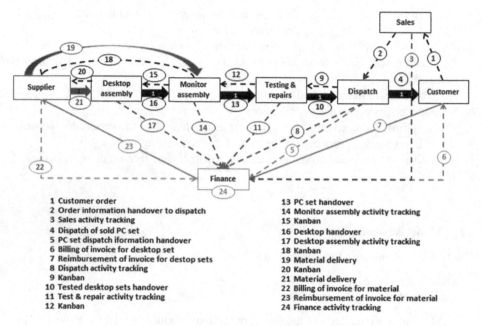

1 Customer order
2 Order information handover to dispatch
3 Sales activity tracking
4 Dispatch of sold PC set
5 PC set dispatch iformation handover
6 Billing of invoice for desktop set
7 Reimbursement of invoice for destop sets
8 Dispatch activity tracking
9 Kanban
10 Tested desktop sets handover
11 Test & repair activity tracking
12 Kanban

13 PC set handover
14 Monitor assembly activity tracking
15 Kanban
16 Desktop handover
17 Desktop assembly activity tracking
18 Kanban
19 Material delivery
20 Kanban
21 Material delivery
22 Billing of invoice for material
23 Reimbursement of invoice for material
24 Finance activity tracking

Fig. 2. Lean production model

Table 5. The results of transformation

Department	Effects of transformation on employees	Cost accounting results	Lean accounting results
Sales	1	−10	2
Main production	−1	10	16
Dispatch	0	0	2
Finance	0	0	0
Total	0	0	20

$$I * P * Q = section\,value\,increase \qquad (1)$$

Where:

I – the effect of the department on the potential price increase (%),
P – the potential price increase,
Q – the number of improved products sold.

The differences between both methods are increasing in case only half of the production capacity is sold. In this case the mass production creates overproduction as the effect of production forecasts. In the same case, in lean production tact time adjustment is realized and two employees are transferred to the improvement of processes as shown in Fig. 3.

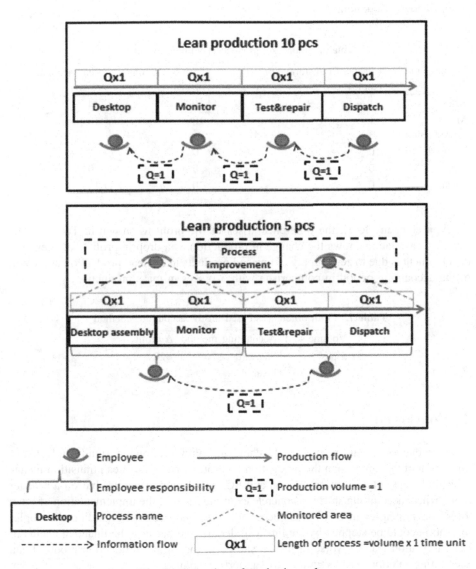

Fig. 3. Reduction of production volume

The impact of the displayed change of the financial results is shown in Table 6.

If production falls to half capacity, cost accounting shows the transformation of mass production to lean production as negative development. This phenomenon is caused by the transfer of employees to the offline process which leads to change from variable costs to fixed costs. Lean accounting shows the change as a positive development with the exception of the sales department that generates loss of 4 units as a result of low production.

Table 6. Impact on production volume reduction

Department	Effects of transformation on employees	Cost accounting results	Lean accounting results
Sales	1	10	−4
Main production	−1	10	18
Dispatch	0	0	1
Finance	0	0	0
Total	0	20	15

At a company level, the difference arises in the profit as shown in Table 7. The standard calculation shows the change in production as a drop in profit. This negative development is due to zero supply of finished products in the lean production at the end of the accounting period in comparison with 5 pieces in mass production.

Table 7. Profit differences based on the accounting method

Volume sold	Accounting method	Δ profit
5 pcs	Standard	−20
	Lean	5

4 Conclusion

Lean production is an example of Sustainable solution allowing significantly better utilization of resources than the production methods used so far. Lean transition means critical change not only in production and SCM tools and principles but on a broader scale, where accounting shift is a concrete example. Even if the implementation of Lean tools and principles in SCM was successful, the final decision regarding the implementation could be stopped by the financial department because the financial results of Lean transition lead to worse results as shown in the simple production model. Lean accounting solution could significantly support accepting the Sustainable SCM concept to support not only competitiveness but the environmentally friendly customer satisfaction concept.

Acknowledgments. The work was supported by the specific university research of Ministry of Education, Youth and Sports of the Czech Republic at SKODA AUTO University No. SGS/2015/02.

References

1. Liker, J.K.: The Toyota Way. McGraw-Hill, New York (2004)
2. Womack, J.P., Jones, D.T., Roos, D.: The Machine That Change the World: The Story of Lean Production. Free Press, New York (2007)
3. Upadhye, N., Deshmukh, S.G., Garg, S.: Lean manufacturing for sustainable development. Global Bus. Manag. Res. **2**, 125–137 (2010)
4. Global Sustainable Development Report: Building the Common Future We Want. Executive Summary, United Nations Department of Economic and Social Affairs (2013). https://sustainabledevelopment.un.org/content/documents/975GSDR%20Executive%20Summary.pdf
5. Kubota, Y.: VW set to overtake Toyota as global auto leader, Reuters (2014). http://www.reuters.com/article/2014/07/29/us-japan-autos-idUSKBN0FY2AM20140729
6. Carvalho, H., Duarte, S., Machado, C.: Lean, agile, resilient and green: divergencies and synergies. Int. J. Lean Six Sigma **2**, 151–179 (2011)
7. Holman, D., Jirsak, P.: Unified theory of SCM competitiveness in 21st century (Principles of paradigmatic change MassSCM > LeanSCM). In: CLC 2013: 3rd Carpathian Logistics Congress, Tanger, Krakow (2013)
8. Asefeso, A.: Lean Accounting. Booktango, Bloomington (2013)
9. Maskell, B., Baggaley, H.B.: Practical Lean Accounting: A Proven System for Measuring and Managing the Lean Enterprise. Productivity Press, New York (2004)
10. Cunningham, J.E., Fiume, E.O., Adams, E.: Real Numbers: Management Accounting in a Lean Organization. Durham, Managing Times Press, New York (2003)
11. Michna, J.: Comparison of selected methods of managerial accounting and lean accounting with respect to ability to support transformation on lean production control. Diploma thesis, SKODA AUTO University, Mlada Boleslav (2015)

Green Supply Chain Design Considering Warehousing and Transportation

Ingo Gestring[(✉)]

HTW Dresden, Friedrich-List-Platz 1, 01069 Dresden, Germany
gestring@htw-dresden.de

Abstract. Green supply chain design considers besides costs and service level as well the environmental impact. There is a trade-off in terms of costs and environmental impact between the size of warehouses and the transport mode and transport frequency. High frequent deliveries with trucks result in high emission during transport, but low emission during the storage process. Less frequent delivery with trains or ships have a lower emission during transport, but the items must be stored for a longer time and so need more space in a warehouse. The consequences are illustrated with a case study. The total CO_2 emission and the eco-efficiency are calculated.

Keywords: CO_2-emission · Warehousing · Transportation · Eco-efficiency · Trade-off

1 Introduction

Supply chain design is in most cases done under costs and service level considerations. If the environmental impact is as well considered then the term green supply chain design is used. The common measurement of the environmental impact is the CO_2 emission. Beside CO_2 different gases have a much higher impact on the global warming then CO_2. Considering the global warming potential of CO_2 as 1, other gases like Methane CH_4 or Nitrous oxide N_2O have a much higher factor than CO_2. The global warming potential of Sulphur hexafluoride SF_6 is 23,900 times higher than that one of CO_2. Therefore the emission is often converted to CO_2-equivalents CO_2e. The different gases of a combustion process are transferred to the CO_2 emission, having the same impact. Besides the atmospheric pollution of different gases, the noise pollution, vibration, accidents and waste are other external impacts of freight transport.

In a transport chain the highest emission takes often place during the transport. Energy savings methods like the use of EURO-6 trucks or alternative fuels have a positive impact on the environment but a negative impact on the costs of a transport chain. This correlation is shown in Fig. 1. If a company wants to be the cost-leader it will probably not consider the environmental impact. Companies which want to green their supply chain have to invest money to reduce the emissions.

The strategic design of logistics networks focusses primarily of the infrastructure and the transportation mode. The infrastructure is described by the facility location problem. There the number of facilities, the location and the capacity of a network node are calculated. This location analysis is well known in operations research.

© ICST Institute for Computer Sciences, Social Informatics and Telecommunications Engineering 2016
A. Leon-Garcia et al. (Eds.): Smart City 2015, LNICST 166, pp. 648–658, 2016.
DOI: 10.1007/978-3-319-33681-7_56

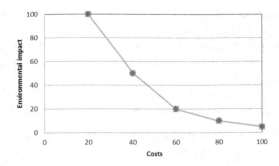

Fig. 1. Trade-off between total costs and environmental impact.

Transporting goods with trains instead of an aircrafts could result in a reduction of the CO_2 emission by the factor of 40. But transportation duration increases and the flexibility of the supply chain decreases.

Different companies have a Green House Gas reduction program. These companies want to lower the CO_2 or CO_2e emission of their supply chain. Therefore a carbon footprinting process has been started at these companies. The carbon footprint can be done in several ways (Fig. 2).

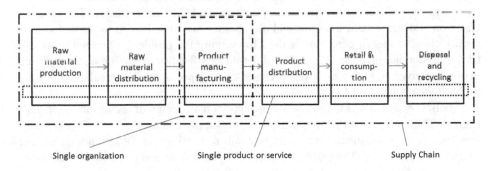

Fig. 2. Carbon Footprinting [9].

Some companies are doing the carbon footprint process for their company or their organization. This is in some cases the easiest way because the needed data for the analysis can be measured within the company having access to the different data. For a single item like jeans the total CO_2 emission can be measured along the supply chain. This starts with the raw material production and distribution and the manufacturing and product distribution. In order to achieve a total life cycle assessment the consumption and the disposal or recycling are also included in the accounting process. The highest level is the carbon footprint of the complete supply chain. Considering various players in different regions of the world, this process is very complex to handle. Various guidelines exist for the carbon footprint measuring and reporting:

- ISO 14067: Greenhouses Gases –Carbon Footprint of Products. Requirements and Guidelines for Quantification and Communication (ISO 14067, 2013)
- The Greenhouse Gas Protocol: A Corporate Accounting and Reporting Standard. Revised Edition (World Business Council for Sustainable Development, World Resources Institute, 2013)
- PAS 2050: Specification for the Assessment of the Life Cycle Greenhouse Gas Emission of Gods and Services (British Standards Institution, 2011)

Worldwide exist more guidelines. Larger companies or industry branches even may use their own methodology to measure the emission.

2 Literature Review

The optimization of the logistic infrastructure is investigated by an increasing number of researchers, Harris et al. [1] investigate the impact of CO_2-emissions of the number of depots in a transport chain and the fill rate of trucks, varying from 60 % to 90 % as well as the total costs. They used the center of gravity approach for the facility location problem. This approach accords well with the originally generated experimental data from a network of the automotive sector. To minimize the costs 2 depots are used, for minimizing the environmental impact 2–3 depots are used.

In another study Harris et al. [2] solved the capacitated facility location problem for costs and the CO_2 emission from transportation and running facilities. The study is based on realistic data of transport and distribution network. For up to ten depots in a supply chain, a special algorithm is used for solving the problem. The total costs and CO_2 emission are given in Fig. 3. The different possibilities of having open or closed depots are given in Fig. 3 by 0: depot closed or 1: depot open. The results correspond to the trade-off given in Fig. 1.

Mallidis et al. [3] investigate the green supply chain design of regions in South-East Europe. They found that the optimization of the supply chain based on CO_2 emissions does not increase substantially the supply chain network costs. Other findings are the sharing of warehouses. The results are lower CO_2 emissions and just a slight increase in the costs compared to dedicated warehouses.

Dekker et al. [4] give a substantial overview about the possibilities of operations research and its application in green supply chain design. Design, planning and control of supply chains are explained under the consideration of transportation, inventory of products and facility decisions. They indicate several areas where environmental aspects could be included in operations research models for logistics.

Aronsson and Brodin [5] discuss the possibility of changing the logistics infrastructure without performance losses in terms of costs and delivery service. Changes of three companies are explained as well as the effects and results. Changes of the transport mode, standardization of load carriers, consolidation of flows are aspects all three companies have in common for cost reduction and reduced emission. The benefit for the companies was that both cost and the environmental impact reduction were possible at the same time.

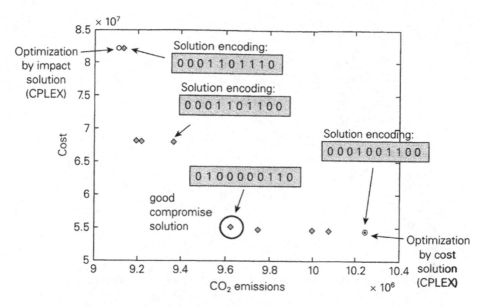

Fig. 3. Environmental impact and total costs for a facility location problem [2].

Elhedhli and Merrick [6] use Lagrangian relaxation to determine the network design under different emission costs. The application is focused on regions that have a carbon tax or cap-and-trade system. For the design network it is suggested that more distribution centers should be integrated in the network to reduce the vehicle travel distances.

Rizet et al. [7] calculate the CO_2 emission from New Zealand to different locations in Europe and compare the results with the emission of the competitive supply chain within Europe. The findings are the dominant influence of the maritime transport from New Zealand to the European location. This transport mode is responsible for over 80 % of the CO_2 emissions of the transport chain considering transportation by ship, truck and storages. For the internal European supply chain in the UK the CO_2 emission of the storage facilities are responsible for up to 60 % and more.

A complete lifecycle assessment is done by Köhler and Steinhilper [8]. For an automotive supplier all necessary data from transport chains, material specification, supplier locations and production technology are generated. The CO_2 balance is generated with the life cycle software SimaPro PHD-version 7.1.8. For three different metal products the main CO_2e emission takes place during the raw material of steel. For these parts only 11 % of the total CO_2e emission comes from logistics whereas the external transport has the highest impact. The internal logistics generates only 1 % of the CO_2e emissions. In Fig. 4 these emission data are shown.

Depending on the supply chain, the balancing method and the mathematical algorithm as well as the system boundaries different results and impacts on the environment are generated and discussed in the literature.

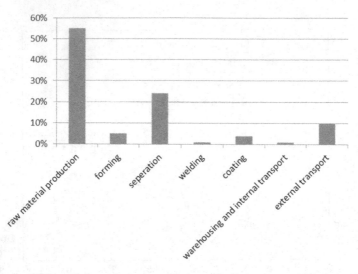

Fig. 4. CO2e emission of an automotive supply chain on a product base [8].

3   Method

The calculation of the impact of the transport volume on the storage size and their impact is done by process of the World Business Council for Sustainable Development. In Fig. 5 the typical approach is given.

Step 1: The objectives of the case study are to identify the influence of the transport mode and frequency on the warehouse capacity and size and on the total environmental impact. The warehouse can consist of a non-cooling and a cooling area. Processes are the transportation by truck, train or ship from a warehouse to another distribution center. The frequency and the capacity of the different transport modes vary and so does the required space in the distribution center.

Step 2: McKinnon and Piecyk [9] suggest different systems boundaries around transport operations for carbon measurement. This is shown in Fig. 6.

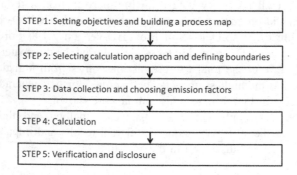

Fig. 5. Steps to calculating the carbon footprint [12].

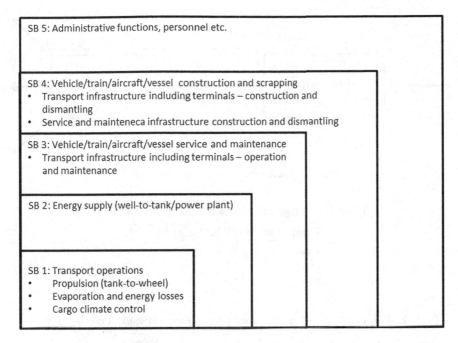

SB 5: Administrative functions, personnel etc.

SB 4: Vehicle/train/aircraft/vessel construction and scrapping
- Transport infrastructure indluding terminals – construction and dismantling
- Service and mainteneca infrastructure construction and dismantling

SB 3: Vehicle/train/aircraft/vessel service and maintenance
- Transport infrastructure including terminals – operation and maintenance

SB 2: Energy supply (well-to-tank/power plant)

SB 1: Transport operations
- Propulsion (tank-to-wheel)
- Evaporation and energy losses
- Cargo climate control

Fig. 6. System boundaries around transport operations for carbon measurement [9].

Emission data from different transportation modes are available. The energy consumption of warehouses is also reported in different publications. So system boundary SB 3 is chosen for the calculation. The SB 1 and SB 2 are related to the transportation solely, SB3 the warehouse operations but not construction and dismantling are integrated (Fig. 7).

In the distribution centre different items are also stored for a specific time. Between the warehouse and the distribution center trucks, trains or ships transport the items. A one-way transportation is considered.

Step 3: The transportation emissions are calculated with the EcotransIT-software from IFEU [10] as well as with average values given in Table 1. EF are the specific emission factors of a transport mode.

For the emission of the distribution center data from Süssenguth [11] are taken. In their investigation 9 different warehouses with and without cooling section are investigated. The average value of the energy consumption of the warehouses is 80 kWh per m^2 and year. The data vary from 40 to almost 140 kWh per m^2 and year. Corresponding to a conversion factor of 0.569 kg CO_2/kWh given by the German federal environmental agency for the year 2014 the emissions are between 21.56 kg CO_2/m^2 year and 75.46 kg CO_2/m^2 year. For the calculation real data from one specific warehouse are taken for the case study.

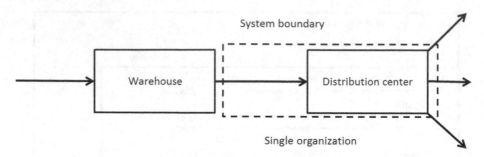

Fig. 7. System boundary of the case study.

Table 1. Average emission factors for the calculation.

Transport mode	EF [CO_2e g/t km]
Train	30
Truck	60
Ship	10

Table 2. CO_2 emission data for the distribution center [11] without cooling section.

Data	Value
Area	28,000 m^2
CO_2 emission per year	672.1 t
Emission factor CO_2 kg per m^2 and year	24.0

4 Results

Step 4: For calculating the CO_2 emissions an activity based approach is used. The emissions of the transportation are given by:

$$CO_2 \text{ emission}_{transport} = \text{weight} \times \text{distance} \times \text{emission factor} \qquad (1)$$

The emissions of warehousing activities in a distribution center are given by:

$$CO_2 \text{ emission}_{distributioncenter} = \text{storage period} \times \text{emission factor} \qquad (2)$$

It is also possible to calculate the CO_2 emission with the size of the warehouse/distribution center:

$$CO_2 \text{ emission}_{distributioncenter} = \text{area} \times \text{emission factor} \qquad (3)$$

For the arbitrary case study the transport between warehouse and distribution center takes place every day per truck, or every week per train or once a month per ship. The distance is 200 km. The lower the transport frequency the higher is the average stock in the distribution center.

Table 3. Data for the calculation.

Data	Train	Truck	Ship
Number of pallets received per year	345,000	345,000	345,000
Number of pallets locations	30,000	10,000	90,000
Utilization factor	80 %	80 %	80 %
Average stock	24,000	8,000	72,000
Weight per pallet [kg]	500	500	500
Value per pallet [€]	750	750	750
Interest rate	7 %	7 %	7 %

First the influence of the loading factor is considered. It is assumed that the truck costs 300.00 € for the transport. If the number of pallets transported by truck is increased from 27 to the maximum load of 33, a decrease in transportation costs of 2.02 € is achieved. Considering an increase in the storage period by 5 days and so additional tied up capital costs by 0.73 €, the total savings are 1.29 € per pallet. The total costs savings are then 445,000 € per year. The emission by transport is decreased as well. The increase of the CO_2 emission of the warehouse is calculated next. Distribution planning has a high impact on the costs and emissions. According to the high amount of transported goods of the case study it is considered in the next calculation that all trucks are fully loaded.

The total CO_2 emissions of the chosen system boundaries are given in Fig. 8 for the distance of 200 km.

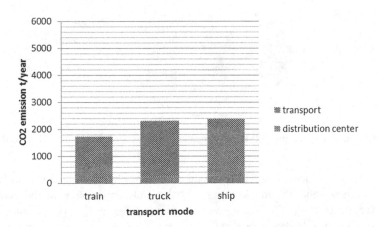

Fig. 8. CO_2 emission for the 200 km distance.

The train has the lowest total CO_2 emission of the transport chain. For truck transport the dominant CO_2 emission is the transport itself. For the slowest transport mode of the ship the size of the distribution center/warehouse matters. Increasing the distance between the two locations the transport the ship benefits due to its low

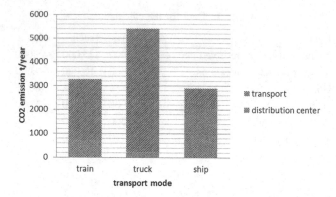

Fig. 9. CO_2 emission for the 500 km distance.

emission during transport. Keeping the size of the stock area the same the results are shown in Fig. 9.

The emission factor per m^2 is assumed to be 24 kg and year. This is compared to other values quite low. If the factor is increased to the upper end of 72 kg CO_2/m^2 year the CO_2 by the factor of three for the distance of 200 km are given in Fig. 10.

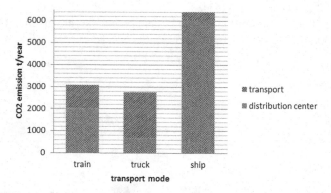

Fig. 10. CO_2 emission for the 200 km distance and an emission factor of 72 kg CO_2/m^2 year.

In this case the truck has the lowest total emission. The investigations are based on real data from warehouses in Germany and the CO_2 emission with the conversion factor of 0.569 kg CO_2/kWh. This conversion factor differs in Europe. Countries with a higher use of renewable energy or atomic energy have a smaller conversion factor. This value could be as low as 0.08 kg CO_2/kWh and so just 15 % of the value in Germany. France has because of their atomic energy plants these kinds of low values. Taking the simple approach from the case study, the green supply chain design would result in different solutions for the size of warehouses and the transport mode in the countries of France and Germany considering CO_2 as the major measure of environmental impact.

Another measure for the environmental impact is the eco-efficiency. This is given by:

$$\text{Eco-efficiency} = \text{value added}/\text{environmental impact added} \qquad (4)$$

The value added is the increase in the value of a product within a process. In this case the added value is the transport from the warehouse to the distribution center and the storing activities before unloading the product on a further transport mode. Assume that the value is 10.00 € per pallet. With the values from Tables 2 and 3 the total CO_2 emission can be calculated per pallet and year. This is the environmental impact added in kg CO_2. By using Eq. 4 the eco-efficiency is given for this transportation and storing process by the values in Table 4.

Table 4. Eco-efficiency for the distance of 200 km.

Transport mode	Value [€/kg CO_2]
Train	2.02
Truck	1.50
Ship	1.46

5 Conclusions

Step 5: The environmental impact of a distribution network of a distribution center and different transport modes is investigated. Warehousing and transportation both must be considered in the carbon footprint accounting. The most important factors are the distance of transportation and the specific emission factor of the building. Taking average values for the CO_2 emission of warehouses can result to wrong recommendations in the supply chain design. The difference between average values and the real consumption can be quite high. Extending the system boundary in the case study to the other warehouse will guide to other solutions in terms of optimal low environmental impact supply structure. All boundaries and assumption have to be well documented.

References

1. Harris, I., Naim, M., Palmer, A., Potter, A., Mumford, C.: Assessing the impact of cost optimization based on infrastructure modelling on CO_2 emissions. Int. J. Prod. Econ. **131**, 313–321 (2011)
2. Harris, I., Mumford, C., Naim, M.: An evolutionary bi-objective approach to the capacitated facility location problem with costs and CO_2 emission. In: 13th Annual Conference on Genetic and Evolutionary Computation, pp. 697–704. ACM (2011)
3. Mallidis, I., Dekker, R., Vlachos, D.: The impact of greening on supply chain design and cost: a case for a developing region. J. Transp. Geogr. **22**, 118–128 (2012)
4. Dekker, R., Bloemhof, J., Mallidis, I.: Operations research for green logistics – an overview of aspects, issues, contributions and challenges. Eur. J. Oper. Res. **219**, 671–679 (2012)
5. Aronsson, H., Brodin, M.H.: The environmental impact of changing logistics structures. Int. J. Logist. Manag. **17**, 394–415 (2006)

6. Elhedhli, S., Merrick, R.: Green supply chain design to reduce carbon emission. Transp. Res. Part D **17**, 370–379 (2012)
7. Rizet, C., Brown, M., Cornelis, E., Leonardi, J.: Assessing carbon footprint and energy efficiency in competing supply chains: review – case studies and benchmarking. Transp. Res. Part D **17**, 293–300 (2012)
8. Köhler, D., Steinhilper, R.: CO_2-Bilanzierung von supply chains. In: Zadek, H., Schulz, R. (eds.) Sustainable Logistics, pp. 48–68. DVV Media Group, Hamburg (2011)
9. McKinnon, A.C., Piecyk, M.I.: Measuring and Management CO2 Emissions of European Chemical Transport. http://www.ccr-zkr.org/temp/wrshp120411/Presentations/1_02_JVerlinden_en.pdf
10. IFEU: EcoTransIT, Ecological transport information tool, environmental methodology and data, Heidelberg. http://www.ecotransit.org
11. Süssenguth, W.: Ermittlung von Energiebilanzen für Logistikzentren. In: Zadek, H., Schulz, R. (eds.) Sustainable Logistics, pp. 82–94. DVV Media Group, Hamburg (2011)
12. McKinnon, A., Browne, M., Piecyk, M., Whiteing, A.: Green Logistics. Kogan Page, London (2015)

The Challenges of Sustainable Logistics in Finland

Jorma Imppola(✉)

School of Business and Culture, Seinäjoki University of Applied Sciences,
Kampusranta 11, 65101 Seinäjoki, Finland
jorma.imppola@seamk.fi

Abstract. This paper will give an overview of the logistic situation in Finland, especially on the sustainability viewpoint. Finland has quite extraordinary logistical situation in both international and national logistics. The need for transportation is significantly higher than any other EU country mostly because the geographical position and national economic structure. Because of these handicaps our transportation performance in both materials and persons is high comparing to other EU countries. This is a significant challenge for sustainable development, which is today one of the cornerstones in EU policies. How to cut down the energy consumption and emissions created in Finland by everyday logistics without distracting the holistic functionality of our society?

Keywords: Logistics · Sustainability · Finland

1 Introduction

Finland's international business environment and thus also its transport situation have changed enormously during the last 25 years. Finland's accession to the European Union and Russia's transformation towards a market economy have induced major changes for Finland. Economic and political integration to Western Europe has led to the EU becoming one of the financial centres of the world. Integration offers Finland a chance to act as a North European regional centre. The role as an mediator between east and west is important to Finland. Significant new opportunities are offered by the Barents Region where the increasing use of natural resources may increase transport operations through Finland and create a basis for new business activities [1].

During the years 1970–2000 has the goods transportation volume increased averagely about 1.7 % per year and personal traffic about 2.5 % per year [2].

Viewed from the continent of Europe, Finland is virtually an island. Vast majority of Finland's foreign trade (about 70 % of the import transport and 90 % of the export transport) is carried on by ship, and the harbours are its principal traffic nodes. The network of ports is indeed a dense one, but this means that most of the ports themselves are small and traffic flows are highly fragmentary. Icebreakers form an important part of the transport infrastructure, eight of these being responsible for assisting freighters and passenger ships into 23 harbours that are kept open all the year round. Given a normal winter, the harbours on the Bothnian Bay require icebreakers to keep them functioning

© ICST Institute for Computer Sciences, Social Informatics and Telecommunications Engineering 2016
A. Leon-Garcia et al. (Eds.): Smart City 2015, LNICST 166, pp. 659–670, 2016.
DOI: 10.1007/978-3-319-33681-7_57

for half the year, from November to May, while these are needed in the Gulf of Finland for about three months [3].

A large (total area 338 145 km^2 of which dry land 304 530 km^2) and low-populated (population of Finland is about 5.5 million inhabitants, which equals to 18 inhabitants per dry land km^2) country like Finland is challenging to organise countrywide distribution in. Population density in Finland can be seen at Fig. 1. Especially when taking into consideration the fact that the population is strongly concentrated in the Southern Finland as seen in Fig. 2.

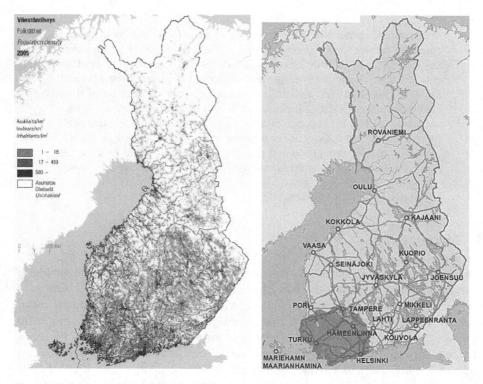

Fig. 1. The population density in Finland [4] (Color figure online)

Fig. 2. Map of Finland, where the most densely populated area having 50 % of the whole population is highlighted [5]. (Color figure online)

Finland has the lowest population density in European Union and it causes many logistic challenges because of long distances in both distribution and travelling as most of the country is inhabited and the same services and utilities ought to be provided to all citizens despite their location. In the Fig. 3 is described the transportation performance and population density in some European countries. There seems to be some correlation between population density and transportation performance.

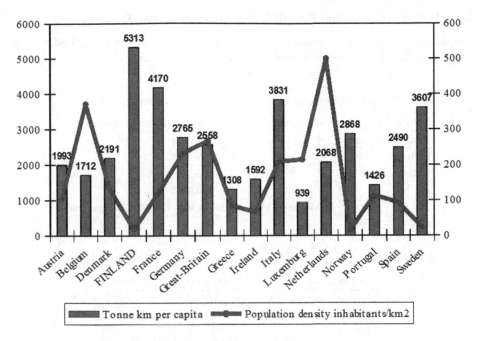

Fig. 3. Transportation volumes per capita and population densities of some European countries [6, 7].

2   Finnish Transport Network and Volumes

The Finnish transport network consists of the infrastructure needed for road, rail, water and air traffic, parts of which belongs to the Trans-European Network. The network of roads and streets amounts to a total of 454 000 km, which comprises 78 000 km of public roads maintained by the National Roads Administration, 26 000 km of streets maintained by municipal and other local authorities, and 350 000 km of private and forestry roads. Finland has about 880 km of motorways. Out of the national and municipal roads about 65 % (50 000 km) are asphalted and about half (41 000 km) are of low utilisation [8].

The rail network amounts to a total of 5 944 km, of which a bit more than half, 3 256 km, is electrified [9]. An evaluation of transit routes between West Europe and Russia shows that western European companies rank the service of the Finnish route highly The route is also easy and reliable and, compared to other routes the loss of goods is minimal [10].

Finland haves a direct railroad connection to Russia (same track width) and railship connection to Sweden and Germany (which requires special rail cars having change-able sets of wheels and wheel set exchange terminals). Also direct truck transport connections exist to Russia and Sweden. Trucks are also transported by ferries to Sweden, Estonia, Poland and Germany.

2.1 Domestic Goods and Passenger Transport Performance

The biggest users of transportation services are construction business, food cluster, forest industry and transito from and to Russia (Tables 1 and 2).

Table 1. The volume of Finnish goods transportation 2012 [11].

Vehicle type	Million tonnes	Million tonne kilometres
Trucks and lorries	294	22 000
Railways	35	9 300
Waterways	8	3 100
All	337	34 400
	Equals to 62 t per capita	Equals to 5 800 tkm per capita

Table 2. The volume of Finnish passenger transportation 2012 [12].

Vehicle type	Million person kilometres
Private passenger cars	65 270
Buses and motor coaches	7 540
Railways	4 040
Airways and others	1 720
All	78 600
	14 550 km per capita

2.2 Import and Export

Finnish import and export transportation quantity was at 2012 about 105 million tonnes. The share of sea transportation was 93 million tonnes and land transportation (lorries and trains) 12 million tonnes. The share of air transport is about 10 % of the total value, but the volume was mere 0.2 million tonnes. Domestic air freight volume was about 7 500 tonnes [11]. International transportation volume equals to about 20 tonnes per capita.

The Finnish port system is operational and its capacity is sufficient for the time being. There are a total of 60 ports and loading berths in Finland. The ports are mainly municipal. Additionally there are some ten substantial private industry ports and numerous small private loading berths. Foreign goods traffic is evenly distributed between the most important ports with emphasis on the southern coast.

The largest municipal ports are located in Helsinki, Kotka, Hamina, Rauma and Pori. Additional large private ports are in Sköldvik (oil refinery), Naantali (oil refinery) and Raahe (steel mill). The ports link railway and sea traffic. Train ferries maintain a service from Turku to Sweden and Germany. The largest transit traffic ports are located in Kotka, Hamina and Helsinki.

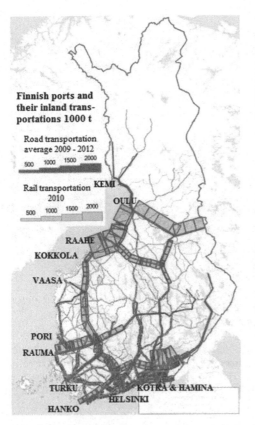

Finnish ports and their inland transportations 1000 t

Road transportation average 2009 - 2012
500 1000 1500 2000

Rail transportation 2010
500 1000 1500 2000

KEMI
OULU
RAAHE
KOKKOLA
VAASA
PORI
RAUMA
TURKU
HELSINKI
HANKO
KOTKA & HAMINA

Fig. 4. Finnish foreign trade material routes and Finnish ports [13]. (Color figure online)

The harsh winter conditions raise the costs of building, maintaining and operating the transport infrastructure in Finland. The penetration of the frost into the ground means that all constructions have to be dimensioned and insulated properly to cope with the problem of freezing (Fig. 4).

Salt has to be dispensed on the roads to prevent icy conditions and this means that protective layers have to be installed in the road structures in areas where the groundwater deposits are located. Snow clearance, sanding and salting and the repair of frost damage are further sources of additional costs. Finland is also one of the few countries allowing the use of studded tires in winter, which causes severe abrasion problem to the road pavement especially on heavily used main roads.

3 Location of Finland in the Northern Hemisphere

The geographical location of Finland in EU is logistically very disadvantageous. The average distance from Finland to Central Europe is about 2 000 km and this means that Finnish companies have to add additional 1 to 2 days extra to delivery time comparing to Central European competitors, not to mention extra costs. The global location is relatively not so disadvantageous than the location in the EU because when the actual distance increases the relative disadvantage gets smaller, which can be seen on the Fig. 5.

The geographical location of Finland creates also some opportunities to increase Finnish international air traffic and especially to increase intercontinental traffic via Finland. The shortest and fastest flight connections from western and central Europe to e.g. Japan and from the American East Coast to the Far East are routed via Finland. Helsinki-Vantaa Airport acts as a node for long distance air traffic.

Logistically speaking Finland is very challenging country to operate in both domestically (low population density causes excessive distribution costs) and European

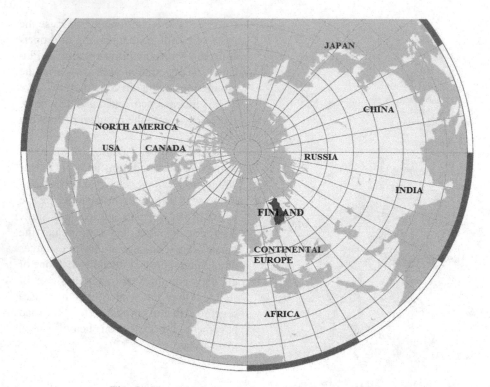

Fig. 5. The northern hemisphere and Finland in it [14].

wide (an additional 2 000 km to the distribution distance comparing to Central European competitors). Globally the location of Finland is not so big a handicap.

4 Sustainability

As described in previous chapters, there is a big need for transportation in Finland mostly because of very low population density and widely inhabited relatively big country. The way of life today requires lots of material to be transported to meet the needs of both industry and population. This all causes very large quantities of materials and passenger transportation needs.

4.1 Distribution Challenge

In Finland the highly developed information technology infrastructure supports the centralisation of distribution. Also geographical and demographical factors support this development. Therefore the basic question has become important: which location(s) may give the most cost effective way (in the long run) to distribute products nationwide?

The centralisation development in Finland has been very drastic during the last decades. As in 70's and early 80's it was normal to have at least 20 local distribution terminals in the case of nationwide distribution the amount of distribution centres is today 1 to 3 and usually distribution centres are also production units. Practically all of the distribution terminals having no production activities have been closed and the distribution has been centralised.

In a centralised system decisions are made at a central location for the entire distribution network. Typically, the objective is to minimise the total cost of the system subject to satisfying some service-level requirements. In a logistics system in which each facility can access only its own information, centralised strategy is not possible. With advances in information technologies, however, all facilities in a centralised system can have access to the same data [15].

By using the results of analysis done by the author at 2000 Finland can be divided into five regions:

(1) Most favourable locations,
(2) Favourable locations,
(3) Average locations,
(4) Unfavourable locations,
(5) Least favourable locations.

As shown in the Fig. 6 logistically favourable locations are strongly concentrated in the Southern Finland. The fact that the Finnish population has quite strongly concentrated into Southern Finland (as seen in Figs. 1 and 2) can be clearly seen from the results. Also the most of the companies dealing today with a nationwide distribution have their main distribution terminals located in area 1, which indicates that the analysis has gave in this case reliable results.

Because the Finnish geographical facts cannot be changed the only ways to change the situation are:

(1) Distribute the population more evenly, which is in the open society like Finland practically impossible and today the trend is quite opposite.

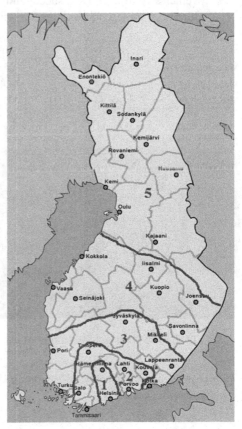

Fig. 6. Finland divided **into** five logistic regions

(2) Change the consumption behaviour of the people

- – with taxation some consumption patterns could be changed,
- – local retail services instead of mega-sized shopping centres would decrease the shopping distances and the use of a private cars could also decrease – some governmental actions against suburban or rural mega shopping centres have already been made.

(3) Increase the distribution vehicle efficiency

- – there is two ways to improve vehicle efficiency: maximise the utility level of the vehicles (two-way-distribution, route optimisation) and increase the vehicle capacity,
- – very efficient route optimisation tools and for example strategic alliances in order to achieve two-way distribution maximising the utility level of the vehicles have been used successfully,
- – Finnish road law allows bigger vehicles (Fig. 7):

	EU average	Finland
Max. length	18.75 m	25.25 m, with special permission 34 m
Max. height	4.00	4.40 m
Max. weight	40–44 t	76 t

Fig. 7. The "Ecotruck" - the biggest allowed 34 m long truck in Finland [16]

(4) Create industrial activity at less favourable areas which are not so dependent on the distribution costs:

- – local markets; then the market area is smaller and local optimisation can be done – recent consumer trends are supporting this approach,
- – international markets, because in this case all locations in Finland are more or less equally unfavourable (look Fig. 5) - most of the Finnish industry is already export-oriented,

- production of products, which have a low transportation cost comparing to its value – nowadays the average value of Finnish import and export is slightly over 1 € per kg, which is surprisingly low.

Nationwide distribution should be organised using favourable locations as distribution centres. Both international and local distribution can be done economically also in disadvantageous areas because all the locations are equally distant internationally and naturally local distribution is not so much dependent on the region.

4.2 Mobility Challenge

During the last decades there has been a significant migration to so called growth centres in Finland. This means, that lots of people has been moved to live on areas, which can provide better working possibilities because of successful industrial companies and offices. Most of these people have found their accommodation from relatively distant suburban living areas which has increased the average pendeling distance.

About 700 000 people (over 25 % of working people) in Finland have their working place outside their living municipality. This is all a result of improved mobility of the Finnish citizens. All the enormous investments to Finnish road infrastructure and automobilisation of Finnish households had led to situation, in which earlier impossible distances between home, work, shopping, school, hobbies, recreation etc. have become everyday reality.

We travel more and more to do our everyday activities because we can, and our society and in a way our modern civilisation has designed to accommodate that. Now, because we can, we **have to** travel long distances for the services and things which used to be near - available on walking or cycling distance. This is the biggest sustainability challenge concerning the modern society mobility.

This is also environmental issue. At 2013 the share of traffic on total energy consumption of Finland was 16.5 % = 182 petajoules (PJ), which equals to 800 l of fuel per capita. The share of traffic was about 40 % of all oil energy used in Finland. The share of traffic has been slightly increasing on recent years [17].

The emissions of vehicles has been reduced since 1970's, but the increasing traffic has been slowing down the total emissions decreasing. The emissions dangerous on health have been decreased significantly. The traffic is still significant source on many emissions – 87 % of carbon monoxide (CO) and about half of hydrocarbon and nitrous oxide emissions come from traffic (Table 3).

Table 3. Traffic emissions in Finland

Emission	1990 (t/a)	2012 (t/a)	Change	Share of road traffic
CO_2	10 900	11 200	+2.8 %	75 %
CO	470	72.5	−84.6 %	87 %
NO_x	134	39	−70.9 %	45 %
HC	68	9.8	−85.6 %	77 %
SO_2	5.3	<0.1	−99.1 %	0.6 %

Road traffic is the most significant source of emission except on SO_2 emissions, which come almost solely from sea transportation [17]. The reason for that is the use of low quality and sulphur rich heavy fuel oil on ship engines. On Baltic Sea the accepted sulphur content of the fuel was decreased to 1 % at 1st of January 2012 and further to 0.1 % at 1st of January 2015. This will cut down SO_2 emissions significantly [18].

In heavy road traffic the gradually tightening motor requirements have cut down emissions and on smaller vehicles improved engine efficiency and catalyst technology have cut down many emissions significantly. Although technical development on emission control has been most successful, is the ever growing traffic negatively compensating this development.

Emissions are just one element of traffic problems, traffic has additional effects like noise pollution, dust, vibration and the space required for roads and parking areas required for more and more cars. Also traffic causes all kinds of solid (junk cars, old tires and accumulators etc.) and liquid (lubrication oils and other auto chemicals) waste, which can be very dangerous if not disposed correctly.

The main problem is the ever increasing volume of traffic – necessary or unnecessary. We must seriously think, is all the traffic necessary, or are we wasting natural resources on needless mobility? Distant working is for example considered as partial solution for this problem. Today in the age of wireless communication many kinds of activities can be done practically at any physical location. This could at least decrease the need for commuting to office every day. Is our working culture ready to accept this?

4.3 Economics Challenge

As the sometimes needless and unsustainable consumption and distribution caused by it increases transportation logistics and its negative effects there is also the economics aspect to keep in mind. Our current economic crisis is partially caused by diminished consumption of goods, which leads to lower demand causing unemployment on manufacturing, distributing and retailing businesses. And this affects negatively on national economy and peoples willingness to consume – and vicious circle is created.

So, what to do – should we keep on consuming despite its unsustainable consequences in order to help the economy to maintain its urge to continuous growth? Can economy based on paradigm of continuous growth co-exist with sustainable development in a world with limited resources? If the continuous growth means more materials and energy to be utilised to manufacture, distribute and retail unnecessary things and gadgets to consumers – it will not work.

But if the growth is achieved by immaterial services, IT-assisted distant working, virtual experiences etc., which require very little or no physical materials or energy to make and distribute, it is very possible.

5 Conclusion

A country like Finland having low population density and high living standards is facing lots of logistic sustainability challenges. Today the unnecessary use of materials and energy is in any case harmful for sustainable development, but in which way we could control or even limit it? Most of these behaviour and consumption decisions we make are voluntary and therefore avoidable. The sustainable awareness is needed and with information and education some progress can be achieved.

The best way to improve sustainability of logistics is to eliminate reasons for unwanted behaviour and practices. Decreasing the need for move things and people with vehicles would be of course the most sustainable way to deal this matter. This is a problem of infrastructure and municipal planning. Today we have a world of big distances to work, school, shopping, leisure etc. - because it is possible. Could we create a world of smaller distances – and with less transportation needs? This would require a change of paradigm in the whole society. It is necessary, but is it possible?

Another very efficient way to improve sustainability in logistics is to improve the fuel efficiency of vehicles and functionality of the infrastructure. Traffic congestions waste both time and fuel and exist because of bottlenecks in the infrastructure. In Finland the congestion situation is much better than in many countries having much bigger population density, but there is no reason for satisfaction, because of very high traffic performance in both goods and persons traffic.

What about the stick instead of the carrots? Should we governmentally/municipally restrict the consumption and travelling behaviour of Finnish peoples in order to decrease the need for traffic? Are the private persons unable to make the sustainable decisions without rules and regulations requiring it? There is very positive examples of restricting rush-hour traffic with city tolls from both London and Stockholm which show that good results can be achieved with restrictions.

Finally the dilemma of economics based on eternal growth and sustainable economics, can it be solved? If we stick on out old habits and behaviour, this dilemma will be absolutely unsolvable. But if we can find a new paradigm to combine our economic system (and logistics as a part of it) and sustainable development and this way change our mode of behaviour very positive results are possible.

References

1. Finnish Ministry of Transport and Communications. https://web.archive.org/web/, http://www.mintc.fi/www/sivut/english/facilities/sivu3.htm. 20041205070816
2. Suomen kuljetusopas (Finnish transportation guide). http://www.kuljetusopas.com/yleistietoa/kuljetussuoritteet/
3. Finnish Ministry of Transport and Communications. https://web.archive.org/web/, http://www.mintc.fi/www/sivut/dokumentit/liikenne/vaylat/li010699307eng.htm. 20050423231731
4. Ääntä vaimentamaan. http://arkisto.eralehti.fi/erablogit/ps-pekka-suuronen/aanta-vaimentamaan-1.aspx
5. Otavan Opisto: Internetix distant learning materials service. http://opinnot.internetix.fi/fi/muikku2materiaalit/peruskoulu/ge/ge3/4_suomen_vaesto/03?C:D=iFzk.iEBD&m:selres=iFzk.iEBD
6. KYAMK University of Applied Sciences. http://www2.kyamk.fi/dl/log03/SSainio2.pdf#page=1&zoom=auto,-305,60
7. The World Bank. http://data.worldbank.org/indicator/EN.POP.DNST

8. The Finnish Transport Agency. http://portal.liikennevirasto.fi/sivu/www/f/liikenneverkko/tiet
9. The Finnish Transport Agency. http://portal.liikennevirasto.fi/sivu/www/f/liikenneverkko/rautatiet
10. Finnish Ministry of Transport and Communications. https://web.archive.org/web/, http://www.mintc.fi/www/sivut/english/facilities/sivu4.htm. 20050724082823
11. The Finnish Transport Agency. http://portal.liikennevirasto.fi/sivu/www/f/liikenneverkko/liikennejarjestelma/tavaraliikenne
12. Statistics Finland. http://www.stat.fi/tup/suoluk/liikenneverkko/suoluk_liikenne_en.htm
13. Sito Ltd. http://www.sito.fi/tyot/suomen-satamien-tavaraliikenteen-takamaat/
14. WANtaroHP. http://members3.jcom.home.ne.jp/civilyarou/gmt_Schmidt/fig_E_north.png
15. Simchi-Levi, D., Kaminsky, P., Simchi-Levi, E.: Designing and Managing the Supply Chain. Irwin McGraw-Hill, Boston (2000)
16. Konepörssi web magazine. http://www.koneporssi.com/uutiset/kesko-mukaan-hct-kokeiluihin/
17. Motiva. http://www.motiva.fi/liikenne/perustietoa_liikenteesta_ja_ymparistosta/liikenteen_energiankulutus_ja_pakokaasupaastot
18. Finnish Shipowners Association. http://www.shipowners.fi/fi/ymparisto/ilmansuojelu%20ja%20ilmastonmuutos/merenkulun%20rikkipaastot

Technology Transfer – Case of Slovak Academic Environment

Jana Kundríková[1]($\boxtimes$), Anna Závodská[2], and Jakub Soviar[1]

[1] Faculty of Management Science and Informatics, University of Žilina,
Univerzitná 8215/1, 010 26 Žilina, Slovakia
{jana.kundrikova, jakub.soviar}@fri.uniza.sk
[2] University Science Park of the University of Žilina,
Univerzitná 8215/1, 010 26 Žilina, Slovakia
anna.zavodska@uvp.uniza.sk

Abstract. Innovativeness and subsequent technology transfer is essential for universities and research institutions in order to remain competitive. However, Slovak universities or research institutions have not been successful in these transfer initiatives. The purpose of this paper is to analyze the current technology transfer activities of the University of Žilina in Žilina as well as propose recommendations in order to ensure further successful and sustainable technology transfer.

Keywords: Technology transfer · Sustainability · Cooperation · Research · University · Slovak universities · University of Žilina

1 Introduction to the Topic

Technology transfer (TT), which is closely related to knowledge transfer (KT), has already become an object of interest in Slovak republic, not only for universities and businessmen, but also for politicians, regions and various research organizations. The main reason is changing view on the role of research and development (R&D) by supporting economic growth of the country or region. TT is able to generate both significant financial and other advantages for all involved subjects, as we can see on examples from USA, Great Britain or Germany [1].

There are several *meanings* of the term TT. It can be understood in one of the following ways [2]:

- as an effort to develop backward countries by providing them technology from developed countries,
- as a movement of technology in the commercial sphere between companies or within one company among its organizational units,
- as a transfer of research and development results into practice, which means also transfer of technology from academic environment to commercial.

There are also various *definitions* of the term TT. Following two definitions are the most accurate. "Technology transfer is a process of transferring scientific results from one organization to another in order to achieve its further development and

© ICST Institute for Computer Sciences, Social Informatics and Telecommunications Engineering 2016
A. Leon-Garcia et al. (Eds.): Smart City 2015, LNICST 166, pp. 671–680, 2016.
DOI: 10.1007/978-3-319-33681-7_58

commercialization. This process usually involves (i) identifying new technologies; (ii) protecting technology through patents and copyrights; (iii) preparing strategies for the development and commercialization, marketing and providing licenses to private companies or creation of new technology start-up companies" [3]. TT is a technical term that means not only transmission of technology. In a broader context, when it comes to the transmission of any knowledge, it is possible to use the term *knowledge transfer*, which is justified by the second definition, which says: "Technology transfer is a process through which is technology extended. TT may or may not have be secured with legally binding agreements, but it includes the transfer of knowledge (through an intermediary) from provider to recipient" [4]. TT can be considered as successful if the recipient is able to use the technology effectively in practice.

TT should be seen as a complex process of applying industrial proprietaries (inventions, technical solutions, designs, etc.), which are results of R&D realized on universities, in economic and social practice for purpose of financial evaluation. The role of universities in TT is to adapt their research and development for the needs of market, while businesses are required to ensure that the final product is produced and placed on the market to customers, eventually to help research organization with research costs.

The technology transfer process is the "process of conducting basic research that is developed into commercializing new technologies" [5]. It consists of numerous complex activities whereby multiple factors influence university performance during the transfer. Process of TT itself can be divided into two main *phases*:

– protection of intellectual property - in this phase the research takes place and is generated the actual subject of intellectual property,
– commercialization - includes especially the choice of a particular method of commercialization and finding partners for its implementation.

Commercialization represents "financial evaluation of intellectual property of the institution" [6]. Depending on how is the intellectual property commercialized, the process of TT can be implemented in several ways, for example joint research, realizing research on order, transfer of intellectual property rights (or sale), licensing, establishing spin-off companies etc. [2].

There are many potential *reasons* for both universities and companies to participate in joint R&D, but there is no general agreement as to which are the most important. Empirical surveys of companies participating in such collaborations, as well as case studies and game theoretic models, processed by the authors in their study [7], point to the following incentives:

– economies of scale in research,
– economies of scope in research,
– ability to finance costly projects,
– avoidance of unnecessary duplication of research,
– risk management,
– access to know-how of the network,
– obtaining a window on related technologies,
– exploitation of partners' complementary positions,

– internalizing the externalities created by research spillovers.

Importance of joint R&D consist in fact that it is a way how to improve competitiveness. R&D is an expensive activity, but it is also an essential source of innovations which bring competitive advantages. Joining resources can overcome costingness of the process and makes possible to perform it more effectively (e.g. Emilia-Romagna High-Tech Network) [8].

One of the main identified *problems* is that although TT or KT occurs frequently, it is often incomplete, or it is just declared [9]. Another important issue is how to organize cooperation between academia and industry so that TT and KT occur and generate benefits for everybody involved in the cooperation.

2 Situation in Slovak Republic

The current situation in Slovakia is in the phase of implementing projects aimed at supporting cooperation between research organizations and business entities. The institution that launched such a project is called *Centre of Science-Technical Information of Slovak republic* (CVTI SR). It is a national information center and also a specialized scientific public library of Slovak Republic focused on technical disciplines and selected areas from natural sciences, economic sciences and humanities established in Bratislava [10]. The name of the project is *National infrastructure for supporting technology transfer in Slovakia* (NITT SK) and is co financed by the European Regional Development Fund (under the Operational Programme Research and Development). The strategic objective of the project is creating and implementing a system of national support of transferring technology and knowledge acquired in R&D activities into economic and social practice in order to promote the development of knowledge-based society. The system of national support of TT and KT involves building a soft infrastructure (a system of support services) and marginally building also physical infrastructure mainly relating to the completion of information systems supporting TT, i.e. realizing professional expertise and support services [11].

There is also *Industrial Property Office* (ÚPV SR) as a part of the TT management scheme in Slovakia on the next level after CVTI SR. The mission of ÚPV SR is to grant protection of industrial property, such as inventions (patents), utility models (so-called small patents), trademarks, designs, topographies of semiconductor products, designations of origin of products, and geographical indications of products. ÚPV SR provides services and products to the public in the field of industrial-legal information and supports the development of technical creativity and its protection, education and popularization of intellectual property [12].

The importance of the national supporting of TT consist in realizing R&D activities based on the specific needs from the business sector, which will result in increased rates of application knowledge and technologies acquired in research activities into industrial practice. The system should also significantly contribute to creation and development of long-term R&D cooperative partnerships of academia and industry [11].

The present condition of science parks in Slovakia could be described as in the stage of building. *Eight science parks* are planned to be built close to *six universities* in

Slovakia. Minister of education signed contracts on co-financing these projects with Slovak University of Technology in Bratislava (STU), Slovak University of Agriculture in Nitra (UNIAG), The Technical University of Košice (TUKE), Comenius University in Bratislava (UK), The University of Žilina in Žilina (UNIZA) and Pavol Jozef Šafárik University in Košice. Signed contracts include multi-source financing with using money from EU funds under the Operational Programme Research and Development, as well as from the state budget [13].

One of the first parks should be university science park *"Campus MTF STU"* built in the area of Material Technology Faculty of the STU in Trnava. The project will build a new scientific infrastructure at the global level focused on the research field of materials engineering, plasma and ion technologies, and automation of industrial processes. STU builds another *University Science Park* in Bratislava, which will have two workplaces. First workplace will deal with research in the field of information and communication technology, electrical engineering, automation and control systems, and nanoelectronics and photonics. The second one will have research oriented on modern technologies - chemistry, industrial biotechnology, the environment and the safety and reliability of buildings [14]. *University Science Park* of UK in Bratislava will operate in the field of molecular medicine, environmental medicine and biotechnology [15].

TUKE together with its partners presented the project *"University Science Park TECHNICOM for innovative applications with the support of knowledge technologies"*, whose main mission is an effective support of active development of applied R&D, innovative culture and competitiveness for concerned and customer organizations of production and services from both public and corporate environment [16]. Science Park will be focused on applied research in information and communication technology, electrical engineering, automation and control systems, mechanical engineering, civil engineering and environmental engineering. TECHNICOM is designed as an intelligent building providing space for start-ups in High-Tech formed by linking teams from universities and practice [17].

The strategic objective of the project *AgroBioTech Research Centre* in UNIAG Nitra is building a complex research, innovation and competence regional center in the field of agronomy, agroecology, biotechnology and bioenergy, which will integrate top applied research through partnerships with Constantine the Philosopher University in Nitra and the Institute of Plant Genetics and Biotechnology of Slovak Academy of Sciences in Nitra [18]. AgroBioTech will consist of three separate centers which will be based on the areas of all three partners within the project [19].

Technical University in Zvolen (TUZVO) also introduced a project of Science Park named *ENVIRO-TECH*, which will deal with complex research of forest ecosystem, research of intelligent usage of wood as the most important renewable raw material through ecological and environmental research and research in the field of environmental and innovation management [20].

UNIZA has also two projects - *University Science Park* [21], and *Research Center* [22], which will be further mentioned in the next chapter.

2.1   Case of UNIZA

The *vision* of UNIZA declared in the Long-term plan of the University of Žilina for the years 2014–2020 is: "the use and recovery of educational and scientific potential on the top European level, the broad development of international cooperation with educational and research organizations, permanent deepening of attachment to social practice" [23] and into its cross-sectional tasks were also included innovation and transfer of knowledge/technology, a technology cooperation, which includes:

– protection of intellectual property (IP),
– creating partnerships and support mechanisms for implementation of research results and innovation in practice (the creation of new business units, incubators etc.),
– applied research supported by partners from practice with direct TT.

Technology transfer at UNIZA was made primarily by enthusiastic research individuals, however most of the time they excluded university from this process. IP protection of these technologies was often lacking so it was hard to ensure that competitors would not copy the solution. UNIZA usually have not known about the transfer initiatives of individual researchers so it could not claim shares in spin-off company or on the solution.

UNIZA's Department of science and research has been responsible for technology transfer of research results. One person has been primarily responsible for the whole technology transfer process at UNIZA. However, there have been no formal rules guiding this person. UNIZA has been lacking documents, mostly directives which would determine e.g. share in spin-off company. Several reasons such as missing directives caused apathy of researchers in technology transfer. Thanks to the NITT SK project universities across Slovakia have been provided by the possibility to gain help with technology transfer for free. NITT SK project has been a big step in increasing the technology transfer awareness among researchers.

In the future UNIZA wants to possess a complex concept supporting the process of TT and KT which would involve all its departments (primarily its faculties and scientific institutes). Therefore is UNIZA realizing projects *University Science Park* (UVP) and *Research Center* (VC), which should bring especially evaluation of the university's potential. To this project is also engaged the Transport Research Institute, Inc. in Žilina (VÚD). Both projects had been preparing for nearly two years and they are mainly financed from the Operational Programme Research and Development. VC and UVP will be built on UNIZA campus [24].

There have already been some organizational units dealing with TT and KT at the University of Žilina. These include the *Institute for Competitiveness and Innovation* (ÚKaI), which main objectives are R&D in High-Tech and transfer of the latest technology, knowledge and innovation from this area in industry (designing methods, strategies, processes and technologies to improve the competitiveness of companies), as well as supporting the development of UNIZA by implementing technological, product and process innovations [25].

There has been only one technology transfer success story – Central European Institute of Technology (CEIT) which is a spin-off of UNIZA. CEIT provides solutions in various areas, e.g. product, technological and process innovation, industrial automation, material innovation and biomedical engineering [26].

Based on our analysis we have identified the following major problems related to UNIZA technology transfer activities:

- lack of department which deals with technology transfer and have experiences with it as it can be seen at any foreign university where it is usually called Center for technology transfer,
- lack of directives which determine the rules of establishing a spin-off company, shares of UNIZA in spin-off company, IP protection, etc.
- lack of success stories that would show researchers that it makes sense to deal with technology transfer,
- focus on basic research more than applied research,
- poor research infrastructure,
- lot of time spent with teaching of students resulting in lack of time for research,
- unwillingness of researchers.

These problems are not new and universities across Slovakia have been aware of them for many years, however, they are still not able to solve them. New EU projects for building science parks and research centers across Slovakia should bring help to universities with all of the mentioned issues.

What should the science park and research centre projects bring and what problems it should solve:

- creation of Centre for technology transfer not only for science park but also for university itself which should help mainly with the problem of lacking department, directives and experienced people who understand technology transfer,
- focus on applied research,
- sufficient research infrastructure by getting excellent technologies which will be procured,
- new buildings where this technology will be placed,
- new excellent researchers,
- decrease in brain drain.

Building of science parks and research centers seemed promising, however, technology transfer have not been done yet. One of the main reasons is that we do not have buildings; they are still under construction so when new technologies arrive we have no place to store them and moreover to use them.

When technologies arrive some might be already obsolete because it takes so much time to specify them when writing the project and then to procure them. Some technologies are getting obsolete so quickly because of the rapid change on the market so researchers will be not be able to come up with an unique idea and be competitive using them.

There is certain time required for researchers to learn how to use new technologies. If they get them at the end of project it might be not possible to immediately produce research results which will be then commercialized. It will take time until some success arrives.

When researchers have no technologies they are not able to do research and they are losing patience.

Moreover, the Ministry of Education, Science, Research and Sport of the Slovak Republic promised new calls for projects which will build on previous experiences and infrastructure so research will be sustainable. However, the Ministry still has not released information about new calls. Therefore many researchers are worried about their future in science parks and research centers.

3 Discussion

Concept of sustainability in socioeconomic area is nowadays well known and used. E.g. sustainability performance of companies could be evaluated [27] in order to analyze and project more efficient solutions (economical, strategical, marketing, etc.). According to Galpin and Whittington "Sustainability now appears to be the strategic imperative of the new millennium and is building momentum similar to the excellence, quality, and reengineering movements of the late 20th century" [28]. They also emphasize that sustainability could be an integral part of corporate strategy with significant impact on its effectiveness. In older work of Dyllick and Hockerts is sustainability defined as integrating element of economic, ecological and social aspects (triple-bottom line) in a corporation [29]. In all above mentioned works is the concept of sustainability oriented on organization's value creation (economic aspect), effective management of stakeholders (economic and social aspect) and on long-term sustainability of an organization in its environment (strategical aspect).

What are the main recommendations for making the technology transfer process in Slovak academic environment sustainable?

- *Partnership.* All strategies and real actions are oriented on development of long-term partnerships between crucial stakeholders [30]. This partnership must be in general beneficial for each partner; relations are based on mutual trust.
- *Management system* strategy and performance are oriented on effective cooperation creation and its sustainability [31, 32].
- *Positive externalities.* Effective cooperation based organizational forms could have significant impact (positive) on its wider socio-economic environment [33, 34].
- *Continuous Innovativeness* will ensure sustainability [33, 34]. This must be also a part of management strategy. Results of R&D activities must be sufficiently innovative in order to be successful in academic area or in commerce market.

The problems experienced at the universities across Slovakia that arose from analysis are considerably complex and therefore their solution requires comprehensive approach. We proposed a set of practical recommendations that are crucial for effective and sustainable technology transfer at universities and research institutions.

- *Willingness of researchers.* Researchers need to have motivation to conduct serious applied research.
- *Motivating directives.* University needs to prepare official formal documents supporting the knowledge transfer process, especially directives determining rules of

establishing a spin-off company by researchers, shares of university in spin-off company, etc.

- *Proper help from university side.* Universities have to make sure they have experts in various fields who can provide sufficient help to researchers when thinking about establishing spin-off company and transferring their research results into practice. These experts should be in the field of IP protection, marketing and sales, finance, law, etc.

- *Sufficient research infrastructure.* Universities should have excellent technologies thanks to the recent projects for building science parks and research centers. When these technologies are procured, researchers should be able to conduct extraordinary research.

- *Less teaching, more time for actual research.* The trend in Slovakia is increasing teaching hours per teacher while decreasing the number of teachers at faculties. This trend results into lack of time for carrying out research.

- *Focus on getting support for performing applied research.* Researchers should be focusing more on getting grants and other forms of support, e.g. sponsorships for their research. Applied research is lagging behind so strengthening the activity focusing on doing research for companies will help to bring money for supporting further research activities and ensuring sustainability in research.

- *Faster publishing of new calls for research projects by the Ministry of Education, Science, Research and Sport of the Slovak Republic.* Ministries have very important role in education. They are responsible for publishing calls for submitting projects. They need to foster the research process by being flexible and fast in publishing calls concerning education and research.

- *Improvement of procurement process which requires changes in law.* Research and technology transfer process would not be easier without encouraging responsible people to propose amendments to law.

4 Conclusions

Slovakia is one of the countries where technology transfer is very poor mostly due to the lack of knowledge and experiences with it as well as awareness about the need of intellectual property protection prior to the actual transfer and commercialization of research results.

There have been extensive debates in Slovakia during the last few years if these problems could be solved by building science parks and research centers where researchers can find the best environment for their research. However, these institutions are not enough for solving the problems we identified from our analysis. Without motivation of researchers to conduct serious applied research which would be then commercialized even the best condition would be negligible. Problems with Slovak law are also negligible. This problem is complex and requires significant changes.

This paper, therefore, investigates the current technology transfer activities at the University of Žilina in Žilina. This investigation shows that although the University of

Žilina in Žilina has a big projects for building the University Science Park and Research Centre, technology transfer activities are not yet sufficiently developed.

Based on our analysis, we proposed set of recommendations for sustainable technology transfer which require not only change at the universities but further changes in law and other related fields.

Acknowledgments. This paper is supported by the following projects: University Science Park of the University of Žilina (ITMS: 26220220184) supported by the Research and Development Operational Program funded by the European Regional Development Fund, and the Slovak scientific grant VEGA 1/0621/14 Marketing management in cooperative environment – Proposal of strategic cooperation management implementation model.

References

1. Basic concepts, tools and approaches to technology transfer in the world - surveillance study (in Slovak). http://nitt.cvtisr.sk/buxus/docs/Studia_II_o_TT_NITT_SK.pdf
2. Intellectual property and technology transfer (in Slovak). http://nptt.cvtisr.sk/buxus/docs/Dusevne_vlastnictvo_a_transfer_technologii_1.pdf
3. AUTM's About Technology Transfer. http://www.autm.net/Tech_Transfer.htm
4. Transfer of Technology. http://unctad.org/en/docs/psiteiitd28.en.pdf
5. Ho, M.H.C., et al.: A new perspective to explore the technology transfer efficiencies in US universities. J. Technol. Transf. **39**, 247–275 (2014)
6. National portal for technology transfer. Word-book (in Slovak). http://nptt.cvtisr.sk/sk/transfertechnologii/slovnik-pojmov.html?page_id=300
7. Tripsas, M., Schrader, S., Sobrero, M.: Discouraging opportunistic behavior in collaborative R&D: a new role for government. Res. Policy **24**, 367–389 (1995)
8. Soviar, J., et al.: Kooperacný manažment. University of Žilina, Žilina (2013)
9. Argote, L., Ingram, P.: Knowledge transfer: a basis for competitive advantage in firms. Organ. Behav. Hum. Decis. Process. **82**, 150–169 (2000)
10. Center of science-technical information SR. Basic information (in Slovak). http://www.cvtisr.sk/cvtisr-vedecka-kniznica/o-cvti-sr/zakladne-informacie.html?page_id=409
11. National infrastructure for supporting technology transfer in Slovakia. About the project (in Slovak). http://nitt.cvtisr.sk/uvodna-stranka/o-projekte.html?page_id=255
12. Industrial Property Office (in Slovak). http://www.patentovat.sk/upv-sr/urad-priemyselneho-vlastnictva-sr/
13. There will be eight science parks in Slovakia (in Slovak). http://www.aktuality.sk/clanok/232509/na-slovensku-vyrastie-osem-vedeckych-parkov/
14. Slovak University of Technology in Bratislava. STU proposed a project of university science park (in Slovak). http://www.stuba.sk/sk/diani-na-stu/prehlad-aktualit/stu-predlozilaprojekt-niverzitneho-vedeckeho-parku.html?page_id=6040
15. Ministry of Education, Science, Research and Sport of the Slovak Republic. The department of education has supported 8 science parks by 6 universities so far (in Slovak). https://www.minedu.sk/rezort-skolstva-doposial-podporil-8-vedeckych-parkov-pri-6-univerzitach/
16. Košice IT valley. TECHNICOM – university science park (in Slovak). http://www.kosiceitvalley.sk/sk/technicom-univerzitny-vedecky-park

17. Technical university of Košice builds a science park for nearly 42 million Euro (in Slovak). http://www.teraz.sk/ekonomika/tu-kosice-buduje-vedecky-park-technicom/99829-clanok. html

18. UNIAG. Building of research centre "AgroBioTech" (in Slovak). http://agrobiotech.uniag. sk/sk/

19. NITRA: Research centre AgroBioTech joins scientific authorities (in Slovak). http://www. piestanskydennik.sk/sita-detail/?tx_kiossita_pi1%5Bdetail%5D=173193

20. TT bulletin. NITT SK 2014 conference – Technology transfer in Slovakia and abroad (in Slovak). http://ttb.cvtisr.sk/bulletiny-2014/4-2014/konferencia-nitt-sk-2014-transfer-technologii-naslovensku-a-v-zahranici.html?page_id=883

21. University Science Park. http://uvp.uniza.sk/en/

22. Research Centre. http://vyskumnecentrum.sk/en/o_nas

23. The University of Žilina. Long-term plan of the University of Žilina for the years 2014–2020. https://www.uniza.sk/document/DZ_2014_2020_7_1_2014.pdf

24. There will be a science park and a research centre near Žilina (in Slovak). http://www.svet-it. sk/2013/05/pri-ziline-vyrastie-vedecky-park-a-vyskumny-ustav/

25. Institute of Competitiveness and Innovations. http://ukai.uniza.sk/o_nas

26. CEIT Group. http://www.ceitgroup.eu/index.php/en

27. Delai, I., Takahashi, S.: Sustainability measurement system: a reference model proposal. Soc. Responsib. J. 7, 438–471 (2011)

28. Galpin, T., Whittington, J.L.: Sustainability leadership: from strategy to results. J. Bus. Strategy 33, 40–48 (2012)

29. Dyllick, T., Hockerts, K.: Beyond the business case for corporate sustainability. Bus. Strategy Environ. 11, 130–141 (2002)

30. Robbins, P.S., Coulter, M.: Management. Grada, Prague (2004)

31. Lafleur, M.: A model for cooperative challenges. In: Cooperative Grocer Network, no. 116 (2005)

32. Vodák, J., Soviar, J., Lendel, V.: The evaluation system proposal of the businesses preparedness for cooperative management implementation. Bus. Theory Pract. 14, 315–322 (2013)

33. Porter, E.M.: Clusters and the new economics of competition. Harv. Bus. Rev. 76, 25–26 (1998)

34. Porter, E.M.: On Competition. Harvard Business School, Boston (1998)

Marketing Communications and Its Sustainable Influence on Different Generations

Michal Varmus[⊠] and Milan Kubina

Faculty of Management Science and Informatics, University of Zilina,
Univerzitná 8215/1, 01026 Žilina, Slovakia
{michal.varmus,milan.kubina}@fri.uniza.sk

Abstract. Trends in marketing communication are time to time changed due to new technologies, social trends and other aspects. Internet and social media are used in marketing communication couple of years and especially they are focused to younger customers. On the other hand recently is growing up group of older customers who are interest in internet buying and as well as in taking information from websites. This paper deals with perception of marketing communications by different generations of customers. On based of the conducted research and review of literature is shown how different generations of customers perceive marketing communication, especially traditional channels and tools versus internet and social media. During the research were used these methods: content analysis, documents study, comparative analysis, process analysis, statistic analysis, empirical research and more. One of the results of the paper is that internet is very crucial in all generations although their loyalty is different.

Keywords: Marketing communications · Generation · Social media · Customer behaviour · Loyalty

1 Introduction

Use and perceptions of marketing communication mix, as was defined a few years ago has nowadays significantly changed. It is no longer appropriate to divide the different communication tools to "traditional" and "non-traditional", mainly due to the fact that originally named the "non-traditional" are more frequency and effective in business practice. To some extent they integrated original instruments of "traditional" communication mix and in today's fast times, full of information and information technology they have significantly higher probability of effective targeting to selected customer segments.

Integrated marketing communication is no longer just an advantage; it is a necessity if company or other organizations want to be successful. Segmentation that is required for correct targeting of campaigns should be treated in great detail, and many companies and organizations use micro segmentation to utilize its resources [21]. The situation today is complicated by the highly dynamic behaviour of customers that is often subject to a change of trend. The new challenge for market is also the gradual formation of a strong group of customers "seniors", which is still significantly

© ICST Institute for Computer Sciences, Social Informatics and Telecommunications Engineering 2016
A. Leon-Garcia et al. (Eds.): Smart City 2015, LNICST 166, pp. 681–691, 2016.
DOI: 10.1007/978-3-319-33681-7_59

undervalued by individual companies, despite the fact that a large group of these customers is not prevent to new consumer trends. On the other hand, there is a segment juniors who still have great influence on customer behavior and their vicinity. All this relates mainly with coming and continuous development of information technologies.

Use of modern information and communication technologies is no longer the domain currently only companies in business sector. The survey of Statistical Office of the Slovak Republic for 2012 shows that almost 80 % of households own a computer and 76 % of households in Slovakia also have access to the Internet and can use its services [19].

Another important factor that affects the communication mix is mobile communication, and in particular the development and use of mobile Internet using by "smart" phones, which also significantly changes the view on the communication mix. Penetration of mobile services in Slovakia have already exceeded 100 % and more and more people are using cell phone just for making calls but also for mobile data services and applications that recently achieved a significant development with the coming of LTE (Long Term Evolution) technology. LTE technology is considered as a modern technology for mobile internet access. Due to achieve the high speed and low delay (latency) LTE network enabling e.g. smooth video transmission in real time, online transmission of content in high quality HD and 3D video content.

Significant phenomenon becomes social networks particularly for the younger generation. There are several social networking sites such as Facebook, Google+, LinkedIn or Twitter that are variously designed respectively, focuses on a different type of content and services. Companies, increasingly in communication with customers also focus on the use of these networks. However the challenge remains to make communication mix and target the desired segment and achieve the desired effect.

1.1 Marketing Communication and Social Media

An interesting topic of the marketing communication is social networks and their impact on customer behaviour. Social Networking Sites are virtual communities where users can create individual public profiles, interact with real-life friends, and meet other people based on shared interests. They are seen as a 'global consumer phenomenon' with an exponential rise in usage within the last few years [11]. Social media marketing is different than traditional methods of marketing; therefore, it requires special attention and strategy building to achieve brand image and loyalty. Social media marketing is related to the consumers [8]. Each application consists of a social network, a set of socially relevant nodes connected by one or more relations [12]. Style of communication and orientation of the people to information and knowledge become one of the dynamically changing areas in recent years. Mainly due to the development of ICT reached various social areas its "virtual" form that resulted to creation of different social networks (Facebook, Google+, Twiter...). From a consumer's perspective, the use of information communication technologies offers a number of benefits, including efficiency, convenience, richer and participative information, a broader selection of products, competitive pricing, cost reduction, and product diversity [4].

The nature and distribution of these connections may vary from web site to web site. Social networks have a significant impact on the possible change in customer behaviour. They give unlimited space for discussion and sharing of customer experience. They also offer scope for rapid dissemination of new special offers.

Scott [15] has developed a number of recommendations as to extract the maximum from the social network for marketing:

- To reach specific audiences. Create the page to hit the audience that the organization needs. It is usually better to reach niche market.
- Being thought leaders. Offer interesting and valuable information that people are looking for. It is always better to show the market advantages of company, or solve customer problems as celebrate own product.
- Be authentic and transparent. Do not attempt to imitate anyone. Do not use dirty practices, because if it breaks, irreparably undermine the reputation of the company.
- Create many links. Make a link to own website and blog as well as on other pages within the industry and network. Everybody loves links - links make the web site.
- Encourage people to contact the organization. Make it so that an organization can be easy to find on the web and it is necessary to respond to e-mails from fans.
- To participate. Create groups and take part in internet discussions. Become the online leader and organizer.
- People have to easily find the organization. The page must be tagged.
- Experiment. Social sites are perfect and there are plenty of opportunities to try new things.

Social Media move the internet a step further. And although it is not known where they lead, one thing is certain, that the marketing and PR on the Web will continue to develop and to take a dramatic turn.

Donn L. Hoffman and Tom Novak of the University of California developed within social media 4Cs model based on higher order objectives [16]:

- Connection,
- Create,
- Consume,
- Control.

Thus social media becomes a hub for market intelligence as marketers begin to understand consumer's purchasing behaviour and gain insight as to why consumers feel the way that they do about certain brands [3]. These opportunities allow the marketer to create dialogue with the consumer, fine tune the marketing message and maintain the brand's presence in online market places [7]. However, as stated Urgeman and Myslivcová [18], it must be borne in mind that currently, social media are already the essential part of companies' communication mix. However, it is necessary to realize that they represent only a part of the modern communication. Companies must neither underestimate, nor overestimate this communication channel. However, if the company wants to be successful, it should include social media in its regular communication portfolio where they belong.

1.2   Loyalty and Customer Behaviour

There are many definitions of loyalty. Aaker [1] defines brand loyalty as the attachment that a customer has to a brand. Grembler and Brown [9] describe different levels of loyalty. Behavioural loyalty is linked to consumer behaviour in the marketplace that can be indicated by number of repeated purchases [10] or commitment to rebuy the brand as a primary choice [13, 14]. Cognitive loyalty which means that a brand comes up first in a consumers' mind, when the need to make a purchase decision arises, that is the consumers' first [3]. According Beyond Philosophy, however, few people realized that loyalty runs hand in hand with emotion. Customer loyalty is the result of consistent positive emotional experience, physical attributes based on the satisfaction and perceived value of experience, which includes product or service [17].

When is building customer loyalty it is about the management of the customer experience that combines physical, emotional experience and value elements into one cohesive experience. Following steps can form customer loyalty:

- Maintaining contact with customers via e-mail marketing, cards and so on.
- Good care of own company's team, so the team will then take good care of their customers.
- To show that the company depends on customers and remember what they like and dislike.
- Acknowledge that they preferred the company against of the competition.
- To figure out how to make customers more successful, happier and more enjoyable.

Through social networks such as Facebook organizations from all sectors collect data on the basis of new connections with their customers. Since customers regularly update their activities, status and life events, such companies are able to respond and adapt their marketing activities aimed at their clients and loyal customers, whether special offers or discounts.

2   Conducted Research

To better understand how customers' perception marketing communications in Slovakia was conducted survey in the form of questionnaires, which included 308 respondents. The survey was conducted in January and February 2014.

2.1   Methodology

In terms of age structure, respondents were divided into three groups: under 25, then from 26 to 50 years and the last group consists of respondents aged over 51 years. The percentage distribution can be seen in the Fig. 1.

From the all respondents was 41 % under the age of 25 years, 45 % of respondents were aged from 26 to 50 years and 14 % of respondents were aged over 51 years. Both genders were represented in like manner. 49 % of women and 51 % of men represented group under 25 years old. 41 % of women and 59 % of men represented category from 26 to 50 years. Ages over 51 years constitutes group of 43 % of women and 57 % of men.

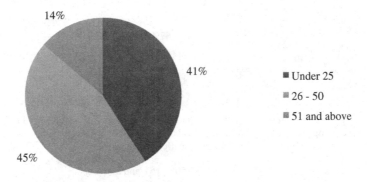

Fig. 1. Age structure of respondents (Color figure online)

2.2 Perceptions of Selected Tools and Channels that Are Using in Marketing Communication

One of the key tasks of the survey was to identify communication tools and channels that the segments often meet. Then which are most credible and which have the greatest influence on shopping behaviour of selected segments.

The survey focused primarily on the following communication tools and channels: advertising on TV, radio advertising, print media, catalogues, outdoor advertising, billboards, leaflets, internet, online advertising, mobile advertising and personal selling, respectively contact face to face.

Within the question "What kind of forms of marketing communication you are experiencing and how often?" the respondents could comment on a number of options based on a scale from "often encounter" to "not at all have not met." Some respondents used the option "do not know" responses.

On the Fig. 2 it can be seen that respondents under the age of 25 years reported that they often meet with internet, resp. online advertising and the advertising on TV. Group of 26–50 years reported very similar, just in the first place it is advertising on TV and then online advertising. Age group 51 and over indicated that they often meet with advertising on TV and with online and outdoor advertising, respectively with leaflets.

One thing is observation of marketing tools and second thing is a trust. We discovered that customers do not trust advertising, as we know it now. All age groups had the negative attitude to all mentioned marketing tools. This is a new trend that brings new challenges to marketers.

2.3 Social Media and Blogs

As was mentioned the social media have played very important role in marketing strategy couple of years. Their influence is bigger and bigger. Most of the marketers like it and use it in their campaigns, especially focused on young customers. In the research we were looking for the opinions of customers on this question.

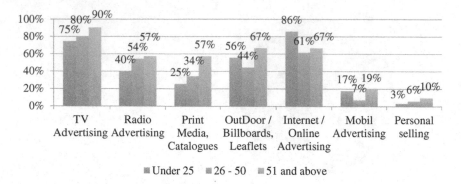

Fig. 2. Most often observed forms of marketing communication (Color figure online)

When we asked if they think that social networks (Facebook, twitter…) play an important role in online marketing, most of the customers confirmed that yes. The results can be seen on Fig. 3.

Of course the most of customers under 25 (63 %) confirmed that social media have important role for sure. But on other hand 43 % of respondents in years 50 and above confirmed that social media probably have important role and 29 % of them confirmed that social media are definitely important.

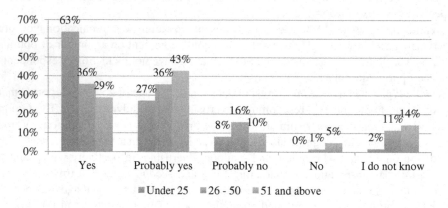

Fig. 3. Importance of social media (Color figure online)

Discussion forums have already an irreplaceable role in online marketing. As can be seen on Fig. 4. Most of the respondents check the discussion forums before they buy something. They are looking for evaluation of products as well. What is surprise, that 71 % of respondents in age 51 and above check that forums. This is something what give another view on online marketing and power of users on internet.

One thing is checking but what is very important is influence of forums. One of the interesting surprise of survey (as is shown on Fig. 5) is that most of the respondents confirmed that they are very influenced by forums (32 % of respondents under 25,

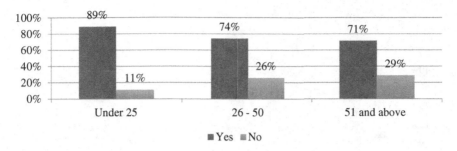

Fig. 4. Checking of discussion forums before buying (Color figure online)

13.46 % of respondents between age 26 and 50, and 6.67 % of respondents in age 51 and above), or probably influenced (almost 59 % of respondents under 25, 84.62 % of respondents between age 26 and 50, and 80 % of respondents in age 51 and above).

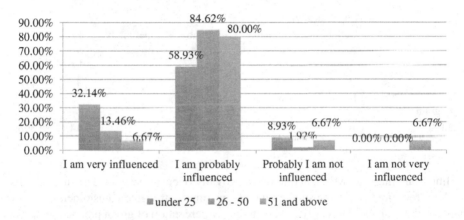

Fig. 5. Influence of discussion forums on buying (Color figure online)

2.4 Loyalty and Change of Purchase

Loyalty is one of the most important things in relationship with customers. Very often happens that both sites (customers vs. seller) understand loyalty by different ways. When were responded asked if they are loyal most of them confirmed that they are (Fig. 6). On the other hand 29 % of respondents under age 25 confirmed, that they are not probably loyal, but only 5 % of respondents under in age 51 and above said that are probably not loyal. It was confirmed, that younger people are more flexible in question of change of customer behaviour.

Loyalty programs are very often joined with loyalty of customers. In Table 1 is confrontation of answers of all respondents in questions if they are loyal and if they are joined in loyalty program. The result as can be seen is very consistent. E.g. 132 respondents who said that are probably loyal confirmed that they are join in loyalty program, against 46 of probably loyal respondents who are not in loyalty program.

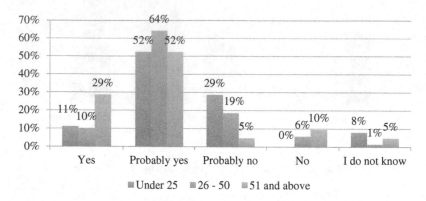

Fig. 6. Loyalty of customers (Color figure online)

Table 1. Loyalty vs. loyalty program

		Loyal customer					Total
		Definitely yes	Probably yes	Probably no	Definitely no	I do not know	
Involved in program	Yes	30	132	40	6	4	212
	No	10	46	24	6	10	96
Total		**40**	**178**	**64**	**12**	**14**	**308**

Important message what can improve the loyalty of customers is the main idea of the hotel or restaurant. Very strong group of customers are green customers. As was mentioned Baksi and Parida [2] in their study. As perception of green practices emerged as a potential factor to perceive green image, employees of firms pursuing eco-friendly marketing should initiate communication with the consumers explaining the green initiatives adopted by them and stating what triggered them to adopt such strategy.

Although the customers think that they are loyal there is still potential to change it. Each customer have different preferences on basis of which they make decisions when buying products and a different degree of sensitivity to changes in purchasing behaviour. Marketing communication significantly affects these preferences. During the survey were respondents asked to comment how much selected factors affect their purchasing.

All customers as can be seen on Fig. 7 are mostly influenced by these factors:

– Current price,
– Brand,
– References from friend,
– References in the discussions forums.

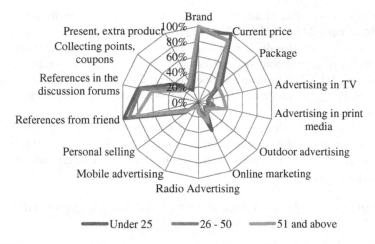

Fig. 7. Influence of selected tools and channels on buying (Color figure online)

The preferences are very similar except references, when 62 % consumers from the group 51 and above confirmed that they are influenced by references in the discussion forums. In contrast to this almost 80 % from other groups confirmed that are influenced by references in the discussion forums. On the other hand 62 % is very high number in group 51 and above, when in last time they were pointed as people who do not know use internet. It is also big challenge for companies.

3 Conclusions and Recommendations

With the coming of new information and communication technologies are changing the principles of marketing communications, as well as the preferences of individual customers. Based on a carried out survey, we can say that all generations to some extent are subject to these changes and adapt their behaviour.

On base the research can be understood that very traditional communication tools such as advertising are still very visible, but they have lower power and impact on customer behaviour. It does not mean that they lost importance in communication mix of any company. Although nowadays the social media are crucial in many communication campaigns the communication strategy has to be well balanced.

As was mentioned in the paper all ages are aware that the online environment plays an important role in the marketing communication, but people over age 51 yet does not capture the trend in the use of social networks.

People want to be loyal, but on other hand they allow to change their attitude when they are confronted mainly with better price or references from friends or in discussion forums. A long time existed presumption that older customers are very loyal and they do not want to change their customer behavior. After conducted survey it is possible say that older people are more loyal than younger but it is not definitely and older people like the change if it brings benefits. According to survey as the biggest motivation to change product is to taste something new.

It is clear that price had power in all times, but references from discussion forums are something new. Mainly if is talked about older generation. It is necessary that company create to space for discussion and recommendations from customers. It does not really matter if the company uses social networks like Facebook or they use forum in own web site. What is important and does matter, that company have all discussions under control. It is great space for feedback and the hotels or organizations have time and mainly spaces for react.

In this area exist still a lot of questions and the answers for them should be sought in next survey. It would be necessary find out other differences and dependencies in each generation for the needs make micro segmentation and better focus to smaller groups of customers.

Acknowledgments. This paper was supported by the Slovak scientific grants VEGA 1/0621/14, VEGA 1/0363/14 and KEGA 035ŽU-4/2013.

References

1. Aaker, D.: Managing Brand Equity: Capitalizing on the Value of a Brand Name. Free Press, New York (1991)
2. Baksi, A.K., Parida, B.B.: Impact of green marketing on perceived image and behavioural intentions of consumers: empirical evidence from restaurant practices. Tour. Int. Multi. J. Tour. **8**, 233–257 (2013)
3. Balakrishnan, B.K., Dahnil, M.I., Yi, W.J.: The impact of social media marketing medium toward purchase intention and brand loyalty among generation Y. Procedia – Soc. Behav. Sci. **148**, 177–185 (2014)
4. Bayo-Moriones, A., Lera-Lopez, F.: A firm-level analysis of determinants of ICT adoption in Spain. Technovation **27**, 352–366 (2007)
5. Beer, D.: Social network(ing) sites...revisiting the story so far: a response to danah boyd & Nicole Ellison. J. Comuput. Mediat. Commun. **2**, 516–529 (2008)
6. Erdogmus, I.E., Cicek, M.: The impact of social media marketing on brand loyalty. Procedia – Soc. Behav. Sci. **58**, 1353–1360 (2012)
7. Evans, D., McKee, J.: Social Media Marketing: The Next Generation of Business Engagement. Wiley, Indiana (2010)
8. Gordhamer, S.: 4 Ways social media is changing business. http://Mashable.com/2009/09/22Social-Media-Business/
9. Gremler, D., Brown, S.W.: The loyalty ripple effect: appreciating the full value of customers. Int. J. Serv. Ind. Manag. **10**, 271–293 (1996)
10. Keller, K.L.: Strategic Brand Management: Building, Measuring and Managing Brand Equity. Prentice Hall, New Jersey (1998)
11. Kuss, D.J., Griffiths, M.D.: Online social networking and addiction - a review of the psychological literature. Int. J. Environ. Res. Public Health **8**, 3528–3552 (2011)
12. Marin, A., Wellman, B.: Social network analysis: an introduction. In: Scott, J., Carrington, P.J. (eds.) The SAGE Handbook of Social Network Analysis, pp. 11–25. Sage, London (2011)
13. Oliver, R.L., Rust, R.T., Varki, S.: Customer delight: foundations, findings, and managerial insight. J. Retail. **73**, 311–336 (1997)

14. Oliver, R.L.: Whence consumer loyalty? J. Mark. **63**, 33–44 (1999)
15. Scott, D.M.: Nové pravidla marketingu a PR. Eastone Books, Bratislava (2010)
16. Solomon, M.R.: Consumer Behavior, Buying, Having, and Being. Pearson Education, Harlow (2013)
17. Understanding the true definition of customer loyalty. http://www.beyondphilosophy.com/customer-experience/customer-loyalty/
18. Urgeman, O., Myslivcová, S.: Model of communication usable for small and medium-sized companies for the consumer communication in social media. E+M Ekon. Manag. = Econ. Manag. **17**, 167–184 (2014)
19. SOSR. Using of information and communication technologies in the SR. http://portal.statistics.sk/files/Sekcie/sek_500/doprava-IKT/publikacia_ikt_sr_2012.pdf
20. Velšič, M.: Sociálne siete na Slovensku. http://www.ivo.sk/buxus/docs//publikacie/subory/Socialne_siete_SR.pdf
21. Vodák, J., Soviar, J., Lendel, V.: The evaluation system proposal of the businesses preparedness for cooperative management implementation. Bus. Theory Pract. **14**, 315–322 (2013)

Sustainable E-marketing of Selected Tourism Subjects from the Mediterranean Through Active Online Reputation Management

František Pollák[1]([✉]), Peter Dorčák[2], Nikola Račeta[3],
and Nella Svetozarovová[4]

[1] Faculty of Management, Department of Marketing and International Trade,
University of Prešov in Prešov, Konštantínova 16, 080 01 Prešov, Slovakia
frank.pollak@acuityeng.com
[2] Faculty of Business Management, University of Economics in Bratislava,
Dolnozemská cesta 1, 852 35 Bratislava, Slovakia
[3] Milenij hoteli d.o.o., Viktora Cara Emina 6, 51410 Opatija, Croatia
[4] Department of Management, Faculty of Management, University of Prešov
in Prešov, Konštantínova 16, 080 01 Prešov, Slovakia

Abstract. The paper discusses the issue of sustainable e-marketing of the selected tourism subjects from Mediterranean through active online reputation management, more specifically it presents the available ways and methods of measuring the phenomenon of online reputation of selected entities operating in the tourism sector on selected market. A thorough multifactor analysis of reputation in the virtual world of the Internet was conducted on a specific sample of entities - all hotels operating in a selected local Mediterranean destination. Taking into account all the relevant factors - entities ratings on major internet sites such as Booking, TripAdvisor a Facebook, these ratings are normalized and then compared against the widespread sentiment analysis. Using a careful statistical testing, relationships between factors are then examined in order to identify and describe basic facts affecting online reputation of selected entities in the hyper competitive market environment of the Internet.

Keywords: Sustainable e-marketing · Online reputation · Reputator · Internet · Destinations

1 Introduction

Reputation is a concept commonly used in marketing management and it generally means an overall presence on the market. From the point of view of Internet we can compare it to leaving footprints. All activities are interconnected and complement one another [1]. Each institution has a reputation or online reputation, whether they want it, or not; the reputation does exist [2]. If an entrepreneurs running their own businesses (or managing an institutions), they should not leave their reputation to chance. It is their ultimate responsibility. Company's reputation is considered to be very valuable asset. As George Washington once said "With a reputation you can do anything without one, nothing" [3]. However, if we consider corporate reputation, its definition is a bit

© ICST Institute for Computer Sciences, Social Informatics and Telecommunications Engineering 2016
A. Leon-Garcia et al. (Eds.): Smart City 2015, LNICST 166, pp. 692–703, 2016.
DOI: 10.1007/978-3-319-33681-7_60

complicated [4]. Balmer and Greyser [5] characterize corporate reputation as such which is created over time based on what the organization did and how it behaved. Company's or corporate reputation only reflects relative standing of the company, both internally with its employees and externally with other stakeholders, in both its competitive and institutional environments. Highhouse defines corporate reputation as a global, stable over time, evaluative judgement about a company that is shared by multiple constituencies [6]. It is a pure reaction of customers, investors, employees and other stakeholders. It is a collective judgement of individual impressions [7].

1.1   The Issue of Reputation in the Context of Trust

Trust fulfils every organisation in a million of different ways. No institution can function without it. Trust is a strong belief that we can rely on someone [8]. Shaw offers alternative definition; he defines the concept of trust as a belief that those on whom we depend will meet our expectations of them [9]. These expectations depend on our critical judgement of other person's responsibility to meet our needs. Generally accepted definition of trust is still missing despite comprehensive studies of philosophers, sociologists and psychologists [10]. It is easier to identify individual features of trust than to determine exactly what it means. We agree, that trust (or symmetrically, distrust) is a particular level of the subjective probability with which an agent assesses that another agent or group of agents will perform a particular action, both before he can monitor such action (or independently of his capacity ever to be able to monitor it) and in a context in which it affects his own action [11] An agent is generally an individual or a thing (entity) which affects the environment or other agents and has characteristic and its own targets which it strives to achieve. The contextuality of trust means that the trust of entity "A" towards entity "B" is always dependent on certain context "C". We'd like to point out the work of Jøsang et al. [12] who deals with "the issue of trust" (in terms of creating trust, establishing credibility and making decisions on the basis of credibility). Trust is an oriented relationship between two parties called the subject and the object. The term oriented is used in the sense of clear distinction of resources (subject) and goals (object) of the relationship. The authors further define two types of trust: Context-independent (reliability trust) - where trust is the subjective probability by which an individual "A" expects that another individual "B" performs a given action on which its welfare depends; and Context-dependent (decision-trust) - Trust is the extent to which one party is willing to depend on something or somebody in a given situation with a feeling of relative security, even though negative consequences are possible.

1.2   Classification of Models Based on Trust and Reputation

Sabater and Sierra in their work Review on Computational Trust and Reputation Models [13] have specified classifications which focus on major models and try to find common features based on which individual classification methods and their categories are designed. Basic classification criterion is the so called model type.

Model type means whether the model works with trust or a reputation.

- models of trust – work only with trust,
- models of reputation – work only with reputation,
- hybrid models – work both with trust and reputation.

According to these authors, models can be classified on the basis of determining the origin of information (knowledge) which is used for the evaluation of reputation, as well as confidence. These include: direct experience, hearsay information, sociological knowledge and prejudice.

1.3   From the Image to the Reputation

Companies and organizations in common have invested large amounts of financial resources and hired agencies and marketing professionals to prepare communication campaigns to support such brand image that would create an incentive for the customers to make purchases [14]. Companies prefer to focus primarily on the image and leave the reputation behind [15]. Image is not a guarantee of positive comments and recommendations. These will only be achieved due to good reputation [14]. In other words, the foundation of modern marketing is not the image which the organization strives to create, but the reputation which it has actually established. As regards the image and reputation, Bennet and Kottasz point out time dimension (time of creation) as the main characteristics which distinguish these two constructs. In other words, organization's image can be created in a short time. Reputation is generated in a longer time frame, and therefore cannot be changed or redirected as quickly as the image [15]. Such an approach is also supported by Jackson [16] who argue that the time of establishment or creation is one of the main differences between the image (short time of creation) and reputation (long time of creation). Fill [17] perceives reputation as wider set of images. He is also of the opinion that changing reputation is more time consuming and difficult while image can be influenced much faster. Therefore, it may be said that reputation and image are not synonymous, as some authors point out, yet they are closely related and interdependent elements. Reputation of any organisation is composed of three forms, i.e. primary, secondary and cyclic. Fombrun and Foss [18] defined reputation as collective assessment of the organization's ability to provide valuable product, service or other value to a group of customers. They have developed a scale that measures corporate reputation, which they call corporate reputation quotient (RQ). RQ is a complex method of measuring corporate reputation [19]. The building of corporate reputation has been primarily attributed to the area of marketing and communication. Nowadays the corporate reputation has been integrated into human resource management and corporate strategy. Reputation is communicated to the public by the organisation's managers [20]. It is generally accepted that reputation begins from the inside out. It is good if the organisation takes care of its reputation, and they emphasized the following factors [18]:

- The Principle of Distinctiveness - Strong reputations result when organizations own a distinctive position in the minds of customers.

- The Principle of Focus - Strong reputations result when organizations focus their actions and communications around a single core theme.
- The Principle of Consistency - Strong reputations result when organizations are consistent in their actions and communications with internal, as well as external environment.
- The Principle of Identity - Strong reputations result when organizations act in ways that are consistent with espoused principles of identity. The main task is that the organizations are perceived as real by its customers and the public.
- The Principle of Transparency - Strong reputations result when organizations are transparent in the way they conduct their affairs. In particular, organizations should be perceived as open and honest in their business activities. Transparency requires communication - a lot of it.

1.4   Reputation in Online Environment

Walsh and Beatty argues that reputation in life and business is everything [19]. It means that reputation is very fragile and one mistake may sometimes cause irreversible damage. This is especially true in the digital world, where radical transparency and demanding customers have the greatest power. If the Internet offers consumers a new way to share information about companies and brands, then it also allows the companies to control information about them [1]. Consumers are able to obtain information on potential suppliers and products, but they can also create new content on the Internet which may affect the perception of other consumers and stakeholders of the respective organization. Negative comments on the Internet can quickly and seriously damage the image and reputation of the brand [21]. eWOM (electronic word of mouth) is an important part of online reputation - this form of communication may be defined as any positive or negative statement made by potential, actual or former customers about a product or organization via the Internet [22]. Loayza [23] presents basic principles of online reputation management which he divides into various segments such as Quick Fix, Long-Lasting, Content Driven and Relationship Driven.

2   Aims and Methods

The paper presents partial results of a complex research of the issue of online reputation, more specifically the ways and methods of its measurements in selected entities operating in the tourism sector. The main objective of the paper is to present options for measuring online reputation of selected entities operating in the tourism sector with an aim to increase their competitiveness through a better understanding of the basic determinants of effective management of online reputation. Based on the current state of the issue theoretical knowledge and bases were accumulated, that provide knowledge base for the subsequent empirical research.

A thorough multifactor analysis of reputation in the virtual world of the Internet was conducted on a specific sample of entities – All hotels operating in a selected local destination (overall 31 hotels). Taking into account all the relevant factors - entities ratings on major internet sites such as Booking, TripAdvisor a Facebook, these ratings are normalized (recalculated to percentages) and then compared against the advanced sentiment analysis (ASA), which provides a relevant perspective on a selected entity through the eyes of a model customer - Internet user. For the purposes of better understanding of relations affecting the reputation of selected entities on the Internet from the perspective of their potential, as well as existing customers, methodology of advanced sentiment analysis is presented as default. In essence, it is a thorough analysis of positions and nature of individual search results of a given entity according to its usual name mediated by the Google search engine. Based on the position in the search these results are awarded points in accordance with a preset matrix (Table 1):

Table 1. Sentiment individual results/position of results [24].

Sentiment/Position of the result	1	2	3	4	5	6	7	8	9	10
Positive sentiment (+)	20	19	18	17	16	15	14	13	12	11
Custom web site of the organization (x)	10	9	8	7	6	5	4	3	2	1
Neutral sentiment ($\pm$)	2	2	2	2	2	2	2	2	2	2
Negative sentiment (−)	−20	−19	−18	−17	−16	−15	−14	−13	−12	−11

A summary of all the results and the positions represents the score of online reputation of the particular entity/subject. As a part of advanced sentiment analysis usual subject name is parallelly testes using the same methodology, where the name is supplemented by the first and most important keyword, in this case "accommodation" and then by the second keyword - "services". The scores are then added up. Compared to the theoretically highest achievable score the total strength of entity's online reputation by advanced sentiment analysis - ASA score is calculated and provided in percentage.[1]

Relations among factors (online reputation score based on the advanced sentiment analysis compared to the indices of reputation offered by the main Internet players, such as Booking, TripAdvisor a Facebook provide as a part of their ratings) were then examined in thorough statistical testing using non-parametrical methods, such as Kendall rank coefficient, or Kruskal–Wallis one-way analysis of variance, in order to identify and describe basic facts affecting online reputation of selected entities in the hypercompetitive market environment of the Internet.

---

[1] For better clarity the methodology is supplemented by the parameter of percentage evaluation of the score relative to the maximum possible number of points obtained within the advanced analysis of sentiment (maximum possible number of points = 465, 1p = 0.215 %).

3 Results and Discussion

Each of the set of selected entities, in this case, all the hotels in the Mediterranean destination of Opatija (located 10 km west from Rijeka, in the Primorje-Gorski Kotar County), try to shape their reputation both within real and virtual world through their management. For the purposes of our research, we focused on the virtual world of the Internet.

3.1 Overview Table of Partial Score

Using the advanced sentiment analysis (ASA), we calculated partial score presenting the power of online reputation of entities based on the nature of the first 10 Google search results. Google and its search results are, however, only one of many ways in which potential customers can access relevant information.

Considering the previous research in the field of tourism, we identified the following other determinants of online reputation (reputators) of tourism entities, in particular:

- ratings from Booking.com,
- ratings from Facebook,
- ratings from Google,
- a ratings from Trip Advisor.

Each of these reputators has its own system which determines the overall score. Booking rates subjects on a scale of 1–10, Google, Facebook and Trip Advisor on a scale of 1–5. For the purposes of further analysis scores of partial reputators were unified and converted into a percentage. Before we analyse the results of statistical testing, based on which we compiled a general formula to calculate total (overall) online reputation of a tourism entity (TOR), it is necessary to expound the specific values and partial score for the analysed subjects through the overview table.

The following table presents partial results - measured values of individual determinants/score of partial reputators of online reputation/as well as score of total (overall) online reputation (Table 2):

Table 2. Overall (total) online reputation.

Rank	Common name of an entity	ASA score (%)	Booking rating (%)	Facebook rating (%)	Google rating (%)	Trip Advisor rating (%)	Number of pages indexed by Google*	TOR** (%)
1.	Hotel Navis	92.5	91	100	0	100	14300	95.9
2.	Hotel Miramar	83.0	0	98	0	100	2340000	93.7
3.	Hotel Royal	82.8	94	100	0	90	13500000	91.7
4.	Hotel Villa Kapetanovic	84.5	89	92	94	90	34200	89.9
5.	Hotel Bevanda	76.1	95	92	0	90	48700	88.3
6.	Hotel Bristol	89.2	88	90	92	80	5 870 000	87.8

(Continued)

Table 2. (*Continued*)

Rank	Common name of an entity	ASA score (%)	Booking rating (%)	Facebook rating (%)	Google rating (%)	Trip Advisor rating (%)	Number of pages indexed by Google*	TOR** (%)
7.	Remisens Premium Hotel Ambasador	84.9	91	92	88	80	69200	87.2
8.	Design Hotel Astoria	91.4	87	88	0	80	187000	86.6
9.	Hotel W.A. Mozart	93.5	82	0	90	80	19800	86.4
10.	Hotel Villa Ariston	80.6	88	0	0	90	60200	86.2
11.	Remisens Premium Villa Ambasador	89.2	89	0	0	80	29900	86.1
12.	Remisens Premium Hotel Kvarner	82.8	91	100	0	70	47200	86.0
13.	Hotel Milenij	80.6	91	90	0	80	88100	85.4
14.	Hotel Agava	80.6	88	92	0	80	62000	85.2
15.	Hotel Continental	78.5	86	100	80	80	4850000	84.9
16.	Hotel Savoy	89.2	88	82	0	80	2780000	84.8
17.	Hotel Sveti Jakov	78.5	90	80	0	90	13100	84.6
18.	Grand Hotel Opatijska Cvijeta	80.6	86	90	80	80	28100	83.3
19.	Hotel Galeb	87.0	83	80	0	80	39400	82.5
20.	Villa Palme	82.8	82	84	0	80	36900	82.2
21.	Remisens Premium Villa Amalia	87.0	87	0	0	70	22600	81.3
22.	Remisens Hotel Admiral	87.0	82	86	78	70	39200	80.6
23.	Grand Hotel Adriatic	76.3	78	86	86	70	213000	79.3
24.	Smart Selection Hotel Imperial	89.0	78	80	0	70	10700	79.3
25.	Smart Selection Hotel Palace Bellevue	85.1	78	0	82	70	15400	78.8
26.	Remisens Hotel Kristal	78.7	80	82	82	70	46300	78.5
27.	Smart Selection Hotel Belvedere	88.4	73	80	0	60	11300	75.4
28.	Hotel Opatija	81.3	71	80	74	60	149000	73.3
29.	Smart Selection Hotel Residenz	82.1	71	0	0	60	4830	71.0
30.	Smart Selection Hotel Istra	77.2	68	0	72	60	13100	69.3
31.	Villa Dubrava	73.7	0	0	0	50	20000	61.9

* Absolute number of Google Indexed Pages containing a commonly used name of the given entity as a keyword; for greater relevance, quotation marks were added around the commonly used name before search.
**Total online reputation (TOR) calculation methodology is presented in the following subchapter.

3.2   Calculation Methodology of Overall Score of Online Reputation

Partial scores of entities from individual reputators were statistically tested in order to determine whether on the chosen significance level there is a statistically significant correlation between scores of entities achieved with various reputators and score achieved through advanced sentiment analysis. Last but not least variables such as the score achieved through the advanced sentiment analysis and the absolute number of pages indexed by Google containing a generally used the name of an entity as the key word were statistically tested. Regarding the link between scores of entities achieved through different reputators and scores achieved through advanced sentiment analysis, statistical testing did not confirm any link between variables on the significance level we selected (Tables 3, 4 and 5).

Table 3. Link between ASA and Booking.

Variables	Kendall tau, level of significance: $p < 0.05$			
	No.	Kendall tau	Z	p-value
ASA and Booking	29	0.031009	0.236155	0.813312

Table 4. Link between ASA and Facebook.

Variables	Kendall tau, level of significance: $p < 0.05$			
	No.	Kendall tau	Z	p-value
ASA and Facebook	23	−0.072394	−0.483722	0.628583

Table 5. Link between ASA and trip advisor.

Variables	Kendall tau, level of significance: $p < 0.05$			
	No.	Kendall tau	Z	p-value
ASA and Trip	31	0.114257	0.903008	0.366522

Regarding the link between scores achieved by means of an extended sentiment analysis and the absolute number of pages indexed by Google, statistical testing did not confirm any link between variables on the significance level we selected (Table 6).

Table 6. Link between ASA and Google Index.

Variables	Kendall tau, level of significance: $p < 0.05$			
	No.	Kendall tau	Z	p-value
ASA and Google index	31	−0.070108	−0.554087	0.579519

On the selected significance level of 5 % the p value is much higher than 0.05. Statistically significant link between the number of pages indexed by Google and the ASA score was not confirmed. Absolute number of pages indexed by Google which include usual name of the given entity as a keyword does not have any statistically significant impact on the level of online reputation ASA score of that entity. The proven argument for the necessity of quality over quantity applies here as well.

For better interpretation we used Kruskal-Wallis nonparametric test of variance analysis for further testing. By using this test we basically test the influence of levels of a selected factor on the variability of values of analysed variable. In our case, the influence of ASA score on partial scores of Booking, Facebook, Trip Advisor was tested. Since the p value is much higher than 0.05, there is no statistically significant link between ASA and other reputators. Graphic interpretation of tested variables (Fig. 1):

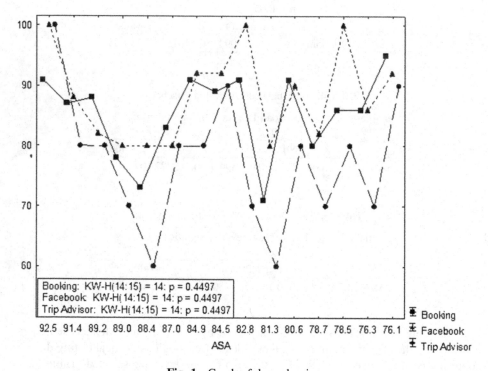

Booking: KW-H(14:15) = 14: p = 0.4497
Facebook: KW-H(14:15) = 14: p = 0.4497
TripAdvisor: KW-H(14:15) = 14: p = 0.4497

92.5 91.4 89.2 89.0 88.4 87.0 84.9 84.5 82.8 81.3 80.6 78.7 78.5 76.3 76.1

ASA

✦ Booking
✦ Facebook
✦ Trip Advisor

Fig. 1. Graph of dependencies.

The scale of assessments of individual entities based on the ASA score is located the x axis, percentage assessment of entities is located on the y axis. Since we have not confirmed any links between variables, we can proceed to the calculation of the total online reputation of a particular entity.

We shall start from the basic relationship we have drawn:

$$TOR = \frac{W_{ASA} \times R_{ASA} + \sum_{i=1}^{n}[W_i \times R_i]}{W_{ASA} + \sum_{i=1}^{n} W_i} \qquad (1)$$

TOR - Total online reputation (%),
R_i - Reputator (% score based on a given *i*-th determinant of online reputation),
R_{ASA} - Reputator ASA (% score based on the advanced sentiment analysis),
W_{ASA} - ASA reputator weight,
W_i - *i*-th reputator weight.

The equation includes specific determinants of online reputation, which we named reputators, and, of course, their weight as variables. The basic reputator is the percentage ASA score, and the equation enables to include any number of other reputators in the calculation.

A reputator can be any determinant which can objectively affect the perceived online reputation of a given entity and at the same time, its value in percentage can be quantified. In our case the scores from Booking.com, Facebook, Google ratings and Trip Advisor ratings were taken into consideration as determinants. For the actual calculation weights of individual reputators need to be determined, which are, by default, determined based on a given entity and a target market. Based on the selected entities and previous research conducted in the field of tourism each of the weights of individual reputators was given the value 1. In this case, the formula for the calculation of the overall online reputation which we set up, can be simplified as follows:

$$TOR = \frac{R_{ASA} + \sum_{i=1}^{n} R_i}{n+1} \tag{2}$$

TOR - Total online reputation (%),
R_i - Reputator (% score based on a given *i*-th determinant of online reputation),
R_{ASA} - Reputator ASA (% score based on the advanced sentiment analysis),
n - number of indicators.

In this case, the value of the overall online reputation of an entity is the arithmetic mean of individual indicators (partial scores of individual reputators).

4 Conclusion

Independent position of the online reputation index ASA based on the advanced analysis of the sentiment, that represents users' views of the model Internet user searching for information through the Google search engine comparing to reputation indices that are provided by the main Internet players, such as Booking, TripAdvisor and Facebook as a part of their ratings, is one of the major finding of the conducted analyses. This only encourages the need for continuing efforts towards building online reputation, not only on the pages of the main players operating directly in the tourism sector, but also towards the main players such as Internet editions of mainstream newspapers, Wikipedia, catalogues, Internet discussions, or notable bloggers. These players will help eliminate neutral, or even negative reputation on the Internet and will thus directly contribute to an increase in competitiveness of active entities, as opposed to their passive competitors.

In general, it might seem at first that the best model of e-marketing of a selected tourism entity consists mainly of active management of its own profiles on two key platforms: Trip Advisor and Booking (of the first five subjects arranged according to TOR score, only one made full use of all four major platforms). From the perspective of spending resources (mainly in the form of time) the possibility of managing a limited number of profiles on selected platforms (and alleged benefiting from the absence of "other profiles" providing the possibility of entity assessment) appears to be optimal. From the perspective of sustainability of this form of e-marketing, however, it was a very short-sighted action. Due to the relatively open nature of the Internet, it is only a matter of time when the missing profiles on the remaining platforms (notably Google and Facebook) will created by entities outside the scope of that entity. In such a case, the given tourism entity loses its direct influence over the active administration of a given profile and authenticity of presented content, thereby exposing itself to the increased risk of getting under unwanted pressure of competition on the increasingly fierce market environment, or even more unwanted pressure potential or actual customers seeking to ensure additional profit from the position of power. It is therefore essentially a necessity to deal with using e-marketing tools. Only a comprehensive approach can result in a sustainability of active e-marketing in a highly competitive tourism (not only) market.

The findings identified by the analysis conducted on the local market (in this case, used as a model example), can be effectively used in any market for the purpose of increasing competitiveness of selected tourism entities. Patterns and variables affecting virtual reputation of these entities are relatively invariable across the global Internet market.

Acknowledgments. This article is one of the partial outputs of the currently solved research grant VEGA No. 1/0145/14 entitled "Online reputation management (ORM) as a tool to increase competitiveness of Slovak SMEs and its utilization in conditions of Central European virtual market".

References

1. Janouch, V.: 333 tipů a triků pro internetový marketing. Computer Press, Brno (2011)
2. Marsden, H.: Guard Your Reputation On-Line. Smartebookshop, Birmingham (2013)
3. Haywood, R.: Manage Your Reputation: How to Plan Public Relations to Build & Protect the Organization's Most Powerful Asset. Kogan Page Publishers, London (2002)
4. Griffin, A.: New Strategies for Reputation Management: Gaining Control of Issues, Crises & Corporate Social Responsibility. Kogan Page Publishers, London (2008)
5. Balmer, J., Greyser, S.: Revealing the Corporation: Perspectives on Identity, Image, Reputation, Corporate Branding and Corporate-level Marketing. Routledge, Oxford (2003)
6. Helm, S., et al.: Reputation Management. Springer, Berlin (2011)
7. Gottschalk, P.: Corporate Social Responsibility, Governance and Corporate Reputation. World Scientific Publishing, New York (2011)
8. Shore, D.A.: The Trust Prescription for Healthcare: Building Your Reputation with Consumers. Health Administration Press, New York (2005)

9. Armstrong, M.: Řízení lidských zdrojů: Najnovější trendy a postupy. Grada Publishing, Prague (2007)
10. Tavakolifard. M.: On some challenges for on-line trust and reputation systems. Thesis, Norwegian University of Science and Technology, Trondheim (2012)
11. Gambetta, D.: Can we trust trust? In: Gambetta, D. (ed.) Trust: Making and Breaking Cooperative Relations, pp. 213–237. University of Oxford, Oxford (2000)
12. Jøsang, A., et al.: Survey of trust and reputation systems for on-line service provision. Decis. Support Syst. **43**, 618–644 (2007)
13. Sabater, J., Sierra, S.: Review on computational trust and reputation models. Artif. Intell. Rev. **24**, 33–60 (2005)
14. Leboff, G.: Sticky marketing – Jak zaujmout, získat a udržet si zákazníky. Management Press, Prague (2011)
15. Smaiziene, I., Jucevicius, R.: Corporate reputation: multidisciplinary richness and search for a relevant definition. Eng. Econ. **2**, 91–101 (2009)
16. Jackson, K.T.: Building Reputational Capital: Strategies for Integrity and Fair Play that Improve the Bottom Line. Oxford University Press, Oxford (2004)
17. Fill, C.: Marketing Communications: Interactivity, Communities and Content. Pearson Education, Harlow (2009)
18. Fombrun, C.J., Foss, C.B.: Developing a reputation quotient. The Gauge **14**, 1–4 (2001)
19. Walsh, G., Beatty, S.: Customer-based corporate reputation of a service firm: scale development and validation. J. Acad. Mark. Sci. **35**, 127–143 (2007)
20. Burke, J., et al.: Corporate Reputation: Managing Opportunities and Threats. Gower Publishing, Farnham (2011)
21. Siano, A., et al.: Exploring the role of on-line consumer empowerment in reputation building. J. Brand Manag. **19**, 57–71 (2011)
22. Henning-Thueau, T., et al.: Electronic word-of-mouth via consumer-opinion platforms: what motivates consumers to articulate themselves on the Internet? J. Interact. Mark. **18**, 38–52 (2004)
23. The Beginner's Guide to Reputation Management: 8 Core Principles of Reputation Management. http://reputationhacks.com/guide-to-reputation-management-3-8-core-principles/
24. Analýza sentimentu výsledkov slovenských firiem. http://www.reputation.sk/wp-content/uploads/2014/02/ORMreport.pdf

Approaches to Analysis of the Green Transport Level

David Staš[✉], Radim Lenort, Pavel Wicher, and David Holman

ŠKODA AUTO University,
Na Karmeli 1457, 293 01 Mladá Boleslav, Czech Republic
{stas,lenort,wicherl,holman}@is.savs.cz

Abstract. The article presents proposals of two approaches for assessing the green transport level in industrial companies and supply chains. As the first approach was designed a methodology for green transport audit, which is suitable for quick view of assessed industrial transport. For more detailed analysis of the green transport level is necessary to use more sophisticated tool then green transport audit. Conceptual framework for assessing the green transport level was designed for this purpose. The framework contains five main phases – preliminary analysis, transport system analysis, selection of assessing parameters, taxonomy development, and evaluation.

Keywords: Green transport · Green transport audit · Green transport level · Assessment

1 Introduction

In recent decades, the performance of economic and non-economic activities has required them to be friendly with the environment. This proactive approach to addressing and eliminating the negative environmental impacts from logistic processes is called green logistics (GL). The potential for an effective implementation of the GL principles can be found in many logistics activities. One of the key areas is the industrial company transport. It is necessary to be able to properly evaluate the green transport level during the implementation of GL and the subsequent process management. The aim of the paper is to summarize results of authors' previous research work in this area. First, green transport audit (GTA) and its methodology will be presented as the starting point for successful implementation of the GL principles. Second, a conceptual framework for measurement, monitoring, and evaluation of an industrial transport will be presented.

2 Methodological Basis

This part presents literature review related to green transport, logistics audit, and recent systems measuring the green transport level as fundamental methodological basis of the proposed methodologies.

© ICST Institute for Computer Sciences, Social Informatics and Telecommunications Engineering 2016
A. Leon-Garcia et al. (Eds.): Smart City 2015, LNICST 166, pp. 704–712, 2016.
DOI: 10.1007/978-3-319-33681-7_61

2.1 Green Transport

Movement towards GL starts with green transport (GT) [1]. Transport in the area of logistics processes is one of the areas having considerable potential within the scope of the implementation of the green practices, since it occupies top positions in negative impacts on the environment. At present, the public has been increasingly aware of a number of negative effects transport produces. They include, primarily, the emissions of CO and CO_2 and other exhaust gases, noise, and, last but not least, congested transport infrastructure.

The current goals of GT are now focused on reducing the fuel consumption (which is closely linked to cutting CO_2 and other exhaust gases), reducing noise, reducing the transport costs, reducing traffic jams and, ultimately, on complying with the legislative restrictions. An active and effective solution of the issues of GT must be seen not only as a challenge, but especially as an opportunity offering the possibility of significant competitive advantage, improving the image of the company in the eyes of the customers, region, state and the general public.

2.2 Logistics Audit

For enhancing the performance of the logistics system, it is necessary to take stock of the efficiency and effectiveness status of various sub-systems of the logistic chain. This process is called logistics audit [2].

Logistics audit is conducted to quantify the opportunity for improvement and to prioritize the initiatives in logistics process improvements [3]. Logistics audit is a periodic audit of a firm's logistics system, with the objective of finding an optimal mix of both cost and customer service [4].

Tvrdoň et al. recommend three subsequent parts for logistics audit performance [5]: (1) Descriptive: summarizing and describing all key parameters, measurable values and practice statuses of the logistics corporate system. (2) Diagnostic: the goal is to analyze to what extent corporate logistics systems are optimized or to what extent these systems meet the practical requirements in the specific company environment. (3) Proposal: it is formulated as an action plan, chronologically sorted activities description.

2.3 Recent Systems Measuring the Green Transport Level

On the basis of the literature review in the area of the conceptual frameworks used for measurement, monitoring, and evaluation of GT level, it can be stated: (1) Assessing the GT level is worldwide processed, described and developed topic, but only from a multinational and national prospect, especially for the area of urban or public transport (see e.g. [6, 7]). (2) The GT is usually included in a broader concept of Sustainable transport, which, apart from the environmental aspects, also deals with the economic and social criteria [8–11]. (3) GT field from the viewpoint of industrial companies or supply chains in the available green and sustainable transport conceptual frameworks is addressed only sporadically and marginally (see e.g. [12]). (4) As a result of different importance of green criteria, their measurement, monitoring, and evaluation should use the principle of weights. Sustainable Highway Self Evaluation Tool using default weights can serve as an example [13].

3 Green Transport Audit

The corner-stone of the proposed methodology is the technique of checklists. Industrial enterprises have two basic practical options how to ensure transport – to have their own car fleet or to use the logistics service providers. A third possibility is the combination of both these options. That is why two types of checklists have been created; taking into account the specific features of both methods of transport. Checklist for the first option is shown in Table 1.

Table 1. Checklist for an industrial company with its own vehicle fleet.

Field	Question
Strategy	1. Are the key suppliers situated near to you?
	2. Is your transport network optimized from the viewpoint of Green indicators?
	3. Do you have a system of monitoring indicators of Green Transport?
	4. Do you have created a partnership platform with all stakeholders?
Management	5. Do you use the concept of fully-loaded direct supplies and milk runs?
	6. Do you use the intermodal transport?
	7. Do your suppliers have an agreement for sharing their warehouses?
	8. Do you plan deliveries with your suppliers /customers?
	9. Do you utilize back rides?
Technology	10. Do you use ICT for transport planning and control?
	11. Do you carry out regular optimization of transport capacity utilization?
	12. Do you use alternative fuels and engines?
	13. Do you innovate your fleet?
	14. Do you use software for route optimization?
	15. Do you use road trains?
	16. Do you use double deck vehicles and other two-level systems?
	17. Do you use one-way pallets or other packages for long transports?
	18. Do you optimize loading /unloading time?
	19. Do you use telematics for efficient transport operations?
	20. Do you carry out careful preventive maintenance of your fleet?
	21. Do you have lighter vehicles?
	22. Do you use engine shutdown during waiting times?
Staff	23. Do you have a motivation system for your drivers to behave green?
	24. Do you carry out green training of your drivers?
	25. Do you select new drivers with regard to the green skills?

The checklists were created on the basis of a detailed research of green best practices used in the area of transport. More than 170 best practices have been analyses altogether. The principal sources of information were [14–19]. Each question in the checklist reflects one best practice. If the question is answered yes, the industrial company uses this best practice.

The questions are divided into four areas, reflecting their essential nature: (1) Strategy – best practices creating the basis of a successful application of other best practices or they have the character of supply chain structural changes. (2) Management – best practices focused on planning and subsequent execution of transport. (3) Technology – technical innovations of the means of transport, equipment, ICT systems and packages. (4) Staff – best practices whose motive power is represented by the people and their skills. The actual checklist evaluation is performed in three levels: (1) Questions – express the level of implementation of a given best practice. (2) Areas – represent the level of implementation of green practices in the individual areas. (3) Overall evaluation – overall level of GT in the evaluated industrial company. An example of the graphical presentation of GTA results is shown in Fig. 1.

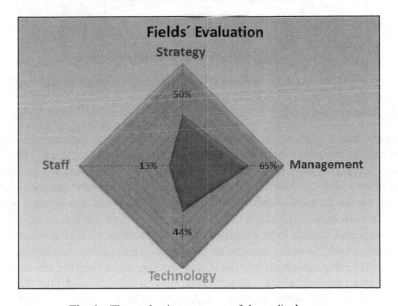

Fig. 1. The evaluation outcome of the audited areas.

4 Conceptual Framework for Assessing the GT Level

For more detailed analysis of the GT level is necessary to use more sophisticated tool then GTA. Conceptual framework for assessing the GT level was designed for this purpose. The main idea of the conceptual framework is based on an assessment of whether and to what extent the given transport system uses the approaches (beast practices) that are generally considered as green. Design conceptual framework includes the stages shown in Fig. 2.

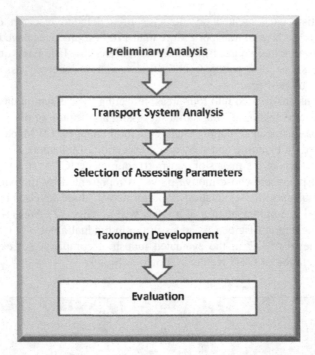

Fig. 2. Conceptual framework for assessing GT level in industrial companies and supply chains.

4.1 Preliminary Analysis

At the beginning, it is necessary to analyze the factors that will determine the manner and focus of the planned evaluation of GT level. The main factors are: (1) Purpose of evaluation – the goal may be to define the current level of GT and the potential for further improvement, to determine the level of GT for the newly designed transport system or the creation of standards for monitoring transport sub-systems within a company or corporation. (2) Scope of evaluation – it defines the part of the industrial company transport system to be evaluated. You can evaluate all transport activities of the company, which, however, requires large resources (especially costs and time). That is why it is preferable to analyze only the mouse negative impacts on the environment. In large industrial companies, the transport system is usually divided into these areas: inbound, internal, and outbound. (3) Availability of information – the method of evaluation will also be affected by the quality and availability of information.

4.2 Transport System Analysis

A good understanding of the transport system is a necessary condition for the evaluation of its green level. Each transport system has certain specific features that need to be taken into account when assessing its green level. The basic examined areas include the transport system structure (type and number of elements, their locations, and mutual links), transport politics (make or buy), transported commodities and their quantity, the used technologies (modes of transport, kinds of pallets and containers, transport capacities), transport planning and control principles and systems.

4.3 Selection of Assessing Parameters

The task at this stage is the selection of key parameters that will be used to evaluate the level of GT. For this purpose, GTA methodology described above can be used (see Table 1). The selection of key parameters is performed in the following steps: (1) The elimination of the best practices that are not related to the used make or buy transport policy – if the industrial company does not use its own fleet, it usually cannot have a direct impact, for example, on the fleet innovation, the introduction of telematics systems and eco-efficient new drivers selection and vice versa. (2) The elimination of the best practices that cannot be implemented for objective reasons – for example, the use of road trains, which is significantly restricted by the legislation of the individual countries. (3) The selection of strategically important best practices – in strategic management, it is necessary to concentrate on a lower number of crucial factors to avoid the fragmentation of limited company resources. This selection can take advantage of a modified matrix [15], which is presented in Fig. 3.

The company should incorporate the remaining best practices into categories presented in the matrix according to the following criteria: (1) Expected emission reduction after increasing the level or the implementation of a best practice in the given company – low or high. (2) Estimated cost of increasing the level or the implementation of a best practice in the given company – low or high. (3) Responsibility to decide on the increase of the level or the implementation of a best practice in the given company: I. In the responsibility of the implementers or II. Limited responsibility of the implementers (e.g. within the responsibility of another company department or corporation). The result is the inclusion of the remaining best practices into one of four categories: (1) Ideal – high reduction of emissions can be achieved at low costs or even cost savings. (2) Economic – only limited reduction of emissions can be achieved at low costs or even cost savings. (3) Ecological – incurring high costs will achieve a high reduction of emissions. (4) Ineffective – incurring high costs brings only a limited

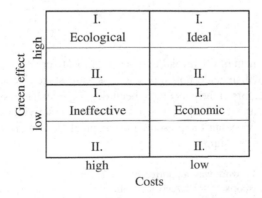

Fig. 3. Matrix for the selection of key parameters.

reduction of emissions. Ideal category should preferably be used to select the key parameters; on the other hand, Ineffective category should not be used at all. At the same time, we prefer the best practices that are within the direct responsibility of the implementers. There are no generally accepted rules for the inclusion of the individual best practices into the matrix, because it is always necessary to consider the individual conditions of the company in question. For one company, the increasing use of transport vehicles can mean relatively large investments in the technological systems with limited emission reduction. In another company, inexpensive organizational measures will lead to significant reduction of emissions.

4.4 Taxonomy Development

The task of taxonomy development is the creation of a system for measuring GT level. It is based on the decomposition of selected parameters into a weighted system of measurable indicators. The indicators may be of qualitative or quantitative nature. It is necessary to assign weight to each indicator. The Analytic Network Process (ANP) designed by Saaty can be used for this purpose. The main procedure of ANP is described in [20]. An example of a network created in Super Decisions software [21] is presented in Appendix.

4.5 Evaluation

The information and the data necessary for determining the indicators are collected during this stage. Using ANP, you can calculate GT level. The evaluation of the results may include: (1) Comparison of the calculated value with the maximum (ideal) and minimum values. (2) Inclusion of the calculated value into the pre-defined categories (low, medium, high GT level). (3) Benchmarking for application of the conceptual framework in other transport systems of the company or in another company. (4) Evaluation of the trend if the GT level evaluation is performed repeatedly. When increasing GT level, it is desirable to focus on the areas and parameters with the highest weight. If these capabilities reach an unsatisfactory level, it is necessary to prepare a plan of actions that will lead to their improvement. If the key parameters reach a sufficient level, it is advisable to prepare a plan of actions in order to maintain them at that level.

5   Conclusion

An efficient management of GT level, however, requires to create a complex conceptual framework, which will include not only the assessing stage, but also execution and control. Thus, the authors of the paper have been dealing with the possible application of the Balanced Scorecard (BSC) approach. Future research activities of the authors will also be focused on extending the presented conceptual framework into the spheres of green logistics and green supply chain.

Acknowledgments. The work was supported by the specific university research of Ministry of Education, Youth and Sports of the Czech Republic at SKODA AUTO University No. SIGA/ 2014/01 and No. SGS/2015/02.

Appendix

Network for application of ANP method created in Super Decisions software.

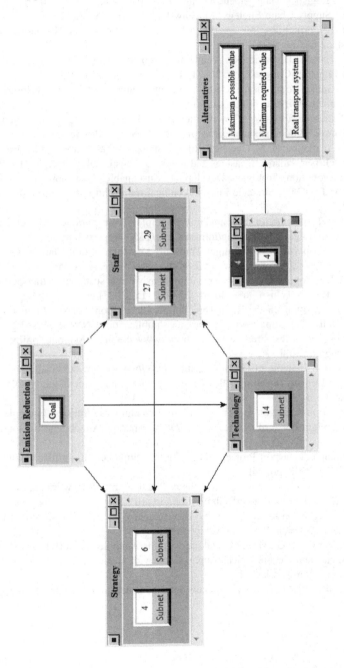

References

1. Emmet, S., Sood, V.: Green Supply Chains: An Action Manifesto. Wiley, Chichester (2010)
2. Sople, V.V.: Logistics Management. Dorling Kindersley, New Delhi (2007)
3. Frazelle, E.: Supply Chain Strategy. McGraw-Hill, New York (2002)
4. Wisner, J.D.: Principles of Supply Chain Management: A Balanced Approach. South-Western, Mason (2012)
5. Tvrdoň, L., Bazala, J., David, R.: A new approach of the logistics audit. In: CLC 2012, Carpathian Logistics Congress, pp. 66–71. TANGER, Ostrava (2012)
6. UNDESA: Guide Book to the Green Economy. https://sustainabledevelopment.un.org/content/documents/GE%20Guidebook.pdf
7. UNEP: Measuring Progress Towards a Green Economy. http://www.unep.org/green economy/Portals/88/documents/research_products/MeasuringProgress.pdf
8. Jeon, C.M., Amekudzi, A.A., Guensler, R.L.: Sustainability assessment at the transportation planning level: performance measures and indexes. Transp. Policy **25**, 10–21 (2013)
9. Texas Transportation Institute: Developing Sustainable Transportation Performance Measures for TxDOT′S Strategic Plan – Technical report. http://tti.tamu.edu/documents/0-5541-1.pdf
10. York Region: Transportation Sustainability Principles: Transportation Master Plan. www.york.ca/Services/Regional+Planning/Infrastracture/TMP_Reports.htm
11. Super Green Supporting EU's Freight Transport Logistics Action Plan on Green, Green Corridors Handbook. http://www.weastflows.eu/media//Supergreen-Project-brief_1.0.pdf
12. Litman, T.: Developing indicators for comprehensive and sustainable transport planning. Transp. Res. Rec. J. Transp. Res. Board **2017**, 10–15 (2007)
13. EEA: Are We Moving in the Right Direction? Indicators on Transport and Environment Integration in the EU. http://www.eea.europa.eu/publications/ENVISSUENo12
14. CLECAT: Logistics Best Practice Guide. http://www.clecat.org/ongoing-projects/logistics-best-practice-guide.html
15. 4flow: Costs and Benefits of Green Logistics. http://www.4flow.de/fileadmin/user_upload/Unternehmen/Logistikforschung/4flow_supply_chain_management_study_2013_-_abbreviated_version.pdf
16. British International Freight Association: Environmental Case Studies- Examples of Good Practice the Freight Forwarding Sector. http://www.bifa.org/_Attachments/Resources/1665_S4.pdf
17. ECR: Sustainable Transport Project – Case Studies. http://ecr-all.org/files/Combined-Case-studies-_v1-8_220508_pro.pdf
18. IRU: Report on Road Transport – Best Industry Practices. http://www.iru.org/en_bookshop_item?_rewrite_sticky=bookshop-display-action&id=10
19. IRU: Second Report on Road Transport – Best Industry Practices. https://www.iru.org/cms-filesystem-action?file=en_Publications/bip04.E.pdf
20. Saaty, T.L., Vargas, L.G.: Decision Making with the Analytic Network Process: Economic, Political, Social and Technological Applications with Benefits, Opportunities, Costs and Risks. Springer, New York (2013)
21. SuperDecisions. http://www.superdecisions.com/super-decisions-an-introduction

Influence of Traffic Congestions on Safety Stock in Company

Juraj Dubovec[(✉)], Jana Makyšová, and Milan Kubina

Faculty of Management Science, University of Žilina,
Univerzitná 8215/1, 010 26 Žilina, Slovakia
{juraj.dubovec,jana.makysova,
milan.kubina}@fri.uniza.sk

Abstract. Traffic intensification in Slovakia is an effect of economic development of the country. Traffic development in limited capacities of road infrastructure produces delays in traffic congestions. Congestions are becoming the problem mostly for companies which has to deal with its serious impact on established supply rules due to the extension of delivery time. This article points to effects of congestions on safety stock level change which is necessary for stabilization of assembling systems.

Keywords: Congestion · Delivery time · Production system stability · Safety stock · Logistics

1 Introduction

Accompaniment of development in Slovakia, as it is in developed countries is an intensification of traffic on the roads which has not only positive effects on mobility, but has also negative influence on environment, on worsening traffic flow, increasing number of car accidents or on road traffic inefficiency.

We would like to concentrate in our article on problem of traffic flow worsening leading to a sharp increase of congestions number on the roads and its influence on safety stock.

In road traffic network which is on the edge of its capacity, even small deviations in traffic volume produce a cascade effect [6].

More non-linearity is striking, more the thing (car) and a function of this thing (transport) are diverging. If traffic is linear, there would be no big difference between situations when stretch of a road is passed by 20.000, 25.000 or 23.000 cars. In case when cars are driving. The difference between the thing and its function will increase depending on uncertainty rate which is present in it. The driving time does not depend on intensity average, but on positive deviation from this state.

2 Traffic Congestions

In the frame of the traffic problem, congestions are conceived as an impassability or a blockage of driving corridor in road traffic [7]. Main reasons of congestions creation on the roads are:

© ICST Institute for Computer Sciences, Social Informatics and Telecommunications Engineering 2016
A. Leon-Garcia et al. (Eds.): Smart City 2015, LNICST 166, pp. 713–718, 2016.
DOI: 10.1007/978-3-319-33681-7_62

– intensity of road traffic,
– insufficient capacity of road network.

There are also additional reasons of congestions creations on roads. They are different, starting by car accidents, technical faults on means of transport, natural phenomenon, maintenance activities etc. When different events producing congestions occur in the same time, there is a synergic effect and congestions are even broader. Also the probability of congestion creation on different stretches of road varies [1].

Consequences of congestions are delays caused by getting stuck in blockage or by use of alternative route which usually has worse parameters than the route disabled by congestion. The dependence between road network loading and the time loss in congestions is presented in Fig. 1.

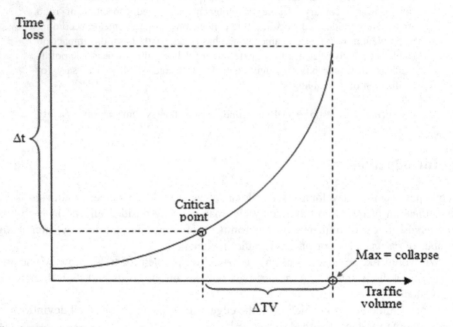

Fig. 1. The graph demonstrating the dependence between traffic volume in the road network and a loss of a time created by congestions on loaded even overloaded road network. Value of Δt presents an addition of delay time due to traffic volume increase by ΔTV. Traffic intensification has an exponential character. On this curve is located a critical point from which even a small addition on traffic volume generates a multiplication of delay in congestions. The point represented on a curve is only illustrative.

Analysis and prognosis of Slovak road administration [2] are not optimist at all in this problem, it is even reversely. In cooperation with Strategic plan of road network development of Slovak republic till the year 2020 [3] it turns out that motor vehicles increase is quicker than the increase of new express roads and highways which aim is to bring the intensity down to an acceptable level. The total number of motor vehicles listed in Slovakia is presented on Fig. 2. It is important to notice, that congestions on roads are not caused only by vehicles registered in Slovakia, but Slovakia is also a country of destination and of transit and so foreign vehicles significantly participate in traffic, mostly vehicles from Czech Republic and from Poland, but also from other countries.

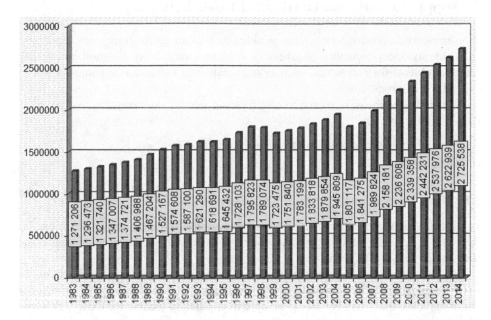

Fig. 2. The graph representing the total number of motor vehicles registered in Slovakia from the year 1983 till the year 2014 [4].

Slovak road administration measures all five years the intensity of road traffic. It is possible to get details of survey methodology is possible on their web pages [2]. Due to realized measurements the highest traffic volume was detected on the bypass of Bratislava directed to Senec where pass more than 100,000 vehicles per day and on the bridge Lafranconi directed to Wien with more than 88,000 vehicles per day. Any other road section in Slovakia did not reach the number 50,000 vehicles per day. The highest increase of traffic volume – 78 % – achieved the road section from Martin to Žilina. Also, this is a road section with very frequent congestions. Executors of this survey say that main roads in Slovakia are congested. And the intensity is increasing each year. Measurement of this year will show how the traffic intensity would change. Figure 2 indicates, that situation in years 2010–2015 got even more complicated and traffic got denser.

It is possible to find an analogy in queueing theory with multiple queueing nodes, while all nodes are not equal. In comparison with road network it is important to consider the fact that there is one optimal queueing node and others are offering solution where at least one parameter is worse. In case that there is a congestion on optimal queueing node, driver can chose another queueing node but he has to take into account more passed kilometers, traffic restrictions (bridges – reduced height, reduced carrier; road quality, sharp turns...) on other queueing node.

Queueing theory provides also an explanation for queue creation, its behavior, and advance in queue.

3 Supply Logistics on Overloaded Road Network

Worsening road network permeability presents complications for companies depending on regularity and punctuality of inventory delivery. Irregularity and non-punctuality causes problems for companies, such as marginal costs increase that company has to expend for its production.

When supply situation related to cost increase occurs, company has two possibilities, how to solve it:

– Time reserve and cost shifting to suppliers (carriers),
– Safety stock increase.

3.1   Time Reserve and Cost Shifting to Suppliers (Carriers)

The simplest solution on the first view is to prepare the shipment earlier that it can hit the road in advance so that potential congestions would not have an influence the deadline of delivery to destination.

But this solution anticipates the increase of costs necessary for material delivery in fixed dates. This includes necessity to procure new motor vehicles, new drivers for motor vehicles, more fuel is used, to procure manipulation technic for loading material on vehicles etc.

Car factories already adopted a kind of supplying principle which allowed them to cut their stocks by 20 % approximately. So they have shifted a part of their costs on suppliers. Car companies will shift their costs related to congestions and potential delays to their suppliers or they will take a part of risk by increasing the level of safety stock.

3.2   Safety Stock Increase

The purpose of safety stock is to increase the stability of system when uncertainty really exists in particular environment. Safety stock should cover random deviations in delivery time. Costs of deficit for productive or assembling stock can have as a consequence the interruption of production or assembling. Sometimes, non-satisfaction of demand is joined to financial sanctions. The size of safety stock is mostly influenced by variability between the supplier and the company which can have two forms. It is a late delivery or a poor quality delivery.

If delivery time is longer due to congestions, companies will have to reevaluate their actual supplying system. Because if the shipment is late because of impassability of the road, company can be obliged to stop the production, and that will produce big financial loss.

Car factories are rare companies in Slovakia functioning under the mode of production stability. That means that they have in their plants only a minimal level of stock (safety stock) and the majority of material is delivered in system Just in Time.

The level of safety stock is set in the way that new material will come in a moment when all material delivered in previous shipment is used. The time from the moment when is reached the level of safety stock giving impulse for ordering new stock to the moment of delivery of ordered stock to the company is exactly calculated and is defined as delivery time (DT). Figure 3 is a graphical presentation of consumption, ordering and delivery process.

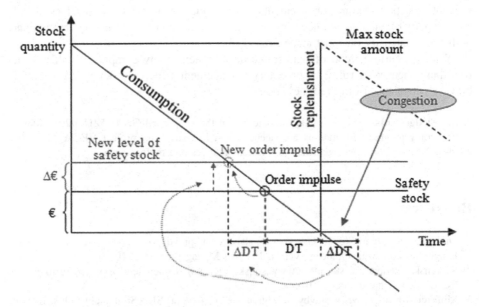

Fig. 3. Model of consumption and stock replenishment in company.

It is obvious that the amount of safety stock is defined in a way to cover the consumption from the moment of ordering to delivery of new shipment. But if the delivery time is longer due to congestion, company will find itself in stock deficit and have no material for production. To eliminate this situation, it is necessary to add the time extending delivery to standard delivery time. This would ensure new delivery at least or before the moment when the safety stock is spent. That means that the impulse for ordering must come early enough to ensure sufficient time for delivery. This leads to safety stock level increase. Having safety stock level increased means that company has to have more sources fixed in its safety stock as it has previously and this would increase marginal costs invested to stabilize the system.

4 Conclusion

Slovakia as one of top car producers in the world faces actually the strengthening of traffic volume. This causes problems to companies which have their production system stabilized like car factories. It is very arduous to reach this state preceded by numerous analysis and optimizations. Paradoxically problems based on road transport intensification are partially caused by car factories them-selves.

Also a Slovak road administration seeks to mitigate the impact of increasing traffic volume through the project *National system of transport information* [5]. This should solve basic problems in the field of security and fluency of traffic on roads of Slovak republic. In accordance with main factual and political aims of European Union and with main missions of Slovak republic, the project creates an environment for a significant reduction of transport accidents and extenuation of its effects on lives, health and property of citizens, at once it participate to diminution of congestion creation and high traffic intensity on most loaded roads [2].

With the current trend of road traffic development many companies will have to reevaluate their exert rules for inventory management which are dependent on reliability of shipments from the time's point of view.

Acknowledgements. This article is the outcome of the project KEGA 035ZU-4/2013 Master degree study program: Operations Management and Logistics and project VEGA 1/0363/14 2014–2017 Innovation management - processes, strategies and performance.

References

1. Ondrejka, R., Jánošíková, G.: Postup stanovenia pravdepodobnosti vzniku dopravnej kongescie ako zdroja spoločenských rizík. Crisis Manag. **1**, 77–82 (2011)
2. Slovenská správa ciest. http://www.ssc.sk/sk/Rozvoj-cestnej-siete/Dopravne-inzinierstvo/Celostatne-scitanie-dopravy-2010.ssc
3. Ministerstvo dopravy, výstavby a regionálneho rozvoja SR: Strategický plán rozvoja dopravnej infraštruktúry SR do roku 2020. http://www.telecom.gov.sk/index/index.php?ids=75682
4. Ministerstvo vnútra SR: Celkový počet evidovaných vozidiel v SR. http://www.minv.sk/?celkovy-pocet-evidovanych-vozidiel-v-sr
5. Ministerstvo dopravy, výstavby a regionálneho rozvoja SR: Program podpory IDS – NSDI. http://www.telecom.gov.sk/index/index.php?ids=75842
6. Schrank, D., Lomax, T.: The 2002 Urban Mobility Report. Texas A&M University Texas Transportation Institute, Texas (2002)
7. Easing the Burden: A Companion Analysis of the Texas Transportation Institute's Congestion Study. STPP, Washington (2001)

SmartCityCom

Place Attachment and Social Communities
in the Concept of Smart Cities

Matej Jaššo and Dagmar Petríková$^{(\boxtimes)}$

Slovak University of Technology in Bratislava,
Vazovova 5, 812 43 Bratislava, Slovakia
{matej.jasso,dagmar_petrikova}@stuba.sk

Abstract. Territorial identity and place attachment are examples of the soft factors in smart cities. Smart cities and communities are also those ones that make more efficient use of physical infrastructure, engage effectively with local people in the process of citizen participation. Every concept of place attachment requires a particular work within the community, its effective transmission to all the members as well as to outward environment. In the sense of place attachment there is the idea of urban gardening that generates uniqueness – specific character of places created by urban gardening contributes to calibration of unique place identity and develops emotional and social ties related to certain place. Urban gardening provides opportunities for social interactions that help residents develop their relationships in community, support community life and develop community and place attachment as well as enhance the quality of urban environment in the smart cities. Urban gardening is often viewed as one of the strategies which can improve urban sustainability and promote sustainable urban development in the smart cities.

Keywords: Territorial identity · Place attachment · Identity · Urbanity · Community life · Spatial planning · Urban sustainability · Urban gardening

1 Introduction

Cities provide the citizens with a number of services and functions to be used in the urban environment. Each of the functions - housing, employment, culture, sociability, leisure time activities, recreation – show evidence of a characteristic structure and also of various needs of current population, with various impacts on the environment. In this regard smart cities and communities are also those ones that make more efficient use of physical infrastructure, engage effectively with local people in local governance and decision with emphasis placed on citizen participation and learn, adapt and innovate and thereby respond more effectively and promptly to changing circumstances by improving the intelligence of the city.

Territorial identity and place attachment are prominent examples of so called soft factors in smart cities. They are very fragile mental structures which cannot be bought, emulated or stealt, but they are significantly contributing to the effectiveness of functioning of any social system based in certain territory. Despite the leading role of the city centres we cannot underestimate the role of the peripheral residential spatial

© ICST Institute for Computer Sciences, Social Informatics and Telecommunications Engineering 2016
A. Leon-Garcia et al. (Eds.): Smart City 2015, LNICST 166, pp. 721–728, 2016.
DOI: 10.1007/978-3-319-33681-7_63

structures in this process. Social cohesion based on the highly profiled identification with the living space and deeply articulated place attachments are the fundamental preconditions of sustainability of any community or settlement structure. Large parts of the Slovak cities and neighbourhoods are covered by residential areas of panel blocks of flats built in the 1970s and in the 1980s. These communities and settlements are often more than 30–40 years old and have become specific places with its own history, social climate and narratives. Unique and specific metatext of almost any Slovak city would remain unfinished without residential areas of panel blocks of flats. These areas have generated specific identity, social cohesion as well as social problems related to them. It is obvious that Slovak panel block housing areas failed to deliver the unique "tomorrow's quality of life" as once declared but on the other hand they never became the completely excluded localities without the vital contacts with the city' organism.

Acceleration of spatial development has generated also the increased probability to face also the negative effects of both the globalization as well as EU integration. Recent economic and financial crisis highlighted this risk and created threats which were not acute even some years ago. Fragile spatial and societal structures have been exposed to huge pressure originated either from international markets, unfavourable demographic prognosis, environmental hazards or another sources of risk. Spatial planning faces the problem of increasingly higher uncertainty of the framework conditions of spatial development as well as necessity to react efficiently and flexibly to unpredictable external and internal shocks like floods, fires, economic disturbances confronted with unpredictable individual behaviour/decisions of multiple stakeholders. These factors represent risks not only for planning, but first of all also for sustainability of spatial development. Spatial planning has been transformed and has become a process of permanent search without any warranty of outcome. Assessment and decision-taking under uncertainty – it's the call of the day [1].

2 Urbanity and Its Interpretations

Urban and metropolitan milieu is an example of ultimate complexity on territorial level. This milieu displays manifold hierarchical and horizontal structures and registers including the contraversions and conflicts. Few of man created systems do include so many variables; do involve so many involved actors. Moore delivers the following overview of the approaches toward the city from the social perspective:

- The city as symbol and carrier of civilization
- The city as land of economic and social opportunity
- The city as an initiating and controlling centre of a region or the nation
- The city as a melting pot versus the city as a mosaic of social worlds
- The city as heterogeneity, variety, diversity, the apex of culture and cosmopolitanism
- The city as a "feast" and the city as electronic stimulation
- The city as a place for transitory, second-hand, superficial contracts, as a place of reserve and indifference, of blasé or even predatory attitudes
- The city as depravity, the alienation of the person from the land, and the subjugation of human values to the machines and commercialism [2].

The common denominator of almost all current approaches is that the main scope of urbanity is shifting from "fulfilling the complexity and hierarchy" to "ability to deliver uniqueness and specificity". New urbanity is arising on the interface of various and manifold contexts (visual, symbolic, narrative, historical, political) etc. The tension "public-private" has been modified: it has been removed to the semi-public places. The role of the professionals (planners, architects) is to redefine the legibility of the place and its sense. The place as a point of meeting, interaction, exchange, transition...Place is becoming a pattern in the "language" of people (Ch. Alexander) and generates specific metatext in the minds of people. Place and space are opportunities for projection and self-realisation – projection of values, ideas, principles, thoughts...On the other hand we are witnesses of certain controversial tendencies: commodification of spaces, privatisation of public spaces (shopping malls, corporate plazas...), fragmentarisation of spatial experiences, globalisation of local contexts (more in [3]). This shift has been reflected also in planning paradigm shift and modification of planning culture: from the system theories ("comprehensive planning") having their roots back in 1950s toward the "incrementalism" of the 1970s and later to "cooperative planning" of 1990s and 2000s [1].

The city of optimal infrastructural performance, social equity and rather normative regulation of spatial conflicts has been replaced by postmodern conceptual approaches enhancing uniqueness, imagery and soft assets [4]. Hierarchical planning cultures based upon the authoritarian decision-making proved to be inefficient and inappropriate when dealing with complex problems of high dynamics and multilateral impacts (see e.g. [1, 5]). Change must be made by those living and acting outside the prevailing paradigm [6]. Planning has been transformed onto rather contingent nature [7] and has become a process of permanent searching without any warranty of outcome. Judgement under uncertainty – is the call of the day. Moreover, spatial planners, urban designers and architects are facing the ambiguity - lack of judgement criteria. Who knows what the stakeholders really want? Smooth, successful and genuine spatial development requires value compatibility and continuity. Integration of different values, basic assumptions and beliefs into a coherent spatial concept is a necessity and ultimate challenge for spatial planners (see [8]). Forester's concept "making sense together" has been completed by Healy's addition "while living differently" [9].

We are confronted with both positive (urban imagery, fun, celebration) and negative (urban anxiety, urban panic) connotations of urban environment. Current urban imagery is fragmented, deteritorialised, heterogeneous, diasporic, split apart...Sense of a place is constantly changing, not necessarily held together and the city is regarded as a partially connected multiplicity [3]. Archetypal perceptional patterns [10] appeared: the crowd as an ocean, skyscrapers as the mountains, the city as jungle, the cars as predators...Revival of mythological contexts represented by e.g. "oceanic feeling" (term of Paul Tillich): the individual in the city is losing its freedom and is led by crowd and the city itself...(see [10]).

3   Identity and Place Attachment

It is generally supposed that highly profiled city/place identity and strong ties of place attachment are of utter importance for social cohesion within the territory [11]. Territorial identity is crucial dimension in the concept of social identity and sense of belonging and identity was one of the weakest points of the big modernist dreams (e.g. Brasilia). Place attachment saturates many psychological needs: the need for security, the need for self-realisation, the need for belonging and structuring the outer environment. Highly profiled identity contributes to the legibility of the place and space. The people are still generally territorial in their behavioural patterns. Slovak communities, mainly in smaller settlements (but even in urban milieu) always displayed rather strong and deep place attachment and deep identification with living place and environment. However, we can conclude from recent surveys (e.g. project Identity of River Basins, see more [12]) that both these phenomena (place attachment and territorial identification) are saturated more by emotional and social identification patterns ("I have grown up here", "my family lives her for decades") than by value based identification patterns ("I am living here because I appreciated the value profile and behaviour of our municipality"). The territorial identification and sense of belonging is rather deep, but in many cases rather monodimensional.

During recent years in Slovakia, our housing and residential estates ceased to be the monolithic sense-less places and have become chronicles of various stories and experiences which overcome sometimes the obsolete and uniform architectural language. It is obvious that the landmarks of identity are never only the physical (architectural) forms but rather the common experience, morals and stories. Identification with the living place goes far beyond the positive distinction (image) and should be based upon the common vision and values, which are present in given territory (environmental values, liberal values…). Urban gardening is in this dimension not only improvement of the physical structures but a unique platform for fostering the sense of community, reflection of place attachment and expression of the need of self-realisation.

Although place attachment and processes of identification with place/territory are growing up from certain given predispositions, they are dynamic phenomena which should be effectively fostered and further developed. Every concept of place attachment requires a precise work within the community, its effective transmission to all the members as well as to outward environment. Direct participation of the inhabitants in this process is very important. The inhabitants are key players in this process – they are both creators of the place identity and also are the key target group in the process of its acceptation and evaluation. In order to ensure the highest quality and effectiveness of the process, it is necessary to approach the place in an interdisciplinary manner and with maximum emphasis on mutual functional and value compatibility of individual participants and the measures proposed. One of the most important conditions is authenticity of the concept.

A very important category in terms of place identity and place attachment is an image of the place. Image is an abstract mental construction representing the subject in minds of audience. Positive image of a place/city means its goodwill, its good reputation or positive emotion appearing by thinking about the subject. The image is also the degree of affinity to subject manifested by significant groups of perceivers. Image in the city with significant presence of urban gardening structures goes far beyond pure visual appearance of green structures: it encapsulate also the values of solidarity, fairness, justice and advanced sense for quality of life.

4   Urban Gardening

Urban gardening is more and more popular leisure time and recreational activity among city inhabitants that offer an opportunity for people from different backgrounds to participate in the activity of gardening and provide themselves with fresh fruit vegetables or herbs and at the same time to develop social relations among community members in the urban environment during the process of regular maintenance. Urban gardening contributes to increase green infrastructure in the city thus improving the quality of the urban environment and at the same time it is also a way of communicating within a city or its suburb. In this way urban gardening is a powerful tool for creating and building up community and fostering a deep place attachment. Urban gardening is an expression of positive values and attitudes towards environment and community. In relation to place attachment, urban gardening generates uniqueness – specific character of places created by urban gardening contributes to calibration of unique place identity and develops emotional and social ties related to certain place. It is a kind of "scene" yielding the stories and tales which secure inner composure of social community.

In towns and cities there is also endless quantity of degraded or underused areas of brownfields that are waiting for more sustainable and sensitive redevelopment. Temporary use of the brownfield areas is an opportunity for a particular type of public space for urban gardening and the potential for community places open to neighbourhood. This phenomenon helps change current understanding of gardens, when gardens are not just enhancing life of the gardeners and the immediate family or close friends but serve as a tool to improve the life of local people and visitors and it is also of educational character, especially for children, who spend their whole life in a city. It gives them possibility to learn more about gardening activities and recognize different kinds of flowers, fruit and vegetables. Neighbourhood spaces and courtyard garden places in particular provide opportunities for social interactions that help residents develop their relationships in community, support community life and develop community and place attachment as well as enhance the quality of urban environment.

Donna Armstrong's survey of 63 community gardens grouped under twenty community garden programs in upstate New York resulted in the description of numerous benefits of gardening:

- Improved social connections, raising awareness and activity of local policy
- Interactions between gardeners' groups through different programs
- Identification of children with cultivated land
- Participation also of lower income households
- Stronger community cohesion – recognition of people on the streets
- Higher knowledge about local actors – easier action initiation process
- Social control of the neighbourhood
- Landscaping attempts not only on the community garden
- Establishment of neighbourhood organizations
- Establishment and maintenance of parks and playgrounds [13]

The quality of the urban environment has also become a crucial component of economic and social regeneration of abandoned and underused sites and brownfields in the cities. This creates not only economic revitalization programmes but also programmes enhancing the quality of life of the urban population. Slovakia in May 2004 had become a Member State of the European Union, which also brought many responsibilities and obligations of Member States in the field of environmental protection and human health. Recently, there is a growing number of activities to promote sustainable urban development and the adoption of several documents and declarations in support of effective strategies that address the development of the urban environment towards meeting its quality for urban population. One of the approaches is the focus on ecosystem services that is part of the Strategy of adaptation to the adverse effects of climate changes in cities. Bratislava as the capital of Slovakia has adopted such a strategy in 2015 and within that context supports creating community gardens on available plots of underused land or brownfields, with environmental and social benefits for the city. Community gardens are often viewed as one of the strategies, which can improve sustainability of urban environment as well as improve health and affect lifestyle of individuals.

5   Urban Gardening in Bratislava

Urban gardening in Bratislava is organised on the basis of voluntary work that has begun under the Pontis foundation. The first attempts of community gardens have been connected with improving the courtyards in the residential areas and the civic initiative "Courtyard" has been established, with the aim to support motivation of the residents to improve public spaces in the community. Within this movement a specific project "Gaps" has started that mapped all the possible community places in the city that can be used for social activities. These community places are the plots that are underused and abandoned and as such are the holes in the urban fabric and can be designated as brownfields suitable for temporary use. Based on these available plots the first activity "mobile gardens" has started where the main motivation for stakeholders to utilise these places has been the opportunity for gardening. Surprisingly, spin-off effect of this activity has brought rich social informal interactions that have been developed while spending time by urban gardening and sharing duties and experiences among local people of various age and nationality. Gradually people started to be involved in other après-gardening activities connected with consuming their own products together and having fun and socialize together up to becoming friends and spending time together in the afternoon and evenings. The next spin-off effect of this activity has been children education in becoming familiar with the type, colour and smell of flowers and vegetables as well as getting practical experience in helping with gardening. Last but not least spin-off effect of this activity have been discussions about current situation on upgrading the outdoor environment in the community and creating semi-public spaces that are important for identification with local community and pro-active behaviour of community members. Participation in urban gardening has generated synergy of the place attachment with the needs of the development of the community.

Now there are 4 types of "mobile gardens" in Bratislava. The first is in the old town in a gap between the block of flats, the second one is on a walkway under the building called Pyramid and it is a combination of a community garden with a café, the third one is in the community close to nature under the slopes of the Lesser Carpathians and this one has extended its scope of gardening also to vineyards and tries to start with community winegrowing. Altogether there are about 276 people involved in these activities. Since these activities have only started two years ago it is quite a success. Urban gardening on the underused plots is based on the lease of the plots for three years that has been guarded by the Pontis foundation. Among the challenges and perspectives in Slovakia, the following ones seem to be most significant:

- Limited research done yet (mapping of vacant spaces)
- Number of vacant/unused plots in cities
- Brownfields as potential space for urban gardening
- Learning from first successful examples: community garden Sasinkova, Bratislava – Old Town, community vine yard and garden Pionierska, Bratislava – Nové Mesto
- Missing complex strategy for public spaces and legal support
- Missing support instruments for attracting gardeners (passportisation of available plots, clear rules,
- Promotion for land owners – usual fear of something new (gardeners will "stay forever", fear of plot degradation, administrational difficulties...)
- Transition of our cities
- And many others.

6 Conclusions

Urban environment can have positive effects on creation and growth of communities as they have the opportunity to build a local identity and a sense of localism around a certain space. Place attachment is a significant factor influencing identification with local community, pro-active behaviour of community members and generates territoriality based not only on routine, but on the social commitment and value consensus among the members of community. In order to utilise the synergy of the place attachment with the needs of the development of the community and space/place overall, it is necessary to foster participative planning culture involving all the actors, making optimal mix between private, public and corporate elements. Special attention must be paid to non-formal tools: cooperation with the communities living in similar environment, introduction of best practice cases to public, building up clusters, non-formal cooperation with the municipality, city and region etc. Community gardens can have a huge impact on this process as well as on the quality of urban life beginning from producing fresh food to strengthening neighbourhood bonds. It can also have positive impacts on distressed neighbourhoods where vacant lots can be converted into community gardens or community green spaces and these improvements can have an effect on residents' perception of safety outdoors, reduction of social problems and cultivation of social responsibility.

References

1. Jaššo, M.: Plánovacie kultúra. In: Finka, M. (ed.) Priestorové plánovanie, pp. 175–196. ROAD Spectra, Bratislava (2011)
2. Pipkin, J.S., Gory, M.E., La Blau, J.R. (eds.): Remaking the City: Social Science Perspectives on Urban Design. State University of New York Press, Albany (1983)
3. Fahmi, W.S.: The Urban incubator: (De) constructive interpretation of heterotopian spatiality and virtual image (ries). First Monday Online, Special Issues 4: Urban Screens: Discovering the Potential of Outdoor Screens for Urban Society (2006)
4. Hain, S.: Der Berliner Städtebaudiskurs als symbolisches Handeln und Ausdruck hegemonialer Interessen. In: WeltTrends, vol. 17, pp. 103–123 (1997)
5. Märker, O., Schmidt-Belz, B.: Online Meditation for Urban and Regional Planning (2000). http://enviroinfo.isep.at/UI%20200/MaerkerO-12.07.2000.el.ath.pdf. Accessed 20 Jan 2008
6. Kuhn, T.: The Structure of Scientific Revolutions, 2nd edn. The University of Chicago Press, Chicago (1970)
7. Keim, K.-D., Jähnke, P., Kühn, M., Liebmann, H.: Transformation der Planungskultur? Ein Untersuchungsansatz im Spiegel stadt- und regionalplanerischer Praxisbeispiele in Berlin-Brandenburg. In: Planungsrundschau – Zeitschrift für Planungstheorie und Planungspolitik, Ausgabe, vol. 6, pp. 126–152 (2002)
8. Jaššo, M., Kubo, L.: Urbánna sémiotika. Spectra – ROAD, Bratislava (2015)
9. Mäntysalo, R.: Approaches to Participation in Urban Planning Theories. In: Zetti, I., Brand, S. (eds.) Rehabilitation of Suburban Areas – Brozzi and Le Piagge Neighbourhoods, pp. 23–38. University of Florence, Firenze (2005)
10. Zlydneva, N.: Urban fun. In: Place and Location. Studies in Environmental Aesthetics and Semiotics III, pp. 139–146 (2003)
11. Kearns, A., Forrest, R.: Social cohesion and multilevel urban governance. Urban Stud. **37**(5–6), 995–1017 (2000)
12. Jaššo, M.: Regional identity – its background and management. In: Petríková, D., Roch, I. (eds.) Flusslandschaften ohne Grenzen - Mitteleuropäische Ansätze zu Management und Förderung landschaftsbezogener Identität, pp. 171–179. ROAD-Spectra, Bratislava (2005)
13. Armstrong, D.: A survey of community gardens in upstate New York: implications for health promotion and community development. Health Place **6**, 319–327 (2000)
14. Petríková, D., Szuhová, J.: The role of networking, innovation and creativity in social responsibility to connect urban and rural environment. In: AESOP Congress, Prague (2015)

Generative Green Building Design, Computational Analysis of the Ecological Algorithm

Martin Uhrík[✉] and Ondrej Kövér

Faculty of Architecture, Slovak University of Technology, Bratislava,
Námestie slobody 19, 812 45 Bratislava, Slovakia
uhrik@stuba.sk, ondrej.kover23@gmail.com

Abstract. The research deals with the building design aimed at meeting the strict ecological criteria set out by the European legislation of 2020 while using the latest digital technologies of parametric designing in the Grasshopper program. Specifically, we have focused on the architectural design stage. Instead of providing purely technological solution, we preferred to use technology as a part of the architectural concept. The goal was to get closer to the zero energy building concept. Parametrization of the technological, aesthetic and organizational part of the building into a single system as well as parametrization of the surrounding environment was chosen as the tool. The research shows one of the options how to extend the building's information model into the conceptual design stage and how to interconnect data with the environment.

Keywords: Ecology · Digital architecture · Grasshopper

1 Introduction

The classic view of the Smart City issue and contribution to improvement of the urban functioning is considered primarily from the city usage point of view. This is also pointed out by the question of Anthony M. Townsend in his book Smart Cities: *How will a building system talk to each other? How can my phone ask a bus where it is going?* [1]. This is a natural starting point because this information aspect may be applied as a new layer to the existing urban structure. This attitude is further justified by the current fast acceleration of the use of information technologies by the common city residents contrasted by the information passivity of the urban environment.

Another view of the problem is the utilisation of data to optimize flows in the urban environment. Some of the examples already implemented include optimization of public transport or distribution of security forces.

However, the aforementioned strategies fail to solve the issue of designing the essential element of the city, which is the building. In our case, we have restricted the assignment to residential architecture located on the outskirts of the city. In particular, we are considering the territory of deteriorating vineyards above the Bratislava district of Rača. The locality is typical for the Central European context of urban development.

© ICST Institute for Computer Sciences, Social Informatics and Telecommunications Engineering 2016
A. Leon-Garcia et al. (Eds.): Smart City 2015, LNICST 166, pp. 729–737, 2016.
DOI: 10.1007/978-3-319-33681-7_64

There is also a difference in similar strategies which are mostly applied to larger agglomerations with more dynamic growth of the urban structure.

When searching for the limits within the building's ecological aspect, we were trying to suppress the purely technological solutions as much as possible and to prefer using technologies as a part of the architectural concept. The solution was directed to simple technologies, already available, used in an innovative way. The goal was to get closer to the zero energy building, the definition of which clarifies our energy goals. *A Zero Energy Building (ZEB) shall mean a building producing (at least) as much energy as it needs for its operation from renewable sources throughout the year. Therefore, the need of primary energy is fully covered by the energy obtained from the environment or from renewable sources in/on/at the building. The coverage is evaluated in annual balance* [2].

Ideological architectural background of sustainable architecture contains social and aesthetic parameters as well as the parameter of environmental quality. This concept was further developed by prof. Keppl in his work Ecological Algorithm of Designing. He defines this issue as follows: *Algorithm is based on the principle of designing in accordance with the environment (idea of bio-climatic architecture - see Ecological architecture) and utilisation of the characteristics of the environment, locality and natural forces, especially the sun and wind, for the benefit of functioning of the object designed* [3].

2   Parametrization of Architecture

The aforementioned starting points form a diverse milieu of relationships and information which has to be considered when designing a building. Compared to the standard architectural practice, there is a number of new factors which shall be considered in designing. Upon reaching a certain amount of data, the human factor loses its ability to meaningfully analyse and interpret information. Utilisation of digital technologies is inevitable.

The procedure required quantification of individual components creating the architectural diagram, inscription thereof into a unified data format, definition of their relations and enabling three-dimensional interpretation of data in architectural form. The whole system has to be interactive (recursive), in order to enable redefinition of input data and thus optimization of the resulting form at any stage.

Since beauty was one of the parameters required, in other words, aesthetic appropriateness of forms in relation to the surrounding environment, we have chosen the Rhinoceros Grasshopper[1] modelling program add-on as a tool. This is a graphical algorithm editor which enables to create generative algorithms. The greatest advantage is the integration into architectural modelling environment. Thus, the outputs are dynamically interpreted in 3d objects which may be further interpreted in perspective imaging. This is a form of graphic programming language which enables standard calculations and thereby integration of various data forms.

---

[1] http://www.grasshopper3d.com/.

Aesthetic Parameter. The Parameter is based on the analysis of the concept of beauty and its definitions. The basis was the analysis of compositions of implemented projects on photographs in a particular environment. Selection was based on known and positively perceived built architectures in similar natural environment. In terms of composition, the mutual ratio of area elements was evaluated: architecture, environment in front of the object, environment behind the object and the sky. The goal was to quantify the ratio of individual elements which creates an aesthetically satisfactory view of architecture in natural environment.

The analyses resulted in a proposal of several material structures with the same volume which are subsequently evaluated in terms of composition and area in the environment, always in three identical points: panoramic view, oncoming view, point in the environment between the matters. All of the views are composed so that the observed object, architecture in our case, is compositionally fitted according to the golden section principle in a frame which has the 16:9 ratio. The process is automated by the script which generates different types of architectural forms in the modelling environment, meeting the given criteria, including evaluation of their aesthetic quality (Figs. 1, 2 and 3).

Fig. 1. Example of architectonic style in countryside: "Monument of Beauty", reproduction of (Ondrej Kövér 2015) original building: Marte. Marte Architects Mountain Cabin, Laternser Valley, Austria (2011).

The Energy Parameter. The energy concept is based on the effort to make the most of the morphology and genius loci of the environment as the potential source for producing energy needed to cover the building's energy consumption.

Energy consumed in the particular residential house with 40 residents may be divided in three units. Energy needed for the domestic hot water (DHW), energy needed for heating and energy needed for the running o household devices. The best way of energy production was searched for these three separate units. This resulted in a complex formula working on the basis of the object's volume and floor area (Fig. 4).

Energy needed for the domestic hot water was acquired by using solar panels. According to the calculations above, 13544 kWh/year is consumed for DHW. According to the research by Krippelová and Peráčková [4], annual consumption of hot water is 16.76 m³ per resident. Consumption of hot water during the year, week and even day is a very fluctuating value. Therefore, it is necessary to have the system dimensioned for the maximum possible water consumption, to be able to cover the water consumption at its maximum value. According to the research, the highest water consumption is on a Sunday, in particular 52 l per person. Considering the number of residents, the reservoir with capacity of 3120 l is needed (consumption × residents × 1.5). According to the formula for preliminary draft of the solar collector surface (number of persons × 1.5), [5] the preliminary surface of collectors needed is 60 m². Considering the values calculated, we recommend to use 6 times the system for water heating with the surface of 8.73 m², reservoir capacity of 500 l, 24 tube collectors (Fig. 5).

The second unit is the energy needed for heating of the building itself. Energy for the building heating forms 33 % (15962 kWh/year) of total energy consumed. When the floor height calculated is 3 m, the total heated volume is 3,224 m³. The boiler

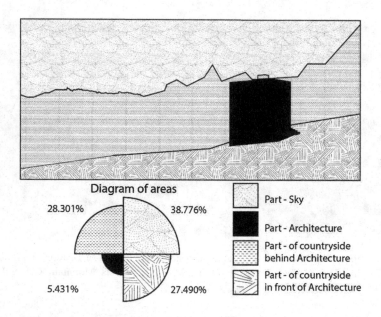

Fig. 2. Evaluation of composition, frame 16:9 (Ondrej Kövér 2015)

output is calculated empirically as the volume of the object in m3 x estimated heat output (20 W/m³, new development, insulated) [6]. These values require a boiler with output of 64 kW. We propose a pellet boiler, with the efficiency factor of 0.92. Obtaining of the raw material for the boiler from the vineyard was also considered, whereby both the transportation cost and the carbon footprint of the fuel used would be decreased. By using the software support, we were able to simulate the vineyard as the

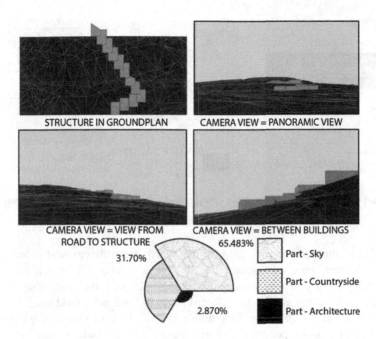

Fig. 3. Generating different types of structure and analysing the composition. Frame 16:9 (Ondrej Kövér 2015).

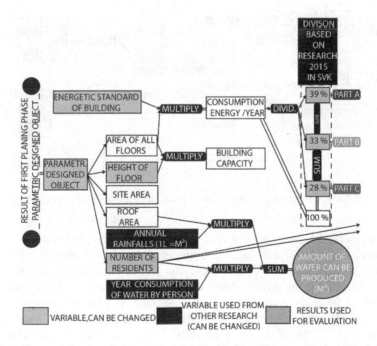

Fig. 4. Interpretation of technical part of the Grasshopper diagram (Ondrej Kövér 2015).

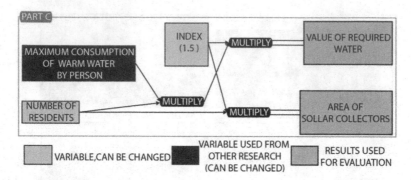

Fig. 5. Part C Energy required for water heating 28 % from all energy required (Ondrej Kövér 2015).

source of different types of fuel, as each material has a different heat value per kilogram. At the same time, the relevant area of vineyard needed for obtaining sufficient volume of fuel for a year was simulated. For example, with the heat value of wooden pallets being 5 kWh/kg, at the boiler effectiveness of 0.92, we would need 3,470 kg of pellets to cover the consumption. Assuming that from 1 m^2 of vineyard, we are able to obtain 0.5 kg of wooden pellets, the vineyard area needed would be 6940 m^2 (Fig. 6).

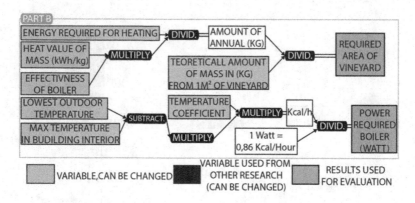

Fig. 6. Part B Energy required for heating 33 % from all required energy (Ondrej Kövér 2015).

The last unit is the energy needed to cover the running of household devices. 39 % of total energy (18865 kWh/year) falls upon household devices. Energy needed to cover devices will be obtained from photovoltaic cells. This calculation was facilitated by the GIS data prepared for the given locality. If we were to cover the full consumption of electric power under the formula (solar panel surface × solar panel output in WP × surface of a single panel × amount of sun energy per 1 m^2 per year * 0.7 loss factor) [7], we would need 290 m^2 of photovoltaic cells. The issue is the uneven power input considering the amount of sunlight both over the day and the year. In case of surpluses,

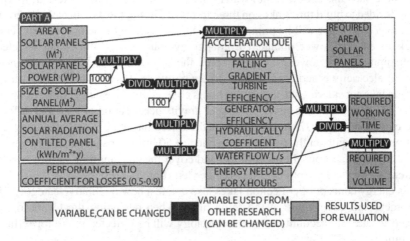

Fig. 7. Part A Energy required for household devices 39 % from all required energy (Ondrej Kövér 2015)

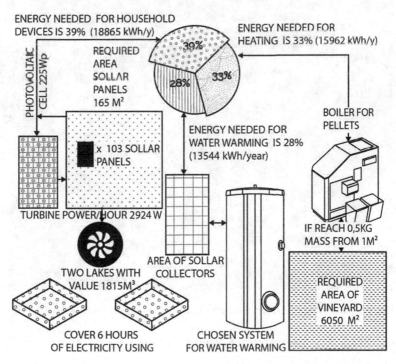

Fig. 8. Diagram of separation and functioning of the energy concept (for 1,075 m² floor area is the energy consumption of 48 372 kWh) Division based on research of standard Slovak housing energy consumption. (Ondrej Kövér 2015).

we can store such unsteadiness into water energy. With respect to the terrain morphology, we decided to build three lakes on three terraces. During the day, in case of surpluses of electric power, water will be pumped from the lowest lake to the highest one. During the lack of electric power obtained from photovoltaic panels, this water is released through piping to the lowest lake and spins the micro-turbine, whereby the needed amount of electricity is acquired. Thanks to the software, it is possible to determine the size of the lake considering the amount of hours covered by this source. For example, we need 10,767 W of energy to cover 5 h, under gravity acceleration of 9.81 and difference in lake elevation of 14.197 m, efficiency of the micro-turbine 0.7 and efficiency of the generator 0.8, we will get the water flow needed of 50 litres per second and the resulting output 2,924 kW per hour. In order to use and cover the consumption of 5 h, two lakes with area of 18 m^2 and depth of 3 m were needed (Fig. 7).

This energy concept of collection lakes also create a new qualitative category of the environment and architecture at the same time. When designing the technology, we also need to take into account how the technology will be reflected in the form (façade) of the building itself (Fig. 8).

Fig. 9. Final architecture of generated apartment house. (Ondrej Kövér 2015).

3 Generated Architecture - Conclusion

Technological solutions such as insulation and building equipment are a part of the building solutions. At present, the research in building technologies is very common and constantly brings us new and better solutions. In our research, we were trying to support architectural solutions of the issue relating to the shape of the building, its orientation and interaction with its immediate surroundings.

The building becomes an organism, is not separated but communicates with the surrounding, which does not only consist of other buildings but the surrounding cultural landscape as well. In order to achieve that the building's communication was not only restricted to the metaphoric level, it was necessary to create a common language whereby the individual parts of the architectural and construction process could communicate with one another. This language consists in parametrization of both technological and architectural parts of the structure as well as parametrization of the environment the architecture is being incorporated in.

At the time, digital architecture has tools to perform such parametrization during early stages of the architectural concept. These data may be further transferred to the project in the BIM environment and subsequently, such information may be integrated into the broader information relations within the city. Buildings communicate not only about their output and production of energy but about their form as well. There is an option to evaluate mutual urban interactions of the buildings, starting with the parking spaces up to the entitlement for sun of the future buildings. The research shows one of the options how to extend the building's information model into the conceptual design stage and how to interconnect data with the environment (Fig. 9).

Acknowledgement. This paper was prepared within the grant project: Architecture and Urban Planning 2020 – towards a zero energy standard, VEGA č. 1/0559/13.

References

1. Townsend, A.M.: Smart Cities: Big Data, Civic Hackers, and the Quest for a New Utopia. W. W. Norton & Company, New York (2013)
2. Krajcsovics, L.: Nulový, plusový, autonómny dom. In: Špaček, R., Pifko, H. (eds.) Rukoväť udržateľnej architektúry, p. 59. SKA, Bratislava (2013)
3. Keppl, J.: Ekologický algoritmus navrhovania. In: Špaček, R., Pifko, H. (eds.) Rukoväť udržateľnej architektúry, pp. 72–79. SKA, Bratislava (2013)
4. Krippelová, Z., Peráčková, J.: Aká je spotreba teplej vody na obyvateľa v bytovom dome? TZB Haustech. Odb. Recenzovaný Časopis Z Obl. TZB Tech. Prostredia. vol. 22, pp. 54–56 (2014)
5. Šebest, D.: Solarne kolektory: ohrev vody. http://www.solarnekolektory.sk/index.php?id=247
6. energia: Ako si vybrať najvhodnejší kotol pre vykurovanie domu? http://energia.dennikn.sk/poradime-vam/zemny-plyn-a-ropa/ako-si-vybrat-najvhodnejsi-kotol-pre-vykurovanie-domu/3996/

Using the Means-Ends Approach
to Understand the Value of Sustainability
on the Property Market

Michal Gluszak[(⊠)] and Małgorzata Zięba

Cracow University of Economics, ul. Rakowicka 27, 31-510 Krakow, Poland
{gluszakm, ziebam}@uek.krakow.pl

Abstract. The paper explores the drivers of business organizations' decisions to locate in sustainable office buildings. This study uses a Means-End Chain (MEC) analysis to investigate tenant decision-making processes in the commercial property market. Fundamental research question was to identify motivations of market participants when they choose to locate in a green buildings, whether they aim for economics benefits or intend to promote themselves as environmentally responsible. First part discusses existing literature referring to benefits of sustainable buildings as perceived by market participants. Next, the development of sustainable office market in Poland has been presented. Finally, the research data and method were discussed along with the findings of the research. The study revealed limited environmental awareness of real estate market participants in Poland. Cost effectiveness of the selected space and corporate image are the values that link their choices to sustainability of the office building.

Keywords: Real estate · Sustainable · Means-End Chain analysis · Green building · Certification

1 Introduction

Incorporation of the concept of sustainable development into built environment results in construction of buildings which are called sustainable, green, high performance, featured by environmentally conscious design, economic use of natural resources at the construction stage, and during exploitation phase, low negative impact on the natural environment and its bio-diversity as well as on the local community, while providing optimal utility for their owners, tenants and other users and satisfying profitability for investors.

Even though there are disputes over the concept of sustainability in built environment [40], there exist some generally accepted definitions; among them the one by Charles Kibert [21]: "(…) sustainable buildings are responsibly created and managed construction environment, complying with the guidelines of natural environment protection and the efficient use of natural resources". But the most common and mainstream definitions are associated with the Brundtland Commission Report [37] and Elkington's [10] conceptualization of sustainable development into business activities.

© ICST Institute for Computer Sciences, Social Informatics and Telecommunications Engineering 2016
A. Leon-Garcia et al. (Eds.): Smart City 2015, LNICST 166, pp. 738–749, 2016.
DOI: 10.1007/978-3-319-33681-7_65

Sustainable buildings are the application of Triple Bottom Line: Profit, People, Planet, concept into business practices in real estate market. The concept assuming that companies should consider economic (economic value created by the company, economic benefit to the surrounding community and society), social (the fair and favorable business practices regarding labor and the community in which the company conducts its business) and environmental (the use of sustainable environmental practices and the reduction of environment footprint) impacts in their practices.

Literature provides a list of key design features of sustainable buildings [1, 12]: (A) responsibility to the environment; (B) efficient use of resources, in particular non-renewable energy and water resources; (C) maximum reduction of refuse, and the practice of recycling; (D) application of "environmentally friendly" materials; (E) flexibility and the possibility to re-adapt the building, its installations and appliances as a way to saving resources and economy; (F) the application of building management systems that monitor and control its appliances and installations in line with the principle of energy and non-renewable resources saving.

Since 2000 we observed diffusion of environmental innovation on the commercial property market [14] and growing competition between multi-criteria certification systems used to measure building sustainability [15].

Even though the definition of sustainability in built environment is disputable, it is generally acknowledged that into the category of a green building fall primarily buildings awarded one of a 'green certificates': BREEAM, LEED, Green Star, DGNB, CASBEE etc. These rating tools were developed to estimate the sustainability of the overall building stock in countries and an individual building, thus making investment and occupancy decisions more conscious for market participants. Even though the certification schemes differ, they have become useful also for the research purposes.

In recent years, the importance of the idea of sustainable development has been noticeably increasing in commercial building industry in Western Europe and United States and the number of sustainable real estate has increased dramatically [7], with extremely high increase of LEED projects worldwide [2], with more than a half companies worldwide projected to undertake green buildings activities (as compared to 13 % in 2009) [41]. Building certification schemes (LEED, Green Star, BREEM, CASBEE) have been successfully used in developed countries, but experienced considerable problems in less mature economies [30].

Eicholtz, Kok and Quigley [9] indicate that there are four basic explanations increasing users propensity to choose sustainable properties (properties with green building certificate). These are as follows: (A) direct economic benefits resulting from lower operating costs and lower energy consumption in those buildings; (B) indirect economic benefits drawn from improved image, increased work efficiency of staff, lower staff turnover, lower absenteeism due to sick building syndrome; (C) risk avoidance which in market conditions translates into the rate of functional and moral deterioration of sustainable building, commercial character of a facility, future changes of energy prices and future institutional and legal changes; (D) ethical conduct related to CSR (Corporate Social Responsibility), responsible property investing, and corporate culture.

According to economic theory, higher utility of office environment should translate into willingness to pay for better work space, and finally higher office rents.

Literature is quite consistent on rent premiums in sustainable office space [11]. Most studies report rent increase in such buildings, by 2–7 % [8], by 5 % [29], by 4–5 % [13], and even from 7 % to 17 % for buildings with Energy Star certificate and LEED ecological certificate, respectively [39], worldwide research, as presented by Stein et al. [35], confirms these economics benefits of green buildings. Several research findings suggest tenants willingness to pay higher rental rates for office space in green buildings, by 12.4 % on average in Poland [43], by average 3 % in Switzerland (2.59 % in private sector, 3.88 % public sector companies) on lease [38].

Most authors also indicate lower costs incurred by the use of sustainable buildings [24, 29, 33]. Especially savings on energy costs convince real estate companies to include green buildings into their portfolios as research in Great Britain demonstrates [5].

Direct economic benefits of sustainable buildings are the drivers of green real estate development but the benefits for employees and marketing and image aspects of investing and occupying 'green' space is gaining on significance considerably.

Sustainability is one of the features influencing the choice of the office by the tenants, others include: location, flexibility, cost, staff needs, external pressure, marketing and availability [22]. Lower operational costs of green buildings were not as important as marketing reasons – to enhance their image and satisfy CSR policies (the case of larger organizations), which choose green office space as this is what customers and 'market' expects and they want to be seen as responsible corporations. In case of smaller organizations, sustainability was declared part of their organizational culture and necessity to lower the maintenance costs. These marketing advantages were also confirmed by research in New Zealand, where the green certificate is seen as providing competitive advantage to investors and developers as well as better work conditions for tenants and together with the existence of a rating systems, the three are main drivers for developments of green buildings [3]. Bond and Perrett's research also confirms the significance of CSR policy, company's image considerations along with environmental considerations in developing plans for involvement in green buildings [3].

Involvement in the ecological building is the way business organizations may pursue to stand out from the competition to create the image of an innovative organization, socially responsible, concerned about the natural environment, setting new trends (USBGC). The research that has been conducted to date contributes to the issue indirectly [9]. Eichholtz et al. [9] noted that CSR influences corporate decisions on property market (e.g. deciding on LEED certified office space). Similarly, non-profit and government organizations display higher propensity to rent office space in an ecological building, guided strongly by legal considerations. The research by Myers et al. [25] proves the difference in motives to choose sustainable buildings between private and public sector, with the latter preferring social and environmental issues over financial reasons. And public companies express higher willingness to pay for leasing space in green buildings [38].

A few countries conducted research on the relationship between CSR and decisions on the property market. To give an example, Hebb et al. [17] indicated growing CSR awareness among developers and institutional investors operating on commercial property market in Canada. Similar research with comparable results was also conducted in European countries [26]. For many companies occupying office space in a green building is a way to communicate their corporate vision to shareholders and a part of

CSR policy that incorporates Environmental, Social and Governance virtues; this mostly refers to institutional investors and financial services, insurance and advertising companies and investors concerned with Responsible Property Investment [5, 27].

The research conducted in 6 U.S. cities, over the importance of green buildings attributes proves that most desired typical green buildings attributes (divided into: environmental, economic, and social as in the Triple Bottom Line) are more important for the tenants' employees, representing 'social' attributes [34]. Findings suggest that green buildings generate more social than economic and environmental benefits from the point of view of their users.

The overview of the latest research worldwide proves there's significant increase in the demand for green office space driven by social responsibility aspects of corporate policies and willingness to provide better workspace, which indirectly generates economic benefits to organizations (wellbeing of employees, higher productivity, lower turnover of employees).

And it is an important finding, further justification of the research on the value of sustainability for the market participants. But still, as Warren-Myers puts it [36]: "without financial justification and viability of the required investment it is likely that the advancement of sustainability in commercial real estate will be limited".

Knowledge of the investors' attitude towards sustainability in Polish real estate market and what arguments justify their choices of green buildings is particularly scarce. It is worth noting that although certification systems for ecological solutions such as LEED, Green Star, BREEM, CASBEE have been applied in highly developed countries, their implementation on nascent property markets such as Poland is relatively rare. That provision includes empirical research which predominantly has been focused on highly developed office space markets. The report authored by Sayce et al. [32] based on 128 papers indicates that till 2009 majority of papers was targeted on the US (28 %), Great Britain (26 %), and Australia (22 %).

2 Green Buildings in Poland

According to the report of Jones Lang LaSalle [20] focused on ecological building in the selected countries of Eastern Europe (Poland, the Czech Republic, Slovakia, Hungary, Romania and the Republic of Serbia), in the first quarter of 2012 there were 670 thousand sq.m. of office space in buildings that received multi-criteria certificates (LEED, BREEM, DGNB). The high share of ecological space within the total office space in the countries of Eastern Europe (as high as 8 % in Prague) finds explanation in the fact that those markets are relatively poorly developed, and the existing volume of such spaces is still negligible in comparison to similar cities in Western Europe. Hence new investment projects make a relatively larger impact on the changes of status quo on the market. That volume is not distributed evenly, and there are four major regional centers with the highest concentration of large ecological building projects, i.e. Prague, Warsaw, Bucharest and Budapest. By the end of 2013 there was over 730 thousand sq.m of certified office space only in Poland and if green office space in Czech Republic, Hungary, Romania and Slovakia are included, there are 1,7 million sq.m. of sustainable office space in Central and Eastern Europe, and this number has been increasing annually [20]. At the beginning of 2014 almost 2.5 million sq. meter of office space was targeting certification (mainly BREAAM, and LEED – second most popular).

Between 2012 and 2014 Warsaw became the hub of ecological building in Eastern Europe (about 550 thousand sq.m/UFA by the end of 2014) taking the place of Prague. Jones Lang Lasalle's report informed that 100 % of office building projects that realized in 2012 have been covered by ecological certification procedure. Even if that estimate were slightly exaggerated, such large dominance of ecological building proves that type of building slowly joins the main stream of office building development in Poland [20].

Further on in our analysis we will focus on the volume of sustainable office space currently available in Poland. According to our assessment, in the first quarter of 2012 approximately 2–3 % of office space available in major cities in Poland (Warsaw, Kraków, Łódź, Wrocław, Poznań, Trójmiasto) is to be found in buildings that have been awarded ecological certificates. Needless to say, that volume is not evenly distributed – similarly to the commercial market, there is a noticeable strong dominance of the central part of Poland (that is Warsaw, the capital city, currently accommodating 50 % of ecologically certified office space).

According to Colliers [6] at the beginning of 2015 there were 47 LEED certified buildings in Poland, 24 of them in Warsaw, 4 in Krakow and the rest in other regional cities (Poznan, Wroclaw, Lodz, Szczecin, Gdansk). At the beginning of 2015 there are 202 BREAAM certified projects, what makes 81 % of green (certified) buildings in Poland). Half of them – 102 building are located in Warsaw, 22 in Krakow and 14 in Poznan.

3 Data and Methods

During the research we conducted 12 semi-structured in-depth interviews from May to August 2011. The research sample were commercial property professionals in Krakow (10) and Warsaw (2). The respondents were employees of consultancy companies specializing in real estate (e.g. Colliers, Knight Frank, FYI), developer companies involved in building green (Buma Group), employees of analytical institutes involved in market research (mrn.pl) and independent consultants in real estate. The interviewees were asked several questions about office space tenants – or more specifically users decisions and beliefs when choosing their office space. Although not expressed explicitly, the main research questions were: (A) are office tenants aware of characteristics (and advantages) of sustainable office space? (B) is sustainability taken into account when making decisions about renting office space, and if so what are the main reasons? (C) do office tenants in Poland value sustainable more than standard buildings? (D) are they willing to pay more for having sustainable working environment?

In order to understand how companies perceive relevant aspects of office space, the Means-End Chain (MEC) model was applied MEC conceptual framework was originally created by Gutman [16] and developed by Reynolds and Gutman [31].

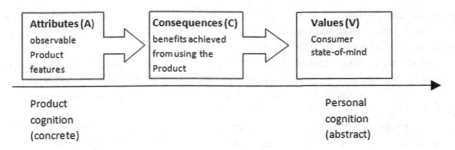

Fig. 1. Means-End Value Chain. Source: Own based on [16]

MEC links sequentially products' attributes (A) to consequences of product use (C) and to ultimate values (V). The A-C-V sequence is called Means-End Chain or Ladder (see Fig. 1).

MEC was successfully used since, when analyzing preferences and values attached to commercial products, but also in the field of architecture and urban design [42]. Lundgren and Lic [23] used MEC to understand housebuyers' needs and preferences, which can support decision-making in product development. In other study MEC was used as a theoretical framework to link customized housing projects attributes and costumers' values [18]. MEC was also applied to understand meanings and attitudes towards sustainability, for example when analyzing growing environmental awareness of clients in restaurants [19]. To authors best knowledge, although several authors tried

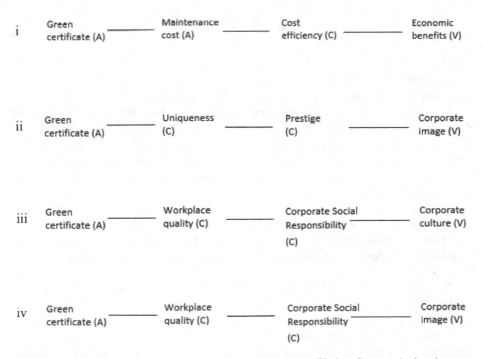

Fig. 2. Theoretical sustainable property Means-End Values Chains. Source: Authors' own

to use qualitative research to analyze the role of sustainability in decision processes of different agents on the commercial property market [22], there is no single paper applying MEC theoretical framework.

Based on literature review (see Sect. 1) we identified hypothetical Means-End Value Chains, that link property sustainability (we used green building certificate as a proxy), their functional consequences and values achieved by companies using office space (see Fig. 2).

To demonstrate how to verify connections between property attributes and end values on an empirical level, we used qualitative research results [2]. In order to elicit A-C-V sequences laddering interviews was used. Laddering is an in-depth one-on-one interviewing technique aimed at understanding of how users translate the attributes into meaningful associations with consequences of their use (direct and indirect), and finally values. The ultimate goal is the construction of a hierarchical value map (HVM) which is used to interpret market preferences.

4 Results and Discussion

In the first phase, interviewees were asked to indicate important factors considered by companies when choosing office space. To analyze the results, we used free-list technique. We analyzed both relative frequency of factors listed, and the order in which factors were listed. To build relative hierarchy of decision factors we constructed Smith's S saliency index [4, p. 21]:

$$S_j = \frac{n - r_j + 1}{n}. \tag{1}$$

where:
  rj - position of element on a free-list
  n - number of elements on a free-list Main text paragraph

According to experts, the most important features to be taken into account when choosing office space is rent (100 % of responses), the location of the building (83 %), the structure and size of the office space (75 %), capacity charge and the media (58 %) and the availability of parking spaces (50 %). Two respondents spontaneously mentioned the architecture, and only one mentioned the green certificate. The results are summarized in Table 1.

The importance of rent and maintenance costs can be attributed to budget constraints. Interviewees were consistent when assessing tenants flexibility in rent terms (1–2 euro/sqm/month). High sensitivity to rent in their opinions was typical to large tenants in the services sector - Business Process Outsourcing (BPO) and Shared Service Centre (SSC).

The size of office space was crucial for large tenants (i.e. tenants willing to rent 5000–10000 sqm of office space), and the office market is quite thin when this constraint is induced. Often, buildings are designed and built to suit for a specific tenant. The importance of location is not necessarily the most important feature and not only connected to the distance from city centre and prestige. In many cases, accessibility

Table 1. List of Means-End concepts

Attributes (A)	Consequences (C)	Values (I)
Rent (N = 12; S = 0,94)	Cost efficiency	Economic
Location (N = 10; S = 0,7)	Prestige	benefits
Structure and area of office space	Flexibility and	Corporate culture
(N = 9; S = 0,69)	options	Corporate image
Maintenance costs (N = 7; S = 0,55)	Workplace quality	
Parking lot (N = 6; S = 0,42)		
Tenant mix (N = 5; S = 0,25)		
Amenities (N = 5; S = 0,36)		
Architecture (N = 2; S = 0,18)		
Green certificate (N = 1; S = 0,33)		

Note: N – number of respondents spontaneously quoting the attribute; S – Smith's Saliency Index
Source: Authors' own

(by public transport - tram in Krakow and metro in Warsaw) and a good connection to the airport is even more important.

An significant conclusion of the qualitative research is that of low ecological awareness of tenants and companies. It is a conclusion that should encourage various institutions to launch educational activities. Low level of environmental consciousness is manifested i.e. by limited recognition of multi-criteria building certification systems; even worldwide applied systems such as LEED and BREEAM. Multinational corporation are basically featured by higher level of environmental awareness and do recognize sustainability criteria, with European companies being mostly familiar with BREEAM system and American ones with LEED.

Experts emphasized that generally tenants are not conscious of real economic benefits and costs of sustainable office space or are even express conviction about higher costs of renting sustainable space.

According to some respondents, there are significant differences between Polish and international companies, when office amenities are concerned. While some of the respondents felt that they were rather derived from the size of the organization (large companies attach greater importance to employees satisfaction and work space comfort), others argued multinational companies are more demanding. Popular expectations in that field are: air conditioning systems, access control, server rooms, recreation space.

Except one, respondents wouldn't spontaneously point green certificate as significant decision-making criteria when selecting the office space/particular building but direct questions about this feature of the building, lead to the conclusion that in practice green certificate has no or low significance (also due to very limited stock of green space in the market), although some companies sending request for proposal required space in a green building. General opinion of all respondents was that tenants – even those declaring interest in the sustainable office space would not be willing to pay (WTP) for it, i.e. they would not bear any additional costs of using green space such as higher rents, costs of moving to other building or participation in modernization costs. Probably tenants would accept temporary burden of modernization into green building.

When asked directly most of respondents admitted that green building certificate can be a factor in selected cases – for examples major international companies (with developed CSR practices). Laddering interview was used to understand the consequences and

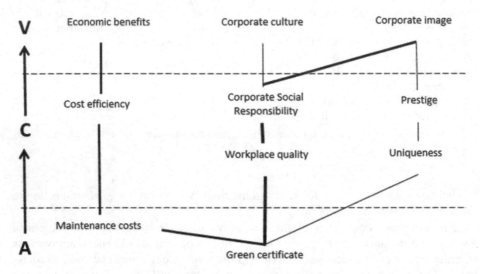

Fig. 3. Hierarchical value map for green certificate. Source: Authors' own. Note: links indicate Means-End Chains found in previous research or suggested in theoretical papers; thick lines indicate MEC identified during interviews.

values linked to the green building certificate (LEED, BREEAM or DGNB), and to verify chains identified in the previous studies (Fig. 3).

Respondents pointed out that environmental awareness (interest in Green Building Certificate) of tenants may be the result of their sensitivity to costs of space (maintenance costs), which is a major feature in space selection process. Basically, economic reasons (cost efficiency) create "green" behavior and raise environmental awareness.

Another chain identified by laddering interviews linked green building certificate with workplace quality (the functional consequence), and reporting related to Corporate Social Responsibility. According to experts interviewed it was not driven by concerns about environment, but rather because of corporate image enhancement practices used by multinational companies operating worldwide. In the same time experts admitted, that only few Polish companies/tenants consciously create the image of environmentally aware and socially responsible organizations.

5   Conclusions

Sustainable construction has been developing in developed countries with significant dynamics since 2000s. Research justifies this development with benefits green buildings provide over conventional buildings. These basically include lower maintenance costs, indirect economic benefits due to improved image of the company-tenant, lower risk related to more sustainable market value of green buildings. Also, data (statistics) proves that market for green buildings has been growing recently in countries of Eastern Europe, and volume of new, sustainable office space, has been increasing significantly. But it is still very limited, and e.g. in Poland only 2–3 % of office space has been awarded ecological certificates (mostly LEED and BREEAM). The market of sustainable office space in Poland is limited and so far, there has been no research focused on demand for green offices and attitudes of users towards sustainability in construction.

Analysis of attitudes of office space users was conducted using existing data - analyzed were studies carried out among Polish companies, and own research was conducted - in-depth interviews carried out on a sample of professionals operating in commercial real estate market. The results were surprisingly consistent and allowed the isolation of the major barriers to development of green building in Poland. These are the following issues: (A) superficial understanding of the ecological issues among Polish enterprises (lower than in other countries in the region); (B) lack of awareness of users on the benefits of the sustainable of construction; (C) lack of conviction among developers and investors about whether to invest in green buildings (especially the demand for and willingness to pay for environmental solutions); (D) costs and financing of sustainable construction; (E) financial crisis has increased uncertainty of investing on the property market and reduced willingness to invest.

Above enumerated barriers, major criteria of office space selection – total costs (maintenance and rent) and generally low level of environmental awareness makes for most important barriers in further development of the sustainable office space volume in Poland.

The methods applied in this research were qualitative, and included semi-structured in-depth interviews. Research sample consisted of Polish real estate market professionals, involved in market research, analysis and investment. The results of MEC analysis allowed to create the hierarchical value map for office space decisions.

From practical point of view, the results indicate clearly the need for education and promotion of ecological solutions in construction and popularizing information on real economic benefits of sustainable space (maintenance costs, rents, value). Potential investors and developers of sustainable office space should appreciate the information that companies selecting sustainable office space are concerned about their image and apply rules of responsible business conduct.

Undoubtedly, there is a need for further research in this field; particularly as this was the first research of the users' attitudes towards sustainable office space in Poland. Research sample should be significantly larger and quantitative methods could be applied to investigate (and possibly measure) more thoroughly attitudes of tenants towards green buildings and ecological issues in their space-selection decisions.

Conclusions of qualitative research on the barriers of diffusion sustainable office buildings in Poland and attitude of tenants towards them are not univocal as the opinions of respondents – experts. Thus, the problem requires further research and more precise methods and techniques; also – bigger research sample.

Acknowledgments. The publication was co-financed from the funds allocated to the Faculty of Economics and International Relations, Cracow University of Economics (Research grant: 052/WE-KEN/01/2015/S/5052).

References

1. Addae-dapaah, K., Hiang, L.K., Yen, N.: Sustainability of sustainable real property development. J. Sustain. Real Estate **1**(1), 203–225 (2009)
2. Belniak, S., Głuszak, M., Zięba, M.: Budownictwo ekologiczne. Aspekty ekonomiczne, 1st edn. Wydawnictwo Naukowe PWN, Warszawa (2013)
3. Bond, S., Perrett, G.: The key drivers and barriers to the sustainable development of commercial property in New Zealand. J. Sustain. Real Estate **4**(1), 48–77 (2012)
4. Borgatti, S.: ANTHROPAC 4.0 Reference Manual. Analytic Technologies, Natick (1996)
5. Chegut, A., Eichholtz, P., Kok, N.: Supply, demand and the value of green buildings. Urban Stud. **51**(1), 22–43 (2013)
6. Colliers International: Zielone Budynki w Polsce 2015. Certyfikacja w liczbach (2015)
7. DeLisle, J., Grissom, T., Högberg, L.: Sustainable real estate: an empirical study of the behavioural response of developers and investors to the LEED rating system. J. Property Investment Finan. **31**(1), 10–40 (2013)
8. Eichholtz, P., Kok, N., Quigley, J.M.: Doing Well by Doing Good Green Office Buildings (No. W08-001). Program on Housing and Urban Policy (2008)
9. Eichholtz, P., Kok, N., Quigley, J.M.: Why companies rent green: CSR and the role of real estate. Acad. Manag. Ann. Meet. Proc. **8**(1), 1–6 (2009)
10. Elkington, J.: Enter the triple bottom line. In: Henriques, A., Richardson, J. (eds.) The Triple Bottom Line: Does it all Add Up?, pp. 1–16. Earthscan, London (2004)
11. Falkenbach, H., Lindholm, A.-L., Schleich, H.: Environmental sustainability: drivers for the real estate investor. J. Real Estate Lit. **18**, 203–223 (2010)
12. Frej, A.B. (ed.): Green Office Buildings: a Practical Guide to Development. Urban land Institute, Washington, D.C. (2005)
13. Fuerst, F., McAllister, P.: Green noise or green value? Measuring the effects of environmental certification on office values. Real Estate Econ. **39**(1), 45–69 (2011)
14. Głuszak, M., Zięba, M.: Dyfuzja innowacji ekologicznych w budownictwie na przykładzie rynku nieruchomości komercyjnych w krajach OECD. Zarządzanie i Finanse **12**(4), 153–166 (2014)
15. Głuszak, M.: Internationalization, competiveness and green building certification in europe. In: Stanek, P., Wach, K. (eds.) Europeanization Processes from the Mesoeconomic Perspective: Industries and Policies, pp. 173–191. Cracow University of Economics, Krakow (2015)
16. Gutman, J.: A means-end chain model based on consumer categorization processes. J. Mark. **46**, 60–72 (1982)
17. Hebb, T., Hamilton, A., Hachigian, H.: Responsible property investing in Canada: factoring both environmental and social impacts in the Canadian real estate market. J. Bus. Ethics **92**, 99–115 (2010)
18. Hentschke, C., Formoso, C., Rocha, C., Echeveste, M.: A method for proposing valued-adding attributes in customized housing. Sustainability **6**(12), 9244–9267 (2014)
19. Jeng, M.-Y., Yeh, T.-M.: The effect of consumer values on the brand position of green restaurants by means-end chain and laddering interviews. Serv. Bus. (2015)
20. Lasalle, J.L.: Offices. Going Green in CEE, 2013/2014 Online. http://www.jll.pl/poland/en-gb/Research/Offices_Going_Green_in_CEE_2014_final.pdf

21. Kibert, C.J.: Sustainable Construction: Green Building Design and Delivery, 1st edn. Wiley, Hoboken (2007)
22. Levy, D., Peterson, G.: The effect of sustainability on commercial occupiers' building choice. J. Property Investment Finan. **31**(3), 267–284 (2013)
23. Lundgren, B.A., Lic, T.: Customers' perspectives on a residential development using the laddering method. J. Hous. Built Environ. **25**(1), 37–52 (2009)
24. Miller, N., Spivey, J., Florance, A.: Does green pay off? J. Real Estate Portfolio Manag. **14**(4), 385–399 (2008)
25. Myers, G., Reed, R., Robinson, J.: Sustainable property - the future of the New Zealand market. Pac. Rim Property Res. J. **14**(3), 298–321 (2008)
26. Nappi-Choulet, I., Décamps, A.: Is sustainability attractive for corporate real estate decisions? In: ESSEC Working Paper. Document de Recherche ESSEC/Centre de Recherche de l'ESSEC (2011)
27. Nelson, A., Rakau, O.: Green buildings. A niche becomes mainstream. Deutsche Bank Res. (2010)
28. Pivo, G., Fisher, J.D.: Investment Returns from Responsible Property Investments: Energy Efficient, Transit-oriented and Urban Regeneration Office Properties in the US from 1998–2007, Working Paper No. WP 08-2 (2008)
29. Pivo, G., Fisher, J.D.: Income, value, and returns in socially responsible office properties. J. Real Estate Res. **32**(3), 243–270 (2010)
30. Reed, R., Bilos, A., Wilkinson, S.: International comparison of sustainable rating tools authors. J. Sustain. Real Estate **1**(1), 1–22 (2009)
31. Reynolds, T.J., Gutman, J.: Laddering theory, method, analysis, and interpretation. J. Advertising Res. **28**, 11–31 (1988)
32. Sayce, S., Sundberg, A., Clements, B.: Is sustainability reflected in commercial property prices: an analysis of the evidence base. RICS, London (2010)
33. Shiers, D.E.: "Green" developments: environmentally responsible buildings in the UK commercial property sector. Property Manag. **18**(5), 352–365 (2000)
34. Simons, R.A., Robinson, S., Lee, E.: Green office buildings: a qualitative exploration of green office building attributes. J. Sustain. Real Estate **6**(1), 211–232 (2014)
35. Stein, M., Braun, W., Villa, M.S.: Monte carlo cash flows and sustainability: how to decide on going green authors. J. Sustain. Real Estate **6**(1), 143–161 (2014)
36. Warren-Myers, G.: The value of sustainability in real estate: a review from a valuation perspective. J. Property Investment Finan. **30**(2), 115–144 (2012)
37. WCED: Our common future. In: UN World Commission on Environment and Development (1987)
38. Wiencke, A.: Willingness to pay for green buildings - empirical evidence from Switzerland. J. Sustain. Real Estate **5**(1), 111–133 (2013)
39. Wiley, J.A., Benefield, J.D., Johnson, K.H.: Green design and the market for commercial office space. J. Real Estate Finan. Econ. **41**(2), 228–243 (2010)
40. Wilkinson, S.J.: Conceptual understanding of sustainability in the Australian property sector. Property Manag. **31**(3), 260–272 (2013)
41. World Green Building Trends: Business Benefits Driving New and Retrofit Market Opportunities in Over 60 Countries. McGraw Hill Construction, New York (2013)
42. Zachariah, Z.B., Bin, M., Jusan, M.: Means-end chain model framework for measuring housing environment choice behavior. J. Civil Eng. Archit. **5**(6), 535–546 (2011)
43. Zieba, M., Belniak, S., Gluszak, M.: Demand for sustainable office space in Poland: the results from a conjoint experiment in Krakow. Property Manag. **31**(5), 404–419 (2013)

Being Smart in Project Management

Karolína Hanulíková$^{(\boxtimes)}$, Marcel Martišek, and Tomáš Uhlík

Institute of Management, Slovak University of Technology in Bratislava,
Vazovova 5, 811 07 Bratislava, Slovakia
hanulikova.karolina@gmail.com,
marcel.martisek@gmail.com, tomas.uhlik@gmail.com

Abstract. This paper describes the real estate development projects and its management from investor's point of view, explaining why the management of such a complicated business in competitive environment needs smart solutions Authors have chosen few of managing tools that help private developers to drive successfully their projects. The paper discuss organization chart of project team, basic division of project timeline into detailed stages, role of relatively new members like foreign architect and external construction manager. Authors are employed in one of the biggest central European development company and they share experience from different projects in Slovakia and Czech Republic.

Keywords: Project management · Real estate development · Construction management · Architect · Optimization

1 Introduction

Nowadays, being smart means to save money. In private business being smart means to earn money. Real estate business in this point of view is the same as other fields of investment. An investor in Real estate sector needs to understand deeply all processes that happen since the plot is bought till the last flat is sold. From the beginning of investment development in Slovakia and Czech Republic, early 90's, developers are learning how to be smart while they manage their projects.

A peculiarity of real estate project is in its diversity. In this kind of projects many different professions take part, execution of these projects takes a lot of time, even the juristic environment and market demand change fast. Management of this process requires tools to execute, control and improve every single step.

With 25 years of experience including the decay caused by the real estate bubble, developers have set up few easy ways how to make their project successful. The complicated and long term projects were split in smaller parts, which are easier to control. To control this smaller parts, sets of rules and models were established. These rules and models are being improved by successes and failures every day and this paper describes only few of them, used by developers nowadays.

1.1 Methods

All of us work for a private investment company, which is active also in real estate development, we are focusing on residential projects. We worked on several projects

© ICST Institute for Computer Sciences, Social Informatics and Telecommunications Engineering 2016
A. Leon-Garcia et al. (Eds.): Smart City 2015, LNICST 166, pp. 750–759, 2016.
DOI: 10.1007/978-3-319-33681-7_66

throughout their all development stages and created several internal documents. Based on our experience and internal company know-how we tried to focus on several topics in this paper. To compose this paper we started by analyzing several books and journals. After this preliminary literature research we tried to look at the project management in bigger picture, as we do in our ordinary profession. For this purpose we synthetized the literature review and tried to point out some smart tools of project management in real estate development.

2 Tools of Smart Project Management

Up until the start of the 20th century, the history of project management was indistinct from the history of techniques or professions. At the beginning the project activity had no specific status. Project management only became a management model in the 1950s and 1960s. At the time, it became independent and standardized, in particular because differences between business sectors were perceived as less important than common preoccupations in managing engineering projects. The standardization of practices and tools was widely encouraged by major contractors who viewed them as a way of rationalizing their efforts. Around the same time, the management of engineering projects began to move towards standardized tools, practices and roles, and the emergence of a true model [1].

Any kind of management needs a tool or tools for execution. And all of them can be optimized. As one of the historically first such tool can be considered the Gantt charts, which were very well established by the mid-1920s as a general production planning tool. Their earlier applications to more general production planning and control problems have been overwhelmed by practical problems and overtaken by technological developments. Computing nowadays offers more powerful techniques for modelling these problems; but Gantt charts still have found a role providing a readily useful interface allowing users to define problems and better understand and accept solutions. Gantt charts remain popular management tools in spite of dating back over a century and in their current primary application to projects they provide an effective means for displaying important information [2].

Speaking about management tools often goes along with approaches to management strategy. There are many different approaches, but Maylor offers very interesting view on this problematics. He characterizes the traditional approach through weak link between project and organisational strategy, lack of co-ordination between partial projects and inevitable resource conflicts. Projects are usually represented by economically important set of activities. In developing the argument for a forward move in the subject area, some underlying problems are identified with the universality of the traditional approach. High-performing firms, taking a radically different approach to strategy, assessment, planning and the subject of project management itself have solved many of these problems. He synthesised these solutions into the "Beyond the Gantt Chart" approach, which is seen as a coherent, co-ordinated, focused and strategy-driven. In contrast to the traditional approach, the BTGC approach focus planning activities not only on planning, but on all activities from planning through to post project activities review and marketing of project performance. Project is perceived as a core business process which draws on similar processes for experience and contains many elements of repetitive work [3].

This chapter is dedicated to several common tools used in real estate development, that have been optimized lately and nowadays provide effective instruments in development and management of the projects.

2.1   Project Stages Model and Organization Chart

Recent progress in project management reveals that projects are becoming more complex and wide-ranging. It leads to fact, that they can no more be held and overseen by one hand. Tendency to develop complexity also implies the need of a variety of very specialized knowledge which is usually not commonly available. Solution is in division of work and awarding subtasks to respective specialists. This solves the demand for skills and on the other hand, induces the new requirement of motivation and coordination [4].

Firstly it is very important to organize development project into smaller stages according to different processes that happen. In every stage different kind of activity is needed and each activity requires different professional with different responsibilities. In Slovakia for example, developers often follow an established model displayed below in Table 1.

At the beginning, it's the development process divided according the Building Code. Some of them are subdivided according criteria that are important to developer like size of internal project team, budget, time, etc.

Organization chart allows to see clearly all the members and relations between them during the project. Investor and his team occupy the first levels of the organization chart. Organization chart described hereafter is only one specific example, but effective and clear.

Partner or owner is the actual money carrier. They make the conceptual and strategic decisions which are executed by his internal team consisting of business development manager and technical project manager. Business development managers not only create and lead the team but they are responsible for whole project financial management, bank relationships and reporting to partner(owner). The internal team members are chosen by Business development manager and their responsibilities are specialized in four sections. The project development section takes care of land preparation, negotiation with local authorities and communication with architects and engineers. Once the plot is prepared for the construction, all permissions are issued and project documentation is finished, the project is taken by the construction management section. Members of CMS start with tendering process and they lead the construction till the permit of use is issued. Internal construction managers often hire an external construction management companies to facilitate work to internal team. Sales or leasing section prepares all marketing strategy with all its products and once the building permit is issued they start with the sale (sometimes the pre-sale starts even without any permission, through reservation contract). Property management section is mostly used in office development. Property managers takeover the building after the

Table 1. Project stages in residential development projects, Slovakia. Source: authors' practice

Stages		Purposes and tasks
1 PREPARATION	Masterplanning	Setting up project strategy. Adjusting the whole scheme massing to meet basic technical requirements (daylight, traffic, etc.), client's Strategic Brief and site constrains. Definition of project phasing strategy, Masterplan and landscape framework.
2 DESIGN	Concept Design	Outline Architectural Concept Design including outline Proposals for structural and building services systems, outline specifications, information for cost planning. Ensures that the project is feasible technically, functionally and financially. Optional solutions provided to the Client.
	Environmental impact assessment	Information feed from Concept Design to EIA consultant.
	Planning Permit Documentation	Formal documents necessary for Full Planning Permission application submitted to Local Authority.
	Schematic Design	Detailed Proposal, full design of the project by the Design Architect including design for structure and building services systems, update of outline specifications and information for cost planning.
	Building Permit Documentation	Final Proposal based on Scheme design. Technical design and specifications sufficient to coordinate all project components and elements of the project and information for statutory standards and construction safety. Building Regulation Approval application submitted to Local Authority.
3 PRE-CONSTRUCTION	Tender Documentation	Based on architectural Leading Details. Preparation of production information in sufficient detail to enable a tender or tenders to be obtained.
	Tender Action	Identification and evaluation of potential contractors and/or specialists for the project.
	Construction Documentation	Preparation of further information for construction required under the building contract.
4 CONSTRUCTION	Construction Administration	Site Supervision, preparation of further information for construction required, review drawings from contractors.
5 USE	Completion	Documenting and handing over the building to the client.

permit of use and they manage processes like maintenance, cleaning and tenants care. Internal team usually consists of 5–10 persons according to its complexity or the stage.

External teams are much bigger, always chosen with many criteria like experience, price, references… The importance to the project and time of their collaboration depends of the specifics of their role in the project. If they serve only as a consultant in a limited area, the collaboration is used to be short. External partner with long term participation on the project are architect and Engineers Company and construction Management Company. Architects give the physical form to the investor's expectation and with all its subordinates create project documentation through all stages of project development. Example of organizational chart showing several levels of the whole project team, internal and external as well, is shown below in Table 2. The role of external construction manager is better described in following chapter.

Table 2. Example of organization chart in residential development projects. Source: authors' practice

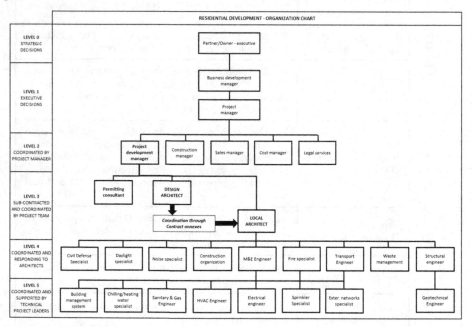

In order to maintain effective communication between the Project Manager, the Design Team, the Investor and later the Contractor it is important that regular meetings are conducted.

Meetings of all types shall be minimized in both duration and frequency. Careful consideration is to be given to the necessary attendee at each meeting. It is an aim that all meetings should have a brief agenda circulated to all participants, the Project

Manager and the Client at least 24 h in advance and that minutes be distributed within 48 h of any meeting and Actions be incorporated into Action Plans.

2.2 Foreign Inspiration

Local habits appear as in architecture as in other parts of our lives. That's why the investors are used to hire foreign architects, lately. To bring fresh ideas and unseen solutions as one of the advantages in a competitive struggle. Foreign architects design only conceptual part of the project like master plans and/or concept and schematic design for example, but the execution part will still be taken by local firms. It is not like there are some foreign architects "stealing" the job from local ones, it is always, or at least should be a win–win cooperation, because foreign architect (also called Design architect) always need some local support of Local architect. If the personal chart and every member's responsibilities are well set up and clear, than the contribution of foreign architect to the success of the project is obvious.

Design Architect. Produces an architectural Concept Design, Schematic Design and Leading Details (architectural part of Tender Documentation), while incorporating all consultants' and local team's technical and legal requests. Design architect retains full aesthetic design control and responsibility through all project Stages.

Local Architect. Is an production Architect – Planning Permit Documentation and Building Permit Documentation. Local Architect is responsible for technical (solutions,

Table 3. Task distribution in different stages. Source: authors' practice

Stages		Design architect	Local architect	Investor
1	Masterplanning	x	s + r	r
2	Concept Design	x	s + r	r
	Environmental Impact Assessment Information Feed	s	x	s
	Planning Permit Documentation	s + r	x	r
	Schematic Design	x	s	r
	Building Permit Documentation	s + r	x	r
3	Tender Documentation	s + r	x	r
	Tender Action	s + r	s + r	x
	Construction Documentation	s + r	x	r
	Changes to documentation incurred by the future owner		x	s + r
4	Construction Administration	s + r	x	s + r
5	Completion		x	s

x – responsible for specific Stage completion

r – review

s – support

construction practice) and legal assistance (planning issues, local Building Code) through Concept Design and Schematic Design Stage to Design Architect.

Local Architect is responsible for detailed co-ordination of architectural and specialist consultant work, production of Tender Documentation and Construction Documentation. Local Architect is responsible for Construction Administration and Project Completion. Local Architect will provide full support to the Client sales and marketing team at the coordination and management of changes incurred by future owners as well. Different responsibilities of Design and Local architect in different project stages are shown below in Tables 3 and 4.

Table 4. Task distribution in different stages. Source: authors' practice

General tasks/responsibilities	Design architect	Local architect	Investor
Project management			x
Design process management and Project Architect team coordination	x*	x*	
Concept team management	x		
Local team management		x	
Contractors communication for design and cost purposes	x*	x*	
Contractors communication for tender purposes	s	s	x
Project meetings attendance	x	x	x
Local authorities communication for design purposes		x	s
Local authorities communication for formal proceedings		s	x
Project Brief definition and updates	s + r	s + r	x
Site survey request - specification of site surveys required to progress design		x	
Site surveys	s	s + r	x
Local authorities constrains conformity	x	x	r
Local Building code and regulations conformity	x	x	
Architecture and Design development	x	s + r	r
Technical development	s + r	x**	r
Value Engineering	x*	x*	r
Cost control	s + r	x	r

x – responsible | * fluctuating depending on project Stage | ** based on concept team solutions
r – review | s – support/shared responsibility

2.2.1 Pros and Cons of Design and Local Architect Cooperation

+ International and skilled know-how
+ Positive PR and marketing
+ "Different" and unprejudiced approach in project design

- Complex and careful choice of foreign architect
- DA do not understand the complexities of doing business in foreign country
- difference in approach between local and foreign firms
- more difficult and complicated in coordination and communication

2.3 Construction Management

Supposing investor as the money carrier, it is very important to him to have an expert support which is motivated by the success of the project, not his own financial profit. Collaboration with a construction management company is based on the Contract of work. Construction manager is as an external member of the project team. His role is to bring smart ideas in the technical field of the project. Construction management and construction managers have many possible roles during the different phases of the project:

- **Project documentation management.** Construction manager is unique administrator of project documentation. He manages and updates all physical and digital files including revisions, controlling the project documentation is complete and in preferred quality. Construction management redistributes the project documentation between all contractors.
- **Project documentation revision.** After the project documentation is submitted, construction managers control its correctness, technical solutions and if needed, they propose better or cheaper options. The construction management check up the project documentation is up to investor's demand.
- **Cost management.** Considering the budget one of the most important piece of development project, its creation and controlling is given to that member of project team which is able to analyze every single input to the project.
- **Financial optimization.** Once issued the project cost plan, construction managers start to optimize it. It's necessary deep knowledge of the project, investor's demand and technical skills to propose savings without reducing quality of the final "product".
- **Tendering process.** One of the most important roles of construction management is during the tendering process. Construction managers prepare the tenders way that every needed piece of the project is bought and it's bought just once. This process must be as transparent as possible, allowing the investor control it anytime and compare it with approved budget. With purpose of cost reduction, the construction managers tender each item of the project with a very low degree of aggregation.
- **Construction control and coordination.** The most important contribution of construction management to the success of the project is during the 4th stage– Construction. CM controls the quality of all works every day. Their goal is to look after the building is being built up to investor's expectation.

Real estate investments with external Construction management require split the construction process in more stages – packages than it is with general contractor. This technique is called "package strategy". The amount of packages depends of the amount of the contractors that are needed. For example, these packages are used:

2010 – Excavation works
2600 – Structural constructions
3000 – Facade
4000 – Internal walls and floors, finishers
6000 – HVAC systems
7000 – Electrical installation
7500 – Elevators
9020 – Infrastructure – external works
9500 – Landscape

This package strategy appears already in the project documentation structure. Every package needs to have its documentation that is given to possible future contractors during the tendering process. Big advantage of this method is in time savings. This approach allows to start the tenders of first packages (Excavation works, structure…) in the beginning of the projection, so the projection of others packages and the tenders of first packages are happening simultaneously. During the construction each contractor is responsible only of his part of "delivery" and possible future complaint about the quality are deeply investigated to figure out who had done it wrong.

2.3.1 Pros and Cons of Building with Construction Management Instead of General Contractor

+ Objective and technically specialized member of the project team
+ Good building quality reputation
+ Absolutely transparent activities of all participants during every stage
+ Investor's control during all stages of the project
+ Time savings
+ Transparent cost planning
- More internal specialized members of project team needed
- The structure of project documentation is more complicated and more extensive, and also more expensive

3 Conclusion

The project management in Slovak and Czech Republic is saturated of many developers from small ones to the bigger ones. All of them use tools to manage their projects. These tools are mostly similar with a low degree of deflection according to the type of project they dedicate, but all of them have in common an intention to have the tools smart. Every failure is a lesson learnt that improves existing tool. In this paper, only few of the tools were mentioned above. Organization chart and project stages structure are permanent type of tool. The foreign architect or external construction managers are considered to be new tools that improved the old set of tools the developers had in past. Nowadays, project management in real estate development isn't perfect process at all. There are still difficulties that increase the risk or possibility to mislead. Therefore new tools are still needed to prevent all this uncertainties that come along with dynamic and changing market demand and environment.

References

1. Garel, G.: A history of project management models: from pre-models to the standard models. Int. J. Proj. Manag. **31**, 663–669 (2013). www.sciencedirect.com/
2. Wilson, M.J.: Gantt charts: a centenary appreciation. Eur. J. Oper. Res. **149**, 430–437 (2003). www.sciencedirect.com/
3. Maylor, H.: Beyond the Gantt chart: project management moving on. Eur. Manag. J. **19**(1), 92–100 (2001)
4. Eber, W., Zimmermann, J.: Mathematical background of key performance indicators for organizational structures in construction and real estate management. Procedia Eng. **85**, 571–580 (2014) www.sciencedirect.com/
5. Building Code no. 50/1975 Zb. on land planning and building regulations

Economic and Social Effects
of Urbanization - Case Study Analysis

Anna Wojewnik-Filipkowska[(⊠)]

Department of Management, Faculty of Investment and Real Estate,
University of Gdansk, Armii Krajowej 101, 81-824 Sopot, Poland
anna.filipkowska@ug.edu.pl

Abstract. The study focuses on the effects of uncontrolled urbanization and
local investment planning on local economy and society. The first part covers
literature review regarding economic and social effects of uncontrolled urbanization. The second part includes description of the investor and its financial
situation. Afterwards, the property under development is described and three
development plans are presented. Finally, the effectiveness evaluation is performed. The research is closed with summary and conclusions. Basic research
methods include literature review, methods of comparison, logical concluding,
and case study. Tools of financial and economic analysis have been used. Based
on cost-benefit analysis (CBA), economic internal rate of return (ERR), economic net present value (ENPV) and benefits to costs ratio (B/C) were calculated. The assumptions for three options of development program meet
conditions in terms of master planning but vary in terms of project effectiveness.
Studying different solutions can help better management and anticipate results of
different development programs for the local economy and society. Since the
proposed framework supports investment evaluation from the perspective of
society, it supports local municipal decision makers. The model may be also an
example of how to evaluate economic and social results of local planning and
may be used as a tool for effectiveness maximization.

Keywords: Urbanization · Development project · Municipality · Cost-benefit
analysis

1 Introduction - Study Justification, Aim, Methodology

A city grows quantitatively and qualitatively. It can change functions of certain areas
within the city itself or in its suburbs. Choosing the most efficient land use, providing
the best possible level of services to inhabitants while retaining the high quality of the
natural environment is a tool for optimization of urban space use and relates to the
qualitative growth. Cities' growth requires then a redesign of the spatial layout, making
decisions on the best possible way, and sequencing of city development. Moreover,
without some capital investment connected with overcoming specific infrastructure
barriers, further development might not possible. The research is then justified by the
recognition of several problems relating to local planning, land speculation, and real
estate function impact on its value. Too little attention is paid to different possible uses

© ICST Institute for Computer Sciences, Social Informatics and Telecommunications Engineering 2016
A. Leon-Garcia et al. (Eds.): Smart City 2015, LNICST 166, pp. 760–773, 2016.
DOI: 10.1007/978-3-319-33681-7_67

of land. In particular, local government should be a stabilizer of the real estate market and take proper action to determine the spatial development of the city through local plan approval. Otherwise, the city may suffer from uncontrolled urbanization and its negative effects. Thus the research fits within an existing trend of the studies relating urbanization, urban sprawl, and smart cities as a response for problems of big cities. It focuses on the effects of uncontrolled urbanization in particular and local investment planning on local economy and society. Yet, the analysis is conducted for relatively small municipality to point out that the mentioned problems of urbanization, urban sprawl and sustainable development are relevant also in that case.

The first part of the research covers brief literature review regarding economic and social effects of uncontrolled urbanization. Second part of research includes description of the investor and its financial situation determining project realization. Afterwards, the property under development is described and three development plans presented. Finally, the effectiveness evaluation of the project within its three options is performed. The research is closed with summary and conclusions.

Basic research methods include literature review, methods of comparison, logical concluding, and case study. Tools of financial and economic analysis has been used. Based on cost-benefit analysis (CBA), economic internal rate of return (ERR), economic net present value (ENPV) and benefits to costs ratio (B/C) were calculated for the three options of the project's development program. CBA is a conceptual framework to evaluate a project and determine its value from a social perspective. Therefore, CBA differs from a direct financial appraisal as it includes benefits and costs to society as a whole (external effects of the project). CBA has the same meaning as economic analysis. It reflects values which society would be willing to pay for a good or service which are not sold on a commercial market. Such aspects are characteristic mainly for public sector service [1]. Hence, economic analysis covers a wider range than financial analysis as external effects may relate to different spheres. If these results cannot be expressed in monetary values, evaluation of the effectiveness should include also qualitative part which is called descriptive for the unmeasurable results. CBA framework involves numerous stages of analysis: defining a alternatives, identification of stakeholders regarding their benefits and costs, calculation of effects and the choice of indicators, quantitative prediction of the effects, the introduction of monetary values for each type of effect, discounting of costs and benefits for the purpose of NPV (net present value) and IRR (internal rate of return), calculation of ENPV (economic net present value) and ERR (economic rate of return) for each of the alternatives, sensitivity analysis, and recommendation.

2 Uncontrolled Urbanization – Literature Review

In the long run, cities cannot fulfil their function as engines of social progress and economic growth unless social balance, ensuring cultural diversity and proper quality of urban design, architecture and environment is not maintained [2]. Cities need visions which are able to cope with their various and dynamic character. To achieve that cooperation of local actors is required, starting with the construction of new urban descriptions which able to propose new objectives and new projects, and to recognise their changes and potentialities [3]. Urbanization applies both to change of the space and people [4]. It is a multi-faceted and extremely complex process which should be considered in several dimensions, including demographic, social, economic, spatial, and functional scopes [5]. Research on urbanization are important as number of cities and urban population grow in all countries of the world [6].

The urbanization process in Poland is legally and formally controlled, however the problem is that not all the participating entities want to use control tools, which results in the negative effects of urbanization [7] and eventually causes that urbanisation is uncontrolled. The most important negative effect of uncontrolled urbanization is spatial chaos which results from conflicts such as between the public and private sector interest [8]. It relates to inadequate social participation in the planning process, as well as the mismanagement of a public-private partnership.

The spatial chaos is directly related to the accidental relationship of housing and infrastructure. This causes difficulties in everyday life by restricting access to means of transport and isolation from social infrastructure services, which are generally located in city centres, or on the outskirts of the metropolis. It may contribute to the exclusions of less well-off inhabitants. It also means extra time getting to work – from housing developments outside the cities to the business centres, which significantly increases previously reduced costs of living. An important consequence of uncontrolled urbanization is then increase in time and cost of commuting.

Inefficient master planning relates to development of residential area. Many municipalities bear (or will bear in the future) huge costs for land re-purchase for roads and technical infrastructure in areas that have been significantly overestimated in the relation to needs of the housing area. The revenues from fees planning are often lost as well. It is a result of speculations on the real estate market. The profits skip the municipality budget and goes to landowners. This phenomenon does not occur in developed countries, where the majority of income that are created by planning, goes to the budgets of municipalities and is used to financing local development [7].

The costs of destruction of housing and infrastructure costs can be also included to negative effects of uncontrolled urbanisation. This applies particularly to areas at risk of flooding and landslides, were an investment is a result of incorrect location decisions, sometimes in violation of applicable law.

Proper planning should limit construction and maintenance costs of the technical infrastructure, while chaotic and scattered layout increases the cost of sewerage systems, water supply, gas, heating, telecommunications, energy, traffic, and lighting. The increase in costs is also generated by excessive amount of small schools, kindergartens, hospitals, where costs are significantly higher than in large institutions. Moreover, human resources are inefficiently used [9].

Finally, the instability of planning, function, and potential localization difficulties increase investment risk and discourage foreign investors. Uncontrolled urbanization creates 'speculative bubble' where prices of land are not linked with good location or infrastructure, but connected with the conviction that eventually all agricultural land is converted into development land of higher value and price. The final effect is that the municipality has to purchase agricultural land for the public investment at market prices, which is significantly overvalued.

The final cost and general development of spatial chaos is a factor of low competitiveness of the municipalities and barrier for investors while master planning should support promoting competitiveness, social and territorial cohesion in Europe and in its cities, and regions [10].

3 The Case Study Analysis

3.1 The Municipality and Its Financial Situation

The Municipality, where the area under development is located, is placed in the centre of low-lying landscape in the north of Poland. The surrounding area is characterised by the lack of natural hills and high level of ground waters. A national road, which is a part of the international route, connects the Municipality with the regional capital city (40 km). Traffic results from regional and national transport aiming warehouses and logistics cents, and high-traffic passenger cars relate to both tourist and business destination in the regional capital city. The main branch of the economy in the Municipality is agriculture and agrotourism. Agriculture land, meadows and pastures are over 80 % of the land in the Municipality. The area is dominated by a very fertile soil, growing wheat, sugar beet, barley, potatoes and oilseed rape. There are also many dairy farms. The average size of farms in the Municipality is much larger than the national average yet agriculture activity in the Municipality constitute only of about 3 % of 1.4 thousand registered entities (while transport and construction is about 26 %). Most of the private entities are single-owned companies not generating job places and the current unemployment rate is 14 %. It is higher than in the region (10.3 %) and in Poland (10.8 %). General demographic situation is characterised by aging and decreasing population (18.0 thousand for 2015).

A primary category that illustrates financial condition of the Municipality is budget balance containing operating and capital balance. Operating balance as the difference

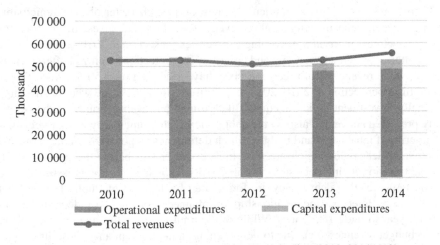

Fig. 1. General financial situation of the Municipality (2010–2014) [12].

between operating revenues and operating expenditure indicates whether the unit is able to cover running expenses with current income without abuse of municipal assets and additional debt [11]. Operating balance and capital revenues indicates the investment possibilities. In other words, surplus of total revenues over operating expenses can be spent on investment. The Fig. 1 illustrates the case for the Municipality.

There was a distressing deficit trend in 2010–2011. Yet, it has stopped and the budget balance has been positive since 2012. Current revenues generated about 87 % of total revenues on average in the studied period 2010–2014, while capital revenues equalled 13 % on average but were generally decreasing. This suggests that the Municipality concentrates on a current performance.

Table 1 shows revenues and expenditures per sections in 2014. The share of revenues from fees and taxes was the greatest, while from agriculture relatively small and tourism - none. The share of social expenditures is the greatest, while agriculture and tourism relatively small.

Table 1. Revenues and expenditures per sections in the Municipality (2014) [12].

Revenues	(%)	Expenditures	(%)
Fees and taxes	38.47 %	Schools and education	35.50 %
Social service	16.52 %	Social service	22.83 %
Housing	8.24 %	Housing	6.81 %
Transport and communication	0.38 %	Transport and communication	3.30 %
Tourism	0.00 %	Tourism	0.41 %
Agriculture	3.16 %	Agriculture	3.20 %
Communal economy	0.13 %	Communal economy	6.49 %
Others	33.00 %	Others	21.44 %
Total	100.00 %	Total	100.00 %

Taking under consideration agriculture and touristic character of the Municipality, and high dependence of Municipality revenues on fees and taxes, the observation relating structure is worrying. According to revenues per section in 2010–2014, revenues in agriculture, communal economy and environment protection stabilized after decrease in 2012, while revenues from fees and taxes have increased over 50 %. According to expenditures per section in 2010–2014, expenditures for agriculture were decreasing.

Finally, investment policy is equally determined by revenue policy of the Municipality presented above, but also by the debt policy. The Municipality is relatively small one in terms of inhabitants and budget, which determines its potential. Table 2 presents fundamental debt ratios which are very high however still below the law limit. The increase of ratio relating debt servicing in 2013 is explained by bonds issue.

The limits relating debt policy are formulated by The Act of Public Finance. The limit of 15 % refers to the relationship of planned repayment of debt during the financial year to budget revenues. While 60 % limit refers to the relationship of total debt to budget revenues. Yet, due to new regulation in public finance these limits have

Table 2. Selected debt ratios of the Municipality (2010–2014) [12].

Item	2010	2011	2012	2013	2014
Debt/own revenues (limit 60 %)	55.09 %	59.80 %	59.63 %	54.34 %	52.20 %
Debt servicing/own revenues	6.19 %	11.07 %	10.96 %	30.09 %	6.03 %
Interests paid/own revenues (limit 15 %)	2.41 %	3.55 %	3.63 %	2.87 %	2.02 %

been replaced by the individual local government individual debt ratio (Art. 242), starting from 2014. Individual debt ratio, calculated along the formula provided in the referred article of law, shows that the limit for debt service was not exceeded for the Municipality in 2014.

3.2 Description of the Property and Development Programs

The Municipality has been looking forward to investors interested in agriculture support and development, particularly food processing and feed factories. The Municipality owns adequate grounds to undertake such activities. A large agricultural area is available for the development. It is placed between arms of the river, which is currently leased by local farmers. The current bridge is in bad condition and roads are not driveable. The general investment idea assumes development of the 180 ha area with the replica of a Dutch town, with hotels, restaurants, bars, offices, shopping and tourist businesses, housing for service and workers. The creation of a replica town is justified by history as Dutch settlers were present in the sixteenth and seventeenth centuries in the area. In addition, museum and model farms relating milk production and its processing, fishing and flowery, are anticipated. The construction of parking lots and small freight trains is also forecasted. The Municipality has signed a number of partnership agreements and letters of intent, yet it is still looking for particular investors interested in the project. Because of poor condition or sometimes lack of technical infrastructure, and level of real estate prices, most investors would rather prefer investing in the outskirts of a larger city. On the other hand, the natural values supports clean and natural agriculture which has become very important recently in the context of sustainable development. Also, relatively high level of unemployment is an important resource for potential investors. Therefore, taking under consideration legal and economic conditions relating to the property as well as financial and demographic condition of the Municipality, the general objective of the project is to attract investors.

It the first stage of the project, development of 60 ha area is planned. The master plan allows following function: housing, retail and service, bio-agriculture and model farms. Due to natural values of the region, the master plan does not allow to implement environmentally harmful projects or investment which can change the landscape significantly. The development program for the area assumes three alternative functional programs:

1. The whole investment area is designated for housing. The Municipality will invest in the technical infrastructure in the area, divide the land into plots of approximately 1.000 m^2, and sell 40 plots per year.

2. The investment area is developed with commercial function of retail and service, and bio-agriculture with model farms. Some processing, feed production, plant biomass is possible in this option. The Municipality assumes sale of the entire within 4 years. The program assumes the site for the hotel with conference facilities, as there is no hotel and no conference space for about 300 people in the Municipality. Single places are offered by local farmers supplementing their basic agriculture activity with agrotourism.
3. The investment area is developed based on above presented two options. The half of the land is designated for the residential function and hotel, and the other half is entitled for retail and service, bio-agriculture and model farms.

3.3   Evaluation Assumptions and Social-Economic Analysis

The evaluation of the project has been performed from the Municipality point of view with respect to the appropriate guidelines [13]. It has been conducted based on the standard method which means that the debt financing the project will be secured and repaid from the project itself. The analysis covers the period associated with sale of the parcels which is 11 years and has been conducted in current prices. The real discounting rate is assumed at the market level of 10 % and has been re-calculated with CPI (consumer price index) to nominal rate of discounting. Macroeconomic assumptions regarding CPI and GNP (gross national product) is based on the forecast of the EBRD (European Bank for Reconstruction and Development). Income tax has been omitted, as municipalities do not pay income tax.

CAPEX (capital expenditures) relates to the construction period and contains land contribution, and realization of the technical infrastructure: roads, water and sewage system, and energy. Replacement investments and capital expenditures during the operation phase are not projected. CAPEX includes VAT (value added tax), as local governments do not have right to VAT deduction. For the comparability of data, PLN (pln) has been converted into EUR (€) at the average rate of €1 = pln4,1021 for the day of the analysis (NBP, 2015-18-07). Table 3 shows assumptions of development program in three described options with applicable CAPEX assessment.

In terms of the revenues, it has been assumed in all cases that the Municipality sells 25 % of all parcels before the start of the investment and hereby fund part of the capital expenditures. Parcels for pre-sale are without technical infrastructure and therefore have been priced with 20 % discount. After pre-sale in '0' year of analysis, in case of residential area, 40 the plots will be sold each year, and the remaining area will be sold within 4 years. OPEX (operational expenditures) includes costs associated with the project promotion and sale of parcels (division of property, valuation, and preparation for sale) and have been expected at 5 % of the revenue from sales as in comparable projects. Other costs do not occur. The Table 4 shows forecast of revenues, costs, and net operating profit for three variants of the project.

Based on the forecasts of EBITDA and own financing, cash flow and financial evaluation have been performed for three alternatives. Cash flows do not include changes in working capital. Internal rate of return (IRR), net present value (NPV), and profitability index (PI) of the project have been calculated. The calculation has been made at the discount rate of 10 %, recalculated to nominal value. According to CBA

Table 3. Project development program and basic financial assumptions. Author's study.

Alternative and value	I	II	III
Area of property under development [m²]	600 000	600 000	600 000
Area of roads and communication [m²]	64 000	24 000	44 000
Area for parcels [m²]	536 000	576 000	556 000
Area for residential investment [m²]	536 000	–	278 000
Area for retail and service, bio-agriculture production, model farms investment [m²]	–	576 000	278 000
Plots for residential investment [no]	536	–	273
Current value of the land used for agriculture [€]	530 948	530 948	530 948
Price of agricultural land to value Municipality's contribution in-kind [€/m²]	0.88	0.88	0.88
Price of land for retail and service, and agriculture production with model farms, no infrastructure [€/m²] (for pre-sale)	4.88	4.88	4.88
Price of land for residential investment, no infrastructure [€/m²] (for pre-sale)	8.19	8.19	8.19
Price of land for retail and service, and agriculture production with model farms [€/m²]	6.09	6.09	6.09
Price of land for residential investment [€/m²]	10.24	10.24	10.24
CAPEX - in-land contribution [€]	530 948	530 948	530 948
CAPEX - roads infrastructure [€]	2 100 225	561 218	1 181 098
CAPEX - water and sewage system, energy [€]	1 585 657	932 419	1 169 894
Total CAPEX [€]	4 216 830	2 024 585	2 881 940
Own financing	100 %	100 %	100 %

framework, selected benefits and costs have been analysed and quantified. The main focus is on the socio-economic impact of the investment project while environmental effects have been skipped. It has been justified by the scope of the research and also according to the master plan, that the investment cannot be harmful to environment.

Following external benefits for the project stakeholders have been identified: additional employment for local society, increase in share of income taxes and property tax for the Municipality, additional income regarding tourism for local entrepreneurship, increase of standard of living for the inhabitants, and finally, perpetuity of the benefits. Here's how the mentioned socio-economic benefits of the project have been calculated.

Additional employment refers to the surplus workers at the time of investment. It is assumed that parcels will be sold systematically. The additional income regarding employment has been assumed at 13 % of the estimated value (CAPEX) of the investments. For housing investment CAPEX is €150.000 per single house and €1.200/m² for remaining area.

Table 4. Revenues, operation costs and EBITDA for three variants of the project. Author's study

Alternative I	0	1	2	3	4	5	6	7	8	9	10
Price [€/m²]	8.19	8.19	8.19	8.19	8.19	8.19	8.19	8.19	8.19	8.19	8.19
CPI	1.60%	1.60%	1.60%	1.60%	1.60%	1.60%	1.60%	1.60%	1.60%	1.60%	1.60%
Price with CPI [€/m²]	8.32	8.46	8.59	8.73	8.87	9.01	9.15	9.30	9.45	9.60	9.75
Number of sold parcels [m²]	134	40	40	40	40	40	40	40	40	40	40
Area sold [m²]	134 000	40 000	40 000	40 000	40 000	40 000	40 000	40 000	40 000	40 000	40 000
Total revenues	**223 029**	**338 205**	**343 617**	**349 114**	**354 700**	**360 376**	**366 142**	**372 000**	**377 952**	**383 999**	**390 143**
OPEX (5%)	**11 151**	**16 910**	**17 181**	**17 456**	**17 735**	**18 019**	**18 307**	**18 600**	**18 898**	**19 200**	**19 507**
EBITDA	**211 878**	**321 295**	**326 436**	**331 659**	**336 965**	**342 357**	**347 834**	**353 400**	**359 054**	**364 799**	**370 636**
Alternative II	**0**	**1**	**2**	**3**	**4**						
Price [€/m²]	4.88	4.88	4.88	4.88	4.88						
CPI	1.60%	1.60%	1.60%	1.60%	1.60%						
Price with CPI [€/m²]	4.95	5.03	5.11	5.20	5.28						
Area sold [m²]	144 000	108 000	108 000	108 000	108 000						
Total revenues	**561 664**	**526 560**	**526 560**	**526 560**	**526 560**						
OPEX (5%)	**28 083**	**26 328**	**26 328**	**26 328**	**26 328**						
EBITDA	**533 580**	**500 232**	**500 232**	**500 232**	**500 232**						
Alternative III	**0**	**1**	**2**	**3**	**4**	**5**	**6**				
Price [€ /m²]	8.19	8.19	8.19	8.19	8.19	8.19	8.19				
CPI	1.60%	1.60%	1.60%	1.60%	1.60%	1.60%	1.60%				
Price with CPI [€/m²]	8.32	8.46	8.59	8.73	8.87	9.01	9.15				
Number of sold parcels [m²]	68.00	40	40	40	40	40	5				
Area sold [m²]	68 000	40 000	40 000	40 000	40 000	40 000	5 000				
Revenues	452 716	338 205	343 617	349 114	354 700	360 376	45 768				
Price [€/m²]	4.88	4.88	4.88	4.88	4.88						
CPI	1.60%	1.60%	1.60%	1.60%	1.60%						
Price with CPI [€/m²]	4.95	5.03	5.11	5.20	5.28						
Area sold [m²]	69 500	52 125	52 125	52 125	52 125						
Revenues	271 081	254 138	254 138	254 138	254 138						
Total revenues	**723 796**	**592 343**	**597 755**	**603 253**	**608 838**	**360 376**	**45 768**				
OPEX (5%)	**36 190**	**29 617**	**29 888**	**30 163**	**30 442**	**18 019**	**2 288**				
EBITDA	**687 607**	**562 726**	**567 867**	**573 090**	**578 397**	**342 357**	**43 479**				

Increase in share of income taxes and property tax for the Municipality relates additional employment and related income. It has been assumed that 70 % of the developers' income relates individuals and 30 % relates companies. Municipalities has share in income taxes which equals 39.34 % for PIT (personal income tax) and 7.61 % for CIT (corporate income tax). Increase of Municipalities' revenues relates also to the

Table 5. Economic analysis of third alternative of the project. Author's study

No.	Benefit		0	1	2	3	4
1.	**Additional employment**						
A.	Number of sold parcels for housing investment		68	40	40	40	40
	CAPEX of 1 investment	150 000	152 400	154 838	157 316	159 833	162 390
	Value of all investments		10 363 200	6 193 536	6 292 633	6 393 315	6 495 608
	Developers' remuneration	13.00%	1 347 216	805 160	818 042	831 131	844 429
B.	Area sold		69 500	52 125	52 125	52 125	52 125
	CAPEX per m2	1 200	1 219	1 239	1 259	1 279	1 299
	Value of all investments		84 734 400	64 567 613	65 600 695	66 650 306	67 716 711
	Developers' remuneration	13.00%	11 015 472	8 393 790	8 528 090	8 664 540	8 803 172.38
C.	**Total remuneration**		12 362 688	9 198 949	9 346 133	9 495 671	9 647 601
2.	**Share in income taxes**						
A.	Personal income increase	70.00%	8 653 881.60	6 439 264.54	6 542 292.77	6 646 969.46	6 753 320.97
	PIT (personal income tax)	20.00%	1 730 776	1 287 853	1 308 459	1 329 394	1 350 664
	Municipality share in PIT	39.34%	680 887	506 641	514 748	522 984	531 351
B.	Corporate income increase	30.00%	3 708 806	2 759 685	2 803 840	2 848 701	2 894 280
	CIT (corporate income tax)	19.00%	704 673	524 340	532 730	541 253	549 913
	Municipal shares in CIT	6.71%	47 284	35 183	35 746	36 318	36 899
C.	Municipality CAPEX		2 350 992				
	Correction of VAT	23.00%	439 616				
D.	**Total**		1 167 787	541 825	550 494	559 302	568 250
3.	**Increase of property value (property tax)**						
A.	Houses (m2) cumulative	200	13 600	21 600	29 600	37 600	45 600
100%		0.17	2 354	3 739	5 123	6 508	7 893
B.	Remaining area cumulative		69 500	121 625	173 750	225 875	278 000
20%	Buildings	5.64	78 376	137 158	195 940	254 723	313 505
100%	Land	0.22	15 248	26 685	38 121	49 557	60 993
	Total		95 978	167 581	239 184	310 787	382 390
4.	**Tourism**						
	Number of events	12	12	12	12	12	12
	Number of participants	60	60	60	60	60	60
	Value of expenses per participant	100	102	103	105	107	108
	Total		73 152	74 322	75 512	76 720	77 947
5.	**Standard of living**						
	Number of inhabitants cumulative	4	272	432	592	752	912
	Ratio of benefits	10%	27.20	43.20	59.20	75.20	91.20
	Days of work absence	3	3	3	3	3	3
	Expenses for medicines	10	10	10	10	11	11
	Number of working days a year	252	252	252	252	252	252
	GDP per day		34	35	36	37	39
	Total		111	115	119	123	127
6.	**Perpetuity**						
	Total value of benefits		13 699 717	9 982 793	10 211 441	10 442 602	10 676 317
	Residual value		-	-	-	-	-
	Total		13 699 717	9 982 793	10 211 441	10 442 602	10 676 317
7.	**Present value of benefits**						
	Total benefits		13 699 717	9 982 793	10 211 441	10 442 602	10 676 317
	Real economic discount rate		1.0000	0.9374	0.8787	0.8237	0.7721
	Present value of benefits		13 699 717	9 357 699	8 972 656	8 601 213	8 243 078
	Present value of benefits cumulative		13 699 717	23 057 415	32 030 071	40 631 285	48 874 363
8.	**Present value of benefits**		55 027 286				

No.	Benefit	5	6	7	8	9	10
1.	**Additional employment**						
A.	Number of sold parcels for housing investment	40	5	-	-	-	-
	CAPEX of 1 investment	164 988	167 628				
	Value of all investments	6 599 537	838 141	-	-	-	-
	Developers' remuneration	857 940	108 958	-	-	-	-
B.	Area sold	-	-				
	CAPEX per m2						
	Value of all investments	-	-	-	-	-	-
	Developers' remuneration	-	-				
C.	**Total remuneration**	**857 940**	**108 958**	-	-	-	-
2.	**Share in income taxes**						
A.	Personal income increase	600 557.91	76 270.85	-	-	-	-
	PIT (personal income tax)	120 112	15 254	-	-	-	-
	Municipality share in PIT	47 252	6 001	-	-	-	-
B.	Corporate income increase	257 382	32 688	-	-	-	-
	CIT (corporate income tax)	48 903	6 211	-	-	-	-
	Municipal shares in CIT	3 281	417	-	-	-	-
C.	Municipality CAPEX						
	Correction of VAT						
D.	**Total**	**50 533**	**6 418**	-		-	-
3.	**Increase of property value (property tax)**						
A.	Houses (m2) cumulative	53 600	54 600	54 600	54 600	54 600	54 600
100%		9 277	9 450	9 450	9 450	9 450	9 450
B.	Remaining area cumulative	278 000	278 000	278 000	278 000	278 000	278 000
20%	Buildings	313 505	313 505	313 505	313 505	313 505	313 505
100%	Land	60 993	60 993	60 993	60 993	60 993	60 993
	Total	**383 775**	**383 948**	**383 948**	**383 948**	**383 948**	**383 948**
4.	**Tourism**						
	Number of events	**12**	**12**	**12**	**12**	**12**	**12**
	Number of participants	**60**	**60**	**60**	**60**	**60**	**60**
	Value of expenses per participant	**110**	**112**	**114**	**115**	**117**	**119**
	Total	**79 194**	**80 462**	**81 749**	**83 057**	**84 386**	**85 736**
5.	**Standard of living**						
	Number of inhabitants cumulative	1 072	1 092	1 092	1 092	1 092	1 092
	Ratio of benefits	107.20	109.20	109.20	109.20	109.20	109.20
	Days of work absence	3	3	3	3	3	3
	Expenses for medicines	11	11	11	12	12	12
	Number of working days a year	252	252	252	252	252	252
	GDP per day	40	42	43	45	46	48
	Total	**131**	**137**	**141**	**146**	**151**	**156**
6.	**Perpetuity**						
	Total value of benefits	1 371 574	579 922	465 838	467 151	468 485	469 840
	Residual value	-	-	-	-	-	7 033 532
	Total	**1 371 574**	**579 922**	**465 838**	**467 151**	**468 485**	**7 503 372**
7.	**Present value of benefits**						
	Total benefits	1 371 574	579 922	465 838	467 151	468 485	7 503 372
	Real economic discount rate	0.7237	0.6784	0.6359	0.5961	0.5588	0.5238
	Present value of benefits	992 668	393 434	296 247	278 479	261 787	3 930 307
	Present value of benefits cumulative	**49 867 031**	**50 260 465**	**50 556 712**	**50 835 192**	**51 096 979**	**55 027 286**

increase in the value of property and property tax. The property tax for houses is €0.17/m² and it has been assumed that average house is 200 m². The property tax for commercially used building is €5.64/m² and €0.22/m² for land. It has been assumed that buildings' average share in the sold area is 20 % while land is 100 %.

Estimates regarding tourism are careful. It has been assumed, that 12 events for 60 people each, will take place every year. The average expenditure on accommodation and food has been presumed at €50 per person. This is an additional income for local entrepreneurship. Tax benefits have been skipped in this case.

Table 6. Present value of selected benefits for the alternative variants. Author's study.

Alternative	I		II		III	
	(€)	(%)	(€)	(%)	(€)	(%)
(1) Additional employment						
Residential investment	8 774 128	48.95 %	n/a	0.00 %	4 852 160	8.82 %
Remaining investment	n/a	n/a	83 521 473	82.71 %	40 310 711	73.26 %
(2) Share in income taxes						
Personal income increase	483 244	2.70 %	4 600 029	4.56 %	2 487 390	4.52 %
Corporate income increase	33 558	0.19 %	319 445	0.32 %	172 734	0.31 %
Correction of VAT	689 230	3.84 %	279 298	0.28 %	439 616	0.80 %
(3) Increase of property value (property tax)						
Residential investment	86 766	0.48 %	n/a	n/a	56 814	0.10 %
Buildings	n/a	n/a	4 136 059	4.10 %	1 996 223	3.63 %
Land	n/a	n/a	804 681	0.80 %	388 370	0.71 %
(4) Tourism	n/a	n/a	564 860	0.56 %	638 012	1.16 %
(5) Standard of living	1 052	0.01 %	n/a	n/a	1 052	0.00 %
(6) Residual value	7 858 296	43.84 %	6 756 730	6.69 %	3 684 202	6.70 %
Present value of benefits	17 926 275	100.00 %	100 982 574	100.00 %	55 027 286	100.00 %

n/a – not applicable

A higher standard of living is achieved due to change of residence from the city to the suburbs. This benefit is unquestionable, yet problematic for its quantification. It has been assumed, that 4 people move with one sold residential plot. Benefits have been carefully assumed only for 10 % of the population. The benefit has been calculated as costs' savings related to work absence of three days which relates to appropriate loss of GBP and costs of medicine of €10 per person.

Economic analysis covers the period of the investment, yet to cover the period afterwards, the residual value of the benefit has been calculated based on the Gordon's model.

Table 5 shows detailed economic analysis for the third alternative as it is a mix of first and second alternative.

The value of above described benefits has been identified and evaluated for each of the three alternatives. The Table 6 shows the results of the analysis.

First alternative's benefits are generated generally by additional employment due to realization of residential investments and due to residual value. It is the weakest alternative. Second alternative offers the highest value of present benefits. The benefit relating additional employment relating implementation of investment in retail and service, agriculture production, and model farm generates about 82 % of the present value of benefits. The last alternative offers major benefits of additional employment of 73 % of total present value of the benefits. Increase of Municipal revenues due to taxes, tourism, and standard of living seems of less importance in all cases. Taking however under consideration Municipal demographic and economic situation, unemployment and migrations are the major Municipality worry. Therefore, based on analysis of present value of benefits, the Municipality should consider not only second, but also third alternative which is shearing benefits from development of residential and commercial area.

4 Discussion and Conclusions

In term of effectiveness analysis, a rational investor will seek to maximize the ENPV, ERR and B/C indicators. Only projects with positive ENPV should be accepted. The ERR should be compared to the required rate of return and investment should be only accepted when IRR is higher than required rate of return. B/C should be accepted only when is higher than 1. The results of calculation of financial metrics: NPV (net present value), IRR (internal rate of return), and PI (profitability index); and economic metrics: ENPV (economic net present value), ERR (economic rate of return), and B/C (benefits to costs) are presented in Table 7.

Table 7. Present value of selected benefits for the alternative variants. Author's study.

Alternative	I	II	III
Total CAPEX	4 216 830	2 024 585	2 881 940
Pre-financing	211 878	533 580	687 607
Investor's capital engagement	4 004 952	1 491 005	2 194 333
NPV	−2 061 823	36 085	−236 206
IRR	−2.54 %	12.90 %	7.17 %
PI	0.49	1.02	0.89
Present value of benefits	17 926 275	100 982 574	55 027 286
ENPV	16 363 208	101 198 272	53 464 219
ERR	237.84 %	Not available	Not available
B/C	33.74	Not available	Not available
Present value of benefits : total CAPEX	425.11 %	885.43 %	622.02 %
ENPV : Total CAPEX	388.05 %	808.23 %	567.78 %

In the case of second and third alternative, it was not possible to calculate ERR or B/C as all present value of economic cash flows were positive and there was no negative cash flow to refer to (value of external benefits exceeded value of CAPEX).

Considering the above, the Municipality should implement second alternative of the investments, for which the metrics for financial efficiency (NPV, IRR, PI) and economic effectiveness (ENPV, ERR, B/C) are the highest. Moreover, also taking under consideration the Municipal Strategy (focused on creating job opportunities, economy diversification and tourism development), and also literature review relating effects of urbanisation, second alternative is the most justified.

The assumptions for three options of development programs meet requirements of master planning but vary in terms of project effectiveness. Studying different alternatives can help towards better management and understanding results of different development programs. The research might be also useful for public managers searching for partners and also private investors looking for opportunities. Since the proposed framework supports investment evaluation from the perspective of society, it supports local municipal decision makers. The model may be also an example of how to evaluate economic and social results of local planning and may be used as a tool for effectiveness maximization.

Local planning is connected with speculation in real estate markets, additionally strengthened by urban sprawl. Wrong or bad planning system, and inadequate public institution intervention may result in more speculative activities in the real estate market. Local planning should then respect general and specific circumstances in which space and land management takes place. These circumstances are: the specific geographic location of the area, political system, socio-economic system, development of a city, shape of the metropolitan area. Any decision contained in the plan means actual and possible changes in the cost/benefit allocation seen from the both economic and social perspective.

References

1. European Commission: Regional and Urban Policy, Guide to Cost-Benefit Analysis of Investment Projects Economic appraisal tool for Cohesion Policy 2014–2020, December 2014. http://ec.europa.eu/regional_policy/sources/docgener/studies/pdf/cba_guide.pdf
2. European Union: Leipzig Charter on Sustainable European Cities. Informal Ministerial Meeting on Urban Development and Territorial Cohesion, Leipzig, 24 May 2007
3. Balducci, A., Fedeli, V.: The state of European cities report: some critical reflections upon urban phenomena in the European union. Urban Res. Pract. 1(3), 240–253 (2008)
4. Smailes, A.E.: The definition and measurement of urbanization. In: Jones, R. (ed.) Essays on World Urbanization. London (1975)
5. Zaremba, P.: Urbanizacja Polski i środowisko człowieka. Wydawnictwo Książka i Wiedza, Warszawa (1974)
6. Bitner, A., Hołyst, R., Fiałkowski, M.: From complex structures to complex processes: percolation theory applied to the formation of a city. Phys. Rev. E 80(3), 037102 (2009)
7. Fundacja Rozwoju Demokracji Lokalne, Instytut Geografii i Przestrzennego Zagospodarowania: Raport o ekonomicznych stratach i społecznych kosztach niekontrolowanej urbanizacji w Polsce, Warszawa (2013). http://www.frdl.org.pl/pliki/frdl/document/zalaczniki_artykuly/Raport%20Ekonomiczny%2029.10.2013%20calosc.pdf
8. Ścisło, M.: Opinie i ekspertyzy na konferencję o ekonomicznych stratach i społecznych kosztach niekontrolowanej urbanizacji w Polsce, Sejm-Sala Kolumnowa (2014)
9. Jażdżewska, I. (ed.): Współczesne procesy urbanizacji i ich skutki. Wydawnictwo Uniwersytetu Łódzkiego, Łódź (2005)
10. Elteges, M.: Liepzig charter on sustainable European cities – a work in progress. Review articles and reports. Eur. Spat. Res. Policy 16(2), 63–78 (2009)
11. Jastrzębska, M.: Zarządzanie długiem jednostek samorządu terytorialnego. Woters Kluwer, Warszawa (2009)
12. Budget Execution Reports 2010–2014
13. Minister Infrastruktury i Rozwoju, Wytyczne w zakresie zagadnień związanych z przygotowaniem projektów inwestycyjnych, w tym projektów generujących dochód i projektów hybrydowych na lata 2014–2020, Warszawa, 18 marca (2015). https://www.funduszeeuropejskie.gov.pl/media/5193/NOWE_Wytyczne_PGD_PH_2014_2020_podpisane.pdf

Involvement of Smart Cities Citizens to Global Cooperation in Research and Education in Space - Architectural and Urban Conditions

Pavel Nahálka$^{(\boxtimes)}$, Eva Oravcová, and Milan Andráš

Faculty of Architecture, Slovak University of Technology,
Námestie Slobody 19, 812 45 Bratislava, Slovakia
{nahalka, oravcova, andras}@fa.stuba.sk

Abstract. The global dimension of human existence is not only perceptible from our communication skills, mobility and our impact on the environment within our planet Earth. If we want be involved in process of Space exploration at least somewhat successfully, it is necessary to responsibly enter into the process of education and research in the smart cities such as Bratislava. Astronomy education and research must to involve a construction of planetariums. Planetarium must be able to educate, enlighten, entertain and inspire to space understanding, so planetariums must be interactive. So if Bratislava is a smart city, it must build such Planetarium.

Keywords: Space exploration · Astronomy education · Planetarium · Planetarium presentation · Interactive

1 Introduction

The world around us is not only ordinarily perceptible surroundings of our human life, it is not only the environment in which we live, work or spend our leisure time. Our living environment has a much broader scope and it also has this broad framework, the impact of our operations. The global dimension of human existence is not only perceptible from our communication skills, mobility and our impact on the human environment within our planet Earth. We are part of a much broader existential framework, and we are increasingly able to get to know him, to interfere into it and influence as well as its present and especially the future. The existence of the human race (present and future) is associated with this framework and it is therefore necessary to take for his influence on the due share of responsibility. This responsibility has its specific projections in our activities, including the expansion of the ability to explore this vast space environment, the processes that take place in it and our place in them.

Space exploration is not just a job narrowcasting top scientists. Discoveries and exploring space through space probes create opportunities relating to the understanding of our past, present and possible future developments and thus affect all of us. New knowledge gained space missions as recently observation of Ceres Dawn explorer, whether culminating overflight of the probe New Horizons in the vicinity of Pluto, the former eighth planet of the solar system, its surprising revelations global layman but

© ICST Institute for Computer Sciences, Social Informatics and Telecommunications Engineering 2016
A. Leon-Garcia et al. (Eds.): Smart City 2015, LNICST 166, pp. 774–782, 2016.
DOI: 10.1007/978-3-319-33681-7_68

also the professional public. Ability to engage as much as possible to research these processes is an essential requirement for every developed, smart society, particularly in the field of scientific and technical cooperation on space programs. Our entry into this research, whether participating in the project Rosetta and its journey to Comet 67P/Churyumov–Gerasimenko, [7] or the status of cooperating state with ESA (European Space Agency), is an example of the positive results of our relationship to space exploration.

2 Learning Space – Astronomy Education

The Exploring the universe is not only the greatest adventure in which human had embarked, but it's also expanding horizons of knowledge to hitherto unforeseen distance. If we want be involved in this process at least somewhat successfully, it is necessary to responsibly enter into the process of education and research in the smart cities such as Bratislava. Its scientific, academic and research capacity it suitable also for the important place in international cooperation in education, enlightenment and understanding of our role in the Today, however, "the conditions for discovering, exploring and learning about the universe especially are not comparable to those, that existed in Bratislava in the 20 s of the 18th century", [8] when an astronomical observations Samuel Mikovíni (about 1686 - March 23, 1750) set up his own observatory in apartment on Laurinska street. Today's night sky of the capital is significantly affected by the disturbing light, known as light pollution, so it is necessary to direct astronomical observations complement by the representation and simulation of space.

Archimedes is credited with the first device demonstrating planetary motions about 250 B.C. Later, Ptolemy's globe is alleged to have even demonstrated the precession of the equinoxes. "The next improvement came with the enlargement of the globes. The most famous, the Gottorf globe constructed in the middle 17th century *(The original globe was built between 1654 to 1664 in Gottorf on request of Frederick III, Duke of Holstein-Gottorp.)*, was about 4 m in diameter, weighed over 3 tons, and could seat several persons inside on a circular bench. The stars were holes in the globe. Other globes like the Gorroro sphere were built, one of the last being the Atwood globe in 1913 for the Museum of the Chicago Academy of Sciences. With a diameter of almost 5 m the Atwood globe shows 692 stars, and a moveable light bulb represents the Sun. Apertures along the ecliptic, which can be uncovered as necessary, represent the planets" [1].

With the coming of the Copernican idea and with advances in instrument - making, various models of the planetary system were constructed as teaching devices. These are called "orreries" in English. The first orrery that was a planetarium of the modern era was produced in 1704, and one was presented to Charles Boyle, 4th Earl of Orrery (28 July 1674–28 August 1731) — whence came the name. The orreries reached their culmination in the large ceiling orreries at Munich (since destroyed), Chapel Hill, and New York. Meanwhile, elaborate astronomical clocks were developed showing various sky events. Thus the stage was set for the entrance of the next advance (Fig. 1).

Orbitoscope, invented about 1912 by Prof. Eduard Hindermann in Basel is generally considered as the first projection device for showing planetary motions.

Fig. 1. Mechanical model demonstrating the Copernican system dating about 1780 [2]

The instrument is driven by springworks and has two planets revolving about a central Sun. A small light bulb on one of the planets projects shadows of the other two objects in the directions they would be seen from that planet, reproducing accurately the retrograde loops and speed changes. This ingenious device is useful for instruction, but of course had many shortcomings.

The idea of realistically reproducing the sky in detail is due to astronomer Max Wolf, involved with the Deutsches Museum. The museum was the brainchild of Oskar von Miller, an engineer interested in all aspects of science. He founded it in 1903, but the opening of a building on an island in the Isar River as its new home in Munich, planned for 1916 was postponed due to the war. The fully constructed museum finally opened in 1925. In 1913, Wolf had suggested to von Miller the idea of a device for his museum which would reproduce not only the stars but also the planetary motions von Miller approached the well-known optical firm of Carl Zeiss in Jena, and they agreed to look into the problem.

About March 1919, Walther Bauersfeld, chief design engineer and later director of Carl Zeiss, hit upon the idea of projection of the celestial objects in a dark room. The original plan had been for some sort of globe similar to that of Gottorf. The new idea[1] simplified things immensely. The mechanism could be on a small scale and easily controllable. In August 1923, a 16 m dome was set up on the roof of the factory in Jena, and the first Model I projector was installed. The "Wonder of Jena" had its first unofficial showings there. Then the instrument was taken down, shipped to the Deutsches Museum, and installed there in a 10 m dome.

The planetarium so impressed many scientific and civic leaders in Germany that in the few years following the first Model I, several other cities ordered and received projectors. Dusseldorf installed a Model I, then replaced it with a Model II which Zeiss

---

[1] Applying also the Rudolf Straubel's concept that the fixed stars should be projected from the central apparatus [3].

had developed in the meantime. (This planetarium had a 30 m dome, one of the largest ever constructed, and totally destroyed in the war.) The Model II (Fig. 2) was the large dumbbell-shaped projector which everyone has since identified with Zeiss.

Fig. 2. Universal projection instrument in the Jena Zeiss Planetarium in 1926 (produced by Zeiss during the 1920s and 1930s) [2]

Even in the 1920 s the first planetariums were built outside Germany (the Rome planetarium opened in 1928, and the Moscow planetarium in 1929). On May 5, 1930, the Adler Planetarium in Chicago greeted its first visitors in US.

Since then, it was built more than 2,000 planetarium equipped with projector devices of different types, sizes, and made by more of manufacturers (about a third of the Zeiss), with more and more sophisticated technology. "Planetariums for decades have been created to serve the cause of astronomical enlightenment-to offer people knowledge and understanding and a sense of place in a universe far bigger than themselves. It's an important role and one that we continue to play-changing, we hope, as times, technology, education, and our view of the universe change" [4].

Construction planetariums in the United States posted the largest growth after 1957. "On October 4th of that year, the Soviet Union successfully launched the first artificial satellite and surprised the free world with its advanced technology. America was shocked out of its complacency, and a few months later placed its own satellite into orbit. And so, the technological contest had begun. America found itself and its educational program wholly inadequate to meet this challenge. It was apparent to the nation's legislators and educators that from that time forward, the United States, by accepting the space challenge, must also accept the responsibility of educating its people to the space environment. Astronomy and space science impregnated almost every field of learning, and an understanding of them became essential to the country's well being. It penetrated the nation's history, economics, foreign policy, and all branches of its science and industry. In the schools, the teachers became victims of the times – totally unprepared to answer the probing questions of the students. Parents were suddenly confronted with the excitement their children found in the drama of the space age, but like their children's teachers, could not nurture the enthusiasm of their inquiring minds… Everyone was getting into the scene with seemingly every community thinking that they needed a planetarium. Also, of the 700 plus **planetariums that had been built** by 1970" [4].

Clearly, planetariums represent one of the biggest and most visible avenues for presenting astronomy and related subjects to the public-surpassable. This gives planetariums an enormous potential for supporting both formal and informal astronomy education. Astronomy education and research compounded by the enormous construction of planetariums, the US showed progresses in this field.

Our society in this field lags far behind, Slovakia is currently operating seven small planetariums (projection dome with a diameter of 8 or 10 m), of which no one in Bratislava. According to the civic association Slovak planetarium: "Bratislava is the only capital city in the European Union, which has no observatory or planetarium. Approximately 600,000 residents in the Bratislava region does not have any public astronomical workplace, although astronomy is a part of the curriculum and visit the planetarium is specifically recommended for students 4th and 9th class of primary schools. Planetarium presentation of geography and astronomy helps students quickly master the valuable and lasting curriculum. The potential for the use of the planetarium is not only almost 500 schools in the Bratislava region, but also for individual visitors, families and tourists. Three-quarters of the more than 100,000 students in Bratislava consists of primary school pupils and secondary school students, so the target group of 4th class elementary school students represents at least 300 excursions every year" [5] to space exploration.

3   Opportunities to Participate in Global Cooperation - Current Issues in the Planetariums Profession

James. G. Manning, President of International Planetarium Society, addressed to the Education Symposium of the Astronomical Society of the Pacific, June 24, 1995: "In defining the role that planetariums play, it's useful to review their strengths. We all know that planetariums can reproduce the night sky for any place on earth on any day of the year for many years past and future, creating a view that simulates the three-dimensional "backyard" sky. And that they can accurately reproduce the apparent motions and cycles of the sky-in speeded-up fashion so people can see what happens over time. But planetariums also create environments that encompass the audience, bringing them into the experience in a way that classroom, book, television or computer screen cannot. They can combine and effectively use audiovisual technology to help create these experiences. And they possess tremendous flexibility in how these audiovisual resources can be used. First and foremost, we strive to educate, in ways ranging from curriculum-based school lessons to popular-level programs. We also strive to enlighten, which I think is not quite the same as to educate; we want people not just to know but to understand and to incorporate this understanding in their lives. And yes, many of us also try to entertain-on the principle that you catch more flies with honey, that learning ought to be fun, and that people probably learn more when they're enjoying themselves. And not least, we strive to inspire. Our time with people is brief, and it is perhaps less important that someone remembers the diameter of Jupiter than that he or she remembers Jupiter as a neat planet, and buys a book or enrolls in a class or comes to the next star party to learn more-or takes time to look for it on the next clear night" [4].

In setting these goals, planetariums operate in all three realms of learning: in the thought-processing of the cognitive realm; increasingly in the psychomotor area as we offer more interactive experiences involving physical action; and we also operate in the affective realm, the realm of feelings, as we encourage greater appreciation and enjoyment of the sky and try to cultivate a sense of the adventure of science. The importance of equipping planetariums in addition to traditional also a digital technology is a clear role today. It's, along with installing other interactive technologies, seat buttons which allow the audience the active participation to events in dome-theater.

The versatility of current combination planetarium is well documented several examples. The staff at the US Air Force Academy Planetarium uses its facility extensively for hands-on lessons of a special kind: Air Force cadet training in topics ranging from aeronautics to survival skills using a compass and the planetarium sky, Jack Dunn at the Mueller Planetarium in Lincoln, Nebraska, US has developed a program for people with visual impairments such as retinitis pigmentosa, using the intense light of lasers to create starfields and visual effects that give them back a night sky they thought was to them lost forever.

The scientific community in planetariums trying to regularly check their sources about the latest information from space to pass on to the public, help each other through organizations such as the International Planetarium Society and its affiliated planetarium associations worldwide. Our opportunities for active participation in this organization are slims without modern planetarium Bratislava.

4   Urban and Architectural Planetarium Solutions Conceivable in Bratislava

The issue of the location of the planetarium in Bratislava dealt teams of students and teachers of the Faculty of Architecture for several times. In 1996 conceivable connection with the planetarium observatory in Koliba – Stráže, who studied with students Pavel Nahálka. Unfortunately, the plot with ideal orientation to cardinal points, with excellent terrain morphology, as a beautiful view has become building plots for luxury villas and not intended for public facilities.

Another combination of features that would allow the positioning of the planetarium in place at the heart of the city was to create a science center. His ability to include other activities such as exhibitions, leisure and education, were investigated since 2005 especially near high schools and universities, and recreational areas. Eva Oravcová with students examined the localization of such buildings, for example on both sides of the Danube River, including the area of the former stone quarry. Suitable we can evaluate student projects according to the position within the city: Trnavské mýto, Šancová, Radlinského, Imricha Karvaša streets and Kollar square.

The teachers from the Institute of Civic Structures with your students in 2015 verified the possibility to build a planetarium with observatory or with research or science center in the area of the Comenius University and Slovak University of Technology in the Mlynská dolina (Fig. 3). This site was chosen along with the civic association Slovak planetariums. Its location is particularly suitable especially in terms of connection to the scientific and educational activities (near the faculties of two universities, Slovak Academy of Sciences, Botanical Garden, Zoo), transport accessibility (motorway exit, urban public transport, cycling and walking routes) and also the appropriate orientation and slope of the terrain.

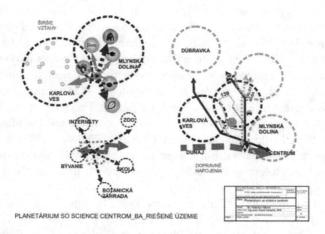

Fig. 3. Student analysis of planetarium site Mlynská Dolina, student Katarina Ješová, tutor Pavel Nahálka, 2015

In this area planetarium or science center could become an important landmark, especially because of its significant architectural form (Fig. 4). It could become a symbol of smart cities, a symbol of technological advancement and international scientific success Bratislava (Fig. 5).

Fig. 4. Study of planetarium architectural form, Alzbeta Komorná student, Pavel Nahálka tutor, 2015

Fig. 5. Study of planetarium architectural form, Alzbeta Komorná student, Pavel Nahálka tutor, 2015

In architecture, the planetarium will dominate in particular the main areas of the building - dome planetarium hall with a diameter of 17 m with 150 scats for spectators with staggered pattern. Estimated hybrid planetarium technology (Optomechanical plus digital projection) should be from the current industry-leading manufacturers (Fig. 6), well known companies that make (or have made) planetarium projectors include Carl Zeiss Jena (Germany), Spitz (US), Goto and Minolta (Japan), Evans & Sutherland (US), and Ohira Tech (Japan).

Fig. 6. Hybrid planetarium technology in Planetarium Johana Palisy, Ostrava, CZ

Planetarium activity is planned for seven days a week in three working daily changes. Integrant of the professional staff work is also the preparation of planetarium operations in cinema, respectively lecture hall, experimentarium space for interactive exhibits, an observatory and observation terrace, scientific laboratory - a space for research training and group experiments, exhibition hall and other spaces.

5 Conclusion: The Necessity of the Involvement Bratislava in the World Network Planetariums

Slovakia is proceeding on the route to successful implementation into the global scientific space community. Slovak Organisation for Space Activities (SOSA) has been active in various types of space activities or space-related activities, including launching of stratospheric balloons, development of the first Slovak suborbital rocket ARDEA or development of spaceflight simulator. SOSA together with technical universities in Bratislava, Košice, and Žilina and handful of private companies are currently developing first Slovak satellite skCUBE, which is planned to be launched in 2016. In February 2015, "Slovakia has signed European Cooperating State (ECS) Agreement with the European Space Agency (ESA) and Slovak scientists already participated on some high-level space projects, e.g. Rosetta mission" [7].

We are lagging behind the popularization of space research and its spread among young people, in particular with regard to the need for international cooperation in technological advances. It is evident that to improve this situation in our nation's capital would help to build a really dignified stand of space science - Planetarium in Bratislava.

References

1. Chartrand, M.R.: A fifty year anniversary of a two thousand year dream [The History of the Planetarium]. American Museum-Hayden Planetarium Central Park West at 81st St. New York, NY 10024. Reprinted from the Planetarian J. Int. Planet. Soc., September 1973
2. Schorcht, V.: Zeiss Planetaria from Jena published by Kombinat VEB Carl Zeiss JENA, p. 66, Ag. 29/259/84, September 1984
3. Ary, M.L: The third stage of planetarium evolution. Planetarian J. Int. Planet. Soc., vol. 3, no. 1–2 (1974)
4. Manning, J.G.: The role of planetariums in astronomy education. An Address to the Education Symposium of the Astronomical Society of the Pacific, 24 June 1995, Reproduced from the Planetarian, vol. 24, no. 4, December 1995
5. Masný, R.: Planetarium Bratislava, assignment the drafting of architectural studies for students of Faculty of Architecture, Civil Association Slovak Planetarium, June 2014. www.planetaria.sk
6. Planetarium projector, from Wikipedia, the free encyclopedia, July 2015. https://en.wikipedia.org/wiki/Planetarium_projector
7. June 2015. http://www.esa.int/Our_Activities/Space_Science/Rosetta/Rosetta_preparing_for_perihelion
8. July 2015. www.planetaria.sk

Knowledge of University Knowledge Workers

Jozef Hvorecký[✉]

Vysoká škola manažmentu, Panónska cesta 17, 85104 Bratislava, Slovakia
jhvorecky@vsm.sk

Abstract. Knowledge workers are expected to possess expert knowledge critical for innovation and progress. For that reason, management of knowledge workers is considered to be a substantial part of knowledge management. Knowledge is always present in explicit and tacit forms. Whilst the explicit knowledge is quite easy to demonstrate, the tacit knowledge is hidden and difficult to observe and measure. In fact, our ability to estimate their proportion is also "tacit". Nevertheless, using a critical analysis, we make an attempt to categorize knowledge-intensive professions by their balance. Such a categorization (which is predominantly tacit as well) could be exploited by human resource managers during selection of knowledge workers for their best fitting positions.

Keywords: Knowledge management · Knowledge workers categorization · Balancing explicit and tacit professional knowledge

1 Introduction

Peter Drucker [1] was the first to use the term knowledge worker. He already pointed to the fact that a portion of knowledge is invisible. Nonaka and Takeuchi [2] then identified two categories of knowledge: explicit (visible) and tacit (hidden in human's brains) Traditional managerial approaches address visible "products" so they do not fit to knowledge workers management. Due to that, Mládková talks about a necessity of introducing specific management methods [3]. At the same time, the range of knowledge-intensive professions varies from research to arts. To simplify designing and developing knowledge worker management, Kess [4] identified six types of knowledge workers pigeonholed by different proportions between their tacit and explicit knowledge.

The author and his colleagues believe that such differentiation is necessary because a big portion of knowledge transfer depends on not-fully-rational factors such as a gift, imagination, creativity, interpersonal communication skills, and others [5]. The most of these "irrational" factors represents individual's traits and, as such, has direct consequences on appropriate and successful exploitation of the person's ideas. And, as a result, on the competitiveness of their organizations. Below, Kess' typology is used as a guide for juxtaposing knowledge worker's types with their appropriate positions. The juxtaposing might facilitate the exploitation of highly-qualified human resources in organizations. Such a practice is not common yet. As the author shows in [6], the Slovak tertiary education often neglects it – leading university positions are often

© ICST Institute for Computer Sciences, Social Informatics and Telecommunications Engineering 2016
A. Leon-Garcia et al. (Eds.): Smart City 2015, LNICST 166, pp. 783–789, 2016.
DOI: 10.1007/978-3-319-33681-7_69

occupied by high quality researchers without relevant tacit knowledge and skills. For that reason, our paper considers the application of Kess' typology to selected academic positions.

2 Kess Typology of Knowledge Workers

Kess [4] defines six types of knowledge workers: Mentor, Coach, Angel, Guru, Politician, and Father.

- Mentor typically has a long and extensive experience of successful business. He/she is willing to share his/her knowledge with younger and less experienced entrepreneurs and managers.
- Coach is a professional with expertise especially in business processes and in their improvement and development. Here, we underline his/her importance to understand informal requirements, e.g. the ability to tailor the process techniques with their operator's qualification and mentality.
- Angel has some financial resources or at least knows where to get these resources for the company. The Angel also knows how to utilize the financial resources that are already within the company.
- Guru has deep professional knowledge about specific areas of expertise. This expertise can be used to products, production, marketing or other processes of the company.
- Politician has knowledge about local, national and even international politics relevant to the business operations.
- Father represents the historical background of the business. In this role the knowledge is strongly combined with the shared "family" values. In our interpretation of the "family" can be any team glued by their shared values.

Our above additions to original Kess typology are in a good relation with his expected proportion of explicit and tacit knowledge. Figure 1 also origins in [1].

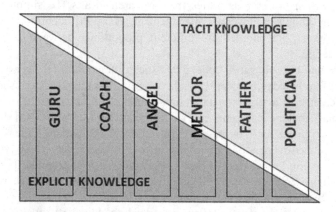

Fig. 1. The proportion of tacit and explicit knowledge in knowledge worker types

First, it is important to admit that "total knowledge" of a knowledge worker (indicated by every particular column in Fig. 1) addresses the knowledge related to the executed position; his/her individual knowledge unrelated to the position is not taken into account. To apply Kess typology in our presumed direction, the suggested reading of Fig. 1 would ignore the total amount of the person's knowledge. It should only consider the proportion between his/her knowledge on one side and the position itself on the other. The most beneficial situation presumes the optimal correspondence between the person's type and the position's requirements.

From this point of view, Guru is a "pure thinker" fully concentrated on his/her field of expertise. During the execution of his/her profession, he/she predominantly rely on his/her expert knowledge – and unlikely on anything else. The amount of the person's knowledge can be tremendous (e.g. knowledge of a top surgeon) but it is primarily tied to the daily routine – whatever the "routine" means. His/her tacit knowledge links to other fields are minimal. A popular picture of a "mad scientist" corresponds this extreme situation in a paramount way.

The Politician's proportions between explicit and tacit knowledge represent the other extreme. For proper execution of his/her function, he/she can hardly rely on deep knowledge from a narrow field. In his/her case, the role of explicit knowledge is overridden by tacit knowledge – qualified guesses about a situation of society, a wider context, business experience, an estimation of opportunities and risks, market trends, innovative methodologies, information, procedures, etc. In addition to that, every Politician must have a good sense for people's qualities. He/she will often act with them and through them. Thus, he/she has to be capable to estimate their capacity, reliability and limits. All by all, his/her tacit knowledge (the ability to "smell" opportunities and risks of planned and executed activities) must be extremal. His dependence on his/her tacit knowledge (e.g. instincts and intuition) is the greatest among all knowledge workers. This type of person is capable to orient him/herself in every situation and to find a way out of troubles.

The characterization of remaining types of knowledge workers can be derived from these two extremes.

Coach must be an expert in a field he/she coaches. In the same time, he/she has to be capable of explaining his/her knowledge and demonstrate his/her skills to his/her less experienced partners to avoid the risk of their misinterpretation. Guru's tacit knowledge is directly related to the field-dependent explicit knowledge. Often, gurus are not ready to share it with anyone else. Compared to them, coaches are supposed to do so. To succeed, their expert knowledge must be enriched by their ability to identify correct and false potential interpretations by trainees as well as by strategies of their perfection.

All remaining four types are transient ones. Both Angel and Coach are supposed to have quite high explicit knowledge in a certain field but their positions lead them out of it. In particular, Angel must be skilled in looking for applications of the given knowledge and in gaining money for putting these application in life. Similarly, Coach must be capable not only to understand the discussed processes but also to modify them in efficient and effective ways and to estimate whether the other people will be capable of accepting them. He/she must also find when to act and how – and when not. Their capacity to understand people's needs moves them closer to Politicians.

Finally, Father is a very specific type – quite distinct from the others - because of his/her very personal relationship to the subject. Even if he/she is not real parent of the company and its staff, he/she feels his/her full "parental" responsibility for them. As a result, he/she so deeply involved in the company matters and bets his/her position into the body's existence. This emotional side moves Fathers even closer to Politicians.

3 Kess Typology and the SECI Diagram

The SECI model [2] describes the transfer between explicit and tacit knowledge and back. It presumes that knowledge develops and is accumulated in cycles. The first letters of the cycle form the cryptonym SECI.

Bearers of tacit knowledge interact with bearers of (possibly different) tacit knowledge during *Socialization*. It is performed by interpersonal communication and/or intrapersonal insights. As such, knowledge gained during socialization is general but quite vague. The same concept can be interpreted differently by different individuals or groups.

To achieve a person-independent knowledge, people try to express their internal understanding of objects and methods in a commonly accepted way using various forms of *Externalization*. Externalized subjects appears in a standardized format legible for all partners. These representations (numbers, texts, graphs, formulas, etc.) create a basis for the wider distribution of knowledge and can be spread over geographic and time barriers.

The pieces of knowledge expressed in their formal notation can be processed using formal rules. Their *Combination* may lead to new pieces of knowledge. Computers and robots are also capable of executing combination incorporated in their controlling programs. On the other hand, a machine-performed combination represents just a part of all actions. Top experts often perform combinations that are beyond computers' capabilities.

In the last stage, people try to interpret the outcomes of their activity and want to comprehend them. Through *Internalization*, the new piece of knowledge becomes an integral part of the individual's knowledge and is at hand for its future application.

Notice that different knowledge worker types can be related to the particular stages of the SECI model. The gurus can be placed into Combination. They are primarily interested in formal manipulations – even their tacit knowledge concentrates on the deep understanding when to apply a particular rule and how to do it in an efficient and effective way.

Coaches are domestics of Internalization. They are interested in transfer of exact knowledge into their trainees' brains and finding appropriate methods for making their internalization easier and faster.

Domestics of Socialization are Politicians. They are keen of information exchange regardless whether it is in a formal or informal way. In a way, its informal version is more appropriate for their aims because it gives them more flexibility.

Mentors are often occupying Externalization because they work on making foggy ideas hidden in our brains more exact and legible by their codification, systematization, classification, etc. A typical example of a mentor is a production line designer. He has to decompose the process into elementary steps which can be performed by the available staff and technology within a minimal time.

4 Kess Typology and University Positions

Universities offer a good study field for our analysis. The most of their employees are knowledge workers with different specifics done by their positions. As we indicated above, personal traits influence the person's inclinations to a certain field of the SECI diagram. Consequently, moves to other positions may lead to the necessity of changing not only working habits but also the entire communication style.

4.1 Gurus

As said above, gurus are pure thinkers concentrated on their fields of expertise. During the execution of their profession, they rely on their expert knowledge. Likely, the most common positions of that kind are in research. Devoted researchers have to be concentrate on their topics – and do not pay attention to anything that could distract their attention. The situation is not so simple today as various research experiments are under supervision of relevant communities e.g. of ecologists or animal protectionists.

The best fitting positions for guru-like personalities are in research. Their explicit knowledge should concentrate on gaining new data on research methods, results of their partners and competitors. They should share their results with their colleagues but they do not always practice it in order to keep their "knowledge power". Their superiors should decide when such conspiracy is appropriate and when not. It is right to stress that the university research should be more open to the public than that of private companies.

4.2 Coaches

Coaches combine their expert knowledge with education or training of less experienced individuals. They have to be top-level specialist in their field but, unlike gurus, they are also interested in the links between their field and the "rest of the World". The familiarity with the links helps them to offer appropriate absent pieces of knowledge to their less experience colleagues. The links should always point to two directions: to the area of origin and to the application of the particular piece of knowledge in it. A good coach should be therefore capable of attracting people to his/her field of expertise.

University educators are a typical example. On one side, they must be high-level experts in their discipline. On the other hand, too narrow orientation to their discipline might discourage less gifted learners. They would not be able to follow their reasoning because they could not bridge it to the world they are familiar with.

4.3 Angels

Angels are often external to the organization they guard or protect. "Internal" angels are the persons taking care of the optimal working conditions for others. At universities, they build appropriate working environment and atmosphere for gurus and coaches for example by taking care of appropriate financing of a particular field. They are actively searching for relevant calls for research and/or educational projects, inform potential candidates, help them in the application preparation, and control their completeness and deadlines etc. Universities which want to prosper should open such positions and assign appropriate persons to them, for example former researchers. Preferably below guru level because gurus are too narrowly oriented.

4.4 Mentors

Compared to coaches, mentors are more oriented to the future. Their efforts should concentrate on building "technology for future". Coaches transfer guru's knowledge to the format acceptable by their potential successors. Mentors make the future coming. At universities, they pave the road to the massive application of the guru's knowledge by designing new study programs, writing textbooks and manuals, building laboratories and so on. They cooperate with coaches who tell them what should be done as well as with angels who facilitate sponsoring. The mentors should also collect information from external sources – research centers and leading universities – in order to design an innovative and competitive university vision and to develop a realistic strategy for its implementation.

4.5 Fathers

Every vision must be adopted by a strong individual (a "father") who will adopt it and consecrate his/her efforts to its implementation and long-term advancement. As Kess [4] stresses, the fathers play their critical role in two moments: during launching the vision and during its depression. In the first case, their enthusiasm can inspire the others and lead them toward new aspirations. In the second one, it can show them the way out of the misery by pointing to new goals that will modify those that became obsolete. The father has to be a strong personality and a passionate leader. The universities should seek the leaders of research and educational teams among fathers.

4.6 Politicians

The key role of politicians is leading their community. To succeed, they should have a clear vision and the capability to attract people to it. They have to be able to explain to every individual what makes their vision important, why it should be implemented and how. They have to be able to build a strong and reliable team of fellows who will implement it. Top management of universities should consist of politicians sharing the same vision and having a strong informal influence on key academicians. In accordance to Mládková [3], knowledge workers can hardly be ordered, they must be invited to collaborate. Every good politician intuitively knows that this is the most appropriate tactic for making strong and durable ties between the followers and the vision.

5 Lessons Learned for Slovak Tertiary Education

The analysis shows that all types of knowledge workers can participate at university life starting from gurus are "pure scientists", coaches as educators, angels as ignitors of development, mentors as its catalysts, fathers as its guards, and politicians as its leaders and coordinators. Universities with an appropriate mechanism for their installations to their relevant positions will move ahead.

Unfortunately, the Slovak University Act [7] prohibits the universities from using their specific mechanism. It introduces a unified model limiting a case-by-case adjustment in selecting "right people for right positions". All Slovak universities' top managers – rectors and deans – must be elected by their academic senates. If the senates consisted only of "fathers", the mechanism might work. As this is rarely the case, the candidates often do not set up their own, distinct visions – they simply follow the Academic Senate's desires. They do not offer the radical progressive vision. Without such a vision, the university will not develop. An infinite loop of stagnation continues.

Even if a progressively-thinking candidate wins, he/she has limited in his activities by the university legislation. The rector is just a formal head of university. The power remains in the Senate's hands. As radical changes often lead to tensions and subordinates' discomfort, the rector can be called-off at any moment. Consequently, the top managers are very cautious to introduce radical changes.

All by all, one can conclude: To make a progress of the Slovak tertiary education system more flexible, the University Act must allow university to function in a more flexible mode and give them an opportunity to organize their human resource policy in accordance to its own goals.

References

1. Drucker, P.F.: Landmarks of Tomorrow, 270 pages. Harper & Row, New York (1957)
2. Nonaka, I., Takeuchi, H.: The Knowledge Creating Company: How Japanese Companies Create the Dynamics of Innovation, 304 pages. Oxford University Press, Oxford (1995)
3. Mládková, L.: Management of Knowledge Workers, 190 pages. IURA Edition, Bratislava (2012)
4. Kess, P.: Knowledge transfusion from external sources to small and medium-sized companies. In: Proceedings of the International conference Human Capital without Borders: Knowledge and Learning for Quality Life Management, Knowledge and Learning, Portorož, Slovenia, 25–27 June 2014
5. Hvorecký, J., Šimúth, J., Lichardus, B.: Managing rational and not-fully-rational knowledge. Acta Polytechnica Hungarica **10**(2), 121–132 (2013)
6. Hvorecký, J.: Testament vedca: kolaps školstva a cesta k jeho oživeniu (Last Will of a Researcher: Collapsing Education and Its Revitalization). Premedia, Bratislava (2015). 120 pages
7. Zákon o vysokých školách č. 131/2002 Z. z. (University Act of the Slovak Republic)

Issues of Hazardous Materials Transport and Possibilities of Safety Measures in the Concept of Smart Cities

Vladimír Adamec[1], Barbora Schüllerová[1(✉)], and Vojtěch Adam[2]

[1] Institute of Forensic Engineering, Brno University of Technology,
Purkyňova 464/118, 612 00 Brno, Czech Republic
{vladimir.adamec,barbora.schullerova}@usi.vutbr.cz
[2] Department of Chemistry and Biochemistry, Mendel University in Brno,
Zemědělská 1, 613 00 Brno, Czech Republic
vojtech.adam@mendelu.cz

Abstract. The transportation of goods and supplies is an essential part of maintaining a functioning urban infrastructure. It also involves the transport of dangerous goods. This type of transportation may especially in the urban areas signify a high risk that may significantly damage the critical infrastructure of the city, if there is an accident and leakage of dangerous chemical substances. The aim is therefore, to minimize the risk and its consequences. The effective instruments are through the identification, analysis and assessment of these risks, searching for critical areas in cities and ensuring the application of prevention and safety measures. This paper aims to introduce the issue of the risks associated with the transportation of hazardous substances in the cities and to propose measures that are in accordance with the concept of Smart Cities, in order to contribute to create of functional communication network, traffic flow in cities and increasing the security of critical infrastructure.

Keywords: Road accident · Hazardous substances · Risk · Human health · Environment · Impact · Smart measure

1 Introduction

Currently, the issue of Smart Cities is the area that requires the attention of many developed countries and in particular their cities. With respect to the mission of Smart Cities the emphasis is on creating an environment that uses different flows and interactions in cities (finance, energy, materials, services, etc.). These processes are becoming smart by the strategic use of information and communication infrastructures and services in the process of the transparent land use planning and management, responsive to the social and economic needs [1]. The solutions and the introduction of these smart systems, it is necessary primarily in cities, which are already currently on the border of technical competence and are not able to adequately meet the service in relation to ensuring a safe supply of energy, transport services, security, etc. [2]. These problems are no longer possible to be solved by conventional means, such as increasing

© ICST Institute for Computer Sciences, Social Informatics and Telecommunications Engineering 2016
A. Leon-Garcia et al. (Eds.): Smart City 2015, LNICST 166, pp. 790–799, 2016.
DOI: 10.1007/978-3-319-33681-7_70

capacity or building new roads. In order to create the concept of Smart Cities it is important to follow the fundamental key areas such as:

- Creating partnerships with key city businesses
- Compliant database with the information about daily operations and processes for long-term planning,
- The use of digital modelling to supply of the physical environment focused on citizens,
- The introduction of digital and communications infrastructure,
- Development and testing new business models and processes [3, 4].

Implementing the concept of Smart Cities should thus be based on strategic planning. One of the current areas is intelligent, ecological, safe and integrated transport. There are currently many projects that are focused on, for example, reducing transport emissions that are in particular associated with the transit traffic in cities [3]. The most serious problem of transport is the contamination of air by the emissions, mainly due to their significant risk to human health, in particular in large cities with a high density of automobile traffic [5]. In recent years, significantly increasing the proportion of transport on air pollution, which leads to increase of participation of the health risks associated with exposure of humans to these pollutants [6, 7]. One of the completely new group of substances flowing in this way into the environment are the platinum group of metals (platinum, palladium, rhodium and ruthenium less commonly iridium), which are part of automotive catalysts [8]. In addition to these negative phenomena, there may also be the potential risks posed by the transportation of hazardous substances, which is not an isolated case in cities. This risk within the Smart Cities is only marginally solved. Considering the possible risk it deserves more attention, especially in relation to the protection of critical infrastructure, population and ability to respond faster and more effectively to the resulting undesirable event.

2 Transport of Hazardous Substances

Transportation of hazardous substances comprises about 4–8 % of the total goods transportation in EU countries. More than 50 % of the contents transported are flammable liquids, mostly in the form of propellant fuel. The second most frequently transported substances are condensed gases under pressure. In some of the European Countries the amount of the volume transported in 2013 increased by nearly 100 % (Estonia, Luxemburg, Great Britain) [9]. The risk of the occurrence of a serious road accident is real in spite of the application of safety and preventive measures, which should aim to minimize this risk. One of the reasons is the increasing variety of the transported hazardous substances [10, 11].

Hazardous chemicals are not only important in their negative properties, but also their other properties, which are within the functions of cities used for various activities which makes their supply so essential. Relevant examples are fuels, gaseous and liquid substances used for disinfection or cooling.

Currently, are the only available summary statistics of accidents with leakage of hazardous substances in the individual countries and their regions. These statistics, however, do not contain especially mentioned data about accidents of the ADR vehicle or vehicles carrying sub-limit volumes in cities.

The importance of the need to reduce the risk of this type of transportation is demonstrated by the experience of the past years (see Table 1), where there have been accidents of vehicles carrying dangerous substances in cities or urban track, which caused serious damage. In this context it should be noted that these failures have in urban areas had more serious consequences than in rural areas. The evacuation of people can significantly impair the function of the affected cities and disrupt the infrastructure.

The accidents may occur particularly in the mobile phase or during loading tasks. In both cases, the level of risk increases with regard to the venue and nature of the event (a dangerous substance was initiated - an explosion, fire, toxicity) [10].

Table 1. Overview of significant hazardous chemical substances accidents [11–15]

Event	Scenario	Damages
11. 7. 1978, Los Alfaques, Spain	The explosion of a truck with propylene near the camp Los Alfaques in the village of San Carlos de la Rápita	216 dead, 200 injures
10. 11. 1979, Mississauga, Canada	The train explosion and leakage of chlorine in populated areas	Evacuation of 200 000 habitants
4. 8. 1981, Montanas, Mexico	The chlorine leak after truck accident	28 dead, 1000 intoxicated, 5000 evacuated
2. 5. 2011, Pilsen, Czech Republic	The fire and explosion pressure cylinders after the accident 2086 kg of acetylene gas, 50 kg of CO2, 240 kg of R-404A, 132 kg of R-407C, 144 kg of R-437A 66 kg R - 417A 66 kg of R-422D 72 kg R - 134A	No injuries. Serious property damage.
7. 5. 2013, Mexico City a City of Pachua, Mexico	The explosion of tank with methane	22 dead, 36 injured, property damage: 30 houses, 20 vehicles
6. 7. 2013, Lac-Mégantic, Canada	The explosion of a freight train with crude oil	42 dead, property damages

Hazardous chemicals have become part of our life to the extent that it is impossible to imagine a modern society where they are not used. Increasing their number, as well as, the amount of transported used, combine to increase the safety requirements for studying the risks arising from the use of these substances, and the emergence of a series of measures to increase security. This is then reflected for example in legislation or requirements for emergency preparedness. Most of the legislative instruments are focused on static sources, which are for example the production and storage of fuel. The emergency plans for the stationary installations are prepared as part of a integrated emergency system, they are under regular review and the situation is constantly monitored. But there is an absence of such measures in connection with the transportation of dangerous goods.

3 Risk of Dangerous Goods Transport in Cities

3.1 Critical Areas in Cities

Especially vulnerable are the urban areas where high numbers of people whether permanent (city centres, businesses, transfer station hubs, hospitals, schools, etc.) or temporary (e.g. Traffic congestion on the centre circuits and in the city centres). Critical places of transport networks can be based on criteria such as: the importance of the road section and the possibility to replace it, the demanding to return the section back into operation, the importance of the section linking a significant portion of urban agglomerations, the links strategic places, traffic intensity, capacity segment, other risks, which is exposed segment [16].

Currently, the movement of dangerous goods by road is coordinated in Czech Republic only through safety signs (B18, B19) according to the European Agreement Concerning the International Carriage of Dangerous Goods by Road (ADR) [17]. In the Czech Republic is the movement of these vehicles limited by prohibition traffic signs especially before some road tunnels where a risk in the event of an accident is especially high. Critical points are particularly important transportation constructions, such as bridges, tunnels, intersections. By the early identification of these critical points can be reduced the level of risk by using prevention and safety measures. Such measures could be, for example, CCTV monitoring sites, prohibiting signs for vehicles carrying dangerous substances or providing short arrival times of rescue. One of the effective tools is the application of risk analysis methods and support software tools that can identify, analyze and evaluate the risk, including modeling of dangerous scenarios development of the situation [10].

3.2 Approaches to Assessing the Environmental Risks of Dangerous Goods Transportation

The identification and assessment of the risks of damage requires a comprehensive system approach, both in terms of acute and chronic risk. While the acute risk effects show immediately, especially at the accident location, identification of the chronic risk effects is a complex and time-consuming process [10]. These risks can manifest themselves, for example in the form of chronic disease on the affected population in the form of respiratory diseases, for example, or the deterioration of environmental quality [5].

It is first necessary to define the area to be evaluated, as well as the definition of the problem situation with the definition phase, during which the leak occurred:

- mobile phase (transportation by road, compulsory safety breaks, checks by state authorities),
- loading tasks (loading, unloading, cleaning the shipping containers etc.).

Besides the hazardous substances mentioned above, there are other factors, internal and external, that affect the extent of an accident, which vary in different transportation phases (climatic conditions, technical condition of the transportation unit, vulnerability of the environment, the physical health and mental condition of the driver etc.). It is, therefore, necessary to define all the aspects of the transport of dangerous chemicals that may be significant risks for the examined process.

3.3   Application of Risk Analysis Methods to Identify Risks in the Urban Areas

Risk Analysis of transportation of hazardous substances by road, not only in the cities, is a very complex problem as for the selection of a suitable methodology. The aim of the analysis is to obtain relevant information describing the identified risks and their importance for the given area. Therefore, it is important to use a combination of methods based on qualitative, semi-quantitative and quantitative approach. A qualitative approach in the first part of the assess process including its components which are related and influence each other. By applying of this approach can to detect even so-called hidden processes, which may occur in connection with the transport of dangerous substances [9]. The quantitative approach allows modelling of the consequences of hazardous substance leakage in specified areas using precise numerical data. In the case of hazardous substance transportation, the scenarios may include fluid leak followed by evaporation, gas leak with immediate dispersion into the atmosphere, flammable liquids with immediate or subsequent initiation. In general, quantitative approaches numerically evaluate the frequency of undesirable manifestation of the risk sources and their consequences. Because the methods of risk analysis cannot be used individually for all phases of transportation, are particularly suitable methods, which are based on a multi-criteria approach used map data and information on where the incident occurred or may occur. Some analytical instruments may have a software form and can be connected to an electronic database of chemicals [18, 19].

The identification of risks should never been underestimated, and so-called black swans that in the case of their full expression may have the fatal consequences should be taken into account. Although it is not easy to predict precisely the occurrence and extent of the impact of events, it is important to ensure sufficient functional background work is undertaken, which is based on the creation of a communication network in preparedness for an immediate response with primary and secondary measures with regard to protecting the human society. It should also include an adequate analysis and assessment of undesirable events with the objective approach, which includes external experiences and the assessment [20, 21].

3.4   Proposal for the Introduction of Smart Risk Minimization Measures

With regard to the possible use of safety measures in cities, it is necessary to introduce smart systems that identify the moving city traffic unit, to warn drivers of ADR vehicles about the route for transportation, communicating with emergency services and warn other drivers and residents in good time in the event of an accident.

One of the possible measures is the identification and monitoring of ADR vehicles in the city or in close proximity or arriving and moving there, can be the use of the existing CCTV system, which is in most cities already widely used. Given that these types of vehicles in cities are moving mostly in order to supply, could then notify the carrier or the recipient of the planned entry of vehicles into the city, and their predicted route. The Integrated Rescue System should be able to monitor vehicle movement and communicate with it in order to prevent undesirable events (e.g. the information about the closures, traffic congestion). Another option is the automatic vehicle identification by marking ADR, as well as for automatic identification of license plates of vehicles [22]. The necessary need for the monitoring of the movement of vehicles transporting hazardous substances are proving by research projects to be solved in Europe and worldwide [23–25]. Applying these measures may be important not only in the area of prevention.

In cases where there is a leakage of dangerous substances, is necessary to avoid movement in the so-called danger zone in which the substance is spread. In this case, it is necessary to transfer early information to drivers through dynamic information panels informing about the incident in the danger zone and allow other drivers to choose alternative routes. The timely information through the visual communication mediated by these panels can be in time to prevent the collapse of transport and enables the rescue services to get to the crash site, to the injured persons. Dynamic information panels would be appropriate to supplement a warning light signalling for the cases of an undesirable situation.

3.5   SWOT Analysis of the Proposed Measures

Due to complexity of some operations based on the eventual implementation to the Smart Cities system, was made the SWOT analysis (see Tables 2 and 3). The aim was to identify internal and external factors that may have a significant impact on decisions about integration of these measures.

Then was selected five or six key points of the internal and external factors on the basis of SWOT analysis. Monitoring of vehicles in ADR, moving in cities, is one of the measures for which it can use existing CCTV systems, which are mainly implemented in the big cities. The weak point of this measure could be in this case an obsolete camera system that is not able to automatically identify ADR vehicles. The threat is from unlabelled vehicles because of the transport of the very low amount of hazardous substances or intentionally substituted vehicles signs. An especially important opportunity in this case is to improve communication among carriers in ADR and rescue services in order to increase safety and security, and to prevent accidents with spills of hazardous substances and ensuring traffic flow.

Table 2. SWOT analysis of the ADR vehicles monitoring in cities

STRENGHTS	WEAKNESSES
• automatic ADR vehicles identification • awareness about of ADR vehicles movement • ability for rapid response to adverse situation • use of existing camera systems (CCTV) location and communication with the drivers of the ADR vehicles • exact location of potentially dangerous goods	• obsolete camera systems (CCTV) • small CCTV coverage • CCTV coverage without automatic identification of the ADR signs • the new system price • absence of the communication equipment with the driver of the ADR vehicle • absence of the solutions in the current legislation
OPPORTUNITIES	THREATS
• increase of safety and security • improvement of the drivers (ADR vehicles) and the integrated rescue system communication • providing of better traffic flow • improve of prevention measures • the annual statistical reports for the evaluation of the critical points • the introductions of these measures into legislation	• ADR vehicles without signs • deliberately poorly labelled ADR vehicles • illegible signs for vehicles • unreported transport in the city • poor communication by the carrier and recipient • disagreement with the Czech and European Union legislation

Table 3. SWOT analysis of the dynamic information panels in cities

STRENGHTS	WEAKNESSES
• rapid transfer of the information • ability of the rescue services and drivers to rapid response to the undesirable situation • communication with drivers and persons around • using and supplementation of the current dynamic information panels • ensure the traffic continuity in cases of the accident and information about alternative routes	• the new system price • the choice of uniform style information for the driver and the other persons • obsolete system that does not allow connections to GSM emergency services • Selection of specific locations for the placement • depending upon the source of energy
OPPORTUNITIES	THREATS
• increase of safety and security and accident prevention • improvement of the drivers (ADR vehicles) and the rescue services communication • ensure of the better traffic flow not only in the cases of the accident • utilization of the information panels not only after the accident cases • the renewable energy use (alternative or additional source of energy for information panels)	• accident in location without information panels • unreadable information • failure of energy resources • broken communication system • delay of the transmission of the information

Another analyzed measure happened to using dynamic of information panels, which are now commonly used for highway or street circuits. Strong point of this measure is the possibility of rapid transfer of information on the undesirable situation, ensuring the traffic flow and prevent the movement of people in the danger zone, where there has been to release of hazardous substances. The weakness point is the difficulty in selecting suitable locations for the placement of these of information panels. The threat is therefore in this context particularly accident in an area without the information panels and movement of people in the danger zone. Special opportunities, like at previous measures increasing safety and the prevention of ensuring the traffic flow and reducing or completely averting undesirable impact in the case the accident. Important is also the opportunity of ensuring of substitute or additional power sources to prevent any malfunction of the system due to power failure.

4 Conclusions

Possibilities of implementation of the Smart Cities concept are very wide and it is a long process. In the paper was highlighted currently little solving issue, which is the transport of hazardous substances in the cities. It is an essential part of maintaining their functional infrastructure. Despite the low probability of traffic accident and leakage of the hazardous substances is the significance of their impact very high. To ensure the prevention and improvement of safety is the important part of communication not only with carriers in ADR, but also with other drivers and people who are moving at place of the accident. Therefore, it is necessary a good knowledge of the transport infrastructure in cities including critical locations. In this paper was, therefore, introduced the basic methodology approach to identify and analyze risks. Proposed the measures, that can be incorporated into the already functional systems in the cities and can be used not only for the purpose of transporting hazardous substances in cities which have been assessed by the elementary SWOT analysis. In the analysis were selected 5–6 key factors that can positively or negatively affect the whole process. The important opportunity is not only improve the communication network between drivers and emergency services but also the possibilities of using so-called green energy, which can be used in both the proposed measures. The aim of this paper was mainly to highlight at the current situation and the need to ensuring the activities in this area. Detailed procedures for removing weaknesses and threats will be the subject of further solutions and research.

References

1. European Commission – Digital Agenda for Europe, Smart Cities. https://ec.europa.eu/digital-agenda/en/smart-cities
2. Matějka, P., Jizba, T., Tvrdý, K.: Člověk a globální komunikace. In: Sborník 11. konference Prezentace projektů, pp. 23–28. CTU in Prague, Faculty of Transportation Science, Prague (2013). (in Czech)

3. Smart Cities magazine. http://www.scmagazine.cz/article/view/173. (in Czech)
4. European Innovation Partnership on Smart Cities and Communities, Strategic Implementation Plan, pp. 2–22. European Comission (2013)
5. Adamec, V., et al.: Doprava, zdraví a životní prostředí. Grada, Prague (2007). (in Czech)
6. Bumbová, A., Adamec, V., Navrátil, J., Ješonková, L., Langerová, A.: Health risk assessment of air pollution caused by polycyclic aromatic hydrocarbons bound to particulate matter smaller than 1 μm. In: International Conference on Development, Energy, Environment, Economics, DEEE 2010, Puerto de la Cruz, Tenerife, Spain, 30 November 2010 through 2 December 2010, Code 85148, pp. 218–223. WSEAS Press, Puerto De La Cruz (2010)
7. Božek, F., Adamec, V., Navrátil, J., Kellner, J., Bumbová, A., Dvořák, J.: Genotoxic risks for population in vicinity of traffic communication caused by PAHs emissions. WSEAS Trans. Environ. Dev. 6(3), 198–207 (2010)
8. Bednarova, I., Mikulaskova, H., Havelkova, B., Strakova, L., Belkova, M., Sochor, J., Hynek, D., Adam, V., Kizek, R.: Study of the influence of platinum, palladium and rhodium on duckweed (Lemna minor). Neuro Endocrinol. Lett. 35, 35–42 (2014)
9. European Commission. European Union, 1995–2013. Eurostat: Statistics Explained. Road freight transport by type of goods (2014). http://ec.europa.eu/eurostat/statistics-explained/index.php/Statistics_Explained:General_disclaimer#Copyright_Notice
10. Schullerova, B., Adamec, V., Balog, K.: The risk of transport and possibility of their assessment. In: Proceedings of the 2nd International Conference on Traffic and Transport Engineering (ICTTE), 27–28 November, pp. 384–391. Scientific Research Center Ltd., Belgrade (2014)
11. Arturson, G.: The los alfaques disaster: a boiling-liquid, expanding-vapour explosion. Burns 7(4), 233–251 (1981)
12. Mannan, S.: Lees' Loss Prevention in the Process Industries: Hazard Identification Assessment and Control. Elsevier, Oxford (2012)
13. Fire Rescue Service of the Czech Republic. http://www.hzscr.cz/clanek/2012-listopad-chovani-tlakovych-lahvi-pri-pozaru.aspx. (in Czech)
14. British Broadcasting Corporation. http://www.bbc.com/news/world-latin-america-22438925
15. British Broadcasting Corporation. http://www.bbc.com/news/world-us-canada-27387287
16. Taylor, M.A.P.: Critical transport infrastructure in urban areas: impacts of traffic incidents assessed using accessibility-based network vulnerability analysis. Growth Change 39(4), 593–616 (2008)
17. UNECE. European Agreement concerning the International Carriage of Dangerous Goods by Road, ADR 2015. http://www.unece.org/trans/danger/publi/adr/adr2015/15contentse.html
18. Aven, T.: Uncertainty in Risk Assessment – The Representation and Treatment of Uncertainties by Probabilistic and Non-Probabilistic Method. Wiley, Chichester (2014)
19. Roosberg, J., Thorsteinsson, D.: Environmental and Health Risk Management for Road Transport of Hazardous Materials. University of Lund, Lund Institute of Technology, Lund (2000)
20. Taleb, N.N.: Black Swan: The Impact of the Highly Improbable. Random House Trade Paperbacks, Westminster (2010)
21. Hanson, D., Ward, T., Ives, N.: Responding to a Black Swan: Principles and Protocols for Responding to Unexpected Catastrophic Events. Ernst & Young, London (2013)
22. Malínek, L.: Automatická identifikace vozidel ADR. CDV, Brno (2010). (in Czech)
23. Novák, L.: ChemLog T&T nastínil možnosti sledování kontejnerů. Dopravni noviny, Prague (2015). (in Czech)

24. Benza, M., Bersani, C., Garbolino, E., Giglio, D., Olampi, S., Sacile, R., Tomasoni, A., Trasforini, E.: A distributed information system prototype to detect and monitor the hazardous material transport on the road in the territory of nice-imperia-ventimiglia. In: 2nd International Conference on Safety and Security Engineering, SAFE 2007, 25 June through 27 June 2007, pp. 327–336. WIT Transactions on Built Environment, Southampton (2007)
25. Zhang, X., Fu, J., Yu, M., Zhang, N., Mei, W.: Research on state monitoring system using the RS485 bus for HAZMAT transportation. In: Proceeding of SPIE – The International Society for Optical Engineering 8th International Symposium on Precision Engineering Measurements and Instrumentation; Chengdu; China, Bellingham, WA, 8 August 2012 through 11 August 2012, 8759, Article No. 875931 (2012)

Changes in the Demographic Structure of the Central City in the Light of the Suburbanization Process (The Study of Poznań)

Maria Trojanek, Justyna Tanaś, and Radosław Trojanek[✉]

Poznań University of Economics, Al. Niepodległości 10, Poznań, Poland
{m.trojanek, justna.tanas, r.trojanek}@ue.poznan.pl

Abstract. The aim of the paper is to identify changes in the age structure of the inhabitants of the Downtown of Poznań and in the housing stock and number of residents in a single flat, taking into consideration the type of construction (in 2008 and 2013).

In the first part of the paper, we presented processes occurring in contemporary Polish cities as well as their causes. We discussed the process of suburbunization – its aspects and implications. In the empirical part, on the basis of data from the resident register of the Ministry of Internal Affairs, we conducted the analysis of the demographic structure of the inhabitants of Poznań and of the structure of buildings located in the Downtown of Poznań.

On the basis of the conducted analysis of changes occurring in the area of the Downtown of Poznań, we may observe that the number of residents in the area of Poznań Downtown decreased by about 20 % in the period under study. The age structure of the inhabitants of the center of the city also changed. The calculated indicators show that the population of the Downtown of Poznań began to be subject to gradual processes of ageing, which should be perceived as a negative phenomenon. In turn, the analysis of housing stock shows that housing conditions in Poznań Downtown improved. This is reflected in the drop in the number of people living in one apartment in this part of the city.

Keywords: Suburbanization · Shrinking city · Demographic structure of the city centre

1 Introduction

The demographic changes we observe in most European Union countries, such as the ageing of societies, the development of suburban zones, and functional and spatial transformation, pose new challenges of an unprecedented scale for local governments. In the period between the two last censuses (2002 and 2011), the balance of migration between urban and rural areas swayed in favor of the latter (for the first time in 50 years). The need arises for the integration of the central city with its neighboring communes. A common policy regarding the provision of public services must be pursued and the coordination of the spatial development of the central city and its surrounding communes is necessary [1].

© ICST Institute for Computer Sciences, Social Informatics and Telecommunications Engineering 2016
A. Leon-Garcia et al. (Eds.): Smart City 2015, LNICST 166, pp. 800–811, 2016.
DOI: 10.1007/978-3-319-33681-7_71

Civilization processes have brought about changes in the functions of city centers. City dwellers began to move to suburbs and areas beyond city borders in order to improve their living standard. This tendency has considerably influenced the process of the depopulation of the city center, which used to play a significant role in the past, e.g. it was a place of living, entertainment and trade. A decrease in the number of inhabitants was determined by various factors (of an endogenous and systemic character) and has a number of multi-criteria implications. It may be analyzed in the macro scale and from the local angle. The ongoing processes of social and spatial transformations in the conditions of a decrease in the size of population (referred to as shrink smart) do not always bear negative consequences. They may also create opportunities for positive changes, such as the improvement of the living standard, owing to, for example, reduced population density per unit of residential area, lower burden for the environment or better transport links. Having in mind the aim of this paper, we shall focus on a single selected aspect of the ongoing socio-economic transformations in the center of Poznań, namely, we will discuss changes in the number and age structure of the inhabitants of Poznań (in 2008 and 2013) as well as changes in the housing stock and number of residents in a single flat, taking into consideration the type of construction.

2 The Concept of Suburbanization and the Indications of This Process

Urbanisation is a process which in a significant way shapes spatial and functional structures of particular areas. In the literature we can most often meet with four basic stages of the process: urbanisation (primary), suburbanisation, de-urbanisation and re-urbanisation. Highly developed countries with advanced urbanisation processes have already experienced all four stages of urbanisation.

With the growth of market economy in Poland, some markets which played a marginal role in the pre-transition economic system have grown in importance. A number of Polish researchers have attempted to seek for relationships between different markets of goods and the economy, effectiveness of investments in different segments of property market [2–6] or identification of suburbanization processes [7].

Beginning from the system transformation in Poland, we may observe de-urbanisation of the population, both from the central areas of the biggest cities and large panel housing estates located in peripheral city districts – to suburban area where new estates of detached houses are built. More wealthy groups migrate from deteriorating central districts to suburbs which, by their distant location from the centre allow for everyday commuting to work in the centre, offering at the same time much better living conditions than in the previous place of living. Density of population in city centres is decreasing while it is increasing in the suburbs, and the balance of migration of the whole urban agglomeration is positive. Intensification of building development in peripheral parts of the city and suburbs results in disappearance of the border between the city and its external area. Agricultural land is converted into industrial, warehousing and storage, trading, residential and sports areas.

Above mentioned features are characteristic for the complex process of suburbanisation. Etymologically, the notion comes from "suburbium", which means peripheral in relation to city or adjacent to its administration borders (closely located) area with residential functions. As R. Fishman writes [8], for the first time the word "suburb" was used in the 14th century by G. Chaucer in a story collection entitled The Canterbury Tales, to define forgotten places around 14th century cities. These were the places where various types of outcasts gathered. The places were despised, therefore "sub" to stress domination of the city (urbia).

In the literature suburbanisation is perceived in three basic spatial contexts:

(a) inside administrative borders of the central city (so called internal suburbanisation, in the vacant for investment areas of the central city),

(b) outside central city borders in the area of so called closer suburban zone – defined as external suburbanisation (urban fringe, suburban zone) characterised by relative spatial continuity of investment;

(c) outside closer suburban zone, in the area of further suburban zone (urban region, urban-rural fringe), with the domination of extensive forms of using the land and similar in landscape to the countryside; in the United States it is defined as ex-urbanisation and in France – as peri-urbanisation [9].

The existing body of literature provides numerous definitions of suburbanization [10–14]. In spatial dimension suburbanisation means dynamic development and increase of intensity of the use of peripheral areas of the cities and their suburban zones where the example is so called urban sprawl.

Suburbanisation process is connected with a number of consequences, both for communes in the suburban zone and for the central city. The consequences may be analysed in three areas: spatial, economic and social. From the point of view of social phenomena, suburbanisation is not a favourable phenomenon. In many aspects it is, however, favourable both for some people (inhabitants of suburban zone), and for businesses (investors).

The process of suburbanization and demographic changes are some of the causes of the shrinkage of cities. The phenomenon of shrinking cities manifests itself in many forms and structures, both in the spatial and time approach [15]. The shrinkage of cities is the process of depopulation, which results in a decrease of the attractiveness of a city as a place for life and development, and in the lack of jobs. We observe a negative birth rate and migration in pursuit for better earnings and improved living conditions. The shrinkage of cities is not only a Polish phenomenon, but it is well known in the whole world [16]. The term "shrinking city" was first used by scholars in 1987. Sociologists Hartmut Häußermann and Walter Siebel first applied the expression "shrinking city" (schrumpfende Stadt) in their book titled "NeueUrbanität". Since then, a lot of definitions of the term – which describe the characteristic features, causes and effects of this phenomenon - have appeared in literature.

This phenomenon we can observe in Poznań agglomeration. The number of inhabitants of the agglomeration of Poznań, the area of which coincides with the administrative area of the Poznański district, is constantly increasing. Between 1995 and 2010, the population growth was 6.92 %. As early as at the beginning of 1990s, we observed a systematic decrease in the number of the inhabitants of Poznań (from 581.2 thousand in 1995 to 551.2 thousand in 2010, which means a drop of 5 % in the size of the population of the city). This decrease is accompanied by a significant increase in the number of people inhabiting the communes of the Poznański district. The population of this district has gone up by nearly 36 % in the past fifteen years. The highest growth is observed in the communes directly neighboring the city of Poznań. In some of these communes, the population has doubled. The positive balance of migration was the main factor responsible for the growth of population size.

Figure 1 shows changes in the size of population in the Poznań agglomeration in the years 1995–2010.

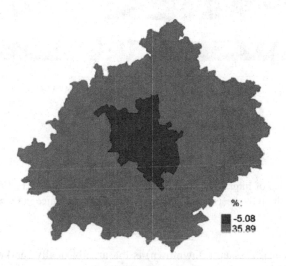

Fig. 1. Changes in the size of population in the Poznań agglomeration in the years 1995–2010. Source: author's own research on the basis of the data from the Central Statistical Office (GUS). (Color figure online)

In the years under study, dwellers of the central city usually migrated to the communes of the Poznański district. The percentage of migrants to these areas grew from 1995 to over 67 % in 2005. In 2010, the influx was a bit slower and the figure was 65 % of the total number of migrants. The percentage of people migrating to the other communes of the Wielkopolskie province and to other provinces was much lower. Not many people emigrated abroad.

Figure 2 shows the directions of migration of the dwellers of Poznań in the years 1995–2010.

3 The Scope of the Study

3.1 The Spatial Scope of the Study

A Downtown is the most densely populated part of a city, offering the widest choice of facilities. It provides a variety of public services and has a mixture of residential and public utility buildings. The most characteristic part of a Downtown is the city center, which constitutes the core of its spatial structure.

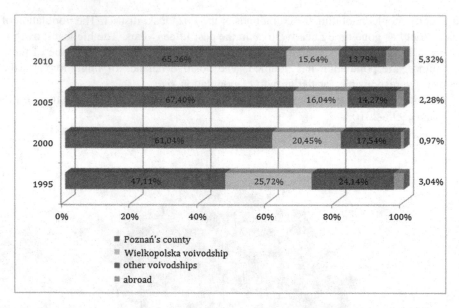

Fig. 2. The directions of migration of the dwellers of Poznań in the years 1995–2010. Source: author's own research on the basis of the data from the Statistical Office in Olsztyn. (Color figure online)

The Downtown of Poznań (Downtown) is the area basically marked by the streets of the so-called 2nd transport frame, consisting of:

- in the west – S. Żeromskiego street, St. Przybyszewskiego street,
- in the south – Hetmańska street,
- in the east – the Warta river, Jana Pawła II street, Podwale street, A. Hlonda street,
- in the north – Szelągowska street, Winogrady street, Pułaskiego street and the Poznań-Szczecin railway (Fig. 3).

Since 2011, there have been seven Estate Councils in the area of Downtown. They are Auxiliary Units of the City of Poznań and they have different share in the area and population of Downtown. As Fig. 4 below shows, the marked area of Downtown is about 1,700 ha in size.

3.2 The Time Scope of the Study

The analysis of changes concerning the population of Downtown, including the age of its inhabitants and changes in the housing stock and number of residents in a single flat, taking into consideration the type of construction, covered the years 2008 and 2013.

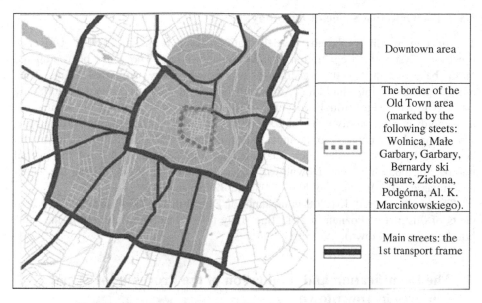

	Downtown area
	The border of the Old Town area (marked by the following steets: Wolnica, Małe Garbary, Garbary, Bernardy ski square, Zielona, Podgórna, Al. K. Marcinkowskiego).
	Main streets: the 1st transport frame

Fig. 3. Poznań Downtown (Downtown) area. (Color figure online)

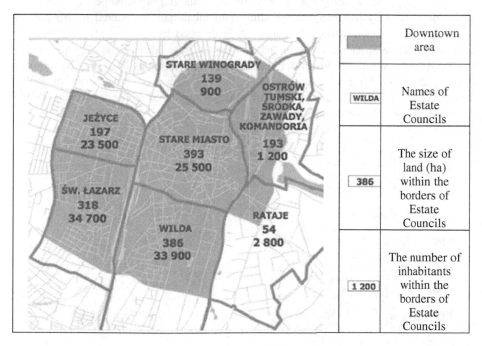

	Downtown area
WILDA	Names of Estate Councils
386	The size of land (ha) within the borders of Estate Councils
1 200	The number of inhabitants within the borders of Estate Councils

Fig. 4. Borders of Estate Councils in the district of Poznań-Downtown in 2012. (Color figure online)

3.3   The Objective Scope of the Study

The data on which we based our deliberations come from the PESEL (Universal Electronic System for Registration of the Population) base. They have been prepared on the basis of data from the registration base of the Ministry of Internal Affairs. They include address points (buildings), in which inhabitants were registered in 2008 and 2013. The data were brought to comparability. Records concerning the number of households occurring only either in 2008 or in 2013 were removed from the data base. This means that, compared to the input base, the number of households in Downtown decreased by about 7,000, which accounted for approximately 14 % of the overall number of households in Downtown as compared with 2008. Thus, the study encompassed 49,101 households in 2008 and 42,396 in 2013.

The study covered 137,208 inhabitants of Downtown in 2008 and 109,423 residents of this part of Poznań in 2013 (the study referred to households from the same buildings in Downtown).

4   The Identification and Evaluation of the Processes of Social Changes in Downtown

When carrying out a comparative analysis of demographic changes occurring in Downtown, we may observe that the number of inhabitants registered in this part of Poznań in the selected years (2008 and 2013) dropped by about 20 %. The biggest decrease of population occurred in the districts o Stare Miasto (24 %) and Jeżyce (21 %). In the district of Grunwald, the number of inhabitants in 2013 was 20 % lower than in 2008. In the period under study, the population of the district of Wilda decreased by 17 %, while the number of residents registered in the apartments of the district of Nowe Miasto dropped by 15 % (Fig. 5).

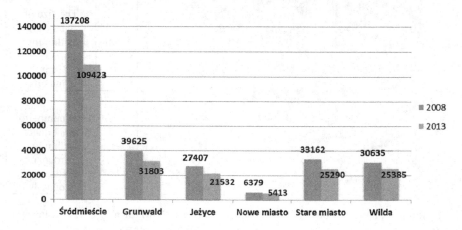

Fig. 5. Changes in the size of the population of Downtown across districts in the years 2008–2013. Source: compiled by the author. (Color figure online)

We may also observe changes in the age structure of the inhabitants of Downtown over the period under study. As Fig. 6 shows, between 2008 and 2013, the number of people in the age groups of 25–39 and 40–64 dropped by, respectively, 3.52 % and 2.05 %. What is worrying is the fact that the number of inhabitants between 18 and 24 fell by 5 % and the population of young people under 17 also decreased, though not as much (by 0.55 %). As it is seen, the number of people over 65 years of age increased by 0.27 % in the period under discussion. The growing number of residents in the age group of 25–64 and a simultaneous decrease in the number of inhabitants under 24 indicate that the population of Downtown is undergoing the gradual process of ageing. This situation is confirmed by Fig. 7, which shows that the percentage of people in the productive and post-productive age in the years under study increased by, respectively, 0.28 % and 0.27 %, with a simultaneous decrease of the percentage of residents in the pre-productive age (0.55 %).

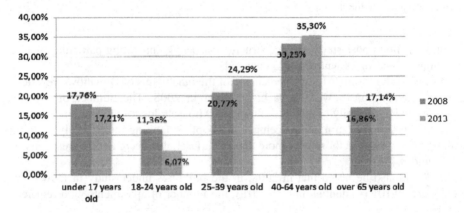

Fig. 6. Changes in the age structure of the inhabitants of Downtown in the years 2008–2013. Source: compiled by the author (Color figure online)

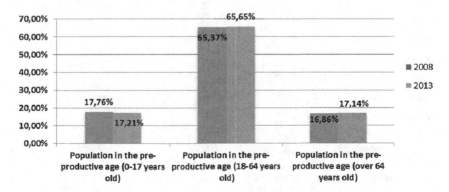

Fig. 7. Changes in the share of particular age groups of the inhabitants of Downtown in the years 2008–2013. Source: compiled by the author. (Color figure online)

It should also be pointed out that in 2008 the number of inhabitants registered in the residential units based in Downtown accounted for 25 % of all residents of Poznań. As the population of Downtown gradually decreased, this figure stood at the level of 20 % in 2013, which may reflect the migration of people from Downtown to other parts of the city and to peripheral areas (Table 1).

Table 1. The number of inhabitants of Downtown compared with the total number of residents of Poznań in 2008 and 2013.

	2008	2013
The population of Downtown	137,208	109,423
The population of Poznań (Statistical Yearbook – data for 2010)	556,722	552,393
The share of the inhabitants of Downtown in the total population of Poznań	25 %	20 %

Source: compiled by the author

In the period under study, the age structure of people inhabiting particular types of buildings located in Downtown also changed.

As Fig. 8 shows, in 2013, the percentage of the inhabitants of Downtown registered in single-family houses was 1.1 % higher than in 2008. The number of residents registered in multi-family buildings with up to 10 households rose even more – by 6 % from 2008 to 2013. In turn, the percentage of people inhabiting multi-family buildings with up to 20 units and those with more than 20 households decreased by, respectively, 3.7 % and 3.4 %.

It should also be noted that in 2008, in the buildings under study in Downtown, there were 49,101 residential units. In 2013, the number of apartments with registered

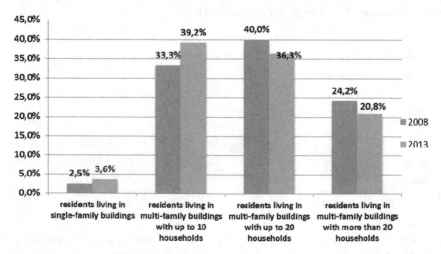

Fig. 8. The percentage of population inhabiting particular types of buildings in 2008 and 2013. Source: compiled by the author. (Color figure online)

inhabitants in this part of Poznań fell to 42,396. It means that the number of households in the buildings under study (equal in both years under consideration) decreased by 14 % (6,705 households).

Moreover, between 2008 and 2013, we observed a drop in the number of people per one apartment based in Downtown. In 2008, the average apartment in this part of Poznań was inhabited by 2.79 people. In 2013, this number fell to 2.58 people per apartment. Therefore, as it is seen, in 2013 an apartment in Downtown was inhabited by 0.21 person less than in 2008.

Figure 9 above shows changes in the average number of residents in an apartment in particular districts from 2008 to 2013. We may observe that the highest number of people per apartment was in the district of Nowe Miasto (2.92 and 2.79 respectively). The lowest figure both in 2008 and 2013 was noted in the district of Wilda (2.74 and 2.55 inhabitants per apartment). The biggest improvement in living conditions was observed in Jeżyce, where in 2013 apartments were inhabited on average by 0.27 person less than in 2008. The situation was also better in the districts of Grunwald and Stare Miasto, where the average number of residents per apartment was smaller by, respectively, 0.21 and 0.2 person. Thus, it may be seen that changes in this respect were the least visible in the area of Nowe Miasto, where in 2013 the average apartment was inhabited by 0.14 person less than in 2008.

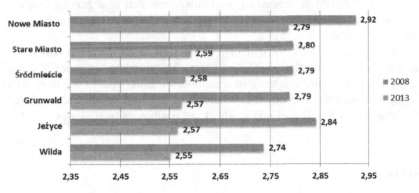

Fig. 9. The average number of people in an apartment in 2008 and 2012 across districts. Source: compiled by the author. (Color figure online)

In order to fully depict changes in the age structure of the inhabitants of Downtown, we should analyze changes in the process under discussion in absolute numbers. In 2013, in comparison to 2008:

- the number of inhabitants in all districts of Downtown decreased, although there were differences in the scale of changes,
- the biggest changes (a decrease) occurred in the districts of Stare Miasto and Grunwald, 7,872 and 7,822 respectively, while the smallest reduction in the number of residents was observed in Nowe Miasto (966),
- the biggest drops were observed in the age groups of 18–24 (a decrease of 8,939) and 40–64 (a decrease of 6,996); these figures reflect highly negative phenomena from the perspective of the functioning of the city,

- if we take into consideration a decrease in the percentage of the population in the pre-productive age (0–17 years of age), a drop in the number of inhabitants in the age group of 0–64 was 23,398 people, which accounts for 85.5 %,
- the number of residents in the post-productive age also decreased (by 4,387 people).

5 Conclusion

The aim of the paper is to identify changes in the age structure of the inhabitants of the Downtown (Downtown) of Poznań and in the housing stock and number of residents in a single flat, taking into consideration the type of construction (in 2008 and 2013). In the light of the above data we may conclude that the percentage of the inhabitants of Downtown in the total number of residents of Poznań in the period from 2008 to 2013 decreased by 5.5 %. Moreover, calculated indicators show that the population of the Downtown of Poznań began to be subject to gradual processes of ageing, which should be perceived as a negative phenomenon. In turn, the analysis of housing stock shows that housing conditions in Poznań Downtown improved. This is reflected in the drop in the number of people living in one apartment in this part of the city.

Our study allows us to evaluate the ongoing changes, although, due to the limited scope of data, it should be treated as preliminary research of a general character. In order to provide full assessment of the processes under discussion, further thorough analyses are required.

The above deliberations are part of a discussion on the ongoing changes in the spatial distribution of functions in the city area. The shrinkage of cities is a problem which has determined the existence of a number of urban centres for over 20 years. Demographic forecasts, the economic situation and overall development trends indicate that this phenomenon will continue to affect the position of many cities in future.

References

1. Tanaś, J., Trojanek, R.: Demographic structural changes in Poznań Downtown: in the light of the processes taking place in the contemporary cities in the years 2008 and 2013. J. Int. Stud. **8**(3), 128–140 (2015)
2. Palicki, S.: Evaluation of urban spatial planning. Actual Probl. Econ. Natl. Acad. Manag. **9** (147), 455–463 (2013)
3. Rącka, I.: Sales of residential properties illustrated with the city of Kalisz. J. Int. Stud. **6**(2), 132–144 (2013)
4. Rącka, I., Palicki, S., Kostov, I.: State and perspectives of the real estate markets' development in the Central-Eastern Europe countries on the example of Poland and Bulgaria. Real Estate Manag. Valuation **23**(2), 77–90 (2015)
5. Trojanek, R.: Fluctuations of dwellings' prices in the biggest cities in Poland during 1996–2011. Actual Probl. Econ. **1–2**, 224–232 (2013)
6. Trojanek, R., Trojanek, M.: Profitability of investing in residential units: the case of the real estate market in Poland in the years 1997–2011. Actual Probl. Econ. **2012**(7), 73–83 (2012)

7. Tanaś, J.: Differentiation of local housing markets in Poznań suburban area. Real Estate Manag. Valuation **3**, 88–98 (2013)
8. Fishman, R.: Bourgeois Utopias: The Rise and Fall of Suburbia, pp. 3–17. Basic Books, New York (1987)
9. Lorens, P. (ed.): Problem suburbanizacji, pp. 17–32. Biblioteka Urbanisty, No. 7, Urbanista, Warsaw (2005)
10. van den Berg, L., Drewett, R., Klaassen, L.H., Rossi, A., Vijverberg, C.H.T.: Urban Europe: A Study of Growth and Decline. Pergamon Press, Oxford (1982)
11. Champion, T.: Urbanization, suburbanization, counterurbanization and reurbanization. In: Paddison, R. (ed.) Handbook of Urban Studies, pp. 143–161. Sage Publications, London (2001)
12. Klaassen, L.H.: Myśl i praktyka ekonomiczna a przestrzeń. Wydawnictwo Uniwersytetu Łódzkiego, Łódź (1988)
13. Zagożdżon, A.: Sieć osadnicza, zmienność i trwałość. In: Jałowiecki, B., Kaltenberg-Kwiatkowska, E. (eds.) Proces urbanizacji i przekształcenia miast w Polsce. Ossolineum, Wrocław-Warszawa (1988)
14. Zuziak, Z.: Strefa podmiejska w architekturze miasta. W stronę nowej architektoniki regionu Miejskiego. In: Lorens, PP. (ed.) Problem suburbanizacji, Biblioteka Urbanisty 7, Urbanista, Warszawa, pp. 17–32 (2005)
15. Haase, A.: No one-size-fits-all. O różnorodności kurczących się miast w Europie. In: Szajewska, N., Lipińska, M. (eds.) Zarządzanie rozwojem miast o zmniejszającej się liczbie mieszkańców (w kontekście perspektywy finansowej 2014 – 2020). Materiały z konferencji zorganizowanej przez Komisję Samorządu Terytorialnego i Administracji Państwowej we współpracy z Ministerstwem Rozwoju Regionalnego i Głównym Urzędem Statystycznym, Kancelaria Senatu, Warszawa, pp. 31–45 (2013)
16. Szajewska, N.: Modele kurczących się miast – wnioski do badań. In: Szajewska, N., Lipińska, M. (eds.) Zarządzanie rozwojem miast o zmniejszającej się liczbie mieszkańców (w kontekście perspektywy finansowej 2014 – 2020). Materiały z konferencji zorganizowanej przez Komisję Samorządu Terytorialnego i Administracji Państwowej we współpracy z Ministerstwem Rozwoju Regionalnego i Głównym Urzędem Statystycznym, Kancelaria Senatu, Warszawa, pp. 31–45 (2013)

Bratislava Towards Achieving the Concept of Smart City: Inspirations from Smart City Vienna

Andrej Adamuscin[✉], Julius Golej, and Miroslav Panik

Slovak University of Technology in Bratislava,
Vazovova 5, 812 43 Bratislava, Slovakia
{andrej.adamuscin, julius.golej,
miroslav_panik}@stuba.sk

Abstract. The concept of smart cities arose against the background of economic and technological changes caused by processes of integration and globalization, which European cities have been forced to face common challenges in the context of competitiveness and sustainable development. These challenges have an observable impact on issues related to the quality of the urban environment such as housing, complete urban infrastructure, commercial sector and their environmental impact. This concept thus includes the overall quality of urban life through the built and unbuilt urban environment, urban economy, social environment, urban culture, human and social capital and participation of citizens in government and the city. In this paper authors are trying to outline the problematic areas of Bratislava to achieve Smart City concept, whereby they take inspiration from the neighboring city of Vienna, which in turn is considered as one of the top smart cities in Europe.

Keywords: Smart city · Bratislava · Vienna · Framework strategy · Renewal

1 Introduction

For the past 20 years Bratislava has undergone many dynamic changes. Disordered and uncontrollable new construction of buildings and renovation of existing housing stock without comprehensive strategy or insufficient implementation support system, both static and dynamic transport should be the main reasons such as these developing processes should be started to meet the highest requirements of contemporary modern European cities.

Bratislava as a sister city of Vienna, from which it is located approximately 64 km could thus in its direction just to take an example from Vienna which is considered among the top European and world smart cities for several years. To achieve this state could be helpful, inter alia, also a project EU-GUGLE and also prepared several concepts such as "Methodology for complex renewal of housing estates with a focus on housing reconstruction" or still uncompleted implementation of transport policy of the city of Bratislava.

© ICST Institute for Computer Sciences, Social Informatics and Telecommunications Engineering 2016
A. Leon-Garcia et al. (Eds.): Smart City 2015, LNICST 166, pp. 812–820, 2016.
DOI: 10.1007/978-3-319-33681-7_72

1.1 Smart City Vienna

The "smartness" of a city describes its ability to bring together all its resources, to effectively and seamlessly achieve the goals and fulfil the purposes it has set itself. In other words, it describes how well all the different city systems, and the people, organizations, finances, facilities and infrastructures involved in each of them, are: individually working efficiently; and acting in an integrated way and coherent way, to enable potential synergies to be exploited and the city to function holistically, and to facilitate innovation and growth [1].

Recent years Vienna has become a leading smart and sustainable European city. The Austrian capital differs from most other metropolises through its good performance in so many areas: housing, public transport and other infrastructure services (e.g. waste separation, Spring Water Mains), education and universities as well as vast urban green spaces. [2] Vienna is the city with the world's best quality of living, according to the Mercer 2014 Quality of Living rankings, in which European cities dominate [3].

For the city of Vienna has been prepared a framework urban development strategy with a view into the 2050. The present Smart City Vienna framework strategy is directed at all target groups of the city: Vienna's citizens, enterprises, non-profit institutions and, last but not least, the public sector itself. [2] Smart City Vienna comprises first and foremost the aim of resource preservation. Development and modification processes in the sectors of energy, mobility, and infrastructure and building management are to dramatically reduce CO_2 emissions by 2050 [2].

In fact Vienna recently created a public private entity, TINA Vienna which is tasked with co-developing smart city strategies and solutions for the city. Nowadays there are prepared more than 100 smart cities projects being developed throughout the city. [4] For example one of the mentioned projects is Citizen Solar Power Plant. With a goal of obtaining 50 % of their energy from renewables by 2030, the city partnered with the local energy provider, Vienna Energy, they developed a crowd-funding model whereby individual citizens can buy half or whole panels and receive a guaranteed return of 3.1 % annually [4].

Vienna is also testing out a range of electric mobility solutions from expanding their charging network from 103 to 440 stations by 2015 to testing EV car sharing and electric bike rentals. Vienna bike sharing program is fully accessible to visitors, not just residents. [5] Another important innovation has been in rezoning dense neighborhoods allowing for zero-parking residential buildings. Residents in these communities commit to not owning a personal vehicle.

Finally, Vienna is renovating a 40 hectare former slaughterhouse district and turning it into a much smarter use: an innovation district focused on media science and technology. By 2016, the city expects 15,000 people to working on startups in the Neu Marx Quarter district. [4] Furthermore, Vienna took the extra step of incorporating the strategy into law to minimize the risk of future mayors throwing the plan out to start over [5].

1.2 Smart City Vienna Framework Strategy

The key goal for 2050 of Smart City Vienna is to offer optimum quality of living, combined with highest possible resource preservation, for all citizens. This can be achieved through comprehensive innovations (shown on Fig. 1).

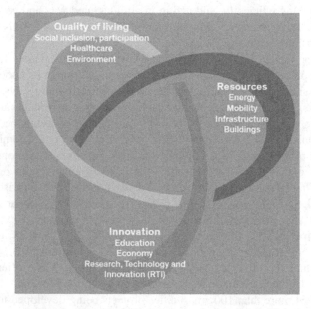

Fig. 1. The smart city Vienna principle [2] p. 17

The present framework strategy describes the key goals and principal approaches chosen to attain them. It represents guidelines for the numerous important specialised strategies of the city that define concrete multiyear plans for such areas as urban planning, climate protection, the future of energy supply or Vienna as an innovation hub [2].

The Smart City Vienna framework strategy is more comprehensive (but not exhaustive), pursues a long-term horizon (2050) and does not offer detailed packages of measures. However, concrete sub-projects with a shorter timeframe will definitely be formulated and implemented [2].

2 Methodology for Smart Cities

According global advisory committee for Smart Cities Benchmarking was developed 62 indicators across the Smart Cities Wheel (shown on Fig. 2).

Each of the six components of the Smart Cities Wheel are assigned a set of indicators reflect an attempt to create a proxy for measuring each of the sub-components of the Wheel. Each component contains 3 subcomponents. Therefore there are 18 total subcomponents in the model, and with 62 indicators, that leaves an average of almost 3.5 indicators per subcomponent (shown on Fig. 3).

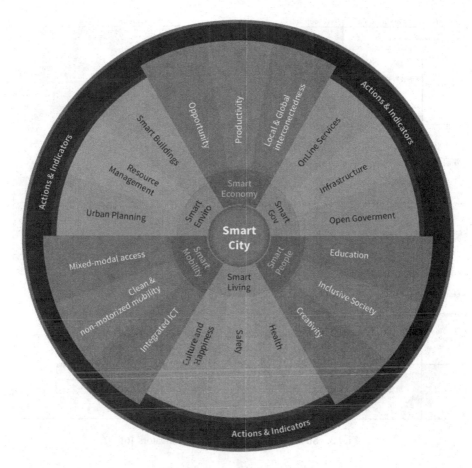

Fig. 2. Smart cities wheel [6]

The data were transformed by using a mathematical formula called a z-score, which permits the comparison of data in different units (e.g. %, tons of GHG emissions, etc.). Each of the 6 components is then assigned a maximum of 15 points and the results are transformed in a way that the highest performing city in each category is assigned 15 points. Thus, if one city were to lead in each of the six components, the city would obtain a maximum score of 90 points. Of the 62, 16 of them are also directly mapped to the new sustainable cities ISO standard (ISO 37120) [6].

2.1 Mercer's Quality of Living

Mercer's Quality of Living reports provide valuable information and hardship premium recommendations for over 460 cities throughout the world, the ranking covers 223 of these cities [3].

Living conditions are analyzed according to 39 factors, grouped in 10 categories:

Dimension	Working Area	Indicator	Description
Environment	Smart Buildings	Sustainability–certified Buildings	Number of LEED or BREAM sustainability certified buildings in the city (Note: if your city uses another standard please indicate)
			% of commercial and industrial buildings with smart meters
			% of commercial buildings with a building automation system
		Smart homes	% of homes (multi–family & single–family) w/ smart meters
	Resources Management	Energy	% of total energy derived from renewable sources (ISO 37120: 7.4)
			Total residential energy use per capita (in kWh/yr) (ISO 37120: 7.1)
			% of municipal grid meeting all of following requirements for smart grid (1.: 2–way communication; 2.) Automated control systems for addressing system outages 3.) real–time information for customers; 4.) Permits distributed generation; 5.) Supports net metering
		Carbon Footprint	Greenhouse gas emissioned measured in tonnes per capita (ISO 37120: 8.5)
		Air quality	Fine Particulate matter 2.5 concentration (µg/m3) (ISO 37120: 8.1)
		Waste Generation	% of city's solid waste that is recycled (ISO 37120: 16.2)
			Total collected municipal solid waste city per capita (in kg) (ISO 37120: 16.3)
		Water consumption	% of commercial buildings with smart water meters
			Total water consumption per capita (litres/day) (ISO 37120: 21.5)
	Sustainable Urban Planning	Climate resilience planning	Does your city have a public climate resilience strategy/plan in place? (Y/N) If yes provide link.
		Density	Population weighted density (average densities of the separate census tracts that make up a metro)
		Green Space per capita	Green areas per 100,000 (in m2) (ISO 37120: 19.1)
Mobility	Efficient Transport	Clean–energy Transport	Kilometers of bicycle paths and lanes per 100,000 (ISO 37120: 18.7)
			# of shared bicycles per capita
			# of shared vehicles per capita.
			# of EV charging stations within the city
	Multi–modal Access	Public Transport	Annual # of public transport trips per capita (ISO 37120: 18.3)
			% non–motorized transport trips of total transport
		Smart cards	Integrated fare system for public transport.
			% of total revenue from public transit obtained via unified smart card systems
	Technology Infrastructure	Access to real–time information	Presence of demand–based pricing (e.g. congestion pricing, variably priced toll lanes, variably priced parking spaces). Y/N
			% of traffic lights connected to real–time traffic management system
			# of public transit services that offer real time information to the public: 1 point for each transit category up to 5 total points (bus, regional train, metro, rapid transit system (e.g. BRT, tram), and sharing modes (e.g. bikesharing, carsharing)
			Availability of multi–modal transit app with at least 3 services integrated (Y/N)
Government	Online services	Online Procedures	% of government services that can be accessed by citizens via web or mobile phone
		Electronic Benefits Payments	Existence of electronic benefit payments (e.g. social security) to citizens (Y/N)
	Infrastructure	WiFi Coverage	Number of WiFi hotspots per km2
		Broadband coverage	% of commercial and residential users with internet download speeds of at least 2 Mbit/s
			% of commercial and residential users with internet download speeds of at least 1 gigabit/s
		Sensor Coverage	# of infrastructure components with installed sensors 1 point for each: traffic, public transit demand, parking, air quality, waste, H2O, public lighting
		Integrated health + safety operations	# of services integrated in a singular operations center leveraging real–time data. 1 point for each: ambulance, emergency/disaster response, fire, police, weather, transit, air quality
	Open Government	Open Data	Open data use
		Open Apps	# of mobile apps available (iPhone) based on open data
		Privacy	Existence of official citywide privacy policy to protect confidential citizen data
Economy	Entrepreneurship & Innovation	New startups	Number of new opportunity–based startups/year
		R + D	% GDP invested in R&D in private sector
		Employment levels	% of persons in full–time employment (ISO 37120: 5.4)
		Innovation	Innovation cities index
	Productivity	GRP per capita	Gross Regional Product per capita (in US$, except in EU, in Euros)
	Local and Global Conexion	Exports	% of GRP based on technology exports
		International Events Hold	Number of international congresses and fairs attendees.
People	Inclusion	Internet–connected Households	% of internet–connected households
		Smart phone penetration	% of residents with smartphone access
		Civic engagement	# of civic engagement activities offered by the municipality last year
			Voter participation in last municipal election (X of eligible voters) (ISO 37120: 11.1)
	Education	Secondary Education	% of students completing secondary education (ISO 37120: 6.3)
		University Graduates	Number of higher education degrees per 100,000 inhabitants (ISO 37120: 6.7)
	Creativity	Foreign–born immigrants	% of population born in a foreign country
		Urban Living Labs	# of officially registered ENOLL living labs
		Creative Industry Jobs	Percentage of labor force (LF) engaged in creative industries
Living	Culture and Well–being	Life Conditions	Percentage of inhabitants with housing deficiency in any of the following 5 areas (potable water, sanitation, overcrowding, deficient material quality, or lacking electricity)
		Gini Index	Gini coefficient of inequality
		Quality of life ranking	Mercer ranking in most recent quality of life survey
		Investment in Culture	% of municipal budget allocated to culture
	Safety	Crime	Violent crime rate per 100,000 population (ISO 37120: 14.5)
		Smart Crime Prevention	# technologies in use to assist with crime prevention, 1 point for each of the following: livestreaming video cameras, taxi apps, predictive crime software technologies
	Health	Single health history	% of residents w/ single, unified health histories facilitating patient and health provider access to complete medical records
		Life Expectancy	Average life expectancy (ISO 37120: 12.1)

Fig. 3. Smart cities benchmarking indicators [6]

- Political and social environment (political stability, crime, law enforcement, etc.)
- Economic environment (currency exchange regulations, banking services)
- Socio-cultural environment (media availability and censorship, limitations on personal freedom)
- Medical and health considerations (medical supplies and services, infectious diseases, sewage, waste disposal, air pollution, etc.)
- Schools and education (standards and availability of international schools)
- Public services and transportation (electricity, water, public transportation, traffic congestion, etc.)
- Recreation (restaurants, theatres, cinemas, sports and leisure, etc.)
- Consumer goods (availability of food/daily consumption items, cars, etc.)
- Housing (rental housing, household appliances, furniture, maintenance services)
- Natural environment (climate, record of natural disasters)

The scores attributed to each factor, which are weighted to reflect their importance to expatriates, allow for objective city-to-city comparisons. The result is a quality of living index that compares relative differences between any two locations evaluated.

For the indices to be used effectively, Mercer has created a grid that allows users to link the resulting index to a quality of living allowance amount by recommending a percentage value in relation to the index [3].

3 Bratislava

Until the fall of former political regime in 1989 was in Slovakia, including Bratislava for several years realized mass production of affordable housing. This construction was marked by the poor quality of buildings, especially as regards their energy performance. This poor technical condition mainly of prefabricated apartment buildings in many cases persists to these days, also thanks to still unrealized coherent concept of housing estates renewal. Renovation of buildings in Bratislava is provided on individual and un-conceptual basis. Renewal is performed only on separate apartment blocks, without connectivity to their immediate surroundings. Despite to this state for Ministry of Transport, Construction and Regional Development has been developed a comprehensive study of housing estate renewal in the recent past: "Methodology for complex renewal of housing estates with a focus on housing reconstruction".

Within this study was developed analysis of the current state of housing estates renewal in Slovakia - architectural, urban, administrative aspects and existing planning tools of complex housing estates renewal. There were analyzed European documents in the field of urban development (Leipzig Charter, Toledo Declaration, the Territorial Agenda 2020, the Europe 2020 Strategy) as well as the research was performed on the selected model of foreign examples. Finally was realized the draft of methodology process of preparing strategic documents for housing estates renewal with emphasis on housing reconstruction at urban level, with an emphasis on an integrated approach and feasibility plans. [7] It should be added that putting this methodology into practice is heavily dependent on a momentary political will.

Now, the Slovak capital has a chance to move forward within a project aimed at demonstrating the feasibility of nearly-zero energy building renovation models. Bratislava is the only eastern European city to participate in the EU-GUGLE project, which stands for European cities serving as a Green Urban Gate towards Leadership in sustainable Energy. The aim of the project is to create a concept of energy performance and securing the energy efficiency of buildings when using them, as well as the reduction of energy intensity within the city's district in which the building is located. In other words, the project will take into consideration not only the reduction of energy consumption in the buildings, but will simultaneously deal with other aspects of a sustainable environment, like the interconnection of the building with public space, green areas and sustainable forms of mobility. The latter includes mass public transport, bicycles and moving on foot. Bratislava was chosen in a strong competition of 45 European cities and the city is cooperating with Vienna in this project, while the Austrian capital is serving as a district leader. Over the five years of the project (2013–2018) Bratislava with other European cities will join efforts to combine the latest research results in smart renovation of groups of buildings at the district level and use this knowledge to renovate the living space. The main task of this project is to bring to Bratislava new, sustainable technologies that will reduce emissions caused especially by heating apartment blocks. Within this project, Bratislava can receive up to €2 million to renovate 40,000 square meters of total floor area, i.e. up to €50 per square meter to cover the costs of the renovation. Out of the total floor area, 20,000 square meters should account for buildings owned by the Bratislava municipality, while the remaining 20,000 square meters should account for privately owned housing represented by owners' associations or apartment block administrators. The European Commission will refund the renovation costs only after the works are completed and have achieved the target parameters [8].

Also very important is the issue of transport infrastructure. Physical lifetime of transport infrastructure depends primarily on the building materials and old design of transport capacities. The materials that were used for its construction currently do not meet the quality requirements due to the infrastructure was not subject to more fundamental recovery process during its lifetime. Moreover, the infrastructure lifetime is significantly influenced by the intensity of its use. Its implementation largely falls within the period of implementation of residential buildings and public facilities in housing estates, when at least in a position of static transport capacitively was sufficient for the then demands.

The issue of parking in Slovakia is a long-term problem, whether in existing buildings or with new development projects where parking costs are only kind of forced expenditure on which developers often want to save money. Bratislava is one of the European metropolises, which seeks for the solution for several decades. Problem that Bratislava was not ready for, is a major building boom which caused a further increase in both passenger and freight transport in the city center. This means that the constantly increasing level of motorization brings to Slovakia and especially in densely populated urban areas around the capital - Bratislava even higher space requirements. That becomes the most valuable quantities especially in the inner-city environment. This fact makes new demands on the urbanization of our cities, the professionalism of solutions to traffic problems and high standards to ensure a quality environment. One of the most serious current problems closely related to urban space in Bratislava is the traffic situation, especially the issue of static traffic [9].

Another important issue in the field of comprehensive transport solutions in Bratislava is the fact that there is insufficient traffic data database and the city does not have sufficient details of current conditions of its urban road network. City of Bratislava is lacking the scheduled surveys and their results, which would be able to determine the disproportion of the current state and predict its development [10].

The list of projects that have an ambition to contribute to the solution of traffic problem in Bratislava is quite long. Solving problems with static traffic in Bratislava could be implemented using comprehensive regulation through traffic signs. In practice this means charging for parking at a time of increased congestion and the designation of paid parking zones with the road signs. Paid parking zones could improve the environment and conditions for non-motorized road users, as well as improving the quality of transport services. One of the solutions to the problems with static traffic could be building a semi recessed and recessed parking, garage houses, increase recessed parking with one or two floors. Addressing of static traffic in different districts of the city lies in cooperation with the magistrate of the capital. Cooperation includes the selection of appropriate areas that would capacitive mean an increase in parking areas for individual districts. Solution of this complex issue could be also implemented through PPP projects. Another solution is a free parking not only on the borders of the city, but also outside, for example in Malacky, Pezinok or Senec. The condition is to create high quality service suburban bus line, which will operate at appropriate intervals. Another solution of problem of static transport in Bratislava could be seen in the construction of smart parking spaces by installing smart parking sensors placed directly on the parking places. Drivers would be allowed to easily find a free parking place and would contribute significantly to the reduction of emissions in the city [9].

Another important issue is the participatory budget of the city and the city districts. Bratislava as the first Slovak city began experimenting with the introduction of participatory budgeting since 2011. Citizens were given the opportunity to decide directly on the reallocation of public finances and on the form of public space and services. Participatory budgeting process takes place throughout the year and is open to all citizens. In the first phase are collected suggestions and ideas from people on the use of public finances. They are then sorted and processed into projects. Since the idea is always more than a means to implement them, citizens must also decide which of their ideas are supported and which are not [11].

It took place at participatory budgeting at the city level for a number of deficiencies and irregularities in recent years. They arise in the event of a communication strategy that would attract as many residents into the process; or administrative support, which would work systematically on the involvement of citizens and work on the drafts; and especially mismatch about the rules for the conduct of participatory budgeting process.

Municipality of Bratislava launches e-governance project in 2015. It is a project of electronic council, which contributes to saving the environment and optimizes the work of the City Office. The official website of the city will be available invitations and materials for meetings, profiles of deputies and information about their individual vote, or resolution of the City Council. The new application will serve all - as citizens, as well as local authorities and the deputies [12].

4   Conclusion

In order to Bratislava achieve the Smart City concept it needs to develop and implement mainly a comprehensive concepts a policies in the field of residential and non-residential buildings, transport infrastructure, technical infrastructure, public spaces but also in the field of sustainable economy and governance. Of course, main condition to achieve this effective sustainable development is the implementation of the latest materials, technologies and innovative concepts in each of these areas, whether in the field of urban development, ICT and construction and architecture, etc. In this would help to Bratislava a generous funding from the European funds, the potential of which the city does not know sufficiently take full advantage. This could help the generous funding from the European funds, the potential of which the city does not know to sufficiently take full advantage. Precisely in these areas Bratislava could take inspiration from the sister city of Vienna, which actual projects and its approaches to them could be considered as an exemplary direction of sustainable development of a modern European city.

References

1. ISO/IEC JTC 1, Information Technology. Smart Cities, Preliminary Report 2014. ISO 2015, Published in Switzerland. http://www.iso.org/iso/smart_cities_report-jtc1.pdf
2. Smart City Wien, Framework Strategy. City of Vienna. Vienna City Administration (2014). ISBN 978-3-902576-91-0
3. 2014 Quality of Living Worldwide City Rankings – MERCER Survey. United States, New York (2014). http://www.mercer.com/newsroom/2014-quality-of-living-survey.html#City-Rankings
4. Cohen, B.: The 10 Smartest Cities In Europe. 2014. Fast Company & Inc, 2015 Mansueto Ventures LLC. http://www.fastcoexist.com/3024721/the-10-smartest-cities-in-europe
5. Cohen, B.: The Smartest Cities In The World. 2014. Fast Company & Inc, 2015 Mansueto Ventures LLC. http://www.fastcoexist.com/3038765/fast-cities/the-smartest-cities-in-the-world
6. Cohen, B.: The Smartest Cities In The World 2015: Methodology. 2014. Fast Company & Inc, 2015 Mansueto Ventures LLC. http://www.fastcoexist.com/3038818/the-smartest-cities-in-the-world-2015-methodology
7. Finka, M., Golej, J., Jamečný, Ľ., Ladzianska, Z., Ondrejička, V., Baloga, M., Schweigert, M., Tóth, A.: Metodika komplexnej obnovy sídlisk s dôrazom na obnovu bytových domov: 1. 2. 3.etapa. Bratislava: STU v Bratislave. Ústav manažmentu, 248 p. (2012)
8. Liptáková, J.: Making Bratislava a Smart City. The Slovak Spectator (2014). http://spectator.sme.sk/c/20049863/making-bratislava-a-smart-city.html
9. Špirková, D., Golej, J., Pánik, M.: The issue of urban static traffic on selected examples in Bratislava in the context of economic sustainability. In: 2014 International Conference on Traffic and Transport Engineerin, ICTTE 2014, Belgrade, Serbia, 27–28 November 2014. ISBN 978–86-916153-1-4
10. Methodology of traffic capacitive impact assessment of investment projects. The Annex to Decision of the Mayor of the capital city of the Slovak Republic, Bratislava. 16 p. (2014)
11. Vittek, P.: Aby aj o peniazoch rozhodovali ľudia. P E R E X, a. s (2014). http://nazory.pravda.sk/osa/clanok/322462-aby-aj-o-peniazoch-rozhodovali-ludia/
12. Samospráva spúšťa digitálne zastupiteľstvo. Hlavné mesto SR Bratislava (2015). http://www.bratislava.sk/samosprava-spusta-digitalne-zastupitelstvo/d-11048590/p1=11049947

Urban Safety as Spatial Quality in Smart Cities

Maroš Finka$^{(\boxtimes)}$, Vladimír Ondrejička, and Ľubomír Jamečný

SPECTRA Centre of Excellence EU, Slovak University of Technology
in Bratislava, Vazovova 5, 812 43 Bratislava, Slovakia
{maros.finka,vladimir.ondrejicka,
lubomir.jamecny}@stuba.sk

Abstract. Urban safety representing one of the most important aspect of spatial quality for human life in urban areas. The concept of smart city has to reflect the fact, that in today's society, where most people live in cities, a man is exposed to different kinds of danger every day. Integration of urban safety into the complex smart urban development strategies is recent challenge not only for a spatial planners. Urban safety assessment methodology, presenting in this article, has a potential to be a base for smart system of urban safety monitoring in urban areas reflecting of local specifics in different categories of settlements.

Keywords: Urban safety · Smart city · Spatial quality · Risks · Perception of safety

1 Introduction

The "smart city" concept is mostly interpreted as the concept of use of information and communication technologies (ICT) to improve quality and performance of urban services, to reduce costs and resource consumption, in some cases to improve the framework for active participation of the citizens. This concerns mostly the implementation of new ICT based technologies in transport, energy sector, water and waste management, communication of the citizens, government services. But the spatial planners following their co-responsibility for sustainable urban life – including every day processes and urban flows as well as short term and long term development processes understand the "smart" dimension of the cities much broader. The growing complexity and dynamics of the development in urban systems with its social, functional and physical subsystems in the combination with growing dynamics of unpredictable external changes (natural disasters, economic shocks, social changes…) brings more and more uncertainty in the decision making and development processes. The crucial quality of the cities nowadays seems to be resilience of urban socio-ecosystems (including natural ecosystems, communities, economic sector, services …), closely connected with their ability to respond to challenges properly, in real time and with low transactional costs. To follow this dictate needs the use of advanced technologies, but this would be not enough. Even their efficient use needs the changes in societal processes, not speaking about the other dimensions of efficient responds. So the smart urban concepts developed by the spatial planners are going behind simple implementation of the information, communication and other technologies into the urban life

© ICST Institute for Computer Sciences, Social Informatics and Telecommunications Engineering 2016
A. Leon-Garcia et al. (Eds.): Smart City 2015, LNICST 166, pp. 821–829, 2016.
DOI: 10.1007/978-3-319-33681-7_73

and development, behind the technology innovations, towards social and institutional innovations. One of important aspects of urban resilience, where the smart innovations seem to be crucial is urban safety.

2 Urban Safety as Spatial Quality

Urban safety as urban spatial quality - addresses physical as well as social environment. Safety belongs to fundamental psychological needs and its absence in the cities is destructive. Since the very beginning of human existence, people had to face tasks to ensure safety for themselves and their beloved ones, it was the motivation for first human settlement development. Nothing has changed on importance of safety in human life during the history. This need persists, although the structure of safety needs and the contexts of this spatial quality have changed with societal development. Basic needs associated with protection against imminent threats resulting from the nature impacts and thus ensuring basic conditions for survival developed via property protection, to the need to ensure the long-term safety sustainable development [1].

The concept of smart city has to reflect the fact, that in today's society, where most people live in cities, a man is exposed to different kinds of danger every day. Concentration of urban population, human activities, unpredictability of human behavior as well as external shocks brought new conflict risks of various functions implemented in the cities. The conflicts results not only from different requirements and interests in the field of land use, but they are linked to the very background of decision making – different value systems of different stakeholders acting on different positions following in many cases contra dictionary goals. This multiplies the problems increasing anonymity, impeded orientation, dynamics and complexity of interdependencies in the functioning and development of the urban settlements, menace of spreading epidemics, fire hazards, as well as social conflicts, etc. The issues of safety and security have thus not retreated on the contrary; they have become particularly important part of life quality, in many aspects directly connected with urban resilience, less and less manageable using standard concepts, approaches and tools [2].

The new impulse for urban safety issues have been not only the terrorist attacks in the USA on 11 September, 2001, but climate change with numerous unexpected natural catastrophes, globalizing war with the extremism, growing technologic dependence of humans and especially of the cities in the combination with growing sensibility on individual failures. Not only political scientists agree on the fact that after them (and the subsequent attacks on the civilian population in the European cities just confirmed this fact), the world has changed even more and the safety issue in the so called western culture becomes even more acute. However, new dimensions related to urban safety also relate to approaching natural resources limits - materials, energy, land and water, with a threat related of inefficient exploitation, unscrupulous interferences in natural environment, global climate change, and food shortages. Large cities and communities, as complex systems, are particularly sensitive and with their quantitative growth and increase in the complexity their vulnerability increases. In these contexts the society has gradually been adjusting its perception of safety and safety moves even higher in real values ranking.

But changes in the system of values in the society also act from the opposite side, as there is change in the perception of a man as a basic reference frame unit for safety assessment in the space. While an "average man" (the so called "Modulor") served as a model for environment creation and assessment of its safety within architecture and urbanism in the past [3], today the most "vulnerable" person is considered as the benchmark group and every environment should be addressed to suit it, including claims for safety - thereby ensuring usability for everyone. Furthermore, subjective requirements of each individual conditioned not only by his physical and mental attributes but also by his social and cultural dimensions are taken into account in a much greater extent.

Safety is a broad area that is difficult to be defined precisely by some borders [4] – there are exactly as many kinds of safety as there are various hazards and threats to a man, even if we restrict the area of dangers only to threats of a man and leaving aside, for example, some ecosystem risks. It is therefore important that the safety issue is to be systematically addressed.

3 Safety Smart Concept

Urban safety is not strictly a new issue, but so far it has been quite little conceptually addressed and there is no single universally applicable and generally acceptable definition, yet. An exact definition, moreover, may vary depending on the country in which the term is used. The expression is composed of two relatively easily understandable words (urban + safety), combination of which, however, leads to formation of a new term whose meaning acquires a wholly new dimension. The general definition of safety or security (see [5, 6]) is no longer sufficient when we discuss the so called urban (city) safety. For this purpose, it is clear that we have to add the "dimension of the city" to the safety/security definition.

Smart concept of urban safety includes a wide range of aspects and activities primarily linked to publicly accessible areas, from crime (prevention) through physical environment safety, accessibility (barrier-free solutions and principles of design for all - "universal design") to institutional and organizational aspects. We define the urban safety (always, unless explicitly stated otherwise) as safety of any kind with respect to a man in any area within the city (urbanised area), where the public has more or less free access without restrictions (i.e. in public spaces, with emphasis on outdoor space), or any kind of man-related safety tied to phenomena and activities in these public areas.

The safety need, as well as the need for psychological well-being, have been essential for man's life quality. This confirms the position of safety in human needs following the American psychologist Abraham Maslow's hierarchy. Safety is placed here in the second position of importance, immediately after satisfaction of the primary biological-physiological needs. Abraham Maslow lined up the human needs in order of importance, thus creating a pyramid whose base consists of physiological needs (breathing, food, sleep, excretion, thermal comfort), other levels are organized in the order of importance (the lower the level, the more important) and it is the safety, emotional needs, the need for recognition, cognitive needs, needs of aesthetics and needs of fulfillment. According to Maslow's theory the needs of a lower level have to be (at least partially) satisfied if needs of a higher (less important) level shall begin to be fulfilled. From this is clear how much safety is important for humans and that it is not only the actual physical safety of human existence, but also a very safe feeling (perception of safety as the quality of the environment), which plays an important role for people's mental well-being and behavior. A man who feels insecure behaves instinctively, irrationally, and such behavior of a larger group of people (sometimes even the behavior of an individual) leads to chaos, resulting often in fatal consequences.

Coordination, harmonization, distribution of human activities in space and time and effort for their conflict-free rational cooperation is one of the objectives of the spatial planning discipline. It is therefore clear that safety must begin to be seen as one of the key components of both life quality and space quality for life and as such, it should be a dominant focus of the spatial planning - in collaboration with other disciplines, particularly architecture and urbanism, which are (from the perspective of urban safety) some kind of extended hands of spatial planning.

We assume that people perceive safety rather as part of the system quality of their environment, not as clearly defined quality of their lives (as evidenced by the fact that the concept of "urban safety" has no unambiguous definition). Safety is generally considered to be an integral part of the environment quality that either "is" or "is not" and not the quality based on individual needs, perception and human activity in space. The safety has been much discussed about on general level, however detailed knowledge and seize are lacking. There are principles for the level of safety to be increased or decreased, but there are not explicit rules (instructions) how to do this within the means of expression of architecture and urbanism. The existing knowledge is partial [7]. Generally, the safety issues are underestimated, the emphasis in examining it in the past was rather put on its economic dimension (e.g. risk-analysis in the insurance sector), followed by other aspects equally important for life quality. Currently the spatial planning with its integrative approach to shaping the space quality and the organization of human activities across the system levels and environment components should be the integrant platform for urban safety issues, both in relation to internal synergy of its aspects, as well as in relation to its systemic relations with other aspects of life quality and space for it.

3.1 Safety Classification

In the complex and coherent concept of smart city the interface between particular modules is of special important. This interface should create a platform for continual flow of information in not aggregated form relevant for the other modules. Speaking about urban safety, this continual exchange between the modules in smart city concept is precondition for efficient proper respond to the changes in the system and external shocks, as well as to safeguard low transactional costs. Important part in this context represents safety classification. Elaborating the classification is an important part of the assessment methodology. It is necessary to be aware that the difference in the priorities between particular security needs in various types of cities and its evolution over time has to be taken into account. Detailed study and benchmarking of these needs across the whole dimensional, functional and spacio-structural scale of the cities is the object of recent research the results of which will further develop the methodology introduced in this paper.

The very concept of safety is related to several domains related to life within the city organism and safety can be further particularized and subdivided by different criteria.

Safety can be classified according to:

- **origin** (e.g. safety situations caused by intentional activity - terrorist act, assault... or safety situations of random origin – e.g. car accident, heavy snow disasters, etc.);
- **spatial dimension** (e.g. safety situation related to a particular area – nightclub, busy crossroad... or without any commitment to a particular area - theft, car crash resulting from driver's carelessness, etc.);
- **time dimension** (e.g. safety situation pertaining to a specific time period - morning traffic jam, night, winter... or without any regard to the time aspect - an accident injury, a random car accident, etc.) [1]

The time dimension of safety can be further sub-divided into:

- **everyday safety** – (daily) safety situations with the potential hazard of a permanent nature – e.g. areas with higher concentrations of people - bus and train stations, subways, city center, areas in the city attractive for tourists...
- **spasmodic safety**:
  - *episodic* - disposable (safety situation happening once, e.g. scaffolds collapse in a construction site during a building reconstruction...)
  - *periodic* (impact situation, but recurring with some frequency, e.g. school year ends, periods of social benefits payment, public holidays, weekends,...) [1].

All categories and classifications of safety and security should also be considered from two perspectives:

- volumes and space without human factor (e.g. building structures safety, historic buildings, medieval walls, natural terrain modifications)
- "Man" in the environment - adding a human element to the environment (socialization, crime, community, human behavior in different situations), threats or rather improving man's safety by another man [1].

Safety can be further divided according to the perception of the receiver into the following categories:

- **objective safety** = safety whose quality is evaluated (evaluable) on the basis of certain objective data (e.g. casualty statistics, number of criminal acts in an area, etc.);
- **subjective safety** = perceptible, it is individual and unique for every person (Fig. 1) [2].

3.2   Options to Measure the Safety Quality

As the universal way of assessing the state of safety in a city currently does not exist, the aim of this publication is to present the proposal of methodology of how the urban

Fig. 1. Procedure basic division of urban safety [1]

safety can be comprehensively and particularly objectively investigated. In such analyses of urban areas four basic elements should be considered:

- volume-spatial composition, especially public spaces (i.e. street spaces, passages, buildings, parks, greenery areas, sports facilities…);
- the human element - people (taking into account differences in age, sex, social status and their communities…);
- technical elements (transport systems, lighting systems, access control elements, elements of spatial orientation…);
- organizational and institutional elements (neighborhoods, safety and emergency services, civic initiatives, unions and associations, etc.) [8].

But how is it possible to cover such a complex problem as the urban safety within space and time? The first step definitely is a detailed drafting of all elements and factors associated with the safety phenomenon. The second step is to describe all the possible safety/security risks that possibly threaten a man in the urban environment. The third step will then consist of searching mutual synergies (interactions) among the environment characteristics and potential risks. If we are able to achieve that no safety phenomenon and, at the same time, no safety risk will be forgotten, this method should exhaustively and comprehensively cover the issues of urban safety - for contemporary needs. In this way we obtain an objective method that is concurrently also sufficiently an open system that can be entered and flexibly modified if needed any time. The versatileness of the whole system is essential as the perception of (urban) safety is constantly changing, the majoritarian behaviour of people is also altering, and new threats and risks appear.

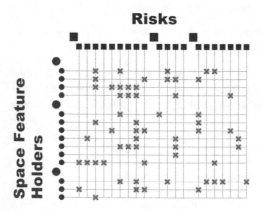

Fig. 2. Procedure simplified diagram of the methodology for assessing urban safety [1]

The proposed method of assessing urban safety (see Fig. 2) can be simply visualized as a large chart that has been created by the intersection of the vertical (y axis) and the horizontal (x axis) levels. The vertical part has been formed by the space feature holders that make up some quality of the environment. The horizontal part of the chart is a list of those risks we come into contact when dealing with urban safety.

It is obvious that we can find quite a number of space feature holders as well as potential safety/security threats in an area. They need to be logically sorted into major categories in the very first stage. For the field of risks they are the following four ones:

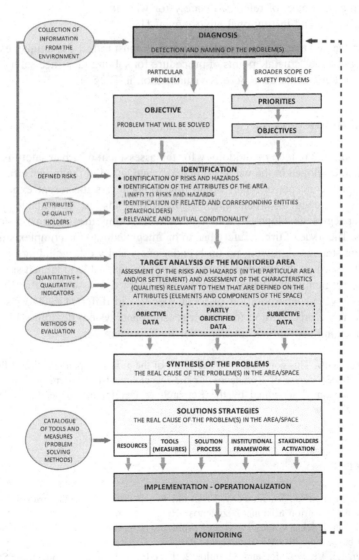

Diag. 1 Procedure for applying the method of assesing the quality of urban safety for solving identified safety threats [1]

A Health risks (endangering human physical condition and/or life);
B Socio-psycho-pathological risks;
C Economic risks and losses on property;
D Energy/resource safety.

The field of space feature holders consists of five main categories as follows:
01 Physical structure (volume and space);
02 Functional structure (space function and management, traffic safety);
03 Man and society (social environment) – a man as a passive or active participant of the environment;
04 Man as an object of reference (safety for whom);
05 Legislative and institutional environment [1].

Despite the fact that the urban safety approach must reflect the uniqueness of each area, there are some "crucial" points of procedure for solving identified safety threats in an area. The logic of the procedure is visualization in Diag. 1.

4 Conclusions

In recent research a unique methodology for the assessment of urban safety is currently being further developed in the whole complexity and tested in the model cities as a part of the complex concepts of smart urban development. As the resent experience has shown, the efficiency of urban safety concept depends on its embeddedness into complex strategies development and management using the system of interrelated smart tools. The issue of urban safety has to be integrated into the complex smart urban development strategies growing up on broader analytical work including urban safety assessment. Based on the developed methodology it is possible to launch smart system of urban safety monitoring based on permanent interactive assessment and evaluation of urban safety and incorporation of local specifics in different categories of settlements. This is the precondition for proper reaction and system flexibility in proposing and implementing appropriate measures for its improvements.

Acknowledgement. This contribution is the result of the project implementation: SPECTRA + No. 26240120002 "Centre of Excellence for the Development of Settlement Infrastructure of Knowledge Economy" supported by the Research & Development Operational Programme funded by the ERDF.

References

1. Finka, M., Ondrejička, V., Jamečný, Ľ., et al.: Bezpečnosť ako kvalita priestoru – úvod do problematiky. Centrum urbánnej bezpečnosti/ROAD, Bratislava (2012)
2. Finka, M., Ondrejička, V. (eds.): Vybrané problémy bezpečnosti sídelného priestoru. Centrum urbánnej bezpečnosti/ROAD, Bratislava (2012)
3. Corbusier, Le: Le Modulor and Modulor 2, 1st edn. Birkhäuser Architecture, Switzerland (2000). ISBN 978-3764361884

4. Zhang, H., Dai, S.: Literature review of safety research in urban planning. Urban Planning Forum, p. 007. ISSN 1000-3363. (2005)
5. Pearrsall, J., Hanks, P. (eds.): The Oxford English Reference Dictionary, vol. 1309, 2nd edn, p. 1271. Oxford University Press, New York (1996). ISBN 0-19-860050-X
6. Skavland Idsø, E., Mejdell Jakobsen, Ø.: Objekt- og informasjonssikkerhet. Metode for risikoog sårbarhetsanalyse, Institutt for produksjons- og kvalitetsteknikk, NTNU. (2000) In: Albrechtsen, E.: Security vs. Safety, p. 2. (2003). http://www.iot.ntnu.no/users/albrecht/rapporter/notat%20safety%20v%20security.pdf>Accessed 14 June 2011
7. Colquhoun, I.: Design Out Crime. Creating Safe and Sustainable Communities, p. 186. Architectural press, Oxford (2004). ISBN 0-7506-5492-9
8. Ondrejička, V.: Koncepčné riešenia bezpečnosti v mestách. In: Finka, M., Ondrejička, V. (eds.) Vybrané problémy bezpečnosti sídelného priestoru, pp. 74–85. Centrum urbánnej bezpečnosti/ROAD, Bratislava (2012)

ENERGY PARK BUILDING 03 – Certified Under Platinum LEED for Core & Shell v2.0

Marzia Morena[1(✉)], Angela Silvia Pavesi[1], and Andrej Adamuščin[2]

[1] ABC Department, Politecnico di Milano, Via Bonardi, 9, 20133 Milan, Italy
{marzia.morena, angela.pavesi}@polimi.it
[2] Slovak University of Technology in Bratislava, Vazovova 5, 812 43
Bratislava, Slovakia
andrej.adamuscin@stuba.sk

Abstract. The Energy Park of Vimercate, just outside Milan, stands as the true answer to all the companies operating in Hi-Tech, telecommunications and IT, and which are planning to rationalize their rents and energy bills while improving the environmental and working conditions of their employees.

The Building 03 of the Energy Park is the first Italian building ever to be issued the LEED Platinum certificate.

There are only six more Platinum-certified buildings in Europe, more precisely in Sweden, Finland, Luxembourg and Germany.

The Building is part of the Technology Park of Vimercate and it was built by SEGRO, an investment and development firm, the European leader in the supply of flexible spaces and business solutions. It is a project for the development of an area that was already known for its industrial/manufacturing vocation, in order to achieve a modern, sustainable transformation that is mandatory if this area is to survive in the future.

The building won the LEED Platinum certificate thanks to the optimum solutions regarding energy consumption, lighting, use of water and of other materials, and thanks to a wide range of strategies aimed at enhancing the sustainability of this structure, which is the subject of this paper.

Keywords: Environmental certification · LEED for Core & Shell · Technology campus · Sustainability · Energy saving · Investment strategies

1 Introduction

In the past decades, manufacturing undertakings have turned from heavy industrial activities that occupied large plots of land, to lighter, smaller and "cleaner" units. Many of these have adapted or based their factories in old industrial buildings, which are unsuitable for the technical and operational realities of the new enterprises.

These industrial buildings, therefore, have to be able to meet the requirements of the activities they host in a more modern fashion.

To prevent these areas from becoming abandoned, a drastic renovation of former industrial factories must be planned to gradually replace the existing buildings [1].

This is exactly what happened in the industrial area of Vimercate, the historical headquarters of Alcatel Lucent and other Italian divisions of multinational companies,

© ICST Institute for Computer Sciences, Social Informatics and Telecommunications Engineering 2016
A. Leon-Garcia et al. (Eds.): Smart City 2015, LNICST 166, pp. 830–841, 2016.
DOI: 10.1007/978-3-319-33681-7_74

which together cover a floor area of approximately 50,000 sqm of office space and research laboratories.

The existing buildings have all the features of old-generation buildings: they are true industrial factories, usually one-floored; they often have a much higher energy consumption than that of "technologically advanced" buildings, and do not meet current working requirements.

1.1   Energy Park: "Green Building" Philosophy as an Investment Strategies

The operation of the Energy Park stemmed from the intention to build highly technological and performing buildings, with a minimum pre-let percentage of 80 %. In the past three years some service buildings were developed, like the multi-storey car park and the kindergarten, while the canteen was renovated; in parallel there came the construction of Building 03, which is now the headquarters of SAP Italia S.p.A. among others, and of Building 04, the headquarters of Esprinet S.p.A. The new Campus of Alcatel Lucent S.p.A. is under development for an overall floor area of 33,000 sqm for office space and research laboratories.

The decision to develop an operation like Energy Park was influenced by the location of the site, which rises in a suburban area endowed with many infrastructures (car parks, shops, motorway junctions, etc.) and located not too far from Milan. This territory has a historical bent to technology, so much so that it is the headquarters of the leading international companies in this business.

The investor is Segro PLC, which has a property portfolio of 5.5 million square meters for a value exceeding six billion euros. Segro PLC ranks among the leading companies in Europe for real estate development and investment.

The company has its offices in England and is listed in the London and Paris Stock Exchanges; it operates in ten countries with over 2,000 clients performing their activities in various fields of the economy: from latest-generation technology parks to office buildings in suburban areas, from logistic platforms to light industry plants.

Segro was able to redevelop an existing industrial area by constructing new-generation "green" buildings without occupying any new parcel of land. The wish to develop a site that is economically viable and environmentally sustainable for the final user was crowned by the grant of the Leed Platinum Certificate to Building 03 (the first building in Italy, and the eighth in Europe), while the pre-certification phase for LEED Platinum is already started for Building 04 and for the Campus of Alcatel Lucent S.p.A. The success of the negotiations aimed at preserving the historical factory of Alcatel inside the same site, which is being turned into a modern Campus, materialized in the rational use of spaces and lower operating costs. Such a highly attractive area with performing buildings has roused the interest of other international companies operating in the same business sector, and which appreciate the Energy Park operation and have therefore based their Italian headquarters here.

The operation was funded directly by Segro PLC.

2 Methodology for LEED Certification

LEED is one of the largest environmental certification systems in the world and has been developed by the U.S. Green Building Council (USGBC). LEED is an abbreviation for Leadership in Energy and Environmental Design [2]. LEED certification provides independent verification of a building or neighborhood's green features, allowing for the design, construction, operations and maintenance of resource-efficient, high-performing, healthy, cost-effective buildings. LEED is the triple bottom line in action, benefiting people, planet and profit [3].

LEED for Core & Shell development is a green building system that was designed to provide a set of performance criteria for certifying the sustainable design and construction of speculative developments and core and shell buildings. Broadly defined, core and shell construction covers base building elements, such as the structure, envelope and building-level systems, such as central HVAC, etc. The LEED for Core and Shell system recognizes that the division between owner and tenant responsibility for certain elements of the building varies between markets [4].

LEED for Core & Shell ratings are awarded according to the following scale [4]:

There are 100 base points; 6 possible Innovation in Design and 4 Regional Priority points
Certified 40–49 points
Silver 50–59 points
Gold 60–79 points
Platinum 80 points and above (Table 1)

Table 1. Key areas with examples of credits used to provide an overall picture of what is assessed in LEED systems [2].

Sustainable sites – Site selection – Alternative transportation – Stromwater design	**Water efficiency** – Water efficient landscaping – Innovative wastewater Technologies – Water use reduction
Indoor environmental quality – Indoor air quality – Low-emitting materials – Lighting – Thermal comfort – Daylight and views	**Materials and resources** – Construction waste management – Materials reuse – Regional materials – Sustainable purchasing
Energy and atmosphere – Optimize energy performance – On site renewable energy – **Green power** – **Energy-efficient building systems**	**Innovation in design** – LEED Accredited Professional – Innovation in design – Exemplary performance
Regional priority – Regional priority	

A certain number of points can be scored in each key area. These points vary depending on which rating system is used [2].

3   The Building 03 Inside the Energy Park of Vimercate

The Building 03, located inside the Energy Park of Vimercate, is the first building in Italy to be issued the LEED Platinum Certificate for Core & Shell.

Garretti Associati, the author of the masterplan, produced the project as well and supervised the construction of Building 03. Sustainability and energy saving were the pillars of this building since the concept stage, when much attention was bestowed on all the elements that are required to favour interaction between the users of the building and other types of users/consumers on the campus. The aim was to offer them a higher quality of life during the time they spend on the workplace (Figs. 1 and 2).

Fig. 1. The whole masterplan of the Energy Park – Garretti Associati

The buildings of the Park rise along a main road backbone, in the fulcrum of which are the buildings providing common functions; along this axis large green islands shape a rhythmic, dynamic morphology that underlines the identity of the area as a "campus".

The Building 03 consists of an underground level serving as a car park, and three levels above the ground as office space. It is composed of two rectangular bodies

Fig. 2. Bird view Energy Park – Garretti Associati

arranged to form an "H". These two bodies are slightly offset to optimise exposure to the sun and are interconnected by two glazed units. Office layout is flexible and can be arranged into three configurations. Technologically, the design choices made for the facade include a frame in pre-engineered reinforced-concrete panels, and ventilated walls with steel (Aluzink) and wood (Holzbau) cladding. Glazed surfaces are protected with a sun screening system and with blinds operated by bio-climate sensors. System and installation networks are integrated in the false ceiling and in the raised floor.

Despite the vocation of the building as office space, meeting areas are present as well in the form of winter gardens with glazed walls located in the central areas (Figs. 3 and 4).

The building was granted the LEED Platinum certificate because of the wealth of its sustainable solutions, the most striking of which being [2]:

- optimization of water resources;
- re-use of demolition debris and use of locally-manufactured materials;
- less issues related to air quality, hence higher environmental wellbeing of the building users;
- special and flexible operation of the temperature control system, which is made available to the users of independent areas as well;
- optimization of natural light;
- the supply of 100 % certified electricity, obtained from renewable sources;
- use of wood with certification of origin and manufacture.

Fig. 3. The outside of Building 03 - Garretti Associati

Fig. 4. The outside of Building 03 - Garretti Associati

The main features of the buildings are listed below:

- min. net height of rooms is 3.00 m;
- the floor load-bearing capacity is suitable to host also laboratories, IT rooms, training rooms, test rooms, an auditorium and much more;
- the façade module is 1.5 m wide;
- the underground park has 95 places with monitored access;
- the efficiency of office space is 84.5 %;
- excellent flexibility for use by a single tenant or multi-tenants;
- special and flexible operation of the temperature control system, which is made available to the users of independent areas as well;
- a wide common courtyard inside the building;
- a triple-height entrance lobby, with stairs taking to the various floors and two lifts;
- storage/archive rooms on the underground level;
- latest generation air-conditioning and heating systems with a condensed heat pump using underground water;
- high efficiency, low energy consumption;
- balanced ratio between opaque parts and transparent parts, with fully glazed elements;
- use of natural materials with a certificate of origin, as is the case of the wood used for the frame of the lobbies and indoor finishes;
- ventilated facades made of prefab reinforced-concrete panels, exterior insulation achieved with rock wool and bored steel sheet;
- the sunscreening system is installed outside the building;

Fig. 5. The inside of Building 03 - Garretti Associati

- glazed openings are equipped with an awning shading system remotely controlled by a BMS system, in order to optimize the natural lighting of rooms;
- re-use of condensation water for garden watering and toilet flush;
- rainfall is conveyed to the water table not to burden the sewer system;
- fewer heat islands to curb the environmental impact on natural micro-climates and on human habitat;
- re-use of demolition debris and use of locally-manufactured materials (Figs. 5 and 6).

Fig. 6. The inside of Building 03 - Garretti Associati

4   A Description of the LEED Approach – Building 03

4.1   Sustainable Sites - 15/15 Points

The building was constructed within the framework of the redevelopment project of a former manufacturing site at Vimercate (MB, Italy), which had been reclaimed of polluting waste before the construction works began. In order to encourage sustainable transportation the project integrated a pre-existing cycle-lane, while bicycle storage areas were created with their relevant changing facilities and showers solely reserved for the occupants. To reduce the negative impact from automobile use, connection with the nearby villages and towns is guaranteed by a private shuttle bus service to integrate the public bus lines that have their stops at a short distance. The project site is well served also by the motorway/orbital road and by county roads.

The "E-mobility Italia" project was implemented on this site too, to promote the use of electricity-driven public transportation means or the rental of electric cars. Preferred parking lots are reserved to low-emission vehicles in the area allocated to the car parks of this Building.

The planned green areas were planted with native and adapted vegetation, in order to safeguard the habitat and promote biodiversity. To ensure occupants' wellbeing and reduce heat islands, the materials chosen for the covers and for external paved surfaces have a low solar reflectance index. Specific measures were adopted to avoid light pollution and some guidelines were drafted to promote the sustainable use of the building by its occupants.

4.2   Water Efficiency - 5/5 Points

In order to reduce potable water consumption and favour the conscious use of water resources, specific design choices were made: the heating and cooling systems of the building use underground water; native trees with low water consumption were planted, and a rainwater storage tank was installed to provide water to toilet flushing and to the irrigation system of the green areas. Buildings are also equipped with timer-controlled faucets with a reduced water flow, or double-flow toilet flushing, both fixtures proving useful in curbing overall water requirement further. Rainfall is also captured on the roofs and re-used for irrigation.

4.3   Energy and Atmosphere - 9/14 Points

A dynamic computer simulation of the energy requirement of each building was performed for both summer and winter. This simulation quantified that the energy cost savings in the first certified building, or Building 03, will be 27.4 % compared with the baseline building performance rating.

The whole core and shell system is optimized by an electronic metering network that separates the energy consumption from lighting, motive power and the mechanical ventilation system with a heat regenerator. The connections to sub-metering equipment for future tenants have been created as well. The buildings are equipped with the BMS (Building Management System), which makes global operation easier and constantly monitors the systems. By means of this system, the user can monitor the single areas of the building in order to improve overall energy savings over time, since temperature control management is flexible to adapt to users and to the duration of use. To deter the release of stratospheric ozone, the HVAC systems use low-pollution refrigerants. An agreement was entered into with a local power supplier to provide the building with electricity produced 100 % from RECs-certified renewable sources; this is to foster the development and use of zero-impact renewable grid technologies. Some photovoltaic installations are on the site, as well. The long side of the building looks west, which allows good capture of the light and of solar energy in the central hours of the day, when the building is going to be used. In order to curb excessive overheating, a sunscreening system was installed along with powered external blinds. The balance between opaque surfaces (the ventilated wall) and clear surfaces (greenhouses and entrance lobbies) is positive to limit energy consumption, and to optimize natural lighting use. To avoid excessive overheating in summer caused by sunbeams, the electrical installation is equipped with a modulation system based on the natural light that penetrates the facility.

4.4 Materials and Resources - 6/11 Points

To reduce the amount of waste produced during the construction process, waste management plans were prepared for the waste produced on the construction site, while specific areas on the site were designated for segregated collection of waste from the construction process. This gave the opportunity to divert all reusable materials to appropriate collection sites, and to recycle and/or salvage a very high percentage of non-hazardous construction and demolition debris. During the construction phase, most of the materials obtained from the demolition of pre-existing factories on the site were reused. To increase use of materials that are manufactured and recycled in the region, the project team selected some building products that are extracted and manufactured within a distance of 800 km from the project site. The team also checked that these products contained a high percentage of recycled content. Construction materials made of wood are certified as being from responsible forest management (FSC and PEFC).

4.5 Indoor Environmental Quality - 6/11 Points

Smoking is prohibited inside each building, and outside them within 8 meters of operable windows and doors, in order to guarantee the minimum performance of air quality and thereby safeguard the health of occupants. Outside the non-smoking boundary some areas were created purposely for smokers. To achieve reduced use of artificial lighting, each building is equipped with the BMS system that automatically adjusts the external shading devices and artificial lighting of rooms and offices in order to maximize daylighting and offer optimal view opportunities. To reduce the presence of pollutants and improve indoor air quality, an air-treatment system has been installed with adjustable airflow depending upon the number of occupants in a room, and upon the concentration of CO_2 in indoor air as is monitored by purpose-made sensors. To promote the comfort and wellbeing of construction workers and building occupants, dirt-absorbing barriers are placed at the entrance points of the building. The adhesives, primers, paints and flooring materials used during the construction comply with the limits for volatile organic compounds (VOC). Moreover in order to reduce the air contaminants inside the building that are odorous, irritating and/or harmful for the comfort and wellbeing of construction workers and building occupants, adequate carpet was installed.

4.6   Innovation in Design - 4/5 Points

The building earned points for its exemplary performance in the conservation of natural areas and in the promotion of biodiversity, and also in the use of local materials and resources with considerable reduction of transportation impacts on the environment.

The project of Building 03 allocates 75 % of the green areas to native vegetation and lawn species; the value of the building products extracted and manufactured within a limited distance is equal to 44.57 % of the overall cost of the construction materials used for the project.

More model performances were achieved with the smart use of groundwater.

4.7   Cost Monitoring

The project's economic sustainability rests both on the design choices made, and on the operational methods applied. LEED certified buildings guarantee energy saving, volume benefits and tax deductions for their owners, final users and enterprises. The volume advantages and tax deductions available to owners depend upon the amount of technological solutions adopted for energy saving (insulation) and use of renewable sources (100 % RECs-certified sources for the production of electricity from renewable sources of energy). The lower water consumption achieved by recovery of rainfall, and lower energy consumption by monitoring the actual energy requirement, have positive repercussions on the building management costs. Also the presence of recycled materials manufactured at a short transportation distance adds to this advantage. During the construction phase work was optimized by monitoring realization costs and times, and requiring a guarantee on the duration of the materials used.

4.8   Social Sustainability

Special attention was placed on the anthropocentric vision of the project, i.e. to create an office-space building where environmental conditions are favourable for workers. The strategies concerning indoor air quality and temperature, visual and sound comfort make the working environment healthier and more pleasant. The presence of green islands and of recreational areas within the building enhance the degree of satisfaction of internal and external users.

5   Conclusion

Sustainable building construction and long-term energy efficiency are among the most important trends in real estate development in Italy. This is confirmed by the amount of certified buildings and buildings that are currently undergoing the certification process. They are increasingly decision driving for investors, developers and end users when selling or leasing commercial spaces [6].

During the projecting and construction of sustainable buildings economic and ecological factors play equally important role as well as quality and durability of the building. In Italy the driving force behind green building construction begin be the developers who attempt to satisfy the demands of real estate investors and mainly tenants.

References

1. Morena, M.: Real Estate Property as a Tool in Territorial Development. Maggioli Editore, Rimini (2010)
2. Heincke, C., Olsson, D., Nillsson, C.: Simply GREEN - a quick guide to energy and environmental assessment certifications of buildings. Swegon Air Academy (2014). ISBN 978-91-977443-5-5
3. The U.S. Green Building Council (USGBC) (2015). http://leed.usgbc.org/leed.html
4. The U.S. Green Building Council (USGBC) (2015). http://www.usgbc.org/Docs/Archive/General/Docs3355.pdf
5. Pavesi, A.S., Verani, E.: Introduzione alla certificazione LEED®: progetto, costruzione, gestione - Ottimizzazione del processo edilizio secondo i principi della sostenibilità. Maggioli Editore, Rimini (2012)
6. Adamuscin, A., Morena, M., Truppi, T.: The importance of sustainable construction of office buildings and its development in Italy and in the Visegrad countries (Mainly in Slovakia). Swiat Nieruchomośсi. World Real Estate J. 90(4) 51–57 (2014). ISSN 1231-8841

Energy-Efficient Buildings in Slovakia: Green Atrium

Miroslav Panik$^{(\boxtimes)}$, Andrej Adamuscin, and Julius Golej

Institute of Management, Slovak University of Technology in Bratislava,
Vazovova 5, 81243 Bratislava, Slovakia
{miroslav_panik, andrej.adamuscin,
julius.golej}@stuba.sk

Abstract. Power management is very necessary, as well as the environment. Construction of low energy and passive houses, however, both of these requirements can be fulfilled. Project Green Atrium is the first passive apartment building in Slovakia that meets the requirements for passive buildings. In many cases also it achieved superior results as desired. Exceptional properties of Green Atrium have been achieved through these parameters: heat consumption for heating, heat transfer coefficient of walls and infiltration through leaks of building.

Keywords: Energy-efficient buildings · Green atrium · Low-energy · Passive buildings

1 Introduction

Low-energy house has a common form of construction especially abroad; it ensures energy efficiency, environmental protection, quality structures and high living comfort. In the Slovak Republic, however, this trend promotes the construction of a very slow pace, despite the fact that construction technologies and theoretical knowledge is not enough. The basic criterion by which we divide the category of energy-efficient homes into several groups is the heat consumption for heating. Compared with a conventional house, which achieves power consumption of 100–195 kWh/(m².a) have energy-efficient homes several times lower power consumption [1].

Slovakia was in January 2006 adopted a law on energy performance of buildings and on amendments to certain laws. It entered into force on 1 January 2008. The law follows the Directive of the European Parliament and of the Council of the European Union 2002/91/EC of 16 December 2002 on the energy performance of buildings. This directive restricts the burning of non-renewable natural resources, thus wants to contribute to a reduction of carbon dioxide. The Directive aims to improve the energy performance of buildings (EPBD) 15 reducing energy consumption for heating, hot water preparation and lighting, taking into account the efficiency of costs incurred for the construction and operation of buildings. A crucial source of energy required for residential buildings in Slovakia combustion of non-renewable natural resources, and thus carbon dioxide emissions [2].

© ICST Institute for Computer Sciences, Social Informatics and Telecommunications Engineering 2016
A. Leon-Garcia et al. (Eds.): Smart City 2015, LNICST 166, pp. 842–850, 2016.
DOI: 10.1007/978-3-319-33681-7_75

Energy consumption of buildings is assessed according to valid STN 73 0540-2/2,002th. Its contents are the requirements of thermal protection and energy label of the building. In this case, it is only a theoretical value, which does not take into account the method of heating, regulation or adequate ventilation. Just adequate ventilation plays a major role in energy-efficient buildings. Today it is known only to control energy consumption for heating buildings, in the future, however, do justice to the control of energy use for cooling, hot water, operation of buildings, construction and operation of buildings [2].

Institute for energy-efficient houses that exists in Slovakia is defined as non-political, voluntary, leisure NGO. The aim of its activities is mainly supporting the construction of passive houses and architecture considerate to the environment, dissemination of information on energy-passive houses between professional and also the general public [2].

Vodiková [1] states that division according to distance energy consumption:

Energy-saving house - with heat consumption 50–70 kWh/(m^2.a). Parameters of the house can be achieved by appropriate austerity measures such as increased thermal envelope values, the targeted use of solar products and reducing energy consumption by installing solar collectors. The heating system is mostly the conventional, performance, and energy consumption, however, are low.

Low-energy house - with heat consumption 15–50 kWh/(m^2.a) requires more action. Of course there should be not only high quality thermal insulation jacket and passive and active use of solar energy as well as mechanical ventilation with heat recovery and air preheating heat or low temperature heating system with a connection to solar collectors. On a proposal from the house requires a clearly defined low-energy system concept with a maximum optimization of the individual components.

Passive house - the heat consumption from 5 to 15 kWh/(m^2.a) has a perfect thermal insulating building envelope. Thanks to mostly do without a conventional heating system. The residual heat demand arising as a result of the natural heat escaping from buildings is mostly provided by heat recovery from the outgoing air recovery. It can also be applied for production of energy from heat pumps, solar energy and biomass. The concept of passive houses projected total energy demand (for heating, hot water and electrical operation) of less than 40 kWh/(m^2.a). 14 heat recovery from solar radiation and the use of ventilation systems with heat recovery in passive houses cover up to 80 % of heat consumption.

Zero house - a house with near-zero energy for heating (0–5 kWh/m^2). It is used therein exclusively local renewable resources. Zero houses in the summer so they can produce excess electricity, which in winter consumption. Stocks of energy are stored either in large-scale solar collectors or photovoltaic panels are used to supply the public network [1].

2   Passive Buildings

Passive House is an advanced variant of the low-energy house. Due to the very low heat demand is there any excess heat. It can be left out expensive heat storage, which saves not only investment but also operating costs. These are then used to improve the thermal insulation and mechanical air exchange [3]. With high isolated system of external walls, three heat-insulating glazing in quality frames decreasing specific heat demand less than 15 kWh/(m^2). The house is passive and is therefore able without heating and hence without expensive storage tank to maintain the required temperature. Designation passive house recalls also its largest source of heat - the sun's radiation, which is obtained dimensioned southern windows passively and instrumentation equipment [3].

Passive House provides pleasant comfort in every season and the clean fresh air in the interior at very low operating costs. Incremental investment cost of the user to return at low operating costs [4].

Hudec [4] sets out the essential features of a passive house:

- orientation of the glass facade to the south,
- compact design without unnecessary breakdowns.
- high quality insulating windows (triple insulation)
- perfect thermal insulation and air tightness of the house,
- quality solution of thermal bridges.
- controlled ventilation using heat recovery,
- classic heating system is missing.

Hudec [4] also states the basic criteria for passive house (values for Central European climatic conditions):

- Specific heat demand for heating $\leq$ 15 kWh/(m^2.a)
- The maximum heat output of 10 W/m^2,
- Heat transfer coefficient of all solid external structures of U $\leq$ 0.15 W/(m^2 K).
- windows with a U-value $\leq$ 0.8 W/(m^2 K) with glass and the value of G $\geq$ 50 %
- tightness in total must not exceed 0.6 times the air changes per hour,
- ventilation heat recovery unit with efficiency greater than 75 %;
- The overall annual primary energy consumption (heating, domestic hot water, ventilation and electrical appliances) must not exceed 120 kWh/(m^2)

The functionality of passive house it is necessary to provide the necessary air tightness of the house envelope. It is necessary to avoid leaks and holes that arises unasked heat transfer. What is important is the use of the ventilation system with a high-efficiency heat recovery. Bad construction project or carelessness can cause heat loss and condensation in structures that result in the breakdown [4].

The standard sets the overall permeability of the building envelope as the total value of the n50 the air exchange rate at a differential pressure of 50 Pa. Airtightness of the building is the greater, the smaller this value. For passive house with forced ventilation with heat recovery is the recovery limit n50, N = 0.6 h^{-1}. At 50 Pa for one hour in a building not designated more air than 60 % of the total volume of the building [4] (Table 1).

The higher the permeability means the higher the heat loss. According to approximate calculations, heat loss caused by marginal permeability in passive houses around 3.5 kWh/(m^2.a). It is in the overall specific heat demand for heating 15 kWh/(m^2.a) a significant part. Interestingly comparison with conventional buildings, which have a natural ventilation value N50, N = 4.5 h−1, which means infiltration of the

Table 1. The recommended total value of the air exchange rate n50 at 50 Pa pressure differential.

Ventilation in the building	N50, N (h−1)
Natural	4,5
Forced	1,5
Forced heat recovery	1

Source: Tywoniak [5, p. 46].

annual loss of about 26 kWh/(m^2.a), it is more than 1.5 times the specific heat for heating a passive house [4].

Typical gaps and air can flow freely from the interior to the exterior; they are erroneously transferred joints of building elements, such as joint window frame with masonry. The moisture flow, which is a structural case exfiltration of indoor air loading, may adversely affect the wetting of the building envelope. This ultimately causes a drastic reduction in the thermal performance of the building envelope and also the formation of mildew and wood decaying fungi [5].

The aim of this paper is to compare whether the first passive apartment house in SR - Green Atrium met the requirements of the applicable standards for passive buildings. The second order to calculate energy savings and return on investment when purchasing an apartment in the building Green atrium.

3   Project Green Atrium

Project Green atrium in Trnava is the first apartment building in passive standard in Slovakia. It is located in a lucrative and popular part of Trnava with major construction of family houses, not far from the centre and also known Trnava natural area – Kameny mlyn.

Multifunctional residential building green atrium consists of two objects. The first object is called reconstruction. brownfield, so the former printing plants. Building type is brick. Architecture based on simple material structure preserving the original shape of the production building [6] (Fig. 1).

3.1   Layout Solution

Green atrium is composed of several functional units. These are apartments, commercial space, administrative space, parking in the basement of the building and common areas for residents of the house, used for joint and private activities - party. In the basement are the underground garage (63 parking spaces), storage areas belonging to apartments, basements and energy core of the building. On the ground floor there are three apartments in the building wing, office space and commercial premises. On the first floor there are three apartments in the building wing, lounge, kitchen and children's play area in the gallery above commercial premises. On the last two floors there are just dwellings in Part A. The flats are mainly small flat, 1, 2 and 3-room. On the roof of a residential building is the "party" room. On the staircase on the roof are a small kitchen and a pergola.

Fig. 1. Green Atrium (Trnava) (Source: Author)

3.2   Technology and Economy

Green building is an atrium planted by a combination of the latest technology the most logical way to save everything, but even makes user experience and minimize energy costs. Green atriums technology in not only energy. The biggest added value of the energy savings is provided through multiple technologies. This is a heat pump with energy piles, photovoltaic panels, cogeneration unit, the combustion gas generates electricity and the waste heat is used for hot water and heating, the wall and ceiling capillary heating and cooling, outdoor blinds and measure all the energy in real time online management. The Green atriums are available courtesy heating and cooling and also the possibility of reheating in a heat recovery unit. Computing the need for heating in the flats is up to 14 kWh/m^2; with the requirement of the standard is 150 kWh/m^2. Ecological aspect of the project is also reflected in the fact that at least 95 % of the original building will recycle material - either reintroduced per fraction and subsequently used. The rest is waste collection.

Heat Pump. The heat pump is a device that the temperature difference and electricity produces heat or cold. Medium pump with different temperatures, and thus one kilowatt of electricity produced 3 to 4 kW of heat. The object is to use the heat pump earth/water. The energy contained in the ground has been used through the so-called energy piles, which are located under the building and at the same time serve as a basis.

Photovoltaic Panels. On the roof of the house are photovoltaic panels, which generate electricity from the sun. This is then distributed to the needs of the heat pump. During a very significant part of the year except coldest months the heating energy produced exclusively from renewable sources.

Recovery Ventilation. Each apartment includes a ventilation unit with heat recovery. This provides tremendous comfort in terms of user characteristics flat. One-ventilated intelligent IT equipment that heat from the exhaust air transmits the supply of fresh air. The result is a perfectly flat vented. This benefit is especially important in the winter months when the open window blows cold air comes to the formation of mold from a lack of ventilation during sleep breathed air in the bedroom. Cost ventilation at an average 70 m^3 of air per hour heat recovery saves 2200 kWh per year, which is around 150 Euros.

Outdoor Blinds. In traditional new multi-dwelling houses are normally provides shielding interior blinds. This solution is significantly cheaper than, as well as developer leaves the problem of shielding the owner of the apartment. But if we want to make it an effective shielding must be shaded from the window. Shielding the interiors had flat does not prevent overheating in the summer months. Exterior blinds are controlled motor and possibly also automatically represent the highest form of protection against overheating apartment in the summer months. The Green atriums blinds can be controlled via mobile phone and smart applications. They can be opened and closed as needed, and for safety reasons e.g. to simulate the presence in the apartment during the holiday.

Measurement and Control. All energies are controlled and measured by a sophisticated system accessible via the Internet. Using Smartphone is possible to continuously accurate overview of how much energy is currently consumed for heating and hot water. Heating and cooling is managed centrally, thus avoiding the fact that someone had turned off the heating and heat their apartment through neighbouring apartments. Apartment owners have the opportunity to fine-tune the final desired temperature in the apartment via regenerative units. No monopoly energy supplier can invoice the loss of the route. Energy in Green atriums is always cheaper than from the network precisely because it is produced with high efficiency and are eliminated any losses.

Partition Walls Between Apartments. The apartments are separated by plasterboard walls, whose composition has been designed specifically for project green atrium. Supporting profiles are filled with sound insulation at a thickness of 75 mm. On the profile of each side plate is fitted Rigips which provides structural strength (this board are commonly used for planting in ATMs). It is then applied to the acoustic panel, which improves the acoustic properties of the wall, and this is equipped with a sound board Activair they absorb from the air volatiles, mainly formaldehyde, thereby improving air quality in the home. This composition of the wall thickness of 150 mm, where are used of a total 6 plates and provides protection against noise above 60 dB. The standard requires 52 db. It is also really solid partition. Noise characteristics also ensures dilation screed from the walls. The inter-residential rungs are not equipped with any sewer or water pipes that impair the properties of the walls, as is common in traditional brick technology.

4 Energy Savings and Calculation of Cost Return

According to the Isover and Rigips, annual energy savings of investing in an apartment in Green atriums compared with normal warmed byte are shown in Tables 2 and 3.

Table 2. Energy savings and calculation of cost return

Flat area m/^{2}:	90 m^2
People in flat:	4
Normally insulated apartment building	
Heating costs:	558,00 €
The cost of hot water:	416,00 €
Cooling costs:	360,00 €
Green Atrium	
Heating costs:	90,75 €
The cost of hot water:	130,00 €
Cooling costs:	54,00 €
Saving	1 059,25 €
Saving on heating:	467,25 €
Saving for hot water:	286,00 €
Saving on cooling:	306,00 €
Price of apartment with parking and cooling Green atriums (€):	124 000,00 €
Price a new apartment with parking and cooling in another house (€):	118 000,00 €
Difference	6 000,00 €
Return on investment in green atrium (years)	5,66

Source: Isover, Rigips, Glassolutions a Rehau.

Table 3. Energy savings and calculation of cost return

Structures property	Measuring unit	Requirement of standard or normal standard	Values obtained in the Green atrium
Heat demand for heating one m^2 apartment	kW/m^2/a	150	13,5
The cost of heating one m^2 apartment	€/m^2	10,2	0,97
Thermal transmittance of walls	W/m^2 K	0,32	0,13
Thermal transmittance of roof	W/m^2 K	0,2	0,1

(Continued)

Table 3. (*Continued*)

Structures property	Measuring unit	Requirement of standard or normal standard	Values obtained in the Green atrium
Heat transfer coefficient of windows	$W/m^2\ K$	1,4	0,77
Infiltration leaks building	n50	8.1	0,6
The amount of water vapour condensation in the roof	$Kg/m^2/a$	0,1	0,0047
Index of air airtightness inter-flat partitions	dB	53	54

Source: Isover, Rigips, Glassolutions a Rehau.

5 Conclusion

Power management is very necessary, as well as the environment. Construction of low energy and passive houses, however, both of these requirements can be fulfilled. Most home energy is spent for heating, hot water, lighting, electrical equipment and cooling. It is the largest part used for heating [7]. Using the available technology, this energy consumption can be reduced. Low-energy construction has in comparison with classical. Many times are better thermal insulation envelope structures. In doing so, quality must be done details and technical work. Windows and large glazed areas are directed to the south, that the use of solar energy. When heating is used heat recovery unit, which heats the incoming air into the room. Construction of low-energy operating cost savings can be made up to two thirds compared to conventional house. Project Green The atrium is the first passive apartment building that meets the requirements for passive buildings. In many cases also it achieved superior results as desired. Green atriums exceptional properties have been achieved parameters: heat consumption for heating, heat transfer coefficient of walls and infiltration leaks building. When comparing energy costs and return on investment in a model example it was calculated return in six years.

References

1. Vodiková, E.: Všetko o nízkoenergetickom dome. JAGA GROUP, s. r. o. (2007), 190 strán, 3krát rone, ISSN: 1335-9142
2. Šopová, J.: Nízkoenergetické domy (2007). http://www.trh.sk/nehnutelnosti/byvanie/198/nizkoenergeticke-domy. Accessed 13 Jan 2010
3. Humm, O.: Nízkoenergetické domy. Grada Publishing, a. s. (1999), 353 strán, ISBN: 80-7169-657-9
4. Hudec, M.: Pasivní rodinný dům – proč a jak stavět. Grada Publishing, a. s. (2008), 108 strán, ISBN: 978-80-247-2555-0
5. Tywoniak, J.: Nízkoenergetické domy. Grada Publishing, a. s. (2005), 193 strán, ISBN: 80-247-1101-X

6. Architektúra, stavebníctvo, bývanie (2014). http://www.asb.sk/architektura/projekty/zelene-atrium-chce-ziskat-leed-platinum?from=rss&utm_content=new_articles%2
7. Ivanicka, K., Zubkova, M., Sindlerova, E., Spirkova, D.: Housing finance in the Slovak Republic and other CEFTA countries. Emergo – J. Transf. Econ. Soc. 3(3), 102–123 (1996)

Influence of Urban Renewal
on the Assessment of Housing Market
in the Context of Sustainable Socioeconomic
City Development

Sławomir Palicki[1(✉)] and Izabela Rącka[2]

[1] Poznań University of Economics and Business, Poznań, Poland
s.palicki@ue.poznan.pl
[2] The President Stanisław Wojciechowski University School of Applied
Sciences in Kalisz, Kalisz, Poland
i.racka@pwsz.kalisz.pl

Abstract. The variability of the urban environment, where the symptoms are observed in terms of spatial, aesthetic, architectural, urban and socio-economic development, seems to be relevant to the functioning of the local real estate market. Housing issue is the vital component of sustainable socioeconomic city development. The perception of the property attractiveness is determined by price-setting attributes such as: building standard, area, utilities, zoning and also location and neighbourhood. The attractiveness of the residential property is manifested in its market value. As a part of the follow-urban transformation, it seems to be important to reconstruct the impact of the neighbourhood changes on the housing market. The authors attempt to explain the ensuing problem on the example of one of the streets in a Polish city – Kalisz, which over the years has gained a new face and market image and simulate changes in the market value of selected properties located on the street, in order to map the influence of changes on the value.

Keywords: Housing market · Property value · Revitalization · Neighbourhood · Kalisz

1 Introduction

Symptoms of changes in the urban environment can be seen in a number of aspects: spatial, aesthetic, architectural, urban and socio-economic. They seem to be relevant to the functioning of local property markets. Perception of property attractiveness by potential buyers depends on evaluation of its vital qualities, whose resultant is an objective economic measure – property market value. This value is affected by all relevant market attributes, which in turn affect a particular property.

Under this study observations focused on revitalization processes in Dobrzecka street in a Polish city, Kalisz, in 2006–2014. The analysis was accompanied by identification of trends and dynamics of changes in the local property market in Kalisz. The choice of the research object was deliberate – within a few years Dobrzecka street gained a new aesthetic face and market image.

© ICST Institute for Computer Sciences, Social Informatics and Telecommunications Engineering 2016
A. Leon-Garcia et al. (Eds.): Smart City 2015, LNICST 166, pp. 851–860, 2016.
DOI: 10.1007/978-3-319-33681-7_76

The main purpose of the study was assumed to be an evaluation and interpretation of the impact of urban transformations upon the economic and social assessment of residential properties. Thus, a possibility was recognized of conscious programming of a sustainable city development taking into account the influence of revitalization processes upon attractiveness of the local property market.

The research procedure employed the principles of a quantity and quality analysis of the property market (including a statistical analysis of phenomenon structure and dynamics), a case study, a comparative analysis, a methodology of property assessment in a comparative approach, a simulation method and a questionnaire. Above all, a market survey was conducted to evaluate the level of value changes and related factors used by various social and trade groups during their assessment.

2   Impact of Changes in the Urban Environment upon the Property Value

Properties are characterized by interdependence which means that by possessing a certain image they affect the surrounding including properties in the close and more distant neighbourhood [1]. The interdependency in the property market also means spatial and functional interrelations. This kind of interaction is explained by concentration of functions in space, influence exerted by development methods, neighbourhood effects, local site development plans and the power of brand [2, 3].

A diagnosis of the sources and essence of the interdependence first led researchers to consider environmental causes of changes in property values. They analyzed impact of air quality and its pollution upon market listings of flat and house prices [4]. Already then the term of externalities began to be used, which determine change in attractiveness of individual premises in the property market [5]. The externalities also include relations caused by neighbourhood of specific assets or limitations. Microlocation may mean a potential asset or a negative circumstance affecting the value depending on the nature and perception of the neighbourhood. Also complexes of properties desired due to popularity usually improve assessment of their surrounding [6]. The most vivid effects can be observed in commercial property markets where interdependence causes more intense investment activity in the neighbourhood (for instance, IKEA, "Old Brewery: in Poznan, "Manufacture" in Lodz) [1, 2]. It is not only connected with investments in the commercial property market, but also in residential and public properties [7, 8]. Studies of the neighbourhood nature and quality consider presence of organized urban greenery and recreational areas (municipal parks or areas accompanying residential estate space) [9, 10]. The widely understood public space and its influence on fluctuations of property value or more generally – on neighbourhood assessment – was analyzed referring to several cities in Poland [11, 12]. The said studies prove that among various types of urban public space centres and representative squares to a large extent determine market aspects of the surrounding development.

In the context of transformations in the property market a lot of attention is dedicated to space transformations, including revitalization processes. The notion of city revitalization combines both revitalization and gentrification. Variety of forms and conceptions of developing European urban space as part of revitalization projects or gentrification phenomena [13] points to conscious attempts of determining interdependence effects in the property market. What is interesting from the point of view of evaluating phenomena accompanying city revitalization is in particular reconstruction of the way it affects the residential and commercial property market [13–20]. The property market plays an important role in attracting both investors and inhabitants. A huge capital consumed by revitalization processes is a barrier to its development. A rapid growth of prices in the property market, especially in the residential one, attracts entities with strong capital which follow a disinvestment strategy (meaning a relatively quick sale at a high price) [21].

The market value is a resultant of attractiveness of perception of important property qualities. Their diagnosis includes attributes related a particular property (such as a standard and technical condition, usable area, plot area, premises location within a building) and other non-related attributes (such as general location, detailed location, neighbourhood nature and quality, available technical infrastructure, designation in the local site development plan). These attributes, called price determining attributes, are defined each time for a market segment where the assessed property falls in. Weights of individual attributes may be assigned by examining customer preferences in a particular property market or by analyzing transactional prices [22, 23]. Relations between city revitalization or functional and quality surrounding transformations and the property market value in Poland are not exhaustively described; they are still open to preliminary analysis. The development level of domestic residential segment suggests a necessity to carefully examine the phenomenon of transmitting revitalization effects in the property market.

3   Changes in the Market Value of Living Premises in Kalisz – A Case Study

3.1   Analysis of the Residential Property Market in Kalisz in 2006–2014

The analysis of the living property market included sale transactions of flats in Kalisz from the beginning of January 2006 to the end of December 2014. 2941 market transactions of flats were analyzed. Between 2006 and 2010 the number of transactions declined, however, in the period considered as crisis in the property market in Poland it grew. Every second flat sold had an area between 30 sq m and 50 sq m (an average size of a property sold in 2006–2014 in Kalisz was 49 sq m).

By examining unit transactional prices a trend formula was created for flats sold in Kalisz between 2006–2014. The linear trend function takes the following form:

$$y = 0.2681x + 2108.81 \tag{1}$$

The average price of one square metre increased month by month by PLN 0.27 and its theoretical value in the period immediately preceding the analysis, i.e. in December 2005, amounted to PLN 2108.81. The average increase of living properties in Kalisz property market in 2006–2014 was found to be 0.39 % monthly. Throughout the entire analysis the average unit price reached 2526 PLN/sq m.

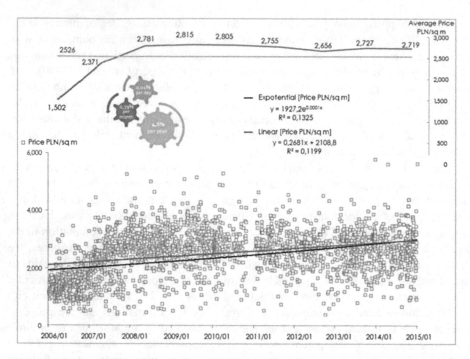

Fig. 1. Average price and price trend [PLN per sq m] of flats in Kalisz from 2006 to 2014.

3.2   Characteristics of the Analyzed Area

Dobrzecka street in Kalisz is about 2.6 km long; it starts near the city centre and reaches the administrative areas of Dobrzec village. The name "Dobrzec" goes back to the oldest tradition of this land and bears a large emotional and historical significance. The first mentions of Dobrzec settlement date 1280.

The street has a non-homogenous nature. Its beginning consists of multi-family residential buildings which are about one hundred years old, built close to each other. In the post-war years they were confiscated from private owners by the State and at that time they were mostly rent tenement blocks. They alternate with other buildings: public services (a blood donor station, social aid centre), manufacturing (former clothes plant). In its middle section the street is built up with warehouses, engineering and service buildings. The end of Dobrzecka street crosses the area of former Dobrzec village, partly transformed into detached house estates, and partly still settlement and farming areas. A particular attention was paid to transformations in the initial sections of the street. This terrain has changed its character in years. Rent tenement houses administrated then and partly now by a municipal company have been regained by previous owners; other ownership transformations have taken place. The first effective action was change of ownership of the property located at 6 Dobrzecka street build up with a shabby living house. Next the building was demolished and in 2006 replaced with a new one.

A parallel step in order to change the street character was replacement of the old living substance at the junction of Dobrzecka and Poznańska streets, where one of

Kalisz housing associations built the first block of flats in 2005 and the second one in 2008. The obsolete petrol station located at the beginning of the street was dismantled in 2007. In the same year the ownership transformation of the property located at 10 Dobrzecka street was finished, which permitted its general repair.

At the same time, some manufacturing areas, which formerly belonged to KALPO Textile Plant, were – upon announcing the company's bankruptcy – bought out by a local investor (a quasi-developer) and transformed into living areas. Construction of a block of flats (flats and apartments) was begun in January 2008 and finished in December 2009. The result was 37 m tall building of 1 overground and 9 underground storeys and 100 flats. In order to build this building, the manufacturing facility was mostly demolished. The only thing left was a raw structure which was subsequently developed and a few storeys were added.

In 2009 the perpetual administrator (PCK) of the property located at 2 Dobrzecka street renovated the building, made the façade, replaced the woodwork and roof.

Recently, renovation of the building at 5 Dobrzecka street was completed. In 2014 the legal status of the property located at 8 Dobrzecka street was regulated. Currently, the third building joining the two living houses owned by a housing association is being built.

3.3   Market Value of the Flats in the Analyzed Area

In to show changes in values of the flats as a result of positive changes in the surrounding, a flat situated in an old tenement house in Dobrzecka Street in Kalisz was valued. The said flat covering 50.0 sq m is situated on the first floor of a short building, consists of two rooms, a kitchen, a bathroom with toilet and a hall. Its market value was determined. Transactions connected with second-hand flats were analyzed, which were located close to the flat and were of a similar technical condition and standard. Based on our own analysis and surveys of preferences among potential buyers in property agencies, basic attributed were identified which determine the property's value as well as their percentage weights. The average annual time trend was found to be 4,6 % in 2006–2014. Therefore, the transactional prices were corrected due to elapsing time. Next, transactions were selected which best correspond to the said flat. For the representative sample, parameters shown in Table 1 were identified.

Table 1. The parameters of a representative sample – flats in Kalisz in 2006 and 2014 [PLN per sq m].

Parameter	Transaction prices 2006	Adjusted prices 2006	Transaction prices 2014	Adjusted prices 2014
Minimum price	489	682	679	691
Average price	1502	2094	2719	2766
Median price	1429	2002	2788	2842
Maximum price	4197	5757	6130	6341
Standard deviation	504	697	704	715
Coefficient of variation	34 %	33 %	26 %	26 %

The most important asset in the calculation was comparison of the market value of the same flat in two situations – the former worse surrounding (picture of Dobrzecka street in 2006) and upon the image transformation of the surrounding (picture of Dobrzecka street in 2014). The property prices which were the reference point in both situations referred to the same moment – 31.12.2014. As a result, it was possible to maintain comparability of all other market conditions. The results of the property assessment were as follows (Fig. 2):

– 83,000 PLN before the surrounding changes (2006),
– 123,000 PLN after the surrounding changes (2014).

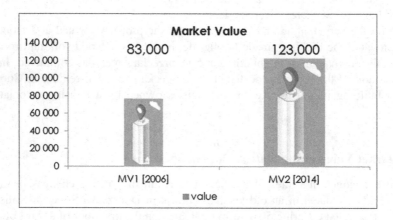

Fig. 2. The value of the flat according to its surrounding in 2006 and 2014 (Prices as on 31.12.2014).

3.4   Perception of Space Transformation in the Analyzed Area by Kalisz Inhabitants

One of the purposes of the study was to collect information about perception of changes in the urban surrounding by Kalisz inhabitants. The questionnaire asked about feelings and knowledge about changes in the city's image within the last ten years and about the trend, visibility and image transformation of Dobrzecka street (from Poznańska to Al. Wojska Polskiego streets). A question was also asked about most likely and desired trends in this area. The survey was designed to recognize and compare knowledge of Kalisz inhabitants about changes in values of the properties located there (Table 2).

The respondents are Kalisz inhabitants belonging to various groups:

– property market specialists (property agents and property surveyors),
– clerks employed in Kalisz City Office,
– students from the The President Stanisław Wojciechowski University School of Applied Sciences in Kalisz,
– inhabitants of Dobrzecka street,
– passer-byes.

Table 2. Number of surveyed inhabitants.

No	Trade group	No of respondents	Share in total
1	Specialists	25	6.6 %
2	Clerks	70	18.4 %
3	Students	43	11.3 %
4	Dobrzecka inhabitants	43	11.3 %
5	Passer-byes	199	52.4 %
	Total	**380**	**100.0 %**

3.5 Survey Results

The respondents were asked to define the image trend within the last decade for the analyzed section of Dobrzecka street. The changes are perceived as common, repeatable and lacking outstanding diversity. Furthermore, Dobrzecka street is evaluated subjectively – despite the changes – as ugly.

When asked about the degree of changes in the image of Dobrzecka street within the last 10 years, the respondents most often gave neutral answers as they thought the street's image changes to some extent (45 %). Few (17 %) considered the changes as visible.

The survey also checked knowledge of trends in flat prices in Kalisz. Kalisz citizens were asked about changes in flat prices in Kalisz within the last ten years including Dobrzecka street. The biggest number of the respondents think that the prices of flats in Kalisz and at Dobrzecka street have been stable, however, almost as large a group said the prices went up. Only 4 % marked a high increase of the prices in Kalisz – 3 % for Dobrzecka street. As many as 22 % of the respondents think that flat prices have gone down in Kalisz.

28 % who say that flat prices in Kalisz have decreased think they have been stable in Dobrzecka street while 19 % think they have gone up. Also every fifth who thinks the prices were generally stable in the city point to their rise in Dobrzecka street.

What is interesting, (compare: Fig. 1) wrong answers about the drop of flat prices in Kalisz within the last 10 years were most frequently given by property agents and clerks. The surveyors, students and passer-byes marked the price increase whereas the inhabitants of Dobrzecka street were convinced of their stabilization.

The respondents were asked to identify which presently existing element is the strongest sign of space changes in the analyzed section of Dobrzecka street. The block of flats dominated the spontaneous answers. Supported answers were similar. Even though 100 new flats were built in the analyzed vicinity, as many as 16 % think the social structure of the street inhabitants has not changed while 35 % think it has been poor (Fig. 3).

Next, they were asked about respondent anticipated and desired trends in that area. Spontaneous answers about the desired trends boiled down to two main options:

- renovation of tenement houses,
- development of transportation infrastructure.

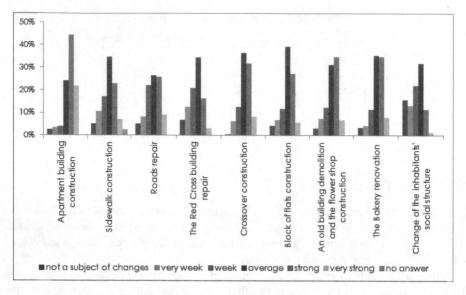

Fig. 3. Accents of changes within Dobrzecka street.

Next, the respondents were offered a few variants of answers regarding the change of Dobrzecka image. The respondents considered the majority of the suggested trends as quite or rather unlikely. The highest score was given to further growth of blocks of flats – renovation of tenement houses (p = 0.49). On the other hand, construction of tall buildings is regarded as slight less likely (p = 0.38). The respondents also pointed to transfer of the current trend to the farther section of the street or adjacent areas as quite probable (p = 0.46). The likelihood of growth of commercial and other functions was estimated by the respondents as p = 0.38 and p = 0.36 respectively.

The last question asked to Kalisz citizens was about their satisfaction with transformations within Dobrzecka street within the last ten years. Most people did not clearly state their attitude to the changes (selected the neutral answer), however, the emotionally burdened answers were mostly positive (Fig. 4). The lowest satisfaction with the changes was shown by property agents and passer-bys; the students are slightly more satisfied. Among the street inhabitants negative scores prevail, which proves their dissatisfaction with the changes.

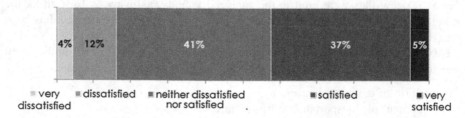

Fig. 4. The level of satisfaction with the changes within Dobrzecka street in the last ten years.

4   Conclusions

The study shows the trends and dynamics of the changes in the market value of the flat located in Kalisz, Dobrzecka street. This area was subject to urban transformations which in 2006–2014 improved the surrounding quality and image and consequently increased attractiveness of the local flat market.

The flat's market value was defined according to its surrounding in 2006 and 2014. Due to the simulations taking into account various states of attractiveness of the analyzed flat, it was assessed that should the surrounding's condition remain relatively low and typical of 2006, its market value would now amount to PLN 83,000. However, the actual improvement of the neighbourhood's image and quality made the value go up to PLN 123,000. Therefore, in the observed period the real appreciation of the said flat increased by 48 %.

This kind of rise, which is to a large extent though not entirely a consequence of the local revitalization, proves a connection between transformations in the space and flat valuation. It illustrates possibilities of stimulating price increase in a property market in areas subject to revitalization.

Consciousness among the respondents of the scale of changes in flat prices is low. They diagnosed the difference slightly higher on the scale for Dobrzecka street than for the whole city. When asked about desired trends of changes in that area, the respondents indicate a necessity to modify the social structure.

Significance of changes in urban space and their market consequences reaches more strongly and quickly to profiteers who seek to multiply their assets through successful investments. General social consciousness is limited and blurred. Typical space users behave inconsistently – they notice accents, evident signs of transformations, however, at the same time they say the transformations cannot be easily noticed. They also cannot see a link between changes in the surrounding with prices of flats. In this way, a surprising mechanism was caught of separation between social and market consciousness. This indicates a gap in consciousness or economic competence in the society which is unable to translate significance of physical changes in the space to their market consequences.

References

1. Kucharska-Stasiak, E.: Nieruchomość w gospodarce rynkowej. PWN, Warszawa (2006)
2. Olbińska, K.: The influence of real estate on its surroundings based on the example of the manufaktura complex in lodz. Real Estate Manage. Valuation 22(4), 5–16 (2014)
3. Polko, A.: Miejski rynek mieszkaniowy i efekty sąsiedztwa, pp. 61–66. AE w Katowicach, Katowice (2005)
4. Ridker, R.G., Henning, I.A.: The determinants of residential property values with special reference to air pollution. Rev. Econ. Stat. 49(2), 246–257 (1967)
5. Mason, G.: Revealing 'space' in spatial externalities: edge-effect externalities and spatial incentives. J. Environ. Econ. Manage. 54(1), 84–99 (2007)

6. Simons, R., Quercia, R., Meric, I.: The value impact on new residential construction and neighborhood disinvestment on residential sales price. J. Real Estate Res. **15**(1/2), 147–161 (1998)
7. Emery, J.: Bullring: a case-study of retail-led urban renewal and its contribution city centre regeneration. J. Retail Leisure Property **5**(2), 121–133 (2006)
8. Trojanek, R., Trojanek, M.: Profitability of investing in residential units: the case of the real estate market in Poland in the years 1997-2011. Actual Probl. Econ. **7**, 73–83 (2012)
9. Gies, E.: The Health Benefits of Parks. The Trust for Public Land, San Fransisco (2006)
10. Matusiak, M.: Przestrzeń publiczna jako czynnik konkurencyjności miast. In: Gaczek, W.M. (ed.) Prace z gospodarki przestrzennej, Zeszyt 161, pp. 51–70. Wydawnictwo Uniwersytetu Ekonomicznego w Poznaniu, Poznań (2010)
11. Palicki, S.: A valuation of public spaces: selected research results. Real Estate Manage. Valuation **21**(1), 19–24 (2013)
12. Tanaś, J.: Differentiation of local housing markets in Poznań suburban area. Real Estate Manage. Valuation **21**(3), 88–98 (2013)
13. Couch, C.: Economic and physical influences on urban regeneration in Europe. In: Couch, C., Fraser, C., Percy, S. (eds.) Urban regeneration in Europe, pp. 166–179. Blackwell Publishing, Oxford (2003)
14. Bryx, M. (ed.): Rynek nieruchomości. Finansowanie rozwoju miast, pp. 34–41. CeDeWu, Warszawa (2013)
15. Budner, W., Palicki, S.: Rewitalizacja obszaru centrum Leszna a handel detaliczny, mpm, Urząd Miasta Leszna (2012)
16. Kaźmierczak, B., Nowak, M., Palicki, S., Pazder, D.: Oceny rewitalizacji. Studium zmian na poznańskiej Śródce. Wydawnictwo Wydziału Nauk Społecznych UAM, Poznań (2011)
17. Palicki, S.: Interakcje przestrzeni publicznej z rynkiem nieruchomości komercyjnych. Przykład śródmiejskiego obszaru Poznania. In: Gaczek, W.M. (ed.) Prace z gospodarki przestrzennej. Zjawiska i procesy współczesnego rozwoju społeczno-gospodarczego, pp. 181-196, Wydawnictwo Uniwersytetu Ekonomicznego w Poznaniu, Poznań (2012)
18. Palicki, S., Rącka, I.: Wpływ odnowy miejskiej na wartość rynkową nieruchomości mieszkaniowych. In: Zeszyty Naukowe Politechniki Śląskiej, Gliwice (in print)
19. Belniak, S.: Rewitalizacja nieruchomości w procesie odnowy miast. Wydawnictwo Uniwersytetu Ekonomicznego w Krakowie, Kraków (2009)
20. Smith, M.M., Henever, C.C.: The impact of housing rehabilitation on local neighborhoods: the case of small community development organizations. Am. J. Econ. Sociol. **70**(1), 51–85 (2011)
21. Trojanek, R.: Fluctuations of dwellings' prices in the biggest cities in Poland during 1996–2011. Actual Probl. Econ. **2**(1–2), 224–231 (2013)
22. Rącka, I.: Czynniki wpływające na wartość nieruchomości gruntowych niezabudowanych o przeznaczeniu mieszkaniowym jednorodzinnym na podstawie analizy kaliskiego rynku nieruchomości w latach 2003–2008. Biuletyn Stowarzyszenia Rzeczoznawców Majątkowych Województwa Wielkopolskiego **3**, 57–67 (2009)
23. Rącka, I.: Sales of residential properties illustrated with the city of Kalisz. J. Int. Stud. **6**(2), 132–144 (2013)

Using Visual Lane Detection to Control Steering in a Self-driving Vehicle

Kevin McFall[(✉)]

Department of Mechatronics Engineering, Kennesaw State University,
1100 South Marietta Parkway, Marietta, GA 30060, USA
kmcfall@kennesaw.edu

Abstract. An effective lane detection algorithm employing the Hough transform and inverse perspective mapping to estimate distances in real space is utilized to send steering control commands to a self-driving vehicle. The vehicle is capable of autonomously traversing long stretches of straight road in a wide variety of conditions with the same set of algorithm design parameters. Better performance is hampered by slowly updating inputs to the steering control system. The 5 frames per second (FPS) using a Raspberry Pi 2 for image capture and processing can be improved to 23 FPS with an Odroid XU3. Even at 5 FPS, the vehicle is capable of navigating structured and unstructured roads at slow speed.

Keywords: Self-driving vehicle · Hough transform · Dynamic threshold · Inverse perspective transform · Temporal integration · Angle control

1 Introduction

It is now generally accepted that self-driving vehicles [1–3] in one form or another are the future of automobile transportation. Every major car manufacturer is exploring autonomous driving [4–8]. Elon Musk, CEO of Tesla Motors, famously stated in 2014 that Tesla's new set of cars to be unveiled in 2015 will be capable of self-driving 90 % of the time [9]. Lane departure warning, adaptive cruise control, and self-parking features are already available on luxury model cars. Understandably, intense research is ongoing to develop algorithms and hardware to make these and more advanced self-driving capabilities sufficiently inexpensive and reliable to be made universally available.

Self-driving vehicles have been pioneered by Google [10] and the DARPA Grand Challenge in 2005 [11–13] and Urban Challenge in 2007 [14–18]. However, the Google car has access to high resolution 3D maps of the world [19] and DARPA Urban Challenge competitors were provided exact digital maps of the course, enabling navigation with limited onboard perception [20]. Commercial systems do not currently have access to such data, requiring robust sensing systems. A wide array of research addresses lane detection [21], but most focus on a particular subtask with few offering quantitative performance evaluation on the full system [20], and even fewer gathering characteristics essential for navigation [22]. This manuscript implements all the requisite functional modules for lane detection [20], and its primary contribution lies in extracting steering commands from the algorithm and using them to control a vehicle

© ICST Institute for Computer Sciences, Social Informatics and Telecommunications Engineering 2016
A. Leon-Garcia et al. (Eds.): Smart City 2015, LNICST 166, pp. 861–873, 2016.
DOI: 10.1007/978-3-319-33681-7_77

on an actual road. In order to avoid the safety issues associated with testing on a full-sized automobile, the 4 ft by 4 ft aluminum-framed vehicle pictured in Fig. 1 was used to test lane detection and steering control.

Fig. 1. Self-driving vehicle used during field tests.

Modalities for lane and road perception include vision, light detection and ranging (LIDAR), geographic information systems (GPS), inertial measurement units (IMU), vehicle dynamics, and radar [20]. Vision is the most common, but LIDAR offers 3D structure of the environment and an active light source to mitigate issues stemming from shadow and darkness. LIDAR devices have been used extensively in the DARPA Grand Challenges, but high cost currently prevents their use from becoming widespread [20]. Accordingly, this work focuses on low-cost camera sensing instead. Lane detection with cameras is generally classified as using color, texture, or edge features to segment the road surface [21]. Among these, edge methods using some version of the Hough transform are one of the most common [22–43].

The main functional modules [20] of successful vision detection systems include: pre-processing, feature extraction, road/lane model fitting, temporal integration, and image to world correspondence. Some research touch only on pre-processing and feature extraction [25, 32, 35, 37, 38] while others apply various road models [22, 24, 31, 42]. A common method for connecting a road/lane model to vehicle position in the real world involves perspective mapping [23, 26–30, 34, 36, 40, 41, 43] which translates image lines to their corresponding locations in real space. Perspective mapping is most often used to reject potential lane lines not parallel to each other, or those indicating impossible lane widths. Temporal integration with the Hough transform, using information from previous image frames, is much less common. This technique can be used to identify a vanishing point [24] or reduce the image's region of interest (ROI) [33, 39]. Temporal integration is essential to the algorithm presented here, by effectively reducing the ROI and allowing accurate localization of the vehicle in real space when only a single lane boundary is detected. Another uncommon but useful technique is to identify a so-called virtual boundary, e.g. the location in the image of an undetected lane boundary using the detected boundary on the other side of the lane [22, 28]. The work here combines all these aspects: using boundary positions from previous frames calculated with the inverse perspective transform to limit the search space, and predicting virtual boundary locations when a boundary is obscured or otherwise not detected.

The vast majority of lane detection research evaluates an algorithm offline using a video feed of previously recorded road images, while some are tested in real-time with a human driving the vehicle. Both of these methods assume the vehicle always travels nearly parallel to the road direction. Deviations of only 5–10° significantly hamper lane detection where one lane boundary can disappear completely from the field of view. With steering controlled autonomously rather than by a human, lane detection can be tested with a full range of representative road images. This work presents a complete system where lane detection is shown sufficient to successfully control steering autonomously in real road conditions.

2 Lane Detection

At the core of the lane detection algorithm is the Hough transform, which evaluates a binary edge image by discretizing all possible lines in the image into an accumulator matrix and counting the edge pixels falling on each line [44]. Accumulator entries with large numbers of pixels falling on them are likely candidates for lane boundaries. A detected line is selected from the candidates by searching for local maxima in the accumulator matrix close to the boundary detected in the previous frame. Essential to the algorithm is determining whether the detected line is to be trusted or not. A detected boundary is trusted if either it has not changed significantly from the position of a trusted boundary in the previous frame, or if the distance in real space between left and right detected boundaries is close to the actual lane width. The inverse perspective transform is used to measure the distance in real space between the two detected lines in the image. A previous version of this algorithm [45] using a MATLAB toolbox for the Hough transform [46] successfully identified lane boundaries in 95 % of the frames tested during an 8 min video of highway driving. The algorithm described here modifies the previous one to use the open source computer vision (OpenCV) library [47, 48] in order to implement it in an embedded system. The remainder of this section presents details of the four functional modules of lane detection, where the road/lane model and real world correspondence are covered together with the inverse perspective transform.

2.1 Image Pre-processing

The acquired image is first converted to grayscale since color is not used in the algorithm. The top half of the image is cropped out since the vanishing point falls at the image center, and the road bed lies in the bottom half image for a camera with zero roll and pitch travelling on a level road. To further reduce the ROI, the remaining bottom half image is split vertically where the left and right lane boundaries are detected independently in the left and right bottom quarters, respectively.

2.2 Feature Extraction

The binary edge image generated with a Canny filter is analyzed using the Hough transform. The HoughLines function in OpenCV returns the accumulator entries comprising the most edge pixels above a given threshold. Variations in road scene, image contrast, quality of road markings, etc. significantly affect proper threshold choice. Allowing `HoughLines` to return too many accumulator entries risks a false positive while too few could miss the actual lane boundary. Returning between 40 and 50 candidate accumulator entries has been found to produce reasonable results for any number of different road situations. The threshold is dynamically updated every frame by decreasing it if fewer than 40 entries are returned and increasing if above 50.

2.3   Temporal Integration

Of the 40 to 50 candidate accumulator entries returned by the Hough transform, the actual lane boundary is expected to be one of the strongest lines. However, selecting the strongest line could result in identifying a windshield wiper, an adjacent boundary on a multiple lane road, or otherwise incorrect line.

Each accumulator entry represents a unique line defined by the perpendicular distance ρ from the top left image corner and its angle θ below the horizontal [44]. The parameters ρ and θ are used as opposed to the more commonplace slope m and intercept b to avoid slope discontinuities from vertical lines. Converting between ρ,θ and m,b parameters is straightforward using standard trigonometry.

The first step in determining which accumulator entry to select involves removing obvious outliers. As in [39], candidates are removed from consideration having values of ρ and θ differing significantly from the line detected in the previous frame. Some processing time could be saved if this step is instead moved to the pre-processing module [33] by negating edge pixels outside the ROI.

Accumulator entries are returned by `HoughLines` in rank order of their strength, which is modified by comparing the Euclidean distances in ρ,θ space between each remaining candidate line and the line detected in the previous frame. The ranking of each candidate is penalized depending on its distance normalized by the standard deviation of the candidate distances. If all candidates identify essentially the same line, none of their rankings will be modified and result in the strongest being detected. When candidates exhibit large dispersion in distance, however, those farther from the previous lane position are increasingly demoted. Standard deviation rather than mean is used for normalization to account for the expectation of some nonzero distance between detected lines from subsequent frames. The winning candidate is determined by the modified rank, and chosen as the "detected" lane boundary line. Whether the detected line is "trusted" depends on results from the inverse perspective transform.

2.4   Inverse Perspective Transform

The road model used assumes driving on a level surface with parallel left and right lane boundaries a known width apart. Comparing detected left and right lines with this model determines whether or not they are trusted as actual lane boundaries.

Camera images follow the central imaging model [44, 45] where a camera is placed at the XYZ origin of the world coordinate axes. The perspective transform projecting point P in real space to its corresponding location p in the image is one-to-one. The inverse perspective transform, however, results in an infinite number of points

P corresponding to any given p. A one-to-one inverse correspondence between image lines and world-coordinate lines does exist assuming the real lines lie in the XZ plane at a fixed $Y = H$ where H is the height of the camera above ground. The distance L of a line in world-coordinates to the camera and the yaw angle ϕ between the line and direction of travel as appears in Fig. 2 are related to the image slope m and intercept b according to

$$L = \frac{H}{\sqrt{\left[2b\tan(\tfrac{1}{2}\psi)\big/N_c\sqrt{1+1/R^2}\right]^2 + m^2}} \quad and \quad \phi = -\tan^{-1}\frac{2b\tan(\tfrac{1}{2}\psi)}{mN_c\sqrt{1+1/R^2}} \quad (1)$$

where ψ is the camera's diagonal angle of view, N_c is the horizontal camera resolution, R is the image aspect ratio, and b is measured in pixels. The angle of view is approximately $50°$ for most cameras.

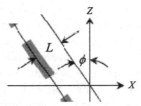

Fig. 2. Definition of lane distance L and yaw angle ϕ for a camera located at the XZ origin and travelling along the Z axis.

Detected road boundary lines are trusted if the L distances for both left and right boundaries add to a value close to the actual lane width. If the detected and actual lane widths do not match, detected boundaries will instead be trusted if they have not changed significantly from the previous frame. Detection of lines in the next frame is dependent on boundaries from the current frame; in case only one boundary in the current frame is trusted, the other virtual boundary is predicted using the inverse of Eq. (1) for an L one lane width away from the trusted line and the same θ. In such a manner, the algorithm continues to operate normally even when one lane boundary is occluded, beyond the field of view, beaten in rank by a nearby spurious line, or detection otherwise fails.

3   Vehicle Hardware and Control

Rather than testing vehicle control on a full-size automobile, a smaller but still road-worthy custom vehicle was designed and built. The smaller vehicle is safer to operate and easier to manage. The aluminum-framed design is relatively stiff and still lightweight, with 25.4 cm wheels sufficiently large to traverse uneven roads and other obstructions. The front drive wheels control steering as well with each motor driven by an independent motor as in [29], while the rear caster wheels are free to swivel.

Both Raspberry Pi and Odroid XU3 microprocessors are explored to provide image capture and processing. The lane detection algorithm is used to generate a steering command which is sent via serial USB communication to an Arduino Uno, which in turn transmits pulse width modulation signals to motor controllers for each drive motor. The Arduino also accepts signals from a radio control (RC) receiver. The transmitter allows for remote control of the vehicle with a kill switch and mode control for manual and autonomous modes. Currently, autonomous mode uses throttle commands from the transmitter and steering commands from the lane detection algorithm. Power is supplied to the microprocessor, Arduino, and RC receiver with a 5 V portable cell phone battery charger, while a 12 V, 7 aH lead-acid battery provides power to the motor controllers.

Standard proportional, integral, derivative (PID) control can be used for self-driving vehicles [49]. Currently a proportional derivative (PD) control output

$$ u = K_1 \left(\frac{1}{2} W_d - L \right) + K_2 \phi + K_3 \Delta \phi \tag{2} $$

is implemented where W_d is the most recent detected lane width, $\Delta \phi$ is the change in ϕ from the previous frame, and the K_i are control gains. An integral term may be introduced later if significant steady state errors in L persist. Values for L and ϕ are based on trusted boundaries only, taking the average of left and right if both are trusted. Initial testing with only proportional gain was unable to maintain a small yaw angle ϕ; the control problem is primarily one of angle rather than position control. Unmitigated increases in ϕ quickly result in loss of one boundary from the field of view and driving over the other boundary. Addition of the K_3 derivative term strengthens steering when turning away from the proper lane direction and dampens it to prevent overcorrection when ϕ is still large but improving. The control gains were tuned to achieve as responsive and smooth steering as possible within the constraints of chatter in L and ϕ and a relatively slow frame rate. The control output u is mapped to integer values between 25 and 125 to be sent to the Arduino as a single byte via USB. Some lane detection research specifically locates the vehicle in lane [42] or provides steering information [22, 50], but none distinguish between error in position vs. error in angle; any successful control scheme must focus primarily on maintaining the proper heading relative to road direction.

4   Field Test Results

The vehicle demonstrates successful navigation on straight paths in the numerous situations appearing in Fig. 3. The gray lines in Fig. 3 are trusted by the algorithm while black indicates lines detected in the previous frame. The top row of numbers report lane distances from the inverse perspective transform with left detected lane boundary (left), right detected boundary (right), and detected lane width (center). The bottom row of numbers displays the yaw angle according to the left (left) and right (right) detected lines, as well as the steering command (center). A command value of 75 represents straight while 25 and 125 request full left and right turns, respectively.

Fig. 3. Various scenes successfully navigated by the vehicle including a 5 ft wide artificial lane in a laboratory setting, hallway, sidewalk, and several different road conditions.

Although relatively simple, the lane detection algorithm is sufficient to traverse stretches of road up to 70 ft long as well as the sidewalks, hallways, and indoor environments in Fig. 3. For a camera level in terms of pitch and roll, the only necessary calibration involves the height of the camera above ground and the lane width. In fact none of these requirements need be specified with much accuracy when applying a simple, single-step calibration process. If any of the parameters are inaccurate, the detected width will differ slightly from its exact width. Before engaging autonomous mode, the road width parameter in the lane detection algorithm can simply be set to the detected lane width to account for any inaccuracies. No fine tuning of algorithm parameters is necessary; the same set of parameters (other than lane width) were used in all locations depicted in Fig. 3.

By changing only the lane width, the vehicle is capable of autonomous control for lanes of widths ranging from 5 to 14 feet, even in highly noisy environments such as the laboratory setting in the top left image of Fig. 3. The wall and nearby equipment introduce additional lines parallel to actual boundaries. In Fig. 4, such a line (white) is falsely detected, but the 6.4 ft measured distance between the trusted (gray) and detected (white) lines falls outside the threshold for the actual 5 ft lane width. Instead, the right lane boundary is sought in the next frame at a position of the virtual boundary (off-white) determined by the perspective transform prediction of a line 5 ft to the right of the trusted line.

Fig. 4. Case where a spurious lane boundary (white) is rejected– the trusted line (gray) is used to predict the location of the rejected lane boundary (off-white) using the perspective transform.

The lane detection algorithm can still benefit from refinement as is apparent in the trusted right lane boundary in Fig. 5 where the detected line represents a shadow rather

Fig. 5. False positive trusted line due to shadow condition.

than the actual lane boundary. Situations with false positive trusted boundaries generally persist for only a few frames, 6 in this case, before correct identification resumes. The valid trusted left boundary reduces the effect of the false positive by averaging in accurate values for L and ϕ with the improper right boundary values. The resulting steering brought the vehicle somewhat closer to the left boundary than desired but still maintained the vehicle safely within the lane.

All field test results used a Raspberry Pi 2 on a Linux operating system for image capture and processing. The 900 MHz quad core ARM cortex in the Raspberry Pi 2 offers a significant improvement over the 700 MHz Raspberry Pi 1. Both versions include support, including a software library, for the Raspberry Pi camera module which connects directly to the board using a ribbon cable. Another single-board computer, the Odroid XU3, is also capable of running Linux and provides even more computing power with a 2.0 GHz quad core Cortex A-15. Both Raspberry Pi and Odroid execute the same Python script, differing only in image capture using the Odroid USB-CAM with the OpenCV `VideoCapture` command rather than the Pi camera and its library. For comparison, the Raspberry Pi is tested both with the Pi camera and the USB-CAM. Table 1 includes frame rates comprised of both image capture and processing for all three microprocessors at two resolutions. Tests have shown that the smaller resolution, with its higher frame rate, offers sufficient resolution for successful boundary detection. Frame rates for the Raspberry Pi are essentially independent of camera selection, and are approximately 5 times slower than using the more powerful Odroid XU3. Future field tests will employ the XU3 exclusively, but have not yet been conducted as existing portable batteries are unable to supply 5 V at the requisite 4 A of current.

Table 1. Comparison of frame rates using different microprocessors.

Resolution	Microprocessor	Camera	Frame rate (FPS)
352 × 288	Raspberry Pi 1	Pi camera	2.2
		USB	1.8
	Raspberry Pi 2	Pi camera	4.5
		USB	5.2
	Odroid XU3	USB	23
640 × 480	Raspberry Pi 1	Pi camera	1.2
		USB	0.83
	Raspberry Pi 2	Pi camera	2.1
		USB	2.4
	Odroid XU3	USB	11

5   Discussion and Future Work

Failure to maintain the vehicle in lane generally does not result from poor lane detection, which is successful even on the curved roads in Fig. 6 as the approximately straight near-field boundaries dominate the image. Rather, inability of the PD control scheme to react to steering commands is the weakest link. Slow frame rates around 5 frames per second (FPS) using the Raspberry Pi 2 are partially to blame, which will be remedied once the XU3 power supply issue is resolved. Chatter in boundary detection such as jumping from one side of a double marked line to another or from curb shoulder to road edge is also problematic for PD control. An inertial measurement unit (IMU) supplying yaw angle and rate should greatly improve time resolution and accuracy of ϕ and $\Delta\phi$. The IMU data and speed from shaft encoders can improve lane detection by incorporating dynamic thresholds for how much a lane boundary is expected to change from frame to frame. Another factor contributing to difficulty with steering control is the inertia required to restore rotated caster wheels when recovering from a turn. Eventually, the vehicle's tank drive steering should be replaced with a steering mechanism similar to that in a standard automobile.

Fig. 6. Successful lane boundary detection on curved roads.

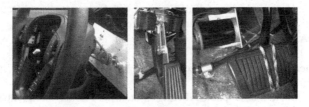

Fig. 7. Motor and servo controlled actuation of steering (left), acceleration (center), and braking (right) to enable drive-by-wire control of a KIA Optima.

The majority of lane detection research does not supply information about computational speed, which is essential for real-time control of autonomous vehicles. Some algorithms are described as fast [24] or real-time [35] but offer no information about computation time, while others report 10 FPS or less [23, 32, 36]. Frame rates between 35 and 100 FPS depending on image complexity are reported [41] at 640×480 resolution on a 3.5 GHz computer. The 50 FPS in [34] at 640×480 using a 2.4 GHz machine likely does not include image capture time as processing was performed offline. An embedded AMD E-350 1.6 GHz dual-core processor operating at 320×240 achieved 21 FPS [27]. The 23 FPS using the Odroid XU3 at 352×288 is comparable to these published frame rates.

The vehicle and lane detection algorithm presented here is successful on structured and unstructured roads with a variety of features including curbs, shoulders, median dividers, and solid or dashed lane markings. Although currently only capable of traversing straight road sections, improvements are already underway to improve the speed and accuracy of inputs to the PD controller to improve performance. This includes encoder and IMU data, and eventually GPS and a scanning laser range finder. Completely successful self-driving vehicles must rely on multiple modalities such as these rather than relying solely on vision [20].

Field testing has so far been restricted to a 4 ft by 4 ft vehicle, but the system will be ported to a KIA Optima. The Optima has already been modified to be drive-by-wire capable as depicted in Fig. 7 where a motor controls steering with a timing belt connected to the steering column (left), servo motors actuate the accelerator pedal (center), and a cable attached to the brake pedal winds around a motor shaft (right). Once the mature self-driving system is developed on the smaller vehicle, it can be adapted to control a full size automobile.

References

1. Mimizuka, K.: FOCUS: Global race to develop self-driving cars heats up. Kyodo News International, Inc., 18 October 2013
2. Miller, M.: Self-driving cars could be the future. Eunice News (LA), 16 October 2013
3. Pultarova, T.: Self-driving selfcharging electric cars ready to roll. Eng. Technol. **9**(12), 10 (2015)
4. Truett, R.: For GM, the self-driving car of the future is also a thing of the past. Automotive News, p. 0040, 15 September 2014
5. Shane, D.: Ford moves closer to self-driving cars with high-tech reveal, (Dubai, United Arab Emirates), 25 February 2014. ArabianBusiness.com
6. Durbin, D.-A.: Honda introduces self-driving car. Associated Press: Worldstream, 09 September 2014
7. Frizell, S.: Here Is Mercedes' Outrageous Vision for the Future of Cars, p. N.PAG, January 2015. Time.com
8. Leggett, D.: US: Audi tests 'piloted driving' systems in Florida. Aroq (Global News), p. 8, August 2014. Just-Auto.com
9. Hays, B.: Musk: Next Tesla cars will self-drive 90 percent of the time. UPI NewsTrack (Consumer Health), October 2014
10. Fox, D.: Google car moves into fast lane. Discover **36**(1), 54 (2015)
11. Mason, R., Radford, J., Kumar, D., Walters, R., Fulkerson, B., Jones, E., Caldwell, D., Meltzer, J., Alon, Y., Shashua, A., Hattori, H., Frazzoli, E., Soatto, S.: The Golem Group/University of California at Los Angeles autonomous ground vehicle in the DARPA Grand Challenge. J. Field Rob. **23**(8), 527–553 (2006)
12. McBride, J., Ivan, J., Rhode, D., Rupp, J., Rupp, M., Higgins, J., Turner, D., Eustice, R.: A perspective on emerging automotive safety applications, derived from lessons learned through participation in the DARPA Grand Challenges. J. Field Rob. **25**(10), 808–840 (2008)

13. Thrun, S., Montemerlo, M., Dahlkamp, H., Stavens, D., Aron, A., Diebel, J., Fong, P., Gale, J., Halpenny, M., Hoffmann, G., Lau, K., Oakley, C., Palatucci, M., Pratt, V., Stang, P., Strohband, S., Dupont, C., Jendrossek, L.-E., Koelen, C., Markey, C., Rummel, C., van Niekerk, J., Jensen, E., Alessandrini, P., Bradski, G., Davies, B., Ettinger, S., Kaehler, A., Nefian, A., Mahoney, P.: Stanley: the robot that won the DARPA Grand Challenge. J. Field Rob. 23(9), 661–692 (2006)
14. Bohren, J., Foote, T., Keller, J., Kushleyev, A., Lee, D., Stewart, A., Vernaza, P., Derenick, J., Spletzer, J., Satterfield, B.: Little ben: the ben franklin racing team's entry in the 2007 DARPA Urban Challenge. J. Field Rob. 25(9), 598–614 (2008)
15. Kammel, S., Ziegler, J., Pitzer, B., Werling, M., Gindele, T., Jagzent, D., Schroder, J., Thuy, M., Goebl, M., von Hundelshausen, F., Pink, O., Frese, C., Stiller, C.: Team AnnieWAY's autonomous system for the 2007 DARPA Urban Challenge. J. Field Rob. 25(9), 615–639 (2008)
16. Sprinkle, J., Eklund, J.M., Gonzalez, H., Grøtli, E.I., Upcroft, B., Makarenko, A., Uther, W., Moser, M., Fitch, R., Durrant-Whyte, H., Sastry, S.S.: Model-based design: a report from the trenches of the DARPA Urban Challenge. Softw. Syst. Model. 8(4), 551 (2009)
17. Thrun, S.: Why we compete in DARPA's Urban Challenge autonomous robot race. Commun. ACM 50(10), 29–31 (2007)
18. Urmson, C., Anhalt, J., Bagnell, D., Baker, C., Bittner, R., Clark, M.N., Dolan, J., Duggins, D., Galatali, T., Geyer, C., Gittleman, M., Harbaugh, S., Hebert, M., Howard, T.M., Kolski, S., Kelly, A., Likhachev, M., McNaughton, M., Miller, N., Peterson, K., Pilnick, B., Rajkumar, R., Rybski, P., Salesky, B., Seo, Y.-W., Singh, S., Snider, J., Stentz, A., "Red" Whittaker, W., Wolkowicki, Z., Ziglar, J., Bae, H., Brown, T., Demitrish, D., Litkouhi, B., Nickolaou, J., Sadekar, V., Zhang, W., Taylor, M., Darms, M., Ferguson, D.: Autonomous driving in urban environments: Boss and the Urban Challenge. J. Field Rob. 25(8), 425–466 (2008)
19. Erico, G.: How google's self-driving car works. IEEE Spectr. 18, 18 October 2011. http://spectrum.ieee.org/automaton/robotics/artificial-intelligence/how-google-self-driving-car-works
20. Hillel, A.B., Lerner, R., Levi, D., Raz, G.: Recent progress in road and lane detection: a survey. Mach. Vis. Appl. 25(3), 727–745 (2012)
21. Yenikaya, S., Yenikaya, G., Düven, E.: Keeping the vehicle on the road- a survey on on-road lane detection systems. ACM Comput. Surv. 46(1), 2 (2013)
22. Umamaheswari, V., Amarjyoti, S., Bakshi, T., Singh, A.: Steering angle estimation for autonomous vehicle navigation using hough and Euclidean transform. In: 2015 IEEE International Conference on Signal Processing, Informatics, Communication and Energy Systems (SPICES), pp. 1–5 (2015)
23. Collado, J.M., Hilario, C., de la Escalera, A., Armingol, J.M.: Adaptative road lanes detection and classification. In: Blanc-Talon, J., Philips, W., Popescu, D., Scheunders, P. (eds.) ACIVS 2006. LNCS, vol. 4179, pp. 1151–1162. Springer, Heidelberg (2006)
24. Liu, H., Guo, Z., Lu, J., Yang, J.: A fast method for vanishing point estimation and tracking and its application in road images. In: 2006 6th International Conference on ITS Telecommunications Proceedings, pp. 106–109 (2006)
25. Thittaporn Ganokratanaa, P.P.: A Hough Transform Based Lane Detection for Driving System (2013)
26. Zhou, S., Jiang, Y., Xi, J., Gong, J., Xiong, G., Chen, H.: A novel lane detection based on geometrical model and Gabor filter. In: 2010 IEEE Intelligent Vehicles Symposium (IV) 2010, pp. 59–64 (2010)
27. Sun, T., Tang, S., Wang, J., Zhang, W.: A robust lane detection method for autonomous car-like robot. In: Fourth International Conference on Intelligent Control and Information Processing (ICICIP) 2013, pp. 373–378 (2013)

28. Jiang, Y., Gao, F., Xu, G.: Computer vision-based multiple-lane detection on straight road and in a curve. In: International Conference on Image Analysis and Signal Processing (IASP) 2010, pp. 114–117 (2010)

29. Pannu, G., Ansari, M., Gupta, P.: Design and implementation of autonomous car using Raspberry Pi. Int. J. Comput. Appl. **113**(9), 22–29 (2015)

30. Seo, D., Jo, K.: Inverse perspective mapping based road curvature estimation. In: IEEE/SICE International Symposium on System Integration (SII) 2014, pp. 480–483 (2014)

31. Wang, J., Gu, F., Zhang, C., Zhang, G.: Lane boundary detection based on parabola model. In: IEEE International Conference on Information and Automation (ICIA) 2010, pp. 1729–1734 (2010)

32. Habib, S., Hannan, M.A.: Lane departure detection and transmisson using hough transform method. Przegląd Elektrotechniczny **R. 89**(5), 141–146 (2013)

33. Wang, J., Wu, Y., Liang, Z., Xi, Y.: Lane detection based on random hough transform on region of interesting. In: IEEE International Conference on Information and Automation (ICIA) 2010, pp. 1735–1740 (2010)

34. Aly, M.: Real time detection of lane markers in urban streets. In: IEEE Intelligent Vehicles Symposium 2008, pp. 7–12 (2008)

35. Assidiq, A.A.M., Khalifa, O.O., Islam, R., Khan, S.: Real time lane detection for autonomous vehicles. In: International Conference on Computer and Communication Engineering, ICCCE 2008, pp. 82–88 (2008)

36. Tan, S., Mae, J.: Real-time lane recognition and position estimation for small vehicle. Internetworking Indonesia J. **5**(2), 3–8 (2013)

37. Lin, H., Kim, H., Lin, C., Chua, L.O.: Road boundary detection based on the dynamic programming and the randomized hough transform. In: International Symposium on Information Technology Convergence, ISITC 2007, pp. 63–70 (2007)

38. Daigavane, P.M., Bajaj, P.R.: Road lane detection with improved canny edges using ant colony optimization. In: 2010 3rd International Conference on Emerging Trends in Engineering and Technology (ICETET) 2010, pp. 76–80 (2010)

39. Ghazali, K., Xiao, R., Ma, J.: Road lane detection using H-maxima and improved hough transform. In: 2012 Fourth International Conference on Computational Intelligence, Modelling and Simulation (CIMSiM) 2012, pp. 205–208 (2012)

40. Xiaoyun, W., Yongzhong, W., Chenglin, W.: Robust lane detection based on gradient-pairs constraint. In: 2011 30th Chinese Control Conference (CCC), pp. 3181–3185 (2011)

41. Huang, J., Liang, H., Wang, Z., Mei, T., Song, Y.: Robust lane marking detection under different road conditions. In: 2013 IEEE International Conference on Robotics and Biomimetics (ROBIO) 2013, pp. 1753–1758 (2013)

42. Batista, M.P., Shinzato, P.Y., Wolf, D.F., Gomes, D.: Lane detection and estimation using perspective image. In: 2014 Joint Conference on Robotics: SBR-LARS Robotics Symposium and Robocontrol (SBR LARS Robocontrol), 2014, pp. 25–30 (2014)

43. Borkar, A., Hayes, M., Smith, M.T.: Robust lane detection and tracking with ransac and Kalman filter. In: 2009 16th IEEE International Conference on Image Processing (ICIP) 2009, pp. 3261–3264 (2009)

44. Corke, P.: Robotics, Vision and Control. Springer, Heidelberg (2011)

45. McFall, K., Tran, D.: Visual lane detection algorithm using the perspective transform. In: Proceedings of the 14th Early Career Technical Conference 2014, vol. 13 (2014)

46. Corke, P.: Machine vision toolbox for MATLAB release 3, January 2015. http://www.petercorke.com/MVTB/vision.pdf. Accessed 12 Mar 2015

47. Pulli, K., Baksheev, A., Kornyakov, K., Erumihov, V.: Real-time computer vision with OpenCV. Commun. ACM **55**(6), 61–69 (2012)

48. Brahmbhatt, S.: Embedded computer vision: running OpenCV programs on the Raspberry Pi. Practical OpenCV, pp. 201–218. Apress, New York (2013)
49. Zhao, P., Chen, J., Song, Y., Tao, X., Tiejuan, X., Mei, T.: Design of a control system for an autonomous vehicle based on adaptive-PID. Int. J. Adv. Rob. Syst. **9**, 1–11 (2012)
50. Shu, T., Zheng, Y., Shi, Z.: Image processing-based wheel steer angle detection. J. Electron. Imaging **22**(4), 043005 (2013)

Environmental Management as Part of a Socially Responsible Behavior in the Volkswagen Group

Marcela Basovnikova[1], Daniela Spirkova[2(✉)], and Roman Dubovy[1]

[1] Mendel University in Brno, Faculty of Business and Economics,
Zemedelska 1, 613 00 Brno, Czech Republic
{xbasovnl, xdubovy}@node.mendelu.cz
[2] Institute of Management, Slovak University of Technology in Bratislava,
Vazovova 5, 812 43 Bratislava, Slovakia
daniela.spirkova@stuba.sk

Abstract. In industrialized countries in the Nineties a fundamental change occurred in a way how companies approach environmental protection. In practice are promoted new tools, associated with creation and protection of the environment, with a significantly preventive character. Awareness of corporate social responsibility for their actions and knowledge of the basic principles of the progressive management system for businesses is becoming a matter of prestige opportunity. One of the advanced business management tools for the protection of the environment is an environmental management system which contributes significantly to improving the environmental performance of the company. Article is devoted to environmental policy and the impact of the application of ISO 14001 according to Environmental Management System within the automotive company Volkswagen Slovakia.

Keywords: Corporate social responsibility · Environmental protection · Automotive industry

1 Introduction

The current situation in the business environment brings a number of risks, which mainly have recently noticed a significant increase, with negative consequences for society as a whole. Climate change, environmental pollution, unfamiliarity of laws, ignoring the social responsibility of organizations towards employees and the community - all this represents only a small part of ethical problems that occur in the global economic environment.

With the question about how to make company's business activities successful for as many people as possible deals the concept of social responsibility.

Corporate Social Responsibility is still the subject of extensive discussions and its concept is still interpreted differently. For now, there is no single known definition. The most famous interpretation is mentioned in the Green Book (European Union): "CSR is the voluntary integration of social and ecological aspects into everyday corporate

© ICST Institute for Computer Sciences, Social Informatics and Telecommunications Engineering 2016
A. Leon-Garcia et al. (Eds.): Smart City 2015, LNICST 166, pp. 874–884, 2016.
DOI: 10.1007/978-3-319-33681-7_78

operations and interactions with corporate" stakeholders "that can be divided into primary, which includes owners, employees, customers, business partners, local communities and environmental NGOs, and secondary, which includes competitors, the public, media, civic and business associations and government institutions.

According Boatrighta [1] CSR is a voluntary transfer of responsibilities that exceeds purely economic (economic) and legal responsibility. World Business Council for Sustainable development defines CSR as "continuous commitment of businesses to behave ethically, contributing to sustainable economic development, while contributing to improving the quality of life of employees and their families, as well as local communities and society as a whole".

According to Kuldova [2] implementation of CSR into corporate activities brings the opportunity to differentiate from the competition. These activities include mainly minimizing the negative impacts on the environment, employee care and support for the region where a given company operates. According to Kunz [3], the social responsibility has purely voluntary nature, therefore has no clearly defined border and thus is linked across a whole range of different disciplines. This is, according to Kunz, also the reason of terminological disunity.

Based on a synthesis of existing knowledge, Archie Caroll contributed in 1979 to development of the concept of social responsibility with his definition: "Social corporate responsibility includes economic, legal, ethical and discretionary (philanthropic) expectations that company against other company has at a particular time" [4]. These expectations reflect responsibility of company in the generally displayed form of pyramid (Fig. 1).

Fig. 1. Structure of Corporate Social Responsibility [4]

The basic responsibility of business takes place in the economic sphere, in the form of production and distribution of goods and services based on knowledge of consumer needs, providing work and fair wages to employees, and at the same time making a profit [5]. From every company is within the legal liability expected to comply with all laws and standards relevant to the country where the enterprise carries on its business activity. This latter kind of responsibility is an ethical responsibility, which represents the company's commitment to behave in line with expectations, which are not regulated by legislation, i.e. so-called activities beyond the law. Within philanthropic responsibilities are contained activities entirely voluntary that enterprise can perform at its own decision and thus support the well-being of the whole society [5].

From the above definitions, we can deduce common ideas that can be considered as the basic principles of CSR. These include: voluntary, the initiative beyond the required legislation, improvement of the quality of life, sustainable development, communication with stakeholders, integration of social and environmental values into everyday business practices. It can thus be said that although there is no single, generally accepted definition of CSR activities can be generally divided into three areas: economic, social and environmental.

2 Materials and Methods

We analyzed a number of standards which help to fill CSR strategy, while we focus on the standards that are used in the automotive industry. The methodology of environmental management is completely covered by ISO 14000, which is a series of environmental management standards developed and published by the International Organization for Standardization (ISO) for organizations. The ISO 14000 standards provide a guideline or framework for organizations that need to systematize and improve their environmental management efforts.

The ISO 14001 standard is the most important standard within the ISO 14000 series. ISO 14001 specifies the requirements of an environmental management system (EMS) for small to large organizations. An EMS is a systemic approach to handling environmental issues within an organization. The ISO 14001 standard is based on the Plan-Check-Do-Review-Improve cycle.

When we processed this paper, we had used statistical data of the central environmental reports from Volkswagen Group as well as annual and environmental reports from Volkswagen Slovakia. For investigating the issue of Corporate Social Responsibility and environmental management system, we used a combination of several scientific methods, approaches (particularly analysis, abstraction, synthesis, induction, deduction, comparison), which allowed mutually coherent knowledge of the facts and investigation processes in all their complexity.

3 Management Systems in the Automotive Industry

For very powerful global industry it is currently considered the automotive industry, which is affected by the challenges and opportunities such as: climate change and the reduction of natural resources, energy security, demographic changes and employment, innovation and new green technologies, development of new economies and markets, etc. All of the above can be also connected with the concept of Corporate Social Responsibility (CSR), which is in the case of the automotive industry closely linked to sustainable development.

There are many norms and standards that help accomplish the strategy of CSR which was created by both government and NGOs. In the automotive industry, current management systems are most frequently certified under ISO 9001, ISO 14001 and

ISO/TS 16949. I Implementation of ISO 9001 is focused on the system quality, respectively to achieve competitive advantage through quality control. ISO 9001 certification demonstrates company commitment to quality. Using of benchmarking - continuous comparison - it is possible to measure the progress of continuous improvement and development of business activities. The standard is not intended purely for the automotive industry, but it can be used in all sectors of production and services. In the case of the automotive industry, this standard is often accompanied by so-called industry standards, such as QS 9000, VDA or (standard which is focused on management system quality of suppliers who ensure serial production for the automotive industry. At the present time it is accepted only to a limited extent, by the suppliers of German automotive industry).

ISO/TS 16949: 2009 is a new departmental standard intended purely for the system of quality management in the automotive industry. Standard replaces ISO/TS 16949 from October 2002 and unifies the requirements for system of quality management in the industry. Standard contains the full text of ISO 9001: 2008 and is supplemented by further specific requirements of the automotive industry. The difference between ISO 9001 and ISO 16949 is mainly in the specific requirements of organizations providing mass production and production of spare parts in the automotive industry which are added to the standard ISO16949. ISO/TS 16949 were developed in cooperation of IATF (International Automotive Task Force) and ISO and its first version was published in 1999.

The latest, most often voluntary used in the automotive industry is the standard ISO 14001, which will be in this part of article described more. Currently, demands of involved parties - stakeholders are constantly increasing, especially on the environmental protection system. The principle of ISO 14001 is therefore to promote environmental protection and pollution prevention. Standard was approved by the European Committee for Standardization (in English CES, in French CEN), which is a non-profit organization dealing mainly with the support of the European economy in global trade, prosperity of the European population and environment.

Interest in this certification increases world widely, which is also confirmed by Figs. 2 and 3. In companies of all kinds nowadays it is more than necessary to achieve and demonstrate their socially responsible behavior especially in the field of environmental management, which companies declare with the legal implementation of those standards.

ISO 14001 [16, 17] is based on the methodology of Plan-Do-Check-Act (PDCA), which can be characterized as follows:

- *Plan*: establish the objectives and processes necessary to deliver results in line with the organization's environmental policy
- *Do*: apply processes
- *Check*: monitor and measure processes in relation to environmental policy, objectives, the targets, legal requirements and other requirements and show results
- *Act*: take actions to continually improve performance of the environmental management system

The standard does not set any specific requirements for the environmental performance of certified companies, but it insists on the need to respect the legislative

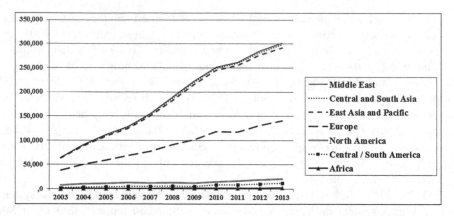

Fig. 2. ISO 14001- Worldwide total in years 2003-2013 [6]

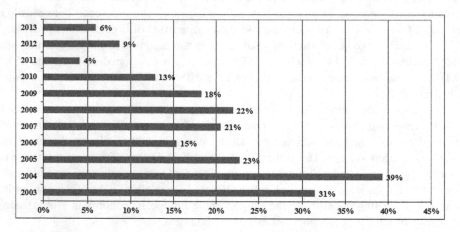

Fig. 3. ISO 14001- World annual growth in years 2003-2013 (in %) [6]

requirements in individual environmental components, which include water, air, soil, waste, etc. The principle is to identify all the factors that may affect the environment and which may be affected by a certified company with its operation. ISO 14001 [16] is therefore possible to implement in all organizations whose goal is to establish, implement, maintain and improve system efficiency and its environmental management system, to make sure of compliance with environmental policy which was announced and last but not least to demonstrate conformity with this International standard. Therefore, if a company is interested in certification according to ISO 14001, it is necessary to meet the following:

- Establishment of environmental policy of the company and consequently acquaint this policy to employees and the public, which is also included into groups of stakeholders;

- Identification of factors that result from company's activities that may have a significant impact on the environment;
- Monitoring the constantly changing conditions related to legal and other environmental requirements in connection with the identified aspects of the company and the reflection of these requirements to the environmental management system;
- In its environmental policy, to establish environmental objectives and values for individual functions and levels of company management;
- To determine the methodology and ways of their implementation to achieve the objectives and targets in connection with the environmental management system;
- Ensure appropriate staff training and corporate communications, both internal as well as external;
- Finally, the company has to monitor and measure the key features of its operation with a focus on the features that can have significant effects on the environment. In case of any disagreement with the legal requirements applicable in the field of environment, it is necessary for the company to make preventive and corrective measures in case of any identified deficiencies, deviations and damages.

According to that environmental protection becomes currently a growing priority, respecting the procedure should be a matter of course for any company thinking of sustainable development.

3.1 Benefits and Barriers of Implementation of Standard ISO 14001

Benefits of implementation of ISO 14001 [7–9] are reported by almost all the authors dealing with environmental management identical, but some authors are dividing it also into internal and external. Internal majority of author's states especially the clarity of environmental costs, early detection of problems related to the environment, the elimination of fees and fines for environmental pollution, prevention of environmental pollution, improve the quality management system, environmental management, etc. The external benefits of implementation are mainly the benefits of competition, the benefits of strengthening good public relations and the confidence of current and future customers. We cannot forget the increasing business credibility, not only for partners and customers, but also for potential investors, banks and public authorities.

For cons (barriers) at the enterprise level, combined with the introduction of Environmental Management System Remtova (2006) considers mainly costs associated with the implementation. It is not only the cost associated with the change of the control system (while in the case of a large operation is the implementation of ISO 14001 more expensive than e.g. ISO 9001) but the costs associated with the payment to an independent certification audit companies. Price for the implementation and subsequent repeating audits, which are done once every three years, is dependent on the size of the company and also on its activities, and it is not low. Some studies also indicate that barriers or constraints at the company level in the implementation of ISO 14001 may be the lack of involvement of the different levels of management, or unfamiliarity of environmental policy among employees. They should be of course very well trained, which implies additional costs associated with implementation. The barrier may also appear as a lack of knowledge of legislation relating to environmental protection which is associated with another additional financial cost in the form of either expansion of staffing, or hiring a specialized company, which deals with this topic.

4 Results and Discussion

Effective tool for environmental protection within Volkswagen Slovakia is Environmental Management System (EMS), which aim is, according to the international standard ISO 14001, to support environmental protection and prevention of pollution in balance with social and economic needs. The introduction and certification of EMS began in in 2002. The synergy between the requirements of environmental protection and sustainable technologies, as well as the instruments of a functioning environmental management system allows to continuously influence the effects of production processes and products for environmental sustainability at the planning stage of products and technologies until the evaluation of the car at the end of its life [10]. As reported by the National Council for Advanced Manufacturing [11], "the sustainable production is defined as production of products that use processes without environment pollution, saving energy and natural resources and is economically stable and safe for employees, society and consumers. Sustainable production includes sustainable products and production processes. This includes production of renewable energy, energy efficiency and related environmental aspects. "Langewalter [12] defines green (environmentally friendly) and sustainable production as a method to create technologies that transforms materials without emission of greenhouse gases, do not use non-renewable and toxic materials and eliminates waste.

The consistent application of ISO 140001 in the analyzed company has an effect on energy saving, sustainable use of water, waste management, prevent the emergence of emissions, reducing the amount and recovery of waste, the use of BAT technologies (Best Available Technologies) which are environmentally friendly, using recycled textile material insulating the noise in the passenger compartment, soundproofing against the noise from junkyard operation, In particular, technical textiles are an important part of a vehicle and are specially developed for the demanding needs of the automotive industry, which is the largest consumer and constitutes 22 % share of all industry sectors in total.

Such sustainable operation building seeks to minimize the negative impact on human health and the environment and thereby contribute to increase productivity of its employees. These buildings not only reflect a reduction of operational costs but also the requirements for sustainable development, promoting legislative and normative changes in regulation (particularly as a result of the directive Performance/Energy EU from 2010/31), in the European Union [13].

In 2013, Volkswagen Slovakia joined to the strategy called Think Blue to achieve with production even greater environmental benefits. The strategy was defined by five indicators:

- fuel consumption
- waste generation
- air emissions
- consumption of water and CO_2.

The seriousness how Volkswagen approaches this strategy has the real results that are for example annual savings of 1 million kWh electricity, 77,000 m^3 of natural gas and 595.8 tons of CO_2 in 2013 [14].

Air quality protection. This is particularly the reduction of emissions (Fig. 4) which are discharged into the atmosphere because of prioritization of paints and materials with low content of pollutants using active separation equipment.

	2009	2010	2011
CO₂ (direct emissions from the combustion of natural gas)	42,403.50	53,193.60	54,396.36
SO₂	0.20	0.25	0.26
NOx	63.79	91.53	121.00
Solid polluting substancess	12.19	21.99	33.27
Volatile organic compounds emitted on bodywork, sollid polluting substances (g/m²)	27.68	34.07	31.15

Fig. 4. Emissions to air in Volkswagen Slovakia in years 2009-2011 [14]

Waste waters (Fig. 5) from plants are treated before being discharged into the watercourse at neutralization stations and central treatment plant, which has a significant environmental impact on the cities in which these water streams are. The emphasis is put on compliance with the permitted levels of pollution discharged with waste waters as well as air emissions. To ensure preventive groundwater protection have been implemented nondestructive tightness testing's of retaining systems and pipelines and all monitored groundwater wells were restored.

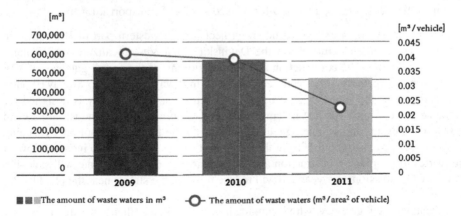

Fig. 5. The amount of waste waters (volume of waste waters depends on the production of vehicles, material consumption and the type of technology. In 2011 it managed to significantly reduce the amount of waste waters due to the reconstruction of wastewater treatment technologies and deployment of best available technologies in the paint shop) [14]

Waste management. The priority is the recovery (recycling) of waste before creating landfills and also separation by types in all operation stations.

Energy efficiency. Energy savings in the amount of 25 % is achieved through external lighting, which is controlled by dusk sensors. Scrap management. Recycled ecological material STERED from the vehicle's interior is of VW is used for soundproofing from the noise of the operation of scrap management. That means the material which previously isolated the noise inside the vehicle, now isolates the noise of the operation.

Further it is the implementation of environmentally friendly production technology directly into the individual plant sectors:

- *Paint shop* - as an example we can give the dry particle separator for cars of New Small Family, which reduces emissions up to 90 % and up to 80 % reduces energy consumption. Volkswagen Slovakia in Bratislava was the first place where was this technology implemented into the serial production for the first time (2011).
- *Body shop* - several machines in the manufacturing process is powered hydraulically. The relevant units are equipped with sump, which protect the subsoil in the event of malfunction against leaking hydraulic fluid. Welding smoke is suctioned and before being discharged into the environment is filtered through appropriate filtering equipment which removes polluting particles. Metals residues that remain from the production of car body are transported for recycling.
- *Assembly line.* During vehicle assembly there arises waste from packaging in which parts were packed. This waste is as a priority used again, respectively it is recovered as secondary material. By separation, adhesive residues and cleaning cloths containing solvents are separated from recyclables.
- *Logistics.* Aspect, which is environment affected by is the production of emissions from transport. This fact is taken into account at the planning and selection of suppliers of each transport session with the consideration of the transport distance from the plant, on which basis positive effects on reducing emissions from production can be achieved. For selected material transport sessions were from mid-2011 deployed gigaliners, which saved 40 % of transport kilometers [14].

For the most important infrastructure project for the western part of Bratislava, in terms of environmental impact on the Devinska Nova Ves (localization VW plant) must be considered the construction and commissioning of the fourth gateway of VW plant. The new gateway is directly connected to highway entrance to Stupava South, which is part of the future of zero bypass of Bratislava. The gateway is designed for entrance and exit only for Just-in-Time deliveries of components of industrial parks in Lozorno, Malacky and Vrable. Direct connection to the highway is not only reducing the number of trucks (about 500) in the urban part of the city, but also increase flow of deliveries to the plant. Construction and commissioning of the new gate will save 446 tons of CO_2 emissions per year and will reduce noise in the streets near the plant by 2.1 decibels.

Creating a new gateway, with its unique frame design, together with other necessary construction works (construction of interchange intersections, road treatment, landscaping, planting of greenery etc.) required the investment of nearly 6 million EUR.

5 Conclusion

The paper emphasizes the importance of introducing an environmental management system and the benefits of its introduction in Volkswagen Slovakia. Benefits from the introduction of an environmental management system contribute to reduce or avoid negative impacts on the environment and the reduction of operation costs (water, electricity, gas, etc.). The priority is compliance with the legal requirements which also affects the reduction of corporate costs by meeting the limits set by the legislation. After the introduction of environmental management systems is generally improved the company's image in the global market, as systems are characterized by a systematic approach to environmental protection at all levels of business. Through this systematic approach the company integrates environmental protection not only to their business strategy, but also into normal operation. This approach can be declared just by ISO 14001 certification, which has been treated and released to support the environment and prevention of its pollution. The benefits from the acquisition of the requirements of ISO 14001, despite the high costs that are associated with implementing this standard, allow the reduction of operating expenses, keeping track of the positive and negative aspects of business on the environment and know how to (in case of negative effects) minimize the such situation. For additional benefits, particularly in relation to raising awareness of the positive activities related to the environment, can be also regarded the reinforcement of good public relations and increased business confidence.

Nowadays, due to continuity of increase and aggressiveness of competition and constantly increasing demands of interested parties - stakeholders, in particular in the system of environmental protection, the certification according to ISO 14001, sooner or later it will be a necessity in almost every large enterprise in all sectors. This fact is evidenced by the fact that enterprises in the European Union with over 500 employees are required to publish reports on what they are doing in the field of sustainable development and Corporate Social Responsibility (CSR).

In conclusion we can say that Volkswagen with its activities in the field of environmental management contributes to a policy of sustainable production of their products, which have a direct impact on reducing pollution, saving energy and natural resources which are economically stable and safe both for the company and for VW consumers. We consider this as a major benefit for VW and also for strategic objectives of Slovak Republic which already since 1990 reduced total emissions by 41 % and with continuation of this trend (based on data from Eurostat) reached in 2014 the best results among all EU member states [18]. The above is documenting the fact that after completing the necessary 14 internal and one external audit of the VW company in 2011, the audit has an internal target of 97 % and was satisfied with the result of 98.22 %.

References

1. Boatright, J.R.: Ethics and the Conduct of Business.6.vyd. New Jersey, Pearson, 463s. (2009)
2. Kuldova, L.: Společenská odpovědnost firem: etické podnikání a sociální odpovědnost v praxi. OPS, Plzeň (2010)

3. Kunz, V.: Společenská odpovědnost firem. Grada, Praha (2012)
4. Carroll, A.B., Buchholty, A.K.: Business and Society: Ethics and Stakeholder Management. South-Western Cengage Learning, Ohio (2008)
5. Gasparikova, V.: Corporate social responsibility. Dissertation thesis. Slovak University of Technology in Bratislava, Slovakia (2014)
6. The ISO Survey of Management System Standard Certifications (1999–2013)
7. Veber, J.: Environmentální management. Praha: Oeconomica, 94 s. (2002)
8. Remtova, K.: Planeta – odborný časopis pro životní prostředí. Dobrovolné environmentální aktivity – orientální příručka pro podniky (2006)
9. Madlova, L.: Nový pohled na společenskou odpovědnost firem: strategická CSR. Nava, Plzeň (2012)
10. Kovacova, L.: Integration Management Tools – Lean Manufacturing and sustainability. In: The 16th International Scientific Conference Trends and Innovative Approaches in Business Processes, Slovakia (2013)
11. National Council for Advanced Manufacturing, http://www.nacfam.org/
12. Langewalter, G. Life is Our Ultimate Customer: From Lean to Sustainability, http://www.zerowaste.org/
13. Adamuščin, A., Morena, M., Truppi, T.: The importance of sustainable construction of office buildings and its development in Italy and in the Visegrad countries (Mainlyin Slovakia). Swiat Nieruchomošci. World of real estate Journal. Vol. 90, No. 4 51–57 (2014)
14. Správa o životnom prostredí 2013. Volkswagen Slovakia (2013)
15. Bureau Veritas Czech Republic, http://www.bureauveritas.cz/
16. Česká technická norma. Systémy environmentálního managementu – Požadavky s návodem pro použití. ČSN EN ISO 14001
17. International Organization for Standartization, http://www.iso.org
18. Golej, J., Pánik, M.: Social issues of housing and its environmental-economic aspects in Slovak Republic. In: SGEM 2014. Energy and Clean Technology : Conference Proceedings of the 14th International Multidisciplinary Scientific GeoConferences SGEM. Albena, Bulgaria, 357–377 (2014)

Improving Urban Noise Monitoring Opportunities via Mobile Crowd-Sensing

Marco Zappatore[1,2(✉)], Antonella Longo[1,2], Mario A. Bochicchio[1],
Daniele Zappatore[1], Alessandro A. Morrone[1], and Gianluca De Mitri[1]

[1] Department of Innovation Engineering, University of Salento,
via Monteroni sn, 73100 Lecce, Italy
{marcosalvatore.zappatore,antonella.longo,
mario.bochicchio}@unisalento.it
[2] Alba Project S.R.L., via Don Luigi Sturzo 36, 73100 Lecce, Italy
{marco.zappatore,antonella.longo}@albaproject.it

Abstract. In the recent years, mobile devices pervasivity has boosted the diffusion of a novel sensing paradigm known as Mobile Crowd Sensing (MCS). In this paper, we propose a MCS-based system exploiting FIWARE middleware platform and allowing users to gather noise measurements (both opportunistically and participatory) in order to perform large-scale, low-cost and sufficiently accurate urban noise monitoring campaigns. Collected measurements are then aggregated, filtered and interpolated in order to provide city managers with an overview of the actual noise pollution levels in their cities. Specific noise abatement measures are suggested to city managers (in terms of both estimated noise reduction and average installation costs). The already performed field tests demonstrated the feasibility of the proposed approach.

Keywords: Mobile Crowd Sensing · Urban noise monitoring · Urban traffic noise abatement measures · Data Warehouse · FIWARE

1 Introduction

In the last decade, wireless communications have shown an unrivalled growth, in both networks and devices, thanks to a series of key technological enablers [1]. Smartphones and tablets are quickly replacing PDAs and laptops as they can offer an unprecedented combination of computational power and embedded sensors (e.g., 3D accelerometers, hygrometers, gyroscopes, magnetometers, etc.). Moreover, novel broadband 4G wireless standards promise up to 1 GB/s transfer speed and high-quality coverage.

The more the users familiarize with mobiles in their everyday activities, the higher grows the possibility to leverage them effectively in order to improve life quality conditions. As described by the Mobile Crowd Sensing (MCS) paradigm [2], mobiles along with their embedded sensors represent very powerful sensing nodes that overcome the limitations of Wireless Sensor Networks (WSNs), since they provide wider coverage areas, greater number of deployable nodes (without requiring any network reconfiguration procedure when new nodes have to be added), more reliable communication and connectivity. Therefore, mobiles can be dynamically scattered across huge

© ICST Institute for Computer Sciences, Social Informatics and Telecommunications Engineering 2016
A. Leon-Garcia et al. (Eds.): Smart City 2015, LNICST 166, pp. 885–897, 2016.
DOI: 10.1007/978-3-319-33681-7_79

areas with heterogeneous sensing purposes and they can acquire contextual awareness opportunistically from the surrounding environment [3]. Similarly, they may improve users' knowledge about specific scientific phenomena and research challenges by engaging them in collaborative, large-scale monitoring experiences that widen the scope of traditional monitoring campaigns [4].

MCS can be applied profitably also in urban scenarios, where citizens can provide information about specific situations occurring around them thanks to their mobiles. Firstly, MCS allows defining innovative services capable of managing contextual information and interacting with user's social and physical situations. Secondly, it makes possible to harvest large and heterogeneous amounts of information from citizens, regarding their continuously evolving urban environments, thus representing a very promising way for city managers to acquire a better awareness of their municipalities without relevant additional costs.

In this research activity, we opted for the urban noise-monitoring scenario, which is gaining relevance in modern cities: several reports from the European Commission address public concerns about how noise can affect the quality of life and encourage local administrators to cope with urban monitoring and planning accordingly.

We propose a system with the following features: (1) users' direct involvement in sensing activities; (2) suggestion of noise abatement interventions to city managers; (3) inclusion of educational aspects; (4) users' opinion collection in order to obtain psychoacoustic measurements (i.e., how sound is perceived by humans [5]). These elements contribute to improve the overall quality of currently available MCS solutions in the noise-monitoring domain (see Sect. 3), which are typically tailored to single user's needs and do not provide any kind of valuable suggestions to city managers.

We designed, developed and tested (in a city from Southern Italy) a prototype of our system that gathers data from mobiles and sends them to a context broker application, which forwards them to a Hadoop-based server farm. These functionalities have been achieved by merging a set of components from the FIWARE middleware [6] to our ad-hoc developed platform. Then, a complete ETL (Extract-Transform-Load) pipeline elaborates and manages collected measurements in a Data Warehouse (DWH) system, for aggregating them w.r.t. sensing location, device type, timestamp, etc. Only freeware and open-source IT solutions have been used to promote knowledge sharing and reuse.

The proposed system is capable of behaving as: (1) a sensing platform; (2) a noise-abatement suggestion system for city authorities; (3) a learning platform for single users (e.g., citizens, students, etc.); (4) a preliminary, low-cost, large-scale and sufficiently accurate monitoring tool suitable to locate areas with potential noise pollution risks where more accurate measurement campaigns can be performed.

The paper is organized as in the following: Sect. 2 describes the actual scenario in terms of noise pollution concerns and Italian noise monitoring regulations. Mobile device pervasivity, MCS paradigm and its application in urban contexts are presented in Sect. 3. The proposed system is detailed in Sect. 4. Section 5 presents the actual outcomes of our research. Section 6 describes conclusions and further developments.

2   Urban Noise: Public Concerns, Health Effects and Regulations

Historically, noise pollution has not been considered similar to other urban pollutants (e.g., chemical or radiological) and still a low number of cities consider noise-related health risks in their policies despite several technical reports by the EU Commission ascertained citizens' concerns about noise pollution issues. According to the 2013 urban mobility report [7], 72 % of Europeans believes that noise represents the fifth most significant problem within cities. This concern reaches even higher values in Italy (83 %), Bulgaria (85 %), Greece (87 %) and Malta (92 %).

As for the Italian situation: only 0.98 % of the cities carried out noise monitoring campaigns in 2013, mainly required directly by citizens (91 %). In 63.2 % of the cases, at least one regulatory threshold was trespassed [8]. In 2014, 52 % of the noise emission controls performed in administrative centers exceeded thresholds, mainly due to high vehicular traffic volumes [9]. Moreover, only 63 % of the Italian administrative centers already complies with acoustic classification plans, as requested by national laws [10].

The necessity of proper noise monitoring activities is enforced also by the outcomes of several scientific research works thoroughly analyzing possible correlations between health effects and noise [11]. The outcomes of a primary exposure to a constant environmental noise source can be classified into acute effects, chronic effects and long term risks [12] but exposure levels vary depending on multiple causes and on individual basis (i.e., some subjects are more noise-sensitive than other ones). Amongst the acute effects, we can enlist: decrease sleep quality and fragmentation; stress and distraction; noise-induced hearing loss (NIHL). Especially in urban scenarios, *noise annoyance* [13] is experienced. It stands for a series of socio-behavioral changes and overall discontent in citizens residing in noisy areas that may determine additional effects (e.g., increased drug consumption, increased number of accidents). Chronic effects entail hypertension, reduced learning and productivity, disruption of endocrine system and diabetes [14]. The long-term risks concern possible heart disease due to cardiovascular system and permanent NIHL [15].

Noise emissions also heavily affect specific categories of subjects or people exhibiting additional health risks: for instance, children living in noisy contexts or attending schools located in dense urban areas show poor performances, stress, decreased learning rates, misbehavior, concentration deficits and scarce reading comprehension [16]. However, despite the documented correlations between health effects and noise, local authorities do not yet implement stable noise monitoring policies due to several factors, such as high equipment costs, scarcity of skilled personnel and lack of environmental awareness, thus determining an overall relevant requests of novel and proper monitoring solutions to tackle these issues.

In order to assess quantitatively and qualitatively the noise exposure, proper measurement scales are needed. One of the widely adopted scale is the A-weighting: it measures the Sound Pressure Level (*SPL*) in units of *dB(A)* [17] and allows measuring the dependence of perceived loudness w.r.t. frequency. Since sounds are typically fluctuating (i.e., they vary in time and have different durations) and since *SPL* is an instantaneous measurement instead, the Equivalent Sound Level $L_{EQ(T)}$ is preferred [17] as the reference exposure descriptor in noise regulations and guidelines. It measures, in $dB(A)$, the steady sound level conveying the same sound energy of the actual time-varying noise source in a given place during a given time window T (where T typically ranges from 30 s to 24 h). In a more simplified explanation, $L_{EQ(T)}$ averages the *SPL* values measured during T, thus smoothing spikes and outliers.

Italian noise regulations [18] classify urban areas into six *acoustic classes* depending on their main usage and building typologies. As reported in Table 1, different threshold $L_{EQ(T)}$ values are provided for each of those classes. In addition, these thresholds are also expressed w.r.t. [10, 19]: time of the day (*diurnal*: 6a.m.–10p.m.; *nocturnal*: 10p.m–6 a.m.); sensor position (*insertion values*: if near the source; *emission values*: if far from the source); road type (w.r.t. vehicle capacity and speed) and age (novel or already existing roads). The Italian laws adopt a precautionary approach, so that the law thresholds that cannot be trespassed (i.e., *limit values*) are always below the noise emission values representing a lower risk or a potential risk for human health (i.e., *quality values* and *attention values*, respectively).

Table 1. $L_{EQ(T)}$ threshold values [10, 18]. Law limits are grayed out. Reference values (15 m from the source): heavy truck 90 dB(A); congested road 80 dB(A); light car traffic 60 dB(A).

Acoustic Class	Limit [dB(A)]		Quality [dB(A)]		Attention [dB(A)]	
	day	night	day	night	day	night
C1. Protected (schools, hospitals)	45	35	47	37	50	40
C2. Residential	50	40	52	42	55	45
C3. Mixed (SOHO, suburban)	55	45	57	47	60	50
C4. Intense human activities	60	50	62	52	65	55
C5. Mainly industrial	65	55	67	57	70	60
C6. Exclusively industrial	65	55	70	70	70	70

3 Mobile Crowd Sensing (MCS) and Its Applications

The most recent analyses for the mobile market forecast that by the end of 2015 mobile cellular subscriptions will reach [20] a worldwide penetration rate of 97 % and 127 % in Western Europe (WE). In Q1 2015, mobile broadband subscriptions reached 535mn in WE only. By the end of the same year, the mobile broadband technology will represent the most dynamic market segment, with a penetration rate of 47 % and an overall network coverage of 69 % of the world population (89 % if we consider the urban population only). The prospected trend for year 2020 is even more evident: worldwide mobile subscriptions will amount 9.2 bn (6.1 bn for smartphones) [20] from the actual 7.1 bn (2.6 bn for smartphones). The increase for WE will amount 140 mn, although the 80 % of new subscriptions will come from Asia Pacific, the Middle East and Africa. As for the mobile traffic growth forecasts, the worldwide monthly data traffic per smartphone amounts 1.05 TB/month for Q1 2015 and it is expected to reach 4.9 TB/month in 2020, with a Compound Annual Growth Rate (CAGR) of 30 % [20].

From a socio-demographic point of view, 90 % of world population over 6 years of age will have a mobile phone by the end of 2020 [20]. In Italy, 59 % of users in the age 16–24 uses smartphones. This percentage increases up to 72 % for individuals ageing 25–34 and 70 % for subjects in the age 35–44 [21].

This success is due to many reasons, such as high data rates, reliable coverage, high Quality of Service, extreme portability, data plans and monthly bills less expensive than fixed-broadband plans. The highest smartphone penetration rates come from youngsters in urban scenarios, since they are the typical early adopters of new technological solutions and they are inclined to use their smartphones to perform many heterogeneous activities (e.g., social networking, audio/video streaming, online shopping, location-based services). Therefore, our application will benefit significantly from its diffusion across youngsters as primary data collectors.

Mobile pervasivity started to be leveraged more than one decade ago, when Burke et al. [22] proposed the notion of *participatory sensing* (PS) to describe how individuals provided with devices capable of collecting and analysing data may become "data source points" without the need of deploying ad-hoc sensor nodes around him and may share local knowledge on a broader scale. The first applications were aimed only at user's self-monitoring in the healthcare sector but they rapidly broadened their scope so that the original definition of PS has been replaced by the Mobile Crowd Sensing (MCS) [2] paradigm, which allows collecting data directly from mobiles more effectively than traditional WSNs. In MCS, users can choose when monitoring an event (*participatory sensing*) or delegate their mobiles to send data automatically (*opportunistic sensing*). *Community monitoring* represents another increasing trend, aiming at involving larger and larger number of participants in sensing campaigns.

These aspects are particularly evident in urban monitoring scenarios, where four main application areas can be considered: (1) mobility-related issues (e.g., traffic monitoring, parking availabilities, road safety control [2]); (2) environmental monitoring (e.g., air [23] and water pollutants [24] control); (3) emergency management (e.g., flood alerting systems [25], earthquake immediate sensing [26]); (4) large-scale events monitoring and planning (e.g., follow groups of people attending festivals [27]).

As for noise monitoring, the majority of MCS applications are for personal use only: they reproduce the main functionalities of Sound Level Meters (SLMs) and allow users to check how loud their surrounding environment is (e.g., Advanced Decibel Meter[1], Sound Meter Pro[2]). However, they do not provide measurement aggregation on a geographical/temporal basis. Very few research works address urban noise mapping, such as the "Ear-Phone" project [28] where smartphones were used to predict outdoor sound levels, "NoiseSPY" [29], which exploited mobiles carried by bicycle couriers to collect noise data in Cambridge, or the "2Loud?" project [30] that uses iPhones to assess nocturnal noise within buildings near highways in Australia. One of their main limitations, however, is that users are only involved as data collectors but no specific platform functionalities are tailored to city managers for improving urban life quality.

---

[1] https://itunes.apple.com/us/app/advanced-decibel-meter/id595718101?mt=8.

[2] https://play.google.com/store/apps/details?id=com.soundmeter.app&hl=it.

4   The Proposed System

The proposed system addresses multiple categories of users: on the one hand, city managers will be provided with a Web application suggesting how to reduce noise levels and where regulatory thresholds are exceeded. On the other hand, mobile users will be allowed not only to collect measurements but also to learn about noise metering and acoustic principles directly on their devices. Our approach also allows overcoming the drawbacks of traditional noise monitoring techniques, which are more accurate but much more expensive. By embedding users' comments, we also can integrate noise socio-acoustic surveys [31] to analyze the noise annoyance.

We followed a Data Warehouse (DWH) approach [32], according to which data are processed in an Extract-Transform-Load (ETL) pipeline: measurements are collected from sensors and then they are cleansed, transformed and stored in order to make them available for final users. Sensor data are suitable to be managed in a multidimensional model: in order to make data management effective, we propose the Dimensional Fact Model (DFM) [32] depicted in Fig. 1A, which also allows us to introduce the corresponding notation. The DFM is a conceptual model whose graphical expressivity and clarity allow representing concepts in a straightforward way, thus easing the comprehension of the multidimensional analyses that can be performed on data. The core element in a DFM is called a *fact* (the rounded box in Fig. 1A): it represents any concept relevant to decision-making processes and which evolves in time; our fact is represented by the noise measurements. Facts are described qualitatively by *fact attributes* and quantitatively by *measures* (i.e., numerical properties or calculations, enlisted in the bottom part of the fact in Fig. 1A). Our measures refer to both *SPL* and maximum/minimum/average $L_{EQ(T)}$. Each analysis coordinate of a fact is called a *dimension* and it consists of several *dimensional attributes* organized as a directed tree departing from the fact (the attributes are the circles connected by lines to the fact in Fig. 1A; the dimension is the root circle). Dimensional attributes qualify the finite domain of their dimension along with its different degrees of granularity (e.g., the temporal dimension can vary from seconds to days, weeks, months; a product is described by its name, series, brand, etc.). In our DFM, the following dimensions have been considered: time (both timestamp and date/month/year); geographical position (latitude, longitude, town, province, region and country); sensor type (external or embedded); device type (model and brand); measurement type; outlier condition. The dimension representing user's annotations refers to the noise source (uniqueness, type, location, annoyance, nuisance and distance from the observer) and it is optional.

As for the platform architecture, we propose an Android-based application to collect noise measurements via mobile-embedded microphones; it mimics a professional SLM and allows users to access a noise regulation repository. The mobile app collects peak, average and current values of *SPL* and $L_{EQ(T)}$ on customizable temporal windows, as required by EU and Italian noise regulations. Measurements are stored locally (short-term history) and sent to the applications hosted on a server farm for data aggregation (both in time and in space) and filtering. The data brokering functionality is achieved by using Orion[3], a Generic Enabler (GE) from FIWARE middleware [6] that offers publishing/subscribing operations on collected data. Another FIWARE GE, namely Cosmos[4], offers HDFS-based persistent storage capabilities in this first system prototype (but alternative implementation strategies are under evaluation). Additional tasks are performed on server side: correlation between annotated and opportunistic measurements or between measurements and vehicular traffic flows.

The logical architecture of the proposed platform has a three-layer structure (Fig. 1B): starting from the bottom, the first layer (data layer) consists of a non-persistent storage solution for mobile-hosted sensor data, the persistent HDFS-based component to host the complete measurement history (implemented via Apache Hive) and a persistent relational DB for noise regulations and guidelines. The second layer has context-brokering capabilities (for managing multiple sensors) as well as data integration, filtering and reporting functionalities (thanks to Pentaho CE[5], a freeware ETL application). The third layer (data presentation) offers a Web app for accessing data reporting and integration results. Mobile devices and a limited number of fixed noise monitoring stations represent data sources. We also developed a Web application for data visualization purposes, specifically tailored to city managers.

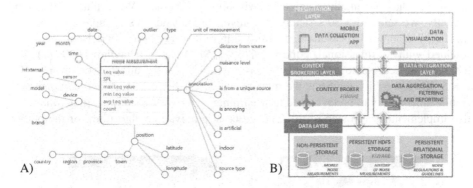

Fig. 1. DFM representation (on the left) and platform logical architecture (on the right).

5 Research Outcomes

The platform has been preliminary tested at our University campus. Subsequently, five students from our faculty performed a field test in a central area of the city of Lecce (Southern Italy). They collected nearly 80 measurements in a 1-h time window by moving across high-traffic hotspots (next to two roundabouts and alongside some 4-lane roads). We will now examine the mobile app at first and then the web app.

---

[3] Orion: http://catalogue.fiware.org/enablers/publishsubscribe-context-broker-orion-context-broker.

[4] Cosmos: http://catalogue.fiware.org/enablers/bigdata-analysis-cosmos.

[5] Pentaho Community Edition: http://community.pentaho.com/projects/data-integration/.

The user interface (UI) of the ad-hoc developed mobile app mimics a professional SLM, thus offering also to unskilled users a way for learning how to manage such kind of equipment as well as to understand which physical quantities are involved in noise monitoring campaigns. Figure 2A depicts the app page for the participatory measurements. Both $L_{EQ(T)}$ and *SPL* values are reported and plotted on a XY graph (users can switch between time and frequency analysis mode by switching on the radio-button placed below the graph area), as well as the selected observation time period *T*. Once the measurement ends, users can choose amongst: (1) starting a new measurement by discarding the current one (round orange button, bottom right corner); (2) sending the measurement (right green button, page bottom); (3) commenting and then sending the measurement (left green button, page bottom).

Figure 2B represents the app page where users can assess noise sources, in terms of: location (indoor/outdoor), nature (artificial/natural), annoyance, estimated distance from the observer, uniqueness, typology (by selecting amongst a set of predefined values such as truck engine, car traffic, construction site, crowd, machinery, etc.). It is also possible to quantify perceived nuisance levels, by activating a slider representing a psychometric 10-value scale [31], and to add free-text comments. The bottom right button allows users to take pictures of the area where noise measurements come from.

Mobiles embed normal directional microphones instead of professional metering equipment, thus potentially hindering measurement accuracy. We evaluated it instrumentally: we selected a 30 s steady, mid-level, broadband noise source and then we repeatedly compared measurements from different smartphone models against data obtained with a professional, portable, Class-1 SLM (i.e., DeltaOhm HD9019). We achieved an acceptable accuracy: data from mobiles were affected on average by a ± 5 dB bias, which confirms the most recent research works [33] and demonstrates mobile amenability to be leveraged as preliminary monitoring stations. In addition, we also implemented, as a step of the ETL process, a univariate algorithm for the outlier

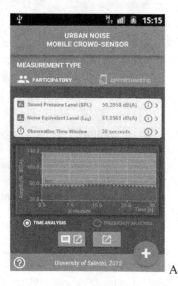 

Fig. 2. Mobile UI: participatory measurements (on the left) and users' comments (on the right).

detection in order to remove measurements having an excessive sound level amplitude in a given temporal window. We opted for a slightly modified version of the Tukey's method [34], which is simple and quite effective with datasets having a not highly skewed lognormal distribution as the ones we achieved during the tests.

We also developed a Web application for city managers: it allows to georeference and visualize measurements coming from a given area as points in a *post map* (i.e., a discrete map where the colour ramp used to represent the measurement location points is directly proportional to the measured $L_{EQ(T)}$ values). Another view (Fig. 3) provides users with the interpolation of measurements achieved in the same area as an *intensity map* (i.e., a surface map where adjacent measurements are interpolated according to a given algorithm in order to compute $L_{EQ(T)}$ values also for those points where no measurements were actually performed). Intensity maps are extremely useful for understanding how noise levels are perceived throughout the urban environment without requiring to scatter all across the city mobile sensors. The rendering of both the maps described so far has been achieved by forwarding measurement data, after the ETL process, towards a CartoDB [35] instance, an open-source, cloud-hosted, geospatial database for map storage and visualization.

In addition, the intensity map offers the possibility to dynamically explore how noise level abatement interventions may impact on actual interpolated $L_{EQ(T)}$ measurements: by selecting from proper dropdown lists a given noise abatement measure, users can see how interpolated values could be reduced accordingly on that area. At this moment, we considered measures addressing traffic noise emissions (since they represent the most relevant cause of urban noise pollution). The system suggests, for each different abatement measures, the corresponding estimated impact on $L_{EQ(T)}$ and estimated average costs, as specified in Table 2. Further combinations and more configuration parameters are also possible for such noise abatement measures: they are actually under investigation in order to be implemented in the next prototype of our platform.

Fig. 3. Web app: intensity map of interpolated L_{EQ} with suggested noise abatement measures (on the right). The interpolation refers to measurements collected within a 1-h time window.

City administrators can revolve to two different categories of interventions for traffic noise abatement: measures pertaining to the noise sources (vehicles, roads, traffic) and measures relating to the noise exposure. As for the first category, since municipalities cannot intervene on specifications of vehicles or tyres, we focused on traffic speed/volumes and road pavement techniques. Low-noise asphalts (e.g., thin-layer, double-layer, porous) are low-cost and significantly effective options for reducing traffic noise [36]. Moreover, they can be applied directly in noise hot spots without requiring any relevant environmental or architectonic modification. Similarly, speed limit enforcements, especially in the range 40-70 km/h, and traffic flow restriction measures are particularly useful, not only in terms of noise reduction but also for air quality and road safety [37]. Typically, such solutions have even lower costs for cities than low-noise asphalts but they may have collateral social costs due to travel time losses. Other possible interventions are vertical (e.g., speed bumps/humps, rumble strips) and horizontal (e.g., roundabouts) traffic calming measures [38]: however, administrators must evaluate their application w.r.t. the specific case since each speed reduction artefact may generate additional noise (e.g., once a vehicle reaches a road hump). Noise barriers are the most suitable solution for reducing noise exposure [39] but their average costs are quite relevant (nearly 300 €/m^2 instead of 20 €/m^2 for low-noise asphalts) and their environmental and visual impact is significant.

Conclusively, as reference values, we recall how a $\pm$ 2 dB(A) variation is barely noticeable by humans, a $\pm$ 3 dB(A) variation is perceptible, a $\pm$ 6 dB(A) is clearly perceived, a $\pm$ 10 dB(A) is perceived as the doubling/halving of the loudness of a sound.

In addition, we also considered privacy issues, in order to reduce concerns from mobile users about their potential tracking or identification. Indeed, any information or metadata capable of identifying the device owner is discarded and users are notified about this when they start the app for the first time. Mobile devices are only indexed thanks to their IMEI (International Mobile Equipment Identity) code, which do not allow going back to respective owners (therefore, mobiles are traceable but their owners are unknown to both platform managers and other application end users).

Table 2. Urban traffic noise abatement measures: expected impact on $L_{EQ(T)}$ and estimated costs (for vehicle speed/flow reduction measures the installation costs per traffic sign are reported).

Urban traffic noise abatement measure	Expected average impact on L_{EQ}	Estimated average cost
Low-noise road pavement installation [36]		
Two-layer porous asphalt	−5/6 dB(A)	29 €/m^2
Thin-layer asphalt	−2/3 dB(A)	22 €/m^2
Porous asphalt	−2/−4 dB(A)	23 €/m^2
Stone mastic asphalt	0/−3 dB(A)	12 €/m^2
Dense asphalt concrete (ref. value)	0 dB(A)	17 €/m^2

(*Continued*)

Table 2. (*Continued*)

Urban traffic noise abatement measure	Expected average impact on L_{EQ}	Estimated average cost
Speed reduction (mixed traffic, normal asphalt) [37]		
From 40 to 30 km/h	−0.3 dB(A)	0.2–20 k€/sign
From 50 to 40 km/h	−1.4 dB(A)	"
From 60 to 50 km/h	−2.1 dB(A)	"
From 70 to 60 km/h	−1.8 dB(A)	"
Mixed traffic flow reduction (normal asphalt) [37]		
10 %	−0.5 dB(A)	"
30 %	−1.6 dB(A)	"
50 %	−3.0 dB(A)	"
75 %	−3.4 dB(A)	"
Traffic calming measures [38]		
Definition of a 30 km/h zone	up to −2 dB(A)	0.2–20 k€/sign
Installation of a roundabout	up to −4 dB(A)	150–350 k€
Night time restriction on heavy vehicles	up to −7 dB(A)	0.2–20 k€/sign
Installation of round-top humps	up to −2 dB(A)	500 €/m²
Installation of flat-top humps	up to +6 dB(A)	500 €/m²
Installation of round speed bumps	up to +2 dB(A)	200 €/m
Installation of multiple sets of rumble strips	up to +6 dB(A)	500 €/set
Interventions on noise exposure [39]		
Noise barrier (depending on height, design, material)	up to −10 dB(A)	200–400 €/m²

6   Conclusions and Further Developments

The Mobile Crowd Sensing (MCS) paradigm can find numerous applications in urban planning, as users can explore systematically their habits or specific events within their cities for achieving more sustainable practices and ways of life. In this paper, a MCS-based platform for gathering noise measurements by using mobile-embedded microphones has been proposed. The platform consists of a mobile app allowing users to perform opportunistic/participatory measurements, a data warehouse system for managing data (storage, aggregation and filtering) and a web app providing city managers with multiple views about collected data. The web app also suggests possible noise abatement measures to city managers. The system has been preliminary tested in a central area of the city of Lecce and it assessed urban noise levels effectively; its deployment in a second city with multiple noise sources (airport, commercial/touristic harbour, railway, highway) is under way. Further improvements are actually under development: evaluating model scalability, introducing new monitoring scenarios (railways, airports), combining multiple noise abatement measures and introducing new setup parameters (city areas, noise barrier materials/shapes).

Acknowledgement. This research activity is part of the EU funded project SP4UM (Grant agreement n. 632853, sub-grant agreement n. 021), within the "frontierCities" FIWARE accelerator.

References

1. Goldsmith, A.: Wireless Communications. Cambridge University Press, Cambridge (2005)
2. Ganti, R.K.: Mobile crowdsensing: current state and future challenges. IEEE Commun. Mag. **49**(11), 32–39 (2011)
3. Heggen, S.: Integrating participatory sensing and informal science education. In: 2012 ACM Conference on Ubiquitous Computing (UbiComp 2012), pp. 552–555 (2012)
4. Guo, B., Yu, Z., Zhou, X., Zhang, D.: From participatory sensing to mobile crowd sensing. In: 2nd IEEE International Workshop on Social and Community Intelligence, pp. 593–598 (2014)
5. Fastl, H.: Psycho-acoustics and sound quality. In: Blauert, J. (ed.) Communication Acoustics, pp. 139–162. Springer, Berlin Heidelberg, Berlin (2005)
6. FIWARE Architecture. https://forge.fiware.org/plugins/mediawiki/wiki/fiware/index.php/FIWARE_Architecture
7. TNS: Attitudes of Europeans towards urban mobility. Wave EB79.4, EC (2013)
8. ISTAT: Qualità dell'Ambiente Urbano (in Italian). Statistical Report, Rome, Italy (2013)
9. ISPRA: X Rapporto Aree Urbane, Ed. 2014 (in Italian), Rome, Italy (2014)
10. LQ 26.10.1995/447 - Legge Quadro sull'Inquinamento Acustico (in Italian) (1995)
11. Goines, L., Hagler, L.: Noise pollution: a modern plague. South Med. J. **100**, 287–294 (2007)
12. Passchier, W., Passchier, W.F.: Noise exposure and public health. Environ. Health Perspect. **108**, 123–131 (2000)
13. WHO - World Health Organization: Methodological Guidance for Estimating the Burden of Disease from Environmental Noise. Report (2012)
14. Soerensen, M., et al.: Long-term exposure to road traffic noise and incident diabetes: a cohort study. Environ. Health Perspect. **121**, 217 (2013)
15. Lewis, R.C., Gershon, R.R., Neitzel, R.L.: Estimation of permanent noise-induced hearing loss in an Urban setting. Environ. Sci. Technol. **47**, 6393–6399 (2013)
16. Stansfeld, S.A., et al.: Aircraft and road traffic noise and children's cognition and health: a cross-national study. Lancet **365**, 1942–1949 (2005)
17. Alton Everest, F., Pohlmann, K.C.: Master Handbook of Acoustics 5th edn. (2009)
18. DPCM 14/11/97 - Determinaz. dei Valori Limite delle Sorgenti Sonore (in Italian) (1997)
19. DPR 30.03.2004/142 (in Italian) (2004)
20. Ericsson: Ericsson Mobility Report. Report EAB-15:026112 Rev. A (2015)
21. Nielsen: The Mobile Consumer - A Global Snapshot. Report (2013)
22. Burke, J., et al.: Participatory sensing. In: WSW 2006, pp. 117–134 (2006)
23. Leonardi, C., et al.: SecondNose. In: NordiCHI 2014, pp. 1051–1054 (2014)
24. Minkman, E., et al.: Citizen science in water quality monitoring: mobile crowd sensing for water management in the Netherlands. In: EWRI 2015, pp. 1399–1408 (2015)

25. Degrossi, L.C., et al.: Flood citizen observatory: a crowdsourcing-based approach for flood risk management in Brazil. In: 26th International Conference on SEKE 2014, pp. 1–6 (2014)
26. Faulkner, M., et al.: Community sense and response systems: your phone as quake detector. Commun. ACM **57**(7), 66–75 (2014)
27. Stopczynski, A., et al.: Participatory bluetooth sensing. In: PERCOM 2013, pp. 242–247 (2013)
28. Rana, R.K., et al.: Ear-phone: an end-to-end participatory urban noise mapping system. In: 9th ACM/IEEE IPSN 2010, pp. 105–116 (2010)
29. Kanjo, E.: NoiseSPY: a real-time mobile phone platform for urban noise monitoring and mapping. Mob. Netw. Appl. **15**(4), 562–574 (2010)
30. Leao, S., Ong, K.L., Krezel, A.: 2Loud?: community mapping of exposure to traffic noise with mobile phones. Envion. Monit. Assess. **186**, 6193–6206 (2014)
31. ISO - International Standards Organization: Assessment of Noise Annoyance by Means of Social and Socio-Acoustics Surveys. Standard ISO/TS 15666:2003 (2003)
32. Golfarelli, M., Rizzi, S.: Data Warehouse Design, 1st edn. McGraw-Hill, New York (2009)
33. Kardous, C.A., Shaw, P.B.: Evaluation of smartphone sound measurement application. J. Acoust. Soc. Am. **135**(4), 186–192 (2014)
34. Hoaglin, D.C., Iglewicz, B., Tukey, J.W.: Performance of some resistant rules for outlier labeling. J. Am. Stat. Assoc. **82**, 1147–1149 (1986)
35. CartoDB (2015). https://cartodb.com (accessed)
36. Alberts, W.: Traffic Noise and Motorway Pavements. Technical report. GRB-61-16, CEDR (2015)
37. Ellebjerg, L.: Noise Reduction in Urban Areas from Traffic and Driver Management - A Toolkit for City Authorities. Project Report - WP Deliv. H.D2, WP H.2, EUKN (2008)
38. Bendtsen, H., et al.: Traffic Management and Noise Reducing Pavements - Recommendations on Additional Noise Reducing Measures (SILVIA Project Report) (2005)
39. Bendtsen, H.: Noise Barrier Design: Danish and Some European Examples. Technical report UCPRC-RP-2010-04, Danish Road Institute - Road Directorate (2010)

Seniors' Life Satisfaction in Regions of the Czech Republic

Martina Rašticová[⊠], Naďa Birčiaková, Ivana Kolářová,
and Kateřina Rampulová

Faculty of Business and Economics,
Mendel University, Zemědělská 1, 61300 Brno, Czech Republic
martina.rasticova@mendelu.cz

Abstract. The main aim of this paper is to analyse the seniors' life satisfaction in 14 Czech regions with respect to the two age groups of seniors – younger (50–65 years) and older (over 65 years) and their gender. The outputs of this study detect the regions with the highest and lowest levels of seniors' satisfaction. The main source of data is the results of the investigation (EU-SILC). The analysis is based on the corresponding methodology. The results of the satisfaction measurements in regions are compared using the cluster analysis, which is a statistical method grouping the Czech Republic regions into clusters. The similarity and correlation in terms of satisfaction between the regions is shown by a dendrogram. The results presented are the first unique probe into the issue of satisfaction of seniors in respective regions of the Czech Republic.

Keywords: Life satisfaction · Seniors · Regions

1 Introduction

1.1 Demographic Developments in the European Union Compared with that of the Czech Republic

The aging of the population will be a key demographic problem in many European countries. Eurostat projections indicate that the aging population will reach an unprecedented level over the following 50 years in 31 European countries [1]. Europe is the continent with the oldest population in the world. Comparable demographic situation in the world can only be found in Japan, where the forecasts for the following 20 years are consistent with the demographic projections in Europe - declining birth rate and declining mortality will, together with a decline in illness and disability, increase longevity. A large number of European countries are even characterized by the lowest birth rate and the highest life expectancy from the global perspective [2].

Eurostat further states that EU27 population will increase (compared to 2010) from 501 million to 525 million in 2035, in 2040 up to 526 million and then it will start to decline to 517 million in 2060. The increasing proportion of the population aged 65+ from 17 % in 2010 to 30 % in 2060 and the share of the population 80+ from 5 % in 2010 to 12 % in 2060 is also expected [3]. The transformation of the mostly young society to the society controlled by older age cohorts takes place throughout the EU. It

© ICST Institute for Computer Sciences, Social Informatics and Telecommunications Engineering 2016
A. Leon-Garcia et al. (Eds.): Smart City 2015, LNICST 166, pp. 898–908, 2016.
DOI: 10.1007/978-3-319-33681-7_80

is obvious that the development along these lines will have an impact on the future social and public policies associated with the aging population and the quality of this age group everyday life. This situation will require major adjustments in many aspects of the society - from the family to the labour market [2].

Even though the society is aging, this phenomenon is not identical across borders and nations. The developed Western nations experience an enormous growth in population age and the birth rate falls. In contrast, the developing countries experience significant fertility rate. The developing countries, however, are aging much faster than the developed countries - in the next 50 years more than 80 % of seniors will live in the developing country (which is 20 % more than in 2005). Thus, the future will not be dominated by modern technologies, but by the global competition of human capital [4].

An increase of the number of inhabitants in the age group 55+ will also take place in the Czech Republic in the coming years. In 2013, this age group was represented by 3,265,972 inhabitants. Until 2023 the representation of this age group should have increased by 330 thousand. In contrast, the development of the part of population in pre-productive age can be considered as steadily evolving [5]. The number of economically dependent people will, due to unfavourable demographic trends, get almost doubled by 2050, in case of the failure to increase the employment of people aged 50+ [6].

1.2 Active Aging

Along with the aforementioned demographic situation the term active aging is increasingly alluded to. The term was defined by WHO as a process that serves to provide optimal opportunities for health, participation and security in society, in order to ensure the highest quality of life for older people. The concept of active aging enables older people to realize their potential for physical, social and mental well-being throughout their lives and to participate in society. At the same time, however, society provides them with adequate protection, security and care in case of need [7].

Life conditions in the old age cannot be separated from the previous stages of life, and health in the old age is largely influenced by the living conditions in both childhood and adulthood. It is important to pay particular attention to the situation of those seniors who were in various ways disadvantaged during their lives. Each of the steps that will be implemented in response to population aging should thus foster intergenerational solidarity and cohesion. MoLSA in its document *Preparing for aging* mentions that for the successful functioning of the concept of active aging it is essential that the people at a young age become interested in this issue, because this is a process that will accompany them during lifetime [8].

The old age represents a moment of development in which some psychological and physical losses are very likely to happen and smooth adaptation to new situation can constitute a key role in successful aging. The factors found to influence life satisfaction include age, gender, income and education levels [9].

Life satisfaction is defined as the satisfaction of psychological and social needs of the individual, while well-being rather reflects the subjective life experience. The term quality of life includes both the above terms. There is a relationship between life satisfaction and state of health, experienced life dissatisfaction thus affects the psychosomatic condition of the individual [10].

The place where one lives is one of the factors influencing life satisfaction. The satisfaction with the quality of the immediate surrounding environment is directly proportional to the level of satisfaction with opportunities for relaxation and rest. A certain influence of environment, living conditions in the city manifests itself in the health of citizens, too [11].

Life satisfaction is also affected by the size of government expenditures, hence the city/village authorities. Effective leadership and management of expenditures have a positive effect on life satisfaction, while satisfaction decreases with lower quality leadership and higher expenditures. The influence is stronger in case of left-wing leadership. Particularly low and middle-income groups, men, feel this. Government capital formation and social expenditures have no significant impact on life satisfaction of citizens [12]. The city is the place where diverse cultures meet and interact. Lifestyle is developing in the city; it is shaped by the cultural aspects, growth of consumption, and a variety of housing concepts [13].

1.3   Czech Seniors in the City and in the Village

Besides population aging there is another significant global trend, and that is the process of urbanization. The number of people living in cities is constantly increasing - more than half the world's population lived in cities in 2007. Along with the growing population in cities, there is also a rising share of people older than 60 who live in these cities. The proportion of older people living in cities in developed countries is around 80 %. In developing countries seniors will make up a quarter of the total urban population in 2050. Aging of population and urbanization are the culmination of successful development of society in the last century [14].

If the cities try to be friendly to the seniors, it is necessary to adapt the infrastructure and services so as they are easily accessible to seniors with their specific needs and abilities.

If old people live in hazardous environment or in environment with physical barriers, it may lead to the fact that they do not get out too often, which leads to isolation, depression, poor physical condition and mobility problems [15].

The process of aging is described as the process of shrinking the area – the area which the individual covers decreases, but there is an increase of contact with the immediate surroundings What is this neighbourhood made up of is becoming increasingly important for seniors, as it is this neighbourhood which determines the quality of his life [16].

According to USAID, 74 % of the total population lives in cities in the Czech Republic [17]. Approximately 74 % of seniors live in the cities in the Czech Republic. The results of their research, which concerns the life of seniors in the three largest cities in the Czech Republic show that 70 % of seniors living in these cities have a generally positive attitude towards the changes happening in their cities. It has also been shown that seniors have relatively low mobility and high bond to their home and its immediate surroundings. From a broader perspective, the life of seniors in cities is found to be positive in terms of good availability of services and shops, but on the other hand it entails specific risks [18].

Gentrification which is one of revitalization processes appears to be one of the problematic factors. City centres are becoming attractive zones which attract economic and cultural capitals into city centres (called Yuppies). Yuppies moving into the central parts of cities increase the attractiveness of these areas, and that brings increasing property prices, rents and nearby services with it, which leads to pushing the original inhabitants - among others, seniors (especially lonely ones) – away from their original homes [19].

The studies dealing with the conditions of seniors' life in different districts of Prague state that the rate of residential satisfaction of seniors is influenced by a combination of physical changes in the environment, functional structure and composition of the population with a strong bond to the place of residence and poor capacity of seniors to adapt to the changes. In these researched sites there is a significant restructuring, which entails a number of positive and negative changes in the lives of seniors. Better conditions for pedestrian movement in central and inner parts of the city and proximity of nature and green areas in housing estates are examples of positive aspects of urban restructuring on the lives of seniors. Reducing seniors' satisfaction with the availability and price levels of basic civic amenities in the city centre belong to the negative effects of restructuring. In all areas surveyed uncertainty of seniors is high in terms of neighbourly assistance because of the frequent replacement of the residents in houses [20].

It is necessary to pay more attention to seniors who live in villages. Urbanization and migration of young people seeking work from villages to cities may cause old people to remain alone in rural areas with limited access to both health and social services [15].

The rural seniors are often at a disadvantage compared with the urban seniors, especially in the view of lower income, lower education and worse access to public transport or health services [21, 22]. The rural seniors tend to be in worse mental and physical condition. Many of them would like to maintain their physical and mental condition, but they cannot find appropriate environment and mentoring for that [23].

The aim of this study is, based on available data (from a database of European Union Statistics on Income and Living Conditions - EU-SILC), to analyse the seniors' life satisfaction in 14 Czech regions with respect to the two age groups of seniors - younger (50–65 years) and older (over 65 years) and gender of seniors. This is the first study of seniors' satisfaction in the Czech regions. We assume that the outputs of this study will allow us to detect the regions with the highest and lowest levels of seniors' satisfaction and will be the basis for further in-depth analysis of life satisfaction and formulation of seniors' satisfaction factors in particular districts and regions of the Czech Republic.

2   Methodology

The main source of data is the results of the investigation (EU-SILC). The analysis will be based on the corresponding methodology and calculations will apply to the last year with available data, therefore, to 2013. 8,434 of senior citizens participated in the survey. The conversion factor for the entire population of the Czech Republic for modular data was used for further work with the data, and Pearson coefficient was applied to test the differences among individual groups of respondents.

Data analysis is focused on seniors' life satisfaction. It is expressed on the scale from 0 to 10 (0 - dissatisfaction, 10 - great satisfaction). It will reveal the total satisfaction of seniors, also with respect to gender and age.

The results of the satisfaction measurements in regions are compared using the cluster analysis, which is a statistical method grouping the Czech Republic regions into clusters. This is hierarchical clustering, which generates a system of subsets. A cluster may be defined by similarities or dissimilarities. Several different approaches exist to measuring distance or similarity. This paper uses the Euclidean distance between two vectors Y and Z:

$$\sqrt{\sum_{i=1}^{k}(y_i - z_i)^2} \tag{1}$$

Objects will be clustered by the distance or similarity using the nearest-neighbour or complete linkage method based on the equation:

$$v(S^h, S^k) = \min(v_{ij}) \\ i \in S^h, j \in S^k, \tag{2}$$

where v is a measure of similarity between clusters, S^h and S^k denoting clusters h and k at a given clustering stage.

The distance between two clusters is determined by the longest distance between two objects each being in a different cluster. The result of a cluster analysis is a dendrogram, which is a cluster diagram. A dendrogram shows, which regions are similar and correlated in terms of satisfaction [24–26]. The calculations of the analysis were done using the Statistica 12 software by Statsoft.

3   Results

In this section we present the differences in life satisfaction in 14 regions of the Czech Republic, the average for the whole country was also calculated. The first chart compares the results of life satisfaction in the whole country and in 14 regions of the Czech Republic with respect to respondents' age (Fig. 1), the respondents were divided into two categories: younger seniors (50–65) and older seniors (65 - over), axis y presents satisfaction rate (0 - dissatisfied/and 8 - satisfied). The results show that seniors, regardless of the exact age, are rather satisfied with life in the Czech Republic (the average for the entire study population of seniors is 6.4). Similar levels of satisfaction were reported even in the other regions, with the exception of regions Karlovy Vary and Pardubice, where the level of satisfaction of seniors was the lowest (Karlovy Vary 5.8, Pardubice 5.6). Conversely, the highest level of satisfaction was expressed by seniors in Liberec (6.7) and Hradec Kralove (6.9). In most regions perception of satisfaction between the two groups of respondents which were surveyed - younger and older - coincided. Larger differences between younger and older seniors were recorded in the Karlovy Vary region, the average satisfaction of younger seniors was 5.5, while the average satisfaction of older seniors reached the level of 6.1. Older seniors were also happier in the Liberec Region (6.7) compared to younger seniors (6.4). Conversely, in the Pardubice region younger seniors (5.9) feel more satisfied than older seniors (5.2). The difference between younger and older respondents was also tested. At the 5 % significance level the difference between the two groups of respondents was confirmed. Positive evaluations expressing that respondents are satisfied or rather satisfied (the range includes items 8, 9, 10) with life in the Czech Republic generally was expressed by less than 55 % of younger and 45 % of older respondents (Pearson coefficient 0.02).

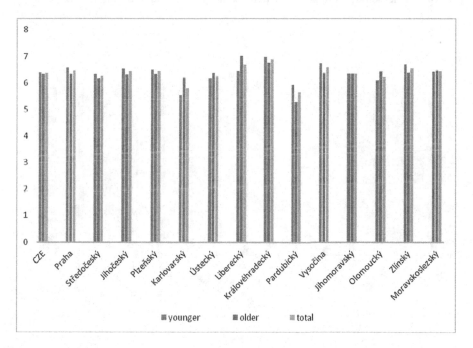

Fig. 1. Overall life satisfaction in respective regions by age (Source: authors. (Notes: translation of axis x: *Praha* – Prague, *Středočeský* – Central Bohemian Region, *Jihočeský* – South Bohemian Region, *Plzeňský* – Pilsen Region, *Karlovarský* – Karlovy Vary Region, *Ústecký* – Usti Region, *Liberecký* – Liberec Region, *Královéhradecký* – Hradec Kralove Region, *Pardubický* – Pardubice Region, *VysoNina* – Highlands Region, *Jihomoravský* – South-Moravian Region, *Olomoucký* – Olomouc Region, *Zlínský* – Zlin Region, *Moravskoslezský* – Moravian-Silesian Region)) (Color figure online)

Furthermore, the results of life satisfaction in the whole Czech Republic and in 14 regions of the Czech Republic with regard to the gender of the respondents were examined (Fig. 2), axis y again shows satisfaction rate (0 - dissatisfied/and 8 - satisfied).

The average results for the whole Czech Republic and for individual regions for all respondents are identical with the previous case (see Fig. 1). In most regions the level of satisfaction between two surveyed groups of respondents - men and women - was identical. Larger differences among seniors with regard to gender were recorded in regions South Bohemia (men - 6.3, women - 6.6), Pilsen (men - 6.2, women - 6.6) and Karlovy Vary (men - 5.6 women - 6.0), the average satisfaction was higher in women than in men in these regions. Only in Hradec Kralove region men (7.1) are happier than women (6.7).

The difference between men and women was also tested. At the 1 % significance level the difference between the two groups of respondents was confirmed. Positive evaluation expressing that respondents are satisfied or rather satisfied (the range includes items 8, 9, 10) with life in the Czech Republic generally was expressed by 55 % of female seniors and 45 % of male seniors (Pearson coefficient 0.01).

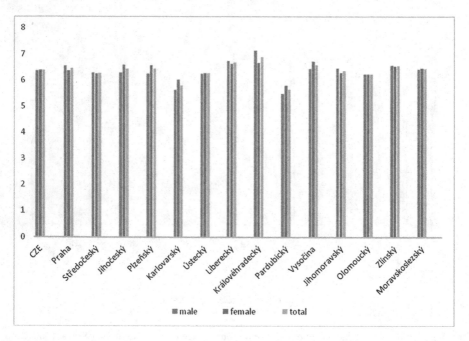

Fig. 2. Overall life satisfaction in respective regions by gender (Source: authors. (Notes: translation of axis x: *Praha* – Prague, *Středočeský* – Central Bohemian Region, *Jihočeský* – South Bohemian Region, *Plzeňský* – Pilsen Region, *Karlovarský* – Karlovy Vary Region, *Ústecký* – Usti Region, *Liberecký* – Liberec Region, *Královéhradecký* – Hradec Kralove Region, *Pardubický* – Pardubice Region, *Vysočina* – Highlands Region, *Jihomoravský* – South-Moravian Region, *Olomoucký* – Olomouc Region, *Zlínský* – Zlin Region, *Moravsko-slezský* – Moravian-Silesian Region)) (Color figure online)

In the group of seniors surveyed cluster analysis of regions was also conducted with respect to life satisfaction in the respective regions. "Cluster analysis groups objects into clusters so that objects belonging to the same cluster were close to each other (similar) and objects belonging to different clusters were distant (different)." 4 It resulted in dendrogram of regions of the Czech Republic. (see Fig. 3).

Looking at the whole chart, it is clear that two clusters are formed on the midlevel of clustering: the right part of dendrogram consists of a cluster of regions Liberec, South Bohemia, Central Bohemia, Hradec Kralove, Usti, and Prague. The central part of dendrogram consists of predominantly Moravian regions: South Moravia, Moravia-Silesia, Olomouc, Zlin, Highlands. Regions Pardubice, Karlovy Vary, and Pilsen stand aside other regions on the left part of dendrogram. With respect to the assessment of life satisfaction in respective regions, it is clear that the right part of dendrogram is formed by regions, where the level of satisfaction was generally described as being higher compared to the central and left parts of dendrogram. The Usti Region which is generally considered to be one of the poorest and economically weakest regions of the Czech Republic is worth mentioning. Cluster analysis, however, merged the Usti Region with the Hradec Kralove region, which was evaluated as a region for rather enjoyable life by all senior groups surveyed. We can therefore assume that life satisfaction in a given region is not only subject to the economic situation in

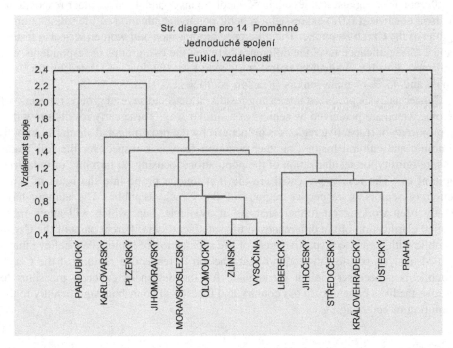

Fig. 3. Dendrogram of the Czech Republic regions based on satisfaction in the senior-citizen group (Source: authors. (Notes: translation of the title: Diagram for 14 variables, Simple link, Euclidean distances; translation of axis y: Link distance; translation of axis x: *Pardubický* – Pardubice Region, *Karlovarský* – Karlovy Vary Region, *Plzeňský* – Pilsen Region, *Jihomoravský* – South-Moravian Region, *Moravskoslezský* – Moravian-Silesian Region, *Olomoucký* – Olomouc Region, *Zlínský* – Zlin Region, *VysoNina* – Highlands Region, *Liberecký* – Liberec Region, *Jihočeský* – South Bohemian Region, *Středočeský* – Central Bohemian Region, *Královéhradecký* – Hradec Kralove Region, *Ústecký* – Usti Region, *Praha* – Prague))

the region, we can only speculate on the reasons for satisfaction. The presented results do not allow us to interpret the facts. In further research, it would be appropriate to analyse the respective factors of satisfaction in detail.

The clustering of Moravian regions and the Highlands offers numerous interpretations, the Moravian regions being close to each other in terms of economy, culture, and history with common features such as observing traditions, religiosity, with the population mostly engaged in farming (Olomouc, Moravia-Silesia Region) and viticulture (South Moravia and Zlin Region), etc.

4 Conclusion

The aim of this study was the analysis of secondary data (from a database of European Union Statistics on Income and Living Conditions - EU-SILC) dealing with the life satisfaction of seniors in 14 Czech regions with respect to two age groups of seniors - younger (50-65 years) and older (over 65 years) and their gender.

The results of the analysis of the different perception of satisfaction among seniors of different ages suggest that less than 55 % of younger and 45 % of older respondents (Pearson coefficient 0.02) expressed a general positive evaluation of life satisfaction in regions of the Czech Republic. The difference among men and women was also tested; at the 1 % significance level the difference between the two groups of respondents was confirmed. Positive evaluation expressing general satisfaction was stated by 55 % of female and 45 % of male seniors (Pearson coefficient 0.01).

Cluster analysis produced interesting results; it detected several groups (clusters) of regions, which are perceived by seniors in a similar way. These early results show that the proximity of respective regions is influenced by the proximity and similarity of both economic and cultural history, another common feature is respect for the folk traditions, religiosity, or secularization of the population, focusing on farming, or industrial tradition etc. The results presented are the first unique probe into the issue of satisfaction of seniors in respective regions of the Czech Republic. The authors have already been working on further analysis of available data, which will allow more detailed clarification of the differences in life satisfaction in different parts of the Czech Republic with regard to respective areas of life satisfaction of seniors. We believe that a detailed analysis of life satisfaction/dissatisfaction in respective regions of the Czech Republic is a necessary initial prerequisite for the design of concrete measures to improve the lives of seniors in our country and that it will contribute significantly to the promotion of active aging.

References

1. Eurostat: The greying of the babyboomers: A century-long view of ageing in European Populations. Statistics in Focus. Eurostat, Statistical Office of the European Union (2011)
2. Walker, A., Maltby, T.: Active ageing: a strategic policy solution to demographic ageing in the European Union. Int. J. Soc. Welf. 21(1), 117–130 (2012). Blackwell Publishing, Oxford

3. Eurostat: Population projections 2010–2060: EU27 population is expected to peak by around 2040. Eurostat, Statistical Office of the European Union (2011)
4. Mahon, J.F., Millar, C.: ManAGEment: the challenges of global age diversity for corporations and governments. J. Organ. Change Manag. 27(4), 553–568 (2014). Emerald Group Publishing
5. Burcin, B., Kučera, T.: Prognóza populačního vývoje České republiky na období 2008–2070. Ministry of Finance of the Czech Republic, Prague (2010)
6. Hovorková, K.: Mají zkušenosti a chuť pracovat. Ve věku 55 a víc moc šancí ale nemají. MF DNES, Prague (2012)
7. World Health Organization: What is active ageing? World Health Organization, Ageing and Life Course Family and Community Health (2015)
8. MoLSA: Příprava na stárnutí. Ministry of Labour and Social Affairs, Prague (2008)
9. Meléndez, J.C., Tomás, J.M., Oliver, A., Navarro, E.: Psychological and physical dimensions explaining life satisfaction among the elderly: a structural model examination. Arch. Gerontol. Geriatr. 48(3), 291–295 (2008). Elsevier Ireland
10. Enkvist, Å., Ekström, H., Elmståhl, S., Osborne, G., Hurling, R.: What factors affect life satisfaction (LS) among the oldest-old? The higher order factor structure of subjective and psychological well-being measures. Arch. Gerontol. Geriatr. 54(1), 140–145 (2012). Elsevier Ireland
11. Křupka, J., Kašparová, M., Jirava, P.: Modelování kvality života pomocí rozhodovacích stromů. E & M Ekonomie a Management 13(3), 130–146. ISSN: 1212-3609
12. Bjørnskov, C., Dreher, A., Fischer, J.: The bigger the better? Evidence of the effect of government size on life satisfaction around the world. Public Choice 130(3–4), 267–292 (2007). Springer Science
13. Franklin, A.: City Life, p. 256. Sage Publication, Ltd. (2010). ISBN: 9780761944768
14. World Health Organization: Global age-friendly cities: a guide. World Health Organization, Ageing and Life Course Family and Community Health (2007)
15. World Health Organization: Active ageing: Policy Framework. Second United Nations World Assembly on Ageing, Madrid (2002)
16. Nair, K.: The physically ageing body and the use of space. In: Andrews, G.J., Phillips, D.R. (eds.) Ageing and Place: Perspectives, Policy, Practice, pp. 110–117. Routledge, New York (2005)
17. USAID: World Population Data Sheet. Population Reference Bureau (2013)
18. Kafková, M.P., Galčanová, L.: Stárnutí městských populací a senioři. Demografie 2, 181–194 (2012). Masaryk University, Brno
19. Sýkora, L.: Gentrifikace: měnící se tvář vnitřních měst. In: Teoretické přístupy a vybrané problémy v současné geografii, pp. 100–119. Department of Social Geography and Regional Development FoS Charles University in Prague, Prague (1993)
20. Temelová, J., Dvořáková, N., Slezáková, A.: Rezidenční spokojenost seniorů v proměňujících se čtvrtích Prahy. Sociální Studia 3, 95–113 (2010). Masaryk University, Brno
21. Bascu, J.R., et al.: Healthy aging in place: supporting rural seniors' health needs. Online J. Rural Nurs. Health Care 12(2), 77–87 (2012). Binghamton University, Binghamton
22. Sylvestre, G., Christopher, G., Snyder, M.: The mobility needs and transportation issues of the aging population in rural Manitoba. Institute of Urban Studies, University of Winnipeg, Winnipeg (2006)

23. Crowther, M.R., Scogin, F.: Johnson Norton, M.: Treating the aged in rural communities: the application of cognitive-behavioural therapy for depression. J. Clin. Psychol. **66**, 502–512 (2010). Wiley Periodicals
24. Hebák, P., Hustopecký, J., Pecáková, I., Kol, A.: Vícerozměrné statistické metody. Informatorium (2005)
25. Hendl, J.: Přehled statistických metod. Portál, Praha (2012)
26. Meloun, M., Militký, J.: Kompendium statistického zpracování dat. Academia, Praha (2006)

Comparison of Historical and Physical Models to Predict Marginal Electricity in the Context of Cloud Optimization

Constant Vallée-Schmitter[1], Thomas Dandres[1], Yves Lemieux[2], and Réjean Samson[1]

[1] CIRAIG/CIRODD, Montréal, Canada
{constant.vallee-schmitter,thomas.dandres,rejean.samson}@polytmtl.ca
[2] Ericsson Canada Inc., Montréal, Canada
yves.lemieux@ericsson.com

Abstract. This paper is an abstract for a *poster* submission for the EAI International Conference on Smart Sustainable City Technologies.

Keywords: Life cycle assessment · Electricity · Data centers

1 Introduction

The ICT sector is growing really fast. To keep up with the ever-increasing need for storage and computation power, companies are building an increasing number of data centres. These data centres require a lot of energy (1.3 % of world electricity in 2010 [1]) to supply power to the servers but also to their cooling systems. This growing demand for energy is becoming an environmental issue. Indeed, the ICT sector was reported, in 2007, to emit 2 % of anthropogenic greenhouse gas emissions (GHG) [2]. For that reason, important efforts are being made to improve energy efficiency of data centres and supply them with low carbon energy.

One reason explaining the need for additional computation power is the emergence of smart technologies. This is especially the case of smart cities that are anticipated to generate a constant flow of data that need to be processed continuously. Indeed, the key component of smart cities is the ability to analyze information in order to make the best decisions for the urban environment in real time. This is now possible thanks to new technologies that enable to collect, transmit, centralize, store and process data.

One idea to reduce the environmental impacts of data centers is to have multiple data centres in different regions and use the one located in the region with the cleanest electric grid mix at anytime. While this approach requires virtual servers migrations it has a great potential for reducing GHG emissions and other environmental impacts. In recent projects, the life cycle assessment methodology has been used to produce environmental indicators for ICT systems [3, 4]. Life cycle assessment (LCA) is a tool to quantify the potential environmental impacts

A. Leon-Garcia et al. (Eds.): Smart City 2015, LNICST 166, pp. 909–910, 2016.
DOI: 10.1007/978-3-319-33681-7

of a product, a service or a policy. The strength of LCA is that it considers several environmental indicators (not just carbon or GHG emissions) and includes all the life cycle stages of projects. Thus, LCA has the ability to catch environmental impact displacement that occur when a life cycle step is improved while another one is deteriorated. However, current modeling of the electricity generation in LCA may lead to biased results. Indeed, in LCA, impacts of regional electric grid mixes are currently computed with yearly production averages. Therefore, from an LCA perspective, the impacts of 1 kWh are the same all year long. In the real world, the mix of the different technologies used to generate electricity changes all the time, depending on the demand, weather, maintenance, etc. This major difference with reality prevents LCA from correctly evaluating the impacts of a technology with a very fluctuating demand for electricity such as ICT. This is even more true when the electricity consumption of this technology is being optimized like in multi regional data centres management approaches. To overcome this issue, temporally disaggregated data of electricity generation were introduced in consequential LCA to build prediction models [4]. Based on historical data of electricity generation in multiple regions of Canada, these historical models were implemented in a Green Sustainable Telco Cloud to minimize GHG emissions by identifying in real-time where the cleanest electricity would be available.

However, these prediction models do not include physical limitations and parameters of the actual electric grids. Adding a significant power demand by turning on a data centre will require a new balance of the grid that is expected t depend on the geographical location and the amplitude of the power demand. If confirmed, the location of the data centre inside a region could also be considered as a parameter of global optimization of the data centre deployment. By producing a simplified model of the Ontario electric grid, it is possible to test if the required electricity to supply the additional power demand of a data centre in Ontario matches the prediction of the historical model previously developed. It is expected that the physical parameters such as the load capacity of lines, geographical disposition or reserve capacity will have consequences on the selection of the marginal sources of electricity that will meet the power demand of the data centre. Therefore, it is anticipated that in a few cases, the historical model might identify marginal electricity that is not available at a given time. Introducing physical constraints to the historical model will help to improve it.

References

1. Koomey, J.: Growth in Data Center Electricity use 2005 to 2010. Analytics Press, Oakland (2011)
2. The Climate Group: SMART 2020: Enabling the low carbon economy in the information age (2008)
3. Maurice, E.: Modélisation temporelle de la consommation électrique en analyse du cycle de vie, appliquée au contexte des TIC (2015)
4. Dandres, T., Farrahi Moghaddam, R., Nguyen, K., Lemieux, Y., Cheriet, M., Samson, R.: Real-time optimization of a Green Sustainable Telco Cloud network of servers using consequential life cycle assessment. SAM 8 Seminar (2014)

How to Address Behavioral Issues in the Environmental Assessment of Complex Systems: Case of a Smart Building

Julien Walzberg[1], Thomas Dandres[1], Mohamed Cheriet[2], and Réjean Samson[1]

[1] CIRAIG/CIRODD - Polytechnique Montreal, University of Montreal, Montreal, Canada
{Julien.Walzberg, Thomas.Dandres, Rejean.Samson}@polymtl.ca
[2] Synchromedia/CIRODD - École de Technologie Supérieure, University of Quebec, Montreal, Canada
Mohamed.Cheriet@etsmtl.ca

Abstract. The life cycle assessment of complex systems such as smart-buildings requires taking into considerations rebound effects caused by human behaviors. This project aims at modelling rebound effects with an agent based model using human behavior theories.

Keywords: Life cycle assessment · Human behaviors · Agent based model · Smart building

1 Introduction

Information and communication technologies (ICT) are believed to possess the potential to reduce greenhouse gases emissions (GHG). Their application to the residential sector – which is responsible for 30 % of global GHG – has aroused numbers of initiatives around the world, at smart-building, smart grid, and smart city levels. The common goal of these initiatives is to help achieving sustainability through energy consumption reduction.

One of these initiatives is the new student dormitory of Ecole de Technologie Supérieure (ETS) in Montreal. The project aims at making the dormitory "smart" by allowing household appliances and systems to be controlled automatically by a mobile cloud of machine to machine (M2M) smart objects.

2 Research Problem

Although reduction of environmental impacts was made possible thanks to virtualization of services and activities, it is stressed by several authors that those benefits might be partially offset by a phenomenon called the "rebound effect" [1]. A good example of rebound effect is teleworking: while a direct positive environmental impact

© ICST Institute for Computer Sciences, Social Informatics and Telecommunications Engineering 2016
A. Leon-Garcia et al. (Eds.): Smart City 2015, LNICST 166, pp. 911–912, 2016.
DOI: 10.1007/978-3-319-33681-7

of working from home part time is a decrease in the need to drive to the workplace, an indirect negative effect can occur if that reduction in the number of commutes is the reason why the household decides to live further from the workplace. In other words, the environmental benefits of part time teleworking may be partially offset by the increased distance between the home and the workplace.

Therefore it is argued that environmental studies of ICT should not be only focused on the technology itself, but also on its utilization. The goal of this project's research is to specifically address the issue of rebound effects on building users when evaluating the environmental impacts of ETS's smart building.

3 Methodology

The approach will use agent-based modeling of the users combined with life cycle assessment (LCA) in order to account for occupants' behaviors in the environmental assessment of the smart building. Agent Based Modelling (ABM) is a technique that has already proved useful for the LCA of complex systems such as biofuel production [2].

This project will use existing theories on consumers behaviors to identify the main variables explaining the choices of an individual regarding the utilization of ICT [3]. Once those variables are well-defined and comforted by a field study, they will be incorporated in an ABM. The model will be built in order to predict the electric consumption of the smart building mentioned above as a function of the values taken by the behavioral variables. Once the consumptions are computed, an LCA will transduce them into impacts. The model will be confronted to the real time data from the smart-building, and optimized to improve the accuracy of the prediction. Finally the ABM will be used to study different scenarios using hypothesis on the behavioral variables.

4 Outcomes

The project will both answer ICT system designers who need to know how their technology is effectively used, as well as address methodological issues currently faced by LCA practitioners regarding sustainable consumption and rebound effects. Finally the methodology developed in this project will be applied to study the expected environmental performance of a smart city.

References

1. Røpke, I., Christensen, T.H.: Energy impacts of ICT – Insights from an everyday life perspective. Telematics Inform. **29**, 348–361 (2012)
2. Davis, C., Nikolić, I., Dijkema, G.P.J.: Integration of life cycle assessment into agent-based modeling. J. Ind. Ecol. **13**, 306–325 (2009)
3. Walters, C.G.: Consumer Behavior: Theory and Practice. R. D. Irwin, Homewood (1974)

A Novel Approach to Enabling Sustainable Actions in the Context of Smart House/Smart City Verticals Using Autonomous, Cloud-Enabled Smart Agents

Reza Farrahi Moghaddam[1], Yves Lemieux[2], and Mohamed Cheriet[1]

[1] Synchromedia Lab/CIRROD, ETS, University of Quebec, Montreal
QC H3C 1K3, Canada
imriss@ieee.org
[2] Ericsson Research Canada, Montreal, QC H4P 2N2, Canada

Abstract. This poster presents a practical application of ICT agents in a use case of smart houses. The proposed solution provides a certain level of accountability from every house. Many resources that the agents may require, such as data storage or specialized analytics, is hosted on high-performance cloud-oriented data and compute centers, such as that of Green Sustainable Telco-grade Clouds (GSTCs).

Keywords: Sustainability · ICT · Smart house · Agents

1 Extended Abstract

Along the global shift from products to services and as a step further, the Information and Communication Technology (ICT) services are replacements for many 'material'-driven services. Considering the limited amount of [natural] resources and also the additional energy and water used in the manufacturing of the material-based products and services, ICT services have a great potential to serve as a 'platform' to transform the world toward dematerialization. However, a non-sustainable ICT would itself cause more damage than benefits. Therefore, the sustainability requirements should cover all elements and components of any ICT solution, for example data centers, network and equipment, in order to ensure a large scale adoption of ICT across the globe. One approach to reduce the possible risk and impact of the complexity on the performance and also sustainability of an ICT solution is shifting toward non-centralized ICT. Non-centralized ICT in particular put an ICT footprint on the customer premises beyond just a user interface, sensor, or actuator. To put more emphasis on this aspect, we introduced the notion of (E)ICT, which stands for (Embedded) Information and Communication Technology, to highlight the importance of embedded parts of any ICT solution. The power of ICT in enabling real-time, long-distance, networked interactions and communications has nominated it an enabler and also a carrier of various disruptive changes for good. This particularly is very important in the context of cities and urban living. As mentioned before, all these benefits could be jeopardized by a non-sustainable

© ICST Institute for Computer Sciences, Social Informatics and Telecommunications Engineering 2016
A. Leon-Garcia et al. (Eds.): Smart City 2015, LNICST 166, pp. 913–914, 2016.
DOI: 10.1007/978-3-319-33681-7

operation of ICT itself. All ICT equipment passes through a complicated path of manufacturing and fabrication along which rare, conflicted minerals and other expensive material are used to build the final equipment. Although a big impact associated to equipment is the energy consumed and the associated GHG emissions, there are other environmental impacts such as those related to toxic material that should be considered in the assessment of sustainability of an ICT solution. Single-goaled visions to ICT for sustainability, such as that focusing only to reduce the GHG emissions, would cause more problems, especially those related to health and wellness. Therefore, Life Cycle Assessment (LCA) of the operation is required to contain all impacts and footprint. There is also an ever increasing growth in the integration of Internet of Things (IoT) and low-cost, low-power sensors in all aspects of life. Although we are far from reaching a technological singularity, the current state of available artificial intelligence and also real-time communications have great potentials to take over a large portion of the workloads especially those related to undesired, undignified tasks.

This poster presents a practical application of ICT agents in a use case of smart houses, where federal regulators govern services of a household particularly in relations with external entities such as utilities. There are various resource flows to a typical household, such as Water, Electricity, Data, Food, and Air (WEDFA) flows, which are highly critical from the sustainability perspective at both local and global levels. Therefore, smart-house solutions have a great potential in reducing not only the primary resource consumptions at a household, they also could minimize secondary, associated resource consumptions occurring within operation and maintenance activities of the utilities. Although deployment of sensing devices and continuous monitoring has been a trend in implementation of generic smart house solutions, there are several concerns that could delay or jeopardize massive adoption of these solutions, particularly the risk factors related to privacy and security along with other concerns related to rapid increase in the number of vendors.

The proposed autonomous, cloud-enabled, agent-based smart house is a potential solution to this chaotic situation. The agent(s), which operate on the house side, control all outgoing data and also all ingoing commands. The generic nature of such an agent, which we call a Federal SmartHouse Regulator, makes it highly compatible with open source and crowd-based paradigms, which increase trust and also pace of development. These federal regulator may govern every service interaction related to a vendor's sensor/actuator, and also may create their own interactions with counterpart agents of the high-level entities, such as those of the utilities, in order to reduce the resource consumption while providing a high-quality experience to the residence along with generating 'value' for them. The main role of these agents is in providing a certain level of accountability from every house which in turn reduces a big amount of uncertainty in capacity planning on the utilities side. Although the intelligence of every agent is recommended to stay within the actual premises of their associated entity, many of the resources that the agents may require, such as data storage or specialized analytics, is hosted on high-performance cloud-oriented data and compute centers, such as that of Green Sustainable Telco-grade Clouds (GSTCs). This is an example of how ICT and its associated services could serve as a dynamic platform for reaching a true realization of networked society where every person and industry is empowered to reach their full potential.

Resource Consumption Assessment for Cloud Middleware

Hicham Abdelfattah, Kim Khoa Nguyen, and Mohamed Cheriet

Laboratoire Synchromedia, École Technologie Superieure, Montréal, QC, Canada
{habdelfattah,knguyen,mohamedcheriet}@synchromedia.ca

1 Introduction

To provide users with relevant information about cloud operation and to be aware of cloud performance, it is essential to understand the cloud system behaviour and analyse the performance of cloud components to pinpoint on its strength and limitations. Infrastructure as Service (IaaS) allows a vision for acquisition and management of physical resources and the elastically, and is expendable to users to add more resources based on immediate needs. This way makes IaaS suitable for companies to deploy and configure their own private Cloud. Some open-source used for private cloud are Nimbus, Eculyptus, OpenStack and others. Facing increasing resource demand, Cloud administrator may either over-provision his cloud or reject a larger portion of requests (which is no longer on-demand). To better afford this kind of user requests a profiling phase is needed to seek which part of code or program uses most resources. Furthermore, this solution helps the administrator support his stack by learning more about his code. It provides an overview of each use case, gives an idea what are strength, leaking and bottleneck parts in order to intervene when it is required. However, a majority of prior research in the field were focused on only on high level, e.g. application layer which is built on the top of architecture models by analysing and monitoring applications performance, using multiple metrics like I/O, CPU, RAM, energy consumption and others. In the application layer, prior work has taken several approaches like instrumenting code, inferring the abnormal behaviour from history logs. In this paper, we investigate the relationship between resource usage and Cloud Middleware performance (OpenStack as an example), which runs in a dedicated server, also to determine the maximal number of instances that could be supported by the stack, and study the impact of those instances on resource usage. It would be beneficial to improve performance prediction and evaluate the success rate of user requests in order to make decision to accept or refuse a user request.

2 Methodology

To overcome this issue, we need to build a deep measurement and profiling framework for private cloud to determine the limitations and strength before using it

© ICST Institute for Computer Sciences, Social Informatics and Telecommunications Engineering 2016
A. Leon-Garcia et al. (Eds.): Smart City 2015, LNICST 166, pp. 915–916, 2016.
DOI: 10.1007/978-3-319-33681-7

in a production chain. We profile OpenStack based on various scenarios to determine the behavior of OpenStack components and to evaluate its performance. We address two questions typically for cloud middleware performance: (i) what is the hottest processes or code region influence on middleware performance?, (ii) how does performance vary regarding different amount of workflow? A number of metrics is considered like number of tenants, number of users per tenant, number of VM, VM image, and VM flavor, which will affect the performance of Cloud Middleware. Experimental design concept, especially factorial technique helps determine which of those metrics influences most on the performance of Cloud Middleware, and then pinpoints limitations and learns how CPU and Program Execution Time (PET) response varies on different amount of load. Our main scenario is to create and delete instances concurrently by creating a number of instances in parallel in order to stretch our stack to maximum and to observe how OpenStack will response. We used Rally as tool for benchmarking. For a given test, we change workload and run it for couple of times (to validate our results). The resulting performance enables us to establish links between the Cloud Middleware metrics and resource usage. This experiment determines the success rate and pinpoints the relationship between cloud Middleware metrics in terms of the successful rate of scenarios with data load variation. The response variable is measured by the success rate in each scenario. For instance, a scenario is defined to create a number of instances and then delete them after building them up (ready to use) and spread those instances on multiple tenants and users. To highlight the bottlenecks and limitation of Cloud Middleware. We simulate a real operational scenario by creating instances and then deleting them after having used. We consider the success rate as the output of the process and the input is (concurrency, tenant, users). Data is then collected to perform a statistical analysis in order to determine the effects of the main factors, and their interactions with the dependent variable (the success rate). We aim to extract the most significant factor(s), determine the relationship between significant main factor(s) and/or interactions and their impact on resource usage using a regression method.

3   Results and Conclusions

Our experiments showed that changing OpenStack configurations can support a larger workload up to 800 instances. The performance of OpenStack is controllable by three metrics which are correlated: the number of compute nodes, the number of running instances, and the number of workers across the Nova Cloud Controller. Also, resources consumed by OpenStack in terms of CPU increase along with the number of instances. The current version of OpenStack cannot support more than 800 instances, and the time required for creating instances increases linearly with the number of instances. In future work, we plan to use XEN and KVM virtualizations in parallel and compare their results obtained with XEN results especially for PTE and CPU load consumption.

Session Based Communication for Vital Machine to Machine Applications

Marc-Olivier Arsenault[1], Hanen Garcia Gamardo[1],
Kim-Khoa Nguyen[2], and Mohamed Cheriet[2]

[1] Ericsson, Montréal, Canada
{marc-olivier.arsenault,
hanen.garciagamardo}@Ericsson.com
[2] École de Techologie Supérieure, Montréal, Canada
{Kim-Khoa.Nguyen,Mohamed.Cheriet}@etsmtl.ca

1 Introduction

Today, machine-to-machine (M2M) communication is often implemented in the tele-com world based on a push and pull mechanism where devices push data to a central database and authorized services retrieve data when they need. There is no stream-oriented mechanism for M2M, which is required by a new class of critical and vital applications such as security monitoring, health and life monitoring, real time recognition, etc. All these applications need a stream-oriented protocol that is control-lable, monitored and secured. In addition, M2M requires an agnostic wide area network (WAN) that receives connections from different underlying access technologies, such as wired or wireless access. Such a network should be provided with a scalable addressing scheme which is auto configured when devices are deployed on the field.

Some previously proposed solutions offered IP Multimedia Subsystem (IMS) ori-ented connectivity, which reuse IMS sessions to connect devices together. These solutions deal partially with the general M2M communication problem by creating a session-based communication but do not really address the aforementioned concerns.

This poster presents a Machine-to-Machine Session Based Communication (MSBC) architecture that provides Telco-grade stream-oriented communications for critical applications and offers security, reliability, network agnostic and scalable addressing scheme.

2 MSBC Architecture

The proposed solution is a multi-tier architecture, composed of three main components: the local gateway (LGW) on the local domain, the M2M Interconnect Server (M2M-IS) in the operator's IMS core and the application service gateway (ASGW) in the M2M services provider domain. We define Connected Thing Identifier (CTID) as a serial number, MAC address or any agreed identity mechanism, which is basically the only identifier recognized in the MSBC network and used not only for getting addressed as destination but for addressing their counterpart on the network as the source of

© ICST Institute for Computer Sciences, Social Informatics and Telecommunications Engineering 2016
A. Leon-Garcia et al. (Eds.): Smart City 2015, LNICST 166, pp. 917–919, 2016.
DOI: 10.1007/978-3-319-33681-7

information. Routing in this network is done via a logical link, called wire, which is a virtual connection between one device and one application server. Such mechanism removes coupling between devices and the application server, exempting the need of network addressing configurations on the devices and the LGW, and so enabling massive deployment of machines.

The MSBC reuses the IMS core with an add-on of an extra service, called the M2M Interconnect Server, which is designed to be deployed in the service layer of an IMS network. It limits the impacts and facilitates the integration on operator's network, and at the same time, it inherits the network agnostic characteristic of the IMS service layer. The deployment process of MSBC, is to find an operator with a configured IMS architecture, add the M2M-IS node, and create subscribers in the operator's HSS with the address of M2M-IS configured by the service trigger.

Communication between components in the MSBC is done through MSRP, which is a de facto stream oriented payload protocol for messaging in IMS and 4G networks. MSRP is a reliable protocol, and secured when using MSRP over TLS. It also offers a reporting mechanism ensuring all the messages were received correctly.

As MSBC is builds on top of IMS, it is network agnostic. As long as you can reach the IMS core, you are able to use the MSBC features. Based on network access technology different behavior can be applied. In case of radio access, communication is encrypted by the underlying network, thus there is no need to encrypt MSRP with TLS. However, in case of local cable access, such precaution needs to be taken. On the other hand, local cable access offers almost free bandwidth compared to radio access, thus more data can be sent, including bandwidth-greedy unimportant updates that were held in standby.

MSBC would therefore be a strategic asset for operators, and even if it could be deployed as an Over the Top service, it will rely on the underlying operator's network to provide QoS avoiding suffer from best effort Internet access. Together with security requirements, the implicit operator's security measures in their access network optimize resource consumption of the explicit TLS fallback mechanism while performing on a public IP connection. Therefore, the MSBC is a more suitable solution for an operator's already enabled IMS network.

3 Experimental Results and Conclusion

A test environment was to simulate the implementation of a real-life use case consisting in a Play Mobil dollhouse where we have added some sensors, motors, actuators and other smart objects. There are 5 service providers; each offers a service to the smart house. Each service comes with some devices. All communication between the devices and the service providers is done via the MSBC's network. Six test scenarios have been carried out: Add/Remove CT; Transmission of data on existing wire; Clean shutdown; Lost connectivity – Watchdog; Switch between LTE and Wi-Fi; Swap from one AS to another (easy migration service provider).

We observed that the MSBC prototype addresses the needs for M2M communication. Furthermore, network agnosticity and addressing capabilities will provide a scalable, secure and efficient solution.

The first version of MSBC has been designed for a traditional deployment of IMS services, but today's technologies evolution challenges this implementation of services as a shortsighted view, and opens the question of what native cloud deployment services are optimal for MSBC. This evolution has been introduced on the MSBC roadmap and will be part of our future work.

Optimization of Energy Consumption in Smart Homes: A New LCA-Based Demand Side Management Program

Alexandre Milovanoff, Thomas Dandres, and Réjean Samson

CIRAIG/CIRODD - Polytechnique Montreal, University of Montreal,
Montreal, Canada
{Alexandre.Milovanoff,Thomas.Dandres,
Rejean.Samson}@polymtl.ca

Abstract. Smart technologies provide new alternatives for sustainability. Forthcoming cities will gather innovations through buildings and grids among others. In the new dormitory of the École de Technologie Supérieure of Montréal, life cycle assessment (LCA) of electricity use measures the relevance of modern demand side management programs (DSM). Subsequently, an environmental indicator is established which provides a more comprehensive and sustainable solution.

Keywords: LCA · Carbon emissions · Electricity generation · DSM

European policies aim at reducing greenhouse gas emissions by 20 % while increasing energy efficiency by 20 % by 2020 and the household sector is believed to have a major role to play in reaching this goal [1]. Accordingly, new solutions for private homes based on information and communication technologies (ICT) are being developed to create smart technologies such as smart buildings or smart grids. This is the case of the new dormitory of the École de Technologie Supérieure of Montréal which will allow household appliances and systems to be controlled automatically by producing a mobile cloud of machine-to-machine (M2M) smart objects. The objectives of this smart home are to increase home automation, facilitate energy management and reduce environmental emissions over the entire building life cycle. Such a building would be efficient through the use of demand-side management (DSM) programs and the deployment of an energy management system (EMS) connected to a smart grid [2].

One of the main objectives of this research is to design a sustainable smart city model for an urban community based on the optimization of the energy consumption through a new kind of DSM focused on an environmental indicator.

DSM is a portfolio of measures that aims to improve the energy system as a whole by reducing the system demand when the supply becomes scarce. Two common DSM programs are currently popular; energy conservation and efficiency programs that intend to preserve energy and Demand/Load response programs [3]. The second strategy uses tools based on dynamic time pricing or time-of-use rates exposed to customers, which allow them to shift their energy usage from high-priced to low-priced periods [4]. But could we know the quality of the electricity consumed if only the price is regarded as the decisional factor? Admittedly, the use of the load as an additional degree of freedom would reduce the contingency margin of the generation installed. Furthermore this knowledge would be particularly relevant for the forthcoming integration of intermittent renewable sources [5]. However, electricity markets are highly complex and the numerous physical constraints of power systems prevent prices from being correlated with environmental emissions.

One way to provide dynamic potential impacts of power consumption would be through life cycle assessment (LCA). Instead of regarding the dynamic emissions factors of the electricity generation, the trades between regions are considered in a dynamic emissions factors of the electricity consumption. The gap among both factors is paramount to understand which are the least damaging periods of electricity use.

The different approaches encompassed in the LCA methodology [6] allow us, first, to assess the impacts of the past use of electricity (attributional approach). Such a perspective provides us information about the environmental issues of DSM during, for example, off-peak hours where an inconvenient and issuing electricity would be traded instead of reduced. Thanks to that, ecological relevancies of various programs of DSM are compared. The second approach, called consequential LCA, is developed in order to identify the marginal emissions associated with a prospective power use [6]. Thus, we assess the response of the power system subject to an increase in use and create a model to predict when the electricity consumption will have the least potential impacts.

Hence, consumers will be aware of the energy sustainability that they decide to use not only through its price but also using an LCA-based indicator. With this DSM program, a smart home would be able to minimize its greenhouse gas emissions or any other of its environmental impacts through a dynamic management of its energy consumption. Moreover, once the model is applied, an LCA of the smart building is conducted to measure its overall impact.

Ultimately, these results could be extended to the case of a smart city in order to measure the decrease of potential environmental impacts the implementation of smart buildings could provide.

References

1. Nordic Energy Perspectives: "Biomass market and potentials," Nordic Energy Perspectives (2009)
2. Saad al-sumaiti, A., Ahmed, M.H., Salama, M.M.A.: Smart home activities: a literature review. Electr. Power Compon. Syst. **42**, 294–305 (2014)
3. Saini, S.: Conservation v. generation: the significance of demand-side management (DSM), its tools and techniques. Refocus **5**, 52–54 (2004)
4. Strbac, G.: Demand side management: benefits and challenges. Energ. Policy **36**, 4419–4426 (2008)
5. Finn, P., O'Connell, M., Fitzpatrick, C.: Reduced usage phase impact using demand side management. In: 2011 IEEE International Symposium on Sustainable Systems and Technology (ISSST), pp. 1–6 (2011)
6. Rehl, T., Lansche, J., Müller, J.: Life cycle assessment of energy generation from biogas—attributional vs. consequential approach. Renew. Sustain. Energy Rev. **16**, 3766–3775 (2012)

RDF-Based Data Integration for Multi-modal Transport Systems

Stefano Braghin, Nuno Lopes, Yiannis Gkoufas, Rudi Verago, Adi Botea,
Michele Berlingerio, and Veli Bicer

IBM Research, Smarter Cities Technology Centre, Dublin, Ireland
stefanob@ie.ibm.com

In many cities, the increasing traffic of private and commercial vehicles is straining the transportation infrastructure, and traffic congestion causes significant losses to the economy. In order to provide robust, efficient and accurate multi-modal travel solutions to users, journey planners require accurate, up-to-date, and integrated data. The PETRA EU FP7 project specifically aims at addressing all these issues. Specifically, one of the goals is to create an integrated platform for Smart Cities allowing data producer and consumers to efficiently exchange information. In this demo we will present a platform allowing to import live transportation data from a city using Resource Description Framework (RDF). This platform is part of the PETRA project and the data collected from the city is then retrieved by the Dynamic Optimisation for Intermodal City Transportation (DOCIT) journey planner in order to provide accurate multi-modal routes in Rome and other cities. Our demo proposes the use of RDF to facilitate not only the integration to a journey planner, but also any tasks related to daily activities performed by city operators, for example adding temporary disruptions of bus routes. The use of RDF for storing General Transit Feed Specification (GTFS) and further data provides several advantages when compared to other type of storage: (i) it simplifies querying and managing the data, allowing to easily expose data to users as Linked Data (ii) it provides a transparent model for combining data from the different GTFS CSV files and other data sources (iii) updates can be performed using a standard language instead of using a custom solution. We will also present the evaluation of some of the queries used by the platform, further demonstrating the performances of the system.

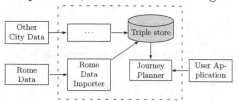

The architecture allows us to leverage the traffic data from cities like Rome and Venice (provided as a data dump in GTFS format along with live updates) in the journey planner via a triple-store. By using RDF as an intermediate representation format and a triple-store, the City Data Importer (CDI) can use SPARQL queries to obtain any necessary data and also perform updates over the stored data (e.g., in case of bus delays). As mentioned, the PETRA project builds on DOCIT that is an integrated system providing a multi-modal journey planner under uncertainty.

© ICST Institute for Computer Sciences, Social Informatics and Telecommunications Engineering 2016
A. Leon-Garcia et al. (Eds.): Smart City 2015, LNICST 166, 922–923, 2016.
DOI: 10.1007/978-3-319-33681-7

DOCIT provides functions such as non-deterministic multi-modal journey plan computation, plan execution monitoring, and re-planning. The demo will consist of live interaction with the system, plus videos of the system in action on sample critical situations.

Author Index

inted in the United States
Bookmasters